MACROECONOMICS

MACROECONOMICS

Seventh Edition

Paul Krugman
Graduate Center of the City University of New York

Robin Wells

Ryan Herzog
Gonzaga University Contributor

worth publishers
Macmillan Learning
New York

Senior Executive Program Manager: **Carolyn Merrill**
Development Manager: **Lukia Kliossis**
Associate Director, Digital Content: **Joshua Hill**
Development Editor: **Melissa Mashburn**
Assessment Manager: **Kristyn Brown**
Media Editor: **Stephanie Sosa**
Editorial Assistant: **Sara Lawler**
Executive Marketing Manager: **Scott Guile**
Marketing Assistant: **Claudia Cruz**
Senior Director, Content Management Enhancement: **Tracey Kuehn**
Executive Managing Editor: **Michael Granger**
Manager, Publishing Services: **Edward Dionne**
Manager, Digital Asset Management: **Jennifer Wetzel**
Production Supervisor: **Brianna Lester**
Director of Design, Content Management: **Diana Blume**
Senior Design Services Manager: **Natasha A. S. Wolfe**
Interior Design: **Lumina Datamatics, Inc.**
Cover Design: **John Callahan**
Art Manager: **Matt McAdams**
Illustration Coordinator: **Janice Donnola**
Executive Permissions Editor: **Cecilia Varas**
Director of Digital Production: **Keri deManigold**
Senior Media Project Manager: **Andrew Vaccaro**
Media Project Manager: **Brian Nobile**
Composition: **Lumina Datamatics, Inc.**
Printing and Binding: **Lakeside Book Company**

ISBN 978-1-319-41593-8 (Paperback)
ISBN 978-1-319-48151-3 (Loose-leaf Edition)
ISBN 978-1-319-54472-0 (International Edition)

Library of Congress Control Number: 2023942605

Printed in the United States of America.

1 2 3 4 5 6   28 27 26 25 24 23

Acknowledgments
*Acknowledgments and copyrights appear on the same page as the text and art selections
they cover; these acknowledgments and copyrights constitute an extension of the
copyright page.*

Worth Publishers
120 Broadway
New York, NY 10271
www.macmillanlearning.com

Achieve for *Macroeconomics*

Engaging Every Student. Supporting Every Instructor. Proven Success. Continued Enhancement.

Achieve for Macroeconomics sets the standard for integrating **activities, assessments,** and **analytics** into your teaching. It brings together all of the features that instructors and students need—an e-book with interactive graphing, LearningCurve adaptive quizzing, and other instructional and application activities, assessments, and extensive instructor resources—in a powerful platform that offers:

- Adaptive quizzing.
- Powerful assessment.
- Deep LMS integration.
- A fully integrated iClicker classroom response system.
- Exciting, enhanced, interactive graphing tools.

Our resources were **co-designed with instructors and students**, using a foundation of **learning research** and rigorous testing. The result is pedagogically superior content, organization, and functionality. Achieve's pre-built assignments engage students both *inside* and *outside* of class. And Achieve is effective for students of *all levels* of motivation and preparedness, whether they are high achievers or need extra support.

Macmillan Learning offers **deep platform integration** of Achieve with all LMS providers, including Blackboard, Brightspace, Canvas, and Moodle. With integration, students can access course content and their grades through one sign-in. And you can pair Achieve with course tools from your LMS, such as discussion boards and chat and Gradebook functionality. LMS integration is also available with Inclusive Access. For more information, visit MacmillanLearning.com /College/US/Solutions/LMS-Integration or talk to your local sales representative.

Achieve was built with **accessibility** in mind. Macmillan Learning strives to create products that are usable by all learners and meet universally applied accessibility standards. In addition to addressing product compatibility with assistive technologies such as screen reader software, alternative keyboard devices, and voice recognition products, we are working to ensure that the content and platforms we provide are fully accessible. For more information visit https:// www.macmillanlearning.com/college/us/our-story/accessibility.

◀ **LearningCurve Adaptive Quizzing** With a game-like interface, this popular and effective quizzing engine offers students a low-stakes way to brush up on concepts and help identify knowledge gaps. Questions are linked to relevant e-book sections, providing both the incentive to read and a framework for an efficient reading experience.

▶ **Enhanced E-Book with Interactive Graphs** The Achieve e-book offers highlighting, bookmarking, and note-taking. Students can download the e-book to read offline or to have it read aloud to them. Achieve allows instructors to assign chapter sections as homework.

The Achieve e-book now features interactive graphs. Students can now engage with economic models to see how components of the graph change as market dynamics change. Every data graph in the text is now interactive, so students can explore live visualizations and improve their data literacy.

Figure 3 | Movement Along the Supply Curve versus Shift of the Supply Curve

Move the point on the graph as directed. The fall in quantity supplied when going from point A to point B reflects a movement along the supply curve: it is the result of a fall in the price of a good. The fall in quantity supplied when going from point A to point C reflects a shift of the supply curve: it is the result of a fall in the quantity supplied at any given price.

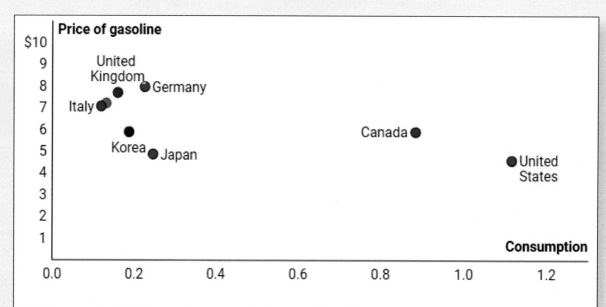

Price is measured in U.S. dollars per gallon; consumption is measured as gallons per capita, per day.

Chart: © Worth Publishers • Get the data • Download image • Data from: World Development Indicators and U.S. Energy Information Administration, 2021

ACTIVITIES

▶ **Interactive Topic Reviews** Interactive Topic Reviews provide students with an overview of key topics from the Principles course. With embedded interactive graphs and assessment, these self-study modules provide students with an immersive and easy-to-use tool. Students can use these reviews at their own pace throughout the course to prep for class, tests, or exams.

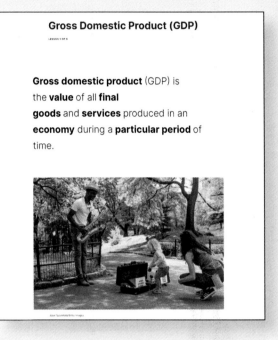

◀ **Problem Video Walkthroughs** These skill-building activities pair sample end-of-chapter problems with targeted feedback and video explanations to help students solve problems step-by-step. This approach allows students to work independently, tests their comprehension of concepts, and prepares them for class and exams.

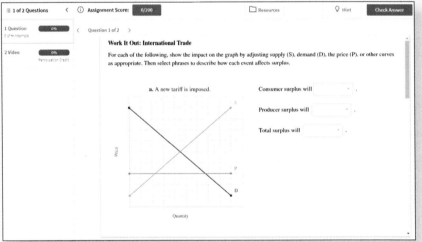

ASSESSMENTS

▶ **End-of-Chapter Questions** Developed by economists active in the classroom, these multistep problems are paired with rich feedback for incorrect and correct responses that guide students through the process of problem solving. These questions also feature our user-friendly graphing tool, designed so students focus entirely on economics and not on how to use the application.

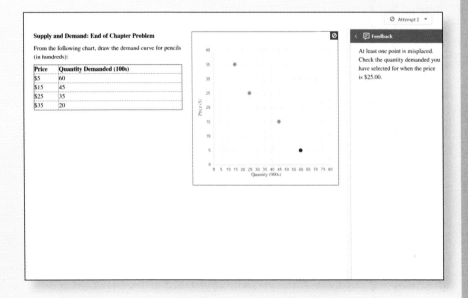

Homework Curated homework problems feature randomly sampled variables and our user-friendly graphing tool. These problems are multistep with a variety of answer inputs—each with detailed and targeted feedback specific to that answer.

Practice Quizzes Designed to be used as a study tool, these quizzes feature multiple-choice questions and allow for multiple attempts as students familiarize themselves with content.

ANALYTICS

◀ **Learning Objectives, Reports, and Insights** Every asset you can assign in Achieve is tagged to specific Learning Objectives. Reporting within Achieve helps students see how they are performing against objectives, and it helps instructors determine if any student, group of students, or the class as a whole needs extra help in specific areas. This enables more efficient and effective instructor interventions.

Achieve provides reports on student activities, assignments, and assessments at the course level, unit level, subunit level, and individual student level, so instructors can identify trouble spots and adjust their efforts accordingly. Within Reports, the Insights section offers snapshots with high-level data on student performance and behavior, to answer such questions as:

- What are the top Learning Objectives to review in this unit?
- What are the top assignments to review?
- What's the range of performance on a particular assignment?
- How many students aren't logging in?

Powerful Support for Instructors

Test Bank This comprehensive Test Bank contains multiple-choice and short-answer questions to help instructors assess students' comprehension, interpretation, and ability to synthesize.

Lecture Slides These brief, interactive, and visually interesting slides are designed to hold students' attention in class with graphics and animations demonstrating key concepts and real-world examples.

Clicker Slides These slides contain questions to incorporate active learning in the classroom. Students can participate by using the iClicker app on their smartphone or laptop.

iClicker Integration With Achieve's seamless integration with iClicker, you can help any student participate — in the classroom or virtually. iClicker's attendance feature gets students in class, then instructors can choose from flexible polling and quizzing options to engage, check understanding, and get feedback from students in real time. iClicker also allows students to participate using laptops, mobile devices, or iClicker remotes — whichever each student prefers. Additionally, we offer Instructor Activity Guides and book-specific iClicker question slides within Achieve to make the most out of your class time. It's no surprise that over a decade after being founded by educators, iClicker still leads the market. And thousands of instructors continue to give every student a voice with our simple, award-winning student engagement solutions.

Instructor's Resource Manual The Instructor's Resource Manual offers instructors teaching materials and tips to enhance the classroom experience, along with chapter objectives, outlines, and suggestions for further reading.

Gradebook Assignment scores are collected into a comprehensive Gradebook providing instructors reporting on individuals and overall course performance.

Customer Support Our Achieve Client Success Specialist Team — dedicated platform experts — provides collaboration, software expertise, and consulting to tailor each course to fit your instructional goals and student needs. Start with a demo at a time that works for you to learn more about how to set up your customized course. Talk to your sales representative or visit https://www.macmillanlearning.com /college/us/contact-us/training-and -demos for more information.

Powerful, Continued Input from the Faculty Advisory Board

We are delighted to partner with the following faculty members who provide us with feedback, insight, and ideas to continually improve Achieve for both students and instructors:

Annette Chamberlain, *Virginia Western Community College*
Christopher Clarke, *Washington State University*
Sherry Jensen, *Salt Lake Community College*
Erika Martinez, *University of South Florida*

Susan McCoy, *Des Moines Area Community College*
Eric Parsons, *University of Missouri*
Aisling Winston, *University of Buffalo*

Pricing and bundling options are available at the Macmillan student store: store.macmillanlearning.com/

WHAT'S NEW IN THE SEVENTH EDITION?

The overwhelming majority of instructors and students use Achieve online courseware for *Macroeconomics*. The new edition offers significant improvements to Achieve. New digital assets in every chapter include:

- **Interactive Topic Reviews.** These tutorials provide students with an overview of key topics from the Principles course. With embedded interactive graphs and assessment, these self-study modules provide students with an immersive and easy-to-use tool. Students can use these reviews at their own pace throughout the course to prep for class, tests, or exams.
- **Interactive graphs.** To help students improve data literacy and understand economic models, Achieve now offers interactive graphs throughout the e-book and in a Graphing Bank. Students can manipulate graphs to simulate market dynamics and to explore historical data, providing a more engaging reading and learning experience.
- **New homework assignments available in Achieve.** Reimagined assessment offers targeted feedback for use in class and as homework assignments. Designed so that students learn by doing the economics, these problems contain multiple question types, including our innovative and intuitive graphing tool that assesses students' understanding of economics and not their use of graphing software. Each chapter offers a new set of assignable, multi-step problems that complement online, auto-graded versions of the end-of-chapter problems.

The seventh edition of the text has new coverage and updates throughout. In particular:

- The **Introduction** features a new opener on adaptation and resilience in the Covid-19 economy and focuses on the economic growth of India during the pandemic.
- **Chapter 1** includes a new Business Case on success of Airbnb.
- **Chapter 3** has a new opener on a day in the life of an Uber driver in San Francisco. This Uber example carries through the rest of the chapter. The chapter now reverses the discussion to cover supply before demand and includes an updated Economics in Action: Holy Guacamole! on Covid's impact on avocado supply.
- **Chapter 4** includes a revised Economics in Action: The Rise and Fall of the Unpaid Intern and the Business Case: A Market Disruptor Gets Disrupted by the Market updated with the impact of Covid on Uber.
- **Chapter 5** includes added coverage of supply chain disruptions during the pandemic and vaccine production and the trade of vaccine components between countries, a new Economics in Action on the effect of tariffs on washing machine prices, which includes a new figure on the consumer price index of major household appliances and an updated

Economics in Action: Trade War, What Is It Good For?, which includes a new figure on the history of U.S./China tariff rates.
- **Chapter 6** features updated coverage of the recession in Greece in the chapter opener and Economics in Action as well as thorough coverage of the Covid recession and subsequent inflation.
- **Chapter 7** features a new chapter opener open on India's growth and a new Economics in Action on Sri Lanka's economic crisis: Trouble in Paradise, as well as updated GDP and CPI data throughout.
- **Chapter 8** analyzes 2022 unemployment and inflation, including a new chapter opener, focus on Covid unemployment, and a new Economics in Action: The Inflation Surge of 2021–2022.
- **Chapter 9** includes coverage of the Inflation Reduction Act, updated climate change content, and the Economics in Action on the productivity paradox now includes the economic implications of ChatGPT and other large language models.
- **Chapter 10** includes an updated Economics in Action: Three Generations of U.S. Interest Rates and a new Business Case: When Tech Stocks Took a Fall.

- **Chapter 11** includes a new chapter opener about the fall in consumer spending during the pandemic: The Shortest Recession Ever.
- **Chapter 12** includes recent coverage of the Fed's response to inflation, a thorough revision of the aggregate demand/aggregate supply to focus on the inflation rate instead of the price level, two new Economics in Action features: (1) Why Aggregate Demand Fell in 2007–2008 and (2) Aggregate Supply in a Time of (Relative) Stability.
- **Chapter 13** features a new opener on the American Rescue Plan and its effect on inflation, updated examples of expansionary and contractionary fiscal policy, an updated Economics in Action: A Tale of Two Stimuli, an updated Global Comparison on the U.S. debt, and a new Business Case: BMW Goes Electric.
- **Chapter 14** includes an updated definition of M1, updated coverage of cryptocurrencies, a new Economics in Action: The Fall of Silicon Valley Bank, updated coverage of Fed tools to include interest on reserve balances and reverse repo to reflect modern monetary policy.
- **Chapter 15** features an updated chapter opener on 2023 interest rate hikes, an updated Economics in Action to cover the Fed raising its target interest rate to fight inflation, new Pitfalls: Interest Rates and the Aggregate Demand Curve.
- **Chapter 16** includes coverage of the early 2020s inflation as a result of the pandemic and the Russia-Ukraine war, an updated Economics in Action: The Spanish Squeeze, and two new Economics in Actions: (1) A Tale of Two Disinflations and (2) Is the Zero Lower Bound History?
- **Chapter 17** figures now cover the inflation rate instead of the price level and includes a new section on The Coronavirus Pandemic and the Economics of Disruption.
- **Chapter 18** has a new chapter opener: Propping up the Turkish Lira and a new Economics in Action: Turkey's Lira Problem.

About the Authors

PAUL KRUGMAN, recipient of the 2008 Nobel Memorial Prize in Economic Sciences, is a faculty member of the Graduate Center of the City University of New York, associated with the Luxembourg Income Study, which tracks and analyzes income inequality around the world. Prior to that, he taught at Princeton University for 14 years. He received his BA from Yale and his PhD from MIT. Before Princeton, he taught at Yale, Stanford, and MIT. He also spent a year on the staff of the Council of Economic Advisers in 1982–1983. His research has included pathbreaking work on international trade, economic geography, and currency crises. In 1991, Krugman received the American Economic Association's John Bates Clark medal. In addition to his teaching and academic research, Krugman writes extensively for nontechnical audiences. He is a regular op-ed columnist for the *New York Times*. His best-selling trade books include *End This Depression Now!, The Return of Depression Economics and the Crisis of 2008*, a history of recent economic troubles and their implications for economic policy, and *The Conscience of a Liberal*, a study of the political economy of economic inequality and its relationship with political polarization from the Gilded Age to the present. His earlier books, *Peddling Prosperity* and *The Age of Diminished Expectations*, have become modern classics.

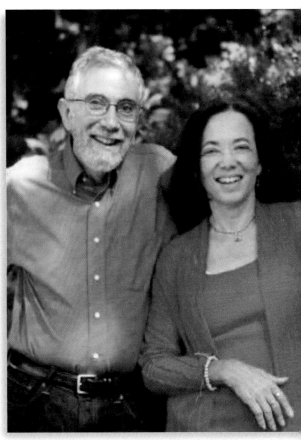

Ligaya Franklin

ROBIN WELLS was a Lecturer and Researcher in Economics at Princeton University. She received her BA from the University of Chicago and her PhD from the University of California at Berkeley; she then did postdoctoral work at MIT. She has taught at the University of Michigan, the University of Southampton (United Kingdom), Stanford, and MIT.

Vision and Story of *Macroeconomics*

This is a text about economics as the study of what people do and how they interact, a study very much informed by real-world experience. These words, this spirit, have served as a guiding principle for us in every edition.

While we were driven to write this book by many small ideas about particular aspects of economics, we also had one big idea: an economics textbook should be built around narratives, many of them pulled from real life, and it should never lose sight of the fact that economics is, in the end, a set of stories about what people do.

Many of the stories economists tell take the form of models—for whatever else they are, economic models are stories about how the world works. But we believe that student understanding of and appreciation for models are greatly enhanced if they are presented, as much as possible, in the context of stories about the real world that both illustrate economic concepts and touch on the concerns we all face living in a world shaped by economic forces. We've carefully updated this edition to be sure our examples are as current as possible, integrating the Covid Recession and covering modern monetary policy.

You'll find a rich array of stories in every chapter, in the chapter openers, Economics in Actions, For Inquiring Minds, Global Comparisons, and Business Cases. As always, we include many new stories and update others. We also integrate an international perspective throughout, more extensively than ever before. We have a new focus on how increases in the economy's potential leads to long-run growth, highlighted as a principle in Chapter 1 then throughout the text.

We also include pedagogical features that reinforce learning. For example, each major section ends with three related elements devised with the student in mind: (1) the Economics in Actions: a real-world application to help students achieve a fuller understanding of concepts they just read about; (2) a Quick Review of key ideas in list form; and (3) Check Your Understanding self-test questions with answers provided to students. Our thought-provoking end-of-chapter problems are another strong feature and are assignable in Achieve with answer-specific feedback. Achieve also offers Problem Video Walkthroughs, offering students tutorials that guide them step-by-step through solving problems that are modeled after the end-of-chapter problems. Discovering Data exercises offer students the opportunity to use interactive graphs to analyze interesting economic questions.

We're most excited by the new interactive graphs that will be available in Achieve in a Graphing Bank and embedded in the e-book. This interactivity will allow students to engage with the models, theory, and data presented in the text. All have been devised with the goal of supporting instructor teaching and student learning in principles of economics courses.

We hope your experience using our product is a good one. Thank you for introducing it into your classroom.

Paul Krugman   Robin Wells

Engaging Students in the Study of *Macroeconomics*

We are committed to the belief that students learn best from a complete textbook program built around narratives, steeped in real life and current events, with a strong emphasis on global matters and with proven technology that supports student success.

Narrative Approach

This is a textbook built around narratives and stories, many pulled from real life. In every chapter, stories are used to teach core concepts and motivate learning.

- To engage students, every chapter begins with a compelling story. What You Will Learn questions help students focus on key concepts in the chapter.
- So students can immediately see economic concepts applied in the real world, Economics in Action applications appear throughout chapters.
- To provide students with an international perspective, the Global Comparison feature uses data and graphs to illustrate why countries reach different economic outcomes.
- So students can see key economic principles applied to real-life business situations, each chapter concludes with a Business Case.

Global Focus

This book is unrivaled in the attention paid to global matters. With unparalleled insight and clarity, the authors use their hallmark narrative approach to take students outside of the classroom and into our global world, starting in the Introduction with a new focus on India's technological and economic growth. We have thoroughly integrated an international perspective into the text, in the numerous applications, cases, and stories and, of course, in the data-based Global Comparison feature.

Technology That Builds Success

Macroeconomics is not just a textbook. Achieve brings all of the best aspects of Krugman/Wells and Macmillan's digital resources together in one place. Built on the best practices in learning sciences, Achieve encourages even stronger student engagement, mastery of the material, and success in the course.

ChatGPT's Power Unleashed: Navigating Learning's Future with Responsibility

Dear Students,

In the fall of 2022, ChatGPT was released, forever changing the landscape of student learning. Since then, new artificial intelligence (AI) platforms have been rapidly developed, making AI the most significant disruptor to learning in our lifetime. It is no surprise that students quickly harnessed the power of ChatGPT. However, as the character Uncle Ben, in the movie *Spider-Man*, famously told Peter Parker, "with great power comes great responsibility." Students must be mindful of university policies and their instructors' rules regarding the use of ChatGPT, as it has the potential to make information gathering easier and, in turn, raise concerns about academic dishonesty.

Iryna Khabliuk/Alamy Stock Photo

We predict that ChatGPT's ability to swiftly find and summarize information will place a greater burden on students. Professors and instructors will expect students to have a deeper understanding of the material, leading to more thoughtful, in-depth, and critical thinking–based questions in the classroom. Therefore, we aim to provide students with a list of best practices they can employ to enhance their learning further.

1. Understanding key terms
ChatGPT can help explain, for example, the difference between nominal GDP and real GDP or the distinction between a change in demand and quantity demanded.

2. Creating a study guide
ChatGPT is excellent at summarizing essential material. You can ask ChatGPT to summarize the key concepts from the elasticity chapter in Microeconomics by Krugman and Wells or the chapter on aggregate expenditures in Macroeconomics.

3. Clarifying answers
Frequently heard in office hours, "I understood the answer in class but don't remember how you got it." Instead of staying confused or waiting until office hours, you can ask ChatGPT. For example, "Why is 'When nobody can be made better off without making someone worse off' the answer to 'Which is the best definition of efficiency?'" Or can you explain "Why, when a car manufacturer from outside the United States builds another car factory in Alabama, the factory is counted as investment in U.S. GDP?"

4. Providing more examples
Although professors strive to create engaging examples, time constraints limit the number of examples covered in class. If you're tired of hearing about pizza and beer, ChatGPT can provide you with more examples demonstrating an increase in demand.

5. Offering additional problems
Many students seek more practice problems before exams. ChatGPT can supply you with a never-ending database of practice problems. Ask ChatGPT for sample problems involving elasticity calculations or solving aggregate expenditure models for short-run equilibrium.

6. Looking up new information

Our economic environment is constantly evolving. Although we update our textbooks, there may be recent developments not covered. ChatGPT can help you stay updated by providing information on current examples of price floors, instances of price collusion, or the economic situation in countries such as Venezuela.

7. Finding reliable data sources

In the past, finding economic data meant laboriously searching through books at the library or scrolling through countless pages in Google. Today, with ChatGPT's assistance, you can quickly discover data sources. For example, if you need data on economic growth in the 1800s, ChatGPT will guide you to the Maddison Project Database, a valuable resource for studying long-run growth.

8. Translating to a different language

For international students learning in English, ChatGPT can clarify information in your native language, helping you better understand the material.

Although the use of ChatGPT and other AI technologies will continue to expand, we urge you to exercise caution. When you seek help from ChatGPT, it may provide more information than necessary or offer slightly different perspectives from your textbook or instructor's teachings. As Bill Gates, the founder of Microsoft, wisely said, "While we're all very dependent on technology, it doesn't always work."

Sincerely,
Your Authors

Acknowledgments

Our deep appreciation and heartfelt thanks go out to **Ryan Herzog** for his hard work and extensive contributions during every stage of this revision. Ryan is an Economics Professor at Gonzaga University in Spokane, Washington. He received his BA from Pacific Lutheran University and his PhD from the University of Oregon. He has demonstrated a passion for teaching and a commitment to research. His research focuses on the effects of business cycle shocks on regional labor markets, international capital mobility, and empirical economic growth models.

Courtesy of Ryan Herzog

Ryan has an engaging classroom style, which combines theoretical concepts with real-world applications to help students develop a deeper understanding of economics. He has received numerous awards for his teaching and mentorship, including the Gonzaga University Exemplary Faculty of the Year. He is a dedicated advisor and mentor to students. Ryan uses the Krugman/Wells Achieve product and has officially joined Paul Krugman, Robin Wells, and Macmillan as **Contributor** on the Seventh Edition. He has worked extensively on the edition's new interactive graphs, end-of-chapter problems, and interactive topic reviews.

Outside of his academic work, Ryan enjoys traveling with his wife, Annie, and two boys, Ben and Landon. He is an avid sports fan.

We must also thank the many people at Worth Publishers for their work on this edition: Chuck Linsmeier, Shani Fisher, Carolyn Merrill, Lukia Kliossis, Melissa Mashburn, Amanda Nava, Joshua Hill, Kristyn Brown, and Stephanie Sosa in editorial. We thank Scott Guile and Travis Long for their enthusiastic and tireless advocacy of this book. Many thanks to the incredible production, design, photo, and media production teams: Tracey Kuehn, Michael Granger, Edward Dionne, Jennifer Wetzel, Diana Blume, Natasha Wolfe, Cecilia Varas, Andrew Vaccaro, and Brian Nobile.

Our deep appreciation and heartfelt thanks to the following reviewers, whose input helped us shape this Seventh Edition.

Morgan Bridge, *Colorado Mesa University*

Daniel Ford, *Southern Maine Community College*

Mark Goldhammer, *Rutgers University—New Brunswick*

Julie H. Gonzalez, *University of California, Santa Cruz*

Mark Holmgren, *Eastern Washington University*

Alexander Katkov, *Johnson & Wales University*

Nakul Kumar, *Northern Virginia Community College—Alexandria*

Michael Manville, *University of California, Los Angeles*

Ling Shao, *Miami University*

Meiping Sun, *Fordham University*

Dhanushka Thamarapani, *California State University, Chico*

Jadrian Wooten, *Virginia Polytechnic Institute and State University*

Brief Contents

Contents

PART 2 Supply and Demand

CHAPTER 3
Supply and Demand / 67

CHAPTER 4
Price Controls and Quotas: Meddling with Markets / 103

CHAPTER 5
International Trade / 131

MACROECONOMICS

Introduction: The Covid-19 Economy

ADAPTATION AND RESILIENCE

THE ECONOMY SINCE MARCH 2020 has been unlike anything experienced before. In spring 2020, the Covid-19 pandemic caused significant parts of the global economy to grind to a halt. Lives and businesses were upended, while local, regional, and federal governments worldwide and in the United States scrambled to respond.

Stuck at home, households sharply curtailed eating in restaurants, visiting gyms, and taking trips, and many workers stopped going to the office. Essentials like toilet paper became hard to find. As people shifted their purchases to items they could use at home — home exercise equipment, toys, patio furniture, computers — shipments of those items from international factories rose significantly, leading to jammed shipping ports and soaring global shipping costs (rising as much as tenfold). Some goods in short supply became wildly expensive — for example, dumbbells began selling for six times their normal price.

Simultaneously, gasoline prices plummeted, alongside office rents, car rental rates, and airfares. While thousands of restaurant, hotel, and airline workers were laid off, nurses saw their wages soar. The U.S. government stepped in to support the incomes of laid-off workers, extended loans to businesses to stave off a potential tidal wave of bankruptcies, and directed the distribution of critical medical equipment. And there were nonmonetary effects, too. On the positive side, pollution and traffic congestion declined significantly. On the negative side, schooling was interrupted for millions of students.

Yet the economic disruptions of 2020–2021, while extreme and unprecedented, weren't random or chaotic. On the contrary, the economy's response to Covid-19 followed clear economic logic — the kind of logic you'll learn from this textbook. Take the example of home exercise equipment. The closure of gyms precipitated a huge increase in demand for home exercise equipment, and a huge increase in demand for shipping containers to transport that equipment from factories in Asia. Economic logic tells us that when demand for a good goes up while supply of it is limited, its price goes up. And that's exactly what happened. The price of dumbbells and other types of exercise equipment and the price of shipping containers shot up. Moreover, economics tells us that people respond to prices: for example, according to economic logic the higher prices for exercise equipment should motivate people with unwanted exercise equipment sitting in their basement to sell it on Craigslist or Facebook Marketplace. And, yes, that's exactly what people did.

So the story of the "Covid-19 Economy" is not one of chaos and failure. Rather, it's a story of adaptation and resilience — adaptations and resilience that were predictable given the logic of economics. For example, where possible, businesses adopted new technologies that allowed their employees to work from home. Laid-off restaurant workers found jobs making meal deliveries. Toilet paper manufacturers switched production from commercial-grade paper (used in restaurants and offices) to residential-grade paper (used in homes) to ease toilet paper shortages in grocery stores. Lower airfares enticed people to take trips. Giant retailers like Home Depot, Walmart, and Costco chartered their own ships to make sure their shelves were stocked with merchandise.

Governments adapted too. To avert further hardship, the U.S. government provided extensive financial aid to people unable to find work (especially those with low incomes), kept businesses from going under, and leveraged its vast purchasing power to obtain and deliver critical medical supplies.

So although Covid-19 was an epidemiological event, economics has a lot to say about the way it affected people's lives. Moreover, it has a lot to say about how the world will function as the threat of Covid-19 recedes.

In this book, you will learn about the principles that govern the economy, even in the midst of disruptive events like pandemics, wars, and natural disasters. Among the questions we will cover are:

- How does our economic system work? That is, how does it manage to deliver goods and services to people?
- How does the economy respond to disruptive events, like a pandemic or technological innovation?
- Why does the economy sometimes go astray, leaving people worse off, such as producing excessive air pollution or high rates of unemployment?
- Why does the economy sometimes need government intervention to make society better off?
- Even in the years without disruptive events, why are there ups and downs in the economy? That is, why does the economy sometimes have a bad year?
- Why is the long run mainly a story of growth and rising living standards despite pandemics, wars, and the like?

Let's take a look at these questions and offer a brief preview of what you will learn in this book. ●

economy a system for coordinating society's productive activities.

economics the social science that studies the production, distribution, and consumption of goods and services.

‖ The Invisible Hand

The speed and effectiveness of the global response to Covid-19 was made far better by major technological innovations. Remote work wouldn't have been possible without modern conferencing software. Food and other supplies wouldn't have arrived on doorsteps without digital barcode technology and internet retailing platforms. And the pandemic was mitigated, though not ended, by the almost miraculous deployment of new vaccines, which not only had to be developed but manufactured on a huge scale.

Where did these innovations come from? You might think they must have come from the world's traditional technological leaders—North America, Western Europe, and Japan. And you'd be mostly right. But some emerging nations also played a major role—India, in particular. The Serum Institute, based in the Indian city of Pune, has been a major exporter of the AstraZeneca Covid-19 vaccine, for example.

Meanwhile, for those who spent some of 2020–2021 working in sweatpants: One of the main teleconferencing platforms many businesses and schools used was Zoom—and although Zoom is a U.S.-based company, it has a large development center in the Indian city of Bangalore. Indeed, Bangalore has emerged as one of the world's prime hubs for information technology.

How did India become an economic player on a global scale? It's still a very poor nation by U.S. or European standards; in 2022, the average worker was paid only about $400 a month. But it has nonetheless gotten vastly better off over the past 40 years.

India's growth can be attributed to vast improvements in its system for coordinating productive activities—the activities that create the goods and services people want and that get them to the people who want them. That kind of system is what we mean when we talk about the **economy.** And **economics** is the social science that studies the production, distribution, and consumption of goods and services.

As recently as 1980, estimates of India's per capita income suggest that it was barely richer than it had been in the early twentieth century. Since then, however, Indian incomes have risen about fivefold, and India has become a major player in some important global industries. It's not just the Covid-19 vaccine; India supplies a large fraction of the world's generic drugs. It's not just Zoom: Bangalore has become a prime hub for information technology, designing software used around the world.

Who planned India's economic rise? Nobody. True, government policies helped create some of the preconditions for economic success. For example, both Pune and Bangalore have benefited from their role as major centers of world-class education. But India's surge has been driven by multinational corporations that saw opportunities to increase their profits, local entrepreneurs who saw new opportunities, and workers moving to growth hubs in pursuit of a better life.

No person or organization was in charge of this transformation. In fact, India's economic rise was made possible by reforms that reduced the government's role in the economy and gave the private sector a freer hand.

In the 1970s, before India began its big rise, the nation's economy was subject to often suffocating government control. Under the so-called "license Raj" ("raj" is the Hindi word for "rule"), businesses needed bureaucratic approval for almost any initiative. Regulations and taxes made it especially costly to buy anything from abroad. Inspired by the example of "command economies" of the former Soviet Union and Maoist China, in which the government told everyone what to

A booming marketplace in today's India.

Soltan Frédéric/Getty Images

do, many Indian politicians of that time believed that extensive government intervention in the economy was the key to prosperity.

Over time, however, it became clear that command economies worked badly. Consumers often couldn't find the goods they wanted, and there were notoriously long lines at shops when desirable goods did show up. Meanwhile, producers often found that nobody wanted what they were capable of producing. Subject to the erratic dictates of bureaucrats, entrepreneurs and businesses were unwilling to invest in new equipment or adopt new technologies. As a result, command economies fell steadily behind the *market economies* of the rest of the world.

In the 1980s, Indian reformers finally admitted that their model wasn't working, and the nation transformed itself into much more of a **market economy,** an economy in which production and consumption are the result of decentralized decisions by firms and individuals. For example, the United States has a market economy. Unlike in the past, in today's India there is no central authority telling people what to produce or deciding what people can consume. Each individual producer makes what they think will be most profitable; each consumer buys what they choose.

If you had never seen a market economy in action, you might imagine that it would be chaotic. After all, nobody is in charge. But market economies are able to coordinate even highly complex activities and reliably provide consumers with the goods and services they want. Indeed, people quite casually trust their lives to the market system: residents of any major city would starve in a few days if the unplanned yet somehow orderly actions of thousands of businesses did not deliver a steady supply of food. In fact, the unplanned "chaos" of a market economy turns out to be far more orderly than the planning of a command economy. And that's why almost every country in the world—North Korea, Cuba, and Venezuela are the only exceptions—has become a market economy.

The benefits of a market economy are not a new discovery. In 1776, in a famous passage in his book *The Wealth of Nations,* the pioneering Scottish economist Adam Smith wrote about how individuals, in pursuing their own interests, often end up serving the interests of society as a whole. Of a businessman whose pursuit of profit makes the entire nation wealthier, Smith wrote: "[H]e intends only his own gain, and he is in this, as in many other cases, led by an invisible hand to promote an end which was no part of his intention." Ever since, economists have used the term **invisible hand** to refer to the way a market economy harnesses the power of self-interest for the good of society.

The study of how individuals make decisions and how these decisions interact is called **microeconomics.** One of the key themes in microeconomics is the validity of Adam Smith's insight: individuals pursuing their own interests often do promote the interests of society as a whole.

So the answer to our first question—"How does our economic system manage to deliver goods and services to people?"—is that self-interest, operating within a market economy—that is, the invisible hand—guides production and consumption decisions to promote society's interests.

But the invisible hand isn't always our friend. It's also important to understand when and why the individual pursuit of self-interest can lead to counterproductive behavior and undesirable outcomes for society. Excessive pollution and traffic congestion are prime examples.

According to Adam Smith, a market economy manages to harness the power of self-interest for the common good.

market economy an economy in which decisions about production and consumption are made by individual producers and consumers.

invisible hand a phrase used by Adam Smith to refer to the way in which an individual's pursuit of self-interest can lead, without the individual intending it, to good results for society as a whole.

microeconomics the branch of economics that studies how people make decisions and how these decisions interact.

‖ My Benefit, Your Cost

In most ways, life in India is immensely better than it was in 1980. Two things have, however, gotten much worse: traffic congestion and air quality. The average speed in Bangalore is only around 12 miles an hour. The air is also very unhealthy, although not as bad as in Delhi, India's capital, where some estimates say that pollution reduces life expectancy by 10 years.

market failure the failure of a market to be efficient.

recession a downturn in the economy.

macroeconomics the branch of economics that is concerned with the overall ups and downs in the economy.

Why do these problems represent failures of the invisible hand? Consider the case of traffic congestion.

When traffic is congested, each driver is imposing a cost on all the other drivers on the road—every driver is literally getting in the way of every other driver. The cost can be substantial: one estimate found that someone driving a car into lower Manhattan on a weekday causes more than three hours of delays to other drivers, and around $160 in monetary losses. Yet when deciding whether or not to drive and instead take public transportation, commuters have no incentive to take the costs they impose on others into account.

Traffic congestion is a familiar example of a much broader problem in market economies: **market failure,** which happens when the individual pursuit of one's own interest, instead of promoting the interests of society as a whole, actually makes society worse off. Another important example of market failure is air pollution, which is all too visible, literally, in India's cities. Water pollution and the overexploitation of natural resources such as fish and forests are variations of the same problem.

Today, the environmental costs of self-interested behavior are huge. As we will discuss later in this book, environmental degradation and climate change caused by pollution are arguably the greatest challenges facing society. The good news, as you will learn when you study microeconomics, is that economic analysis can be used to diagnose cases of market failure and to devise solutions. Economic analysis shows that government intervention is called for in the presence of extensive market failures like environmental degradation and climate change. And as we know now, government intervention has been critical in responding to Covid-19.

Good Times, Bad Times

India has become an enormous economic powerhouse. One somewhat ironic consequence of India's rise is that people around the world sometimes suffer when India finds itself in economic difficulties because the nation is both a major supplier of some crucial goods—like medicine—and a major source of demand for other countries' products.

India was hit hard by Covid-19, which was responsible for millions of deaths as well as a severe economic contraction. While the cause of this setback was unusual, occasional troubled periods are a regular feature of modern economies. The fact is that the economy does not always run smoothly: it experiences fluctuations, a series of ups and downs. By middle age, a typical American will have experienced three or four downs, known as **recessions.** The U.S. economy experienced recessions, some serious, in 1973, 1981, 1990, 2001, 2007, and 2020. During a recession, wages stagnate, jobs are hard to find, and millions of workers may be laid off.

Like market failure, recessions are a fact of life; but also like market failure, they are a problem for which economic analysis offers some solutions. Recessions are one of the main concerns of the branch of economics known as **macroeconomics,** which is concerned with the overall ups and downs of the economy. If you study macroeconomics, you will learn how economists explain recessions and how government policies can be used to minimize the damage from economic fluctuations.

Despite the occasional recession, however, over the long run the stories of all major economies contain many more ups than downs. And that long-run ascent is the subject of our final question.

Onward and Upward

The overall standard of living of the average resident of Bangalore, while immensely higher than it was in 1980, is still pretty low by U.S. standards.

"Remember, an economic boom is usually followed by an economic kaboom."

But then, the United States wasn't always as rich as it is today. Indeed, at the beginning of the twentieth century, most Americans lived under conditions that we would now think of as extreme poverty. Only 10% of homes had flush toilets, only 8% had central heating, only 2% had electricity, and almost nobody had a car, let alone a washing machine or air conditioning. But over the course of the following century, the United States achieved a remarkable rise in living standards that ultimately led to the great wealth that we see around us today.

Such comparisons are a stark reminder of how much lives around the world have been changed by **economic growth,** the increasing ability of the economy to produce goods and services, leading to higher living standards. Why does the economy grow over time? And why does economic growth occur faster in some places and times than in others? These are key questions for economics, because economic growth is a good thing, for many, as the citizens of India can attest, and most of us want more of it. But economic growth does come with some costs.

Despite benefiting the vast majority of people, economic growth has always created losers as well as winners as fast-growing, emerging sectors of the economy eclipse those of the past. For example, Mumbai has become home to wealthy Indians and the headquarters of many Indian companies. This development has made the city a very expensive place to live, displacing many poorer residents.

The environment is another potential loser. Unless sufficient attention is paid to achieving *sustainable long-run economic growth*—economic growth over the long run that balances protection of the environment with improved living standards for current and future generations—the risk of catastrophic environmental change increases and we will all lose. Today, the goal of balancing the production of goods and services with the health of the environment is a hotly debated policy topic. Economic analysis has a key role to play here because environmental degradation is often a result of market failure.

Economics isn't a list of answers; rather, it's a discipline, a means for understanding. In an unpredictable and changing world, economics provides a framework to understand how individuals function, how they adapt and respond. Now, more than ever, an economics education is a critical element in giving individuals, firms, governments, and society the ability to respond successfully to the opportunities and challenges ahead. So let's not waste time.

economic growth the growing ability of the economy to produce goods and services, leading to higher living standards.

KEY TERMS

Economy, p. 2
Economics, p. 2
Market economy, p. 3

Invisible hand, p. 3
Microeconomics, p. 3
Market failure, p. 4

Recession, p. 4
Macroeconomics, p. 4
Economic growth, p. 5

1 > First Principles

THERE WAS A TIME when most of the world's college students were located in wealthy Western nations. Today, however, the number of college students in developing countries like China and India is rapidly overtaking the number in the United States and Western Europe. In fact, China already has more students enrolled in college than the United States does.

And what are these students studying? A variety of subjects, of course. But regardless of the region of the world, a lot of students will be studying economics.

Regardless of where in the world you study, the basic principles of economics are the same.

You might wonder, however, whether the economics being taught at, say, Shanghai University or the University of Mumbai bears much resemblance to the economics being taught in U.S. colleges. After all, there are big differences between nations in levels of income, political institutions, and the problems they face. Doesn't this mean that the economics in these countries is different, too?

The answer is, yes and no. "Yes," because different circumstances and history affect what both students and practitioners need to know. That's why there are international editions of this textbook. Canada, for example, is different enough from the United States to warrant its own edition with explanations about Canadian economic issues and institutions.

The answer is also "no" because much of the material covered in basic economics is the same wherever you are around the world. The reason for this is that all economics is based on a set of common principles that apply to many different issues, regardless of the particular setting.

Some of these principles involve *individual choice* — for economics is, first of all, about the choices that individuals make. Do you save your money and take the bus or do you buy a car? Do you keep your old phone or upgrade to a new one? These decisions involve *making a choice* from a limited number of alternatives — limited because no one can have everything that they want. Every question in economics at its most basic level involves individuals making choices.

But to understand how an economy works, you need to understand more than how individuals make choices. None of us are like the fictional Robinson Crusoe, living alone on an island. Every person must make decisions in an environment that is shaped by the decisions of others. So in this chapter we will learn about four principles of economics that guide the choices made by individuals.

Indeed, in a modern economy even the simplest decisions you make — say, what to have for breakfast — are shaped by the decisions of thousands of other people, from the banana grower in Costa Rica who decided to grow the fruit you eat to the farmer in Iowa who provided the corn in your cornflakes.

Because each of us in a market economy depends on so many others — and they, in turn, depend on us — our choices interact. So although all economics at a basic level is about individual choice, in order to understand how market economies behave we must also understand *economic interaction* — how my choices affect your choices, and vice versa. To that end, in this chapter you will study the four principles that govern how individual choices interact in the economy.

Although many important economic interactions can be understood by looking at the markets for individual goods (like the market for corn), when we consider the economy as a whole, we see that it is composed of an enormous number of markets for individual goods, and these many markets interact. As a result, the larger economy experiences ups and downs. In order to understand economy-wide interactions, in this chapter we will study the three principles that underlie their behavior.

These 11 principles are the basis of all economic analysis. They form the common ground of economics. And they apply just as much in Shanghai or Mumbai as they do in Omaha or Atlanta. •

WHAT YOU WILL LEARN

- What four principles guide the choices made by individuals?
- What four principles govern how individual choices interact?
- What three principles illustrate economy-wide interactions?

7

Principles That Underlie Individual Choice: The Core of Economics

Every economic issue involves, at its most basic level, **individual choice**— decisions by an individual about what to do and what not to do. In fact, you might say that it isn't economics if it isn't about choice.

Take Walmart or Amazon. There are thousands of different products available, and it is extremely unlikely that you—or anyone else—could afford to buy everything you might want to have. And anyway, there's only so much space in your dorm room or apartment. So will you buy another bookcase or a mini-refrigerator? Given limitations on your budget and your living space, you must choose which products to buy and which to leave on the shelf.

The fact that those products are on the shelf in the first place involves choice—the store manager chose to put them there, and the manufacturers of the products chose to produce them. All economic activities involve individual choice.

Four economic principles underlie the economics of individual choice, as shown in Table 1. We'll now examine each of these principles.

Principle #1: Choices Are Necessary Because Resources Are Scarce

You can't always get what you want. Many of us would like to have a big beautiful house or apartment in a great location, a new car or two, and vacations in exotic locations each year. But even in a rich country like the United States, not many families can afford all that. So they must make choices—like whether to go to Disney World this year or buy a better car, or whether to move to the city where housing is expensive, or accept a longer commute in order to live where housing prices are cheaper.

Limited income isn't the only thing that keeps us from having everything we want. Time is also in limited supply: there are only 24 hours in a day. Choosing to spend time on one activity means choosing not to spend time on something else—studying for an exam means forgoing a night spent watching a movie. Indeed, many people faced with the limited number of hours in the day are willing to trade money for time. For example, local convenience stores typically charge higher prices than a regular supermarket. But they fulfill a valuable role by catering to time-pressed customers who would rather pay more than travel farther to the supermarket.

This leads us to our first principle of individual choice:

> *People must make choices because resources are scarce.*

A **resource** is anything that can be used to produce something else. Lists of the economy's resources usually begin with land, labor (the time of workers), capital (machinery, buildings, and other man-made productive assets), and human capital (the educational achievements and skills of workers). A resource is **scarce** when there's not enough of the resource available to satisfy all the ways a society wants to use it.

There are many scarce resources. These include natural resources that come from the physical environment, such as minerals, lumber, and petroleum. There is also a limited quantity of human resources, such as labor, skill, and intelligence. And in a growing world economy with a rapidly increasing human population, even clean air and water have become scarce resources.

Just as individuals must make choices, the scarcity of resources means that society as a whole must make choices. One way a society with a market economy makes choices is by allowing them to emerge from many individual choices. For example, Americans as a group have only so many hours in a week. How many of those hours will be spent traveling to supermarkets to get lower prices, rather

---

TABLE 1 Principles of Individual Choice

1. People must make choices because resources are scarce.
2. The opportunity cost of an item—what you must give up in order to get it—is its true cost.
3. "How much" decisions require making trade-offs at the margin: comparing the costs and benefits of doing a little bit more of an activity versus doing a little bit less.
4. People respond to incentives, exploiting opportunities to make themselves better off.

Ben Heys/Shutterstock

Resources are scarce.

individual choice the decision by an individual of what to do, which necessarily involves a decision of what not to do.

resource something that can be used to produce something else; includes natural resources (from the physical environment) and human resources (labor, skill, intelligence).

scarce in short supply; a resource is scarce when there is not enough of the resource available to satisfy all the various ways a society wants to use it.

than saving time by shopping at local convenience stores? The answer is the sum of individual decisions: each of the millions of individuals in the economy makes a choice about where to shop, and the overall choice is simply the sum of those individual decisions.

opportunity cost the real cost of an item: what you must give up in order to get it.

Principle #2: The True Cost of Something Is Its Opportunity Cost

It is the last term before you graduate, and your class schedule allows you to take only one elective. There are two, however, that you really want to take: Data Visualization Basics and Introduction to Wildlife Conservation.

Suppose you decide to take the Intro to Wildlife Conservation course. What's the cost of that decision? It is, primarily, the fact that you can't take the Data Visualization class, your next best alternative choice. Economists call that kind of cost—what you must give up in order to get an item you want—the **opportunity cost** of that item. This leads us to our second principle of individual choice:

> *The opportunity cost of an item—what you must give up in order to get it—is its true cost.*

So the opportunity cost of taking the Intro to Wildlife Conservation class includes the benefit you would have derived from the Data Visualization class.

The concept of opportunity cost is crucial to understanding individual choice because, in the end, all costs are opportunity costs. That's because every choice you make means forgoing some other alternative.

Sometimes critics claim that economists are concerned only with costs and benefits that can be measured in dollars and cents. But that is not true. Much economic analysis involves cases like our electives example, where it costs no extra tuition to take one elective course instead of another—that is, there is no direct monetary cost. Nonetheless, the elective you choose has an opportunity cost—the other desirable elective course that you must forgo because time limits permit you to take only one. More specifically, the opportunity cost of a choice is what you forgo by not choosing your next best alternative.

You might think that opportunity cost is an add-on—that is, something *additional* to the monetary cost of an item. But it isn't. Suppose that an elective class costs an additional $750. Now there is a monetary cost to taking Intro to Wildlife Conservation. Is the opportunity cost of taking that course something separate from that monetary cost?

Yes, it is. Consider that you will have to spend that $750 no matter which class you take. So what you give up to take Intro to Wildlife Conservation is still the Data Visualization class—you have to spend that $750 either way. But what if the Data Visualization class is free? In that case, what you give up to take the Intro to Wildlife Conservation class is the benefit from the data visualization class *plus* the benefit you could have gained from spending the $750 on other things.

Either way, the real cost of taking your preferred class is what you must give up to get it. As you expand the set of decisions that underlie each choice—whether to take an elective or not, whether to finish this term or not, whether to drop out or not—you'll realize that all costs are ultimately opportunity costs.

Sometimes the money you have to pay for something is a good indication of its opportunity cost. But many times it is not.

One very important example of how poorly monetary cost can indicate opportunity cost is the cost of attending college. Tuition and housing are major monetary expenses for most

Jalen Lewis understood the concept of opportunity cost.

David Dow/Getty Images

students; but even if they were free, attending college would still be an expensive proposition because most college students, if they were not in college, would have a job. By going to college, then, students *forgo* the income they could have earned if they had worked instead. This means that the opportunity cost of attending college is what you pay for tuition and housing plus the forgone income you would have earned in a job.

It's easy to see that the opportunity cost of going to college is especially high for people who could be earning a lot during what would otherwise have been their college years. That is why star athletes and successful entrepreneurs often skip or leave college early.

Principle #3: "How Much" Is a Decision at the Margin

Some of the decisions we make involve an "either–or" choice—for example, you decide either to go to college or to begin working; you decide either to take economics or something else. But other important decisions involve "how much" choices—for example, if you are taking both economics and chemistry this semester, you must decide how much time to spend studying for each. When it comes to understanding "how much" decisions, economics has an important insight to offer: "how much" is a decision made at the margin.

Suppose you are taking both economics and chemistry. And suppose you are a pre-med student, so your grade in chemistry matters more to you than your grade in economics. Should you spend *all* your study time on chemistry and wing it on the economics exam? Probably not; even if you think your chemistry grade is more important, you should put some effort into studying economics.

Spending more time studying chemistry involves a benefit (a higher expected grade in that course) and a cost (you could have spent that time doing something else, such as studying to get a higher grade in economics). That is, your decision involves a **trade-off**—a comparison of costs and benefits.

How do you decide this kind of "how much" question? The typical answer is that you make the decision a bit at a time, by asking how you should spend the next hour. If both exams are the next day, you will spend the night reviewing your notes for both courses. At 6:00 P.M., you decide that it's a good idea to spend at least an hour on each course. At 8:00 P.M., you decide you need to spend another hour on each course. At 10:00 P.M., you are getting tired and figure you have one more hour to study before bed. Do you study chemistry or economics? If you are pre-med, it's likely to be chemistry; if you are a business major, it's likely to be economics.

Note how you've made the decision to allocate your time: at each point the question is whether or not to spend *one more hour* on either course. In deciding whether to spend that hour studying chemistry, you weigh the costs (an hour forgone of studying economics or an hour forgone of sleeping) versus the benefits (a likely increase in your chemistry grade). As long as the benefit of studying chemistry for one more hour outweighs the cost, you should choose to study for that additional hour.

Decisions of this type—whether to do a bit more or a bit less of an activity, like what to do with your next hour, your next dollar, and so on—are **marginal decisions.** This brings us to our third principle of individual choice:

> *"How much" decisions require making trade-offs at the margin: comparing the costs and benefits of doing a little bit more of an activity versus doing a little bit less.*

The study of such decisions is known as **marginal analysis.** Many of the questions that we face in real life involve marginal analysis: How many minutes should I exercise? How many hours should I work? What is an acceptable rate of negative side effects from a new medicine? Marginal analysis plays a central role in economics because it is the key to deciding "how much" of an activity to do.

trade-off a comparison of costs and benefits of doing something.

marginal decision a decision made at the "margin" of an activity to do a bit more or a bit less of that activity.

marginal analysis the study of marginal decisions.

Principle #4: People Respond to Incentives, Exploiting Opportunities to Make Themselves Better Off

While listening to the news one day, the authors heard a great tip about cheap parking in Manhattan. At the time, garages in the Wall Street area charged as much as $30 per day. But according to this news report, some people had found a better way: instead of parking in a garage, they had their oil changed at the Manhattan Jiffy Lube for $19.95—and they keep your car all day!

An incentive that cuts waste: Shoppers switch to reusable shopping bags when charged a fee for disposable bags at checkout.

It's a great story, but unfortunately it turned out not to be true—in fact, there is no Jiffy Lube in Manhattan. But if there were, you can be sure there would be a lot of oil changes there. Why? Because when people are offered opportunities to make themselves better off, they take them—and if they could find a way to park their car all day for $19.95 rather than $30, they would.

In this example, economists say that people are responding to an **incentive**—an opportunity to make themselves better off, which leads to our fourth principle of individual choice:

> *People respond to incentives, exploiting opportunities to make themselves better off.*

When you try to predict how individuals will behave in an economic situation, it is a very good bet that they will respond to incentives—that is, exploit opportunities to make themselves better off. Furthermore, individuals will *continue* to exploit these opportunities until they have been fully exhausted. If there really were a Manhattan Jiffy Lube and an oil change really were a cheap way to park your car, we can safely predict that before long the waiting list for oil changes would be weeks, if not months.

In fact, the principle that people will exploit opportunities to make themselves better off is the basis of *all* predictions by economists about individual behavior.

In fact, economists tend to be skeptical of any attempt to change behavior that *doesn't* change incentives. For example, a plan aimed at reducing traffic in Manhattan that doesn't offer Manhattan-bound drivers an incentive, like a financial reward, for not driving, or that isn't accompanied by a penalty for driving, is unlikely to succeed. Likewise, a plan that calls on manufacturers to reduce pollution voluntarily probably won't be effective. In contrast, a plan that gives them a financial reward to reduce pollution is a lot more likely to succeed because it has changed their incentives.

So are we ready to do economics? Not yet—because most of the interesting things that happen in the economy are the result not merely of individual choices but of the way in which individual choices interact.

ECONOMICS >> *in Action*
The Cost of Marriage: China's One-Child Policy Created Millions of Lonely Bachelors

China is the most populous country on Earth, with over 1,440,000,000 people, as of 2021. That's over *one billion four hundred forty million* people. And trends in Chinese demographics have shifted the cost of marriage over time—specifically, the cost of finding a bride for Chinese bachelors.

In the 1970s, China was very poor and had an already large and growing population. Concerned that it would be unable to adequately provide care for so

incentive anything that offers rewards to people to change their behavior.

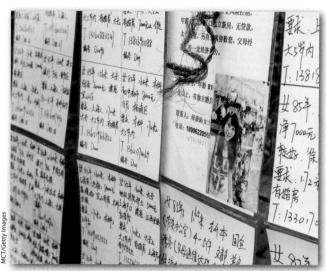

The cost of finding a bride is quite high for millions of men in China.

many people, the Chinese government introduced a one-child policy that restricted most couples to only one child and imposed penalties on those who defied the mandate. By 2021, the average number of children per Chinese woman had fallen to 1.7, from more than 5 before the policy was introduced in 1978. And in big Chinese cities like Beijing and Shanghai, the fertility rate is the lowest in the world—about 0.7. This is well below the replacement fertility rate of 2.1, the minimum rate necessary to maintain the population, and implies that the Chinese population will shrink over time.

But the one-child policy has led to an unfortunate unintended consequence on the balance between the sexes in the population. Until recently China was overwhelmingly rural. Because of the physical demands of farming, sons were strongly preferred over daughters. In addition, tradition dictated that sons, not daughters, took care of elderly parents. The effect of the one-child policy was to greatly increase the perceived cost to a Chinese family of a female child. As a result, while some female infants were given up for adoption abroad, many simply "disappeared" during the first year of life, victims of neglect and mistreatment as Chinese families were determined that their only child be a son. The Nobel Prize–winning economist Amartya Sen calculated that there were millions of "missing women" in Asia due to the perceived higher cost of female children, with estimates running from 45 million to 100 million missing women.

The number of boys in China has outpaced the number of girls for 20 years. Today, there are nearly 34 million *excess* males in the population compared to females. That's the equivalent of the entire population of California—men who will never find wives from among their fellow Chinese.

As of 2019, within the age group of 10- to 19-year-olds, there were 120 males for every 100 women, with projections that there will be as many as 190 young men per 100 young women by 2050. So, although the Chinese government officially ended the one-child policy in 2015, the consequences will endure for decades.

Not surprisingly, some Chinese bachelors are eager to meet eligible women from abroad—particularly from nearby countries such as Vietnam, Laos, and Cambodia that don't have a problem with gender imbalance. And enterprising eligible women from those countries are coming to China to find husbands. Marriage brokers have sprung up in these countries to address the situation in China. For example, one Chinese bachelor, Liu Hua, found happiness with Lili, a Cambodian woman who came to China to find a husband. Before meeting Lili, Liu lived in a village with 60 bachelors and only 2 single women. He ended up paying deposits ranging from $5,000 to $40,000 to three families in nearby villages for the opportunity to date their daughters (not all of which was refunded when the matches didn't work out). He eventually paid a $15,000 broker's fee to marry Lili. Happily married, they now have two children—a boy *and* a girl.

>> Quick Review

- All economic activities involve **individual choice.**
- People must make choices because **resources** are **scarce.**
- The real cost of something is its **opportunity cost**—what you must give up to get it. All costs are opportunity costs. Monetary costs are sometimes a good indicator of opportunity costs, but not always.
- Many choices involve not *whether* to do something but *how much* of it to do. "How much" choices call for making a **trade-off** at the margin. The study of **marginal decisions** is known as **marginal analysis.**
- Because people exploit opportunities to make themselves better off, **incentives** can change people's behavior.

>> Check Your Understanding 1-1
Solutions appear at back of book.

1. Explain how each of the following illustrates one of the four principles of individual choice.
   a. You are on your third trip to a restaurant's all-you-can-eat dessert buffet and are feeling very full. Although it would cost you no additional money, you forgo a slice of coconut cream pie but have a slice of chocolate cake.
   b. Even if there were more resources in the world, there would still be scarcity.
   c. Different teaching assistants teach several Economics 101 tutorials. Those taught by the teaching assistants with the best reputations fill up quickly, with spaces left unfilled in the ones taught by assistants with poor reputations.

d. To decide how many hours per week to exercise, you compare the health benefits of one more hour of exercise to the effect on your grades of one less hour spent studying.

2. You make $45,000 per year at your current job with Whiz Kids Consultants. You are considering a job offer from Brainiacs, Inc., that will pay you $50,000 per year. Which of the following are elements of the opportunity cost of accepting the new job at Brainiacs, Inc.?
   a. The increased time spent commuting to your new job
   b. The $45,000 salary from your old job
   c. The more spacious office at your new job

Interaction: How Economies Work

An economy is a system for coordinating the productive activities of many people. In a market economy like we live in, coordination takes place without any coordinator: each individual makes their own choices.

Yet those choices are by no means independent of one another: each individual's opportunities, and hence choices, depend to a large extent on the choices made by other people. So to understand how a market economy behaves, we have to examine this **interaction** in which my choices affect your choices, and vice versa.

When studying economic interaction, we quickly learn that the end result of individual choices may be quite different from what any one individual intends. Consider the case of farmers in the United States, who, over the past century have adopted new farming techniques and crop strains that have reduced their costs and increased their yields. The end result of each farmer trying to increase their own income has actually been to drive many farmers out of business. Because U.S. farmers have been so successful at producing larger yields, agricultural prices have steadily fallen, reducing the incomes of many farmers, and as a result fewer people find farming worth doing. That is, an individual farmer who plants a better variety of corn is better off, but when many farmers plant a better variety of corn, the result may be to make farmers as a group worse off.

There are four principles underlying the economics of interaction. These principles are summarized in Table 2 and we will now examine each one.

Principle #5: There Are Gains from Trade

Why do the choices I make interact with the choices you make? A family could try to take care of all its own needs—growing its own food, sewing its own clothing, providing itself with entertainment. But trying to live that way would be very hard.

The key to a much better standard of living for everyone is **trade,** in which people divide tasks among themselves and each person provides a good or service that other people want in return for different goods and services that they want.

The reason we have an economy, not many self-sufficient individuals, is that there are **gains from trade:** by dividing tasks and trading, two people (or 6 billion people) can each get more of what they want than they could get by being self-sufficient. This leads us to our fifth principle:

There are gains from trade.

Gains from trade arise from this division of tasks, which economists call **specialization**—a situation in which different people each engage in a different task, specializing in those tasks that they are good at performing. The advantages of specialization, and the resulting gains from trade, were the starting point for

interaction (of choices) my choices affect your choices, and vice versa; a feature of most economic situations. The results of this interaction are often quite different from what the individuals intend.

trade the practice, in a market economy, in which individuals provide goods and services to others and receive goods and services in return.

gains from trade gains achieved by dividing tasks and trading; in this way people can get more of what they want through trade than they could if they tried to be self-sufficient.

specialization the situation in which each person specializes in the task that they are good at performing.

TABLE 2 Principles of Interaction of Individual Choices

5. There are gains from trade.

6. Markets move toward equilibrium.

7. Resources should be used efficiently to achieve society's goals.

8. Markets usually lead to efficiency, but when they don't, government intervention can improve society's welfare.

"I hunt and they gather—otherwise, we couldn't make ends meet."

Adam Smith's 1776 book *The Wealth of Nations,* which many regard as the beginning of economics as a discipline.

Smith's book begins with a description of an eighteenth-century pin factory where, rather than each of the 10 workers making a pin from start to finish, each worker specialized in one of the many steps in pin-making:

> One man draws out the wire, another straights it, a third cuts it, a fourth points it, a fifth grinds it at the top for receiving the head; to make the head requires two or three distinct operations; to put it on, is a particular business, to whiten the pins is another; it is even a trade by itself to put them into the paper; and the important business of making a pin is, in this manner, divided into about eighteen distinct operations. . . . Those ten persons, therefore, could make among them upwards of forty-eight thousand pins in a day. But if they had all wrought separately and independently, and without any of them having been educated to this particular business, they certainly could not each of them have made twenty, perhaps not one pin a day. . . .

The same principle applies when we look at how people divide tasks among themselves and trade in an economy. *The economy, as a whole, can produce more when each person specializes in a task and trades with others.*

The benefits of specialization are the reason a person typically chooses only one career. It takes many years of study and experience to become a physician or a commercial pilot. Many physicians might well have had the potential to become excellent pilots, and vice versa. But it is very unlikely that anyone who decided to pursue both careers would be as good at both as someone who decided at the beginning to specialize in a single field. So it is to everyone's advantage that individuals specialize in their careers.

Markets allow a physician and a pilot to specialize in their own fields. Because markets for commercial flights and for medical care exist, a physician is assured that she can find a flight and a pilot is assured that he can find a physician. As long as individuals know that they can find the goods and services they want in the market, they are willing to forgo self-sufficiency and to specialize. But what assures people that markets will deliver what they want? The answer to that question leads us to our next principle of how individual choices interact.

DANIEL SLIM/Getty Images

Witness equilibrium in action on the checkout line.

equilibrium an economic situation in which no individual would be better off doing something different.

Principle #6: Markets Move Toward Equilibrium

It's a busy afternoon at the supermarket; there are long lines at the checkout counters. Then one of the previously closed cash registers opens. What happens right away, of course, is a rush to that register. After a couple of minutes, however, things will have settled down. Shoppers will have rearranged themselves so that the line at the newly opened register is about the same length as the lines at all the other registers.

How do we know this? We know from our fourth principle that people will exploit opportunities to make themselves better off. People will rush to the newly opened register to save time standing in line. The rushing around will stop when shoppers can no longer improve their position by switching lines—that is, when the opportunities to make themselves better off have all been exploited.

A story about supermarket checkout lines may seem to have little to do with how individual choices interact, but in fact it illustrates an important principle. A situation in which individuals cannot make themselves better off by doing something different—the situation in which all the checkout lines are the same length—is what economists call an **equilibrium.** An economic situation is in equilibrium when no individual would be better off doing something different.

Recall the story about the mythical Jiffy Lube, where it was supposedly cheaper to leave your car for an oil change than to pay for parking. If the opportunity had really existed and people were still paying $30 to park in garages, the situation would *not* have been an equilibrium. And that should have been a giveaway that the story couldn't be true. In reality, people would have seized an opportunity to park cheaply, just as they seize opportunities to save time at the checkout line. And in so doing they would have eliminated the opportunity! Either it would have become very hard to get an appointment for an oil change or the price of a lube job would have increased to the point that it was no longer an attractive option (unless you really needed an oil change). This brings us to our sixth principle:

> *Because people respond to incentives, markets move toward equilibrium.*

As we will see, markets usually reach equilibrium through changes in prices, which rise or fall until no opportunities for individuals to make themselves better off remain.

The concept of equilibrium is extremely helpful in understanding economic interactions because it provides a way to cut through the sometimes complex details of those interactions. To understand what happens when a new line opens at a supermarket, you don't need to worry about exactly how shoppers rearrange themselves, which register just opened, and so on. What you need to know is that any time there is a change, the situation will move to an equilibrium.

The fact that markets move toward equilibrium is why we can depend on them to work in a predictable way. In fact, we can trust markets to supply us with the essentials of life. For example, people who live in cities can be sure that the supermarket shelves will always be fully stocked. Why? Because if some merchants who distribute food *didn't* make deliveries, a big profit opportunity would be created for any merchant who did—and there would be a rush to supply food, just like the rush to a newly opened cash register.

So the market ensures that food will always be available for city dwellers. And, returning to our fifth principle, this allows city dwellers to be city dwellers—to specialize in doing city jobs rather than living on farms and growing their own food.

A market economy, as we have seen, allows people to achieve gains from trade. But how do we know how well such an economy is doing? The next principle gives us a standard to use in evaluating an economy's performance.

Principle #7: Resources Should Be Used Efficiently to Achieve Society's Goals

You are attending a lecture in a classroom that is too small for the number of students—many of your fellow classmates are standing or sitting on the floor—despite the fact that large, empty classrooms are available nearby. You would be correct to say that this is no way to run a college. Economists would call this an *inefficient* use of resources. But if an inefficient use of resources is undesirable, just what does it mean to use resources *efficiently?*

You might imagine that the efficient use of resources has something to do with money, maybe that it is measured in dollars-and-cents terms. But in economics, as in life, money is only a means to other ends. The measure that economists really care about is not money but people's happiness or welfare. Economists say that *an economy's resources are used efficiently when they are used in a way that has fully exploited all opportunities to make everyone better off.* Put another way: an economy is **efficient** if it takes all opportunities to make some people better off without making other people worse off.

efficient description of a market or economy that takes all opportunities to make some people better off without making other people worse off.

Sometimes equity trumps efficiency.

In our classroom example, there clearly was a way to make everyone better off—move the lecture to a larger room. Students attending the lecture would be made better off without hurting anyone else at the college. This result would be an efficient use of the college's resources. Assigning the course to the smaller classroom was an inefficient use of those resources.

When an economy is efficient, it is producing the maximum gains from trade possible given the resources available. Why? Because there is no way to rearrange how resources are used so that everyone can be made better off. When an economy is efficient, one person can be made better off by rearranging how resources are used *only* by making someone else worse off.

In our example, if all larger classrooms were already occupied, the college would actually have been run efficiently: to make your class better off by moving it to a larger classroom would displace other students already in a larger room. Those students would be made worse off by a move.

We can now state our seventh principle:

> *Resources should be used as efficiently as possible to achieve society's goals.*

Should policy makers always strive to achieve economic efficiency? Well, not quite, because efficiency is only a means to achieving society's goals. Sometimes efficiency may conflict with a goal that society has deemed worthwhile to achieve. For example, in most societies, people also care about issues of fairness, or **equity.** And there is typically a trade-off between equity and efficiency: policies that promote equity often come at a cost of decreased efficiency in the economy, and vice versa.

To see this, consider the case of disabled-designated parking spaces in public parking lots. Many people have difficulty walking due to age or disability, so it seems only fair to assign closer parking spaces specifically for their use. You may have noticed, however, that a certain amount of inefficiency is involved. To ensure that a parking space is always available should a disabled person want one, there are typically more such spaces available than there are disabled people who want one. As a result, desirable parking spaces are unused. (And the temptation for nondisabled people to use them is so great that drivers must be dissuaded by fear of getting a ticket.)

So, short of hiring parking valets to allocate spaces, there is a conflict between *equity*, making life "fairer" for disabled people, and *efficiency*, making sure that all opportunities to make people better off have been fully exploited by never letting close-in parking spaces go unused.

Exactly how far policy makers should go in promoting equity over efficiency is a difficult question that goes to the heart of the political process. As such, it is not a question that economists can answer. What is important for economists, however, is always to seek to use the economy's resources as efficiently as possible in the pursuit of society's goals, whatever those goals may be.

Principle #8: Markets Usually Lead to Efficiency, But When They Don't, Government Intervention Can Improve Society's Welfare

There is no branch of the U.S. government entrusted with ensuring the general economic efficiency of our market economy—we don't have agents tasked with checking that brain surgeons aren't plowing fields or that Minnesota farmers aren't trying to grow oranges. The government doesn't need to enforce the efficient use of resources, because in most cases the invisible hand does the job. As explained in the Introduction, the *invisible hand* refers to how a market economy harnesses the power of self-interest for the good of society.

The incentives built into a market economy ensure that resources are usually put to good use and that opportunities to make people better off are not wasted.

equity fairness; everyone gets their fair share. Since people can disagree about what is "fair," equity is not as well defined a concept as efficiency.

If a college were known for its habit of crowding students into small classrooms while large classrooms went unused, its enrollment would soon drop, putting the jobs of its administrators at risk. The "market" for college students would respond in a way that induces administrators to run the college efficiently.

A detailed explanation of why markets are usually very good at making sure that resources are used efficiently will have to wait until we have studied how markets actually work. But the most basic reason is that in a market economy, in which individuals are free to choose what to consume and what to produce, people normally take opportunities for mutual gain—that is, gains from trade.

If people encounter an opportunity to make themselves better off, they will take advantage of it. And that is exactly what defines efficiency: all the opportunities to make some people better off without making other people worse off have been exploited. We have now arrived at the first half of our eighth principle:

> ### Because people exploit gains from trade, markets usually lead to efficiency.

However, there are exceptions to this principle that markets are generally efficient. In cases of *market failure,* the individual pursuit of self-interest found in markets makes society worse off—that is, the market outcome is inefficient.

Consider the nature of the market failure caused by traffic congestion—commuters driving to work have no incentive to take into account the cost that their actions inflict on other drivers in the form of increased traffic congestion.

Possible remedies to this situation include charging tolls, subsidizing the cost of public transportation, and taxing gasoline sales to individual drivers. These remedies would change the incentives of would-be drivers, motivating them to drive less. But they also share another feature: each relies on government intervention in the market, which leads to the second half of this principle:

> ### When markets don't achieve efficiency, government can intervene to improve society's welfare.

An appropriately designed government policy can sometimes move society closer to an efficient outcome by changing how society's resources are used. And, as we will see next, short of instances of market failure, the general rule is that markets are a remarkably good way of organizing an economy.

ECONOMICS >> *in Action*
Wait, Then Hurry Up, and Wait Again

In a densely populated city like New York, very few people own cars. New Yorkers have typically relied on subways and buses, local taxis, or walking to get where they needed to go. Yet each of these forms of transportation has drawbacks: the subway is often plagued with delays, buses can be slow, taxis are expensive and hard to find during peak travel times, and walking long distances takes time and isn't optimal in bad weather.

Unsurprisingly, the market for transportation changed dramatically with the arrival of ride-hailing services like Uber and Lyft, which have become wildly popular in cities like New York. Hopping into an Uber has been seen as a way to get where you need to go more quickly. In 2019, there were more than 80,000 Uber-affiliated vehicles in New York City, providing an average of 700,000 rides per day. Correspondingly, the number of New Yorkers taking public transportation has declined.

Yet the popularity of ride-hailing services has created one significant drawback. With so many more vehicles on the street, traffic congestion has increased dramatically. A recent study found that in nine large densely populated

The fundamental law of traffic congestion is an example of equilibrium in action.

metropolitan areas (Boston, Chicago, Los Angeles, Miami, New York, Philadelphia, San Francisco, Seattle, and Washington, DC), there was an overall increase of 160% in driving on city streets. New York City transportation officials describe the city as "crippled" by traffic congestion, and they point to a 40% reduction in travel speeds in the borough of Manhattan.

It's an outcome that traffic planners find predictable. Thanks to the new ride-hailing apps that induce more driving and have led to an influx of new cars on city streets, commuters looking for a quick trip in a cab are finding their travel time has increased, making the bus, subway, or walking appealing travel options once again. With commuting times more or less back where they started before ride-hailing services appeared, a new equilibrium has been reached in which travel times across all modes of available transport are unchanged. This predictable outcome resembles what traffic planners call the *fundamental law of traffic congestion:* if a city builds more roads, this induces more driving, and this increase in traffic continues until a new equilibrium is reached, with commuting times more or less back where they started. Whether it's a new ride-hailing app or newly built roads that induces more driving, the ultimate result is that a new equilibrium is reached in which travel times across all modes of transportation are unchanged.

For those who hoped that ride-hailing services would make commuting faster and easier, this result is discouraging. It is, however, a good illustration of the importance of thinking about equilibrium.

>> Quick Review

• Most economic situations involve the **interaction** of choices, sometimes with unintended results. In a market economy, interaction occurs via **trade** between individuals.

• Individuals trade because there are **gains from trade,** which arise from **specialization.** Markets usually move toward **equilibrium** because people exploit gains from trade.

• To achieve society's goals, the use of resources should be **efficient.** But **equity,** as well as efficiency, may be desirable in an economy. There is often a trade-off between equity and efficiency.

• Except for certain well-defined exceptions, markets are normally efficient. When markets fail to achieve efficiency, government intervention can improve society's welfare.

>> Check Your Understanding 1-2
Solutions appear at back of book.

1. Explain how each of the following illustrates one of the four principles of interaction.
   a. At a college tutoring co-op, students can arrange to provide tutoring in subjects they are good in (like economics) in return for receiving tutoring in subjects they struggle with (like philosophy).
   b. The local municipality imposes a law that requires bars and nightclubs near residential areas to keep their noise levels below a certain threshold.
   c. To provide better care for low-income patients, the local municipality has decided to close some underutilized neighborhood clinics and shift funds to the main hospital.
   d. On Amazon, used textbooks of a given title with approximately the same level of wear and tear sell for about the same price.

2. Which of the following describes an equilibrium situation? Which does not? Explain your answer.
   a. The restaurants across the street from the university dining hall serve better-tasting and cheaper meals than those served at the university dining hall. The vast majority of students continue to eat at the dining hall.
   b. You currently take the subway to work. Although taking the bus is cheaper, the ride takes longer. So you are willing to pay the higher subway fare in order to save time.

‖ Economy-Wide Interactions

The economy as a whole—the macroeconomy—has its ups and downs. For example, in 2007 the U.S. economy entered a severe recession in which millions of people lost their jobs, while those who remained employed saw their wages stagnate. It took seven years — until May 2014 — for the number of Americans employed to return to its pre-recession level, but wages didn't recover until 2016.

Over time, the behavior of the macroeconomy is a lot like a drive through a mountain range. The trip isn't one continuous upward climb to a destination at high altitude. Instead, you will drive over hills and valleys, with short-term ups and downs during your journey, as you slowly, but inevitably, ascend to your destination.

In the short run, the overall economy experiences ups and downs: good economic times (recoveries) alternate with bad economic times (recessions), with a cycle lasting an average of 7 to 10 years. However, over the long run, a period of at least 10 years, the economy grows larger and larger. A graph of the total amount of goods and services the economy produces over time would show a line that looks a lot like our car ride: lots of squiggles up and down, but, over time, the line reaches upward.

To understand why the macroeconomy cycles between recessions and recoveries, but also achieves economic growth over time, we need to look at economy-wide interactions. And understanding the big picture of the economy requires three more economic principles, which are summarized in Table 3.

TABLE 3 Principles of Economy-Wide Interactions
9. One person's spending is another person's income.
10. Overall spending sometimes gets out of line with the economy's productive capacity; when it does, government policy can change spending.
11. Increases in the economy's potential lead to economic growth over time.

Principle #9: One Person's Spending Is Another Person's Income

Between 2005 and 2011, including a deep recession, U.S. home construction plunged more than 60% because builders found it increasingly hard to make sales. At first, the damage was limited to the construction industry. But over time the slump spread throughout the economy, with consumer spending falling across the board.

But why should a fall in home construction mean empty stores in the shopping malls? After all, malls are where families, not builders, do their shopping.

The answer is that lower spending on construction led to lower incomes throughout the economy. People who had been employed either directly in construction, producing goods and services builders need (like roofing shingles), or in producing goods and services new homeowners need (like new furniture), either lost their jobs or were forced to take pay cuts. And as incomes fell, so did spending by consumers. This example illustrates our ninth principle:

One person's spending is another person's income.

In a market economy, people make a living selling things — including their labor — to other people. If some group in the economy decides, for whatever reason, to spend more, the incomes of other groups will rise. If some group decides to spend less, the incomes of other groups will fall.

And a chain reaction of changes in spending behavior tends to have repercussions that spread economy-wide. For example, a fall in consumer spending at shopping malls leads to reduced family incomes; families respond by reducing their own spending, which leads to another round of income cuts; and so on. These repercussions play an important role in our understanding of recessions and recoveries.

Principle #10: Overall Spending Sometimes Gets Out of Line with the Economy's Productive Capacity; When It Does, Government Policy Can Change Spending

The coronavirus pandemic which began in 2020 harkened back to a period in the 1930s, known as the Great Depression. Then, as now, a collapse in spending by consumers and businesses led to a plunge in overall spending. In both periods, the plunge in spending led to very high unemployment.

What economists learned from the Great Depression is that overall spending—the amount of goods and services that consumers and businesses want to buy—sometimes doesn't match the amount of goods and services the economy is capable of producing. In the 1930s, as in the Covid lockdown period of 2020 to 2021, spending fell far short of what was needed to keep U.S. workers employed, and the result was a severe economic slump.

It's also possible for overall spending to be too high. In that case, the economy experiences *inflation*, a rise in prices throughout the economy. This rise in prices occurs when the amount that people want to buy outstrips the supply, leading producers to raise their prices and still find willing buyers.

When the economy experiences either shortfalls in spending or excesses in spending, government policies can be used to address the imbalances, which leads to our tenth principle:

> *Overall spending sometimes gets out of line with the economy's productive capacity; when it does, government policy can change spending.*

The U.S. government spends a lot, on everything from military equipment to health care. Moreover, it can choose to spend more or less, depending upon the state of the economy. Likewise, the government can vary how much it collects in taxes, which in turn affects how much income consumers and businesses have to spend. And the government's control of the quantity of money in circulation gives it another powerful tool with which to affect total spending. Government spending, taxes, and control of money are the tools of *macroeconomic policy*.

Modern governments deploy macroeconomic policy tools in an effort to balance overall spending in the economy, trying to steer it between the perils of recession and inflation. These efforts aren't always successful—recessions still happen, as do periods of inflation. But it's widely believed that aggressive efforts to sustain spending in 2008 and 2009 helped prevent the financial crisis of 2008 from turning into a full-blown depression. And in 2020, Congress passed a $4 trillion relief package for U.S. workers and businesses to cushion the blow from the coronavirus pandemic. In 2022, partly as a result of the large increases in government spending, the economy suffered through the highest inflation in over 40 years.

Principle #11: Increases in the Economy's Potential Lead to Economic Growth Over Time

Today's economy is different from the economy of 20 years ago, and drastically different from the economy of a century ago. These changes are due to *economic growth*, the increase in living standards over time. Economic growth has made the United States and other countries far richer over time. Like a car climbing up a mountain range, despite the valleys and hills along the way, the overall path of the economy has been upward in the long run, as Figure 1 illustrates.

What accounts for this growth? It is due to the emergence of new technologies and increases in the resources available for production—resources like land, labor, and machinery. As a result, the economy's *potential*, the total amount of goods and services it can produce, rises and leads to higher living standards. For example, in 1820, 80% of U.S. workers were engaged in farming; now, that figure is 2%. Yet there is a far greater quantity and variety of food available now than 200 years ago. The increased mechanization and technological sophistication of agriculture—humongous tractors and satellite imaging—are changes to the resources available for production. As a result, the economy's potential has risen: U.S. farmers can now produce vastly more than before and U.S. consumers can now consume vastly more than before.

We have now arrived at our eleventh and final principle:

> *Increases in the economy's potential lead to economic growth over time.*

FIGURE 1   Growth in the U.S. Economy Over Time

The overall path of the U.S. economy for the last 200 years, from 1800 to 2000, has been upward, with the inevitable short-term ups and downs along the way.

Y-axis measures real GDP per capita, a measure of economic growth

Data from: Maddison Project Database, version 2020. Jutta Bolt, Robert Inklaar, Hermong de Jong, and Jan Luiten van Zandem (2020).

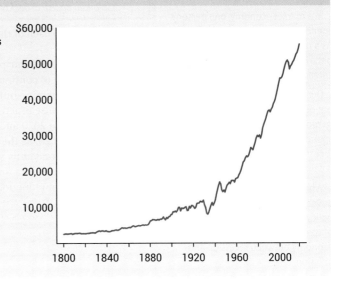

While economic growth has benefitted a vast number of people, the increase in living standards are usually unequally distributed among a country's residents in the short term. In fact, at any given time, an increase in the economy's potential typically creates *winners and losers.*

For example, over the past 20 years, technological advancements have revolutionized the way we produce energy in the United States. New drilling techniques have made natural gas abundant, and alternative energy sources such as solar and wind power have emerged. These new sources of energy, which pollute less than older sources such as coal, benefit both the economy and the environment—they are the winners in our example. But at the same time, the reduced demand for coal has hurt communities where mining has been a primary source of employment, creating losers.

Yet, in a dynamic market economy, losers won't always stay losers. Remember Principle #4: People usually respond to incentives. It implies that unemployed coal miners will eventually migrate to other sectors of the economy where they can find work. They may, for example, become solar panel installers. However, because it takes time for workers to make such a transition (and it may be impossible for older workers), we can also see why Principle #9 applies: Government intervention can improve society's welfare. Government assistance programs can provide a cushion for dislocated workers.

In the end, just as increases in an economy's potential lead to economic growth over time, economic growth inevitably leads to fundamental economic and social change. With these changes come questions (and debates) that are as relevant today as they were back in the eighteenth century when Adam Smith penned *The Wealth of Nations*—questions about equity, the role of government, and appropriate macroeconomic policy remedies.

With advances in technology and greater resources, farmers today produce far more than they did 100 years ago.

>> Quick Review

• In a market economy, one person's spending is another person's income. As a result, changes in spending behavior have repercussions that spread through the economy.

• Overall spending sometimes gets out of line with the economy's capacity to produce goods and services. When spending is too low, the result is a recession. When spending is too high, it causes inflation.

• When spending is out of line, governments can use macroeconomic policy tools to affect the overall level of spending in an effort to steer the economy between recession and inflation.

• Despite the economy's ups and downs, increases in the economy's potential lead to economic growth in the long term, while creating winners and losers in the short term.

>> Check Your Understanding 1-3

Solutions appear at back of book.

1. Explain how each of the following illustrates one of the three principles of economy-wide interactions.

   a. The price of solar panels has fallen by nearly 99% over the past 40 years. Prices are projected to continue falling over the next 30 years.

   b. The economic shutdown in 2020 caused unemployment to soar. In response, the White House urged Congress to pass a package of temporary spending increases and tax cuts in 2020 and 2021.

   c. During 2020, as the coronavirus pandemic raged, people drove less. Gasoline companies responded by sharply cutting production of gasoline. In cities in oil-producing states like Alaska and Texas, restaurants and other consumer businesses experienced significant reductions in their sales.

Airbnb: How Three Guys and an Air Mattress Revolutionized the Lodging Industry

Mikel Taboada/Getty Images

It started out as just a way to pay the rent. In 2007, roommates Joe Gebbia and Brian Chesky found themselves without enough money to pay the rent on their San Francisco apartment. But they had a bright idea. Knowing that there was a convention in town and a shortage of hotel rooms for participants, Gebbia and Chesky figured they could make a little money by providing a place to sleep. So they arranged three air mattresses on the floor and created a website airbedandbreakfast.com. It worked: They made $80 per night and enough money to pay their rent.

Realizing they were onto something that could be a lot bigger than just help in paying the rent, Gebbia and Chesky brought in an old friend, Nathan Blecharczyk as a partner. The three developed a business plan for Airbnb.com, and the rest is history—a very lucrative history. Fourteen years later, the market value of the company was more than $107 billion in December 2021 (that's right—"b" for billion).

It wasn't an easy journey. Early on, the three partners needed investors in the company to provide the funds to build its booking website, hire customer service reps, and advertise. So in 2008, they pitched their idea to 15 investment groups—and received 15 rejections. Refusing to give up, the three partners pitched their services at another conference in 2008 where there was, yet again, a shortage of hotel rooms. A prestigious startup incubator Y Combinator finally recognized the company's potential and gave them the backing to grow the company. One investor who passed up the opportunity to invest in Airbnb now ruefully says, "We couldn't wrap our heads around air mattresses on the living room floor as the next hotel room."

Y Combinator saw that Airbnb's success lay in its ability to spot exploitable opportunities for itself and for its customers. Gebbia, Chesky, and Blecharczyk understood that the internet could bring together those with spare bedrooms (or spare air mattresses) with travelers looking for an alternative to high-priced hotels. While some travelers prefer the security of staying at a well-known hotel chain, some are happy to take a chance on staying in someone's spare bedroom or renting an entire house in order to benefit from a lower price, a better location, or more space. In essence, Airbnb found a way to make everyone better off—including itself since it charges a small fee for each booking it facilitates.

Yet, in 2020, Airbnb's future was at risk. When Covid-19 hit in 2020, virtually all travel came to a screeching halt. The company's 2020 revenue was less than half of its 2019 revenue and it was forced to lay off 25% of its staff. Caught between guests who cancelled their stays and demanded refunds, and hosts who needed the money to stay afloat, the company struggled to respond as its losses escalated. The company's total value fell by half from its 2017 level and industry observers questioned whether it would survive.

The future of Airbnb, and the hosts who relied on it to make money, depended largely on how quickly travel would rebound and whether they had the funds to survive until then. In March 2020, in response to the pandemic, the U.S. Congress passed a federal relief act that provided loans, unemployment assistance, and tax assistance to small business owners such as Airbnb hosts. Likewise, U.S. airlines were saved from bankruptcy by a federal aid package of more than $50 billion. Federal government actions such as early procurement and distribution of Covid-19 vaccines, as well as the issuance of safety guidelines for travel, created the environment for a rebound in U.S. travel in the second half of 2021.

By fall 2021, Airbnb had largely recovered from the pandemic as customers returned to travelling and were reassured by Airbnb's cleaning protocols and ease of social distancing. Moreover, its huge data gathering capability gave it the ability to quickly capitalize on how the market for lodging was swiftly changing in the wake of the pandemic. The company pronounced, "Stays of longer than a few days started increasing as work-from-home became work-from-any-home on Airbnb. We believe the lines between travel and living are blurring, and the global pandemic has accelerated the ability to live anywhere."

QUESTION FOR THOUGHT

1. Explain how each of the 11 principles of economics is illustrated in this case.

SUMMARY

1. All economic analysis is based on a set of basic principles that apply to three levels of economic activity. First, we study how individuals make choices; second, we study how these choices interact; and third, we study how the economy functions overall.

2. Everyone has to make choices about what to do and what *not* to do. **Individual choice** is the basis of economics—if it doesn't involve choice, it isn't economics.

3. The reason choices must be made is that **resources**—anything that can be used to produce something else—are **scarce.** Individuals are limited in their choices by money and time; economies are limited by their supplies of human and natural resources.

4. Because you must choose among limited alternatives, the true cost of anything is what you must give up to get it—all costs are **opportunity costs.**

5. Many economic decisions involve questions not of "whether" but of "how much"—how much to spend on some good, how much to produce, and so on. Such decisions must be made by performing a **trade-off** *at the margin*—by comparing the costs and benefits of doing a bit more or a bit less. Decisions of this type are called **marginal decisions,** and the study of them, **marginal analysis,** plays a central role in economics.

6. The study of how people *should* make decisions is also a good way to understand actual behavior. Individuals usually respond to **incentives**—exploiting opportunities to make themselves better off.

7. The next level of economic analysis is the study of **interaction**—how my choices depend on your choices, and vice versa. When individuals interact, the end result may be different from what anyone intends.

8. Individuals interact because there are **gains from trade:** by engaging in the **trade** of goods and services with one another, the members of an economy can all be made better off. **Specialization**—each person specializes in the task they are good at—is the source of gains from trade.

9. Because individuals usually respond to incentives, markets normally move toward **equilibrium**—a situation in which no individual can make himself or herself better off by taking a different action.

10. An economy is **efficient** if all opportunities to make some people better off without making other people worse off are taken. Resources should be used as efficiently as possible to achieve society's goals. But efficiency is not the sole way to evaluate an economy: **equity,** or fairness, is also desirable, and there is often a trade-off between equity and efficiency.

11. Markets usually lead to efficiency, with some well-defined exceptions. But when markets fail and do not achieve efficiency, government intervention can improve society's welfare.

12. Because people in a market economy earn income by selling things, including their own labor, one person's spending is another person's income. As a result, changes in spending behavior can spread throughout the economy.

13. Overall spending in the economy can get out of line with the economy's productive capacity. Spending below the economy's productive capacity leads to a recession; spending in excess of the economy's productive capacity leads to inflation. When overall spending gets out of line, governments can use macroeconomic policy tools to steer the economy between recession and inflation.

14. Increases in the economy's potential lead to economic growth over time. Although economic growth leads to higher living standards for everyone over time, in the short run, increases in the economy's potential lead to both winners and losers.

KEY TERMS

Individual choice, p. 8
Resource, p. 8
Scarce, p. 8
Opportunity cost, p. 9
Trade-off, p. 10

Marginal decision, p. 10
Marginal analysis, p. 10
Incentive, p. 11
Interaction, p. 13
Trade, p. 13

Gains from trade, p. 13
Specialization, p. 13
Equilibrium, p. 14
Efficient, p. 15
Equity, p. 16

PROBLEMS

1. In each of the following situations, identify which of the 11 principles is at work.

   a. You choose to purchase your textbooks online rather than pay a higher price for the same books through your college bookstore.

   b. On your spring break trip, your budget is limited to $35 a day.

   c. To help reduce traffic congestion, many states have adopted congestion pricing. Under this program, drivers are charged more to use express lanes during peak rush hour.

   d. Congress passes an infrastructure bill to help construction workers who were left jobless after the last recession.

   e. You buy a used textbook from your roommate. Your roommate uses the money to pay for a Spotify subscription.

   f. You decide how many cups of coffee to have when studying the night before an exam by considering how much more work you can do by having another cup versus how jittery it will make you feel.

   g. There is limited lab space available to do the project required in Chemistry 101. The lab supervisor assigns lab time to each student based on when that student is able to come.

   h. You realize that you can graduate a semester early by forgoing a semester of study abroad.

   i. At the student center, there is a bulletin board on which people advertise used items for sale, such as bicycles. Once you have adjusted for differences in quality, all the bikes sell for about the same price.

   j. You are better at performing lab experiments, and your lab partner is better at writing lab reports. So the two of you agree that you will do all the experiments and she will write up all the reports.

   k. Amazon announces a program to develop a drone delivery system in place of traditional ground shipping.

2. Describe some of the opportunity costs when you decide to do the following:

   a. Attend college instead of taking a job

   b. Watch a movie instead of studying for an exam

   c. Ride the bus instead of driving your car

3. Kim needs to buy a textbook for the next economics class. The price at the college bookstore is $65. One website offers it for $55, and another site, for $57. All prices include sales tax. The accompanying table indicates the typical shipping and handling charges for the textbook ordered online.

Shipping method	Delivery time	Charge
Standard shipping	3–7 days	$3.99
Second-day air	2 business days	8.98
Next-day air	1 business day	13.98

   a. What is the opportunity cost of buying online instead of at the bookstore? Note that if you buy the book online, you must wait to get it.

   b. Show the relevant choices for Kim. What determines which of these options Kim will choose?

4. Use the concept of opportunity cost to explain the following.

   a. More people choose to get graduate degrees when the job market is poor.

   b. More people choose to do their own home repairs when the economy is slow and hourly wages are down.

   c. There are more parks in suburban than in urban areas.

   d. Convenience stores, which have higher prices than supermarkets, cater to busy people.

   e. Fewer students enroll in classes that meet before 10:00 A.M.

5. For the following examples, state how you would use the principle of marginal analysis to make a decision.

   a. Deciding how many days to wait before doing your laundry

   b. Deciding how much time to spend researching before writing your term paper

   c. Deciding how many bags of chips to eat

   d. Deciding how many class lectures to skip

6. This morning you made the following individual choices: you bought a bagel and coffee at the local café, you drove to school in your car during rush hour, and you typed your course notes for your roommate because she was texting in class—in return for which she will do your laundry for a month. For each of these actions, describe how your individual choices interacted with the individual choices made by others. Were other people left better off or worse off by your choices in each case?

7. The Hatfield family lives on the east side of the Hatatoochie River, and the McCoy family lives on the west side. Each family's diet consists of fried chicken and corn-on-the-cob, and each is self-sufficient, raising their own chickens and growing their own corn. Explain the conditions under which each of the following would be true.

   a. The two families are made better off when the Hatfields specialize in raising chickens, the McCoys specialize in growing corn, and the two families trade.

   b. The two families are made better off when the McCoys specialize in raising chickens, the Hatfields specialize in growing corn, and the two families trade.

8. Which of the following situations describes an equilibrium? Which does not? If the situation does not describe an equilibrium, what would an equilibrium look like?

   a. Many people regularly commute from the suburbs to downtown Pleasantville. Due to traffic congestion, the trip takes 30 minutes via highway but only 15 minutes via side streets.

b. At the intersection of Main and Broadway are two gas stations. One station charges $3.00 per gallon for regular gas and the other charges $2.85 per gallon. Customers can get service immediately at the first station but must wait in a long line at the second.

c. Every student enrolled in Economics 101 must also attend a weekly tutorial. This year there are two sections offered: section A and section B, which meet at the same time in adjoining classrooms and are taught by equally competent instructors. Section A is overcrowded, with people sitting on the floor and often unable to see what is written on the board at the front of the room. Section B has many empty seats.

9. For each of the following, explain whether you think the situation is efficient or not. If it is not efficient, why not? What actions would make it efficient?

a. Electricity is included in the rent at your dorm. Some residents in your dorm leave lights, computers, and appliances on when they are not in their rooms.

b. Although they cost the same amount to prepare, the cafeteria in your dorm consistently provides too many dishes that diners don't like, such as tofu casserole, and too few dishes that diners do like, such Pad Thai.

c. The enrollment for a particular course exceeds the spaces available. Some students who need to take this course to complete their major are unable to get a space even though others who are taking it as an elective do get a space.

10. Discuss the efficiency and equity implications of each of the following. How would you go about balancing the concerns of equity and efficiency in these areas?

a. The government pays the full tuition for every college student to study whatever subject they wish.

b. When people lose their jobs, the government provides unemployment benefits until they find new ones.

11. Governments often adopt certain policies in order to promote efficiency in society. For each of the following policies, determine what the incentive is and what behavior the government wishes to promote. In each case, why do you think the market is inefficient and why the government might wish to change people's behavior, rather than allow their actions to be solely determined by individual choice?

a. A tax of $5 per pack is imposed on cigarettes.

b. The government pays parents $100 when their child is vaccinated for measles.

c. The government pays college students to tutor children from low-income families.

d. The government imposes a tax on the amount of air pollution that a company discharges.

12. In each of the following situations, explain how government intervention could improve society's welfare by changing people's incentives. In what sense is the market going wrong?

a. Pollution from auto emissions has reached unhealthy levels.

b. Everyone in Woodville would be better off if streetlights were installed in the town. But no individual resident is willing to pay for installation of a streetlight in front of their house because it is impossible to recoup the cost by charging other residents for the benefit they receive from it.

13. Tim Geithner, a former U.S. Treasury secretary, has said, "The recession that began in late 2007 was extraordinarily severe. But the actions we took at its height to stimulate the economy helped arrest the free fall, preventing an even deeper collapse and putting the economy on the road to recovery." Which two of the three principles of economy-wide interaction are at work in this statement?

14. A sharp downturn in the U.S. housing market in August 2007 reduced the income of many who worked in the home construction industry. One news source reported that wire transfer businesses were likely to suffer because many construction workers are foreign nationals who regularly send part of their wages back to relatives in their home countries via wire transfers. With this information, use one of the principles of economy-wide interaction to trace the train of events that explains how reduced spending for U.S. home purchases is likely to affect the performance of the economies in the home countries of these workers.

15. Following the financial crisis of 2008, U.S. consumers cut back on new car purchases. In response to the decline in car sales, Congress passed the program "Cash for Clunkers," which allowed consumers to trade in their old car and receive a cash stipend to purchase a new vehicle. Which principle of economy-wide interactions is at work here?

16. Self-driving cars, also known as autonomous vehicles, will require little or no human input to operate safely. A recent report claims that these vehicles will cost the U.S. economy 4 million jobs but also add nearly $800 billion in annual output. Explain how autonomous vehicles increase potential output and contribute to economic growth. Identify the winners and losers in the development of autonomous vehicles.

Economic Models: Trade-offs and Trade

FROM KITTY HAWK TO DREAMLINER

BOEING'S 787 DREAMLINER was the result of an aerodynamic revolution—a super-efficient airplane designed to cut airline operating costs and the first to use superlight composite materials.

To ensure that the Dreamliner was sufficiently lightweight and aerodynamic, it underwent over 15,000 hours of wind tunnel tests, resulting in subtle design changes that improved its performance, making it more fuel efficient and less pollutant emitting than existing passenger jets. In fact, some budget airlines such as Norwegian

Ross D. Franklin/AP Images

Bettmann/Getty Images

The Wright brothers' model made modern airplanes, including the Dreamliner, possible.

Air (Europe's third-largest budget airline) have been offering transatlantic flights at half the price of their rivals, expecting that the super-fuel-efficient Dreamliner will shrink fuel costs enough to make their discount strategy profitable.

The first flight of the Dreamliner was a spectacular advance from the 1903 maiden voyage of the Wright Flyer, the first successful powered airplane, in Kitty Hawk, North Carolina. Yet the Boeing engineers—and all aeronautical engineers—owe an enormous debt to the Wright Flyer's inventors, Wilbur and Orville Wright.

What made the Wrights truly visionary was their invention of the wind tunnel, an apparatus that let them experiment with many different designs for wings and control surfaces. Doing experiments with a miniature airplane, inside a wind tunnel the size of a shipping crate, gave the Wright Brothers the knowledge that would make heavier-than-air flight possible.

Neither a miniature airplane inside a packing crate nor a miniature model of the Dreamliner inside Boeing's state-of-the-art Transonic Wind Tunnel is the same thing as an actual aircraft in flight. But each is a very useful *model* of a flying plane—a simplified representation of the real thing that can be used to answer crucial questions, such as how much lift a given wing shape will generate at a given airspeed.

Needless to say, testing an airplane design in a wind tunnel is cheaper and safer than building a full-scale version and hoping it will fly. More generally, models play a crucial role in almost all scientific research—economics very much included.

In fact, you could say that economic theory consists mainly of a collection of models, a series of simplified representations of economic reality that allow us to understand a variety of economic issues.

In this chapter, we'll look at three economic models that are crucially important in their own right and illustrate why such models are so useful. We'll conclude with a look at how economists actually use models in their work. ●

WHAT YOU WILL LEARN

- What are economic **models** and why are they so important to economists?
- How do three simple models—the **production possibility frontier, comparative advantage,** and the **circular-flow diagram**—help us understand how modern economies work?
- Why is an understanding of the difference between **positive economics** and **normative economics** important for the real-world application of economic principles?
- Why do economists sometimes disagree?

model a simplified representation of a real situation that is used to better understand real-life situations.

other things equal assumption in the development of a model, the assumption that all other relevant factors remain unchanged.

‖ Models in Economics: Some Important Examples

A **model** is any simplified representation of reality that is used to better understand real-life situations. But how do we create a simplified representation of an economic situation?

One possibility—an economist's equivalent of a wind tunnel—is to find or create a real but simplified economy. Take, for example, an economist who wants to know how an increase in the government-mandated minimum wage would affect the U.S. economy. It would be impossible to do an experiment that involved raising the minimum wage across the country and seeing what happens. Instead, the economist will observe the effects of a smaller economy that is raising its minimum wage (like Virginia did in 2022) and then extrapolate those results to the larger U.S. economy.

Another possibility is to simulate the workings of the economy on a computer. For example, when changes in tax law are proposed, government officials use *tax models*—large mathematical computer programs—to assess how the proposed changes would affect different types of people.

Models are important because their simplicity allows economists to focus on the effects of only one change at a time. That is, they allow us to hold everything else constant and study how one change affects the overall economic outcome.

So an important assumption when building economic models is the **other things equal assumption,** which means that all other relevant factors remain unchanged.

But you can't always find or create a small-scale version of the whole economy, and a computer program is only as good as the data it uses. (Programmers have a saying: "garbage in, garbage out.") For many purposes, the most effective form of economic modeling is the construction of "thought experiments": simplified, hypothetical versions of real-life situations.

We used the example of how customers checking out at a supermarket rearrange themselves when a new cash register opens to illustrate the concept of equilibrium in Chapter 1. Although we didn't say it, this is an example of a simple model—an imaginary supermarket, in which many details, like what customers were buying, are ignored. This simple model can be used to answer a "what if" question: for example, what if another cash register were to open?

As this checkout story shows, it is possible to describe and analyze a useful economic model in plain English. However, because much of economics involves changes in quantities—in the price of a product, the number of units produced, or the number of workers employed in its production—economists often find that using some mathematics helps clarify an issue. In particular, a numerical example, a simple equation, or—especially—a graph can be key to understanding an economic concept.

Whatever form it takes, a good economic model can be a tremendous aid to understanding. We'll now look at three simple but important economic models and what they tell us.

- First, we will look at the *production possibility frontier*, a model that helps economists think about the trade-offs every economy faces.

- We then turn to *comparative advantage*, a model that clarifies the principle of gains from trade—trade both between individuals and between countries.

- We will also examine the *circular-flow diagram*, a schematic representation that helps us understand how flows of money, goods, and services are channeled through the economy.

Throughout this chapter, and the entire book, we will make considerable use of graphs to represent mathematical relationships. If you are already familiar with how graphs are used, you can skip the appendix to this chapter, which provides a

brief introduction to the use of graphs in economics. If not, this would be a good time to read the appendix on graphing.

production possibility frontier a model that illustrates the trade-offs facing an economy that produces only two goods. It shows the maximum quantity of one good that can be produced for any given quantity produced of the other.

Trade-offs: The Production Possibility Frontier

The first principle of economics we introduced in Chapter 1 is that resources are scarce and, as a result, any economy faces trade-offs—whether it's an isolated group of a few dozen hunter-gatherers or the nearly 7.8 billion people making up the twenty-first-century global economy. No matter how lightweight the Boeing Dreamliner is, no matter how efficient Boeing's assembly line, producing Dreamliners means using resources that therefore can't be used to produce something else.

To think about the trade-offs that face any economy, economists often use the model known as the **production possibility frontier.** The idea behind this model is to improve our understanding of trade-offs by considering a simplified economy that produces only two goods. This simplification enables us to show the trade-off graphically.

Suppose, for a moment, that the United States was a one-company economy, with Boeing its sole employer and aircraft its only product. But there would still be a choice of what kinds of aircraft to produce—say, Dreamliners versus small commuter jets. Figure 1 shows a hypothetical production possibility frontier representing the trade-off this one-company economy would face. The frontier—the line in the diagram—shows the maximum quantity of small jets that Boeing can produce per year *given* the quantity of Dreamliners it produces per year, and vice versa. That is, it answers questions of the form, "What is the maximum quantity of small jets that Boeing can produce in a year if it also produces 9 (or 15, or 30) Dreamliners that year?"

There is a crucial distinction between points *inside* or *on* the production possibility frontier (the shaded area) and *outside* the frontier. If a production point lies inside or on the frontier—like point *C*, at which Boeing produces 20 small jets and 9 Dreamliners in a year—it is feasible. After all, the frontier tells us that if Boeing produces 20 small jets, it could also produce a maximum of 15 Dreamliners that year, so it could certainly make 9 Dreamliners.

FIGURE 1 The Production Possibility Frontier

The production possibility frontier illustrates the trade-offs Boeing faces in producing Dreamliners and small jets. It shows the maximum quantity of one good that can be produced given the quantity of the other good produced. Here, the maximum quantity of Dreamliners manufactured per year depends on the quantity of small jets manufactured that year, and vice versa. Boeing's feasible production is shown by the area *inside* or *on* the curve. Production at point *C* is feasible but not efficient. Points *A* and *B* are feasible and efficient in production, but point *D* is not feasible.

However, a production point that lies outside the frontier—such as the hypothetical production point *D*, where Boeing produces 40 small jets and 30 Dreamliners—isn't feasible. Boeing can produce 40 small jets and no Dreamliners, *or* it can produce 30 Dreamliners and no small jets, but it can't do both.

In Figure 1, the production possibility frontier intersects the horizontal axis at 40 small jets. This means that if Boeing dedicated all its production capacity to making small jets, it could produce 40 small jets per year but could produce no Dreamliners. The production possibility frontier intersects the vertical axis at 30 Dreamliners. This means that if Boeing dedicated all its production capacity to making Dreamliners, it could produce 30 Dreamliners per year but no small jets.

The figure also shows less extreme trade-offs. For example, if Boeing's managers decide to make 20 small jets this year, they can produce at most 15 Dreamliners; this production choice is illustrated by point *A*. And if Boeing's managers decide to produce 28 small jets, they can make at most 9 Dreamliners, as shown by point *B*.

Thinking in terms of a production possibility frontier simplifies the complexities of reality. The real-world U.S. economy produces millions of different goods. Even Boeing can produce more than two different types of planes. Yet it's important to realize that even in its simplicity, this stripped-down model gives us important insights about the real world.

By simplifying reality, the production possibility frontier helps us understand some aspects of the real economy better than we could without the model: efficiency, opportunity cost, and economic growth.

Efficiency   First of all, the production possibility frontier is a good way to illustrate the general economic concept of *efficiency*. Recall from Chapter 1 that an economy is efficient if there are no missed opportunities—there is no way to make some people better off without making other people worse off.

One key element of efficiency is that there are no missed opportunities in production—there is no way to produce more of one good without producing less of other goods. As long as Boeing operates on its production possibility frontier, its production is efficient. At point *A*, 15 Dreamliners are the maximum quantity feasible given that Boeing has also committed to producing 20 small jets; at point *B*, 9 Dreamliners are the maximum number that can be made given the choice to produce 28 small jets; and so on.

But suppose for some reason that Boeing was operating at point *C*, making 20 small jets and 9 Dreamliners. In this case, it would not be operating efficiently and would therefore be *inefficient:* it could be producing more of both planes.

Although we have used an example of the production choices of a one-firm, two-good economy to illustrate efficiency and inefficiency, these concepts also carry over to the real economy, which contains many firms and produces many goods. If the economy as a whole could not produce more of any one good without producing less of something else—that is, if it is on its production possibility frontier—then we say that the economy is *efficient in production*.

If, however, the economy could produce more of some things without producing less of others—which typically means that it could produce more of everything—then it is inefficient in production. For example, an economy in which large numbers of workers are involuntarily unemployed is clearly inefficient in production. And that's a bad thing because these workers could be employed in the production of more useful goods and services.

Although the production possibility frontier helps clarify what it means for an economy to be efficient in production, it's important to understand that efficiency in production is only *part* of what's required for the economy as a whole to be efficient. Efficiency also requires that the economy allocate its resources so that consumers are as well off as possible. If an economy does this, we say that it is *efficient in allocation*.

To see why efficiency in allocation is as important as efficiency in production, notice that points *A* and *B* in Figure 1 both represent situations in which the economy is efficient in production, because in each case it can't produce more of one good without producing less of the other. But these two situations may not be equally desirable from society's point of view. Suppose that society prefers to have more small jets and fewer Dreamliners than at point *A;* say, it prefers to have 28 small jets and 9 Dreamliners, corresponding to point *B*. In this case, point *A* is inefficient in allocation from the point of view of the economy as a whole because it would rather have Boeing produce at point *B* instead of point *A*.

This example shows that efficiency for the economy as a whole requires *both* efficiency in production and efficiency in allocation: to be efficient, an economy must produce as much of each good as it can given the production of other goods. It must also produce the mix of goods that people want to consume and deliver those goods to the right people. An economy that gives small jets to international airlines and Dreamliners to commuter airlines serving small rural airports is inefficient, too.

In the real world, command economies, such as the former Soviet Union, are notorious for inefficiency in allocation. For example, it was common for consumers to find stores well stocked with items few people wanted but lacking basics such as soap and toilet paper.

Opportunity Cost The production possibility frontier is also useful as a reminder of the fundamental point that the true cost of any good isn't the money it costs to buy it, but what must be given up in order to get that good — the *opportunity cost*. If, for example, Boeing decides to change its production from point *A* to point *B*, it will produce 8 more small jets but 6 fewer Dreamliners. So the opportunity cost of 8 small jets is 6 Dreamliners — the 6 Dreamliners that must be forgone in order to produce 8 more small jets. This means that each small jet has an opportunity cost of $6/8 = 3/4$ of a Dreamliner.

Is the opportunity cost of an extra small jet in terms of Dreamliners always the same, no matter how many small jets and Dreamliners are currently produced? In the example illustrated by Figure 1, the answer is yes. If Boeing increases its production of small jets from 28 to 40, the number of Dreamliners it produces falls from 9 to 0. So Boeing's opportunity cost per additional small jet is $9/12 = 3/4$ of a Dreamliner, the same as it was when Boeing went from 20 small jets produced to 28.

However, the fact that in this example the opportunity cost of a small jet in terms of a Dreamliner is always the same is a result of an assumption we've made, an assumption that's reflected in how Figure 1 is drawn. Specifically, whenever we assume that the opportunity cost of an additional unit of a good doesn't change regardless of the output mix, the production possibility frontier is a straight line.

Moreover, as you might have already guessed, the slope of a straight-line production possibility frontier is equal to the opportunity cost — specifically, the opportunity cost for the good measured on the horizontal axis in terms of the good measured on the vertical axis. In Figure 1, the production possibility frontier has a *constant slope* of $-3/4$, implying that Boeing faces a *constant opportunity cost* for 1 small jet equal to $3/4$ of a Dreamliner. (A review of how to calculate the slope of a straight line is found in this chapter's appendix.) This is the simplest case, but the production possibility frontier model can also be used to examine situations in which opportunity costs change as the mix of output changes.

Figure 2 illustrates a different assumption, a case in which Boeing faces *increasing opportunity cost*. Here, the more small jets it produces, the more costly it is to produce yet another small jet in terms of forgone production of a Dreamliner. And the same holds true in reverse: the more Dreamliners Boeing produces, the more costly it is to produce yet another Dreamliner in terms of forgone production of small jets. For example, to go from producing zero small jets to producing 20, Boeing has to forgo producing 5 Dreamliners. That is, the opportunity cost of those 20 small jets is 5 Dreamliners. But to increase its production of small jets to 40 — that is, to produce an additional 20 small jets — it must forgo producing 25 more Dreamliners, a much higher opportunity cost. As you can see in Figure 2, when opportunity costs are increasing rather than constant, the production possibility frontier is a bowed-out curve rather than a straight line.

FIGURE 2 Increasing Opportunity Cost

The bowed-out shape of the production possibility frontier reflects increasing opportunity cost. In this example, to produce the first 20 small jets, Boeing must forgo producing 5 Dreamliners. But to produce an additional 20 small jets, Boeing must forgo manufacturing 25 more Dreamliners.

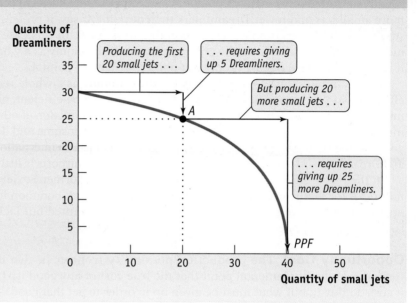

Although it's often useful to work with the simple assumption that the production possibility frontier is a straight line, economists believe that in reality opportunity costs are typically increasing. When only a small amount of a good is produced, the opportunity cost of producing that good is relatively low because the economy needs to use only those resources that are especially well suited for its production.

For example, if an economy grows only a small amount of corn, that corn can be grown in places where the soil and climate are perfect for corn-growing but less suitable for growing anything else, like wheat. So growing that corn involves giving up only a small amount of potential wheat output. Once the economy grows a lot of corn, however, land that is well suited for wheat but isn't so great for corn must be used to produce corn anyway. As a result, the additional corn production involves sacrificing considerably more wheat production. In other words, as more of a good is produced, its opportunity cost typically rises because well-suited inputs are used up and less adaptable inputs must be used instead.

Economic Growth Finally, the production possibility frontier helps us understand what it means to talk about *economic growth*. In the Introduction, we defined the concept of economic growth as *the growing ability of the economy to produce goods and services.* As we saw, economic growth is one of the fundamental features of the real economy. But are we really justified in saying that the economy has grown over time? After all, although the U.S. economy produces more of many things than it did a century ago, it produces less of other things—for example, horse-drawn carriages. Production of many goods, in other words, is actually down. So how can we say for sure that the economy as a whole has grown?

The answer is illustrated in Figure 3, where we have drawn two hypothetical production possibility frontiers for the economy. In them we have assumed once again that everyone in the economy works for Boeing and, consequently, the economy produces only two goods, Dreamliners and small jets. Notice how the two curves are nested, with the one labeled "Original *PPF*" lying completely inside the one labeled "New *PPF*." Now we can see graphically what we mean by economic growth of the economy: economic growth means an *expansion of the economy's production possibilities;* that is, the economy *can* produce more of everything.

For example, if the economy initially produces at point *A* (25 Dreamliners and 20 small jets), economic growth means that the economy could move to point *E* (30 Dreamliners and 25 small jets). *E* lies outside the original frontier; so in the

FIGURE 3 Economic Growth

Economic growth results in an *outward shift* of the production possibility frontier because production possibilities are expanded. The economy can now produce more of everything. For example, if production is initially at point *A* (25 Dreamliners and 20 small jets), economic growth means that the economy could move to point *E* (30 Dreamliners and 25 small jets).

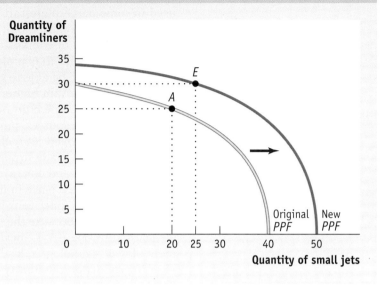

production possibility frontier model, growth is shown as an outward shift of the frontier.

What can lead the production possibility frontier to shift outward? There are basically two sources of economic growth. One is an increase in the economy's **factors of production,** the resources used to produce goods and services. Economists usually use the term *factor of production* to refer to a resource that is not used up in production. For example, in traditional airplane manufacture workers used riveting machines to connect metal sheets when constructing a plane's fuselage; the workers and the riveters are factors of production, but the rivets and the sheet metal are not. Once a fuselage is made, a worker and riveter can be used to make another fuselage, but the sheet metal and rivets used to make one fuselage cannot be used to make another.

factors of production the resources used to produce goods and services.

Broadly speaking, the main factors of production are the resources: land, labor, physical capital, and human capital. Land is a resource supplied by nature; labor is the economy's pool of workers; physical capital refers to created resources such as machines and buildings; and human capital refers to the educational achievements and skills of the labor force, which enhance its productivity. Of course, each of these is actually a broad category rather than a single factor: land in North Dakota is very different from land in Florida.

To see how adding to an economy's factors of production leads to economic growth, suppose that Boeing builds another construction hangar that allows it to increase the number of planes—small jets or Dreamliners or both—it can produce in a year. The new construction hangar is a factor of production, a resource Boeing can use to increase its yearly output. How many more planes of each type Boeing will produce is a management decision that will depend on, among other things, customer demand. But we can say that Boeing's production possibility frontier has shifted outward because it can now produce more small jets without reducing the number of Dreamliners it makes, or it can make more Dreamliners without reducing the number of small jets produced.

The four factors of production: land, labor, physical capital, and human capital.

technology the technical means for producing goods and services.

The other source of economic growth is progress in **technology,** the technical means for the production of goods and services. Composite materials had been used in some parts of aircraft before the Boeing Dreamliner was developed. But Boeing engineers realized that there were large additional advantages to building a whole plane out of composites. The plane would be lighter, stronger, and have better aerodynamics than a plane built in the traditional way. It would therefore have longer range, be able to carry more people, and use less fuel, in addition to being able to maintain higher cabin pressure. So in a real sense Boeing's innovation—a whole plane built out of composites—was a way to do more with any given amount of resources, pushing out the production possibility frontier.

Because improved jet technology has pushed out the production possibility frontier, it has made it possible for the economy to produce more of everything, not just jets and air travel. Over the past 30 years, the biggest technological advances have taken place in information technology, not in construction or food services. Yet some Americans have chosen to buy bigger houses and eat out more than they used to because the economy's growth has made it possible to do so. As we learned in Chapter 1, increases in the economy's potential, like the development of new technologies, lead to economic growth over time.

The production possibility frontier is a very simplified model of an economy. Yet it teaches us important lessons about real-life economies. It gives us our first clear sense of what constitutes economic efficiency, it illustrates the concept of opportunity cost, and it makes clear what economic growth is all about.

Comparative Advantage and Gains from Trade

Another of the 11 principles of economics described in Chapter 1 is the principle of *gains from trade*—the mutual gains that individuals can achieve by specializing in doing different things and trading with one another. Our second illustration of an economic model is a particularly useful model of gains from trade—trade based on *comparative advantage.*

One of the most important insights in all of economics is that there are gains from trade: it makes sense to produce the things you're especially good at producing and to buy from other people the things you aren't as good at producing. This would be true even if you could produce everything for yourself: even if a brilliant brain surgeon *could* repair her own dripping faucet, it's probably a better idea for her to call in a professional plumber.

How can we model the gains from trade? Let's stay with our aircraft example and once again imagine that the United States is a one-company economy where everyone works for Boeing, producing airplanes. Let's now assume, however, that the United States has the ability to trade with Brazil—another one-company economy where everyone works for the Brazilian aircraft company Embraer, which is, in the real world, a successful producer of small commuter jets. (If you fly from one major U.S. city to another, your plane is likely to be a Boeing, but if you fly into a small city, the odds are good that your plane will be an Embraer.)

In our example, the only two goods produced are large jets and small jets. Both countries could produce both kinds of jets. But as we'll see in a moment, they can gain by producing different things and trading with each other. For the purposes of this example, let's return to the simpler case of straight-line production possibility frontiers. America's production possibilities are represented by the production possibility frontier in panel (a) of Figure 4, which is similar to the production possibility frontier in Figure 1. According to this diagram, the United States can produce 40 small jets if it makes no large jets and can manufacture 30 large jets if it produces no small jets. Recall that this means that the slope of the U.S. production possibility frontier is $-\frac{3}{4}$: its opportunity cost of 1 small jet is $\frac{3}{4}$ of a large jet.

Panel (b) of Figure 4 shows Brazil's production possibilities. Like the United States, Brazil's production possibility frontier is a straight line, implying a constant opportunity cost of a small jet in terms of large jets. Brazil's production possibility

FIGURE 4 Production Possibilities for Two Countries

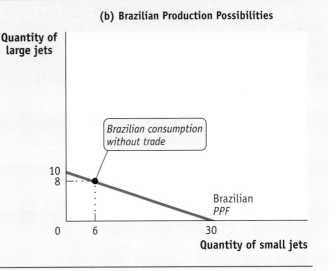

Here, both the United States and Brazil have a constant opportunity cost of small jets, illustrated by a straight-line production possibility frontier. For the United States, each small jet has an opportunity cost of ¾ of a large jet. Brazil has an opportunity cost of a small jet equal to ⅓ of a large jet.

frontier has a constant slope of – ⅓. Brazil can't produce as much of anything as the United States can: at most it can produce 30 small jets or 10 large jets. But it is relatively better at manufacturing small jets than the United States; whereas the United States sacrifices ¾ of a large jet per small jet produced, for Brazil the opportunity cost of a small jet is only ⅓ of a large jet. Table 1 summarizes the two countries' opportunity costs of small jets and large jets.

Now, the United States and Brazil could each choose to make their own large and small jets, not trading any of them and consuming only what each produced within its own country. (A country "consumes" an airplane when it is owned by a domestic resident.) Let's suppose that the two countries start out this way and make the consumption choices shown in Figure 4: in the absence of trade, the United States produces and consumes 16 small jets and 18 large jets per year, while Brazil produces and consumes 6 small jets and 8 large jets per year.

But is this the best the two countries can do? No, it isn't. Given that the two producers—and therefore the two countries—have different opportunity costs, the United States and Brazil can strike a deal that makes both of them better off.

Table 2 shows how such a deal works: the United States specializes in the production of large jets, manufacturing 30 per year, and sells 10 to Brazil. Meanwhile, Brazil specializes in the production of small jets, producing 30 per year, and sells 20

TABLE 1 U.S. and Brazilian Opportunity Costs of Small Jets and Large Jets

	U.S. opportunity cost	Brazilian opportunity cost
1 small jet	¾ large jet >	⅓ large jet
1 large jet	4⁄3 small jets <	3 small jets

TABLE 2 How the United States and Brazil Gain from Trade

		Without trade		With trade		Gains from trade
		Production	Consumption	Production	Consumption	
United States	**Large jets**	18	18	30	20	+2
	Small jets	16	16	0	20	+4
Brazil	**Large jets**	8	8	0	10	+2
	Small jets	6	6	30	10	+4

FIGURE 5 Comparative Advantage and Gains from Trade

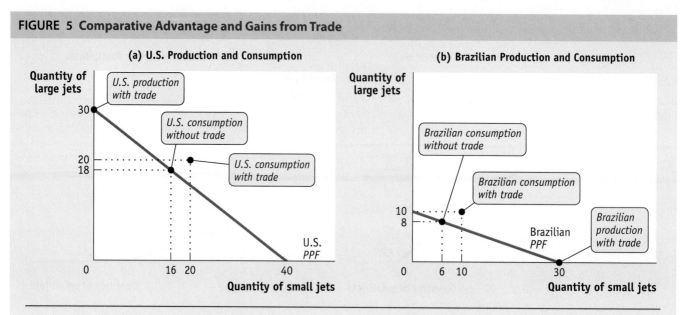

By specializing and trading, the United States and Brazil can produce and consume more of both large jets and small jets. The United States specializes in manufacturing large jets, its comparative advantage, and Brazil — which has an *absolute* disadvantage in both goods but a *comparative* advantage in small jets — specializes in manufacturing small jets. With trade, both countries can consume more of both goods than either could without trade.

to the United States. The result is shown in Figure 5. The United States now consumes more of both small jets and large jets than before: instead of 16 small jets and 18 large jets, it now consumes 20 small jets and 20 large jets. Brazil also consumes more, going from 6 small jets and 8 large jets to 10 small jets and 10 large jets. As Table 2 also shows, both the United States and Brazil reap gains from trade, consuming more of both types of planes than they would have without trade.

Both countries are better off when they each specialize in what they are good at and trade. It's a good idea for the United States to specialize in the production of large jets because its opportunity cost of a large jet is smaller than Brazil's: $\frac{4}{3} < 3$. Correspondingly, Brazil should specialize in the production of small jets because its opportunity cost of a small jet is smaller than the United States: $\frac{1}{3} < \frac{3}{4}$.

What we would say in this case is that the United States has a comparative advantage in the production of large jets and Brazil has a comparative advantage in the production of small jets. A country has a **comparative advantage** in producing something if the opportunity cost of that production is lower for that country than for other countries. The same concept applies to firms and people: a firm or an individual has a comparative advantage in producing something if their opportunity cost of production is lower than for others.

One point of clarification before we proceed further. You may have wondered why the United States traded 10 large jets to Brazil in return for 20 small jets. Why not some other deal, like trading 10 large jets for 12 small jets? The answer to that question has two parts. First, there may indeed be other trades that the United States and Brazil might agree to. Second, there are some deals that we can safely rule out—one like 10 large jets for 10 small jets.

To understand why, reexamine Table 1 and consider the United States first. Without trading with Brazil, the U.S. opportunity cost of a small jet is $\frac{3}{4}$ of a large jet. So it's clear that the United States will not accept any trade that requires it to give up more than $\frac{3}{4}$ of a large jet for a small jet. Trading 10 large jets in return for 12 small jets would require the United States to pay an opportunity cost of $\frac{10}{12} = \frac{5}{6}$ of a large jet for a small jet. Because $\frac{5}{6}$ is greater than $\frac{3}{4}$, this is a deal that the

comparative advantage the advantage a country has in producing a good or service if its opportunity cost of producing the good or service is lower than other countries' cost. Likewise, an individual has a comparative advantage in producing a good or service if their opportunity cost of producing the good or service is lower than it is for other people.

United States would reject. Similarly, Brazil won't accept a trade that gives it less than $\frac{1}{3}$ of a large jet for a small jet.

The point to remember is that the United States and Brazil will be willing to trade only if the "price" of the good each country obtains in the trade is less than its own opportunity cost of producing the good domestically. Moreover, this is a general statement that is true whenever two parties—countries, firms, or individuals—trade voluntarily.

While our story clearly simplifies reality, it teaches us some very important lessons that apply to the real economy, too.

First, the model provides a clear illustration of the gains from trade: through specialization and trade, both countries produce more and consume more than if they were self-sufficient.

Second, the model demonstrates a very important point that is often overlooked in real-world arguments: each country has a comparative advantage in producing something. This applies to firms and people as well: *everyone has a comparative advantage in something, and everyone has a comparative disadvantage in something.*

Crucially, in our example it doesn't matter if, as is probably the case in real life, American workers are just as good as or even better than Brazilian workers at producing small jets. Suppose that the United States is actually better than Brazil at all kinds of aircraft production. In that case, we would say that the United States has an **absolute advantage** in both large-jet and small-jet production: in an hour, an American worker can produce more of either a large jet or a small jet than a Brazilian worker. You might be tempted to think that in that case the United States has nothing to gain from trading with the less productive Brazil.

But we've just seen that the United States can indeed benefit from trading with Brazil because *comparative, not absolute, advantage is the basis for mutual gain.* It doesn't matter whether it takes Brazil more resources than the United States to make a small jet; what matters for trade is that for Brazil the opportunity cost of a small jet is lower than the U.S. opportunity cost. So Brazil, despite its absolute disadvantage, even in small jets, has a comparative advantage in the manufacture of small jets. Meanwhile the United States, which can use its resources most productively by manufacturing large jets, has a comparative *dis*advantage in manufacturing small jets.

Comparative Advantage and International Trade, in Reality

Look at the label on a manufactured good sold in the United States, and there's a good chance you will find that it was produced in some other country—in China, or Japan, or even in Canada. On the other side, many U.S. industries sell a large fraction of their output overseas. This is particularly true of agriculture, high technology, and entertainment.

absolute advantage the advantage a country has in producing a good or service if the country can produce more output per worker than other countries. Likewise, an individual has an absolute advantage in producing a good or service if they are better at producing it than other people. Having an absolute advantage is not the same thing as having a comparative advantage.

PITFALLS

MISUNDERSTANDING COMPARATIVE ADVANTAGE

Students do it, pundits do it, and politicians do it all the time: they confuse *comparative advantage* with *absolute advantage.* For example, back in the 1980s, when the U.S. economy seemed to be lagging behind that of Japan, news commentators could be heard warning that if we didn't improve our productivity, we would soon have no comparative advantage in anything.

What those commentators meant was that we would have no *absolute advantage* in anything—that there might come a time when the

Japanese were better at everything than we were. (It didn't turn out that way, but that's another story.) And they had the idea that in that case we would no longer be able to benefit from trade with Japan.

But just as Brazil, in our example, was able to benefit from trade with the United States (and vice versa) despite the fact that the United States was better at manufacturing both large and small jets, in real life nations can still gain from trade even if they are less productive in all industries than the countries they trade with.

GLOBAL COMPARISON PAJAMA REPUBLICS

A terrible industrial disaster made headlines when a building that housed five clothing factories collapsed in Bangladesh in 2013, killing more than a thousand garment workers trapped inside. Attention soon focused on the substandard working conditions in those factories, as well as the many violations of building codes and safety procedures — including those required by Bangladeshi law — that set the stage for the tragedy.

While this disaster provoked a justified outcry, it also highlighted the remarkable rise of Bangladesh's clothing industry, which has become a major player in world markets — second only to China in total exports — and a desperately needed source of income and employment in a very poor country.

It's not that Bangladesh has especially high productivity in clothing manufacturing. In fact, estimates by the consulting firm McKinsey and Company suggest that it's about a quarter less productive than China. Rather, it has even lower productivity in other industries, giving it a comparative advantage in clothing manufacturing. This is typical in poor countries, which often rely heavily on clothing exports during the early phases of their economic development. An official from one such country once joked, "We are not a banana republic — we are a pajama republic."

The figure plots the per capita income of several such "pajama republics" (the total income of the country divided by the size of the population) against the share of total exports accounted for by clothing; per capita income is measured as a percentage of the U.S.

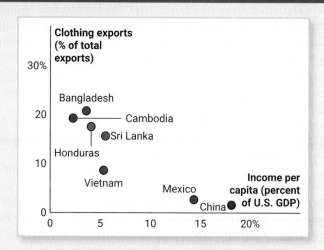

level in order to give you a sense of just how poor these countries are. As you can see, they are very poor indeed — and the poorer they are, the more they depend on clothing exports.

It's worth pointing out, by the way, that relying on clothing exports is not necessarily a bad thing, despite tragedies like the one in Bangladesh. Indeed, Bangladesh, although still desperately poor, is more than four and a half times as rich as it was two decades ago, when it began its dramatic rise as a clothing exporter. (Also see the upcoming Economics in Action on Bangladesh.)

Data from: The World Bank

Should all this international exchange of goods and services be celebrated, or is it cause for concern? Politicians and the public often question the desirability of international trade, arguing that the nation should produce goods for itself rather than buying them from foreigners. Industries around the world demand protection from foreign competition: Japanese farmers want to keep out American rice, American steelworkers want to keep out Chinese steel. And these demands are often supported by public opinion.

Economists, however, have a very positive view of international trade. Why? Because they view it in terms of comparative advantage. As we learned from our example of American large jets and Brazilian small jets, international trade benefits both countries. Each country can consume more than if it doesn't trade and remains self-sufficient. Moreover, these mutual gains don't depend on each country being better than other countries at producing one kind of good. Even if one country has, say, higher output per worker in both industries—that is, even if one country has an absolute advantage in both industries—there are still gains from trade. The following Global Comparison illustrates just this point.

Transactions: The Circular-Flow Diagram

The model economies that we've studied so far—each containing only one firm—are huge simplifications. We've also greatly simplified trade between the United States and Brazil, assuming that they engage only in the simplest of economic transactions, **barter**, in which one party directly trades a good or service for another good or service without using money. In a modern economy, simple barter is rare: usually people trade goods or services for money—pieces of colored

barter trade in the form of the direct exchange of goods or services for other goods or services that people want.

paper with no inherent value—and then trade those pieces of colored paper for the goods or services they want. That is, they sell goods or services and buy other goods or services.

And they both sell and buy a lot of different things. The U.S. economy is a vastly complex entity, with more than 100 million workers employed by millions of companies, producing millions of different goods and services. Yet you can learn some very important things about the economy by considering the simple graphic shown in Figure 6, the **circular-flow diagram.** This diagram represents the transactions that take place in an economy by two kinds of flows around a circle: flows of physical things such as goods, services, labor, or raw materials in one direction, and flows of money that pay for these physical things in the opposite direction. In this case the physical flows are shown in blue, the money flows in gold.

The simplest circular-flow diagram illustrates an economy that contains only two kinds of inhabitants: **households** and **firms.** A household consists of either an individual or a group of people (usually, but not necessarily, a family) that share their income. A firm is an organization that produces goods and services for sale—and that employs members of households.

As you can see in Figure 6, there are two kinds of markets in this simple economy. On the left side, there are **markets for goods and services** in which households buy the goods and services they want from firms. This produces a flow of goods and services to households and a return flow of money to firms.

On the right side, there are **factor markets** in which firms buy the resources they need to produce goods and services. Recall from earlier that the main factors of production are land, labor, physical capital, and human capital.

The factor market most of us know best is the labor market, in which workers sell their services. In addition, we can think of households as owning and selling the other factors of production to firms. For example, when a firm buys physical capital in the form of machines, the payment ultimately goes to the households that own the machine-making firm. In this case, the transactions occur in the *capital market,* the market in which capital is bought and sold. As we'll examine in detail later, factor markets ultimately determine an economy's **income distribution,** how the total income created in an economy is allocated between less skilled workers, highly skilled workers, and the owners of capital and land.

circular-flow diagram a diagram that represents the transactions in an economy by two kinds of flows around a circle: flows of physical things such as goods or labor in one direction and flows of money to pay for these physical things in the opposite direction.

household a person or a group of people that share their income.

firm an organization that produces goods and services for sale.

markets for goods and services markets in which firms sell goods and services that they produce to households.

factor markets markets in which firms buy the resources they need to produce goods and services.

income distribution the way in which total income is divided among the owners of the various factors of production.

FIGURE 6 The Circular-Flow Diagram

This diagram represents the flows of money and of goods and services in the economy. In the markets for goods and services, households purchase goods and services from firms, generating a flow of money to the firms and a flow of goods and services to the households. The money flows back to households as firms purchase factors of production from the households in factor markets.

The circular-flow diagram ignores a number of real-world complications in the interests of simplicity. A few examples:

- In the real world, the distinction between firms and households isn't always that clear-cut. Consider a small, family-run business—a farm, a shop, a small hotel. Is this a firm or a household? A more complete picture would include a separate box for family businesses.

- Many of the sales that firms make are not to households but to other firms; for example, steel companies sell mainly to other companies such as auto manufacturers, not to households. A more complete picture would include these flows of goods, services, and money within the business sector.

- The figure doesn't show the government, which in the real world diverts quite a lot of money out of the circular flow in the form of taxes but also injects a lot of money back into the flow in the form of spending.

Figure 6, in other words, is by no means a complete picture either of all the types of inhabitants of the real economy or of all the flows of money and physical items that take place among these inhabitants.

Despite its simplicity, however, the circular-flow diagram is a very useful aid to thinking about the economy.

ECONOMICS >> *in Action*
Rich Nation, Poor Nation

Try taking off your clothes—at a suitable time and in a suitable place, of course—and taking a look at the labels inside that say where they were made. It's a very good bet that much, if not most, of your clothes were manufactured overseas, in a country that is much poorer than the United States—say, in El Salvador, Sri Lanka, or Bangladesh.

Why are these countries so much poorer than we are? The immediate reason is that their economies are much less *productive*—firms in these countries are just not able to produce as much from a given quantity of resources as comparable firms in the United States or other wealthy countries. Why countries differ so much in productivity is a deep question—indeed, one of the main questions that preoccupy economists. But in any case, the difference in productivity is a fact.

But if the economies of these countries are so much less productive than ours, how is it that they make so much of our clothing? Why don't we do it for ourselves?

The answer is "comparative advantage." Just about every industry in Bangladesh is much less productive than the corresponding industry in the United States. But the productivity difference between rich and poor countries varies across goods; it is very large in the production of sophisticated goods like aircraft but not that large in the production of simpler goods like clothing. So Bangladesh's position with regard to clothing production is like Embraer's position with respect to producing small jets: it's not as good at it as Boeing, but it's the thing Embraer does comparatively well.

Although Bangladesh is at an absolute disadvantage compared with the United States in almost everything, it has a comparative advantage in clothing production. This means that both the United States and Bangladesh are able to consume more because they specialize in producing different things, with Bangladesh supplying our clothes and the United States supplying Bangladesh with more sophisticated goods.

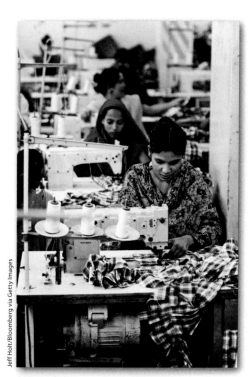

Although less productive than the American economy, Bangladesh's economy has a comparative advantage in clothing production.

>> Check Your Understanding 2-1
Solutions appear at back of book.

1. True or false? Explain your answer.
   a. An increase in the amount of resources available to Boeing for use in producing Dreamliners and small jets does not change its production possibility frontier.
   b. A technological change that allows Boeing to build more small jets for any amount of Dreamliners built results in a change in its production possibility frontier.
   c. The production possibility frontier is useful because it illustrates how much of one good an economy must give up to get more of another good regardless of whether resources are being used efficiently.

2. In Italy, an automobile can be produced by 8 workers in one day and a washing machine by 3 workers in one day. In the United States, an automobile can be produced by 6 workers in one day and a washing machine by 2 workers in one day.
   a. Which country has an absolute advantage in the production of automobiles? In washing machines?
   b. Which country has a comparative advantage in the production of washing machines? In automobiles?
   c. What pattern of specialization results in the greatest gains from trade between the two countries?

3. Using Table 1, explain why the United States and Brazil are willing to engage in a trade of 10 large jets for 15 small jets.

4. Use the circular-flow diagram to explain how an increase in the amount of money spent by households results in an increase in the number of jobs in the economy. Describe in words what the circular-flow diagram predicts.

Using Models

We have now seen how economic analysis is mainly a matter of creating models that draw on a set of basic principles but add some more specific assumptions that allow the modeler to apply those principles to a particular situation. But what do economists actually *do* with their models?

Positive versus Normative Economics

Imagine that you are an economic adviser to the governor of your state. What kinds of questions might the governor ask you to answer?

Well, here are three possible questions:

1. How much revenue will the tolls on the state turnpike yield next year?
2. How much would that revenue increase if the toll were raised from $1 to $1.50?
3. Should the toll be raised, bearing in mind that a toll increase will reduce traffic and air pollution near the road but will impose some financial hardship on frequent commuters?

There is a big difference between the first two questions and the third one. The first two are questions about facts. Your forecast of next year's toll collection will be proved right or wrong when the numbers actually come in. Your estimate of the impact of a change in the toll is a little harder to check—revenue depends on other factors besides the toll, and it may be hard to disentangle the causes of any change in revenue. Still, in principle there is only one right answer.

But the question of whether tolls should be raised may not have a "right" answer—two people who agree on the effects of a higher toll could still disagree about whether raising the toll is a good idea. For example, someone who lives near the turnpike but doesn't commute on it will care a lot about noise and air

positive economics the branch of economic analysis that describes the way the economy actually works.

normative economics the branch of economic analysis that makes prescriptions about the way the economy should work.

forecast a simple prediction of the future.

pollution but not so much about commuting costs. A regular commuter who doesn't live near the turnpike will have the opposite priorities.

This example highlights a key distinction between two roles of economic analysis. Analysis that tries to answer questions about the way the world works, which have definite right and wrong answers, is known as **positive economics.** In contrast, analysis that involves saying how the world *should* work is known as **normative economics.** To put it another way, positive economics is about description; normative economics is about prescription.

Positive economics occupies most of the time and effort of the economics profession. And models play a crucial role in almost all positive economics. As we mentioned earlier, the U.S. government uses a computer model to assess proposed changes in national tax policy, and many state governments have similar models to assess the effects of their own tax policy.

It's worth noting that there is a subtle but important difference between the first and second questions we imagined the governor asking. Question 1 asked for a simple prediction about next year's revenue—a **forecast.** Question 2 was a "what if" question, asking how revenue would change if the tax law were changed. Economists are often called upon to answer both types of questions, but models are especially useful for answering "what if" questions.

The answers to such questions often serve as a guide to policy, but they are still predictions, not prescriptions. That is, they tell you what will happen if a policy were changed; they don't tell you whether or not that result is good.

Suppose your economic model tells you that the governor's proposed increase in highway tolls will raise property values in communities near the road but will hurt people who must use the turnpike to get to work. Does that make this proposed toll increase a good idea or a bad one? It depends on whom you ask. As we've just seen, someone who is very concerned with the communities near the road will support the increase, but someone who is very concerned with the welfare of drivers will feel differently. That's a value judgment—it's not a question of economic analysis.

Still, economists often do engage in normative economics and give policy advice. How can they do this when there may be no "right" answer?

One answer is that economists are also citizens, and we all have our opinions. But economic analysis can often be used to show that some policies are clearly better than others, regardless of anyone's opinions.

Suppose that policies A and B achieve the same goal, but policy A makes everyone better off than policy B—or at least makes some people better off without making other people worse off. Then A is clearly more efficient than B. That's not a value judgment: we're talking about how best to achieve a goal, not about the goal itself.

For example, two different policies have been used to help low-income families obtain housing: rent control, which limits the rents landlords are allowed to charge, and rent subsidies, which provide families with additional money to pay rent. Almost all economists agree that subsidies are the more efficient policy. And so the great majority of economists, whatever their personal politics, favor subsidies over rent control.

When policies can be clearly ranked in this way, then economists generally agree. But it is no secret that economists sometimes disagree.

When and Why Economists Disagree

Economists have a reputation for arguing with each other. Where does this reputation come from, and is it justified?

One important answer is that media coverage tends to exaggerate the real differences in views among economists. If nearly all economists agree on an issue—for example, the proposition that rent controls lead to housing shortages—reporters and editors are likely to conclude that it's not a story worth covering, leaving the professional consensus unreported. But an issue on which prominent economists take opposing sides—for example, whether cutting taxes right now would help the economy—makes a news story worth reporting. So you hear much more about the areas of disagreement within economics than you do about the large areas of agreement.

It is also worth remembering that economics is, unavoidably, often tied up in politics. On a number of issues powerful interest groups know what opinions they want to hear; they therefore have an incentive to find and promote economists who profess those opinions, giving these economists a prominence and visibility out of proportion to their support among their colleagues.

While the appearance of disagreement among economists exceeds the reality, it remains true that economists often *do* disagree about important things. For example, some well-respected economists argue vehemently that the U.S. government should replace the income tax with a *value-added tax* (a national sales tax, which is the main source of government revenue in many European countries). Other equally respected economists disagree. Why this difference of opinion?

One important source of differences lies in values: as in any diverse group of individuals, reasonable people can differ. In comparison to an income tax, a value-added tax typically falls more heavily on people of modest means. So an economist who values a society with more social and income equality for its own sake will tend to oppose a value-added tax. An economist with different values will be less likely to oppose it.

A second important source of differences arises from economic modeling. Because economists base their conclusions on models, which are simplified representations of reality, two economists can legitimately disagree about which simplifications are appropriate—and therefore arrive at different conclusions.

Suppose that the U.S. government were considering introducing a value-added tax. Economist A may rely on a model that focuses on the administrative costs of tax systems—that is, the costs of monitoring, processing papers, collecting the tax, and so on. This economist might then point to the well-known high costs of administering a value-added tax and argue against the change. But economist B may think that the right way to approach the question is to ignore the administrative costs and focus on how the proposed law would change savings behavior. This economist might point to studies suggesting that value-added taxes promote higher consumer saving, a desirable result.

Because the economists have used different models—that is, made different simplifying assumptions—they arrive at different conclusions. And so the two economists may find themselves on different sides of the issue.

ECONOMICS >> *in Action*
When Economists Agree

"If all the economists in the world were laid end to end, they still couldn't reach a conclusion," goes an economist joke. But do economists really disagree that much? Not according to an ongoing survey. The Booth School of Business at the University of Chicago has assembled a panel of 51 economists, all with

These four economists are on the panel (clockwise from top left): Cecilia Rouse of Princeton, David Cutler of Harvard, Hilary Hoynes of UC Berkeley, and Raj Chetty of Harvard.

exemplary professional reputations, representing a mix of regions, schools, and political affiliations. They are regularly polled on questions of policy or political interest, often ones on which there are bitter divides among politicians or the general public.

Yet the survey shows much more agreement among economists than rumor would have it, even on supposedly controversial topics. For example, 98% of economists agreed that society would be better off if the cost of emitting carbon dioxide, which leads to greenhouse gases, was raised significantly. A slightly smaller percentage (82%) disagreed with the proposition that rent control increases the supply of quality, affordable housing.

In the first case, the panel overwhelmingly agreed with a position widely considered liberal in American politics, while in the second case they agreed with one widely considered politically conservative.

Disagreements tended to involve untested economic policies. There was, for example, an almost even split over whether the long-term impact of new policies forgiving student loan debt in 2022 would cause substantially higher tuition at some universities. Ideology played a limited role in these disagreements: Economists known to be liberals did have slightly different positions, on average, from those known to be conservatives, but the differences weren't nearly as large as those among the general public.

So economists do disagree quite a lot on some issues, especially in macroeconomics. But there is a large area of common ground.

>> Quick Review

• **Positive economics** — the focus of most economic research — is the analysis of the way the world works, in which there are definite right and wrong answers. It often involves making **forecasts. Normative economics,** which makes prescriptions about how things *ought to be,* inevitably involves value judgments.

• Economists do disagree — though not as much as legend has it — for two main reasons. One, they may disagree about which simplifications to make in a model. Two, economists may disagree — like everyone else — about values.

>> Check Your Understanding 2-2

Solutions appear at back of book.

1. Which of the following is a positive statement? Which is a normative statement?
   a. Society should take measures to prevent people from engaging in dangerous personal behavior.
   b. People who engage in dangerous personal behavior impose higher costs on society through higher medical costs.

2. True or false? Explain your answer.
   a. Policy choice A and policy choice B attempt to achieve the same social goal. Policy choice A, however, results in a much less efficient use of resources than policy choice B. Therefore, economists are more likely to agree on choosing policy choice B.
   b. When two economists disagree on the desirability of a policy, it's typically because one of them has made a mistake.

Efficiency, Opportunity Cost, and the Logic of Lean Production

Daniel Acker/Bloomberg/Getty Images

In January 2020, the Boeing 777X, an update to the widely popular 777, took its maiden flight. The 777X was the product of what Boeing calls its *advanced manufacturing* process. With it, Boeing extended its extremely successful process known as *lean production* to newer production methods, such as robotics.

Lean manufacturing, pioneered by Toyota Motors of Japan, is based on the practice of having parts arrive on the factory floor just as they are needed for production. This reduces the amount of parts Boeing holds in inventory as well as the amount of the factory floor needed for production. To help move from lean production to advanced manufacturing Boeing has turned to Toyota, hiring some of their top engineers.

Boeing first adopted lean manufacturing in 1999 in the manufacture of the 737, the most popular commercial airplane. By 2005, after constant refinement, it achieved a 50% reduction in the time it takes to produce a plane and a nearly 60% reduction in parts inventory. An important feature is a continuously moving assembly line, moving products from one assembly team to the next at a steady pace and eliminating the need for workers to wander across the factory floor from task to task or in search of tools and parts.

Toyota's lean production techniques have been the most widely adopted, revolutionizing manufacturing worldwide. In simple terms, lean production is focused on organization and communication. Workers and parts are organized so as to ensure a smooth and consistent workflow that minimizes wasted effort and materials. Lean production is also designed to be highly responsive to changes in the desired mix of output—for example, quickly producing more SUVs and fewer sedans according to changes in customer demand.

Toyota's methods were so successful that they transformed the global auto industry and severely threatened once-dominant American automakers. Until the 1980s, the "Big Three"—Chrysler, Ford, and General Motors—dominated the American auto industry, with virtually no foreign-made cars sold in the United States. In the 1980s, however, Toyotas became increasingly popular due to their high quality and relatively low price—so popular that the Big Three eventually prevailed upon the U.S. government to protect them by restricting the sale of Japanese autos in the United States. Over time, Toyota responded by building assembly plants in the United States, bringing along its lean production techniques, which then spread throughout American manufacturing.

QUESTIONS FOR THOUGHT

1. What is the opportunity cost associated with having a worker wander across the factory floor from task to task or in search of tools and parts?

2. Explain how lean manufacturing improves the economy's efficiency in allocation.

3. Before lean manufacturing innovations, Japan mostly sold consumer electronics to the United States. How did lean manufacturing innovations alter Japan's comparative advantage vis-à-vis the United States?

4. How do you think the shift in the location of Toyota's production from Japan to the United States has altered the pattern of comparative advantage in automaking between the two countries?

SUMMARY

1. Almost all economics is based on **models,** "thought experiments" or simplified versions of reality, many of which use mathematical tools such as graphs. An important assumption in economic models is the **other things equal assumption,** which allows analysis of the effect of a change in one factor by holding all other relevant factors unchanged.

2. One important economic model is the **production possibility frontier.** It illustrates *opportunity cost* (showing how much less of one good can be produced if more of the other good is produced); *efficiency* (an economy is efficient in production if it produces on the production possibility frontier and efficient in allocation if it produces the mix of goods and services that people want to consume); and *economic growth* (an outward shift of the production possibility frontier). There are two basic sources of growth: an increase in **factors of production**—resources such as land, labor, capital, and human capital, inputs that are not used up in production—and improved **technology.**

3. Another important model is **comparative advantage,** which explains the source of gains from trade between individuals and countries. Everyone has a comparative advantage in something—some good or service in which that person has a lower opportunity cost than everyone else. But it is often confused with **absolute advantage,** an ability to produce a particular good or service better than anyone else. This confusion leads some to erroneously conclude that there are no gains from trade between people or countries.

4. In the simplest economies people **barter**—trade goods and services for one another—rather than trade them for money, as in a modern economy. The **circular-flow diagram** represents transactions within the economy as flows of goods, services, and money between **households** and **firms.** These transactions occur in **markets for goods and services** and **factor markets,** markets for factors of production—land, labor, physical capital, and human capital. The circular-flow diagram is useful in understanding how spending, production, employment, income, and growth are related in the economy. Ultimately, factor markets determine the economy's **income distribution,** how an economy's total income is allocated to the owners of the factors of production.

5. Economists use economic models for both **positive economics,** which describes how the economy works, and for **normative economics,** which prescribes how the economy *should* work. Positive economics often involves making **forecasts.** Economists can determine correct answers for positive questions but typically not for normative questions, which involve value judgments. The exceptions are when policies designed to achieve a certain objective can be clearly ranked in terms of efficiency.

6. There are two main reasons economists disagree. One, they may disagree about which simplifications to make in a model. Two, economists may disagree—like everyone else—about values.

KEY TERMS

Model, p. 28
Other things equal assumption, p. 28
Production possibility frontier, p. 29
Factors of production, p. 33
Technology, p. 34
Comparative advantage, p. 36

Absolute advantage, p. 37
Barter, p. 38
Circular-flow diagram, p. 39
Household, p. 39
Firm, p. 39
Markets for goods and services, p. 39

Factor markets, p. 39
Income distribution, p. 39
Positive economics, p. 42
Normative economics, p. 42
Forecast, p. 42

PRACTICE QUESTIONS

1. Penelope Pundit, an economics reporter, states that the European Union (EU) is increasing its productivity very rapidly in all industries. She claims that this productivity advance is so rapid that output from the EU in these industries will soon exceed that of the United States and, as a result, the United States will no longer benefit from trade with the EU.

   a. Do you think Penelope Pundit is correct or not? If not, what do you think is the source of her mistake?

   b. If the EU and the United States continue to trade, what do you think will characterize the goods that the EU sells to the United States and the goods that the United States sells to the EU?

2. The inhabitants of the fictional economy of Atlantis use money in the form of cowry shells. Draw a circular-flow diagram showing households and firms. Firms produce potatoes and fish, and households buy potatoes and fish. Households also provide the land and labor to firms. Identify where in the flows of cowry shells or physical things (goods and services, or resources) each of the following impacts would occur. Describe how this impact spreads around the circle.

   a. A devastating hurricane floods many of the potato fields.

   b. A very productive fishing season yields a very large number of fish caught.

   c. The inhabitants of Atlantis discover Shakira and spend several days a month at dancing festivals.

3. An economist might say that colleges and universities "produce" education, using faculty members and students as inputs. According to this line of reasoning, education is then "consumed" by households. Construct a circular-flow diagram to represent the sector of the economy devoted to college education: colleges and universities represent firms, and households both consume education and provide faculty and students to universities. What are the relevant markets in this diagram? What is being bought and sold in each direction? What would happen in the diagram if the government decided to subsidize 50% of all college students' tuition?

4. A representative of the U.S. clothing industry made the following statement: "Workers in Asia often work in sweatshop conditions earning only pennies an hour. American workers are more productive and as a result earn higher wages. In order to preserve the dignity of the American workplace, the government should enact legislation banning imports of low-wage Asian clothing."

   a. Which parts of this quote are positive statements? Which parts are normative statements?

   b. Is the policy that is being advocated consistent with the preceding statements about the wages and productivities of American and Asian workers?

   c. Would such a policy make some Americans better off without making any other Americans worse off? That is, would this policy be efficient from the viewpoint of all Americans?

   d. Would Asian workers earning low wages benefit from or be hurt by such a policy?

5. Evaluate the following statement: "It is easier to build an economic model that accurately reflects events that have already occurred than to build an economic model to forecast future events." Do you think this is true or not? Why? What does this imply about the difficulties of building good economic models?

6. Economists who work for the government are often called on to make policy recommendations. Why do you think it is important for the public to be able to differentiate normative statements from positive statements in these recommendations?

PROBLEMS

1. Two important industries on the island of Bermuda are fishing and tourism. According to data from the Food and Agriculture Organization of the United Nations and the Bermuda Department of Statistics, 315 registered fishermen in Bermuda caught 497 metric tons of marine fish. And 2,446 people employed by hotels produced 580,209 hotel stays (measured by the number of visitor arrivals). Suppose that this production point is efficient in production. Assume also that the opportunity cost of 1 additional metric ton of fish is 2,000 hotel stays and that this opportunity cost is constant (the opportunity cost does not change).

   a. If all 315 registered fishermen were to be employed by hotels (in addition to the 2,446 people already working in hotels), how many hotel stays could Bermuda produce?

   b. If all 2,446 hotel employees were to become fishermen (in addition to the 315 fishermen already working in the fishing industry), how many metric tons of fish could Bermuda produce?

   c. Draw a production possibility frontier for Bermuda, with fish on the horizontal axis and hotel stays on the vertical axis, and label Bermuda's actual production point.

2. According to data from the U.S. Department of Agriculture's National Agricultural Statistics Service, 124 million acres of land in the United States were used for wheat or corn farming in a recent year. Of those 124 million acres, farmers used 50 million acres to grow 2.158 billion bushels of wheat and 74 million acres to grow 11.807 billion bushels of corn. Suppose that U.S. wheat and corn farming is efficient in production. At that production point, the opportunity cost of producing 1 additional bushel of wheat is 1.7 fewer bushels of corn. However, because farmers have increasing opportunity costs, additional bushels of wheat have an opportunity cost greater than 1.7 bushels of corn. For each of the following production points, decide whether that production point is (i) feasible and efficient in production, (ii) feasible but not efficient in production, (iii) not feasible, or (iv) unclear as to whether or not it is feasible.

   a. Farmers use 40 million acres of land to produce 1.8 billion bushels of wheat, and they use 60 million acres of land to produce 9 billion bushels of corn. The remaining 24 million acres are left unused.

   b. From their original production point, farmers transfer 40 million acres of land from corn to wheat production. They now produce 3.158 billion bushels of wheat and 10.107 bushels of corn.

c. Farmers reduce their production of wheat to 2 billion bushels and increase their production of corn to 12.044 billion bushels. Along the production possibility frontier, the opportunity cost of going from 11.807 billion bushels of corn to 12.044 billion bushels of corn is 0.666 bushel of wheat per bushel of corn.

3. In the ancient country of Roma, only two goods, spaghetti and meatballs, are produced. There are two tribes in Roma, the Tivoli and the Frivoli. By themselves, the Tivoli each month can produce either 30 pounds of spaghetti and no meatballs, or 50 pounds of meatballs and no spaghetti, or any combination in between. The Frivoli, by themselves, each month can produce 40 pounds of spaghetti and no meatballs, or 30 pounds of meatballs and no spaghetti, or any combination in between.

a. Assume that all production possibility frontiers are straight lines. Draw one diagram showing the monthly production possibility frontier for the Tivoli and another showing the monthly production possibility frontier for the Frivoli. Show how you calculated them.

b. Which tribe has the comparative advantage in spaghetti production? In meatball production?
   In A.D. 100, the Frivoli discover a new technique for making meatballs that doubles the quantity of meatballs they can produce each month.

c. Draw the new monthly production possibility frontier for the Frivoli.

d. After the innovation, which tribe now has an absolute advantage in producing meatballs? In producing spaghetti? Which has the comparative advantage in meatball production? In spaghetti production?

4. One July, the United States sold aircraft worth $1 billion to China and bought aircraft worth only $19,000 from China. During the same month, however, the United States bought $83 million worth of men's pants, shorts, and jeans from China but sold only $8,000 worth of pants, shorts, and jeans to China. Using what you have learned about how trade is determined by comparative advantage, answer the following questions.

a. Which country has the comparative advantage in aircraft production? In production of pants, shorts, and jeans?

b. Can you determine which country has the absolute advantage in aircraft production? In production of pants, shorts, and jeans?

5. You are in charge of allocating residents to your dormitory's baseball and basketball teams. You are down to the last four people, two of whom must be allocated to baseball and two to basketball. The accompanying table gives each person's batting average and free-throw average.

Name	Batting average	Free-throw average
Taylor	70%	60%
Nico	50%	50%
Annie	10%	30%
Ryan	80%	70%

a. Explain how you would use the concept of comparative advantage to allocate the players. Begin by establishing each player's opportunity cost of free throws in terms of batting average.

b. Why is it likely that the other basketball players will be unhappy about this arrangement but the other baseball players will be satisfied? Nonetheless, why would an economist say that this is an efficient way to allocate players for your dorm's sports teams?

6. Your roommate plays loud music most of the time; you, however, would prefer more peace and quiet. You suggest that they buy some headphones. Your roommate responds that although they would be happy to use headphones, they have many other things that they would prefer to spend money on right now. You discuss this situation with a friend who is an economics major. The following exchange takes place:

Friend: How much would it cost to buy headphones?
You: $15.
Friend: How much do you value having some peace and quiet for the rest of the semester?
You: $30.
Friend: It is efficient for you to buy the headphones and give them to your roommate. You gain more than you lose; the benefit exceeds the cost. You should do that.
You: It just isn't fair that I have to pay for the headphones when I'm not the one making the noise.

a. Which parts of this conversation contain positive statements and which parts contain normative statements?

b. Construct an argument supporting your viewpoint that your roommate should be the one to change their behavior. Similarly, construct an argument from the viewpoint of your roommate that you should be the one to buy the headphones. If your dormitory has a policy that gives residents the unlimited right to play music, whose argument is likely to win? If your dormitory has a rule that a person must stop playing music whenever a roommate complains, whose argument is likely to win?

7. Are the following statements true or false? Explain your answers.

a. "When people must pay higher taxes on their wage earnings, it reduces their incentive to work" is a positive statement.

b. "We should lower taxes to encourage more work" is a positive statement.

c. Economics cannot always be used to completely decide what society ought to do.

d. "The system of public education in this country generates greater benefits to society than the cost of running the system" is a normative statement.

e. All disagreements among economists are generated by the media.

8. The mayor of Gotham City, worried about a potential epidemic of deadly influenza this winter, asks an economic adviser the following series of questions. Determine whether a question requires the economic adviser to make a positive assessment or a normative assessment.

a. How much vaccine will be in stock in the city by the end of November?

b. If we offer to pay 10% more per dose to the pharmaceutical companies providing the vaccines, will they provide additional doses?

c. If there is a shortage of vaccine in the city, whom should we vaccinate first—the elderly or the very young? (Assume that a person from one group has an equal likelihood of dying from influenza as a person from the other group.)

d. If the city charges $25 per shot, how many people will pay?

e. If the city charges $25 per shot, it will make a profit of $10 per shot, money that can go to pay for inoculating poor people. Should the city engage in such a scheme?

9. The Observatory of World Complexity (oec.world) presents data for nearly all countries and products traded in the global economy. Use this website to answer the following questions:

a. Using the search box, find the two countries that have a comparative advantage in producing soybeans.

b. What does Australia have a comparative advantage producing?

c. What is the value of Bangladesh's exports? Approximately what percent of Bangladesh's exports are textiles (clothing)?

d. Search products for "Planes, Helicopters and/or Spacecraft." Analyze the table showing exports and imports by country. Many countries show up as both large exporters and importers. Using the concept of comparative advantage explain how it's possible to be both an exporter and importer of airplanes.

10. A recent study published in the journal of *Work, Employment, and Society* found that, "Women with children reduced housework from 18 to 14 hours a week as they went from earning zero to half of the household income. But after passing her husband's salary, a woman's home tasks increased to nearly 16 hours a week, the analysis found. In contrast, a man's housework ranged from six to eight hours a week when he was the primary breadwinner but then declined as his wife out-earned him." Use the concepts of opportunity cost and comparative advantage to explain how households can come to a more efficient allocation of working and household chores.

11. Atlantis is a small, isolated island in the South Atlantic. The inhabitants grow potatoes and catch fish. The accompanying table shows the maximum annual output combinations of potatoes and fish that can be produced. Obviously, given their limited resources and available technology, as they use more of their resources for potato production, there are fewer resources available for catching fish.

Maximum annual output options	Quantity of potatoes (pounds)	Quantity of fish (pounds)
A	1,000	0
B	800	300
C	600	500
D	400	600
E	200	650
F	0	675

a. Draw a production possibility frontier with potatoes on the horizontal axis and fish on the vertical axis illustrating these options, showing points *A–F.*

b. Can Atlantis produce 500 pounds of fish and 800 pounds of potatoes? Explain. Where would this point lie relative to the production possibility frontier?

c. What is the opportunity cost of increasing the annual output of potatoes from 600 to 800 pounds?

d. What is the opportunity cost of increasing the annual output of potatoes from 200 to 400 pounds?

e. Can you explain why the answers to parts c and d are not the same? What does this imply about the slope of the production possibility frontier? ∎

Graphs in Economics

Getting the Picture

When reading about economics in the *Wall Street Journal* or in your economics textbook, you will see many graphs. Visual images can make it much easier to understand verbal descriptions, numerical information, or ideas. In economics, graphs are the type of visual image used to facilitate understanding. So, you need to be familiar with how to interpret and construct these visual aids. This appendix explains how to do this.

Graphs, Variables, and Economic Models

One reason to attend college is that a bachelor's degree provides access to higher paying jobs. Additional degrees, such as MBAs or law degrees, increase earnings even more. If you were to read an article about the relationship between educational attainment and income, you would probably see a graph showing the income levels for workers with different amounts of education. And this graph would depict the idea that, in general, more education increases income.

This graph, like most of those in economics, would depict the relationship between two economic variables. A **variable** is a quantity that can take on more than one value, such as the number of years of education a person has, the price of a can of soda, or a household's income.

As you learned in Chapter 2, economic analysis relies heavily on *models*, simplified descriptions of real situations. Most economic models describe the relationship between two variables, simplified by holding constant other variables that may affect the relationship.

For example, an economic model might describe the relationship between the price of a can of soda and the number of cans of soda that consumers will buy, assuming that everything else affecting consumers' purchases of soda stays constant. This type of model can be described mathematically or verbally, but illustrating the relationship in a graph makes it easier to understand, as you'll see next.

How Graphs Work

Most graphs in economics are based on a grid built around two perpendicular lines that show the values of two variables, helping you visualize the relationship between them. Let's see how this works.

Two-Variable Graphs

Figure A-1 shows a typical two-variable graph. It illustrates the data in the accompanying table on outside temperature and the number of sodas a typical vendor can expect to sell at a baseball stadium during one game. The first column shows the values of outside temperature (the first variable) and the second column shows the values of the number of sodas sold (the second variable). Five combinations or pairs of the two variables are shown, each denoted by *A* through *E* in the third column.

Now let's turn to graphing the data in this table. In any two-variable graph, one variable is called the *x*-variable and the other is called the *y*-variable. Here we have

variable a quantity that can take on more than one value.

FIGURE A-1 Plotting Points on a Two-Variable Graph

The data from the table are plotted where outside temperature (the independent variable) is measured along the horizontal axis and number of sodas sold (the dependent variable) is measured along the vertical axis. Each of the five combinations of temperature and sodas sold is represented by a point: A, B, C, D, and E. Each point in the graph is identified by a pair of values. For example, point C corresponds to the pair (40, 30) — an outside temperature of 40°F (the value of the x-variable) and 30 sodas sold (the value of the y-variable).

horizontal axis the horizontal number line of a graph along which values of the x-variable are measured; also referred to as the **x-axis.**

vertical axis the vertical number line of a graph along which values of the y-variable are measured; also referred to as the **y-axis.**

origin the point where the axes of a two-variable graph meet.

causal relationship the relationship between two variables in which the value taken by one variable directly influences or determines the value taken by the other variable.

independent variable the determining variable in a causal relationship.

dependent variable the determined variable in a causal relationship.

made outside temperature the x-variable and number of sodas sold the y-variable. The solid horizontal line in the graph is called the **horizontal axis or x-axis,** and values of the x-variable—outside temperature—are measured along it. Similarly, the solid vertical line in the graph is called the **vertical axis or y-axis,** and values of the y-variable—number of sodas sold—are measured along it.

At the **origin,** the point where the two axes meet, each variable is equal to zero. As you move rightward from the origin along the x-axis, values of the x-variable are positive and increasing. As you move up from the origin along the y-axis, values of the y-variable are positive and increasing.

You can plot each of the five points A through E on this graph by using a pair of numbers—the values that the x-variable and the y-variable take on for a given point. In Figure A-1, at point C, the x-variable takes on the value 40 and the y-variable takes on the value 30. You plot point C by drawing a line straight up from 40 on the x-axis and a horizontal line across from 30 on the y-axis. We write point C as (40, 30). We write the origin as (0, 0).

Looking at point A and point B in Figure A-1, you can see that when one of the variables for a point has a value of zero, it will lie on one of the axes. If the value of the x-variable is zero, the point will lie on the vertical axis, like point A. If the value of the y-variable is zero, the point will lie on the horizontal axis, like point B.

Most graphs that depict relationships between two economic variables represent a **causal relationship,** a relationship in which the value taken by one variable directly influences or determines the value taken by the other variable. In a causal relationship, the determining variable is called the **independent variable;** the variable it determines is called the **dependent variable.** In our example of soda sales, the outside temperature is the independent variable. It directly influences the number of sodas that are sold, the dependent variable in this case.

By convention, we put the independent variable on the horizontal axis and the dependent variable on the vertical axis. Figure A-1 is constructed consistent with this convention; the independent variable (outside temperature) is on the horizontal axis and the dependent variable (number of sodas sold) is on the vertical axis.

An important exception to this convention is in graphs showing the economic relationship between the price of a product and quantity of the product: although price is generally the independent variable that determines quantity, it is always measured on the vertical axis.

Curves on a Graph

Panel (a) of Figure A-2 contains some of the same information as Figure A-1, with a line drawn through the points *B, C, D,* and *E.* Such a line on a graph is called a **curve,** regardless of whether it is a straight line or a curved line. If the curve that shows the relationship between two variables is a straight line, or linear, the variables have a **linear relationship.** When the curve is not a straight line, or nonlinear, the variables have a **nonlinear relationship.**

A point on a curve indicates the value of the *y*-variable for a specific value of the *x*-variable. For example, point *D* indicates that at a temperature of 60°F, a vendor can expect to sell 50 sodas. The shape and orientation of a curve reveal the general nature of the relationship between the two variables. The upward tilt of the curve in panel (a) of Figure A-2 means that vendors can expect to sell more sodas at higher outside temperatures.

When variables are related this way—that is, when an increase in one variable is associated with an increase in the other variable—the variables are said to have

curve a line on a graph, which may be curved or straight, that depicts a relationship between two variables.

linear relationship the relationship between two variables in which the slope is constant and therefore is depicted on a graph by a curve that is a straight line.

nonlinear relationship the relationship between two variables in which the slope is not constant and therefore is depicted on a graph by a curve that is not a straight line.

FIGURE A-2 Drawing Curves

(a) Positive Linear Relationship

(b) Negative Linear Relationship

The curve in panel (a) illustrates the relationship between the two variables, outside temperature and number of sodas sold. The two variables have a positive linear relationship: positive because the curve has an upward tilt, and linear because it is a straight line. It implies that an increase in the *x*-variable (outside temperature) leads to an increase in the *y*-variable (number of sodas sold). The curve in panel (b) is also a straight line, but it tilts downward. The two variables here, outside temperature and number of hot drinks sold, have a negative linear relationship: an increase in the *x*-variable (outside temperature) leads to a decrease in the *y*-variable (number of hot drinks sold). The curve in panel (a) has a horizontal intercept at point *B,* where it hits the horizontal axis. The curve in panel (b) has a vertical intercept at point *J,* where it hits the vertical axis, and a horizontal intercept at point *M,* where it hits the horizontal axis.

positive relationship a relationship between two variables in which an increase in the value of one variable is associated with an increase in the value of the other variable. It is illustrated by a curve that slopes upward from left to right.

negative relationship a relationship between two variables in which an increase in the value of one variable is associated with a decrease in the value of the other variable. It is illustrated by a curve that slopes downward from left to right.

horizontal intercept the point at which a curve hits the horizontal axis; it indicates the value of the x-variable when the value of the y-variable is zero.

vertical intercept the point at which a curve hits the vertical axis; it shows the value of the y-variable when the value of the x-variable is zero.

slope a measure of how steep a line or curve is. The slope of a line is measured by "rise over run"—the change in the y-variable between two points on the line divided by the change in the x-variable between those same two points.

a **positive relationship.** It is illustrated by a curve that slopes upward from left to right. Because this curve is also linear, the relationship between outside temperature and number of sodas sold illustrated by the curve in panel (a) of Figure A-2 is a positive linear relationship.

When an increase in one variable is associated with a decrease in the other variable, the two variables are said to have a **negative relationship.** It is illustrated by a curve that slopes downward from left to right, like the curve in panel (b) of Figure A-2. Because this curve is also linear, the relationship it depicts is a negative linear relationship. Two variables that might have such a relationship are the outside temperature and the number of hot drinks a vendor can expect to sell at a baseball stadium.

Return for a moment to the curve in panel (a) of Figure A-2 and you can see that it hits the horizontal axis at point B. This point, known as the **horizontal intercept,** shows the value of the x-variable when the value of the y-variable is zero. In panel (b) of Figure A-2, the curve hits the vertical axis at point J. This point, called the **vertical intercept,** indicates the value of the y-variable when the value of the x-variable is zero.

A Key Concept: The Slope of a Curve

The **slope** of a curve is a measure of how steep it is and indicates how sensitive the y-variable is to a change in the x-variable. In our example of outside temperature and the number of cans of soda a vendor can expect to sell, the slope of the curve would indicate how many more cans of soda the vendor could expect to sell with each 1 degree increase in temperature. Interpreted this way, the slope gives meaningful information. Even without numbers for x and y, it is possible to arrive at important conclusions about the relationship between the two variables by examining the slope of a curve at various points.

The Slope of a Linear Curve

Along a linear curve the slope, or steepness, is measured by dividing the *rise* between two points on the curve by the *run* between those same two points. The rise is the amount that y changes, and the run is the amount that x changes. Here is the formula:

$$\frac{\text{Change in } y}{\text{Change in } x} = \frac{\Delta y}{\Delta x} = \text{Slope}$$

In the formula, the symbol Δ (the Greek uppercase delta) stands for *change in*. When a variable increases, the change in that variable is positive; when a variable decreases, the change in that variable is negative.

The slope of a curve is positive when the rise (the change in the y-variable) has the same sign as the run (the change in the x-variable). That's because when two numbers have the same sign, the ratio of those two numbers is positive. The curve in panel (a) of Figure A-2 has a positive slope: along the curve, both the y-variable and the x-variable increase.

The slope of a curve is negative when the rise and the run have different signs. That's because when two numbers have different signs, the ratio of those two numbers is negative. The curve in panel (b) of Figure A-2 has a negative slope: along the curve, an increase in the x-variable is associated with a decrease in the y-variable.

Figure A-3 illustrates how to calculate the slope of a linear curve. Let's focus first on panel (a). From point A to point B, the value of the y-variable changes from 25 to 20 and the value of the x-variable changes from 10 to 20. So the slope of the line between these two points is:

$$\frac{\text{Change in } y}{\text{Change in } x} = \frac{\Delta y}{\Delta x} = \frac{-5}{10} = -\frac{1}{2} = -0.5$$

FIGURE A-3 Calculating the Slope

(a) Negative Constant Slope

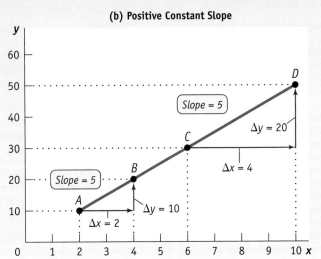

(b) Positive Constant Slope

Panels (a) and (b) show two linear curves. Between points *A* and *B* on the curve in panel (a), the change in *y* (the rise) is −5 and the change in *x* (the run) is 10. So the slope from *A* to *B* is $\frac{\Delta y}{\Delta x} = \frac{-5}{10} = -\frac{1}{2} = -0.5$, where the negative sign indicates that the curve is downward sloping. In panel (b), the curve has a slope from *A* to *B* of $\frac{\Delta y}{\Delta x} = \frac{10}{2} = 5$. The slope from *C* to *D* is $\frac{\Delta y}{\Delta x} = \frac{20}{4} = 5$. The slope is positive, indicating that the curve is upward sloping. Furthermore, the slope between *A* and *B* is the same as the slope between *C* and *D*, making this a linear curve. The slope of a linear curve is constant: it is the same regardless of where it is measured along the curve.

Because a straight line is equally steep at all points, the slope of a straight line is the same at all points. In other words, a straight line has a constant slope. You can check this by calculating the slope of the linear curve between points *A* and *B* and between points *C* and *D* in panel (b) of Figure A-3.

Between *A* and *B*: $\frac{\Delta y}{\Delta x} = \frac{10}{2} = 5$

Between *C* and *D*: $\frac{\Delta y}{\Delta x} = \frac{20}{4} = 5$

Horizontal and Vertical Curves and Their Slopes

When a curve is horizontal, the value of the *y*-variable along that curve never changes—it is constant. Everywhere along the curve, the change in *y* is zero. Now, zero divided by any number is zero. So, regardless of the value of the change in *x*, the slope of a horizontal curve is always zero.

If a curve is vertical, the value of the *x*-variable along the curve never changes—it is constant. Everywhere along the curve, the change in *x* is zero. This means that the slope of a vertical curve is a ratio with zero in the denominator. A ratio with zero in the denominator is equal to infinity—that is, an infinitely large number. So the slope of a vertical curve is equal to infinity.

A vertical or a horizontal curve has a special implication: it means that the *x*-variable and the *y*-variable are unrelated. Two variables are unrelated when a change in one variable (the independent variable) has no effect on the other variable (the dependent variable). Or to put it a slightly different way, two variables are unrelated when the dependent variable is constant regardless of the value of the independent variable. If, as is usual, the y-variable is the dependent variable, the curve is horizontal. If the dependent variable is the x-variable, the curve is vertical.

The Slope of a Nonlinear Curve

A **nonlinear curve** is one in which the slope changes as you move along it. Panels (a), (b), (c), and (d) of Figure A-4 show various nonlinear curves. Panels (a) and (b) show nonlinear curves whose slopes change as you move along them, but the slopes always remain positive. Although both curves tilt upward, the curve in panel (a) gets steeper as you move from left to right in contrast to the curve in panel (b), which gets flatter.

A curve that is upward sloping and gets steeper, as in panel (a), is said to have *positive increasing* slope. A curve that is upward sloping but gets flatter, as in panel (b), is said to have *positive decreasing* slope.

When we calculate the slope along these nonlinear curves, we obtain different values for the slope at different points. How the slope changes along the curve determines the curve's shape. For example, in panel (a) of Figure A-4, the slope of the curve is a positive number that steadily increases as you move from left to right, whereas in panel (b), the slope is a positive number that steadily decreases.

The slopes of the curves in panels (c) and (d) are negative numbers. Economists often prefer to express a negative number as its **absolute value,** which is the value of the negative number without the minus sign. In general, we denote the absolute value of a number by two parallel bars around the number; for example, the absolute value of –4 is written as $|-4| = 4$.

In panel (c), the absolute value of the slope steadily increases as you move from left to right. The curve therefore has *negative increasing* slope. And in panel (d), the absolute value of the slope of the curve steadily decreases along the curve. This curve therefore has *negative decreasing* slope.

Calculating the Slope Along a Nonlinear Curve

We've just seen that along a nonlinear curve, the value of the slope depends on where you are on that curve. So how do you calculate the slope of a nonlinear curve? We will focus on two methods: the *arc method* and the *point method*.

The Arc Method of Calculating the Slope An arc of a curve is some piece or segment of that curve. For example, panel (a) of Figure A-4 shows an arc consisting of the segment of the curve between points *A* and *B*. To calculate the slope along a nonlinear curve using the arc method, you draw a straight line between the two end-points of the arc. The slope of that straight line is a measure of the average slope of the curve between those two endpoints.

You can see from panel (a) of Figure A-4 that the straight line drawn between points *A* and *B* increases along the x-axis from 6 to 10 (so that $\Delta x = 4$) as it increases along the y-axis from 10 to 20 (so that $\Delta y = 10$). Therefore, the slope of the straight line connecting points *A* and *B* is:

$$\frac{\Delta y}{\Delta x} = \frac{10}{4} = 2.5$$

This means that the average slope of the curve between points *A* and *B* is 2.5.

Now consider the arc on the same curve between points *C* and *D*. A straight line drawn through these two points increases along the x-axis from 11 to 12

FIGURE A-4 Nonlinear Curves

(a) Positive Increasing Slope

Positive slope gets steeper.

Slope = 15

$\Delta y = 15$

D

Slope = 2.5

C

B

A

$\Delta x = 1$

$\Delta y = 10$

$\Delta x = 4$

(b) Positive Decreasing Slope

Slope = $1\frac{2}{3}$

D

Slope = 10

C

$\Delta y = 5$

$\Delta x = 3$

B

$\Delta y = 10$

A

Positive slope gets flatter.

$\Delta x = 1$

(c) Negative Increasing Slope

$\Delta x = 3$

A

$\Delta y = -10$

Negative slope gets steeper.

B

Slope = $-3\frac{1}{3}$

$\Delta x = 1$

C

$\Delta y = -15$

Slope = -15

D

(d) Negative Decreasing Slope

$\Delta x = 1$

A

$\Delta y = -20$

Negative slope gets flatter.

Slope = -20

B

$\Delta x = 3$

C

$\Delta y = -5$

Slope = $-1\frac{2}{3}$

D

In panel (a), the slope of the curve from A to B is $\dfrac{y}{x} = \dfrac{10}{4} = 2.5$, and from C to D it is $\dfrac{\Delta y}{\Delta x} = \dfrac{15}{1} = 15$. The slope is positive and increasing; the curve gets steeper as you move to the right. In panel (b), the slope of the curve from A to B is $\dfrac{\Delta y}{\Delta x} = \dfrac{10}{1} = 10$, and from C to D it is $\dfrac{\Delta y}{\Delta x} = \dfrac{5}{3} = 1\dfrac{2}{3}$. The slope is positive and decreasing; the curve gets flatter as you move to the right. In panel (c), the slope from A to B is $\dfrac{\Delta y}{\Delta x} = \dfrac{-10}{3} = -3\dfrac{1}{3}$, and from C

to D it is $\dfrac{\Delta y}{\Delta x} = \dfrac{-15}{1} = -15$. The slope is negative and increasing; the curve gets steeper as you move to the right. And in panel (d), the slope from A to B is $\dfrac{\Delta y}{\Delta x} = \dfrac{-20}{1} = -20$, and from C to D it is $\dfrac{\Delta y}{\Delta x} = \dfrac{-5}{3} = -1\dfrac{2}{3}$. The slope is negative and decreasing; the curve gets flatter as you move to the right. The slope in each case has been calculated by using the arc method — that is, by drawing a straight line connecting two points along a curve. The average slope between those two points is equal to the slope of the straight line between those two points.

($\Delta x = 1$) as it increases along the y-axis from 25 to 40 ($\Delta y = 15$). So the average slope between points C and D is:

$$\frac{\Delta y}{\Delta x} = \frac{15}{1} = 15$$

Therefore, the average slope between points C and D is larger than the average slope between points A and B. These calculations verify what we have already

tangent line a straight line that just touches, or is tangent to, a nonlinear curve at a particular point; the slope of the tangent line is equal to the slope of the nonlinear curve at that point.

maximum the highest point on a nonlinear curve, where the slope of the curve changes from positive to negative.

minimum the lowest point on a nonlinear curve, where the slope of the curve changes from negative to positive.

observed—that this upward-tilted curve gets steeper as you move from left to right and therefore has positive increasing slope.

The Point Method of Calculating the Slope   The point method calculates the slope of a nonlinear curve at a specific point on that curve. Figure A-5 illustrates how to calculate the slope at point *B* on the curve. First, we draw a straight line that just touches the curve at point *B*. Such a line is called a **tangent line:** the fact that it just touches the curve at point *B* and does not touch the curve at any other point on the curve means that the straight line is *tangent* to the curve at point *B*. The slope of this tangent line is equal to the slope of the nonlinear curve at point *B*.

You can see from Figure A-5 how the slope of the tangent line is calculated. From point *A* to point *C*, the change in *y* is 15 and the change in *x* is 5, generating a slope of

$$\frac{\Delta y}{\Delta x} = \frac{15}{5} = 3$$

By the point method, the slope of the curve at point *B* is equal to 3.

A natural question to ask at this point is which method should I use—the arc method or the point method—in calculating the slope of a nonlinear curve? The answer depends on the curve itself and the data used to construct it.

Use the arc method when you don't have enough information to be able to draw a smooth curve. For example, suppose that in panel (a) of Figure A-4 you have only the data represented by points *A*, *C*, and *D* and don't have the data represented by point *B* or any of the rest of the curve. Clearly, then, you can't use the point method to calculate the slope at point *B;* you would have to use the arc method to approximate the slope of the curve in this area by drawing a straight line between points *A* and *C*.

But if you have sufficient data to draw the smooth curve shown in panel (a) of Figure A-4, then you could use the point method to calculate the slope at point *B*—and at every other point along the curve as well.

Maximum and Minimum Points

The slope of a nonlinear curve can change from positive to negative or vice versa. When the slope of a curve changes from positive to negative, it creates what is called a *maximum* point of the curve. When the slope of a curve changes from negative to positive, it creates a *minimum* point.

Panel (a) of Figure A-6 illustrates a curve in which the slope changes from positive to negative as you move from left to right. When *x* is between 0 and 50, the slope of the curve is positive. At *x* equal to 50, the curve attains its highest point—the largest value of *y* along the curve. This point is called the **maximum** of the curve. When *x* exceeds 50, the slope becomes negative as the curve turns downward. Many important curves in economics, such as the curve that represents how the profit of a firm changes as it produces more output, are hill-shaped like this.

In contrast, the curve shown in panel (b) of Figure A-6 is U-shaped: it has a slope that changes from negative to positive. At *x* equal to 50, the curve reaches its lowest point—the smallest value of *y* along the curve. This point is called the **minimum** of the curve. Various important curves in economics are U-shaped like this.

FIGURE A-5 Calculating the Slope Using the Point Method

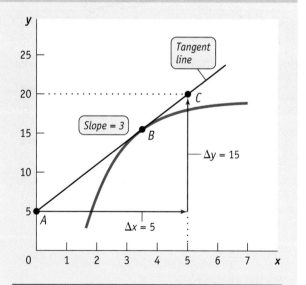

Here a tangent line has been drawn, a line that just touches the curve at point *B*. The slope of this line is equal to the slope of the curve at point *B*. The slope of the tangent line, measuring from *A* to *C*, is $\frac{\Delta y}{\Delta x} = \frac{15}{5} = 3.$

FIGURE A-6 Maximum and Minimum Points

Panel (a) shows a curve with a maximum point, the point at which the slope changes from positive to negative. Panel (b) shows a curve with a minimum point, the point at which the slope changes from negative to positive.

Calculating the Area Below or Above a Curve

It is useful to know how to measure the size of the area below or above a curve. For the sake of simplicity, we'll only calculate the area below or above a linear curve.

How large is the shaded area below the linear curve in panel (a) of Figure A-7? First note that this area has the shape of a right triangle. A right triangle is a triangle that has two sides that make a right angle with each other. We will refer to one of these sides as the *height* of the triangle and the other side as the *base* of the triangle. For our purposes, it doesn't matter which of these two sides we refer to as the base and which as the height.

Calculating the area of a right triangle is straightforward: multiply the height of the triangle by the base of the triangle, and divide the result by 2. The height of the triangle in panel (a) of Figure A-7 is 10 − 4 = 6. And the base of the triangle is 3 − 0 = 3. So the area of that triangle is:

$$\frac{6 \times 3}{2} = 9$$

How about the shaded area above the linear curve in panel (b) of Figure A-7? We can use the same formula to calculate the area of this right triangle. The height of the triangle is 8 − 2 = 6. And the base of the triangle is 4 − 0 = 4. So the area of that triangle is:

$$\frac{6 \times 4}{2} = 12$$

Graphs That Depict Numerical Information

Graphs are also a convenient way to summarize and display data without assuming some underlying causal relationship. Graphs that simply display numerical information are called *numerical graphs.*

FIGURE A-7 Calculating the Area Below and Above a Linear Curve

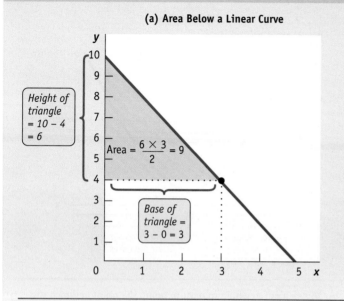

(a) Area Below a Linear Curve

(b) Area Above a Linear Curve

The area above or below a linear curve forms a right triangle. The area of a right triangle is calculated by multiplying the height of the triangle by the base of the triangle, and dividing the result by

2. In panel (a), the area of the shaded triangle is $6 \times \dfrac{3}{2} = 9$. In panel (b), the area of the shaded triangle is $6 \times \dfrac{4}{2} = 12$.

FIGURE A-8 Time-Series Graph

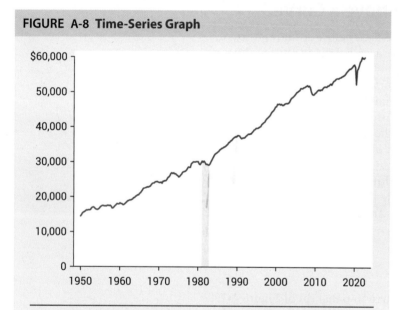

Time-series graphs show successive dates on the *x*-axis and values for a variable on the *y*-axis. This time-series graph shows real gross domestic product per capita, a measure of a country's standard of living, in the United States from 1950 to early 2022.

Real GDP per capita in chained 2012 dollars on *y*-axis

Data from: Bureau of Economic Analysis and Federal Reserve Bank of St. Louis

time-series graph a two-variable graph that has dates on the horizontal axis and values of a variable that occurred on those dates on the vertical axis.

Here we will consider four types of numerical graphs: *time-series graphs, scatter diagrams, pie charts,* and *bar graphs.* These are widely used to display real, empirical data about different economic variables because they often help economists and policy makers identify patterns or trends in the economy. But it's important to be aware of both the usefulness and the limitations of numerical graphs to avoid misinterpreting them or drawing unwarranted conclusions from them.

Types of Numerical Graphs

You have probably seen graphs that show what has happened over time to economic variables such as the unemployment rate or stock prices. A **time-series graph** has successive dates on the horizontal axis and the values of a variable that occurred on those dates on the vertical axis.

For example, Figure A-8 shows real gross domestic product (GDP) per capita—a rough measure of a country's standard of living—in the United States from 1950 to 2022. A line connecting the points that correspond to real GDP per capita for each calendar quarter during those years gives a clear idea of the overall trend in the standard of living over these years.

Figure A-9 is an example of a different kind of numerical graph. It represents information from a sample of 180 countries on the standard of living, again measured by GDP per capita, and the amount of carbon emissions per capita, a measure of environmental pollution. Each point here indicates an average resident's standard of living and their annual carbon emissions for a given country.

The points lying in the upper right of the graph, which show combinations of a high standard of living and high carbon emissions, represent economically advanced countries such as the United States. (The country with the highest carbon emissions, at the top of the graph, is Qatar.) Points lying in the bottom left of the graph, which show combinations of a low standard of living and low carbon emissions, represent economically less advanced countries such as Afghanistan and Sierra Leone.

The pattern of points indicates that there is a positive relationship between living standard and carbon emissions per capita: on the whole, people create more pollution in countries with a higher standard of living.

This type of graph is called a **scatter diagram,** in which each point corresponds to an actual observation of the x-variable and the y-variable. In scatter diagrams, a curve is typically fitted to the scatter of points; that is, a curve is drawn that approximates as closely as possible the general relationship between the variables. As you can see, the fitted line in Figure A-9 is upward sloping, indicating the underlying positive relationship between the two variables. Scatter diagrams are often used to show how a general relationship can be inferred from a set of data.

A **pie chart** shows the share of a total amount that is accounted for by various components, usually expressed in percentages. For example, Figure A-10 is a pie chart that depicts the education levels of workers who in 2021 were paid the federal minimum wage or less. As you can see, the majority of workers paid at or below the minimum wage had no college degree. Approximately 15% of workers who were paid at or below the minimum wage had a bachelor's degree or higher.

scatter diagram a graph that shows points that correspond to actual observations of the x- and y-variables; a curve is usually fitted to the scatter of points to indicate the trend in the data.

pie chart a circular graph that shows how some total is divided among its components, usually expressed in percentages.

FIGURE A-9 Scatter Diagram

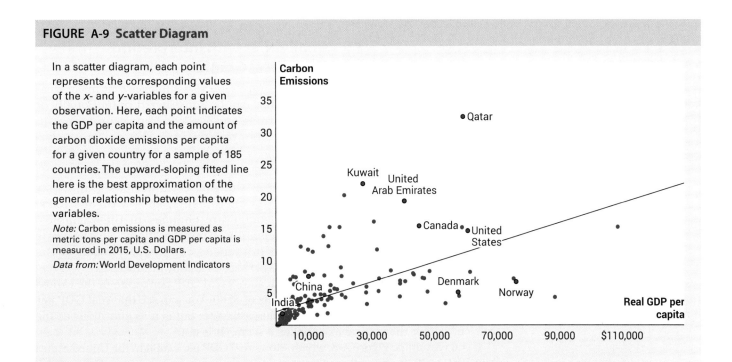

In a scatter diagram, each point represents the corresponding values of the x- and y-variables for a given observation. Here, each point indicates the GDP per capita and the amount of carbon dioxide emissions per capita for a given country for a sample of 185 countries. The upward-sloping fitted line here is the best approximation of the general relationship between the two variables.

Note: Carbon emissions is measured as metric tons per capita and GDP per capita is measured in 2015, U.S. Dollars.

Data from: World Development Indicators

FIGURE A-10 Pie Chart

A pie chart shows the percentages of a total amount that can be attributed to various components. This pie chart shows the percentages of workers with given education levels who were paid at or below the federal minimum wage in 2021. (Numbers may not add to 100 due to rounding.)

Data from: Bureau of Labor Statistics

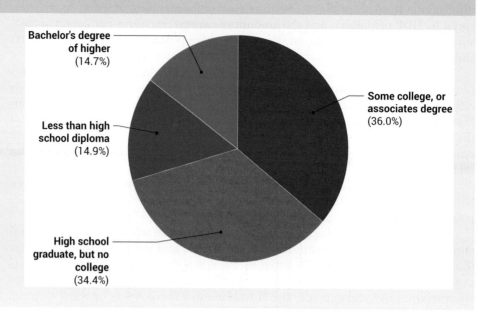

Bachelor's degree of higher (14.7%)

Some college, or associates degree (36.0%)

Less than high school diploma (14.9%)

High school graduate, but no college (34.4%)

FIGURE A-11 Bar Graph

A bar graph measures a variable by using bars of various heights or lengths. This bar graph shows the percent change in GDP per capita (measured in 2010 dollars) for the United States, China, and Peru.

Data from: The World Bank, World Development Indicators

bar graph a graph that uses bars of varying heights or lengths to show the comparative sizes of different observations of a variable.

Bar graphs use bars of various heights or lengths to indicate values of a variable. In the bar graph in Figure A-11, the bars show the percent change in GDP per capita from 2020 to 2021 for the United States, China, and Peru. Exact values of the variable that is being measured may be written at the end of the bar, as in this figure. For instance, GDP per capita for China increased by 8.0% between 2020 and 2021. But even without the precise values, comparing the heights or lengths of the bars can give useful insight into the relative magnitudes of the different values of the variable.

Challenges with Interpreting Numerical Graphs

Although graphs are visual images that make ideas or information easier to understand, they can be constructed (intentionally or unintentionally) in ways that are misleading and can lead to inaccurate conclusions. This section addresses some difficulties you may have when you are analyzing graphs.

Features of Construction When evaluating a numerical graph, pay close attention to the scale, or size of increments, shown on the axes. Small increments tend to visually exaggerate changes in the variables, whereas large increments tend to visually diminish them. So the scale used in construction of a graph can influence your interpretation of the significance of the changes it illustrates—perhaps in an unwarranted way.

Take, for example, Figure A-12, which shows real GDP per capita in the United States from 1981 to 1982 using increments of $500. You can see that real GDP per capita fell from $30,335 to $29,205. A decrease, sure, but is it as enormous as the scale chosen for the vertical axis makes it seem? It is not.

If you reexamine Figure A-8, which shows real GDP per capita in the United States from 1950 to 2022, you will see that it includes the same data shown in Figure A-12.

FIGURE A-12 Interpreting Graphs: The Effect of Scale

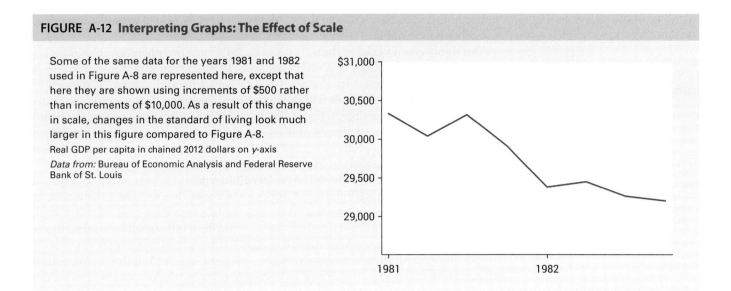

Some of the same data for the years 1981 and 1982 used in Figure A-8 are represented here, except that here they are shown using increments of $500 rather than increments of $10,000. As a result of this change in scale, changes in the standard of living look much larger in this figure compared to Figure A-8.

Real GDP per capita in chained 2012 dollars on *y*-axis

Data from: Bureau of Economic Analysis and Federal Reserve Bank of St. Louis

But, Figure A-8 is constructed with a scale having increments of $10,000 rather than $500. From it you can see that the fall in real GDP per capita from 1981 to 1982 was, in fact, relatively insignificant.

In fact, the story of real GDP per capita—a measure of the standard of living—in the United States is mostly a story of ups, not downs. This comparison shows that if you are not careful to factor in the choice of scale in interpreting graphs, you can arrive at very different, and possibly incorrect, conclusions.

Related to the choice of scale is the use of *truncation* in constructing a graph. An axis is **truncated** when part of the range is omitted. This is indicated by two slashes (//) in the axis near the origin. You can see that the vertical axis of Figure A-12 has been truncated—some of the range of values from 0 to $29,000 have been omitted. Truncation saves space in the presentation of a graph and allows smaller increments to be used in constructing it. As a result, changes in the variable depicted on a graph that has been truncated appear larger compared to a graph that has not been truncated and that uses larger increments.

You must also consider exactly what a graph is illustrating. For example, in Figure A-11, you should recognize that what is being shown are *percent* changes in GDP per capita, not *numerical* changes. The growth rate for Peru increased by the highest percentage, 12.0% in this example. If you were to confuse numerical changes with percent changes, you would erroneously conclude the country with the greatest change in GDP per capita was Peru.

In fact, a correct interpretation of Figure A-11 shows that the greatest dollar change in GDP per capita was for the United States: GDP per capita increased by $3,220 for the United States, which is greater than the increase in GDP per capita for China, which is $830 in this example. Although there was a higher percentage increase in GDP per capita for China, the dollar increase for China from 2020 to 2021 was smaller than the change for the United States, leading to a smaller change in GDP per capita for China than the United States. The same can be said for Peru, where GDP per capita grew by 12.0%, but resulted in a relatively smaller, $698, increase in actual GDP per capita.

Omitted Variables From a scatter diagram that shows two variables moving either positively or negatively in relation to each other, it is easy to conclude that there is a causal relationship. But relationships between two variables are not always due to direct cause and effect. Quite possibly an observed relationship

truncated cut; in a truncated axis, some of the range of values are omitted, usually to save space.

omitted variable an unobserved variable that, through its influence on other variables, creates the erroneous appearance of a direct causal relationship among those variables.

reverse causality the error committed when the true direction of causality between two variables is reversed, and the independent variable and the dependent variable are incorrectly identified.

between two variables is due to the *unobserved* effect of a third variable on each of the other two variables.

An unobserved variable that, through its influence on other variables, creates the erroneous appearance of a direct causal relationship among those variables is called an **omitted variable.** For example, in New England, a greater amount of snowfall during a given week will typically cause people to buy more snow shovels. It will also cause people to buy more de-icer fluid. But if you omitted the influence of the snowfall and simply plotted the number of snow shovels sold versus the number of bottles of de-icer fluid sold, you would produce a scatter diagram that showed an upward tilt in the pattern of points, indicating a positive relationship between snow shovels sold and de-icer fluid sold.

To attribute a causal relationship between these two variables, however, is misguided. More snow shovels sold do not cause more de-icer fluid to be sold, or vice versa. They move together because they are both influenced by a third, determining, variable—the weekly snowfall, which is the omitted variable in this case.

So before assuming that a pattern in a scatter diagram implies a cause-and-effect relationship, it is important to consider whether the pattern is instead the result of an omitted variable. Or to put it another way: correlation is not causation.

Reverse Causality Even when you are confident that there is no omitted variable and that there is a causal relationship between two variables shown in a numerical graph, you must also be sure to avoid making the mistake of **reverse causality**—coming to an erroneous conclusion about which is the dependent and which is the independent variable by reversing the true direction of causality between the two variables.

For example, imagine a scatter diagram that depicts the grade point averages (GPAs) of 20 of your classmates on one axis and the number of hours that each classmate spends studying on the other. A line fitted between the points will probably have a positive slope, showing a positive relationship between GPA and hours of studying. We could reasonably infer that hours spent studying is the independent variable and that GPA is the dependent variable. But you could make the error of reverse causality: you could infer that a high GPA causes a student to study more, whereas a low GPA causes a student to study less.

As you've just seen, it is important to understand how graphs can mislead or be interpreted incorrectly. Policy decisions, business decisions, and political arguments are often based on interpretation of the types of numerical graphs we've just discussed. Problems of misleading features of construction, omitted variables, and reverse causality can lead to important and undesirable consequences.

PROBLEMS

1. Study the four accompanying diagrams. Consider the following statements and indicate which diagram matches each statement. Which variable would appear on the horizontal and which on the vertical axis? In each of these statements, is the slope positive, negative, zero, or infinity?

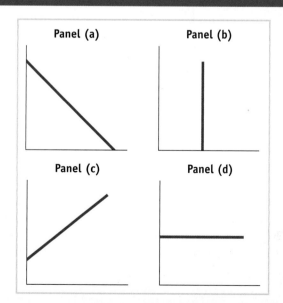

Panel (a)   Panel (b)
Panel (c)   Panel (d)

a. If the price of movies increases, fewer consumers go to see movies.

b. More experienced workers typically have higher incomes than less experienced workers.

c. Whatever the temperature outside, Americans consume the same number of tacos per day.

d. Consumers buy more frozen yogurt when the price of ice cream goes up.

e. Research finds no relationship between the number of diet books purchased and the number of pounds lost by the average dieter.

f. Regardless of its price, Americans buy the same quantity of salt.

2. During the Reagan administration, economist Arthur Laffer argued in favor of lowering income tax rates in order to increase tax revenues. Like most economists, he believed that at tax rates above a certain level, tax revenue would fall because high taxes would discourage some people from working and that people would refuse to work at all if they received no income after paying taxes. This relationship between tax rates and tax revenue is graphically summarized in what is widely known as the Laffer curve. Plot the Laffer curve relationship assuming that it has the shape of a nonlinear curve. The following questions will help you construct the graph.

a. Which is the independent variable? Which is the dependent variable? On which axis do you therefore measure the income tax rate? On which axis do you measure income tax revenue?

b. What would tax revenue be at a 0% income tax rate?

c. The maximum possible income tax rate is 100%. What would tax revenue be at a 100% income tax rate?

d. Estimates now show that the maximum point on the Laffer curve is (approximately) at a tax rate of 80%. For tax rates less than 80%, how would you describe the relationship between the tax rate and tax revenue, and how is this relationship reflected in the slope? For tax rates higher than 80%, how would you describe the relationship between the tax rate and tax revenue, and how is this relationship reflected in the slope?

3. In the accompanying figures, the numbers on the axes have been lost. All you know is that the units shown on the vertical axis are the same as the units on the horizontal axis.

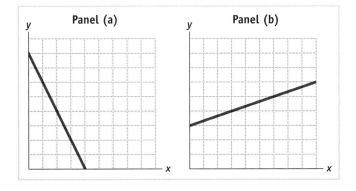

a. In panel (a), what is the slope of the line? Show that the slope is constant along the line.

b. In panel (b), what is the slope of the line? Show that the slope is constant along the line.

4. Answer each of the following questions by drawing a schematic diagram.

a. Taking measurements of the slope of a curve at three points farther and farther to the right along the horizontal axis, the slope of the curve changes from –0.3, to –0.8, to –2.5, measured by the point method. Draw a schematic diagram of this curve. How would you describe the relationship illustrated in your diagram?

b. Taking measurements of the slope of a curve at five points farther and farther to the right along the horizontal axis, the slope of the curve changes from 1.5, to 0.5, to 0, to –0.5, to –1.5, measured by the point method. Draw a schematic diagram of this curve. Does it have a maximum or a minimum?

5. For each of the accompanying diagrams, calculate the area of the shaded right triangle.

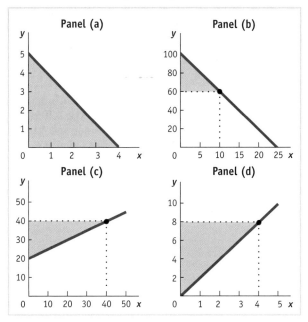

6. The base of a right triangle is 10, and its area is 20. What is the height of this right triangle?

7. The accompanying table shows the relationship between workers' hours of work per week and their hourly wage rate. Apart from the fact that they receive a different hourly wage rate and work different hours, these five workers are otherwise identical.

Name	Quantity of labor (hours per week)	Wage rate (per hour)
Akiko	30	$15
Ben	35	30
Cameron	37	45
Diego	36	60
Emily	32	75

a. Which variable is the independent variable? Which is the dependent variable?

b. Draw a scatter diagram illustrating this relationship. Draw a (nonlinear) curve that connects the points. Put the hourly wage rate on the vertical axis.

c. As the wage rate increases from $15 to $30, how does the number of hours worked respond according to the relationship depicted here? What is the average slope of the curve between Akiko's and Ben's data points using the arc method?

d. As the wage rate increases from $60 to $75, how does the number of hours worked respond according to the relationship depicted here? What is the average slope of the curve between Diego's and Emily's data points using the arc method?

8. An insurance company has found that the severity of property damage in a fire is positively related to the number of firefighters arriving at the scene.

a. Draw a diagram that depicts this finding with number of firefighters on the horizontal axis and amount of property damage on the vertical axis. What is the argument made by this diagram? Suppose you reverse what is measured on the two axes. What is the argument made then?

b. Should the insurance company ask the city to send fewer firefighters to any fire in order to reduce its payouts to policy holders?

9. This table illustrates annual salaries and income tax owed by five individuals. Despite receiving different annual salaries and owing different amounts of income tax, these five individuals are otherwise identical.

Name	Annual salary	Annual income tax owed
Mila	$22,000	$3,304
Jayden	63,000	14,317
Aria	3,000	454
Logan	94,000	23,927
Saeed	37,000	7,020

a. If you were to plot these points on a graph, what would be the average slope of the curve between the points for Jayden's and Logan's salaries and taxes using the arc method? How would you interpret this value for slope?

b. What is the average slope of the curve between the points for Aria's and Mila's salaries and taxes using the arc method? How would you interpret that value for slope?

c. What happens to the slope as salary increases? What does this relationship imply about how the level of income taxes affects a person's incentive to earn a higher salary?

10. Studies have found a relationship between a country's yearly rate of economic growth and the yearly rate of increase in airborne pollutants. It is believed that a higher rate of economic growth allows a country's residents to have more cars and travel more, thereby releasing more airborne pollutants.

a. Which variable is the independent variable? Which is the dependent variable?

b. Suppose that in the country of Sudland, when the yearly rate of economic growth fell from 3.0% to 1.5%, the yearly rate of increase in airborne pollutants fell from 6% to 5%. What is the average slope of a nonlinear curve between these points using the arc method?

c. Assume that when the yearly rate of economic growth rose from 3.5% to 4.5%, the yearly rate of increase in airborne pollutants rose from 5.5% to 7.5%. What is the average slope of a nonlinear curve between these two points using the arc method?

d. How would you describe the relationship between the two variables here? ■

3 Supply and Demand

A DAY IN THE LIFE OF AN UBER DRIVER

IT'S 4:25 IN THE MORNING and Rey wakes up to the buzzing of a phone alarm. Rey lives in Sacramento but spent the night 100 miles away, sleeping on the passenger seat of his car in the rideshare lot of San Francisco Airport.

It's the second of 14 days that Rey plans to spend in the San Francisco Bay Area driving for Uber. Rey is up early, hoping that the rainy weather will increase the demand for rides. When more people are looking for rides on any given day, Uber raises the price of any given ride. Rey makes more money to take back to Sacramento.

Rey is just one of many who travel from outside the Bay Area to work as drivers for ride-hailing companies Uber and Lyft. "It gets real busy early in the morning. I got early people catching flights, getting ready to go to work. Once you figure out how it works, you can make some money. But you gotta be ready to get out there on the hustle," said

Rey, checking the map of San Francisco on the Uber app. The app shows areas of red where there are more people seeking rides than drivers. In those areas, Uber's dynamic pricing model delivers higher rates. That means more money in drivers' pockets for every mile driven.

Rey sets out for the Mission District in San Francisco, picking up a woman who has to be at work by 5 A.M. Rey knows the morning commute period well because he has been traveling from Sacramento to San Francisco to work as an Uber driver for nearly four years. "I will run probably until one o'clock this afternoon. Nine straight hours. And then I will shut down. Take a break," said Rey. "Everybody comes to San Francisco to work because there is a very high demand. The Bay Area has the highest rates, period."

In fact, drivers come from as far away as Los Angeles to work in San Francisco, a distance of nearly 400 miles. Why? According to Rey, more Los Angelenos own cars and drive themselves to work, to school, and to the airport. So significantly fewer people are looking for rides and the rates are lower.

Rey makes about $65,000 a year after subtracting expenses, but he notes "You actually have to put in 12, 13, 14 hours out of a day to make really good money like we used to make, before so many drivers from other areas came to the Bay Area." Rey wishes Uber drivers could get the same rates in Sacramento as they get in San Francisco. Then they wouldn't have to spend so much time away from home.

But Rey likes the flexibility and independence that driving for Uber provides. He decides when to start and end each shift and when he's made enough money. On this particular day, Rey stops driving around noon and takes a break to go to the bank

Kanawa_Studio/Getty Images

and then to the gym for a shower and a few hours of relaxation. By midafternoon, he is back at the airport rideshare lot waiting for a passenger. The lot is nearly full of ride-hailing drivers, and Rey waits until nearly four in the afternoon before getting a fare to start the second shift of the day.

After a six-hour shift, Rey returns to the airport lot at about 10 P.M. to sleep. After waiting a bit, Rey is able to find a parking spot not directly under the glare of the flood lights, grabs a pillow and blanket from the trunk, and settles down again in the passenger's seat.

"I will get started again in the morning," Rey said, going offline on the Uber app.

Rey's experience as an Uber driver illustrates key aspects of the supply of and demand for rides in the Bay Area. But what does *supply and demand* mean? Many people use the terms as a sort of catchphrase to mean "the laws of the marketplace at work." To economists, however, the concept of supply and demand has a precise meaning: it is a *model of how a market behaves* that is extremely useful for understanding many — but not all — markets.

In this chapter, we lay out the pieces that make up the *supply and demand model,* put them together, and show you how this model can be used. ●

WHAT YOU WILL LEARN

- What is a **competitive market?**
- What are **supply** and **demand curves?**
- How do supply and demand curves lead to an **equilibrium price** and **equilibrium quantity** in the market?
- What are **shortages** and **surpluses** and why do price movements eliminate them?

Supply and Demand: A Model of a Competitive Market

Economists call the people who interact in a market "buyers" and "sellers." Buyers are the people looking to consume a good or service, while sellers are the people looking to provide a good or service. A market arises when buyers and sellers come together to transact a given type of good or service. If we apply those concepts to our opening example of an Uber driver's day in San Francisco, the people wanting to take a ride—that is consuming the service of being driven—are the buyers. Uber drivers like Rey, people offering their services of providing rides, are the sellers. The market for rides in San Francisco arises as buyers wanting rides and sellers providing rides transact with one another. (In this example, they are interacting via the Uber platform.)

The market for rides in San Francisco is an example of a particular type of market known as a *competitive market*. A **competitive market** is a market in which there are many buyers and sellers of the same good or service. More precisely, the key feature of a competitive market is that no individual's actions have a noticeable effect on the price at which the good or service is sold. It's important to understand, however, that this is not an accurate description of every market.

For example, it's not an accurate description of the market for carbonated soft drinks. That's because in this market, Coca-Cola and Pepsi account for such a large proportion of total sales that they are able to influence the price at which their beverages are bought and sold. But it is an accurate description of the market for rides in San Francisco as there are many drivers willing to provide the service. If Rey takes the day off, the prices of Uber rides that day will not be affected. That's because Rey is only one of many, many Uber drivers in San Francisco. He represents only a small fraction of the total number of rides offered on any given day. As a result, neither Rey's absence nor his presence can influence the prices at which Uber rides are bought and sold.

It's a little hard to explain why competitive markets are different from other markets until we've seen how a competitive market works. So let's take a rain check—we'll return to that issue at the end of this chapter. For now, let's just say that it's easier to model competitive markets than other markets. When taking an exam, it's always a good strategy to begin by answering the easier questions. In this book, we're going to do the same thing. So we will start with competitive markets.

When a market is competitive, its behavior is well described by the **supply and demand model.** And because many markets are competitive, the supply and demand model is a very useful one indeed.

There are five key elements in this model:

- The *supply curve*
- The *demand curve*
- The set of factors that cause the supply curve to shift and the set of factors that cause the demand curve to shift
- The *market equilibrium,* which includes the *equilibrium price* and *equilibrium quantity*
- The way the market equilibrium changes when the supply curve or demand curve shifts

To understand the supply and demand model, we will examine each of these elements.

The Supply Curve

To simplify our discussion, let's assume that every Uber ride in San Francisco covers the same number of miles. Therefore, every ride is identical. If you were asked the question, "How many Uber rides will drivers want to provide on any given day in San Francisco?" you might think the way to answer the question is to multiply the number of drivers by the total number of rides they can provide in a day. Yet this will almost certainly give you the wrong answer. Why? Because as Rey's story illustrates, how many rides an Uber driver provides depends on the price they receive per ride. When the price per ride in San Francisco goes up, the number of rides Uber drivers are willing to provide also goes up. As we learned in Rey's story, the number of rides goes up when the prices go up because: (1) drivers like Rey are willing to work more hours, and (2) more drivers come to San Francisco from other locations that have lower prices, like Sacramento or Los Angeles. In general, the amount of any good or service a seller wants to provide depends on the price. The higher the price, the more of the good or service sellers want to provide; alternatively, the lower the price, the less of the good or sellers want to provide.

So the answer to the question, "How many Uber rides will drivers want to provide on any given day in San Francisco?" depends on the price of a ride. If you don't yet know what the price will be, you can start by making a table of how many rides Uber drivers will want to provide at a number of different prices. Such a table is known as a *supply schedule*. This, in turn, can be used to draw a *supply curve*, which is one of the key elements of the supply and demand model.

The Supply Schedule and the Supply Curve

A **supply schedule** is a table showing how much of a good or service sellers will want to provide at different prices. At the right of Figure 1, we show a hypothetical supply schedule for Uber rides. (This is a hypothetical supply schedule and doesn't use actual data on the supply of Uber rides.) According to the table, at a price of $12.50 per ride, drivers are willing to produce only 800 rides. At $12.75 per ride,

supply schedule a list or table showing how much of a good or service producers will supply at different prices.

FIGURE 1 The Supply Schedule and the Supply Curve

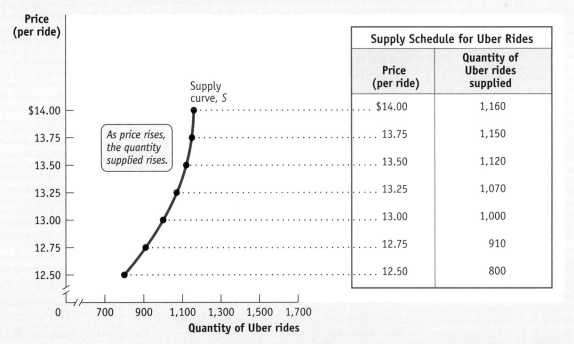

Supply Schedule for Uber Rides	
Price (per ride)	Quantity of Uber rides supplied
$14.00	1,160
13.75	1,150
13.50	1,120
13.25	1,070
13.00	1,000
12.75	910
12.50	800

The supply schedule for rides yields the corresponding supply curve, which shows how much of a good or service sellers are willing to sell at any given price. The supply curve and the supply schedule reflect the fact that supply curves are usually upward-sloping: other things equal, the quantity supplied rises when the price rises.

they're willing to provide 910 rides. At $13, they're willing to provide 1,000 rides, and so on. The higher the price, the more rides Uber drivers are willing to provide. So, as the price rises, the **quantity supplied** of rides—the actual amount drivers are willing to provide at some specific price—also rises.

The graph in Figure 1 is a visual representation of the information in the table. (You might want to review the discussion of graphs in economics in the appendix to Chapter 2.) The vertical axis shows the price of a ride and the horizontal axis shows the quantity of rides. Each point on the graph corresponds to one of the entries in the table. The curve that connects these points is a **supply curve.** A supply curve is a graphical representation of the supply schedule, another way of showing the relationship between the quantity supplied and price.

Suppose that the price of a ride rises from $12.50 to $14.00; we can see that the quantity of rides that drivers are willing to provide rises from 800 to 1,160. This is the normal situation for a supply curve, that a higher price leads to a higher quantity supplied. This means that supply curves normally slope upward: *other things equal*, the higher the price being offered, the more of any good or service sellers are willing to sell.

Shifts of the Supply Curve

In March 2021, Ned Eames, an Uber driver in San Francisco, decided to call it quits despite being offered significantly higher fares. And he wasn't alone: across the country, Uber drivers had been quitting in droves even in the face of uniformly higher fares. How can we reconcile this with the fact that the quantity supplied normally rises as price goes up?

The answer lies in the crucial phrase *other things equal*. During early 2021, other things were definitely not equal to times before. Concerned about catching Covid-19 from their passengers, significant numbers of Uber drivers were unwilling to drive regardless of the fact that fares were rising as people started venturing out again. According to the blog Rideshare Guy, Uber drivers turned to food and package delivery apps like UberEats and DoorDash because those gigs, although lower paying than driving passengers for Uber, felt safer.

Figure 2 illustrates this phenomenon using the supply schedule and supply curve for rides. (As before, the numbers in Figure 2 are hypothetical.)

The table in Figure 2 shows two supply schedules. The first is the supply schedule for rides before the pandemic, the same as shown in Figure 1. The second is the supply schedule for rides during the pandemic. It differs from the prepandemic schedule because significant numbers of Uber drivers were unwilling to drive during the pandemic, leading to a fall in the quantity of rides supplied at any given price. So at each price the pandemic schedule shows a lower quantity supplied than the prepandemic schedule. For example, the quantity of rides drivers wanted to offer at a price of $13 per ride fell from 1,000 to 850 rides per day; the quantity for sale at $13.25 per ride went from 1,070 to 910, and so on.

What is clear from this example is that the changes that occurred as a result of the pandemic generated a *new* supply schedule, one in which the quantity supplied was lower at any given price than in the original supply schedule. The two curves in Figure 2 show the same information graphically. As you can see, the pandemic schedule corresponds to a new supply curve, S_2, that is to the left of the prepandemic schedule, S_1. Notice that S_2 lies to the left of S_1, a reflection of the fact that quantity supplied fell at any given price as a result of the pandemic. This **shift of the supply curve** shows the change in the quantity supplied at any given price, represented by the change in position of the original supply curve S_1 to its new location at S_2.

It's crucial to draw a distinction between such shifts of the supply curve and **movements along the supply curve**—changes in the quantity supplied arising from a change in price. Figure 3 illustrates the difference. The movement from

quantity supplied the actual amount of a good or service producers are willing to sell at some specific price.

supply curve a graphical representation of the supply schedule, showing the relationship between quantity supplied and price.

shift of the supply curve a change in the quantity supplied of a good or service at any given price. It is represented by the change of the original supply curve to a new position, denoted by a new supply curve.

movement along the supply curve a change in the quantity supplied of a good that results from a change in the good's price.

FIGURE 2 A Fall in Supply

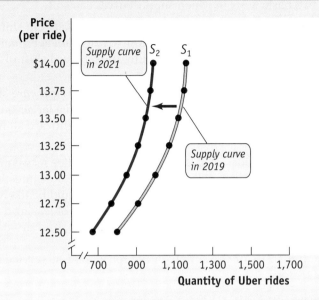

Supply Schedules for Uber Rides		
Price (per ride)	Quantity of Uber rides supplied	
	In 2019	In 2021
$14.00	1,160	990
13.75	1,150	975
13.50	1,120	950
13.25	1,070	910
13.00	1,000	850
12.75	910	770
12.50	800	720

In 2021, the coronavirus pandemic led to a fall in the supply of Uber rides — a fall in the quantity supplied at any given price. This is represented by two supply schedules: one showing the prepandemic supply, when drivers were not reluctant to drive due to the fear of infection, and the other showing the pandemic supply, when drivers were reluctant to drive — and their corresponding supply curves. The fall in supply shifts the supply curve to the left.

point A to point B is a movement along the supply curve: the quantity supplied falls along S_1 due to a fall in price. Here, a fall in price from $13.50 to $13.00 leads to a fall in the quantity supplied from 1,120 rides to 1,000 rides. But the quantity supplied can also fall when the price is unchanged if there is a fall in supply—a leftward shift of the supply curve. This is shown by the leftward shift of the supply curve from S_1 to S_2. Holding the price constant at $13.50, the quantity supplied falls from 1,120 rides at point A on S_1 to 950 rides at point C on S_2.

FIGURE 3 Movement Along the Supply Curve versus Shift of the Supply Curve

The fall in quantity supplied when going from point A to point B reflects a movement along the supply curve: it is the result of a fall in the price of a good. The fall in quantity supplied when going from point A to point C reflects a shift of the supply curve: it is the result of a fall in the quantity supplied at any given price.

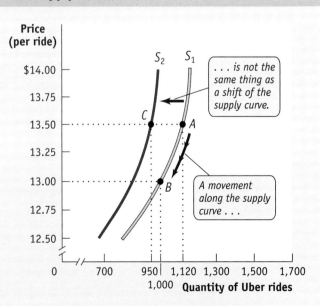

input a good or service used to produce another good or service.

Understanding Shifts of the Supply Curve

Figure 4 illustrates the two basic ways in which supply curves can shift.

1. When economists talk about a decrease in supply, they mean a *leftward* shift of the supply curve: at any given price, sellers are willing to sell a smaller quantity of the good or service than before. This is shown by the leftward shift of the original supply curve S_1 to curve S_2.

2. When economists talk about an increase in supply, they mean a *rightward* shift of the supply curve: at any given price, sellers are willing to sell a larger quantity of the good or service than before. This is shown by the rightward shift of the original supply curve S_1 to curve S_3.

What caused the supply curve for rides to shift during the pandemic? As we mentioned earlier, fewer drivers were willing to provide rides due to fear of infection. If you think about it, you can come up with other factors that would be likely to shift the supply curve for rides. For example, suppose that the cost of leasing a car falls. This will induce some people to quit their jobs, lease a car, and drive for Uber. As a result, the supply of rides increases.

Economists believe that shifts of the supply curve for a good or service are mainly the result of five factors:

- Changes in input prices
- Changes in the prices of related goods or services
- Changes in technology
- Changes in expectations
- Changes in the number of sellers

Changes in Input Prices   To produce output, you need inputs. For example, to make vanilla ice cream, you need vanilla beans, cream, sugar, and so on. An **input** is any good or service that is used to produce another good or service. Inputs, like outputs, have prices. And an increase in the price of an input makes the production of the final good more costly for those who produce and sell it. So sellers are less willing to supply the final good at any given price, and the supply curve shifts to the left. That is, supply falls. For example, a surge in the price of semiconductor chips in 2021 forced U.S. automakers to slash their production

---

FIGURE 4 Shifts of the Supply Curve

Any event that reduces supply shifts the supply curve to the left, reflecting a fall in the quantity supplied at any given price. Any event that increases supply shifts the supply curve to the right, reflecting an increase in the quantity supplied at any given price.

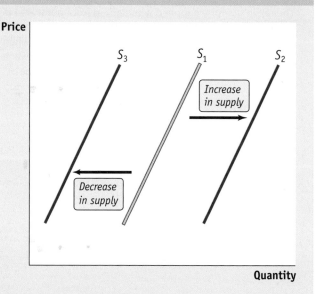

PITFALLS

SUPPLY VERSUS QUANTITY SUPPLIED

When economists say "an increase in supply," they mean a rightward shift of the supply curve, and when they say "a decrease in supply," they mean a leftward shift of the supply curve — that is, when they're being careful and speaking accurately.

In ordinary speech most of us, professional economists included, use the words *supply* and *demand* casually. For example, an economist might say "the supply of Airbnb lodgings has doubled over the past 10 years, partly because of rising rental rates" when they really mean that the *quantity supplied* has doubled.

It's okay to be a bit sloppy in ordinary conversation. But when you're doing economic analysis, it's important to make the distinction between changes in the quantity supplied, which involve movements along a supply curve, and shifts of the supply curve (see Figure 3). Sometimes students end up writing something like this: "If supply increases, the price will go down, but that will lead to a fall in supply, which pushes the price up . . ." and then go around in circles.

By making a clear distinction between changes in *supply*, which mean shifts of the supply curve, and changes in *quantity supplied*, which means movement along the supply curve, you can avoid a lot of confusion.

of new cars. In the case of Uber rides, the sudden increase in gas prices following the Russian invasion of Ukraine would cause supply to shift.

Similarly, a fall in the price of an input makes the production of the final good less costly for sellers. They are more willing to supply the good at any given price, and the supply curve shifts to the right. That is, supply increases.

Changes in the Prices of Related Goods or Services A single seller often produces a mix of goods rather than a single product. For example, an oil refinery produces gasoline from crude oil, but it also produces heating oil and other products from the same raw material. Likewise, a gig worker can sell their furniture moving services on TaskRabbit, deliver meals on DoorDash, or provide rides on Uber. When a seller is capable of providing several products, the quantity of any one good or service it is willing to supply at any given price depends on the prices of its other co-produced goods.

This effect can run in either direction. An oil refiner will supply less gasoline at any given price when the price of heating oil rises, shifting the supply curve for gasoline to the left. But it will supply more gasoline at any given price when the price of heating oil falls, shifting the supply curve for gasoline to the right. This means that gasoline and other co-produced oil products are *substitutes in production* for refiners. Similarly, Task-Rabbiting, DoorDashing, and Uber-Driving are substitutes in production for many gig workers.

In contrast, due to the nature of the production process, other goods can be *complements in production*. Take the case of beer, which produces a lot of useful leftover products in its brewing. Marmite, a uniquely British condiment spread (reported to taste like soy sauce and look like used motor oil) is made from the yeast by-products of beer brewing. Similarly, leftover grain is used for making pet biscuits, animal feed, and granola bars. So the higher price a beer brewery can get for its beer, the more willing it will be to produce not only beer, but also the by-products of beer brewing. As a result, the by-products of beer brewing are a complements in production of beer.

Changes in Technology Changes in technology affect the supply curve. Consider the technological advances that made the Uber and Lyft ride-sharing apps possible. Before smartphones, the only way for a commuter to get a ride was to call a taxi company — if they were fortunate enough to live in a location that had a taxi company. Now that apps enable drivers and riders to quickly and efficiently find one another via their smartphones, the number of drivers offering rides has exploded. In general, technological improvements reduce the seller's cost of producing a good or service. (In this example, new apps installed on smartphones reduced the cost to drivers of finding commuters who want rides.) As a result, supply increases and the supply curve shifts to the right. Another important technological change is the use of GPS mapping apps like Google Maps, Waze, or Apple Maps. These maps automatically update driving directions and guide the driver to the most efficient route. The driver saves time and money, enabling them to supply more rides.

individual supply curve a graphical representation of the relationship between quantity supplied and price for an individual producer.

Changes in Expectations Changes in expectations can shift the supply curve leftward or rightward. When sellers have some choice about when they put their good up for sale, changes in the expected future price of the good can lead a supplier to supply less or more of the good today.

Suppose that Rey is trying to schedule their work for the week, and the weather forecast is for several days of rain beginning tomorrow in San Francisco. As discussed at the beginning of the chapter, Rey knows that rainy days will result in more rides requested at higher fares. Given this expectation for rainy weather and higher prices tomorrow, Rey chooses to take time off today to do laundry and clean the car. That is, Rey makes a decision to reduce the supply of rides today in order to supply more rides in the future, when there will be more rides requested and higher prices.

In general, the choice a seller makes between selling the good now or saving it and selling it later depends on a comparison of the current price and the expected future price. This example illustrates how changes in expectations can alter supply: an increase in the anticipated future price of a good or service reduces supply today, a leftward shift of the supply curve. But a fall in the anticipated future price increases supply today, a rightward shift of the supply curve.

Changes in the Number of Producers Changes in the number of producers affect the supply curve. Let's examine the **individual supply curve,** by looking at panel (a) in Figure 5. The individual supply curve shows the relationship between quantity supplied and price for an individual seller. For example, suppose that panel (a) of Figure 5 shows the quantity of rides that Rey will supply per year at any given price. Then S_{Rey} is Rey's individual supply curve.

FIGURE 5 Individual Supply Curves and the Market Supply Curve

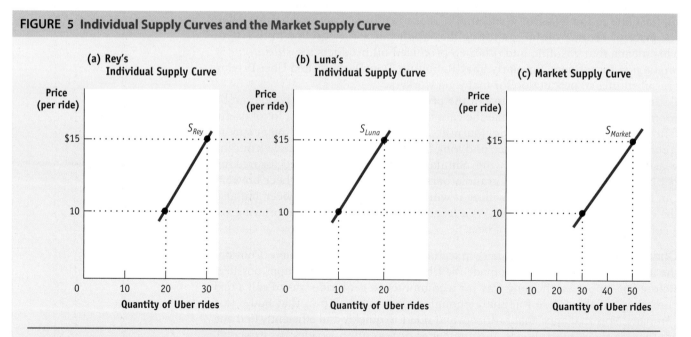

Let's assume that Rey and Luna are the only two drivers in the market for Uber rides. Panel (a) shows Rey's individual supply curve: the number of rides he will offer per day at any given price. Panel (b) shows Luna's individual supply curve. Given that Rey and Luna are the only two sellers, the *market supply curve,* which shows the quantity of rides offered by all sellers at any given price, is shown in panel (c). The market supply curve is the *horizontal sum* of the individual supply curves of all sellers. In this case, at any given price, the quantity supplied by the market is the sum of the quantities supplied by Rey and Luna. For example, at a price of $15 per ride, Rey offers 30 rides per day and Luna offers 20 rides per day. So the quantity supplied by the market is 50 rides per day, as seen on the market supply curve, S_{Market}.

Clearly, the quantity supplied by the market at any given price is larger when Luna is also a driver than it would be if Rey were the only driver. The quantity supplied at any given price would be even larger if we added a third driver, then a fourth, and so on. So an increase in the number of drivers leads to an increase in supply.

For a review of the factors that shift supply, see Table 1.

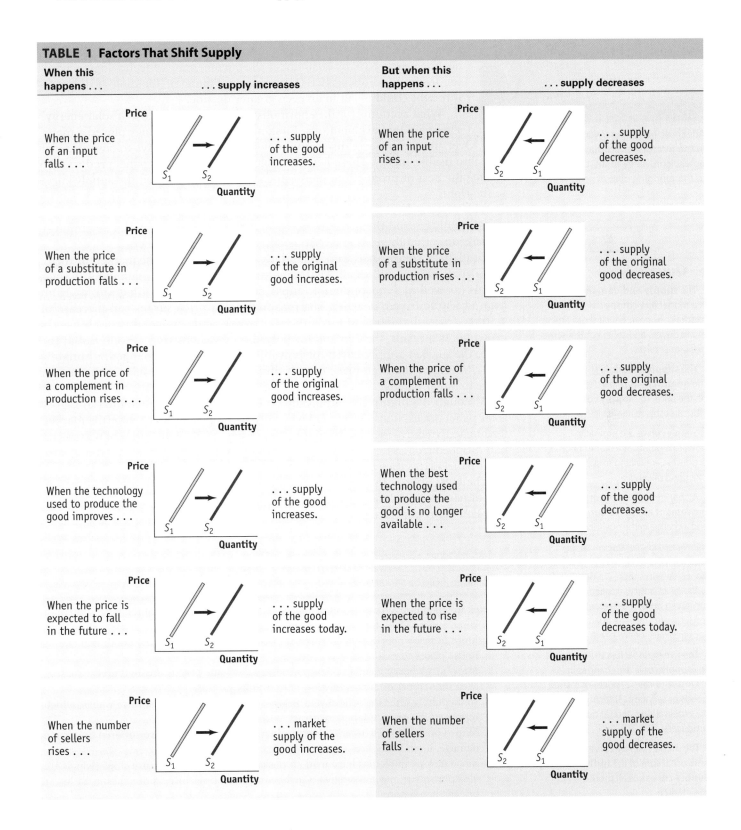

TABLE 1 Factors That Shift Supply

When this happens . . .	. . . supply increases	But when this happens . . .	. . . supply decreases
When the price of an input falls . . .	. . . supply of the good increases.	When the price of an input rises . . .	. . . supply of the good decreases.
When the price of a substitute in production falls . . .	. . . supply of the original good increases.	When the price of a substitute in production rises . . .	. . . supply of the original good decreases.
When the price of a complement in production rises . . .	. . . supply of the original good increases.	When the price of a complement in production falls . . .	. . . supply of the original good decreases.
When the technology used to produce the good improves . . .	. . . supply of the good increases.	When the best technology used to produce the good is no longer available . . .	. . . supply of the good decreases.
When the price is expected to fall in the future . . .	. . . supply of the good increases today.	When the price is expected to rise in the future . . .	. . . supply of the good decreases today.
When the number of sellers rises . . .	. . . market supply of the good increases.	When the number of sellers falls . . .	. . . market supply of the good decreases.

ECONOMICS >> *in Action*
The Plunging Cost of Solar Panels

Advances in technology and a change in the number of producers of polysilicon, a key input, contributed to the plunging cost of solar panels.

The cost of solar panels has fallen by a stunning 99% over the past 40 years, making large-scale generation of solar energy an even more economical choice than more conventional forms of energy, such as coal-generated power. The lower cost of solar panels accounts for the proliferation of skyward-facing blue rectangles visible all across the United States. And, the cost of solar panels is projected to keep falling. Costs are projected to decline nearly 63% by 2050 under the current state of technology, according to the BloombergNEF (New Energy Finance). Technological breakthroughs could result in an even greater decline.

What accounts for the enormous reductions in the cost of solar energy? There are two explanations. First, advances in technology played a major part. Over time, engineers discovered new, more efficient ways to convert solar rays into usable energy. These new technologies allowed solar panel producers to reduce the cost of production, increasing supply, which shifted the supply curve to the right.

The second driver of the plunge in solar panel prices began with an event that actually caused the price to increase: a change in the cost of a key input—polysilicon—that then led to a change in the number of producers.

Until 2008, solar panels were still relatively expensive and the market for them, while growing, was still small. That same year, polysilicon, the main input in solar panels (as well as semiconductor chips), surged to $475 per kilogram, up from around $30 four years earlier. The reason for this price surge—an increase of 1,500%—was that demand for both solar panels and semiconductor chips was growing. As a result, the demand for polysilicon was growing as well. But at the time, the market supply curve for polysilicon remained unchanged, ultimately contributing to the high price of polysilicon and a leftward shift in the supply curve for solar panels.

Although the high price of polysilicon in 2008 initially contributed to higher solar panel prices, it also prompted new polysilicon producers to enter the market, leading to a massive increase in supply. As a result, by 2014, the price of polysilicon had dropped from $475 to under $16 as the market supply curve shifted outward. Solar panel prices then dropped further and sales increased.

The U.S. Energy Information Administration estimated that in 2022 nearly half of new power plant capacity would be powered by solar energy. The amount of solar energy generated increased more than 100-fold from 2008 to 2022.

>> Quick Review

- The **supply and demand model** is a model of a **competitive market** — one in which there are many buyers and sellers of the same good or service.

- The **supply schedule** shows how the **quantity supplied** depends on the price. The **supply curve** illustrates this relationship.

- Supply curves are normally upward-sloping: at a higher price, producers are willing to supply more of a good or service.

- A change in price results in a **movement along the supply curve** and a change in the quantity supplied.

- Increases or decreases in supply lead to **shifts of the supply curve.** An increase in supply is a rightward shift: the quantity supplied rises for any given price. A decrease in supply is a leftward shift: the quantity supplied falls for any given price.

- The five main factors that can shift the supply curve are changes in (1) **input** prices, (2) prices of related goods or services, (3) technology, (4) expectations, and (5) number of producers.

- The market supply curve is the horizontal sum of the **individual supply curves** of all producers in the market.

>> Check Your Understanding 3-1
Solutions appear at back of book.

1. Explain whether each of the following events represents (i) a *shift of* the supply curve or (ii) a *movement along* the supply curve.
   a. More homeowners put their houses up for sale during a real estate boom that causes house prices to rise.
   b. Many strawberry farmers open temporary roadside stands during harvest season, even though prices are usually low at that time.
   c. Immediately after the school year begins, fast-food chains must raise wages, which represent the price of labor, to attract workers.
   d. Many construction workers temporarily move to areas that have suffered hurricane damage, lured by higher wages.
   e. Since new technologies have made it possible to build larger cruise ships (which are cheaper to run per passenger), Caribbean cruise lines offer more cabins, at lower prices, than before.

The Demand Curve

Some commuters have more money to spend, or have more urgent needs to get to their destinations. Some live and work close to public transportation; others do not. So just as the number of rides that Uber drivers are willing to offer depends on price, the number of Uber rides that commuters want to take—the **quantity demanded**—also depends on the price they must pay.

The Demand Schedule and the Demand Curve

The table in Figure 6 shows how the quantity of Uber rides demanded varies with the price—that is, it shows a hypothetical **demand schedule** for rides.

A demand schedule works the same way as the supply schedule shown in Figure 1: in this case, the table shows the number of Uber rides commuters are willing to buy at different prices on a given day in San Francisco. At $13 per ride, commuters will want to purchase 1,200 rides that day. If the price is $13.25 per ride, they will want to buy only 1,070 rides; if the price is only $12.75 per ride, they will want to buy 1,380 rides. The higher the price, the fewer the rides that commuters will want to purchase. So, as the price rises, the quantity demanded of Uber rides—the actual amount consumers are willing to buy at some specific price—falls.

In the same way that a supply schedule can be represented graphically by a supply curve, a demand schedule can be represented by a **demand curve.** Note that the demand curve shown in Figure 6 slopes downward. This reflects the inverse relationship between price and the quantity demanded: a higher price reduces the quantity demanded, and a lower price increases the quantity demanded. As price

quantity demanded the actual amount of a good or service consumers are willing to buy at some specific price.

demand schedule a list or table showing how much of a good or service consumers will want to buy at different prices.

demand curve a graphical representation of the demand schedule. It shows the relationship between quantity demanded and price.

FIGURE 6 The Demand Schedule and the Demand Curve

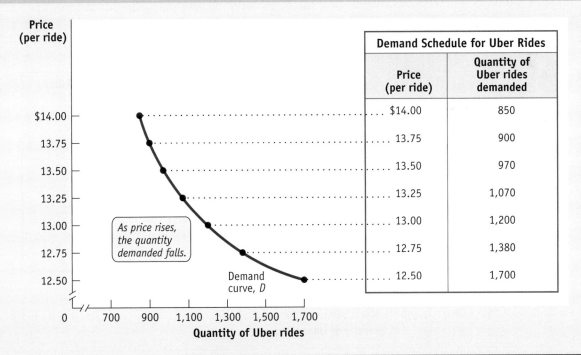

Demand Schedule for Uber Rides	
Price (per ride)	Quantity of Uber rides demanded
$14.00	850
13.75	900
13.50	970
13.25	1,070
13.00	1,200
12.75	1,380
12.50	1,700

The demand schedule for rides yields the corresponding demand curve, which shows how much of a good or service consumers want to buy at any given price. The demand curve and the demand schedule reflect the law of demand: as price rises, the quantity demanded falls. Similarly, a fall in price raises the quantity demanded. As a result, the demand curve is downward-sloping.

law of demand the principle that a higher price for a good or service, other things equal, leads people to demand a smaller quantity of that good or service.

shift of the demand curve a change in the quantity demanded at any given price, represented graphically by the shift of the original demand curve to a new position, denoted by a new demand curve.

falls, we move down the demand curve and quantity demanded increases. And as price increases, we move up the demand curve and quantity demanded falls.

In the real world, demand curves almost always *do* slope downward. (The exceptions are so rare that for practical purposes we can ignore them.) Generally, the proposition that a higher price for a good, *other things equal*, leads people to demand a smaller quantity of that good is so reliable that economists are willing to call it a "law"—the **law of demand.**

Shifts of the Demand Curve

In 2021, the average price of an Uber ride in cities like San Francisco and New York were much lower than they had been in 2019, yet ridership was down by 75%. How can we reconcile this fact with the law of demand, which says that a higher price reduces the quantity demanded, other things equal?

Again, similar to the supply curve, the answer lies in the crucial phrase *other things equal*. In this case, other things weren't equal: between 2019 and 2021, the coronavirus pandemic hit. Far fewer people were leaving their homes in major cities; and those that were, were reluctant to get in a car with a stranger. Just as a change in supply schedules leads to a shift of the supply curve, a change in demand schedules leads to a **shift of the demand curve**—a change in the quantity demanded at any given price. This is shown in Figure 7 by the shift of the demand curve before the pandemic, D_1, to its new position during the pandemic, D_2. Notice that D_2 lies to the left of D_1, a reflection of the fact that quantity demanded falls at any given price. (As before, the numbers in Figure 7 are hypothetical.)

The table in Figure 7 shows two demand schedules. The first is the demand schedule before the pandemic, the same as shown in Figure 6, and corresponding to demand curve D_1. The second is the demand schedule during the pandemic,

---

FIGURE 7 A Decrease in Demand

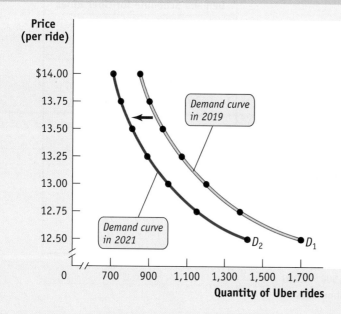

Demand Schedules for Uber Rides		
Price (per ride)	Quantity of Uber rides demanded	
	In 2019	In 2021
$14.00	850	710
13.75	900	750
13.50	970	810
13.25	1,070	890
13.00	1,200	1,000
12.75	1,380	1,150
12.50	1,700	1,420

A strong economy is one factor that increases the demand for Uber rides — a rise in the quantity demanded at any given price. This is represented by the two demand schedules — one showing the demand in 2019 when the economy was strong, the other showing the demand in 2021 during the pandemic — and their corresponding demand curves. The decrease in demand shifts the demand curve to the left.

GLOBAL COMPARISON PAY MORE, PUMP LESS

For a real-world illustration of the law of demand, consider how gasoline consumption varies according to the prices consumers pay at the pump. Because of high taxes, gasoline and diesel fuel are nearly twice as expensive in most European countries and in many East Asian countries than in the United States. According to the law of demand, this should lead Europeans to buy less gasoline than Americans — and they do. As you can see from the figure, per person, Europeans consume significantly less fuel as Americans, mainly because they drive smaller cars with better mileage. For comparison, on average fuel consumption in Italy is less than 1/10 of the United States.

Prices aren't the only factor affecting fuel consumption, but they're probably the main cause of the difference between European and U.S. fuel consumption per person.

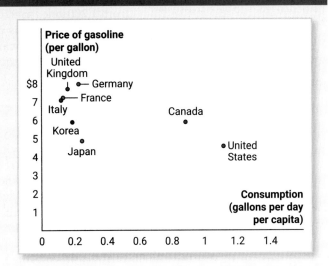

Price is measured in dollars per gallon, consumption is in gallons per capita, per day.

Data from: World Development Indicators and U.S. Energy Information Administration, 2021

corresponding to demand curve D_2. As the figure shows, the pandemic leads to a fall in the quantity of rides demanded at any given price. So at each price the pandemic schedule shows a smaller quantity demanded than the prepandemic schedule. For example, due to the pandemic, the quantity of rides commuters wanted to buy at a price of $13 per ride decreased from 1,200 to 1,000 on any given day; the quantity demanded at $13.25 per ride went from 1,070 to 890, and so on.

As in the analysis of supply, it's crucial to draw a distinction between such shifts of the demand curve and **movements along the demand curve** — changes in the quantity demanded arising from a change in price. We can see this difference in Figure 8. The movement from point *A* to point *B* is a movement along

movement along the demand curve a change in the quantity demanded of a good that results from a change in the good's price.

FIGURE 8 Movement Along the Demand Curve versus Shift of the Demand Curve

The fall in quantity demanded when going from point *A* to point *B* reflects a movement along the demand curve: it is the result of a rise in the price of a good. The fall in quantity demanded when going from point *A* to point *C* reflects a shift of the demand curve: it is the result of a fall in the quantity demanded at any given price.

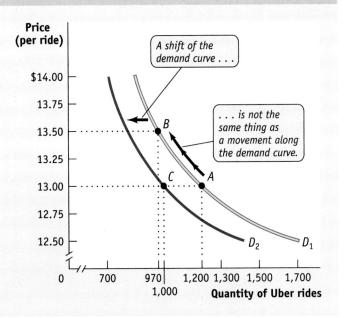

substitutes pairs of goods for which a rise in the price of one of the goods leads to an increase in the demand for the other good.

the demand curve: the quantity demanded falls along D_1 due to a rise in price. Here, a rise in price from $13 to $13.50 leads to a fall in the quantity demanded from 1,200 rides to 970. But the quantity demanded can also fall when the price is unchanged if there is a fall in demand—a leftward shift of the supply curve. This is shown by the leftward shift of the supply curve from D_1 to D_2. Holding the price constant at $13, the quantity demanded falls from 1,200 at point A on D_1 to 1,000 at point C on D_2.

Understanding Shifts of the Demand Curve

Figure 9 illustrates the two basic ways in which demand curves can shift. When economists talk about a "fall in demand," they mean a *leftward* shift of the demand curve: at any given price, buyers demand a smaller quantity of the good than before. This is shown in Figure 9 by the leftward shift of the original demand curve D_1 to D_2. And when economists talk about an "increase in demand," they mean a *rightward* shift of the demand curve: at any given price, buyers demand a larger quantity of the good than before. This is represented by the rightward shift of D_1 to D_3.

Economists believe that there are five principal factors that shift the demand curve for a good or service (though as with supply, there are other possible causes):

- Changes in the prices of related goods or services
- Changes in income
- Changes in tastes
- Changes in expectations
- Changes in the number of buyers

Although this list is not exhaustive, it contains the five most important factors that can shift demand curves. When we say that the quantity of a good or service demanded falls as its price rises, *other things equal*, we are in fact stating that the factors that shift demand are remaining unchanged. Let's now explore how those factors shift the demand curve.

Changes in the Prices of Related Goods or Services Public transportation is what economists call a *substitute* for Uber rides. A pair of goods are **substitutes**

FIGURE 9 Shifts of the Demand Curve

Any event that increases demand shifts the demand curve to the right, reflecting a rise in the quantity demanded at any given price. Any event that decreases demand shifts the demand curve to the left, reflecting a fall in the quantity demanded at any given price.

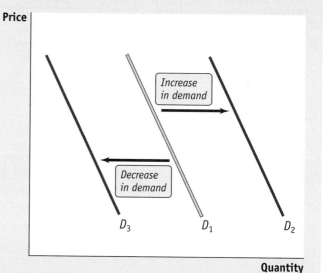

if a rise in the price of one good (Uber rides) makes buyers more likely to buy the other good (public transportation). In San Francisco, if Uber fares are too high, many potential riders will choose to ride BART (Bay Area Rapid Transit). Substitutes are usually goods that in some way serve a similar function: dairy milk and soy milk, muffins and doughnuts, a Ford car and a General Motors car, Uber and BART. A rise in the price of the alternative good (public transportation) induces some buyers to purchase the original good (Uber rides) *instead* of the substitute, shifting demand for the original good to the right.

But sometimes a rise in the price of one good makes consumers *less* willing to buy another good. Such pairs of goods are known as **complements.** Complements are usually goods that in some sense are consumed together: smartphones and apps, coffee and a breakfast burrito, cars and gasoline. Because consumers like to consume a good and its complement together, a change in the price of one of the goods will affect the demand for its complement. In particular, when the price of one good rises, the demand for its complement decreases, shifting the demand curve for the complement to the left. So, for example, when the price of gasoline rises significantly, the demand for gas-guzzling cars falls.

complements pairs of goods for which a rise in the price of one good leads to a decrease in the demand for the other good.

normal good a good for which a rise in income increases the demand for that good — the "normal" case.

inferior good a good for which a rise in income decreases the demand for the good.

Changes in Income
Rashida, a well-paid news presenter, takes an Uber every morning. However, when she was a poorly paid intern, she took public transportation to work. The difference was, of course, down to her income. Rashida purchases more Uber rides now that her income is higher. People consume more of *most* goods at any given price as their incomes go up.

Why do we say that people are likely to purchase more of "*most* goods," rather than purchase more of "*all* goods"? Most goods are **normal goods** — the demand for them increases when consumer income rises. However, the demand for some products falls when income rises. Goods for which demand decreases when income rises are known as **inferior goods.** For example, notice that Rashida's demand for public transportation fell when her income went up. An inferior good — like public transportation — is considered less desirable than more expensive alternatives — like taking an Uber or driving oneself. It is worth noting that in some cities, like San Francisco, Washington D.C., or New York, many people will choose to take public transportation due to traffic congestion or to support climate change initiatives. But in general, when they can afford to, people stop buying an inferior good and switch their consumption to the preferred, more expensive alternative. So when a good is inferior, a rise in income shifts the demand curve to the left. And, not surprisingly, a fall in income shifts the demand curve to the right.

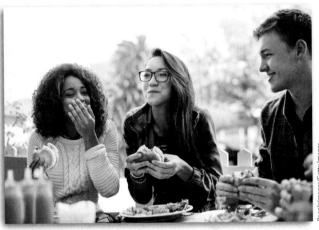

Consumption of normal goods increases when incomes increase, benefiting businesses like casual dining restaurants, but at the expense of fast-food outlets.

Another example of the difference between normal and inferior goods is the comparison of so-called casual-dining restaurants such as Chipotle or Olive Garden and fast-food chains such as Burger King or McDonald's. When their incomes rise, Americans tend to eat out more at casual-dining restaurants. However, some of that increased dining out comes at the expense of fast-food venues — to some extent, people visit McDonald's less often once they can afford to move upscale. So casual dining is a normal good, whereas fast-food consumption appears to be an inferior good.

Changes in Tastes
Why do people want what they want? Fortunately, we don't need to answer that question — we just need to acknowledge that people have certain preferences, or tastes, that determine what they choose to consume and that these tastes can change. Economists usually lump together changes in demand

individual demand curve a graphical representation of the relationship between quantity demanded and price for an individual consumer.

due to trends, beliefs, cultural shifts, and so on under the heading of changes in tastes or preferences.

For example, not so long ago the culturally acceptable range of hair styles and men's facial hair was much more limited. Men's hair was to be kept close-cropped, while beards and moustaches were very rarely seen. Women with curly hair had to keep it straightened (and they certainly couldn't wear pants). Fortunately, those days are gone. Today, people feel free to wear man-buns, full beards, and fulsome curly hair. Pants are more the norm for women than skirts.

Economists have relatively little to say about the social and cultural forces that influence consumers' tastes. However, a change in tastes does have a predictable impact on demand. When tastes change in favor of a good, more people want to buy it at any given price, so the demand curve shifts to the right. When tastes change against a good, fewer people want to buy it at any given price, so the demand curve shifts to the left.

Changes in Expectations When consumers have some choice about when to make a purchase, current demand for a good is often affected by expectations about its future price. For example, savvy shoppers often wait for seasonal sales—say, buying next year's holiday decorations during the post-holiday markdowns. In this case, expectations of a future drop in price lead to a decrease in demand today. Alternatively, expectations of a future rise in price are likely to cause an increase in demand today.

Expected changes in future income can also lead to changes in demand: if you expect your income to rise in the future, you will typically borrow today and increase your demand for certain goods; if you expect your income to fall in the future, you are likely to save today and reduce your demand for some goods.

Changes in the Number of Buyers Another factor that can cause a change in demand is a change in the number of buyers of a good or service. For example, an increase in the population of San Francisco will lead to an increase in the number of commuters wanting to purchase Uber rides.

Just as changes in the number of sellers affect the supply curve, changes in the number of buyers affect the demand curve. An **individual demand curve** shows the relationship between quantity demanded and price for a given buyer. Let's examine individual demand curves by looking at Figure 10 on page 84. Panel (a) of Figure 10 shows the quantity of rides that Rashida will demand on a given day. $D_{Rashida}$ is Rashida's individual demand curve.

Let's assume that the only other buyer in San Francisco on that given day is Terry, and Terry's demand curve is represented by panel (b) in Figure 10. Given that Rashida and Terry are the only two buyers, the *market demand curve*, which shows the quantity of rides demanded by all buyers at any given price on that day, is shown in panel (c). The market demand curve is the *horizontal sum* of the individual demand curves of all consumers. In this case, at any given price, the quantity demanded by the market is the sum of the quantities demanded by Rashida and Terry.

Clearly, the quantity demanded by the market at any given price is larger with Terry present than it would be if Rashida were the only buyer. The quantity demanded at any given price would be even larger if we added a third consumer, then a fourth, and so on. So an increase in the number of buyers leads to an increase in demand.

For a review of the factors that shift demand, see Table 2.

TABLE 2 Factors That Shift Demand

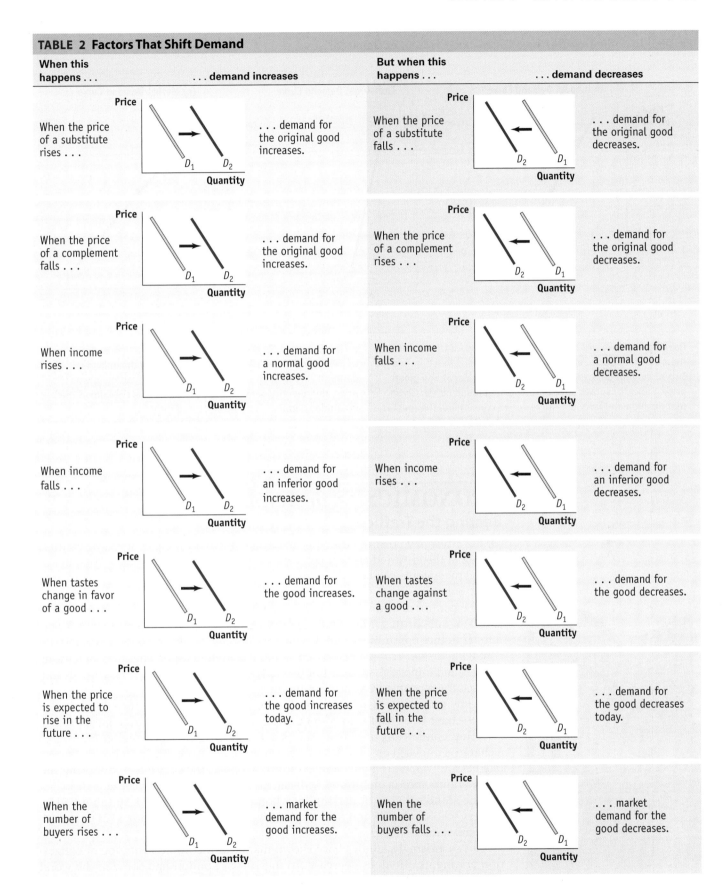

When this happens . . .	. . . demand increases	But when this happens . . .	. . . demand decreases
When the price of a substitute rises . . .	. . . demand for the original good increases.	When the price of a substitute falls . . .	. . . demand for the original good decreases.
When the price of a complement falls . . .	. . . demand for the original good increases.	When the price of a complement rises . . .	. . . demand for the original good decreases.
When income rises . . .	. . . demand for a normal good increases.	When income falls . . .	. . . demand for a normal good decreases.
When income falls . . .	. . . demand for an inferior good increases.	When income rises . . .	. . . demand for an inferior good decreases.
When tastes change in favor of a good . . .	. . . demand for the good increases.	When tastes change against a good . . .	. . . demand for the good decreases.
When the price is expected to rise in the future . . .	. . . demand for the good increases today.	When the price is expected to fall in the future . . .	. . . demand for the good decreases today.
When the number of buyers rises . . .	. . . market demand for the good increases.	When the number of buyers falls . . .	. . . market demand for the good decreases.

FIGURE 10 Individual Demand Curves and the Market Demand Curve

Rashida and Terry are the only two consumers of Uber rides in the market. Panel (a) shows the Rashida's individual demand curve: the number of rides she will buy per year at any given price. Panel (b) shows Terry's individual demand curve. Given that Rashida and Terry are the only two consumers, the *market demand curve*, which shows the quantity of rides demanded by all consumers at any given price, is shown in panel (c). The market demand curve is the *horizontal sum* of the individual demand curves of all consumers. In this case, at any given price, the quantity demanded by the market is the sum of the quantities demanded by Rashida and Terry.

ECONOMICS >> *in Action*
Beating the Traffic

All big cities have traffic problems, and many local authorities try to discourage driving in the crowded city center. If we think of an auto trip to the city center as a good that people consume, we can use the economics of demand to analyze anti-traffic policies.

One common strategy is to reduce the demand for auto trips by lowering the prices of substitutes. Many metropolitan areas subsidize bus and rail service, hoping to lure commuters out of their cars. An alternative is to raise the price of complements: several major U.S. cities impose high taxes on commercial parking garages and impose short time limits on parking meters, both to raise revenue and to discourage people from driving into the city.

A few major cities—including Singapore, London, Oslo, Stockholm, and Milan—have been willing to adopt a direct and politically controversial approach: reducing congestion by raising the price of driving. Under *congestion pricing*, a charge is imposed on cars entering the city center during business hours. Drivers buy passes, which are then debited electronically as they drive by monitoring stations. Compliance is monitored with cameras that photograph license plates.

The standard cost of driving into London is currently £11.50 (about $15). Drivers who don't pay and are caught pay a fine of £130 (about $171) for each transgression.

Not surprisingly, studies have shown that after the implementation of congestion pricing, traffic does decrease. In the 1990s, London had some of the worst traffic in Europe. The introduction of its congestion charge in 2003 immediately reduced traffic in the city center by about 15%. Fifteen years later, by 2018, the

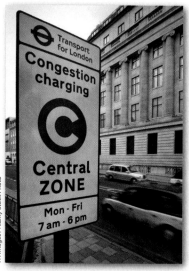

Cities can reduce traffic congestion by raising the price of driving.

policy was still working, as traffic volumes are still 25% lower than they were in the late 1990s. And there has been increased use of substitutes, such as public transportation, bicycles, and ride-hailing. From 2001 to 2011, bike trips in London increased by 79%, and bus usage was up by 30%.

And less congestion led not just to fewer accidents, but to a lower *rate* of accidents as fewer cars jostled for space. One study found that from 2000 to 2010 the number of accidents per mile driven in London fell by 40%. Stockholm experienced effects similar to those in London: traffic fell by 22% in 2013 compared with pre-congestion charge levels, transit times fell by one-third to one-half, and air quality measurably improved. A 2018 article found that serious childhood asthma attacks declined significantly in Stockholm after the congestion charge was imposed.

Congestion pricing is now getting the attention of city planners in the United States. New York City became the first U.S. city to implement congestion pricing, with Los Angeles, Seattle, and Portland, Oregon, currently considering plans to do the same.

>> Check Your Understanding 3-2
Solutions appear at back of book.

1. Explain whether each of the following events represents (i) a *shift of* the demand curve or (ii) a *movement along* the demand curve.
   a. A store owner finds that customers are willing to pay more for umbrellas on rainy days.
   b. When Circus Cruise Lines offered reduced prices for summer cruises in the Caribbean, their number of bookings increased sharply.
   c. People buy more long-stem roses the week of Valentine's Day, even though the prices are higher than at other times during the year.
   d. A sharp rise in the price of gasoline leads many commuters to join carpools in order to reduce their gasoline purchases.

>> Quick Review
- The **demand schedule** shows how the **quantity demanded** changes as the price changes. A **demand curve** illustrates this relationship.
- The **law of demand** asserts that a higher price reduces the quantity demanded. Thus, demand curves normally slope downward.
- An increase in demand leads to a rightward **shift of the demand curve:** the quantity demanded rises for any given price. A decrease in demand leads to a leftward shift: the quantity demanded falls for any given price. A change in price results in a change in the quantity demanded and a **movement along the demand curve.**
- The five main factors that can shift the demand curve are changes in (1) the price of a related good, such as a **substitute** or a **complement,** (2) income, such as a **normal** or **inferior** good, (3) tastes, (4) expectations, and (5) the number of consumers.
- The market demand curve is the horizontal sum of the **individual demand curves** of all consumers in the market.

Supply, Demand, and Equilibrium

We have now covered the first three key elements in the supply and demand model: the demand curve, the supply curve, and the set of factors that shift each curve. The next step is to put these elements together to show how they can be used to predict the actual price at which the good is bought and sold, as well as the actual quantity transacted.

What determines the price at which a good or service is bought and sold? What determines the quantity transacted of the good or service? In Chapter 1, we learned the general principle that *markets move toward equilibrium,* a situation in which no individual would be better off taking a different action. In the case of a competitive market, we can be more specific: a competitive market is in equilibrium when the price has moved to a level at which the quantity of a good demanded equals the quantity of that good supplied. At that price, no individual seller could make themselves better off by offering to sell either more or less of the good and no individual buyer could make themselves better off by offering to buy more or less of the good. In other words, at the market equilibrium, price has moved to a level that exactly matches the quantity demanded by consumers to the quantity supplied by sellers.

The price that matches the quantity supplied and the quantity demanded is the **equilibrium price;** the quantity bought and sold at that price is the **equilibrium quantity.** The equilibrium price is also known as the **market-clearing price:** it is the price that "clears the market" by ensuring that every buyer willing

equilibrium price the price at which the market is in equilibrium, that is, the quantity of a good or service demanded equals the quantity of that good or service supplied; also referred to as the market-clearing price.

equilibrium quantity the quantity of a good or service bought and sold at the equilibrium (or market-clearing) price.

market-clearing price the price at which the market is in equilibrium, that is, the quantity of a good or service demanded equals the quantity of that good or service supplied; also referred to as the equilibrium price.

to pay that price finds a seller willing to sell at that price, and vice versa. So how do we find the equilibrium price and quantity?

Finding the Equilibrium Price and Quantity

The easiest way to determine the equilibrium price and quantity in a market is by putting the supply curve and the demand curve on the same diagram. Since the supply curve shows the quantity supplied at any given price and the demand curve shows the quantity demanded at any given price, the price at which the two curves cross is the equilibrium price: the price at which quantity supplied equals quantity demanded.

Figure 11 combines the supply curve from Figure 1 and the demand curve from Figure 6. They *intersect* at point *E*, which is the equilibrium of this market; $13 is the equilibrium price and 1,000 rides is the equilibrium quantity.

Let's confirm that point *E* fits our definition of equilibrium. At a price of $13.25 per ride, Uber drivers are willing to provide 1,070 on a given day and commuters want to buy 1,070 rides on that day. So at the price of $13.25 per ride, the quantity of rides supplied equals the quantity demanded. Notice that at any other price the market would not clear: every willing buyer would not be able to find a willing seller, or vice versa. More specifically, if the price were more than $13.25, the quantity supplied would exceed the quantity demanded; if the price were less than $13.25, the quantity demanded would exceed the quantity supplied.

The model of supply and demand, then, predicts that given the demand and supply curves shown in Figure 11, 1,070 will be purchased at a price of $13.25 per ride. But how can we be sure that the market will arrive at the equilibrium price? We begin by answering three simple questions:

1. Why do all sales and purchases in a market take place at the same price?
2. Why does the market price fall if it is above the equilibrium price?
3. Why does the market price rise if it is below the equilibrium price?

FIGURE 11 Market Equilibrium

Market equilibrium occurs at point *E*, where the supply curve and the demand curve intersect. In equilibrium, the quantity demanded is equal to the quantity supplied. In this market, the equilibrium price is $13.25 per ride and the equilibrium quantity is 1,070 rides.

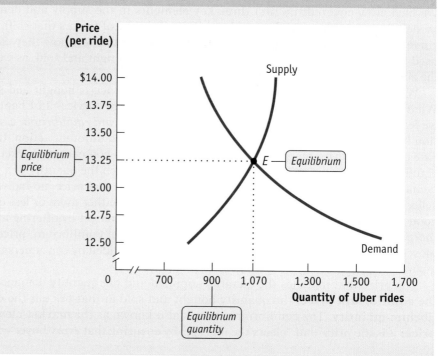

1. Why Do All Sales and Purchases in a Market Take Place at the Same Price?

There are some markets in which the same good can sell for many different prices, depending on who is selling or who is buying. For example, have you ever bought a souvenir in a tourist trap and then seen the same item on sale somewhere else for a lower price? Because tourists don't know which shops offer the best deals and don't have time for comparison shopping, sellers in tourist areas can charge different prices for the same good.

But in any market in which both buyers and sellers have been around for some time, sales and purchases tend to converge at a generally uniform price, so we can safely talk about *the* market price. It's easy to see why. Suppose a seller offered a potential buyer a price noticeably above what the buyer knew other people to be paying. The buyer would clearly be better off shopping elsewhere—unless the seller were prepared to offer a better deal.

Conversely, a seller would not be willing to sell for significantly less than the amount they knew most buyers were paying; they would be better off waiting to get a more reasonable customer. So in any well-established, ongoing market, all sellers receive and all buyers pay approximately the same price. This is what we call the *market price*.

2. Why Does the Market Price Fall If It Is Above the Equilibrium Price?

Suppose the supply and demand curves are as shown in Figure 11 but the market price is above the equilibrium level of $13.25—say, $13.75. This situation is illustrated in Figure 12. Why can't the price stay there?

As the figure shows, at a price of $13.75 there would be more rides offered than commuters wanted to buy: 1,150 rides versus 900 rides. The difference of 250 rides is the **surplus**—also known as the *excess supply*—of rides at $13.25.

This surplus means that some Uber drivers are frustrated: at the current price, they cannot find commuters who want to purchase their rides. The surplus offers an incentive for those frustrated would-be drivers to offer a lower price in order to poach business from other drivers and entice more commuters to buy. The result

surplus the excess of a good or service that occurs when the quantity supplied exceeds the quantity demanded; surpluses occur when the price is above the equilibrium price.

" YEAH, BUT ALL WE HAVE TO SELL IS ONE GLASS ! "

FIGURE 12 Price Above Its Equilibrium Level Creates a Surplus

The market price of $13.75 is above the equilibrium price of $13.25. This creates a surplus: at a price of $13.75, Uber drivers would like to sell 1,150 rides but consumers want to buy only 900 rides, so there is a surplus of 250 rides. This surplus will push the price down until it reaches the equilibrium price of $13.25.

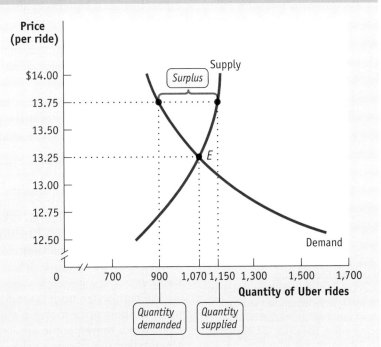

FIGURE 13 Price Below Its Equilibrium Level Creates a Shortage

The market price of $12.75 is below the equilibrium price of $13.25. This creates a shortage: commuters want to buy 1,380 rides, but only 910 are offered, so there is a shortage of 470 rides. This shortage will push the price up until it reaches the equilibrium price of $13.25.

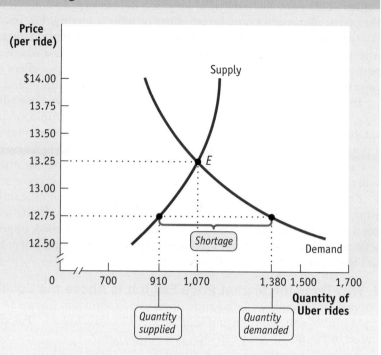

3. Why Does the Market Price Rise If It Is Below the Equilibrium Price?

Now suppose the price is below its equilibrium level—say, at $12.75 per ride, as shown in Figure 13. In this case, the quantity demanded, 1,380 rides, exceeds the quantity supplied, 910 rides, implying that there are commuters who cannot find rides: there is a **shortage**, also known as an *excess demand*, of 470 rides.

When there is a shortage, there are frustrated would-be commuters—people who want to purchase rides but cannot find willing drivers at the current price. In this situation, either buyers will offer more than the prevailing price or sellers will realize that they can charge higher prices. Either way, the result is to drive up the prevailing price.

This bidding up of prices happens whenever there are shortages—and there will be shortages whenever the price is below its equilibrium level. So, the market price will always rise if it is below the equilibrium level.

Using Equilibrium to Describe Markets

We have now seen that a market tends to have a single price, the equilibrium price. If the market price is above the equilibrium level, the ensuing surplus leads buyers and sellers to take actions that lower the price. And if the market price is below the equilibrium level, the ensuing shortage leads buyers and sellers to take actions that raise the price. So the market price always *moves toward* the equilibrium price, the price at which there is neither surplus nor shortage.

We can better understand a key feature of the Uber app now that we have analyzed how price moves a market to equilibrium. Recall that at times and locations when more people are looking for rides than are currently available, what Uber called their "surge pricing mechanism," now their dynamic pricing, raises

shortage the insufficiency of a good or service that occurs when the quantity demanded exceeds the quantity supplied; shortages occur when the price is below the equilibrium price.

of this price cutting will be to push the prevailing price down until it reaches the equilibrium price. So the price of a good will fall whenever there is a surplus—that is, whenever the market price is above its equilibrium level.

the price of any given ride. In other words, Uber's dynamic pricing model works in the same way that a market-clearing price works in a competitive market. When the demand for rides outstrips the supply, raising the price has the effect of (1) reducing the quantity of rides demanded; and (2) increasing the quantity of rides supplied. (The quantity of rides supplied increases as existing drivers work longer hours and as drivers from other locations are drawn in.) Once the quantity demanded equals the quantity supplied, the price stabilizes—that is, it has reached the market-clearing level. Conversely, when the number of rides offered at a location is greater than the number of rides demanded, price falls until equilibrium is reached.

ECONOMICS >> *in Action*
The Price of Admission

The market equilibrium, so the theory goes, is pretty egalitarian because the equilibrium price applies to everyone. That is, all buyers pay the same price—the equilibrium price—and all sellers receive that same price. But is this realistic?

The market for concert tickets is an example that seems to contradict the theory—there's one price at the box office, and there's another price (typically much higher) for the same event online where people who already have tickets resell them. For example, compare the box office price for a Taylor Swift concert in Seattle, Washington, in July 2023 to the StubHub.com price for seats in the same location: $125.00 versus a minimum of $500.00.

The competitive market model determines the price you pay for concert tickets.

Puzzling as this may seem, there is no contradiction once we take opportunity costs and tastes into account. For major events, buying tickets from the box office can mean waiting in very long "digital" lines. Ticket buyers who use online resellers have decided that the opportunity cost of their time is too high to spend waiting in line. And tickets for major events being sold at face value by online box offices often sell out within minutes. In this case, some people who want to go to the concert badly but have missed out on the opportunity to buy cheaper tickets from the online box office are willing to pay the higher online reseller price.

Not only that, but by comparing prices across sellers for seats close to one another, you can see that markets really do move to equilibrium. For example, for a seat in Section 304, Row Q, StubHub's price was $602.00 while SeatGeek's price for a nearby seat was $582.00. As the competitive market model predicts, units of the same good will end up selling for approximately the same price.

In fact, e-commerce has made markets move to equilibrium more quickly by doing the price comparisons for you. The website SeatGeek compares ticket prices across more than 100 ticket resellers, allowing customers to instantly choose the best deal. Tickets that are priced lower than those of competitors will be snapped up, while higher priced tickets will languish unsold.

Tickets on StubHub can sell for less than the face value for events with little appeal, while they can skyrocket for events in high demand. For example, in 2022, the average ticket price on StubHub for the Super Bowl was more than $9,800. The prior year, one fan paid more than $85,000 for a single seat to watch Tom Brady win his last Super Bowl championship. Even StubHub's chief executive said the site is "the embodiment of supply-and-demand economics."

So the theory of competitive markets isn't just speculation. If you want to experience it for yourself, try buying tickets to a concert or an NBA championship.

>> Check Your Understanding 3-3
Solutions appear at back of book.

1. In the following three situations, the market is initially in equilibrium. Explain the changes in either supply or demand that result from each event. After each event described below, does a surplus or shortage exist at the original equilibrium price? What will happen to the equilibrium price as a result?
   a. Due to wildfires in the area, 2021 was a down year for California wine-grape growers, who saw grape production fall by 5%.
   b. After a hurricane, Florida hoteliers often find that many people cancel their upcoming vacations, leaving them with empty hotel rooms.
   c. After a heavy snowfall, many people want to buy second-hand snowblowers at the local home improvement store.

|| Changes in Supply and Demand

The huge fall in the price of the average Uber ride from 2019 to 2020 may have come as a shock to Uber drivers, but it was no surprise to those who understand how a competitive market operates. Predictably, the huge drop in commuters caused by the arrival of coronavirus lockdown measures reduced the equilibrium price by reducing the demand for Uber rides.

In fact, from 2019 to 2022, the growth and ebb of the pandemic caused the supply curve as well as the demand curve for Uber rides to shift multiple times. In order to simplify our analysis, let's first consider cases in which only one curve shifted but not the other. Then we will consider cases in which both the supply curve and the demand curve shift.

We have seen that when a curve shifts, the equilibrium price and quantity change. We will now concentrate on exactly how the shift of a curve alters the equilibrium price and quantity.

What Happens When the Demand Curve Shifts

Figure 14 shows the effect of the drop in demand in 2020 on the market for Uber rides. Point E_1 shows the equilibrium corresponding to the original demand curve, with P_1 the equilibrium price and Q_1 the equilibrium quantity bought and sold.

FIGURE 14 Equilibrium and Shifts of the Demand Curve

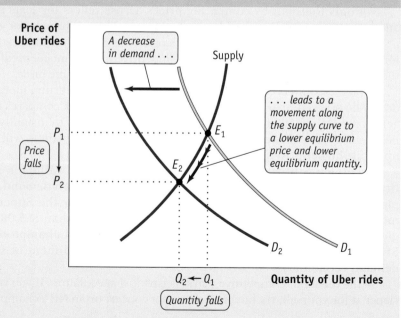

The original equilibrium in the market for Uber rides is at E_1, at the intersection of the supply curve and the original demand curve, D_1. The fall in demand by commuters in 2020, as the pandemic hit, shifted the demand curve leftward to D_2. A surplus of rides existed at the original price, P_1, causing both the price and quantity supplied to fall, a movement along the supply curve. A new equilibrium was reached at E_2, with a lower equilibrium price, P_2, and a lower equilibrium quantity, Q_2. When demand for a good or service falls, the equilibrium price and the equilibrium quantity of the good or service both fall as well.

A fall in demand is indicated by a *leftward* shift of the demand curve from D_1 to D_2. At the original market price P_1, this market is no longer in equilibrium: a surplus occurs because the quantity supplied exceeds the quantity demanded. So the price of rides falls and generates a decrease in the quantity supplied, a downward *movement along the supply curve*. A new equilibrium is established at point E_2, with a lower equilibrium price, P_2, and lower equilibrium quantity, Q_2. This sequence of events reflects a general principle: *When demand for a good or service falls, the equilibrium price and the equilibrium quantity of the good or service both fall.*

What would happen in the reverse case, a rise in the demand for rides? This is in fact what happened in mid-2021, as vaccinated commuters returned to work and a strong economic recovery raised their incomes. The demand curve shifted to the *right*, creating a shortage of rides at the original price as the quantity demanded exceeded the quantity supplied. The increase in price leads to an increase in the quantity supplied, resulting in a higher equilibrium price and a higher equilibrium quantity. *When demand for a good or service increases, the equilibrium price and the equilibrium quantity of the good or service both increase as well.*

To summarize how a market responds to a change in demand: *A fall in demand leads to a fall in both the equilibrium price and the equilibrium quantity. An increase in demand leads to an increase in both the equilibrium price and the equilibrium quantity.*

What Happens When the Supply Curve Shifts

In normal times (that is, periods not in the midst of pandemic), it's easier to predict changes in supply than changes in demand for most goods and services. Physical factors that affect supply, like weather or the availability of inputs, are easier to get a handle on than the fickle tastes that often cause demand shifts. Still, with supply as with demand, what we can best predict are the *effects* of shifts of the supply curve.

As we mentioned earlier, over the course of the pandemic years of 2019 to 2022, the supply curve as well as the demand curve for Uber rides shifted. As the experiences of Ned Eames illustrated, by the spring of 2021, increasingly fearful of becoming infected and given the plentiful availability of delivery jobs, many Uber drivers across the country called it quits.

Figure 15 shows how this shift affected the market equilibrium. The original prepandemic equilibrium is at E_1, the point of intersection of the original

FIGURE 15 Equilibrium and Shifts of the Supply Curve

The original equilibrium in the market is at E_1. An increase in the unwillingness of sellers to provide the good at any given price causes a fall in the supply of Uber rides and shifts the supply curve leftward from S_1 to S_2. A new equilibrium is established at E_2, with a higher equilibrium price, P_2, and a lower equilibrium quantity, Q_2.

prepandemic supply curve, S_1, with an equilibrium price P_1 and equilibrium quantity Q_1. By the spring of 2021, supply decreases and S_1 shifts *leftward* to S_2. Compared with the prepandemic equilibrium at price P_1, the fall in supply creates a shortage of rides and the market is no longer in equilibrium. This shortage causes a rise in price and a fall in the quantity demanded, a *downward movement along the demand curve*. The new equilibrium is at E_2, with an equilibrium price P_2 and an equilibrium quantity Q_2. In the new equilibrium E_2, the price is higher and the equilibrium quantity is lower than before. This can be stated as a general principle: *When supply of a good or service falls, the equilibrium price of the good or service increases and the equilibrium quantity of the good or service falls.*

What happens to the market when supply falls? A fall in supply leads to a *leftward* shift of the supply curve. At the original price a shortage now exists. As a result, the equilibrium price rises and the quantity demanded falls. This describes what happened to the market for Uber rides after the economic shutdown in spring 2020. We can formulate a general principle: *When supply of a good or service decreases, the equilibrium price of the good or service rises and the equilibrium quantity of the good or service falls.*

To summarize how a market responds to a change in supply: *An increase in supply leads to a fall in the equilibrium price and a rise in the equilibrium quantity. A decrease in supply leads to a rise in the equilibrium price and a fall in the equilibrium quantity.*

Simultaneous Shifts of Supply and Demand Curves

Even absent a pandemic, supply curves and demand curves for many goods and services shift quite often because the economic environment continually changes. So it's important that we understand what happens when *both* the demand and supply curves shift at the same time.

Figure 16 illustrates two examples of simultaneous shifts. In both panels there is a decrease in supply — that is, a leftward shift of the supply curve from S_1 to S_2 — representing, for example, Uber drivers switching to delivery jobs. Notice that the leftward shift in panel (a) is smaller than the one in panel (b): we can suppose that panel (a) represents a smaller number of Uber drivers quitting, while panel (b) represents a larger number.

Both panels show a decrease in demand — that is, a leftward shift from D_1 to D_2. Also notice that the leftward shift in panel (a) is relatively larger than the one in panel (b): we can suppose that panel (a) reflects the effect on demand of a sharp fall in the number of people commuting while panel (b) reflects the effect of a less extreme fall.

This reflects actual events by the summer of 2021. Demand for rides was still smaller relative to the prepandemic level. Yet, by the summer of 2021, many people had been vaccinated. Tired of being stuck inside their homes and apartments, and feeling protected against the virus, people started to go out more frequently and the demand for rides increased from spring 2021 levels. At the same time, former Uber drivers were still delivering meals and packages rather than offering rides. As a result, in comparison to prepandemic levels, panel (b) shows a decrease in supply that is large relative to the decrease in demand, so the equilibrium quantity falls as the equilibrium price rises.

In both cases, the equilibrium quantity falls from Q_1 to Q_2 as the equilibrium moves from E_1 to E_2. But what happens to the equilibrium price? In panel (a), the decrease in demand is large relative to the decrease in supply, and the equilibrium price falls as a result. In panel (b), the decrease in supply is large relative to the decrease in demand, and the equilibrium price rises as a result. That is, when both demand and supply decrease, the actual quantity bought and sold will fall but

FIGURE 16 Simultaneous Shifts of the Demand and Supply Curves

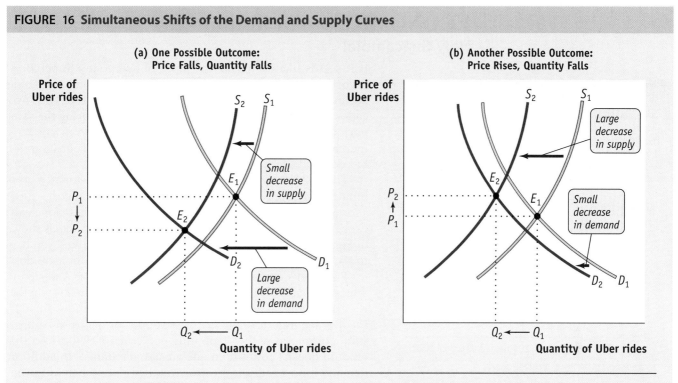

In panel (a), there is a simultaneous leftward shift of the demand curve and a leftward shift of the supply curve. This broadly reflects what actually happened in the market for Uber rides by the spring of 2021, relative to the prepandemic market. Here the decrease in demand is relatively larger than the decrease in supply, so the equilibrium quantity falls as the equilibrium price also falls. In panel (b), there is also a simultaneous shift leftward of the demand curve as well as of the supply curve. Note, however, that the leftward shift of the demand curve in panel (b) is smaller than the leftward shift in panel (a).

the change in equilibrium price can go either way depending on *how much* the demand and supply curves have shifted.

Can we safely make any predictions about the changes in price and quantity when supply and demand shift in the same direction? As our example shows, the change in quantity bought and sold can be predicted, but the change in price is ambiguous. The two possible outcomes when the supply and demand curves shift in the same direction are as follows:

- When both demand and supply increase, the equilibrium quantity rises but the change in equilibrium price is ambiguous.
- When both demand and supply decrease, the equilibrium quantity falls but the change in equilibrium price is ambiguous.

But what happens when supply and demand shift in opposite directions? Then we can't predict what the ultimate effect will be on the quantity bought and sold. What we can say is that a curve that shifts a disproportionately greater distance than the other curve will have a disproportionately greater effect on the quantity bought and sold. That said, we can make the following prediction about the outcome when the supply and demand curves shift in opposite directions:

- When demand decreases and supply increases, the equilibrium price falls but the change in the equilibrium quantity is ambiguous.
- When demand increases and supply decreases, the equilibrium price rises but the change in the equilibrium quantity is ambiguous.

ECONOMICS >> *in Action*
Holy Guacamole!

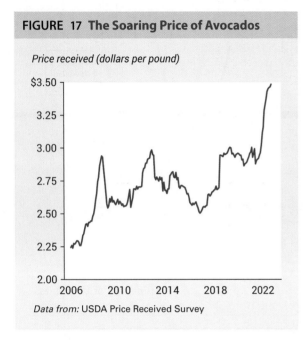

FIGURE 17 The Soaring Price of Avocados

Price received (dollars per pound)

Data from: USDA Price Received Survey

If it seems like each year the price of everyone's Super Bowl favorite — a big bowl of guacamole — has gone up, that's because, well, it has. In early 2022, a 20-pound box of Hass avocados from Mexico cost $6.29 more than it did during the same period in 2021. Over the past 20 years, avocado prices have increased nearly eightfold. Meanwhile, per capita consumption has doubled over the past 10 years.

The 2022 record-breaking price increase was due to a combination of supply problems — soaring production costs, labor shortages, and supply chain backlogs. However, that alone can't explain the long-run upward trend of avocado prices that is shown in Figure 17. To understand the forces behind that trend you have to examine both demand and supply in the market for avocados.

First, let's consider demand. Year after year, Americans' appetite (demand) for all things avocado has grown — whether it's guacamole, avocado toast, or avocado smoothies. In 2021, the average American ate nearly 9 pounds of the fresh fruit per year, compared with 1.1 pounds per year in 1990. (And that amount doesn't count premade guacamole items.) In addition, demand for avocados is growing in other places such as Europe and China. These changes in tastes have shifted the demand curve rightward over time.

Second, there's supply. Owing to the coronavirus pandemic, production costs have soared. Fertilizer prices in 2022 are three times higher than the year before. Labor and energy costs are higher. Transportation costs are also higher due to a shortage of truckers. These higher production costs shifted the supply curve leftward.

Inevitably, an increase in demand coupled with a sharp fall in supply leads to sharply rising prices for avocados. It's economic logic, after all. Until demand falls, or supply rises, or both, the price of satisfying America's avocado cravings will remain high. As one industry observer stated "There just aren't enough [avocados] to meet demand, which has driven prices higher. Avocados are 100% more expensive than they were a year ago."

However, there's a bright spot on the horizon for avocado lovers. At some point, pandemic-induced production problems will dissipate and give growers (and their crops) a boost. So keep your tortilla chips on hand and ready for dipping.

>> Quick Review

• Changes in the equilibrium price and quantity in a market result from shifts of the supply curve, the demand curve, or both.

• An increase in demand increases both the equilibrium price and the equilibrium quantity. A decrease in demand decreases both the equilibrium price and the equilibrium quantity.

• An increase in supply drives the equilibrium price down but increases the equilibrium quantity. A decrease in supply raises the equilibrium price but reduces the equilibrium quantity.

• Fluctuations in markets involve shifts of both the supply and demand curves. When they shift in the same direction, the change in equilibrium quantity is predictable but the change in equilibrium price is not. When they shift in opposite directions, the change in equilibrium price is predictable but the change in equilibrium quantity is not. When there are simultaneous shifts of the demand and supply curves, the curve that shifts the greater distance has a greater effect on the change in equilibrium price and quantity.

>> Check Your Understanding 3-4
Solutions appear at back of book.

1. For each of the following, determine (i) the market in question; (ii) whether a shift in demand or supply occurred, the direction of the shift, and what induced the shift; and (iii) the effect of the shift on the equilibrium price and the equilibrium quantity.
   a. As U.S. gasoline prices fall, more people buy large cars.
   b. As technological innovation has lowered the cost of recycling used paper, fresh paper made from recycled stock is used more frequently.
   c. When a local cable company offers cheaper on-demand films, local movie theaters have more unfilled seats.

2. When a new, faster computer chip is introduced, demand for computers using the older, slower chips decreases. Simultaneously, computer makers increase their production of computers containing the old chips in order to clear out their stocks of old chips.
   a. Draw two diagrams of the market for computers containing the old chips: one in which the equilibrium quantity falls in response to these events and one in which the equilibrium quantity rises.
   b. What happens to the equilibrium price in each diagram?

‖ **Competitive Markets — and Others**

Earlier in this chapter, we defined a competitive market and explained that the supply and demand framework is a model of competitive markets. But why does it matter whether or not a market is competitive? Now that we've seen how the supply and demand model works, we can offer some explanation.

To understand why competitive markets are different from other markets, compare the problems facing two individuals: a wheat farmer who must decide whether to grow more wheat and the president of a giant aluminum company — say, Alcoa — who must decide whether to produce more aluminum.

For the wheat farmer, the question is simply whether the extra wheat can be sold at a price high enough to justify the extra production cost. The farmer need not worry about whether producing more wheat will affect the price of the wheat they were already planning to grow. That's because the wheat market is competitive. There are thousands of wheat farmers, and one farmer's decision will not impact the market price.

But for the Alcoa executive, the aluminum market is *not* competitive. There are only a few big producers, including Alcoa, and each of them is well aware that its actions *do* have a noticeable impact on the market price. This adds a whole new level of complexity to the decisions producers have to make. Alcoa can't decide whether or not to produce more aluminum just by asking whether the additional product will sell for more than it costs to make. The company also has to ask whether producing more aluminum will drive down the market price and reduce its *profit,* its net gain from producing and selling its output.

When a market is competitive, individuals can base decisions on less complicated analyses than those used in a noncompetitive market. This in turn means that it's easier for economists to build a model of a competitive market than of a noncompetitive market.

This doesn't mean that economic analysis has nothing to say about noncompetitive markets. On the contrary, economists can offer some very important insights into how other kinds of markets work. But those insights require other models.

BUSINESS CASE

Uber Gives Riders a Lesson in Supply and Demand

JEENAH MOON/The New York Times/Redux

Two young entrepreneurs, Garrett Camp and Travis Kalanick, created Uber in 2009 to alleviate a common frustration: how to find a taxi when you need to get somewhere and there aren't any taxis available. In densely populated cities like New York City, finding a taxi is relatively easy on most days—stand on a corner, stick out your arm, and before long a taxi will stop to pick you up. And you know exactly what taxi fare rates will be before you step into the car, because they are set by city regulators.

But at other times, it can be difficult to find a taxi, and you can wait a very long time for one—for example, on rainy days or during rush hour. As you wait, you will probably notice empty taxis passing you by—drivers who have quit working for the day and are headed home. Moreover, there are times when it is simply impossible to hail a taxi—such as during a snowstorm or on New Year's Eve.

Uber was created to address this problem. Using an app, Uber connects people who want a ride to drivers with cars. It also registers drivers, sets fares, and automatically collects payment from a registered rider's credit card. Uber then keeps 25% of the fare, with the rest going to the driver. As of 2021, Uber was operating in over 10,000 cities across 71 countries, and booked $17.4 billion in rides.

Studies have shown that Uber fares are either roughly equal to or less than regular taxi fares during normal driving hours. The qualification *during normal driving hours* is important because at other times Uber's rates fluctuate. When there are more people looking for a ride than cars available, Uber uses what it calls *dynamic pricing (originally termed surge pricing):* setting the rate higher until everyone who wants a car at the going price can get one. For example, during a snowstorm or on New Year's Eve, Uber rides cost around 9 to 10 times the standard price. Enraged, some Uber customers have accused it of price gouging.

But according to their founders, Uber's dynamic pricing is simply a method of keeping customers happy because the surge price is calculated to leave as few people as possible without a ride. As Kalanick explains, "We do not own cars nor do we employ drivers. Higher prices are required to get cars on the road and keep them on the road during the busiest times." However, with more drivers joining Uber's fleet, drivers are finding that it takes longer hours to make sufficient income. So in cities like San Diego where passengers have limited access to taxi services, Uber drivers have banded together to take "synchronized breaks" during peak hours, such as Saturday nights. These breaks cause prices to surge, which prompts the drivers to jump into their cars. Clearly these Uber drivers know how supply and demand works.

QUESTIONS FOR THOUGHT

1. What accounts for the fact that before Uber's arrival, there were typically enough taxis available for everyone who wanted one on good weather days, but not enough available on bad weather days?

2. How does Uber's dynamic pricing solve the problem? Assess Kalanick's claim that the price is set to leave as few people possible without a ride.

3. Use a supply and demand diagram to illustrate how Uber drivers can cause prices to surge by taking coordinated breaks. Why is this strategy unlikely to work in New York, a large city with an established fleet of taxis?

SUMMARY

1. The **supply and demand model** illustrates how a **competitive market,** one with many buyers and sellers, none of whom can influence the market price, works.

2. The **supply schedule** shows the **quantity supplied** at each price and is represented graphically by a **supply curve.** Other things equal, supply curves usually slope upward.

3. A **movement along the supply curve** occurs when a price change leads to a change in the quantity supplied. When economists talk of increasing or decreasing supply, they mean **shifts of the supply curve**—a change in the quantity supplied at any given price. An increase in supply causes a rightward shift of the supply curve. A decrease in supply causes a leftward shift.

4. There are five main factors that shift the supply curve:
   - A change in **input** prices
   - A change in the prices of related goods and services
   - A change in technology
   - A change in expectations
   - A change in the number of producers

5. The market supply curve for a good or service is the horizontal sum of the **individual supply curves** of all producers in the market.

6. The **demand schedule** shows the **quantity demanded** at each price and is represented graphically by a **demand curve.** The **law of demand** says that demand curves slope downward; that is, a higher price for a good or service leads people to demand a smaller quantity.

7. A **movement along the demand curve** occurs when a price change leads to a change in the quantity demanded. When economists talk of increasing or decreasing demand, they mean **shifts of the demand curve**—a change in the quantity demanded at any given price. An increase in demand causes a rightward shift of the demand curve. A decrease in demand causes a leftward shift.

8. There are five main factors that shift the demand curve:
   - A change in the prices of related goods or services, such as **substitutes** or **complements**
   - A change in income: when income rises, the demand for **normal goods** increases and the demand for **inferior goods** decreases
   - A change in tastes
   - A change in expectations
   - A change in the number of consumers

9. The market demand curve for a good or service is the horizontal sum of the **individual demand curves** of all consumers in the market.

10. The supply and demand model is based on the principle that the price in a market moves to its **equilibrium price,** or **market-clearing price,** the price at which the quantity demanded is equal to the quantity supplied. This quantity is the **equilibrium quantity.** When the price is above its market-clearing level, there is a **surplus** that pushes the price down. When the price is below its market-clearing level, there is a **shortage** that pushes the price up.

11. An increase in demand increases both the equilibrium price and the equilibrium quantity; a decrease in demand has the opposite effect. An increase in supply reduces the equilibrium price and increases the equilibrium quantity; a decrease in supply has the opposite effect.

12. Shifts of the demand curve and the supply curve can happen simultaneously. When they shift in opposite directions, the change in equilibrium price is predictable but the change in equilibrium quantity is not. When they shift in the same direction, the change in equilibrium quantity is predictable but the change in equilibrium price is not. In general, the curve that shifts the greater distance has a greater effect on the changes in equilibrium price and quantity.

KEY TERMS

PRACTICE QUESTIONS

1. In the market for automobiles explain how demand responds to (i) an increase in the price of automobiles today and (ii) an expected increase in the future price of automobiles.

2. Explain why the following statement is misleading: "Apple increases supply of watches following an unexpected increase in demand."

3. In each of the following, what is the mistake that underlies the statement? Explain the mistake in terms of supply and demand and the factors that influence them.

   a. Consumers are illogical because they are buying more Starbucks beverages in 2022 despite the fact that Starbucks has raised prices 10 to 30 cents per drink.

   b. Consumers are illogical because they buy less at Cost-U-Less Warehouse Superstore when their incomes go up.

   c. Consumers are illogical for buying an iPhone 14 when an iPhone 13 costs less.

4. Two students are debating the effects of an expected decline in future home prices. One student claims that a decline in home prices will increase the total quantity of homes while the other student claims that the quantity of homes will decline. Which student is correct? Explain. Be sure to discuss how expected price changes shift demand and/or supply.

PROBLEMS

1. A survey conducted by YouGov revealed that chocolate is the most popular flavor of ice cream in the United States. For each of the following, indicate the possible effects on demand, supply, or both as well as equilibrium price and quantity of chocolate ice cream.

   a. A severe drought in the Midwest causes dairy farmers to reduce the number of milk-producing cattle in their herds by a third. These dairy farmers supply cream that is used to manufacture chocolate ice cream.

   b. A new report by the American Medical Association reveals that chocolate does, in fact, have significant health benefits.

   c. The discovery of cheaper synthetic vanilla flavoring lowers the price of vanilla ice cream.

   d. New technology for mixing and freezing ice cream lowers manufacturers' costs of producing chocolate ice cream.

2. In a supply and demand diagram, draw the shift of the demand curve for hamburgers in your hometown due to the following events. In each case, show the effect on equilibrium price and quantity.

   a. The price of tacos increases.

   b. All hamburger sellers raise the price of their french fries.

   c. Income falls in town. Assume that hamburgers are a normal good for most people.

   d. Income falls in town. Assume that hamburgers are an inferior good for most people.

   e. Burger King starts a 2-for-1 offer on the Impossible Whopper (a meatless alternative).

3. The market for many goods changes in predictable ways according to the time of year, in response to events such as holidays, vacation times, seasonal changes in production, and so on. Using supply and demand, explain the change in price in each of the following cases. Note that supply and demand may shift simultaneously.

   a. Lobster prices usually fall during the summer peak lobster harvest season, despite the fact that people like to eat lobster during the summer more than at any other time of year.

   b. The price of a Christmas tree is lower after Christmas than before but fewer trees are sold.

   c. The price of a round-trip ticket to Paris on Air France falls by more than $200 after the end of school vacation in September. This happens despite the fact that generally worsening weather increases the cost of operating flights to Paris, and Air France therefore reduces the number of flights to Paris at any given price.

4. Show in a diagram the effect on the demand curve, the supply curve, the equilibrium price, and the equilibrium quantity of each of the following events.

   a. The market for hotel rooms in your town

   Case 1: The wages of housekeepers go up.

   Case 2: A major political convention will be held in your town, attracting many visitors from across the country.

   b. The market for Los Angeles Rams cotton T-shirts

   Case 1: The Rams win the Super Bowl.

   Case 2: The price of cotton increases.

   c. The market for bagels

   Case 1: People realize that bagels are high in calories and sugar.

   Case 2: People have less time to cook breakfast in the morning.

   d. The market for the Krugman and Wells economics textbook

   Case 1: Your professor makes it required reading for all of their students.

   Case 2: Printing costs for textbooks are lowered by the use of synthetic paper.

5. Let's assume that each person in the United States consumes an average of 37 gallons of soft drinks (nondiet) at an average price of $2 per gallon and that the U.S. population is 330 million. At a price of $1.50 per gallon, each individual consumer would demand 50 gallons of soft drinks. From this information about the individual demand schedule, calculate the market demand schedule for soft drinks for the prices of $1.50 and $2 per gallon.

6. Suppose that the supply schedule of Maine lobsters is as follows:

Price of lobster (per pound)	Quantity of lobster supplied (pounds)
$25	800
20	700
15	600
10	500
5	400

Suppose that Maine lobsters can be sold only in the United States. The U.S. demand schedule for Maine lobsters is as follows:

Price of lobster (per pound)	Quantity of lobster demanded (pounds)
$25	200
20	400
15	600
10	800
5	1,000

a. Draw the demand curve and the supply curve for Maine lobsters. What are the equilibrium price and quantity of lobsters?

Now suppose that Maine lobsters can be sold in France. The French demand schedule for Maine lobsters is as follows:

Price of lobster (per pound)	Quantity of lobster demanded (pounds)
$25	100
20	300
15	500
10	700
5	900

b. What is the demand schedule for Maine lobsters now that French consumers can also buy them? Draw a supply and demand diagram that illustrates the new equilibrium price and quantity of lobsters. What will happen to the price at which fishermen can sell lobster? What will happen to the price paid by U.S. consumers? What will happen to the quantity consumed by U.S. consumers?

7. Find the flaws in reasoning in the following statements, paying particular attention to the distinction between shifts of and movements along the supply and demand curves. Draw a diagram to illustrate what actually happens in each situation.

a. "A technological innovation that lowers the cost of producing a good might seem at first to result in a reduction in the price of the good to consumers. But a fall in price will increase demand for the good, and higher demand will send the price up again. It is not certain, therefore, that an innovation will really reduce price in the end."

b. "A study shows that eating a clove of garlic a day can help prevent heart disease, causing many consumers to demand more garlic. This increase in demand results in a rise in the price of garlic. Consumers, seeing that the price of garlic has gone up, reduce their demand for garlic. This causes the demand for garlic to decrease and the price of garlic to fall. Therefore, the ultimate effect of the study on the price of garlic is uncertain."

8. The following table shows a demand schedule for a normal good.

Price	Quantity demanded
$23	70
21	90
19	110
17	130

a. Do you think that the increase in quantity demanded (say, from 90 to 110 in the table) when price decreases (from $21 to $19) is due to a rise in consumers' income? Explain clearly (and briefly) why or why not.

b. Now suppose that the good is an inferior good. Would the demand schedule still be valid for an inferior good?

c. Lastly, assume you do not know whether the good is normal or inferior. Devise an experiment that would allow you to determine which one it was. Explain.

9. In recent years, the number of car producers in China has increased rapidly. In fact, China now has more car brands than the United States. In addition, car sales have climbed every year and automakers have increased their output at even faster rates, causing fierce competition and a decline in prices. At the same time, Chinese consumers' incomes have risen. Assume that cars are a normal good. Draw a diagram of the supply and demand curves for cars in China to explain what has happened in the Chinese car market.

10. Aaron Judge is a star hitter for the New York Yankees baseball team. He is close to breaking the major league record for home runs hit during one season, and it is widely anticipated that in the next game he will break that record. As a result, tickets for the team's next game have been a hot commodity. But today it is announced that, due to a knee injury, he will not in fact play in the team's next game. Assume that season ticket-holders are able to resell their tickets if they wish. Use supply and demand diagrams to explain your answers to parts a and b.

a. Show the case in which this announcement results in a lower equilibrium price and a lower equilibrium quantity than before the announcement.

b. Show the case in which this announcement results in a lower equilibrium price and a higher equilibrium quantity than before the announcement.

c. What accounts for whether case a or case b occurs?

d. Suppose that a scalper had secretly learned before the announcement that Aaron Hank would not play in the next game. What actions do you think he would take?

11. Fans of music often bemoan the high price of concert tickets. One superstar has argued that it isn't worth hundreds, even thousands, of dollars to see them perform. Let's assume this star sold out arenas around the country at an average ticket price of $75.

a. How would you evaluate the argument that ticket prices are too high?

b. Suppose that due to this star's protests, ticket prices were lowered to $50. In what sense is this price too low? Draw a diagram using supply and demand curves to support your argument.

c. Suppose the superstar really wanted to bring down ticket prices. Since they control the supply of their services, what would you recommend they do? Explain using a supply and demand diagram.

d. Suppose this performer's next album was a total dud. Do you think they would still have to worry about ticket prices being too high? Why or why not? Draw a supply and demand diagram to support your argument.

e. Suppose the performer announced that their next tour was going to be their last. What effect would this likely have on the demand for and price of tickets? Illustrate with a supply and demand diagram.

12. After several years of decline, the market for handmade acoustic guitars is making a comeback. These guitars are usually made in small workshops employing relatively few highly skilled luthiers. Assess the impact on the equilibrium price and quantity of handmade acoustic guitars as a result of each of the following events. In your answers, indicate which curve(s) shift(s) and in which direction.

a. Environmentalists succeed in having the use of Brazilian rosewood banned in the United States, forcing luthiers to seek out alternative, more costly woods.

b. A foreign producer reengineers the guitar-making process and floods the market with identical guitars.

c. Music featuring handmade acoustic guitars makes a comeback as audiences tire of heavy metal and alternative rock music.

d. The country goes into a deep recession and the income of the average American falls sharply.

13. *Demand twisters:* Sketch and explain the demand relationship in each of the following statements.

a. I would never buy a Taylor Swift album! You couldn't even give me one for nothing.

b. I generally buy a bit more coffee as the price falls. But once the price falls to $2 per pound, I'll buy out the entire stock of the supermarket.

c. I spend more on orange juice even as the price rises. (Does this mean that I must be violating the law of demand?)

d. Due to a tuition rise, most students at a college find themselves with less disposable income. Almost all of them eat more frequently at the school cafeteria and less often at restaurants, even though prices at the cafeteria have risen, too. (This one requires that you draw both the demand and the supply curves for school cafeteria meals.)

14. Will Shakespeare is a struggling playwright in sixteenth-century London. As the price he receives for writing a play increases, he is willing to write more plays. For the following situations, use a diagram to illustrate how each event affects the equilibrium price and quantity in the market for Shakespeare's plays.

a. The playwright Christopher Marlowe, Shakespeare's chief rival, is killed in a bar brawl.

b. The bubonic plague, a deadly infectious disease, breaks out in London.

c. To celebrate the defeat of the Spanish Armada, Queen Elizabeth declares several weeks of festivities, which involves commissioning new plays.

15. This year, the small town of Middling experiences a sudden doubling of the birth rate. After three years, the birth rate returns to normal. Use a diagram to illustrate the effect of these events on the following.

a. The market for an hour of babysitting services in Middling this year

b. The market for an hour of babysitting services 14 years into the future, after the birth rate has returned to normal, by which time children born today are old enough to work as babysitters

c. The market for an hour of babysitting services 30 years into the future, when children born today are likely to be having children of their own

16. Use a diagram to illustrate how each of the following events affects the equilibrium price and quantity of pizza.

a. The price of mozzarella cheese rises.

b. The health hazards of hamburgers are widely publicized.

c. The price of tomato sauce falls.

d. The incomes of consumers rise, and pizza is an inferior good.

e. Consumers expect the price of pizza to fall next week.

17. Although he was a prolific artist, Pablo Picasso painted only 1,000 canvases during his "Blue Period." Picasso is now dead, and all of his Blue Period works are currently on display in museums and private galleries throughout Europe and the United States.

a. Draw a supply curve for Picasso Blue Period works. Why is this supply curve different from ones you have seen?

b. Given the supply curve from part a, the price of a Picasso Blue Period work will be entirely dependent on what factor(s)? Draw a diagram showing how the equilibrium price of such a work is determined.

c. Suppose rich art collectors decide that it is essential to acquire Picasso Blue Period art for their collections. Show the impact of this on the market for these paintings.

18. Draw the appropriate curve in each of the following cases. Is it like or unlike the curves you have seen so far? Explain.

a. The demand for cardiac bypass surgery, given that the government pays the full cost for any patient

b. The demand for elective cosmetic plastic surgery, given that the patient pays the full cost

c. The supply of reprints of Annie Leibovitz photographs

19. In 2022, the price of oil reached a 10-year high. For drivers, the cost of driving increased significantly as gasoline prices soared (drivers in many states paid more than $5 per gallon). For the airline industry, the cost of operation also increased significantly because jet fuel is a major expense.

a. Draw a supply and demand diagram that illustrates the effect of a rise in the price of jet fuel on the supply of air travel.

b. Draw a supply and demand diagram that illustrates the effect of a rise in the price of oil on the demand for air travel. (*Hint:* Think about this in terms of the substitutes for air travel, like driving.)

c. Put the diagrams from parts a and b together. What happens to the equilibrium price and quantity of air travel?

Despite the increase in the cost of flying, many more Americans still chose to fly to their destinations during 2022 as incomes rose, Covid lockdowns ended, and people splurged on vacations that had been postponed during the pandemic.

d. Using your results from part c, modify your diagram to illustrate an outcome in which the equilibrium price of air travel rises as people take more vacations by air.

20. The shutdowns that occurred during the pandemic affected many industries, perhaps none more than the automobile market. New automobile production depends directly on a producer's ability to source semi-conductor chips, most of which are manufactured in China. Using a supply and demand model, explain how the Covid-19 shutdowns affected each of the new and used car market:

a. Many new car dealers were having difficulty finding inventory, many buyers waited months to receive their cars.

b. Prices for used cars soared. By early 2022, the average used car had increased by more than 50%, over $10,000, from their 2020 values.

21. According to a study published in *JAMA Pediatrics*, nearly 15% of all babies born in the United States have a cow's milk allergy, more suffer from lactose intolerance. Parents are forced to purchase expensive hypoallergenic formulas that are more gentle on a baby's digestive system. At the onset of the pandemic, worried Covid-19 would shut down production facil-ities, parents started panic buying. This caused a widespread shortage. By early 2022, the situation worsened when the Food and Drug Administration recalled several Similac brands, including the hypo-allergenic Alimentum, due to a possible bacterial contamination. As a result of the contamination, the largest manufacturing facility in Sturgis, Michigan was forced closed.

a. There are few substitutes for hypoallergenic baby formula, parents are forced to pay almost any price. What would the demand curve for baby formula look like and why?

b. Assume relatively steep demand and supply curves, draw a demand and supply graph for hypoallergenic baby formula during the early part of the pandemic.

c. On the same diagram, show the effects of shutting down the large manufacturing facility. What happens to price and quantity? To keep the hypoallergenic formula affordable, many companies did not raise prices, how would this affect the market?

d. To help alleviate the empty store shelves, the Biden Administration temporarily removed all taxes on international baby formula and announced Operation Fly Formula which would transport formula from countries all over the world.

22. The accompanying table gives the annual U.S. demand and supply schedules for pickup trucks.

Price of truck	Quantity of trucks demanded (millions)	Quantity of trucks supplied (millions)
$20,000	20	14
25,000	18	15
30,000	16	16
35,000	14	17
40,000	12	18

a. Plot the demand and supply curves using these schedules. Indicate the equilibrium price and quantity on your diagram.

b. Suppose the tires used on pickup trucks are found to be defective. What would you expect to happen in the market for pickup trucks? Show this on your diagram.

c. Suppose that the U.S. Department of Transportation imposes costly regulations on manufacturers that cause them to reduce supply by one-third at any given price. Calculate and plot the new supply schedule and indicate the new equilibrium price and quantity on your diagram. ■

Price Controls and Quotas: Meddling with Markets

A BRONX TALE

STEPHANIE KIRNON WAS WORRIED. How would she, a landlord, afford the $29,000 needed to repair the leaky roof of the building she owns in the Bronx, a borough of New York City? In contrast, Gloribel Castillo, a tenant in a nearby apartment building, was relieved, knowing that she would no longer have to worry about affording her monthly rent.

The source of this contrast was a tightening of rent-control regulations. These laws prevent landlords from raising rents or evicting tenants in rent-controlled apartments without permission from a city agency. In 2019, New York State made it much more difficult for landlords to obtain that permission. The revised regulations also prohibit landlords from switching apartments from rent-controlled to unregulated status. Once apartments are unregulated, landlords can charge much higher market rents.

Tenant groups, who had lobbied hard for these regulatory changes, cheered. Many

While tenant Gloribel Castillo (left) cheered the tightening of New York rent-control laws, landlord Stephanie Kirnon (right) worried she would now be unable to afford necessary building repairs.

of their members were considered working class, like Gloribel, a hotel cleaner who worked two shifts in order to pay the rent on her rent-controlled apartment. For decades, the Bronx has been home to working-class and lower-income New Yorkers. But the Bronx has been undergoing *gentrification* — less desirable locations became more desirable as people with higher incomes move in, and lower income residents are forced out. As a result, rents have increased. Until the tighter restrictions were adopted, tenants in rent-controlled apartments faced the very real possibility that landlords would find a loophole in the law to raise their rents or evict them.

Another group also benefited from the new tighter regulations: owners of unregulated apartments. Now that it was illegal to shift rent-controlled apartments to unregulated status, there would be fewer unregulated apartments available. As a result, the rents for unregulated apartments would rise. But landlords of rent-controlled buildings, like Stephanie Kirnon, were facing a real bind. The tightened regulations made it harder to afford the necessary renovations and maintenance.

What will the future hold for Bronx residents? In the 1970s, when rent-control laws had been applied very strictly, many buildings were abandoned as landlords were unable to charge rents high enough to cover their costs. The Bronx declined dramatically during these years: there was a shortage of inhabitable apartments and crime soared as empty buildings were used for nefarious purposes. Only time will tell whether the Bronx will become a tenant's paradise or revert to being a tenant's nightmare.

Rent control is a type of *market intervention*, a policy imposed by government to prevail over the market forces of supply and demand — in this case, over the market forces of the supply and demand for rental

apartments in the Bronx. Although rent-control laws were introduced during World War II in many major American cities to protect the interests of tenants, the problems they created led most cities to discard them — with New York City and San Francisco being notable exceptions. Recently, a form of rent control has been making a comeback as the states of Oregon and California have adopted statewide limitations on the annual rate of rent increase as demand for housing in those states has outstripped supply.

As we will learn in this chapter, when a government tries to dictate either a market price or a market quantity that's different from the equilibrium price or quantity, the market will strike back in predictable ways. A shortage of apartments is one example of what happens when the logic of the market is defied: a market intervention like rent control keeps the price of apartment rentals below market equilibrium level, creating the shortage and other serious problems. And, as we'll see, those problems inevitably create winners and losers.

Although there are specific winners and losers from market intervention, we will learn how and why society as a whole loses — a result that has led economists to be generally skeptical of market interventions except in certain well-defined situations. ●

WHAT YOU WILL LEARN

- What is a market intervention and why are **price controls** and **quantity controls** the two main forms it takes?

- Who benefits and who loses from market interventions?

- Why are economists often skeptical of market interventions? And why do governments undertake market interventions even though they create losses to society?

price controls legal restrictions on how high or low a market price may go.

price ceiling a maximum price sellers are allowed to charge for a good or service; a form of price control.

price floor a minimum price buyers are required to pay for a good or service; a form of price control.

Why Governments Control Prices

As we know from Chapter 3, a market moves to equilibrium—the market price moves to the level at which the quantity supplied equals the quantity demanded. But this equilibrium price does not necessarily please either buyers or sellers.

After all, buyers would always like to pay less if they could. Sometimes they can make a strong moral or political case for this, such as when the equilibrium rental rates are not affordable for an average working person. In that case, a government might well be under pressure to impose limits on the rents landlords can charge.

Similarly, sellers would always like to get higher prices. Sometimes they can make a strong moral or political case for this, such as when the equilibrium wage rate for a worker who sells their labor in the labor market results in an income below the poverty level. In that case, a government might well be pressured to require employers to pay a rate no lower than some specified minimum wage.

So there are often strong political demands for governments to intervene in markets with powerful interests often making a compelling case that market intervention in their favor is "fair." When a government intervenes to regulate prices, we say that it imposes **price controls.** These controls typically take the form either of an upper limit, a **price ceiling,** or a lower limit, a **price floor.**

However, it's not that easy to tell a market what to do. When a government tries to legislate prices—whether it legislates them down by imposing a price ceiling or up by imposing a price floor—there are certain predictable and often unpleasant side effects.

Yet, there are two important caveats to consider. First, we assume in this chapter that the markets in question are efficient before price controls are imposed. But markets can sometimes be inefficient—for example, when a market is dominated by a monopolist, a single seller has the power to influence the market price. When markets are inefficient, price controls don't necessarily cause problems and can potentially move markets closer to efficiency. Second, government intervention can be justified on the basis of equity and social welfare when crises occur. For example, during the coronavirus pandemic of 2020–2021, there weren't enough ventilators available for everyone who might need one. If there had been a free market for ventilators, the price of a ventilator would have skyrocketed and only the well-off would have been able to afford one.

Price Ceilings

Aside from rent control, there are not many price ceilings in the United States today. But at times they have been widespread. Price ceilings are typically imposed during crises—wars, harvest failures, natural disasters—because these events often lead to sudden price increases that hurt many people but produce big gains for a lucky few.

The U.S. government imposed ceilings on many prices during World War II: the war sharply increased demand for raw materials, such as aluminum and steel, and price controls prevented those with access to these raw materials from earning huge profits. Price controls on oil were imposed in 1973, when an embargo by Arab oil-exporting countries seemed likely to generate huge profits for U.S. oil companies. After Hurricane Ian hit southwest Florida in 2022, the state received over 1,300 complaints of alleged price gouging and has paid restitution to over 100 of those complaints.

Rent control in New York is, as we mention in the opening story, a legacy of World War II: it was imposed because wartime production led to an economic boom that increased demand for apartments at a time when the labor and raw materials that might have been used to build them were being used to win the war instead. Although most price controls were removed soon after the war ended, New York's rent limits were retained and gradually extended to buildings not previously covered, leading to some very strange situations.

You can rent a one-bedroom apartment in Manhattan on fairly short notice—if you are able and willing to pay several thousand dollars a month and live in a less desirable area. Yet some people pay only a small fraction of this for comparable apartments, and others pay hardly more for bigger apartments in the most desirable locations.

Aside from producing great deals for some renters, however, what are the broader consequences of New York's rent-control system? To answer this question, we turn to the model we developed in Chapter 3: the supply and demand model.

Modeling a Price Ceiling

To see what can go wrong when a government imposes a price ceiling on an efficient market, consider Figure 1, which shows a simplified model of the market for apartments in New York. For the sake of simplicity, we imagine that all apartments are exactly the same and would rent for the same price in an unregulated market.

The table in Figure 1 shows the demand and supply schedules; the demand and supply curves are shown on the left. We show the quantity of apartments on the horizontal axis and the monthly rent per apartment on the vertical axis. You can see that in an unregulated market the equilibrium would be at point *E:* 2 million apartments would be rented for $1,000 each per month.

Now suppose that the government imposes a price ceiling, limiting rents to a price below the equilibrium price—say, no more than $800.

Figure 2 shows the effect of the price ceiling, represented by the line at $800. At the enforced rental rate of $800, landlords have less incentive to offer apartments, so they won't be willing to supply as many as they would at the equilibrium

---

FIGURE 1 The Market for Apartments in the Absence of Price Controls

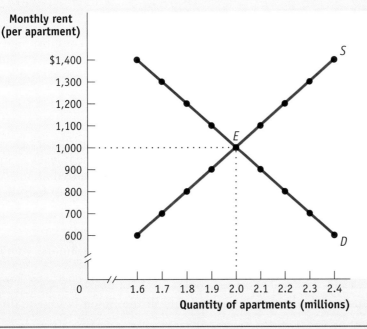

Monthly rent (per apartment)	Quantity of apartments (millions)	
	Quantity demanded	Quantity supplied
$1,400	1.6	2.4
1,300	1.7	2.3
1,200	1.8	2.2
1,100	1.9	2.1
1,000	2.0	2.0
900	2.1	1.9
800	2.2	1.8
700	2.3	1.7
600	2.4	1.6

Without government intervention, the market for apartments reaches equilibrium at point *E* with a market rent of $1,000 per month and 2 million apartments rented.

FIGURE 2 The Effects of a Price Ceiling

The black horizontal line represents the government-imposed price ceiling on rents of $800 per month. This price ceiling reduces the quantity of apartments supplied to 1.8 million, point *A*, and increases the quantity demanded to 2.2 million, point *B*. This creates a persistent shortage of 400,000 units: 400,000 people who want apartments at the legal rent of $800 but cannot get them.

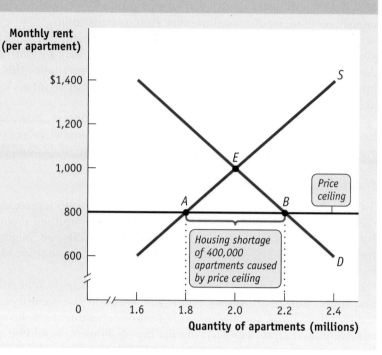

rate of $1,000. They will choose point *A* on the supply curve, offering only 1.8 million apartments for rent, 200,000 fewer than in the unregulated market.

At the same time, more people will want to rent apartments at a price of $800 than at the equilibrium price of $1,000; as shown at point *B* on the demand curve, at a monthly rent of $800 the quantity of apartments demanded rises to 2.2 million, 200,000 more than in the unregulated market and 400,000 more than are actually available at the price of $800. So there is now a persistent shortage of rental housing: at that price, 400,000 more people want to rent than are able to find apartments.

Do price ceilings always cause shortages? No. If a price ceiling is set above the equilibrium price, it won't have any effect. Suppose that the equilibrium rental rate on apartments is $1,000 per month and the city government sets a ceiling of $1,200. Who cares? In this case, the price ceiling won't be *binding*—it won't actually constrain market behavior—and it will have no effect.

How a Price Ceiling Causes Inefficiency

The housing shortage shown in Figure 2 is not merely annoying: like any shortage induced by price controls, it can be seriously harmful because it leads to inefficiency. In other words, there are gains from trade that go unrealized.

Rent control, like all price ceilings, creates inefficiency in at least four distinct ways.

1. It reduces the quantity of apartments rented below the efficient level.
2. It typically leads to inefficient allocation of apartments among would-be renters.
3. It leads to wasted time and effort as people search for apartments.
4. It leads landlords to maintain apartments in inefficiently low quality or condition.

In addition to inefficiency, price ceilings give rise to illegal behavior as people try to circumvent them. We'll now look at each of these inefficiencies caused by price ceilings.

FIGURE 3 A Price Ceiling Causes Inefficiently Low Quantity

A price ceiling reduces the quantity supplied below the market equilibrium quantity. Because buyers can't buy more units of a good than sellers are willing to sell, a price ceiling reduces the quantity of a good bought and sold.

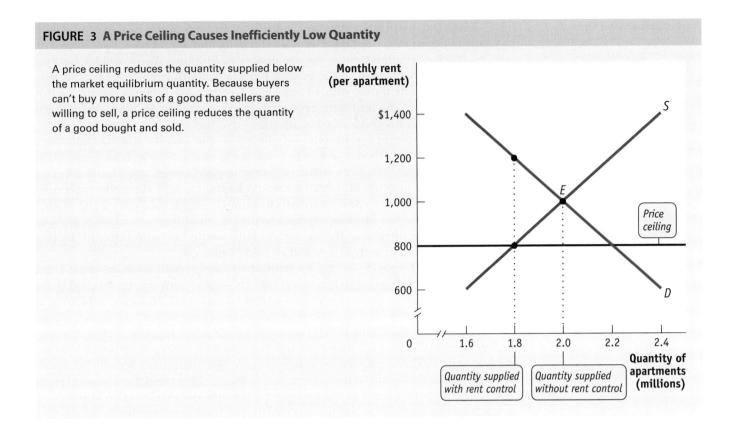

Inefficiently Low Quantity Because a price ceiling reduces the price of a good, it reduces the quantity that sellers are willing to supply. In addition, buyers can't buy more units of a good than sellers are willing to sell. So a price ceiling reduces the quantity of a good bought and sold below the market equilibrium quantity.

Because rent controls reduce the number of apartments supplied, they reduce the number of apartments rented, too. The low quantity sold is an inefficiency due to missed opportunities: price ceilings prevent mutually beneficial transactions from occurring, transactions that would benefit both buyers and sellers. Figure 3 shows the inefficiently low quantity of apartments supplied with rent control.

Inefficient Allocation to Consumers Rent control doesn't just lead to too few apartments being available. It can also lead to misallocation of the apartments that are available: people who badly need a place to live may not be able to find an apartment, but some apartments may be occupied by people with much less urgent needs.

In the case shown in Figure 2, 2.2 million people would like to rent an apartment at $800 per month, but only 1.8 million apartments are available. Of those 2.2 million who are seeking an apartment, some want one badly and are willing to pay a high price to get it. Others either have a less urgent need and are only willing to pay a low price, perhaps because they have alternative housing, or simply don't have enough income and can't afford to pay more than $800 per month.

An efficient allocation of apartments would reflect these differences: people who really want an apartment will get one and people who aren't all that eager to find an apartment, or can't afford one, won't. In an inefficient distribution of apartments, the opposite will happen: some people who are not especially interested in finding an apartment will get one and others who are very eager to find an apartment won't.

Because people usually get apartments through luck or personal connections under rent control, it generally results in an **inefficient allocation to consumers** of the few apartments available.

inefficient allocation to consumers a form of inefficiency in which some people who want the good badly and are willing to pay a high price don't get it, and some who care relatively little about the good and are only willing to pay a low price do get it; often a result of a price ceiling.

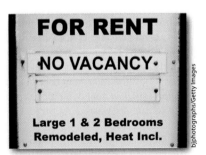

A price ceiling like rent control leads to inefficiency in the market for rental apartments.

wasted resources a form of inefficiency in which people expend money, effort, and time to cope with the shortages caused by a price ceiling.

To see the inefficiency involved, consider the plight of the Lees, a family with young children who have no alternative housing and would be willing to pay up to $1,500 for an apartment—but are unable to find one. Also consider George, a retiree who lives most of the year in Florida but still has a lease on the New York apartment he moved into 40 years ago. George pays $800 per month for this apartment, but if the rent were even slightly more—say, $850—he would give it up and stay with his children when he visits New York.

This allocation of apartments—George has one and the Lees do not—is a missed opportunity: there is a way to make the Lees and George both better off at no additional cost. The Lees would be happy to pay George, say, $1,200 a month to sublease his apartment, which he would happily accept since the apartment is worth no more than $849 a month to him. George would prefer the money he gets from the Lees to keeping his apartment; the Lees would prefer to have the apartment rather than the money. So both would be made better off by this transaction—and nobody else would be made worse off.

Generally, if people who really want apartments could sublease them from people who are less eager to live there, both those who gain apartments and those who trade their occupancy for money would be better off. However, subletting is illegal under rent control because it would occur at prices above the price ceiling.

The fact that subletting is illegal doesn't mean it never happens. In fact, chasing down illegal subletting is a major business for New York private investigators who are hired to prove that the legal tenants in rent-controlled apartments actually live somewhere else, and have sublet their apartments at two or three times the controlled rent.

This subletting leads to the emergence of a shadow market (also known as a black market), which we will discuss shortly. For now, just note that landlords and legal agencies actively discourage the practice. As a result, the problem of inefficient allocation of apartments remains.

Wasted Resources Another reason a price ceiling causes inefficiency is that it leads to **wasted resources**: people expend money, effort, and time to cope with the shortages caused by the price ceiling. Back in 1979, U.S. price controls on gasoline led to shortages that forced millions of Americans to wait in lines at gas stations for hours each week. The opportunity cost of the time spent in gas lines—the wages not earned, the leisure time not enjoyed—constituted wasted resources from the point of view of consumers and of the economy as a whole.

Because of rent control, the Lees will spend all their spare time for several months searching for an apartment, time they would rather have spent working or in family activities. That is, there is an opportunity cost to the Lees' prolonged search for an apartment—the leisure or income they had to forgo.

FOR INQUIRING MINDS Mumbai's Rent-Control Millionaires

Mumbai, India, like New York City, has rent-controlled apartments. Currently, about 60% of apartments in Mumbai's city center are rent-controlled. Although Mumbai is half a world away from New York City, the economics of rent control works just the same: rent control leads to shortages, low quality, inefficient allocation to consumers, wasted resources, and shadow markets.

Mumbai landlords, who often pay more in taxes and maintenance than what they receive in rent, sometimes simply abandon their properties to decay. And a shadow market in rent-controlled apartments thrives in Mumbai as old tenants sell the right to occupy apartments to new tenants.

And, like many major cities, New York included, Mumbai has its "rent-control millionaires." One renter lived in a 2,600 square foot apartment paying just $20 per month in an area where apartments not under rent control often go for $2,000 a month. He refused to leave when his roof collapsed, and after three years of negotiations was paid $2.5 million by a developer to vacate the apartment so that a luxury building could be constructed. Similarly, in recent years, three New York City tenants were paid $25 *million* by a property developer to move from their rent-controlled apartments.

With its shortage of land for development, and its desirability as a place to live for the rapidly expanding number of high-income Indians, Mumbai has thousands of rent-controlled tenants who have become millionaires upon vacating their apartments.

If the market for apartments worked freely, the Lees would quickly find an apartment at the equilibrium rent of $1,000, leaving them time to earn more or to enjoy themselves—an outcome that would make them better off without making anyone else worse off. Again, rent control creates missed opportunities.

Inefficiently Low Quality Yet another way a price ceiling creates inefficiency is by causing goods to be of inefficiently low quality. **Inefficiently low quality** means that sellers offer low-quality goods at a low price even though buyers would rather have higher quality and would be willing to pay a higher price for it.

Again, consider rent control. Landlords have no incentive to provide better conditions because they cannot raise rents to cover their repair costs but are able to find tenants easily. In many cases, tenants would be willing to pay much more for improved conditions than it would cost for the landlord to provide them—for example, upgrading an outdated electrical system that cannot safely run air conditioners or computers. But any additional payment for such improvements would be legally considered a rent increase, which is prohibited.

Indeed, rent-controlled apartments are notoriously badly maintained, rarely painted, subject to frequent electrical and plumbing problems, sometimes even hazardous to inhabit. As one manager of a Manhattan building described: "At unregulated apartments we'd do most things that the tenants requested. But on the rent-regulated units, we did absolutely only what the law required. . . . We had a perverse incentive to make those tenants unhappy." This whole situation is a missed opportunity—some tenants would be happy to pay for better conditions, and landlords would be happy to provide them for payment. But such an exchange would occur only if the market were allowed to operate freely.

Shadow Markets In addition to these four inefficiencies there is a final aspect of price ceilings: the incentive they provide for illegal activities, specifically the emergence of **shadow markets (also known as black markets).** We have already described one kind of shadow market activity—illegal subletting by tenants. But it does not stop there. Clearly, there is a temptation for a landlord to say to a potential tenant, "Look, you can have the place if you slip me an extra few hundred in cash each month"—and for the tenant to agree if they are one of those people who would be willing to pay much more than the maximum legal rent.

So, what's wrong with shadow markets? In general, it's a bad thing if people break any law, because it encourages disrespect for the law in general. Worse yet, in this case illegal activity worsens the position of those who are honest. If the Lees are scrupulous about upholding the rent-control law but other people—who may need an apartment less than the Lees—are willing to bribe landlords or grab illegal sublets, the Lees may never find an apartment.

Yet shadow markets can diminish *some* of the inefficiency of rent control. For example, if George allows the Lees to sublet his rent-controlled apartment (a shadow market deal since it is illegal), society is better off (as are the Lees) than if there were no deal. But in the end, society as a whole is made worse off by the presence of a shadow market relative to a market that is completely free of rent control.

So Why Are There Price Ceilings?

We have seen three common results of price ceilings:

- A persistent shortage of the good
- Inefficiency arising from this persistent shortage in the form of inefficiently low quantities transacted, inefficient allocation of the good to consumers, resources wasted in searching for the good, and the inefficiently low quality of the good offered for sale
- The emergence of illegal, shadow market activity

inefficiently low quality a form of inefficiency in which sellers offer low-quality goods at a low price even though buyers would prefer a higher quality at a higher price; often a result of a price ceiling.

shadow market a market in which goods or services are bought and sold illegally, either because it is illegal to sell them at all or because the prices charged are legally prohibited by a price ceiling; also known as a black market.

Given these unpleasant consequences of price ceilings, why do governments still sometimes impose them? Why does rent control, in particular, persist in New York?

One answer is that although price ceilings may have adverse effects, they do benefit some people. In practice, New York's rent-control rules—which are more complex than our simple model—hurt most residents but give a small minority of renters much cheaper housing than they would get in an unregulated market. And those who benefit from the controls are typically better organized and more vocal than those who are harmed by them.

Also, when price ceilings have been in effect for a long time, buyers may not have a realistic idea of what would happen without them. In our earlier example, the rental rate in an unregulated market (Figure 1) would be only 25% higher than in the regulated market (Figure 2): $1,000 instead of $800. But how would renters know that? Indeed, they might have heard about shadow market transactions at much higher prices—the Lees or some other family paying George $1,200 or more—and would not realize that these shadow market prices are much higher than the price that would prevail in a fully unregulated market.

A last answer is that government officials often do not understand supply and demand analysis! It is a great mistake to suppose that economic policies in the real world are always sensible or well informed.

ECONOMICS >> *in Action*
How Price Controls in Venezuela Proved Disastrous

By all accounts, Venezuela is a rich country as one of the world's top producers of oil. But despite its wealth, price controls have so distorted its economy that the country is struggling to feed its citizens and provide health care. Necessities like toilet paper, rice, coffee, corn, flour, milk, and meat are chronically lacking. Hospitals operate without basic supplies and with broken equipment.

Venezuela's food shortages show how price controls disproportionately hurt the people they were designed to benefit.

Today, Venezuelans line up for hours to purchase price-controlled goods at state-run stores, but often came away empty handed. "Empty shelves and no one to explain why a rich country has no food. It's unacceptable," said Jesús López, a 90-year-old farmer.

The origins of the shortages can be traced to policies espoused by Venezuela's former president, Hugo Chávez. First elected in 1998 on a platform that promised to favor the poor and working classes over the country's economic elite, Chávez implemented price controls on basic foodstuffs. Prices were set so low that farmers reduced production, so that by 2006 shortages were severe. As a result, Venezuela went from being self-sufficient in food in 1998 to importing more than 70% of its food. By 2019, researchers had documented widespread weight loss and increasing malnutrition among Venezuelans with significant numbers of children suffering from stunted growth and anemia.

At the same time, generous government programs for the poor and working class created higher demand. The reduced supply of goods due to price controls combined with higher demand led to sharply rising prices for shadow market goods that, in turn, generated even greater demand for goods sold at the controlled prices. Smuggling became rampant, as a bottle of milk sold across the border in Colombia for seven or eight times the controlled price in Venezuela. Not surprisingly, fresh milk was rarely seen in Venezuelan markets.

The irony of the situation is that the policies put in place to help the poor and working classes have disproportionately hurt them. The minimum monthly wage allows Venezuelans to afford only 24 eggs, three-quarters of a pizza, or half a burger on the shadow market. People are spending up to 12 hours at a time in line to purchase basic foodstuffs. As one shopper in a low-income area said, "It fills me with rage to have to spend the one free day I have wasting my time for a bag of rice. I end up paying more at the resellers [the shadow market]. In the end, all these price controls proved useless."

The lack of basic necessities—food and medicine—coupled with soaring crime has led to a mass exodus of more than 3 million people from Venezuela to neighboring countries. As one woman said, "I'm leaving with nothing. But I have to do this. Otherwise, we will just die hungry here."

>> Check Your Understanding 4-1

Solutions appear at back of book.

1. On game days, homeowners near Middletown University's stadium used to rent parking spaces in their driveways to fans at a going rate of $11. A new town ordinance now sets a maximum parking fee of $7. Use the accompanying supply and demand diagram to explain how each of the following corresponds to a price-ceiling concept.

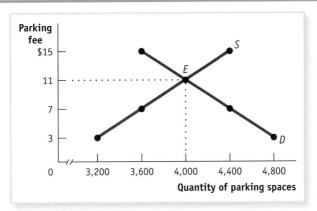

    a. Some homeowners now think it's not worth the hassle to rent out spaces.
    b. Some fans who used to carpool to the game now drive alone.
    c. Some fans can't find parking and leave without seeing the game.
    Explain how each of the following adverse effects arises from the price ceiling.
    d. Some fans now arrive several hours early to find parking.
    e. Friends of homeowners near the stadium regularly attend games, even if they aren't big fans. But some serious fans have given up because of the parking situation.
    f. Some homeowners rent spaces for more than $7 but pretend that the buyers are non-paying friends or family.

2. True or false? Explain your answer. A price ceiling below the equilibrium price of an otherwise efficient market does the following:
    a. Increases quantity supplied
    b. Makes some people who want to consume the good worse off
    c. Makes all producers worse off

‖ Price Floors

Sometimes governments intervene to push market prices up instead of down. *Price floors* have been widely legislated for agricultural products, such as wheat and milk, as a way to support the incomes of farmers. Historically, there were also price floors—legally mandated minimum prices—on such services as trucking and air travel, although these were phased out by the U.S. government in the 1970s.

If you have ever worked in a fast-food restaurant, you are likely to have encountered a price floor: governments in the United States and many other countries maintain a lower limit on the hourly wage rate of a worker's labor; that is, a floor on the price of labor called the **minimum wage.**

Just like price ceilings, price floors are intended to help some people but generate predictable and undesirable side effects. Figure 4 shows hypothetical supply and demand curves for butter. Left to itself, the market would move to equilibrium at point *E*, with 10 million pounds of butter bought and sold at a price of $1 per pound.

Now suppose that the government, in order to help dairy farmers, imposes a price floor on butter of $1.20 per pound. Its effects are shown in Figure 5, where

minimum wage a legal floor on the wage rate, which is the market price of labor.

FIGURE 4 The Market for Butter in the Absence of Government Controls

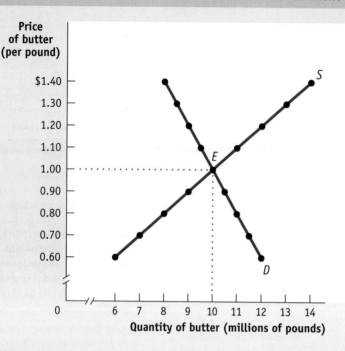

Price of butter (per pound)	Quantity of butter (millions of pounds)	
	Quantity demanded	Quantity supplied
$1.40	8.0	14.0
1.30	8.5	13.0
1.20	9.0	12.0
1.10	9.5	11.0
1.00	10.0	10.0
0.90	10.5	9.0
0.80	11.0	8.0
0.70	11.5	7.0
0.60	12.0	6.0

Without government intervention, the market for butter reaches equilibrium at a price of $1 per pound with 10 million pounds of butter bought and sold.

FIGURE 5 The Effects of a Price Floor

The black horizontal line represents the government imposed price floor of $1.20 per pound of butter. The quantity of butter demanded falls to 9 million pounds, and the quantity supplied rises to 12 million pounds, generating a persistent surplus of 3 million pounds of butter.

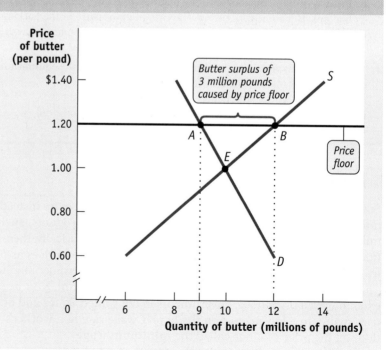

the line at $1.20 represents the price floor. At a price of $1.20 per pound, producers would want to supply 12 million pounds (point *B* on the supply curve) but consumers would want to buy only 9 million pounds (point *A* on the demand curve). So the price floor leads to a persistent surplus of 3 million pounds of butter.

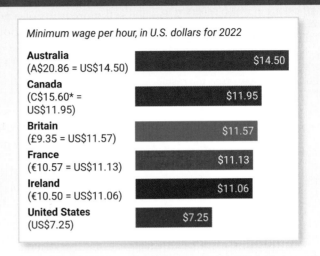

GLOBAL COMPARISON   CHECK OUT OUR LOW, LOW WAGES!

The minimum wage rate in the United States, as you can see in this graph, is actually quite low compared with that in other rich countries. Since minimum wages are set in national currency—the British minimum wage is set in British pounds, the French minimum wage is set in euros, and so on—the comparison depends on the exchange rate on any given day. As of 2022, Australia had a minimum wage twice as high as the U.S. rate, with Canada, France, Ireland, and Britain not far behind.

You can see one effect of this difference in the supermarket checkout line. In the United States there is usually someone to bag your groceries—someone typically paid the minimum wage or at best slightly more. In Europe, where hiring a bagger is a lot more expensive, you're almost always expected to do the bagging yourself.

Data from: Organization for Economic Cooperation and Development (OECD).

*The Canadian minimum wage varies by province from C$13.00 to C$15.60

Does a price floor always lead to an unwanted surplus? No. Just as in the case of a price ceiling, the floor may not be binding—that is, it may be irrelevant. If the equilibrium price of butter is $1 per pound but the floor is set at only $0.80, the floor has no effect.

But suppose that a price floor is binding: what happens to the unwanted surplus? The answer depends on government policy. In the case of agricultural price floors, governments buy up unwanted surplus. As a result, the U.S. government, for example, has at times found itself warehousing thousands of tons of butter, cheese, and other farm products. The government then has to find a way to dispose of these unwanted goods.

Some countries pay exporters to sell products at a loss overseas; this is standard procedure for the European Union. The United States gives surplus food away to citizens in need as well as to schools, which use the products in school lunches. In some cases, governments have actually destroyed the surplus production.

When the government is not prepared to purchase the unwanted surplus, a price floor means that would-be sellers cannot find buyers. This is what happens when there is a price floor on the wage rate paid for an hour of labor, the minimum wage: when the minimum wage is above the equilibrium wage rate, some people who are willing to work—that is, sell labor—cannot find buyers—that is, employers—willing to give them jobs.

How a Price Floor Causes Inefficiency

The persistent surplus that results from a price floor creates missed opportunities—inefficiencies—that resemble those created by the shortage that results from a price ceiling. Like a price ceiling, a price floor creates inefficiency in at least four ways:

1. It causes inefficiently low quantity.
2. It leads to an inefficient allocation of sales among sellers.
3. It leads to a waste of resources.
4. It leads to sellers providing an inefficiently high-quality level.

In addition to inefficiency, like a price ceiling, a price floor leads to illegal behavior as people break the law to sell below the legal price.

inefficient allocation of sales among sellers a form of inefficiency in which sellers who would be willing to sell a good at the lowest price are unable to make sales while sales go to sellers who are only willing to sell at a higher price; often the result of a price floor.

Inefficiently Low Quantity Because a price floor raises the price of a good to consumers, it reduces the quantity of that good demanded; because sellers can't sell more units of a good than buyers are willing to buy, a price floor reduces the quantity of a good bought and sold below the market equilibrium quantity. Notice that this is the *same* effect as a price ceiling. You might be tempted to think that a price floor and a price ceiling have opposite effects, but both have the effect of reducing the quantity of a good bought and sold (see the accompanying Pitfalls).

As in the case of a price ceiling, the low quantity sold is an inefficiency due to missed opportunities: price floors prevent mutually beneficial transactions from occurring, transactions that would benefit both buyers and sellers. Figure 6 shows the inefficiently low quantity of butter sold with a price floor on the price of butter.

Inefficient Allocation of Sales Among Sellers Like a price ceiling, a price floor can lead to *inefficient allocation*—in this case, an **inefficient allocation of sales among sellers:** sellers who are willing to sell at the lowest price are unable to make sales, while sales go to sellers who are only willing to sell at a higher price.

PITFALLS

CEILINGS, FLOORS, AND QUANTITIES

A price ceiling pushes the price of a good *down*. A price floor pushes the price of a good *up*. So it's easy to assume that the effects of a price floor are the opposite of the effects of a price ceiling. In particular, if a price ceiling reduces the quantity of a good bought and sold, doesn't a price floor increase the quantity?

No, it doesn't. In fact, both floors and ceilings reduce the quantity bought and sold. Why? When the quantity of a good supplied isn't

equal to the quantity demanded, the actual quantity sold is determined by the "short side" of the market—whichever quantity is less. If sellers don't want to sell as much as buyers want to buy, it's the sellers who determine the actual quantity sold, because buyers can't force unwilling sellers to sell. If buyers don't want to buy as much as sellers want to sell, it's the buyers who determine the actual quantity sold, because sellers can't force unwilling buyers to buy.

FIGURE 6 A Price Floor Causes Inefficiently Low Quantity

A price floor reduces the quantity demanded below the market equilibrium quantity. Because sellers can't sell more units of a good than buyers are willing to buy, a price floor reduces the quantity of a good bought and sold.

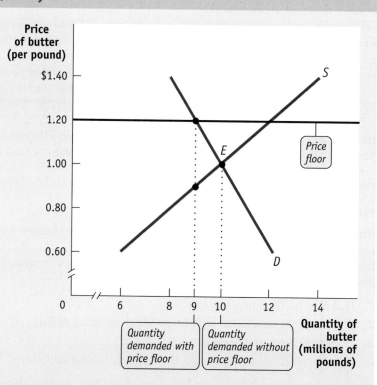

One example of the inefficient allocation of selling opportunities caused by a price floor is the "two-tier" labor market found in many European countries that emerged in the 1980s and persists to this day. A high minimum wage led to a two-tier labor system, composed of the fortunate who had good jobs in the formal labor market, and the rest who were locked out without any prospect of ever finding a good job.

Either unemployed or underemployed in dead-end jobs in the shadow market for labor, the unlucky ones are disproportionately young, from the ages of 18 to early 30s. Although eager for good jobs in the formal sector and willing to accept less than the minimum wage—that is, willing to sell their labor for a lower price—it is illegal for employers to pay them less than the minimum wage. For example, in 2021, unemployment for young Italian workers stood at nearly 30%.

The inefficiency of unemployment and underemployment is compounded as generations of young people are unable to get adequate job training, develop careers, and save for their future. These young people are also more likely to engage in crime. The worst hit countries—such as Greece, Spain, Italy, and France—have seen many of their best and brightest young people emigrate, leading to a permanent reduction in the future performance of their economies.

Wasted Resources Also like a price ceiling, a price floor generates inefficiency by *wasting resources.* The most graphic examples involve government purchases of the unwanted surpluses of agricultural products caused by price floors. The surplus production is sometimes destroyed, which is pure waste; in other cases, the stored produce goes, as officials euphemistically put it, "out of condition" and must be thrown away.

Price floors also lead to wasted time and effort. Consider the minimum wage. Would-be workers who spend many hours searching for jobs, or waiting in line in the hope of getting jobs, play the same role in the case of price floors as hapless families searching for apartments in the case of price ceilings.

Inefficiently High Quality Again like price ceilings, price floors lead to inefficiency in the quality of goods produced.

We saw that when there is a price ceiling, suppliers produce products that are of inefficiently low quality: buyers prefer higher-quality products and are willing to pay for them, but sellers refuse to improve the quality of their products because the price ceiling prevents their being compensated for doing so. This same logic applies to price floors, but in reverse: suppliers offer goods of **inefficiently high quality.**

How can this be? Isn't high quality a good thing? Yes, but only if it is worth the cost. Suppose that suppliers spend a lot to make goods of very high quality but that this quality isn't worth much to consumers, who would rather receive the money spent on that quality in the form of a lower price. This represents a missed opportunity: suppliers and buyers could make a mutually beneficial deal in which buyers got goods of lower quality for a much lower price.

A good example of the inefficiency of excessive quality comes from the days when transatlantic airfares were set artificially high by international treaty. Forbidden to compete for customers by offering lower ticket prices, airlines instead offered expensive services, like lavish in-flight meals that went largely uneaten—an especially wasteful practice, considering that what passengers really wanted was less food and lower airfares.

Since the deregulation of U.S. airlines in the 1970s, American passengers have experienced a large decrease in ticket prices accompanied by a decrease in the quality of in-flight service—smaller seats, lower-quality food, and so on. Everyone complains about the service—but thanks to lower fares, the number of people flying on U.S. carriers has grown from 130 billion passenger miles when deregulation began to over one trillion in 2022.

Illegal Activity In addition to the four inefficiencies we analyzed, like price ceilings, price floors provide incentives for illegal activity. For example, in countries

inefficiently high quality a form of inefficiency in which sellers offer high-quality goods at a high price even though buyers would prefer a lower quality at a lower price; often the result of a price floor.

where the minimum wage is far above the equilibrium wage rate, workers desperate for jobs sometimes agree to work off the books for employers who conceal their employment from the government—or bribe the government inspectors.

So Why Are There Price Floors?

To sum up, a price floor creates various negative side effects:

- A persistent surplus of the good
- Inefficiency arising from the persistent surplus in the form of inefficiently low quantity transacted, inefficient allocation of sales among sellers, wasted resources, and an inefficiently high level of quality offered by suppliers
- The temptation to engage in illegal activity, particularly bribery and corruption of government officials

So why do governments impose price floors when they have so many negative side effects? The reasons are similar to those for imposing price ceilings. Government officials often disregard warnings about the consequences of price floors either because they believe that the relevant market is poorly described by the supply and demand model or, more often, because they do not understand the model. Above all, just as price ceilings are often imposed because they benefit some influential buyers of a good, price floors are often imposed because they benefit some influential sellers.

ECONOMICS >> *in Action*
The Rise and Fall of the Unpaid Intern

"We have an opening for a part-time unpaid intern, which could lead to a full-time unpaid internship."

Aaron Bacall/www.Cartoonstock.com

The best-known example of a price floor is the minimum wage. Most economists believe, however, that the minimum wage has relatively little effect on the overall job market in the United States, mainly because the floor is set so low. In 1964, the U.S. minimum wage was 53% of the average wage of blue-collar production workers; by 2022, it had fallen to about 25%. However, there is one sector of the U.S. job market where it appears that the minimum wage can indeed be binding: the market for interns.

Starting in 2011, a spate of lawsuits brought by former unpaid interns claiming they were cheated out of wages brought the matter to public attention. A common thread in these complaints was that interns were assigned grunt work with no educational value, such as tracking lost cell phones. In other cases, unpaid interns complained that they were given the work of full-salaried employees. And many of those lawsuits proved successful, with several companies forced to negotiate multimillion-dollar settlements with their former unpaid interns. For example, Condé Nast Publications settled for $5.8 million, Sirius SatelliteXM Radio settled for $1.3 million, and Viacom Media settled for $7.2 million. Now these companies pay their interns for their work.

In 2018, the U.S. Department of Labor, the agency that formulates federal labor laws, issued a directive stating that unless their programs can clearly demonstrate an educational component such as course credit, companies have to pay their interns minimum wage or shut down their programs altogether. Companies have clearly taken notice and acted accordingly, either by shutting down their internship programs, by turning internships into paying positions, or by collaborating with schools to offer academic credit for unpaid work.

Yet the tension that arises from the presence of a binding minimum wage is still present in the case of internships. As of 2022, around 40% of internships were unpaid, offering valuable training and education as legally required. And because they are unpaid, lower income students are disproportionately unable to take such positions. Yet imposing a minimum wage might force some companies to eliminate internship programs altogether. In contrast, interns working at companies whose programs do not offer academic benefits but pay the minimum wage have clearly benefited.

>> Check Your Understanding 4-2

Solutions appear at back of book.

1. The state legislature mandates a price floor for gasoline of P_F per gallon. Assess the following statements and illustrate your answer using the figure provided.

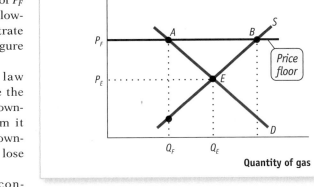

   a. Proponents of the law claim it will increase the income of gas station owners. Opponents claim it will hurt gas station owners because they will lose customers.
   b. Proponents claim consumers will be better off because gas stations will provide better service. Opponents claim consumers will be generally worse off because they prefer to buy gas at cheaper prices.
   c. Proponents claim that they are helping gas station owners without hurting anyone else. Opponents claim that consumers are hurt and will end up doing things like buying gas in a nearby state or on the shadow market.

>> Quick Review

• The most familiar price floor is the **minimum wage.** Price floors are also commonly imposed on agricultural goods.

• A price floor above the equilibrium price benefits successful sellers but causes predictable adverse effects such as a persistent surplus, which leads to four kinds of inefficiencies: deadweight loss from inefficiently low quantity, **inefficient allocation of sales among sellers,** wasted resources, and **inefficiently high quality.**

• Price floors encourage illegal activity, such as workers who work off the books, often leading to official corruption.

‖ Controlling Quantities

In the 1930s, New York City instituted a system of licensing for taxicabs: only taxis with a "medallion" were allowed to pick up passengers, hailing them from the street. Because this system was intended to assure quality, medallion owners were supposed to maintain certain standards, including safety and cleanliness. A total of 11,787 medallions were issued, with taxi owners paying $10 for each medallion.

In 1995, there were still only 11,787 licensed taxicabs in New York, even though the city had meanwhile become the financial capital of the world, a place where hundreds of thousands of people in a hurry tried to hail a cab every day. By 2022, the number of licensed cabs had risen to only 13,587. And up until a few years ago, this restriction on the number of New York City taxi medallions made them a very valuable item: if you wanted to operate a taxi in the city, you had to lease a medallion from someone or buy one.

Yet restrictions on the number of taxis induced people to try to circumvent them, eventually leading to the emergence of mobile-app-based car services like Uber and Lyft. Their cars aren't hailed from the street like taxis—in fact, their drivers are forbidden from picking up riders from the street. Instead, riders arrange trips on their smartphones, directing available drivers to their location. Of course, the ubiquity of smartphones also contributed to the emergence of these car services.

Since 2013, Uber and Lyft have fundamentally altered the market for car rides in New York City and most other major cities. But let's postpone the discussion of

Quotas increased the value of taxi medallions on the streets of NYC.

those effects until we learn more about how the market worked when only licensed taxicabs could operate.

A taxi medallion is a form of **quantity control,** or **quota,** by which the government regulates the quantity of a good that can be bought and sold rather than the price at which it is transacted. It is another way that government intervenes in markets along with price ceilings and price floors. The total amount of the good that can be transacted under the quantity control is called the **quota limit.** Typically, the government limits quantity in a market by issuing **licenses;** only people with a license can legally supply the good.

A taxi medallion is just such a license. The government of New York City limited the number of taxi rides that can be sold by limiting the number of taxis to only those who hold medallions. More generally, quantity controls, or quotas, set an upper limit on the quantity of a good that can be transacted. For example, quotas have been used frequently to limit the size of the catch of endangered fish stocks. In this case, quotas are implemented for good economic reasons: to protect endangered fish stocks.

But some quotas are implemented for bad economic reasons, typically for the purpose of enriching the quota holder. For example, quantity controls introduced to address a temporary problem such as assuring that only safe and clean taxis are allowed to operate, become difficult to remove later, once the problem has disappeared, because quota holders benefit from them and exert political pressure.

The Anatomy of Quantity Controls

Before the arrival of Uber and Lyft, a New York taxi medallion was worth a lot of money—averaging several hundred thousand dollars. To understand why a New York taxi medallion was worth so much money in those days, we consider a simplified version of the market for taxi rides, shown in Figure 7. Just as we assumed in the analysis of rent control that all apartments are the same, we now suppose that all taxi rides are the same—ignoring the real-world complication that some taxi rides are longer, and so more expensive, than others.

The table in the figure shows supply and demand schedules. The equilibrium—indicated by point E in the figure and by the shaded entries in the table—is a fare of $5 per ride, with 10 million rides taken per year. (You'll see in a minute why we present the equilibrium this way.)

In this example, the New York medallion system limits the number of taxis, but each taxi driver can offer as many rides as they can manage. To simplify our analysis, however, we will assume that a medallion system limits the number of taxi rides that can legally be given to 8 million per year.

Until now, we have derived the demand curve by answering questions of the form: "How many taxi rides will passengers want to take if the price is $5 per ride?" But it is possible to reverse the question and ask instead: "At what price will consumers want to buy 10 million rides per year?" The price at which consumers want to buy a given quantity—in this case, 10 million rides at $5 per ride—is the **demand price** of that quantity. You can see from the demand schedule in Figure 7 that the demand price of 6 million rides is $7 per ride, the demand price of 7 million rides is $6.50 per ride, and so on.

Similarly, the supply curve represents the answer to questions of the form: "How many taxi rides would taxi drivers supply at a price of $5 each?" But we can also reverse this question to ask: "At what price will suppliers be willing to supply 10 million rides per year?" The price at which suppliers will supply a given quantity—in this case, 10 million rides at $5 per ride—is the **supply price** of that quantity. We can see from the supply schedule in Figure 7 that the supply price of

quantity control an upper limit, set by the government, on the quantity of some good that can be bought or sold; also referred to as a quota.

quota an upper limit, set by the government, on the quantity of some good that can be bought or sold; also referred to as a quantity control.

quota limit the total amount of a good under a quota or quantity control that can be legally transacted.

license the right, conferred by the government or an owner, to supply a good.

demand price the price of a given quantity at which consumers will demand that quantity.

supply price the price of a given quantity at which producers will supply that quantity.

FIGURE 7 **The Market for Taxi Rides in the Absence of Government Controls**

Fare (per ride)	Quantity of rides (millions per year)	
	Quantity demanded	Quantity supplied
$7.00	6	14
6.50	7	13
6.00	8	12
5.50	9	11
5.00	10	10
4.50	11	9
4.00	12	8
3.50	13	7
3.00	14	6

Without government intervention, the market reaches equilibrium with 10 million rides taken per year at a fare of $5 per ride.

6 million rides is $3 per ride, the supply price of 7 million rides is $3.50 per ride, and so on.

Now we are ready to analyze a quota. We have assumed that the city government limits the quantity of taxi rides to 8 million per year. Medallions, each of which carries the right to provide a certain number of taxi rides per year, are made available to selected people in such a way that a total of 8 million rides will be provided. Medallion-holders may then either drive their own taxis or rent their medallions to others for a fee.

Figure 8 shows the resulting market for taxi rides, with the black vertical line at 8 million rides per year representing the quota limit. Because the quantity of rides is limited to 8 million, consumers must be at point *A* on the demand curve, corresponding to the shaded entry in the demand schedule: the demand price of 8 million rides is $6 per ride. Meanwhile, taxi drivers must be at point *B* on the supply curve, corresponding to the shaded entry in the supply schedule: the supply price of 8 million rides is $4 per ride.

But how can the price received by taxi drivers be $4 when the price paid by taxi riders is $6? The answer is that in addition to the market in taxi rides, there is also a market in medallions. Medallion-holders may not always want to drive their taxis: they may be ill or on vacation. Those who do not want to drive their own taxis will sell the right to use the medallion to someone else.

So we need to consider two sets of transactions here, and so two prices: (1) the transactions in taxi rides and the price at which these will occur, and (2) the transactions in medallions and the price at which these will occur. It turns out that since we are looking at two markets, the $4 and $6 prices will both be right.

To see how this all works, consider two imaginary New York taxi drivers, Ali and Jean. Ali has a medallion but can't use it because he's recovering from a severely sprained wrist. So he's looking to rent his medallion out to someone else. Jean doesn't have a medallion but would like to rent one. Furthermore, at any point in time there are many other people like Jean who would like to rent a

FIGURE 8 Effect of a Quota on the Market for Taxi Rides

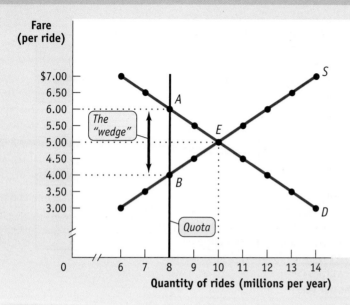

Fare (per ride)	Quantity of rides (millions per year)	
	Quantity demanded	Quantity supplied
$7.00	6	14
6.50	7	13
6.00	8	12
5.50	9	11
5.00	10	10
4.50	11	9
4.00	12	8
3.50	13	7
3.00	14	6

The table shows the demand price and the supply price corresponding to each quantity: the price at which that quantity would be demanded and supplied, respectively. The city government imposes a quota of 8 million rides by selling licenses for only 8 million rides, represented by the black vertical line. The price paid by consumers rises to $6 per ride, the demand price of 8 million rides, shown by point A.

The supply price of 8 million rides is only $4 per ride, shown by point B. The difference between these two prices is the quota rent per ride, the earnings that accrue to the owner of a license. The quota rent drives a wedge between the demand price and the supply price and discourages mutually beneficial transactions.

wedge the difference between the demand price of the quantity transacted and the supply price of the quantity transacted for a good when the supply of the good is legally restricted. Often created by a quantity control, or quota. The price paid by buyers ends up being higher than that received by sellers.

quota rent the difference between the demand price and the supply price at the quota limit; this difference, the earnings that accrue to the license-holder from ownership of the right to sell the good, is equal to the market price of the license when the licenses are traded.

medallion. Suppose Ali agrees to rent his medallion to Jean. To make things simple, assume that any driver can give only one ride per day and that Ali is renting his medallion to Jean for one day. What rental price will they agree on?

To answer this question, we need to look at the transactions from the viewpoints of both drivers. Once she has the medallion, Jean knows she can make $6 per day—the demand price of a ride under the quota. And she is willing to rent the medallion only if she makes at least $4 per day—the supply price of a ride under the quota. So Ali cannot demand a rent of more than $2—the difference between $6 and $4. And if Jean offered Ali less than $2—say, $1.50—there would be other eager drivers willing to offer him more, up to $2. So, in order to get the medallion, Jean must offer Ali at least $2. Since the rent can be no more than $2 and no less than $2, it must be exactly $2.

It is no coincidence that $2 is exactly the difference between $6, the demand price of 8 million rides, and $4, the supply price of 8 million rides. In every case in which the supply of a good is legally restricted, there is a **wedge** between the demand price of the quantity transacted and the supply price of the quantity transacted.

This wedge, illustrated by the double-headed arrow in Figure 8, has a special name: the **quota rent.** It is the earnings that accrue to the license-holder from ownership of a valuable commodity, the license. In the case of Ali and Jean, the quota rent of $2 goes to Ali because he owns the license, and the remaining $4 from the total fare of $6 goes to Jean.

Figure 8 also illustrates the quota rent in the market for New York taxi rides. The quota limits the quantity of rides to 8 million per year, a quantity at which the demand price of $6 exceeds the supply price of $4. The wedge between these two prices, $2, is the quota rent that results from the restrictions placed on the quantity of taxi rides in this market.

But wait a second. What if Ali doesn't rent out his medallion? What if he uses it himself? Doesn't this mean that he gets a price of $6? No, not really. Even if Ali doesn't rent out his medallion, he could have rented it out, which means that the medallion has an *opportunity cost* of $2: if Ali decides to use his own medallion and drive his own taxi rather than renting his medallion to Jean, the $2 represents his opportunity cost of not renting out his medallion. That is, the $2 quota rent is now the rental income he forgoes by driving his own taxi.

In effect, Ali is in two businesses—the taxi-driving business and the medallion-renting business. He makes $4 per ride from driving his taxi and $2 per ride from renting out his medallion. It doesn't make any difference that in this particular case he has rented his medallion to himself! So under quantity controls, the medallion is a valuable asset regardless of whether the medallion owner uses it or rents it out to others. In 2010, before the rise of Uber and Lyft effectively eliminated the quantity controls, New York taxi medallions were trading for around $500,000. Notice, by the way, that quotas—like price ceilings and price floors—don't always have a real effect. If the quota were set at 12 million rides—that is, above the equilibrium quantity in an unregulated market—it would have no effect because it would not be binding.

The Costs of Quantity Controls

Like price controls, quantity controls can have some predictable and undesirable side effects. The first is the by-now-familiar problem of inefficiency due to missed opportunities: quantity controls prevent mutually beneficial transactions from occurring, transactions that would benefit both buyers and sellers.

Looking back at Figure 8, you can see that starting at the quota limit of 8 million rides, New Yorkers would be willing to pay at least $5.50 per ride when 9 million rides are offered, 1 million more than the quota, and that taxi drivers would be willing to provide those rides as long as they got at least $4.50 per ride. These are rides that would have taken place if there were no quota limit.

The same is true for the next 1 million rides: New Yorkers would be willing to pay at least $5 per ride when the quantity of rides is increased from 9 to 10 million, and taxi drivers would be willing to provide those rides as long as they got at least $5 per ride. Again, these rides would have occurred without the quota limit.

Only when the market has reached the unregulated market equilibrium quantity of 10 million rides are there no "missed-opportunity rides." The quota limit of 8 million rides has caused 2 million "missed-opportunity rides."

Generally, *as long as the demand price of a given quantity exceeds the supply price, there is a missed opportunity*. A buyer would be willing to buy the good at a price that the seller would be willing to accept, but such a transaction does not occur because it is forbidden by the quota.

And because there are transactions that people would like to make but are not allowed to, quantity controls generate an incentive to circumvent them. In the days before Uber and Lyft, a substantial number of unlicensed taxis simply defied the law and picked up passengers without a medallion. These unregulated, unlicensed taxis contributed to a disproportionately large share of accidents.

However, Uber and Lyft cars legally circumvent the restriction that a car without a medallion can't be hailed from the street. As of 2023, Uber had approximately 80,000 cars in New York City, significantly more than the 13,587 licensed taxicabs.

Clearly, the quantity restriction on New York City taxicabs has been substantially undermined. In effect, the quota line in Figure 8 has shifted rightward, closer to the equilibrium quantity, with the entry of Uber and Lyft.

In the past few years, as quota rents to owners of a taxi medallion have fallen, the prices of taxi medallions have fallen significantly as well. In 2021, the price of a New York City taxi medallion had fallen to under $80,000. By the end of 2022, prices had rebounded to nearly $150,000. But still a steep fall from the $500,000 price tag in 2010. In sum, quantity controls typically create the following undesirable side effects:

- Inefficiencies, or missed opportunities, in the form of mutually beneficial transactions that don't occur
- Incentives for illegal activities

ECONOMICS >> *in Action*
Crabbing, Quotas, and Saving Lives in Alaska

Alaskan king and snow crabs are considered delicacies worldwide. And crab fishing is one of the most important industries in the Alaskan economy. So many were justifiably concerned when, in the early 1980s, the annual crab catch fell by 90% due to overfishing. In response, marine biologists set a *total allowable catch quota system*, which limited the amount of crab that could be harvested annually in order to allow the crab population to return to a healthy, sustainable level.

Notice, by the way, that the Alaskan crab quota is an example of a quota that was justified by broader economic and environmental considerations—unlike the New York City taxicab quota, which has long since lost any economic rationale. Another important difference is that, unlike New York City taxicab medallions, owners of Alaskan crab boats did not have the ability to buy or sell individual quotas. So although depleted crab stocks eventually recovered with the total catch quota system in place, there was another, unintended and deadly consequence.

The Alaskan crabbing season is fairly short, running roughly from October to January, and it can be further shortened by bad weather. Within a few years, Alaskan crab fishermen were engaging in "fishing derbies." To stay within the quota limit when the crabbing season began, boat crews rushed to fish for crab in dangerous, icy, rough water, straining to harvest in a few days a haul that could be worth several hundred thousand dollars. As a result, boats often became overloaded and capsized, making Alaskan crab fishing one of the most dangerous jobs, with an average of 7.3 deaths a year, about 80 times the fatality rate for an average worker. And after the brief harvest, the market for crab was flooded with supply, lowering the prices fishermen received.

So fishery regulators instituted another quota system called *quota share*—aimed at protecting Alaska's crabbers and crabs. Under individual quota share, each boat received a quota to fill during the three-month season. Moreover, the individual quotas could be sold or leased. These changes transformed the industry as owners of bigger boats bought the individual quotas of smaller boats, shrinking the number of crabbing boats dramatically. Bigger boats are much less likely to capsize, improving crew safety.

In addition, by extending the fishing season, the quota-share system boosted the crab population and crab prices. With more time to fish, fishermen could make sure that juvenile and female crabs were returned to the sea rather than harvested. And with a longer fishing season, the catch comes to market more gradually, eliminating the downward plunge in prices when supply hits the market. Predictably, an Alaskan crab fisherman earns more money under the quota-share system than under the total catch quota system.

The quota-share system protects Alaska's crab population and saves the lives of crabbers.

Discovery Network/Kobal/Shutterstock

>> Check Your Understanding 4-3

Solutions appear at back of book.

1. Suppose that the supply and demand for taxi rides is given by Figure 7 but the quota is set at 6 million rides instead of 8 million. Find the following and indicate them on Figure 7.
   a. The price of a ride
   b. The quota rent
   c. Suppose the quota limit on taxi rides is increased to 9 million. What happens to the quota rent?

2. Assume that the quota limit is 8 million rides. Suppose demand decreases due to a decline in tourism. What is the smallest parallel leftward shift in demand that would result in the quota no longer having an effect on the market? Illustrate your answer using Figure 7.

A Market Disruptor Gets Disrupted by the Market

Michael Nagle/Bloomberg/Getty Images

In 2021, Uber benefited from increased demand for UberEats. But 2022 was an ugly year for them. Looks like net income could end up worse than during the early stages of the pandemic as people cut back on both ride-sharing and home delivery. Even before the Covid pandemic, Uber had suffered significant falls in the annual growth rate in the number of rides provided. These results have led some observers to question the company's long-term viability.

For a company that had been the darling of the high-tech business world, the massive losses, year after year, have been humbling. Investors had believed that only one company—namely Uber—would come to dominate the ride-hailing industry and it would be very profitable. What has gone so wrong?

Uber was the brainchild of two friends, Travis Kalanick and Garrett Camp, conceived after a difficult search for a taxi in Paris. When it launched in 2010 in San Francisco,

Uber was the first company to enable ride hailing via a smartphone app. It provided easy access to lower-priced cab rides. Uber expanded rapidly, eventually extending its reach to over 600 cities worldwide. The company focused, in particular, on expansion in cities where the existing taxi market was highly regulated and restricted. Ridership grew explosively, so that by 2019 Uber was completing nearly 14 million rides each day.

But Uber's success did not go unnoticed. Seeing the opportunity to make money, some people wanted to become Uber drivers while others wanted to start up rival companies. In 2012, for example, Lyft launched a competing service. In Latin America, China, and India, home-grown challengers emerged. Uber responded by rolling out costly initiatives. For example, to keep its ridership high, Uber began subsidizing rides—that is, it provided discount codes and coupons that lowered the price of rides below the actual cost of providing them.

Whether Uber can ever fulfill its early promise—turning its losses around, recapturing its high growth rates of the past, and ultimately become profitable—remains to be seen.

QUESTIONS FOR THOUGHT

1. How did quantity controls for taxi rides contribute to Uber's high rates of growth in its early years?

2. Based on what you've learned in the chapter, explain whether Uber's recent difficulties were predictable or the result of bad luck.

3. How likely is it that Uber can regain its past high rates of growth?

4. How has the allocation of surplus changed in this market over time? Who benefitted when Uber began competing with existing taxi companies? Who benefited when rival ride-hailing companies began competing with Uber?

SUMMARY

1. Even when a market is efficient, governments often intervene to pursue greater fairness or to please a powerful interest group. Interventions can take the form of **price controls** or quantity controls, both of which generate predictable and undesirable side effects consisting of various forms of inefficiency and illegal activity.

2. A **price ceiling,** a maximum market price below the equilibrium price, benefits successful buyers but creates persistent shortages. Because the price is maintained below the equilibrium price, the quantity demanded is increased and the quantity supplied is decreased compared to the equilibrium quantity. This leads to predictable problems: inefficiently low quantity transacted, **inefficient allocation to consumers, wasted resources,** and **inefficiently low quality.** It also encourages illegal activity as people turn to **shadow markets** to get the good. Because of these problems, price ceilings have generally lost favor as an economic policy tool. However, price ceilings can be justified when the market is inefficient or when a natural disaster leads to shortages that, if left to a free market, would greatly diminish equity and social welfare.

3. A **price floor,** a minimum market price above the equilibrium price, benefits successful sellers but creates persistent surplus. Because the price is maintained above the equilibrium price, the quantity demanded is decreased and the quantity supplied is increased compared to the equilibrium quantity. This leads to predictable problems: inefficiently low quantity transacted, **inefficient allocation of sales among sellers,** wasted resources, and **inefficiently high quality.** It also encourages illegal activity and shadow markets. The most well-known kind of price floor is the **minimum wage,** but price floors are also commonly applied to agricultural products.

4. **Quantity controls,** or **quotas,** limit the quantity of a good that can be bought or sold. The quantity allowed for sale is the **quota limit.** The government issues **licenses** to individuals, the right to sell a given quantity of the good. The owner of a license earns a **quota rent,** earnings that accrue from ownership of the right to sell the good. It is equal to the difference between the **demand price** at the quota limit, what consumers are willing to pay for that quantity, and the **supply price** at the quota limit, what suppliers are willing to accept for that quantity. Economists say that a quota drives a **wedge** between the demand price and the supply price; this wedge is equal to the quota rent. Quantity controls lead to inefficiencies in the form of mutually beneficial transactions that do not occur; they also encourage illegal activity.

KEY TERMS

Price controls, p. 104
Price ceiling, p. 104
Price floor, p. 104
Inefficient allocation to consumers, p. 107
Wasted resources, p. 108
Inefficiently low quality, p. 109

Shadow market, p. 109
Minimum wage, p. 111
Inefficient allocation of sales among sellers, p. 114
Inefficiently high quality, p. 115
Quantity control, p. 118
Quota, p. 118

Quota limit, p. 118
License, p. 118
Demand price, p. 118
Supply price, p. 118
Wedge, p. 120
Quota rent, p. 120

PRACTICE QUESTIONS

1. Oregon recently became the first state to adopt legislation capping housing rents statewide. Explain how Oregon's policy will affect landlords, renters, and the quality of rental units available.

2. In your state, the minimum wage is $12 per hour. Yet, you notice that many fast-food restaurants have posted help wanted signs for jobs paying $15 per hour. What does this tell you about the minimum wage and the availability of restaurant work in your town?

3. Many Washington State residents and politicians are concerned about the declining salmon population, a primary food source for local wildlife, including the endangered orca whale. To protect the salmon population from overfishing, politicians are considering two policies. The first is a binding price ceiling in the market for salmon. The second policy is a quota: permits would be sold to those who fish commercially in order to restrict their salmon catch. As events have unfolded, it's become clear that politicians tend to favor the quota system while those who catch fish for a living prefer a price ceiling. Why do you think this is the case?

PROBLEMS

1. In order to appeal to voters, the mayor of Gotham City decides to lower the price of taxi rides. Assume, for simplicity, that all taxi rides are the same distance and therefore cost the same. The accompanying table shows the demand and supply schedules for taxi rides.

Fare (per ride)	Quantity of rides (millions per year)	
	Quantity demanded	Quantity supplied
$7.00	10	12
6.50	11	11
6.00	12	10
5.50	13	9
5.00	14	8
4.50	15	7

a. Assume that there are no restrictions on the number of taxi rides that can be supplied (there is no medallion system). Find the equilibrium price and quantity.

b. Suppose that the mayor sets a price ceiling at $5.50. How large is the shortage of rides? Illustrate with a diagram. Who loses and who benefits from this policy?

c. Suppose that the stock market crashes and, as a result, people in Gotham City are poorer. This reduces the quantity of taxi rides demanded by 6 million rides per year at any given price. What effect will the mayor's new policy have now? Illustrate with a diagram.

d. Suppose that the stock market rises and the demand for taxi rides returns to normal (that is, returns to the demand schedule given in the table). The mayor now decides to ingratiate himself with taxi drivers. He announces a policy in which operating licenses are given to existing taxi drivers; the number of licenses is restricted such that only 10 million rides per year can be given. Illustrate the effect of this policy on the market, and indicate the resulting price and quantity transacted. What is the quota rent per ride?

2. In the late eighteenth century, the price of bread in New York City was controlled, set at a predetermined price above the market price.

a. Draw a diagram showing the effect of the policy. Did the policy act as a price ceiling or a price floor?

b. What kinds of inefficiencies were likely to have arisen when the controlled price of bread was above the market price? Explain in detail.

One year during this period, a poor wheat harvest caused a leftward shift in the supply of bread and therefore an increase in its market price. New York bakers found that the controlled price of bread in New York was below the market price.

c. Draw a diagram showing the effect of the price control on the market for bread during this one-year period. Did the policy act as a price ceiling or a price floor?

d. What kinds of inefficiencies do you think occurred during this period? Explain in detail.

3. In 2019, the U.S. House of Representatives approved a new farm bill modifying the price supports for dairy farmers. The new program, the Dairy Margin Coverage, supports dairy farmers when the margin between feed costs and milk prices falls below $0.08 per pound. Suppose that current feed costs are $0.10 per pound, which means the program creates a price floor for milk at $0.18 per pound. At that price, in 2019, the quantity of milk supplied is 240 billion pounds, and the quantity demanded is 140 billion pounds. To support the price of milk at the price floor, the U.S. Department of Agriculture (USDA) has to buy up 100 billion pounds of surplus milk. The supply and demand curves in the following diagram illustrate the market for milk.

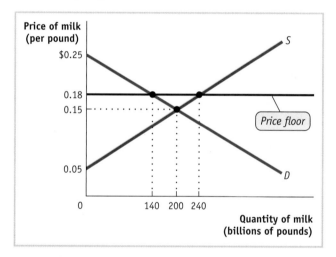

a. In the absence of a price floor, how much consumer surplus is created? How much producer surplus? What is the total surplus (producer surplus plus consumer surplus)?

b. With the price floor at $0.18 per pound of milk, consumers buy 140 billion pounds of milk. How much consumer surplus is created now?

c. With the price floor at $0.18 per pound of milk, producers sell 240 billion pounds of milk (some to consumers and some to the USDA). How much producer surplus is created now?

d. How much money does the USDA spend to buy surplus milk?

e. Taxes must be collected to pay for the purchases of surplus milk by the USDA. As a result, total surplus is reduced by the amount the USDA spent buying surplus milk. Using your answers from parts b, c, and d, what is the total surplus when there is a price floor? How does this total surplus compare to the total surplus without a price floor from part a?

4. The accompanying table shows hypothetical demand and supply schedules for milk per year. The U.S. government decides that the incomes of dairy farmers should be maintained at a level that allows the traditional family dairy farm to survive. So it implements a price floor of $1 per pint by buying surplus milk until the market price is $1 per pint.

Price of milk (per pint)	Quantity of milk (millions of pints per year)	
	Quantity demanded	Quantity supplied
$1.20	550	850
1.10	600	800
1.00	650	750
0.90	700	700
0.80	750	650

a. How much surplus milk will be produced as a result of this policy?

b. What will be the cost to the government of this policy?

c. Since milk is an important source of protein and calcium, the government decides to provide the surplus milk it purchases to elementary schools at a price of only $0.60 per pint. Assume that schools will buy any amount of milk available at this low price. But parents now reduce their purchases of milk at any price by 50 million pints per year because they know their children are getting milk at school. How much will the dairy program now cost the government?

d. Explain how inefficiencies in the form of inefficient allocation to sellers and wasted resources arise from this policy.

5. European governments tend to make greater use of price controls than does the U.S. government. For example, the French government sets minimum starting yearly wages for new hires who have completed *le bac,* a certification roughly equivalent to a high school diploma. The demand schedule for new hires with *le bac* and the supply schedule for similarly credentialed new job seekers are given in the accompanying table. The price here—given in euros, the currency used in France—is the same as the yearly wage.

Wage (per year)	Quantity demanded (new job offers per year)	Quantity supplied (new job seekers per year)
€45,000	200,000	325,000
40,000	220,000	320,000
35,000	250,000	310,000
30,000	290,000	290,000
25,000	370,000	200,000

a. In the absence of government interference, what are the equilibrium wage and number of graduates hired per year? Illustrate with a diagram. Will there be anyone seeking a job at the equilibrium wage who is unable to find one—that is, will there be anyone who is involuntarily unemployed?

b. Suppose the French government sets a minimum yearly wage of €35,000. Is there any involuntary unemployment at this wage? If so, how much? Illustrate with a diagram. What if the minimum wage is set at €40,000? Also illustrate with a diagram.

c. Given your answer to part b and the information in the table, what do you think is the relationship between the level of involuntary unemployment and the level of the minimum wage? Who benefits from such a policy? Who loses? What is the missed opportunity here?

6. In many European countries, high minimum wages have led to high levels of unemployment and underemployment, and a two-tier labor system. In the formal labor market, workers have good jobs that pay at least the minimum wage. In the informal or shadow market for labor, workers have poor jobs and receive less than the minimum wage.

a. Draw a demand and supply diagram showing the effect of the imposition of a minimum wage on the overall market for labor, with wage on the vertical axis and hours of labor on the horizontal axis. Your supply curve should represent the hours of labor offered by workers according to the wage, and the demand curve should represent the hours of labor demanded by employers according to the wage. What type of shortage is created? Illustrate on your diagram the size of the shortage.

b. Assume that the imposition of the high minimum wage causes a contraction in the economy so that employers in the formal sector cut their production and their demand for workers. Illustrate the effect of this on the overall market for labor. What happens to the shortage? Illustrate with a diagram.

c. Assume that the workers who cannot get a job paying at least the minimum wage move into the informal labor market where there is no minimum wage. What happens to the size of the informal market for labor as a result of the economic contraction? What happens to the equilibrium wage in the informal labor market? Illustrate with a supply and demand diagram for the informal market.

7. For the last 85 years, the U.S. government has used price supports to provide income assistance to American farmers. To implement these price supports, at times the government has used price floors, which it maintains by buying up the surplus farm products. At other times, it has used target prices, a policy by which the government gives the farmer an amount equal to the difference between the market price and the target price for each unit sold. Consider the market for corn depicted in the accompanying diagram.

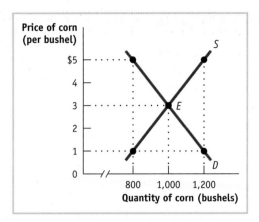

a. If the government sets a price floor of $5 per bushel, how many bushels of corn are produced? How many are purchased by consumers? By the government? How much does the program cost the government? How much revenue do corn farmers receive?

b. Suppose the government sets a target price of $5 per bushel for any quantity supplied up to 1,000 bushels. How many bushels of corn are purchased by consumers and at what price? By the government? How much does the program cost the government? How much revenue do corn farmers receive?

c. Which of these programs (in parts a and b) costs corn consumers more? Which program costs the government more? Explain.

d. Is one of these policies less inefficient than the other? Explain.

8. The waters off the North Atlantic coast were once teeming with fish. But because of overfishing by the commercial fishing industry, the stocks of fish became seriously depleted. In 1991, the National Marine Fisheries Service of the U.S. government implemented a quota to allow fish stocks to recover. In 2016, the quota limited the amount of swordfish caught per year by all U.S.-licensed fishing boats to 7 million pounds. As soon as the U.S. fishing fleet had met the quota limit, the swordfish catch was closed down for the rest of the year. The accompanying table gives the hypothetical demand and supply schedules for swordfish caught in the United States per year.

Price of swordfish (per pound)	Quantity of swordfish (millions of pounds per year)	
	Quantity demanded	Quantity supplied
$20	6	15
18	7	13
16	8	11
14	9	9
12	10	7

a. Use a diagram to show the effect of the quota on the market for swordfish in 1991. In your diagram, illustrate the deadweight loss from inefficiently low quantity.

b. How do you think fishermen will change how they fish in response to this policy?

9. In Maine, you must have a license to harvest lobster commercially; these licenses are issued yearly. The state of Maine is concerned about the dwindling supplies of lobsters found off its coast. The state fishery department has decided to place a yearly quota of 80,000 pounds of lobsters harvested in all Maine waters. It has also decided to give licenses this year only to those fishermen who had licenses last year. The accompanying diagram shows the demand and supply curves for Maine lobsters.

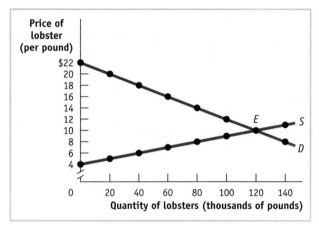

a. In the absence of government restrictions, what are the equilibrium price and quantity?

b. What is the *demand price* at which consumers wish to purchase 80,000 pounds of lobsters?

c. What is the *supply price* at which suppliers are willing to supply 80,000 pounds of lobsters?

d. What is the *quota rent* per pound of lobster when 80,000 pounds are sold?

e. Explain a transaction that benefits both buyer and seller but is prevented by the quota restriction.

10. The Venezuelan government has imposed a price ceiling on the retail price of roasted coffee beans. The accompanying diagram shows the market for coffee beans. In the absence of price controls, the equilibrium is at point E, with an equilibrium price of P_E and an equilibrium quantity bought and sold of Q_E.

a. Show the consumer and producer surplus before the introduction of the price ceiling.

After the introduction of the price ceiling, the price falls to P_C and the quantity bought and sold falls to Q_C.

b. Show the consumer surplus after the introduction of the price ceiling (assuming that the consumers with the highest willingness to pay get to buy the available coffee beans; that is, assuming that there is no inefficient allocation to consumers).

c. Show the producer surplus after the introduction of the price ceiling (assuming that the producers with the lowest cost get to sell their coffee beans; that is, assuming that there is no inefficient allocation of sales among producers).

d. Using the diagram, show how much of what was producer surplus before the introduction of the price ceiling has been transferred to consumers as a result of the price ceiling.

11. The accompanying diagram shows data from the U.S. Bureau of Labor Statistics on the average price of an airline ticket in the United States from 1975 until 1985, adjusted to eliminate the effect of *inflation* (the general increase in the prices of all goods over time). In 1978, the U.S. Airline Deregulation Act removed the price floor on airline fares, and it also allowed the airlines greater flexibility to offer new routes.

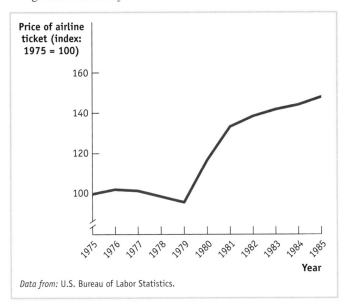

Data from: U.S. Bureau of Labor Statistics.

a. Looking at the data on airline ticket prices in the diagram, do you think the price floor that existed before 1978 was binding or nonbinding? That is, do you think it was set above or below the equilibrium price? Draw a supply and demand diagram, showing where the price floor that existed before 1978 was in relation to the equilibrium price.

b. Most economists agree that the average airline ticket price per mile traveled actually *fell* as a result of the Airline Deregulation Act. How might you reconcile that view with what you see in the diagram?

12. Many college students attempt to land internships before graduation to burnish their resumes, gain experience in a chosen field, or try out possible careers. The hope shared by all of these prospective interns is that they will find internships that pay more than typical summer jobs, such as waiting tables or flipping burgers.

a. With wage measured on the vertical axis and number of hours of work on the horizontal axis, draw a supply and demand diagram for the market for interns in which the minimum wage is nonbinding at the market equilibrium.

b. Assume that a market downturn reduces the demand for interns by employers. However, many students are willing and eager to work in unpaid internships. As a result, the new market equilibrium wage is equal to zero. Draw another supply and demand diagram to illustrate this new market equilibrium.

13. Suppose it is decided that rent control in New York City will be abolished and that market rents will now prevail. Assume that all rental units are identical and so are offered at the same rent. To address the plight of residents who may be unable to pay the market rent, an income supplement will be paid to all low-income households equal to the difference between the old controlled rent and the new market rent.

a. Use a diagram to show the effect on the rental market of the elimination of rent control. What will happen to the quality and quantity of rental housing supplied?

b. Use a second diagram to show the additional effect of the income-supplement policy on the market. What effect does it have on the market rent and quantity of rental housing supplied in comparison to your answers to part a?

c. Are tenants better or worse off as a result of these policies? Are landlords better or worse off? Is society as a whole better or worse off?

d. From a political standpoint, why do you think cities have been more likely to resort to rent control rather than a policy of income supplements to help low-income people pay for housing? ◼

5 International Trade

THE EVERYWHERE PHONE

WHAT DO AMERICANS DO with their time? The answer is that they largely spend it staring at small screens. In 2023, the average American spent five hours and 24 minutes a day looking at a smartphone (especially an iPhone) or a tablet, slightly more time than they spent watching TV.

Where do these small screens come from? Specifically, where does an iPhone come from?

Bloomberg/Getty Images

Hero Images Inc./Alamy Stock Photo

The production and consumption of smartphones are examples of today's hyperglobal world with its soaring levels of international trade.

Apple, which sells the iPhone, is a U.S. company. But if you said that iPhones come from the United States you're mostly wrong: Apple develops products, but contracts almost all of the manufacturing of those products to other companies that are mainly located overseas. But it's not really right to answer "China," either, even though that's where iPhones are assembled. Assembly is the last phase of iPhone production, in which the pieces are put together in the familiar metal-and-glass case.

In fact, a study of the iPhone X estimated that of the average wholesale price of about $800 per phone, less than $25 stayed in the Chinese economy. A substantially larger amount went to South Korean manufacturers, who supplied the display and memory chips. There were also substantial outlays for raw materials, which are sourced all over the world. And the biggest share of the price — more than half — consisted of Apple's profit margin, which was largely a reward for research, development, and design.

So where do iPhones come from? Lots of places. And the case of the iPhone isn't unusual: the car you drive, the clothing you wear, even the food you eat are generally the end products of complex supply chains that span the globe. Large-scale international trade like this isn't new. It was fairly common by the early twentieth century. In recent decades, however, new technologies for transportation and communication have interacted with pro-trade policies to produce an era of *hyperglobalization* in which international trade has soared thanks to complex chains of production like the one that puts an iPhone in front of your nose.

In 2021–2022, Americans got a harsh lesson in how important global supply chains have become when those chains faced disruption as a result of the Covid-19 pandemic. For a time, shortages of shipping containers and congestion at major ports translated into soaring prices and/or delayed delivery for many items, from cars to garage doors. Normally, however, these supply chains make the world economy much more productive and, as a result, richer than it would be if each country tried to be self-sufficient. And it isn't just the world as a whole that benefits from international trade: it's almost certain that every country benefits, too. But international trade is nonetheless controversial, because it sometimes hurts particular groups *within* countries. For these reasons, we must have a full picture of international trade to understand how national economies work.

This chapter examines the economics of international trade. We start from the model of comparative advantage, which, as we saw in Chapter 2, explains why there are gains from international trade. We will briefly recap that model here, then turn to a more detailed examination of the causes and consequences of globalization. •

WHAT YOU WILL LEARN

- What is comparative advantage and why does it lead to international trade?
- What are the sources of comparative advantage?
- Who gains and who loses from international trade?
- Why do **trade protections** like **tariffs** and **import quotas** create inefficiency?
- Why do governments engage in trade protection and how do **international trade agreements** counteract this?

imports goods and services purchased from other countries.

exports goods and services sold to other countries.

‖ Comparative Advantage and International Trade

The United States buys smartphones—and many other goods and services—from other countries. At the same time, it sells many goods and services to other countries. Goods and services purchased from abroad are **imports;** goods and services sold abroad are **exports.**

As illustrated by the opening story, international trade plays an increasingly important role in the world economy. Panel (a) of Figure 1 shows the ratio of goods crossing national borders to *world GDP*—the total value of goods and services produced in the world as a whole—since 1870. As you can see, the long-term trend has been upward, although there have been some periods of declining trade—for example, the sharp but brief dip in trade during the global financial crisis of 2008 and its aftermath.

Panel (b) illustrates imports and exports as a percentage of GDP for a number of countries. It shows that foreign trade is significantly more important for many other countries than it is for the United States.

Foreign trade isn't the only way countries interact economically. In the modern world, investors from one country often invest funds in another nation; many companies are multinational, with subsidiaries operating in several countries; and a growing number of people work in a country different from the one in which

---

FIGURE 1 The Growing Importance of International Trade

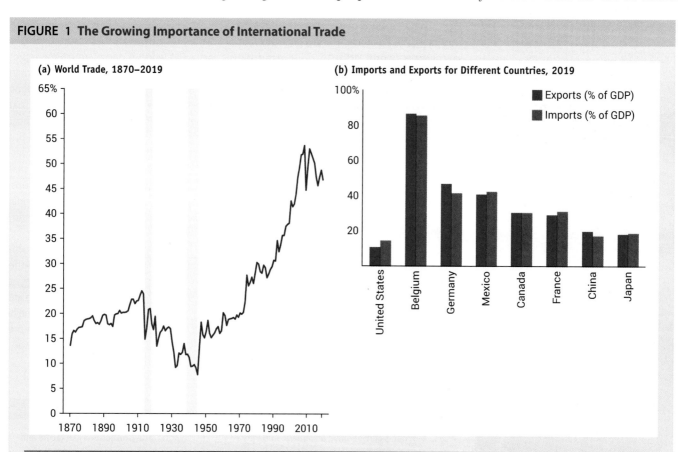

(a) World Trade, 1870–2019

(b) Imports and Exports for Different Countries, 2019

Panel (a) shows the long-term history of the ratio of world trade to world production. The trend has been generally upward, thanks to technological progress in transportation and communication, although there was a long setback during the period between the two world wars. Panel (b) demonstrates that international trade is significantly more important to many other countries than it is to the United States.

Percent of World GDP on *y*-axis. Data are for 62 countries that represent 90% of world GDP.

Data from: [panel (a)] Klasing, M. J., and P. Milionis, "Quantifying the Evolution of World Trade, 1870–1949," *Journal of International Economics* 92, no. 1 (2013): 185–197; and Feenstra, Robert C., Robert Inklaar, and Marcel P. Timmer, "The Next Generation of the Penn World Table," *American Economic Review* 105, no. 10 (2015): 3150–3182, available for download at www.ggdc.net/pwt; [panel (b)] World Development Indicators.

they were born. The growth of all these forms of economic linkages among countries is often called **globalization.**

Globalization isn't a new phenomenon. As you can see from panel (a) of Figure 1, there was rapid growth in trade between 1870 and the beginning of World War I, as railroads and steamships made shipping goods long distances faster and cheaper, effectively shrinking the world. This growth of trade was accompanied by large-scale international investment and migration. However, globalization went into reverse for almost 40 years after World War I, as governments imposed limits on trade. And by several measures, globalization didn't return to 1913 levels until the 1980s.

Since then, however, there has been a further dramatic increase in international linkages, sometimes referred to as **hyperglobalization.** The manufacture of iPhones and other high-tech goods, which often involve supply chains of production that span the globe, is an example of hyperglobalization. Each stage of a good's production takes place in a different country—all made possible by advances in communication and transportation technology. (For a real-life example, see this chapter's business case.)

One big question in international economics is whether hyperglobalization will continue in the decades ahead. As you can see from looking closely at Figure 1, the big rise in the ratio of exports to world GDP leveled off around 2005. Since then, many reports have appeared about companies deciding that the money they saved by buying goods from suppliers thousands of miles away is more than offset by the disadvantages of long shipping times and other inconveniences. (Even before the pandemic disrupted shipping, it took around two weeks for a container ship from China to arrive in California, and a month to reach the East Coast.) As a result, there has been some movement toward *reshoring*, bringing production closer to markets.

Thanks to cheap and fast ways of transporting goods, extremely high levels of international trade are a feature of today's economy.

More recently, international disputes over trade have heated up, and governments may once again impose the kind of restrictions on trade that caused globalization to decline after World War I. Although international trade is likely to remain important to world economies, it is possible that hyperglobalization may become less prevalent than it is today.

To understand why international trade occurs and why economists believe it is beneficial to the economy, we will first review the concept of comparative advantage.

Production Possibilities and Comparative Advantage, Revisited

To produce phones, any country must use resources—land, labor, and capital— that could have been used to produce other things. The opportunity cost of that phone is the potential production of other goods a country must forgo to produce it.

In some cases, it's easy to see why the opportunity cost of producing a good is especially low in a given country. Consider, for example, shrimp—much of which now comes from seafood farms in Vietnam and Thailand. It's a lot easier to produce shrimp in Vietnam, where the climate is nearly ideal and there's plenty of coastal land suitable for shellfish farming, than it is in the United States.

Conversely, other goods are not produced as easily in Vietnam as in the United States. For example, Vietnam doesn't have the base of skilled workers and technological know-how that makes the United States so good at producing high-technology goods. So the opportunity cost of a ton of shrimp, in terms of other goods such as aircraft, is much less in Vietnam than it is in the United States.

In other cases, the trade-off is less obvious. For example, it is as easy to assemble smartphones in the United States as in China. And Chinese electronics workers

globalization the phenomenon of growing economic linkages among countries.

hyperglobalization the phenomenon of extremely high levels of international trade.

Ricardian model of international trade a model that analyzes international trade under the assumption that opportunity costs are constant.

are, if anything, less productive than their U.S. counterparts. But Chinese workers are even less productive than U.S. workers in other areas, such as automobile and chemical production. So we say that China has a comparative advantage in producing smartphones. Let's repeat the definition of comparative advantage from Chapter 2: *A country has a comparative advantage in producing a good or service if the opportunity cost of producing the good or service is lower for that country than for other countries.*

Employing a Chinese worker to assemble phones is more productive than employing a U.S. worker to assemble phones because the U.S. worker can be even more productively employed elsewhere. That is, the opportunity cost of smartphone assembly in China is less than it is in the United States.

Notice that we said the opportunity cost of phone *assembly*. As we've seen, most of the value of a "Chinese made" phone actually comes from other countries. For the sake of exposition, however, let's ignore that complication and consider a hypothetical case in which China makes phones from scratch.

Figure 2 provides a hypothetical numerical example of comparative advantage in international trade. We assume that only two goods are produced and consumed, phones and Caterpillar heavy trucks. (The United States doesn't export many ordinary trucks, but Caterpillar, which makes earth-moving equipment, is a major exporter.) And we assume that there are only two countries in the world, the United States and China. The figure shows hypothetical production possibility frontiers for the United States and China.

As in Chapter 2, we simplify the model by assuming that the production possibility frontiers are straight lines, as shown in Chapter 2, Figure 1, rather than the more realistic bowed-out shape in Chapter 2, Figure 2. The straight-line shape implies that the opportunity cost of a phone in terms of trucks in each country is constant—it does not depend on how many units of each good the country produces. The analysis of international trade under the assumption that opportunity costs are constant, which makes production possibility frontiers straight lines, is known as the **Ricardian model of international trade,** named after the English

FIGURE 2 Comparative Advantage and the Production Possibility Frontier

The U.S. opportunity cost of 1 million phones in terms of trucks is 1,000: for every 1 million phones, 1,000 trucks must be forgone. The Chinese opportunity cost of 1 million phones in terms of trucks is 250: for every additional 1 million phones, only 250 trucks must be forgone. As a result, the United States has a comparative advantage in truck production, and China has a comparative advantage in phone production. In autarky, each country is forced to consume only what it produces: 50,000 trucks and 50 million phones for the United States; 25,000 trucks and 100 million phones for China.

economist David Ricardo, who introduced this analysis in the early nineteenth century.

In Figure 2, we show a situation in which the United States can produce 100,000 trucks if it produces no phones, or 100 million phones if it produces no trucks. Thus, the slope of the U.S. production possibility frontier, or *PPF*, is −100,000/100 = −1,000. That is, to produce an additional million phones, the United States must forgo the production of 1,000 trucks. Likewise, to produce one more truck, the United States must forgo 1,000 phones (equal to 1 million phones divided by 1,000 trucks).

Similarly, China can produce 50,000 trucks if it produces no phones or 200 million phones if it produces no trucks. Thus, the slope of China's *PPF* is −50,000/200 = −250. That is, to produce an additional million phones, China must forgo the production of 250 trucks. Likewise, to produce one more truck, China must forgo 4,000 phones (1 million phones divided by 250 trucks).

Historically, countries have almost always traded with each other. Yet economists find it helpful as a first step to illustrate the choices a country would make if it were unable to engage in international trade. Economists use the term **autarky** to refer to a situation in which a country does not trade with other countries. In our example, we assume that in autarky the United States chooses to produce and consume 50 million phones and 50,000 trucks. We also assume that in autarky China produces 100 million phones and 25,000 trucks.

The trade-offs facing the two countries when they don't trade are summarized in Table 1. As you can see, the United States has a comparative advantage in the production of trucks because it has a lower opportunity cost in terms of phones than China has: producing a truck costs the United States only 1,000 phones, while it costs China 4,000 phones. Correspondingly, China has a comparative advantage in phone production: 1 million phones costs only 250 trucks, while it costs the United States 1,000 trucks.

autarky a situation in which a country does not trade with other countries.

TABLE 1 U.S. and Chinese Opportunity Costs of Phones and Trucks

	U.S. opportunity cost		Chinese opportunity cost
1 million phones	1,000 trucks	>	250 trucks
1 truck	1,000 phones	<	4,000 phones

As we learned in Chapter 2, each country can do better by engaging in trade than it could by not trading. A country can accomplish this by specializing in the production of the good in which it has a comparative advantage and exporting that good, while importing the good in which it has a comparative disadvantage.

Let's see how this works.

The Gains from International Trade

Figure 3 illustrates how both countries can gain from specialization and trade, by showing a hypothetical rearrangement of production and consumption that allows *each* country to consume more of *both* goods. Again, panel (a) represents the United States and panel (b) represents China. In each panel, we indicate again the autarky production and consumption assumed in Figure 2.

Once trade becomes possible, however, everything changes. With trade, each country can move to producing only the good in which it has a comparative advantage—trucks for the United States and phones for China. Because the world production of both goods is now higher than in autarky, trade makes it possible for each country to consume more of both goods.

Table 2 sums up the changes as a result of trade and shows why both countries can gain. The left part of the table shows the autarky situation, before trade, in which each country must produce the goods it consumes. The right part of the table shows what happens as a result of trade. After trade, the United States specializes in the production of trucks, producing 100,000 trucks and no phones; China specializes in the production of phones, producing 200 million phones and no trucks.

The result is a rise in total world production of both goods. As you can see in the table, there are gains from trade to both countries:

• The United States can consume both more trucks (12,500 more) and phones (25 million more) than before, even though it no longer produces phones, because it can import phones from China.

FIGURE 3 The Gains from International Trade

Trade increases world production of both goods, allowing both countries to consume more. Here, each country specializes its production as a result of trade: the United States concentrates on producing trucks, and China concentrates on producing phones. Total world production of both goods rises, which means that it is possible for both countries to consume more of both goods.

TABLE 2 How the United States and China Gain from Trade

		In autarky		With trade		
		Production	Consumption	Production	Consumption	Gains from trade
United States	Million phones	50	50	0	75	+25
	Trucks	50,000	50,000	100,000	62,500	+12,500
China	Million phones	100	100	200	125	+25
	Trucks	25,000	25,000	0	37,500	+12,500

- China can also consume more of both goods (12,500 more trucks and 25 million more phones), even though it no longer produces trucks, because it can import trucks from the United States.

The key to this mutual gain is the fact that trade liberates both countries from self-sufficiency—from the need to produce the same mixes of goods they consume. Because each country can concentrate on producing the good in which it has a comparative advantage, total world production rises, making a higher standard of living possible in both nations.

In this example, we have simply assumed the post-trade consumption bundles of the two countries. In fact, the consumption choices of a country reflect both the preferences of its residents and the *relative prices*—the prices of one good in terms of another in international markets. Although we have not explicitly given the price of trucks in terms of phones, that price is implicit in our example: China sells the United States the 75 million phones the United States consumes in return for the 37,500 trucks China consumes, so 1 million phones are traded for 500 trucks. This tells us that the price of a truck on world markets must be equal to the price of 2,000 phones.

One requirement that the relative price must satisfy is that no country pays a relative price greater than its opportunity cost of obtaining the good in autarky.

That is, the United States won't pay more than 1,000 trucks for 1 million phones from China, and China won't pay more than 4,000 phones for each truck from the United States. Once this requirement is satisfied, the actual relative price in international trade is determined by supply and demand—and we'll turn to supply and demand in international trade in the next section. However, first let's look more deeply into the nature of the gains from trade.

Comparative Advantage versus Absolute Advantage

It's easy to accept the idea that Vietnam and Thailand have a comparative advantage in shrimp production: they have a tropical climate that's better suited to shrimp farming than the climate of the United States, and they have a lot of usable coastal area. So the United States imports shrimp from Vietnam and Thailand. But as we have seen in the case of cell phone assembly, the gains from trade often depend on *comparative advantage,* rather than on absolute advantage. It would take less labor to assemble a phone in the United States than in China. That is, the productivity of Chinese electronics workers is less than that of their U.S. counterparts. But what determines comparative advantage is not the amount of resources used to produce a good but the opportunity cost of that good—in this case, the quantity of other goods forgone in order to produce a phone. And the opportunity cost of phones is lower in China than in the United States.

The tropical climate of Thailand gives them a comparative advantage in shrimp production.

Here's how it works: Chinese workers have low productivity compared with U.S. workers in the electronics industry. But Chinese workers have even lower productivity compared with U.S. workers in other industries. Because Chinese labor productivity in industries other than electronics is relatively very low, producing a phone in China, even though it takes a lot of labor, does not require forgoing the production of large quantities of other goods.

In the United States, the opposite is true: very high productivity in other industries (such as automobiles) means that assembling electronic products in the United States, even though it doesn't require much labor, requires sacrificing lots of other goods. So the opportunity cost of producing electronics is less in China than in the United States. Despite its lower labor productivity, China has a comparative advantage in the production of many consumer electronics, although the United States has an absolute advantage.

The source of China's comparative advantage in consumer electronics is reflected in global markets by the wages Chinese workers are paid. That's because a country's wage rates, in general, reflect its labor productivity. In countries where labor is highly productive in many industries, employers are willing to pay high wages to attract workers, so competition among employers leads to an overall high wage rate. In countries where labor is less productive, competition for workers is less intense and wage rates are correspondingly lower.

As the Global Comparison shows, there is indeed a strong relationship between overall levels of productivity and wage rates around the world. Because China has generally low productivity, it has a relatively low wage rate. Low wages, in turn, give China a cost advantage in producing goods where its productivity is only moderately low, like consumer electronics. As a result, it's cheaper to produce these goods in China than in the United States.

Popular Misconceptions Arising from Misunderstanding Comparative Advantage

The kind of trade that takes place between low-wage, low-productivity economies like China and high-wage, high-productivity economies like the United States gives rise to two common misperceptions:

- The *pauper labor fallacy* is the belief that when a country with high wages imports goods produced by workers who are paid low wages, it must hurt the standard of living of workers in the importing country.

GLOBAL COMPARISON **PRODUCTIVITY AND WAGES AROUND THE WORLD**

Is it true that both the pauper labor argument and the sweatshop labor argument are fallacies? Yes, it is. The real explanation for low wages in poor countries is low overall productivity.

The graph shows estimates of labor productivity, measured by the value of output (GDP) per worker, and wages, measured by the hourly compensation of the average worker, for several countries in 2021. Both productivity and wages are expressed as percentages of U.S. productivity and wages; for example, productivity and wages in Japan were 57% and 59%, respectively, of their U.S. levels. You can see the strong positive relationship between productivity and wages. The relationship isn't perfect. For example, Iceland has higher wages than its productivity might lead you to expect. But simple comparisons of wages give a misleading sense of labor costs in poor countries: their low wage advantage is mostly offset by low productivity.

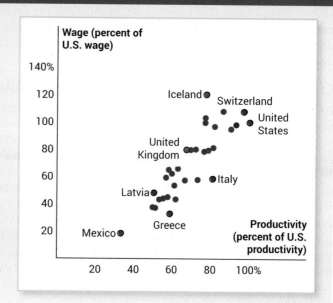

Data from: The OECD and the World Bank, World Development Indicators.

- The *sweatshop labor fallacy* is the belief that trade must be bad for workers in poor exporting countries because those workers are paid very low wages by our standards.

Both fallacies miss the nature of gains from trade: it's to the advantage of both countries if the poorer, lower-wage country exports goods in which it has a comparative advantage, even if its cost advantage in these goods depends on low wages. That is, both countries are able to achieve a higher standard of living through trade.

It's particularly important to understand that buying a good made by someone who is paid much lower wages than most U.S. workers doesn't necessarily imply that you're taking advantage of that person. It depends on the alternatives. Because workers in poor countries have low productivity across the board, they are offered low wages whether they produce goods exported to the United States or goods sold in local markets. A job that looks terrible by rich-country standards can be a step up for someone in a poor country.

International trade that depends on low-wage exports can nonetheless raise the exporting country's standard of living. This is especially true of very-low-wage nations. For example, Bangladesh and similar countries would be much poorer than they are—their citizens might even be starving—if they weren't able to export goods such as clothing based on their low wage rates.

Sources of Comparative Advantage

International trade is driven by comparative advantage, but where does comparative advantage come from? Economists who study international trade have found three main sources of comparative advantage: international differences in *climate*, international differences in *factor endowments*, and international differences in *technology*.

Differences in Climate One key reason the opportunity cost of producing shrimp in Vietnam and Thailand is less than in the United States is that shrimp need warm water—Vietnam has plenty of that, but the United States doesn't. In general, differences in climate play a significant role in international trade. Tropical countries export tropical products like coffee, sugar, bananas, and shrimp. Countries in the temperate zones export crops like wheat and corn. Some trade is even driven by the difference in seasons between the northern and southern hemispheres: winter deliveries of Chilean grapes have become commonplace in U.S. and European supermarkets.

Differences in Factor Endowments The United States does more trade with Canada than with any other country (China comes in second). Among other things, Canada sells us a lot of forest products—lumber and products derived from lumber, like pulp and paper. These exports don't reflect the special skill of Canadian lumberjacks. Canada has a comparative advantage in forest products because its forested area is much greater compared to the size of its labor force than the ratio of forestland to the labor force in the United States.

Forestland, like labor and capital, is a *factor of production:* an input used to produce goods and services. (Recall from Chapter 2 that the factors of production are land, labor, physical capital, and human capital.) Due to history and geography, the mix of available factors of production differs among countries, providing an important source of comparative advantage. The relationship between comparative advantage and factor availability is described in an influential model of international trade, the *Heckscher–Ohlin model,* developed by two Swedish economists in the first half of the twentieth century.

Two key concepts in the model are *factor abundance* and *factor intensity.* Factor abundance refers to how large a country's supply of a factor is relative to its supply of other factors. **Factor intensity** refers to the ranking of goods according to which factor is used in relatively greater quantities in production compared to other factors. So oil refining is a capital-intensive good because it tends to use a high ratio of capital to labor, but phone production is a labor-intensive good because it tends to use a high ratio of labor to capital.

According to the **Heckscher–Ohlin model,** *a country that has an abundant supply of a factor of production will have a comparative advantage in goods whose production is intensive in that factor.* So a country that has a relative abundance of capital will have a comparative advantage in capital-intensive industries such as oil refining, but a country that has a relative abundance of labor will have a comparative advantage in labor-intensive industries such as phone production.

The basic intuition behind this result is simple and based on opportunity cost.

- The opportunity cost of a given factor—the value that the factor would generate in alternative uses—is low for a country when it is relatively abundant in that factor.

- Relative to the United States, China has an abundance of low-skilled labor.

- As a result, the opportunity cost of the production of low-skilled, labor-intensive goods is lower in China than in the United States.

World trade in clothing is the most dramatic example of the validity of the Heckscher–Ohlin model in practice. Clothing production is a labor-intensive activity: it doesn't take much physical capital, nor does it require a lot of human capital in the form of highly educated workers. So you would expect labor-abundant countries such as China and Bangladesh to have a comparative advantage in clothing production. And they do.

The fact that international trade is the result of differences in factor endowments helps explain another fact: international specialization of production is often *incomplete.* That is, a country often maintains some domestic production of a good that it imports. A good example is British trade in oil. Britain imports most of the petroleum it consumes, mainly from Norway, which has huge offshore reserves. But Britain has some offshore reserves of its own, mostly off the coast of Scotland, so it's a significant oil producer itself.

A greater endowment of forestland gives Canada a comparative advantage in forest products.

factor intensity a measure of which factor is used in relatively greater quantities than other factors in production. For example, oil refining is capital-intensive compared to auto seat production because oil refiners use a higher ratio of capital to labor than do producers of auto seats.

Heckscher–Ohlin model a model of international trade in which a country has a comparative advantage in a good whose production is intensive in the factors that are abundantly available in that country.

FOR INQUIRING MINDS *How Scale Effects Drive International Trade*

Most analyses of international trade focus on how differences between countries — differences in climate, factor endowments, and technology — create national comparative advantage. While comparative advantage is the single most significant cause of international trade, economists have also pointed out another reason for international trade: the role of *increasing returns to scale*.

Production of a good is characterized by increasing returns to scale if the productivity of labor and other resources used in production rise with the quantity of output. For example, in an industry characterized by increasing returns to scale, increasing output by 10% might require only 8% more labor and 9% more raw materials.

One dramatic recent example of how increasing returns drive international trade was the production of innovative Covid-19 vaccines. The components of these vaccines are produced in expensive, highly specialized facilities; it would have made no sense to build one of these facilities in every country. Instead, a few facilities served the whole world. For example, when Pfizer rolled out its vaccine it relied on lipid nanoparticles (don't ask) produced at only two sites, one in Alabama and the other in Britain. Delivering the vaccines required shipping these lipids to a handful of other sites for the next stage of the process, then to a handful of "fill and finish" locations, then on to medical facilities around the world. Since many of these shipments crossed national boundaries, they gave rise to substantial international trade.

The financial services industry is another example of international trade generated by increasing returns. The industry is dominated by a relatively small number of very large banks. These banks also find it advantageous to cluster in the same location in order to facilitate face-to-face interaction on deals, as well as to have access to a large pool of skilled workers. As a result, the world financial industry is dominated by banks located in two cities — New York and London.

Increasing returns also explain the large amount of trade that takes place between countries that have similar natural endowments of resources. Forestland aside, the United States and Canada don't look very different in terms of technology or resources. Yet they export huge quantities of manufactured goods to each other. The reason is that increasing returns lead each country to specialize in producing a limited range of products and to import the goods it doesn't produce. Increasing returns to scale probably play an especially large role in the trade in manufactured goods between advanced countries, which is about 25% of the total value of world trade.

In our supply and demand analysis in the next section, we'll consider incomplete specialization by a country to be the norm. We should emphasize, however, that the fact that countries often incompletely specialize does not in any way change the conclusion that there are gains from trade.

Differences in Technology In the 1970s and 1980s, Japan became by far the world's largest exporter of automobiles, selling large numbers to the United States and the rest of the world. Japan's comparative advantage in automobiles wasn't the result of climate. Nor can it easily be attributed to differences in factor endowments: aside from a scarcity of land, Japan's mix of available factors is quite similar to that in other advanced countries. Instead, Japan's comparative advantage in automobiles was based on the superior production techniques developed by its manufacturers, which allowed them to produce more cars with a given amount of labor and capital than their American or European counterparts.

Japan's comparative advantage in automobiles was a case of comparative advantage caused by differences in technology — the techniques used in production.

The causes of differences in technology are somewhat mysterious. Sometimes they seem to be based on knowledge accumulated through experience — for example, Switzerland's comparative advantage in watches reflects a long tradition of watchmaking. Sometimes they are the result of a set of innovations that for some reason occur in one country but not in others.

Technological advantage, however, is often transitory. By adopting *lean production* (techniques designed to improve manufacturing productivity through increased efficiency), U.S. auto manufacturers closed much of the gap in productivity with their Japanese competitors. Similarly, Europe's aircraft industry eventually closed a comparable gap with the U.S. aircraft industry. At any given point in time, however, differences in technology are a major source of comparative advantage.

ECONOMICS >> *in Action*
How Hong Kong Lost Its Shirts

The rise of Hong Kong was one of the most improbable-sounding economic success stories of the twentieth century. When a communist regime took over China in 1949, Hong Kong—which was at that time still a British colony—became in effect a city without a hinterland, largely cut off from economic relations with the territory just over the border. Until that point, the people of Hong Kong had made a living largely by serving as a point of entry into China. However, after the city became cut off from China, it did not languish. Instead, Hong Kong prospered to such an extent that today the city—now returned to China, but governed as a special autonomous region—has a GDP per capita comparable to that of the United States.

Much of Hong Kong's ascent was the result of its clothing industry. In 1980, Hong Kong's garment and textile sectors employed almost 450,000 workers, close to 20% of total employment on the island. These workers overwhelmingly made apparel—shirts, trousers, dresses, and more—for export, especially to the United States.

More recently, the Hong Kong clothing industry has fallen sharply—in fact, it has almost disappeared and along with it, Hong Kong's apparel exports. Figure 4 shows Hong Kong's share of U.S. apparel imports since 1989, along with the share of a relative newcomer to the industry, Bangladesh. As you can see, Hong Kong has more or less dropped off the chart, while Bangladesh's share has risen significantly.

Why did Hong Kong lose its comparative advantage in making clothing? It wasn't because the city's garment workers became less productive. Instead, it was because the city got better at other things. Apparel production is a labor-intensive, relatively low-tech industry; comparative advantage in that industry has historically always rested with poor, labor-abundant economies. Hong Kong no longer fits that description; Bangladesh does. Hong Kong's garment industry was a victim of the city's success.

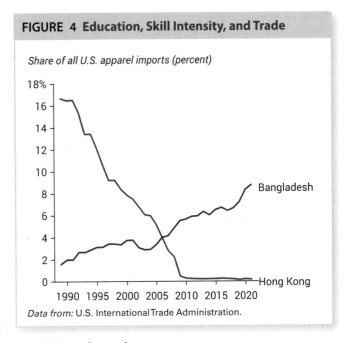
FIGURE 4 Education, Skill Intensity, and Trade

Share of all U.S. apparel imports (percent)

Data from: U.S. International Trade Administration.

>> *Check Your Understanding* 5-1
Solutions appear at back of book.

1. In the United States, the opportunity cost of 1 ton of corn is 50 bicycles. In China, the opportunity cost of 1 bicycle is 0.01 ton of corn.
   a. Determine the pattern of comparative advantage.
   b. In autarky, the United States can produce 200,000 bicycles if no corn is produced, and China can produce 3,000 tons of corn if no bicycles are produced. Draw each country's production possibility frontier assuming constant opportunity cost, with tons of corn on the vertical axis and bicycles on the horizontal axis.
   c. With trade, each country specializes its production. The United States consumes 1,000 tons of corn and 200,000 bicycles; China consumes 3,000 tons of corn and 100,000 bicycles. Indicate the production and consumption points on your diagrams, and use them to explain the gains from trade.

2. Explain the following patterns of trade using the Heckscher–Ohlin model.
   a. France exports wine to the United States, and the United States exports movies to France.
   b. Brazil exports shoes to the United States, and the United States exports shoe-making machinery to Brazil.

>> *Quick Review*

• **Imports** and **exports** account for a growing share of the U.S. economy and the economies of many other countries.

• The growth of international trade and other international linkages is known as **globalization.** Extremely high levels of international trade are known as **hyperglobalization.**

• International trade is driven by comparative advantage. **The Ricardian model of international trade** shows that trade between two countries makes both countries better off than they would be in **autarky**—that is, there are gains from international trade.

• The main sources of comparative advantage are international differences in climate, factor endowments, and technology.

• The **Heckscher–Ohlin model** shows how comparative advantage can arise from differences in factor endowments: goods differ in their **factor intensity,** and countries tend to export goods that are intensive in the factors they have in abundance.

domestic demand curve a demand curve that shows how the quantity of a good demanded by domestic consumers depends on the price of that good.

domestic supply curve a supply curve that shows how the quantity of a good supplied by domestic producers depends on the price of that good.

‖ Supply, Demand, and International Trade

Simple models of comparative advantage are helpful for understanding the fundamental causes of international trade. However, to analyze the effects of international trade at a more detailed level and to understand trade policy, it helps to return to the supply and demand model. We'll start by looking at the effects of imports on domestic producers and consumers, then turn to the effects of exports.

The Effects of Imports

Figure 5 shows the U.S. market for phones, ignoring international trade for a moment. It introduces a few new concepts: the *domestic demand curve*, the *domestic supply curve*, and the domestic or autarky price.

The **domestic demand curve** shows how the quantity of a good demanded by residents of a country depends on the price of that good. Why "domestic"? Because people living in other countries may demand the good, too. Once we introduce international trade, we need to distinguish between purchases of a good by domestic consumers and purchases by foreign consumers. So the domestic demand curve reflects only the demand of residents of our own country.

Similarly, the **domestic supply curve** shows how the quantity of a good supplied by producers inside our own country depends on the price of that good. Once we introduce international trade, we need to distinguish between the supply of domestic producers and foreign supply—supply brought in from abroad.

In autarky, with no international trade in phones, the equilibrium in this market would be determined by the intersection of the domestic demand and domestic supply curves, point A. The equilibrium price of phones would be P_A, and the equilibrium quantity of phones produced and consumed would be Q_A. As always, both consumers and producers gain from the existence of the domestic market. In autarky, consumer surplus would be equal to the area of the blue-shaded triangle in Figure 5. Producer surplus would be equal to the area of the red-shaded triangle. And total surplus would be equal to the sum of these two shaded triangles.

Now let's imagine opening up this market to imports. To do this, we must make an assumption about the supply of imports. The simplest assumption, which we will adopt here, is that unlimited quantities of phones can be purchased from abroad at a fixed price. The price at which a good can be bought or sold abroad is

---

FIGURE 5 Consumer and Producer Surplus in Autarky

In the absence of trade, the domestic price is P_A, the autarky price at which the domestic supply curve and the domestic demand curve intersect. The quantity produced and consumed domestically is Q_A. Consumer surplus is represented by the blue-shaded area, and producer surplus is represented by the red-shaded area.

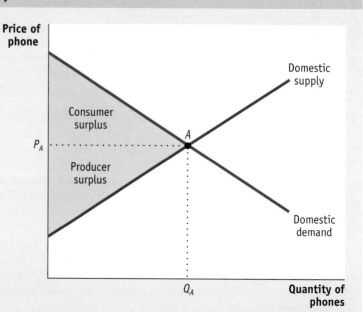

known as the **world price.** Figure 6 shows a situation in which the world price of a phone, P_W, is lower than the price of a phone that would prevail in the domestic market in autarky, P_A.

world price the price at which that good can be bought or sold abroad.

Given that the world price is below the domestic price of a phone, it is profitable for importers to buy phones abroad and resell them domestically. The imported phones increase the supply of phones in the domestic market, driving down the domestic market price. Phones will continue to be imported until the domestic price falls to a level equal to the world price.

The result is shown in Figure 6. Because of imports, the domestic price of a phone falls from P_A to P_W. The quantity of phones demanded by domestic consumers rises from Q_A to Q_D, and the quantity supplied by domestic producers falls from Q_A to Q_S. The difference between the domestic quantity demanded and the domestic quantity supplied, $Q_D - Q_S$, is filled by imports.

Now let's turn to the effects of imports on consumer surplus and producer surplus. Because imports of phones lead to a fall in their domestic price, consumer surplus rises and producer surplus falls. Figure 7 shows how this works. We label four areas: W, X, Y, and Z. The autarky consumer surplus we identified in Figure 5 corresponds to W, and the autarky producer surplus corresponds to the sum of X and Y. The fall in the domestic price to the world price leads to an increase in consumer surplus; it increases by X and Z, so consumer surplus now equals the sum of W, X, and Z. At the same time, producers lose X in surplus, so producer surplus now equals only Y.

The table in Figure 7 summarizes the changes in consumer and producer surplus when the phone market is opened to imports. Consumers gain surplus equal to the areas $X + Z$. Producers lose surplus equal to X. So the sum of producer and consumer surplus—the total surplus generated in the phone market—increases by Z. As a result of trade, consumers gain and producers lose, but the gain to consumers exceeds the loss to producers.

This is an important result. We have just shown that opening up a market to imports leads to a net gain in total surplus, which is what we should have expected given the proposition that there are gains from international trade.

However, we have also learned that although the country as a whole gains, some groups—in this case, domestic producers of phones—lose as a result of

---

FIGURE 6 The Domestic Market with Imports

Here the world price of phones, P_W, is below the autarky price, P_A. When the economy is opened to international trade, imports enter the domestic market, and the domestic price falls from the autarky price, P_A, to the world price, P_W. As the price falls, the domestic quantity demanded rises from Q_A to Q_D and the domestic quantity supplied falls from Q_A to Q_S. The difference between domestic quantity demanded and domestic quantity supplied at P_W, the quantity $Q_D - Q_S$, is filled by imports.

FIGURE 7 The Effects of Imports on Surplus

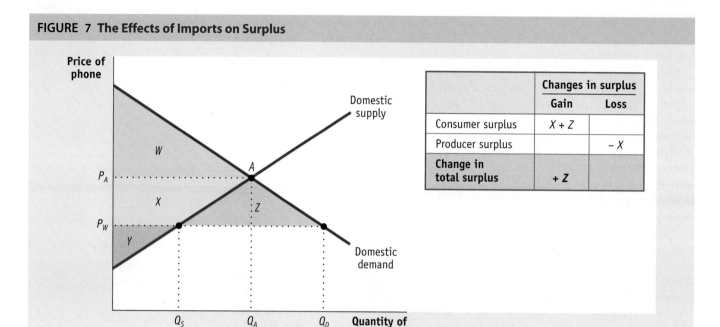

	Changes in surplus	
	Gain	Loss
Consumer surplus	$X + Z$	
Producer surplus		$-X$
Change in total surplus	**$+Z$**	

When the domestic price falls to P_W as a result of international trade, consumers gain additional surplus (areas $X + Z$) and producers lose surplus (area X). Because the gains to consumers outweigh the losses to producers, there is an increase in the total surplus in the economy as a whole (area Z).

international trade. As we'll see shortly, the fact that international trade creates losers as well as winners is crucial for understanding the politics of trade policy.

We turn next to the case in which a country exports a good.

The Effects of Exports

Figure 8 shows the effects on a country when it exports a good, in this case trucks. For this example, we assume that unlimited quantities of trucks can be sold abroad at a given world price, P_W, which is higher than the price that would prevail in the domestic market in autarky, P_A.

The higher world price makes it profitable for exporters to buy trucks domestically and sell them overseas. The purchases of domestic trucks drive the domestic price up until it is equal to the world price. As a result, the quantity demanded by domestic consumers falls from Q_A to Q_D and the quantity supplied by domestic producers rises from Q_A to Q_S. This difference between domestic production and domestic consumption, $Q_S - Q_D$, is exported.

Like imports, exports lead to an overall gain in total surplus for the exporting country but also create losers as well as winners. Figure 9 shows the effects of truck exports on producer and consumer surplus. In the absence of trade, the price of each truck would be P_A. Consumer surplus in the absence of trade is the sum of areas W and X, and producer surplus is area Y. As a result of trade, price rises from P_A to P_W, consumer surplus falls to W, and producer surplus rises to $Y + X + Z$. So producers gain $X + Z$, consumers lose X, and, as shown in the table accompanying the figure, the economy as a whole gains total surplus in the amount of Z.

We have learned, then, that imports of a particular good hurt domestic producers of that good but help domestic consumers, whereas exports of a particular good hurt domestic consumers of that good but help domestic producers. In each case, the gains are larger than the losses.

FIGURE 8 The Domestic Market with Exports

Here the world price, P_W, is greater than the autarky price, P_A. When the economy is opened to international trade, some of the domestic supply is now exported. The domestic price rises from the autarky price, P_A, to the world price, P_W. As the price rises, the domestic quantity demanded falls from Q_A to Q_D and the domestic quantity supplied rises from Q_A to Q_S. The portion of domestic production that is not consumed domestically, $Q_S - Q_D$, is exported.

FIGURE 9 The Effects of Exports on Surplus

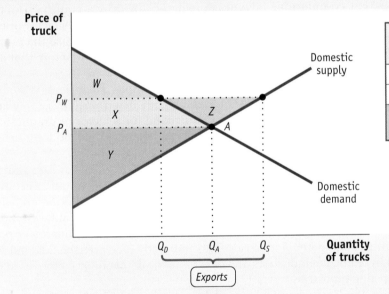

	Changes in surplus	
	Gain	**Loss**
Consumer surplus		– X
Producer surplus	X + Z	
Change in total surplus	**+ Z**	

When the domestic price rises to P_W as a result of trade, producers gain additional surplus (area X + Z) but consumers lose surplus (area X). Because the gains to producers outweigh the losses to consumers, there is an increase in the total surplus in the economy as a whole (area Z).

International Trade and Wages

So far we have focused on the effects of international trade on producers and consumers in a particular industry. For many purposes, this is a very helpful approach. However, producers and consumers are not the only parts of society affected by trade; the owners of factors of production are also affected. In particular, the owners of labor, land, and capital employed in producing goods that are exported, or goods that compete with imported goods, can be deeply affected by trade.

Moreover, the effects of trade aren't limited to just those industries that export or compete with imports because *factors of production can often move between industries*. So now we turn our attention to the long-run effects of international trade on income distribution — how a country's total income is allocated among its various factors of production.

To begin our analysis, consider the position of Mia, who is initially employed as an accountant in an industry that is shrinking as a result of growing international trade. Suppose, for example, that she works in the U.S. apparel (clothing) industry, which formerly employed millions of people but has largely been displaced by imports from low-wage countries. Mia is likely to find a new job in another industry, such as health care, which has been expanding rapidly over time. How will the move affect her earnings?

The answer is, there probably won't be much effect. According to the U.S. Bureau of Labor Statistics, accountants earn roughly the same amount in health care that they do in what's left of the apparel industry — about $65,000 a year. So we shouldn't think of Mia as a producer of apparel who is hurt by competition from imports. Instead, we should think of her as a worker with particular skills who is affected by imports — mainly by the extent to which those imports change the wages of accountants in the economy as a whole.

The wage rate of accountants is a *factor price* — the price employers have to pay for the services of a factor of production. One key question about international trade is how it affects factor prices — not just narrowly defined factors of production like accountants, but broadly defined factors such as capital, unskilled labor, and college-educated labor.

Earlier in this chapter, we described the Heckscher–Ohlin model of trade, which states that comparative advantage is determined by a country's factor endowment. This model also suggests how international trade affects factor prices in a country: compared to autarky, international trade tends to raise the prices of factors that are abundantly available and reduce the prices of factors that are scarce.

We won't work this out in detail, but the idea is simple. The prices of factors of production, like the prices of goods and services, are determined by supply and demand. If international trade increases the demand for a factor of production, that factor's price will rise; if international trade reduces the demand for a factor of production, that factor's price will fall.

Now think of a country's industries as consisting of both **exporting industries,** which produce goods and services that are sold abroad, and **import-competing industries,** which produce goods and services that compete with goods and services that are imported from abroad. Compared with autarky, international trade leads to higher production in exporting industries and lower production in import-competing industries. This indirectly increases the demand for factors used by exporting industries and decreases the demand for factors used by import-competing industries.

In addition, the Heckscher–Ohlin model shows that a country tends to export goods that are intensive in factors that are abundant in that country and to import goods that are intensive in factors that are scarce. *So international trade tends to increase the demand for factors that are more abundant in a country compared with other countries, and to decrease the demand for factors that are more scarce in a country compared with other countries. As international trade grows, the prices of abundant factors tend to rise, and the prices of scarce factors tend to fall.*

In other words, international trade tends to redistribute income toward a country's abundant factors and away from its less abundant factors.

U.S. exports tend to be human-capital-intensive (such as high-tech design and Hollywood movies) while U.S. imports tend to be unskilled-labor-intensive (such as phone assembly and clothing production). This suggests that the effect of international trade on the U.S. factor markets is to raise the wage rate of highly

exporting industries industries that produce goods and services that are sold abroad.

import-competing industries industries that produce goods and services that are also imported.

educated U.S. workers, who already have relatively high incomes, and reduce the wage rate of unskilled U.S. workers, who already have relatively low wages.

This effect has been a source of much concern in recent years. Wage inequality—the gap between the wages of high-paid and low-paid workers—has increased substantially over the past 40 years. Some economists believe that growing international trade is an important factor in that trend.

But keep in mind another phenomenon: trade reduces the income inequality between countries as poor countries improve their standard of living by exporting to rich countries.

The effects of trade on wages in the United States have generated considerable controversy in recent years. Most economists who have studied the issue agree that growing imports of labor-intensive products from newly industrializing economies, and the export of high-technology goods in return, have helped cause a widening wage gap between highly educated and less educated workers in the United States. However, most economists believe that it is only one of several forces explaining the growth in U.S. wage inequality.

ECONOMICS >> *in Action*
The China Shock

If you go into a Walmart or other large store and look at the labels on the products, it can seem as if everything is made in China these days. That's not really true, but we do buy a lot from China, which supplies almost a quarter of U.S. imported goods.

This is a fairly recent phenomenon. Imports from China, though growing, were small until the late 1990s when they took a great leap upward. In 2000, imports from China were less than 1% of U.S. national income but by 2007 they were more than 2%, after which they began to level off. The surge in Chinese imports corresponded to a change in the structure of the global economy—in particular, a transfer of production and transportation technology from advanced countries to China. China's admittance to the World Trade Organization, a global institution for regulating international trade, also contributed to the surge, known as the *China Shock*.

We have seen that international trade often creates losers as well as winners. In this case, the surge in imports from China was good for U.S. consumers, who paid less for many goods. The price of clothing, in particular, fell about 10% during the China Shock, even as overall consumer prices rose about 25%. It was, however, hard on some U.S. industries. Producers of clothing, furniture, and some electronic goods suddenly faced greatly increased competition. The losers were U.S. companies that produced those goods, many of which were forced to close plants and lay off workers.

Several estimates of the effects of the China Shock indicate that as many as a million manufacturing jobs may have been lost to imports from China from 2000 to 2007. These job losses were offset by job gains elsewhere: overall U.S. employment rose by 5 million over the period. But the communities experiencing job gains weren't the same as those experiencing job losses, and some communities were hard hit as shown in Figure 10.

FIGURE 10 The Effect of Chinese Imports on Employment in the U.S. Furniture Industry

Total nonfarm employment (index 2000 = 100)

Hickory, NC

United States

2000 2001 2002 2003 2004 2005 2006 2007

Data from: U.S. Census and the Federal Reserve Bank of St. Louis.

For example, increased imports from China were probably the main reason the U.S. furniture industry lost around 150,000 jobs between 2000 and 2007, even as overall U.S. employment rose. For the overall U.S. economy, this wasn't that big a deal: almost 2 million U.S. workers are laid off every month, even in good times. But for communities like Hickory, North Carolina, where one in six workers were employed in the furniture industry, the consequences were devastating. Not only were furniture workers laid off, but additional jobs were lost as these workers stopped spending in the local economy. As Figure 10 shows, overall employment fell sharply and stagnated in the Hickory area even as it rose in the nation as a whole.

>> *Check Your Understanding* **5-2**
Solutions appear at back of book.

1. Due to a strike by truckers, trade in food between the United States and Mexico is halted. In autarky, the price of Mexican grapes is lower than that of U.S. grapes. Using a diagram of the U.S. domestic demand curve and the U.S. domestic supply curve for grapes, explain the effect of the strike on the following.
   a. U.S. grape consumers' surplus
   b. U.S. grape producers' surplus
   c. U.S. total surplus
2. What effect do you think the strike will have on Mexican grape producers? Mexican grape pickers? Mexican grape consumers? U.S. grape pickers?

‖ The Effects of Trade Protection

Ever since David Ricardo laid out the principle of comparative advantage in the early nineteenth century, most economists have advocated **free trade.** That is, they have argued that government policy should not attempt either to reduce or to increase the levels of exports and imports that occur naturally as a result of supply and demand.

Despite the free-trade arguments of economists, however, many governments use taxes and other restrictions to limit imports. Less frequently, governments offer subsidies to encourage exports. Policies that limit imports, usually with the goal of protecting domestic producers in import-competing industries from foreign competition, are known as **trade protection** or simply as **protection.**

Let's look at the two most common protectionist policies, *tariffs* and *import quotas,* then turn to the reasons governments follow these policies.

The Effects of a Tariff

A **tariff** is a form of excise tax, levied only on sales of imported goods. For example, the U.S. government could declare that anyone bringing phones for sale into the country must pay a tariff of $100 per unit. In the distant past, tariffs were an important source of government revenue because they were relatively easy to collect. But in the modern world, tariffs are usually intended to discourage imports and protect import-competing domestic producers, and not levied as a source of government revenue.

A tariff raises both the price received by domestic producers and the price paid by domestic consumers. Suppose, for example, that our country imports phones, and a phone costs $200 on the world market. As we saw earlier, under free trade the domestic price would also be $200. But if a tariff of $100 per unit is imposed, the domestic price will rise to $300, because it won't be profitable to import phones unless the price in the domestic market is high enough to compensate importers for the cost of paying the tariff.

FIGURE 11 The Effect of a Tariff

A tariff raises the domestic price of the good from P_W to P_T. The domestic quantity demanded shrinks from Q_D to Q_{DT}, and the domestic quantity supplied increases from Q_S to Q_{ST}. As a result, imports — which had been $Q_D - Q_S$ before the tariff was imposed — shrink to $Q_{DT} - Q_{ST}$ after the tariff is imposed.

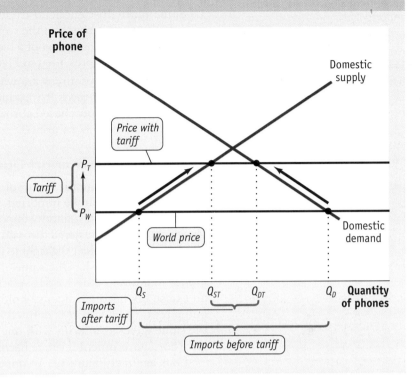

Figure 11 illustrates the effects of a tariff on imports of phones. As before, we assume that P_W is the world price of a phone. Before the tariff is imposed, imports have driven the domestic price down to P_W, so that pre-tariff domestic production is Q_S, pre-tariff domestic consumption is Q_D, and pre-tariff imports are $Q_D - Q_S$.

Now suppose that the government imposes a tariff on each phone imported. As a consequence, it is no longer profitable to import phones unless the domestic price received by the importer is greater than or equal to the world price plus the tariff. So the domestic price rises to P_T, which is equal to the world price, P_W, plus the tariff. Domestic production rises to Q_{ST}, domestic consumption falls to Q_{DT}, and imports fall to $Q_{DT} - Q_{ST}$.

A tariff, then, raises domestic prices, leading to increased domestic production and reduced domestic consumption compared to the situation under free trade. Figure 12 shows three effects:

1. The higher domestic price increases producer surplus, a gain equal to area A.
2. The higher domestic price reduces consumer surplus, a reduction equal to the sum of areas A, B, C, and D.
3. The tariff yields revenue to the government. How much revenue? The government collects the tariff — which, remember, is equal to the difference between P_T and P_W on each of the $Q_{DT} - Q_{ST}$ units imported. So total revenue is $(P_T - P_W) \times (Q_{DT} - Q_{ST})$. This is equal to area C.

The welfare effects of a tariff are summarized in the table in Figure 12. Producers gain, consumers lose, and the government gains. But consumer losses are greater than the sum of producer and government gains, leading to a net reduction in total surplus equal to areas $B + D$.

An excise tax creates inefficiency, or deadweight loss, because it prevents mutually beneficial trades from occurring. In the case of a tariff, the deadweight loss imposed on society is equal to the loss in total surplus represented by areas $B + D$.

import quota a legal limit on the quantity of a good that can be imported.

Tariffs generate deadweight losses because they create inefficiencies in two ways:

1. Some mutually beneficial trades go unexploited: some consumers who are willing to pay more than the world price, P_W, do not purchase the good, even though P_W is the true cost of a unit of the good to the economy. The cost of this inefficiency is represented in Figure 12 by area D.

2. The economy's resources are wasted on inefficient production: some producers whose cost exceeds P_W produce the good, even though an additional unit of the good can be purchased abroad for P_W. The cost of this inefficiency is represented in Figure 12 by area B.

The Effects of an Import Quota

An **import quota,** another form of trade protection, is a legal limit on the quantity of a good that can be imported. For example, a U.S. import quota on Chinese phones might limit the quantity imported each year to 50 million units. Import quotas are usually administered through licenses: a number of licenses are issued, each giving the license-holder the right to import a limited quantity of the good each year.

A quota on sales has the same effect as an excise tax, with one difference: the money that would otherwise have accrued to the government as tax revenue under an excise tax becomes license-holders' revenue under a quota—also known as quota rents. (*Quota rent* is defined in Chapter 4.) Similarly, an import quota has the same effect as a tariff, with one difference: the money that would otherwise have been government revenue becomes quota rents to license-holders.

Look again at Figure 12. An import quota that limits imports to $Q_{DT} - Q_{ST}$ will raise the domestic price of phones by the same amount as the tariff we considered

FIGURE 12 A Tariff Reduces Total Surplus

	Changes in surplus	
	Gain	Loss
Consumer surplus		$-(A + B + C + D)$
Producer surplus	A	
Government revenue	C	
Change in total surplus		$-(B + D)$

When the domestic price rises as a result of a tariff, producers gain additional surplus (area A), the government gains revenue (area C), and consumers lose surplus (areas $A + B + C + D$).

Because the losses to consumers outweigh the gains to producers and the government, the economy as a whole loses surplus (areas B and D).

previously. That is, it will raise the domestic price from P_W to P_T. However, area C will now represent quota rents rather than government revenue.

Who receives import licenses and so collects the quota rents? In the case of U.S. import protection, the answer may surprise you: the most important import licenses—mainly for clothing, and to a lesser extent for sugar—are granted to foreign governments.

Because the quota rents for most U.S. import quotas go to foreigners, the cost to the nation of such quotas is larger than that of a comparable tariff (a tariff that leads to the same level of imports). In Figure 12, the net loss to the United States from such an import quota would be equal to areas $B + C + D$, the difference between consumer losses and producer gains.

ECONOMICS >> *in Action*
No Spin: The Effects of Tariffs on Washing Machine Prices

U.S. law grants the president authority to impose tariffs unilaterally, without going to Congress, under certain circumstances. This authority was intended to allow prompt responses to trade challenges without opening up a political process that, history shows, tends to be rife with special-interest politics. In general, presidents have used this authority sparingly. However, in 2018 President Donald Trump moved to impose high tariffs on multiple countries and multiple products. One of the first of these tariffs, imposed in February 2018, was on imported washing machines. This tariff started at 20%, rising to 50% by the end of 2018. It was reduced but not eliminated in February 2019.

Some of the president's statements seemed to imply that he believed foreign exporters, not U.S. consumers, would be paying these tariffs.

Market data, however, showed rising consumer prices for the goods subjected to tariffs. Figure 13 shows the consumer price index for major household appliances—a category in which washing machines are an important component. After years of gradual decline, these prices shot up after the tariff was imposed, then came down when the tariff was reduced. If you're wondering about the surge in prices after 2020, that wasn't about tariffs but about Covid-related supply disruptions.

Which prices rose? As you would expect from the analysis in Figure 11, consumer prices of both domestically produced and imported washing machines rose. Perhaps more surprisingly, prices of some other appliances, such as dryers,

---

FIGURE 13 Washing Machine Tariffs Raised Consumer Prices

The washing machine tariff, then, played out much the same way standard analysis would have predicted. Producers of import-competing goods — U.S. appliance manufacturers — gained. Consumers were hurt.

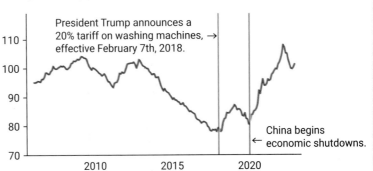

Data from: Bureau of Labor Statistics.

also rose even though they weren't subject to tariffs, probably because most consumers buy a washing machine and a dryer at the same time.

Did the tariffs also lead, as Figure 11 would predict, to higher domestic production? Yes: some foreign manufacturers relocated production to the United States, and overall employment in the industry rose. However, these job gains appear to have been small compared with the burden on consumers—about $1.5 billion in consumer costs generated only about 1,800 jobs, implying a cost per job of more than $800,000.

>> **Check Your Understanding 5-3**

Solutions appear at back of book.

1. Suppose the world price of butter is $0.50 per pound and the domestic price in autarky is $1.00 per pound. Use a diagram similar to Figure 10 to show the following.
   a. If there is free trade, domestic butter producers want the government to impose a tariff of no less than $0.50 per pound. Compare the outcome with a tariff of $0.25 per pound.
   b. What happens if a tariff greater than $0.50 per pound is imposed?
2. Suppose the government imposes an import quota rather than a tariff on butter. What quota limit would generate the same quantity of imports as a tariff of $0.50 per pound?

‖ The Political Economy of Trade Protection

We have seen that international trade produces mutual benefits to the countries that engage in it. We have also seen that tariffs and import quotas, although they produce winners as well as losers, reduce total surplus. Yet many countries continue to impose tariffs and import quotas as well as to enact other protectionist measures.

To understand why trade protection takes place, we will first look at some common justifications for protection. Then we will look at the politics of trade protection. Finally, we will look at an important feature of trade protection in today's world: tariffs and import quotas are the subject of international negotiation and are policed by international organizations.

Arguments for Trade Protection

Advocates for tariffs and import quotas offer three common arguments:

1. The *national security* argument is based on the proposition that overseas sources of goods are vulnerable to disruption in times of international conflict. A country should protect domestic suppliers of crucial goods with the aim to be self-sufficient in the production of those goods. For example, during the coronavirus pandemic of 2020, 90% of medical masks used in the United States were produced overseas. As a result, masks were in extremely short supply and rose sharply in price as countries scrambled for supplies of this critical good.

2. The *job creation* argument points to the additional jobs created in import-competing industries as a result of trade protection. Economists argue that these jobs are offset by the jobs lost elsewhere, such as industries that use imported inputs and now face higher input costs. But noneconomists don't always find this argument persuasive.

3. The *infant industry* argument, often raised in newly industrializing countries, holds that new industries require a temporary period of trade protection to get established. For example, in the 1950s many countries in Latin America imposed tariffs and import quotas on manufactured goods, in an effort to switch from their traditional role as exporters of raw materials to a new status as industrial countries.

In theory, the argument for infant industry protection can be compelling, particularly in high-tech industries that increase a country's overall skill level. Reality, however, is more complicated: it is most often industries that are politically influential that gain protection. In addition, governments tend to be poor predictors of the best emerging technologies. Finally, it is often very difficult to wean an industry from protection when it should be mature enough to stand on its own.

The Politics of Trade Protection

In reality, much trade protection has little to do with the arguments just described. Instead, it reflects the political influence of import-competing producers.

We've seen that a tariff or import quota leads to gains for import-competing producers and losses for consumers. Producers, however, usually have much more influence over trade policy decisions. The producers who compete with imports of a particular good are usually a smaller, more cohesive group than the consumers of that good.

For example, in 2018, the U.S. government imposed a 30% tariff on imports of solar panels, many of which come from China. While it helped U.S. producers, who employed about 2,000 workers, it hurt a much larger group, including tens of thousands of solar panel installers, whose business was hurt when panels became more expensive, leading to a decline in new installations. However, the voices of panel producers were heard much more clearly in Washington than the voices of concern from those who buy panels or install them.

It would be nice to say that the main reason trade protection isn't more extensive is that economists have convinced governments of the virtues of free trade. A more important reason, however, is the role of *international trade agreements.*

International Trade Agreements and the World Trade Organization

When a country engages in trade protection, it hurts two groups. We've already addressed the adverse effect on domestic consumers, but protection also hurts foreign export industries. This means that countries care about one another's trade policies: the Canadian lumber industry, for example, has a strong interest in keeping U.S. tariffs on forest products low.

Because countries care about one anothers' trade policies, they enter into **international trade agreements:** treaties in which a country promises to engage in less trade protection against the exports of another country in return for a promise by the other country to do the same for its own exports. International trade agreements are especially important as a way to head off potential **trade wars,** in which countries impose tariffs and other protectionist measures against other countries' products in an attempt to force them to make policy concessions. Most world trade is now governed by such agreements.

Some international trade agreements involve just two countries or a small group of countries. For example, in 1993 the United States, Canada, and Mexico joined together in the **North American Free Trade Agreement, or NAFTA.** By 2008, NAFTA had removed most barriers to trade among the three nations. In 2018, the countries negotiated a revised agreement, the **United States-Mexico-Canada Agreement or USMCA,** which made some changes but kept the main structure of NAFTA intact. For simplicity's sake, we will refer to the current trade agreement as NAFTA-USMCA.

Most European countries are part of an even more comprehensive agreement, the **European Union,** or **EU.** Unlike members of NAFTA-USMCA, the 27 members of the EU agree to charge the same tariffs on goods imported from non-EU countries. The EU also sets rules on policies other than trade, most notably requiring that each member nation freely accept migrants from any other member, while collecting fees from member nations to pay for things like agricultural subsidies. These

international trade agreements treaties in which a country promises to engage in less trade protection against the exports of other countries in return for a promise by other countries to do the same for its own exports.

trade war occurs when countries deliberately try to impose pain on their trading partners, as a way to extract policy concessions.

North American Free Trade Agreement (NAFTA) a trade agreement among the United States, Canada, and Mexico. Revised in 2018 as USMCA.

United States-Mexico-Canada Agreement or USMCA a revised trade agreement between the United States, Canada, and Mexico to replace NAFTA.

European Union (EU) a customs union among 27 European nations.

World Trade Organization (WTO)
an international organization of member countries that oversees international trade agreements and rules on disputes between countries over those agreements.

rules and fees are often unpopular and controversial. In June 2016, Britain held a referendum on whether to leave the EU—a proposal popularly known as *Brexit* (short for "British exit"), which was approved by a narrow majority of voters.

There are also global trade agreements covering most of the world. Such global agreements are overseen by the **World Trade Organization, or WTO,** an international organization composed of member countries—164 of them currently, accounting for the bulk of world trade. The WTO plays two roles:

1. It provides the framework for the massively complex negotiations involved in a major international trade agreement (the full text of the last major agreement, approved in 1994, was 24,000 pages long).

2. The WTO resolves disputes between its members that typically arise when one country claims that another country's policies violate its previous agreements.

An example of the WTO at work is the dispute between the United States and Brazil over U.S. subsidies to its cotton farmers. These subsidies, in the amount of $3 billion to $4 billion a year, are illegal under WTO rules. Brazil argued that they artificially reduced the price of U.S. cotton on world markets and hurt Brazilian cotton farmers. In 2005, the WTO ruled against the United States and in favor of Brazil, and the United States responded by cutting some export subsidies on cotton. However, in 2007 the WTO ruled that the United States had not done enough to fully comply, such as eliminating government loans to cotton farmers. In 2010, after Brazil threatened, in turn, to impose import tariffs on U.S.-manufactured goods, the two sides agreed to a framework for the solution to the cotton dispute.

The WTO rules do allow trade protection under certain circumstances. One such circumstance occurs when the foreign competition is "unfair" under certain technical criteria. Trade protection is also allowed as a temporary measure when a sudden surge of imports threatens to disrupt a domestic industry. For example, although both Vietnam and Thailand are members of the WTO, the United States has, on and off, imposed tariffs on shrimp imports from these countries.

The WTO is sometimes, with great exaggeration, described as a world government. In fact, it has no army, no police, and no direct enforcement power. The grain of truth in that description is that when a country joins the WTO, it agrees to accept the organization's judgments—and these judgments apply not only to tariffs and import quotas but also to domestic policies that the organization considers trade protection disguised under another name. So in joining the WTO a country does give up some of its sovereignty.

Challenges to Globalization

The forward march of globalization over the past century is generally considered a major political and economic success because it has brought rising living standards to hundreds of millions of people. But it is also true that many people, including some economists and policy makers, are having second thoughts about globalization. These second thoughts arise largely from the decline of manufacturing in richer countries and *offshore outsourcing* that jeopardizes the jobs of nonmanufacturing workers, once considered immune from foreign competition.

The Decline of Manufacturing We have seen that international trade has an effect on factor prices, particularly wages. Forty years ago, U.S. imports from poorer countries consisted mostly of raw materials and goods that depended upon the climate, like bananas and coffee beans. So U.S. wages were relatively unaffected by international trade. But that is no longer the case. Today many of the manufactured goods consumed in the United States are imported from poorer countries. As a result, international trade now has a much larger effect on income inequality in the United States.

Trade with Asia has raised the greatest concerns among those who study the effect of international trade on wage levels in rich countries. China, despite its rapid economic growth and rising wages in recent years, is still a very low-wage country compared with the United States. Its hourly compensation in manufacturing is approximately 10% of the U.S. level. Other manufacturing exporters, such as India, Bangladesh, and Vietnam, have wage levels less than half of China's. As we discussed earlier in the chapter, it's clear that imports from these countries have placed downward pressure on the wages of less skilled U.S. workers and possibly contributed to income inequality.

Outsourcing Chinese exports to the United States overwhelmingly consist of labor-intensive manufactured goods. However, some U.S. workers have also found themselves facing a new form of international competition. *Outsourcing,* in which a company hires another company to perform a task, such as running the corporate computer system, is a long-standing business practice. Until recently, however, outsourcing was normally done locally, with a company hiring another company in the same city or country.

offshore outsourcing the practice in which businesses hire people in another country to perform various tasks.

Now, modern telecommunications increasingly make it possible to engage in **offshore outsourcing,** in which businesses hire people in another country to perform various tasks. The classic example is call centers: the person answering the phone when you call a company's help line may well be in India, which has taken the lead in attracting offshore outsourcing. Offshore outsourcing has also spread to fields such as software design and even health care: the radiologist examining your X-rays, like the person giving you computer help, may be on another continent.

Offshore outsourcing has the potential to disrupt the job prospects of millions of U.S. workers.

The threat of offshore outsourcing differs from the threat posed by large-scale imports of manufactured goods from poorer countries. By and large, offshore outsourcing hits higher-skilled U.S. workers who imagined their jobs were safe from foreign competition. An example is U.S. computer programmers, many of whom have had their jobs outsourced to India or Eastern Europe. Although offshore outsourcing still accounts for a relatively small portion of international trade, some economists have warned that millions or even tens of millions of workers in rich countries may face unpleasant surprises in the not-too-distant future—workers such as bookkeepers, claims adjusters, and mortgage processors.

Do these challenges of globalization undermine the argument that international trade is a good thing? The great majority of economists would argue that the gains from trade protection still exceed the losses. However, as international trade has grown and job losses in vulnerable sectors have mounted, the politics of international trade has become increasingly difficult and has led to calls for protectionist trade policies. In this debate it's important to understand that government programs, such as unemployment benefits, easily accessible health care, and retraining projects, can reduce the opposition to free trade by helping cushion the losses of those hurt by trade.

ECONOMICS >> *in Action*
Trade War, What Is It Good For?

There are, as we've seen, a number of reasons countries sometimes impose tariffs and other restrictions on imports, and these measures often hurt other countries as well as domestic consumers. However, we generally only use the term *trade war* when hurting foreigners isn't a side effect of tariffs, but their purpose—that is, when tariffs are imposed to inflict damage on another country in an attempt to force it to make concessions of some kind.

In 2019, the United States and China engaged in a classic trade war by levying tariffs on each other's exports.

FIGURE 14 An Escalating Trade War

This really was a trade war in the classic sense. At one point, in 2020 it appeared that China might have blinked: in what the U.S. administration called a "historic" trade agreement, China promised to purchase an additional $200 billion of U.S. goods and services. By the end of 2021, however, it was clear that China had done essentially nothing to make good on that promise.

US-China tariff rates toward each other and rest of world (ROW)

••• Chinese tariffs on ROW exports
— Chinese tariffs on US exports
— US tariffs on Chinese exports ••• US tariffs on ROW exports

Data from: Peterson Institute for International Economics, Chad P. Brown

>> *Quick Review*

• The three major justifications for trade protection are national security, job creation, and the infant industry argument.

• Despite the deadweight losses, import protections are often imposed because groups representing import-competing industries are more influential than groups of consumers.

• To further trade liberalization, countries engage in **international trade agreements.** An important purpose of these agreements is to head off the possibility of **trade wars.** Some agreements are among a small number of countries, such as the **North American Free Trade Agreement (NAFTA)** and the **European Union (EU).** The current version of NAFTA is known as **NAFTA-USMCA.** The **World Trade Organization (WTO)** oversees global trade agreements and referees trade disputes between members.

• Resistance to globalization has emerged in response to a surge in imports of manufacturing goods from poorer countries and the threat of **offshore outsourcing** many jobs that were once considered safe from foreign competition.

A classic example is the "chicken war" that broke out between the United States and Europe more than half a century ago. In 1964, the United States imposed a 25% tariff on imports of light trucks—a category that today includes most pickups and SUVs. The purpose of the tariff was to put pressure on the European community to eliminate a tariff it had placed on U.S. exports of frozen chicken, which surged with the rise of factory farming. Incredibly, this dispute was never resolved: that 25% tariff remains in place.

Historically, however, trade wars in which countries try to inflict pain have been fairly rare. Before the 1930s, the United States and other countries generally ignored the effects of their trade policies on other countries; since World War II trade wars have mostly been prevented by international trade agreements.

That may, however, be changing. Since 2017, the U.S. government has imposed tariffs on a wide variety of goods and trading partners, with the explicit aim of forcing other countries to change their policies, and some of the countries have responded with tariffs of their own that are explicitly meant to cause pain here.

By far the most important part of this tariff increase was the imposition, in 2018 and 2019, of tariffs ranging from 15% to 25% on a wide range of Chinese exports to the United States. China retaliated with tariffs on some U.S. products, especially agricultural goods, in a clear attempt to raise the political costs of current U.S. policy, for example by hurting U.S. farmers. Figure 14 shows how the two countries' tariffs evolved over time.

At the time of writing, it was unclear when or how this trade war might be resolved. And the case of the "chicken war" of 1964 suggests that the effects of the trade conflict might last for a very long time.

>> *Check Your Understanding* 5-4
Solutions appear at back of book.

1. In 2017, the United States imposed a tariff on steel imports from a number of countries. Steel is an input in a large number and variety of U.S. industries. Explain why political lobbying to eliminate these tariffs is more likely to be effective than political lobbying to eliminate tariffs on consumer goods such as sugar or clothing.

2. Over the years, the WTO has increasingly found itself adjudicating trade disputes that involve not just tariffs or quota restrictions but also restrictions based on quality, health, and environmental considerations. Why do you think this has occurred? What method would you, as a WTO official, use to decide whether a quality, health, or environmental restriction is in violation of a free-trade agreement?

Li & Fung: From Guangzhou to You

Bloomberg/Getty Images

It's a very good bet that as you read this, you're wearing something manufactured in Asia. And if you are, it's also a good bet that the Hong Kong company Li & Fung was involved in getting your garment designed, produced, and shipped to your local store. From Levi's to Walmart, Li & Fung is a critical conduit from factories around the world to the shopping mall nearest you.

The company was founded in 1906 in Guangzhou, China. According to Victor Fung, the company's chairman, his grandfather's "value added" was that he spoke English, which allowed him to serve as an interpreter in business deals between Chinese and foreigners. When Mao's Communist Party seized control in mainland China, the company moved to Hong Kong. As Hong Kong's market economy took off during the 1960s and 1970s, Li & Fung grew as an export broker, bringing together Hong Kong manufacturers and foreign buyers.

However, the real transformation of the company came as Asian economies grew and changed. Hong Kong's rapid growth led to rising wages, making Li & Fung increasingly uncompetitive in garments, its main business. So the company reinvented itself: rather than being a simple broker, it became a "supply chain manager." It would not only allocate production of a good to a manufacturer, it would break the allocations of inputs down according to steps in the production process and then allocate final assembly of the good among its 12,000+ suppliers around the globe. Sometimes production would be done in sophisticated economies like those of Hong Kong or even Japan, where high wages reflect high quality and productivity. Sometimes production would be done in less advanced economies such as that of mainland China or Thailand, where labor is less productive but also cheaper.

For example, suppose you own a U.S. retail chain and want to sell garment-washed blue jeans. Rather than simply arrange for production of the jeans, Li & Fung will work with you on design, providing you with the latest production and style information such as what materials and colors are trendy. After the design has been finalized, Li & Fung will arrange for the creation of a prototype, find the most cost-effective way to manufacture it, and then place an order on your behalf. Li & Fung might secure fabric made in Korea and dyed in Taiwan, and then have the jeans assembled in Thailand or mainland China. And because production takes place in so many locations, Li & Fung provides transport logistics as well as quality control.

Li & Fung has been enormously successful. In 2023, the company had an estimated worth of over $35 billion, with offices and distribution centers in more than 50 countries.

You might ask, by the way, how Li & Fung has been affected by the U.S.-China trade war. The answer is that U.S. tariffs on Chinese exports hurt one important aspect of the company's business, but also opened other opportunities. Li & Fung has been helping U.S. customers shift to alternative sources, such as Vietnam and Bangladesh; it has also been helping customers in Europe and other locations take advantage of the low prices offered by Chinese suppliers shut out of U.S. markets.

QUESTIONS FOR THOUGHT

1. Why do you think it was profitable for Li & Fung to go beyond brokering exports to becoming a supply chain manager, breaking down the production process and sourcing the inputs from various suppliers across many countries?

2. What principle do you think underlies Li & Fung's decisions on how to allocate production of a good's inputs and its final assembly among various countries?

3. Why do you think a retailer prefers to have Li & Fung arrange international production of its jeans rather than purchase them directly from a jeans manufacturer in mainland China?

4. What is the source of Li & Fung's success? Is it based on human capital, on ownership of a natural resource, or on ownership of capital?

SUMMARY

1. International trade is of growing importance to the United States and of even greater importance to most other countries. International trade, like trade among individuals, arises from comparative advantage: the opportunity cost of producing an additional unit of a good is lower in some countries than in others. Goods and services purchased from abroad are **imports;** those sold abroad are **exports.** Foreign trade, like other economic linkages between countries, has been growing rapidly, a phenomenon called **globalization. Hyperglobalization,** the phenomenon of extremely high levels of international trade, has occurred as advances in communication and transportation technology have allowed supply chains of production to span the globe.

2. The **Ricardian model of international trade** assumes that opportunity costs are constant. It shows that there are gains from trade: two countries are better off with trade than in **autarky.**

3. In practice, comparative advantage reflects differences between countries in climate, factor endowments, and technology. The **Heckscher–Ohlin model** shows how differences in factor endowments determine comparative advantage: goods differ in **factor intensity,** and countries tend to export goods that are intensive in the factors they have in abundance.

4. The **domestic demand curve** and the **domestic supply curve** determine the price of a good in autarky. When international trade occurs, the domestic price is driven to equality with the **world price,** the price at which the good is bought and sold abroad.

5. If the world price is below the autarky price, a good is imported. This leads to an increase in consumer surplus, a fall in producer surplus, and a gain in total surplus. If the world price is above the autarky price, a good is exported. This leads to an increase in producer surplus, a fall in consumer surplus, and a gain in total surplus.

6. International trade leads to expansion in **exporting industries** and contraction in **import-competing industries.** This raises the domestic demand for abundant factors of production, reduces the demand for scarce factors, and so affects factor prices, such as wages.

7. Most economists advocate **free trade,** but in practice many governments engage in **trade protection.** The two most common forms of **protection** are tariffs and quotas. In rare occasions, export industries are subsidized.

8. A **tariff** is a tax levied on imports. It raises the domestic price above the world price, hurting consumers, benefiting domestic producers, and generating government revenue. As a result, total surplus falls. An **import quota** is a legal limit on the quantity of a good that can be imported. It has the same effects as a tariff, except that the revenue goes not to the government but to those who receive import licenses.

9. Although several popular arguments have been made in favor of trade protection, in practice the main reason for protection is probably political: import-competing industries are well organized and well informed about how they gain from trade protection, while consumers are unaware of the costs they pay. Still, U.S. trade is fairly free, mainly because of the role of **international trade agreements,** in which countries agree to reduce trade protection against one another's exports. Trade agreements also help prevent **trade wars.** The **North American Free Trade Agreement (NAFTA), USMCA,** and the **European Union (EU)** cover a small number of countries. In contrast, the **World Trade Organization (WTO)** covers a much larger number of countries, accounting for the bulk of world trade. It oversees trade negotiations and adjudicates disputes among its members.

10. Many concerns have been raised about the effects of globalization. One issue is the increase in income inequality due to the surge in manufacturing imports from poorer countries over the past 20 years particularly countries in Asia. Another concern is the increase in **offshore outsourcing,** as many jobs that were once considered safe from foreign competition have been moved abroad.

KEY TERMS

1. Evaluate the following statement: is it true, false, or uncertain? "The United States can produce more tomatoes and avocados compared to Mexico, therefore there is no need for the United States to trade with Mexico for these goods."

2. In the context of supply and demand under international trade, when will a country decide to export a particular good? Import a good? Who gains and loses under each decision?

3. In 2018, the United States announced 25% tariffs on avocados imported from Mexico. Supporters of the tariff claimed that the increased price would be paid by Mexico. Evaluate the validity of this claim. (*Hint:* Use a figure in the chapter to support your conclusion.)

1. Both Canada and the United States produce lumber and footballs with constant opportunity costs. The United States can produce either 10 tons of lumber and no footballs, or 1,000 footballs and no lumber, or any combination in between. Canada can produce either 8 tons of lumber and no footballs, or 400 footballs and no lumber, or any combination in between.

   a. Draw the U.S. and Canadian production possibility frontiers in two separate diagrams, with footballs on the horizontal axis and lumber on the vertical axis.

   b. In autarky, if the United States wants to consume 500 footballs, how much lumber can it consume? Label this point *A* in your diagram. Similarly, if Canada wants to consume 1 ton of lumber, how many footballs can it consume in autarky? Label this point *C* in your diagram.

   c. Which country has the absolute advantage in lumber production?

   d. Which country has the comparative advantage in lumber production?

   Suppose each country specializes in the good in which it has the comparative advantage, and there is trade.

   e. How many footballs does the United States produce? How much lumber does Canada produce?

   f. Is it possible for the United States to consume 500 footballs and 7 tons of lumber? Label this point *B* in your diagram. Is it possible for Canada at the same time to consume 500 footballs and 1 ton of lumber? Label this point *D* in your diagram.

2. For each of the following trade relationships, explain the likely source of the comparative advantage of each of the exporting countries.

   a. The United States exports software to Venezuela, and Venezuela exports oil to the United States.

   b. The United States exports airplanes to China, and China exports clothing to the United States.

   c. The United States exports wheat to Colombia, and Colombia exports coffee to the United States.

3. According to data from the U.S. Census Bureau, since 2000, the value of U.S. imports of men's and boy's shirts from China has more than tripled from a relatively small $227 million in 2000 to $869 million in 2018. What prediction does the Heckscher–Ohlin model make about the wages received by labor in China?

4. Shoes are labor-intensive and satellites are capital-intensive to produce. The United States has abundant capital. China has abundant labor. According to the Heckscher–Ohlin model, which good will China export? Which good will the United States export? In the United States, what will happen to the price of labor (the wage) and to the price of capital?

5. Before the North American Free Trade Agreement (NAFTA) gradually eliminated import tariffs on goods, the autarky price of tomatoes in Mexico was below the world price and in the United States was above the world price. Similarly, the autarky price of poultry in Mexico was above the world price and in the United States was below the world price. Draw diagrams with domestic supply and demand curves for each country and each of the two goods. (You will need to draw four diagrams, total.) As a result of NAFTA, the United States now imports tomatoes from Mexico and the United States now exports poultry to Mexico. How would you expect the following groups to be affected?

   a. Mexican and U.S. consumers of tomatoes. Illustrate the effect on consumer surplus in your diagram.

   b. Mexican and U.S. producers of tomatoes. Illustrate the effect on producer surplus in your diagram.

   c. Mexican and U.S. tomato workers.

   d. Mexican and U.S. consumers of poultry. Illustrate the effect on consumer surplus in your diagram.

   e. Mexican and U.S. producers of poultry. Illustrate the effect on producer surplus in your diagram.

   f. Mexican and U.S. poultry workers.

6. The accompanying table indicates the U.S. domestic demand schedule and domestic supply schedule for commercial jet airplanes. Suppose that the world price of a commercial jet airplane is $100 million.

Price of jet (millions)	Quantity of jets demanded	Quantity of jets supplied
$120	100	1,000
110	150	900
100	200	800
90	250	700
80	300	600
70	350	500
60	400	400
50	450	300
40	500	200

a. In autarky, how many commercial jet airplanes does the United States produce, and at what price are they bought and sold?

b. With trade, what will the price for commercial jet airplanes be? Will the United States import or export airplanes? How many?

7. The accompanying table shows the U.S. domestic demand schedule and domestic supply schedule for oranges. Suppose that the world price of oranges is $0.30 per orange.

Price of orange	Quantity of oranges demanded (thousands)	Quantity of oranges supplied (thousands)
$1.00	2	11
0.90	4	10
0.80	6	9
0.70	8	8
0.60	10	7
0.50	12	6
0.40	14	5
0.30	16	4
0.20	18	3

a. Draw the U.S. domestic supply curve and domestic demand curve.

b. With free trade, how many oranges will the United States import or export?

Suppose that the U.S. government imposes a tariff on oranges of $0.20 per orange.

c. How many oranges will the United States import or export after introduction of the tariff?

d. In your diagram, shade the gain or loss to the economy as a whole from the introduction of this tariff.

8. The U.S. domestic demand schedule and domestic supply schedule for oranges was given in Problem 7. Suppose that the world price of oranges is $0.30. The United States introduces an import quota of 3,000

oranges and assigns the quota rents to foreign orange exporters.

a. Draw the domestic demand and supply curves.

b. What will the domestic price of oranges be after introduction of the quota?

c. Illustrate the area representing the quota rent on your graph. What is the value of the quota rents that foreign exporters of oranges receive?

9. The Observatory of Economic Complexity (OEC) is a data visualization that models international trade data among countries. Go to the website at atlas.media.mit.edu to answer the following questions.

a. Start by entering United States in the search bar. After selecting United States, scroll down and find historical data. In 2020, what was the largest exported good (in dollars) for the United States? What was the value of exports for "Planes, Helicopters, and/or Spacecraft"? What was the largest imported good for the United States?

b. Repeat the steps above for Brazil. In 2020, what was the largest exported good for Brazil? What was the value of exports for, "Planes, Helicopters, and/or Spacecraft"? What was the largest imported good for the Brazil?

c. On the left sidebar click on the link "Explore on Visualization Page." On the new page, in the left sidebar select "Exports," under "Country" select "Brazil," under "Partner" select "United States," and then "Build Visualization." What is the total value of Brazilian exports to the United States? What is Brazil's largest exported good (in dollars) compared to the United States? What type of goods does Brazil generally export to the United States? What is the value of exports related to "Planes, Helicopters, and/or Spacecraft"?

d. Now repeat the steps from part c for exports from the United States to Brazil. Change "Country" to "United States," change "Partner" to "Brazil," and select "Build Visualization." What is the total value of exports from the United States to Brazil? What is the United States' largest export (in dollars) to Brazil? What types of goods does the United States export to Brazil? What is the value of exports related to "Planes, Helicopters, and/or Spacecraft"?

10. Comparative advantage creates an opportunity for less productive economies like Bangladesh to trade with more productive economies like the United States. Using the OEC website from Problem 9, how much did Bangladesh export to the United States? What was its largest export to the United States? In general, what type of goods did Bangladesh export to the United States?

11. Once again, using the OEC website from Problems 9 and 10, identify which country has a comparative advantage for each of the following goods. For each good, include the country's share of global exports and the total dollar value of that share.

a. Computers

b. Maple syrup

c. Soybeans

d. Cocoa beans

e. Diamonds

12. Over the past five years, the United States has become the world's largest producer of natural gas. But gas producers have struggled to find methods to liquefy natural gas so that it can be exported across the Atlantic. Enter Cheniere Energy, a Houston-based natural gas company that has developed a natural gas export terminal located on the Sabine Pass leading into the Gulf of Mexico. The terminal will give U.S. companies access to markets all over the world.

   a. Explain how the development of a natural gas export terminal will affect the market for natural gas in the United States.

   b. Assuming natural gas prices are $3.00 per BTU, illustrate the effect of an export terminal on the demand for natural gas in the United States. Explain your findings.

   c. Assuming natural gas prices in Europe are $6.00 per BTU, draw a diagram to illustrate how the development of a natural gas terminal in the United States will affect supply and demand in the natural gas market for Europe. Explain your findings.

   d. How will the exporting of natural gas from the United States to Europe affect consumers and producers in both places?

13. 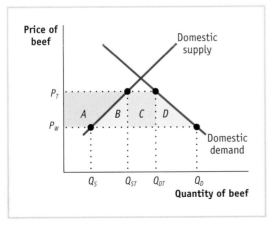 Access the Discovering Data exercise for Chapter 5, Problem 13 online to answer the following questions.

   a. Rank the states in order of exports to China. Rank in order of most to fewest exports.

   b. Calculate the growth in exports from 2002 to 2015 for each state.

   c. As a percent of total exports, rank the states in order of most to fewest exports to China.

   d. Explain the pattern of trade with China.

14. The accompanying diagram illustrates the U.S. domestic demand curve and domestic supply curve for beef.

The world price of beef is P_W. The United States currently imposes an import tariff on beef, so the price of beef is P_T. Congress decides to eliminate the tariff. In terms of the areas marked in the diagram, answer the following questions.

   a. With the elimination of the tariff what is the gain/loss in consumer surplus?

   b. With the elimination of the tariff what is the gain/loss in producer surplus?

   c. With the elimination of the tariff what is the gain/loss to the government?

   d. With the elimination of the tariff what is the gain/loss to the economy as a whole?

15. As the United States has opened up to trade, it has lost many of its low-skill manufacturing jobs, but it has gained jobs in high-skill industries, such as the software industry. Explain whether the United States as a whole has been made better off by trade.

16. The United States is highly protective of its agricultural (food) industry, imposing import tariffs, and sometimes quotas, on imports of agricultural goods. This chapter presented three arguments for trade protection. For each argument, discuss whether it is a valid justification for trade protection of U.S. agricultural products.

17. In World Trade Organization (WTO) negotiations, if a country agrees to reduce trade barriers (tariffs or quotas), it usually refers to this as a *concession* to other countries. Do you think that this terminology is appropriate?

18. Producers in import-competing industries often make the following argument: "Other countries have an advantage in production of certain goods purely because workers abroad are paid lower wages. In fact, U.S. workers are much more productive than foreign workers. So import-competing industries need to be protected." Is this a valid argument? Explain your answer.

19. Assume Saudi Arabia and the United States face the production possibilities for oil and cars shown in the accompanying table.

Saudi Arabia		United States	
Quantity of oil (millions of barrels)	Quantity of cars (millions)	Quantity of oil (millions of barrels)	Quantity of cars (millions)
0	4	0	10.0
200	3	100	7.5
400	2	200	5.0
600	1	300	2.5
800	0	400	0

   a. What is the opportunity cost of producing a car in Saudi Arabia? In the United States? What is the opportunity cost of producing a barrel of oil in Saudi Arabia? In the United States?

Price of beef / Domestic supply / P_T / A B C D / P_W / Domestic demand / Q_S Q_{ST} Q_{DT} Q_D / **Quantity of beef**

b. Which country has the comparative advantage in producing oil? In producing cars?

c. Suppose that in autarky, Saudi Arabia produces 200 million barrels of oil and 3 million cars; and suppose that the United States produces 300 million barrels of oil and 2.5 million cars. Without trade, can Saudi Arabia produce more oil *and* more cars? Without trade, can the United States produce more oil *and* more cars?

Suppose now that each country specializes in the good in which it has the comparative advantage, and the two countries trade. Also assume that for each country the value of imports must equal the value of exports.

d. What is the total quantity of oil produced? What is the total quantity of cars produced?

e. Is it possible for Saudi Arabia to consume 400 million barrels of oil and 5 million cars and for the United States to consume 400 million barrels of oil and 5 million cars?

f. Suppose that, in fact, Saudi Arabia consumes 300 million barrels of oil and 4 million cars and the United States consumes 500 million barrels of oil and 6 million cars. How many barrels of oil does the United States import? How many cars does the United States export? Suppose a car costs $10,000 on the world market. How much, then, does a barrel of oil cost on the world market? ∎

Consumer and Producer Surplus

The concepts of *consumer surplus* and *producer surplus* are extremely useful for analyzing a wide variety of economic issues. They let us calculate how much benefit producers and consumers receive from the existence of a market. They also allow us to calculate how the welfare of consumers and producers is affected by changes in market prices. Such calculations play a crucial role in evaluating economic policies, and they are especially useful in understanding the effects of trade.

All we need in order to calculate consumer surplus are the demand and supply curves for a good. That is, the supply and demand model isn't just a model of how a competitive market works—it's also a model of how much consumers and producers gain from participating in that market. Our starting point is the market for used sneakers. More importantly for us, it is useful for developing the concepts of consumer and producer surplus.

Consumer Surplus and the Demand Curve

Let's look at the market for used sneakers, starting with the buyers. The key point, as we'll see in a minute, is that the demand curve is derived from their tastes or preferences—and that those same preferences also determine how much they gain from the opportunity to buy used sneakers.

Willingness to Pay and the Demand Curve

A used pair of Nike Dunks is not as good as a new pair. The soles may be a little worn, and they might be a bit smelly. How much this bothers you depends on your preferences. Some potential buyers would prefer to buy the used pair even if it is only slightly cheaper than a new one; others would buy the used pair only if it is considerably cheaper.

Let's define a potential buyer's **willingness to pay** as the maximum price at which they would buy a good, in this case a used pair of sneakers. An individual won't buy the good if it costs more than this amount but is eager to do so if it costs less. If the price is just equal to an individual's willingness to pay, they are indifferent between buying and not buying.

Table A-1 shows five potential buyers of a used pair of sneakers that costs $100 new, listed in order of their willingness to pay. At one extreme is Aisha, who will buy a used pair even if the price is as high as $59. Ben is less willing to have a

Potential buyer	Willingness to pay	Price paid	Individual consumer surplus = Willingness to pay – Price paid
Aisha	$59	$30	$29
Ben	45	30	15
Chloe	35	30	5
Darsh	25	—	—
Elena	10	—	—
All buyers			**Total consumer surplus = $49**

TABLE A-1 Consumer Surplus If the Price of a Used Pair of Sneakers = $30

willingness to pay the maximum price at which a consumer is prepared to pay for a good.

individual consumer surplus the net gain to an individual buyer from the purchase of a good; equal to the difference between the buyer's willingness to pay and the price paid.

total consumer surplus the sum of the individual consumer surpluses of all the buyers of a good in a market.

consumer surplus a term often used to refer both to individual consumer surplus and to total consumer surplus.

used pair and will buy one only if the price is $45 or less. Chloe is willing to pay only $35 and Darsh, only $25. And Elena, who really doesn't like the idea of used sneakers, will buy a pair only if it costs no more than $10.

How many of these five students will actually buy a pair of used sneakers? It depends on the price. If the price of a used pair is $55, only Aisha buys one; if the price is $40, Aisha and Ben both buy used pairs, and so on. So the information in the table on willingness to pay also defines the *demand schedule* for used sneakers.

Willingness to Pay and Consumer Surplus

Suppose that the SneakersX website has several pairs of used sneakers available at a price of $30. In that case Aisha, Ben, and Chloe will buy used pairs. Do they gain from their purchases, and if so, how much?

The answer, shown in Table A-1, is that each student who purchases a pair does achieve a net gain but that the amount of the gain differs among students.

Aisha would have been willing to pay $59, so her net gain is $59 – $30 = $29. Ben would have been willing to pay $45, so his net gain is $45 – $30 = $15. Chloe would have been willing to pay $35, so her net gain is $35 – $30 = $5. Darsh and Elena, however, won't be willing to buy a used pair at a price of $30, so they neither gain nor lose.

The net gain that a buyer achieves from the purchase of a good is called that buyer's **individual consumer surplus.** What we learn from this example is that whenever a buyer pays a price less than their willingness to pay, the buyer achieves some individual consumer surplus.

The sum of the individual consumer surpluses achieved by all the buyers of a good is known as the **total consumer surplus** achieved in the market. In Table A-1, the total consumer surplus is the sum of the individual consumer surpluses achieved by Aisha, Ben, and Chloe: $29 + $15 + $5 = $49.

Economists often use the term **consumer surplus** to refer to both individual and total consumer surplus. We will follow this practice; it will always be clear in context whether we are referring to the consumer surplus achieved by an individual or by all buyers.

Total consumer surplus can be represented graphically. As explained in Chapter 3, we can use the demand schedule to derive the market demand curve shown in Figure A-1. Because we are considering only a small number of consumers, this curve doesn't look like the smooth demand curves of Chapter 3, where markets contained hundreds or thousands of consumers. Instead, this demand curve is stepped, with alternating horizontal and vertical segments.

Each horizontal segment or step corresponds to one potential buyer's willingness to pay. Each step in that demand curve is one pair of sneakers wide and represents one consumer. For example, the height of Aisha's step is $59, her willingness to pay. This step forms the top of a rectangle, with $30—the price she actually pays for a pair of sneakers—forming the bottom. The area of Aisha's rectangle, ($59 – $30) × 1 = $29, is her consumer surplus from purchasing one pair at $30. So the individual consumer surplus Aisha gains is the *area of the dark blue rectangle* shown in Figure A-1.

In addition to Aisha, Ben, and Chloe will also each buy a pair when the price is $30. Like Aisha, they benefit from their purchases, though not as much, because they each have a lower willingness to pay. Figure A-1 also shows the consumer surplus gained by Ben and Chloe; again, this can be measured by the areas of the appropriate rectangles. Darsh and Elena, because they do not buy sneakers at a price of $30, receive no consumer surplus.

The total consumer surplus achieved in this market is just the sum of the individual consumer surpluses received by Aisha, Ben, and Chloe. So total consumer surplus is equal to the combined area of the three rectangles—the entire shaded area in Figure A-1. Another way to say this: total consumer surplus is equal to the area below the demand curve but above the price.

FIGURE A-1 Consumer Surplus in the Used Sneakers Market

At a price of $30, Aisha, Ben, and Chloe each buy a pair of sneakers but Darsh and Elena do not. Aisha, Ben, and Chloe receive individual consumer surpluses equal to the difference between their willingness to pay and the price, illustrated by the areas of the shaded rectangles. Both Darsh and Elena have a willingness to pay less than $30, so they are unwilling to buy a pair in this market; they receive zero consumer surplus. The total consumer surplus is given by the entire shaded area — the sum of the individual consumer surpluses of Aisha, Ben, and Chloe — equal to $29 + $15 + $5 = $49.

This illustrates the following general principle: *The total consumer surplus generated by purchases of a good at a given price is equal to the area below the demand curve but above that price.* The same principle applies regardless of the number of consumers.

For large markets, such as the market for smartphones that was used in the chapter, this graphical representation of consumer surplus becomes extremely helpful. Consider, for example, the sales of iPhones to millions of potential buyers. Each potential buyer has a maximum price that they are willing to pay. With so many potential buyers, the demand curve will be smooth, like the one shown in Figure A-2.

FIGURE A-2 Consumer Surplus

The demand curve for iPhones is smooth because there are many potential buyers. At a price of $500, 1 million iPhones are demanded. The consumer surplus at this price is equal to the shaded area: the area below the demand curve but above the price. This is the total net gain to consumers generated from buying and consuming iPhones when the price is $500.

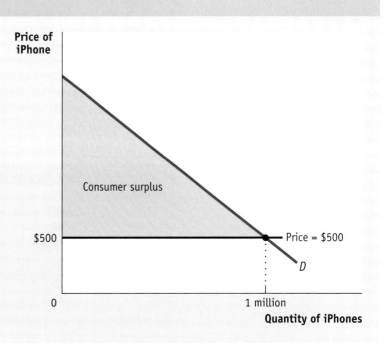

cost (of seller) the lowest price at which a seller is willing to sell a good.

Suppose that at a price of $500, a total of 1 million iPhones are purchased. How much do consumers gain from being able to buy those 1 million iPhones? We could answer that question by calculating the consumer surplus of each individual buyer and then adding these numbers up to arrive at a total. But it is much easier just to look at Figure A-2 and use the fact that total consumer surplus is equal to the shaded area. As in our original example, consumer surplus is equal to the area below the demand curve but above the price. (To refresh your memory on how to calculate the area of a right triangle, see the appendix to Chapter 2.)

Producer Surplus and the Supply Curve

Just as some buyers of a good would have been willing to pay more for their purchase than the price they actually pay, some sellers of a good would have been willing to sell it for less than the price they actually receive. So just as there are consumers who receive consumer surplus from buying in a market, there are producers who receive producer surplus from selling in a market.

Cost and Producer Surplus

Consider a group of sneaker aficionados who are potential sellers of used. Because they have different preferences, the various potential sellers differ in the price at which they are willing to sell their sneakers. Table A-2 shows the prices at which several different students would be willing to sell. Andrew is willing to sell a pair as long as he can get at least $5; Brianna won't sell unless she can get at least $15; Carlos, unless he can get $25; Desiree, unless she can get $35; Eli, unless he can get $45.

The lowest price at which a potential seller is willing to sell has a special name in economics: it is called the seller's **cost.** So Andrew's cost is $5, Brianna's is $15, and so on.

Using the term *cost*, which people normally associate with the monetary cost of producing a good, may sound a little strange when applied to sellers of used sneakers. The students don't have to manufacture the shoes, so it doesn't cost the student who sells used sneakers anything to make that pair available for sale, does it?

Yes, it does. A student who sells a pair of sneakers won't have it later, as part of their personal collection. So there is an *opportunity* cost to selling sneakers, even if the owner doesn't wish to wear them anymore. And remember that one of the basic principles of economics is that the true measure of the cost of doing something is always its opportunity cost. That is, the real cost of something is what you must give up to get it.

So it is good economics to talk of the minimum price at which someone will sell a good as the "cost" of selling that good, even if they doesn't spend any money to make the good available for sale. Of course, in most real-world markets the sellers are also those who produce the good and therefore *do* spend money to make

TABLE A-2 Producer Surplus When the Price of a Used Pair of Sneakers = $30			
Potential seller	Cost	Price received	Individual producer surplus = Price received − Cost
Andrew	$5	$30	$25
Brianna	15	30	15
Carlos	25	30	5
Desiree	35	—	—
Eli	45	—	—
All sellers			Total producer surplus = $45

it available for sale. In this case, the cost of making the good available for sale includes monetary costs, but it may also include other opportunity costs.

Getting back to the example, suppose that Andrew sells his pair for $30. Clearly he has gained from the transaction: he would have been willing to sell for only $5, so he has gained $25. This net gain, the difference between the price he actually gets and his cost—the minimum price at which he would have been willing to sell—is known as his **individual producer surplus.**

As in the case of consumer surplus, we can add the individual producer surpluses of sellers to calculate the **total producer surplus,** the total net gain to all sellers in the market. Economists use the term **producer surplus** to refer to either individual or total producer surplus. Table A-2 shows the net gain to each of the students who would sell a used pair of sneakers at a price of $30: $25 for Andrew, $15 for Brianna and $5 for Carlos. The total producer surplus is $25 + $15 + $5 = $45.

As with consumer surplus, the producer surplus gained by those who sell sneakers can be represented graphically. Just as we derived the demand curve from the willingness to pay of different consumers, we derive the supply curve from the cost of different producers. The step-shaped curve in Figure A-3 shows the supply curve implied by the cost shown in Table A-2. Each step in that supply curve is one pair wide and represents one seller. The height of Andrew's step is $5, his cost. This forms the bottom of a rectangle, with $30, the price he actually receives for his pair, forming the top. The area of this rectangle, ($30 – $5) × 1 = $25, is his producer surplus. So the producer surplus Andrew gains from selling his pair of sneakers is the *area of the red rectangle* shown in the figure.

Let's assume that on the SneakersX website there are willing buyers for all the used sneakers that sellers are willing to sell at a price of $30. Then, in addition to Andrew, Brianna and Carlos will also sell their pairs. They will also benefit from their sales, though not as much as Andrew, because they have higher costs. Andrew, as we have seen, gains $25. Brianna gains a smaller amount: since her cost is $15, she gains only $15. Carlos gains even less, only $5.

Again, as with consumer surplus, we have a general rule for determining the total producer surplus from sales of a good: *The total producer surplus from sales of a good at a given price is the area above the supply curve but below that price.*

individual producer surplus the net gain to an individual seller from selling a good; equal to the difference between the price received and the seller's cost.

total producer surplus the sum of the individual producer surpluses of all the sellers of a good in a market.

producer surplus a term often used to refer both to individual producer surplus and to total producer surplus.

FIGURE A-3 Producer Surplus in the Used Sneaker Market

At a price of $30, Andrew, Brianna, and Carlos each sell a pair of sneakers but Desiree and Eli do not. Andrew, Brianna, and Carlos get individual producer surpluses equal to the difference between the price and their cost, illustrated here by the shaded rectangles. Desiree and Eli each have a cost that is greater than the price of $30, so they are unwilling to sell a pair of sneakers and so receive zero producer surplus. The total producer surplus is given by the entire shaded area, the sum of the individual producer surpluses of Andrew, Brianna, and Carlos, equal to $25 + $15 + $5 = $45.

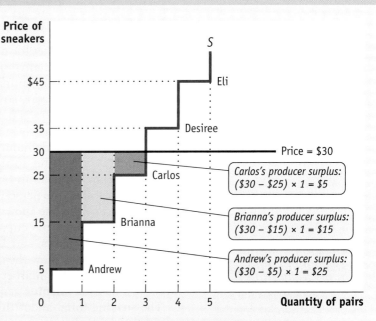

FIGURE A-4 Producer Surplus

Here is the supply curve for wheat. At a price of $5 per bushel, farmers supply 1 million bushels. The producer surplus at this price is equal to the shaded area: the area above the supply curve but below the price. This is the total gain to producers — farmers in this case — from supplying their product when the price is $5.

This rule applies both to examples like the one shown in Figure A-3, where there are a small number of producers and a step-shaped supply curve, and to more realistic examples, where there are many producers and the supply curve is smooth.

Consider, for example, the supply of wheat. Figure A-4 shows how producer surplus depends on the price per bushel. Suppose that, as shown in the figure, the price is $5 per bushel and farmers supply 1 million bushels. What is the benefit to the farmers from selling their wheat at a price of $5? Their producer surplus is equal to the shaded area in the figure—the area above the supply curve but below the price of $5 per bushel.

∥ The Gains from Trade

Let's return to the market for used sneakers on the website SneakersX. But now let's assume there are many potential buyers and sellers, so the market is competitive. Let's line up incoming consumers who are potential buyers in order of their willingness to pay, so that the person with the highest willingness to pay for a pair of sneakers is potential buyer number 1, the person with the next highest willingness to pay is number 2, and so on. Then we can use their willingness to pay to derive a demand curve like the one in Figure A-5.

Similarly, we can line up those who already own pairs of sneakers and are therefore potential sellers in order of their cost—starting with the person with the lowest cost, then the person with the next lowest cost, and so on—to derive a supply curve like the one shown in the same figure.

As we have drawn the curves, the market reaches equilibrium at a price of $30 per pair of sneakers, and 1,000 pairs are bought and sold at that price. The two shaded triangles show the consumer surplus (blue) and the producer surplus (red) generated by this market. The sum of consumer and producer surplus is known as the **total surplus** generated in a market.

The striking thing about this picture is that both consumers and producers gain—that is, both consumers and producers are better off because there is a

total surplus the total net gain to consumers and producers from trading in a market; it is the sum of the producer surplus and the consumer surplus.

FIGURE A-5 Total Surplus

In the market for used sneakers, the equilibrium price is $30 and the equilibrium quantity is 1,000 pairs. Consumer surplus is given by the blue area, the area below the demand curve but above the price. Producer surplus is given by the red area, the area above the supply curve but below the price. The sum of the blue and the red areas is total surplus, the total benefit to society from the production and consumption of the good.

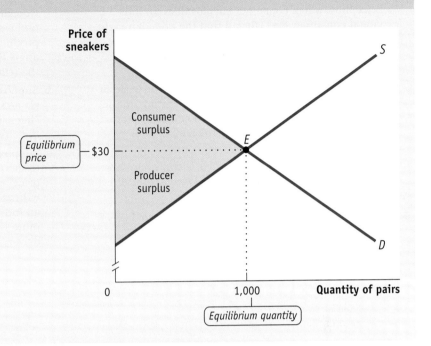

market in this good. But this should come as no surprise—it illustrates another core principle of economics that you learned about in earlier chapters: *There are gains from trade.* These gains from trade are the reason everyone is better off participating in a market economy than they would be if each individual tried to be self-sufficient.

PROBLEMS

1. Determine the amount of consumer surplus generated in each of the following situations.

   a. Bo goes to the clothing store to buy a new T-shirt, for which he is willing to pay up to $10. He picks out one he likes with a price tag of exactly $10. When he is paying for it, he learns that the T-shirt has been discounted by 50%.

   b. Alberto goes to the music store hoping to find a used copy of Nirvana's *Nevermind* for up to $30. The store has one copy of the record selling for $30, which he purchases.

   c. After soccer practice, Stephany is willing to pay $2 for a bottle of mineral water. The 7-Eleven sells mineral water for $2.25 per bottle, so she declines to purchase it.

2. Determine the amount of producer surplus generated in each of the following situations.

   a. Conner lists his old Lionel electric trains on eBay. He sets a minimum acceptable price, known as his reserve price, of $75. After five days of bidding, the final high bid is exactly $75. He accepts the bid.

   b. So-Hee advertises her car for sale in the used-car section of the student newspaper for $2,000, but she

is willing to sell the car for any price higher than $1,500. The best offer she gets is $1,200, which she declines.

   c. Sanjay likes his job so much that he would be willing to do it for free. However, his annual salary is $80,000.

3. You are the manager of Fun World, a small amusement park. The accompanying diagram shows the demand curve of a typical customer at Fun World.

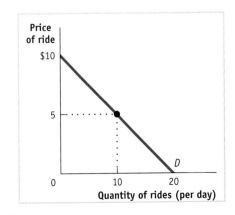

a. Suppose that the price of each ride is $5. At that price, how much consumer surplus does an individual consumer get? (Recall that the area of a right triangle is ½ × the height of the triangle × the base of the triangle.)

b. Suppose that Fun World considers charging an admission fee, even though it maintains the price of each ride at $5. What is the maximum admission fee it could charge? (Assume that all potential customers have enough money to pay the fee.)

c. Suppose that Fun World lowered the price of each ride to zero. How much consumer surplus does an individual consumer get? What is the maximum admission fee Fun World could charge?

4. The accompanying diagram illustrates a taxi driver's individual supply curve (assume that each taxi ride is the same distance).

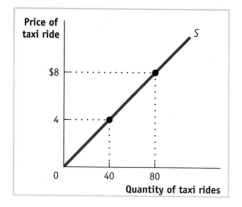

a. Suppose the city sets the price of taxi rides at $4 per ride, and at $4 the taxi driver is able to sell as many taxi rides as they desire. What is this taxi driver's producer surplus? (Recall that the area of a right triangle is ½ × the height of the triangle × the base of the triangle.)

b. Suppose that the city keeps the price of a taxi ride set at $4, but it decides to charge taxi drivers a "licensing fee." What is the maximum licensing fee the city could extract from this taxi driver?

c. Suppose that the city allowed the price of taxi rides to increase to $8 per ride. Again assume that, at this price, the taxi driver sells as many rides as they are willing to offer. How much producer surplus does an individual taxi driver now get? What is the maximum licensing fee the city could charge this taxi driver?

6

Macroeconomics: The Big Picture

GREEK TRAGEDIES

CONSTANTINE KAKOYIANNIS, an engineer, grew up in Greece. But these days he lives in Dusseldorf, Germany. He's one of many Greeks who have settled there since 2010, so many that Dusseldorf has become known as a "mini-Athens."

Why did he and so many others leave home? Because there were no jobs. In 2016, when Kakoyiannis left, Greece's *unemployment rate* — the percentage of those looking for work who couldn't find it — was 24%. As of December 2022, unemployment in Greece had fallen but was still 12.7%. For the sake of comparison, in the United States the unemployment rate was only 3.5%.

Yet Greece hasn't always had sky-high unemployment. In 2007 the unemployment rate was only about 8%. Greece was still poorer than northern European countries like Germany, but it had been doing relatively well, and Greeks were feeling optimistic about their prospects.

Greek citizens in Germany, where the jobs are.

Felix Brüggemann/The New York Times/Redux Pictures

Then Greece plunged into a severe economic downturn — a *recession* — which led to a collapse in employment. Many businesses went bust and people suffered economic hardship. And Greece wasn't alone. After 2007, much of the world, including the United States, plunged into a deep recession, which came to be known as the *Great Recession*. By the beginning of 2023, the United States had not only recovered from the Great Recession but also the economic shutdown from the Covid-19 pandemic, while some parts of Europe, Greece in particular, had not.

Yet, as bad as things were during the Great Recession, the global economy had seen much worse. Beginning in 1929, a severe global economic slump known as the *Great Depression* hit and lasted over a decade, until the start of World War II in 1940. The Great Recession was less severe than the Great Depression for many reasons. But one significant factor was that economists had learned something about what to do from the earlier catastrophe. As the Great Depression began in 1929, political leaders and their economic advisers had no idea what policies might help or hinder recovery.

Microeconomics, which is concerned with the consumption and production decisions of individual consumers and producers and with the allocation of scarce resources among industries, was already a well-developed branch of economics. But *macroeconomics,* which focuses on the behavior of the economy as a whole, was still in its infancy. In contrast, by 2007 macroeconomics had advanced enough that economists knew what needed to be done when the Great Recession hit.

In normal economic times, when there is no recession or depression, workers who lose their jobs are able to find employment somewhere else. However, the Great Depression was no normal time: in the United States the unemployment rate hit 23% and the value of the economy's output (GDP) fell by 26%. Economists realized that they needed to understand the nature of the catastrophe that had overtaken the United States and much of the rest of the world in order to extricate themselves, as well as to learn how to avoid such economic disasters in the future. To this day, the effort to understand economic slumps and find ways to prevent them is at the core of macroeconomics. Over time, however, macroeconomics has broadened its reach to encompass a number of other subjects, such as long-run economic growth, inflation, and international macroeconomics.

This chapter offers an overview of macroeconomics. We start with a general description of the difference between macroeconomics and microeconomics, then briefly describe some of the field's major concerns. •

WHAT YOU WILL LEARN

- What is the difference between macroeconomics and microeconomics?
- What are **business cycles** and why do policy makers try to diminish their severity?
- How does **long-run economic growth** determine a country's standard of living?
- What are **inflation** and **deflation,** and why is **price stability** preferred?
- Why does **international macroeconomics** matter, and how do economies interact through **trade deficits** and **trade surpluses?**

The Nature of Macroeconomics

Macroeconomics differs from microeconomics by focusing on the behavior of the economy as a whole.

Macroeconomic Questions

Table 1 lists some typical economic questions from the perspectives of microeconomists in the left column, and macroeconomists in the right column. By comparing the questions, you can begin to get a sense of the difference between microeconomics and macroeconomics.

TABLE 1 Microeconomic versus Macroeconomic Questions	
Microeconomic Questions	**Macroeconomic Questions**
Should I go to business school or take a job right now?	How many people are employed in the economy as a whole this year?
What determines the salary Google offers to Cherie Camajo, a new MBA?	What determines the overall salary levels paid to workers in a given year?
What determines the cost to a university or college of offering a new course?	What determines the overall level of prices in the economy as a whole?
What government policies should be adopted to make it easier for low-income students to attend college?	What government policies should be adopted to promote employment and growth in the economy as a whole?
What determines whether Citibank opens a new office in Shanghai?	What determines the overall trade in goods, services, and financial assets between the United States and the rest of the world?
Why was there a shortage of toilet paper during the coronavirus pandemic?	How did a fall in consumer spending during the pandemic affect overall employment?

As these questions illustrate, microeconomics focuses on how decisions are made by individuals and firms and the consequences of those decisions. For example, we use microeconomics to determine how much it would cost a university or college to offer a new course, including the instructor's salary, the cost of class materials, and so on. The school can then decide whether to offer the course by weighing the costs and benefits.

Macroeconomics, in contrast, examines the *overall* behavior of the economy—how the actions of all the individuals and firms in the economy interact to produce a particular economy-wide level of economic performance. For example, macroeconomics is concerned with the general level of prices in the economy and how high or how low that level is relative to the general level of prices last year, rather than with the price of one particular good or service.

You might imagine that macroeconomic questions can be answered simply by adding up microeconomic answers. For example, the model of supply and demand introduced in Chapter 3 tells us how the equilibrium price of an individual good or service is determined in a competitive market. So you might think that applying supply and demand analysis to every good and service in the economy, then summing the results, is the way to understand the overall level of prices in the economy as a whole.

But that is incorrect: although basic concepts such as supply and demand are essential to macroeconomics, answering macroeconomic questions requires an additional set of tools and an expanded frame of reference.

Macroeconomics: The Whole Is Greater Than the Sum of Its Parts

If you drive on a highway, you probably know what a rubbernecking traffic jam is and why it is so annoying. Someone pulls over to the side of the road, perhaps to fix a flat tire, and, pretty soon, a long traffic jam occurs as drivers slow down to take a look.

What makes it so annoying is that the length of the traffic jam is greatly out of proportion to the minor event that precipitated it. Because some drivers hit their brakes to rubberneck, the drivers behind them must also hit their brakes, those behind them must do the same, and so

Just as individual actions on the road can unintentionally lead to a traffic jam, individual actions in the economy can produce an unintended macroeconomic effect.

on. The accumulation of all the individual hitting of brakes eventually leads to a long, wasteful traffic jam as each driver slows down a little bit more than the driver ahead. In other words, each person's response leads to an amplified response by the next person.

Understanding rubbernecking gives us some insight into one very important way in which macroeconomics differs from microeconomics: many thousands or millions of individual actions compound upon one another to produce an outcome that isn't simply the sum of those individual actions.

Consider, for example, what macroeconomists call the *paradox of thrift:* when families and businesses are worried about the possibility of economic hard times, they prepare by cutting their spending. This reduction in spending depresses the economy as consumers spend less and businesses react by laying off workers. As a result, families and businesses may end up worse off than if they hadn't tried to act responsibly by cutting their spending.

This is a paradox because seemingly virtuous behavior—preparing for hard times by saving more—ends up harming everyone. The flip-side to this story is that when families and businesses are feeling optimistic about the future, they spend more today. This stimulates the economy, leading businesses to hire more workers, which further expands the economy. Seemingly profligate behavior leads to good times for all.

A key insight of macroeconomics, then, is that the combined effect of individual decisions can have results that are very different from what any one individual intended, results that are sometimes perverse. The behavior of the macroeconomy is, indeed, greater than the sum of individual actions and market outcomes.

Macroeconomics: Theory and Policy

To a much greater extent than microeconomists, macroeconomists are concerned with questions about *policy*, about what the government can do to make macroeconomic performance better. This policy focus was strongly shaped by history, in particular by the Great Depression of the 1930s.

Before the 1930s, economists tended to regard the economy as **self-regulating:** they believed that problems such as unemployment would be corrected through the working of the "invisible hand" and that government attempts to improve the economy's performance would be ineffective at best—and would probably make things worse.

The Great Depression changed all that. The sheer scale of the catastrophe, which left a quarter of the U.S. workforce without jobs and threatened the political stability of many countries, created a demand for action. It also led to a major effort on the part of economists to understand economic slumps and find ways to prevent them.

In 1936 the British economist John Maynard Keynes (pronounced "canes") published *The General Theory of Employment, Interest, and Money,* a book that transformed macroeconomics. According to **Keynesian economics,** a depressed economy is the result of inadequate spending. In addition, Keynes argued that government intervention can help a depressed economy through *monetary policy* and *fiscal policy.* **Monetary policy** uses changes in the quantity of money to alter interest rates, which in turn affect the level of overall spending. **Fiscal policy** uses changes in taxes and government spending to affect overall spending.

In general, Keynes established the idea that managing the economy is a government responsibility. Keynesian ideas continue to have a strong influence on both economic theory and public policy: during the Great Recession and economic shutdown from Covid-19, Congress, the White House, and the Federal Reserve (a quasi-governmental agency that manages U.S. monetary policy) took steps to fend off an economic slump that were clearly Keynesian in spirit, as described in the following Economics in Action.

self-regulating economy describes an economy in which problems such as unemployment are resolved without government intervention, through the working of the invisible hand, and in which government attempts to improve the economy's performance would be ineffective at best, and would probably make things worse.

Keynesian economics a school of thought emerging out of the works of John Maynard Keynes; according to Keynesian economics, a depressed economy is the result of inadequate spending and government intervention can help a depressed economy through monetary policy and fiscal policy.

monetary policy changes in the quantity of money in circulation designed to alter interest rates and affect the level of overall spending.

fiscal policy changes in government spending and taxes designed to affect overall spending.

"If you wear it like this you can't see any economic forecasts."

Matt Pritchett/The Daily Telegraph

ECONOMICS >> *in Action*
A Tale of Two Crises

The past two decades have not been peaceful for the world economy. In fact, there have been two severe economic slumps. The first began in 2008, when problems

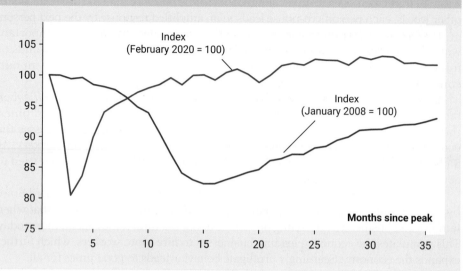

FIGURE 1 World Industrial Output in Two Slumps

The world economy suffered major slumps beginning in 2008, in the wake of a global financial crisis, and in 2020, as the coronavirus pandemic disrupted normal life while causing widespread deaths. In both cases industrial production eventually recovered, but recovery after 2020 was much faster, at least in part because of a much larger fiscal response.

Note: World industrial production includes mining, manufacturing, electricity, gas and steam and air-conditioning.

Data from: OECD (2023), Industrial production (indicator).

in the world financial system—banks and other institutions whose activities play a crucial role in facilitating business worldwide—were disrupted by a collapse of confidence in the aftermath of widespread bad investments. The second began in early 2020, when normal business activity was disrupted by the coronavirus pandemic and the emergency measures taken to limit Covid-19's spread. Figure 1 shows world industrial production, by month, in the aftermath of the two crises.

Both crises had huge economic costs. However, the patterns of these costs over time were very different. The 2008 slump took some time to have its full effect, but recovery was also painfully slow. The Covid-19 slump, by contrast, hit very hard at first, but the world experienced a rapid, "V-shaped" recovery. Why the difference?

One answer is that the 2008 crisis was the culmination of years of excess, which left behind major financial problems, especially high levels of debt that families ran up to buy homes during what turned out to have been a huge bubble—an era of unrealistically high prices—in the housing market. On the eve of the Covid crisis, by contrast, both families and businesses were in pretty good shape.

Another answer is that world leaders learned some lessons from the sluggish recovery after 2008, which was widely attributed to an inadequate policy response. Although governments used fiscal policy to limit the downturn after 2008, the increase in spending fell short of what many economists considered necessary, and was withdrawn relatively quickly. The policy response to the Covid crisis, by contrast, was huge. The U.S. government, in particular, spent so much money aiding families and businesses that household incomes, adjusted for inflation, actually rose even during a period when tens of millions of workers were temporarily unemployed.

In fact, many although not all economists believe that the government response to Covid was excessive, helping to cause a surge in the cost of living during 2021 and 2022, although this surge may also have reflected lingering disruptions from the pandemic and other events, especially Russia's invasion of Ukraine. But few economists disagree with the proposition that a strong fiscal response was appropriate, and that the rapid recovery in world production was good news despite other problems.

>> Check Your Understanding 6-1

Solutions appear at back of book.

1. Which of the following questions involve microeconomics, and which involve macroeconomics? In each case, explain your answer.
   a. Why did consumers switch to smaller cars in 2008?
   b. Why did overall consumer spending slow down in 2008?

>> Quick Review

• Microeconomics focuses on decision making by individuals and firms and the consequences of the decisions made. Macroeconomics focuses on the overall behavior of the economy.

• The combined effect of individual actions can have unintended consequences and lead to worse or better macroeconomic outcomes for everyone.

• Before the 1930s, economists tended to regard the economy as **self-regulating.** After the Great Depression, **Keynesian economics** provided the rationale for government intervention through **monetary policy** and **fiscal policy** to help a depressed economy.

  c. Why did the standard of living rise more rapidly in the first generation after World War II than in the second?
  d. Why have starting salaries for students with economics degrees risen sharply as of late?
  e. What determines the choice between rail and road transportation?
  f. Why did laptops get much cheaper between 2000 and 2017?
  g. Why did inflation fall in the 2010s?

2. In 2008, problems in the financial sector led to a drying up of credit around the country: home-buyers were unable to get mortgages, students were unable to get student loans, car-buyers were unable to get car loans, and so on.
  a. Explain how the drying up of credit can lead to compounding effects throughout the economy and result in an economic slump.
  b. If you believe the economy is self-regulating, what would you advocate that policy makers do?
  c. If you believe in Keynesian economics, what would you advocate that policy makers do?

⫿ The Business Cycle

The Great Depression was by far the worst economic crisis in U.S. history. Although the economy managed to avoid catastrophe in the decades that followed, it has experienced many ups and downs.

It's true that the ups have consistently been bigger than the downs: a chart of any of the major numbers used to track the U.S. economy shows a strong upward trend over time. For example, panel (a) of Figure 2 shows total U.S. private-sector employment (the total number of jobs offered by private businesses) measured along the left vertical axis, with the data given by the purple line. The graph also

FIGURE 2 U.S. Growth, Interrupted, 1985–2023

Panel (a) shows two important economic numbers, the industrial production index and total private-sector employment. Both numbers grew substantially from 1985 to 2023, but they didn't grow steadily. Instead, both suffered from downturns associated with recessions, which are indicated by the shaded areas in the figure. Panel (b) emphasizes those downturns by showing the annual rate of change of industrial production and employment,

that is, the percentage increase over the past year. The simultaneous downturns in both numbers during the recessions are clear.

Data from: (a) Federal Reserve Bank of St. Louis; Bureau of Economic Analysis; and Bureau of Labor Statistics. (b) Federal Reserve Bank of St. Louis

Note: Gray bars indicate periods of recessions

shows the index of industrial production (a measure of the total output of U.S. factories) measured along the right vertical axis, with the data given by the red line. Both private-sector employment and industrial production were much higher at the end of this period than at the beginning, and in most years both measures rose.

But they didn't rise steadily. As you can see from the figure, there were four periods—in the early 1990s, in the early 2000s, beginning in late 2007, and again in 2020—when both employment and industrial output stumbled. Panel (b) emphasizes these stumbles by showing the *rate of change* of employment and industrial production over the previous year. For example, the percent change in employment for October 2009 was –0.6 because employment in October 2009 was 0.6% lower than it had been in October 2008. The big downturns stand out clearly. What's more, a detailed look at the data makes it clear that in each period the stumble wasn't confined to only a few industries: in each downturn, just about every sector of the U.S. economy cut back on production and on the number of people employed.

The economy's forward march, in other words, isn't smooth. And the uneven pace of the economy's progress, its ups and downs, is one of the main preoccupations of macroeconomics.

Charting the Business Cycle

Figure 3 shows a stylized representation of the way the economy evolves over time. The vertical axis shows either employment or an indicator of how much the economy is producing, such as industrial production or *real gross domestic product (real GDP)*, a measure of the economy's overall output that we'll learn about in Chapter 7. As the data in Figure 2 suggest, these two measures tend to move together. Their common movement is the starting point for a major theme of macroeconomics: the economy's alternation between short-run downturns and upturns.

A widespread downturn, in which output and employment in many industries fall, is called a **recession** (sometimes referred to as a *contraction*). Recessions are officially declared by the National Bureau of Economic Research, or NBER (discussed in the upcoming For Inquiring Minds), and are indicated by the shaded areas in Figure 2. When the economy isn't in a recession, when most economic numbers are following their normal upward trend, the economy is said to be in an **expansion** (sometimes referred to as a *recovery*).

The alternation between recessions and expansions is known as the **business cycle.** The point in time at which the economy shifts from expansion to recession is known as a **business-cycle peak;** the point at which the economy shifts from recession to expansion is known as a **business-cycle trough.**

recessions a downturn in the economy when output and employment are falling; also referred to as a contraction.

expansions a period of economic upturn in which output and employment are rising; most economic numbers are following their normal upward trend; also referred to as a recovery.

business cycle the short-run alternation between economic downturns, known as recessions, and economic upturns, known as expansions.

business-cycle peak the point in time at which the economy shifts from expansion to recession.

business-cycle trough the point in time at which the economy shifts from recession to expansion.

FIGURE 3 The Business Cycle

This is a stylized picture of the business cycle. The vertical axis measures either employment or total output in the economy. Periods when these two variables turn down are *recessions;* periods when they turn up are *expansions.* The point at which the economy turns down is a *business-cycle peak;* the point at which it turns up again is a *business-cycle trough.*

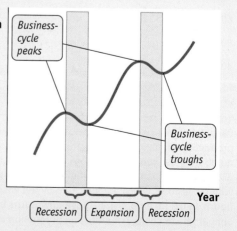

The business cycle is an enduring feature of the economy. Table 2 shows the official list of business-cycle peaks and troughs. As you can see, there have been recessions and expansions for at least the past 160 years. Whenever there is a prolonged expansion, as there was in the 1960s and again in the 1990s, books and articles come out proclaiming the end of the business cycle. Such proclamations have always been proved wrong: the cycle always comes back.

The Pain of Recession

Not many people complain about the business cycle when the economy is expanding. Recessions, however, create a great deal of pain.

The most important effect of a recession is its effect on the ability of workers to find and hold jobs. The most widely used indicator of conditions in the labor market is the *unemployment rate*. We'll explain how that rate is calculated in Chapter 8, but for now it's enough to say that a high unemployment rate tells us that jobs are scarce and a low unemployment rate tells us that jobs are easy to find.

Figure 4 shows the unemployment rate. As you can see, the U.S. unemployment rate surged during and after each recession but eventually fell during periods of expansion.

Because recessions cause many people to lose their jobs and make it hard to find new ones, they reduce the standard of living of households across the country. Recessions are usually associated with a rise in the number of people living below the poverty line, an increase in the number of people who lose their homes because they can't afford the mortgage payments, and a fall in the percentage of Americans with health insurance coverage. But workers are not the only group that suffers during a recession. Recessions are also bad for firms: profits fall during recessions, and many small businesses fail.

All in all, then, recessions are bad for almost everyone. Can anything be done to reduce their frequency and severity?

TABLE 2 The History of the Business Cycle

Business-cycle peak	Business-cycle trough
no prior data available	December 1854
June 1857	December 1858
October 1860	June 1861
April 1865	December 1867
June 1869	December 1870
October 1873	March 1879
March 1882	May 1885
March 1887	April 1888
July 1890	May 1891
January 1893	June 1894
December 1895	June 1897
June 1899	December 1900
September 1902	August 1904
May 1907	June 1908
January 1910	January 1912
January 1913	December 1914
August 1918	March 1919
January 1920	July 1921
May 1923	July 1924
October 1926	November 1927
August 1929	March 1933
May 1937	June 1938
February 1945	October 1945
November 1948	October 1949
July 1953	May 1954
August 1957	April 1958
April 1960	February 1961
December 1969	November 1970
November 1973	March 1975
January 1980	July 1980
July 1981	November 1982
July 1990	March 1991
March 2001	November 2001
December 2007	June 2009
February 2020	April 2020

Data from: National Bureau of Economic Research.

FIGURE 4 The U.S. Unemployment Rate, 1988–2022

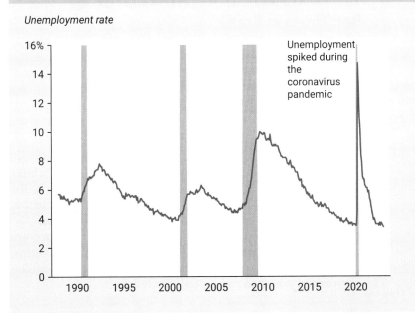

The unemployment rate, a measure of joblessness, rises sharply during recessions and usually falls during expansions.
Data from: Bureau of Labor Statistics.

You may be wondering exactly how recessions and expansions are defined. The truth is that there are no exact definitions!

In many countries, economists adopt the rule that a recession is a period of at least two consecutive quarters (a quarter is three months) during which the total output of the economy shrinks. The two-consecutive-quarters requirement is designed to avoid classifying brief hiccups in the economy's performance, with no lasting significance, as recessions.

Sometimes, however, this seems too strict. For example, three months of sharply declining output, then three months of slightly positive growth, then another three months of rapid decline, should surely be considered a recession.

In the United States, the task of determining when a recession begins and ends is assigned to an independent panel of experts at the National Bureau of Economic Research (NBER). This panel looks at a variety of economic indicators, then makes a judgment call.

Sometimes this judgment is controversial. In fact, there is lingering controversy if the U.S. economy entered a recession at the start of 2022. By the second quarter of 2022, the U.S. economy had posted two consecutive quarters of negative GDP growth. While the media was determined to label the economy in a recession, economists, almost unanimously, held steadfast in their view the economy was not in a recession. Economists were proven correct as revised data on GDP showed continued growth and while unemployment continued to fall.

"I can't move in with my parents. They moved in with my grandparents."

Taming the Business Cycle

Modern macroeconomics largely came into being as a response to the worst recession in history—the 43-month downturn that began in 1929 and continued into 1933, ushering in the Great Depression. The havoc wreaked by the 1929–1933 recession spurred economists to search both for understanding and for solutions: they wanted to know how such things could happen and how to prevent them.

As explained earlier, the work of John Maynard Keynes suggested that monetary and fiscal policies could be used to mitigate the effects of recessions, and to this day governments turn to Keynesian policies when recession strikes. Later work, notably that of another great macroeconomist, Milton Friedman, led to a consensus that it's important to rein in booms as well as to fight slumps. So modern policy makers try to "smooth out" the business cycle. They haven't been completely successful, as a look back at Figure 2 makes clear. It's widely believed, however, that policy guided by macroeconomic analysis has helped make the economy more stable.

Although the business cycle has historically played a crucial role in fostering development of the field, macroeconomists are also concerned with other issues such as long-run growth, inflation and deflation, and international imbalances, which we examine next.

FIGURE 5 The Tale of Two Recoveries

Real GDP index (pre-recession peak = 100)

Data from: Federal Reserve Bank of St. Louis and OECD, "Main Economic Indicators — complete database."

ECONOMICS >> *in Action*
Bad Times in Brazil

The Great Recession afflicted almost all the world's economies, although some suffered more than others. Sometimes, however, individual countries have their own macroeconomic troubles. Five years after the 2007–2009 U.S. recession ended, Brazil—the economic powerhouse of Latin America, often hailed as a country on the rise—entered a recession far worse than anything the United States had experienced in the last half century.

Figure 5 compares real GDP, a measure of the economy's total output, in the U.S. Great Recession and Brazil's later slump. In each case we measure output as a percentage of the maximum output just before recession struck. As you can see, Brazil's slump was much deeper and lasted much longer.

What caused Brazil's slump? It seems to have been a combination of a fall in the prices of some goods, like soybeans, that Brazil sells on world markets, and a pullback by Brazilian consumers, who had run up too much debt.

GLOBAL COMPARISON   RECESSIONS, HERE AND THERE

This figure shows unemployment in two of the world's biggest economies: the United States and the euro area, the group of European countries that share a common currency, the euro. As you can see, both economies saw unemployment surge in 2008–2009 and again in 2020.

More or less simultaneous recessions in different countries are, in fact, quite common. But that doesn't mean that economies always or even usually move in lockstep. As you can see from the figure, unemployment in the United States began steadily falling from 2010 onward, although more slowly than most would have liked. But the euro area experienced a second surge in unemployment from 2011 to late 2012, widely attributed by economists to a wrong turn in economic policy. It was only after 2013 that Europe began to see steadily falling unemployment.

What we learn, then, is that the business cycle is to some extent an international phenomenon. But individual countries can diverge from each other for a variety of reasons, including differences in policy and in the underlying structure of their economies.

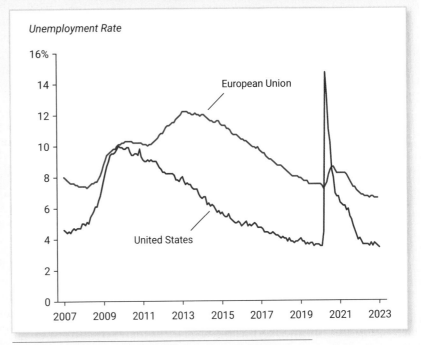

Data from: Federal Reserve Bank of St. Louis and Bureau of Labor Statistics.

But why was the slump so severe? A large part of the answer is that Brazil, unlike the United States in 2007 and after, didn't take policy steps to minimize the downturn. Instead of cutting interest rates and increasing government spending, Brazil did the opposite. Brazil had reasons for these policies, largely political ones, but nonetheless the policies still had the effect of causing a much deeper downturn than experienced in the United States.

>> Check Your Understanding 6-2

Solutions appear at back of book.

1. Why do we talk about business cycles for the economy as a whole, rather than just talking about the ups and downs of particular industries?

2. Describe who gets hurt in a recession, and how.

> **>> Quick Review**
>
> • The **business cycle**, the short-run alternation between **recessions** and **expansions**, is a major concern of modern macroeconomics.
>
> • The point at which expansion shifts to recession is a **business-cycle peak.** The point at which recession shifts to expansion is a **business-cycle trough.**

‖ Long-Run Economic Growth

In 1960, Americans believed, correctly, that they were better off than the citizens of any other nation, past or present. Yet as Figure 6 shows, they were, on average, still quite poor by modern standards. Few than half of households had washing machines, and very few people had air conditioning. Home computers first became available in the early 1980s; widespread internet access didn't come until after 2000, and access didn't get fast enough to permit streamed entertainment until much later. The era of the smartphone didn't begin until the first iPhone was introduced in 2007. And so on.

Why are the vast majority of Americans today able to afford conveniences that many Americans lacked in the past? The answer is **long-run economic growth,** the sustained rise in the quantity of goods and services the economy produces. This sustained rise, in turn, reflects one of our basic principles of economics: Increases in the economy's potential lead to economic growth over time.

long-run economic growth the sustained rise in the quantity of goods and services the economy produces.

FIGURE 6 The Fruits of Long-Run Growth in the United States

Percent of homes with product

■ 1960 ■ 2019

Americans have become able to afford many more material goods over time thanks to long-run economic growth.

Data from: U.S. Census.

FIGURE 7 Economic Growth, the Long View

Real GDP per capita (2011 dollars)

■ United Kingdom ■ United States

Over the long run, real GDP per capita has increased in both Britain and the United States. For about 300 years, real GDP per capita was greater in Britain. But early in the twentieth century, the United States surpassed Britain, becoming the richer country.

Data from: Maddison Data Project, revision 2022.

Figure 7 shows estimates of real GDP per capita, a measure of total output per person, for two countries—the United States and Britain—for selected years going back to the Middle Ages. Both countries have experienced an enormous long-run rise in production per person, dwarfing the ups and downs of the business cycle.

Two points are, however, worth noting:

1. Long-run economic growth is a modern invention: Britain wasn't any richer in 1650 than it was two centuries earlier, and overall world incomes didn't start rising until around 1870.

2. Countries don't necessarily grow at the same rate. Britain was once substantially richer than the United States, but it was overtaken by the rapidly growing new nation after 1875.

Long-run economic growth is fundamental to many of the most pressing economic questions today. Responses to key policy questions, such as the country's ability to bear the future costs of government programs such as Social Security and Medicare, depend in part on how fast the U.S. economy grows over the next few decades.

More broadly, the public's sense that the country is making progress depends crucially on success in achieving long-run growth. When growth slows, as it did in the 1970s, it can generate a national mood of pessimism. In particular, *long-run growth per capita*—a sustained upward trend in output per person—is the key to higher wages and a rising standard of living. A major concern of macroeconomics—and the theme of Chapter 9—is trying to understand the forces behind long-run growth.

Long-run growth is an even more urgent concern in poorer, less developed countries. In these countries, which would like to achieve a higher standard of living, the question of how to accelerate long-run growth is the central concern of economic policy.

As we'll see, macroeconomists don't use the same models to think about long-run growth that they use to think about the business cycle. It's important to keep both sets of models in mind, because what is good in the long run can be bad in the short run, and vice versa. For example, we've already mentioned the paradox of thrift: an attempt by households to increase their savings can cause a recession. But a higher level of savings, as we'll see in Chapter 10, plays a crucial role in encouraging long-run economic growth.

ECONOMICS >> *in Action*
A Tale of Two Countries

Many countries have experienced long-run growth, but not all have done equally well. One of the most informative contrasts is between Canada and Argentina, two countries that, at the beginning of the twentieth century, seemed to be in a good economic position.

From today's vantage point, it's surprising to realize that Canada and Argentina looked rather similar before World War I. Both were major exporters of agricultural products; both attracted large numbers of European immigrants; both also attracted large amounts of European investment, especially in the railroads that opened up their agricultural hinterlands. Economic historians believe that the average level of per capita income was comparable in the two countries as late as the 1930s.

After World War II, however, Argentina's economy performed poorly, largely due to political instability and bad macroeconomic policies. Argentina experienced several periods of extremely high inflation, during which the cost of living soared. Meanwhile, Canada made steady progress. Thanks to the fact that Canada has achieved sustained long-run growth since 1930, but Argentina has not, Canada's standard of living today is almost as high as that of the United States—and is about two and a half times as high as Argentina's.

> **inflation** a rise in the overall level of prices.

> **deflation** a fall in the overall level of prices.

>> Check Your Understanding 6-3
Solutions appear at back of book.

1. Many poor countries have high rates of population growth. What does this imply about the long-run growth rates of overall output that they must achieve in order to generate a higher standard of living per person?

2. Argentina used to be as rich as Canada; now it's much poorer. Does this mean that Argentina is poorer than it was in the past? Explain.

> ## >> Quick Review
> • Because the U.S. economy has achieved **long-run economic growth**, Americans live much better than they did a half-century or more ago.
>
> • Long-run economic growth is crucial for many economic concerns, such as a higher standard of living or financing government programs. It's especially crucial for poorer countries.

Inflation and Deflation

In November 2021, the average private-sector worker in the United States was paid $31.23 an hour. By November 2022, hourly earnings were $32.82—an increase of 5.1%. That's a pretty decent raise, right?

But wait. The cost of living was rising, too. In fact, most things Americans buy became considerably more expensive over the course of that year. Figure 8 compares the percentage increase in hourly earnings between November 2021 and November 2022 with the increases in the cost of some major types of consumer spending. As you can see, the average worker's paycheck went farther in terms of some goods—used car prices, which were very high in 2021 in part because of pandemic-related disruption to supply, fell, and clothing prices rose relatively slowly—but less far in terms of others. Overall, the official U.S. government estimate of the cost of living rose 7.1%, more than wiping out the average worker's wage gains.

The point is that between 2021 and 2022 the economy experienced substantial **inflation:** a rise in the overall level of prices. Understanding the causes of inflation and its opposite, **deflation**—a fall in the overall level of prices—is another main concern of macroeconomics.

The Causes of Inflation and Deflation

You might think that changes in the overall level of prices are just a matter of supply and demand. For example, higher gasoline prices reflect the higher price of crude oil, and higher crude oil

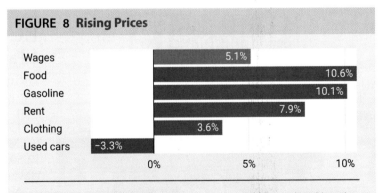

FIGURE 8 Rising Prices

Wages	5.1%
Food	10.6%
Gasoline	10.1%
Rent	7.9%
Clothing	3.6%
Used cars	-3.3%

Between November 2021 and November 2022, U.S. workers' hourly earnings rose by 5.1%. But the cost of some major types of consumer spending also rose, some by more. Overall, the rising cost of living more than offset the rise in the average U.S. worker's wage.
Data from: Bureau of Labor Statistics.

price stability a situation in which the overall cost of living is changing slowly or not at all.

prices reflect such factors as the exhaustion of major oil fields, growing demand from China and other emerging economies as more people grow rich enough to buy cars, and so on. Can't we just add up what happens in each of these markets to find out what happens to the overall level of prices?

No, because supply and demand can only explain why a particular good or service becomes more expensive *relative to other goods and services.* It can't explain why, for example, the price of chicken has risen over time in spite of the fact that chicken production has become more efficient and chicken has become substantially cheaper compared to other goods.

What causes the overall level of prices to rise or fall? As we'll learn in Chapter 8, in the short run, movements in inflation are closely related to the business cycle. When the economy is depressed and jobs are hard to find, inflation tends to fall; when the economy is booming, inflation tends to rise. For example, prices of most goods and services fell sharply during the Great Depression.

In the long run, by contrast, the overall level of prices is mainly determined by changes in the money supply, the total quantity of assets that can be readily used to make purchases. As we'll see in Chapter 16, hyperinflation, in which prices rise by thousands or hundreds of thousands of percent, invariably occurs when governments print money to pay a large part of their bills.

The Pain of Inflation and Deflation

Both inflation and deflation can pose problems for the economy. Let's look at two examples.

First, inflation discourages people from holding onto cash, because cash loses value over time if the overall price level is rising. That is, the amount of goods and services you can buy with a given amount of cash falls. In extreme cases, people stop holding cash altogether and turn to barter.

Second, deflation can cause the reverse problem. If the price level is falling, cash gains value over time. In other words, the amount of goods and services you can buy with a given amount of cash increases. So holding on to cash becomes more attractive than investing in new factories and other productive assets. This can deepen a recession.

We'll describe other costs of inflation and deflation in Chapters 8 and 16. For now, let's just note that, in general, economists regard **price stability**—in which the overall level of prices is changing only slowly—as a desirable goal. From around 1990 to 2020, prices were sufficiently stable in the United States to satisfy most macroeconomists. But the price surge of 2021–2022 caused a great deal of anxiety, and led to urgent policy efforts to bring inflation back under control.

Even though a burger costs 10 times more than it did when McDonald's first opened, it's still a good bargain compared to other consumer goods.

ECONOMICS >> *in Action*
A Fast (Food) Measure of Inflation

The original McDonald's opened in 1948. It offered fast service—it was, indeed, the original fast-food restaurant. And it was also very inexpensive: hamburgers cost $0.15, $0.25 with fries. By 2023, a hamburger at a typical McDonald's cost more than 10 times as much, about $2.50. Has McDonald's lost touch with its fast-food roots? Have burgers become luxury cuisine?

No—in fact, compared with other consumer goods, a burger is a better bargain today than it was in 1948. Burger prices were about 10 times as high in 2023 as they were in 1948. But the consumer price index, the most widely used measure of the cost of living, was about 13 times as high in 2023 as it was in 1948.

>> *Check Your Understanding* **6-4**
Solutions appear at back of book.

1. Which of these sound like inflation, which sound like deflation, and which are ambiguous?
   a. Gasoline prices are up 10%, food prices are down 20%, and the prices of most services are up 1–2%.
   b. Gas prices have doubled, food prices are up 50%, and most services seem to be up 5% or 10%.
   c. Gas prices haven't changed, food prices are way down, and services have gotten cheaper, too.

International Imbalances

The United States is an **open economy:** an economy that trades goods and services with other countries. There have been times when that trade was more or less balanced—when the United States sold about as much to the rest of the world as it bought. But this isn't one of those times.

In 2021, the United States ran a big **trade deficit**—that is, the value of the goods and services U.S. residents bought from the rest of the world was a lot larger than the value of the goods and services U.S. producers sold to customers abroad. Meanwhile, some other countries were in the opposite position, selling much more to foreigners than they bought.

Figure 9 shows the exports and imports of goods for three important economies in 2021. As you can see, the United States imported much more than it exported, but Germany and China did the reverse: they each ran a **trade surplus.** A country runs a trade surplus when the value of the goods and services it buys from the rest of the world is smaller than the value of the goods and services it sells abroad.

Was the U.S. trade deficit a sign that something was wrong with our economy—that we weren't able to make things that people in other countries wanted to buy? No, not really. Trade deficits and their opposite, trade surpluses, are macroeconomic phenomena. They're the result of situations in which the whole is very different from the sum of its parts. You might think that countries with highly productive workers or widely desired products and services to sell run trade surpluses and countries with unproductive workers or poor-quality products and services to sell run trade deficits. But the reality is that there's no simple relationship between the success of an economy and whether it runs trade surpluses or trade deficits.

In Chapter 2 we learned that international trade is the result of comparative advantage: countries export goods they're relatively good at producing and import goods they're not as good at producing. That's why the United States exports wheat and imports coffee. What the concept of comparative advantage doesn't explain, however, is why the value of a country's imports is sometimes much larger than the value of its exports, or vice versa.

So what does determine whether a country runs a trade surplus or a trade deficit? Later on we'll learn the surprising answer: the determinants of the overall balance between exports and imports lie in decisions about savings and investment spending—spending on goods like machinery and factories that are in turn used to produce goods and services for consumers. Countries with high investment spending relative to savings run trade deficits; countries with low investment spending relative to savings run trade surpluses.

>> *Quick Review*
• A dollar today doesn't buy what it did in 1980, because the prices of most goods have risen. This rise in the overall price level has wiped out most if not all of the wage increases received by the typical American worker over the past 40 years.

• One area of macroeconomic study is in the overall level of prices. Because either **inflation** or **deflation** can cause problems for the economy, economists typically advocate maintaining **price stability.**

open economy an economy that trades goods and services with other countries.

trade deficit the deficit that results when the value of the goods and services bought from foreigners is more than the value of the goods and services sold to consumers abroad.

trade surplus the surplus that results when the value of goods and services bought from foreigners is less than the value of the goods and services sold to them.

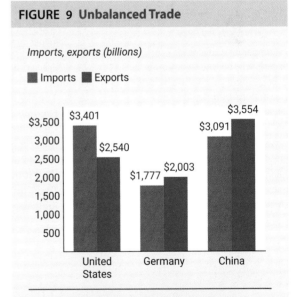

FIGURE 9 Unbalanced Trade

In 2021, the goods and services the United States bought from other countries were worth considerably more than the goods and services we sold abroad. Germany and China were in the reverse position. Trade deficits and trade surpluses reflect macroeconomic forces, especially differences in savings and investment spending.

Data from: World Development Indicators.

ECONOMICS >> *in Action*
Greece's Costly Surplus

In 1999, Greece took a momentous step: it gave up its national currency, the drachma, in order to adopt the euro, a shared currency intended to promote closer economic and political union among the nations of Europe. How did this affect Greece's international trade?

FIGURE 10 Greece's Current Account Balance, 1999–2022

Data from: OECD, Main Economic Indicators.

Figure 10 shows Greece's current account balance—a broad definition of its trade balance—from 2000 to 2022. A negative current account balance, as shown here, means the country is running a trade deficit. As you can see, after Greece switched to the euro it began running large trade deficits, which at their peak equaled almost 16% of the total value of goods and services Greece produced. After 2008, however, the trade deficit began shrinking rapidly, and by 2013 Greece was running a surplus.

Did this mean that Greece's economy was doing badly in the mid-2000s, and better thereafter? Just the opposite. When Greece adopted the euro, foreign investors became highly optimistic about its prospects, and money poured into the country, fueling rapid economic expansion. Unfortunately, this optimism eventually evaporated, and the inflows of foreign capital dried up. One consequence was that Greece could no longer run large trade deficits, and after the early 2010s was usually forced to run large surpluses. Another consequence was a severe recession, leading to a scarcity of jobs—the scarcity that led Constantine Kakoyiannis, the engineer we mentioned at the start of this chapter, to give up and move to Germany.

>> Quick Review

• Comparative advantage can explain why an **open economy** exports some goods and services and imports others, but it can't explain why a country imports more than it exports, or vice versa.

• **Trade deficits** and **trade surpluses** are macroeconomic phenomena, determined by decisions about investment spending and savings.

>> Check Your Understanding 6-5
Solutions appear at back of book.

1. Which of the following reflect comparative advantage, and which reflect macroeconomic forces?
   a. Thanks to the development of huge oil sands in the province of Alberta, Canada has become an exporter of oil and an importer of manufactured goods.
   b. Like many consumer goods, the Apple iPad is assembled in China, although many of the components are made in other countries.
   c. Since 2002, Germany has been running huge trade surpluses, exporting much more than it imports.
   d. The United States, which had roughly balanced trade in the early 1990s, began running large trade deficits later in the decade, as the technology boom took off.

GM Survives

G.J. McCARTHY/Tribune News Service/ARLINGTON/TX/USA/ Newscom

Once upon a time, General Motors (GM) was widely regarded as the world's greatest corporation. It was the largest employer in the United States; its success was so bound up with that of the nation as a whole that in 1953 its CEO declared that "what was good for our country was good for General Motors, and vice versa. The difference did not exist."

By 2008, however, GM was not the company it had been. It no longer dominated the U.S. car market, thanks in part to rising competition from foreign automakers. It had high "legacy" costs resulting from contracts to pay pensions and health benefits to retired workers. And the company was bleeding cash, losing more than $30 billion in 2008. It seemed possible that GM would not just declare formal bankruptcy, failing to pay its debts, but that it would go into actual liquidation, shutting down as a business.

GM executives appealed to the government for help and got it: the federal government provided almost $50 billion in cash, receiving in return majority ownership of the company.

There was intense negative reaction to this bailout, with many critics predicting that the company would be unable to come back, and that the aid provided to GM would be money down the drain. In the end, however, GM did stage a comeback, returning to profitability. By 2010, it repaid its federal loans, and eventually the U.S. government sold all the stock it had acquired, although the price it got for that stock left taxpayers with a $10 billion overall loss.

Why was GM able to survive and become profitable again? The company did undertake a number of cost-cutting measures. But the main secret of its turnaround was that 2008 was an exceptionally bad year for the auto industry, and that things improved dramatically in the years that followed.

The key point is that car sales are very sensitive to the state of the economy. When the economy as a whole stumbles, and workers have either lost their jobs or are worried about future job loss, they tend to postpone buying a new car. Figure 11 shows total U.S. sales of light vehicles (which includes both passenger cars and SUVs) over the past several decades. As you can see, sales plunged dramatically—around 40%—during the Great Recession, far more than the economy as a whole. It was predictable, however, that sales would surge again if and when the economy recovered.

The prospect of rapid growth in sales if the economy recovered is what made bailing out GM in 2009 a better bet than looking at the company's losses might have suggested. Despite its comeback, the company is nothing like the colossus it once was. But it has survived.

QUESTIONS FOR THOUGHT

1. While sales of many goods fell during the Great Recession, cars took a much bigger hit than groceries. Why?

2. Looking at Figure 11, you can see that car sales fell much less during the previous two recessions than they did during the Great Recession. What might explain the difference?

3. General Motors, somewhat unusually for U.S. firms outside the banking industry, has consistently employed a highly regarded economist, who among other things helps the economy make forecasts. (As of 2019 the position was held by Elaine Buckberg, a former student of one of the authors.) Why do you think GM might place a higher priority on economic analysis than, say, Walmart would?

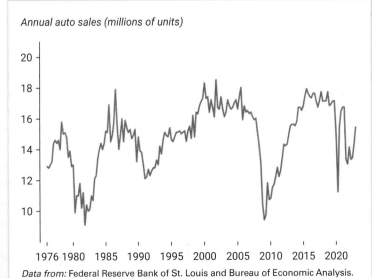

FIGURE 11 Automobile and Light Truck Sales, 1976–2023

Annual auto sales (millions of units)

Data from: Federal Reserve Bank of St. Louis and Bureau of Economic Analysis.

SUMMARY

1. Macroeconomics is the study of the behavior of the economy as a whole, which can be different from the sum of its parts. Macroeconomics differs from microeconomics in the type of questions it tries to answer. Macroeconomics also has a strong policy focus: **Keynesian economics**, which emerged during the Great Depression, advocates the use of **monetary policy** and **fiscal policy** to fight economic slumps. Prior to the Great Depression, the economy was thought to be **self-regulating.**

2. One key concern of macroeconomics is the **business cycle**, the short-run alternation between **recessions**, periods of falling employment and output, and **expansions**, periods of rising employment and output. The point at which expansion turns to recession is a **business-cycle peak.** The point at which recession turns to expansion is a **business-cycle trough.**

3. Another key area of macroeconomic study is **long-run economic growth**, the sustained upward trend in the economy's output over time. Long-run economic growth is the force behind long-term increases in living standards and is important for financing some economic programs. It is especially important for poorer countries.

4. When the prices of most goods and services are rising, so that the overall level of prices is going up, the economy experiences **inflation.** When the overall level of prices is going down, the economy is experiencing **deflation.** In the short run, inflation and deflation are closely related to the business cycle. In the long run, prices tend to reflect changes in the overall quantity of money. Because both inflation and deflation can cause problems, economists and policy makers generally aim for **price stability.**

5. Although comparative advantage explains why **open economies** export some things and import others, macroeconomic analysis is needed to explain why countries run **trade surpluses** or **trade deficits.** The determinants of the overall balance between exports and imports lie in decisions about savings and investment spending.

KEY TERMS

Self-regulating economy, p. 173
Keynesian economics, p. 173
Monetary policy, p. 173
Fiscal policy, p. 173
Recession, p. 176
Expansion, p. 176

Business cycle, p. 176
Business-cycle peak, p. 176
Business-cycle trough, p. 176
Long-run economic growth, p. 179
Inflation, p. 181
Deflation, p. 181

Price stability, p. 182
Open economy, p. 183
Trade deficit, p. 183
Trade surplus, p. 183

PRACTICE QUESTIONS

1. The U.S. Department of Labor reports statistics on employment and earnings that are used as key indicators by many economists to gauge the health of the economy. Figure 4 plots historical data on the unemployment rate each month. Noticeably, the numbers were high during the recessions in the early 1990s, in 2001, in the aftermath of the Great Recession, 2007–2009, and during the pandemic.

   a. Locate the latest data on the national unemployment rate. (*Hint:* Go to the Bureau of Labor Statistics at www.bls.gov, in the search bar enter "Employment Situation Summary," and select the subsequent page.)

   b. Compare the current numbers with those during the early 1990s, 2001, and following the shutdown in March 2022, as well as with the periods of relatively high economic growth just before the recessions. Are the current numbers indicative of a recessionary trend?

2. In the 1990s, there were some dramatic economic events that came to be known as the *Asian financial crisis.* A decade later similar events came to be known as the *global financial crisis.* The accompanying figure shows the growth rate of real GDP in the United States and Japan from 1996 to 2021. Using the graph, explain why the two sets of events are referred to this way.

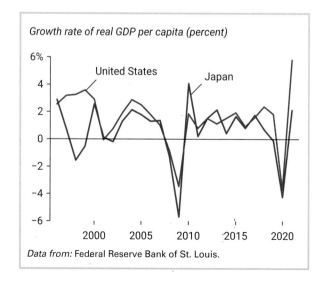

Data from: Federal Reserve Bank of St. Louis.

3. The accompanying figure illustrates the trade deficit of the United States since 1987. The United States has been consistently and, on the whole, increasingly importing more goods than it has been exporting. One of the countries it runs a trade deficit with is China. Which of the following statements are valid possible explanations of this fact? Explain.

a. Many products, such as televisions, that were formerly manufactured in the United States are now manufactured in China.

b. The wages of the average Chinese worker are far lower than the wages of the average American worker.

c. Investment spending in the United States is high relative to its level of savings.

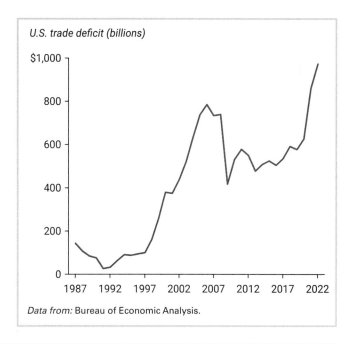

U.S. trade deficit (billions)

Data from: Bureau of Economic Analysis.

PROBLEMS

1. Which of the following questions are relevant for the study of macroeconomics and which for microeconomics?

a. How will tips change when a large manufacturing plant near a restaurant closes?

b. What will happen to spending by consumers when the economy enters a downturn?

c. How will the price of oranges change when a late frost damages Florida's orange groves?

d. How will wages at a manufacturing plant change when its workforce is unionized?

e. What will happen to U.S. exports as the dollar becomes less expensive in terms of other currencies?

f. What is the relationship between a nation's unemployment rate and its inflation rate?

2. When one person saves more, that person's wealth is increased, meaning that they can consume more in the future. But when everyone saves more, everyone's income falls, meaning that everyone must consume less today. Explain this seeming contradiction.

3. Before the Great Depression, the conventional wisdom among economists and policy makers was that the economy is largely self-regulating.

a. Is this view consistent or inconsistent with Keynesian economics? Explain.

b. What effect did the Great Depression have on conventional wisdom?

c. Contrast the response of policy makers during the 2007–2009 recession to the actions of policy makers during the Great Depression. What would have been the likely outcome of the 2007–2009 recession if

policy makers had responded in the same fashion as policy makers during the Great Depression?

4. How do economists in the United States determine when a recession begins and when it ends? How do other countries determine whether or not a recession is occurring?

5. Access the Discovering Data exercise for Chapter 6, Problem 5 online to answer the following questions.

a. What was real GDP per capita for Canada and Argentina in 1950?

b. How much did real GDP per capita increase for Canada and Argentina from 1950 through 2021?

c. Calculate the relative income difference between Canada and Argentina in 1950.

d. Calculate the relative income difference between Canada and Argentina in 2021.

6. Access the Discovering Data exercise for Chapter 6, Problem 6 online to answer the following questions.

a. What was the percentage decline in industrial production for Greece from 2007 to 2009? What was it from 2007 to 2016?

b. What country had the largest decline in industrial production from 2007 to 2009? Rank the countries, in order, from the largest decline in industrial production to the smallest.

c. Find the decline in industrial production from 2007 to 2009 for each of the countries.

d. What country experienced the fastest recovery from the financial crisis? The slowest recovery?

e. How long did it take Germany to fully recover from the financial crisis? How long did it take the United States?

7. a. What three measures of the economy tend to move together during the business cycle? Which way do they move during an upturn? During a downturn?

b. Who in the economy is hurt during a recession? How?

c. How did Milton Friedman alter the consensus that had developed in the aftermath of the Great Depression on how the economy should be managed? What is the current goal of policy makers in managing the economy?

8. Why do we consider a business-cycle expansion different from long-run economic growth? Why do we care about the size of the long-run growth rate of real GDP relative to the size of the growth rate of the population?

9. In 1798, Thomas Malthus's *Essay on the Principle of Population* was published. In it, he wrote: "Population, when unchecked, increases in a geometrical ratio. Subsistence increases only in an arithmetical ratio. … This implies a strong and constantly operating check on population from the difficulty of subsistence." Malthus was saying that the growth of the population is limited by the amount of food available to eat; people will live at the subsistence level forever. Why didn't Malthus's description apply to the world after 1800?

10. Each year, *The Economist* publishes data on the price of the Big Mac in different countries and exchange rates. The accompanying table shows some data from 2007 and 2022. Use this information to answer the following questions.

	2007		2022	
Country	Price of Big Mac (in local currency)	Price of Big Mac (in U.S. dollars)	Price of Big Mac (in local currency)	Price of Big Mac (in U.S. dollars)
Argentina	peso8.25	$2.65	peso590.0	$4.57
Canada	C$3.63	$3.08	C$6.77	$5.25
Euro area	€2.94	$3.82	€4.65	$4.77
Japan	¥280	$2.31	¥390	$2.83
United States	$3.22	$3.22	$5.77	$5.77

a. Where was it cheapest to buy a Big Mac in U.S. dollars in 2007?

b. Where was it cheapest to buy a Big Mac in U.S. dollars in 2022?

c. Using the increase in the local currency price of the Big Mac in each country to measure the percent change in the overall price level from 2007 to 2022, which nation experienced the most inflation? Did any of the nations experience deflation?

11. College tuition has risen significantly in the past few decades. For the sake of this problem, let's assume that during the past 20 years the cost of college, including total tuition, room, and board paid by full-time undergraduate students went from $2,871 to $16,789 at public institutions, a 485% price increase, and from $6,330 to $33,716 at private institutions, a 433% increase. Over the same time, average personal income after taxes rose from $9,785 to $39,409 per year, an increase of 302%. Have these tuition increases made it more difficult for the average student to afford college tuition? ∎

7 GDP and the CPI: Tracking the Macroeconomy

 ## INDIA HITS THE BIG TIME

IN THIS BOOK'S INTRODUCTION, we mentioned the important role India now plays in the development of information technology, including the technology that helped many people cope with the disruptions of the Covid-19 pandemic. India is still a relatively poor country, but its economy has grown significantly since, say, 1980. By some measures India's economy is now the fourth largest in the world, after China, the United States, and Japan, bigger than any nation in Europe.

But what does it mean to have the fourth largest economy in the world? If you compare India with the United States, you find that they do quite different things. India, for example, produces a lot of clothing, while the U.S. clothing industry has largely disappeared. On the other hand, the United States produces around half of the world's passenger jets, while India is just getting into the aircraft industry. So you might think that trying to compare the sizes of the two economies would be a matter of comparing apples and oranges — well, pajamas and Boeings, but you get the idea.

Reinier Snijders/EyeEm/Getty Images

India has become an economic superpower, surpassing any nation in Europe.

In fact, however, economists routinely do compare the sizes of economies across both space and time — for example, they compare the size of the U.S. economy with that of India, and they also compare the size of the U.S. economy today with its size in the past. They do this using a measure known as *gross domestic product,* or *GDP,* the total value of goods and services produced in a country, and a closely related measure, *real GDP,* which corrects GDP for price changes. When number-crunchers say that one country's economy has overtaken the other's, they mean that India's real GDP has surpassed that of the United States (or that the United States' real GDP has surpassed that of India).

GDP and real GDP are two of the most important measures used to track the macroeconomy — that is, to quantify movements in the overall level of output and prices. Measures like GDP and *price indexes* play an important role in formulating economic policy, since policy makers need to know what's going on, and anecdotes are no substitute for hard data. Measures are also important for business decisions — to such an extent that, as the Business Case at the end of the chapter illustrates, corporations and other players seek independent estimates when they don't trust official numbers.

In this chapter, we explain how macroeconomists measure key aspects of the economy. We first explore ways to measure the economy's total output and total income. We then turn to the problem of how to measure the level of prices and the change in prices in the economy. ●

WHAT YOU WILL LEARN

- How do economists use aggregate measures to track the performance of the economy?
- What is **gross domestic product,** or **GDP,** and how is it calculated?
- What is the difference between **real GDP** and **nominal GDP,** and why is real GDP the appropriate measure of real economic activity?
- What is a **price index,** and how is it used to calculate the **inflation rate?**

national income and product accounts (national accounts) a method of calculating and keeping track of consumer spending, sales of producers, business investment spending, government purchases, and a variety of other flows of money between different sectors of the economy.

government purchases of goods and services total purchases by federal, state, and local governments on goods and services.

consumer spending household spending on goods and services from domestic and foreign firms.

investment spending spending on productive physical capital—such as machinery and construction of buildings—and on changes to inventories.

exports goods and services sold to other countries.

imports goods and services purchased from other countries.

‖ The National Accounts

Almost all countries calculate a set of numbers known as the *national income and product accounts.* In fact, the accuracy of a country's accounts is a remarkably reliable indicator of its state of economic development—in general, the more reliable the accounts, the more economically advanced the country. When international economic agencies seek to help a less developed country, typically the first order of business is to send a team of experts to audit and improve the country's accounts.

In the United States, these numbers are calculated by the Bureau of Economic Analysis, a division of the U.S. government's Department of Commerce. The **national income and product accounts,** often referred to simply as the **national accounts,** keep track of the spending of consumers, the sales of producers, business investment spending, government purchases, and a variety of other flows of money between different sectors of the economy. Let's see how they work.

Following the Money: The Expanded Circular-Flow Diagram

To understand the principles behind the national accounts, it helps to look at Figure 1, which is an expanded version of the circular-flow diagram we introduced in Chapter 2 (see Figure 6 in that chapter). Figure 1 shows the flows of money through the economy. For the purposes of this chapter, however, we will focus only on the left side of the diagram, where green arrows represent the "real" economy—flows of money associated with the production and sales of goods and services. We'll turn to the "financial" economy, represented by the blue arrows, in Chapter 10—borrowing, lending, and other money flows—that are crucial but have only an indirect effect on production.

As Figure 1 shows, spending on goods and services—flows of money *into* the markets for goods and services—comes from four distinct kinds of buyers:

1. Governments at the local, state, and federal level spend tax revenue in two broad areas: **government purchases of goods and services** like education or defense, where the government buys things for its own use, and *transfer payments* like Social Security, where the government gives money to households. For now, in this chapter, we will focus only on government purchases.

2. Households—that's your family, ours, and tens of millions of others. Households engage in **consumer spending** by purchasing goods and services through the markets for goods and services from firms or imports from the rest of the world.

3. Firms—firms buy goods and services from each other when they engage in **investment spending,** spending on productive capital, such as machinery and construction of buildings.

4. Rest of the world—a fourth source of spending comes from **exports,** goods and services sold to residents of other countries.

All four of these money flows involve spending on goods and services. However, some of the goods and services purchased by a country's residents are produced abroad. For example, many consumer goods sold in the United States are made in India. Goods and services that are purchased by households, governments, or firms, but produced by residents of another country, are known as **imports.** The purchase of imports leads to a flow of money *out* of the market for goods and services and *out* of the economy.

Suppose we add up consumer spending on goods and services, investment spending, government purchases of goods and services, and the value of exports, then subtract the value of imports. This gives us a measure of the overall market value of the goods and services the economy produces. That measure has a name: it's a country's *gross domestic product.* But before we can formally define gross

FIGURE 1 An Expanded Circular-Flow Diagram: The Flows of Money Through the Economy

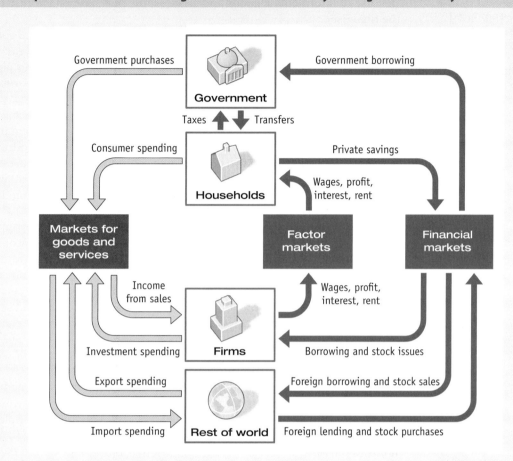

A circular flow of money connects the four sectors of the economy: government, households, firms, and the rest of the world, via three types of markets: markets for goods and services, factor markets, and financial markets. Money flows from firms to households in the form of wages, profit, interest, and rent through the factor markets. Households use that money to pay taxes to the government, to save it in the form of private savings that flows to the financial markets, or to pay for consumer spending on goods and services from firms or imports from the rest of the world. The government uses tax revenue to purchase goods and services from firms or the rest of the world. It can also use tax revenue to transfer money to households in the form of subsidies or the social safety net (Social Security or unemployment insurance payments, for example). Firms use the money they receive from the financial markets via borrowing or issuing stocks or bonds to pay for investment spending, which involves spending on goods and services such as machinery and building construction, which will increase their production in the future. Finally, the rest of the world purchases the economy's exports. To understand national income accounting, we focus on the flows to and from the markets for goods and services, which represent the "real" economy, shown on the left side of the diagram, in orange. The right side of the diagram, in blue, represents the "financial" economy, which we will examine in Chapter 10.

domestic product, or GDP, we have to examine an important distinction between classes of goods and services: the difference between *final goods and services,* on one side, and *intermediate goods and services* on the other.

Gross Domestic Product

A consumer's purchase of a new car from a dealer is one example of a sale of **final goods and services:** goods and services sold to the final, or end, user. But an automobile manufacturer's purchase of steel from a steel foundry or glass from a glassmaker is an example of purchasing **intermediate goods and services:**

final goods and services goods and services sold to the final, or end, user.

intermediate goods and services goods and services—bought from one firm by another firm—that are inputs for production of final goods and services.

gross domestic product (GDP) the total value of all final goods and services produced in the economy during a given period, usually a year.

aggregate spending the total flow of funds into markets for domestically produced final goods and services; the sum of consumer spending, investment spending, government purchases of goods and services, and exports minus imports.

goods and services that are inputs for production of final goods and services. In the case of intermediate goods and services, the purchaser—another firm—is *not* the final user.

Gross domestic product, or **GDP,** is the total value of all *final goods and services* produced in an economy during a given period, usually a year. In 2022 the GDP of the United States was $25,464 billion, or about $76,333 per person. If you are an economist trying to construct a country's national accounts, *one way to calculate GDP is to calculate it directly: survey firms and add up the total value of their production of final goods and services.* We'll soon explain why intermediate goods, and some other types of goods as well, are not included in the calculation of GDP.

But adding up the total value of final goods and services produced isn't the only way of calculating GDP. There are two other ways. One way is based on total spending on final goods and services. Since GDP is equal to the total value of final goods and services produced in the economy, it must also equal the flow of funds received by firms from sales in the goods and services market.

If you look again at the circular-flow diagram in Figure 1, you will see the arrow going from markets for goods and services to firms. The flow of funds out of the markets for goods and services to firms is equal to the total flow of funds into the markets for goods and services from other sectors. And as you can see from Figure 1, the total flow of funds into the markets for goods and services is total or **aggregate spending** on domestically produced final goods and services—the sum of consumer spending, investment spending, government purchases of goods and services, and exports minus imports. *So a second way of calculating GDP is to add up aggregate spending on domestically produced final goods and services in the economy.*

The third way of calculating GDP is based on total income earned in the economy. Firms, and the factors of production that they employ, are owned by households. So firms must ultimately pay out what they earn to households. The flow from firms to the factor markets is the factor income paid out by firms to households in the form of wages, profit, interest, and rent. Since all the income earned by firms belongs to someone—if it doesn't go to workers or bondholders, it counts as profits that accrue to shareholders—the value of the flow of factor income from firms to households must be equal to the flow of money into firms from the markets for goods and services. And this last value, we know, is the total value of production in the economy—GDP.

Why is GDP equal to the total value of factor income paid by firms in the economy to households? Because each sale in the economy must accrue to someone as income—either as wages, profit, interest, or rent. *So a third way of calculating GDP is to sum the total factor income earned by households from firms in the economy.*

"You wouldn't think there'd be much money in potatoes, chickens, and woodchopping, but it all adds up."

Calculating GDP

We've just explained the three methods for calculating GDP:

1. Survey and add up total value of all final goods and services produced.
2. Add up aggregate spending on all domestically produced goods and services in the economy.
3. Add up the total factor income earned by households from firms in the economy.

Government statisticians use all three methods. To illustrate how these three methods work, we will consider a simplified hypothetical economy, shown in Figure 2. This economy consists of three firms—National Motors, Inc., which produces one car per year; National Steel, Inc., which produces the steel that goes into the car; and National Ore, Inc., which mines the iron ore that goes into the steel. So GDP is $21,500, the value of the one car per year the economy produces.

FIGURE 2 Calculating GDP

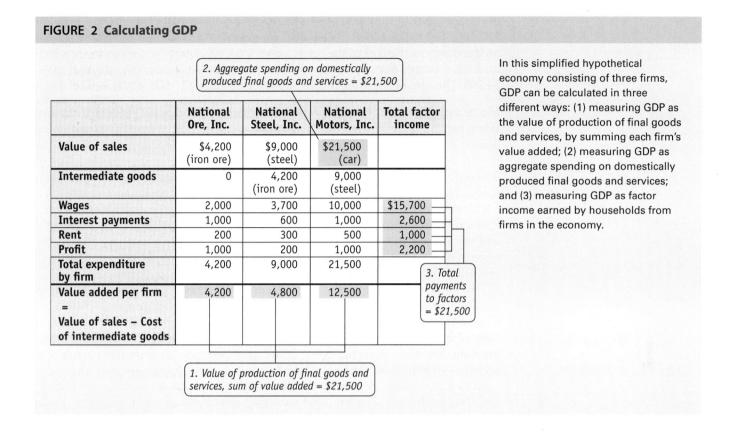

2. Aggregate spending on domestically produced final goods and services = $21,500

	National Ore, Inc.	National Steel, Inc.	National Motors, Inc.	Total factor income
Value of sales	$4,200 (iron ore)	$9,000 (steel)	$21,500 (car)	
Intermediate goods	0	4,200 (iron ore)	9,000 (steel)	
Wages	2,000	3,700	10,000	$15,700
Interest payments	1,000	600	1,000	2,600
Rent	200	300	500	1,000
Profit	1,000	200	1,000	2,200
Total expenditure by firm	4,200	9,000	21,500	
Value added per firm = Value of sales − Cost of intermediate goods	4,200	4,800	12,500	

3. Total payments to factors = $21,500

1. Value of production of final goods and services, sum of value added = $21,500

In this simplified hypothetical economy consisting of three firms, GDP can be calculated in three different ways: (1) measuring GDP as the value of production of final goods and services, by summing each firm's value added; (2) measuring GDP as aggregate spending on domestically produced final goods and services; and (3) measuring GDP as factor income earned by households from firms in the economy.

Let's look at how the three different methods of calculating GDP yield the same result.

Measuring GDP as the Value of Production of Final Goods and Services

The first method for calculating GDP is to add up the value of all the final goods and services produced in the economy—a calculation that excludes the value of intermediate goods and services. Why are intermediate goods and services excluded? After all, don't they represent a very large and valuable portion of the economy?

To understand why only final goods and services are included in GDP, look at the simplified economy described in Figure 2. Should we measure the GDP of this economy by adding up the total sales of the iron ore producer, the steel producer, and the auto producer? If we did, we would in effect be counting the value of the steel twice—once when it is sold by the steel plant to the auto plant, and again when the steel auto body is sold to a consumer as a finished car. And we would be counting the value of the iron ore *three* times—once when it is mined and sold to the steel company, a second time when it is made into steel and sold to the auto producer, and a third time when the steel is made into a car and sold to the consumer.

So counting the full value of each producer's sales would cause us to count the same items several times and artificially inflate the calculation of GDP. For example, in Figure 2, the total value of all sales, intermediate and final, is $34,700: $21,500 from the sale of the car, plus $9,000 from the sale of the steel, plus $4,200 from the sale of the iron ore. Yet we know that GDP is only $21,500. The way we avoid double-counting is to count only each producer's **value added** in the calculation of GDP: the difference between the value of its sales and the value of the intermediate goods and services it purchases from other businesses.

That is, we subtract the cost of inputs—the intermediate goods—at each stage of the production process. In this case, the value added of the auto producer is

value added (of a producer) the value of a producer's sales minus the value of its purchases of intermediate goods and services.

Steel is an intermediate good because it is sold to other product manufacturers, such as automakers, and rarely to final buyers, such as consumers.

the dollar value of the cars it manufactures *minus* the cost of the steel it buys, or $12,500. The value added of the steel producer is the dollar value of the steel it produces *minus* the cost of the ore it buys, or $4,800. Only the ore producer, which we have assumed doesn't buy any inputs, has value added equal to its total sales, $4,200. The sum of the three producers' value added is $21,500, equal to GDP.

Measuring GDP as Spending on Domestically Produced Final Goods and Services Another way to calculate GDP is by adding up aggregate spending on domestically produced final goods and services. That is, GDP can be measured by the flow of funds into firms. Like the method that estimates GDP as the value of domestic production of final goods and services, this measurement must be carried out in a way that avoids double-counting.

In terms of our steel and auto example, we don't want to count both consumer spending on a car (represented in Figure 2 by $21,500, the sales price of the car) and the auto producer's spending on steel (represented in Figure 2 by $9,000, the price of a car's worth of steel). If we counted both, we would be counting the steel embodied in the car twice.

We solve this problem by counting only the value of sales to *final buyers*, such as consumers, firms that purchase investment goods, the government, or foreign buyers. In other words, to avoid double-counting of spending, we omit sales of inputs from one business to another when estimating GDP using spending data. You can see from Figure 2 that aggregate spending on final goods and services—the finished car—is $21,500.

As we've already pointed out, the national accounts *do* include investment spending by firms as a part of final spending. That is, an auto company's purchase of steel to make a car isn't considered a part of final spending, but the company's purchase of new machinery for its factory *is* considered a part of final spending. What's the difference? Steel is an input that is used up in production; machinery will last for a number of years. Since purchases of capital goods that will last for a considerable time aren't closely tied to current production, the national accounts consider such purchases a form of final sales.

In later chapters, we will make use of the proposition that GDP is equal to aggregate spending on domestically produced goods and services by final buyers. We will also develop models of how final buyers decide how much to spend. With that in mind, we'll now examine the types of spending that make up GDP.

FOR INQUIRING MINDS **Our Imputed Lives**

An old line says that when a person marries the household cook, GDP falls. And it's true: when someone provides services for pay, those services are counted as a part of GDP. But the services family members provide to each other are not. Some economists have produced alternative measures that try to "impute" the value of household work — that is, assign an estimate of what the market value of that work would have been if it had been paid for. But the standard measure of GDP doesn't contain that imputation.

GDP estimates do, however, include an imputation for the value of owner-occupied housing. That is, if you buy the home you were formerly renting, GDP does not go down. It's true that because you no longer pay rent to your landlord, the landlord no longer sells a service to you — namely, use of the house or apartment. But the statisticians make an estimate of what you would have paid if you rented your dwelling, whether it's an apartment or a house. For the purposes of the statistics, it's as if you were renting from yourself.

If you think about it, this makes a lot of sense. In a country like the United States, the pleasure we derive from owning a home is an important part of the standard of living. So to be accurate, estimates of GDP must take into account the value of housing that is

The value of the services that family members provide to each other is not counted as part of GDP.

occupied by owners as well as the value of rental housing.

Look again at the markets for goods and services in the circular-flow diagram in Figure 1, and you will see that one component of sales by firms is consumer spending. Let's denote consumer spending with the symbol C. Figure 1 also shows three other components of sales: sales of investment goods to other businesses, or investment spending, which we will denote by I; government purchases of goods and services, which we will denote by G; and sales to foreigners—that is, exports—which we will denote by X.

In reality, not all of this final spending goes toward domestically produced goods and services. We must take account of spending on imports, which we will denote by IM. Income spent on imports is income not spent on domestic goods and services—it is income that has "leaked" across national borders. So to accurately value domestic production using spending data, we must subtract out spending on imports to arrive at spending on domestically produced goods and services. Putting this all together gives us the following equation, which breaks GDP down by the four sources of aggregate spending:

(1) $GDP = C + I + G + X - IM$

We'll be seeing a lot of Equation 1 in later chapters.

Measuring GDP as Factor Income Earned from Firms in the Economy A final way to calculate GDP is to add up all the income earned by factors of production from firms in the economy—the wages earned by labor; the interest paid to those who lend their savings to firms and the government; the rent earned by those who lease their land or structures to firms; and dividends, the profits paid to the shareholders, the owners of the firms' physical capital.

Figure 2 shows how this calculation works for our simplified economy. The numbers shaded in the column at far right show the total wages, interest, and rent paid by all these firms as well as their total profit. Summing up all of these items yields total factor income of $21,500—again, equal to GDP.

PITFALLS

GDP: WHAT'S IN AND WHAT'S OUT

It's easy to confuse what is included in and excluded from GDP. For example, investment spending—spending on productive physical capital (including construction of residential and commercial structures), and changes to inventories (goods and raw materials held to facilitate business operations)—is included in GDP. But spending on intermediate goods and services, like the steel used to make cars, is not. Why?

The answer is that we only include items that are newly produced (unlike, say, used cars), and aren't used up in production (like the steel in new cars). Here's a table summarizing what's in or out.

IN	OUT
Investment spending	**Spending on intermediate goods and services**
Spending on productive physical capital (including construction of residential and commercial structures) and changes to inventories	Inputs for production of final goods and services
Capital spending	**Used goods**
Considered part of investment spending	To include them would be to double-count: counting them once when sold as new and again when sold as used
Domestically produced final goods and services	**Financial assets like stocks and bonds**
Includes capital goods and new construction of structures produced by firms (also includes owner-occupied home-based businesses like child care provided by households, and educational and other such services provided by the government)	They don't represent either the production or the sale of final goods and services: a *bond* represents a promise to repay with interest; a *stock* represents a proof of ownership
	Import spending
	Spending on goods and services produced outside the country are not part of domestic production and are excluded

We won't emphasize factor income as much as the other two methods of calculating GDP. It's important to keep in mind, however, that all the money spent on domestically produced goods and services generates factor income to households.

The Components of GDP   Now that we know how GDP is calculated in principle, let's see what it looks like in practice.

Figure 3 shows the first two methods of calculating GDP side by side. The height of each bar above the horizontal axis represents the GDP of the U.S. economy in 2022: $25,464 billion. Each bar is divided to show the breakdown of that total in terms of where the value was added and how the money was spent.

In the left bar in Figure 3, we see the breakdown of GDP by value added according to sector, the first method of calculating GDP. Of the $25,464 billion, $19,592 billion consisted of value added by businesses. Another $3,145 billion of value added was added by households and institutions; a large part of that was the imputed services of owner-occupied housing, described in the For Inquiring Minds "Our Imputed Lives." Finally, $2,727 billion consisted of value added by government, in the form of military, education, and other government services.

The right bar in Figure 3 corresponds to the second method of calculating GDP, showing the breakdown by the four types of aggregate spending. The total length of the right bar is longer than the total length of the left bar, a difference of $974 billion (which, as you can see, is the amount by which the right bar extends below the horizontal axis). That's because the total length of the right bar represents total spending in the economy, spending on both domestically produced and foreign-produced final goods and services. Within the bar, consumer spending (*C*), which is 68.2% of GDP, dominates overall spending.

FIGURE 3 U.S. GDP in 2022: Two Methods of Calculating GDP

The two bars show two equivalent ways of calculating GDP. The height of each bar above the horizontal axis represents $26,438 billion, U.S. GDP in 2022. The right bar shows the breakdown of GDP according to the value added of each sector of the economy: government, households, and firms. The left bar shows the breakdown of GDP according to the four types of aggregate spending: $C + I + G + X - IM$. The left bar has a total length of $26,438 billion + $974 billion = $27,412 billion. The $974 billion shown as the area extending below the horizontal axis, is the amount of total spending absorbed by net exports, which were negative in 2022. (Numbers may not add due to rounding.)

Note: Billions of current dollars measured on *y*-axis.

Data from: Bureau of Economic Analysis.

Investment Spending
I = $4,631 (18.2%)

Government purchases
G = $4,447 (17.5%)

Net Exports
$X - IM$ = −$974 (−3.8%)

Consumer spending
C = $17,360 (68.2%)

Value added by business
= $19,592 (76.9%)

Value added by households
= $3,145 (12.4%)

Value added by government
= $2,727 (10.7%)

But some of that spending was absorbed by foreign-produced goods and services. In 2022, **net exports,** the difference between the value of exports and the value of imports (*X – IM* in Equation 1) was negative—the United States was a net importer of foreign goods and services. The 2022 value of *X – IM* was –$974 billion, or –3.8% of GDP. Thus, a portion of the right bar extends below the horizontal axis by $974 billion to represent the amount of total spending that was absorbed by net imports and so did not lead to higher U.S. GDP. Investment spending (*I*) constituted 18.2% of GDP; government purchases of goods and services (*G*) constituted 17.5% of GDP.

net exports the difference between the value of exports and the value of imports. A positive value for net exports indicates that a country is a net exporter of goods and services; a negative value indicates that a country is a net importer of goods and services.

What GDP Tells Us

We've now seen the various ways that gross domestic product is calculated. But what does the measurement of GDP tell us?

The most important use of GDP is as a measure of the size of the economy. For example, suppose you want to compare the economies of different nations. A natural approach is to compare their GDPs. For example, in 2022 India's GDP was $3.5 trillion, somewhat less than the GDP of Germany, Europe's largest economy, which came in at $4.0 trillion.

But wait—didn't we open this chapter by stating that by some measures, India's economy is bigger than that of any European nation? Well, it turns out that one must be careful when using GDP numbers in comparing countries, and especially when making comparisons over time. That's because part of the increase in the value of GDP over time represents increases in the *prices* of goods and services rather than an increase in output. For example, U.S. GDP was $8,578 billion in 1997 and had nearly tripled to $25,464 billion by 2022. But the U.S. economy didn't actually triple in size over that period. To measure actual changes in aggregate output, we need a modified version of GDP that is adjusted for price changes, known as *real GDP.*

A similar issue arises when comparing Germany and India, because many goods and services sold inside India are much cheaper than they are in Germany, and estimates that take this into account find that India's real GDP is bigger than the unadjusted number suggests. We'll see next how real GDP is calculated.

>> Check Your Understanding 7-1
Solutions appear at back of book.

1. Explain why the three methods of calculating GDP produce the same estimate of GDP.

2. What are the various sectors to which firms make sales? What are the various ways in which households are linked with other sectors of the economy?

3. Consider the first row of Figure 2 and suppose you mistakenly believed that total value added was $30,500, the sum of the sales price of a car and a car's worth of steel. What items would you be counting twice?

‖ Real GDP: A Measure of Aggregate Output

The U.S. economy had a pretty good year in 2022: the nation gained 4.8 million jobs, while the unemployment rate fell from 3.9% to 3.5%. It was certainly a better year than 1975, when by the late fall a severe recession reduced employment by 2 million and sent unemployment soaring. Strange to say, however, gross domestic product rose slightly faster in 1975 (10.1%) than it did in 2022 (7.5%). How is that possible? The answer is that back in 1975 GDP was rising for a bad reason—inflation, which raised the prices of the goods and services America produced—not because the economy was actually growing. Inflation, while high in 2022, was still considerably lower than 1975, so the rise in GDP really did correspond to economic progress.

aggregate output the total quantity of final goods and services the economy produces for a given time period, usually a year. Real GDP is the numerical measure of aggregate output typically used by economists.

real GDP the total value of all final goods and services produced in the economy during a given year, calculated using the prices of a selected base year.

nominal GDP the value of all final goods and services produced in the economy during a given year, calculated using the prices current in the year in which the output is produced.

In order to accurately measure the economy's growth, we need a measure of **aggregate output:** the total quantity of final goods and services the economy produces. The measure that is used for this purpose is known as *real GDP*. By tracking real GDP over time, we avoid the problem of changes in prices distorting the value of changes in production of goods and services over time. Let's look first at how real GDP is calculated, then at what it means.

Calculating Real GDP

To understand how real GDP is calculated, imagine an economy in which only two goods, apples and oranges, are produced and in which both goods are sold only to final consumers. The outputs and prices of the two fruits for two consecutive years are shown in Table 1.

The first thing we can say about these data is that the value of sales increased from year 1 to year 2. In the first year, the total value of sales was (2,000 billion × $0.25) + (1,000 billion × $0.50) = $1,000 billion; in the second it was (2,200 billion × $0.30) + (1,200 billion × $0.70) = $1,500 billion, which is 50% larger. But it is also clear from the table that this increase in the dollar value of GDP overstates the real growth in the economy. Although the quantities of both apples and oranges increased, the prices of both apples and oranges also rose. So part of the 50% increase in the dollar value of GDP from year 1 to year 2 simply reflects higher prices, not higher production of output.

To estimate the true increase in aggregate output produced, we have to ask: how much would GDP have gone up if prices had *not* changed? To answer this question, we need to find the value of output in year 2 expressed in year 1 prices. In year 1, the price of apples was $0.25 each and the price of oranges $0.50 each. So year 2 output *at year 1 prices* is (2,200 billion × $0.25) + (1,200 billion × $0.50) = $1,150 billion. And output in year 1 at year 1 prices was $1,000 billion. So in this example GDP measured in year 1 prices rose 15%—from $1,000 billion to $1,150 billion.

Now we can define **real GDP:** it is the total value of final goods and services produced in the economy during a year, calculated as if prices had stayed constant at the level of some given base year. A real GDP number always comes with information about what the base year is.

A GDP number that has not been adjusted for changes in prices is calculated using the prices in the year in which the output is produced. Economists call this measure **nominal GDP,** GDP at current prices. If we had used nominal GDP to measure the true change in output from year 1 to year 2 in our apples and oranges example, we would have overstated the true growth in output: we would have claimed it to be 50%, when in fact it was only 15%. By comparing output in the two years using a common set of prices—the year 1 prices in this example—we are able to focus solely on changes in the quantity of output by eliminating the influence of changes in prices.

TABLE 1 Calculating GDP and Real GDP in a Simple Economy

	Year 1	Year 2
Quantity of apples (billions)	2,000	2,200
Price of apple	$0.25	$0.30
Quantity of oranges (billions)	1,000	1,200
Price of orange	$0.50	$0.70
GDP (billions of dollars)	$1,000	$1,500
Real GDP (billions of year 1 dollars)	$1,000	$1,150

Table 2 shows a real-life version of our apples and oranges example. The second column shows nominal GDP in 2002, 2012, and 2022. The third column shows real GDP for each year in 2012 dollars. For 2012, the two numbers are the same. But real GDP in 2002 expressed in 2012 dollars was higher than nominal GDP in 2002, reflecting the fact that prices were in general higher in 2012 than 2002. Real GDP in 2022 expressed in 2012 dollars, however, was less than nominal GDP in 2022 because prices in 2012 were lower than in 2022.

TABLE 2 Nominal versus Real GDP in 2002, 2012, and 2022

	Nominal GDP (billions of current dollars)	Real GDP (billions of 2012 dollars)
2002	$10,929	$13,488
2012	16,254	16,254
2022	$25,464	$20,015

You might have noticed that there is an alternative way to calculate real GDP using the data in Table 1. Why not measure it using the prices of year 2 rather than year 1 as the base-year prices? This procedure seems equally valid. According to that calculation, real GDP in year 1 at year 2 prices is (2,000 billion × $0.30) + (1,000 billion × $0.70) = $1,300 billion; real GDP in year 2 at year 2 prices is $1,500 billion, the same as nominal GDP in year 2. So using year 2 prices as the base year, the growth rate of real GDP is equal to ($51,500 billion – $1,300 billion)/ $1,300 billion = 0.154, or 15.4%. This is slightly higher than the figure we got from the previous calculation, in which year 1 prices were the base-year prices. In that calculation, we found that real GDP increased by 15%. Neither answer, 15.4% versus 15%, is more "correct" than the other.

In reality, the government economists who put together the U.S. national accounts have adopted a method known as chain-linking to measure the change in real GDP; they use the average between the GDP growth rate calculated using an early base year and the GDP growth rate calculated using a late base year. As a result, U.S. statistics on real GDP are always expressed in **chained dollars.**

What Real GDP Doesn't Measure

GDP, nominal or real, is a measure of a country's aggregate output. Other things equal, a country with a larger population will have higher GDP simply because there are more people working. So if we want to compare GDP across countries but want to eliminate the effect of differences in population size, we use the measure **GDP per capita**—GDP divided by the size of the population, equivalent to the average GDP per person.

Real GDP per capita can be a useful measure in some circumstances, such as in a comparison of labor productivity between countries. However, despite the fact that it is a rough measure of the average real output per person, real GDP per capita has well-known limitations as a measure of a country's living standards. Every once in a while economists are accused of believing that growth in real GDP per capita is the only thing that matters—that is, thinking that increasing real GDP per capita is a goal in itself. In fact, economists rarely make that mistake; the idea that economists care only about real GDP per capita is a sort of urban legend.

Let's take a moment to be clear about why a country's real GDP per capita is not a sufficient measure of human welfare in that country and why growth in real GDP per capita is not an appropriate policy goal in itself.

One way to think about this is to say that an increase in real GDP means an expansion in the economy's production possibility frontier. Because the economy has increased its productive capacity, society can achieve more things. But whether society actually makes good use of that increased potential to improve living standards is another matter. To put it in a slightly different way, your income may be higher this year than last year, but whether you use that higher income to improve your quality of life is your choice.

Real GDP per capita, then, is a measure of an economy's average aggregate output per person. A country with a high GDP can afford for its citizens to be healthy, to be well educated, and in general, to have a good quality of life. But there is not a one-to-one match between GDP and the quality of life.

chained dollars method of calculating real GDP that splits the difference between growth rates calculated using early base years and the growth rate calculated using a late base year.

GDP per capita GDP divided by the size of the population; equivalent to the average GDP per person.

ECONOMICS >> *in Action*
Trouble in Paradise

Travel writers sometimes describe Sri Lanka, an island of spectacular natural beauty, as paradise. But it's also a real country whose 22 million people, like people anywhere, need to make a living. And in 2022, it was a nation experiencing its worst economic crisis since achieving independence in 1948. In particular, shortages of crucial imports, especially fuel and fertilizer, were having devastating

GLOBAL COMPARISON GDP AND THE MEANING OF LIFE

"I've been rich and I've been poor," the actress Mae West famously declared. "Believe me, rich is better." But is the same true for countries?

This figure shows two pieces of information for a number of countries: how rich they are, as measured by GDP per capita, and how people assess their well-being. Well-being was measured by a Gallup world survey that asked people to rate how satisfied they were with their lives on a scale of 0 to 10. The figure seems to tell us three things:

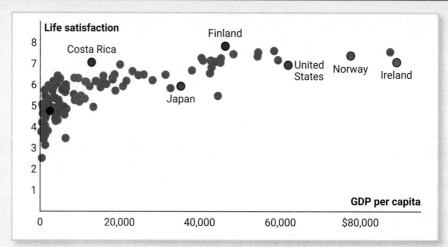

1. *Rich is better.* Richer countries on average have a higher well-being than poor countries.
2. *Money matters less as you grow richer.* As GDP rises, the average gain in life satisfaction per extra dollar gets smaller and smaller. Going from per capita GDP of $20,000 to $40,000 seems to produce no more gain than going from $10,000 to $20,000.

3. *Money isn't everything.* Costa Ricans, whose nation is only middle-income, seem more satisfied with their lives than citizens of much richer countries, like Japan.

These results are consistent with the observation that high GDP per capita makes it easier to achieve a good life but that countries aren't equally successful in taking advantage of that possibility.

Note: Life satisfaction measured as country average from 0 to 10 (Cantril Ladder (0 = worst; 10 = best); GDP per capita (constant 2015 international $).
Data from: World Happiness Report (2021); World Bank.

---

effects on production. Economic discontent led to huge protests, and the president fled the country.

But how could this be? After all, Sri Lanka's GDP rose rapidly in 2022, up 34% from its level in 2021.

The answer was that this was the growth in *nominal* GDP, and one of Sri Lanka's problems was high inflation. *Real* GDP fell by more than 8% in 2022.

Sri Lanka's woes therefore offer a good example of why it's important to distinguish between nominal and real GDP. They also demonstrate the importance of measuring inflation carefully—something that, as we explain in this chapter's Business Case, some governments don't do.

>> Check Your Understanding 7-2

Solutions appear at back of book.

1. Assume there are only two goods in the economy, french fries and onion rings. In 2022, 1,000,000 servings of french fries were sold at $0.40 each and 800,000 servings of onion rings at $0.60 each. From 2022 to 2023, the price of french fries rose by 25% and the servings sold fell by 10%; the price of onion rings fell by 15% and the servings sold rose by 5%.
   a. Calculate nominal GDP in 2022 and 2023. Calculate real GDP in 2023 using 2022 prices.
   b. Why would an assessment of growth using nominal GDP be misguided?
2. From 2016 to 2022, the price of electronic equipment fell dramatically and the price of housing rose dramatically. What are the implications of this in deciding whether to use 2016 or 2022 as the base year in calculating 2018 real GDP?

>> Quick Review

• To determine the actual growth in **aggregate output,** we calculate **real GDP** using prices from some given base year. In contrast, **nominal GDP** is the value of aggregate output calculated with current prices. U.S. statistics on real GDP are always expressed in **chained dollars.**

• Real **GDP per capita** is a measure of the average aggregate output per person. But it is not a sufficient measure of human welfare, nor is it an appropriate goal in itself, because it does not reflect important aspects of living standards within an economy.

Price Indexes and the Aggregate Price Level

By the end of 2022, drivers had something to celebrate: gasoline prices had tumbled to an average of $3.09 per gallon, down 40% from their peak, a year earlier. But while driving was getting cheaper, having someplace to live when you arrived was getting more expensive: by the end of 2022, average rents were 7.5% higher than they had been when gas was its most expensive. So was the cost of living going up or down?

Clearly, there was a need for a single number summarizing what was happening to consumer prices. Just as macroeconomists find it useful to have a single number representing the overall level of output, they also find it useful to have a single number representing the overall level of prices: the **aggregate price level.** Yet a huge variety of goods and services are produced and consumed in the economy. How can we summarize the prices of all these goods and services with a single number? The answer lies in the concept of a *price index*—a concept best introduced with an example.

Market Baskets and Price Indexes

Suppose that a frost in Florida destroys most of the citrus harvest. As a result, the price of an orange rises from $0.20 to $0.40, the price of a grapefruit rises from $0.60 to $1.00, and the price of a lemon rises from $0.25 to $0.45. How much has the price of citrus fruit increased?

One way to answer that question is to state three numbers—the changes in prices for oranges, grapefruit, and lemons. But this is a very cumbersome method. Rather than having to recite three numbers in an effort to track changes in the prices of citrus fruit, we would prefer to have some kind of overall measure of the *average* price change.

To measure average price changes for consumer goods and services, economists track changes in the cost of a typical consumer's *consumption bundle*—the typical basket of goods and services purchased before the price changes. A hypothetical consumption bundle, used to measure changes in the overall price level, is known as a **market basket.** Suppose that before the frost a typical consumer bought 200 oranges, 50 grapefruit, and 100 lemons over the course of a year, our market basket for this example.

Table 3 shows the pre-frost and post-frost cost of this market basket. Before the frost, it cost $95; after the frost, the same bundle of goods cost $175. Since $175/$95 = 1.842, the post-frost basket costs 1.842 times the cost of the pre-frost basket, a cost increase of 84.2%. In this example, the average price of citrus fruit has increased 84.2% since the base year as a result of the frost, where the base year is the initial year used in the measurement of the price change.

aggregate price level a single number that represents the overall price level for final goods and services in the economy.

market basket a hypothetical consumption bundle of consumer purchases of goods and services, used to measure changes in overall price level.

price index a measure of the cost of purchasing a given market basket in a given year, where that cost is normalized so that it is equal to 100 in the selected base year; a measure of overall price level.

TABLE 3 Calculating the Cost of a Market Basket

	Pre-frost	Post-frost
Price of orange	$0.20	$0.40
Price of grapefruit	0.60	1.00
Price of lemon	0.25	0.45
Cost of market basket (200 oranges, 50 grapefruit, 100 lemons)	(200 × $0.20) + (50 × $0.60) + (100 × $0.25) = $95.00	(200 × $0.40) + (50 × $1.00) + (100 × $0.45) = $175.00

Economists use the same method to measure changes in the overall price level over time. For example, to measure the change in the overall price level from 2010 (the base year) to 2022, they compare the cost of purchasing the market basket in 2010 to the cost in 2022. So they *normalize* the measure of the aggregate price level, meaning that they set the cost of the market basket equal to 100 in the chosen base year. Working with a market basket and a base year, and after normalizing, we arrive at a **price index,** a normalized measure of the overall price level. It is always cited along with the year for which the aggregate price level is being measured and the base year. A price index can be calculated using the following formula:

(2) $\text{Price index in a given year} = \dfrac{\text{Cost of market basket in a given year}}{\text{Cost of market basket in base year}} \times 100$

In our example, the citrus fruit market basket cost $95 in the base year, the year before the frost. So by Equation 2 we define the price index for citrus fruit

inflation rate the annual percent change in a price index—typically the consumer price index. The inflation rate is positive when the aggregate price level is rising (inflation) and negative when the aggregate price level is falling (deflation).

consumer price index (CPI) a measure of prices; calculated by surveying market prices for a market basket intended to represent the consumption of a typical urban American family of four. The CPI is the most commonly used measure of prices in the United States.

as (cost of market basket in a given year/$95) × 100, yielding an index of 100 for the period before the frost and 184.2 after the frost. You should note that the price index for the base year always results in a price index equal to 100. This is because the price index in the base year is equal to: (cost of market basket in base year/cost of market basket in base year) × 100 = 100.

Thus, the price index makes it clear that the average price of citrus has risen 84.2% as a consequence of the frost. Because of its simplicity and intuitive appeal, the method we've just described is used to calculate a variety of price indexes to track average price changes among a variety of different groups of goods and services. For example, the *consumer price index*, which we'll discuss shortly, is the most widely used measure of the aggregate price level, the overall price level of final consumer goods and services across the economy.

Price indexes are also the basis for measuring inflation. The **inflation rate** is the annual percent change in an official price index. The inflation rate from year 1 to year 2 is calculated using the following formula, where we assume that year 1 and year 2 are consecutive years:

$$(3) \quad \text{Inflation rate} = \frac{\text{Price index in year 2} - \text{Price index in year 1}}{\text{Price index in year 1}} \times 100$$

Typically, a news report that cites "the inflation rate" is referring to the annual percent change in the consumer price index.

The Consumer Price Index

The most widely used measure of prices in the United States is the **consumer price index** (often referred to simply as the **CPI**), which is intended to show how the cost of all purchases by a typical urban family has changed over time. It is calculated by surveying market prices for a market basket that is constructed to represent the consumption of a typical family of four living in a typical U.S. city. The base period for the index is currently 1982–1984; that is, the index is calculated so that the average of consumer prices in 1982–1984 is 100.

The market basket used to calculate the CPI is far more complex than the three-fruit market basket we just described. In fact, to calculate the CPI, the Bureau of Labor Statistics sends its employees out to survey supermarkets, gas stations, hardware stores, and so on—some 23,000 retail outlets in 87 cities. Every month it tabulates about 80,000 prices, on everything from romaine lettuce to a medical check-up.

Figure 4 shows the weight of major categories in the consumer price index as of February 2023. For example, motor fuel, mainly gasoline, accounted for 3.3%

FIGURE 4 The Makeup of the Consumer Price Index in 2023

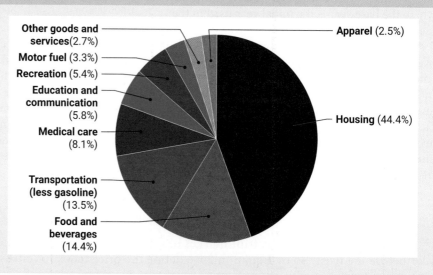

This chart shows the percentage shares of major types of spending in the CPI as of February 2023. Housing, food, transportation, and motor fuel made up about 76% of the CPI market basket. (Numbers don't add to 100% due to rounding.)
Data from: Bureau of Labor Statistics.

FIGURE 5 The CPI, 1913–2022

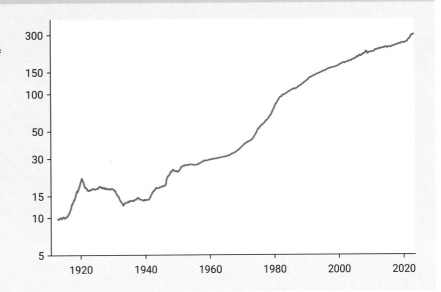

Since 1940, the CPI has risen steadily. But the annual percentage increases in recent years have been much smaller than those of the 1970s and early 1980s. (The vertical axis is measured on a logarithmic scale so that equal percent changes in the CPI have the same slope.)
Data from: Bureau of Labor Statistics.

of the CPI. On the other hand, housing accounted for more than 44% of the CPI. So that 40% plunge in gasoline prices would have reduced the CPI by roughly 1.3%(0.40 × 3.3%), while the smaller percentage rise in housing costs of 7.5% actually had a bigger positive effect on the overall price index of 3.3%(0.075 × 44.4%).

Figure 5 shows how the CPI has changed since measurement began in 1913. Since 1940, the CPI has risen steadily, although its annual percent increases in recent years have been much smaller than those of the 1970s and early 1980s. (A logarithmic scale is used so that equal percent changes in the CPI have the same slope.)

The United States is not the only country that calculates a consumer price index. In fact, nearly every country has one. As you might expect, the market baskets that make up these indexes differ quite a lot from country to country. In low-income countries, where people must spend a high proportion of their income just to feed themselves, food makes up a large share of the price index. Among high-income countries, differences in consumption patterns lead to differences in the price indexes: the Japanese price index puts a larger weight on raw fish and a smaller weight on beef than ours does, and the French price index puts a larger weight on wine.

Other Price Measures

There are two other price measures that are also widely used to track economy-wide price changes. One is the **producer price index** (or **PPI,** which used to be known as the *wholesale price index*). As its name suggests, the PPI measures the cost of a typical basket of goods and services—containing raw commodities such as steel, electricity, coal, and so on—purchased by producers. Because commodity producers are relatively quick to change prices when they perceive a change in overall demand for their goods, the PPI often responds to inflationary or deflationary pressures more quickly than the CPI. As a result, a change in the PPI is often regarded as an early warning signal of changes in the inflation rate.

The other widely used price measure is the *GDP deflator;* it isn't exactly a price index, although it serves the same purpose. Recall in our discussion of Table 2 we distinguished between *nominal GDP* (GDP in current prices) and *real GDP* (GDP calculated using the prices of a base year). The **GDP deflator** for a given year is equal to 100 times the ratio of nominal GDP for that year to real GDP for that year. Since real GDP is currently expressed in 2012 dollars, the GDP deflator for

producer price index (PPI) a measure of the cost of a typical basket of goods and services purchased by producers. Because these commodity prices respond quickly to changes in demand, the PPI is often regarded as a leading indicator of changes in the inflation rate.

GDP deflator a price measure for a given year that is equal to 100 times the ratio of nominal GDP to real GDP in that year.

FIGURE 6 The CPI, the PPI, and the GDP Deflator

As the figure shows, the three different measures of inflation, the PPI (orange), the CPI (green), and the GDP deflator (blue), usually move closely together. Each reveals a drastic acceleration of inflation during the 1970s and a return to relative price stability in the 1990s. With the exception of a brief period of deflation in 2009, prices were stable until they surged in 2021 following the Covid-19 pandemic.

Data from: Bureau of Labor Statistics; Bureau of Economic Analysis.

2012 is equal to 100. If nominal GDP doubles but real GDP does not change, the GDP deflator indicates that the aggregate price level doubled.

Perhaps the most important point about the different inflation rates generated by these three measures of prices is that they usually move closely together (although the PPI tends to fluctuate more than either of the other two measures). Figure 6 shows the annual percent changes in the three indexes since 1930. By all three measures, the U.S. economy experienced deflation during the early years of the Great Depression, inflation during World War II, accelerating inflation during the 1970s, a return to relative price stability in the 1990s and a renewed surge in 2021–2022. Notice, by the way, the dramatic ups and downs in producer prices even when other measures were relatively stable; this reflects large swings in energy and food prices, which play a much bigger role in the PPI than they do in either the CPI or the GDP deflator.

ECONOMICS >> *in Action*
Indexing to the CPI

Although GDP is a very important number for shaping economic policy, official statistics on GDP don't have a direct effect on people's lives. The CPI, by contrast, has a direct and immediate impact on millions of Americans.

The reason is that many payments are tied, or *indexed*, to the CPI—the amount paid rises or falls when the CPI rises or falls.

The practice of indexing payments to consumer prices goes back to the dawn of the United States as a nation. In 1780, the Massachusetts State Legislature recognized that the pay of its soldiers fighting the British needed to be increased because of inflation that occurred during the Revolutionary War. The legislature adopted a formula that made a soldier's pay proportional to the cost of a market basket that consisted of 5 bushels of corn, $68\frac{4}{7}$ pounds of beef, 10 pounds of sheep's wool, and 16 pounds of shoe leather.

Today, 65 million people receive payments from Social Security, a national retirement program that accounts for almost a quarter of current total federal spending—more than the defense budget. The amount of an individual's Social

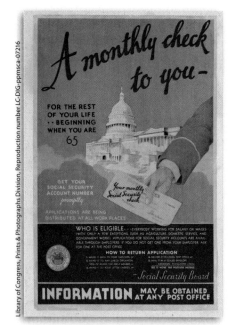

A small change in the CPI has large consequences for those dependent on Social Security payments.

Security payment is determined by a formula that reflects each person's previous payments into the system and other factors. In addition, all Social Security payments are adjusted each year to offset any increase in consumer prices over the previous year. The CPI is used to calculate the official estimate of the inflation rate used to adjust these payments yearly. So every percentage point added to the official estimate of the rate of inflation adds 1% to the checks received by tens of millions of individuals.

Other government payments, such as disability benefits, are also indexed to the CPI. In addition, income tax brackets, the bands of income levels that determine a taxpayer's income tax rate, are indexed to the CPI. (Individuals in a higher income bracket pay a higher income tax rate in a progressive tax system like ours.) Indexing also extends to the private sector, where some private contracts, including some wage settlements, contain cost-of-living allowances (called COLAs) that adjust payments in proportion to changes in the CPI.

Because the CPI plays such an important and direct role in people's lives, it's a politically sensitive number. The Bureau of Labor Statistics, which calculates the CPI, takes great care in collecting and interpreting price and consumption data. It uses a complex method in which households are surveyed to determine what they buy and where they shop, and a carefully selected sample of stores are surveyed to get representative prices.

>> Check Your Understanding 7-3

Solutions appear at back of book.

1. Consider Table 3 but suppose that the market basket is composed of 100 oranges, 50 grapefruit, and 200 lemons. How does this change the pre-frost and post-frost price indexes? Explain. Generalize your explanation to how the construction of the market basket affects the price index.

2. For each of the following events, how would an economist using a 10-year-old market basket create a bias in measuring the change in the cost of living today?
   a. A typical family owns more cars than it would have a decade ago. Over that time, the average price of a car has increased more than the average prices of other goods.
   b. Virtually no households had broadband internet access 20 years ago. Now many households have it, and the price has regularly fallen each year.

3. The consumer price index in the United States (base period 1982–1984) was 280.88 in 2021 and 298.99 in 2022. Calculate the inflation rate from 2021 to 2022.

Paying for a Heads-Up on Inflation

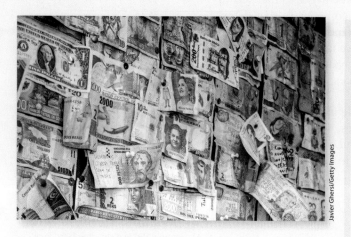

Javier Ghersi/Getty Images

Normally we rely on governments to produce key economic statistics. But what if you can't trust the government's numbers? That's what happened in Argentina from 2007 to 2016, where it was common knowledge that the government was manipulating the data to make inflation look lower than it really was. In response, researchers at MIT and Harvard created what they called The Billion Prices Project, using online prices to create their own measures of inflation, first for Argentina, then for a number of other countries, including the United States. The researchers found that by the middle of 2015 inflation in Argentina had risen to nearly 27.18%, but official measures showed an annual inflation rate of 14.85%. The story was a bit different for the United States. While official inflation measures reported an inflation rate of 0.17%, the project reported an annual inflation rate of –0.60%.

The Billion Prices Project played a surprisingly important role in the U.S. economic debate around

2011–2012. At the time a number of prominent commentators were claiming that official U.S. measures of consumer prices were understating the true rate of inflation. One way to see whether this was really happening was to compare the official inflation rate with the independently calculated Billion Prices measure. As it happened, there was very little difference between the two measures; the U.S. government was, in fact, reporting the numbers honestly.

But if the government numbers are okay, who needs an independent private inflation measure? The answer is that the Billion Prices measure, which is based on online data, can track inflation more or less in real time, unlike the CPI, which is only released once a month.

And there is, it turns out, a market for early reads on the inflation rate. PriceStats, a company owned by State Street Bank, uses Billion Prices data to produce real-time inflation estimates, which are made available to customers—mainly businesses—who pay a subscription fee. PriceStats data give you a heads-up on inflation trends, a few weeks before everyone else has the official data. And people are willing to pay for that heads-up.

QUESTIONS FOR THOUGHT

1. Why do you think the government of Argentina might have wanted to pretend that inflation was lower than it really was?

2. If researchers can produce a pretty good inflation measure just using online data, why do we need the elaborate process used to create the CPI?

3. Elaborating on Question 2, what things might the Billion Prices index miss? Think about what we said about the weights of various goods in the CPI.

SUMMARY

1. Economists keep track of the flows of money between sectors with the **national income and product accounts**, or **national accounts**. Demand for goods and services comes from **consumer spending, investment spending**, and **government purchases of goods and services. Exports** generate an inflow of funds into the country from the rest of the world, but **imports** lead to an outflow of funds to the rest of the world.

2. **Gross domestic product**, or **GDP**, measures the value of all **final goods and services** produced in the economy. It does not include the value of **intermediate goods and services**, but it does include **net exports** ($X - IM$). It can be calculated in three ways: add up the **value added** by all producers; add up all spending on domestically produced final goods and services, leading to the equation $GDP = C + I + G + X - IM$, also known as **aggregate spending;** or add up all the income paid by domestic firms to factors of production. These three methods are equivalent because in the economy as a whole, total income paid by domestic firms to factors of production must equal total spending on domestically produced final goods and services.

3. **Real GDP** is the value of the final goods and services produced calculated using the prices of a selected base year. Except in the base year, real GDP is not the same as **nominal GDP,** the value of **aggregate output** calculated using current prices. Analysis of the growth rate of aggregate output must use real GDP because doing so eliminates any change in the value of aggregate output due solely to price changes. Real **GDP per capita** is a measure of average aggregate output per person but is not in itself an appropriate policy goal. U.S. statistics on real GDP are always expressed in **chained dollars.**

4. To measure the **aggregate price level,** economists calculate the cost of purchasing a **market basket. A price index** is the ratio of the current cost of that market basket to the cost in a selected base year, multiplied by 100.

5. The **inflation rate** is the yearly percent change in a price index, typically based on the **consumer price index,** or **CPI,** the most common measure of the aggregate price level. A similar index for goods and services purchased by firms is the **producer price index,** or **PPI.** Finally, economists also use the **GDP deflator,** which measures the price level by calculating the ratio of nominal GDP to real GDP times 100.

KEY TERMS

PRACTICE QUESTIONS

1. Go to the Bureau of Labor Statistics home page at www.bls.gov. Click on the "Economic Releases" tab and then click on "Major Economic Indicators" in the drop-down menu that appears. Once on the "Major Economic Indicators" page, click on "Consumer Price Index." On that page, under "Table of Contents," click on "Table 1: Consumer Price Index for All Urban Consumers." Using the "unadjusted" figures, determine what the CPI was for the previous month. How did it change from the previous month? How does the CPI compare to the same month one year ago?

2. Explain the difference between intermediate and investment goods. Are intermediate and investment goods included in GDP? Explain.

3. Analyze the following statement: "GDP has increased by 2% from last year. This is a good indicator of economic well-being as it represents an average increase in incomes."

4. Using Figure 4, explain how the current weighting of the CPI index could lead to either over or understating the actual inflation rate for your household.

PROBLEMS

1. Below is a simplified circular-flow diagram for the economy of Micronia. (Note that there is no investment spending and no transfers in Micronia.)

   a. What is the value of GDP in Micronia?

   b. What is the value of net exports?

   c. What is the value of disposable income?

   d. Does the total flow of money out of households—the sum of taxes paid and consumer spending—equal the total flow of money into households?

   e. How does the government of Micronia finance its purchases of goods and services?

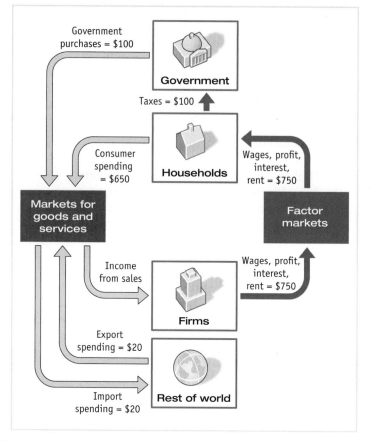

2. A more complex circular-flow diagram for the economy of Macronia is shown below.

   a. What is the value of GDP in Macronia?

   b. What is the value of net exports?

   c. What is the value of disposable income?

   d. Does the total flow of money out of households—the sum of taxes paid, consumer spending, and private savings—equal the total flow of money into households?

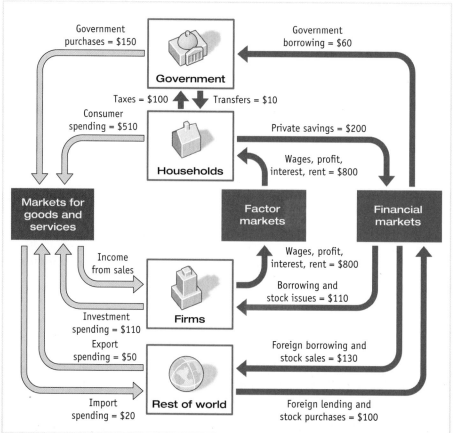

3. The components of GDP in the accompanying table were produced by the Bureau of Economic Analysis.

Category	Components of GDP in 2022 (billions of dollars)
Consumer spending	
Durable goods	$2,184.7
Nondurable goods	3,754.9
Services	11,420.8
Private investment spending	
Fixed investment spending	4,472.0
Nonresidential	3,345.1
Structures	648.2
Equipment and intellectual property products	1,374.3
Residential	1,126.9
Change in private inventories	159.0
Net exports	
Exports	2,979.6
Imports	3,953.9
Government purchases of goods and services and investment spending	
Federal	1,646.7
National defense	924.9
Nondefense	721.7
State and local	2,800.7

a. Calculate 2022 consumer spending.

b. Calculate 2022 private investment spending.

c. Calculate 2022 net exports.

d. Calculate 2022 government purchases of goods and services and government investment spending.

e. Calculate 2022 gross domestic product.

f. Calculate 2022 consumer spending on services as a percentage of total consumer spending.

g. Calculate 2022 exports as a percentage of imports.

h. Calculate 2022 government purchases on national defense as a percentage of federal government purchases of goods and services.

4. The small economy of Pizzania produces three goods (bread, cheese, and pizza), each produced by a separate company. The bread and cheese companies produce all the inputs they need to make bread and cheese, respectively. The pizza company uses the bread and cheese from the other companies to make its pizzas. All three companies employ labor to help produce their goods, and the difference between the value of goods sold and the sum of labor and input costs is the firm's profit. The accompanying table summarizes the activities of the three companies when all the bread and cheese produced are sold to the pizza company as inputs in the production of pizzas.

	Bread company	Cheese company	Pizza company
Cost of inputs	$0	$0	$50 (bread) 35 (cheese)
Wages	15	20	75
Value of output	50	35	200

a. Calculate GDP as the value added in production.

b. Calculate GDP as spending on final goods and services.

c. Calculate GDP as factor income.

5. In the economy of Pizzania (from Problem 4), bread and cheese produced are sold both to the pizza company for inputs in the production of pizzas and to consumers as final goods. The accompanying table summarizes the activities of the three companies.

	Bread company	Cheese company	Pizza company
Cost of inputs	$0	$0	$50 (bread) 35 (cheese)
Wages	25	30	75
Value of output	100	60	200

a. Calculate GDP as the value added in production.

b. Calculate GDP as spending on final goods and services.

c. Calculate GDP as factor income.

6. Which of the following transactions will be included in GDP for the United States?

a. Coca-Cola builds a new bottling plant in the United States.

b. Delta sells one of its existing airplanes to Korean Air.

c. Ms. Moneybags buys an existing share of Disney stock.

d. A California winery produces a bottle of Chardonnay and sells it to a customer in Montreal, Canada.

e. An American buys a bottle of French perfume in Tulsa.

f. A book publisher produces too many copies of a new book; the books don't sell this year, so the publisher adds the surplus books to inventories.

7. Access the Discovering Data exercise for Chapter 7, Problem 7 online to answer the following questions.

a. What was GDP for the United States last year?

b. Calculate the absolute change in U.S. GDP between last year and the year before.

c. Which component of GDP was the largest last year? Which was the smallest? What is the most recent year in which net exports were positive?

d. What happened to the size of government spending during the 1940s? What factors likely caused the shift?

e. How has each of the four components, as a percent of GDP, changed since the 1940s?

8. The accompanying table shows data on nominal GDP (in billions of dollars), real GDP (in billions of 2012 dollars), and population (in thousands) of the United States in 1972, 1982, 1992, 2002, 2012, and 2022. The U.S. price level rose consistently over the period 1972–2022.

Year	Nominal GDP (billions of dollars)	Real GDP (billions of 2012 dollars)	Population (thousands)
1972	$1,279	$5,387	209,924
1982	3,344	6,810	232,218
1992	6,520	9,691	256,922
2002	10,929	13,488	287,955
2012	16,254	16,254	314,725
2022	25,464	20,015	333,595

a. Why is real GDP greater than nominal GDP for all years until 2012 and lower for 2022?

b. Calculate the percent change in real GDP from 1972 to 1982, 1982 to 1992, 1992 to 2002, 2002 to 2012, and 2012 to 2022. Which period had the highest growth rate?

c. Calculate real GDP per capita for each of the years in the table.

d. Calculate the percent change in real GDP per capita from 1972 to 1982, 1982 to 1992, 1992 to 2002, 2002 to 2012, and 2012 to 2022. Which period had the highest growth rate?

e. How do the percent change in real GDP and the percent change in real GDP per capita compare? Which is larger? Do we expect them to have this relationship?

9. Eastland College is concerned about the rising price of textbooks that students must purchase. To better identify the increase in the price of textbooks, the dean asks you, the Economics Department's star student, to create an index of textbook prices. The average student purchases three English, two math, and four economics textbooks per year. The prices of these books are given in the accompanying table.

	2020	2021	2022
English textbook	$100	$110	$114
Math textbook	140	144	148
Economics textbook	160	180	200

a. What is the percent change in the price of an English textbook from 2020 to 2022?

b. What is the percent change in the price of a math textbook from 2020 to 2022?

c. What is the percent change in the price of an economics textbook from 2020 to 2022?

d. Using 2021 as a base year, create a price index for these books for all years.

e. What is the percent change in the price index from 2020 to 2022?

10. The consumer price index, or CPI, measures the cost of living for a typical urban household by multiplying the price for each category of expenditure (housing, food, and so on) times a measure of the importance of that expenditure in the average consumer's market basket and summing over all categories. However, using data from the CPI, we can see that changes in the cost of living for different types of consumers can vary a great deal. Let's compare the cost of living for a hypothetical retired person and a hypothetical college student. Let's assume that the market basket of a retired person is allocated in the following way: 10% on housing, 15% on food, 5% on transportation, 60% on medical care, 0% on education, and 10% on recreation. The college student's market basket is allocated as follows: 5% on housing, 15% on food, 20% on transportation, 0% on medical care, 40% on education, and 20% on recreation. The accompanying table shows the January 2023 CPI for each of the relevant categories.

	CPI January 2023
Housing	202.2
Food	205.1
Transportation	180.9
Medical care	238
Education	135.6
Recreation	149.5

Calculate the overall CPI for the retired person and for the college student by multiplying the CPI for each of the categories by the relative importance of that category to the individual and then summing each of the categories. The CPI for all items in January 2023 was 188.5. How do your calculations for a CPI for the retired person and the college student compare to the overall CPI?

11. The accompanying table provides the annual real GDP (in billions of 2012 dollars) and nominal GDP (in billions of dollars) for the United States.

a. Calculate the GDP deflator for each year.

b. Use the GDP deflator to calculate the inflation rate for all years except 2016.

	2016	2017	2018	2019	2020	2021	2022
Real GDP (billions of 2012 dollars)	17,680	18,077	18,609	19,036	18,509	19,610	20,015
Nominal GDP (billions of dollars)	18,695	19,477	20,533	21,381	21,060	23,315	25,464

12. The accompanying table contains two price indexes for the years 2020, 2021, and 2022: the GDP deflator and the CPI. For each price index, calculate the inflation rate from 2020 to 2021 and from 2021 to 2022.

Year	GDP deflator	CPI
2020	114.7	260.5
2021	121.7	278.8
2022	129.5	296.8

13. Access the Discovering Data exercise for Chapter 7, Problem 13 online to answer the following questions.

a. What was the CPI for the United States last year?

b. What was the inflation rate, the percent change in the CPI, from 2021 to 2022? From 1989 to 1990?

c. Which component of CPI grew the fastest from 1983 through 2022? The slowest?

d. CPI measured by the BLS is most likely to be overstated for which group of people? Understated?

e. Calculate your personal CPI index.

14. The economy of Britannica produces three goods: computers, pens, and pizza. The accompanying table shows the prices and output of the three goods for the years 2018, 2019, and 2020.

a. What is the percent change in production of each of the goods from 2018 to 2019 and from 2019 to 2020?

b. What is the percent change in prices of each of the goods from 2018 to 2019 and from 2019 to 2020?

c. Calculate nominal GDP in Britannica for each of the three years. What is the percent change in nominal GDP from 2018 to 2019 and from 2019 to 2020?

d. Calculate real GDP in Britannica using 2018 prices for each of the three years. What is the percent change in real GDP from 2018 to 2019 and from 2019 to 2020?

Year	Computers		Pens		Pizza	
	Price	Quantity	Price	Quantity	Price	Quantity
2018	$900	10	$10	100	$15	2
2019	1,000	10.5	12	105	16	2
2020	1,050	12	14	110	17	3

8 Unemployment and Inflation

A TERRIFIC, TERRIBLE YEAR

IT WAS THE BEST OF TIMES, IT WAS THE WORST OF TIMES.
Okay, it was not quite the absolute best or the absolute worst. But 2022 was, by some measures, one of the best years the U.S. economy has had in decades. By other measures, it was one of the worst.

Macroeconomic policy usually focuses mainly on trying to mitigate the two great evils of macroeconomics, high unemployment and high inflation. High unemployment incurs human and economic waste because willing workers can't find jobs. High inflation undermines the monetary system through rapidly rising prices. So the two principal goals of macroeconomic policy are low unemployment and price stability, usually defined as a low but positive rate of inflation.

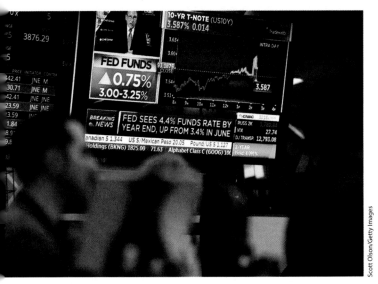

Scott Olson/Getty Images

The chair of the Federal Reserve balances the goals of low unemployment and price stability when deciding whether to give the economy more gas or hit the brakes. Powell chose to raise interest rates in 2022.

In 2022, the U.S. economy did very well on the unemployment front. A large majority of Americans told pollsters that it was a good time to find a quality job; workers were quitting jobs at unusually high rates, a sign that they felt good about the prospects of finding other employment. And the official rate of unemployment ended the year at 3.5%, very low by historical standards.

The inflation news, however, wasn't good. Although gasoline prices, which surged early in 2022, had come down substantially by year's end, food was still expensive, and the overall rate of inflation as measured by the Consumer Price Index was 6.4%, well above the 2% inflation that is the normal goal of policymakers.

And key policymakers — in this case the Federal Reserve, which is the U.S. *central bank*, and controls key interest rates — felt compelled to do something about inflation. The Fed began raising interest rates in March 2022; by the end of the year it had increased rates almost 4.5 percentage points, and seemed likely to keep raising them further in the months ahead. Almost all observers expected that these rate hikes would reduce inflation, which did indeed seem to be slowing, but many also expected them to reduce job creation and drive up the rate of unemployment, perhaps sharply. ●

WHAT YOU WILL LEARN

- How is **unemployment** measured and how is the **unemployment rate** calculated?
- What is the significance of the unemployment rate for the economy?
- What is the relationship between the unemployment rate and economic growth?
- What factors determine the **natural rate of unemployment?**
- What are the economic costs of inflation?
- How do inflation and deflation create winners and losers?
- Why do policy makers try to maintain a stable rate of inflation?

employment the total number of people currently employed for pay in the economy, either full time or part time.

unemployment the total number of people who are actively looking for work but aren't currently employed.

labor force the sum of employment and unemployment; that is, the number of people who are currently working plus the number of people who are currently looking for work.

The Unemployment Rate

Figure 1 shows the U.S. unemployment rate; as you can see, unemployment soared during the Great Recession of 2007–2009 and fell only gradually in the years that followed, and spiked again in spring 2020 as a result of the Covid-19 crisis. What did the elevated unemployment rate mean, and why was it such a big factor in people's lives? To understand why policy makers pay so much attention to employment and unemployment, we need to understand how they are both defined and measured.

Defining and Measuring Unemployment

It's easy to define employment: you're employed if and only if you have a job. **Employment** is the total number of people currently employed, either full time or part time.

Unemployment, however, is a more subtle concept. Just because a person isn't working doesn't mean that we consider that person unemployed. For example, only a minority of Americans over 65 are still working—but the majority of seniors who aren't working have chosen to retire, many of them receiving checks from Social Security. We wouldn't consider someone who has settled into a comfortable, well-earned retirement to be unemployed. In November 2022, there were also 12 million Americans under the age of 65 receiving Social Security checks because they were disabled, most of them unable to work. Again, although they weren't working, we don't consider them to be unemployed.

The U.S. Census Bureau, the federal agency tasked with collecting data on unemployment, considers the unemployed only to be those who are "jobless, looking for jobs, and available for work." Retired people don't count because they aren't looking for jobs; the disabled don't count because they aren't available for work. More specifically, an individual is considered unemployed if they don't currently have a job and have been actively seeking a job during the past four weeks. So **unemployment** is defined as the total number of people who are actively looking for work but aren't currently employed.

A country's **labor force** is the sum of employment and unemployment—that is, of people who are currently working and people who are currently looking for

FIGURE 1 The U.S. Unemployment Rate, 1948–2023

The unemployment rate has fluctuated widely over time. It always rises during recessions, which are shown by the shaded bars. It usually, but not always, falls during periods of economic expansion.
Data from: Bureau of Labor Statistics; National Bureau of Economic Research.

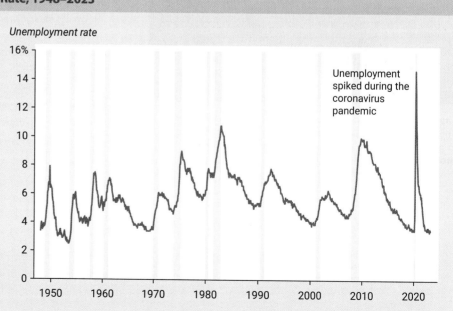

work, respectively. The **labor force participation rate,** defined as the percentage of the working-age population that is in the labor force, is calculated as follows:

(1) Labor force participation rate = $\dfrac{\text{Labor force}}{\text{Population age 16 and older}} \times 100$

The **unemployment rate,** defined as the percentage of the total number of people in the labor force who are unemployed, is calculated as follows:

(2) Unemployment rate = $\dfrac{\text{Number of unemployed workers}}{\text{Labor force}} \times 100$

To estimate the numbers that go into calculating the unemployment rate, the U.S. Census Bureau carries out a monthly survey called the Current Population Survey, which involves interviewing a random sample of approximately 60,000 American households. People are asked whether they are currently employed. If they are not employed, they are asked whether they have been looking for a job during the past four weeks. The results are then scaled up, using estimates of the total population, to estimate the total number of employed and unemployed Americans.

The Significance of the Unemployment Rate

In general, the unemployment rate is a good although imperfect indicator of how easy or difficult it is to find a job given the current state of the economy. You can see this by the strong correlation between the unemployment rate and other indicators of job market conditions, like the *quit rate*—the fraction of workers voluntarily leaving their jobs in any given month. In April 2020, with jobs temporarily scarce because many businesses had been shut down by the coronavirus pandemic, the unemployment rate was 14.7%—and very few workers were quitting, because someone who left a job had little assurance of finding another. By late 2021, with unemployment back down to 4%, the quit rate had nearly doubled.

Although the unemployment rate is a good indicator of current labor market conditions, it's not a literal measure of the percentage of people who want a job but can't find one. That's because in some ways the unemployment rate exaggerates the difficulty people have in finding jobs. But in other ways, the opposite is true—a low unemployment rate can conceal deep frustration over the lack of job opportunities.

How the Unemployment Rate Can Overstate the True Level of Unemployment
If you are searching for work, it's normal to take at least a few weeks to find a suitable job. Yet a worker who is quite confident of finding a job, but has not yet accepted a position, is counted as unemployed. As a consequence, the unemployment rate never falls to zero, even in boom times when jobs are plentiful. Even in the buoyant labor market of December 2022, when it was easy to find work, the unemployment rate was still 3.5%. Later in this chapter, we'll discuss in greater depth the reasons that measured unemployment persists even when jobs are abundant.

How the Unemployment Rate Can Understate the True Level of Unemployment
Frequently, people who would like to work but aren't working still don't get counted as unemployed. In particular, an individual who has given up looking for a job for the time being because there are no jobs available—say, a laid-off steelworker in a deeply depressed steel town—isn't counted as unemployed because they have not been searching for a job during the previous four weeks. Individuals who want to work but have told government researchers that they aren't currently searching because they see little prospect of finding a job

labor force participation rate the percentage of the population age 16 or older that is in the labor force.

unemployment rate the percentage of the total number of people in the labor force who are unemployed, calculated as unemployment/(unemployment + employment).

FIGURE 2 Alternative Measures of Unemployment, 1996–2023

The unemployment number usually quoted in the news media counts someone as unemployed only if that person has been looking for work during the past four weeks. Broader measures also count discouraged workers, marginally attached workers, and the underemployed. These broader measures show a higher unemployment rate, but they move closely in parallel with the standard rate.

Data from: Bureau of Labor Statistics.

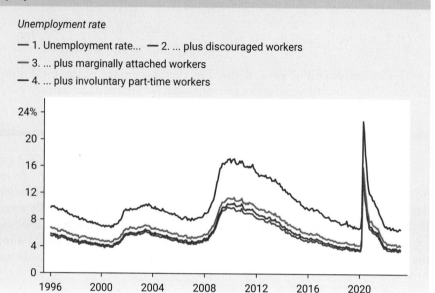

given the state of the job market are called **discouraged workers.** Because it does not count discouraged workers, the measured unemployment rate may understate the percentage of people who want to work but are unable to find jobs.

Discouraged workers are part of a larger group—**marginally attached workers.** These are people who say they would like to have a job and have looked for work in the recent past but are not currently looking for work. They are also not included when calculating the unemployment rate. Finally, another category of workers who are frustrated in their ability to find work but aren't counted as unemployed are the **underemployed:** workers who would like to find full-time jobs but are currently working part time "for economic reasons"—that is, they can't find a full-time job. Again, they aren't counted in the unemployment rate.

The *Bureau of Labor Statistics* is the federal agency that calculates the official unemployment rate. It also calculates broader "measures of labor underutilization" that include the three categories of frustrated workers. Figure 2 shows what happens to the measured unemployment rate once discouraged workers, other marginally attached workers, and the underemployed are counted. The broadest measure of unemployment and underemployment, known as *U-6,* is the sum of these three measures plus the unemployed. It is substantially higher than the rate usually quoted by the news media. But U-6 and the unemployment rate move very much in parallel, so changes in the unemployment rate remain a good guide to what's happening in the overall labor market, including frustrated workers.

Finally, it's important to realize that the unemployment rate varies greatly among demographic groups. Other things equal, jobs are generally easier to find for more experienced workers and for workers during their prime working years, that is, from ages 25 to 54. For younger workers, as well as workers nearing retirement age, jobs are typically harder to find, other things equal.

Figure 3 shows unemployment rates for different groups in 2000, when the overall unemployment rate was low by historical standards, in 2010, when the rate was high in the aftermath of the Great Recession, and in February 2023, when it had come down to pre-crisis levels from before the pandemic. As you can see, the unemployment rate for Black workers is consistently much higher than the national average; the unemployment rate for White teenagers (ages 16–19) is normally even higher; and the unemployment rate for Black teenagers is higher still. (Bear in mind that a teenager isn't considered unemployed, even if they aren't working, unless that

discouraged workers individuals who want to work but who have stated to government researchers that they aren't currently searching for a job because they see little prospect of finding one given the state of the job market.

marginally attached workers nonworking individuals who say they would like a job and have looked for work in the recent past but are not currently looking for work.

underemployment the number of people who work part time because they cannot find full-time jobs.

FIGURE 3 Unemployment Rates of Different Groups in 2000, 2010, and 2023

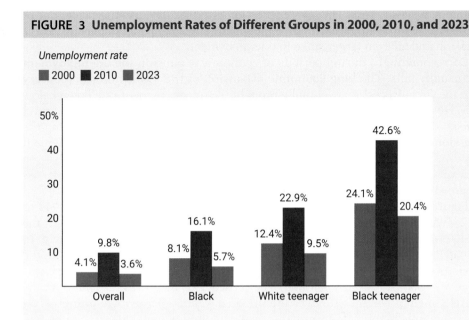

Unemployment rate
■ 2000 ■ 2010 ■ 2023

Unemployment rates vary greatly among different demographic groups. For example, although the overall unemployment rate in February 2023 was 3.5%, the unemployment rate among Black teenagers was 20.4%. As a result, even during periods of low overall unemployment, unemployment remains a serious problem for some groups.

Data from: Bureau of Labor Statistics.

teenager is looking for work but can't find it.) So even at times when the overall unemployment rate is relatively low, jobs are hard to find for some groups.

So you should interpret the unemployment rate as an indicator of overall labor market conditions, not as an exact measure of the percentage of people unable to find jobs. The unemployment rate is, however, a very good indicator: its ups and downs closely reflect economic changes that have a significant impact on people's lives. Let's turn now to the causes of these fluctuations.

Growth and Unemployment

Compared to Figure 1, Figure 4 shows the U.S. unemployment rate over a somewhat shorter period, from 1979 through 2023. The shaded bars represent periods of recession. As you can see, during every recession, without exception, the

FIGURE 4 Unemployment and Recessions, 1979–2023

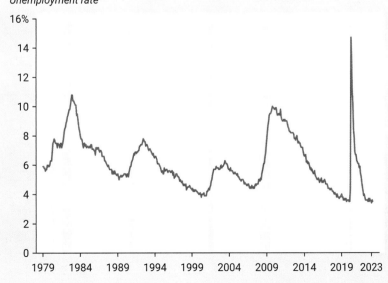

Unemployment rate

This figure shows a close-up of the unemployment rate for the past three decades, with the shaded bars indicating recessions. It's clear that unemployment always rises during recessions and *usually* falls during expansions. But in both the early 1990s and the early 2000s, unemployment continued to rise for some time after the recession was officially declared over.

Data from: Bureau of Labor Statistics; National Bureau of Economic Research.

unemployment rate rose. The severe recession of 2007–2009, like the earlier one of 1981–1982, led to a large rise in unemployment. The 2020 pandemic led to both a recession and an even larger spike in unemployment.

Correspondingly, during periods of economic expansion the unemployment rate usually falls. The long economic expansion of the 1990s and the recovery from the Great Recession eventually brought the unemployment rate down below 4.0%. However, it's important to recognize that *economic expansions aren't always periods of falling unemployment.* Look at the periods immediately following the recessions of 1990–1991 and 2001 in Figure 4. In each case, the unemployment rate continued to rise for more than a year after the recession was officially over. The explanation in both cases is that although the economy was growing, it was not growing fast enough to reduce the unemployment rate.

Figure 5 is a scatter diagram showing U.S. data for the period from 1949 to 2022. (We exclude the coronavirus period, when unusual factors distorted the normal relationship.) The horizontal axis measures the annual rate of growth in real GDP—the percent by which each year's real GDP changed compared to the previous year's real GDP. (Notice that there were 10 years in which growth was negative—that is, real GDP shrank.) The vertical axis measures the *change* in the average unemployment rate over the previous year in percentage points—last year's unemployment rate minus this year's unemployment rate. Each dot represents the observed growth rate of real GDP and change in the unemployment rate for a given year. For example, in 2000 the average unemployment rate fell to 4.0% from 4.2% in 1999; this is shown as a value of –0.2 along the vertical axis for the year 2000. Over the same period, real GDP grew by 4.1%; this is the value shown along the horizontal axis for the year 2000.

The downward trend of the scatter diagram in Figure 5 shows that there is a generally strong negative relationship between growth in the economy and the rate of unemployment. Years of high growth in real GDP were also years in which

FIGURE 5 Growth and Changes in Unemployment, 1949–2022

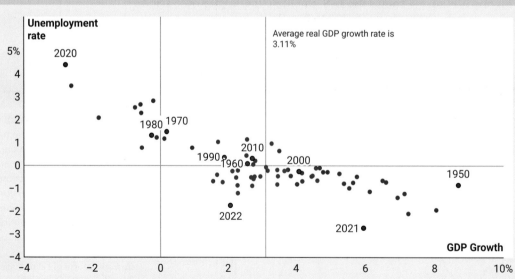

Each dot shows the growth rate of the economy and the change in the unemployment rate for a specific year between 1949 and 2022. For example, in 2000 the economy grew 4.1% and the unemployment rate fell 0.2 percentage points, from 4.2% to 4.0%. In general, the unemployment rate fell when growth was above its average rate of 3.11% a year and rose when growth was below average. Unemployment always rose when real GDP fell.

Data from: Bureau of Labor Statistics; Bureau of Economic Analysis.

the unemployment rate fell, and years of low or negative growth in real GDP were years in which the unemployment rate rose.

The vertical line in Figure 5 at the value of 3.11% indicates the average growth rate of real GDP over the period from 1949 to 2022. Points lying to the right of the vertical line are years of above-average growth. In these years, the value on the vertical axis is usually negative, meaning that the unemployment rate fell. That is, years of above-average growth were usually years in which the unemployment rate was falling. Conversely, points lying to the left of this vertical line were years of below-average growth. In these years, the value on the vertical axis is usually positive, meaning that the unemployment rate rose. That is, years of below-average growth were usually years in which the unemployment rate was rising.

A period in which real GDP is growing at a below-average rate and unemployment is rising is called a **jobless recovery** or a *growth recession*. Since 1990, there have been four recessions, three of which were followed by a period of jobless recovery. But true recessions, periods when real GDP falls, are especially painful for workers. As illustrated by the points to the left of the vertical line at 0 in Figure 5 (representing years in which the real GDP growth rate is negative), falling real GDP is always associated with a rising rate of unemployment, causing a great deal of hardship for families.

jobless recovery a period in which real GDP growth rate is positive but the unemployment rate is still rising.

ECONOMICS >> *in Action*
Opportunity Knocks

Do you need a college degree to get a well-paying job? It definitely helps. But sometimes opportunity knocks even for those without a BA. A 2019 article in the *Wall Street Journal* highlighted the good fortune of Cassandra Eaton, a 23-year-old high school graduate in Biloxi, Mississippi. After leaving school, Ms. Eaton was employed by a day-care center that paid $8.25 an hour. But by early 2019, she was making $18.90 an hour as an apprentice welder at a nearby shipyard.

No doubt Ms. Eaton did much to earn her new position, but there were a lot of stories like hers in 2019: many employers were willing to hire and train workers they might not have been interested in a few years earlier. Why? Because the job market was very good, and employers couldn't afford to be choosy. That *Wall Street Journal* article was titled "Inside the hottest job market of the past half century."

Figure 6 illustrates the point, showing unemployment rates for adults over age 25 with high school and college degrees respectively over the period from 2007 to 2023. Adults without a college degree always have somewhat higher unemployment than their more credentialed peers, but the gap depends a lot on the overall state of employment. In the terrible job market of 2010, with overall unemployment near 10%, the gap was huge. In fact, some commentators warned that the United States was suffering from a "skills gap," with many workers lacking the qualifications the modern economy requires.

By 2019, however, overall unemployment was below 4%, and unemployment among

FIGURE 6   Unemployment Rate for College and High School Graduates, 2007–2023

Data from: Bureau of Labor Statistics.

workers who only had a high school degree was only modestly higher than for the college-educated. To the extent that there was still a skills gap, employers themselves were trying to close it by giving workers the training they needed.

The moral of the story is that the state of the labor market, which the unemployment rate helps us track, makes a huge difference in peoples' lives, even those who stay employed.

>> Check Your Understanding 8-1

Solutions appear at back of book.

1. Suppose employment websites develop new software that enables job-seekers to find suitable jobs more quickly and employers to better screen potential employees. What effect will this have on the unemployment rate over time? Also suppose that these websites encourage job-seekers who had given up their searches to begin looking again. What effect will this have on the unemployment rate?

2. In which of the following cases is a worker counted as unemployed? Explain.
   a. Rosa, an older worker who has been laid off and who gave up looking for work months ago
   b. Anthony, a schoolteacher who is not working during his three-month summer break
   c. Kanako, an investment banker who has been laid off and is currently searching for another position
   d. Sergio, a classically trained musician who can only find work playing for local parties
   e. Natasha, a graduate student who went back to school because jobs were scarce

3. Which of the following are consistent with the observed relationship between growth in real GDP and changes in the unemployment rate as shown in Figure 5? Which are not?
   a. A rise in the unemployment rate accompanies a fall in real GDP.
   b. An exceptionally strong business recovery is associated with a greater percentage of the labor force being employed.
   c. Negative real GDP growth is associated with a fall in the unemployment rate.

The Natural Rate of Unemployment

Fast economic growth tends to reduce the unemployment rate. So how low can the unemployment rate go? You might be tempted to say zero, but that isn't feasible. Over the past half-century, the national unemployment rate has never dropped below 2.9%.

During boom times, how can there be so much unemployment even when many employees are actively searching for work? To answer this question, we need to examine the nature of labor markets and why they normally lead to substantial measured unemployment even when jobs are plentiful. Our starting point is the observation that even in the best of times, jobs are constantly being created and destroyed.

"At this point, I'm just happy to still have a job."

Job Creation and Job Destruction

Even during good times, most Americans know someone who has lost a job. In November 2022, the U.S. unemployment rate was only 3.5%, very low by historical standards. Yet in that month there were 5.9 million *job separations*—terminations of employment that occur because a worker is either fired or quits voluntarily.

There are many reasons for such job loss. One is structural change in the economy: industries rise and fall as new technologies emerge and consumers' tastes change. For example, employment in coal mining has declined to a small fraction of its one-time high due to both automation and a switch to other sources of energy. However, structural change also brings the creation of new jobs: employment in solar power surged after 2010 as a combination of rapidly improving technology and tax incentives led to a rapid growth in the use of solar panels.

Poor management performance or bad luck at individual companies also leads to job loss for employees. For example, in early 2018, J.C. Penney announced the closure of 140 stores and offered early retirement to 6,000 workers. In the same year, Toys "R" Us closed 735 stores, causing 31,000 layoffs. Meanwhile, online retailers like Amazon continued to expand, building distribution centers all over the country.

Continual job creation and destruction are features of modern economies, making a naturally occurring amount of unemployment inevitable. Within this naturally occurring amount, there are two types of unemployment—*frictional* and *structural*.

Frictional Unemployment

When a worker loses a job involuntarily due to job destruction, that worker often doesn't take the first new job offered. For example, suppose a skilled programmer, laid off because their software company's product line was unsuccessful, sees an online job posting for a receptionist. The programmer might apply and get the receptionist job—but that would be foolish. Instead, they should take the time to look for a job that takes advantage of their skills and pays accordingly. In addition, individual workers are constantly leaving jobs voluntarily, typically for personal reasons—family moves, dissatisfaction, and better job prospects elsewhere.

Economists say that workers who spend time looking for employment are engaged in **job search.** If all workers and all jobs were alike, job search wouldn't be necessary; if information about jobs and workers was perfect, job search would be very quick. In practice, however, it's normal for a worker who loses a job, or a young worker seeking a first job, to spend at least a few weeks searching.

Frictional unemployment is unemployment due to the time workers spend in job search. A certain amount of frictional unemployment is inevitable due to the constant process of economic change. As we just mentioned, during the low-unemployment month of November 2022 there were nonetheless almost 6 million job separations, in which workers left or lost their jobs. Total employment grew because these separations were more than offset by an even larger number of hires. Inevitably, some of the workers who left or lost their jobs spent at least some time unemployed, as did some of the workers newly entering the labor force.

Figure 7 shows the average monthly flows of workers among three states: employed, unemployed, and not in the labor force during February 2023. What

job search the time spent by workers in looking for employment.

frictional unemployment unemployment due to time workers spend in job search.

FIGURE 7 Labor Market Flows in February 2023

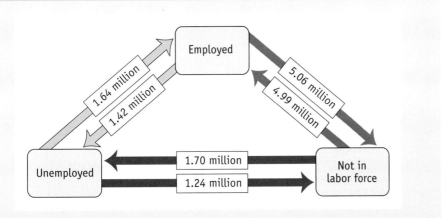

Even in February 2023, a low-unemployment month, large numbers of workers moved into and out of both employment and unemployment.
Data from: Bureau of Labor Statistics.

FIGURE 8 Distribution of the Unemployed by Duration of Unemployment, February 2023

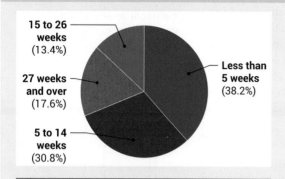

15 to 26 weeks (13.4%)

27 weeks and over (17.6%)

Less than 5 weeks (38.2%)

5 to 14 weeks (30.8%)

When the unemployment rate is low, most unemployed workers are unemployed for only a short period. In February 2023, 38.2% of the unemployed had been unemployed for less than 5 weeks and 69% for less than 15 weeks. The short duration of unemployment for most workers suggests that much of the unemployment was frictional. (Total may not add up to 100 due to rounding.)

Data from: Bureau of Labor Statistics.

the figure suggests is how much churning is constantly taking place in the labor market. An inevitable consequence of that churning is a significant number of workers who haven't yet found their next job—that is, frictional unemployment.

A limited amount of frictional unemployment is relatively harmless and may even be a good thing. The economy is more productive if workers take the time to find jobs that are well matched to their skills, and workers who are unemployed for a brief period while searching for the right job don't experience great hardship. In fact, when there is a low unemployment rate, periods of unemployment tend to be quite short, suggesting that much of the unemployment is frictional.

Figure 8 shows the composition of unemployment in February 2023. Approximately 38% of the unemployed had been unemployed for less than 5 weeks, and only 31% had been unemployed for 15 or more weeks. Only about one in five unemployed workers were considered to be *long-term unemployed*—those unemployed for 27 or more weeks.

In periods of higher unemployment, however, workers tend to be jobless for longer periods of time, suggesting that the amount of frictional unemployment is small relative to the amount of unemployment arising from the downturn in the business cycle. Figure 9 shows the fraction of the unemployed who had been out of work for 6 months or more from 2020 to 2022. It jumped to more than 40% during the pandemic-induced slump, but fell quickly as the economy recovered.

Structural Unemployment

Frictional unemployment exists even when the number of people seeking jobs is equal to the number of jobs being offered—that is, the existence of frictional unemployment doesn't mean that there is a surplus of labor. Sometimes, however, there is a *persistent surplus* of job-seekers in a particular labor market, even when the economy is at the peak of the business cycle. There may be more workers

FIGURE 9 Percentage of Unemployed U.S. Workers Who Had Been Unemployed for Six Months or Longer, 2020–2022

Before the coronavirus pandemic, relatively few U.S. workers had been unemployed for long periods. However, the percentage of long-term unemployed shot up during 2020, only to come down as the economy recovered.

Data from: Bureau of Labor Statistics.

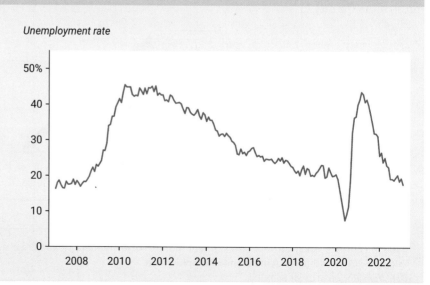

FIGURE 10 The Effect of a Minimum Wage on a Labor Market

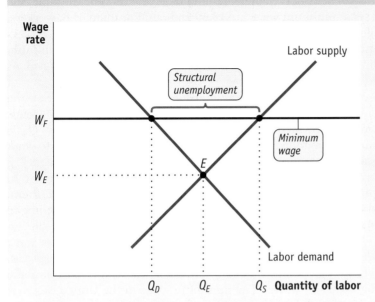

When the government sets a minimum wage, W_F, that exceeds the market equilibrium wage rate in that market, W_E, the number of workers who would like to work at that minimum wage, Q_S, is greater than the number of workers demanded at that wage rate, Q_D. This surplus of labor is structural unemployment.

with a particular skill than there are jobs available using that skill, or there may be more workers in a particular geographic region than there are jobs available in that region. **Structural unemployment** is unemployment that results when there are more people seeking jobs in a particular labor market than there are jobs available at the current wage rate. Economists try to gauge the level of structural unemployment in an economy by looking at the level of unemployment at the peak of the business cycle.

The supply and demand model tells us that the price of a good, service, or factor of production tends to move toward an equilibrium level that matches the quantity supplied with the quantity demanded. This is equally true, in general, of labor markets. Figure 10 shows a typical market for labor. The downward-sloping labor demand curve indicates that when the price of labor—the wage rate—increases, employers demand less labor. The upward-sloping labor supply curve indicates that when the price of labor increases, more workers are willing to supply labor at the prevailing wage rate. These two forces coincide to lead to an equilibrium wage rate for any given type of labor in a particular location. That equilibrium wage rate is shown as W_E.

Even at the equilibrium wage rate W_E, there will still be some frictional unemployment. That's because there will always be some workers engaged in job search even when the number of jobs available is equal to the number of workers seeking jobs. But there wouldn't be any structural unemployment in this labor market. *Structural unemployment occurs when the wage rate is, for some reason, persistently above W_E.* Several factors can lead to a wage rate in excess of W_E, the most important being *minimum wages, unions, efficiency wages,* the side effects of government policies, and mismatches between employees and employers.

Minimum Wages A **minimum wage** is a government-mandated floor on the wage rate. In the United States, the federally mandated minimum wage in 2023 was $7.25 an hour. A number of state and local

structural unemployment unemployment that results when there are more people seeking jobs in a particular labor market than there are jobs available at the current wage rate, even when the economy is at the peak of the business cycle.

minimum wage a legal floor on the wage rate, which is the market price of labor.

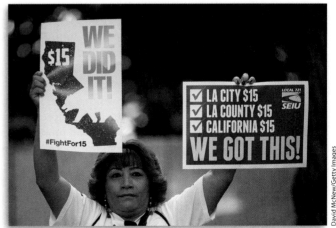

California's minimum wage reached $15 in 2022.

governments also determine the minimum wage within their jurisdictions, typically for the purpose of setting it higher than the federal level. For example, the city of Seattle has set a minimum wage at $18.69 an hour. For many U.S. workers, the minimum wage is irrelevant; the market equilibrium wage for these workers is well above the national price floor. But for less-skilled workers, the minimum wage can be binding—that is, it raises their wage above the equilibrium level. As a result, it can lead to structural unemployment.

Figure 10 shows the effect of a binding minimum wage. In this market, the minimum wage is W_F, which is above the equilibrium wage rate, W_E. This leads to a persistent surplus in the labor market: the quantity of labor supplied, Q_S, is larger than the quantity demanded, Q_D. In other words, more people want to work than can find jobs at the minimum wage, leading to structural unemployment.

Given that minimum wages—that is, binding minimum wages—can lead to structural unemployment, you might wonder why governments impose them. The rationale is to help ensure that people who work can earn enough income to afford at least a minimally adequate standard of living.

Furthermore, although economists broadly agree that a high minimum wage has the employment-reducing effects shown in Figure 10, there is widespread, although not universal, agreement that this isn't a good description of how the U.S. minimum wage actually works. The minimum wage in the United States is quite low compared with that in other wealthy countries, and as already noted, it isn't binding for the vast majority of workers.

In addition, research suggests that minimum wage increases do not seem to be associated with employment declines and may actually lead to higher employment when, as was the case in the United States at one time, the minimum wage is low compared to average wages. They argue that firms employing a large percentage of workers in a particular market can keep wages low by restricting their hiring. Under these conditions, a moderate rise in the minimum wage will not lead to a loss of jobs. Most economists, however, agree that a sufficiently high minimum wage *does* lead to structural unemployment.

Unions The actions of **unions,** organizations of workers that bargain collectively with employers to raise wages and improve living standards of their members, can have effects similar to those of minimum wages, leading to structural unemployment. By bargaining collectively for all of a firm's workers, unions can often win higher wages from employers than workers would have obtained by bargaining individually. This process, known as *collective bargaining,* is intended to tip the scales of bargaining power more toward workers and away from employers. Labor unions exercise bargaining power by threatening firms with a *labor strike,* a collective refusal to work. The threat of a strike can have serious consequences for firms. In such cases, workers acting collectively can exercise more power than they could if acting individually.

Employers have acted to counter the bargaining power of unions by threatening and enforcing *lockouts*—periods in which union workers are locked out and rendered unemployed—while hiring replacement workers.

When workers have increased bargaining power, they tend to demand and receive higher wages. Unions also bargain over benefits, such as health care and pensions, which we can think of as additional wages. Indeed, economists who study the effects of unions on wages find that unionized workers earn higher wages and more generous benefits than non-union workers with similar skills. The result of these increased wages can be the same as the result of a minimum wage: labor unions push the wage that workers receive above the equilibrium wage. Like a binding minimum wage, this leads to structural unemployment. In the United States, however, due to a low level of unionization, the amount of unemployment generated by union demands is likely to be very small. And in countries such as Germany and Japan, unions and management collaborate on devising more efficient work practices that support higher equilibrium wages.

union an organization of workers that bargains collectively with employers to raise wages and improve working conditions.

Efficiency Wages Actions by firms can contribute to structural unemployment. Firms may choose to pay **efficiency wages**—wages that employers set above the equilibrium wage rate as an incentive for their workers to perform better.

Employers may feel the need for such incentives for several reasons. For example, employers often have difficulty observing directly how hard an employee works. They can, however, elicit more work effort by paying above-market wages: employees receiving these higher wages are more likely to work harder to ensure that they aren't fired, which would cause them to lose their higher wages.

For example, in 2022, the average hourly worker at Costco made nearly $25 per hour, while the average worker at Walmart made only $17 per hour. As a result, Costco's employees were reported to be more satisfied with their jobs, more productive, and less likely to search for better opportunities elsewhere.

When many firms pay efficiency wages, the result is a pool of workers who want jobs but can't find them. With Costco paying efficiency wages, a lot of workers are willing to work at Costco but not Walmart. So the use of efficiency wages by firms may lead to structural unemployment.

Side Effects of Government Policies In addition, government policies designed to help workers who lose their jobs can lead to structural unemployment as an unintended side effect. Most economically advanced countries provide benefits to laid-off workers as a way to tide them over until they find a new job. In the United States, these benefits typically replace only about 45% of a worker's income and expire after 26 weeks. (Benefits were extended in some cases to 99 weeks during the period of high unemployment in 2009–2011). In other countries, particularly in Europe, benefits are more generous and last longer. The drawback to this generosity is that it reduces a worker's incentive to quickly find a new job. During the 1980s, it was often argued that unemployment benefits in some European countries were one of the causes of *Eurosclerosis,* persistently high unemployment that afflicted a number of European economies.

Mismatches Between Employees and Employers It takes time for workers and firms to adjust to shifts in the economy. The result can be a mismatch between what employees have to offer and what employers are looking for. A skills mismatch is one form; for example, in the aftermath of the housing bust of 2009, there were more construction workers looking for jobs than there were jobs available. Another form is geographic, as is the case in the "eastern heartland" regions that, as described in Economics in Action, have been left behind by economic change. Until the mismatch is resolved through a big enough fall in wages of the surplus workers to induce retraining or relocation, there will be structural unemployment.

The Natural Rate of Unemployment

Because some frictional unemployment is inevitable and because many economies also suffer from structural unemployment, a certain amount of unemployment is normal, or "natural." Actual unemployment fluctuates around this normal level. The **natural rate of unemployment** is the normal unemployment rate around which the actual unemployment rate fluctuates. It is the rate of unemployment that arises from the effects of frictional plus structural unemployment.

Cyclical unemployment is the deviation of the actual rate of unemployment from the natural rate; that is, it is the difference between the actual and natural rates of unemployment. As the name suggests, cyclical unemployment is the share of unemployment that arises from the downturns of the business cycle.

We'll see in Chapter 16 that an economy's natural rate of unemployment is a critical policy variable because a government cannot keep the unemployment rate persistently below the natural rate without leading to accelerating inflation.

efficiency wages wages that employers set above the equilibrium wage rate as an incentive for workers to deliver better performance.

natural rate of unemployment the normal unemployment rate around which the actual unemployment rate fluctuates; the unemployment rate that arises from the effects of frictional and structural unemployment.

cyclical unemployment the difference between the actual rate of unemployment and the natural rate of unemployment due to downturns in the business cycle.

We can summarize the relationships between the various types of unemployment as follows:

(3) Natural unemployment = Frictional unemployment + Structural unemployment

(4) Actual unemployment = Natural unemployment + Cyclical unemployment

Perhaps because of its name, people often imagine that the natural rate of unemployment is a constant that doesn't change over time and can't be affected by government policy. Neither proposition is true. Let's take a moment to stress two facts:

1. The natural rate of unemployment changes over time.
2. It can be affected by government policies.

Changes in the Natural Rate of Unemployment

Private-sector economists and government agencies need estimates of the natural rate of unemployment both to make forecasts and to conduct policy analyses. Almost all these estimates show that the U.S. natural rate rises and falls over time. For example, the Congressional Budget Office, the independent agency that conducts budget and economic analyses for Congress, believes that the U.S. natural rate of unemployment (the CBO in 2021 renamed this to the noncyclical rate of unemployment) was 5.3% in 1950, rose to 6.3% by the end of the 1970s, but fell to 4.4% by 2023. In December 2022, the Federal Reserve, which makes projections about the future natural rate, left its projection unchanged at between 3.8% and 4.3%, despite the economic effects during and after the Covid-19 crisis. European countries have experienced even larger swings in their natural rates of unemployment.

What causes the natural rate of unemployment to change? The most important factors are changes in labor force characteristics, changes in labor market institutions, and changes in government policies. Let's look briefly at each factor.

Changes in Labor Force Characteristics
In February 2023, the rate of unemployment in the United States was 3.6%. Young workers, however, had much higher unemployment rates: 11.1% for teenagers and 6.9% for workers aged 20 to 24. Workers aged 25 to 54 had an unemployment rate of only 3.1%.

In general, unemployment rates tend to be lower for experienced than for inexperienced workers. Because experienced workers tend to stay in a given job longer than do inexperienced ones, they have lower frictional unemployment. Also, because older workers are more likely than young workers to be family breadwinners, they have a stronger incentive to find and keep jobs. One reason the natural rate of unemployment rose during the 1970s was a large rise in the number of new workers—children of the post–World War II baby boom, as well as a rising percentage of women, entered the labor force. As Figure 11 shows, both the percentage of the labor force less than 25 years old and the percentage of women in the labor force grew rapidly in the 1970s. By the end of the 1990s, however, the share of women in the labor force had leveled off, and the percentage of workers under 25 had fallen sharply. As a result, the labor force as a whole is more experienced today than it was in the 1970s, one likely reason that the natural rate of unemployment is lower today than in the 1970s.

Changes in Labor Market Institutions
As we pointed out earlier, unions that negotiate wages above the equilibrium level can be a source of structural unemployment. Some economists believe that the high natural rate of unemployment in Europe is caused, in part, by strong labor unions. In the United States, a sharp fall in union membership after 1980 may have been one reason the natural rate of unemployment fell between the 1970s and the 1990s.

FIGURE 11 The Changing Makeup of the U.S. Labor Force, 1950–2023

In the 1970s, the percentage of women in the labor force rose rapidly, as did the percentage of those under age 25. These changes reflected the entry of large numbers of women into the paid labor force for the first time and the fact that baby boomers were reaching working age. The natural rate of unemployment may have risen because many of these workers were relatively inexperienced. Today, the labor force is much more experienced, which is one possible reason the natural rate has fallen since the 1970s.

Data from: Bureau of Labor Statistics.

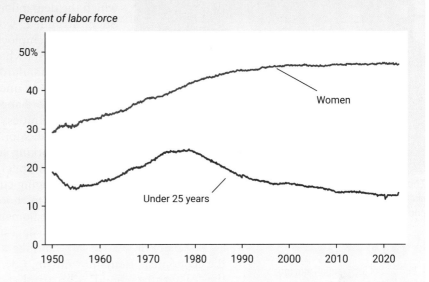

Other institutional changes may also be at work. For example, some labor economists believe that temporary employment agencies have reduced frictional unemployment by helping match workers to jobs. Likewise, the proliferation of gig economy companies like Uber and TaskRabbit has reduced frictional and structural unemployment by making it easier for workers to earn money quickly and accept wages below a minimum wage, if it is binding.

Technological change, coupled with labor market institutions, can also affect the natural rate of unemployment. Technological change tends to increase the demand for skilled workers who are familiar with the relevant technology and reduce the demand for unskilled workers. Economic theory predicts that wages should increase for skilled workers and decrease for unskilled workers as technology advances. But if wages for unskilled workers cannot go down—say, due to a binding minimum wage—increased structural unemployment, and therefore a higher natural rate of unemployment, will result during periods of faster technological change.

Changes in Government Policies A high minimum wage can cause structural unemployment. Generous unemployment benefits can increase both structural and frictional unemployment as workers feel less pressured financially to immediately accept a job. So government policies intended to help workers can have the undesirable side effect of raising the natural rate of unemployment.

Some government policies, however, may reduce the natural rate. Two examples are job training and employment subsidies. *Job-training programs* are supposed to provide unemployed workers with skills that widen the range of jobs they can perform. *Employment subsidies* are payments either to workers or to employers that provide a financial incentive to accept or offer jobs.

ECONOMICS >> *in Action*
Men Not Working

The United States is a vast country: California is as far from Maine as France is from Siberia. Yet we often talk as if the whole country constituted a single labor market. And to be fair, American workers often move to wherever the jobs are.

The decline in employment in traditionally male-dominated sectors hit some regions harder than others, and has contributed to a surge in social problems.

But not all workers are able or willing to move. This creates problems for workers who find themselves stuck in a region in which the demand for labor has declined, for whatever reason. Such "stranded" workers are especially likely to suffer from structural unemployment.

Economists who study this issue generally prefer *not* to look at the standard unemployment rate, because people are only counted as unemployed if they're actively seeking work, which may not happen in places that persistently lack employment opportunities. Instead, recent research tends to focus on a different indicator: the percentage of men in what are usually the prime working years, ages 25 to 54, who aren't working.

Why men specifically, rather than adults in general? Despite changing cultural norms, U.S. men remain less likely than women to choose voluntarily to be stay-at-home parents, caregivers, or homemakers. So when you see large numbers of prime-aged men not working, it suggests a troubled labor market.

So where do we see large numbers of men not working? Mainly in a region the economists Benjamin Austin, Edward Glaeser, and Lawrence Summers call the "eastern heartland"—an arc that runs from western Pennsylvania down to Alabama and Mississippi.

A few decades ago, many of this region's residents were still employed in traditional sectors like farming, coal mining, and industries like steel that were closely linked to coal. Since the 1970s, however, those traditional sources of employment have declined, while employers in rising "knowledge-based" industries tend to prefer large metropolitan areas with highly educated workforces.

The result appears to be persistent high structural unemployment in the troubled region. In West Virginia, for example, only 75% of prime-aged men are working, compared with almost 90% in growing states like New Jersey and Texas.

Sadly, the lack of job opportunities in the eastern heartland appears to be contributing to a variety of social problems, including opioid addiction. Most grimly, the region has seen a surge in mortality, via what the economists Anne Case and Angus Deaton call "deaths of despair"—deaths from suicide, alcohol, and drugs. This demonstrates another reason the state of the job market matters: job opportunities aren't just about money, they're about dignity.

>> Quick Review

• Because of job creation and job destruction, as well as voluntary job separations, some level of unemployment is natural.

• **Frictional unemployment** occurs because unemployed workers engage in **job search,** making some amount of unemployment inevitable.

• A variety of factors — **minimum wages, unions, efficiency wages,** the side effects of government policies such as unemployment benefits, and mismatches between employees and employers — lead to **structural unemployment** by raising wages above their market equilibrium level.

• Frictional plus structural unemployment equals natural unemployment, yielding a **natural rate of unemployment.** In contrast, **cyclical unemployment** changes with the business cycle. Actual unemployment is equal to the sum of natural unemployment and cyclical unemployment.

• The natural rate of unemployment can shift over time, due to changes in labor force characteristics, changes in institutions, and changes in government policies. Government policies designed to help workers are believed to be one reason for high natural rates of unemployment in Europe.

>> Check Your Understanding 8-2

Solutions appear at back of book.

1. Explain the following statements.
   a. Frictional unemployment is higher when the pace of technological advance quickens.
   b. Structural unemployment is higher when the pace of technological advance quickens.
   c. Frictional unemployment accounts for a larger share of total unemployment when the unemployment rate is low.

2. Why does collective bargaining have the same general effect on unemployment as a minimum wage? Illustrate your answer with a diagram.

3. Suppose that at the peak of the business cycle the United States dramatically increases benefits for unemployed workers. Explain what will happen to the natural rate of unemployment.

‖ Inflation and Deflation

As we mentioned in the opening story, macroeconomic policy makers are usually focused on two big evils, unemployment and inflation. It's easy to see why high unemployment is a problem. But why is inflation something to worry about? The answer is that inflation can impose costs on the economy—but not in the way most people think.

The Level of Prices Doesn't Matter …

The most common complaint about *inflation*, which is an increase in the price level, is that it makes everyone poorer—after all, a given amount of money buys less. But inflation does not make everyone poorer. To see why, it's helpful to imagine what would happen if the United States did something other countries have done from time to time—replacing the dollar with a new currency.

An example of this kind of currency conversion happened in 2002, when France, like a number of other European countries, replaced its national currency, the franc, with the new pan-European currency, the euro. People turned in their franc coins and notes, and received euro coins and notes in exchange, at a rate of precisely 6.55957 francs per euro. At the same time, all contracts were restated in euros at the same rate of exchange. For example, if a French citizen had a home mortgage debt of 500,000 francs, this became a debt of 500,000/6.55957 = 76,224.51 euros. If a worker's contract specified that they should be paid 100 francs per hour, it became a contract specifying a wage of 100/6.55957 = 15.2449 euros per hour, and so on.

You could imagine doing the same thing in the case of the dollar, replacing the dollar with a "new dollar" at a rate of exchange of, say, 7 to 1. If you owed $140,000 on your home, that would become a debt of 20,000 new dollars. If you had a wage rate of $14 an hour, it would become 2 new dollars an hour, and so on. This would bring the overall U.S. price level back to about what it was in 1962, when John F. Kennedy was president.

So would everyone be richer as a result because prices would be only one-seventh as high? Of course not. Prices would be lower, but so would wages and incomes in general. If you cut a worker's wage to one-seventh of its previous value, but also cut all prices to one-seventh of their previous level, the worker's **real wage**—the wage rate divided by the price level—hasn't changed. In fact, bringing the overall price level back to what it was during the Kennedy administration would have no effect on overall purchasing power because doing so would reduce income exactly as much as it reduced prices.

Conversely, the rise in prices that has actually taken place since the early 1960s hasn't made the United States poorer because it has also raised incomes by the same amount: **real incomes**—incomes divided by the price level—haven't been affected by the rise in overall prices.

The moral of this story is that the *level* of prices doesn't matter: the rise in prices in the U.S. economy over the past 50 years hasn't made us any poorer.

… But the Rate of Change of Prices Does

The conclusion that the level of prices doesn't matter might seem to imply that the inflation rate doesn't matter either. But that's not true.

To see why, it's crucial to distinguish between the *level of prices* and the *inflation rate:* the percent increase in the overall level of prices per year. Recall from Chapter 7 that the inflation rate is defined as follows:

$$\text{Inflation rate} = \frac{\text{Price index in year 2} - \text{Price index in year 1}}{\text{Price index in year 1}} \times 100$$

Figure 12 highlights the difference between the price level and the inflation rate in the United States over the past half-century, with the price level measured along the left vertical axis and the inflation rate measured along the right vertical axis. In the 2000s, the overall level of prices in the United States was much higher than it had been in 1960—but that, as we've learned, didn't matter. The inflation rate in the 2000s, however, was much lower than in the 1970s—and that almost certainly made the economy richer than it would have been if high inflation had continued.

real wage the wage rate divided by the price level.

real income income divided by the price level.

FIGURE 12 The Price Level versus the Inflation Rate, 1960–2023

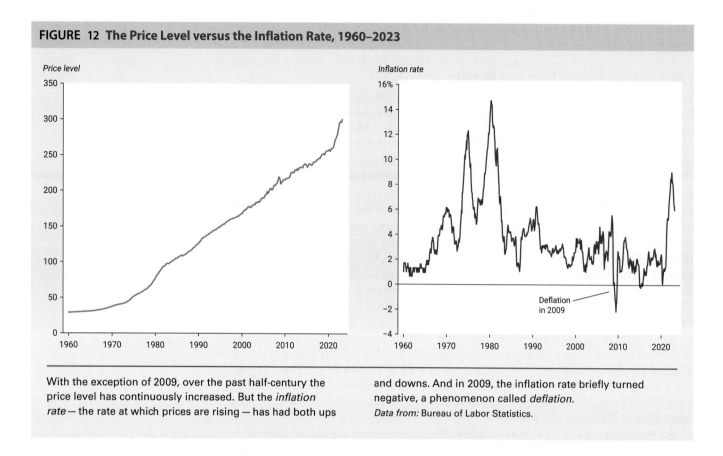

With the exception of 2009, over the past half-century the price level has continuously increased. But the *inflation rate* — the rate at which prices are rising — has had both ups and downs. And in 2009, the inflation rate briefly turned negative, a phenomenon called *deflation*.

Data from: Bureau of Labor Statistics.

Economists believe that high rates of inflation impose significant economic costs as resources are wasted. The most important of these costs are *shoe-leather costs, menu costs,* and *unit-of-account costs.* We'll discuss each in turn.

Shoe-Leather Costs People hold money — cash in their wallets and bank deposits — for convenience in making transactions. A high inflation rate, however, discourages people from holding money because the purchasing power of the cash in your wallet and the funds in your bank account steadily erode as the overall level of prices rises. This leads people to move funds into assets they believe will hold value and to reduce the amount of money they hold, often at considerable economic cost. For example, when Venezuelan inflation hit around 1 million percent in 2018, meaning that prices more than doubled every month, people began holding cigarettes and electronic currency (like Bitcoin) instead of Venezuelan currency.

During the most famous of all inflations, the German *hyperinflation* of 1921–1923, merchants employed runners to take their cash to the bank many times a day to convert it into something that would hold its value, such as a stable foreign currency. Hyperinflation occurs when prices rise by 50% or more per month, making an annual inflation rate of around 13,000%. In such cases, to avoid having the purchasing power of their money eroded, people use up valuable resources, such as the labor of the German runners, that could be used productively elsewhere. During the German hyperinflation, so many banking transactions were taking place that the number of employees at German banks nearly quadrupled — from around 100,000 in 1913 to 375,000 in 1923.

More recently, Brazil experienced hyperinflation during the early 1990s; during that episode, the Brazilian banking sector grew so large that it accounted for 15% of GDP, more than twice the size of the financial sector in the United States measured as a share of GDP. The large increase in the Brazilian banking sector needed to cope with the consequences of inflation, which represented a loss of real resources to its society.

Increased costs of transactions caused by inflation are known as **shoe-leather costs,** an allusion to the wear and tear caused by the extra running around that takes place when people are trying to avoid holding money. Shoe-leather costs are substantial in economies with very high inflation, as anyone who has lived in such an economy—say, one suffering inflation of 100% or more per year—can attest. Most estimates suggest, however, that the shoe-leather costs of inflation at the rates seen in the United States—which in peacetime has never had inflation above 15%—are quite small.

shoe-leather costs (of inflation) the increased costs of transactions caused by inflation.

menu cost the real cost of changing a listed price.

Menu Costs In a modern economy, most of the things we buy have a listed price. There's a price listed under each item on a supermarket shelf, a price listed for goods sold on any online retailer's website, such as Amazon or Zappos, and a price listed for each dish on a restaurant's menu. Changing a listed price has a real cost, called a **menu cost.** Although the potential burden imposed by menu costs has diminished in advanced economies as more sales have shifted online and prices can be changed electronically, they still exist. For example, to change prices in a supermarket or a clothing store requires sending clerks to change the listed price with each item. In the face of inflation, of course, firms are forced to change prices more often than they would if the aggregate price level was more or less stable. This means higher costs for the economy as a whole.

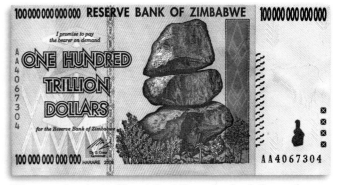

When one hundred trillion dollar bills are in circulation as they were in Zimbabwe, menu costs are substantial.

In times of very high inflation, menu costs can be substantial. During the Brazilian inflation of the early 1990s, for instance, supermarket workers reportedly spent half of their time replacing old price stickers with new ones. When inflation is high, merchants may decide to stop listing prices in terms of the local currency and use either an artificial unit—in effect, measuring prices relative to one another—or a more stable currency, such as the U.S. dollar. This is exactly what the Israeli real estate market began doing in the mid-1980s: prices were quoted in U.S. dollars, even though payment was made in Israeli shekels. And this is also what happened in Zimbabwe when, in May 2008, official estimates of the inflation rate reached 1,694,000%. By 2009, the government had suspended the Zimbabwean dollar, allowing Zimbabweans to buy and sell goods using foreign currencies. Menu costs are also present in low-inflation economies, but they are not severe. In low-inflation economies, businesses might update their prices only sporadically—not daily or even more frequently, as is the case in high-inflation or hyperinflation economies.

Unit-of-Account Costs In the Middle Ages, contracts were often specified "in kind": tenants might, for example, be obliged to provide their landlord with a certain number of cattle each year (the phrase *in kind* actually comes from an ancient word for *cattle*). This may have made sense at the time, but it would be an awkward way to conduct modern business. Instead, we state contracts in monetary terms: renters owe a certain number of dollars per month, a company that issues a bond promises to pay the bondholder the dollar value of the bond when it comes due, and so on. We also tend to make our economic calculations in dollars: a family planning its budget, or a small business owner trying to figure out how well the business is doing, makes estimates of the amount of money coming in and going out.

This role of the dollar as a basis for contracts and calculation is called the *unit-of-account* role of money. It's an important aspect of the modern economy. Yet it's a role that can be degraded by inflation, which causes the purchasing power of

unit-of-account costs (of inflation) costs arising from the way inflation makes money a less reliable unit of measurement.

interest rate the price, calculated as a percentage of the amount borrowed, charged by the lender.

nominal interest rate the interest rate in dollar terms.

real interest rate the nominal interest rate minus the inflation rate.

a dollar to change over time—a dollar next year is worth less than a dollar this year. The effect, many economists argue, is to reduce the quality of economic decisions: the economy as a whole makes less efficient use of its resources because of the uncertainty caused by changes in the unit of account, the dollar. The **unit-of-account costs** of inflation are the costs arising from the way inflation makes money a less reliable unit of measurement.

Unit-of-account costs may be particularly important in the tax system because inflation can distort the measures of income on which taxes are collected. Here's an example: assume that the inflation rate is 10%, so the overall level of prices rises 10% each year. Suppose that a business buys an asset, such as a piece of land, for $100,000, then resells it a year later for $110,000. In a fundamental sense, the business didn't make a profit on the deal: in real terms, it got no more for the land than it paid for it. But U.S. tax law would say that the business made a capital gain of $10,000, and it would have to pay taxes on that phantom gain.

During the 1970s, when the United States had relatively high inflation, the distorting effects of inflation on the tax system were a serious problem. Some businesses were discouraged from productive investment spending because they found themselves paying taxes on phantom gains. Meanwhile, some unproductive investments became attractive because they led to phantom losses that reduced tax bills. When inflation fell in the 1980s—and tax rates were reduced—these problems became much less important.

Winners and Losers from Inflation

As we've just learned, a high inflation rate imposes costs on the economy through a waste of resources. In addition, inflation can produce winners and losers within the economy. The main reason inflation sometimes helps some people while hurting others is that economic transactions often involve contracts that extend over a period of time, such as loans, and these contracts are normally specified in nominal—that is, in dollar—terms.

In the case of a loan, the borrower receives a certain amount of funds at the beginning, and the loan contract specifies the *interest rate* on the loan and when it must be paid off. The **interest rate** is the return a lender receives for allowing borrowers the use of their savings for one year, calculated as a percentage of the amount borrowed.

But what that dollar is worth in real terms—that is, in terms of purchasing power—depends greatly on the rate of inflation over the intervening years of the loan. Economists summarize the effect of inflation on borrowers and lenders by distinguishing between the *nominal* interest rate and the *real* interest rate. The **nominal interest rate** is the interest rate in dollar terms—for example, the interest rate on a student loan. The **real interest rate** is the nominal interest rate minus the rate of inflation. For example, if a loan carries an interest rate of 8%, but there is 5% inflation, the real interest rate is 8% – 5% = 3%.

When a borrower and a lender enter into a loan contract, the contract is normally written in dollar terms—that is, the interest rate it specifies is a nominal interest rate. But each party to a loan contract has an expectation about the future rate of inflation and therefore an expectation about the real interest rate on the loan. If the actual inflation rate is *higher* than expected, borrowers gain at the expense of lenders: borrowers will repay their loans with funds that have a lower real value than had been expected. Conversely, if the inflation rate is *lower* than expected, lenders will gain at the expense of borrowers: borrowers must repay their loans with funds that have a higher real value than had been expected.

In the modern United States, home mortgages are the most important source of gains and losses from inflation. While some mortgage interest rates are linked to the inflation rate, the vast majority are not, creating big winners and losers when inflation rates have changed unexpectedly. Americans who took out mortgages in the early 1970s quickly found the real cost of their payments reduced by higher-than-expected inflation. In contrast, those who took out mortgages in the early 1990s lost. The inflation rate fell to lower-than-expected levels in the following years and raised the cost of their payments.

Because gains for some and losses for others result from inflation that is either higher or lower than expected, yet another problem arises: uncertainty about the future inflation rate discourages people from entering into any form of long-term contract. This is an additional cost of high inflation, because high rates of inflation are usually unpredictable. In countries with high and uncertain inflation, long-term loans are rare, which makes it difficult in many cases to make long-term investments.

One last point: unexpected *deflation*—a surprise fall in the price level—creates winners and losers, too. Between 1929 and 1933, as the U.S. economy plunged into the Great Depression, the consumer price index fell by 35%. This meant that debtors, including many farmers and homeowners, saw a sharp rise in the real value of their debts, which led to widespread bankruptcy and helped create a banking crisis, as lenders found their customers unable to pay back their loans. And as you can see in Figure 12, deflation occurred again in 2009, when the inflation rate fell to –2% at the trough of a deep recession. Like the Great Depression (but to a much lesser extent), the unexpected deflation of 2009 imposed heavy costs on debtors. We will discuss the effects of deflation in more detail in Chapter 16.

disinflation the process of bringing down inflation that has become embedded in expectations.

Inflation Is Easy. Disinflation Is Hard.

There is not much evidence that a rise in the inflation rate from 2% to 5% would do a great deal of harm to the economy. Still, policy makers generally move forcefully to bring inflation back down when it moves above 2% or 3%. Why? Because experience shows that bringing the inflation rate down—a process called **disinflation**—is very difficult and costly once a higher rate of inflation has become well established in the economy.

Figure 13 shows what happened during two major episodes of disinflation in the United States, in the mid-1970s and in the early 1980s. The horizontal axis shows the unemployment rate. The vertical axis shows *core inflation* over the previous year, a measure that excludes volatile food and energy prices and is widely considered a better measure of underlying inflation than overall consumer prices. Each marker represents the inflation rate and the unemployment rate for one month. In each episode, unemployment and inflation followed a sort of clockwise spiral, with high inflation gradually falling in the face of an extended period of very high unemployment.

FIGURE 13 The Cost of Disinflation

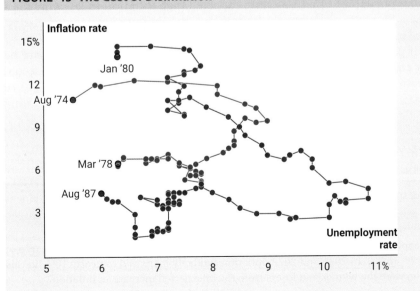

There were two major periods of disinflation in modern U.S. history, in the mid-1970s and the early 1980s. This figure shows the track of the unemployment rate and the core inflation rate, which excludes food and energy, during these two episodes. In each case bringing inflation down required a temporary but very large increase in the unemployment rate, demonstrating the high cost of disinflation.
Data from: Bureau of Labor Statistics.

According to many economists, these periods of high unemployment that temporarily depressed the economy were necessary to reduce inflation that had become deeply embedded in the economy. The best way to avoid having to put the economy through a wringer to reduce inflation, however, is to avoid having a serious inflation problem in the first place. So, as a form of preventive medicine for the economy, policy makers respond forcefully to signs that inflation may be accelerating.

ECONOMICS >> *in Action*
The Inflation Surge of 2021–2022

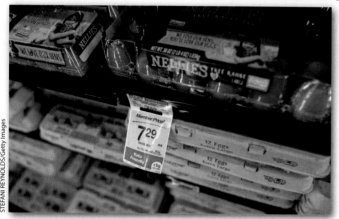

Prices of eggs drastically rose in 2022 due to a shortage of eggs from an avian flu outbreak.

STEFANI REYNOLDS/Getty Images

After several decades of low inflation, the United States experienced a sudden inflation surge during 2021–2022, with annual inflation peaking at almost 10%. The causes of that inflation surge were a matter of widespread dispute, even among economists, although most analyses stressed both the economic disruptions caused by the coronavirus and the policy response, which involved very large federal aid to distressed households and businesses and probably caused overall demand in the economy to surge at a time when pandemic disruptions were limiting supply. We'll discuss the episode at length in Chapter 13.

The public was, understandably, disturbed by the sudden departure from price stability; surveys showed a sharp drop in consumer confidence. But did the 2021–2022 inflation surge have large economic costs? Believe it or not, the answer is probably no.

Some price increases definitely caused hardship. Notably, the price of gasoline temporarily soared to about $5 a gallon, a financial burden on many families, and prices of many foods—especially eggs—also shot up. However, these price increases probably had little to do with overall inflation. Instead, they were driven largely by special events, notably the war between Russia and Ukraine (Russia is a major oil producer, and both countries are important grain producers) and an outbreak of avian flu that killed many chickens.

There were, however, few signs of the traditional costs of inflation. Notably, there was no clear indication that the unit-of-account function of the dollar had been seriously degraded. Financial markets, which can in effect make bets about future inflation, showed that investors expected high inflation to last only for a year or two. Surveys of consumers found the same thing: most people believed that price stability would return fairly soon.

Even if price stability was going to return, however, would getting there be extremely costly, as it was in the 1980s? At the time this edition was written, economists were still arguing about this question. However, early indications were reassuring: inflation seemed to have peaked in mid-2022, then began coming down rapidly without a large rise in unemployment.

>> *Quick Review*

• The **real wage** and **real income** are unaffected by the level of prices.

• Inflation, like unemployment, is a major concern of policy makers — so much so that in the past they have accepted high unemployment as the price of reducing inflation.

• While the overall level of prices is irrelevant, high rates of inflation impose real costs on the economy: **shoe-leather costs, menu costs,** and **unit-of-account costs.**

• The **interest rate** is the return a lender receives for use of their funds for a year. The **real interest rate** is equal to the **nominal interest rate** minus the inflation rate. As a result, unexpectedly high inflation helps borrowers and hurts lenders. With high and uncertain inflation, people will often avoid long-term investments.

• **Disinflation** is very costly, so policy makers try to avoid getting into situations of high inflation in the first place.

>> *Check Your Understanding* 8-3
Solutions appear at back of book.

1. The widespread use of technology has revolutionized the banking industry, making it much easier for customers to access and manage their assets. Does this mean that the shoe-leather costs of inflation are higher or lower than they used to be?

2. Most people in the United States have grown accustomed to a modest inflation rate of around 2% to 3%. In 2021 and 2022, inflation suddenly increased to nearly 10%. In this case, who were the winner and losers from the unexpected increase in inflation?

TaskRabbit

STEPHEN LAM/REUTERS/Newscom

"Moving is the worst. Yard work is the worst. Building IKEA furniture is the worst." So began a 2015 report on TaskRabbit, a company founded in 2008 (under the name RunMyErrand), that helps people hire others to do their chores. As of 2019 there were about 140,000 of these freelancers, whom the company calls Taskers, and TaskRabbit operated in 53 U.S. cities, Great Britain, and Canada.

Why would becoming a Tasker seem appealing to some workers? The great majority of Taskers are part-time workers, who want flexibility in their employment; the company's pitch to potential Taskers contains the slogan "Earn money your way," and features testimonials from workers who combined employment with parenting, careers in the arts, and so on.

Working part time for a variety of clients isn't a new phenomenon. On urban street corners across the United States, workers still line up early each morning in the hope of getting day jobs in industries like construction, where the need for workers fluctuates, sometimes unpredictably. For more skilled workers, there are numerous online resources as well as temporary staffing agencies, like Allegis Group, that provide workers on a subcontracting basis, from a few days to months at a time. And some people still find temporary jobs by calling numbers listed in classified ads, or even going door to door.

But TaskRabbit—founded the year after Apple introduced its first iPhone—tries to use the ubiquity of smartphones to simplify the process. Originally it was set up as a kind of auction market, in which potential employers and workers placed bids, but since 2014 it has relied on a streamlined system that is very similar to the way car services like Uber or Lyft match riders with willing drivers. TaskRabbit's app let those seeking help make their needs known simply by tapping on one of a few common chores; potential workers can then offer to do jobs that match the locations and skills they have put in their profiles, again simply by tapping on jobs that appear on their smartphones. (They have already specified their hourly rate.) The process takes a lot less time and effort than standing on street corners, pounding the pavement, or performing online job searches.

How big a deal are enterprises like TaskRabbit? Some observers suggest that we're seeing the rise of a *gig economy*, in which large numbers of people freelance, moving from job to job rather than being formal employees of a large firm. There's probably some hype in these pronouncements, but real change does seem to be happening. So far, however, there isn't a lot of evidence for a major shift in the nature of employment.

QUESTIONS FOR THOUGHT

1. How is the matching of job-seekers and employers through services like TaskRabbit likely to affect frictional unemployment?

2. What is the likely effect of such services on the number of people considered to be in the labor force?

3. Some analysts suggest that most freelancers have other jobs, and only do gig economy work on the side. How does that statement help explain the lack of clear evidence for a growing gig economy?

SUMMARY

1. The two principal objectives of macroeconomic policy are price stability (a low, but positive, level of inflation) and low unemployment.

2. **Employment** is the number of people employed; **unemployment** is the number of people unemployed and actively looking for work. Their sum is equal to the **labor force,** and the **labor force participation rate** is the percentage of the population age 16 or older who is in the labor force.

3. The **unemployment rate,** the percentage of the labor force that is unemployed and actively looking for work, can both overstate and understate the true level of unemployment. It can overstate because it counts as unemployed those who are continuing to search for a job despite having been offered one. It can understate because it ignores frustrated workers, such as **discouraged workers, marginally attached workers,** and the **underemployed.** In addition, the unemployment rate varies greatly among different groups in the population; it is typically higher for younger workers and for workers near retirement age than for workers in their prime working years.

4. There is a negative relationship between the growth rate of GDP and the change in unemployment. During a recession, when the GDP growth rate is less than zero, unemployment rises; the deeper the recession, the greater the rise in unemployment. During a strong expansion, when the GDP growth rate is above average, unemployment falls; the stronger the expansion, the greater the fall in unemployment. A **jobless recovery** occurs when the GDP growth rate is positive but below average, resulting in rising unemployment.

5. Job creation and destruction, as well as voluntary job separations, lead to natural unemployment, composed of **frictional unemployment** and **structural unemployment. Job search** leads to frictional unemployment. Structural unemployment arises when the prevailing wage rate is above the equilibrium wage rate, resulting in persistent unemployment. It is due to a number of factors, such as **minimum wages, unions, efficiency wages,** government policies, and mismatch between employers and employees. As a result, the **natural rate of unemployment,** the sum of frictional and structural unemployment, is well above zero, even when jobs are plentiful.

6. The actual unemployment rate is equal to the natural rate of unemployment, the share of unemployment that is independent of the business cycle, plus **cyclical unemployment,** the share of unemployment that depends on fluctuations in the business cycle.

7. The natural rate of unemployment changes over time, largely in response to changes in labor force characteristics, labor market institutions, and government policies.

8. Inflation does not, as many assume, make everyone poorer by raising the level of prices. That's because wages and incomes are adjusted to take into account a rising price level, leaving **real wages** and **real income** unaffected. However, a high inflation rate imposes overall costs on the economy: **shoe-leather costs, menu costs,** and **unit-of-account costs.**

9. Inflation can produce winners and losers within the economy, because long-term contracts are generally written in dollar terms. The **interest rate** specified in a loan is typically a **nominal interest rate,** which differs from the **real interest rate** due to inflation. A higher-than-expected inflation rate is good for borrowers and bad for lenders. A lower-than-expected inflation rate is good for lenders and bad for borrowers.

10. Many believe policies that depress the economy and produce high unemployment are necessary to reduce embedded inflation. Because **disinflation** is very costly, policy makers try to prevent inflation from becoming excessive in the first place.

KEY TERMS

Employment, p. 214
Unemployment, p. 214
Labor force, p. 214
Labor force participation rate, p. 215
Unemployment rate, p. 215
Discouraged workers, p. 216
Marginally attached workers, p. 216
Underemployment, p. 216
Jobless recovery, p. 219

Job search, p. 221
Frictional unemployment, p. 221
Structural unemployment, p. 223
Minimum wage, p. 223
Union, p. 224
Efficiency wages, p. 225
Natural rate of unemployment, p. 225
Cyclical unemployment, p. 225
Real wage, p. 229

Real income, p. 229
Shoe-leather costs, p. 231
Menu costs, p. 231
Unit-of-account costs, p. 232
Interest rate, p. 232
Nominal interest rate, p. 232
Real interest rate, p. 232
Disinflation, p. 233

PRACTICE QUESTIONS

1. Each month, usually on the first Friday of the month, the Bureau of Labor Statistics releases the Employment Situation Summary for the previous month. Go to www.bls.gov and find the latest report. On the Bureau of Labor Statistics home page, at the top of the page, select the "Economic Releases" tab, find "Latest Releases," and select "Employment Situation." You will find the Employment Situation Summary listed at the top. How does the current unemployment rate compare to the rate one month earlier? How does the current unemployment rate compare to the rate one year earlier?

2. In 2018, the Bureau of Labor Statistics released the report "Contingent and Alternative Employment Arrangements," which included independent contractors, those in the gig economy. The report found 16.5 million people working in contingent or independent jobs. Surprisingly, the share of all workers classified as either contingent or independent contractors had declined from 11.5% in 2005 to 10.7% in 2017. The BLS report stated, "The government figures only count workers whose gig arrangements are their main job, and only includes those who've worked in that job in the last week." In what ways did the BLS understate the reported numbers? Who was likely being omitted from these calculations?

PROBLEMS

1. In general, how do changes in the unemployment rate vary with changes in real GDP? After several quarters of a severe recession, explain why we might observe a decrease in the official unemployment rate. Explain why we could see an increase in the official unemployment rate after several quarters of a strong expansion.

2. In each of the following situations, what type of unemployment is Melanie facing?

a. After completing a complex programming project, Melanie is laid off. Her prospects for a new job requiring similar skills are good, and she has signed up with a programmer placement service. She has passed up offers for low-paying jobs.

b. When Melanie and her co-workers refused to accept pay cuts, her employer outsourced their programming tasks to workers in another country. This phenomenon is occurring throughout the programming industry.

c. Due to the current slump, Melanie has been laid off from her programming job. Her employer promises to rehire her when business picks up.

3. Part of the information released in the Employment Situation Summary concerns how long individuals have been unemployed. Go to www.bls.gov to find the latest report. Use the same technique as in Practice Questions Problem 1 to find the Employment Situation Summary. Near the end of the Employment Situation, click on Table A-12, titled "Unemployed persons by duration of unemployment." Use the seasonally adjusted numbers to answer the following questions.

a. How many workers were unemployed less than 5 weeks? What percentage of all unemployed workers do these workers represent? How do these numbers compare to the previous month's data?

b. How many workers were unemployed for 27 or more weeks? What percentage of all unemployed workers do these workers represent? How do these numbers compare to the previous month's data?

c. How long has the average worker been unemployed (average duration, in weeks)? How does this compare to the average for the previous month's data?

d. Comparing the latest month for which there are data with the previous month, has the problem of long-term unemployment improved or deteriorated?

4. A country's labor force is the sum of the number of employed and unemployed workers. The accompanying table provides data on the size of the labor force and the number of unemployed workers for different regions of the United States.

Region	Labor force (thousands)		Unemployed (thousands)	
	December 2021	December 2022	December 2021	December 2022
Northeast	28,617	28,865	1,389	1,116
South	60,446	61,753	2,094	2,077
Midwest	34,539	34,845	1,256	1,250
West	38,627	39,318	1,579	1,566

Data from: Bureau of Labor Statistics.

a. Calculate the number of workers employed in each of the regions in December 2021 and December 2022. Use your answers to calculate the change in the total number of workers employed between December 2021 and December 2022.

b. For each region, calculate the growth in the labor force from December 2021 to December 2022.

c. Compute unemployment rates in the different regions of the country in December 2021 and December 2022.

d. What can you infer about the fall in unemployment rates over this period? Was it caused by a net gain in the number of jobs or by a large fall in the number of people seeking jobs?

5. 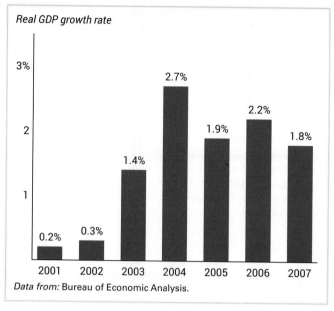 Access the Discovering Data exercise for Chapter 8, Problem 5 online to answer the following questions.

a. What is the current federal minimum wage?

b. In what year was the federal minimum wage last increased?

c. What is the current value for the real minimum wage?

d. In what year was the real minimum wage the highest? The lowest?

e. In general, since 1970, how has the purchasing power of the minimum wage changed over time?

6. In which of the following cases is it more likely for efficiency wages to exist? Why?

a. Jane and her boss work as a team selling ice cream.

b. Jane sells ice cream without any direct supervision by her boss.

c. Jane speaks Korean and sells ice cream in a neighborhood in which Korean is the primary language. It is difficult to find another worker who speaks Korean.

7. How will the following changes affect the natural rate of unemployment?

a. The government reduces the time during which an unemployed worker can receive unemployment benefits.

b. More teenagers focus on their studies and do not look for jobs until after college.

c. Greater access to the internet leads both potential employers and potential employees to use the internet to list and find jobs.

d. Union membership declines.

8. With its tradition of a job for life for most citizens, Japan once had a much lower unemployment rate than that of the United States; from 1960 to 1995, the unemployment rate in Japan exceeded 3% only once. However, since the crash of its stock market in 1989 and slow economic growth in the 1990s, the job-for-life system has broken down and unemployment rose to more than 5% in 2003.

a. Explain the likely effect of the breakdown of the job-for-life system in Japan on the Japanese natural rate of unemployment.

b. As the accompanying diagram shows, the rate of growth of real GDP picked up in Japan after 2001 and before the global economic crisis of 2007–2009. Explain the likely effect of this increase in real GDP growth on the unemployment rate. Was the likely cause of the change in the unemployment rate during this period a change in the natural rate of unemployment or a change in the cyclical unemployment rate?

Real GDP growth rate

9. In the following examples, is inflation creating winners and losers at no net cost to the economy or is inflation imposing a net cost on the economy? If a net cost is being imposed, which type of cost is involved?

a. When inflation is expected to be high, workers get paid more frequently and make more trips to the bank.

b. Lanwei is reimbursed by her company for her work-related travel expenses. Sometimes, however, the company takes a long time to reimburse her. So when inflation is high, she is less willing to travel for her job.

c. Hector has a mortgage with a fixed nominal interest rate of 6% that he took out five years ago. Over the years, the inflation rate has crept up unexpectedly to its present level of 7%.

d. In response to unexpectedly high inflation, the manager of Cozy Cottages of Cape Cod must reprint and resend expensive color brochures correcting the price of rentals this season.

10. The accompanying diagram shows the interest rate on one-year loans and inflation from 2005 to 2022 in the economy of Albernia. When would one-year loans have been especially attractive and why?

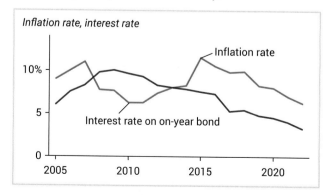

Inflation rate, interest rate

11. The accompanying table provides the inflation rate in the year 2008 and the average inflation rate over the period 2009–2021 for seven different countries.

Country	Inflation rate in 2008	Average inflation rate in 2009–2021
Brazil	5.68%	5.74%
China	5.93	2.20
France	2.81	1.03
Indonesia	10.23	4.26
Japan	1.38	0.23
Turkey	10.44	10.50
United States	3.84	1.79

Data from: IMF.

a. Given the expected relationship between average inflation and menu costs, rank the countries in descending order of menu costs using average inflation over the period 2009–2021.

b. Rank the countries in order of inflation rates that most favored borrowers with 10-year loans that were taken out in 2008. Assume that the loans were agreed upon with the expectation that the inflation rate for 2009 to 2021 would be the same as the inflation rate in 2008.

c. Did borrowers who took out 10-year loans in Japan gain or lose overall versus lenders? Explain.

12. 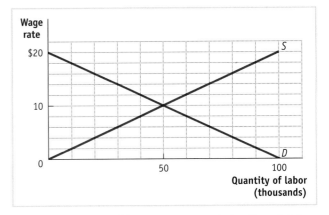 Access the Discovering Data exercise for Chapter 8, Problem 12 online to answer the following questions.

a. What is the current level of employment for individuals without a high school diploma?

b. How much has employment changed for high school graduates from 2010 through 2022?

c. Since 2010, which education group has experienced the largest increase in employment?

d. Since the end of the Great Recession in 2009, how has employment changed for the different education levels? Calculate the net gain (or loss) of jobs for each category to answer.

e. What percent of the employed had a bachelor's degree in January 1992? What percent has a bachelor's degree today?

f. Calculate the change in the share of employment by education level since 1992.

13. The accompanying diagram shows the inflation rate in the United Kingdom from 1980 to 2021.

a. Between 1980 and 1985, policy makers in the United Kingdom worked to lower the inflation rate. What would you predict happened to unemployment between 1980 and 1985?

b. Policy makers in the United Kingdom react forcefully when the inflation rate rises above a target rate of 2%. Why would it be harmful if inflation rose from 2.5% (the level in 2021) to, say, a level of 5%?

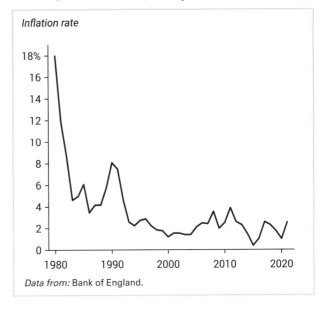

Data from: Bank of England.

14. There is only one labor market in Profunctia. All workers have the same skills, and all firms hire workers with these skills. Use the accompanying diagram, which shows the supply of and demand for labor, to answer the following questions. Illustrate each answer with a diagram.

a. What is the equilibrium wage rate in Profunctia? At this wage rate, what are the level of employment, the size of the labor force, and the unemployment rate?

b. If the government of Profunctia sets a minimum wage equal to $12, what will be the level of employment, the size of the labor force, and the unemployment rate?

c. If unions bargain with the firms in Profunctia and set a wage rate equal to $14, what will be the level of employment, the size of the labor force, and the unemployment rate?

d. If the concern for retaining workers and encouraging high-quality work leads firms to set a wage rate equal to $16, what will be the level of employment, the size of the labor force, and the unemployment rate? ■

9 Long-Run Economic Growth

THE SMOG OF PROSPERITY

DELHI, THE CAPITAL OF INDIA, has terrible air quality — which is a bad thing. But it's a by-product of a very good thing: the remarkable growth of India's economy over the past few decades.

Until around 1980, India's economic story was one of disappointment: living standards weren't much higher than they had been when the nation won independence in 1947. But after 1980 the economy took off. India is still very poor by U.S. or European standards, but it has a rapidly growing middle class, which can finally afford the things middle-class families tend to want everywhere: bigger houses, household appliances like washing machines and, of course, cars.

As recently as 2001 India had only 53 motor vehicles per 1,000 inhabitants, around a tenth as many as in advanced countries. By 2019, however, that number had more than quadrupled.

Hence the air quality problem. The streets of Delhi, which has 18 million residents, are now clogged with cars and trucks; the city is also surrounded with factories producing consumer goods and power plants supplying the electricity to run them.

And all these cars, factories, and power plants emit spectacular amounts of pollution. In November 2017, visibility in much of Delhi dropped to a few feet, and health experts said that just being

outdoors during the Great Smog of Delhi was the equivalent of smoking 50 cigarettes a day. Nor was this a one-time event. In November 2019 another extended period of severe pollution forced the city to close all its schools.

As we said, however, Delhi's air quality crisis is a by-product of a very good thing, economic success. And if the experience of other countries is any guide, India will eventually bring its air pollution under control. Beijing, the capital of China, is even bigger than Delhi, with considerably more cars, and it used to have a severe air quality problem, too. But China, which has had even more economic success than India, has begun to put effective pollution controls in place, and this has helped literally clear the air. Meanwhile, China's living standards have continued to rise.

And despite the pollution, India's recent history is a hugely impressive example of *long-run economic growth* — a sustained increase in output per capita. True, India is still a relatively poor country; but that's only because other nations began the process of long-run economic growth many decades ago. In the case of the United States and European countries, long-run economic growth began more than a century and a half ago.

Many economists have argued that long-run economic growth — why it happens and how to achieve it — is the single most important issue in macroeconomics because of its direct effect on living standards.

In this chapter, we present some facts about long-run growth, look at the factors that economists believe determine the pace at which long-run growth takes place, and examine how government policies can help or hinder growth. We will also address questions about the environmental sustainability of long-run growth. ●

Rapid, uncontrolled economic growth has resulted in much higher living standards in places like Delhi, but at the cost of very high levels of pollution.

DOMINIQUE FAGET/Getty Images

WHAT YOU WILL LEARN

- Why is long-run economic growth measured as the increase in real GDP per capita? How has real GDP per capita changed over time in different countries?

- Why is **productivity** the key to long-run economic growth? How is productivity driven by **physical capital**, **human capital**, and **technological progress**?

- Why do long-run growth rates differ so much among countries?

- How does growth vary among several important regions of the world? Why does the **convergence hypothesis** apply to economically advanced countries?

- How do scarcity of natural resources and environmental degradation pose a challenge to **sustainable long-run economic growth**?

Comparing Economies Across Time and Space

Before we analyze the sources of long-run economic growth, it's useful to have a sense of just how much the U.S. economy has grown over time and how large the gaps are between wealthy countries like the United States and countries that have yet to achieve comparable growth. So let's take a look at the numbers.

Real GDP per Capita

The key statistic used to track economic growth is *real GDP per capita*—real GDP divided by the population size. We focus on GDP because, as we learned in Chapter 7, GDP measures the total value of an economy's production of final goods and services as well as the income earned in that economy in a given year. We use *real* GDP because we want to separate changes in the quantity of goods and services from the effects of a rising price level. We focus on real GDP *per capita* because we want to isolate the effect of changes in the population. For example, other things equal, an increase in the population lowers the standard of living for the average person—there are now more people to share a given amount of real GDP. An increase in real GDP that only matches an increase in population leaves the average standard of living unchanged.

Although we also learned that growth in real GDP per capita should not be a policy goal in and of itself, it does serve as a very useful summary measure of a country's economic progress over time. Figure 1 shows real GDP per capita for the United States, India, and China, measured in 2011 dollars, from 1900 to 2018. The vertical axis is drawn on a logarithmic scale so that equal percent changes in real GDP per capita across countries are the same size in the graph.

To give a sense of how much the U.S. economy grew during the last century, Table 1 shows real GDP per capita at selected years, expressed two ways: as a percentage of the 1900 level and as a percentage of the 2018 level. In 1920, the U.S. economy already produced 126% as much per person as it did in 1900. In 2018, it produced 688% as much per person as it did in 1900, almost a sevenfold increase.

FIGURE 1 Economic Growth in the United States, India, and China over the Past Century

Real GDP per capita from 1900 to 2018, measured in 2011 dollars, is shown for the United States, India, and China. Equal percent changes in real GDP per capita are drawn the same size. As the steeper slopes of the lines representing China and India show, since 1980 India and China had a much higher growth rate than the United States. The standard of living achieved in the United States in 1900 was attained by China in 2008. As of 2018, India's standard of living is still below that of the United States in 1900. Note that the break in China data from 1940 to 1950 is due to war.

Data from: Maddison Project Database, version 2020. Jutta Bolt, Robert Inklaar, Herman de Jong, and Jan Luiten van Zanden (2018), "Rebasing 'Maddison': New income comparisons and the shape of long-run economic development," Maddison Project Working Paper 10.

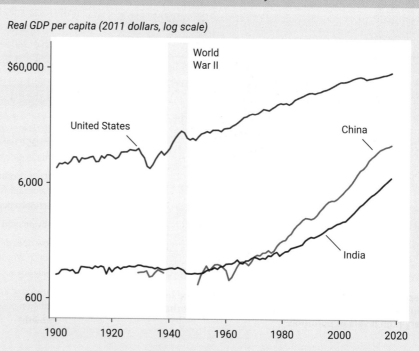

Alternatively, in 1900 the U.S. economy produced only 15% as much per person as it did in 2018.

The income of the typical family normally grows more or less in proportion to per capita income. For example, a 1% increase in real GDP per capita corresponds, roughly, to a 1% increase in the income of the median or typical family—a family at the center of the income distribution. In 2018, the median U.S. household had an income of about $63,000. Since Table 1 tells us that real GDP per capita in 1900 was only 15% of its 2018 level, a typical family in 1900 probably had a purchasing power only 15% as large as the purchasing power of a typical family in 2018. That's around $9,450 in 2018 dollars, representing a standard of living that we would now consider severe poverty. Today's typical American family, if transported back to the United States of 1900, would feel quite a lot of deprivation.

Many people in the world have a standard of living equal to or lower than that of the average American of many generations ago. That's the message about China and India in Figure 1: despite dramatic economic growth in China over the last four decades and the more recent acceleration of economic growth in India, China's per capita GDP is only about as high as America's was in 1930, while India is roughly at our level in 1900.

You can get a sense of how poor much of the world remains by looking at Figure 2, a map of the world in which countries are classified according to their 2021 levels of GDP per capita, in U.S. dollars. As you can see, in large parts of the world, people have very low incomes. Generally speaking, the countries of Europe and North America, as well as a few in the Pacific, have high incomes. Many Asian countries, including China and India, have experienced rapid economic growth, moving them into the middle-income categories. Africa, however, is dominated by countries with GDP less than $4,255 per capita. In fact, about 25% of the world's people live in countries with a lower standard of living than the United States had a century ago.

Growth Rates

How did the United States manage to produce seven times as much real GDP per person in 2018 than in 1900? A little bit at a time. Long-run economic growth

TABLE 1 U.S. Real GDP per Capita

Year	Percentage of 1900 real GDP per capita	Percentage of 2018 real GDP per capita
1900	100%	15%
1920	126	18
1940	149	22
1960	225	33
1980	368	54
2000	571	83
2018	688	100

Data from: Maddison Project Database, version 2018. Jutta Bolt, Robert Inklaar, Herman de Jong, and Jan Luiten van Zanden (2018), "Rebasing 'Maddison': New income comparisons and the shape of long-run economic development," Maddison Project Working Paper 10.

FIGURE 2 Incomes Around the World, 2021

Although the countries of Europe and North America — along with a few in the Pacific — have high incomes, much of the world is still very poor. Today, about a quarter of the world's population lives in countries with a lower standard of living than the United States had a century ago.

Data from: World Development Indicators, World Bank.

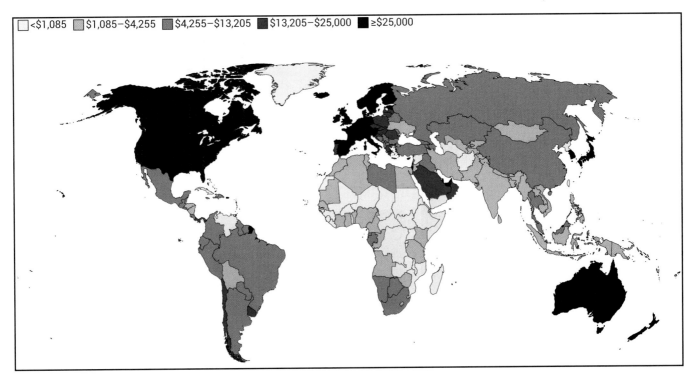

<$1,085 $1,085–$4,255 $4,255–$13,205 $13,205–$25,000   ≥$25,000

Rule of 70 a mathematical formula that states that the time it takes real GDP per capita, or any other variable that grows gradually over time, to double is approximately 70 divided by that variable's annual growth rate.

is normally a gradual process in which real GDP per capita grows at most a few percent per year. From 1900 to 2018, real GDP per capita in the United States increased an average of 1.7% each year.

To have a sense of the relationship between the annual growth rate of real GDP per capita and the long-run change in real GDP per capita, it's helpful to keep in mind the **Rule of 70,** a mathematical formula that tells us how long it takes real GDP per capita, or any other variable that grows gradually over time, to double. The approximate answer is:

(1) Number of years for variable to double $= \dfrac{70}{\text{Annual growth rate of variable}}$

(Note that the Rule of 70 can only be applied to a positive growth rate.) So, if real GDP per capita grows at 1% per year, it will take 70 years to double. If it grows at 2% per year, it will take only 35 years to double. In the case of the United States, since 1900 real GDP per capita rose a little less than 2%, at 1.7% per year.

Applying the Rule of 70 to this information implies that it should have taken 41 years for real GDP per capita to double; it would take 123 years—three periods of 41 years each—for U.S. real GDP per capita to double three times. That is, the Rule of 70 implies that over the course of 123 years, U.S. real GDP per capita should have increased by a factor of $2 \times 2 \times 2 = 8$. And this does turn out to be a pretty good approximation of reality. Between 1900 and 2018—a period of 118 years—real GDP per capita rose just under eightfold.

Figure 3 shows the average annual rate of growth of real GDP per capita for selected countries from 1980 to 2021. Some countries were notable success stories: for example, China, though still quite poor, has made spectacular progress. India, although not matching China's performance, has also achieved impressive growth. The same is true for Bangladesh, as discussed in the following Economics in Action.

Some countries, though, have had very disappointing growth. Argentina was once considered a wealthy nation. In the early years of the twentieth century, it was in the same league as the United States and Canada. But since then it has lagged far behind more dynamic economies. And still others, like Zimbabwe, have slid backward.

What explains these differences in growth rates? To answer that question, we need to examine the sources of long-run economic growth, which we turn to next.

FIGURE 3 Comparing Recent Growth Rates

The average annual rate of growth of real GDP per capita from 1980 to 2021 is shown here for selected countries. China and, to a lesser extent, India and Ireland achieved impressive growth. The United States and France had moderate growth. Once considered an economically advanced country, Argentina had more sluggish growth. Still others, such as Zimbabwe, slid backward.

Data from: World Development Indicators.

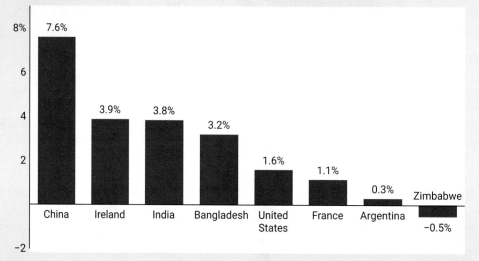

Average annual rate of growth of real GDP per capita (1980–2021)

China 7.6%, Ireland 3.9%, India 3.8%, Bangladesh 3.2%, United States 1.6%, France 1.1%, Argentina 0.3%, Zimbabwe −0.5%

PITFALLS

CHANGE IN LEVEL VERSUS RATE OF CHANGE

When studying economic growth, it's important to understand the difference between a *change in level* and a *rate of change*. When we say that real GDP "grew," economists mean that the *level* of real GDP increased at a certain point in time. For example, we might say that U.S. real GDP grew during 2022 by $405 billion.

But statements about economic growth over a period of years almost always refer to changes in the growth rate. For example, if we knew the level of U.S. real GDP in 2021, we could also represent the amount of 2022 growth in terms of a rate of change. For example, if U.S.

real GDP in 2021 had been $19,610 billion, then U.S. real GDP in 2022 would have been $19,610 billion + $405 billion = $20,015 billion. We could calculate the rate of change, or the growth rate, of U.S. real GDP during 2022 as: (($20,015 billion − $19,610 billion)/$19,610 billion) × 100 = ($405 billion/$19,610 billion) × 100 = 2.1%. So when we say that "U.S. growth fell during the 1970s," we mean that the U.S. growth rate of real GDP was lower in the 1970s compared to the 1960s. When we say that "growth accelerated during the early 1990s," we mean that the growth rate increased year after year in the early 1990s — for example, going from 3% to 3.5% to 4%.

ECONOMICS >> *in Action*
An Economic Breakthrough in Bangladesh

Western news media rarely mention Bangladesh: it's not a political hot spot, it doesn't have oil, and it's overshadowed by its immense neighbor, India. Yet it is home to more than 160 million people—and although it is still very poor, it is nonetheless one of the greatest economic success stories of the past generation.

As recently as the 1980s, real GDP per capita in Bangladesh—which achieved independence from Pakistan in 1971, after a brutal war—was barely higher than it had been in 1950, when the country was so poor that it literally lived on the edge of starvation. In the early 1990s, however, the nation began a process of political and economic reform, making the transition from military rule to democracy, freeing up markets, and achieving monetary and fiscal stability. And growth took off, most notably with the rise of Bangladesh as a major exporter of clothing to Western markets. Real GDP per capita tripled over the period from 1990 to 2021. Other measures also showed dramatic improvements in the quality of life: life expectancy rose by a dozen years, child mortality fell by 70%, and school enrollment rose sharply, especially for girls.

Make no mistake, Bangladesh is still incredibly poor by U.S. standards. Wages are very low although rising, while working conditions are often terrible and dangerous—a point highlighted in 2013, when a factory complex collapsed, killing more than a thousand workers. But compared with its own past, Bangladesh has achieved a lot of progress—and demonstrated that economic growth brings real human benefits, too.

Although Bangladesh remains a very poor country, a high growth rate has improved living standards over the last 25 years.

Michael Runkel/AGE Fotostock

>> Check Your Understanding 9-1

Solutions appear at back of book.

1. Why do economists use real GDP per capita to measure economic progress rather than some other measure, such as nominal GDP per capita or real GDP?

2. Apply the Rule of 70 to the data in Figure 3 to determine how many years it will take each of the countries listed there (except Zimbabwe) to double its real GDP per capita. Would India's real GDP per capita exceed that of the United States in the future if growth rates remain as shown in Figure 3? Why or why not?

3. Although China and India currently have growth rates much higher than the U.S. growth rate, the typical Chinese or Indian household is far poorer than the typical American household. Explain why.

>> Quick Review

• Economic growth is measured using real GDP per capita.

• In the United States, real GDP per capita increased eightfold since 1900, resulting in a large increase in living standards.

• Many countries have real GDP per capita much lower than that of the United States. About 25% of the world's population has living standards worse than those existing in the United States in the early 1900s.

• The long-term rise in real GDP per capita is the result of gradual growth. The **Rule of 70** tells us how many years at a given annual rate of growth it takes to double real GDP per capita.

• Growth rates of real GDP per capita differ substantially among nations.

labor productivity output per worker; also referred to as simply productivity. Increases in labor productivity are the only source of long-run economic growth.

productivity output per worker; a shortened form of the term *labor productivity.*

physical capital human-made resources such as buildings and machines.

human capital the improvement in labor created by the education and knowledge embodied in the workforce.

‖ The Sources of Long-Run Growth

One of our fundamental principles of economics is that *increases in economic potential lead to economic growth over time.* More specifically, long-run economic growth depends almost entirely on one ingredient: rising *productivity.* However, a number of factors affect the growth of productivity. Let's look first at why productivity is the key ingredient and then examine what affects it.

The Crucial Importance of Productivity

Sustained economic growth occurs only when the amount of output produced by the average worker increases steadily. The term **labor productivity,** or **productivity** for short, is used to refer either to output per worker or, in some cases, to output per hour. (The number of hours worked by an average worker differs to some extent across countries, although this isn't an important factor in the difference between living standards in, say, India and the United States.) For the economy as a whole, productivity—output per worker—is simply real GDP divided by the number of people working.

You might wonder why we say that higher productivity is the only source of long-run growth. Can't an economy also increase its real GDP per capita by putting more of the population to work? The answer is, yes, but …

For short periods of time, an economy can experience a burst of growth in output per capita by putting a higher percentage of the population to work. That happened in the United States during World War II, when millions of women who previously worked only in the home entered the paid workforce. The percentage of adult civilians employed outside the home rose from 50% in 1941 to 58% in 1944, and you can see the resulting bump in real GDP per capita during those years in Figure 1.

Over the longer run, however, the rate of employment growth is never very different from the rate of population growth. Over the course of the twentieth century, for example, the population of the United States rose at an average rate of 1.2% per year and employment rose 1.4% per year. Real GDP per capita rose 1.7% per year; of that, 1.5%—that is, almost 90% of the total—was the result of rising productivity. In general, overall real GDP can grow because of population growth, but any large increase in real GDP *per capita* must be the result of increased output *per worker.* That is, it must be due to higher productivity.

So increased productivity is the key to long-run economic growth. But what leads to higher productivity?

Explaining Growth in Productivity

There are three main reasons why the average U.S. worker today produces far more than their counterpart a century ago. First, the modern worker has far more *physical capital,* such as machinery and office space, to work with. Second, the modern worker is much better educated and so possesses much more *human capital.* Finally, modern firms have the advantage of a century's *technological progress.*

Let's look at each of these three sources of productivity growth.

Increases in Physical Capital Economists define **physical capital** as manufactured resources such as buildings and machines. Physical capital makes workers more productive. For example, a worker operating a backhoe can dig a lot more feet of trench per day than one equipped only with a shovel.

The average U.S. private-sector worker today is backed up by nearly $400,000 worth of physical capital—far more than a U.S. worker had 100 years ago and far more than the average worker in most other countries has today.

Increase in Human Capital It's not enough for a worker to have good equipment—they must also know what to do with it. **Human capital** refers to the improvement in labor created by the education and knowledge embodied in the workforce.

The human capital of the United States has increased dramatically over the past century. A century ago, although most Americans were able to read and write, very few had an extensive education. In 1910, only 13.5% of Americans over 25 had graduated from high school and only 3% had four-year college degrees. By 2022, the percentages were 91% and 37%, respectively. It would be impossible to run today's economy with a population as poorly educated as the U.S. populace a century ago.

Analyses based on *growth accounting,* described later in this chapter, suggest that education—and its effect on productivity—is an even more important determinant of growth than increases in physical capital.

Technological Progress Probably the most important driver of productivity growth is **technological progress,** which is broadly defined as an advance in the technical means of the production of goods and services. We'll see shortly how economists measure the impact of technology on growth. Workers today are able to produce more than those in the past, even with the same amount of physical and human capital, because technology has advanced over time. It's important to realize that economically important technological progress need not be flashy or rely on cutting-edge science.

Historians have noted that past economic growth has been driven not only by major inventions, such as the railroad or the semiconductor chip, but also by thousands of modest innovations, such as the precut cardboard boxes used to deliver practically everything we order online, which were invented in 1890, and the Post-it® note, introduced in 1980, which has had surprisingly large benefits for office productivity.

Experts attribute much of a productivity surge that took place in the United States from about 1995 to 2005 to new technology adopted by service-producing companies like Walmart rather than to high-technology companies.

Accounting for Growth: The Aggregate Production Function

Productivity is higher, other things equal, when workers are equipped with more physical capital, more human capital, better technology, or any combination of the three. But can we put numbers to these effects? To do this, economists make use of estimates of the **aggregate production function,** which shows how productivity depends on the quantities of physical capital per worker and human capital per worker as well as the state of technology.

In general, all three factors tend to rise over time, as workers are equipped with more machinery, receive more education, and benefit from technological advances. What the aggregate production function does is allow economists to disentangle the effects of these three factors on overall productivity.

An example of an aggregate production function applied to real data comes from a 2015 study by Keting Shen, Jing Wang, and John Whalley comparing growth in the United States, India, and China from 1979 (when China began a major shift toward becoming a market economy) to 2008. One of their production functions took the form:

GDP per worker = $T \times$ (Physical capital per worker)$^{1/3} \times$ (Human capital per worker)$^{2/3}$

where T represented an estimate of the level of technology, and they related human capital to years of education. Over this period, China moved well up the scale, from GDP per capita only 2% that of the United States to 9% that of the United States (a number that had risen to around 18%). Most of this relative growth, they found, was due to an increase in China's relative T, from around 10% that of the United States to 25% that of the United States.

technological progress an advance in the technical means of production of goods and services.

aggregate production function a hypothetical function that shows how productivity (real GDP per worker) depends on the quantities of physical capital per worker and human capital per worker as well as the state of technology.

diminishing returns to physical capital in an aggregate production function when the amount of human capital per worker and the state of technology are held fixed, each successive increase in the amount of physical capital per worker leads to a smaller increase in productivity.

In analyzing historical economic growth, economists have discovered a crucial fact about the estimated aggregate production function: it exhibits **diminishing returns to physical capital.** That is, when the amount of human capital per worker and the state of technology are held fixed, each successive increase in the amount of physical capital per worker leads to a smaller increase in productivity.

Figure 4 and the table to its right give a hypothetical example of how the level of physical capital per worker might affect the level of real GDP per worker, holding human capital per worker and the state of technology fixed. In this example, we measure the quantity of physical capital in dollars.

To see why the relationship between physical capital per worker and productivity exhibits diminishing returns, think about how the availability of farm equipment affects the productivity of farmworkers. A little bit of equipment makes a big difference: a worker equipped with a tractor can do much more than a worker without one. And a worker using more expensive equipment will, other things equal, be more productive: a worker with a $40,000 tractor will normally be able to cultivate more farmland in a given amount of time than a worker with a $20,000 tractor because the more expensive machine will be more powerful, perform more tasks, or both.

But will a worker with a $40,000 tractor, holding human capital and technology constant, be twice as productive as a worker with a $20,000 tractor? Probably not: there's a huge difference between not having a tractor at all and having even an inexpensive tractor; there's much less difference between having an inexpensive tractor and having a better tractor. And we can be sure that a worker with a $200,000 tractor won't be 10 times as productive: a tractor can be improved only

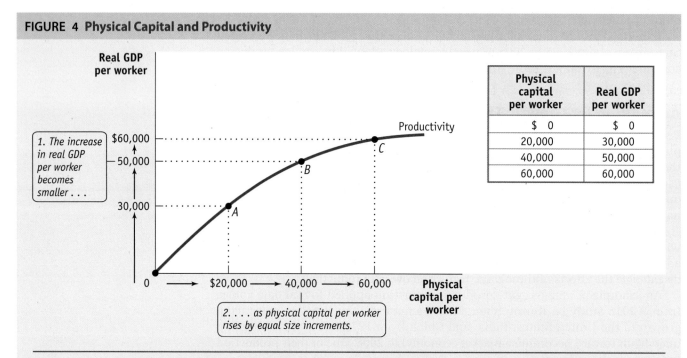

FIGURE 4 Physical Capital and Productivity

Physical capital per worker	Real GDP per worker
$ 0	$ 0
20,000	30,000
40,000	50,000
60,000	60,000

The aggregate production function shows how, in this case, holding human capital per worker and technology fixed, productivity increases as physical capital per worker rises. Other things equal, a greater quantity of physical capital per worker leads to higher real GDP per worker but is subject to diminishing returns: each successive addition to physical capital per worker produces a smaller increase in productivity. Starting at the origin, 0, a $20,000 increase in physical capital per worker leads to an increase in real GDP per worker of $30,000, indicated by point A. Starting from point A, another $20,000 increase in physical capital per worker leads to an increase in real GDP per worker but only of $20,000, indicated by point B. Finally, a third $20,000 increase in physical capital per worker leads to only a $10,000 increase in real GDP per worker, indicated by point C.

so much. Because the same is true of other kinds of equipment, the aggregate production function shows diminishing returns to physical capital.

Diminishing returns to physical capital imply a relationship between physical capital per worker and output per worker like the one shown in Figure 4. As the productivity curve for physical capital and the accompanying table illustrate, more physical capital per worker leads to more output per worker. But each $20,000 increment in physical capital per worker adds less to productivity.

As you can see from the table, there is a big payoff for the first $20,000 of physical capital: real GDP per worker rises by $30,000. The second $20,000 of physical capital also raises productivity, but not by as much: real GDP per worker goes up by only $20,000. The third $20,000 of physical capital raises real GDP per worker by only $10,000. By comparing points along the curve you can also see that as physical capital per worker rises, output per worker also rises—but at a diminishing rate.

Going from the origin at 0 to point *A*, a $20,000 increase in physical capital per worker, leads to an increase of $30,000 in real GDP per worker. Going from point *A* to point *B*, a second $20,000 increase in physical capital per worker, leads to an increase of only $20,000 in real GDP per worker. And from point *B* to point *C*, a $20,000 increase in physical capital per worker, increased real GDP per worker by only $10,000.

It's important to realize that diminishing returns to physical capital is an "other things equal" phenomenon: additional amounts of physical capital are less productive *when the amount of human capital per worker and the technology are held fixed*. Diminishing returns may disappear if we increase the amount of human capital per worker, or improve the technology, or both at the same time the amount of physical capital per worker is increased.

For example, a worker with a $40,000 tractor who has also been trained in the most advanced cultivation techniques may in fact be more than twice as productive as a worker with only a $20,000 tractor and no additional human capital.

But diminishing returns to any one input—regardless of whether it is physical capital, human capital, or number of workers—is a pervasive characteristic of production. Typical estimates suggest that in practice a 1% increase in the quantity of physical capital per worker increases output per worker by only one-third of 1%, or 0.33%.

In practice, all the factors contributing to higher productivity rise during the course of economic growth: both physical capital and human capital per worker increase, and technology advances as well. To disentangle the effects of these factors, economists use **growth accounting,** which estimates the contribution of each major factor in the aggregate production function to economic growth. For example, suppose the following are true:

- The amount of physical capital per worker grows 3% per year.
- According to estimates of the aggregate production function, each 1% rise in physical capital per worker, holding human capital and technology constant, raises output per worker by one-third of 1%, or 0.33%.

growth accounting accounting that estimates the contribution of each of the major factors (physical and human capital, labor, and technology) in the aggregate production function.

PITFALLS

IT MAY BE DIMINISHED . . . BUT IT'S STILL POSITIVE!

As we've seen, the term *diminishing returns to physical capital* means that when holding the amount of human capital per worker and the technology fixed, each successive increase in the amount of physical capital per worker results in a smaller increase in real GDP per worker.

But avoid falling into a common trap. The term does not mean that real GDP per worker will eventually fall as more and more physical

capital is added. What happens instead is that the increase in real GDP per worker will get smaller and smaller, while remaining at or above zero. So an increase in physical capital per worker never reduces productivity.

But due to diminishing returns, at some point, increasing the amount of physical capital per worker will no longer produce an economic payoff. At this point, the increase in output will be so small that it's not worth the cost of the additional physical capital.

In that case, we would estimate that growing physical capital per worker is responsible for 3% × 0.33 = 1 percentage point of productivity growth per year. A similar but more complex procedure is used to estimate the effects of growing human capital. The procedure is more complex because there aren't simple dollar measures of the quantity of human capital.

Growth accounting allows us to calculate the effects of greater physical and human capital on economic growth. But how can we estimate the effects of technological progress? We do so by estimating what is left over after the effects of physical and human capital have been taken into account. For example, let's imagine that there was no increase in human capital per worker so that we can focus on changes in physical capital and in technology.

In Figure 5, the lower curve shows the same hypothetical relationship between physical capital per worker and output per worker shown in Figure 4. Let's assume that this was the relationship given the technology available in 1950. The upper curve also shows a relationship between physical capital per worker and productivity, but this time given the technology available in 2020. (We've chosen a 70-year stretch to allow us to use the Rule of 70.) The 2020 curve is shifted up compared to the 1950 curve because technologies developed over the previous 70 years make it possible to produce more output for a given amount of physical capital per worker than was possible with the technology available in 1950. (Note that the two curves are measured in constant dollars.)

Let's assume that between 1950 and 2020 the amount of physical capital per worker tripled from $20,000 to $60,000. If this increase in physical capital per worker had taken place without any technological progress, the economy would have moved from A to C: output per worker would have risen, but only from $30,000 to $60,000, or 1% per year (using the Rule of 70 tells us that a 1% growth rate over 70 years doubles output). In fact, however, the economy moved from A

FIGURE 5 Technological Progress and Productivity Growth

Technological progress raises productivity at any given level of physical capital per worker, and therefore shifts the aggregate production function upward. Here we hold human capital per worker fixed. We assume that the lower curve (the same curve as in Figure 4) reflects technology in 1950 and the upper curve reflects technology in 2020. Holding technology and human capital fixed, tripling physical capital per worker from $20,000 to $60,000 leads to a doubling of real GDP per worker, from $30,000 to $60,000. This is shown by the movement from point A to point C, reflecting an approximately 1% per year rise in real GDP per worker. In reality, technological progress raised productivity at any given level of physical capital — shown here by the upward shift of the curve — and the actual rise in real GDP per worker is shown by the movement from point A to point D. Real GDP per worker grew 2% per year, leading to a quadrupling during the period. The extra 1% in growth of real GDP per worker is due to higher total factor productivity.

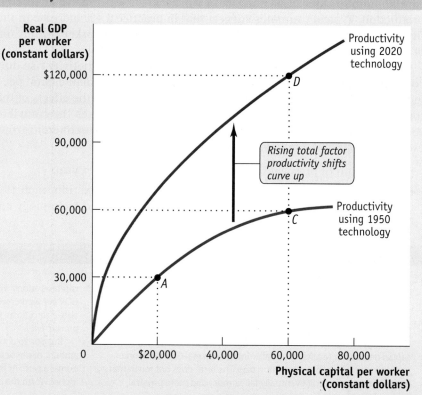

to *D:* output rose from \$30,000 to \$120,000, or 2% per year. There was an increase in both physical capital per worker and technological progress, which shifted the aggregate production function.

In this case, 50% of the annual 2% increase in productivity—that is, 1% in annual productivity growth—is due to higher **total factor productivity,** the amount of output that can be produced with a given amount of factor inputs. So when total factor productivity increases, the economy can produce more output with the same quantity of physical capital, human capital, and labor.

Increases in total factor productivity are central to a country's economic growth. And economists believe that technological progress drives increases in total factor productivity. By reducing the limitations imposed on growth by a given amount of physical capital, technological progress is crucial to economic growth. The Bureau of Labor Statistics estimates the growth rate of both labor productivity and total factor productivity for nonfarm businesses in the United States. According to the Bureau's estimates, over the period from 1948 to 2022 U.S. labor productivity rose 2.1% per year. Less than half of that rise, approximately 49%, is explained by increases in physical and human capital per worker; the rest is explained by rising total factor productivity—that is, by technological progress.

In the United States, labor productivity and total factor productivity have risen continuously for at least two centuries, although the rate of increase has varied a lot over time. For example, productivity growth was very high for a generation after World War II, doubling living standards in a single generation. Since then, productivity growth has been much slower, despite impressive innovations like computers, smartphones, and social media.

What About Natural Resources?

In our discussion so far, we haven't mentioned natural resources, which certainly have an effect on productivity. Other things equal, countries that are abundant in valuable natural resources, such as highly fertile land or rich mineral deposits, have higher real GDP per capita than less fortunate countries.

The most obvious modern example is the Middle East, where enormous oil deposits have made a few sparsely populated countries very rich. For example, the United Arab Emirates (UAE) has about the same level of real GDP per capita as Germany, but the UAE's wealth is based on oil, not manufacturing, the source of Germany's high output per worker.

But other things are often not equal. In the modern world, natural resources are a much less important determinant of productivity than human or physical capital for the great majority of countries. For example, some nations with very high real GDP per capita, such as Japan, have very few natural resources, while some resource-rich nations, such as Nigeria (which has sizable oil deposits), are very poor.

Historically, natural resources played a much more prominent role in determining productivity. In the nineteenth century, the countries with the highest real GDP per capita were those abundant in rich farmland and mineral deposits: the United States, Canada, Argentina, and Australia. As a consequence, natural resources figured prominently in the development of economic thought.

In a famous book published in 1798, *An Essay on the Principle of Population,* the English economist Thomas Malthus made the fixed quantity of land in the world the basis of a pessimistic prediction about future productivity. As population grew, he pointed out, the amount of land per worker would decline. And this, other things equal, would cause productivity to fall.

His view, in fact, was that improvements in technology or increases in physical capital would lead only to temporary improvements in productivity because they would always be offset by the pressure of rising population and more workers on

total factor productivity the amount of output that can be produced with a given amount of factor inputs.

the supply of land. In the long run, he concluded, the great majority of people were condemned to living on the edge of starvation. Only then would death rates be high enough and birth rates low enough to prevent rapid population growth from outstripping productivity growth.

It hasn't turned out that way, although many historians believe that Malthus's prediction of stagnant productivity was valid for much of human history. Population pressure probably did prevent large productivity increases until the eighteenth century. But in the time since Malthus wrote his book, any negative effects on productivity from population growth have been far outweighed by other, positive factors—advances in technology, increases in human and physical capital, and the opening up of enormous amounts of cultivable land in the New World.

It remains true, however, that we live on a finite planet, with limited supplies of resources such as oil and limited ability to absorb environmental damage. We address the concerns these limitations pose for economic growth in the final section of this chapter.

ECONOMICS >> *in Action*
The Rise, Fall, and Return of the Productivity Paradox

We live in an era of revolutionary technological change—or that's what everyone says. And to be fair, there are good reasons for the excitement. After all, your smartphone is thousands of times faster and can store millions of times more data than the computers available to the astronauts who landed on the moon. But is the dramatic increase in computing power translating into equally dramatic economic growth? Economists have been asking that question for decades—and the answer still isn't clear.

Modern information technology began in the 1970s, with the introduction of the first microprocessor—in effect, a whole computer taking the form of tiny transistors and circuits etched on a piece of silicon. Spectacular increases in computing power have transformed how we use and disseminate information. The 1980s brought personal computers, replacing hulking machines that had to be programmed with punch cards, and the first cell phones. The 1990s brought the internet. With the twenty-first century came broadband, smartphones (the first iPhone was introduced in 2007), video streaming, and more.

You might have expected these developments to produce an explosion in total factor productivity. In fact, however, as Figure 6 shows, total factor productivity grew much more rapidly in the generation that followed World War II than it has since. Economists sometimes refer to this disconnect between what looks like rapid technological progress and actual productivity as the "productivity paradox."

True, there was a decade, from 1996 to 2005, when information technology finally seemed to be paying off, and the paradox seemed to be disappearing. Much of this rise came in the service sector, especially retailing, where stores like Walmart achieved major gains in efficiency by using real-time information from cash registers to manage inventory, ordering, and other seemingly mundane aspects of their business. But progress slowed again and remains sluggish even now.

The truth is that nobody knows why modern technology doesn't seem to be doing more for the economy. As we noted in the text, however, a lot of real-world progress comes from

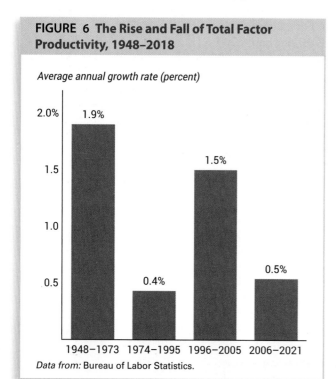

FIGURE 6 The Rise and Fall of Total Factor Productivity, 1948–2018

Average annual growth rate (percent)

Data from: Bureau of Labor Statistics.

technologies that aren't at all flashy, like precut cardboard boxes. Maybe the flip side of this observation is that an era of flashy new technologies isn't necessarily one of rapid progress across the economy as a whole.

In which case, how should we think about the economic implications of ChatGPT and other "large language models," which burst on the scene as this edition was being written? These models are often referred to as artificial intelligence or AI, although many experts will tell you that they aren't truly intelligent in the way a person is—in a way what they do is more like a superpowered version of autocorrect than actual thinking.

Still, they're impressive, one might even say flashy, because these models can deliver coherent responses, drawing on many sources, to questions asked in natural language. So what economic impact will they have? According to one analyst, "Artificial intelligence (AI) has the potential to affect the economy in various ways." Who was that analyst? Nobody: we asked ChatGPT "How will AI affect the economy?" and that was the opening sentence of its reply.

So will AI lead to large productivity increases? Will it displace large numbers of workers, and/or create large numbers of new jobs? It's much too soon to tell.

>> Check Your Understanding 9-2

Solutions appear at back of book.

1. Predict the effect of each of the following events on the growth rate of productivity.
   a. The amounts of physical and human capital per worker are unchanged, but there is significant technological progress.
   b. The amount of physical capital per worker grows at a steady pace, but the level of human capital per worker and technology are unchanged.

2. Output in the economy of Erewhon has grown 3% per year over the past 30 years. The labor force has grown at 1% per year, and the quantity of physical capital has grown at 4% per year. The average education level hasn't changed. Estimates by economists say that each 1% increase in physical capital per worker, other things equal, raises productivity by 0.3%. (*Hint:* % change in (*X/Y*) = % change in *X* − % change in *Y*.)
   a. How fast has productivity in Erewhon grown?
   b. How fast has physical capital per worker grown?
   c. How much has growing physical capital per worker contributed to productivity growth? What percentage of productivity growth is that?
   d. How much has technological progress contributed to productivity growth? What percentage of productivity growth is that?

3. Multinomics, Inc. is a large company with many offices around the country. It has just adopted a new computer system that will affect virtually every function performed within the company. Why might a period of time pass before employees' productivity is improved by the new computer system? Why might there be a temporary decrease in employees' productivity?

>> Quick Review

• Long-run increases in living standards arise almost entirely from growing **labor productivity,** often simply referred to as **productivity.**

• An increase in **physical capital** is one source of higher productivity, but it is subject to **diminishing returns to physical capital.**

• **Human capital** and **technological progress** are also sources of increases in productivity.

• The **aggregate production function** is used to estimate the sources of increases in productivity. **Growth accounting** has shown that rising **total factor productivity,** interpreted as the effect of technological progress, is central to long-run economic growth.

• Natural resources are less important today than physical and human capital as sources of productivity growth in most economies.

‖ Why Growth Rates Differ

In 1800, according to estimates by the economic historian Angus Maddison, Mexico's real GDP per capita was 1.5 times greater than Japan. Today, Japan has higher real GDP per capita than most European nations and Mexico is a relatively poor country, though by no means among the poorest. The difference? Over the long run—since 1800—real GDP per capita grew at 1.7% per year in Japan but at only 1.1% per year in Mexico. Today Japan's real GDP per capita is 2.5 times greater than Mexico.

As this example illustrates, even small differences in growth rates have large consequences over the long run. So why do growth rates differ across countries and across periods of time?

Explaining Differences in Growth Rates

As we've seen, economies with rapid growth tend to add physical capital, increase their human capital, or experience rapid technological progress. Striking economic success stories, like Japan in the 1950s and 1960s or China more recently, tend to be countries that do all three:

1. Rapidly add to their physical capital through high savings and investment spending.
2. Increase their human capital by improving their educational institutions.
3. Make fast technological progress through research and development.

Evidence also points to the importance of government policies and practices in fostering the sources of growth. We'll look at the role of government as well.

Savings and Investment Spending One reason for differences in growth rates between countries is that some countries are increasing their stock of physical capital much more rapidly than others, through high rates of investment spending. In the 1960s, Japan was the fastest-growing major economy. It also spent a much higher share of its GDP on investment goods than did other major economies. In recent years, China has been the fastest-growing major economy, and it similarly spends a very large share of its GDP on investment goods. In 2021, investment spending was 42% of China's GDP, compared with only 21% in the United States.

Where does the money for high investment spending come from? It comes from savings. In the next chapter, we'll analyze how financial markets channel savings into investment spending. For now, however, the key point is that investment spending must be paid for either out of savings from domestic households or by savings from foreign households—that is, an inflow of foreign capital.

Foreign capital has played an important role in the long-run economic growth of some countries, including the United States, which relied heavily on foreign funds during its early industrialization. For the most part, however, countries that invest a large share of their GDP are able to do so because they have high domestic savings. In fact, China in 2021 saved an even higher percentage of its GDP than it invested at home. The extra savings were invested abroad, largely in the United States.

Education Just as countries differ substantially in the rate at which they add to their physical capital, there have been large differences in the rate at which countries add to their human capital through education.

A case in point is the comparison between Argentina and China. In both countries the adult literacy rate has risen steadily over time, but it has risen much faster in China.

Figure 7 shows the percentage of people over the age of 15 who can both read and write in China, which we have highlighted as an example of spectacular long-run growth, and in Argentina, a country whose growth has been disappointing. Thirty-five years ago, Argentina had a much more educated population, while many Chinese were still illiterate. Today, the average educational level and adult literacy rate in China is still slightly below

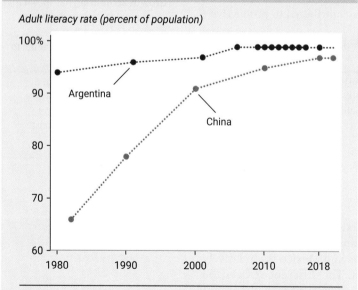

FIGURE 7 China's Students Are Catching Up, 1980–2020

Adult literacy rate (percent of population)

Although China still lags behind Argentina in adult literacy, it is rapidly catching up. China's success at adding human capital is one key to the spectacular rise in its long-run growth rate in recent decades.

Data from: World Development Indicators, World Bank.

that in Argentina—but that's mainly because there are still many elderly adults in China who never received basic education. In terms of secondary and tertiary education, China has outstripped once-rich Argentina.

Research and Development The advance of technology is a key force behind economic growth. What drives technological progress?

Scientific advances make new technologies possible. To take the most spectacular example in today's world, the semiconductor chip—which is the basis for all modern information technology—could not have been developed without the theory of quantum mechanics in physics.

But science alone is not enough: scientific knowledge must be translated into useful products and processes. And that often requires devoting a lot of resources to **research and development,** or **R&D,** spending to create new technologies and apply them to practical use.

Although some research and development is conducted by governments, much R&D is paid for by the private sector. The United States became the world's leading economy in large part because U.S. businesses were among the first to make systematic research and development a part of their operations. In fact, back in 1875 Thomas Edison created the first modern industrial research laboratory.

Developing new technology is one thing; applying it is another. There have often been notable differences in the pace at which different countries take advantage of new technologies. For example, since 2000, Italy has suffered a significant decline in its total factor productivity, while the United States has moved ahead (see the Economics in Action on Italy at the end of this section). The sources of these national differences are the subject of a great deal of economic research.

The Role of Government in Promoting Economic Growth

Governments can play an important role in promoting—or blocking—all three sources of long-term economic growth: physical capital, human capital, and technological progress. They can either affect growth directly through subsidies to factors that enhance growth or by creating an environment that either fosters or hinders growth.

Government policies can increase the economy's growth rate through the following six channels.

1. Government Subsidies to Infrastructure Governments play an important direct role in building **infrastructure:** roads, power lines, ports, information networks, and other large-scale physical capital projects that provide a foundation for economic activity. Although some infrastructure is provided by private companies, much of it is either provided by the government or requires a great deal of government regulation and support.

China offers a spectacular example of a country that uses public spending on infrastructure to promote economic growth. Infrastructure spending on everything from roads to high-speed rail amounts to about 8% of China's GDP, four times the percentage in the United States. In fact, China spends more on infrastructure than Western Europe and North America combined.

Poor infrastructure, such as a power grid that frequently fails and cuts off electricity, is a major obstacle to economic growth in many countries. To provide good infrastructure, an economy must not only be able to afford it, but it must also have the political discipline to maintain it.

Perhaps the most crucial infrastructure is something we, in an advanced country, rarely think about: basic public health measures in the form of a clean water supply and disease control. Poor health infrastructure is a major obstacle to economic growth in poor countries, especially those in Africa.

2. Government Subsidies to Education In contrast to physical capital, which is mainly created by private investment spending, much of an economy's human

research and development (R&D) spending to create new technologies and prepare them for practical use.

infrastructure physical capital, such as roads, power lines, ports, information networks, and other parts of an economy, that provides the underpinnings, or foundation, for economic activity.

capital is the result of government spending on education. In the United States, various levels of government fund the bulk of primary and secondary education. Government funding subsidizes a significant share of higher education as well: over 70% of students attend public colleges and universities. In addition, the federal government significantly subsidizes research performed at private colleges and universities.

Differences in the rate at which countries add to their human capital largely reflect government policy. As we saw in Figure 7, the adult literacy rate in China has been increasing more rapidly than in Argentina. This isn't because China is richer than Argentina; until recently, China was, on average, poorer than Argentina. Instead, it reflects the fact that the Chinese government has made education and raising the literacy rate high priorities.

3. Government Subsidies to R&D
Technological progress is largely the result of private initiative. But in the more advanced countries, important R&D is done by government agencies as well. For example, the internet grew out of a system, the Advanced Research Projects Agency Network (ARPANET), created by the U.S. Department of Defense, then extended to educational institutions by the National Science Foundation.

4. Maintaining a Well-Functioning Financial System
Governments play an important indirect role in making high rates of private investment spending possible. Both the amount of savings and the ability of an economy to direct savings into productive investment spending depend on the economy's institutions, especially its financial system. A well-regulated and well-functioning financial system is very important for economic growth because in most countries it is the principal way in which savings are channeled into investment spending.

If a country's citizens trust their banks, they will place their savings in bank deposits, which the banks will then lend to their business customers. But if people distrust their banks, they will hoard gold or foreign currency, keeping their savings in safe deposit boxes or under the mattress, where it cannot be turned into productive investment spending. A well-functioning financial system requires appropriate government regulation to assure depositors that their funds are protected from loss.

5. Protection of Property Rights
Property rights are the legal rights held by owners of valuable items to dispose of those items as they choose. A subset, *intellectual property rights*, are the rights of innovators to accrue the rewards of their innovations. The state of property rights generally, and intellectual property rights in particular, are important factors in explaining differences in growth rates across economies. Why? Because no one would bother to spend the effort and resources required to innovate if someone else could appropriate that innovation and capture the rewards. So, for innovation to flourish, intellectual property rights must receive protection.

Sometimes protecting property rights is accomplished by the nature of the innovation: it may be too difficult or expensive to copy. But, generally, the government has to protect intellectual property rights. A *patent* is a government-created temporary monopoly given to innovators for the use or sale of their innovations. It's a temporary rather than permanent monopoly because while it's in society's interests to give innovators an incentive to invent, it's also in society's interest to eventually encourage competition.

6. Political Stability and Good Governance
There's not much point in investing in a business if rioting mobs are likely to destroy it, or in saving your money if someone with political connections can steal it. Political stability and good governance (including the protection of property rights) are essential ingredients in fostering economic growth in the long run.

"I'm thinking of giving this up to campaign for orderly, competent government."

Matt Pritchett/The Daily Telegraph

Long-run economic growth in successful economies, like that of the United States, has been possible because there are good laws, institutions that enforce those laws, and a stable political system that maintains those institutions. The law must say that your property is really yours so that someone else can't take it away. The courts and the police must be honest so that they can't be bribed to ignore the law. And the political system must be stable so that laws don't change capriciously.

Americans take these preconditions for granted, but they are by no means guaranteed. Aside from the disruption caused by war or revolution, many countries find that their economic growth suffers due to corruption among the government officials who should be enforcing the law. For example, until 1991 the Indian government imposed many bureaucratic restrictions on businesses, which often had to bribe government officials to get approval for even routine activities—a tax on business, in effect. Economists have argued that a reduction in this burden of corruption was one reason India experienced a surge of economic growth after 1990 that continues to this day.

Even when the government isn't corrupt, excessive government intervention can be a brake on economic growth. If large parts of the economy are supported by wasteful government subsidies, protected from imports, subject to unnecessary monopolization, or otherwise insulated from competition, productivity tends to suffer because of a lack of incentives. As we'll see in the next section, excessive government intervention is one often-cited explanation for slow growth in Latin America.

ECONOMICS >> *in Action*
What's the Matter with Italy?

Italy was once considered a remarkable economic success story. A century ago it was still a poor country—so poor that in the late nineteenth and early twentieth century millions of Italians emigrated to the United States and other destinations in search of a better life. After World War II, however, Italy experienced decades of rapid growth, with real GDP per capita quadrupling between 1950 and 1990.

By the end of that growth spurt, as you can see from Figure 8, Italy was nearly as rich as the United Kingdom, the nation that had led the Industrial Revolution.

But at that point Italian growth stalled. Real GDP per capita was stagnant after the late 1990s, and began falling after 2008, as Italy's economy suffered a severe downturn as a result of the European debt crisis. What went wrong?

Part of the answer involves slow growth of the factors of production. Italy's low birth rate has meant a rapidly aging population, with a declining percentage of working-age adults. Italy has also lagged in education, with the lowest college-educated share of the population in the European Union. Italy also seems to be having trouble taking advantage of technological progress. In fact, measured total factor productivity in Italy has declined since 2000. Why?

Some economists suggest that the explanation may lie in its business culture.

FIGURE 8 Real GDP per Capita for Italy and the United Kingdom, 1960–2021

Real GDP per capita (2015 dollars)

[Line graph showing Real GDP per capita from 1960 to 2018. The vertical axis ranges from $0 to $50,000 in increments of $10,000. Two lines are plotted: the United Kingdom line rises from about $15,000 in 1960 to nearly $48,000 around 2018 before dropping. The Italy line rises from about $10,000 in 1960 to about $32,000, leveling off after the late 1990s and declining after 2008.]

Data from: The World Bank.

In particular, Italian management practices have been widely criticized because promotion and financial rewards all too often reflect seniority rather than performance, giving few incentives to adopt new technology and best business practices.

Underlying this low-performance culture may be a lack of effective competition in many markets, which means that even badly run companies can stay in business indefinitely. The absence of competition within the Italian economy points to a government policy failure, perhaps arising from the relationship between established firms and government being too cozy. In an economy dominated by established firms, there's little incentive to invest or innovate. Italy's troubles show that even countries with a history of economic success can stumble. Achieving sustained economic growth, it turns out, isn't easy.

>> **Check Your Understanding 9-3**

Solutions appear at back of book.

---

1. Explain the link between a country's growth rate, its investment spending as a percent of GDP, and its domestic savings.

2. U.S. centers of academic biotechnology research have closer connections with private biotechnology companies than do their European counterparts. What effect might this have on the pace of innovation and development of new drugs in the United States versus Europe?

3. During the 1990s, in the former Soviet Union a lot of property was seized and controlled by those in power. How might this have affected the country's growth rate at that time? Explain.

‖ Success, Disappointment, and Failure

As Figure 2 illustrates, rates of long-run economic growth differ quite a lot around the world. We'll now look at three regions of the world that have had quite different experiences with economic growth over the last several decades. We've chosen these three regions—East Asia, Latin America, and Africa—because they illustrate the challenges of sustained productivity growth.

Figure 9 shows trends since 1960 in real GDP per capita in 2015 dollars for three countries: Argentina, Nigeria, and South Korea. (As in Figure 1, the vertical axis is drawn in logarithmic scale.) We have chosen these countries because each is a particularly striking example of what has happened in its region. South Korea's amazing rise is part of a broad "economic miracle" in East Asia. Argentina's slow progress, interrupted by repeated setbacks, is more or less typical of the disappointing growth that has characterized Latin America. Like Argentina, Nigeria has also had little growth in real GDP until 2000. Since then both countries have fared better.

East Asia's Miracle

In 1960, South Korea was a very poor country. In fact, in 1960 its real GDP per capita was lower than that of India today. But, as you can see from Figure 9, beginning in the early 1960s South Korea began an extremely rapid economic ascent: real GDP per capita grew about 7% per year for more than 30 years. Today South Korea, though still somewhat poorer than Europe or the United States, looks very much like an economically advanced country.

South Korea's economic growth is unprecedented in history: it took the country only 35 years to achieve growth that required centuries elsewhere. Yet South Korea is only part of a broader phenomenon, often referred to as the East Asian economic miracle. High growth rates first appeared in South Korea, Taiwan, Hong Kong, and Singapore but then spread across the region, most notably to

FIGURE 9 Success and Disappointment

Real GDP per capita from 1960 to 2021, measured in 2015 dollars, is shown for Argentina, South Korea, and Nigeria, using a logarithmic scale. South Korea and some other East Asian countries have been highly successful at achieving economic growth. Argentina, like much of Latin America, has had several setbacks, slowing its growth. Nigeria's standard of living in 2021 was only barely higher than it had been in 1960, an experience shared by many African countries. Neither Argentina nor Nigeria exhibited much growth over the 61-year period, although both have had significantly higher growth in recent years.

Data from: World Development Indicators.

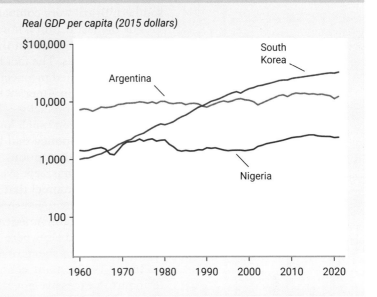

Real GDP per capita (2015 dollars)

China. Since 1975, the whole region has increased real GDP per capita by 6% per year, more than three times the U.S. historical rate of growth.

How have the Asian countries achieved such high growth rates? The answer is that all of the sources of productivity growth have been firing on all cylinders. Very high savings rates, the percentage of GDP that is saved nationally in any given year, have allowed the countries to significantly increase the amount of physical capital per worker. Very good basic education has permitted a rapid improvement in human capital. And these countries have experienced substantial technological progress.

Why were such high rates of growth unheard of in the past? Most economic analysts think that East Asia's growth spurt was possible because of its *relative* backwardness. That is, by the time that East Asian economies began to move into the modern world, they could benefit from adopting the technological advances that had been generated in technologically advanced countries such as the United States.

In 1900, the United States could not have moved quickly to a modern level of productivity because much of the technology that powers the modern economy, from jet planes to computers, hadn't been invented yet. In 1970, South Korea probably still had lower labor productivity than the United States had in 1900, but it could rapidly upgrade its productivity by adopting technology that had been developed in the United States, Europe, and Japan over the previous century. This was aided by a huge investment in human capital through widespread schooling.

The East Asian experience demonstrates that economic growth can be especially fast in countries that are playing catch-up to other countries with higher GDP per capita. On this basis, many economists have suggested a general principle known as the **convergence hypothesis.** It says that differences in real GDP per capita among countries tend to narrow over time because countries that start with lower real GDP per capita tend to have higher growth rates.

However, starting with a relatively low level of real GDP per capita is no guarantee of rapid growth, as the examples of Latin America and Africa both demonstrate.

Latin America's Disappointment

In 1900, Latin America was not considered an economically backward region. Natural resources, including both minerals and cultivable land, were abundant. Some

convergence hypothesis a principle of economic growth that holds that international differences in real GDP per capita tend to narrow over time because countries that start with lower real GDP per capita tend to have higher growth rates.

countries, notably Argentina, attracted millions of immigrants from Europe in search of a better life. Measures of real GDP per capita in Argentina, Uruguay, and southern Brazil were comparable to those in economically advanced countries.

For the last century, however, growth in Latin America has been disappointing. As Figure 9 shows in the case of Argentina, growth has been disappointing for many decades. The fact that South Korea is now much richer than Argentina would have seemed inconceivable a few generations ago.

Why did Latin America stagnate? Comparisons with East Asian success stories suggest several factors. The rates of savings and investment spending in Latin America have been much lower than in East Asia, partly as a result of irresponsible government policy that has eroded savings through high inflation, bank failures, and other disruptions. Education—especially broad basic education—has been underemphasized: even Latin American nations rich in natural resources often failed to channel that wealth into their educational systems. And political instability, leading to irresponsible economic policies, has taken a toll.

In addition, Latin America has been unable to grow through the adoption of technology developed elsewhere. This has led to chronic disappointment among Latin Americans in their standard of living, which has further fueled political instability.

In the 1980s, many economists came to believe that Latin America was suffering from excessive government intervention in markets. They recommended opening the economies to imports, selling off government-owned companies, and, in general, freeing up individual initiative. The hope was that this would produce an East Asian–type economic surge. So far, however, only one Latin American nation, Chile, has achieved sustained rapid growth.

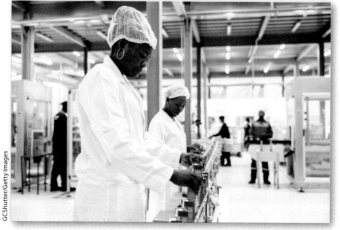

Slow economic growth in sub-Saharan Africa has led to extreme poverty for many of its people, but there are signs of hope as GDP of some countries, such as Nigeria, has turned upward over the past two decades.

Africa's Troubles and Promise

Africa south of the Sahara is home to more than 1 billion people, more than three times the population of the United States. On average, they are very poor, nowhere close to U.S. living standards 100 or even 200 years ago. In fact, real GDP per capita in sub-Saharan Africa actually fell 13% from 1980 to 1994, although it has recovered since then. However, since 1995, growth rates across most of Africa have been much higher, averaging about 5% a year if the big economies of Nigeria, Angola, and South Africa are excluded. What explains the dramatic turnaround?

First and foremost, many African countries have tackled the problem of political instability. In the years after 1975, large parts of Africa experienced devastating civil wars (often with outside powers backing rival sides) that killed millions of people and made productive investment spending impossible. The threat of war and general anarchy also inhibited other important preconditions for growth, such as education and provision of basic infrastructure.

Property rights are also a major problem. The lack of legal safeguards means that property owners are often subject to extortion because of government corruption, making them averse to owning property or improving it. This is especially damaging in a country that is very poor.

While many economists see political instability and government corruption as the leading causes of underdevelopment in Africa, some—most notably Jeffrey Sachs of Columbia University and the United Nations—believe the opposite. They argue that Africa is politically unstable because it is poor. And Africa's poverty, they go on to claim, stems from its extremely unfavorable geographic conditions—much of the continent is landlocked, hot, infested with tropical diseases, and cursed with poor soil.

Sachs, along with economists from the World Health Organization, has high-lighted the importance of health problems in Africa. In poor countries, worker productivity is often severely hampered by malnutrition and disease. In particular, tropical diseases such as malaria can only be controlled with an effective public health infrastructure, something that is lacking in much of Africa. Economists are studying certain regions of Africa to determine whether modest amounts of aid given directly to residents for the purposes of increasing crop yields, reducing malaria, and increasing school attendance can produce self-sustaining gains in living standards.

Although the example of African countries represents a warning that long-run economic growth cannot be taken for granted, there are some signs of hope. As we saw in Figure 9, Nigeria's per capita GDP, after decades of stagnation, turned upward after 2000, and it achieved an average annual growth rate of 2.5% from 2000 to 2021.

Left Behind by Growth?

Historically, rising real GDP per capita has translated into rising real income for the great majority of a nation's residents. However, there's no guarantee that this will happen. One of the principles we laid out in Chapter 1 is that economic change often produces losers as well as winners, and this is true of the changes that come with long-run economic growth. Gains from long-run economic growth may be very unequally distributed, and in some cases significant shares of the population may see their incomes fall even while the overall income of the nation is rising.

This isn't just a theoretical possibility. In the United States, and to a lesser extent in other wealthy countries, the share of income going to families near the top of the income distribution, and especially to the 1% of families with the

---

GLOBAL COMPARISON **LAGGING REGIONS IN RICH COUNTRIES**

Growing regional disparities aren't a uniquely U.S. problem. On the contrary, similar forces — economic trends that appear to favor large, highly educated metropolitan areas over rural and older industrial areas — are clearly at work in virtually all wealthy nations. In Britain, London's economy has surged while the old coal-mining and industrial towns of England's northeast have struggled. France presents a similar contrast between greater Paris and the coal-and-steel belt of the country's north. Italy has long been divided between a wealthy north and a poor south, especially in Sicily. More than 30 years after the fall of the Berlin Wall, the former East Germany remains poorer than the rest of the country.

Comparing regional disparities across countries is tricky, because we don't define regions the same way: the United States collects data for states and metropolitan areas, while European data are based on the "Nomenclature des Unités territoriales statistiques" — yes, NUTS. For what it's worth, however, the figure, which shows real GDP of several countries' poorest region as a percent of the national average, suggests that regional disparities are similar

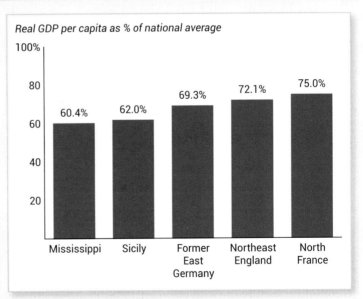

Real GDP per capita as % of national average

across the Western world, and if anything slightly bigger in the United States.

Data from: Nomenclature des Unités territoriales statistiques and Bureau of Economic Analysis.

FIGURE 10 The Growing Income Divide, 1953–2021

In the United States, from 1953 through 1980, both real per capita GDP and the real income of the median family grew at nearly identical rates because the distribution of income was quite stable. After 1980, however, the share of national income going to the richest Americans rose significantly. And while real GDP per capita continued to grow, real median income — the income earned by families in the middle of the income distribution — lagged behind. This means that since 1980 many of those families in the middle have been left behind by economic growth.

Data from: U.S. Census; FRED.

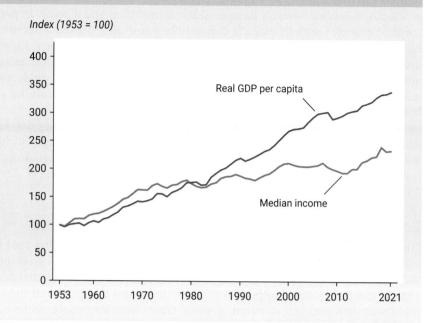

highest incomes, has grown substantially since 1980. Figure 10 shows one consequence of this rise in inequality. The figure compares the growth since 1953 of real per capita GDP in the United States and the real income of the *median family* — the family at the exact middle of the income scale, with half of all families richer and half poorer. Both numbers are shown as indexes, with 1953 = 100.

Until 1980, the two numbers grew at nearly the same rate because the distribution of income was quite stable. After 1980, however, a growing share of income went to a relatively small number of people at the top. As a result, the income of the median family — which arguably reflects the experience of the typical American — rose much more slowly than real GDP per capita. Many U.S. families, in other words, were to some extent left behind by economic growth.

Nor was it simply individual families that were left behind by recent growth. Whole regions have been left behind, reversing a historical trend toward convergence. For most of the twentieth century, the poorest U.S. states, mainly in the south, experienced faster growth than the nation as a whole, so that regional income disparities steadily narrowed. In recent decades, however, gaps have been widening again, with high-income metropolitan areas pulling away both from rural areas and smaller cities that used to be hubs of manufacturing.

Figure 11 illustrates this point by comparing the growth in real GDP per capita since 1997 in two states: Massachusetts, a rich state thanks to the concentration of technology and finance in and around Boston, and Kentucky, where traditional economic mainstays like coal mining and agriculture have been in decline. Even in 1997 Kentucky was poorer than Massachusetts, with real GDP per capita around 25% lower. But the gap between the states has drastically widened since then.

The fact that some regions of the United States are lagging even as the national economy as a whole grows is disturbing in itself. What makes it even more disturbing is that lagging regions appear to be suffering from significant social problems that go beyond merely monetary losses. In these regions, a high fraction of adults in their prime working years are without jobs, although they aren't all counted as unemployed, because some have given up even searching for work. And perhaps as a consequence of the lack of employment opportunities, these regions also suffer disproportionately from what the economists Anne Case and Angus Deaton

FIGURE 11 The Income Gap Between Rich and Poor States, 1997–2021

In recent decades, high-income states have widened the gap with poorer states. From 1997 through 2021, gross domestic product in Massachusetts has grown by nearly 50% compared with only 10% growth for Kentucky. In 1997, per capita income in Massachusetts was 31% greater than Kentucky, by 2021 the gap had widened to nearly 75%.

Data from: U.S. Census; FRED.

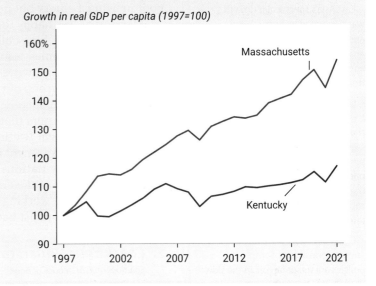

have called "deaths of despair": mortality caused by drug overdoses, suicide, and alcohol.

It is important, however, to acknowledge two qualifications to this somewhat downbeat note about growth in the United States. First, in the broad sweep of history it is still true that economic growth raises the standard of living of the great majority of the population. Second, it would be wrong to imagine that global economic growth, even in recent decades, has mainly benefited a well-off minority. On the contrary, as explained in the Economics in Action below, from a worldwide perspective the most conspicuous aspect of recent growth has been the rise of a *global middle class*—rapidly rising incomes among hundreds of millions of previously poor people in China and other emerging economies.

ECONOMICS >> *in Action*
Global Winners and Losers

Within the United States, the gains from economic growth since around 1980 have been unevenly distributed. Incomes at the top have soared, but incomes of most families have grown much more slowly. As a result, inequality has risen.

But is the same true for the world as a whole? No, the global picture is more complicated. In fact, even the question "Is global inequality rising or falling?" turns out to not be very meaningful. Inequality *within* many countries, especially in richer nations, has gone up. But inequality *between* nations has gone down, thanks to rapid growth in China, India, and other countries that used to be very poor.

One helpful way to think about who benefits from global growth is to divide the world's population into four groups: the untouched, the developing-country middle class, the advanced-country working class, and the global elite.

At the bottom there are still a large number of people, perhaps as many as 2 billion, who have yet to be touched by long-run economic growth. Most of sub-Saharan Africa, and even some parts of both China and India, still have per capita incomes not much higher than they had a century ago.

Above this group, however, is another large group, more than 1 billion strong, of people in China, India, and other rapidly growing economies who were very poor in living memory but now constitute a rapidly rising global middle class.

The story is less happy for the next group, the working class in advanced countries — for example, blue-collar workers in the United States. This group still has above-average incomes compared with the world as a whole, but as we've seen, these incomes have grown slowly since around 1980.

Finally, a small group of very well-off people, mostly but not entirely in wealthy nations, has seen big income gains.

Many analysts argue that this uneven pattern of gains is an important source of social and political friction. The rise of the global middle class, while it represents a huge improvement in human welfare, has also eroded the once-dominant position of wealthy nations in the world economic system, helping to explain such developments as the emergence of trade conflict between the United States and China. And the working class in wealthy countries feels left behind, possibly contributing to a populist backlash.

>> Check Your Understanding 9-4
Solutions appear at back of book.

1. Some economists think the high rates of growth of productivity achieved by many Asian economies cannot be sustained. Why might they be right? What would have to happen for them to be wrong?

2. Based on Figure 9 and the discussion in this section, which regions would you predict to follow the convergence hypothesis? Why?

3. Some economists think the best way to help African countries is for wealthier countries to provide more funds for basic infrastructure. Others think this policy will have no long-run effect unless African countries have the financial and political means to maintain this infrastructure. What policies would you suggest?

Is World Growth Sustainable?

Earlier in the chapter, we described the views of Thomas Malthus, the late-eighteenth-century economist who warned that the pressure of population growth would tend to limit the standard of living. Malthus was right about the past: for around 58 centuries, from the origins of civilization until his own time, limited land supplies effectively prevented any large rise in real incomes per capita. Since then, however, technological progress and rapid accumulation of physical and human capital have allowed the world to defy Malthusian pessimism.

But will this always be the case? Some skeptics have expressed doubt about whether **sustainable long-run economic growth** is possible — that is, growth that can continue in the face of the limited supply of natural resources and, perhaps even more important, given the negative effects of past economic growth on the environment.

Natural Resources and Growth, Revisited

"Neo-Malthusian" theories — claims that economic growth will be severely limited by lack of resources — have emerged at intervals ever since modern long-run economic growth began. In 1865, the British economist William Stanley Jevons wrote an influential book warning that reserves of coal, which fueled the Industrial Revolution, might soon be exhausted. In 1972, a famous report by a group called the Club of Rome warned that shortages of natural resources in general would lead to collapsing growth. In the early 2000s, there were widespread concerns about "peak oil," a crisis that would supposedly be brought on by the exhaustion of world oil supplies.

So far, however, none of these warnings have proved accurate, largely because technological advances have circumvented previous limits. For example, since 2005 there have been dramatic developments in energy production, with large amounts of previously unreachable oil and gas extracted through fracking and with a huge decline in the cost of electricity generated by wind and solar power.

Most, though not all, economists believe that modern economies can almost always find ways to work around limits on the supply of natural resources. One reason for this optimism is the fact that resource scarcity leads to high resource prices. These high prices, in turn, provide strong incentives to conserve the scarce resource and find alternatives. For example, after the sharp oil price increases of the 1970s, U.S. consumers turned to smaller, more fuel-efficient cars as U.S. industry greatly intensified its efforts to reduce energy bills.

Given such responses to prices, economists generally tend to see resource scarcity as a problem that modern economies handle fairly well and not as a fundamental limit to long-run economic growth. Environmental issues, however, pose a more difficult problem for economies because dealing with them requires effective political action.

Economic Growth and the Environment

Economic growth, other things equal, tends to increase the adverse impact of human activity on the environment, including an increase in pollution, the loss of wildlife habitats, the extinction of species, and reduced biodiversity. As we saw in this chapter's opening story, India's economic growth has also brought a spectacular increase in air pollution in its cities.

In analyzing economic growth and its environmental impact, it is useful to distinguish between *local* environmental degradation, which affects a geographically limited area, and *global* environmental degradation, which is far-reaching, with worldwide impact. As we'll see, it has proven to be far more difficult to address global environmental degradation and, in particular, the problem of *climate change*.

In fact, the improved air quality in the cities of today's advanced economies indicates that local environmental harm can be greatly reduced when there is sufficient political will and resources are devoted to finding a solution. As described in the Economics in Action below, in recent years China has dramatically improved air quality in its major cities while continuing to achieve rapid economic growth.

However, taking policy action to limit *climate change* — changes in Earth's climate brought about by human activity, including pollution — has been much more difficult to organize, for several reasons.

There is broad scientific consensus that burning fossil fuels — coal, oil, and natural gas — leads to increasing levels of carbon dioxide in the atmosphere. Carbon dioxide is a type of *greenhouse gas*. Such gases trap the sun's energy, raising the planet's temperature, and lead to shifts in weather patterns, which, in turn, impose high human, economic, and environmental costs. These costs include extreme weather, rising sea levels that increase the risk of flooding, the disruption of agriculture, including crop failures, and more. A recent estimate put the cost of unmitigated climate change at 20% of world gross domestic product by 2100. Moreover, these costs tend to fall more heavily on poor countries.

The problem of climate change is linked to economic growth: the larger the economy, the more homes, factories, and vehicles, will have to be powered, typically by burning fossil fuels. At present, world energy consumption is overwhelmingly dependent upon fossil fuels, which account for 82% of total consumption, while clean, renewable sources account for only 11%, with nuclear energy supplying the balance. Why? Because historically, fossil fuels have been cheaper to use. This mix is changing, in large part because solar and wind power have become much cheaper. The United Kingdom, which led the Industrial Revolution with an economy powered mainly by coal, now gets more than a quarter of its energy from low-carbon sources, especially wind power. But the rise of low-carbon energy hasn't been fast enough to prevent continuing rise in global emissions of greenhouse gases; because these gases accumulate in the atmosphere, the current trajectory will lead to large-scale climate change over the decades ahead. Can anything be done to limit the damage?

Until recently, effective action against climate change was stymied by several factors. One factor was the perception that reducing carbon emissions would be costly, and it was difficult to persuade voters to accept short-term economic costs in return for long-term environmental benefits. This was especially true because the costs of greenhouse gas emissions, unlike those of, say, smog, generally aren't obvious to the naked eye. Scientists tell us that climate change increases the severity of disasters like coastal flooding and severe droughts, but it's difficult to tie any one disaster to specific emissions.

Another political problem is that climate change is a global issue, so that many of the benefits from any one country's actions will accrue to other nations. It's a lot easier to persuade residents of California, for example, to accept pollution controls that reduce smog in Los Angeles than to get them to accept policies whose benefits may take the form of reduced flooding in Pakistan and fewer droughts in East Africa.

Recently, however, the prospects for effective action on climate change may have improved, thanks to changes in both technology and in political strategy.

On one side, rapid technological progress in renewable energy has eliminated much if not all of the historical cost advantage of fossil fuels. It now looks possible that in the quite near future many economies will be able to generate the bulk of their electricity from wind and solar power and use this cleanly generated electricity to run electric cars, heat houses, and so on. In other words, a low-emission economy now looks within reach without requiring any major changes in lifestyle.

These technological possibilities, in turn, suggest that major emissions reductions can be achieved by offering carrots rather than using sticks. That is, instead

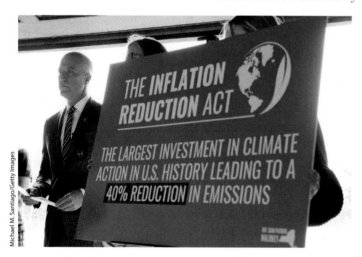

Michael M. Santiago/Getty Images

of using regulations and/or taxes to discourage burning fossil fuels, governments can encourage green energy with things like subsidies and tax credits for the purchase of electric vehicles. Such policies might be perceived by voters as benefits rather than costs, and therefore be easier to implement.

Indeed, in 2022 the United States enacted major climate legislation — misleadingly titled the Inflation Reduction Act — that relied almost entirely on green energy subsidies to reduce greenhouse gas emissions. The legislation was also sold with the promise that it would help create new jobs, especially manufacturing jobs in economically depressed regions.

At the time of writing many experts on climate policy were quite optimistic about the Inflation Reduction Act, arguing that it would greatly reduce emissions with little if any negative impact on economic growth. If they are right, and other countries implement similar policies, concerns about the sustainability of economic growth will be much diminished.

ECONOMICS >> *in Action*
China's War on Pollution

Beijing, the capital of China, is even bigger than New Delhi: the metropolitan area is home to 24 million people. And not long ago it was synonymous with air pollution. In 2014, when the city was host to Asia-Pacific Economic Cooperation

(APEC), a high-profile international forum, the authorities imposed temporary pollution controls that literally cleared the air for a while; this was such a rare occurrence at the time that residents coined the term "APEC blue" for the unusual appearance of natural-colored skies.

In that same year, however, the Chinese government declared a longer-term "war on pollution." This involved a number of measures, including restrictions on coal burning and the closing of some of the oldest, most polluting plants; restrictions on highly polluting vehicles in major cities; and the introduction of highly subsidized electric buses.

As Beijing pivots to electric vehicles, the air is beginning to clear.

These measures worked: the air got a lot cleaner. Beijing's air is still much worse than air in, say, greater New York, which has a similar population; pollution hovers between "moderate" and "unhealthy." But it's far better than it was.

The striking thing is that China achieved this significant reduction in air pollution while remaining one of the world's fastest-growing economies. Chinese real GDP grew 53% between 2014 and 2021, or 6.3% a year, even as the air got steadily clearer. In other words, long-term economic growth can go along with an improving environment.

>> Check Your Understanding 9-5

Solutions appear at back of book.

1. Are economists typically more concerned about the limits to growth imposed by environmental degradation or those imposed by resource scarcity? Explain, noting the role of negative externalities (costs imposed by individuals or firms on others without the requirement to pay compensation), in your answer.

2. What is the link between greenhouse gas emissions and growth? What is the expected effect on growth from emissions reduction? Why is international burden sharing of greenhouse gas emissions reduction a contentious problem?

>> Quick Review

• Economists generally believe that environmental degradation poses a major challenge to **sustainable long-run economic growth.** They also generally believe that modern economies can find ways to alleviate limits to growth from natural resource scarcity through the price response that promotes conservation and the creation of alternatives.

• Economic growth tends to harm the environment unless actions are taken to protect it. Local environmental degradation can be addressed through political will and resources. Global environmental degradation is harder to address because it requires cooperation across many countries.

• The accumulation of greenhouse gases, a by-product of burning fossil fuels, has led to climate change, the raising of Earth's temperature. In order to avert the impact of climate change, effective government intervention is required.

• Developed countries and large countries that are rapidly growing need to shift from a heavy reliance on fossil fuels to using clean, energy sources like solar and wind power. This will come at a modest cost to the rise in real GDP per capita, a cost that is falling as technological innovation in clean energy sources advances.

• U.S. legislation passed in 2022, which tries to encourage the use of green energy through subsidies and tax credits, may show the way toward making economic growth environmentally sustainable.

Raising the Bar(code)

Luke Sharrett/Bloomberg/Getty Images

When we think about innovation and technological progress, we tend to focus on the dramatic changes: cars replacing horses and buggies, electric light bulbs replacing gaslights, computers replacing adding machines and typewriters. However, much more progress is incremental and almost invisible to most people, yet has huge effects over time. Consider, for example, the simple bar-code scanner.

Bar codes were first used commercially in 1974, when a 10-pack of Wrigley's chewing gum was rung up with a scanner produced by the National Cash Register Corporation (now NCR Corp). Since then bar codes and their two-dimensional descendants—visual patterns that are meaningless to human eyes but are instantly recognizable by scanners and smartphones—have become ubiquitous, used to identify and route everything from shipping containers to airline passengers.

The benefits from machine-readable labels are enormous, extending well beyond what consumers in the checkout line can see. For example, retailers use them to continuously track sales, telling them when to reorder merchandise and restock shelves, what to keep in their warehouses, how productive individual workers are, and more. Grocery retailing is a labor-intensive industry, and economists estimate that the adoption of bar-code technology reduced labor costs by as much as 40%. Ultimately, bar-code technology helped drive the computerization of the entire retail industry.

And this story isn't over. A growing number of retailers offer self-checkout, where customers scan items themselves and pay electronically. Some stores offer smartphone apps that offer even more convenience by letting customers scan items as they put them into the shopping cart.

You might think, then, that NCR, which remains a major player in point-of-service technologies like scanners, ATMs, and so forth, made a fortune from its leading role in this technology revolution. But while the company has done well, scanner sales in the early years weren't enormous: the adoption of bar-code scanners was relatively slow compared with the spread of smartphones a couple of decades later. Only about a third of supermarkets adopted them in the first decade after that historic pack of gum.

Why? To realize the full potential of bar-code technology, both retailers and firms had to spend substantial money up front to buy the scanners and the information-processing systems they served. Equally important, manufacturers had to install the equipment to put bar codes on their products. This created a chicken-and-egg problem, with retailers waiting to have more scanner-readable products available and manufacturers waiting for more scanner-ready stores.

Over time this problem was resolved as retailers and manufacturers made the necessary investments, setting the stage for widespread use of information technology. In fact, during the productivity surge from 1995 to 2005, retailing was one of the leading sources of overall productivity growth in the U.S. economy.

Adoption was slower in Europe. In the United States, big stores were the first to install scanners, and the technology fostered greater concentration of retailing at the expense of small, mom-and-pop stores that couldn't afford to implement scanner technology. In Europe, however, government policies—especially land-use policy—protected these stores.

Eventually, however, Europe began to follow the trend, too. Bar-code technology has spread from the United States to become almost universal, at least in advanced economies.

QUESTIONS FOR THOUGHT

1. Bar-code technology spurred a lot of investment in retailing. How did it alter the retailing production function? What would a similar amount of investment have accomplished without the new technology?

2. The spread of bar codes was delayed in the United States because everyone was waiting for someone else to move. What policy could have been adopted to address the delays? Would it have been a good idea?

3. Use the case to explain why international growth rates vary.

4. Despite initial barriers, bar codes have spread globally. What does this imply about differences in economic growth across countries?

SUMMARY

1. Growth is measured as changes in real GDP per capita in order to eliminate the effects of changes in the price level and changes in population size. Levels of real GDP per capita vary greatly around the world: about a quarter of the world's population lives in countries that are still poorer than the United States was in 1900. GDP per capita in the United States is about eight times as high as it was in 1900.

2. Growth rates of real GDP per capita also vary widely. According to the **Rule of 70,** the number of years it takes for real GDP per capita to double is equal to 70 divided by the annual growth rate of real GDP per capita.

3. The key to long-run economic growth is rising **labor productivity,** or just **productivity,** which is output per worker. Increases in productivity arise from increases in **physical capital** per worker and **human capital** per worker as well as **technological progress.** The **aggregate production function** shows how real GDP per worker depends on these three factors. Other things equal, there are **diminishing returns to physical capital:** holding human capital per worker and technology fixed, each successive addition to physical capital per worker yields a smaller increase in productivity than the one before. Equivalently, more physical capital per worker results in a lower, but still positive, increase in productivity. **Growth accounting,** which estimates the contribution of each factor to a country's economic growth, has shown that rising **total factor productivity,** the amount of output produced from a given amount of factor inputs, is key to long-run growth. It is usually interpreted as the effect of technological progress. In contrast to earlier times, natural resources are a less significant source of productivity growth in most countries today.

4. The large differences in countries' growth rates are largely due to differences in their rates of accumulation of physical and human capital as well as differences in technological progress. Although inflows of foreign savings from abroad help, a prime factor is differences in domestic savings and investment spending rates, since most countries that have high investment spending on physical capital finance it by high domestic savings. Technological progress is largely a result of **research and development,** or **R&D.**

5. Governments can help or hinder growth. Government policies that directly foster growth are subsidies to **infrastructure,** particularly public health infrastructure, subsidies to education and R&D, and maintenance of a well-functioning financial system that channels savings into investment spending, education, and R&D. Governments can enhance the environment for growth by protecting property rights (particularly intellectual property rights through patents), by being politically stable and by providing good governance. Poor governance includes corruption and excessive government intervention.

6. The world economy contains examples of success and failure in the effort to achieve long-run economic growth. East Asian economies have done many things right and achieved very high growth rates. The low growth rates of Latin American and African economies over many years led economists to believe that the **convergence hypothesis,** the claim that differences in real GDP per capita across countries narrow over time, fits the data only when factors that affect growth, such as education, infrastructure, and favorable government policies and institutions, are held equal across countries. In recent years, there has been an uptick in growth among some Latin American and sub-Saharan African countries, largely due to a boom in commodity exports.

7. Not only is economic growth uneven across countries, there are many cases where economic growth is uneven within countries. In the United States, this is shown by a divergence in mean and median per capita income, highlighted by the growing income divide between rich and poor states.

8. Economists generally believe that environmental degradation pose a major challenge to **sustainable long-run economic growth.** Addressing the problem will require effective governmental intervention.

9. Climate change is linked to growth and there is broad consensus that government action is needed to address it. To avert the impact of climate change, countries will need to shift from a heavy reliance on fossil fuel to using clean, renewable energy sources. This will come at a modest cost to the rise in real GDP per capita, a cost that is falling as technological innovation in clean energy sources advances.

KEY TERMS

PRACTICE QUESTIONS

1. The accompanying table shows data from the World Bank, World Development Indicators, for real GDP per capita in 2015 U.S. dollars for Argentina, Ghana, South Korea, and the United States for 1960, 1980, 2000, and 2021.

a. Complete the table by expressing each year's real GDP per capita as a percentage of its 1960 and 2021 levels.

b. How does the growth in living standards from 1960 to 2021 compare across these four nations? What might account for these differences?

	Argentina			Ghana			South Korea			United States		
	Real GDP per capita (2015 dollars)	Percentage of		Real GDP per capita (2015 dollars)	Percentage of		Real GDP per capita (2015 dollars)	Percentage of		Real GDP per capita (2015 dollars)	Percentage of	
Year		1960 real GDP per capita	2021 real GDP per capita		1960 real GDP per capita	2021 real GDP per capita		1960 real GDP per capita	2021 real GDP per capita		1960 real GDP per capita	2021 real GDP per capita
1960	$7,410	?	?	$1,108	?	?	$1,027	?	?	$19,135	?	?
1980	10,271	?	?	897	?	?	4,056	?	?	31,162	?	?
2000	10,673	?	?	1,020	?	?	16,992	?	?	48,746	?	?
2021	12,402	?	?	2,015	?	?	32,731	?	?	61,856	?	?

2. The country of Androde is currently using Method 1 for its production function. By chance, scientists stumble onto a technological breakthrough that will enhance Androde's productivity. This technological breakthrough is reflected in another production function, Method 2. The accompanying table shows combinations of physical capital per worker and output per worker for both methods, assuming that human capital per worker is fixed.

Method 1		Method 2	
Physical capital per worker	Real GDP per worker	Physical capital per worker	Real GDP per worker
0	0.00	0	0.00
50	35.36	50	70.71
100	50.00	100	100.00
150	61.24	150	122.47
200	70.71	200	141.42
250	79.06	250	158.11
300	86.60	300	173.21
350	93.54	350	187.08
400	100.00	400	200.00
450	106.07	450	212.13
500	111.80	500	223.61

a. Using the data in the accompanying table, draw the two production functions in one diagram. Androde's current amount of physical capital per worker is 100. In your figure, label that point A.

b. Starting from point A, over a period of 70 years, the amount of physical capital per worker in Androde rises to 400. Assuming Androde still uses Method 1, in your diagram, label the resulting point of production B. Using the Rule of 70, calculate by how many percent per year output per worker has grown.

c. Now assume that, starting from point A, over the same period of 70 years, the amount of physical capital per worker in Androde rises to 400, but that during that time period, Androde switches to Method 2. In your diagram, label the resulting point of production C. Using the Rule of 70, calculate by how many percent per year output per worker has grown now.

d. As the economy of Androde moves from point A to point C, what share of the annual productivity growth is due to higher total factor productivity?

3. The Bureau of Labor Statistics regularly releases the "Productivity and Costs" report for the previous month. Go to www.bls.gov and find the latest report. (On the Bureau of Labor Statistics home page, from the tab "Subjects," select the link to "Productivity: Labor Productivity & Costs"; then, from the heading "LPC News Releases," find the most recent "Productivity and Costs" report.) What were the percent changes in business and nonfarm business productivity for the previous quarter? How does the percent change in that quarter's productivity compare to the percent change from the same quarter a year ago?

4. Why would you expect real GDP per capita in California and Pennsylvania to exhibit convergence but not in California and Baja California, a state of Mexico that borders the United States? What changes would allow California and Baja California to converge?

5. According to the Organization of the Petroleum Exporting Countries, the proven oil reserves existing in the world in 2021 consisted of 1,554 billion barrels. In that year, the U.S. Energy Information Administration reported that the world daily oil production was 101.6 million barrels a day.

a. At this rate, for how many years will the proven oil reserves last? Discuss the Malthusian view in the context of the number you just calculated.

b. In order to do the calculation in part a, what did you assume about the total quantity of oil reserves over time? About oil prices over time? Are these assumptions consistent with the Malthusian view on resource limits?

c. Discuss how market forces may affect the amount of time the proven oil reserves will last, assuming that no new oil reserves are discovered and that the demand curve for oil remains unchanged.

PROBLEMS

1. The following table shows the average annual growth rate in real GDP per capita for Argentina, Ghana, and South Korea using data from the World Bank, World Development Indicators, for the past few decades.

	Average annual growth rate of real GDP per capita		
Years	**Argentina**	**Ghana**	**South Korea**
1970–1980	1.04%	2.54%	7.45%
1980–1990	2.29	0.51	8.73
1990–2000	2.74	1.81	6.14
2000–2010	2.42	3.03	4.12
2010–2020	1.76	3.56	2.11

a. For each 10-year period and for each country, use the Rule of 70 where possible to calculate how long it would take for that country's real GDP per capita to double.

b. Suppose that the average annual growth rate that each country achieved over the period 2010–2020 continues indefinitely into the future. Starting from 2021, use the Rule of 70 to calculate, where possible, the year in which a country will have doubled its real GDP per capita.

2. The following table provides approximate statistics on per capita income levels and growth rates for regions defined by income levels. According to the Rule of 70, starting in 2021 the high-income countries are projected to double their per capita GDP in approximately 70 years, in 2091. Throughout this question, assume constant growth rates for each of the regions are equal to their average value between 2000 and 2021.

Region	Real GDP per capita (2021)	Average annual growth rate of real GDP per capita (2000–2021)
High-income countries	$42.540	0.73%
Middle-income countries	5,631	3.28
Low-income countries	780	0.76

Data from: World Bank.

a. Calculate the ratio of per capita GDP in 2021 of the following:
  i. Middle-income to high-income countries
  ii. Low-income to high-income countries
  iii. Low-income to middle-income countries

b. Calculate the number of years it will take the low-income and middle-income countries to double their per capita GDP.

c. Calculate the per capita GDP of each of the regions in 2091. (*Hint:* How many times does their per capita GDP double in 70 years, the number of years from 2021 to 2091?)

d. Repeat part a with the projected per capita GDP in 2091.

e. Compare your answers to parts a and d. Comment on the change in economic inequality between the regions.

3. What roles do physical capital, human capital, technology, and natural resources play in influencing long-run economic growth of aggregate output per capita?

4. How have U.S. policies and institutions influenced the country's long-run economic growth?

5. Over the next 100 years, real GDP per capita in Groland is expected to grow at an average annual rate of 2.0%. In Sloland, however, growth is expected to be somewhat slower, at an average annual growth rate of 1.5%. If both countries have a real GDP per capita today of $20,000, how will their real GDP per capita differ in 100 years? [*Hint:* A country that has a real GDP today of x and grows at $y\%$ per year will achieve a real GDP of $x \times (1 + (y/100))^z$ in z years. We assume that $0 \leq y \leq 100$.]

6. The accompanying table shows data from the World Bank, World Development Indicators, for real GDP per capita (2015 U.S. dollars) in France, Japan, the United Kingdom, and the United States in 1960 and 2021. Complete the table. Have these countries reduced the income gap with the United States?

	1960		2021	
	Real GDP per capita (2015 dollars)	Percentage of U.S. real GDP per capita	Real GDP per capita (2015 dollars)	Percentage of U.S. real GDP per capita
France	$11,170	?	$38,046	?
Japan	6,261	?	35,291	?
United Kingdom	14,915	?	45,102	?
United States	19,135	?	61,856	?

7. The accompanying table shows data from the World Bank, World Development Indicators for real GDP per capita (2015 U.S. dollars) for Argentina, Ghana, South Korea, and the United States in 1960 and 2021. Complete the table. Have these countries caught up economically?

	1960		2021	
	Real GDP per capita (2015 dollars)	Percentage of U.S. real GDP per capita	Real GDP per capita (2015 dollars)	Percentage of U.S. real GDP per capita
Argentina	$7,410	?	$12,402	?
Ghana	1,108	?	2,015	?
South Korea	1,027	?	32,731	?
United States	19,135	?	61,856	?

8. Access the Discovering Data exercise for Chapter 9 online to answer the following questions.

   a. What was the ratio of Japanese GDP per capita relative to the United States in 1950 and 1991?

   b. Why has Japan's GDP caught up to that of the United States?

   c. Rank the countries in order of richest to poorest (with 1 being the richest) in 1960 and 2020?

   d. What was the ratio of GDP per capita for Spain relative to the United States in 1960 and 2020?

   e. Which two countries experienced the fastest rate of convergence from 1960 through 2020?

   f. Why are lower income countries, like Korea in 1960, able to grow faster than rich countries?

   g. If countries continue along a similar path, will Japan, Korea, Chile, or Spain be the first country to reach the level of real GDP per capita in the United States?

9. The accompanying table shows the annual growth rate for the years 2000–2019 in per capita emissions of carbon dioxide (CO_2) and the annual growth rate in real GDP per capita for selected countries.

Country	2000–2019 Average annual growth rate	
	Real GDP per capita	CO_2 emissions per capita
Argentina	0.93%	0.25%
Bangladesh	4.74	6.44
Canada	0.92	−0.43
China	8.40	5.71
Germany	1.20	−1.28
Ireland	3.10	−2.26
Japan	0.73	−0.46
Mexico	0.59	−0.40
Nigeria	2.87	−1.74
South Africa	1.42	1.16
South Korea	3.33	1.03
United Kingdom	1.02	−2.83
United States	1.16	−1.74

Data from: Energy Information Administration; World Bank.

   a. Rank the countries in terms of their growth in CO_2 emissions, from highest to lowest. What five countries have the highest growth rate in emissions? What five countries have the lowest growth rate in emissions?

   b. Now rank the countries in terms of their growth in real GDP per capita, from highest to lowest. What five countries have the highest growth rate? What five countries have the lowest growth rate?

   c. Would you infer from your results that CO_2 emissions are linked to growth in output per capita?

   d. Do high growth rates necessarily lead to high CO_2 emissions?

10. You are hired as an economic consultant to the countries of Albernia and Brittania. Each country's current relationship between physical capital per worker and output per worker is given by the curve labeled "Productivity$_1$" in the accompanying diagram. Albernia is at point A and Brittania is at point B.

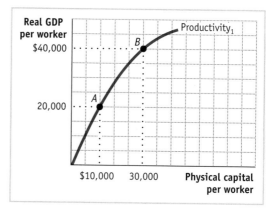

   a. In the relationship depicted by the curve Productivity$_1$, what factors are held fixed? Do these countries experience diminishing returns to physical capital per worker?

   b. Assuming that the amount of human capital per worker and the technology are held fixed in each country, can you recommend a policy to generate a doubling of real GDP per capita in Albernia?

   c. How would your policy recommendation change if the amount of human capital per worker could be changed? Assume that an increase in human capital doubles the output per worker when physical capital per worker equals $10,000. Draw a curve on the diagram that represents this policy for Albernia. ■

10

Savings, Investment Spending, and the Financial System

PAYING FOR A HIDDEN EMPIRE

AMAZON.COM IS THE WORLD'S LARGEST and most famous online retailer. Millions of people routinely visit its website to buy everything from books to electronics to pet supplies. You click a mouse or tap your smartphone, and soon — sometimes the next day — the item you want shows up at your door, seemingly untouched by human hands.

Bloomberg/Getty Images

Through the financial system, Amazon obtained billions of dollars to finance its expansion, making it the world's largest online retailer.

But the impression one sometimes has of a disembodied organization that summons consumer goods out of thin air is misleading: Amazon is by no means a virtual company. Behind those convenient online interactions and deliveries lies a vast, if mostly hidden, physical empire of server farms handling data and warehouses. In fact, that network of physical facilities is widely regarded as a key factor in Amazon's success. According to one recent analysis, Amazon has more than 300 warehouses ("fulfillment centers," in Amazon-speak) that employ 450,000 workers; the majority of the U.S. population lives within 20 miles of one of these centers.

The existence of these warehouses, so close to major markets and containing a huge inventory of popular products, is what allows the firm to offer one- or two-day delivery on many items. And this superiority in distribution — some of you may have purchased this textbook from Amazon! — gives the company a big competitive advantage.

We don't know exactly how much Amazon has spent to build this hidden physical empire, but the cost has surely run to many billions of dollars. Where did that money come from?

Not from reinvestment of the company's profits: Amazon, founded in 1994, basically earned no profits until 2016. But the company was able to convince outside investors that it would eventually become highly profitable. And the prospect of future profits was enough to bring in large amounts of money from outside investors.

Some of these investors bought equity — essentially shares in those expected future profits. In a move that was unusual for tech companies but was standard practice for many traditional companies, Amazon also, early in its history, sold debt: promises to pay investors a fixed amount each year, whatever happens. Those debt sales were controversial at the time, but are now widely viewed as having given Amazon a crucial advantage over competitors, who weren't able to make the same kind of investment in physical plant, especially those in warehouses.

Amazon, then, was able to get the money it needed for massive investment spending long before that spending could yield financial results. It was, in a way, a kind of financial miracle. But while Amazon is an exceptional case, the same kind of financial miracle happens all the time in modern economies.

The long-run growth we analyzed in the previous chapter depends crucially on a set of markets and institutions, collectively known as the *financial system,* that channels the funds of savers into productive investment spending. Without this system, businesses like Amazon would not be able to purchase much of the physical capital that is an important source of productivity growth. And savers would be forced to accept a lower return on their funds.

Historically, financial systems channeled funds into investment spending projects such as railroads and factories. Today, financial systems channel funds into new sources of growth such as green technology, social media, and investments in human capital. Without a well-functioning financial system, a country will suffer stunted economic growth.

In this chapter, we begin by focusing on the economy as a whole. We will examine the relationship between savings and investment spending. Next, we go behind this relationship and analyze the financial system, the means by which savings is transformed into investment spending.

We'll see how the financial system works by creating assets, markets, and institutions that increase the welfare of both savers (those with funds to invest) and borrowers (those with investment spending projects to finance). Finally, we examine the behavior of financial markets and why they often resist economists' attempts at explanation. ●

WHAT YOU WILL LEARN

- What is the relationship between savings and investment spending?
- How does the **loanable funds market** match savers with borrowers?
- What are the purposes of the four principal types of **financial assets: loans,** bonds, stocks, and **bank deposits?**

- How do **financial intermediaries** help investors achieve **diversification?**
- What are the competing views about how asset prices are determined and why asset market fluctuations can be a source of macroeconomic instability?

savings–investment spending identity an accounting fact that states that savings and investment spending are always equal for the economy as a whole.

Matching Up Savings and Investment Spending

We learned in the previous chapter that two of the essential ingredients in economic growth are increases in the economy's levels of *human capital* and *physical capital*. Human capital is largely provided by governments through public education. (In countries with a large private education sector, like the United States, private post-secondary education is also an important source of human capital.) But physical capital, with the exception of infrastructure, is mainly created through private investment spending—that is, spending by firms rather than by the government.

Who pays for private investment spending? In some cases, it's the people or corporations that actually do the spending—for example, a family that owns a business might use its own savings to buy new equipment or a new building, or a corporation might reinvest some of its own profits to build a new factory. In the modern economy, however, individuals and firms that create physical capital often do it with other people's money—money that they borrow or raise by selling stock.

You may recall Chapter 7, Figure 1, which showed an extended version of the circular flow of funds through the economy. In Chapter 7, we focused on the left side of that diagram, the orange arrows showing flows of money into and out of the markets for goods and services. In this chapter, we focus on the blue arrows on the right side of the diagram, specifically those flowing into and out of the *financial markets,* markets in which the government, firms, and individuals trade not goods but promises to pay in the future.

To understand financial markets and how investment spending is financed, we need to look first at how savings and investment spending are related for the economy as a whole. Then we will examine how savings are allocated among investment spending projects.

The Savings–Investment Spending Identity

The most basic point to understand about savings and investment spending is that they are always equal. This is not a theory; it's a fact of accounting called the **savings–investment spending identity.**

To see why the savings–investment spending identity must be true, let's look again at the national income accounting that we learned in Chapter 7. Recall that GDP is equal to total spending on domestically produced final goods and services, and that we can write the following equation (which is the same as Chapter 7, Equation 1):

(1) $GDP = C + I + G + X - IM$

where C is spending by consumers, I is investment spending, G is government purchases of goods and services, X is the value of exports to other countries, and IM is spending on imports from other countries.

The Savings–Investment Spending Identity in a Closed Economy

In a closed economy, there are no exports or imports. So $X = 0$ and $IM = 0$, which makes Equation 1 simpler. As we learned in Chapter 7, the overall income of this simplified economy would, by definition, equal total spending. Why? Recall one of the basic principles of economics from Chapter 1, that one person's spending is another person's income: the only way people can earn income is by selling something to someone else, and every dollar spent in the economy creates income for somebody. This is represented by Equation 2: on the left, GDP represents total income earned in the economy, and on the right, $C + I + G$ represents total spending in the economy:

(2) $\quad\quad GDP = C + I + G$

Total income = Total spending

Now, what can be done with income? It can either be spent on consumption—consumer spending (C) plus government purchases of goods and services (G)—or saved (S). So it must be true that:

(3)   GDP $= C + G + S$

Total income = Consumption spending + Savings

where S is savings. Meanwhile, as Equation 2 tells us, total spending consists of either consumption spending ($C + G$) or investment spending (I):

(4)   GDP $= C + G + I$

Total income = Consumption spending + Investment spending

Putting Equations 3 and 4 together, we get:

(5) $C + G + S = C + G + I$

Consumption spending + Savings = Consumption spending + Investment spending

Subtract consumption spending ($C + G$) from both sides, and we get:

(6) $S = I$

Savings = Investment spending

As we said, then, it's a basic accounting fact that savings equals investment spending for the economy as a whole.

Now, let's take a closer look at savings. Households are not the only parties that can save in an economy. In any given year, the government can save, too, if it collects more tax revenue than it spends. When this occurs, the difference is called a **budget surplus** and is equivalent to savings by government.

If, alternatively, government spending exceeds tax revenue, there is a **budget deficit**—a negative budget surplus. In this case, we often say that the government is *dissaving:* by spending more than its tax revenues, the government is engaged in the opposite of savings. One way to finance a budget deficit is by borrowing. **Government borrowing** is the total amount of funds borrowed by federal, state, and local governments in the financial markets.

We'll define the term **budget balance** to refer to both cases, with the understanding that the budget balance can be positive (a budget surplus) or negative (a budget deficit). The budget balance is defined as:

(7) $S_{Government} = T - G - TR$

where T is the value of tax revenues and TR is the value of government transfers. The budget balance is equivalent to savings by government—if it's positive, the government is saving; if it's negative, the government is dissaving. **National savings,** which we just called savings, for short, is equal to the sum of the budget balance and private savings, where private savings is disposable income (income plus government transfers minus taxes) minus consumption. It is given by:

(8) $S_{National} = S_{Government} + S_{Private}$

So Equations 6 and 8 tell us that, in a closed economy, the savings–investment spending identity has the following form:

(9) $S_{National} = I$

National savings = Investment spending

The Savings–Investment Spending Identity in an Open Economy

In an open or international economy, goods and money can flow into and out of the country. This changes the savings–investment spending identity because savings need not be spent on investment spending projects in the same country in which the savings are generated. That's because the savings of people who live in any

budget surplus the difference between tax revenue and government spending when tax revenue exceeds government spending; saving by the government in the form of a budget surplus is a positive contribution to national savings.

budget deficit the difference between tax revenue and government spending when government spending exceeds tax revenue; dissaving by the government in the form of a budget deficit is a negative contribution to national savings.

government borrowing the total amount of funds borrowed by federal, state, and local governments in the financial markets.

budget balance the difference between tax revenue and government spending. A positive budget balance is referred to as a budget surplus; a negative budget balance is referred to as a budget deficit.

national savings the sum of private savings and the government's budget balance; the total amount of savings generated within the economy.

one country can be used to finance investment spending that takes place in other countries. So any given country can receive *inflows* of funds—foreign savings that finance investment spending in that country. Any given country can also generate *outflows* of funds—domestic savings that finance investment spending in another country.

The net effect of international inflows and outflows of funds on the total savings available for investment spending in any given country is known as the **net capital inflow** into that country, equal to the total inflow of foreign funds minus the total outflow of domestic funds to other countries. Like the budget balance, a net capital inflow can be negative—that is, more capital can flow out of a country than flows into it. In recent years, the United States has experienced a consistent positive net capital inflow from foreigners, who view our economy as an attractive place to put their savings. In 2022, for example, net capital inflows into the United States were $994.7 billion.

It's important to note that, from a national perspective, a dollar generated by national savings and a dollar generated by capital inflow are not equivalent. Yes, they can both finance the same dollars' worth of investment spending. But any dollar borrowed from a saver must eventually be repaid with interest. A dollar that comes from national savings is repaid with interest to someone domestically—either a private party or the government.

But a dollar that comes as capital inflow must be repaid with interest to a foreigner. So a dollar of investment spending financed by a capital inflow comes at a higher *national* cost—the interest that must eventually be paid to a foreigner—than a dollar of investment spending financed by national savings.

The fact that a net capital inflow represents funds borrowed from foreigners is an important aspect of the savings–investment spending identity in an international economy. Consider an individual who spends more than their income; that person must borrow the difference from others. Similarly, a country that spends more on imports than it earns from exports must borrow the difference from foreigners. And that difference, the amount of funds borrowed from foreigners, is the country's net capital inflow. As we explain more fully in Chapter 18, this means the net capital inflow into a country is equal to the difference between imports and exports:

(10) $$NCI = IM - X$$
Net capital inflow = Imports – Exports

Rearranging Equation 1 we get:

(11) $I = (GDP - C - G) + (IM - X)$

Using Equation 3 we know that $GDP - C - G$ is equal to national savings, so that:

(12) $I = S_{National} + (IM - X) = S_{National} + NCI$
Investment spending = National savings + Net capital inflow

So the application of the savings–investment spending identity to an economy that is open to inflows or outflows of capital means that investment spending is equal to savings, where savings is equal to national savings *plus* net capital inflow. That is, in an economy with a positive net capital inflow, some investment spending is funded by the savings of foreigners. And in an economy with a negative net capital inflow (that is, more capital is flowing out than flowing in), some portion of national savings is funding investment spending in other countries.

U.S. investment spending in 2022 totaled $5,489.6 billion. Private savings totaled $5,027.5 billion, and government savings equaled –$333.9 billion, leading to national savings of $4,693.6 billion. Net capital inflow was $994.7 billion. Notice that these numbers don't quite add up. Because data collection isn't perfect, there is a statistical discrepancy of –$198.8 billion, the amount that national

net capital inflow the total inflow of funds into a country minus the total outflow of funds out of a country.

FIGURE 1 The Savings–Investment Spending Identity in Open Economies: The United States and Germany, 2021

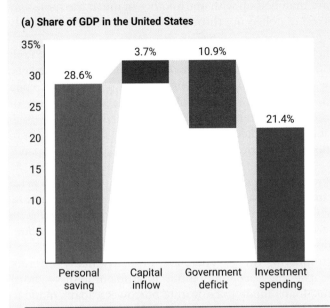

(a) Share of GDP in the United States

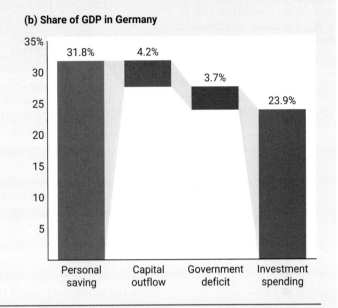

(b) Share of GDP in Germany

U.S. investment spending in 2021 (equal to 21.4% of GDP) was financed by a combination of private savings (28.6% of GDP) and a capital inflow (3.7% of GDP), which were partially offset by a government budget deficit (10.9% of GDP). German investment spending in 2021 (equal to 23.9% of GDP) was financed by a combination of private savings (31.8% of GDP) which was partially offset by a capital outflow (4.2% of GDP) and a government budget deficit (3.7% of GDP). Bars may not equal due to statistical discrepancy.

Data from: International Monetary Fund.

savings plus net capital inflow exceeded investment spending. We know this is a data error because the savings–investment spending identity must hold.

Figure 1 shows what the savings–investment spending identity looked like in 2021 for two of the world's major economies, those of the United States and Germany. To make the two economies easier to compare, we've measured savings and investment spending as percentages of GDP. In each panel, the blue bars on the right show total investment spending and the multicolored bars on the left show the components of savings. U.S. investment spending was 21.4% of GDP, financed by a combination of private savings (28.6% of GDP) and positive net capital inflow (3.7% of GDP) and partly offset by a government budget deficit (–10.9% of GDP). German investment spending was higher as a percentage of GDP, at 23.9%. It was financed by a higher level of private savings as a percentage of GDP (31.8%), but was offset by a government budget deficit (–4.2% of GDP) and a negative capital inflow or capital outflow (–4.2% of GDP).

The economy's savings finance its investment spending. But how are these funds that are available for investment spending allocated among various projects? That is, what determines which projects get financed (such as Amazon's fulfillment centers) and which don't? We'll see shortly that funds get allocated to investment spending projects using a familiar method: by the market, via supply and demand.

The Market for Loanable Funds

For the economy as a whole, savings always equals investment spending. In a closed economy, savings is equal to national savings. In an international or open economy, savings is equal to national savings plus capital inflow. At any given time, however, savers, the people with funds to lend, are usually not the same as

loanable funds market a hypothetical market that brings together those who want to lend money (savers) and those who want to borrow (firms with investment spending projects).

borrowers, the people who want to borrow to finance their investment spending. How are savers and borrowers brought together?

Savers and borrowers are matched up with one another in much the same way producers and consumers are matched up: through markets governed by supply and demand.

To understand this, it helps to consider a somewhat simplified version of reality. In the actual economy, there are a large number of different financial markets. These include markets for *bonds* and *loans,* which are both promises to pay a fixed amount whatever happens, and for *stocks,* which give investors a share of future profits. However, economists often work with a simplified model in which they assume that there is just one market that brings together those who want to lend money (savers) and those who want to borrow (firms with investment spending projects).

This hypothetical market is known as the **loanable funds market.** The price that is determined in the loanable funds market is the interest rate, denoted by *r*. As we noted in Chapter 8, loans typically specify a nominal interest rate. So although we call *r* "the interest rate," it is with the understanding that *r* is a nominal interest rate—an interest rate that is unadjusted for inflation.

We're not quite done simplifying things. There are, in reality, many different kinds of interest rates, because there are many different kinds of loans—short-term loans, long-term loans, loans made to corporate borrowers, loans made to governments, and so on. In the interest of simplicity, we'll ignore those differences and assume that there is only one type of loan.

OK, now we're ready to analyze how savings and investment get matched up.

The Demand for Loanable Funds Figure 2 illustrates a hypothetical demand curve for loanable funds, *D,* which slopes downward. On the horizontal axis, we show the quantity of loanable funds demanded. On the vertical axis, we show the interest rate, which is the "price" of borrowing. But why does the demand curve for loanable funds slope downward?

To answer this question, consider what a firm is doing when it engages in investment spending—say, by buying new equipment. Investment spending

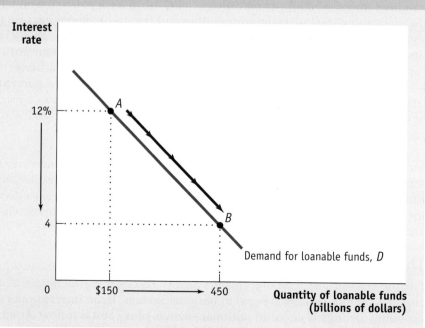

FIGURE 2 The Demand for Loanable Funds

The demand curve for loanable funds slopes downward: the lower the interest rate, the greater the quantity of loanable funds demanded. Here, reducing the interest rate from 12% to 4% increases the quantity of loanable funds demanded from $150 billion to $450 billion.

means laying out money right now, expecting that this outlay will lead to higher profits at some point in the future. In fact, however, the promise of a dollar 5 or 10 years from now is worth less than an actual dollar right now. So an investment is worth making only if it generates a future return that is *greater* than the monetary cost of making the investment today. How much greater?

To answer that, we need to take into account the present value of the future return the firm expects to get. We examine the concept of *present value* in the accompanying For Inquiring Minds. Then, in the chapter's appendix, we show how the concept of present value can be applied to dollars earned multiple years in the future. The appendix also addresses how present value is used to calculate the prices of shares of stock and bonds.

In present value calculations, we use the interest rate to determine how the value of a dollar in the future compares to the value of a dollar today. But the fact is that future dollars are worth less than a dollar today, and they are worth even less when the interest rate is higher.

FOR INQUIRING MINDS   Using Present Value

An understanding of the concept of present value shows why the demand curve for loanable funds slopes downward. A simple way to grasp the essence of present value is to consider an example that illustrates the difference in value between having a sum of money today and having the same sum of money a year from now.

Suppose that exactly one year from today you will graduate, and you want to reward yourself by taking a trip that will cost $1,000. In order to have $1,000 a year from now, how much do you need today? It's not $1,000, and the reason why has to do with the interest rate.

Let's call the amount you need today X. We'll use r to represent the interest rate you receive on funds deposited in the bank. If you put X into the bank today and earn interest rate r on it, then after one year, the bank will pay you $X \times (1+r)$. If what the bank will pay you a year from now is equal to $1,000, then the amount you need today is:

$$X \times (1+r) = \$1,000$$

You can apply some basic algebra to find that:

$$X = \$1,000/(1+r)$$

Notice that the value of X depends on the interest rate r, which is always greater than 0. This fact implies that X *is always less than* $1,000. For example, if $r = 5\%$ (that is, $r = 0.05$), then $X = \$952.38$. In other words, having $952.38 today is equivalent to having $1,000 a year from now when the interest rate is 5%. That is, $952.38 is the value of $1,000 today given an interest rate of 5%.

Now we can define the *present value* of X: it is the amount of money needed today in order to receive X in the future given the interest rate. In this numerical example, $952.38 is the present value of $1,000 received one year from now given an interest rate of 5%.

The concept of present value also applies to decisions made by firms. Think about a firm that has two potential investment projects in mind, each of which will yield $1,000 a year from now. However, each project has different initial costs — say, one requires that the firm borrow $900 right now and the other requires that the firm borrow $950. Which, if any, of these projects is worth borrowing money to finance and undertake?

The answer depends on the interest rate, which determines the present value of $1,000 a year from now. If the interest rate is 10%, the present value of $1,000 delivered a year from now is $909. In other words, at an interest rate of 10%, a $909 loan requires a repayment of $1,000 in a year's time. A loan less than $909 requires a repayment less than $1,000, while a loan of more than $909 requires a repayment of more than $1,000. So only the first project, which has an initial cost of less than $909, is profitable, because its return in a year's time is more than the amount of the loan repayment.

With an interest rate of 10%, the return on any project costing more than $909 is less than the amount the firm has to repay on its loan and is therefore unprofitable. If the interest rate is only 5%, however, the present value of $1,000 rises to $952. At this interest rate, both projects are profitable,

because $952 exceeds both projects' initial cost. So a firm will borrow more and engage in more investment spending when the interest rate is lower.

Meanwhile, similar calculations will be taking place at other firms. So a lower interest rate will lead to higher investment spending in the economy as a whole: the demand curve for loanable funds slopes downward.

When making financial decisions, individuals and firms must always keep in mind that having $1,000 today is worth more than having $1,000 a year from now.

The intuition behind present value calculations is simple. The interest rate measures the opportunity cost of investment spending that results in a future return: instead of spending money on an investment spending project, a company could simply put the money into the bank and earn interest on it. And the higher the interest rate, the more attractive it is to simply put money into the bank and let it earn interest instead of investing it in an investment spending project.

In other words, the higher the interest rate, the higher the opportunity cost of investment spending. And, the higher the opportunity cost of investment spending, the lower the number of investment spending projects firms want to carry out, and therefore the lower the quantity of loanable funds demanded. It is this insight that explains why the demand curve for loanable funds is downward sloping.

When businesses engage in investment spending, they spend money right now in return for an expected payoff in the future. To evaluate whether a particular investment spending project is worth undertaking, a business must compare the present value of the future payoff with the current cost of that project. If the present value of the future payoff is greater than the current cost, a project is profitable and worth investing in. If the interest rate falls, then the present value of any given project rises, so more projects pass that test. If the interest rate rises, then the present value of any given project falls, and fewer projects pass that test.

So total investment spending, and hence the demand for loanable funds to finance that spending, is negatively related to the interest rate. Thus, the demand curve for loanable funds slopes downward. You can see this in Figure 2. When the interest rate falls from 12% to 4%, the quantity of loanable funds demanded rises from $150 billion (point *A*) to $450 billion (point *B*).

The Supply of Loanable Funds   Figure 3 shows a hypothetical supply curve for loanable funds, *S*. Again, the interest rate plays the same role that the price plays in ordinary supply and demand analysis. But why is this curve upward sloping?

The answer is that loanable funds are supplied by savers, and savers incur an opportunity cost when they lend to a business: the funds could instead be spent on consumption — say, a nice vacation. Whether a given saver becomes a lender by making funds available to borrowers depends on the interest rate received in return. By saving your money today and earning interest on it, you are rewarded

---

FIGURE 3 The Supply of Loanable Funds

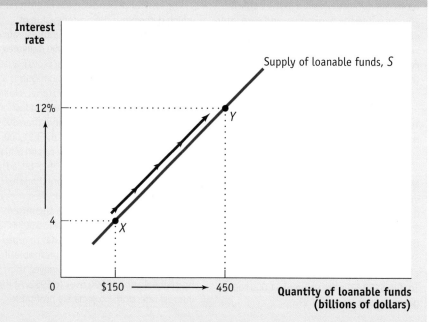

The supply curve for loanable funds slopes upward: the higher the interest rate, the greater the quantity of loanable funds supplied. Here, increasing the interest rate from 4% to 12% increases the quantity of loanable funds supplied from $150 billion to $450 billion.

with higher consumption in the future when the loan you made is repaid with interest. So it is a good assumption that more people are willing to forgo current consumption and make a loan to a borrower when the interest rate is higher.

As a result, our hypothetical supply curve of loanable funds slopes upward. In Figure 3, lenders will supply $150 billion to the loanable funds market at an interest rate of 4% (point X); if the interest rate rises to 12%, the quantity of loanable funds supplied will rise to $450 billion (point Y).

The Equilibrium Interest Rate The interest rate at which the quantity of loanable funds supplied equals the quantity of loanable funds demanded is called the **equilibrium interest rate.** As you can see in Figure 4, the equilibrium interest rate, r^*, and the total quantity of lending, Q^*, are determined by the intersection of the supply and demand curves, at point E.

Here, the equilibrium interest rate is 8%, at which $300 billion is lent and borrowed. In this equilibrium, only investment spending projects that are profitable if the interest rate is 8% or higher are funded. Projects that are profitable only when the interest rate falls below 8% are not funded. Correspondingly, only lenders who are willing to accept an interest rate of 8% or less will have their offers to lend funds accepted; lenders who demand an interest rate higher than 8% do not have their offers to lend accepted.

Figure 4 shows how the market for loanable funds matches up desired savings with desired investment spending: in equilibrium, the quantity of funds that savers want to lend is equal to the quantity of funds that firms want to borrow. The figure also shows that this match-up is efficient, in two senses. First, the right investments get made: the investment spending projects that are actually financed have higher payoffs (in terms of present value) than those that do not get financed. Second, the right people do the saving and lending: the savers who actually lend funds are willing to lend for lower interest rates than those who do not.

The insight that the loanable funds market leads to an efficient use of savings, although drawn from a highly simplified model, has important implications for real life. As we'll see shortly, it is the reason that a well-functioning financial system increases an economy's long-run economic growth rate.

> **equilibrium interest rate** a situation where the interest rate at which the quantity of loanable funds supplied equals the quantity of loanable funds demanded.

FIGURE 4 Equilibrium in the Loanable Funds Market

At the equilibrium interest rate, the quantity of loanable funds supplied equals the quantity of loanable funds demanded. Here, the equilibrium interest rate is 8%, with $300 billion of funds lent and borrowed. Lenders who demand an interest rate of 8% or lower have their offers of loans accepted; those who demand a higher interest rate do not. Projects that are profitable at an interest rate of 8% or higher are funded; those that are profitable only when the interest rate falls below 8% are not.

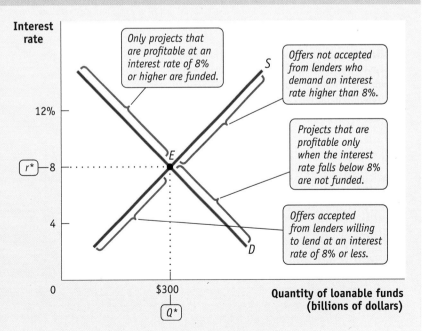

Before we get to that, let's look at how the market for loanable funds responds to shifts of demand and supply. As in the standard model of supply and demand, where the equilibrium price changes in response to shifts of the demand or supply curves, here, the equilibrium interest rate changes when there are shifts of the demand curve for loanable funds, the supply curve for loanable funds, or both.

Shifts of the Demand for Loanable Funds   Let's start by looking at the causes and effects of changes in demand.

The factors that can cause the demand curve for loanable funds to shift include the following:

1. *Changes in perceived business opportunities.* A change in beliefs about the pay-off of investment spending can increase or decrease the amount of desired spending at any given interest rate. For example, during the 1990s there was great excitement over the business possibilities created by the internet, which had just begun to be widely used. As a result, businesses rushed to buy computer equipment, put fiber-optic cables in the ground, launch websites, and so on. This shifted the demand for loanable funds to the right. By 2001, the failure of many dot-com businesses had led to disillusionment with technology-related investment; this shifted the demand for loanable funds back to the left.

2. *Changes in government borrowing.* A government runs a budget deficit when, in a given year, it spends more than it receives. A government that runs budget deficits can be a major source of demand for loanable funds. For example, in 2009 the U.S. federal government was running a budget deficit in excess of $1.413 trillion, but by 2016 the federal deficit had been cut by $1 trillion to a little more than $330 billion. The federal government greatly reduced its borrowing needs. This change in the federal budget position had the effect, other things equal, of shifting the demand curve for loanable funds to the left.

Figure 5 shows the effects of an increase in the demand for loanable funds. S is the supply of loanable funds, and D_1 is the initial demand curve. The initial equilibrium interest rate is r_1. An increase in the demand for loanable funds means that the quantity of funds demanded rises at any given interest rate, so the demand curve shifts rightward to D_2. As a result, the equilibrium interest rate rises to r_2.

FIGURE 5 An Increase in the Demand for Loanable Funds

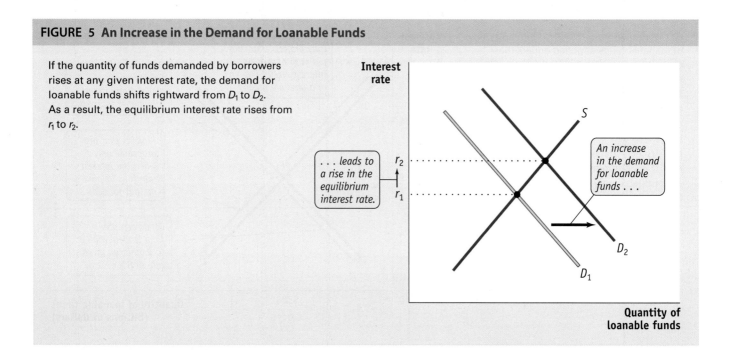

If the quantity of funds demanded by borrowers rises at any given interest rate, the demand for loanable funds shifts rightward from D_1 to D_2. As a result, the equilibrium interest rate rises from r_1 to r_2.

... leads to a rise in the equilibrium interest rate.

An increase in the demand for loanable funds ...

The fact that an increase in the demand for loanable funds leads, other things equal, to a rise in the interest rate has one especially important implication: it tells us that increasing or persistent government budget deficits are cause for concern because an increase in the government's deficit shifts the demand curve for loanable funds to the right, which leads to a higher interest rate. If the interest rate rises, businesses will cut back on their investment spending.

So, other things equal, a rise in the government budget deficit tends to reduce overall investment spending. Economists call the negative effect of government budget deficits on investment spending **crowding out.** Concerns about crowding out are one key reason to worry about increasing or persistent budget deficits.

However, it's important to add a qualification here: crowding out may not occur if the economy is depressed. When the economy is operating far below full employment, government spending can lead to higher incomes, and these higher incomes lead to increased savings at any given interest rate. Higher savings allows the government to borrow without raising interest rates. Many economists believe, for example, that the large budget deficits that the U.S. government ran from 2008 to 2013 in the face of a depressed economy caused little if any crowding out.

crowding out the negative effect of budget deficits on private investment, which occurs because government borrowing drives up interest rates.

Shifts of the Supply of Loanable Funds Like the demand for loanable funds, the supply of loanable funds can shift. Among the factors that can cause the supply of loanable funds to shift are the following:

1. *Changes in private savings behavior.* A number of factors can cause the level of private savings to change at any given interest rate. For example, as the economy recovered from and concerns of increased inflation, households cut back on spending. From April 2020 to February 2023, the personal saving rate, savings as a percent of disposable income, decreased to 5% from about 33%. This had the effect of shifting the supply curve of loanable funds to the left.

2. *Changes in net capital inflows.* Capital flows into and out of a country can change as investors' perceptions of that country change. For example, Greece experienced large net capital inflows after the creation of the euro, Europe's common currency, in 1999, because investors believed that Greece's adoption of the euro as its currency had made it a safe place to put their funds. By 2009, however, worries about the Greek government's solvency (and the discovery that it had been understating its debt) led to a collapse in investor confidence, and the net inflow of funds dried up. The effect of shrinking capital inflows was to shift the supply curve in the Greek loanable funds market to the left.

   In the mid-2000s, the United States received large net capital inflows, with much of the money coming from China and the Middle East. Those inflows helped fuel a big increase in residential investment spending—newly constructed homes—from 2003 to 2006. As a result of the bursting of the U.S. housing bubble in 2006–2007 and the subsequent deep recession, those inflows declined, but by 2021, following the pandemic, capital inflows were starting to return to levels last seen in the housing bubble.

Figure 6 shows the effects of an increase in the supply of loanable funds. D is the demand for loanable funds, and S_1 is the initial supply curve. The initial equilibrium interest rate is r_1. An increase in the supply of loanable funds means that the quantity of funds supplied rises at any given interest rate, so the supply curve shifts rightward to S_2. As a result, the equilibrium interest rate falls to r_2.

A Global Market for Loanable Funds? As we've noted, international capital flows can be an important influence on interest rates. What determines these capital flows? Most of the time, capital flows from countries where interest rates are relatively low to countries where interest rates are relatively high. And the result of these flows is to raise interest rates where they were low, and reduce rates where they were high.

FIGURE 6 An Increase in the Supply of Loanable Funds

If the quantity of funds supplied by lenders rises at any given interest rate, the supply of loanable funds shifts rightward from S_1 to S_2. As a result, the equilibrium interest rate falls from r_1 to r_2.

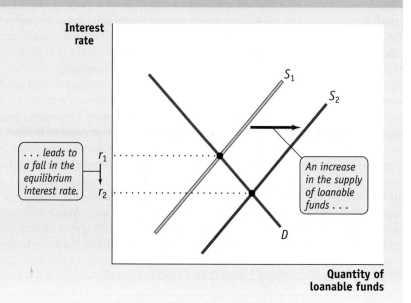

... leads to a fall in the equilibrium interest rate.

An increase in the supply of loanable funds ...

global loanable funds market a situation in which international capital flows are so large that they equalize interest rates across countries.

For some purposes, it is useful to think about what would happen if this process went all the way—if international capital flows were so large that they had the effect of completely equalizing interest rates across countries. In that case, we could talk about a **global loanable funds market.**

Figure 7 shows how such a market would work. We imagine a world consisting of only two countries, the United States and Britain. Panel (a) shows the loanable funds market in the United States, where the equilibrium in the absence of international capital flows is at point E_{US}, with an interest rate of 6%. Panel (b) shows the loanable funds market in Britain, where the equilibrium in the absence of international capital flows is at point E_B, with an interest rate of 2%.

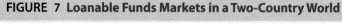

FIGURE 7 Loanable Funds Markets in a Two-Country World

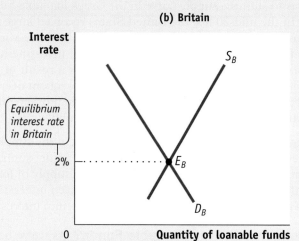

Here we show two countries, the United States and Britain, each with its own loanable funds market. The equilibrium interest rate is 6% in the U.S. market but only 2% in the British market. This creates an incentive for capital to flow from Britain to the United States.

Will the actual interest rate in the United States remain at 6% and that in Britain at 2%? Not if it is easy for British residents to make loans to Americans. In that case, British lenders, attracted by high U.S. interest rates, will send some of their loanable funds to the United States. This capital inflow will increase the quantity of loanable funds supplied to American borrowers, pushing the U.S. interest rate down. It will also reduce the quantity of loanable funds supplied to British borrowers, pushing the British interest rate up. So international capital flows will narrow the gap between U.S. and British interest rates.

Let's further suppose that British lenders consider a loan to an American to be just as good as a loan to one of their own compatriots, and that U.S. borrowers regard a debt to a British lender as no more costly than a debt to a U.S. lender. In that case, the flow of funds from Britain to the United States will continue until the gap between their interest rates is eliminated. In other words, when residents of the two countries believe that foreign assets and foreign liabilities are as good as domestic ones, then international capital flows will equalize the interest rates in the two countries.

Figure 8 shows how an international equilibrium in the loanable funds market arises. In this case, the equilibrium interest rate is 4% in both the United States and Britain. At this interest rate, the quantity of loanable funds demanded by U.S. borrowers exceeds the quantity of loanable funds supplied by U.S. lenders. This gap is filled by "imported" funds—a capital inflow from Britain. At the same time, the quantity of loanable funds supplied by British lenders is greater than the quantity of loanable funds demanded by British borrowers. This excess is "exported" in the form of a capital outflow to the United States. A global loanable funds market arises as the two markets are in equilibrium at a common interest rate of 4%. At that rate, the total quantity of loans demanded by borrowers across the two markets is equal to the total quantity of loans supplied by lenders across the two markets.

In short, international flows of capital are like international flows of goods and services. Capital moves from places where it would be cheap in the absence

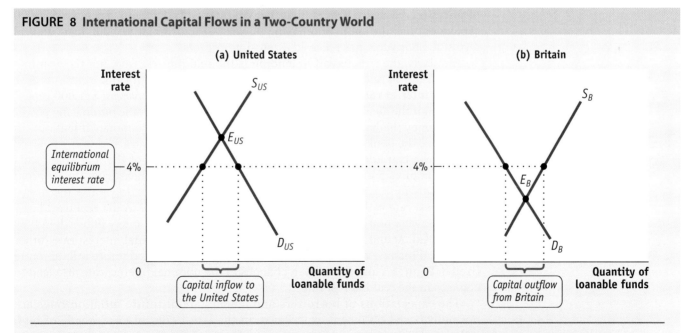

FIGURE 8 International Capital Flows in a Two-Country World

British lenders lend to borrowers in the United States, leading to equalization of interest rates at 4% in both countries. At that rate, U.S. borrowing exceeds U.S. lending; the difference is made up by capital inflows to the United States. Meanwhile, British lending exceeds British borrowing; the excess is a capital outflow from Britain.

of international capital flows to places where it would be expensive in the absence of such flows.

In practice, this picture is complicated by various factors. In particular, countries use different currencies—the United States uses dollars, Britain uses pounds—and when you compare the interest rate on loans in dollars with the rate on loans in pounds, you need to take into account the possibility that the value of a pound in dollars can change over time. Still, the concept of a global market for loanable funds is very useful for some purposes, and we will return to this concept in later chapters.

Inflation and Interest Rates Anything that shifts either the supply of loanable funds curve or the demand for loanable funds curve changes the interest rate. Historically, major changes in interest rates have been driven by many factors, including changes in government policy and technological innovations that created new investment opportunities.

However, arguably the most important factor affecting interest rates over time—the main reason, for example, that interest rates today are much lower than they were in the late 1970s and early 1980s—is changing expectations about future inflation, which shift both the supply and the demand for loanable funds.

To understand the effect of expected future inflation on interest rates, recall our discussion in Chapter 8 of the way inflation creates winners and losers—for example, the way that higher than expected U.S. inflation in the 1970s and 1980s reduced the real value of homeowners' mortgages, which was good for the homeowners but bad for the banks. We also learned that economists summarize the effect of inflation on borrowers and lenders by distinguishing between the *nominal interest rate* and the *real interest rate,* where the difference is:

$$\text{Real interest rate} = \text{Nominal interest rate} - \text{Inflation rate}$$

The true cost of borrowing is the real interest rate, not the nominal interest rate. To see why, suppose a firm borrows $10,000 for one year at a 10% nominal interest rate. At the end of the year, it must repay $11,000—the amount borrowed plus the interest. But suppose that over the course of the year the average level of prices increases by 10%, so that the real interest rate is zero. Then the $11,000 repayment has the same purchasing power as the original $10,000 loan. In real terms, the borrower has received a zero-interest loan.

Similarly, the true payoff to lending is the real interest rate, not the nominal interest rate. Suppose that a bank makes a $10,000 loan for one year at a 10% nominal interest rate. At the end of the year, the bank receives an $11,000 repayment. But if the average level of prices rises by 10% per year, the purchasing power of the money the bank gets back is no more than that of the money it lent out. In real terms, the bank has made a zero-interest loan.

Now we can add an important detail to our analysis of the loanable funds market. Figures 5 and 6 are drawn with the vertical axis measuring the *nominal interest rate for a given expected future inflation rate.* Why do we use the nominal interest rate rather than the real interest rate? Because in the real world neither borrowers nor lenders know what the future inflation rate will be when they make a deal. Actual loan contracts therefore specify a nominal interest rate rather than a real interest rate. Because we are holding the expected future inflation rate fixed in Figures 5 and 6, however, changes in the nominal interest rate also lead to changes in the real interest rate.

The expectations of borrowers and lenders about future inflation rates are normally based on recent experience. In the late 1970s, after a decade of high inflation, borrowers and lenders expected future inflation to be high. By the late 1990s, after a decade of fairly low inflation, borrowers and lenders expected future inflation to be low. And these changing expectations about future inflation had a

FIGURE 9 The Fisher Effect

D_0 and S_0 are the demand and supply curves for loanable funds when the expected future inflation rate is 0%. At an expected inflation rate of 0%, the equilibrium nominal interest rate is 4%. An increase in expected future inflation pushes both the demand and supply curves upward by 1 percentage point for every percentage point increase in expected future inflation. D_{10} and S_{10} are the demand and supply curves for loanable funds when the expected future inflation rate is 10%. The 10 percentage point increase in expected future inflation raises the equilibrium nominal interest rate to 14%. The expected real interest rate remains at 4%, and the equilibrium quantity of loanable funds also remains unchanged.

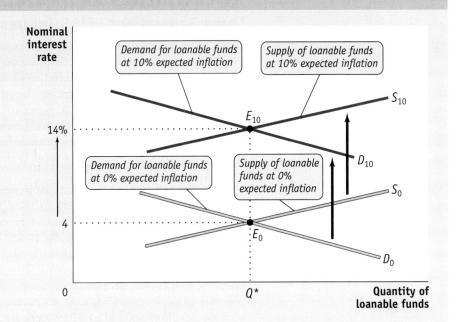

strong effect on the nominal interest rate, largely explaining why nominal interest rates were much lower in the early years of the twenty-first century than they were in the early 1980s.

Let's look at how changes in the expected future rate of inflation are reflected in the loanable funds model.

In Figure 9, the curves S_0 and D_0 show the supply and demand for loanable funds given that the expected future rate of inflation is 0%. In that case, equilibrium is at E_0, and the equilibrium nominal interest rate is 4%. Because expected future inflation is 0%, the equilibrium expected real interest rate over the life of the loan is also 4%.

Now suppose that the expected future inflation rate rises to 10%. The demand curve for loanable funds shifts upward to D_{10}: borrowers are now willing to borrow as much at a nominal interest rate of 14% as they were previously willing to borrow at 4%. That's because with a 10% inflation rate, a 14% nominal interest rate corresponds to a 4% real interest rate.

Similarly, the supply curve of loanable funds shifts upward to S_{10}: lenders require a nominal interest rate of 14% to persuade them to lend as much as they would previously have lent at 4%. The new equilibrium is at E_{10}: the result of an expected future inflation rate of 10% is that the equilibrium nominal interest rate rises from 4% to 14%.

This situation can be summarized as a general principle, known as the **Fisher effect** (after the U.S. economist Irving Fisher, who proposed it in 1930): *the expected real interest rate is unaffected by changes in expected future inflation.*

According to the Fisher effect, an increase in expected future inflation drives up the nominal interest rate, where each additional percentage point of expected future inflation drives up the nominal interest rate by 1 percentage point. The central point is that both lenders and borrowers base their decisions on the expected real interest rate. As a result, a change in the expected rate of inflation does not affect the equilibrium quantity of loanable funds or the expected real interest rate; all it affects is the equilibrium nominal interest rate.

Fisher effect the principle by which an increase in expected future inflation drives up the nominal interest rate, leaving the expected real interest rate unchanged.

ECONOMICS >> *in Action*
Three Generations of U.S. Interest Rates

There have been some large movements in U.S. interest rates dating back to the 1950s. These movements clearly show how both changes in expected future inflation and changes in the expected return on investment spending move interest rates.

Panel (a) of Figure 10 illustrates the first effect. It shows the average interest rate on bonds issued by the U.S. government—specifically, bonds for which the government promises to repay the full amount after 10 years—from 1953 to 2020, along with the rate of consumer price inflation over the same period. As you can see, the big story about interest rates is the way they soared in the 1970s, before coming back down in the 1980s.

It's not hard to see why that happened: inflation shot up during the 1970s, leading to widespread expectations that high inflation would continue. And as we've seen, a higher expected inflation rate raises the equilibrium interest rate. As the inflation rate came down in the 1980s, so did expectations of future inflation, and this brought interest rates down as well.

Panel (b) illustrates the second effect: changes in the expected return on investment spending and interest rates, with a "close-up" of interest rates and an estimate of expected inflation from 2000 to 2019. (We stop the data at that point, because developments after 2019 were strongly affected by the coronavirus pandemic and the policy response, which we discuss in Chapter 13.) Interest rates fell sharply over that period, from more than 5% in the early 2000s to 2% to 3% in the late 2010s. Yet expected inflation didn't fall very much. What happened instead seems to have been a decline in perceived investment returns. Economists are still debating the causes of this decline, although many point to a slowdown in the rate of growth in the working-age population, which has reduced the need for new housing, office buildings, and other forms of capital.

Throughout this whole process, total savings was equal to total investment spending, and the rise and fall of the interest rate played a key role in matching lenders with borrowers.

FIGURE 10 Changes in U.S. Expected Inflation and Interest Rates

(a) From 1953 to 2020

(b) From 2000 to 2020

Note: Interest and inflation rate (measured in percent) on *y*-axis.
Data from: (a) Federal Reserve Bank of St. Louis. (b) Federal Reserve Bank of St. Louis; Federal Reserve Bank of Cleveland.

>> Check Your Understanding 10-1

Solutions appear at back of book.

1. Use a diagram of the loanable funds market to illustrate the effect of the following events on the equilibrium interest rate and investment spending.
   a. An economy is opened to international movements of capital, and a net capital inflow occurs.
   b. Retired people generally save less than working people at any interest rate. The proportion of retired people in the population goes up.

2. Explain what is wrong with the following statement: "Savings and investment spending may not be equal in the economy as a whole because when the interest rate rises, households will want to save more money than businesses will want to invest."

3. Suppose that expected inflation rises from 3% to 6%.
   a. How will the real interest rate be affected by this change?
   b. How will the nominal interest rate be affected by this change?
   c. What will happen to the equilibrium quantity of loanable funds?

The Financial System

A well-functioning financial system that brings together the funds of investors and the vision of entrepreneurs has made the rise of Amazon possible. But to think that this is an exclusively modern phenomenon would be misguided. Financial markets raised the funds that were used to develop colonial markets in India, to build canals across Europe, and to finance the Napoleonic wars in the eighteenth and early nineteenth centuries. Capital inflows financed the early economic development of the United States, funding investment spending in mining, railroads, and canals. In fact, many of the principal features of financial markets and assets have been well understood in Europe and the United States since the eighteenth century. These features are no less relevant today. So let's begin by understanding exactly what is traded in financial markets.

Financial markets are where households invest their current savings and their accumulated savings, or **wealth,** by purchasing *financial assets.* A **financial asset** is a paper claim that entitles the buyer to future income from the seller. For example, when a saver lends funds to a company, the loan is a financial asset sold by the company that entitles the lender (the buyer of the financial asset) to future income from the company.

A household can also invest its current savings or wealth by purchasing a **physical asset,** a tangible object that can be used to generate future income such as a preexisting house or preexisting piece of equipment. Purchasing a physical asset gives the owner the right to dispose of the object as they wish (for example, rent it or sell it).

Recall that the purchase of a financial or physical asset is typically called investing. So if you purchase a preexisting piece of equipment—say, a used airliner—you are investing in a physical asset. In contrast, if you spend funds that *add* to the stock of physical capital in the economy—say, purchasing a newly manufactured airplane—you are engaging in investment spending.

If you get a loan from your local bank—say, to buy a new car—you and the bank are creating a financial asset: your loan. A *loan* is one important kind of financial asset in the real world, one that is owned by the lender—in this case, your local bank. In creating that loan, you and the bank are also creating a **liability,** a requirement to pay income in the future.

So although your loan is a financial asset from the bank's point of view, it is a liability from your point of view. In addition to loans, there are three other important kinds of financial assets: *stocks, bonds,* and *bank deposits.* Because a financial asset is a claim to future income that someone has to pay, it is also someone

financial markets the banking, stock, and bond markets, which channel private savings and foreign lending into investment spending, government borrowing, and foreign borrowing.

wealth (of a household) the value of accumulated savings.

financial asset a paper claim that entitles the buyer to future income from the seller. Loans, stocks, bonds, and bank deposits are types of financial assets.

physical asset a claim on a tangible object that can be used to generate future income.

liability a requirement to pay income in the future.

transaction costs the expenses of negotiating and executing a deal that often prevent a mutually beneficial trade from occurring.

financial risk uncertainty about future outcomes that involve financial losses or gains.

else's liability. We'll explain in detail shortly who bears the liability for each type of financial asset.

These four types of financial assets—loans, stocks, bonds, and bank deposits—exist because the economy has developed a set of specialized markets, like the stock market and the bond market, and specialized institutions, like banks, that facilitate the flow of funds from lenders to borrowers. Taken together, these institutions and markets are known as the financial system.

A well-functioning financial system is a critical ingredient in achieving long-run growth because it encourages greater savings and investment spending. It also ensures that savings and investment spending are undertaken efficiently. To understand how this occurs, we first need to know what tasks the financial system needs to accomplish. Then we can see how the job gets done.

Three Tasks of a Financial System

Our earlier analysis of the loanable funds market ignored three important problems facing borrowers and lenders: *transaction costs, risk,* and the desire for *liquidity.* The three tasks of a financial system are to reduce these problems in a cost-effective way that enhances the efficiency of financial markets and makes it more likely that lenders and borrowers will make mutually beneficial trades—trades that make society as a whole richer. We'll turn now to examining how financial assets are designed and how institutions are developed to cope with these problems.

Task 1: Reducing Transaction Costs The expenses of actually putting together and executing a deal are known as **transaction costs.** For example, arranging a loan requires spending time and money negotiating the terms of the deal, verifying the borrower's ability to pay, drawing up and executing legal documents, and so on.

Suppose a large business decided that it wanted to raise $1 billion for investment spending. No individual would be willing to lend that much. And negotiating individual loans from thousands of different people, each willing to lend a modest amount, would impose very large total costs because each individual transaction would incur a cost. Total costs would be so large that the entire deal would probably be unprofitable for the business.

Fortunately, that's not necessary: when large businesses want to borrow money, they either go to a bank or sell bonds in the bond market. Obtaining a loan from a bank avoids large transaction costs by involving only a single borrower and a single lender. We'll explain more about how bonds work in the next section. For now, it is enough to know that the principal reason a bond market exists is to allow companies to borrow large sums of money without incurring large transaction costs.

Task 2: Reducing Risk Another problem that real-world borrowers and lenders face is **financial risk,** uncertainty about future outcomes that involve financial losses or gains. Financial risk, or simply risk, is a problem because the future is uncertain, containing the potential for losses as well as gains. For example, owning and driving a car entails the financial risk of a costly accident. Most people view potential losses and gains in an *asymmetrical* way: most people experience the loss in welfare from losing a given amount of money more intensely than they experience the increase in welfare from gaining the same amount of money.

A person who is more sensitive to a loss than to a gain of an equal dollar amount is called *risk-averse.* Most people are risk-averse, although to differing degrees. For example, people who are wealthy are typically less risk-averse than those who are not so well-off.

A well-functioning financial system helps people reduce their exposure to risk, which risk-averse people would like to do. Suppose the owner of a business expects to make a greater profit if they buy additional capital equipment, but they aren't completely sure that this greater profit will happen. The business owner could pay for the equipment by using their savings or selling their house. But if the profit is significantly less than expected, the business owner will have lost savings, a house, or both. That is, the owner would be exposed to a lot of risk due to uncertainty about how well or poorly the business performs. (This is why business owners, who typically have a significant portion of their own personal wealth tied up in their businesses, are usually more tolerant of risk than the average person.)

So, being risk-averse, this business owner wants to share the risk of purchasing new capital equipment with someone, even if that requires sharing some of the profit if all goes well. A business owner can do this by selling shares of the company to other people and using the money received from selling shares, rather than money from the sale of other assets, to finance the equipment purchase. By selling shares in the company, the business owner reduces personal losses if the profit is less than expected: the owner won't have lost any other assets. But if things go well, the shareholders earn a share of the profit as a return on their investment.

By selling a share of the business, the owner has achieved *diversification:* the owner has been able to invest in several things in a way that lowers total risk. The owner has maintained their investment in their bank account, a financial asset; in ownership of their house, a physical asset; and in ownership of the unsold portion of their business, a financial asset. These investments are likely to carry some risk of their own; for example, the bank may fail or the house may burn down (though in the modern United States it is likely that the business owner is partly protected against these risks by insurance).

But even in the absence of insurance, the business owner is better off having maintained investments in these different assets because their different risks are *unrelated,* or *independent, events.* This means, for example, that the house is no more likely to burn down if the business does poorly and that the bank is no more likely to fail if the house burns down.

To put it another way, if one asset performs poorly, it is very likely that the other assets will be unaffected and, as a result, the total risk of loss has been reduced. But if the business owner had invested all their wealth in their business, the owner would have faced the prospect of losing everything if the business had performed poorly. By engaging in **diversification**—investing in several assets with unrelated, or independent, risks—our business owner has lowered the total risk of loss.

The desire of individuals to manage and reduce their total risk by engaging in diversification is why we have stocks and a stock market, as we'll explain in detail in the next section.

Task 3: Providing Liquidity   The financial system also exists to provide investors with *liquidity,* a concern that—like risk—arises because the future is uncertain. Suppose that, having made a loan, a lender suddenly finds themself in need of cash—say, to meet a medical emergency. Unfortunately, if that loan was made to a business that used it to buy new equipment, the business cannot repay the loan on short notice to satisfy the lender's need to recover the money. Knowing in advance that there is a danger of needing to get the money back before the term of the loan is up, our lender might be reluctant to lock up the money by lending it to a business.

An asset is **liquid** if it can be quickly converted into cash with relatively little loss of value, **illiquid** if it cannot. As we'll see, stocks and bonds are a partial answer to the problem of liquidity. Banks provide an additional way for individuals to hold liquid assets and still finance illiquid investment spending projects, such as buying capital equipment for a business.

To help lenders and borrowers make mutually beneficial deals, then, the economy needs ways to reduce transaction costs, to reduce and manage risk through diversification, and to provide liquidity. How does it achieve these tasks?

diversification investment in several different assets with unrelated, or independent, risks, so that the possible losses are independent events.

liquid describes an asset that can be quickly converted into cash with relatively little loss of value.

illiquid describes an asset that cannot be quickly converted into cash with relatively little loss of value.

loan a lending agreement between an individual lender and an individual borrower. Loans are usually tailored to the individual borrower's needs and ability to pay but carry relatively high transaction costs.

default the failure of a bond issuer to make payments as specified by the bond contract.

loan-backed securities assets created by pooling individual loans and selling shares in that pool.

Types of Financial Assets

Recall that in the modern economy there are four main types of financial assets: *loans, bonds, stocks,* and *bank deposits.* In addition, financial innovation has allowed the creation of a wide range of *loan-backed securities.* Each asset serves a somewhat different purpose. We'll examine loans, bonds, stocks, and loan-backed securities now, reserving our discussion of bank deposits until the following section.

Loans A lending agreement made between an individual lender and an individual borrower is a **loan.** Most people encounter loans in the form of a student loan or a bank loan to finance the purchase of a car or a house. And small businesses usually use bank loans to buy new equipment.

The good aspect of loans is that a given loan is usually tailored to the needs of the borrower. Before a small business can get a loan, it usually has to discuss its business plans, its profits, and so on with the lender. This results in a loan that meets the borrower's needs and ability to pay.

The bad aspect of loans is that making a loan to an individual person or a business typically involves a lot of transaction costs, such as the cost of negotiating the terms of the loan, investigating the borrower's credit history and ability to repay, and so on. To minimize these costs, large borrowers such as major corporations and governments often take a more streamlined approach: they sell (or issue) bonds.

Bonds An IOU issued by a borrower is known as a bond. Normally, the seller of the bond promises to pay a fixed sum of interest each year and to repay the principal—the value stated on the face of the bond—to the owner of the bond on a particular date. So a bond is a financial asset from its owner's point of view and a liability from its issuer's point of view.

A bond issuer sells a number of bonds with a given interest rate and maturity date to whoever is willing to buy them, a process that avoids costly negotiation of the terms of a loan with many individual lenders.

Bond purchasers can acquire information free of charge on the quality of the bond issuer, such as the bond issuer's credit history, from bond-rating agencies rather than incurring the expense of investigating it themselves. A particular concern for investors is the possibility of **default,** the risk that the bond issuer will fail to make payments as specified by the bond contract. Once a bond's risk of default has been rated, it can be sold on the bond market as a more or less standardized product, one with clearly defined terms and quality. In general, bonds with a higher default risk must pay a higher interest rate to attract investors.

Another important advantage of bonds is that they are easy to resell. This provides liquidity to bond purchasers. Indeed, a bond will often pass through many hands before it finally comes due. Loans, in contrast, are much more difficult to resell because, unlike bonds, they are not standardized: they differ in size, quality, terms, and so on. This makes them a lot less liquid than bonds.

Loan-Backed Securities Assets created by pooling individual loans and selling shares in that pool (a process called *securitization*) are called **loan-backed securities.** This type of asset has become extremely popular over the past two decades. While mortgage-backed securities—in which thousands of individual home mortgages are pooled and shares are sold to investors—are the best-known example, securitization has also been widely applied to student loans, credit card loans, and auto loans.

These loan-backed securities are traded on financial markets like bonds; they are preferred by investors because they provide more diversification and liquidity than individual loans. However, with so many loans packaged together, it can be difficult to assess the true quality of the asset. That difficulty came to haunt investors during the financial crisis of 2008, when the bursting of the housing bubble led to widespread defaults on mortgages and large losses for holders of supposedly "safe" mortgage-backed securities, pain that spread throughout the entire financial system.

Stocks A share in the ownership of a company is a stock. A share of stock is a financial asset from its owner's point of view and a liability from the company's point of view. Not all companies sell shares of their stock; privately held companies are owned by an individual or a few partners, who get to keep all of the company's profit. Most large companies, however, do sell stock. For example, Microsoft has nearly 8 billion shares outstanding; if you buy one of those shares, you are entitled to one eight billionth of the company's profit, as well as 1 of 8 billion votes on company decisions.

Why does Microsoft, historically a very profitable company, allow you to buy a share in its ownership? Why didn't Bill Gates and Paul Allen, the two founders of Microsoft, keep complete ownership for themselves and just sell bonds for their investment spending needs? The reason, as we have just learned, is risk: few individuals are risk-tolerant enough to face the risk involved in being the sole owner of a large company.

Reducing the risk that business owners face, however, is not the only way in which the existence of stocks improves society's welfare: it also improves the welfare of investors who buy stocks. Shareowners are able to enjoy the higher returns over time that stocks generally offer in comparison to bonds. Over the past century, stocks have typically yielded about 7% after adjusting for inflation; bonds have yielded only about 2%. But as investment companies warn you, "past performance is no guarantee of future results."

And there is a downside: owning the stock of a given company is riskier than owning a bond issued by the same company. Why? Loosely speaking, a bond is a promise while a stock is a hope: by law, a company must pay what it owes its lenders before it distributes any profit to its shareholders. And if the company should fail (that is, be unable to pay its interest obligations and declare bankruptcy), its physical and financial assets go to its bondholders—its lenders—while its shareholders generally receive nothing. So although a stock generally provides a higher return to an investor than a bond, it also carries higher risk.

But the financial system has devised ways to help investors as well as business owners simultaneously manage risk and enjoy somewhat higher returns. It does that through the services of institutions known as *financial intermediaries.*

Financial Intermediaries

A **financial intermediary** is an institution that transforms funds gathered from many individuals into financial assets. The most important types of financial intermediaries are *mutual funds, pension funds, life insurance companies,* and *banks.* About three-quarters of the financial assets Americans own are held through these intermediaries rather than directly.

Mutual Funds As we've seen, owning shares of a company entails accepting risk in return for a higher potential reward. But it should come as no surprise that stock investors can lower their total risk by engaging in diversification. By owning a *diversified portfolio* of stocks—a group of stocks in which risks are unrelated to, or offset by, one another—rather than concentrating investment in the shares of a single company or a group of related companies, investors can reduce their risk.

In addition, financial advisers, aware that most people are risk-averse, almost always advise their clients to diversify not only their stock portfolio but also their entire wealth by holding other assets in addition to stock—assets such as bonds and cash. (And, for good measure, to have plenty of insurance in case of accidental losses.)

financial intermediary an institution, such as a mutual fund, pension fund, life insurance company, or bank, that transforms the funds it gathers from many individuals into financial assets.

TABLE 1 Vanguard 500 Index Fund, Top Holdings (as of March 2023)

Company	Percent of mutual fund assets invested in a company
Apple Inc.	6.62%
Microsoft Corp.	5.58
Amazon.com Inc.	2.51
NVIDIA Corp.	1.74
Tesla Inc.	1.66
Berkshire Hathaway Inc. Class B	1.65
Alphabet Inc. Class A	1.62
Alphabet Inc. Class C	1.44
Exxon Mobil Corp.	1.36
UnitedHealth Group Inc.	1.34

Data from: Morningstar.

However, for individuals who don't have a large amount of money to invest—say, $1 million or more—building a diversified stock portfolio can incur high transaction costs (particularly fees paid to stockbrokers) because they are buying a few shares of a lot of companies. Fortunately for such investors, *mutual funds* help solve the problem of achieving diversification without high transaction costs.

A **mutual fund** is a financial intermediary that creates a stock portfolio by buying and holding shares in companies and then selling shares of the stock portfolio to individual investors. By buying these shares, investors with a relatively small amount of money to invest can indirectly hold a diversified portfolio, achieving a better return for any given level of risk than they could otherwise achieve. Table 1 shows an example of a diversified mutual fund, the Vanguard 500 Index Fund. It shows the percentage of investors' money invested in the stocks of the largest companies in the mutual fund's portfolio.

Many mutual funds also perform market research on the companies they invest in. This is important because there are thousands of stock-issuing U.S. companies (not to mention foreign companies), each differing in terms of its likely profitability, dividend payments, and so on. It would be extremely time-consuming and costly for an individual investor to do adequate research on even a small number of companies. Mutual funds save transaction costs by doing this research for their customers.

The mutual fund industry represents a huge portion of the modern U.S. economy, not just of the U.S. financial system. In total, U.S. mutual funds had assets of $29.6 trillion at the end of 2022. In 2022, the largest mutual fund company was Blackrock with $10.1 trillion in assets in mutual funds. Vanguard is the second largest with $8.1 trillion.

We should mention, by the way, that mutual funds charge fees for their services. These fees are quite small for mutual funds that simply hold a diversified portfolio of stocks without trying to pick winners. But the fees charged by mutual funds that claim to have special expertise in investing your money can be quite high.

Pension Funds and Life Insurance Companies In addition to mutual funds, many Americans have holdings in **pension funds,** nonprofit institutions that collect the savings of their members and invest those funds in a wide variety of assets, providing their members with income when they retire. Although pension funds are subject to some special rules and receive special treatment for tax purposes, they function much like mutual funds. They invest in a diverse array of financial assets, allowing their members to achieve more cost-effective diversification and market research than they would be able to achieve individually. At the end of 2022, pension funds in the United States held more than $26.3 trillion in assets.

Americans also have substantial holdings in the policies of **life insurance companies,** which guarantee a payment to the policyholder's beneficiaries (typically, the family) when the policyholder dies. By enabling policyholders to cushion their beneficiaries from financial hardship arising from their death, life insurance companies also improve welfare by reducing risk.

Banks Recall the problem of liquidity: other things equal, people want assets that can be readily converted into cash. Bonds and stocks are much more liquid than physical assets or loans, yet the transaction cost of selling bonds or stocks to meet a sudden expense can be large. Furthermore, for many small and moderate-size companies, the cost of issuing bonds and stocks is too large given the modest amount of money they seek to raise. A *bank* is an institution that helps resolve the conflict between lenders' needs for liquidity and the financing needs of borrowers who don't want to use the stock or bond markets.

mutual fund a financial intermediary that creates a stock portfolio by buying and holding shares in companies and then selling shares of this portfolio to individual investors.

pension fund a type of mutual fund that holds assets in order to provide retirement income to its members.

life insurance company a financial intermediary that sells policies guaranteeing a payment to a policyholder's beneficiaries when the policyholder dies.

GLOBAL COMPARISON   CORPORATE BONDS IN THE UNITED STATES AND THE EURO AREA

A business that wants to borrow funds could do this two ways: by selling bonds to investors or by getting loans from banks. There are advantages and disadvantages to each strategy.

On the one hand, issuing bonds tends to be cheaper than borrowing from a bank, because it eliminates the middleman. Also, banks often place conditions on loans, restricting the borrower's freedom to conduct its business as it chooses. On the other hand, bank loans can be less risky than issuing bonds. If a borrower gets into difficulty, its bank will typically be supportive, offering more time to repay if a good plan is in place to fix their problems. Bond holders are much less flexible.

It's a tough choice — and interestingly, companies in the United States and their counterparts in Europe generally make different choices. The figure shows the value of bonds issued by nonfinancial corporations in the United States and in the euro area, the group of European countries using the euro as a common currency, both expressed as a percentage of GDP in 2022. U.S. companies issue more bonds than their European counterparts, who rely much more on bank borrowing.

Why the difference? Generally, U.S. companies are more inclined to take risks. Also, European households are more inclined than

U.S. households to leave large sums in bank accounts. As a result, European banks have more money to lend than their U.S. counterparts.

Data from: BIS Statistics Explorer.

A bank works by first accepting funds from *depositors:* when you put your money in a bank, you are essentially becoming a lender by lending the bank your money. In return, you receive credit for a **bank deposit**—a claim on the bank, which is obliged to give you your cash if and when you demand it. So a bank deposit is a financial asset owned by the depositor and a liability of the bank that holds it.

A bank, however, keeps only a fraction of its customers' deposits in the form of ready cash. Most of its deposits are lent out to businesses, buyers of new homes, and other borrowers. These loans come with a long-term commitment by the bank to the borrower: as long as the borrower makes their payments on time, the loan cannot be recalled by the bank and converted into cash. So a bank enables those who wish to borrow for long lengths of time to use the funds of those who wish to lend but simultaneously want to maintain the ability to get their cash back on demand.

More formally, a **bank** is a financial intermediary that provides liquid financial assets in the form of deposits to lenders and uses their funds to finance the illiquid investment spending needs of borrowers. In essence, a bank is engaging in a kind of mismatch: lending for long periods of time while subject to the condition that its depositors could demand their funds back at any time. How can it manage that?

The bank counts on the fact that, on average, only a small fraction of its depositors will want their cash at the same time. On any given day, some people will make withdrawals and others will make new deposits; these will roughly cancel each other out. So the bank needs to keep only a limited amount of cash on hand to satisfy its depositors.

In addition, if a bank becomes financially incapable of paying its depositors, individual bank deposits are guaranteed to depositors up to $250,000 by the Federal Deposit Insurance Corporation, or FDIC, a federal agency. This reduces the risk to a depositor of holding a bank deposit, in turn reducing the incentive to withdraw funds if concerns about the financial state of the bank should arise. So, under normal conditions, banks need to hold only a fraction of their depositors' cash.

bank deposit a claim on a bank that obliges the bank to give the depositor their cash when demanded.

bank a financial intermediary that provides liquid assets in the form of bank deposits to lenders and uses those funds to finance the illiquid investments or investment spending needs of borrowers.

By reconciling the needs of savers for liquid assets with the needs of borrowers for long-term financing, banks play a key economic role. As the following Economics in Action explains, the creation of a well-functioning banking system seems to be an important condition for economic success.

ECONOMICS >> *in Action*
Banks, Success, and South America

Reforms to the financial system made banking safer in Chile, fueling growth.

REUTERS/Rodrigo Garrido

Argentina, as we noted in Chapter 9, is a notable example of disappointing long-run economic growth. In the early twentieth century, it was considered a rich country, but GDP per capita has grown only slowly since then. And in the past few decades Argentina has fallen well behind some of its neighbors, especially Chile, Latin America's biggest economic success story. As recently as 1990, Argentina was slightly richer than Chile, but since then Chile's GDP per capita has risen at an annual rate of 3.2%, versus only 1.4% in Argentina, so that Chile is now about 50% richer than its neighbor.

What explains this difference in fortunes? There are surely multiple reasons, but financial development is probably an important factor. After a banking crisis in the early 1980s, Chile implemented reforms that made banks safer, encouraging savers to increase deposits and allowing rapid growth in loans to the private sector. Argentina, by contrast, continued to experience a series of banking crises, as well as bouts of inflation that eroded the real value of deposits.

The result is that there is vastly more financial intermediation in Chile than in Argentina. Economists often use domestic credit to the private sector, measured as a percentage of GDP, as a rough measure of the amount of financial intermediation in an economy. In advanced countries with well-developed financial institutions, this number typically ranges between 100% and 200%. In 2020, Chile's domestic credit was 125% of GDP, similar to that of advanced countries. In Argentina, the number was only 16%, indicating an economy with very limited financial intermediation. This probably means that Chile is doing a much better job than its once-richer neighbor of channeling its savings into productive investments.

>> Check Your Understanding 10-2
Solutions appear at back of book.

1. Rank the following assets in terms of (i) level of transaction costs, (ii) level of risk, (iii) level of liquidity.
   a. A bank deposit with a guaranteed interest rate
   b. A share of a highly diversified mutual fund, which can be quickly sold
   c. A share of the family business, which can be sold only if you find a buyer and all other family members agree to the sale
2. What relationship would you expect to find between the level of development of a country's financial system and its level of economic development? Explain in terms of the country's level of savings and level of investment spending.

‖ Financial Fluctuations

We've learned that the financial system is an essential part of the economy; without stock markets, bond markets, and banks, long-run economic growth would be hard to achieve. Yet the news isn't entirely good: the financial system sometimes doesn't function well and instead is a source of instability in the short run.

In fact, the financial consequences of a sharp fall in housing prices became a major problem for economic policy makers starting in the summer of 2007. By the fall of 2008, it was clear that the U.S. economy faced a severe slump as it adjusted to the consequences of greatly reduced home values, and unemployment stayed elevated for years. We could easily write a whole book on asset market fluctuations. In fact, many people have. Here, we briefly discuss the causes of asset price fluctuations.

The Demand for Stocks

Once a company issues shares of stock to investors, those shares can then be resold to other investors in the stock market. And thanks to cable TV and the internet, you can easily spend all day watching stock market fluctuations—the movement up and down of the prices of individual stocks—as well as summary measures of stock prices like the Dow Jones Industrial Average. These fluctuations reflect changes in supply and demand by investors. But what causes the supply and demand for stocks to shift?

Remember that stocks are financial assets: they are shares in the ownership of a company. Unlike a good or service, whose value to its owner comes from its consumption, the value of an asset comes from its ability to generate higher future consumption of goods or services.

A financial asset allows higher future consumption in two ways. First, many financial assets provide regular income to their owners in the form of interest payments or dividends. But many companies don't pay dividends; instead, they retain their earnings to finance future investment spending. Investors purchase non-dividend-paying stocks in the belief that they will earn income from selling the stock in the future at a profit, the second way of generating higher future income. Even in the cases of a bond or a dividend-paying stock, investors will not want to purchase an asset that they believe will sell for less in the future than today, because such an asset will reduce their wealth when they sell it.

So the value of a financial asset today depends on investors' beliefs about the future value or price of the asset. If investors believe that it will be worth more in the future, they will demand more of the asset today at any given price; consequently, today's equilibrium price of the asset will rise. Conversely, if investors

---

FOR INQUIRING MINDS   How Now, Dow Jones?

Financial news reports often lead with the day's stock market action, as measured by changes in the Dow Jones Industrial Average, the S&P 500, and the NASDAQ.

All three are stock market indices. Like the consumer price index, they are numbers constructed as a summary of average prices—in this case, prices of stocks.

- The Dow, created by the financial analysis company Dow Jones, is an index of the prices of stock in 30 leading companies.

- The S&P 500 is an index of 500 companies, created by Standard and Poor's, another financial company.

- The NASDAQ is compiled by the National Association of Securities Dealers, which trades the stocks of smaller new companies.

Because these indices contain different groups of stocks, they track somewhat different things. The Dow, because it contains only 30 of the largest companies, tends to reflect traditional business powerhouses. The NASDAQ is heavily influenced by technology stocks. The S&P 500, a broad measure, is in between.

These indexes give investors a quick, snapshot view of how stocks from certain sectors of the economy are doing. And the price of a stock embodies investors' expectations about the future prospects of the underlying company. By implication, an index composed of stocks drawn from companies in a particular sector embodies investors' expectations of the future prospects of that sector of the economy.

The numbers tell the tale.

Tetra Images/AGE Fotostock

believe the asset will be worth less in the future, they will demand less today at any given price; consequently, today's equilibrium price of the asset will fall. Today's stock prices will change according to changes in investors' expectations about future stock prices.

Suppose an event occurs that leads to a rise in the expected future price of a company's shares—say, for example, Apple announces that it forecasts higher than expected profitability due to torrential sales of the latest version of the iPhone. Demand for Apple shares will increase. At the same time, existing shareholders will be less willing to supply their shares to the market at any given price, leading to a decrease in the supply of Apple shares. And as we know, an increase in demand or a decrease in supply (or both) leads to a rise in price.

Alternatively, suppose that an event occurs that leads to a fall in the expected future price of a company's shares—say, Home Depot announces that it expects lower profitability because a slump in home sales has depressed the demand for home improvements. Demand for Home Depot shares will decrease. At the same time, supply will increase because existing shareholders will be more willing to supply their Home Depot shares to the market. Both changes lead to a fall in the stock price.

So stock prices are determined by the supply and demand for shares—which, in turn, depend on investors' expectations about the future stock price.

Stock prices are also affected by changes in the attractiveness of substitute assets, like bonds. As we learned early on, the demand for a particular good decreases when purchasing a substitute good becomes more attractive—say, due to a fall in its price. The same lesson holds true for stocks: when purchasing bonds becomes more attractive due to a rise in interest rates, stock prices will fall. And when purchasing bonds becomes less attractive due to a fall in interest rates, stock prices will rise.

The Demand for Other Assets

Everything we've just said about stocks applies to other assets as well, including physical assets. Consider the demand for commercial real estate—office buildings, shopping malls, and other structures that provide space for business activities. An investor who buys an office building does so for two reasons. First, because space in the building can be rented out, the owner of the building receives income in the form of rent. Second, the investor may expect the building to rise in value, meaning that it can be sold at a higher price at some future date.

As in the case of stocks, the demand for commercial real estate also depends on the attractiveness of substitute assets, especially bonds. When interest rates rise, the demand for commercial real estate decreases; when interest rates fall, the demand for commercial real estate increases.

Most Americans don't own commercial real estate. Only half of the population owns any stock, even indirectly through mutual funds, and for most of those people, stock ownership is well under $50,000. However, at the end of 2022 about 66% of American households owned another kind of asset: their own homes. What determines housing prices?

You might wonder whether home prices can be analyzed the same way we analyze stock prices or the price of commercial real estate. After all, stocks pay dividends, commercial real estate yields rents, but when a family lives in its own home, no money changes hands.

In economic terms, however, that doesn't matter very much. To a large extent, the benefit of owning your own home is the fact that you don't have to pay rent to someone else—or, to put it differently, it's as if you were paying rent to yourself. In fact, the U.S. government includes *implicit rent*—an estimate of the amount that homeowners, in effect, pay to themselves—in its estimates of GDP. The amount people are willing to pay for a house depends in part on the implicit rent they expect to receive from that house.

The demand for housing, like the demand for other assets, also depends on what people expect to happen to future prices: they're willing to pay more for a house if they believe they can sell it at a higher price sometime in the future.

Last but not least, the demand for houses depends on interest rates: a rise in the interest rate increases the cost of a mortgage and leads to a decrease in housing demand; a fall in the interest rate reduces the cost of a mortgage and causes an increase in housing demand.

All asset prices, then, are determined by a similar set of factors. But we haven't yet fully answered the question of what determines asset prices because we haven't explained what determines investors' *expectations* about future asset prices.

Asset Price Expectations

There are two principal competing views about how asset price expectations are determined. One view, which comes from traditional economic analysis, emphasizes the rational reasons why expectations *should* change. The other, widely held by market participants and also supported by some economists, emphasizes the irrationality of market participants.

The Efficient Markets Hypothesis Suppose you were trying to assess what Home Depot's stock is really worth. To do this, you would look at the *fundamentals,* the underlying determinants of the company's future profits. These would include factors like the changing shopping habits of the U.S. public and the prospects for home remodeling. You would also want to compare the earnings you could expect to receive from Home Depot with the likely returns on other financial assets, such as bonds.

According to one view of asset prices, the value you would come up with after a careful study of this kind would, in fact, turn out to be the price at which Home Depot stock is already selling in the market. Why? Because all publicly available information about Home Depot's fundamentals is already embodied in its stock price. Any difference between the market price and the value suggested by a careful analysis of the underlying fundamentals indicates a profit opportunity to smart investors, who then sell Home Depot stock if it looks overpriced and buy it if it looks underpriced.

The **efficient markets hypothesis** is the general form of this view; it means that asset prices always embody all publicly available information. One implication of the efficient markets hypothesis is that at any point in time, stock prices are fairly valued: they reflect all currently available information about fundamentals. So they are neither overpriced nor underpriced.

Another implication of the efficient markets hypothesis is that the prices of stocks and other assets should change only in response to new information about the underlying fundamentals. Since new information is by definition unpredictable—if it were predictable, it wouldn't be new information—movements in asset prices are also unpredictable. As a result, the movement of, say, stock prices will follow a **random walk**—the general term for the movement over time of an unpredictable variable.

The efficient markets hypothesis plays an important role in understanding how financial markets work. Most investment professionals and many economists, however, regard it as an oversimplification. Investors, they claim, aren't that rational.

Irrational Markets? Many people who actually trade in the markets, such as individual investors and professional money managers, are skeptical of the efficient markets hypothesis. They believe that markets often behave irrationally and that a smart investor can engage in successful *market timing*—buying stocks when they are underpriced and selling them when they are overpriced.

Although economists are generally skeptical about claims that there are surefire ways to outsmart the market, many have also challenged the efficient

efficient markets hypothesis a principle of asset price determination that holds that asset prices embody all publicly available information. The hypothesis implies that stock prices should be unpredictable, or follow a random walk, since changes should occur only in response to new information about fundamentals.

random walk the movement over time of an unpredictable variable.

FOR INQUIRING MINDS Behavioral Finance

Individuals often make irrational—sometimes predictably irrational—choices that leave them worse off economically than would other, feasible alternatives. People also have a habit of repeating the same decision-making mistakes. This kind of behavior is the subject of *behavioral economics,* which includes the rapidly growing subfield of *behavioral finance,* the study of how investors in financial markets often make predictably irrational choices. In fact, the 2013 Nobel Prize in Economics was awarded to Yale professor Robert Shiller (along with two others), for his work showing how financial markets exhibit clear signs of irrationality.

Like most people, investors depart from rationality in systematic ways. In particular, they are prone to

- *Overconfidence:* having a misguided faith that they are able to spot a winning stock
- *Loss aversion:* being unwilling to sell an unprofitable asset and accept the loss
- A *herd mentality:* buying an asset when its price has already been driven high and selling it when its price has already been driven low

This irrational behavior raises an important question: can investors who *are* rational make a lot of money at the expense of those investors who aren't—for example, by buying a company's stock if irrational fears make it cheap?

The answer to this question is sometimes yes and sometimes no. Some professional investors have made huge profits by

betting against irrational moves in the market—buying when there is irrational selling and selling when there is irrational buying. For example, the billionaire hedge fund manager John Paulson made $4 billion by betting against subprime mortgages during the U.S. housing bubble of 2007–2008 because he understood that these financial assets were being sold at inflated prices.

But sometimes even a rational investor cannot profit from market irrationality. For example, a money manager has to obey customers' orders to buy or sell even when those actions are irrational. Likewise, it can be much safer for professional money managers to follow the herd: if they do that and their investments go badly, they have the career-saving excuse that no one foresaw a problem.

But if they've gone against the herd and their investments go south, they are likely to be fired for making poor choices. So rational investors can even exacerbate the irrational moves in financial markets.

Some observers of historical trends

hypothesize that financial markets alternate between periods of complacency and forgetfulness, which breed bubbles as investors irrationally believe that prices can only go up, followed by a crash, which in turn leads investors to avoid financial markets altogether and renders asset prices irrationally cheap.

Clearly, the events of the past 20 years, with a huge housing bubble followed by extreme turmoil in financial markets, have given researchers in the area of behavioral finance a lot of material to work with.

markets hypothesis. It's important to understand, however, that finding particular examples where the market got it wrong does not disprove the efficient markets hypothesis. If the price of Home Depot stock plunges from $40 to $10 because of a sudden change in buying patterns, this doesn't mean that the market was inefficient in originally pricing the stock at $40. The fact that buying patterns were about to change wasn't publicly available information, so it wasn't embodied in the earlier stock price.

Serious challenges to the efficient markets hypothesis focus instead either on evidence of systematic misbehavior of market prices or on evidence that individual investors don't behave in the way the theory suggests. For example, some economists believe they have found strong evidence that stock prices fluctuate more than can be explained by news about fundamentals.

Others believe they have strong evidence that individual investors behave in systematically irrational ways. For example, people seem to expect that a stock that has risen in the past will keep on rising, even though the efficient markets hypothesis tells us there is no reason to expect this. The same appears to be true of other assets, especially housing: the great housing bubble, discussed in the Economics in Action that follows this section, arose in large part because homebuyers assumed that home prices would continue rising in the future.

Asset Prices and Macroeconomics

How should macroeconomists and policy makers deal with the fact that asset prices fluctuate a lot and that these fluctuations can have important economic effects? This question has become one of the major problems facing macroeconomic policy.

On one side, policy makers are reluctant to assume that the market is wrong—that asset prices are either too high or too low. In part, this reflects the efficient markets hypothesis, which says that any information that is publicly available is already accounted for in asset prices. More generally, it's hard to make the case that government officials are better judges of appropriate prices than private investors who are putting their own money on the line.

On the other side, the past 25 years were marked by not one but two huge asset bubbles, each of which created major macroeconomic problems when it burst. In the late 1990s, the prices of technology stocks, including but not limited to dot-com internet firms, soared to hard-to-justify heights. When the bubble burst, these stocks lost, on average, two-thirds of their value in a short time, helping to cause the 2001 recession and a period of high unemployment. A few years later there was a major bubble in housing prices. The collapse of this bubble in 2008 triggered a severe financial crisis followed by a deep recession, and the lingering effects of the crisis afflicted the U.S. economy years later.

These events have prompted much debate over whether and how to limit financial instability. We discuss financial regulation and the efforts to make it more effective in Chapter 14.

ECONOMICS >> *in Action*
The Rise and Fall of Mortgage Delinquencies

For the past 40 years about a quarter of U.S. investment spending, on average, has been "residential fixed investment": building places for people to live. Because these are mainly single-family homes or condos rather than apartment buildings, families must come up with large sums to purchase their dwellings, and relatively few people can afford to pay cash.

Instead, home purchases are typically paid for by taking out a mortgage—a loan from a bank or other financial intermediary that gives the lender the right to seize your house if you fail to make scheduled payments. That might sound like a risky proposition for the borrower; what if one or more members of the family lose their jobs or face unexpected medical expenses, and can't keep up the payments? In practice, however, "delinquencies"—missed payments—are normally rare, affecting only about 1 mortgage in 40. One reason the rate is so low is that families in financial difficulties can often sell their houses and pay off their loans.

As panel (a) of Figure 11 shows, however, there was a huge surge in mortgage delinquencies from 2007 to 2010, at which point almost one in eight families was missing payments. This period of widespread mortgage delinquencies lasted several years, before beginning a gradual decline. As of 2022, delinquencies were back down to normal historical levels.

What happened? As panel (b) of Figure 11 shows, there was a dramatic increase in mortgage debt between 2000 and 2007, which was closely associated with a period of rapidly rising home prices. Both borrowers and lenders believed that it was safe for homebuyers to borrow more than in the past, because rising prices would make it easy to sell houses and repay loans even if borrowers experienced financial difficulties.

As it turned out, however, the big rise in home prices was a bubble—and the bursting of the bubble provoked a severe recession, which led to high unemployment and greater financial distress. So delinquencies surged.

FIGURE 11 Debt and Delinquencies

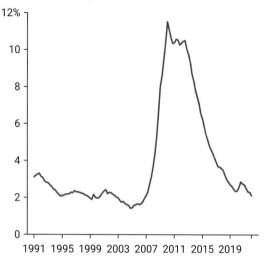

(a) Percent of Delinquencies

Data from: Board of Governors of the Federal Reserve System.

(b) Percent of GDP

Data from: Bureau of Economic Analysis and Board of Governors of the Federal Reserve System.

Eventually, as you can see in the figure, reduced borrowing and economic recovery reduced the level of mortgage debt relative to income, and delinquencies returned to more or less normal levels.

>> *Check Your Understanding* **10-3**

Solutions appear at back of book.

1. What is the likely effect of each of the following events on the stock price of a company? Explain your answers.
   a. The company announces that although profits are low this year, it has discovered a new line of business that will generate high profits next year.
   b. The company announces that although it had high profits this year, those profits will be less than had been previously announced.
   c. Other companies in the same industry announce that sales are unexpectedly slow this year.
   d. The company announces that it is on track to meet its previously forecast profit target.

2. Assess the following statement: "Although many investors may be irrational, it is unlikely that over time they will behave irrationally in exactly the same way—such as always buying stocks the day after the Dow has risen by 1%."

When Tech Stocks Took a Fall

Xinhua/Alamy Stock Photo

We began this chapter with the example of Amazon, which succeeded by making use of the power of financial markets: stock sales and borrowing allowed it to build a huge distribution system. By providing all this cash, markets were in effect engaged in a gigantic act of faith, believing that Amazon, even though it was currently losing money, could eventually deliver big profits.

For the most part, this act of faith was rewarded. Amazon did in fact become highly profitable, and those who bought in early did very well. But Amazon investors experienced some setbacks along the way. Notably, Amazon stock fell sharply between late 2021 and the end of 2022, losing roughly half its value. Why?

For the most part, the fall in Amazon stock didn't reflect concerns about Amazon's business. How do we know that? Because a number of other companies, from Microsoft to Tesla, also saw their stock prices fall.

Earlier in this chapter, we mentioned that many people track the stock market through three major indexes, of which NASDAQ is generally considered to reflect most closely what it happening to technology companies. Well, the NASDAQ experienced a large, year-long decline starting in late 2021, with the timing closely matching Amazon's slide.

So what caused a broad decline in tech stocks? The main answer, almost surely, was a rise in interest rates. Investors expect companies like Amazon to make a lot of money for many years; but as we've seen, the value of future profits today—their *present value*—depends in part on interest rates. And interest rates rose a lot between late 2021 and late 2022, for reasons that we'll discuss later in this book, when we get to the role of monetary policy in fighting inflation.

The point is that investors didn't lose faith in Amazon's ability to stay profitable far into the future, but they began placing a lower value on far-future profits. Of course, they wouldn't have been willing to pay as much for Amazon stock in, for example, early 2021 if they'd known that interest rates would rise so much. But as the old saying goes, predictions are hard, especially about the future.

QUESTIONS FOR THOUGHT

1. Using the concept of present value, explain how low interest rates from 2009 to 2021 helped boost the price of Amazon stock.

2. By early 2023, it had become apparent the Amazon overinvested in expanding their warehouse capacity. Using the concept of present value, explain how a slowdown in consumer spending will adversely affect Amazon's share price.

3. Using the loanable funds market, explain how an increase in expected inflation affects the supply and demand for loanable funds and subsequently Amazon's stock price.

SUMMARY

1. Investment in physical capital is necessary for long-run economic growth. So in order for an economy to grow, it must channel savings into investment spending.

2. According to the **savings–investment spending identity,** savings and investment spending are always equal for the economy as a whole. The government is a source of savings when it runs a positive **budget balance,** also known as a **budget surplus;** it is a source of dissavings when it runs a negative budget balance, also known as a **budget deficit.** One way a government can finance a budget deficit is by borrowing. **Government borrowing** is the total amount of funds borrowed by federal, state, and local governments in the financial markets. In a closed economy, savings is equal to **national savings,** the sum of private savings plus the budget balance. In an open or international economy, savings is equal to national savings plus **net capital inflow** of foreign savings. When a negative net capital inflow occurs, some portion of national savings is funding investment spending in other countries.

3. The hypothetical **loanable funds market** shows how loans from savers are allocated among borrowers with investment spending projects. At the **equilibrium interest rate,** the quantity of loans demanded equals the quantity of loans offered. Only those investment projects with an expected return greater or equal to the equilibrium interest rate are funded. By showing how gains from trade between lenders and borrowers are maximized, the loanable funds market shows why a well-functioning financial system leads to greater long-run economic growth. Increasing or persistent government budget deficits can lead to **crowding out:** higher interest rates and reduced investment spending. Changes in perceived business opportunities and in government borrowing shift the demand curve for loanable funds; changes in private savings and capital inflows shift the supply curve.

4. In order to evaluate a project in which the return, X, is realized in the future, you must transform X into its present value using the interest rate, r. The present value of \$1 received one year from now is \$$1/(1+r)$, the amount of money you must lend out today to have \$1 one year from now. The present value of a given project rises as the interest rate falls and falls as the interest rate rises. This tells us that the demand curve for loanable funds is downward sloping.

5. Capital flows narrow differences in interest rates across countries by flowing from low interest rate countries to high interest rate countries. When flows are large, a **global loanable funds market** arises in which interest rates are equalized across countries.

6. Because neither borrowers nor lenders can know the future inflation rate, loans specify a nominal interest rate rather than a real interest rate. For a given expected future inflation rate, shifts of the demand and supply curves of loanable funds result in changes in the underlying real interest rate, leading to changes in the nominal interest rate. According to the **Fisher effect,** an increase in expected future inflation raises the nominal interest rate one-to-one so that the expected real interest rate remains unchanged.

7. **Financial markets** are where households invest their current savings or **wealth**—their accumulated savings—by purchasing assets. Assets come in the form of either a **financial asset,** a paper claim that entitles the buyer to future income from the seller, or a **physical asset,** a tangible object that can generate future income. A financial asset is also a **liability** from the point of view of its seller. There are four main types of financial assets: loans, bonds, stocks, and **bank deposits.** Each of them serves a different purpose in addressing the three fundamental tasks of a financial system: reducing **transaction costs**—the cost of making a deal; reducing **financial risk**—uncertainty about future outcomes that involves financial gains and losses; and providing **liquid** assets—assets that can be quickly converted into cash without much loss of value (in contrast to **illiquid** assets, which are not easily converted).

8. Although many small and moderate borrowers use bank **loans** to fund investment spending, larger companies typically issue bonds. Bonds with a higher risk of **default** must typically pay a higher interest rate. Business owners reduce their risk by selling stock. Although stocks usually generate a higher return than bonds, investors typically wish to reduce their risk by engaging in **diversification,** owning a wide range of assets whose returns are based on unrelated, or independent, events. Most people are risk-averse, more sensitive to a loss than to an equal-size gain. **Loan-backed securities,** a recent innovation, are assets created by pooling individual loans and selling shares of that pool to investors. Because they are more diversified and more liquid than individual loans, bonds are preferred by investors. It can be difficult, however, to assess a bond's quality.

9. **Financial intermediaries**—institutions such as **mutual funds, pension funds, life insurance companies,** and **banks**—are critical components of the financial system. Mutual funds and pension funds allow small investors to diversify, and life insurance companies reduce risk.

10. A bank allows individuals to hold liquid bank deposits that are then used to finance illiquid loans. Banks can

perform this mismatch because on average only a small fraction of depositors withdraw their funds at any one time. A well-functioning banking sector is a key ingredient of long-run economic growth.

11. Asset market fluctuations can be a source of short-run macroeconomic instability. Asset prices are determined by supply and demand as well as by the desirability of competing assets, like bonds: when the interest rate rises, prices of stocks and physical assets such as real estate generally fall, and vice versa. Expectations drive the supply of and demand for assets: expectations of higher future prices push today's asset prices higher, and expectations of lower future prices drive them lower. One view of how expectations are formed is the **efficient markets hypothesis,** which holds that the prices of assets embody all publicly available information. It implies that fluctuations are inherently unpredictable—they follow a **random walk.**

12. Many market participants and economists believe that, based on actual evidence, financial markets are not as rational as the efficient markets hypothesis claims. Such evidence includes the fact that stock price fluctuations are too great to be driven by fundamentals alone. Likewise, policy makers do not believe that markets always behave rationally or that they can outsmart them.

KEY TERMS

Savings–investment spending identity, p. 274
Budget surplus, p. 275
Budget deficit, p. 275
Government borrowing, p. 275
Budget balance, p. 275
National savings, p. 275
Net capital inflow, p. 276
Loanable funds market, p. 278
Equilibrium interest rate, p. 281
Crowding out, p. 283
Global loanable funds market, p. 284

Fisher effect, p. 287
Financial markets, p. 289
Wealth, p. 289
Financial asset, p. 289
Physical asset, p. 289
Liability, p. 289
Transaction costs, p. 290
Financial risk, p. 290
Diversification, p. 291
Liquid, p. 291
Illiquid, p. 291

Loan, p. 292
Default, p. 292
Loan-backed securities, p. 292
Financial intermediary, p. 293
Mutual fund, p. 294
Pension fund, p. 294
Life insurance company, p. 294
Bank deposit, p. 295
Bank, p. 295
Efficient markets hypothesis, p. 299
Random walk, p. 299

PRACTICE QUESTIONS

1. Explain why equilibrium in the loanable funds market maximizes efficiency.

2. How would you respond to a friend who claims that the government should eliminate all purchases that are financed by borrowing because such borrowing crowds out private investment spending?

3. What are the important types of financial intermediaries in the U.S. economy? What are the primary assets of these intermediaries, and how do they facilitate investment spending and saving?

PROBLEMS

1. Given the following information about the closed economy of Brittania, what is the level of investment spending and private savings, and what is the budget balance? What is the relationship among the three? Is national savings equal to investment spending? There are no government transfers.

| GDP = $1,000 million | T = $50 million |
| C = $850 million | G = $100 million |

2. Given the following information about the international economy of Regalia, what is the level of investment spending and private savings, and what are the budget balance and net capital inflow? What is the relationship among the four? There are no government transfers. [*Hint:* Net capital inflow equals the value of imports (*IM*) minus the value of exports (*X*).]

GDP = $1,000 million	G = $100 million
C = $850 million	X = $100 million
T = $50 million	IM = $125 million

3. The accompanying table shows the percentage of GDP accounted for by private savings, investment spending, and net capital inflow in the economies of Capsland

and Marsalia. Capsland is currently experiencing a positive net capital inflow and Marsalia, a negative net capital inflow. What is the budget balance (as a percentage of GDP) in both countries? Are Capsland and Marsalia running a budget deficit or surplus?

	Capsland	Marsalia
Investment spending as a percentage of GDP	20%	20%
Private savings as a percentage of GDP	10	25
Net capital inflow as a percentage of GDP	5	-2

4. Assume the economy is open to capital inflows and outflows and therefore net capital inflow equals imports (IM) minus exports (X). Calculate each of the following.

a. X = $125 million
   IM = $80 million
   Budget balance = -$200 million
   I = $350 million

   Calculate private savings.

b. X = $85 million
   IM = $135 million
   Budget balance = $100 million
   Private savings = $250 million

   Calculate I.

c. X = $60 million
   IM = $95 million
   Private savings = $325 million
   I = $300 million

   Calculate the budget balance.

d. Private savings = $325 million
   I = $400 million
   Budget balance = $10 million

   Calculate $IM - X$.

5. The government is running a budget balance of zero when it decides to increase education spending by $200 billion and finance the spending by selling bonds. The accompanying diagram shows the market for loanable funds before the government sells the bonds. Assume that there are no capital inflows or outflows. How will the equilibrium interest rate and the equilibrium quantity of loanable funds change? Is there any crowding out in the market?

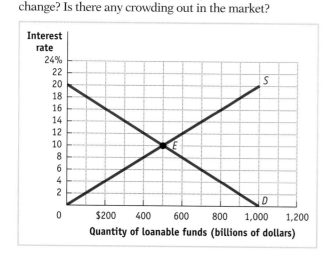

6. Congress estimated that the cost of increasing support and expanding pre-kindergarten education and infant and toddler child care would cost $28 billion in 2014. Since the U.S. government was running a budget deficit at the time, assume that the new pre-K funding was financed by government borrowing, which increases the demand for loanable funds without affecting supply. This question considers the likely effect of this government expenditure on the interest rate.

a. Draw typical demand (D_1) and supply (S_1) curves for loanable funds without the cost of the expanded pre-K programs accounted for. Label the vertical axis "Interest rate" and the horizontal axis "Quantity of loanable funds." Label the equilibrium point (E_1) and the equilibrium interest rate (r_1).

b. Now draw a new diagram with the cost of the expanded pre-K programs included in the analysis. Shift the demand curve in the appropriate direction. Label the new equilibrium point (E_2) and the new equilibrium interest rate (r_2).

c. How does the equilibrium interest rate change in response to government expenditure on the expanded pre-K programs? Explain.

7. Lynn agrees to lend Boris $10,000, which Boris will repay with interest in one year. They agree to a nominal interest rate of 8%, reflecting a real interest rate of 3% on the loan and a commonly shared expected inflation rate of 5% over the next year.

a. If the inflation rate is actually 4% over the next year, how does that lower-than-expected inflation rate affect Boris and Lynn? Who is better off?

b. If the actual inflation rate is 7% over the next year, how does that affect Boris and Lynn? Who is better off?

8. Using the accompanying diagram, explain what will happen to the market for loanable funds when there is a fall of 2 percentage points in the expected future inflation rate. How will the change in the expected future inflation rate affect the equilibrium quantity of loanable funds?

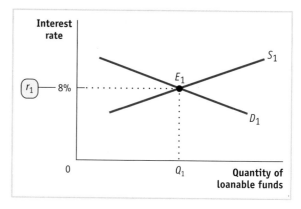

9. The accompanying diagram shows data for the interest rate on 10-year euro area government bonds and inflation rate for the euro area from 1997 through early 2023, as reported by the European Central Bank. How would you describe the relationship between the two? How does the pattern compare to that of the United States in Figure 10?

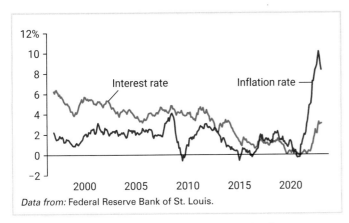

Data from: Federal Reserve Bank of St. Louis.

10. For each of the following, is it an example of investment spending, investing in financial assets, or investing in physical assets?

   a. Rupert, a wealthy investor, buys 100 shares of existing Coca-Cola stock.

   b. Rhonda, the star of a blockbuster film franchise, spends $10 million to buy a mansion built in the 1970s.

   c. Rhonda's costar, Ronald, spends $10 million to build a new mansion with a view of the Pacific Ocean.

   d. Rawlings builds a new plant to make catcher's mitts.

   e. Russia buys $100 million in U.S. government bonds.

11. Explain how a well-functioning financial system increases savings and investment spending, holding the budget balance and any capital flows fixed.

12. Explain the effect on a company's stock price today of each of the following events, other things held constant.

   a. The interest rate on bonds falls.

   b. Several companies in the same sector announce surprisingly higher sales.

   c. A change in the tax law passed last year reduces this year's profit.

   d. The company unexpectedly announces that due to an accounting error, it must amend last year's accounting statement and reduce last year's reported profit by $5 million. It also announces that this change has no implications for future profits.

13. Sallie Mae is a quasi-governmental agency that packages individual student loans into pools of loans and sells shares of these pools to investors as Sallie Mae bonds.

   a. What is this process called? What effect will it have on investors compared to situations in which they could only buy and sell individual student loans?

   b. What effect do you think Sallie Mae's actions will have on the ability of students to get loans?

   c. Suppose that a very severe recession hits and, as a consequence, many graduating students cannot get jobs and default on their student loans. What effect

will this have on Sallie Mae bonds? Why is it likely that investors now believe Sallie Mae bonds to be riskier than expected? What will be the effect on the availability of student loans?

14. Access the Discovering Data activity for Chapter 10, Problem 14 online.

   a. What is the relationship between domestic investment and national saving? How has the relationship changed over time?

   b. Calculate the difference between investment and national saving in 2008, 2014, and 2019. What does the value represent?

   c. Using the loanable funds framework, predict what would happen to interest rates in 2008, 2014, and 2019.

15. Access the Discovering Data activity for Chapter 10, Problem 15 online.

   a. In what year did the United States last run a government surplus?

   b. Calculate the deficit as a percent of GDP in 1971, 1983, 1992, 2003, and 2010. What year had the largest deficit as a percent of GDP?

   c. How would you describe the relationship between government debt and long-term interest rates?

   d. Have larger deficits increased the crowding out of private investment?

16. Use the market for loanable funds shown in the accompanying diagram to explain what happens to private savings, private investment spending, and the interest rate if each of the following events occur. Assume that there are no capital inflows or outflows.

   a. The government reduces the size of its deficit to zero.

   b. At any given interest rate, consumers decide to save more. Assume the budget balance is zero.

   c. At any given interest rate, businesses become very optimistic about the future profitability of investment spending. Assume the budget balance is zero.

Toward a Fuller Understanding of Present Value

In this appendix, we will show how you can expand the use of present value calculations to understand how businesses make investment spending decisions and how investors determine the prices of existing financial assets like stocks and bonds. We begin by showing how to apply present value calculations for one-year and multiyear projects. Then we show how to calculate the present value of a project that has revenues and costs arising in the future. Finally, we use present value to calculate the prices of financial assets like bonds and stocks.

The key point to keep in mind is that when businesses engage in investment spending, the lower the equilibrium interest rate, the greater the payoff from a project, other things equal. As a result, when the interest rate falls, more businesses will spend on investment projects. Likewise, consider an existing financial asset like a stock or bond that promises to deliver payments to its owner in the future. When the equilibrium interest rate falls, the value today of those promised future payments goes up. As a result, the prices of those existing financial assets will rise in financial markets.

How to Calculate the Present Value of One-Year Projects

Recall that the symbol r represents the interest rate, either as a percentage or decimal (that is, $r = 5\% = 0.05$). Rather than work with units of $1,000, we will calculate present value for the simplest case, units of $1.

If you lend X, at the end of one year you will receive:

(A-1) $X \times (1 + r) =$ Amount received at end of year in return for lending X

From Equation A-1, we can calculate how much you would have to lend today in order to receive $1 a year from now. To do that we set Equation A-1 equal to $1 and solve for X:

(A-2) $X \times (1 + r) = \$1$

Solving for X by dividing both sides of Equation A-2 by $(1 + r)$ gives:

(A-3) $X = \$1/(1 + r)$

As we explained in the chapter, X is the present value of $1 given an interest rate of r: it is the amount of money you would need today in order to generate a given amount of money one year from now given the interest rate r. Because r is greater than zero, X is less than $1; $1 to be delivered in the future is worth less than $1 delivered today.

Also recall from the chapter that as the interest rate goes up, the present value of a dollar delivered in the future falls. For example, the present value of $1 when $r = 0.02$ is $\$1/(1 + 0.02) = \$1/1.02 = \$0.98$, and the present value of $1 when $r = 0.10$ is $\$1/(1 + 0.10) = \$1/1.10 = \$0.91$.

How to Calculate the Present Value of Multiyear Projects

Let's represent the value of $1 to be received two years from now as X_{2yrs}. If you lend out X_{2yrs} today for two years, you will receive:

(A-4) $X_{2yrs} \times (1 + r)$ at the end of one year

which you then reinvest to receive:

(A-5) $X_{2yrs} \times (1 + r) \times (1 + r) = X_{2yrs} \times (1 + r)^2$ at the end of two years

From Equation A-5, we can calculate how much you would have to lend today in order to receive $1 two years from now:

(A-6) $X_{2yrs}(1 + r)^2 = \$1$

To solve for X_{2yrs}, divide both sides of Equation A-6 by $(1 + r)^2$ to arrive at:

(A-7) $X_{2yrs} = \$1/(1 + r)^2$

For example, if $r = 0.10$, then $X_{2yrs} = \$1/(1.10)^2 = \$1/1.21 = \$0.83$.

Equation A-7 points the way toward the general expression for present value, where $1 is paid after N years. It is:

(A-8) $X_{Nyrs} = \$1/(1 + r)^N$

In other words, the present value of $1 to be received N years from now is equal to $\$1/(1 + r)^N$.

How to Calculate the Present Value of Projects with Revenues and Costs

Suppose you have to choose one of three projects to undertake. Project A gives you an immediate payoff of $100. Project B costs you $10 now and pays $115 a year from now. Project C gives you an immediate payoff of $119 but requires you to pay $20 a year from now. We will assume that $r = 0.10$.

In order to compare these three projects, you must evaluate costs and revenues that are expended or realized at different times. It is here, of course, that the concept of present value is extremely handy: by using present value to convert any dollars realized in the future into today's value, you can factor out differences in time. Once differences in time are factored out, you can compare the three projects by calculating each one's *net present value*, the present value of current and future revenues minus the present value of current and future costs. The best project to undertake is the one with the highest net present value.

Table A-1 shows how to calculate the net present value of each of the three projects. The second and third columns show how many dollars are realized and when they are realized; costs are indicated by a minus sign. The fourth column shows the equations used to convert the flows of dollars into their present value, and the fifth column shows the actual amounts of the total net present value for each of the three projects.

For instance, to calculate the net present value of project B, you need to calculate the present value of $115 received one year from now. The present value of $1 received one year from now is $\$1/(1 + r)$. So the present value of $115 received one year from now is $115 \times \$1/(1 + r) = \$115/(1 + r)$. The net present value of project

TABLE A-1 The Net Present Value of Three Hypothetical Projects

Project	Dollars realized today	Dollars realized one year from today	Present value formula	Net present value given $r = 0.10$
A	$100	—	$100	$100.00
B	−$10	$115	−$10 + $115/(1 + r)	$94.55
C	$119	−$20	$119 − $20/(1 + r)	$100.82

B is the present value of current and future revenues minus the present value of current and future costs: $-\$10 + \$115/(1 + r)$.

From the fifth column, we can immediately see that, at an interest rate of 10%, project C is the best project. It has the highest net present value, $100.82, which is higher than the net present value of project A ($100) and much higher than the net present value of project B ($94.55).

This example shows how important the concept of present value is. If we had failed to use the present value calculations and had instead simply added up the revenues and costs, we would have been misled into believing that project B was the best project and C was the worst one.

How to Calculate the Price of a Bond Using Present Value

In Chapters 7 and 10, we learned that a buyer of a bond is entitled to receive a fixed sum of interest each year over the life of the bond and, at the end, a repayment of *principal* (the face value of the bond: the amount lent when the bond was issued). Let's illustrate how we can use present value to price a bond with a simple example.

Suppose that today you are offered the chance to purchase a bond issued by Facebook. It was issued two years ago to mature in seven years' time. That is, it pays interest for seven years total, at the end of which the principal is repaid. As of today, then, the bond will pay interest for five more years. Assume that the principal on this Facebook bond is $1,000. Also assume that when it was issued it paid an interest rate of 6%, equal to the current market equilibrium interest rate at the time. So the amount of interest that the owner of this bond receives every year is $1,000 \times 0.06 = \$60$. This annual interest payment is known generally as the *coupon*.

To determine today's price of this bond we need to calculate the present value of the future interest payments from this bond based on *today's* market equilibrium interest rate. Suppose that the market equilibrium interest rate has dropped from 6% when the bond was issued two years ago to 5% today. Then the present value of this bond is equal to the present value of the annual $60 coupon for the remaining five years plus the present value of the repayment of the $1,000 principle at the end of the five years:

(A-9) At today's market equilibrium $r = 5\%$,
$$\text{Present value} = \$60/(1 + 0.05) + \$60/(1 + 0.05)^2 + \$60/(1 + 0.05)^3$$
$$+ \$60/(1 + 0.05)^4 + \$60/(1 + 0.05)^5 + \$1,000/(1 + 0.05)^5$$
$$= \$1,043.30$$

(Your calculated value may be slightly different due to rounding error.)

This means that, as of today, you should be willing to pay no more than $1,043.30 for this Facebook bond. At a higher price, you would be better off spending your $1,043.30 on a newly issued bond that pays an interest rate of 5% for the next five years. This example illustrates a general rule: when determining the price of a preexisting bond, the interest rate used to calculate that price is the *current market equilibrium interest rate* (5% in this example), not the interest rate that was current when the bond was originally issued (6% in this example).

To gain further understanding, let's calculate what the present value of that same bond would be today if the equilibrium interest rate had not fallen and had instead remained at 6%:

(A-10) At market equilibrium $r = 6\%$,
$$\text{Present value} = \$60/(1 + 0.06) + \$60/(1 + 0.06)^2 + \$60/(1 + 0.06)^3$$
$$+ \$60/(1 + 0.06)^4 + \$60/(1 + 0.06)^5 + \$1,000/(1 + 0.06)^5$$
$$= \$1,000.00$$

(Again, your calculated value may be slightly different due to rounding error.)

Equation A-10 illustrates a general principle: when the current market equilibrium interest rate is unchanged from when the bond was issued, then the present value of the bond is equal to its face value, regardless of how many periods are left until it matures. You can check this for yourself by recalculating the present value for the bond when $r = 6\%$ and four years are left to maturity. Your answer should be approximately $1,000.00.

By comparing Equations A-9 and A-10, you can see that the price of the bond goes up when the market equilibrium interest rate falls. Conversely, the price of a bond falls when the market equilibrium interest rate goes up.

In the real world, there is an additional complicating factor when pricing a bond: risk. Some bonds are riskier than others because the bond issuer is perceived to be less likely to repay bondholders in full. A high-risk bond will sell at a lower price than a low-risk bond with the same maturity, face value, and annual coupon payments. That lower price compensates the owners of the high-risk bond for the risk they face of not being repaid in full.

Ignoring the problem of risk, the general formula for bond pricing is as follows, where n is the number of years to maturity, C is the annual coupon, F is the face value, and i is the current market equilibrium interest rate on comparable bonds:

(A-11) $\text{Bond price} = C/(1+i) + C/(1+i)^2 + \cdots + C(1+i)^{n-1} + C(1+i)^n + F(1+i)^n$

We can conclude that when the market interest rate on comparable bonds rises, the price of existing bonds falls; when the market interest rate on comparable bonds falls, the price of existing bonds rises.

How to Calculate the Price of a Share of Stock Using Present Value

While a bond entitles its owner to interest payments, a share of stock entitles its owner to a share of the company's profits. That's because a share of stock represents ownership of a portion of the company. As we explained in Chapter 7, a share of a company's profits paid to a shareholder is called a *dividend*. So a share entitles its owner to a series of payments of future dividends, and we can use the present value formula to find the price of a share of stock:

(A-12) $\text{Stock price} = \text{Dividend}/(1+r) + \text{Dividend}/(1+r)^2 + \text{Dividend}/(1+r)^3 + \cdots$

In the formula, r is the interest rate in the market for loanable funds. Unlike the formula for a bond price in Equation A-11, there is no end date, n, in the formula for a stock because a share entitles its owner to dividend payments indefinitely.

It's possible to simplify Equation A-12 if we assume that the company's profits grow at a constant rate every year, and its dividends grow at a constant rate. Then the stock price formula becomes:

(A-13) $\text{Stock price} = \text{Dividend}/(r - \text{Growth rate})$

Like bond pricing, stock pricing comes with real-world complicating factors for investors to consider: First, dividends paid by most businesses are highly variable (much more than bond payments) because profits vary from year to year. So stock prices are based upon *expected* future dividend payments. Second, the stock market is affected by rumors, fads, and other types of irrational behavior, so stock prices fluctuate far more than bond prices.

PROBLEMS

1. You have won the state lottery. There are two ways in which you can receive your prize. You can either have $1 million in cash now, or you can have $1.2 million that is paid out as follows: $300,000 now, $300,000 in one year's time, $300,000 in two years' time, and $300,000 in three years' time. The interest rate is 20%. How would you prefer to receive your prize?

2. The drug company Pfizer is considering whether to invest in the development of a new cancer drug. Development will require an initial investment of $10 million now; beginning one year from now, the drug will generate annual profits of $4 million for three years.

   a. If the interest rate is 12%, should Pfizer invest in the development of the new drug? Why or why not?

   b. If the interest rate is 8%, should Pfizer invest in the development of the new drug? Why or why not?

3. Suppose that a major city's main thoroughfare, which is also an interstate highway, will be completely closed to traffic for two years, from January 2020 to December 2021, for reconstruction at a cost of $535 million.

If the construction company were to keep the highway open for traffic during construction, the highway reconstruction project would take much longer and be more expensive. Suppose that construction would take four years if the highway were kept open, at a total cost of $800 million. The state department of transportation had to make its decision in 2019, one year before the start of construction (so that the first payment was one year away). So the department of transportation had the following choices:

   i. Close the highway during construction, at an annual cost of $267.5 million per year for two years.

   ii. Keep the highway open during construction, at an annual cost of $200 million per year for four years.

   a. Suppose the interest rate is 10%. Calculate the present value of the costs incurred under each plan. Which reconstruction plan is less expensive?

   b. Now suppose the interest rate is 80%. Calculate the present value of the costs incurred under each plan. Which reconstruction plan is now less expensive? ■

11

Income and Expenditure

THE SHORTEST RECESSION EVER

IN FEBRUARY 2020, it more or less suddenly became apparent that the world was facing its biggest outbreak of infectious disease since the influenza pandemic of 1918. The coronavirus spread through airborne transmission — although medical experts didn't immediately realize that — and could make its victims extremely ill, sometimes causing death. And in the early months, there didn't seem to be any way to reduce the risk of contracting Covid-19 other than limiting contact with other people.

Concerns about the coronavirus inevitably had major economic effects. Most notably, many people in the United States and in other countries stopped going out to eat and stopped inessential travel, reflecting both government policy — many cities and states imposed partial lockdowns on activities considered risky — and personal caution. Real consumer spending on "food services and accommodations" — roughly speaking, restaurants and hotels — fell 40% between late 2019 and mid-2020, causing 8 million workers in leisure and hospitality to lose their jobs.

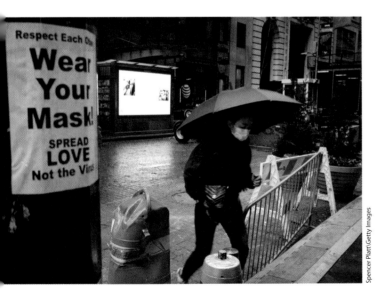

Spencer Platt/Getty Images

A recession was inevitable as the coronavirus pandemic brought the U.S. economy to a standstill.

At the time, many economists and businesspeople feared that these huge job losses would be the prelude to a much broader economic downturn. That is, they feared that the slump would spread from "high-contact" businesses that consumers were temporarily avoiding to the economy as a whole.

As it turned out, these fears proved mostly false. The United States did experience a sharp recession starting in February 2020 — but it was the shortest recession in history, officially ending after only two months. For the most part, large job losses were contained to economic activities directly affected by concerns about infection.

This relatively happy outcome had a lot to do with the fact that the U.S. government provided extensive financial support to workers and businesses. We'll discuss how *fiscal policy* works in Chapter 13. For now, however, let's talk about why, in the absence of that support, fears of a wider, deeper slump might well have come true.

The business cycle is often driven by ups or downs in one particular kind of spending — in the case of the pandemic that would have been consumer spending on high-contact services, although the most common driver of recessions and recoveries is changes in investment spending. These first-round changes in spending then lead to changes in consumer spending, which magnify — or, as economists usually say, *multiply* — the effect of the initial changes on the economy as a whole.

In this chapter, we'll study how this process works, showing how *multiplier* analysis helps us understand the business cycle. As a first step, we introduce the concept of the multiplier informally. ●

WHAT YOU WILL LEARN

- What is the importance of the **multiplier,** which summarizes how initial changes in spending lead to further changes?
- What is the **aggregate consumption function?**
- How do expected future income and aggregate wealth affect consumer spending?
- What determines investment spending and why do we need to distinguish between **planned investment spending** and **unplanned inventory investment?**
- How does the inventory adjustment process move the economy to a new equilibrium after a change in demand?
- Why is investment spending considered a leading indicator of the future state of the economy?

‖ The Multiplier: An Informal Introduction

Why were many economists worried about the broader effects of Covid-19? Because they feared a sort of chain reaction in which an initial rise or fall in aggregate spending leads to changes in income, which lead to further changes in aggregate spending, and so on. Let's examine that chain reaction more closely, this time thinking through the effects of changes in aggregate spending in the economy as a whole.

For the sake of this analysis, we'll initially make four simplifying assumptions that will have to be reconsidered later.

1. We assume that *producers are willing to supply additional output at a fixed price.* That is, if consumers or businesses buying investment goods decide to spend an additional $1 billion, that will translate into the production of $1 billion worth of additional goods and services without driving up the overall level of prices. As a result, *changes in aggregate spending translate into changes in aggregate output,* as measured by real GDP. As we'll learn in the next chapter, this assumption isn't too unrealistic in the short run, but it needs to be changed when we think about the long-run effects of changes in demand.

2. We take the interest rate as given.

3. We assume that there is no government spending and no taxes.

4. We assume that exports and imports are zero (in a later section, we'll see how to bring trade back).

Given these simplifying assumptions, consider what happens if there is an initial change in spending. Let's put the pandemic example on one side, and consider a more typical event: a surge in investment. For example, imagine that businesses responded to the initial economic shutdown by reducing investment spending on new production facilities by extra $100 billion this year.

The direct effect of this fall in investment spending will be to decrease income and the value of aggregate output by the same amount. That's because each dollar spent on investment translates into a dollar's worth of income for construction workers, producers of equipment, and so on. If the process stopped there, the fall in investment spending would decrease overall income by exactly $100 billion.

But the process doesn't stop there. The fall in aggregate output leads to a decline in disposable income that flows to households in the form of profits and wages. The fall in households' disposable income leads to a further decline in consumer spending, which, in turn, induces firms to reduce output yet again. This generates another fall in disposable income, which leads to another round of consumer spending declines, and so on. So there are multiple rounds of reduction in aggregate output.

How large is the total effect on aggregate output if we sum the effect from all these rounds of spending cuts? To answer this question, we need to introduce the concept of the **marginal propensity to consume,** or **MPC:** the increase in consumer spending when disposable income rises by $1. When consumer spending changes because of a rise or fall in disposable income, *MPC* is the change in consumer spending divided by the change in disposable income:

$$(1) \quad MPC = \frac{\Delta \text{ Consumer spending}}{\Delta \text{ Disposable income}}$$

where the symbol Δ (delta) means "change in." For example, if consumer spending goes up by $6 billion when disposable income goes up by $10 billion, *MPC* is $6 billion/$10 billion = 0.6.

Because consumers normally spend part but not all of an additional dollar of disposable income, *MPC* is a number between 0 and 1. The additional disposable income that consumers don't spend is saved; the **marginal propensity to save,** or **MPS,** is the fraction of an additional dollar of disposable income that is saved. *MPS* is equal to $1 - MPC$.

marginal propensity to consume (MPC) the increase in consumer spending when disposable income rises by $1. Because consumers normally spend part but not all of an additional dollar of disposable income, *MPC* is between 0 and 1.

marginal propensity to save (MPS) the fraction of an additional dollar of disposable income that is saved; *MPS* is equal to 1 – *MPC*.

Because we assumed that there are no taxes and no international trade, each $1 increase in aggregate spending increases both real GDP and disposable income by $1. So the $100 billion rise in investment spending initially increases real GDP by $100 billion. This leads to a second-round rise in consumer spending, which increases real GDP by a further $MPC \times \$100$ billion. It is followed by a third-round rise in consumer spending of $MPC \times MPC \times \$100$ billion, and so on. After an infinite number of rounds, the total effect on real GDP is:

$$
\begin{aligned}
&\text{Increase in investment spending} & = && \$100 \text{ billion} \\
+ \;&\text{Second-round increase in consumer spending} & = \; MPC \;\; &\times& \$100 \text{ billion} \\
+ \;&\text{Third-round increase in consumer spending} & = \; MPC^2 \;\; &\times& \$100 \text{ billion} \\
+ \;&\text{Fourth-round increase in consumer spending} & = \; MPC^3 \;\; &\times& \$100 \text{ billion}
\end{aligned}
$$

$$\text{Total increase in real GDP} = (1 + MPC + MPC^2 + MPC^3 + \cdots) \times \$100 \text{ billion}$$

So the $100 billion increase in investment spending sets off a chain reaction in the economy. The net result of this chain reaction is that a $100 billion increase in investment spending leads to a change in real GDP that is a *multiple* of the size of that initial change in spending.

How large is this multiple? It's a mathematical fact that an infinite series of the form $1 + x + x^2 + x^3 + \cdots$, where x is between 0 and 1, is equal to $1/(1 - x)$. So the total effect of a $100 billion increase in investment spending, I, taking into account all the subsequent increases in consumer spending (and assuming no taxes and no international trade), is given by:

(2) Total increase in real GDP from a $100 billion rise in I

$$= \frac{1}{1 - MPC} \times \$100 \text{ billion}$$

Let's consider a numerical example in which $MPC = 0.6$: each $1 in additional disposable income causes a $0.60 rise in consumer spending. In that case, a $100 billion increase in investment spending raises real GDP by $100 billion in the first round. The second-round increase in consumer spending raises real GDP by another $0.6 \times \$100$ billion, or $60 billion. The third-round increase in consumer spending raises real GDP by another $0.6 \times \$60$ billion, or $36 billion. Table 1 shows the successive stages of increases, where "..." means the process goes on an infinite number of times. In the end, real GDP rises by $250 billion as a consequence of the initial $100 billion rise in investment spending:

$$\frac{1}{0.6} \times \$100 \text{ billion} = 2.5 \times \$100 \text{ billion} = \$250 \text{ billion}$$

Notice that even though there are an infinite number of rounds of expansion of real GDP, the total rise in real GDP is limited to $250 billion. The reason is that at each stage some of the rise in disposable income "leaks out" because it is saved. How much of an additional dollar of disposable income is saved depends on MPS, the marginal propensity to save.

We've described the effects of a change in investment spending, but the same analysis can be applied to any other change in aggregate spending—such as a sudden drop in consumer spending on restaurants. The important thing is to distinguish between the initial change in aggregate spending, before real GDP changes, and the additional change in aggregate spending caused by the change in real GDP as the chain reaction unfolds. For example, suppose that a boom in housing prices makes consumers feel richer and that, as a result, they become willing to spend more at any given level of disposable income. This will lead to an initial rise in consumer spending, before real GDP rises. But it will also lead to second and later rounds of higher consumer spending as real GDP rises.

TABLE 1   Rounds of Increases in Real GDP When $MPC = 0.6$

Rounds	Increase in real GDP (billions)	Total increase in real GDP (billions)
First	$100	$100
Second	60	160
Third	36	196
Fourth	21.6	217.6
...	...	...
Final	0	250

autonomous change in aggregate spending an initial rise or fall in aggregate spending at a given level of real GDP.

multiplier the ratio of total change in real GDP caused by an autonomous change in aggregate spending to the size of that autonomous change.

An initial rise or fall in aggregate spending at a given level of real GDP is called an **autonomous change in aggregate spending.** It's autonomous—which means self-governing—because it's the cause, not the result, of the chain reaction we've just described. Formally, the **multiplier** is the ratio of the total change in real GDP caused by an autonomous change in aggregate spending to the size of that autonomous change.

If we let ΔAAS stand for autonomous change in aggregate spending and ΔY stand for the change in real GDP, then the multiplier is equal to $\Delta Y/\Delta AAS$. And we've already seen how to find the value of the multiplier. Assuming no taxes and no trade, the change in real GDP caused by an autonomous change in spending is:

$$(3) \quad \Delta Y = \frac{1}{1 - MPC} \times \Delta AAS$$

So the multiplier is:

$$(4) \quad \text{Multiplier} = \frac{\Delta Y}{\Delta AAS} = \frac{1}{1 - MPC}$$

Notice that the size of the multiplier depends on *MPC*. If the marginal propensity to consume is high, so is the multiplier. This is true because the size of *MPC* determines how large each round of expansion is compared with the previous round. To put it another way, the higher *MPC* is, the less disposable income leaks out into savings at each round of expansion.

In later chapters, we'll use the concept of the multiplier to analyze the effects of fiscal and monetary policies. We'll also see that the formula for the multiplier changes when we introduce various complications, including taxes and foreign trade. First, however, we need to look more deeply at what determines consumer spending.

ECONOMICS >> *in Action*
To Shale and Back

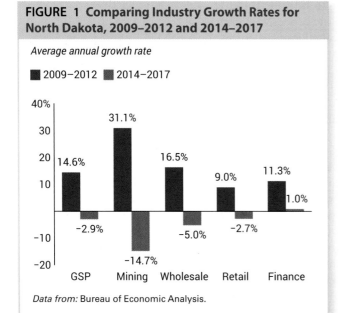

FIGURE 1 Comparing Industry Growth Rates for North Dakota, 2009–2012 and 2014–2017

Average annual growth rate

■ 2009–2012 ■ 2014–2017

Data from: Bureau of Economic Analysis.

For most of America, recovery from the severe recession of 2007–2009 was disappointingly slow. But a few parts of the country experienced rapid growth—and none more rapid than North Dakota, whose economy grew 60% between 2009 and 2012. That's an annual growth rate of almost 15%, almost five times the growth of the U.S. economy as a whole.

There's no mystery about the North Dakota boom: it was all about shale oil. Fracking made it possible to extract oil from the Bakken shale, which underlies the state. Oil companies and other investors rushed in, along with thousands of oil-field workers, more than doubling the output of the mining sector in just two years.

But as Figure 1 shows, mining and related industries weren't the only sectors growing fast. North Dakota also saw much faster growth than other states in a number of areas, notably retail and wholesale trade, banking, and utilities. Why?

The answer was the multiplier. As high-paying shale-related jobs surged, so did consumer spending—much of which ended up in the hands of local shops, bank branches, companies supplying electricity and heating oil, and so on. These local suppliers, in turn, hired more workers, whose incomes added to consumer spending and fed additional rounds of expansion.

Obviously this extraordinary growth couldn't last. In fact, the shale boom came to an abrupt end in late 2014, as falling oil prices led to a drastic slowdown: mining employment in North Dakota fell more than 50% between October 2014 and July 2016, which had a ripple effect throughout the state's economy. But the boom was fun while it lasted, and it also gave an excellent example of the multiplier at work.

>> Check Your Understanding 11-1

Solutions appear at back of book.

1. Explain why a decline in investment spending caused by a change in business expectations leads to a fall in consumer spending.

2. What is the multiplier if the marginal propensity to consume is 0.5? What is it if *MPC* is 0.8?

3. As a percentage of GDP, savings accounts for a larger share of the economy in the country of Scania compared to the country of Amerigo. Which country is likely to have the larger multiplier? Explain.

‖ Consumer Spending

Should you splurge on a restaurant meal or save money by eating at home? Should you buy a new car and, if so, how expensive a model? Should you redo that bathroom or live with it for another year? In the real world, households are constantly confronted with such choices—not just about the consumption mix but also about how much to spend in total.

These choices, in turn, have a powerful effect on the economy: consumer spending normally accounts for two-thirds of total spending on final goods and services. In particular, as we've just seen, the decision about how much of an additional dollar in income to spend—the marginal propensity to consume—determines the size of the multiplier, which determines the ultimate effect on the economy of autonomous changes in spending.

But what determines how much consumers spend?

Current Disposable Income and Consumer Spending

The most important factor affecting a family's consumer spending is its current disposable income—income after taxes are paid and government transfers are received. It's obvious from daily life that people with high disposable incomes on average drive more expensive cars, live in more expensive houses, and spend more on meals and clothing than people with lower disposable incomes. And the relationship between current disposable income and spending is clear in the data.

The Bureau of Labor Statistics (BLS) collects annual data on family income and spending. Families are grouped by levels of before-tax income, and after-tax income for each group is also reported. Since the income figures include transfers from the government, what the BLS calls a household's after-tax income is equivalent to its current disposable income.

> **>> Quick Review**
>
> • A change in investment spending arising from a change in expectations starts a chain reaction in which the initial change in real GDP leads to changes in consumer spending, leading to further changes in real GDP, and so on. The total change in aggregate output is a multiple of the initial change in investment spending.
>
> • Any **autonomous change in aggregate spending,** a change in spending that is not caused by a change in real GDP, generates the same chain reaction. The total size of the change in real GDP depends on the size of the **multiplier.** Assuming that there are no taxes and no trade, the multiplier is equal to $1/(1-MPC)$, where **MPC** is the **marginal propensity to consume.** The total change in real GDP, ΔY, is equal to $1/(1-MPC) \times \Delta AAS$.

People with lower disposable incomes may avoid higher-priced brand-name goods in favor of generics that cost less.

Richard Levine/Alamy Stock Photo

FIGURE 2 Current Disposable Income and Consumer Spending for U.S. Households in 2021

For each income group of households, average current disposable income in 2021 is plotted versus average consumer spending in 2021. For example, the middle income group, with current disposable income of $46,506 to $78,259, is represented by point A (the red point), indicating a household average current disposable income of $60,957 and average household consumer spending of $55,914. The data clearly show a positive relationship between current disposable income and consumer spending: families with higher current disposable income have higher consumer spending.

Data from: Bureau of Labor Statistics.

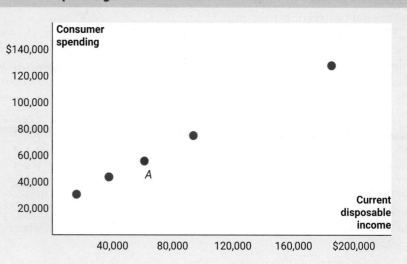

Figure 2 is a scatter diagram illustrating the relationship between household current disposable income and household consumer spending for American households by income group in 2021. For example, the red point shows that in 2021 the middle fifth of the population had an average current disposable income of $60,957 and average spending of $55,914. The pattern of the dots slopes upward from left to right, making it clear that households with higher current disposable income had higher consumer spending.

It's very useful to represent the relationship between an individual household's current disposable income and its consumer spending with an equation. The **consumption function** is an equation showing how an individual household's consumer spending varies with the household's current disposable income. The simplest version of a consumption function is a linear equation:

(5) $c = a + MPC \times yd$

where lowercase letters indicate variables measured for an individual household.

In this equation, c is individual household consumer spending and yd is individual household current disposable income. Recall that MPC, the marginal propensity to consume, is the amount by which consumer spending rises if current disposable income rises by $1. Finally, a is a constant term—individual household *autonomous consumer spending,* the amount of spending a household would have if it had zero disposable income. We assume that a is greater than zero because a household with zero disposable income is able to fund some consumption by borrowing or using its savings.

Notice, by the way, that we're using y for income. That's standard practice in macroeconomics, even though *income* isn't actually spelled "yncome." The reason is that I is reserved for investment spending.

Recall that we expressed MPC as the ratio of a change in consumer spending to the change in current disposable income. We've rewritten it for an individual household as Equation 6:

(6) $MPC = \Delta c/\Delta yd$

Multiplying both sides of Equation 6 by Δyd, we get:

(7) $MPC \times \Delta yd = \Delta c$

Equation 7 tells us that when yd goes up by $1, c goes up by $MPC \times $1.

Figure 3 shows what Equation 5 looks like graphically, plotting yd on the horizontal axis and c on the vertical axis. Individual household autonomous consumer

consumption function an equation showing how an individual household's consumer spending varies with the household's current disposable income.

FIGURE 3 The Consumption Function

The consumption function relates a household's current disposable income to its consumer spending. The vertical intercept, *a*, is individual household autonomous consumer spending: the amount of a household's consumer spending if its current disposable income is zero. The slope of the consumption function line, *cf*, is the marginal propensity to consume, or *MPC*: of every additional $1 of current disposable income, *MPC* × $1 is spent.

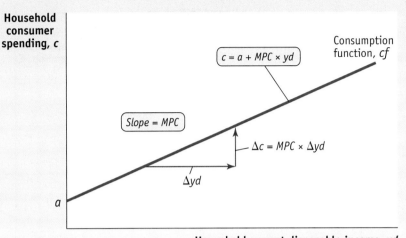

Household consumer spending, *c*

$c = a + MPC \times yd$

Consumption function, *cf*

Slope = *MPC*

$\Delta c = MPC \times \Delta yd$

Δyd

a

Household current disposable income, *yd*

spending, *a*, is the value of *c* when *yd* is zero—it is the vertical *intercept* of the consumption function, *cf*. *MPC* is the *slope* of the line, measured by rise over run. If current disposable income rises by Δyd, household consumer spending, *c*, rises by Δc. Since *MPC* is defined as $\Delta c/\Delta yd$, the slope of the consumption function is:

(8) Slope of consumption function
   = Rise over run
   = $\Delta c/\Delta yd$
   = *MPC*

In reality, actual data has never fit Equation 5 perfectly, but the fit can be pretty good. Figure 4 shows the data from Figure 2 again, together with a line drawn to fit the data as closely as possible. According to the data on households' consumer spending and current disposable income, the best estimate of *a* is $21,622 and of *MPC* is 0.58. So the consumption function fitted to the data is:

$$c = \$21,622 + 0.58 \times yd$$

FIGURE 4 A Consumption Function Fitted to Data

The data from Figure 2 are reproduced here, along with a line drawn to fit the data as closely as possible. For U.S. households in 2021, the best estimate of the average household's autonomous consumer spending, *a*, is $21,622 and the best estimate of *MPC* is 0.58.

Data from: Bureau of Labor Statistics.

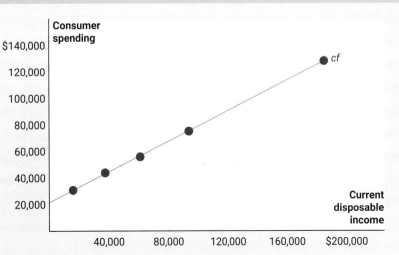

Consumer spending

$140,000
120,000
100,000
80,000
60,000
40,000
20,000

cf

Current disposable income

40,000   80,000   120,000   160,000 $200,000

FIGURE 5 Shifts of the Aggregate Consumption Function

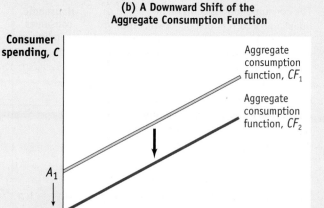

Panel (a) illustrates the effect of an increase in expected aggregate future disposable income. Consumers will spend more at every given level of aggregate current disposable income, *YD*. As a result, the initial aggregate consumption function CF_1, with aggregate autonomous consumer spending A_1, shifts up to a new position at CF_2 and aggregate autonomous consumer spending A_2. An increase in aggregate wealth will also shift the aggregate consumption function up.

Panel (b), in contrast, illustrates the effect of a reduction in expected aggregate future disposable income. Consumers will spend less at every given level of aggregate current disposable income, *YD*. Consequently, the initial aggregate consumption function CF_1, with aggregate autonomous consumer spending A_1, shifts down to a new position at CF_2 and aggregate autonomous consumer spending A_2. A reduction in aggregate wealth will have the same effect.

That is, the data suggest a marginal propensity to consume of approximately 0.60. This implies that the marginal propensity to save (*MPS*)—the amount of an additional $1 of disposable income that is saved—is approximately 0.40, and the multiplier is approximately 1/0.40 = 2.50.

It's important to realize that Figure 4 shows a *microeconomic* relationship between the current disposable income of individual households and their spending on goods and services. However, macroeconomists assume that a similar relationship holds *for the economy as a whole:* that there is a relationship, called the **aggregate consumption function,** between aggregate current disposable income and aggregate consumer spending. We'll assume that it has the same form as the household-level consumption function:

(9) $C = A + MPC \times YD$

Here, *C* is aggregate consumer spending (called just "consumer spending"); *YD* is aggregate current disposable income (called, for simplicity, just "disposable income"); and *A* is aggregate autonomous consumer spending, the amount of consumer spending when *YD* equals zero. This is the relationship represented in Figure 5 by *CF*, analogous to *cf* in Figure 3.

Shifts of the Aggregate Consumption Function

The aggregate consumption function shows the relationship between disposable income and consumer spending for the economy as a whole, other things equal. When things other than disposable income change, the aggregate consumption function shifts. There are two principal causes of shifts of the aggregate consumption function: changes in expected future disposable income and changes in aggregate wealth.

aggregate consumption function the relationship for the economy as a whole between aggregate current disposable income and aggregate consumer spending.

Changes in Expected Future Disposable Income Suppose you land a really good, well-paying job on graduating from college in May—but the job, and the paychecks, won't start until September. So your disposable income hasn't risen yet. Even so, it's likely that you will start spending more on final goods and services right away—maybe buying nicer work clothes than you originally planned—because you know that higher income is coming.

Conversely, suppose you have a good job but learn that the company is planning to downsize your division, raising the possibility that you may lose your job and have to take a lower-paying one somewhere else. Even though your disposable income hasn't gone down yet, you might well cut back on spending even while still employed, to save for a rainy day.

Both of these examples show how expectations about future disposable income can affect consumer spending. The two panels of Figure 5, which plot disposable income against consumer spending, show how changes in expected future disposable income affect the aggregate consumption function. In both panels, CF_1 is the initial aggregate consumption function. Panel (a) shows the effect of good news: information that leads consumers to expect higher disposable income in the future than they did before.

Consumers will now spend more at any given level of current disposable income, YD, corresponding to an increase in A, aggregate autonomous consumer spending, from A_1 to A_2. The effect is to shift the aggregate consumption function up, from CF_1 to CF_2. Panel (b) shows the effect of bad news: information that leads consumers to expect lower disposable income in the future than they did before. Consumers will now spend less at any given level of current disposable income, YD, corresponding to a fall in A from A_1 to A_2. The effect is to shift the aggregate consumption function down, from CF_1 to CF_2.

In a famous 1957 book, *A Theory of the Consumption Function*, Milton Friedman showed that taking the effects of expected future income into account explains an otherwise puzzling fact about consumer behavior. If we look at consumer spending during any given year, we find that people with high current income save a larger fraction of their income than those with low current income. (This is obvious from the data in Figure 4: people with higher incomes spend considerably less than their income; those with lower incomes spend more than their income.) You might think this implies that the overall savings rate will rise as the economy grows and average current incomes rise; in fact, however, this hasn't happened.

Friedman pointed out that when we look at individual incomes in a given year, there are systematic differences between current and expected future income that create a positive relationship between current income and the savings rate. On one side, people with low current incomes are often having an unusually bad year. For example, they may be workers who have been laid off but will probably find new jobs eventually. They are people whose expected future income is higher than their current income, so it makes sense for them to have low or even negative savings. On the other side, people with high current incomes in a given year are often having an unusually good year. For example, they may have investments that happened to do extremely well. They are people whose expected future income is lower than their current income, so it makes sense for them to save most of their windfall.

When the economy grows, by contrast, current and expected future incomes rise together. Higher current income tends to lead to higher savings today, but higher expected future income tends to lead to less savings today. As a result, there's a weaker relationship between current income and the savings rate.

Friedman argued that consumer spending ultimately depends mainly on the income people expect to have over the long term rather than on their current income. This argument is known as the *permanent income hypothesis*.

Changes in Aggregate Wealth Imagine two individuals, Maria and Mark, both of whom expect to earn $30,000 this year. Suppose, however, that they have different histories. Maria has been working steadily for the past 10 years, owns her own home, and has $200,000 in the bank. Mark is the same age as Maria, but he has been in and out of work, hasn't managed to buy a house, and has very little in savings. In this case, Maria has something that Mark doesn't have: *wealth*. Even though they have the same disposable income, other things equal, you'd expect Maria to spend more on consumption than Mark. That is, wealth has an effect on consumer spending.

The effect of wealth on spending is emphasized by an influential economic model of how consumers make choices about spending versus saving called the *life-cycle hypothesis*. According to this hypothesis, consumers plan their spending over a lifetime, not just in response to their current disposable income. As a result, people try to smooth their consumption over their lifetimes—they save some of their current disposable income during their years of peak earnings (typically occurring during a worker's 40s and 50s) and during their retirement live off the wealth they accumulated while working.

We won't go into the details of this hypothesis but will simply point out that it implies an important role for wealth in determining consumer spending. For example, a middle-aged couple who have accumulated a lot of wealth—who have paid off the mortgage on their house and already own plenty of stocks and bonds—will, other things equal, spend more on goods and services than a couple who have the same current disposable income but still need to save for their retirement.

Because wealth affects household consumer spending, changes in wealth across the economy can shift the aggregate consumption function. A rise in aggregate wealth—say, because of a booming stock market—increases the vertical intercept *A*, aggregate autonomous consumer spending. This, in turn, shifts the aggregate consumption function up in the same way as does an expected increase in future disposable income. A decline in aggregate wealth—say, because of a fall in housing prices as occurred in 2008—reduces *A* and shifts the aggregate consumption function down.

ECONOMICS >> *in Action*
Famous First Forecasting Failures

The Great Depression created modern macroeconomics. It also gave birth to the modern field of *econometrics*—the use of statistical techniques to fit economic models to empirical data. The aggregate consumption function was one of the first things econometricians studied. And, sure enough, they quickly experienced one of the first major failures of economic forecasting: consumer spending after World War II was much higher than estimates of the aggregate consumption function based on prewar data would have predicted.

Figure 6 tells the story. Panel (a) shows aggregate data on disposable income and consumer spending from 1929 to 1941, measured in billions of 2012 dollars. A simple linear consumption function, in panel (a) seems to fit the data very well. And many economists thought this relationship would continue to hold in the future. But panel (b) shows what actually happened in later years. The points in red at the left are the data from the Great Depression shown in panel (a). The points in blue at the right are data from 1946 to 1960. (Data from 1942 to 1945 aren't included because rationing during World War II prevented consumers from spending normally.)

The solid black line in the panel (b), is the consumption function fitted to 1929–1941 data. As you can see, post–World War II consumer spending was much higher than the relationship from the Depression years would have predicted. For example, in 1960 consumer spending was 13.5% higher than the level predicted by the consumption function from the Great Depression.

FIGURE 6 Changes in the Aggregate Consumption Function Over Time

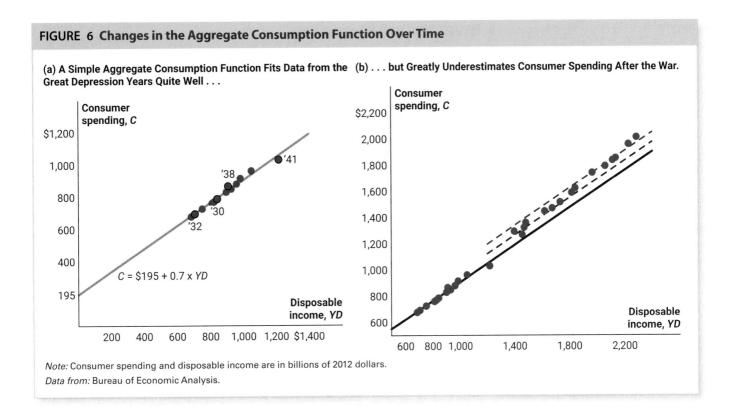

(a) A Simple Aggregate Consumption Function Fits Data from the Great Depression Years Quite Well . . .

(b) . . . but Greatly Underestimates Consumer Spending After the War.

Note: Consumer spending and disposable income are in billions of 2012 dollars.

Data from: Bureau of Economic Analysis.

Why was extrapolating from the earlier relationship so misleading? The answer is that from 1946 onward, both expected future disposable income and aggregate wealth were steadily rising. Consumers grew increasingly confident that the Great Depression wouldn't reemerge and that the post–World War II economic boom would continue. At the same time, wealth was steadily increasing. As indicated by the dashed blue and purple lines in panel (b), the increases in expected future disposable income and in aggregate wealth shifted the aggregate consumption function up a number of times.

In macroeconomics, failure—whether of economic policy or of economic prediction—often leads to intellectual progress. The embarrassing failure of early estimates of the aggregate consumption function to predict post–World War II consumer spending led to important progress in our understanding of consumer behavior.

>> Check Your Understanding 11-2

Solutions appear at back of book.

1. Suppose the economy consists of three people: Angelina, Felicia, and Marina. The table shows how their consumer spending varies as their current disposable income rises by $10,000.
   a. Derive each individual's consumption function, where *MPC* is calculated for a $10,000 change in current disposable income.
   b. Derive the aggregate consumption function.

Current disposable income	Consumer spending		
	Angelina	Felicia	Marina
$0	$8,000	$6,500	$7,250
10,000	12,000	14,500	14,250

2. Suppose that problems in the capital markets make consumers unable either to borrow or to put money aside for future use. What implication does this have for the effects of expected future disposable income on consumer spending?

>> Quick Review

• The **consumption function** shows the relationship between an individual household's current disposable income and its consumer spending.

• The **aggregate consumption function** shows the relationship between disposable income and consumer spending across the economy. It can shift due to changes in expected future disposable income and changes in aggregate wealth.

planned investment spending
the investment spending that firms intend to undertake during a given period. Planned investment spending may differ from actual investment spending due to unplanned inventory investment.

‖ Investment Spending

Although consumer spending is much larger than investment spending, booms and busts in investment spending tend to drive the business cycle. In fact, most recessions originate as a fall in investment spending. Figure 7 illustrates this point; it shows the annual percent change of investment spending and consumer spending in the United States, measured in real terms, during seven recessions from 1973 to 2020. As you can see, swings in investment spending are much more dramatic than those in consumer spending. Even amidst the economic shutdowns during the Covid-19 pandemic, investment spending fell considerably more than consumer spending. In addition, due to the multiplier process, economists believe that declines in consumer spending are usually the result of a process that begins with a slump in investment spending. Soon we'll examine in more detail how a slump in investment spending generates a fall in consumer spending through the multiplier process.

Before we do that, however, let's analyze the factors that determine investment spending, which are somewhat different from those that determine consumer spending. The most important ones are the interest rate and expected future real GDP. We'll also revisit a fact that we noted in Chapter 10: the level of investment spending businesses *actually* carry out is sometimes not the same level as **planned investment spending,** the investment spending that firms *intend* to undertake during a given period.

Planned investment spending depends on three principal factors that we'll analyze next.

1. The interest rate
2. The expected future level of real GDP
3. The current level of production capacity

First, we'll analyze the effect of the interest rate.

1. The Interest Rate and Investment Spending

Interest rates have their clearest effect on one particular form of investment spending: spending on residential construction—that is, on the construction of

---

FIGURE 7 Fluctuations in Investment Spending and Consumer Spending

The bars illustrate the annual percent change in investment spending and consumer spending during six recent recessions. As the lengths of the bars show, swings in investment spending were much larger in percentage terms than those in consumer spending. This pattern has led economists to believe that recessions typically originate as a slump in investment spending.
Data from: Bureau of Economic Analysis.

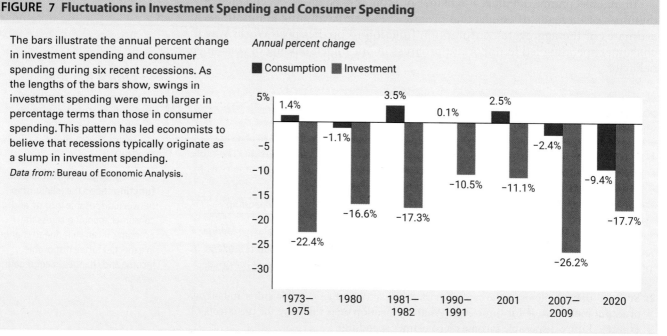

homes. The reason is straightforward: home builders only build houses they think they can sell, and houses are more affordable—and so more likely to sell—when the interest rate is low.

Consider a family that needs to borrow $350,000 to buy a new house. At an interest rate of 6.5%, a 30-year home mortgage will mean payments of $2,212 per month. At an interest rate of 4.0%, those payments would be only $1,722 per month, making houses significantly more affordable.

Interest rates also affect other forms of investment spending. Firms with investment spending projects will only go ahead with a project if they expect a rate of return higher than the cost of the funds they would have to borrow to finance that project. As we saw in Chapter 10, if the interest rate rises, fewer projects will pass that test, and as a result investment spending will be lower.

You might think that the trade-off a firm faces is different if it can fund its investment project with its past profits rather than through borrowing. Past profits used to finance investment spending are called *retained earnings*. But even if a firm pays for investment spending out of retained earnings, the trade-off it must make in deciding whether or not to fund a project remains the same because it must take into account the opportunity cost of its funds. For example, instead of purchasing new equipment, the firm could lend out the funds and earn interest. The forgone interest earned is the opportunity cost of using retained earnings to fund an investment project.

So the trade-off the firm faces when comparing a project's rate of return to the market interest rate has not changed when it uses retained earnings rather than borrowed funds, which means that regardless of whether a firm funds investment spending through borrowing or retained earnings, a rise in the market interest rate makes any given investment project less profitable.

Conversely, a fall in the interest rate makes some investment projects that were unprofitable before profitable at the now lower interest rate. So some projects that had been unfunded before will be funded now.

So planned investment spending—spending on investment projects that firms voluntarily decide whether or not to undertake—is negatively related to the interest rate. Other things equal, a higher interest rate leads to a lower level of planned investment spending.

2. Expected Future Real GDP, Production Capacity, and Investment Spending

Suppose a firm has enough capacity to continue to produce the amount it is currently selling but doesn't expect its sales to grow in the future. Then it will engage in investment spending only to replace existing equipment and structures that wear out or are rendered obsolete by new technologies. But if, instead, the firm expects its sales to grow rapidly in the future, it will find its existing production capacity insufficient for its future production needs. So the firm will undertake investment spending to meet those needs. This implies that, other things equal, firms will undertake more investment spending when they expect their sales to grow.

Now suppose that the firm currently has considerably more capacity than necessary to meet current production needs. Even if it expects sales to grow, it won't have to undertake investment spending for a while—not until the growth in sales catches up with its excess capacity. This illustrates the fact that, other things equal, the current level of productive capacity has a negative effect on investment spending: other things equal, the higher the current capacity, the lower the investment spending.

If we combine the effects on investment spending of both growth in expected future sales and the size of current production capacity, we can see one situation in which we can be reasonably sure that firms will undertake high levels of

accelerator principle the proposition that a higher growth rate in real GDP results in a higher level of planned investment spending, and a lower growth rate in real GDP leads to lower planned investment spending.

inventories stocks of goods and raw materials held to facilitate business operations.

inventory investment the value of the change in total inventories held in the economy during a given period. Unlike other types of investment spending, inventory investment can be negative if inventories fall.

unplanned inventory investment an unintended swing in inventory that occurs when actual sales are higher or lower than expected sales.

actual investment spending the sum of planned investment spending and unplanned inventory investment.

investment spending: when they expect sales to grow rapidly. In that case, even excess production capacity will soon be used up, leading firms to resume investment spending.

What is an indicator of high expected growth of future sales? It's a high expected future growth rate of real GDP. A higher expected future growth rate of real GDP results in a higher level of planned investment spending, but a lower expected future growth rate of real GDP leads to lower planned investment spending. This relationship is summarized in a proposition known as the **accelerator principle.** Generally, the effects of the accelerator principle play an important role in *investment spending slumps,* periods of low investment spending.

3. Inventories and Unplanned Investment Spending

Most firms maintain **inventories,** stocks of goods held to satisfy future sales. Firms hold inventories so they can quickly satisfy buyers—a consumer can purchase an item off the shelf rather than waiting for it to be manufactured. In addition, businesses often hold inventories of their inputs to be sure they have a steady supply of necessary materials and spare parts. At the end of December 2022, the overall value of inventories in the U.S. economy was estimated at $2.48 trillion, just under 10% of GDP.

A firm that increases its inventories is engaging in a form of investment spending. Suppose, for example, that the U.S. auto industry produces 800,000 cars per month but sells only 700,000. The remaining 100,000 cars are added to the inventory at auto company warehouses or car dealerships, ready to be sold in the future. **Inventory investment** is the value of the change in total inventories held in the economy during a given period. Unlike other forms of investment spending, inventory investment can actually be negative. If, for example, the auto industry reduces its inventory over the course of a month, we say that it has engaged in negative inventory investment.

To understand inventory investment, think about a manager stocking the canned goods section of a supermarket. The manager tries to keep the store fully stocked so that shoppers can almost always find what they're looking for. But the manager does not want the shelves too heavily stocked because shelf space is limited and products can spoil. Similar considerations apply to many firms and typically lead them to manage their inventories carefully.

However, sales fluctuate. And because firms cannot always accurately predict sales, they often find themselves holding more or less inventories than they had intended. These unintended swings in inventories due to unforeseen changes in sales are called **unplanned inventory investment.** They represent investment spending, positive or negative, that occurred but was unplanned.

So in any given period, **actual investment spending** is equal to planned investment spending plus unplanned inventory investment. If we let $I_{Unplanned}$ represent unplanned inventory investment, $I_{Planned}$ represent planned investment spending, and I represent actual investment spending, then the relationship among all three can be represented as:

(10) $I = I_{Unplanned} + I_{Planned}$

To see how unplanned inventory investment can occur, let's continue to focus on the auto industry and make the following assumptions. First, let's assume that the industry must determine each month's production volume in advance, before it

When the economy slumps, as it did in 2009, consumer spending plunges and inventory—such as cars at auto dealers—goes unsold, leading to a rise in unplanned inventory investment.

Alexander Chaikin/Shutterstock

knows the volume of actual sales. Second, let's assume that it anticipates selling 800,000 cars next month and that it plans neither to add to nor subtract from existing inventories. In that case, it will produce 800,000 cars to match anticipated sales.

Now imagine that next month's actual sales are less than expected, only 700,000 cars. As a result, the value of 100,000 cars will be added to investment spending as unplanned inventory investment.

The auto industry will, of course, eventually adjust to this slowdown in sales and the resulting unplanned inventory investment. The industry will probably cut next month's production volume in order to reduce inventories.

In fact, economists who study macroeconomic variables in an attempt to determine the future path of the economy pay careful attention to changes in inventory levels. Rising inventories typically indicate positive unplanned inventory investment and a slowing economy, as sales are less than had been forecast. Falling inventories typically indicate negative unplanned inventory investment and a growing economy, as sales are greater than forecast.

In the next section, we will see how production adjustments in response to fluctuations in sales and inventories ensure that the value of final goods and services actually produced is equal to desired purchases of those final goods and services.

ECONOMICS >> *in Action*
Business Investment in the Great Recession

Between December 2007 and June 2009, the U.S. economy experienced its worst economic downturn since the 1930s. Almost all economists agree that the principal driver of the Great Recession was the housing market: as a huge housing bubble deflated, residential investment—construction of new housing—plunged, and falling home values also reduced consumer wealth and therefore consumption spending.

But the Great Recession wasn't just about residential investment. As Figure 8 shows, nonresidential investment—which basically consists of business spending on new factories, office parks, warehouses, and so on—also plunged. Why?

The answer is that the sharp fall in residential investment and consumer spending left U.S. businesses with a great deal of *excess capacity*, as shown by the orange line

FIGURE 8 Nonresidential Investment and Firm Capacity

Note: Y-axis is annual percent change of nonresidential investment or percent of capacity.
Data from: Federal Reserve Board of Governors and Bureau of Economic Analysis.

in Figure 8. That is, because people weren't buying as much as before, there were many idle assembly lines, empty offices, unused space in warehouses, and so on. And since businesses weren't using the capacity they had, they saw little reason to build more.

As a result, a sharp drop in housing construction led to a further drop in non-housing investment, deepening the recession.

The good news is that once the economy stabilized and began growing again, excess business capacity was put back in use, and soon businesses began investing again.

>> Check Your Understanding 11-3

Solutions appear at back of book.

1. For each event, explain whether planned investment spending or unplanned inventory investment will change and in what direction.
   a. An unexpected increase in consumer spending
   b. A sharp rise in the cost of business borrowing
   c. A sharp increase in the economy's growth rate of real GDP
   d. An unanticipated fall in sales

2. Historically, investment spending has experienced more extreme upward and downward swings than consumer spending. Why do you think this is so? (*Hint:* Consider the marginal propensity to consume and the accelerator principle.)

3. Consumer spending was sluggish in late 2007, and economists worried that an *inventory overhang*—a high level of unplanned inventory investment throughout the economy—would make it difficult for the economy to recover anytime soon. Explain why an inventory overhang might, like the existence of too much production capacity, depress current economic activity.

The Income–Expenditure Model

Earlier in this chapter, we described how autonomous changes in spending—such as a fall in investment spending when a housing bubble bursts—lead to a multistage process through the actions of the multiplier that magnifies the effect of these changes on real GDP. We will now examine this multistage process more closely.

We'll see that the multiple rounds of changes in real GDP are accomplished through changes in the amount of output produced by firms—changes that they make in response to changes in their inventories. We'll come to understand why inventories play a central role in macroeconomic models of the economy in the short run as well as why economists pay particular attention to the behavior of firms' inventories when trying to understand the likely future state of the economy.

Before we begin, let's quickly recap the assumptions underlying the multiplier process.

1. *Changes in overall spending lead to changes in aggregate output.* We assume that producers are willing to supply additional output at a fixed price level. As a result, changes in spending translate into changes in output rather than moving the overall price level up or down. A fixed aggregate price level also implies that there is no difference between nominal GDP and real GDP. So we can use the two terms interchangeably in this chapter.

2. *The interest rate is fixed.* We'll take the interest rate as predetermined and unaffected by the factors we analyze in the model. As in the case of the aggregate price level, what we're really doing here is leaving the determinants of the interest rate outside the model. As we'll see, the model can still be used to study the effects of a change in the interest rate.

3. *Taxes, government transfers, and government purchases are all zero.*

4. *Exports and imports are both zero.*

In all subsequent chapters, we will drop the assumption that the aggregate price level is fixed. The Chapter 13 appendix addresses how taxes affect the multiplier process. We'll discuss how foreign trade enters the picture briefly later in this chapter, and bring it fully into the model in Chapter 18.

Planned Aggregate Spending and Real GDP

In an economy with no government and no foreign trade, there are only two sources of aggregate spending: consumer spending, C, and investment spending, I. And since we assume that there are no taxes or transfers, aggregate disposable income is equal to GDP (which, since the aggregate price level is fixed, is the same as real GDP): the total value of final sales of goods and services ultimately accrues to households as income. So in this highly simplified economy, there are two basic equations of national income accounting:

(11) $GDP = C + I$

(12) $YD = GDP$

As we learned earlier, the aggregate consumption function shows the relationship between disposable income and consumer spending. Let's continue to assume that the aggregate consumption function is of the same form as in Equation 9:

(13) $C = A + MPC \times YD$

In our simplified model, we will also assume planned investment spending, $I_{Planned}$, is fixed.

We need one more concept before putting the model together: **planned aggregate spending,** the total amount of planned spending in the economy. Unlike firms, households don't take unintended actions like unplanned inventory investment. So planned aggregate spending is equal to the sum of consumer spending and planned investment spending. We denote planned aggregate spending by $AE_{Planned}$, so:

(14) $AE_{Planned} = C + I_{Planned}$

The level of planned aggregate spending in a given year depends on the level of real GDP in that year. To see why, let's look at a specific example, shown in Table 2. We assume that the aggregate consumption function is:

(15) $C = 300 + 0.6 \times YD$

Real GDP, YD, C, $I_{Planned}$, and $AE_{Planned}$ are all measured in billions of dollars, and we assume that the level of planned investment, $I_{Planned}$, is fixed at $500 billion per year. The first column shows possible levels of real GDP. The second column shows disposable income, YD, which in our simplified model is equal to real GDP. The third column shows consumer spending, C, equal to $300 billion plus 0.6 times disposable income, YD. The fourth column shows planned investment spending, $I_{Planned}$, which we have assumed is $500 billion regardless of the level of real GDP. Finally, the last column shows planned aggregate spending, $AE_{Planned}$, the sum of aggregate consumer spending, C, and planned investment spending, $I_{Planned}$. (To economize on notation, we'll assume that it is understood from now on that all the variables in Table 2 are measured in billions of dollars per year.)

As you can see, a higher level of real GDP leads to a higher level of disposable income: every 500 increase in real GDP raises YD by 500, which in turn raises C by $500 \times 0.6 = 300$ and $AE_{Planned}$ by 300.

Figure 9 illustrates the information in Table 2 graphically. Real GDP is measured on the horizontal axis. *CF* is the aggregate consumption function; it shows how consumer spending depends on real GDP. $AE_{Planned}$, the planned aggregate spending line, corresponds to the aggregate consumption function shifted up by 500 (the amount of $I_{Planned}$). It shows how planned aggregate spending depends on real GDP. Both lines have a slope of 0.6, equal to *MPC*, the marginal propensity to consume.

But this isn't the end of the story. Table 2 reveals that real GDP equals planned aggregate spending, $AE_{Planned}$, only when the level of real GDP is at 2,000. Real GDP does not equal $AE_{Planned}$ at any other level. Is that possible? Didn't we learn in Chapter 7, with the circular-flow diagram, that total spending on final goods and services in the economy is equal to the total value of output of final goods and services? The answer is that for *brief* periods of

planned aggregate spending
the total amount of planned spending in the economy; includes consumer spending and planned investment spending.

TABLE 2 Equilibrium When Real *GDP* = *YD* = $AE_{Planned}$

Real GDP	YD	C	$I_{Planned}$	$AE_{Planned}$
		(billions of dollars)		
$0	$0	$300	$500	$800
500	500	600	500	1,100
1,000	1,000	900	500	1,400
1,500	1,500	1,200	500	1,700
2,000	2,000	1,500	500	2,000
2,500	2,500	1,800	500	2,300
3,000	3,000	2,100	500	2,600
3,500	3,500	2,400	500	2,900

FIGURE 9 The Aggregate Consumption Function and Planned Aggregate Spending

The lower line, *CF*, is the aggregate consumption function constructed from the data in Table 2. The upper line, $AE_{Planned}$, is the planned aggregate spending line, also constructed from the data in Table 2. It is equivalent to the aggregate consumption function shifted up by \$500 billion, the amount of planned investment spending, $I_{Planned}$.

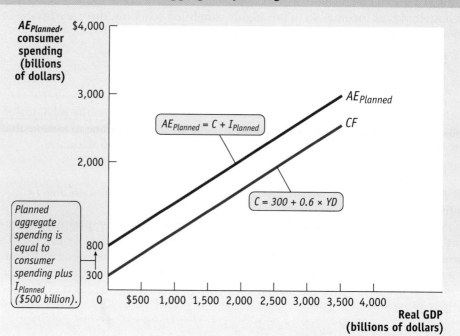

$AE_{Planned} = C + I_{Planned}$

$C = 300 + 0.6 \times YD$

Planned aggregate spending is equal to consumer spending plus $I_{Planned}$ (\$500 billion).

---

time, planned aggregate spending can differ from real GDP because of the role of *unplanned* aggregate spending—$I_{Unplanned}$, unplanned inventory investment.

But as we'll see next, the economy moves over time to a situation in which there is no unplanned inventory investment, a situation called *income–expenditure equilibrium*. And when the economy is in income–expenditure equilibrium, planned aggregate spending on final goods and services equals aggregate output.

Income–Expenditure Equilibrium

For all but one value of real GDP shown in Table 2, real GDP is either more or less than $AE_{Planned}$, the sum of consumer spending and *planned* investment spending. For example, when real GDP is 1,000, consumer spending, *C*, is 900 and planned investment spending is 500, making planned aggregate spending 1,400. This is 400 *more* than the corresponding level of real GDP. Now consider what happens when real GDP is 2,500; consumer spending, *C*, is 1,800 and planned investment spending is 500, making planned aggregate spending only 2,300, which is 200 *less* than real GDP.

As we've just explained, planned aggregate spending can be different from real GDP only if there is unplanned inventory investment, $I_{Unplanned}$, in the economy. Let's examine Table 3, which includes the numbers for real GDP and for planned aggregate spending from Table 2. It also includes the levels of unplanned inventory investment, $I_{Unplanned}$, that each combination of real GDP and planned aggregate spending implies. For example, if real GDP is 2,500, planned aggregate spending is only 2,300. This 200 excess of real GDP over $AE_{Planned}$ must consist of positive unplanned inventory investment. This can happen only if firms have overestimated sales and produced too much, leading to unintended additions to inventories.

More generally, any level of real GDP in excess of 2,000 corresponds to a situation in which firms are producing more than consumers and other firms want to purchase, creating an unintended increase in inventories.

TABLE 3 Equilibrium When $I_{Unplanned} = 0$

Real GDP	$AE_{Planned}$	$I_{Planned}$
(billions of dollars)		
\$0	\$800	-\$800
500	1,100	-600
1,000	1,400	-400
1,500	1,700	-200
2,000	2,000	0
2,500	2,300	200
3,000	2,600	400
3,500	2,900	600

Conversely, a level of real GDP below 2,000 implies that planned aggregate spending is *greater* than real GDP. For example, when real GDP is 1,000, planned aggregate spending is much larger, at 1,400. The 400 excess of $AE_{Planned}$ over real GDP corresponds to negative unplanned inventory investment equal to –400. More generally, any level of real GDP below 2,000 implies that firms have underestimated sales, leading to a negative level of unplanned inventory investment in the economy.

By putting together Equations 10, 11, and 14, we can summarize the general relationships among real GDP, planned aggregate spending, and unplanned inventory investment as follows:

(16) $GDP = C + I$

$\qquad = C + I_{Planned} + I_{Unplanned}$

$\qquad = AE_{Planned} + I_{Unplanned}$

So whenever real GDP exceeds $AE_{Planned}$, $I_{Unplanned}$ is positive; whenever real GDP is less than $AE_{Planned}$, $I_{Unplanned}$ is negative.

But firms will act to correct their mistakes. We've assumed that they don't change their prices, but they *can* adjust their output. Specifically, they will reduce production if they have experienced an unintended rise in inventories or increase production if they have experienced an unintended fall in inventories. And these responses will eventually eliminate the unanticipated changes in inventories and move the economy to a point at which real GDP is equal to planned aggregate spending.

Staying with our example, if real GDP is 1,000, negative unplanned inventory investment will lead firms to increase production, leading to a rise in real GDP. In fact, this will happen whenever real GDP is less than 2,000—that is, whenever real GDP is less than planned aggregate spending. Conversely, if real GDP is 2,500, positive unplanned inventory investment will lead firms to reduce production, leading to a fall in real GDP. This will happen whenever real GDP is greater than planned aggregate spending.

The only situation in which firms won't have an incentive to change output in the next period is when aggregate output, measured by real GDP, is equal to planned aggregate spending in the current period, an outcome known as **income–expenditure equilibrium.** In Table 3, income–expenditure equilibrium is achieved when real GDP is 2,000, the only level of real GDP at which unplanned inventory investment is zero. From now on, we'll denote the real GDP level at which income–expenditure equilibrium occurs as Y^* and call it the **income–expenditure equilibrium GDP.**

Figure 10 illustrates the concept of income–expenditure equilibrium graphically. Real GDP is on the horizontal axis and planned aggregate spending, $AE_{Planned}$, is on the vertical axis. There are two lines in the figure. The solid line is the planned aggregate spending line. It shows how $AE_{Planned}$, equal to $C + I_{Planned}$, depends on real GDP; it has a slope of 0.6, equal to the marginal propensity to consume, *MPC*, and a vertical intercept equal to $A + I_{Planned}$ (300 + 500 = 800). The dashed line, which goes through the origin with a slope of 1 (often called a 45-degree line), shows all the possible points at which planned aggregate spending is equal to real GDP.

This line allows us to easily spot the point of income–expenditure equilibrium, which must lie on both the 45-degree line and the planned aggregate spending line. So the point of income–expenditure equilibrium is at *E*, where the two lines cross. And the income–expenditure equilibrium GDP, Y^*, is 2,000—the same outcome we derived in Table 3.

Now consider what happens if the economy isn't in income–expenditure equilibrium. We can see from Figure 10 that whenever real GDP is less than Y^*, the planned aggregate spending line lies above the 45-degree line and $AE_{Planned}$ exceeds real GDP. In this situation, $I_{Unplanned}$ is negative: as shown in the figure, at

income–expenditure equilibrium a situation in which aggregate output, measured by real GDP, is equal to planned aggregate spending and firms have no incentive to change output.

income–expenditure equilibrium GDP the level of real GDP at which real GDP equals planned aggregate spending.

FIGURE 10 Income–Expenditure Equilibrium

Income–expenditure equilibrium occurs at E, the point where the planned aggregate spending line, $AE_{Planned}$, crosses the 45-degree line. At E, the economy produces real GDP of $2,000 billion per year, the only point at which real GDP equals planned aggregate spending, $AE_{Planned}$, and unplanned inventory investment, $I_{Unplanned}$, is zero. This is the level of income–expenditure equilibrium GDP, Y^*. At any level of real GDP less than Y^*, $AE_{Planned}$ exceeds real GDP. As a result, unplanned inventory investment, $I_{Unplanned}$, is negative and firms respond by increasing production. At any level of real GDP greater than Y^*, real GDP exceeds $AE_{Planned}$. Unplanned inventory investment, $I_{Unplanned}$, is positive and firms respond by reducing production.

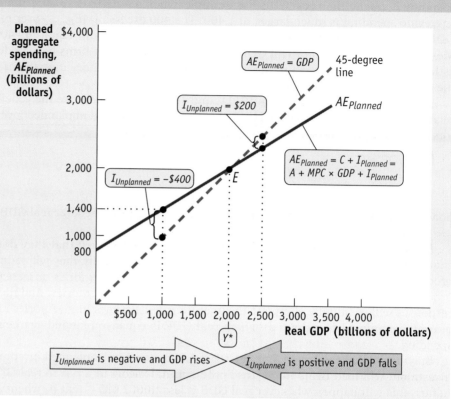

a real GDP of 1,000, $I_{Unplanned}$ is −400. As a consequence, real GDP will rise. In contrast, whenever real GDP is greater than Y^*, the planned aggregate expenditure line lies below the 45-degree line. Here, $I_{Unplanned}$ is positive: as shown, at a real GDP of 2,500, $I_{Unplanned}$ is 200. The unanticipated accumulation of inventory leads to a fall in real GDP.

The type of diagram shown in Figure 10, which identifies income–expenditure equilibrium as the point at which the planned aggregate spending line crosses the 45-degree line, has a special place in the history of economic thought. Known as the **Keynesian cross,** it was developed by Paul Samuelson, one of the greatest economists of the twentieth century (as well as a Nobel Prize winner), to explain the ideas of John Maynard Keynes, the founder of macroeconomics as we know it.

The Multiplier Process and Inventory Adjustment

We've just learned about a very important feature of the macroeconomy: when planned spending by households and firms does not equal the current aggregate output by firms, this difference shows up in changes in inventories. The response of firms to those inventory changes moves real GDP over time to the point at which real GDP and planned aggregate spending are equal. That's why, as we mentioned earlier, changes in inventories are considered a leading indicator of future economic activity.

Now that we understand how real GDP moves to achieve income–expenditure equilibrium for a given level of planned aggregate spending, let's turn to understanding what happens when there is *a shift of the planned aggregate spending line.* How does the economy move from the initial point of income–expenditure equilibrium to a new point of income–expenditure equilibrium? And what are the possible sources of changes in planned aggregate spending?

Keynesian cross a diagram that identifies income–expenditure equilibrium as the point where the planned aggregate spending line crosses the 45-degree line.

In our simple model, there are only two possible sources of a shift of the planned aggregate spending line: a change in planned investment spending, $I_{Planned}$, or a shift of the aggregate consumption function, CF. For example, a change in $I_{Planned}$ can occur because of a change in the interest rate. (Remember, we're assuming that the interest rate is fixed by factors that are outside the model. But we can still ask what happens when the interest rate changes.) A shift of the aggregate consumption function (that is, a change in its vertical intercept, A) can occur because of a change in aggregate wealth—say, due to a rise in house prices. When the planned aggregate spending line shifts—when there is a change in the level of planned aggregate spending at any given level of real GDP—there is an autonomous change in planned aggregate spending.

Recall that an autonomous change in planned aggregate spending is a change in the desired level of spending by firms, households, and government at any given level of real GDP (although we've assumed away the government for the time being). How does an autonomous change in planned aggregate spending affect real GDP in income–expenditure equilibrium?

Table 4 and Figure 11 start from the same numerical example we used in Table 3 and Figure 10. They also show the effect of an autonomous increase in planned aggregate spending of 400—what happens when planned aggregate spending is 400 higher at each level of real GDP.

Look first at Table 4. Before the autonomous increase in planned aggregate spending, the level of real GDP at which planned aggregate spending is equal to real GDP, Y^*, is 2,000. After the autonomous change, Y^* has risen to 3,000. The same result is visible in Figure 11. The initial income–expenditure equilibrium is at E_1, where Y_1^* is 2,000. The autonomous rise in planned aggregate spending shifts the planned aggregate spending line up, leading to a new income–expenditure equilibrium at E_2, where Y_2^* is 3,000.

The fact that the rise in income–expenditure equilibrium GDP, from 2,000 to 3,000, is much larger than the autonomous increase in aggregate spending, which is only 400, has a familiar explanation: the multiplier process. In the specific example we have just described, an autonomous increase in planned aggregate spending of 400 leads to an increase in Y^* from 2,000 to 3,000, a rise of 1,000. So the multiplier in this example is 1,000/400 = 2.5.

We can examine in detail what underlies the multistage multiplier process by looking more closely at Figure 11. First, starting from E_1, the autonomous increase in planned aggregate spending leads to a gap between planned aggregate spending and real GDP. This is represented by the vertical distance between X, at 2,400, and E_1, at 2,000. This gap illustrates an unplanned fall in inventory investment: $I_{Unplanned}$ = −400. Firms respond by increasing production, leading to a rise in real GDP from Y_1^*. The rise in real GDP translates into an increase in disposable income, YD.

That's the first stage in the chain reaction. But it doesn't stop there—the increase in YD leads to a rise in consumer spending, C, which sets off a second-round rise in real GDP. This in turn leads to a further rise in disposable income and consumer spending, and so on. And we could play this process in reverse: an autonomous fall in aggregate spending will lead to a chain reaction of reductions in real GDP and consumer spending.

We can summarize these results in an equation, where $\Delta AAE_{Planned}$ represents the autonomous change in $AE_{Planned}$, and $\Delta Y^* = Y_2^* - Y_1^*$, the subsequent change in income–expenditure equilibrium GDP:

(17) $\Delta Y^* = \text{Multiplier} \times \Delta AAE_{Planned} = \dfrac{1}{1 - MPC} \times \Delta AAE_{Planned}$

TABLE 4 Real GDP Before and After Autonomous Spending Increases by 400 (MPC = 0.6)

Real GDP	$AE_{Planned}$ before autonomous change	$AE_{Planned}$ after autonomous change
	(billions of dollars)	
$0	$800	$1,200
500	1,100	1,500
1,000	1,400	1,800
1,500	1,700	2,100
2,000	2,000	2,400
2,500	2,300	2,700
3,000	2,600	3,000
3,500	2,900	3,300
4,000	3,200	3,600

FIGURE 11 The Multiplier

This figure illustrates the change in Y^* caused by an autonomous increase in planned aggregate spending. The economy is initially at equilibrium point E_1 with an income–expenditure equilibrium GDP, Y_1^*, equal to 2,000. An autonomous increase in $AE_{Planned}$ of 400 shifts the planned aggregate spending line upward by 400. The economy is no longer in income–expenditure equilibrium: real GDP is equal to 2,000 but $AE_{Planned}$ is now 2,400, represented by point X. The vertical distance between the two planned aggregate spending lines, equal to 400, represents $I_{Unplanned} = -400$ — the negative inventory investment that the economy now experiences. Firms respond by increasing production, and the economy eventually reaches a new income–expenditure equilibrium at E_2 with a higher level of income–expenditure equilibrium GDP, Y_2^*, equal to 3,000.

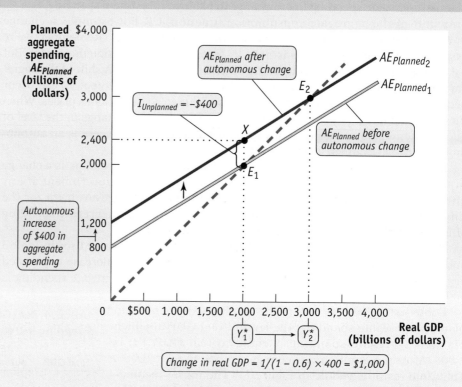

Recalling that the multiplier, $1/(1 - MPC)$, is greater than 1, Equation 17 tells us that the change in income–expenditure equilibrium GDP, ΔY^*, is several times larger than the autonomous change in planned aggregate spending, $\Delta AAE_{Planned}$. It also helps us recall an important point: because the marginal propensity to consume is less than 1, each increase in disposable income and each corresponding increase in consumer spending is smaller than in the previous round. That's because at each round some of the increase in disposable income leaks out into savings.

As a result, although real GDP grows at each round, the increase in real GDP diminishes from each round to the next. At some point, the increase in real GDP is negligible, and the economy converges to a new income–expenditure equilibrium GDP at Y_2^*.

The Paradox of Thrift In an earlier chapter, we mentioned the paradox of thrift to illustrate the fact that in macroeconomics the outcome of many individual actions can generate a result that is different from and worse than the simple sum of those individual actions. In the paradox of thrift, households and firms cut their spending in anticipation of future tough economic times. These actions depress the economy, leaving households and firms worse off than if they hadn't acted virtuously to prepare for tough times. It is called a paradox because what's usually "good" (saving to provide for your family in hard times) is "bad" (because it can make everyone worse off).

Using the multiplier, we can now see exactly how this scenario unfolds. Suppose that there is a slump in

Lavish spending after a slump makes everyone better off thanks to the multiplier effect.

consumer spending or investment spending, or both, just like the slump in residential construction investment spending leading up to the 2007–2009 recession. This causes a fall in income–expenditure equilibrium GDP that is several times larger than the original fall in spending. The fall in real GDP leaves consumers and producers worse off than they would have been if they hadn't cut their spending.

Conversely, prodigal behavior is rewarded: if consumers or producers increase their spending, the resulting multiplier process makes the increase in income–expenditure equilibrium GDP several times larger than the original increase in spending. So lavish spending makes consumers and producers better off than if they had been cautious spenders.

It's important to realize that our result that the multiplier is equal to $1/(1 - MPC)$ depends on the simplifying assumption that there are no taxes or transfers, so that disposable income is equal to real GDP. In the Chapter 13 appendix, we'll bring taxes into the picture, which makes the expression for the multiplier more complicated and the multiplier itself smaller.

But the general principle we just learned remains valid: an autonomous change in planned aggregate spending leads to a change in income–expenditure equilibrium GDP, both directly and through an induced change in consumer spending.

As we've seen, declines in planned investment spending are usually the major factor causing recessions, because historically they have been the most common source of autonomous reductions in aggregate spending. The tendency of the consumption function to shift upward over time, which as noted earlier in the Economics in Action, "Famous First Forecasting Failures," means that autonomous changes in both planned investment spending and consumer spending play important roles in expansions. But regardless of the source, there are multiplier effects in the economy that magnify the size of the initial change in aggregate spending.

What About Exports and Imports?

The simple version of the income–expenditure model that we have just laid out assumes that there is no international trade. But, as you may have noticed, the opening story for this chapter deviates in an important way from this simple version of the model. The coronavirus pandemic not only shutdown domestic industries, but also stopped international travel, which is included an important export for many countries. And in a basic sense the boom in North Dakota, described in an earlier Economics in Action, also involved trade—North Dakota's shale oil is sold to other states and countries, not to local consumers.

So how does bringing exports and imports back in change the story? The answer is that the basic multiplier story continues to work, with two modifications.

First, income earned from exports is a source of spending on domestically produced goods and services, just like consumption and investment. A rise in exports then leads to an increase in the demand for consumer goods, which leads to a further increase in income, and so on, exactly the way an increase in investment spending leads via the multiplier process to an economic expansion.

Second, the multiplier process itself is made somewhat weaker thanks to foreign trade: when consumer spending rises or falls, part of that change is reflected in changes in spending on imports, which don't affect a nation's own income. Suppose, for example, that U.S. consumer spending rises by $1 billion. If the United States didn't engage in foreign trade, all of that rise in spending would translate directly into a rise in U.S. GDP. In reality, however, a significant part of the total—say $200 million—will be a rise in spending on goods produced in Canada, Mexico, China, or elsewhere. And this spending *isn't* part of U.S. GDP. As economists sometimes put it, part of any spending change "leaks" abroad.

The effect of this leakage is to reduce the size of the multiplier. The extent to which the multiplier falls depends on how much of an additional dollar of spending falls on imports rather than domestic goods—the *marginal propensity to import*. In the case of the United States, which is a very large economy with only limited international trade, leaks from imports have only a modest effect on the size of the multiplier. In small countries that engage in a lot of trade, trade may greatly reduce the multiplier.

One final point about the effect of trade: it creates interdependence among national economies, because each country's exports are some other country's imports. Suppose that the U.S. economy enters a recession. This will lead, other things equal, to a decline in the amount we spend on goods produced in Canada, which means a decline in Canadian exports. And this spillover will tend to drag Canada's economy down, too. More broadly, the trade links between economies are one reason business cycles are often international, even global, in scope: many countries tend to have recessions and recoveries at the same time.

One thing is important to realize, however, about exports and imports: while they can change the size of the multiplier, they don't change the fundamental story about how aggregate spending rises and falls.

ECONOMICS >> *in Action*
Inventories and the End of a Recession

A very clear example of the role of inventories in the multiplier process took place in late 2001, as that year's recession came to an end. The driving force behind the recession was a slump in business investment spending. It took several years before investment spending bounced back in the form of a housing boom. By late 2001, the economy had begun to recover, largely due to an increase in consumer spending—especially on durable goods such as automobiles.

Initially, this increase in consumer spending caught manufacturers by surprise. Figure 12 shows changes in real GDP, real consumer spending, and real inventories in each quarter of 2001 and 2002. Notice the surge in consumer spending in the fourth quarter of 2001. Initially, it didn't lead to significant GDP growth because it was offset by a plunge in inventories. But in the first quarter of 2002, producers greatly increased their production, leading to a jump in real GDP.

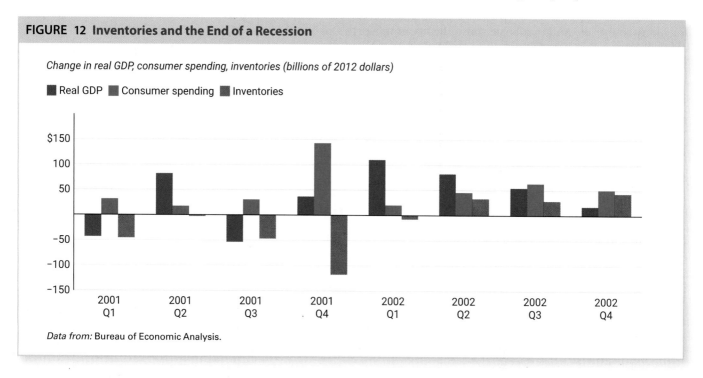

FIGURE 12 Inventories and the End of a Recession

Change in real GDP, consumer spending, inventories (billions of 2012 dollars)

■ Real GDP ■ Consumer spending ■ Inventories

Data from: Bureau of Economic Analysis.

>> Check Your Understanding 11-4

Solutions appear at back of book.

1. Although economists believe that recessions typically begin as slumps in investment spending, they also believe that consumer spending eventually slumps during a recession. Explain why.

2. **a.** Use a diagram like Figure 11 to show what happens when there is an autonomous fall in planned aggregate spending. Describe how the economy adjusts to a new income–expenditure equilibrium.

   b. Suppose Y^* is originally $500 billion, the autonomous reduction in planned aggregate spending is $300 million ($0.3 billion), and $MPC = 0.5$. Calculate Y^* after such a change.

What's Good for America Is Good for GM

Bill Pugliano/Getty Images

With the economy in a steep nosedive in 2009, the U.S. government took many stabilization measures, some of which were highly controversial. The decision to use taxpayer's funds to bail out General Motors, which was teetering on the edge of bankruptcy, was among the most controversial. To keep the company afloat, the U.S. government gave it $49.5 billion in loans that were then converted into stock, giving the government temporary ownership of 61% of the company.

General Motors—or GM, as it was often called in its heyday—was once a U.S. icon, so dominant that in the 1950s the company's president, who had been nominated as Secretary of Defense, famously claimed that any conflict of interest was inconceivable: "I thought what was good for our country was good for General Motors, and vice versa."

By 2009, the fate of GM and the fate of the United States seemed less intertwined. Still, the case for the bailout rested crucially on the belief that GM's problems weren't entirely self-made, that the company was in trouble because the U.S. economy was in trouble, and that national recovery would make a big difference to the automaker's fortune, too.

On the face of it, this interdependence wasn't entirely obvious: the 2007–2009 recession was driven by a housing bust and troubles in the banking sector, not by developments in the auto industry. But multiplier effects had indeed led to a plunge in auto sales, as shown in Figure 13. And sure enough, as the economy began to recover, auto sales made up most of their lost ground, with GM sharing in the industry's resurgence.

Did saving GM justify the bailout? The company's recovery meant that taxpayers got most of their money back—but not all of

it. Recall that the government loan of almost $50 billion was converted into GM stock. Over time, the government sold off its stake for roughly $40 billion—leaving taxpayers with a $10 billion loss.

Defenders of the bailout nonetheless declared it a success, because it resuscitated the U.S. auto industry and saved many jobs, not just in the auto companies and their suppliers, but in the many businesses whose sales depend on the incomes of workers employed in the auto industry. In the summer of 2009, the unemployment rate in Michigan, still the U.S. automotive heartland, rose above 14%—but it then began a rapid decline, falling below the national average to 4.5% by the summer of 2016. Few would argue that the speedy recovery in employment in Michigan would have happened without the auto bailout.

In the end, GM bounced back because the U.S. economy recovered; what was good for America was indeed still good for General Motors. And what was good for General Motors was clearly good for Michigan—and maybe, arguably, for the United States as a whole.

QUESTIONS FOR THOUGHT

1. Why did a national slump that began with housing affect companies like General Motors?

2. Why was it reasonable in June 2009 to predict that auto sales would improve in the near future?

3. How does this story about General Motors help explain how a slump in housing—a relatively small part of the U.S. economy—could produce such a deep national recession?

FIGURE 13 U.S. Auto Sales 2000–2020

Auto sales (millions)

Data from: Data Federal Reserve Bank of St. Louis and Bureau of Economic Analysis.

SUMMARY

1. An **autonomous change in aggregate spending** leads to a chain reaction in which the total change in real GDP is equal to the **multiplier** times the initial change in aggregate spending. The size of the multiplier, 1/(1 − *MPC*), depends on the **marginal propensity to consume, MPC,** the fraction of an additional dollar of disposable income spent on consumption. The larger the *MPC*, the larger the multiplier, and the larger the change in real GDP for any given autonomous change in aggregate spending. The **marginal propensity to save, MPS,** is equal to 1 − *MPC*.

2. The **consumption function** shows how an individual household's consumer spending is determined by its current disposable income. The **aggregate consumption function** shows the relationship for the entire economy. According to the life-cycle hypothesis, households try to smooth their consumption over their lifetimes. As a result, the aggregate consumption function shifts in response to changes in expected future disposable income and changes in aggregate wealth.

3. **Planned investment spending** depends negatively on the interest rate and on existing production capacity; it depends positively on expected future real GDP. The **accelerator principle** says that investment spending is greatly influenced by the expected growth rate of real GDP.

4. Firms hold **inventories** of goods so that they can satisfy consumer demand quickly. **Inventory investment** is positive when firms add to their inventories, negative when they reduce them. Often, however, changes in inventories are unintended. They arise when expected sales and actual sales don't match. The result is unplanned inventory investment. **Actual investment spending** is the sum of planned investment spending and unplanned inventory investment.

5. In **income–expenditure equilibrium, planned aggregate spending,** which in a simplified model with no government and no trade is the sum of consumer spending and planned investment spending, is equal to real GDP. At the **income–expenditure equilibrium GDP,** or *Y**, unplanned inventory investment is zero. When planned aggregate spending is larger than *Y**, unplanned inventory investment is negative; there is an unanticipated reduction in inventories and firms increase production. When planned aggregate spending is less than *Y**, unplanned inventory investment is positive; there is an unanticipated increase in inventories and firms reduce production. The **Keynesian cross** shows how the economy self-adjusts to income–expenditure equilibrium through inventory adjustments.

6. After an autonomous change in planned aggregate spending, the inventory adjustment process moves the economy to a new income–expenditure equilibrium. The change in income–expenditure equilibrium GDP arising from an autonomous change in spending is equal to $(1/(1 − MPC)) \times \Delta AAE_{Planned}$.

7. When trade is introduced, the basic multiplier story continues to work but it is modified in two ways: first, income earned from exports is a source of spending on domestically produced goods and services, just like consumption and investment; and second, imports reduce the size of the multiplier.

KEY TERMS

Marginal propensity to consume (*MPC*), p. 316
Marginal propensity to save (*MPS*), p. 316
Autonomous change in aggregate spending, p. 318
Multiplier, p. 318
Consumption function, p. 320
Aggregate consumption function, p. 322
Planned investment spending, p. 326
Accelerator principle, p. 328
Inventories, p. 328
Inventory investment, p. 328
Unplanned inventory investment, p. 328
Actual investment spending, p. 328
Planned aggregate spending, p. 331
Income–expenditure equilibrium, p. 333
Income–expenditure equilibrium GDP, p. 333
Keynesian cross, p. 334

PRACTICE QUESTIONS

1. Explain how each of the following actions will affect the level of planned investment spending and unplanned inventory investment. Assume the economy is initially in income–expenditure equilibrium.

   a. The Federal Reserve raises the interest rate.
   b. There is a rise in the expected growth rate of real GDP.
   c. A sizable inflow of foreign funds into the country lowers the interest rate.
   d. A large economic shutdown of nonessential businesses causes a significant reduction in consumer spending.

2. The chapter introduced a linear consumption function, which assumes the marginal propensity to consume is equal at all levels of disposable income. Yet many research studies show that *MPC* varies across income levels. Would you expect *MPC* to be greater for lower or higher income groups? How would relaxing the assumption of a constant *MPC*, allowing it to vary across income groups, change the multiplier?

PROBLEMS

1. Due to an increase in consumer wealth, there is a $40 billion autonomous increase in consumer spending in the economies of Westlandia and Eastlandia. Assuming that the aggregate price level is constant, the interest rate is fixed in both countries, and there are no taxes and no foreign trade, complete the accompanying tables to show the various rounds of increased spending that will occur in both economies if the marginal propensity to consume is 0.5 in Westlandia and 0.75 in Eastlandia. What do your results indicate about the relationship between the size of *MPC* and the multiplier?

	Westlandia		
Rounds	Incremental change in GDP		Total change in GDP
1	$\Delta C = 40 billion		?
2	$MPC \times \Delta C =$	?	?
3	$MPC \times MPC \times \Delta C =$	?	?
4	$MPC \times MPC \times MPC \times \Delta C =$	?	?
...		...	...
Total change in GDP	$(1/(1 - MPC)) \times \Delta C = ?$		

	Eastlandia		
Rounds	Incremental change in GDP		Total change in GDP
1	$\Delta C = 40 billion		?
2	$MPC \times \Delta C =$	?	?
3	$MPC \times MPC \times \Delta C =$	?	?
4	$MPC \times MPC \times MPC \times \Delta C =$	?	?
...		...	...
Total change in GDP	$(1/(1 - MPC)) \times \Delta C = ?$		

2. Assuming that the aggregate price level is constant, the interest rate is fixed, and there are no taxes and no foreign trade, what will be the change in GDP if the following events occur?

   a. There is an autonomous increase in consumer spending of $25 billion; the marginal propensity to consume is 2/3.

   b. Firms reduce investment spending by $40 billion; the marginal propensity to consume is 0.8.

   c. The government increases its purchases of military equipment by $60 billion; the marginal propensity to consume is 0.6.

3. Economists observed the only five residents of a very small economy and estimated each one's consumer spending at various levels of current disposable income. The accompanying table shows each resident's consumer spending at three income levels.

Individual consumer spending by	Individual current disposable income		
	$0	$20,000	$40,000
Andre	$1,000	$15,000	$29,000
Barbara	2,500	12,500	22,500
Casey	2,000	20,000	38,000
Declan	5,000	17,000	29,000
Elena	4,000	19,000	34,000

   a. What is each resident's consumption function? What is *MPC* for each resident?

   b. What is the economy's aggregate consumption function? What is *MPC* for the economy?

4. From 2017 to 2022, Eastlandia experienced large fluctuations in both aggregate consumer spending and disposable income, but wealth, the interest rate, and expected future disposable income did not change. The accompanying table shows the level of aggregate consumer spending and disposable income in millions of dollars for each of these years. Use this information to answer the following questions.

Year	Disposable income (millions of dollars)	Consumer spending (millions of dollars)
2017	$100	$180
2018	350	380
2019	300	340
2020	400	420
2021	375	400
2022	500	500

   a. Plot the aggregate consumption function for Eastlandia.

   b. What is *MPC*? What is *MPS*?

   c. What is the aggregate consumption function?

5. The Bureau of Economic Analysis reported that, in real terms, overall consumer spending increased by $376.2 billion in 2022.

   a. If *MPC* is 0.50, by how much will real GDP change in response?

   b. If there are no other changes to autonomous spending other than the increase in consumer spending in part a, and unplanned inventory investment, $I_{Unplanned}$, decreased by $100 billion, what is the change in real GDP?

c. GDP at the end of 2022 was $20,014.1 billion. If GDP were to increase by the amount calculated in part b, what would be the percent increase in GDP?

6. During the early 2000s, the Case–Shiller U.S. Home Price Index, a measure of average home prices, rose continuously until it peaked in March 2006. From March 2006 to May 2009, the index lost 32% of its value. Meanwhile, the stock market experienced similar ups and downs. From March 2003 to October 2007, the Standard and Poor's 500 (S&P 500) stock index, a broad measure of stock market prices, almost doubled, from 800.73 to a high of 1,565.15. From that time until March 2009, the index fell by almost 60%, to a low of 676.53. How do you think the movements in home prices both influenced the growth in real GDP during the first half of the decade and added to the concern about maintaining consumer spending after the collapse in the housing market that began in 2006? To what extent did the movements in the stock market hurt or help consumer spending?

7. How will planned investment spending change as the following events occur?

a. The interest rate falls as a result of Federal Reserve policy.

b. The U.S. Environmental Protection Agency decrees that corporations must upgrade or replace their machinery in order to reduce their emissions of sulfur dioxide.

c. Baby boomers begin to retire in large numbers and reduce their savings, resulting in higher interest rates.

8. In an economy with no government and no foreign sectors, autonomous consumer spending is $250 billion, planned investment spending is $350 billion, and the marginal propensity to consume is 2/3.

a. Plot the aggregate consumption function and planned aggregate spending.

b. What is unplanned inventory investment when real GDP equals $600 billion?

c. What is Y^*, income–expenditure equilibrium GDP?

d. What is the value of the multiplier?

e. If planned investment spending rises to $450 billion, what will be the new Y^*?

9. An economy has a marginal propensity to consume of 0.5, and Y^*, income–expenditure equilibrium GDP, equals $500 billion. Given an autonomous increase in planned investment of $10 billion, show the rounds of increased spending that take place by completing the accompanying table. The first and second rows are filled in for you. In the first row, the increase of planned investment spending of $10 billion raises real GDP and YD by $10 billion, leading to an increase in consumer spending of $5 billion ($MPC \times$ change in disposable income) in row 2, raising real GDP and YD by a further $5 billion.

Rounds	Change in $I_{Planned}$ or C	Change in real GDP	Change in YD
	(billions of dollars)		
1	$\Delta I_{Planned} = \$10.00$	$10.00	$10.00
2	$\Delta C = \$5.00$	$5.00	$5.00
3	$\Delta C = ?$	?	?
4	$\Delta C = ?$	?	?
5	$\Delta C = ?$	?	?
6	$\Delta C = ?$	?	?
7	$\Delta C = ?$	?	?
8	$\Delta C = ?$	?	?
9	$\Delta C = ?$	?	?
10	$\Delta C = ?$	?	?

a. What is the total change in real GDP after the 10 rounds? What is the value of the multiplier? What would you expect the total change in Y^* to be based on the multiplier formula? How do your answers to the first and third questions compare?

b. Redo the table starting from round 2, assuming MPC is 0.75. What is the total change in real GDP after 10 rounds? What is the value of the multiplier? As the marginal propensity to consume increases, what happens to the value of the multiplier?

10. Although the United States is one of the richest nations in the world, it is also the world's largest debtor nation. We often hear that the problem is the nation's low savings rate. Suppose policy makers attempt to rectify this by encouraging greater savings in the economy. What effect will their successful attempts have on real GDP?

11. The U.S. economy slowed significantly in early 2008, and policy makers were extremely concerned about growth. To boost the economy, Congress passed several relief packages (the Economic Stimulus Act of 2008 and the American Recovery and Reinvestment Act of 2009) that combined would deliver about $700 billion in government spending. Assume, for the sake of argument, that this spending was in the form of payments made directly to consumers. The objective was to boost the economy by increasing the disposable income of American consumers.

a. Calculate the initial change in aggregate consumer spending as a consequence of this policy measure if MPC in the United States is 0.5. Then calculate the resulting change in real GDP arising from the $700 billion in payments.

b. Illustrate the effect on real GDP with the use of a graph depicting the income–expenditure equilibrium. Label the vertical axis "Planned aggregate spending, $AE_{Planned}$" and the horizontal axis "Real GDP." Draw two planned aggregate expenditure curves ($AE_{Planned1}$ and $AE_{Planned2}$) and a 45-degree line to show the effect of the autonomous policy change on the equilibrium.

12. Access the Discovery Data exercise for Chapter 11, Problem 12 online.

  a. Calculate the marginal propensity to consume for the United States from 2002 through 2022.

  b. Find the change in real exports of goods and services from 2008 to 2009 and 2021 to 2022.

  c. Using *MPC* from part a, calculate the multiplier and the effect of a change in real exports from part b on real GDP.

13. Access the Discovering Data exercise for Chapter 11, Problem 13 online.

  a. The United Kingdom and most of Europe suffered from the Long Depression from 1873 to 1896. Calculate *MPC* in the United Kingdom using data from 1830 through 1900.

  b. Find the change in real investment expenditures from 1877 to 1880 and 1883 to 1886.

  c. Using the multiplier from part a, calculate multiplier and the effect of a change in real exports from part b on real GDP. How does your calculation compare with the actual change in real GDP?

14. a. The accompanying table shows gross domestic product (GDP), disposable income (YD), consumer spending (C), and planned investment spending ($I_{Planned}$) in an economy. Assume there is no government or foreign sector in this economy. Complete the table by calculating planned aggregate spending ($AE_{Planned}$) and unplanned inventory investment ($I_{Unplanned}$).

  b. What is the aggregate consumption function?

  c. What is Y*, income–expenditure equilibrium GDP?

  d. What is the value of the multiplier?

  e. If planned investment spending falls to $200 billion, what will be the new Y*?

  f. If autonomous consumer spending rises to $200 billion, what will be the new Y*?

GDP	YD	C	$I_{Planned}$	$AE_{Planned}$	$I_{Unplanned}$
		(billions of dollars)			
$0	$0	$100	$300	?	?
400	400	400	300	?	?
800	800	700	300	?	?
1,200	1,200	1,000	300	?	?
1,600	1,600	1,300	300	?	?
2,000	2,000	1,600	300	?	?
2,400	2,400	1,900	300	?	?
2,800	2,800	2,200	300	?	?
3,200	3,200	2,500	300	?	?

Deriving the Multiplier Algebraically

This appendix shows how to derive the multiplier algebraically. First, recall that in this chapter planned aggregate spending, $AE_{Planned}$, is the sum of consumer spending, C, which is determined by the consumption function, and planned investment spending, $I_{Planned}$. That is, $AE_{Planned} = C + I_{Planned}$. Rewriting this equation to express all its terms fully, we have:

(A-1) $AE_{Planned} = A + MPC \times YD + I_{Planned}$

Because there are no taxes or government transfers in this model, disposable income is equal to GDP, so Equation A-1 becomes:

(A-2) $AE_{Planned} = A + MPC \times GDP + I_{Planned}$

The income–expenditure equilibrium GDP, Y^*, is equal to planned aggregate spending:

(A-3) $Y^* = AE_{Planned}$
$$= A + MPC \times Y^* + I_{Planned}$$
in income – expenditure equilibrium

Just two more steps. Subtract $MPC \times Y^*$ from both sides of Equation A-3:

(A-4) $Y^* - MPC \times Y^* = Y^* \times (1 - MPC) = A + I_{Planned}$

Finally, divide both sides by $(1 - MPC)$:

(A-5) $Y^* = \dfrac{A + I_{Planned}}{1 - MPC}$

Equation A-5 tells us that a \$1 autonomous change in planned aggregate spending—a change in either A or $I_{Planned}$—causes a \$1/(1 − MPC) change in income–expenditure equilibrium GDP, Y^*. The multiplier in our simple model is therefore:

(A-6) Multiplier $= 1/(1 - MPC)$

PROBLEMS

1. Complete the following table by calculating the value of the multiplier and identifying the change in Y^* due to the change in autonomous spending. How does the value of the multiplier change with the marginal propensity to consume?

MPC	Value of multiplier	Change in spending	Change in Y*
0.5	?	$\Delta C = +\$50$ million	?
0.6	?	$\Delta I = -\$10$ million	?
0.75	?	$\Delta C = -\$25$ million	?
0.8	?	$\Delta I = +\$20$ million	?
0.9	?	$\Delta C = -\$2.5$ million	?

2. In an economy without government purchases, transfers, or taxes, and without imports or exports, aggregate autonomous consumer spending is \$500 billion, planned investment spending is \$250 billion, and the marginal propensity to consume is 0.5.

   a. Write the expression for planned aggregate spending as in Equation A-1.

   b. Solve for Y^* algebraically.

   c. What is the value of the multiplier?

   d. How will Y^* change if autonomous consumer spending falls to \$450 billion?

12 Aggregate Demand and Aggregate Supply

A TOUGH CALL IN 2021

UNEMPLOYMENT AND INFLATION are the two great evils of macroeconomics, and policy makers do their best to keep both under control. Sometimes, however, this task isn't straightforward, as we learned in Chapter 8: policies to control inflation can worsen unemployment and policies aimed at reducing unemployment can cause inflation. So at times it's hard to know whether inflation or unemployment poses the bigger risk to the economy.

Policy makers at the Federal Reserve, also known as the Fed, found themselves facing such a quandary in summer 2021. The economy was recovering from the brief but severe pandemic recession of 2020; by June 2021, more than a year after the recession ended, the unemployment rate was still 5.9%, far above its prepandemic level of around 3.5%. But inflation, which had been low for decades, had suddenly jumped: consumer prices were 2.1% higher in June than they had been three months earlier, which meant that inflation at an annual rate was running above 8%. So should the Fed keep its policies unchanged, allowing unemployment to keep falling, or should it slam on the brakes in an attempt to bring inflation back down?

At the time, the Fed decided to hold off. Fed officials believed that much of the inflation reflected temporary disruptions caused, directly or indirectly, by the pandemic. In particular, consumers who feared infection had shifted their spending away from in-person services toward goods — for example, fitness-oriented Americans were staying away from gyms but buying lots of exercise equipment — and the shift had overwhelmed the complex supply chains that, for example, bring goods from factories in Asia to consumers in California. Fed officials believed that these supply-chain snarls would soon be straightened out, and that inflation would come down of its own accord.

By early 2022, however, the Fed had changed its assessment. Inflation stayed high for much longer than expected and also broadened, affecting many goods and services that weren't obviously suffering from supply disruptions. It began to look, in other words, as if much of the inflation problem wasn't being caused by inadequate supply; instead, it reflected excessive demand. In March 2022, the Fed began hitting the brakes, raising interest rates in an attempt to discourage private spending, even while acknowledging that its actions might well cause increased unemployment.

How did Fed officials get it wrong in 2021? (They may not have been completely wrong: inflation did come down significantly in late 2022 as those supply chains finally got unsnarled.) The answer is that macroeconomic troubles can be caused by different types of shocks, and sometimes it's hard to know which type of shock you're facing. Some economic crises, like the Great Recession of 2007–2009, are caused by *demand shocks*. Others, like the combined inflation and recession of 1979–1980, are caused by *supply shocks*. In summer 2021, the Fed believed that it was mostly facing a temporary supply shock; by spring 2022, it had decided that it also had to deal with a large demand shock.

In this chapter, we will discuss the *AD–AS model* to distinguish between these two kinds of shocks, and how they affect the economy. We'll proceed in three steps. First, we'll develop the concept of *aggregate demand*. Then we'll develop the parallel concept of *aggregate supply*. Finally, we'll put the two concepts together. ●

Shipping containers sit stacked on the *Ever Lively* container ship at the Port of Los Angeles on October 25, 2021 in San Pedro, California.

Mario Tama/Getty Images

WHAT YOU WILL LEARN

- How does the **aggregate demand curve** illustrate the relationship between inflation and the quantity of aggregate output demanded?
- How does the **aggregate supply curve** illustrate the relationship between inflation and the quantity of aggregate output supplied?
- Why is the aggregate supply curve different in the short run compared to the long run?
- How is the *AD–AS model* used to analyze economic fluctuations?
- How can monetary policy and fiscal policy stabilize the economy?

aggregate demand curve a graphical representation that shows the relationship between the inflation rate and the quantity of aggregate output demanded by households, firms, the government, and the rest of the world. The aggregate demand curve has a negative slope as the inflation rate declines the quantity of aggregate demand increases.

‖ Aggregate Demand

The United States, along with most of the rest of the world, experienced a severe recession between late 2007 and early 2009. This so-called Great Recession, the great majority of economists agree, was the result of a massive negative demand shock. What does that mean? In Chapter 3, we explained that when economists talk about a fall in the demand for a particular good or service, they're referring to a leftward shift of the demand curve. Similarly, when economists talk about a negative demand shock to the economy as a whole, they're referring to a leftward shift of the **aggregate demand curve,** a curve that shows the relationship between inflation and the quantity of aggregate output demanded by households, firms, the government, and the rest of the world.

Figure 1 shows an aggregate demand curve. It's hypothetical, although it's meant to be a somewhat realistic picture of what the curve might look like in 2024 (after this edition went to press), based on consensus economic forecasts and statistical relationships estimated on past data. The horizontal axis shows the total quantity of domestic goods and services demanded, measured in 2012 dollars. We use real GDP to measure aggregate output and will often use the two terms interchangeably.

The vertical axis shows the inflation rate, measured by the annual rate of change of the GDP deflator. With these variables on the axes, we can draw a curve, *AD*, showing how much aggregate output would have been demanded at any given inflation rate. Point A on the curve corresponds to a consensus forecast (from the Survey of Professional Forecasters) made in early 2023; at that point, the forecasters expected real GDP in 2024 to be $20.5 trillion in 2012 dollars, and inflation to be 2.3%.

The aggregate demand curve in Figure 1 is downward sloping, indicating a negative relationship between the inflation rate and the quantity of aggregate output demanded. A higher inflation rate, other things equal, reduces the quantity of aggregate output demanded; a lower inflation rate, other things equal, increases the quantity of aggregate output demanded. According to Figure 1, if inflation in 2024 turned out to be 4.3% instead of 2.3%, the total quantity of domestic final

---

FIGURE 1 The Aggregate Demand Curve

The aggregate demand curve shows the relationship between the inflation rate and the real GDP. The curve is downward sloping as a lower inflation rate, other things equal, increase the quantity of aggregate demand. The AD curve drawn below represents the forecast of professional forecasters for 2024. Point A represents their prediction for 2024, real GDP will be $20.5 trillion with inflation equal to 2.3%.

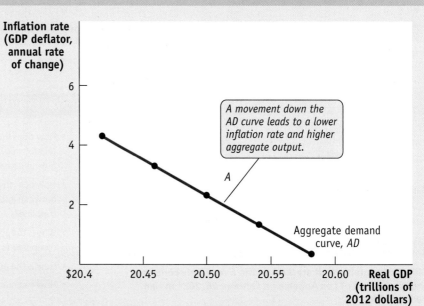

goods and services demanded would be about $20.4 trillion in 2012 dollars instead of $20.5 trillion.

The first key question about the aggregate demand curve is: why should the curve be downward sloping?

Why Is the Aggregate Demand Curve Downward Sloping?

In Figure 1, the curve *AD* is downward sloping. Why? Recall the basic equation of national income accounting:

(1) $GDP = C + I + G + X - IM$

where *C* is consumer spending, *I* is investment spending, *G* is government purchases of goods and services, *X* is exports to other countries, and *IM* is imports. If we measure these variables in constant dollars—that is, in prices of a base year—then $C + I + G + X - IM$ is the quantity of domestically produced final goods and services demanded during a given period. *G* is decided by the government, but the other variables are private-sector decisions. To understand why the aggregate demand curve slopes downward, we need to understand why a rise in the inflation rate reduces *C*, *I*, and $X - IM$.

You might think that the downward slope of the aggregate demand curve is a natural consequence of the *law of demand* defined back in Chapter 3. That is, because the demand curve for any one good is downward sloping, isn't it natural that the demand curve for aggregate output is also downward sloping? This turns out, however, to be a misleading parallel. The demand curve for any individual good shows how the quantity demanded depends on the price of that good, *holding the prices of other goods and services constant*. The main reason the quantity of a good demanded falls when the price of that good rises—that is, the quantity of a good demanded falls as we move up the demand curve—is that people switch their consumption to other goods and services.

But when we consider movements up or down the aggregate demand curve, we're considering *a simultaneous change in the prices of all final goods and services*. Furthermore, changes in the composition of goods and services in consumer spending aren't relevant to the aggregate demand curve: if consumers decide to buy fewer clothes but more cars, this doesn't necessarily change the total quantity of final goods and services they demand.

Why, then, does a rise in the inflation rate lead to a fall in the quantity of all domestically produced final goods and services demanded? The main answer, economists believe, lies in the *interest rate effect* of higher overall prices, which depends on the special role money plays in the economy.

Economists use the term *money* in its narrowest sense to refer to cash and bank accounts on which people can use a debit card and write checks. People and firms hold money because it reduces the cost and inconvenience of making transactions. But at any given point in time, there is a limited amount of money in circulation; people who want to increase their holdings of money must borrow or sell other assets. As a result, the supply of money strongly affects interest rates in the short run.

What determines the money supply? We'll discuss this topic at length in Chapter 14, but what you need to know at this point is that in modern economies the quantity of money is basically determined by a monetary authority or *central bank* such as the Federal Reserve in the United States, the European Central Bank in Europe, the Reserve Bank of China, and so on. Control over the money supply gives central banks the ability to set interest rates. And when inflation is high, central banks normally raise interest rates, which they believe will help limit future inflation.

In Chapter 10, we learned that a rise in the interest rate reduces investment spending because it makes the cost of borrowing higher. It also reduces consumer spending because households save more of their disposable income. So a rise in inflation depresses investment spending, *I*, and consumer spending, *C*, via its effect on interest rates.

We'll have a lot more to say about money and interest rates in Chapter 15 on monetary policy. We'll also see, in Chapter 18, which covers international macroeconomics, that a higher interest rate indirectly tends to reduce exports (*X*) and increase imports (*IM*). For now, the important point is that the aggregate demand curve is downward sloping due to the interest rate effect of a change in the inflation rate.

The Aggregate Demand Curve and the Income–Expenditure Model

In the preceding chapter, we introduced the *income–expenditure model*, which shows how the economy arrives at *income–expenditure equilibrium*. Now we've introduced the aggregate demand curve, which relates the overall demand for goods and services to the overall rate of inflation. How do these concepts fit together?

Recall that one of the assumptions of the income–expenditure model is that the aggregate price level is fixed, which implies the inflation rate is also fixed. We now drop that assumption. We can still use the income–expenditure model, however, to ask what aggregate spending would be *at any given inflation rate*, which is precisely what the aggregate demand curve shows. So the *AD* curve is actually derived from the income–expenditure model. Economists sometimes say that the income–expenditure model is "embedded" in the *AD–AS* model.

Figure 2 shows, once again, how income–expenditure equilibrium is determined. Real GDP is on the horizontal axis; real planned aggregate spending is on the vertical axis. Other things equal, planned aggregate spending, equal to consumer spending plus planned investment spending, rises with real GDP. This is illustrated by the upward-sloping lines $AE_{Planned_1}$ and $AE_{Planned_2}$. Income–expenditure equilibrium, as we learned in Chapter 11, is at the point where the line representing planned aggregate spending crosses the 45-degree line. For example, if $AE_{Planned_1}$ is the relationship between real GDP and planned aggregate

FIGURE 2 How Changes in the Inflation Rate Affect Income–Expenditure Equilibrium

Income–expenditure equilibrium occurs at the point where the curve $AE_{Planned}$, which shows real aggregate planned spending, crosses the 45-degree line. A fall in the inflation rate causes the $AE_{Planned}$ curve to shift from $AE_{Planned_1}$ to $AE_{Planned_2}$, leading to a rise in income–expenditure equilibrium GDP from Y_1 to Y_2.

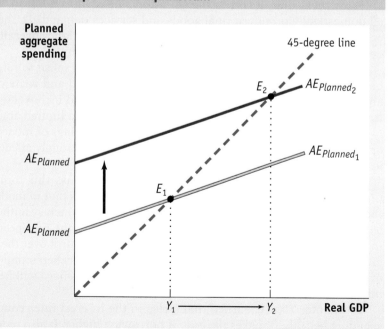

FIGURE 3 The Income–Expenditure Model and the Aggregate Demand Curve

Figure 2 shows how a fall in the inflation rate shifts the planned aggregate spending curve up, leading to a rise in real GDP. Here we see that same result as a movement along the aggregate demand curve. If the inflation rate falls from π_1 to π_2, real GDP rises from Y_1 to Y_2. The *AD* curve is therefore downward sloping.

A movement down the AD curve leads to a lower inflation rate and higher aggregate output.

spending, then income–expenditure equilibrium is at point E_1, corresponding to a level of real GDP equal to Y_1.

We've just seen, however, that changes in the inflation rate change the level of planned aggregate spending *at any given level of real GDP*. This means that when the inflation rate changes, the $AE_{Planned}$ curve shifts. For example, suppose that the inflation rate falls. As a result of the interest rate effect, the fall in inflation will lead to higher planned aggregate spending at any given level of real GDP. So the $AE_{Planned}$ curve will shift up, as illustrated in Figure 2 by the shift from $AE_{Planned_1}$ to $AE_{Planned_2}$. The increase in planned aggregate spending leads to a multiplier process that moves the income–expenditure equilibrium from point E_1 to point E_2, raising real GDP from Y_1 to Y_2.

Figure 3 shows how this result can be used to derive the aggregate demand curve. In Figure 3, we show a fall in the inflation rate from π_1 to π_2. We see in Figure 2 that a fall in inflation would lead to an upward shift of the $AE_{Planned}$ curve and hence a rise in real GDP. We can see this same result in Figure 3 as a movement along the *AD* curve: as the inflation rate falls, real GDP rises from Y_1 to Y_2. Income–expenditure equilibrium occurs at the point where the curve $AE_{Planned}$, which shows real aggregate planned spending, crosses the 45-degree line. A fall in the inflation rate causes the $AE_{Planned}$ curve to shift from $AE_{Planned_1}$ to $AE_{Planned_2}$, leading to a rise in income–expenditure equilibrium GDP from Y_1 to Y_2.

So the aggregate demand curve doesn't replace the income–expenditure model. Instead, it's a way to summarize what the income–expenditure model says about the effects of changes in the inflation rate.

In practice, economists often use the income–expenditure model to analyze short-run economic fluctuations, even though strictly speaking it should be seen as a component of a more complete model. In the short run, in particular, this is usually a reasonable shortcut.

Shifts of the Aggregate Demand Curve

In Chapter 3, where we introduced the analysis of supply and demand in the market for an individual good or service, we stressed the importance of the distinction between *movements along* the demand curve and *shifts of* the demand curve. The same distinction applies to the aggregate demand curve. Figure 1 shows a

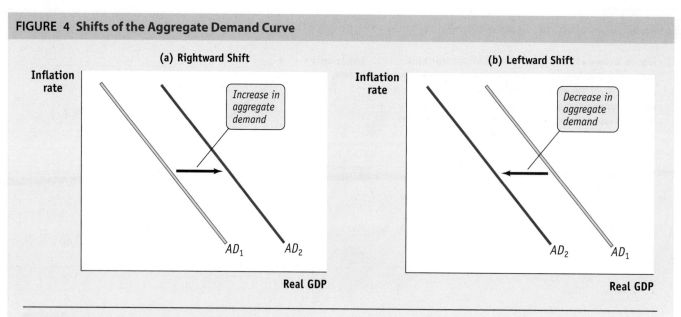

FIGURE 4 Shifts of the Aggregate Demand Curve

(a) Rightward Shift

Inflation rate

Increase in aggregate demand

AD_1 AD_2

Real GDP

(b) Leftward Shift

Inflation rate

Decrease in aggregate demand

AD_2 AD_1

Real GDP

Panel (a) shows the effect of events that increase the quantity of aggregate output demanded at any given inflation rate, such as improvements in business and consumer expectations or increased government spending. Such changes shift the aggregate demand curve to the right, from AD_1 to AD_2.

Panel (b) shows the effect of events that decrease the quantity of aggregate output demanded at any given inflation rate, such as a fall in wealth caused by a stock market decline. This shifts the aggregate demand curve leftward from AD_1 to AD_2.

movement along the aggregate demand curve, a change in the aggregate quantity of goods and services demanded as the inflation rate changes.

But there can also be *shifts of* the aggregate demand curve, changes in the quantity of goods and services demanded at any given inflation rate, as shown in Figure 4. When we talk about an increase in aggregate demand, we mean a shift of the aggregate demand curve to the right, as shown in panel (a) by the shift from AD_1 to AD_2. A rightward shift occurs when the quantity of aggregate output demanded increases at any given inflation rate. A decrease in aggregate demand means that the AD curve shifts to the left, as in panel (b). A leftward shift implies that the quantity of aggregate output demanded falls at any given inflation rate.

A number of factors can shift the aggregate demand curve. Among the most important factors are changes in expectations, changes in wealth, and the size of the existing stock of physical capital. In addition, both fiscal and monetary policy can shift the aggregate demand curve. All five factors set the multiplier process in motion. By causing an initial rise or fall in real GDP, they change disposable income, which leads to additional changes in aggregate spending, which lead to further changes in real GDP, and so on. For an overview of factors that shift the aggregate demand curve, see Table 1.

Changes in Expectations Both consumer spending and planned investment spending depend in part on people's expectations about the future. Consumers base their spending not only on the income they have now but also on the income they expect to have in the future. Firms base their planned investment spending not only on current conditions but also on the sales they expect to make in the future. As a result, changes in expectations can push consumer spending and planned investment spending up or down. If consumers and firms become more optimistic, aggregate spending rises; if they become more pessimistic, aggregate spending falls.

In fact, short-run economic forecasters pay careful attention to surveys of consumer and business sentiment. In particular, forecasters watch the Consumer

TABLE 1 Factors That Shift Aggregate Demand

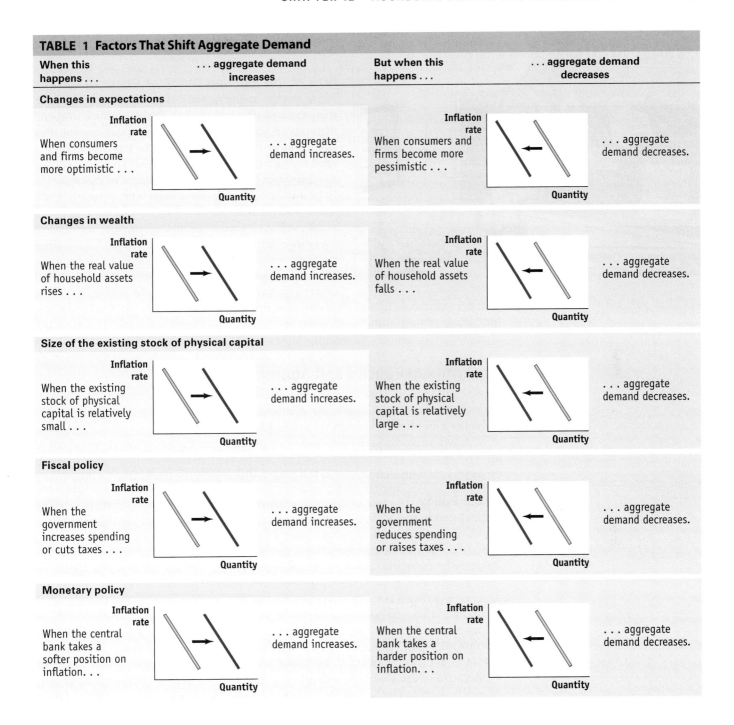

When this happens . . .	. . . aggregate demand increases	But when this happens . . .	. . . aggregate demand decreases
Changes in expectations			
When consumers and firms become more optimistic . . .	. . . aggregate demand increases.	When consumers and firms become more pessimistic . . .	. . . aggregate demand decreases.
Changes in wealth			
When the real value of household assets rises . . .	. . . aggregate demand increases.	When the real value of household assets falls . . .	. . . aggregate demand decreases.
Size of the existing stock of physical capital			
When the existing stock of physical capital is relatively small . . .	. . . aggregate demand increases.	When the existing stock of physical capital is relatively large . . .	. . . aggregate demand decreases.
Fiscal policy			
When the government increases spending or cuts taxes . . .	. . . aggregate demand increases.	When the government reduces spending or raises taxes . . .	. . . aggregate demand decreases.
Monetary policy			
When the central bank takes a softer position on inflation. . .	. . . aggregate demand increases.	When the central bank takes a harder position on inflation. . .	. . . aggregate demand decreases.

Confidence Index, a monthly measure calculated by The Conference Board, and the Michigan Consumer Sentiment Index, a similar measure calculated by the University of Michigan.

Changes in Wealth Consumer spending depends in part on the value of household assets. When the real value of these assets rises, the purchasing power they embody also rises, leading to an increase in aggregate spending. For example, in the 1990s there was a significant rise in the stock market that increased aggregate demand. And when the real value of household assets falls (because of a stock market crash, for instance), the purchasing power they embody is reduced and aggregate demand also falls. The stock market crash of 1929 was a significant factor leading to the Great Depression. Similarly, a sharp decline in real estate values

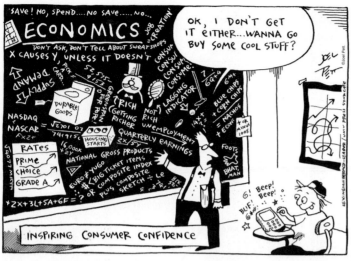

was a major factor depressing consumer spending during the 2007–2009 recession.

Size of the Existing Stock of Physical Capital

Firms engage in planned investment spending to add to their stock of physical capital. Their incentive to spend depends in part on how much physical capital they already have: the more they have, the less they will feel a need to add more, other things equal. The same applies to other types of investment spending. For example, if a large number of houses have been built in recent years, this will depress the demand for new houses and, as a result, will also tend to reduce residential investment spending. In fact, that's part of the reason for the deep slump in residential investment spending that began in 2006. The housing boom of the previous few years had created an oversupply of houses: by spring 2009, the inventory of unsold houses on the market was equal to more than 14 months of sales, and prices of new homes had fallen more than 25% from their peak. This gave the construction industry little incentive to build even more homes.

Government Policies and Aggregate Demand

One of the key insights of macroeconomics is that the government can have a powerful influence on aggregate demand and that, in some circumstances, this influence can be used to improve economic performance.

The two main ways the government can influence the aggregate demand curve are through fiscal policy and monetary policy. We'll briefly discuss their influence on aggregate demand, leaving a full-length discussion for upcoming chapters.

Fiscal Policy The use of either government spending—government purchases of final goods and services and government transfers—or tax policy to stabilize the economy is known as fiscal policy. In practice, governments often respond to recessions by increasing spending, cutting taxes, or both. They often respond to inflation by reducing spending or increasing taxes.

The effect of government purchases of final goods and services, G, on the aggregate demand curve is *direct* because government purchases are themselves a component of aggregate demand. So an increase in government purchases shifts the aggregate demand curve to the right and a decrease shifts it to the left. History's most dramatic example of how increased government purchases affect aggregate demand was the effect of wartime government spending during World War II.

Because of the war, U.S. federal purchases surged 400%. This increase in purchases is usually credited with ending the Great Depression. In the 1990s, Japan used large public works projects—such as government-financed construction of roads, bridges, and dams—in an effort to increase aggregate demand in the face of a slumping economy. Similarly, in 2009, in the wake of the Great Recession, the United States began spending more than $100 billion on infrastructure projects such as improving highways, bridges, public transportation, and more, to stimulate overall spending.

In contrast, changes in either tax rates or government transfers influence the economy *indirectly* through their effect on disposable income. A lower tax rate means that consumers get to keep more of what they earn, increasing their disposable income. An increase in government transfers also increases consumers' disposable income. In either case, this increases consumer spending and shifts the aggregate demand curve to the right. A higher tax rate or a reduction in transfers reduces the amount of disposable income received by consumers. This reduces consumer spending and shifts the aggregate demand curve to the left.

During the onset of the coronavirus pandemic in 2020, many businesses closed, requiring the federal government to implement an unprecedented economic relief package. It included transfer payments through unemployment insurance for those laid off and a one-time tax rebate of $1,200 to individuals earning less than $75,000 with an extra $500 per child dependent. These measures were designed to stabilize consumer spending, preventing a further decline in aggregate demand, minimizing the economic shock from the virus.

Monetary Policy We opened this chapter by talking about the dilemma facing the Federal Reserve in 2021. The Fed controls monetary policy—its control of the money supply gives it strong influence over interest rates, which affect overall spending. Indeed, in the modern economy the tendency of the Fed and its counterparts in other countries to raise interest rates in the face of inflation is the main reason the aggregate demand curve is downward sloping. But how high the Fed sets rates in the face of a given level of inflation can change. The most famous case came in 1979, when the Fed, under the leadership of Paul Volcker, decided to give fighting inflation much higher priority than it had before. The result was a sharp rise in interest rates and a sharp fall in aggregate demand.

Nothing equally drastic has happened since. But investors keep close watch on the Fed, carefully parsing speeches by Fed officials, in an attempt to figure out the Fed's likely future behavior, because this behavior can have major effects on the aggregate demand curve.

"No player may move, collect money, or buy anything."

Matt Pritchett/The Daily Telegraph

ECONOMICS >> *in Action*
Why Aggregate Demand Fell in 2007–2008

The U.S. economy experienced its worst economic slump since the Great Depression between the end of 2007 and the middle of 2009—the slump in 2020 was severe but much shorter. Almost all economists agree that the Great Recession was caused by a fall in aggregate demand. But what lay behind that fall?

The immediate cause was that a huge housing bubble burst in 2006, leading to a roughly 30% decline in average U.S. home prices. This plunge in housing prices, in turn, reduced aggregate demand through two channels.

First, Americans' wealth took a big hit: for many people, the value of their house is their biggest asset, and the price plunge caused the value of homeowners' equity to plunge by $5 trillion, which in turn reduced consumer spending through the wealth effect.

Second, residential investment spending—housing construction—is a large part of overall investment spending, and it too plunged with the housing bust. At the peak of the housing boom, housing starts, that is, the beginning of home construction, was running at about 2 million units per year. By spring 2009, that number was down to less than 500,000.

So both consumption and investment spending plunged, shifting the AD curve drastically to the left.

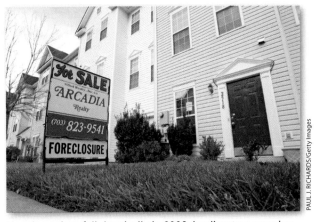

Housing prices fell drastically in 2006, leading to a massive reduction in consumer spending in the years immediately following.

PAUL J. RICHARDS/Getty Images

>> Check Your Understanding 12-1

Solutions appear at back of book.

1. Determine the effect on aggregate demand of each of the following events. Explain whether it represents a movement along the aggregate demand curve (up or down) or a shift of the curve (leftward or rightward).

>> **Quick Review**

• The **aggregate demand curve** is downward sloping because of the interest rate effect of a change in inflation.

• The aggregate demand curve shows how income–expenditure equilibrium GDP changes when inflation changes.

• Changes in consumer spending caused by changes in wealth and expectations about the future shift the aggregate demand curve. Changes in investment spending caused by changes in expectations and by the size of the existing stock of physical capital also shift the aggregate demand curve.

• Fiscal policy affects aggregate demand directly through government purchases and indirectly through changes in taxes or government transfers. Monetary policy affects aggregate demand through changes in the interest rate corresponding to any given inflation rate.

a. A rise in the interest rate caused by a change in monetary policy
b. A rise in the interest rate caused by higher inflation
c. News of a worse-than-expected job market next year
d. A fall in tax rates
e. A rise in the real value of assets in the economy due to a surge in real estate values

‖ Aggregate Supply

Between late 2007 and the middle of 2009, there was a sharp fall in aggregate demand—a reduction in the quantity of goods and services demanded at any given inflation rate. One consequence of the economy-wide decline in demand was a fall in inflation. The GDP deflator rose 2.6% in 2007, but only 0.1% in 2009. A second consequence was a decline in the output of most goods and services: by the middle of 2009, real GDP was 6% below its precrisis trend. A third consequence, closely tied to the fall in real GDP, was a surge in the unemployment rate from 5% to 10%.

The association between the plunge in real GDP and the plunge in inflation wasn't an accident. Between 2007 and 2009, the U.S. economy was moving down its **aggregate supply curve,** which shows the relationship between the economy's inflation rate and the total quantity of final goods and services, or aggregate output, producers are willing to supply. (As you will recall, we use real GDP to measure aggregate output. So we'll often use the two terms interchangeably.) More specifically, between 2007 and 2009 the U.S. economy moved down its *short-run aggregate supply curve.*

The Short-Run Aggregate Supply Curve

The period from 2007 to 2009 demonstrated that there is a positive relationship in the short run between the inflation rate and the quantity of aggregate output supplied. That is, a rise in the inflation rate is associated with a rise in the quantity of aggregate output supplied, other things equal; a fall in the inflation rate is associated with a fall in the quantity of aggregate output supplied, other things equal. To understand why this positive relationship exists, consider the most basic question facing a producer: is producing a unit of output profitable or not? Let's define profit per unit:

(2) Profit per unit of output =
   Price per unit of output – Production cost per unit of output

Thus, the answer to the question depends on whether the price the producer receives for a unit of output is greater than or less than the cost of producing that unit of output. At any given point in time, many of the costs producers face are fixed per unit of output and can't be changed for an extended period of time. Typically, the largest source of inflexible production cost is the wages paid to workers. *Wages* here refers to all forms of worker compensation, such as employer-paid health care and retirement benefits in addition to earnings.

Wages are typically an inflexible production cost because the dollar amount of any given wage paid, called the **nominal wage,** is often determined by contracts that were signed some time ago. And even when there are no formal contracts, there are often informal agreements between management and workers, making companies reluctant to change wages in response to economic conditions. For example, companies usually will not reduce wages during poor economic times—unless the downturn has been particularly long and severe—for fear of generating worker resentment. Correspondingly, they typically won't raise wages during better economic times—until they are at risk of losing workers to competitors—because they don't want to encourage workers to routinely demand higher wages.

aggregate supply curve a graphical representation that shows the relationship between the inflation rate and the total quantity of aggregate output supplied.

nominal wage the dollar amount of any given wage paid.

As a result of both formal and informal agreements, then, the economy is characterized by **sticky wages:** nominal wages that are slow to fall even in the face of high unemployment and slow to rise even in the face of labor shortages. It's important to note, however, that nominal wages cannot be sticky forever: ultimately, formal contracts and informal agreements will be renegotiated to take into account changed economic circumstances.

To understand how the fact that many costs are fixed in nominal terms gives rise to an upward-sloping short-run aggregate supply curve, it's helpful to know that prices are set somewhat differently in different kinds of markets. In *perfectly competitive markets,* producers take prices as given; in *imperfectly competitive markets,* producers have some ability to choose the prices they charge. In both kinds of markets, there is a short-run positive relationship between prices and output, but for slightly different reasons.

Let's start with the behavior of producers in perfectly competitive markets; remember, they take the price as given. Imagine that, for some reason, the inflation rate falls, which means that the price received by the typical producer of a final good or service is lower than they were expecting. Because many production costs are fixed in the short run, production cost per unit of output doesn't fall by the same proportion as the unexpected lower price received by the firm So the profit per unit of output declines, leading perfectly competitive producers to reduce the quantity supplied in the short run.

On the other hand, suppose that for some reason the inflation rate is higher than expected. As a result, the typical producer receives a higher price for its final good or service. Again, many production costs are fixed in the short run, so production cost per unit of output doesn't rise by the same proportion as the unexpected higher price received by the firm. And since the typical perfectly competitive producer takes the inflation rate as given, profit per unit of output rises and output increases.

Now consider an imperfectly competitive producer that is able to set its own price. If there is a rise in the demand for this producer's product, it will be able to sell more at any given price. Given stronger demand for its products, it will probably choose to increase its prices as well as its output, as a way of increasing profit per unit of output. In fact, industry analysts often talk about variations in an industry's *pricing power:* when demand is strong, firms with pricing power are able to raise prices—and they do.

sticky wages nominal wages that are slow to fall even in the face of high unemployment and slow to rise even in the face of labor shortages.

FIGURE 5 The Short-Run Aggregate Supply Curve

The short-run aggregate supply curve shows the relationship between the inflation rate and the quantity of aggregate output supplied in the short run, the period in which many production costs such as nominal wages are fixed. It is upward sloping because a higher inflation rate leads to higher profit per unit of output and higher aggregate output given fixed nominal wages.

A movement down the SRAS curve leads to disinflation and lower aggregate output.

FOR INQUIRING MINDS **What's Truly Flexible, What's Truly Sticky**

Most macroeconomists agree that the picture shown in Figure 5 is correct: there is, other things equal, a positive short-run relationship between inflation and aggregate output. But many would argue that the details are a bit more complicated.

So far we've stressed a difference in the behavior of inflation and the behavior of nominal wages. That is, we've said that prices are flexible but nominal wages are sticky in the short run. Although this assumption is a good way to explain why the short-run aggregate supply curve is upward sloping, empirical data on wages and prices don't wholly support a sharp distinction between

flexible prices of final goods and services and sticky nominal wages.

On one side, some nominal wages are in fact flexible even in the short run because some workers are not covered by a contract or informal agreement with their employers. For example, nonsupervisory workers in the leisure and hospitality sector often don't have long-term contracts, and many were laid off during the worst of the coronavirus pandemic. When normal life began to resume, employers in that sector were desperate to rehire workers, and wages in that sector rose 17.5% in 2021, only to level off in 2022.

On the other side, some prices of final goods and services are sticky rather than

flexible. For example, some firms, particularly the makers of luxury or name-brand goods, are reluctant to cut prices even when demand falls. Instead they prefer to cut output even if their profit per unit hasn't declined.

These complications, as we've said, don't change the basic picture. When inflation falls, some producers cut output because the nominal wages they pay are sticky. And some producers don't cut their prices in the face of reduced demand, preferring instead to reduce their output. In both cases, the positive relationship between inflation and aggregate output is maintained. So, in the end, the short-run aggregate supply curve is still upward sloping.

short-run aggregate supply curve a graphical representation that shows the positive relationship between the inflation rate and the quantity of aggregate output supplied that exists in the short run, the time period when many production costs, particularly nominal wages, can be taken as fixed. The short-run aggregate supply curve has a positive slope because a rise in the inflation rate leads to a rise in profits, and therefore output, when production costs are fixed.

Conversely, if there is a fall in demand, firms will normally try to limit the fall in their sales by cutting prices.

Both the responses of firms in perfectly competitive industries and those of firms in imperfectly competitive industries lead to an upward-sloping relationship between aggregate output and the inflation rate. The positive relationship between inflation and aggregate output in the short run is illustrated by an upward-sloping **short-run aggregate supply curve.** Along this curve, producers are willing to supply final goods and services during the time period when many production costs, particularly nominal wages, can be taken as fixed. Figure 5 shows a hypothetical short-run aggregate supply curve, *SRAS*, whose slope is based on the observed behavior of U.S. inflation in the two decades before the pandemic, described in the Economics in Action at the end of this section. On the horizontal axis is aggregate output (or, equivalently, real GDP)—the total quantity of final goods and services supplied in the economy—measured in 2012 dollars. On the vertical axis is the inflation rate as measured by the GDP deflator.

Shifts of the Short-Run Aggregate Supply Curve

The fall in inflation during the 2007–2009 recession was a movement *along* the short-run aggregate supply curve. But there can also be *shifts of* the short-run aggregate supply curve, as shown in Figure 6. Panel (a) shows a *decrease in short-run aggregate supply*—a leftward shift of the short-run aggregate supply curve. Aggregate supply decreases when producers reduce the quantity of aggregate output they are willing to supply at any given inflation rate. Panel (b) shows an *increase in short-run aggregate supply*—a rightward shift of the short-run aggregate supply curve. Aggregate supply increases when producers increase the quantity of aggregate output they are willing to supply at any given inflation rate.

To understand why the short-run aggregate supply curve can shift, it's important to recall that producers make output decisions based on their profit per unit of output. The short-run aggregate supply curve illustrates the relationship between inflation and aggregate output: because some production costs are fixed in the short run, a change in inflation leads to a change in producers' profit per unit of output and, in turn, leads to a change in aggregate output.

But other factors besides the overall inflation can affect profit per unit and, in turn, aggregate output. It is changes in these other factors that will shift the short-run aggregate supply curve.

FIGURE 6 Shifts of the Short-Run Aggregate Supply Curve

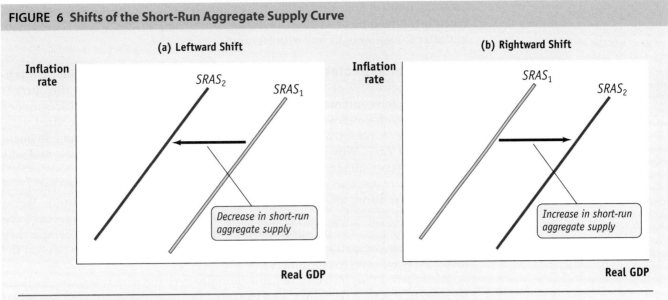

Panel (a) shows a decrease in short-run aggregate supply: the short-run aggregate supply curve shifts leftward from $SRAS_1$ to $SRAS_2$, and the quantity of aggregate output supplied at any given inflation rate falls. Panel (b) shows an increase in short-run aggregate supply: the short-run aggregate supply curve shifts rightward from $SRAS_1$ to $SRAS_2$, and the quantity of aggregate output supplied at any given inflation rate rises.

To develop some intuition, suppose that something happens that raises production costs—say, an increase in the price of oil. At any given price of output, a producer now earns a smaller profit per unit of output. As a result, producers reduce the quantity supplied at any given inflation rate, and the short-run aggregate supply curve shifts to the left. If, in contrast, something happens that lowers production costs—say, a jump in worker productivity—a producer now earns a higher profit per unit of output at any given price of output. This leads producers to increase the quantity of aggregate output supplied at any given inflation rate, and the short-run aggregate supply curve shifts to the right.

Now we'll discuss some of the important factors that affect producers' profit per unit and so can lead to shifts of the short-run aggregate supply curve. These factors include changes in commodity prices, changes in expected inflation, and changes in productivity.

Changes in Commodity Prices The inflation shock of 2021–2022 came after four decades of relatively low inflation. But economists and policy makers hadn't forgotten an early inflationary period—the high inflation of the 1970s and early 1980s. The origins of that inflationary period lay largely in a sharp and sustained increase in the price of a very important commodity—oil. The high price of oil sharply raised costs for producers around the world.

A *commodity* is a standardized input bought and sold in bulk quantities. An increase in the price of a commodity, such as oil, raises production costs across the economy and reduces the quantity of aggregate output supplied at any given overall inflation rate. This shifts the aggregate supply curve to the left. Conversely, a decline in commodity prices reduces production costs, leading to an increase in the quantity supplied at any given inflation rate and a rightward shift of the short-run aggregate supply curve.

Why isn't the influence of commodity prices already captured by the short-run aggregate supply curve? The main answer is that the prices of commodities can sometimes change drastically due to industry-specific shocks to supply. Most recently (at the time of writing), prices of natural gas, oil, and wheat soared globally after Russia went to war with Ukraine.

Changes in Expectations At the beginning of the 1980s, unions still represented about 21% of U.S. private-sector workers—three times the current number—and economic observers paid close attention to the contracts unions negotiated with employers. In 1981, on average, new contracts specified 9.2% annual wage increases, a big number, especially considering that unemployment was high, at 7.6%. Why were workers demanding such big wage hikes, and why were employers willing to grant them?

The answer was that in 1981 most people expected the high inflation rates that had prevailed during the late 1970s to continue into the indefinite future. Workers therefore sought big wage increases to keep up with what they expected to be a rapidly rising cost of living; employers were willing to go along because they expected their competitors to be raising prices, giving them room to pass on the increased wage costs to consumers.

As it turned out, inflation fell substantially over the next few years, initially because of a severe recession, and expected inflation eventually fell too. Most economists believe that this decline in expected inflation shifted the aggregate supply curve to the right: workers began demanding smaller wage hikes and firms engaged in smaller price increases at any given level of aggregate output, so that the economy was eventually able to emerge from recession with a much lower inflation rate.

So expected inflation can be a major factor shifting the aggregate supply curve. As a result, both policy makers and economists have recently paid a lot of attention to surveys that ask consumers and firms how much inflation they expect in the future. At the time of writing, these surveys were mostly reassuring, suggesting that expected inflation hadn't gone up much despite the surge in actual inflation. But there was no guarantee that expectations would remain "anchored" in this way.

Changes in Productivity An increase in productivity means that a worker can produce more units of output with the same quantity of inputs. For example, the introduction of bar-code scanners in retail stores greatly increased the ability of a single worker to stock, inventory, and resupply store shelves. As a result, the cost to a store of "producing" a dollar of sales fell, profit rose, and the quantity supplied increased. (Think of Walmart and the increase in the number of its stores as an increase in aggregate supply.) So a rise in productivity, whatever the source, increases producers' profits per unit produced and shifts the short-run aggregate supply curve to the right.

Conversely, a fall in productivity—say, due to new regulations that require workers to spend more time filling out forms—reduces the number of units of output a worker can produce with the same quantity of inputs. Consequently, the cost per unit of output rises, leading to a fall in profit per unit produced, and a fall in quantity supplied, shifting the short-run aggregate supply curve to the left.

For a summary of the factors that shift the short-run aggregate supply curve, see Table 2.

The Long-Run Aggregate Supply Curve

We've just seen that in the short run a fall in inflation leads to a decline in the quantity of aggregate output supplied, while a rise in inflation leads to a rise in the quantity of aggregate output supplied, because many wages and some prices are sticky in the short run. But there are good reasons to believe that neither wages nor prices are sticky in the long run. This greatly alters the long-run relationship

TABLE 2 Factors That Shift Aggregate Supply

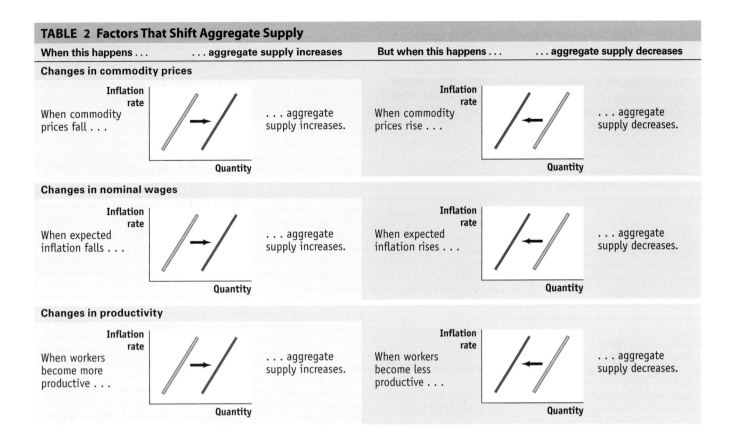

When this happens . . .	. . . aggregate supply increases	But when this happens . . .	. . . aggregate supply decreases
Changes in commodity prices			
When commodity prices fall . . .	. . . aggregate supply increases.	When commodity prices rise . . .	. . . aggregate supply decreases.
Changes in nominal wages			
When expected inflation falls . . .	. . . aggregate supply increases.	When expected inflation rises . . .	. . . aggregate supply decreases.
Changes in productivity			
When workers become more productive . . .	. . . aggregate supply increases.	When workers become less productive . . .	. . . aggregate supply decreases.

between inflation and aggregate supply. Indeed, most economists believe that in the long run—with certain caveats—inflation has *no* effect on the quantity of aggregate output supplied.

To see why, let's conduct a thought experiment. Imagine that you could wave a magic wand—or maybe a magic bar-code scanner—and raise *all prices* in the economy by 20% at the same time. If this happened in one year, that would mean a 20% inflation rate. By "all prices" we mean the prices of all inputs, including nominal wages, as well as the prices of final goods and services. What would happen to aggregate output, given that all input prices, including nominal wages, have gone up by 20%?

The answer is: nothing. Consider Equation 2 again: each producer would receive a higher price for its product, but costs would rise by the same proportion. As a result, every unit of output profitable to produce after the change in prices would have been profitable to produce before the change in prices. So an equal proportional change in *all* prices in the economy has no effect on the economy's aggregate output. In other words, the inflation rate in this hypothetical case has no effect on the quantity of aggregate output supplied.

In reality, of course, no one can change all prices by the same proportion at the same time. But now, we'll consider the *long run, the period of time in which all prices, including production costs such as nominal wages, are fully flexible.* In the long run, inflation has the same effect as someone changing all prices by the same proportion. *As a result, the level of inflation does not change the quantity of aggregate output supplied in the long run.* That's because changes in the inflation rate, which is composed of prices of final goods and services, will be accompanied by equal proportional changes in *all* input prices, including nominal wages.

The **long-run aggregate supply curve,** illustrated in Figure 7 by the curve *LRAS*, shows the relationship between inflation and the quantity of aggregate output supplied that holds when all prices, including nominal wages, are fully

long-run aggregate supply curve a graphical representation that shows the relationship between the inflation rate and the quantity of aggregate output supplied that would exist if all prices, including nominal wages, were fully flexible. The long-run aggregate supply curve is vertical because the inflation rate has no effect on aggregate output in the long run; in the long run, aggregate output is determined by the economy's potential output.

FIGURE 7 The Long-Run Aggregate Supply Curve

The long-run aggregate supply curve shows the quantity of aggregate output supplied when all prices, including nominal wages, are flexible. It is vertical at potential output, Y_P, because in the long run a change in the inflation rate has no effect on the quantity of aggregate output supplied.

flexible. The long-run aggregate supply curve is vertical because when prices are fully flexible inflation has *no* effect on aggregate output. At an inflation rate of 2%, the quantity of aggregate output supplied is $25 trillion in 2012 dollars. If inflation were 5% instead, the quantity of aggregate output supplied would still be $25 trillion in 2012 dollars.

It's important to understand not only that the *LRAS* curve is vertical but also that its position along the horizontal axis represents a significant measure. The horizontal intercept in Figure 7 ($25 trillion in 2012 dollars, where *LRAS* touches the horizontal axis) is the economy's **potential output,** Y_P: the level of real GDP the economy would produce if all prices, including nominal wages, were fully flexible.

In reality, the actual level of real GDP is almost always either above or below potential output. We'll see why later in this chapter, when we discuss the *AD–AS* model. Still, an economy's potential output is an important number because it defines the trend around which actual aggregate output fluctuates from year to year.

In the United States, the Congressional Budget Office, or CBO, estimates annual potential output for the purpose of federal budget analysis. In Figure 8, the CBO's estimates of U.S. potential output from 1990 to 2022 are represented by the orange line and the actual values of U.S. real GDP over the same period are represented by the blue line.

As you can see, U.S. potential output has risen steadily over time—implying a series of rightward shifts of the *LRAS* curve. What has caused these rightward shifts? The answer lies in the factors related to long-run growth that we discussed in Chapter 9, such as increases in physical capital and human capital as well as technological progress. Over the long run, as the size of the labor force and the productivity of labor both rise, the level of real GDP that the economy is capable of producing also rises. Indeed, one way to think about long-run economic growth is that it is the growth in the economy's potential output. We generally think of the long-run aggregate supply curve as shifting to the right over time as an economy experiences long-run growth.

potential output the level of real GDP the economy would produce if all prices, including nominal wages, were fully flexible.

FIGURE 8 Actual and Potential Output, 1990 to 2022

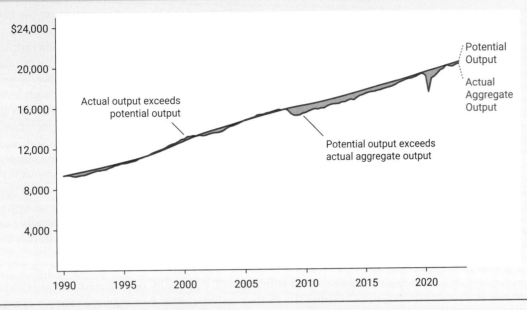

This figure shows the performance of actual and potential output in the United States from 1990 to 2022. The orange line shows estimates of U.S. potential output, produced by the Congressional Budget Office, and the blue line shows actual aggregate output. As shown, significant shortfalls occurred in the recessions of the early 1990s and after 2000. Actual aggregate output was significantly above potential output

in the boom of the late 1990s, and a huge shortfall occurred after the recession of 2007–2009. Another shortfall occurred in the second quarter of 2020, when the coronavirus pandemic caused economic activity to decline at an annualized rate in excess of 30%.

Data from: Congressional Budget Office, Bureau of Economic Analysis, Federal Bank of St. Louis.

From the Short Run to the Long Run

As you can see in Figure 8, the economy normally produces more or less than potential output: actual aggregate output was below potential output in the early 1990s, above potential output in the late 1990s, below potential output for most of the 2000s, and significantly below potential output after the recession of 2007–2009 and during the coronavirus pandemic. So the economy is normally on its short-run aggregate supply curve—but not on its long-run aggregate supply curve. So why is the long-run curve relevant? Does the economy ever move from the short run to the long run? And if so, how?

The first step to answering these questions is to understand that the economy is always in one of only two states with respect to the short-run and long-run aggregate supply curves. It can be on both curves simultaneously by being at a point where the curves cross (as in the few years in Figure 8 in which actual aggregate output and potential output roughly coincided). Or it can be on the short-run aggregate supply curve but not the long-run aggregate supply curve (as in the years in which actual aggregate output and potential output *did not* coincide).

But that is not the end of the story. If the economy is on the short-run but not the long-run aggregate supply curve, the short-run aggregate supply curve will shift over time until the economy is at a point where both curves cross—a point where actual aggregate output is equal to potential output.

PITFALLS

WHAT THE LONG RUN REALLY MEANS

We've used the term *long run* in two different contexts. In an earlier chapter, we focused on *long-run economic growth:* growth that takes place over decades. In this chapter, we introduced the *long-run aggregate supply curve,* which depicts the economy's potential output: the level of aggregate output that the economy would produce if all prices, including nominal wages, were fully flexible. It might seem that we're using the same term, *long run,* for two different concepts. But we aren't: these two concepts are really the same thing.

Because the economy always tends to return to potential output in the long run, actual aggregate output *fluctuates around* potential output, rarely getting too far from it. As a result, the economy's rate of growth over long periods of time—say, decades—is very close to the rate of growth of potential output. And potential output growth is determined by the factors we analyzed in the chapter on long-run economic growth. So that means that the "long run" of long-run growth and the "long run" of the long-run aggregate supply curve coincide.

Figure 9 illustrates how this process works. In both panels, *LRAS* is the long-run aggregate supply curve, *SRAS*₁ is the initial short-run aggregate supply curve, and the inflation rate is at π_1. In panel (a), the economy starts at the initial production point, A_1, which corresponds to a quantity of aggregate output supplied, Y_1, that is higher than potential output, Y_P. Producing an aggregate output level (such as Y_1) that is higher than potential output (Y_P) is possible only because expected inflation hasn't caught up with actual inflation. Until this upward adjustment in occurs, producers are earning high profits and producing a high level of output. But workers and employers will eventually take expected inflation into account when setting wages, as they did in 1981, and this will shift the short-run aggregate supply curve leftward. Eventually it will be in a new position, such as *SRAS*₂. (Later in this chapter, we'll show where the short-run aggregate supply curve ends up. As we'll see, that depends on the aggregate demand curve as well.)

In panel (b), the initial production point, A_1, corresponds to an aggregate output level, Y_1, that is lower than potential output, Y_P. Producing an aggregate output level (such as Y_1) that is lower than potential output (Y_P) is possible only because nominal wages are running ahead of prices. Until wage growth has declined, producers are earning low (or negative) profits and producing a low level of output. An aggregate output level lower than potential output means high unemployment. Again, however, low inflation will eventually be reflected in wages (which actually happened during the 1980s), and the short-run aggregate supply curve will be in a new position, such as *SRAS*₂.

We'll see shortly that these shifts of the short-run aggregate supply curve will normally return the economy to potential output in the long run. We say "normally" because there is a caveat: many although not all macroeconomists believe that the economy can remain depressed, even in the long run, if inflation is very low or negative. We'll explain this caveat later.

FIGURE 9 From the Short Run to the Long Run

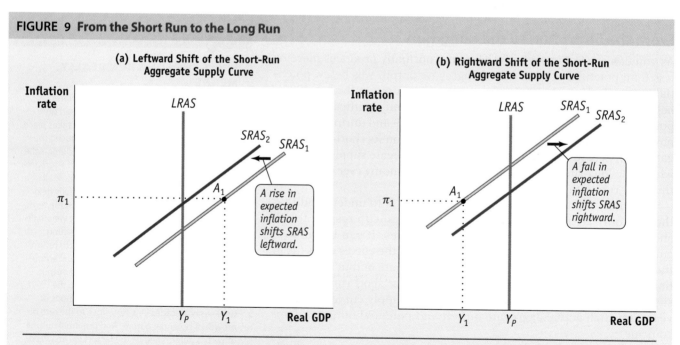

In panel (a), the initial short-run aggregate supply curve is *SRAS*₁. At the inflation rate π_1, the quantity of aggregate output supplied, Y_1, exceeds potential output, Y_P. Eventually, expected inflation will rise, leading to a leftward shift of the short-run aggregate supply curve from *SRAS*₁ to *SRAS*₂. In panel (b), the reverse happens: at the inflation rate π_1 the quantity of aggregate output supplied is less than potential output. Expected inflation eventually falls, leading to a rightward shift of the short-run aggregate supply curve.

ECONOMICS >> *in Action*
Aggregate Supply in a Time of (Relative) Stability

We mentioned in the text that the slope of the hypothetical short-run aggregate supply curve in Figure 5 was based on actual observation of the prepandemic U.S. economy. So it might be of interest to see what kind of evidence economists actually use both to justify the concept of the aggregate supply curve and to assess quantitative relationships.

As it happens, the two decades that preceded the Covid-19 pandemic are a relatively good period for observing the aggregate supply curve. There were large shocks to aggregate demand, especially during the 2007–2009 recession and its aftermath. But the factors that shift aggregate supply were relatively quiet. There were some ups and downs in oil prices, but these can be mostly corrected for by using a measure of inflation that excludes energy prices. Surveys suggest that expected inflation was stable at about 2% for the whole period. And although there were some fluctuations in productivity, there was neither a huge boom nor a huge bust.

So Figure 10 shows what the aggregate supply curve seems to have looked like over the period from 2001 to 2019, using annual data; each point corresponds to one year. The horizontal axis shows the *output gap*—the percentage difference between real GDP and potential real GDP as estimated by the Congressional Budget Office. The vertical axis shows the Federal Reserve's preferred measure of inflation, the percentage change in the personal consumption expenditure deflator excluding food and energy.

There's a clear positive correlation between the output gap and inflation; the line shows the statistically fitted relationship. Obviously the correlation isn't perfect: there were years when inflation was substantially lower or higher than the fitted line would have predicted. But that's not surprising: the economy is an extremely complex system, and there are always factors at work that a simple

FIGURE 10 The Aggregate Supply Curve Before the Pandemic

Note: Inflation rate is measured as the annual percent change in personal consumption expenditure deflator less food and energy. Output gap is measured as the percentage difference between real GDP and potential real GDP.

Data from: Congressional Budget Office; Bureau of Economic Analysis; Federal Reserve Bank of St. Louis.

statistical model won't capture. Overall, however, the data did seem to support the notion of an upward-sloping aggregate supply curve.

One point worth noting, however, is that the fitted line is fairly flat, with an extra percentage point of GDP adding only about 1/6 of a percentage point to inflation. This historically flat relationship was one reason the Fed was caught by surprise by how quickly inflation rose in 2021–2022, a story we'll tell at greater length in Chapter 16.

>> Check Your Understanding 12-2

Solutions appear at back of book.

1. Determine the effect on short-run aggregate supply for each of the following events. Explain whether it represents a movement along the *SRAS* curve or a shift of the *SRAS* curve.
   a. A rise in the consumer price index (CPI) leads producers to increase output.
   b. A fall in the price of oil leads producers to increase output.
   c. A rise in legally mandated retirement benefits paid to workers leads producers to reduce output.

2. Suppose the economy is initially at potential output and the quantity of aggregate output supplied increases. What information would you need to determine whether this was due to a movement along the *SRAS* curve or a shift of the *LRAS* curve?

‖ The *AD–AS* Model

From 2007 to 2009, the U.S. economy moved down the short-run aggregate supply curve as the inflation fell. But that isn't always the story behind economic slumps. The 1979–1980 recession, many economists believe, was largely a story of moving up the aggregate demand curve. And as we suggested in our opening story, inflation in 2021–2022 was complicated, probably involving shifts in both aggregate demand and aggregate supply.

So to understand the behavior of the economy, we must put the aggregate supply curve and the aggregate demand curve together. The result is the **AD–AS model,** the basic model we use to understand economic fluctuations.

Short-Run Macroeconomic Equilibrium

We'll begin our analysis by focusing on the short run. Figure 11 shows the aggregate demand curve and the short-run aggregate supply curve on the same diagram.

FIGURE 11 The *AD–AS* Model

The *AD–AS* model combines the aggregate demand curve and the short-run aggregate supply curve. Their point of intersection, E_{SR}, is the point of short-run macroeconomic equilibrium where the quantity of aggregate output demanded is equal to the quantity of aggregate output supplied. π_E is the short-run equilibrium inflation rate, and Y_E is the short-run equilibrium level of aggregate output.

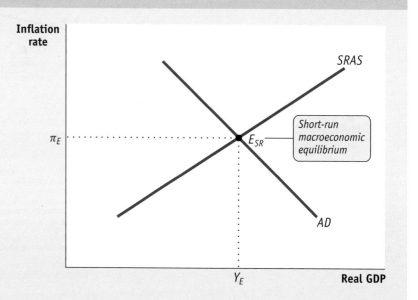

The point at which the *AD* and *SRAS* curves intersect, E_{SR}, is the **short-run macroeconomic equilibrium:** the point at which the quantity of aggregate output supplied is equal to the quantity demanded by domestic households, businesses, the government, and the rest of the world. The inflation rate at E_{SR}, π_E, is the **short-run equilibrium inflation rate.** The level of aggregate output at E_{SR}, Y_E, is the **short-run equilibrium aggregate output.**

We saw in the supply and demand model that a shortage of any individual good causes its market price to rise but a surplus of the good causes its market price to fall. These forces ensure that the market reaches equilibrium. The same logic applies to short-run macroeconomic equilibrium. If inflation is above its equilibrium level, the quantity of aggregate output supplied exceeds the quantity of aggregate output demanded. This leads to a fall in the inflation rate and pushes it toward its equilibrium level.

If inflation is below its equilibrium level, the quantity of aggregate output supplied is less than the quantity of aggregate output demanded. This leads to a rise in the inflation rate, again pushing it toward its equilibrium level. In the discussion that follows, we'll assume that the economy is always in short-run macroeconomic equilibrium.

Short-run equilibrium aggregate output and the short-run equilibrium inflation rate can change either because of shifts of the *AD* curve or because of shifts of the *SRAS* curve. Let's look at each case in turn.

Shifts of Aggregate Demand: Short-Run Effects

An event that shifts the aggregate demand curve, such as a change in expectations or wealth, the effect of the size of the existing stock of physical capital, or the use of fiscal or monetary policy, is known as a **demand shock.** The 2007–2009 slump, often called the Great Recession, was caused by a negative demand shock, the collapse of wealth and investment following the bursting of a massive housing bubble. The Great Depression that began in 1929 was also the result of a negative demand shock, on an even bigger scale. The Depression was ended by a positive demand shock—the huge increase in government purchases during World War II.

Figure 12 shows the short-run effects of negative and positive demand shocks. A negative demand shock shifts the aggregate demand curve, *AD*, to the left, from

short-run macroeconomic equilibrium the point at which the quantity of aggregate output supplied is equal to the quantity demanded.

short-run equilibrium inflation rate the inflation rate in the short-run macroeconomic equilibrium.

short-run equilibrium aggregate output the quantity of aggregate output produced in short-run macroeconomic equilibrium.

demand shock an event that shifts the aggregate demand curve. A positive demand shock is associated with higher demand for aggregate output at any inflation rate and shifts the curve to the right. A negative demand shock is associated with lower demand for aggregate output at any inflation rate and shifts the curve to the left.

FIGURE 12 Demand Shocks

(a) A Negative Demand Shock

(b) A Positive Demand Shock

A demand shock shifts the aggregate demand curve, moving the inflation rate and aggregate output in the same direction. In panel (a), a negative demand shock shifts the aggregate demand curve leftward from AD_1 to AD_2, reducing inflation from π_1 to π_2 and aggregate output from Y_1 to Y_2. In panel (b), a positive demand shock shifts the aggregate demand curve rightward, increasing inflation from π_1 to π_2 and aggregate output from Y_1 to Y_2.

supply shock an event that shifts the short-run aggregate supply curve. A negative supply shock raises production costs and reduces the quantity supplied at any inflation rate, shifting the curve leftward. A positive supply shock decreases production costs and increases the quantity supplied at any inflation rate, shifting the curve rightward.

AD_1 to AD_2, as shown in panel (a). The economy moves down along the $SRAS$ curve from E_1 to E_2, leading to lower short-run equilibrium aggregate output and a lower short-run equilibrium inflation rate. A positive demand shock shifts the aggregate demand curve, AD, to the right, as shown in panel (b). Here, the economy moves up along the $SRAS$ curve, from E_1 to E_2. This leads to higher short-run equilibrium aggregate output and a higher short-run equilibrium inflation rate. Demand shocks cause aggregate output and inflation to move in the same direction.

Shifts of the *SRAS* Curve

An event that shifts the short-run aggregate supply curve, such as a change in commodity prices, expected inflation, or productivity, is known as a **supply shock.** A *negative* supply shock raises production costs and reduces the quantity producers are willing to supply at any given inflation rate, leading to a leftward shift of the short-run aggregate supply curve. The U.S. economy experienced severe negative supply shocks following disruptions to world oil supplies in 1973 and 1979.

In contrast, a *positive* supply shock reduces production costs and increases the quantity supplied at any given inflation rate, leading to a rightward shift of the short-run aggregate supply curve. The United States experienced a positive supply shock between 1995 and 2000, when the increasing use of the internet and other information technologies caused productivity growth to surge.

The effects of a negative supply shock are shown in panel (a) of Figure 13. The initial equilibrium is at E_1, with inflation π_1 and aggregate output Y_1. The disruption in the oil supply causes the short-run aggregate supply curve to shift to the left, from $SRAS_1$ to $SRAS_2$. As a consequence, aggregate output falls and inflation rises, an upward movement along the AD curve. At the new equilibrium, E_2, the

FIGURE 13 Supply Shocks

A supply shock shifts the short-run aggregate supply curve, moving the inflation rate and aggregate output in opposite directions. Panel (a) shows a negative supply shock, which shifts the short-run aggregate supply curve leftward and causes *stagflation* — lower aggregate output and a higher inflation rate. Here the short-run aggregate supply curve shifts from $SRAS_1$ to $SRAS_2$, and the economy moves from E_1 to E_2.

Inflation rises from π_1 to π_2 and aggregate output falls from Y_1 to Y_2. Panel (b) shows a positive supply shock, which shifts the short-run aggregate supply curve rightward, generating higher aggregate output and a lower inflation rate. The short-run aggregate supply curve shifts from $SRAS_1$ to $SRAS_2$, and the economy moves from E_1 to E_2. Inflation falls from π_1 to π_2 and aggregate output rises from Y_1 to Y_2.

short-run equilibrium inflation rate, π_2, is higher, and the short-run equilibrium aggregate output level, Y_2, is lower than before.

The combination of higher inflation and falling aggregate output shown in panel (a) has a special name: **stagflation,** for "stagnation plus inflation." Stagflation is unpleasant: falling aggregate output leads to rising unemployment, while the purchasing power of consumers is squeezed by inflation. Stagflation in the 1970s created a mood of economic pessimism and deeply affected those who lived through it. It also, as we'll see, poses a dilemma for policy makers.

A positive supply shock, shown in panel (b), has exactly the opposite effects. A rightward shift of the *SRAS* curve from $SRAS_1$ to $SRAS_2$ results in a rise in aggregate output and a fall in inflation, a downward movement along the *AD* curve. The favorable supply shocks of the late 1990s led to a combination of full employment and declining inflation. That is, the inflation rate fell compared with the long-run trend. This combination produced, for a time, a great wave of national optimism.

The distinctive feature of supply shocks, both negative and positive, is that, unlike demand shocks, they cause inflation and aggregate output to move in *opposite* directions.

There's another important contrast between supply shocks and demand shocks. As we've seen, monetary policy and fiscal policy enable the government to shift the *AD* curve, meaning that governments are in a position to create the kinds of shocks shown in Figure 12. It's much harder for governments to shift the *AS* curve. Are there good policy reasons to shift the *AD* curve? We'll turn to that question soon. First, however, let's look at the difference between short-run macroeconomic equilibrium and *long-run macroeconomic equilibrium.*

stagflation the combination of inflation and falling aggregate output.

Long-Run Macroeconomic Equilibrium

Figure 14 combines the aggregate demand curve with both the short-run and long-run aggregate supply curves. The aggregate demand curve, *AD*, crosses the short-run aggregate supply curve, *SRAS*, at E_{LR}. Here we assume that enough time has elapsed that the economy is also on the long-run aggregate supply curve, *LRAS*.

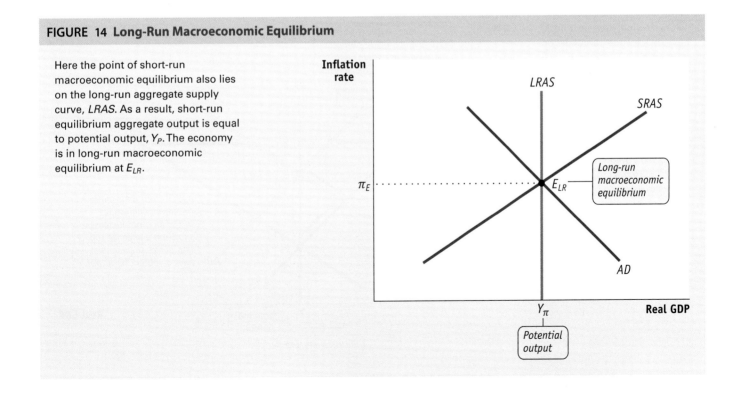

FIGURE 14 Long-Run Macroeconomic Equilibrium

Here the point of short-run macroeconomic equilibrium also lies on the long-run aggregate supply curve, *LRAS*. As a result, short-run equilibrium aggregate output is equal to potential output, Y_P. The economy is in long-run macroeconomic equilibrium at E_{LR}.

long-run macroeconomic equilibrium the point at which the short-run macroeconomic equilibrium is on the long-run aggregate supply curve; so short-run equilibrium aggregate output is equal to potential output.

recessionary gap the gap that exists when aggregate output is below potential output.

As a result, E_{LR} is at the intersection of all three curves—*SRAS*, *LRAS*, and *AD*. So short-run equilibrium aggregate output is equal to potential output, Y_P. Such a situation, in which the point of short-run macroeconomic equilibrium is on the long-run aggregate supply curve, is known as **long-run macroeconomic equilibrium.**

To see the significance of long-run macroeconomic equilibrium, let's consider what happens if a demand shock moves the economy away from long-run macroeconomic equilibrium. In Figure 15, we assume that the initial aggregate demand curve is AD_1 and the initial short-run aggregate supply curve is $SRAS_1$. So the initial macroeconomic equilibrium is at E_1, which lies on the long-run aggregate supply curve, *LRAS*. The economy, then, starts from a point of short-run and long-run macroeconomic equilibrium, and short-run equilibrium aggregate output equals potential output at Y_1.

Now suppose that for some reason—such as a sudden worsening of business and consumer expectations—aggregate demand falls and the aggregate demand curve shifts leftward to AD_2. This results in a lower equilibrium inflation rate at π_2 and a lower equilibrium aggregate output level at Y_2 as the economy settles in the short run at E_2. The short-run effect of such a fall in aggregate demand is what the U.S. economy experienced in 2007–2009: falling inflation and falling aggregate output.

Aggregate output in this new short-run equilibrium, E_2, is below potential output. When this happens, the economy faces a **recessionary gap.** A recessionary gap inflicts a great deal of pain because it corresponds to high unemployment.

But this isn't the end of the story. In our discussion of factors that shift the AS curve, we noted that expected future inflation can play an important role. As we've just seen, a negative aggregate demand shock leads to lower inflation; this lower inflation rate will eventually be reflected in workers' and employers' expectations, causing the short-run aggregate supply curve to shift gradually to the right over time. This process continues until $SRAS_1$ reaches its new position at

---

FIGURE 15 Short-Run versus Long-Run Effects of a Negative Demand Shock

In the long run the economy is self-correcting: demand shocks have only a short-run effect on aggregate output. Starting at E_1, a negative demand shock shifts AD_1 leftward to AD_2. In the short run the economy moves to E_2 and a recessionary gap arises: inflation declines from π_1 to π_2, aggregate output declines from Y_1 to Y_2, and unemployment rises. But in the long run expected inflation falls, and $SRAS_1$ shifts rightward to $SRAS_2$. Aggregate output rises from Y_2 to Y_1, even as inflation declines further to π_3. Long-run macroeconomic equilibrium is eventually restored at E_3.

FIGURE 16   Short-Run versus Long-Run Effects of a Positive Demand Shock

Starting at E_1, a positive demand shock shifts AD_1 rightward to AD_2, and the economy moves to E_2 in the short run. This results in an inflationary gap as aggregate output rises from Y_1 to Y_2, inflation rises from π_1 to π_2, and unemployment falls to a low level. In the long run, $SRAS_1$ shifts leftward to $SRAS_2$ as expected inflation rises. Aggregate output falls back to Y_1, inflation rises further to π_3, and the economy self-corrects as it returns to long-run macroeconomic equilibrium at E_3.

1. An initial positive demand shock . . .

3. . . . until an eventual rise in nominal wages in the long run reduces short-run aggregate supply and moves the economy back to potential output.

2. . . . increases the inflation rate and aggregate output and reduces unemployment in the short run . . .

Inflationary gap

$SRAS_2$, bringing the economy to equilibrium at E_3, where AD_2, $SRAS_2$, and $LRAS$ all intersect. At E_3, the economy is back in long-run macroeconomic equilibrium; it is back at potential output Y_1 but at a lower inflation rate, π_3. In the end, the economy is *self-correcting*.

What if, instead, there was an increase in aggregate demand? The results are shown in Figure 16, where we again assume that the initial aggregate demand curve is AD_1 and the initial short-run aggregate supply curve is $SRAS_1$, so that the initial macroeconomic equilibrium, at E_1, lies on the long-run aggregate supply curve, $LRAS$. Initially, then, the economy is in long-run macroeconomic equilibrium.

Now suppose that aggregate demand rises, and the AD curve shifts rightward to AD_2. This results in a higher inflation rate π_2 and a higher aggregate output level, at Y_2, as the economy settles in the short run at E_2. Aggregate output in this

---

FOR INQUIRING MINDS   Is Long-Run Aggregate Supply Actually Vertical?

The *AD–AS* model says that the economy will eventually return to full employment after a negative demand shock, but at a lower rate of inflation. But many economists would offer a caveat: the economy may not be self-correcting if the required inflation rate is too low, especially if it's negative—that is, if the end point would involve deflation.

Why? Even when the economy is at more or less full employment, there are always some workers who find their skills in limited demand,

because their industry is in decline, technology has displaced their jobs, or any of a variety of reasons. To maintain full employment, the wages of these workers need to grow more slowly than average. But when inflation is very low, that might require actual wage reductions.

And there is abundant evidence that cutting wages in dollars—as opposed to wage growth slower than inflation, which happens often—is very hard to achieve, a phenomenon known as *downward nominal wage*

rigidity. Surveys suggest, in particular, that employers avoid wage cuts, even when they can easily hire new workers, because they believe that such cuts hurt workforce morale.

This means that achieving potential output at a very low rate of inflation may not be possible. Indeed, concerns about this issue are one reason the Federal Reserve and its counterparts abroad generally aim for an inflation rate of 2%, not zero, probably making nominal wage cuts largely unnecessary.

inflationary gap the gap that exists when aggregate output is above potential output.

output gap the percentage difference between actual aggregate output and potential output.

self-correcting describes an economy in which shocks to aggregate demand affect aggregate output in the short run but not in the long run.

new short-run equilibrium is above potential output, and unemployment is low in order to produce this higher level of aggregate output. When this happens, the economy experiences an **inflationary gap.**

As in the case of a recessionary gap, the story doesn't end here. Higher inflation will eventually be reflected in higher expected inflation, shifting the short-run aggregate supply curve up. This process continues until $SRAS_1$ reaches its new position at $SRAS_2$, bringing the economy to equilibrium at E_3, where AD_2, $SRAS_2$, and $LRAS$ all intersect. At E_3, the economy is back in long-run macroeconomic equilibrium. It is back at potential output, but at a higher inflation rate, π_3. Again, the economy is self-correcting in the long run.

To summarize the analysis of how the economy responds to recessionary and inflationary gaps, we can focus on the **output gap,** the percentage difference between actual aggregate output and potential output. We already used this concept in the Economics in Action. The formula for calculating the output gap is:

$$\textbf{(3)} \quad \text{Output gap} = \frac{\text{Actual aggregate output} - \text{Potential output}}{\text{Potential output}} \times 100$$

Our analysis says that the output gap always tends toward zero.

If there is a recessionary gap, so that the output gap is negative, expected inflation eventually falls, moving the economy back to potential output and bringing the output gap back to zero. If there is an inflationary gap, so that the output gap is positive, expected inflation rises, also moving the economy back to potential output and again bringing the output gap back to zero. So in the long run the economy is **self-correcting:** shocks to aggregate demand affect aggregate output in the short run but not in the long run.

ECONOMICS >> *in Action*
Supply Shocks versus Demand Shocks in Practice

How often do supply shocks and demand shocks, respectively, cause recessions? The verdict of most, though not all, macroeconomists is that recessions are mainly caused by demand shocks. But when a negative supply shock does happen, the resulting recession tends to be particularly severe.

Let's get specific. Between World War II and the coronavirus recession of 2020, which was really in a class of its own, there were twelve recessions in the United States. However, two of these, in 1980 and 1981–1982, are often treated as a single *double-dip recession* (that is, a recession followed by a temporary recovery, then followed by another recession), bringing the total number down to eleven. Of these eleven recessions, only two—the recession of 1973–1975 and the double-dip recession of 1980–1982—showed the distinctive combination of falling aggregate output and a surge in inflation that we call stagflation. In each case, the cause of the supply shock was political turmoil in the Middle East—the Arab–Israeli war of 1973 and the Iranian revolution of 1979—that disrupted world oil supplies and sent oil prices skyrocketing. In fact, economists sometimes refer to the two slumps as "OPEC I" and "OPEC II," after the Organization of the Petroleum Exporting Countries, the world oil cartel. The Great Recession that began in 2007 and lasted until 2009 was at least partially exacerbated, if not partially caused, by a spike in oil prices.

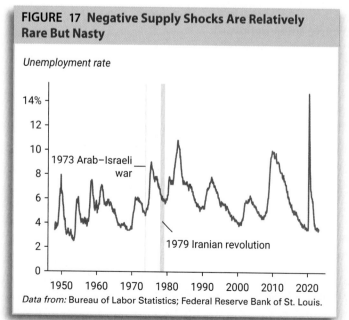

FIGURE 17 Negative Supply Shocks Are Relatively Rare But Nasty

Unemployment rate

1973 Arab–Israeli war

1979 Iranian revolution

Data from: Bureau of Labor Statistics; Federal Reserve Bank of St. Louis.

So eight of eleven postwar recessions were purely the result of demand shocks, not supply shocks. The few supply-shock recessions, however, were the worst as measured by the unemployment rate. Figure 17 shows the U.S. unemployment rate since 1948, with the dates of the 1973 Arab–Israeli war and the 1979 Iranian revolution marked on the figure. Some of the highest unemployment rates since World War II came after these big negative supply shocks.

There's a reason the aftermath of a supply shock tends to be particularly severe for the economy: macroeconomic policy has a much harder time dealing with supply shocks than with demand shocks. We'll see in a moment why supply shocks present such a problem.

Solutions appear at back of book.

1. Describe the short-run effects of each of the following shocks on inflation and on aggregate output.
   a. The government sharply increases the minimum wage, raising the wages of many workers.
   b. Solar energy firms launch a major program of investment spending.
   c. Congress raises taxes and cuts spending.
   d. Severe weather destroys crops around the world.

2. A rise in productivity increases potential output, but some worry that demand for the additional output will be insufficient even in the long run. How would you respond?

Macroeconomic Policy

We've just seen that the economy is self-correcting in the long run: it will eventually trend back to potential output. Most macroeconomists believe, however, that the process of self-correction typically takes a long time. In particular, if aggregate output is below potential output, the economy can suffer an extended period of depressed aggregate output and high unemployment before it returns to normal.

This belief is the background to one of the most famous quotations in economics: John Maynard Keynes's declaration, "In the long run we are all dead." We explain the context in which he made this remark in the upcoming For Inquiring Minds.

Economists usually interpret Keynes as having recommended that governments not wait for the economy to correct itself. Instead, it is argued by many economists, but not all, that the government should use monetary and fiscal policy to get the economy back to potential output in the aftermath of a shift of the aggregate demand curve. This is the rationale for an active **stabilization policy,** which is the use of government policy to reduce the severity of recessions and rein in excessively strong expansions.

Can stabilization policy improve the economy's performance? If we reexamine Figure 8, the answer certainly appears to be yes. Under active stabilization policy, the U.S. economy returned to potential output in 1996 after an approximately five-year recessionary gap. Likewise, in 2001 it also returned to potential output after an approximately four-year inflationary gap. These periods are much shorter than the decade or more that economists believe it would take for the economy to self-correct in the absence of active stabilization policy. In fact, recovery from the Great Recession took longer—seven years—partly because of political constraints on fiscal policy. By contrast, the economy recovered very fast from the 2020 pandemic shock, probably in part because of very supportive government policy—although this fast recovery was marred by a surge in inflation. However, as we'll see shortly, the ability to improve the economy's performance is not always guaranteed. It depends on the kinds of shocks the economy faces.

stabilization policy the use of government policy to reduce the severity of recessions and to rein in excessively strong expansions. There are two main tools of stabilization policy: monetary policy and fiscal policy.

FOR INQUIRING MINDS Keynes and the Long Run

The British economist Sir John Maynard Keynes (1883–1946), probably more than any other single economist, created the modern field of macroeconomics. We'll look at his role, and the controversies that still swirl around some aspects of his thought, in a later chapter on macroeconomic events and ideas. But for now let's just look at his most famous quote.

In 1923, Keynes published *A Tract on Monetary Reform,* a small book on the economic problems of Europe after World War I. In it, he decried the tendency of many of his colleagues to focus on how things work out in the long run — as in the long-run

macroeconomic equilibrium we have just analyzed — while ignoring the often very painful and possibly disastrous things that can happen along the way. Here's a fuller version of the quote:

This long run is a misleading guide to current affairs. In the long run we are all dead. Economists set themselves too easy, too useless a task if in tempestuous seasons they can only tell us that when the storm is long past the sea is flat again.

Keynes focused the attention of economists of his day on the short run.

Policy in the Face of Demand Shocks

Imagine that the economy experiences a negative demand shock, like the one shown in Figure 15. As we've discussed in this chapter, monetary and fiscal policy shift the aggregate demand curve. If policy makers react quickly to the fall in aggregate demand, they can use monetary or fiscal policy to shift the aggregate demand curve back to the right. And if policy were able to perfectly anticipate shifts of the aggregate demand curve, it could short-circuit the whole process shown in Figure 15. Instead of going through a period of low aggregate output and falling prices, the government could manage the economy so that it would stay at E_1.

Why might a policy that short-circuits the adjustment shown in Figure 15 and maintains the economy at its original equilibrium be desirable? For two reasons.

1. The temporary fall in aggregate output that would happen without policy intervention is a bad thing, particularly because such a decline is associated with high unemployment.

2. As explained in Chapter 8, price stability, which in practice normally means inflation of about 2%, is generally regarded as a desirable goal. So preventing an undesirable fall in the inflation rate, perhaps going all the way to deflation, is a good thing.

Does this mean that policy makers should always act to offset declines in aggregate demand? Not necessarily. As we'll see in later chapters, some policy measures to increase aggregate demand, especially those that increase budget deficits, may have long-term costs in terms of lower long-run growth. Furthermore, as our opening story made clear, in the real world policy makers aren't perfectly informed, and the effects of their policies aren't perfectly predictable. This creates the danger that stabilization policy will do more harm than good; that is, attempts to stabilize the economy may end up creating more instability. We'll describe the long-running debate over macroeconomic policy in Chapter 17. Despite these qualifications, most economists believe that a good case can be made for using macroeconomic policy to offset major negative shocks to the *AD* curve.

Should policy makers also try to offset positive shocks to aggregate demand? It may not seem obvious that they should. After all, even though inflation may be a bad thing, isn't more output and lower unemployment a good thing? Not necessarily.

Most economists now believe that any short-run gains from an inflationary gap must be paid back later. So policy makers today usually try to offset positive as well as negative demand shocks. For reasons we'll explain in Chapter 15, attempts to eliminate recessionary gaps and inflationary gaps usually rely on monetary rather than fiscal policy. In 2007 and 2008, the Fed sharply cut interest rates in an attempt to head off a rising recessionary gap; earlier in the decade, when the U.S. economy seemed headed for an inflationary gap, it raised interest rates to generate the opposite effect.

But how should macroeconomic policy respond to supply shocks?

Responding to Supply Shocks

Back in panel (a) of Figure 13 we showed the effects of a negative supply shock: in the short run such a shock leads to lower aggregate output but higher inflation. As we've noted, policy makers can respond to a negative *demand* shock by using monetary and fiscal policy to return aggregate demand to its original level. But what can or should they do about a negative *supply* shock?

In contrast to the aggregate demand curve, there are no easy policies that shift the short-run aggregate supply curve. That is, there is no government policy that can easily affect producers' profitability and so compensate for shifts of the short-run aggregate supply curve. So the policy response to a negative supply shock cannot aim to simply push the curve that shifted back to its original position.

And if you consider using monetary or fiscal policy to shift the aggregate demand curve in response to a supply shock, the right response isn't obvious. Two bad things are happening simultaneously: a fall in aggregate output, leading to a rise in unemployment, *and* a rise in the inflation rate. Any policy that shifts the aggregate demand curve helps one problem only by making the other worse. If the government acts to increase aggregate demand and limit the rise in unemployment, it reduces the decline in output but causes even more inflation. If it acts to reduce aggregate demand, it curbs inflation but causes a further rise in unemployment.

It's a trade-off with no good answer. In the end, the United States and other economically advanced nations suffering from the supply shocks of the 1970s eventually chose to stabilize prices even at the cost of higher unemployment. As we were writing this edition, policy makers were grappling with the question of whether they might have to do the same to rein in the inflation that followed the Covid-19 pandemic.

ECONOMICS >> *in Action*
Is Stabilization Policy Stabilizing?

We've described the theoretical rationale for stabilization policy as a way of responding to demand shocks. But does stabilization policy actually stabilize the economy? We can try to answer this question by looking at the long-term historical record.

Before World War II, the U.S. government didn't really have a stabilization policy, largely because macroeconomics as we know it didn't exist, and there was no consensus about what to do. Since World War II, and especially since 1960, active stabilization policy has become standard practice.

So, has the economy actually become more stable since the government began trying to stabilize it? The answer is a qualified yes. It's qualified for two reasons. One is that data from the pre–World War II era are less reliable than modern data. The other is that both the severe and protracted slump that began in 2007 and the surge in inflation after 2021 have shaken confidence in the effectiveness of government policy. Still, there seems to have been a reduction in the size of fluctuations.

Figure 18 shows the number of unemployed as a percentage of the nonfarm labor force since 1890. (We focus

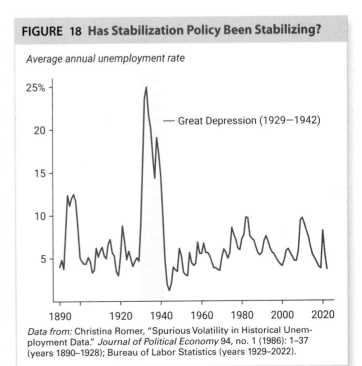

FIGURE 18 Has Stabilization Policy Been Stabilizing?

Average annual unemployment rate

— Great Depression (1929–1942)

Data from: Christina Romer, "Spurious Volatility in Historical Unemployment Data." *Journal of Political Economy* 94, no. 1 (1986): 1–37 (years 1890–1928); Bureau of Labor Statistics (years 1929–2022).

on nonfarm workers because farmers, though they often suffer economic hardship, are rarely reported as unemployed.) Even ignoring the huge spike in unemployment during the Great Depression, unemployment seems to have varied a lot more before World War II than after. It's also worth noticing that the peaks in postwar unemployment, in 1975, 1982, and to some extent in 2010 and 2020, corresponded to major supply shocks—the kind of shock for which stabilization policy has no good answer.

It's possible that the greater stability of the economy reflects good luck rather than policy. But on the face of it, the evidence suggests that stabilization policy is indeed stabilizing.

>> Check Your Understanding 12-4

Solutions appear at back of book.

1. Suppose someone says, "Using monetary or fiscal policy to pump up the economy is counterproductive—you get a brief high, but then you have the pain of inflation."
   a. Explain what this means in terms of the *AD–AS* model.
   b. Is this a valid argument against stabilization policy? Why or why not?

2. In 2008, in the aftermath of the collapse of the housing bubble and a sharp rise in the price of commodities, particularly oil, there was much internal disagreement within the Fed about how to respond, with some advocating lowering interest rates and others contending that this would set off a rise in inflation. Explain the reasoning behind each one of these views in terms of the *AD–AS* model.

The Rise and Fall of Carvana

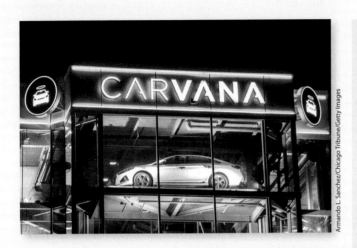

Armando L. Sanchez/Chicago Tribune/Getty Images

The inflation surge that troubled the Fed in 2021–2022 was unusually complicated. It clearly wasn't a pure aggregate demand shock, although high levels of government spending that aimed to insulate vulnerable workers from the financial effects of the pandemic probably fed inflation. But there were also shocks to aggregate supply, many of them linked to the pandemic but with additional factors at play. In particular, there was a global shortage of semiconductor chips, which hobbled the supply of new automobiles.

Say what? Well, modern cars — actually, modern almost everything — have chips in them. And in 2020–2022, there weren't enough of the particular chips needed by the auto industry, limiting production.

With new cars scarce, the market for used cars boomed; used car prices rose more than 50% between May 2020 and February 2022. This was very good news for companies specializing in used-car sales, especially the online retailer Carvana, which briefly experienced high profits and saw its stock price soar from early 2020 through the middle of 2021.

This illustrates a general principle: even things that are clearly bad for the economy as a whole, such as an adverse shock to aggregate supply, can produce some big winners.

Unfortunately for Carvana, the bad times that were good for its business didn't last. As chip shortages began to ease, auto production began rising, and used-car prices and sales slid; Carvana soon found itself experiencing large losses. At the time of writing, its stock was down 94% from its peak, and there was widespread speculation that the company might go bankrupt.

QUESTIONS FOR THOUGHT

1. Why do you think used car prices fell in 2007–2009 but rose in 2021–2022?

2. What does this say about the causes of economic problems in each case?

3. Shipping companies also earned high profits in 2021. Why do you think this happened?

SUMMARY

1. The **aggregate demand curve** shows the relationship between inflation and the quantity of aggregate output demanded.

2. The aggregate demand curve is downward sloping mainly because of the interest rate effect of higher inflation: higher inflation causes central banks to raise interest rates, leading to a fall in investment spending and consumer spending.

3. The aggregate demand curve shifts because of changes in wealth, changes in expected inflation, and the effect of the size of the existing stock of physical capital. Policy makers can use fiscal policy and monetary policy to shift the aggregate demand curve.

4. The **aggregate supply curve** shows the relationship between inflation and the quantity of aggregate output supplied.

5. The **short-run aggregate supply curve** is upward sloping because **nominal wages** are **sticky** in the short run: a higher inflation rate leads to higher profit per unit of output and increased aggregate output in the short run.

6. Changes in commodity prices, expected inflation, and productivity lead to changes in producers' profits and shift the short-run aggregate supply curve.

7. In the long run, all prices, including nominal wages, are flexible and the economy produces at its **potential output.** If actual aggregate output exceeds potential output, expected inflation will eventually rise and aggregate output will fall. If potential output exceeds actual aggregate output, expected inflation will eventually fall and aggregate output will rise. So the **long-run aggregate supply curve** is vertical at potential output.

8. In the *AD–AS model,* the intersection of the short-run aggregate supply curve and the aggregate demand curve is the point of **short-run macroeconomic equilibrium.** It determines the **short-run equilibrium inflation rate** and the level of **short-run equilibrium aggregate output.**

9. Economic fluctuations occur because of a shift of the aggregate demand curve (a *demand shock*) or the short-run aggregate supply curve (a *supply shock*). A **demand shock** causes inflation and aggregate output to move in the same direction as the economy moves along the short-run aggregate supply curve. A **supply shock** causes them to move in opposite directions as the economy moves along the aggregate demand curve. A particularly nasty occurrence is **stagflation**—inflation and falling aggregate output—which is caused by a negative supply shock.

10. Demand shocks have only short-run effects on aggregate output because the economy is **self-correcting** in the long run. In a **recessionary gap,** an eventual fall in expected inflation moves the economy to **long-run macroeconomic equilibrium,** where aggregate output is equal to potential output. In an **inflationary gap,** an eventual rise in expected inflation moves the economy to long-run macroeconomic equilibrium. We can use the **output gap,** the percentage difference between actual aggregate output and potential output, to summarize how the economy responds to recessionary and inflationary gaps. Because the economy tends to be self-correcting in the long run, the output gap always tends toward zero.

11. The high cost—in terms of unemployment—of a recessionary gap and the future adverse consequences of an inflationary gap lead many economists to advocate active **stabilization policy:** using fiscal or monetary policy to offset demand shocks. There can be drawbacks, however, because such policies may contribute to a long-term rise in the budget deficit and crowding out of private investment, leading to lower long-run growth. Also, poorly timed policies can increase economic instability.

12. Negative supply shocks pose a policy dilemma: a policy that counteracts the fall in aggregate output by increasing aggregate demand will lead to higher inflation, but a policy that counteracts inflation by reducing aggregate demand will deepen the output slump.

KEY TERMS

PRACTICE QUESTIONS

1. Your study partner is confused by the upward-sloping short-run aggregate supply curve and the vertical long-run aggregate supply curve. How would you explain the differences?

2. Suppose that in Wageland all workers sign annual wage contracts each year on January 1. No matter what happens to prices of final goods and services during the year, all workers earn the wage specified in their annual contract. This year, prices of final goods and services fall unexpectedly after the contracts are signed. Answer the following questions using a diagram and assume that the economy starts at potential output.

   a. In the short run, how will the quantity of aggregate output supplied respond to the fall in prices?

   b. What will happen when firms and workers renegotiate their wages?

3. The Conference Board publishes the Consumer Confidence Index (CCI) every month based on a survey of 5,000 representative U.S. households. It is used by many economists to track the state of the economy. A press release by the Board on March 31, 2023, stated: "The Conference Board Consumer Confidence Index slightly increased in March, following an increase in February. The Index now stands at 104.2 (1985 = 100), up from 103.2 in February."

   a. As an economist, is this news encouraging for economic growth?

   b. Explain your answer to part a with the help of the AD–AS model. Draw a typical diagram showing two equilibrium points (E_1) and (E_2). Label the vertical axis "Inflation rate" and the horizontal axis "Real GDP." Assume that all other major macroeconomic factors remain unchanged.

   c. How should the government respond to this news if the economy is below potential output? If it is above potential output?

PROBLEMS

1. A fall in the value of the dollar against other currencies makes U.S. final goods and services cheaper to foreigners even though the U.S. price level and subsequent inflation rate stays the same. As a result, foreigners demand more U.S. aggregate output. Your study partner says that this represents a movement down the aggregate demand curve because foreigners are demanding more in response to a lower price. You, however, insist that this represents a rightward shift of the aggregate demand curve. Who is right? Explain.

2. The economy is at point A in the accompanying diagram. Suppose that the inflation rate rises from π_1 to π_2. How will aggregate supply adjust in the short run and in the long run to the increase in the inflation rate? Illustrate with a diagram.

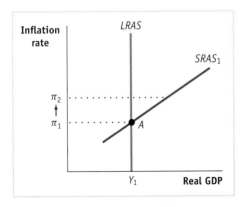

3. Suppose the economy is operating below potential output and as a result interest rates are close to zero.

What happens to the interest rate effect of a change in inflation rates if a further decline in the inflation rate doesn't lower interest rates? What happens to the slope of the aggregate demand curve? Will it still slope downward? Explain.

4. Suppose that the economy is currently at potential output. Also suppose that you are an economic policy maker and that a college economics student asks you to rank, if possible, your most preferred to least preferred type of shock: positive demand shock, negative demand shock, positive supply shock, negative supply shock. How would you rank them and why?

5. Explain whether the following government policies affect the aggregate demand curve or the short-run aggregate supply curve and how.

   a. The government reduces the minimum nominal wage.

   b. The government increases Temporary Assistance for Needy Families (TANF) payments, government transfers to families with dependent children.

   c. To reduce the budget deficit, the government announces that households will pay much higher taxes beginning next year.

   d. The government reduces military spending.

6. In Wageland, all workers sign annual wage contracts each year on January 1. In late January, a new computer operating system is introduced that increases labor productivity dramatically. Explain how Wageland will move from one short-run macroeconomic equilibrium to another. Illustrate with a diagram.

7. There were two major shocks to the U.S. economy in 2007, leading to the severe recession of 2007–2009. One shock was related to oil prices; the other was the slump in the housing market. This question analyzes the effect of these two shocks on GDP using the *AD–AS* framework.

   a. Draw typical aggregate demand and short-run aggregate supply curves. Label the horizontal axis "Real GDP" and the vertical axis "Inflation rate." Label the equilibrium point E_1, the equilibrium quantity Y_1, and equilibrium inflation rate π_2.

   b. Data taken from the Department of Energy indicate that the average price of crude oil in the world increased from $54.63 per barrel on January 5, 2007, to $92.93 on December 28, 2007. Would an increase in oil prices cause a demand shock or a supply shock? Redraw the diagram from part a to illustrate the effect of this shock by shifting the appropriate curve.

   c. The Housing Price Index, published by the Office of Federal Housing Enterprise Oversight, calculates that U.S. home prices fell by an average of 3.0% in the 12 months between January 2007 and January 2008. Would the fall in home prices cause a supply shock or demand shock? Redraw the diagram from part b to illustrate the effect of this shock by shifting the appropriate curve. Label the new equilibrium point E_3, the equilibrium quantity Y_3, and equilibrium inflation rate π_3.

   d. Compare the equilibrium points E_1 and E_3 in your diagram for part c. What was the effect of the two shocks on real GDP and the inflation rate (increase, decrease, or indeterminate)?

8. Using aggregate demand, short-run aggregate supply, and long-run aggregate supply curves, explain the process by which each of the following economic events will move the economy from one long-run macroeconomic equilibrium to another. Illustrate with diagrams. In each case, what are the short-run and long-run effects on the inflation rate and aggregate output?

   a. There is a decrease in households' wealth due to a decline in the stock market.

   b. The government lowers taxes, leaving households with more disposable income, with no corresponding reduction in government purchases.

9. Using aggregate demand, short-run aggregate supply, and long-run aggregate supply curves, explain the process by which each of the following government policies will move the economy from one long-run macroeconomic equilibrium to another. Illustrate with diagrams. In each case, what are the short-run and long-run effects on the inflation rate and aggregate output?

   a. There is an increase in taxes on households.

   b. There is an increase in the quantity of money, that is made independent of the inflation rate.

   c. There is an increase in government spending.

10. The economy is in short-run macroeconomic equilibrium at point E_1 in the accompanying diagram. Based on the diagram, answer the following questions.

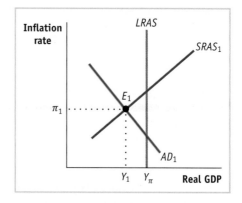

   a. Is the economy facing an inflationary or a recessionary gap?

   b. What policies can the government implement that might bring the economy back to long-run macroeconomic equilibrium? Illustrate with a diagram.

   c. If the government did not intervene to close this gap, would the economy return to long-run macroeconomic equilibrium? Explain and illustrate with a diagram.

   d. What are the advantages and disadvantages of the government implementing policies to close the gap?

11. In the accompanying diagram, the economy is in long-run macroeconomic equilibrium at point E_1 when an oil shock shifts the short-run aggregate supply curve to $SRAS_2$. Based on the diagram, answer the following questions.

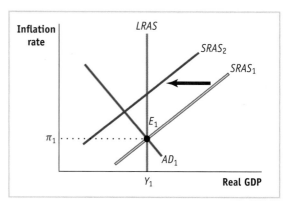

   a. How do the inflation rate and aggregate output change in the short run as a result of the oil shock? What is this phenomenon known as?

   b. What fiscal or monetary policies can the government use to address the effects of the supply shock? Use a diagram that shows the effect of policies chosen to address the change in real GDP. Use another diagram to show the effect of policies chosen to address the change in the inflation rate.

c. Why do supply shocks present a dilemma for government policy makers?

12. The late 1990s in the United States were characterized by substantial economic growth, a significant increase in real GDP, with low inflation. Explain this experience using aggregate demand and aggregate supply curves. Illustrate with a diagram.

13. In each of the following cases, in the short run, determine whether the events cause a shift of a curve or a movement along a curve. Determine which curve is involved and the direction of the change.

a. As a result of an increase in the value of the dollar in relation to other currencies, U.S. producers now pay less in dollar terms for foreign steel, a major commodity used in production.

b. An increase in the quantity of money by the Fed increases the quantity of money that people wish to lend, lowering interest rates.

c. Greater union activity leads to higher nominal wages.

d. A fall in the inflation rate increases the purchasing power of households' and firms' money holdings. As a result, they borrow less and lend more. ∎

13 Fiscal Policy

A STIMULUS TOO FAR?

2020 was the year of the coronavirus — a rapidly spreading virus that quickly infected millions around the world, in some cases requiring weeks of intensive care and in all too many cases proving fatal. The pandemic also had devastating effects on the economy, leading to the steepest decline in employment and output ever recorded. However, the U.S. government attempted to mitigate the amount of hardship with a $2 trillion relief package, the CARES Act, which provided aid to the newly unemployed additional cash payments to many families, and aid to businesses.

By early 2021 the economy had partially recovered. The unemployment rate, which peaked at 14.7% in April 2020, was down to 6.1% in February 2021. This was, however, still well above the roughly 3.5% rate that prevailed in late 2019, and many Americans

THE AMERICAN RESCUE PLAN

Signed into law in March 2021, the American Rescue Plan was intended to reduce hardship and stimulate overall spending.

Kent Nishimura/Getty Images

were still experiencing financial stress caused by pandemic-related disruptions.

In response to these continuing difficulties, in March 2021 President Joe Biden, who had taken office in January, signed the American Rescue Plan (ARP), a $1.9 trillion bill that combined an extension of the CARES Act's financial aid to individuals, especially the unemployed and low-income families with children, with aid to education and assistance to state and local governments. The bill was largely intended to reduce hardship, but it also stimulated overall spending.

So while the ARP was in part about disaster relief, it was also an example of *fiscal policy:* changes in taxes and government spending to stabilize the economy by shifting the aggregate demand curve. In this case the fiscal policy was *expansionary*, designed to shift the aggregate demand curve *out;* fiscal policies that shift the aggregate demand curve *in* are *contractionary*.

Fiscal policy is often controversial. When in 2009 the government engaged in expansionary fiscal policy — the so-called Obama stimulus — to fight the recession that followed the 2008 financial crisis, some believed it was a mistake to increase government spending at a time of widespread distress. One member of Congress spoke for many when he declared that the government should spend *less* in hard times: "American families are tightening their belts, but they don't see government tightening its belt." There were also concerns that the new spending would widen the budget deficit. But most economists believe that expansionary fiscal policy is appropriate when the economy is depressed.

The qualification — "when the economy is depressed" — is important. Many economists who had supported the Obama stimulus, including some who warned that it was too small, criticized the ARP and/or warned

that it was much too big. Were they being inconsistent? In reality, no: in early 2009 the U.S. economy was deeply depressed and was heading further downward. By contrast, in early 2021 the economy was growing, and many estimates suggested that the ARP was more than enough to restore full employment, in which case it could prove counterproductive. While there is still debate about how much the ARP did in fact contribute to inflation, which accelerated greatly in late 2021 and remained high into 2023, there is broad agreement among economists that stimulus that is either excessive or delivered at the wrong time is likely to be counterproductive to the economy.

In this chapter, we'll see how fiscal policy fits into the models of economic fluctuation we studied in Chapters 11 and 12. We will also see why budget deficits and government debt can be problems, and why short-run and long-run considerations can pull fiscal policy in opposite directions. •

WHAT YOU WILL LEARN

- What is fiscal policy and why is it an essential tool in managing economic fluctuations?

- Which policies constitute **expansionary fiscal policy** and which constitute **contractionary fiscal policy**?

- Why does fiscal policy have a multiplier effect and how is this effect influenced by **automatic stabilizers**?

- Why do governments calculate the **cyclically adjusted budget balance**?

- Why can a large **public debt** and **implicit liabilities** of the government be a cause for concern?

‖ Fiscal Policy: The Basics

Modern governments in economically advanced countries spend a great deal of money and collect a lot in taxes. Figure 1 shows government spending and tax revenue as percentages of GDP for a selection of high-income countries in 2022. As you can see, the French government sector is relatively large, accounting for more than half of the French economy. The government of the United States plays a smaller role in the economy than those of Canada, Japan, and most European countries. But that role is still sizable, with the government playing a major role in the U.S. economy. As a result, changes in the federal budget—changes in government spending or in taxation—can have large effects on the U.S. economy.

To analyze these effects, we begin by showing how taxes and government spending affect the economy's flow of income. Then we can see how changes in spending and tax policy affect aggregate demand.

Taxes, Purchases of Goods and Services, Government Transfers, and Borrowing

In Chapter 7, Figure 1, we showed the circular flow of income and spending in the economy as a whole. One of the sectors represented in that figure was the government. Funds flow *into* the government in the form of taxes and government borrowing; funds flow *out* in the form of government purchases of goods and services and government transfers to households.

What kinds of taxes do Americans pay, and where does the money go? Figure 2 shows the composition of U.S. tax revenue in 2022. Taxes, of course, are required payments to the government. In the United States, taxes are collected at the national level by the federal government; at the state level by each state government; and at local levels by counties, cities, and towns. At the federal level, the taxes that generate the greatest revenue are income taxes on both personal income and corporate profits as well as *social insurance* taxes, which we'll explain shortly. At the state and local levels, the picture is more complex: these governments rely on a mix of sales taxes, property taxes, income taxes, and fees of various kinds.

Overall, taxes on personal income and corporate profits accounted for 48.1% of total government revenue in 2022; social insurance taxes accounted for 22.1%; and a variety of other taxes, collected mainly at the state and local levels, accounted for the rest.

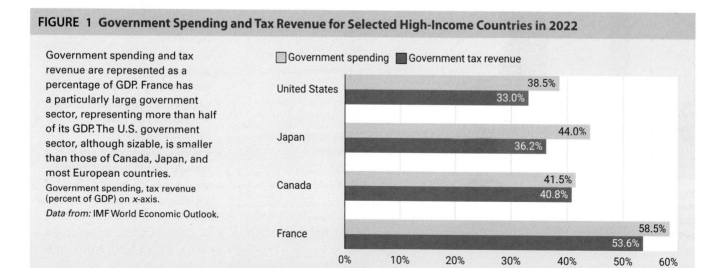

FIGURE 1 Government Spending and Tax Revenue for Selected High-Income Countries in 2022

Government spending and tax revenue are represented as a percentage of GDP. France has a particularly large government sector, representing more than half of its GDP. The U.S. government sector, although sizable, is smaller than those of Canada, Japan, and most European countries.

Government spending, tax revenue (percent of GDP) on x-axis.

Data from: IMF World Economic Outlook.

Figure 3 shows the composition of total U.S. government spending in 2022, which takes two broad forms. One form is purchases of goods and services. This includes everything from ammunition for the military to the salaries of public school teachers (who are treated in the national accounts as providers of a service—education). The big items here are national defense and education. The category "Other goods and services" consists mainly of state and local spending on a variety of services, from police and firefighters to highway construction and maintenance.

The other form of government spending is government transfers, which are payments by the government to households for which no good or service is provided in return. In the United States, as well as in Canada and Europe, government transfers represent a very large proportion of the budget. Most U.S. government spending on transfer payments is accounted for by the following four programs:

- Social Security, which provides guaranteed income to older Americans, disabled Americans, and the surviving spouses and dependent children of deceased or retired beneficiaries

- Medicare, which covers much of the cost of health care for Americans aged 65 or older

- Medicaid, which covers much of the cost of health care for Americans with low incomes

- The Affordable Care Act (ACA), which seeks to make health insurance available and affordable to all Americans

The term **social insurance** is used to describe government programs that are intended to protect families against economic hardship. These include Social Security, Medicare, Medicaid, and the ACA, as well as smaller programs such as unemployment insurance and food stamps. The ACA works through a system of regulated private insurance markets, subsidies, and an expansion of Medicaid eligibility and is much smaller than the other three large programs. Social insurance programs in the United States are largely paid for with special, dedicated taxes on wages—the social insurance taxes mentioned earlier. The ACA is an exception: it is funded mainly by special taxes on high incomes.

How do tax policy and government spending affect the economy? The answer is that taxation and government spending have a strong effect on total aggregate spending in the economy.

The Government Budget and Total Spending

Let's revisit the basic equation of national income accounting:

(1) GDP = $C + I + G + X - IM$

The left-hand side of this equation is GDP, the value of all final goods and services produced in the economy. The right-hand side is aggregate spending, total spending on final goods and services produced in the economy. It is the sum of

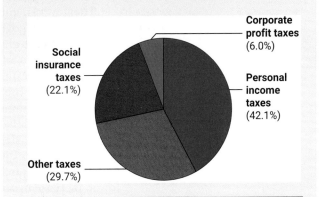

FIGURE 2 Sources of Tax Revenue in the United States, 2022

Personal income taxes, taxes on corporate profits, and social insurance taxes account for most government tax revenue. The rest is a mix of property taxes, sales taxes, and other sources of revenue. (Percentages may not add to 100 due to rounding.)
Data from: Bureau of Economic Analysis.

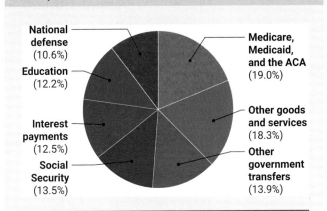

FIGURE 3 Government Spending in the United States, 2022

The two types of government spending are purchases of goods and services and government transfers. The biggest items in government purchases are national defense and education. The biggest items in government transfers are Social Security, Medicare, Medicaid, and the Affordable Care Act. (Percentages do not add to 100 due to rounding.)
Data from: Bureau of Economic Analysis.

social insurance government programs—like Social Security, Medicare, unemployment insurance, and food stamps—intended to protect families against economic hardship.

consumer spending (*C*), investment spending (*I*), government purchases of goods and services (*G*), and the value of exports (*X*) minus the value of imports (*IM*). It includes all the sources of aggregate demand.

The government directly controls one of the variables on the right-hand side of Equation 1: government purchases of goods and services (*G*). But that's not the only effect fiscal policy has on aggregate spending in the economy. Through changes in taxes and transfers, it also influences consumer spending (*C*) and, in some cases, investment spending (*I*).

To see why the budget affects consumer spending, recall that *disposable income*, the total income households have available to spend, is equal to the total income they receive from wages, dividends, interest, and rent, *minus* taxes, *plus* government transfers. So either an increase in taxes or a reduction in government transfers *reduces* disposable income. And a fall in disposable income, other things equal, leads to a fall in consumer spending. Conversely, either a decrease in taxes or an increase in government transfers *increases* disposable income. And a rise in disposable income, other things equal, leads to a rise in consumer spending.

The government's ability to affect investment spending is a more complex story, which we won't discuss in detail. The important point is that the government taxes profits, and changes in the rules that determine how much a business owes can increase or reduce the incentive to spend on investment goods.

Because the government itself is one source of spending in the economy, and because taxes and transfers can affect spending by consumers and firms, the government can use changes in taxes or government spending to *shift the aggregate demand curve*. And as we saw in Chapter 12, there are sometimes good reasons to shift the aggregate demand curve.

Expansionary and Contractionary Fiscal Policy

Why would the government want to shift the aggregate demand curve? Because it wants to close either a recessionary gap, created when aggregate output falls below potential output, or an inflationary gap, created when aggregate output exceeds potential output.

FIGURE 4 Expansionary Fiscal Policy Can Close a Recessionary Gap

The economy is in short-run macroeconomic equilibrium at E_1, where the aggregate demand curve, AD_1, intersects the *SRAS* curve. However, it is not in long-run macroeconomic equilibrium. At E_1, there is a recessionary gap of $Y_P - Y_1$. An expansionary fiscal policy — an increase in government purchases of goods and services, a reduction in taxes, or an increase in government transfers — shifts the aggregate demand curve rightward. It can close the recessionary gap by shifting AD_1 to AD_2, moving the economy to a new short-run macroeconomic equilibrium, E_2, which is also a long-run macroeconomic equilibrium.

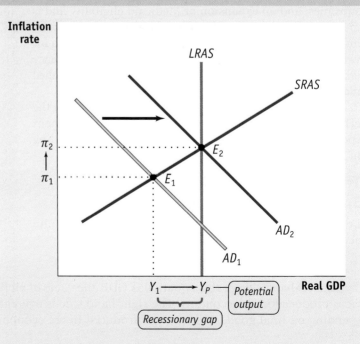

Figure 4 shows the case of an economy facing a recessionary gap. *SRAS* is the short-run aggregate supply curve, *LRAS* is the long-run aggregate supply curve, and AD_1 is the initial aggregate demand curve. At the initial short-run macroeconomic equilibrium, E_1, aggregate output is Y_1, below potential output, Y_P. What the government would like to do is increase aggregate demand, shifting the aggregate demand curve rightward to AD_2. This would increase aggregate output, making it equal to potential output. Fiscal policy that increases aggregate demand, called **expansionary fiscal policy,** normally takes one of three forms:

1. An increase in government purchases of goods and services
2. A cut in taxes
3. An increase in government transfers

The American Rescue Plan consisted mainly of transfers: a one-time check for $1,400 for Americans earning less than $75,000 a year, an extension of expanded unemployment benefits that had been enacted during the worst of the pandemic, and a similar extension of special tax credits for low-income families with children. It also included some increase in spending on health care and aid to state governments.

Figure 5 shows the opposite case—an economy facing an inflationary gap. Again, *SRAS* is the short-run aggregate supply curve, *LRAS* is the long-run aggregate supply curve, and AD_1 is the initial aggregate demand curve. At the initial equilibrium, E_1, aggregate output is Y_1, above potential output, Y_P. As we'll explain in later chapters, policy makers often try to head off inflation by eliminating inflationary gaps. To eliminate the inflationary gap shown in Figure 5, fiscal policy must reduce aggregate demand and shift the aggregate demand curve leftward to AD_2. This reduces aggregate output and makes it equal to potential output. Fiscal policy that reduces aggregate demand, called **contractionary fiscal policy,** is the opposite of expansionary fiscal policy. It is implemented in three possible ways:

1. A reduction in government purchases of goods and services
2. An increase in taxes
3. A reduction in government transfers

expansionary fiscal policy fiscal policy that increases aggregate demand by increasing government purchases, decreasing taxes, or increasing transfers.

contractionary fiscal policy fiscal policy that reduces aggregate demand by decreasing government purchases, increasing taxes, or decreasing transfers.

FIGURE 5 Contractionary Fiscal Policy Can Close an Inflationary Gap

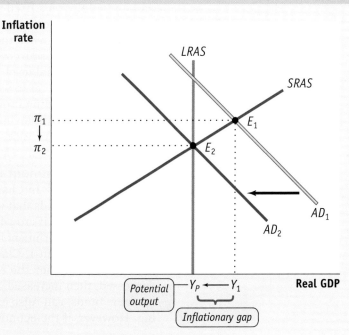

The economy is in short-run macroeconomic equilibrium at E_1, where the aggregate demand curve, AD_1, intersects the *SRAS* curve. But it is not in long-run macroeconomic equilibrium. At E_1, there is an inflationary gap of $Y_1 - Y_P$. A contractionary fiscal policy — such as reduced government purchases of goods and services, an increase in taxes, or a reduction in government transfers — shifts the aggregate demand curve leftward. It closes the inflationary gap by shifting AD_1 to AD_2, moving the economy to a new short-run macroeconomic equilibrium, E_2, which is also a long-run macroeconomic equilibrium.

A classic example of contractionary fiscal policy occurred in 1968, when U.S. policy makers grew worried about rising inflation. President Lyndon Johnson imposed a temporary 10% surcharge on taxable income—everyone's income taxes were increased by 10%. He also tried to scale back government purchases of goods and services, which had risen dramatically because of the cost of the Vietnam War. There were also some significant tax increases in the Inflation Reduction Act, enacted in 2022, although the bill also included spending increases and was probably expansionary overall.

Can Expansionary Fiscal Policy Actually Work?

In practice, the use of fiscal policy—in particular, the use of expansionary fiscal policy in the face of a recessionary gap—is often controversial. We'll examine the origins of these controversies in detail in Chapter 17. But for now, let's quickly summarize the major points of the debate over expansionary fiscal policy, so we can understand when the critiques are justified and when they are not.

There are three main arguments against the use of expansionary fiscal policy.

1. Government spending always crowds out private spending.
2. Government borrowing always crowds out private investment spending.
3. Government budget deficits lead to reduced private spending.

The first of these claims is wrong in principle, but it has nonetheless played a prominent role in public debates. The second is valid under some, but not all, circumstances. The third argument, although it raises some important issues, isn't a good reason to believe that expansionary fiscal policy doesn't work.

Claim 1: "Government Spending Always Crowds Out Private Spending."
Some claim that expansionary fiscal policy can never raise aggregate spending and therefore can never raise aggregate income, with reasons that go something like this: "Every dollar that the government spends is a dollar taken away from the private sector. So any rise in government spending must be offset by an equal fall in private spending." In other words, every dollar spent by the government *crowds out*, or displaces, a dollar of private spending.

But the statement is wrong because it assumes that resources in the economy are always fully employed and, as a result, the aggregate income earned in the economy is always a fixed sum—which isn't true. In reality, whether or not government spending crowds out private spending depends on the state of the economy. In particular, when the economy is suffering from a recessionary gap, there are unemployed resources in the economy, and output (and therefore income) is below its potential level. Expansionary fiscal policy during these periods puts unemployed resources to work and generates higher spending and higher income. Government spending crowds out private spending only when the economy is operating at full employment. So the argument that expansionary fiscal policy always crowds out private spending is wrong in principle.

Claim 2: "Government Borrowing Always Crowds Out Private Investment Spending."
In Chapter 10, we discussed the possibility that government borrowing uses funds that would have otherwise been used for private investment spending—that is, it crowds out private investment spending. So how valid is the argument that government borrowing always reduces private investment spending?

Much like Claim 1, Claim 2 is wrong because whether crowding out occurs depends on whether the economy is depressed or not. If the economy is not depressed, then increased government borrowing, by increasing the demand for loanable funds, can raise interest rates and crowd out private investment spending. However, if the economy is depressed, crowding out is much less likely to occur. When the economy is at far less than full employment, a fiscal expansion will lead to higher incomes, which in turn leads to increased savings at any given interest rate. This larger pool of savings allows the government to borrow without driving up interest rates. The 2009 stimulus was a case in point: despite high levels of government borrowing, U.S. interest rates stayed near historic lows. In the end, government borrowing crowds out private investment spending only when the economy is operating at full employment.

On the other hand, the ARP, much of whose impact came after the economy was probably at or even above full employment, probably did contribute to rising interest rates and may have crowded out some private investment spending, especially housing construction.

Claim 3: "Government Budget Deficits Lead to Reduced Private Spending."

Other things equal, expansionary fiscal policy leads to a larger budget deficit and greater government debt. And higher debt will eventually require the government to raise taxes to pay it off. So, according to the third argument against expansionary fiscal policy, consumers, anticipating that they must pay higher taxes in the future to pay off today's government debt, will cut their spending today in order to save money. This argument, first made by nineteenth-century economist David Ricardo, is known as *Ricardian equivalence*. It is an argument often taken to imply that expansionary fiscal policy will have no effect on the economy because farsighted consumers will undo any attempts at expansion by the government. (And will also undo any contractionary fiscal policy, for that matter.)

In reality, however, it's doubtful that consumers behave with such foresight and budgeting discipline. Most people, when provided with extra cash (generated by fiscal expansion), will spend at least some of it. So even fiscal policy that takes the form of temporary tax cuts or transfers of cash to consumers probably does have an expansionary effect.

Moreover, it's possible to show that even with Ricardian equivalence, a temporary rise in government spending that involves direct purchases of goods and services—such as a program of road construction—would still lead to a boost in total spending in the near term. That's because even if consumers cut back their current spending in anticipation of higher future taxes, their reduced spending will take place over an extended period as consumers save over time to pay the future tax bill. Meanwhile, the additional government spending will be concentrated in the near future, when the economy needs it.

So although the effects emphasized by Ricardian equivalence may reduce the impact of fiscal expansion, the claim that it makes fiscal expansion completely ineffective is neither consistent with how consumers actually behave nor a reason to believe that increases in government spending have no effect. So, in the end, it's not a valid argument against expansionary fiscal policy.

In Sum The extent to which we should expect expansionary fiscal policy to work depends on the circumstances. When the economy has a recessionary gap—as it did when the 2009 stimulus was passed—economics tells us that this is just the kind of situation in which expansionary fiscal policy helps the economy. However, when the economy is already closing in on full employment, as appears to have been the case in 2021, when the ARP went into effect, expansionary fiscal policy can lead to crowding out, an overheated economy, and higher inflation.

A Cautionary Note: Lags in Fiscal Policy

Looking back at Figures 4 and 5, it may seem obvious that the government should actively use fiscal policy—always adopting an expansionary fiscal policy when the economy faces a recessionary gap and always adopting a contractionary fiscal policy when the economy faces an inflationary gap. But many economists caution against an extremely active stabilization policy, arguing that a government that tries too hard to stabilize the economy—through either fiscal policy or monetary policy—can end up making the economy less stable.

We'll leave discussion of the warnings associated with monetary policy to Chapter 15. In the case of fiscal policy, one key reason for caution is that there are important *time lags* between when the policy is decided upon and when it is implemented. To understand the nature of these lags, consider the three things that have to happen before the government increases spending to fight a recessionary gap.

1. The government has to realize that the recessionary gap exists: economic data take time to collect and analyze, and recessions are often recognized only months after they have begun. Although the Great Recession is generally considered to have begun in December 2007, as late as September 2008 some economists were still questioning whether the recession was real.

2. The government has to develop a spending plan, which can itself take months, particularly if politicians take time debating how the money should be spent and passing legislation.

3. It takes time to spend money. For example, a road construction project begins with activities such as surveying that don't involve spending large sums. It may be quite some time before the big spending begins. The Recovery Act was passed in the first quarter of 2009, but much of its effect on federal spending, especially purchases of goods and services, didn't come until 2011.

Because of these lags, an attempt to increase spending to fight a recessionary gap may take so long to get going that the economy has already recovered on its own. In fact, the recessionary gap may have turned into an inflationary gap by the time expansionary fiscal policy takes effect. In that case, expansionary fiscal policy will make things worse instead of better.

Nightman1965/Shutterstock

In making fiscal policy, timing is crucial.

This doesn't mean that fiscal policy should never be actively used. In early 2009, there was good reason to believe that the slump facing the U.S. economy would be both deep and long and that a fiscal stimulus designed to arrive over the next year or two would almost surely push aggregate demand in the right direction. In fact, as we'll see later in this chapter, the 2009 stimulus arguably faded out too soon, leaving the economy still deeply depressed when it ended. But the problem of lags makes the actual use of both fiscal and monetary policy harder than you might think from a simple analysis like the one we have just given.

ECONOMICS >> *in Action*
A Tale of Two Stimuli

There were some broad similarities between the Obama stimulus of 2009 and the ARP of 2021. Yet many economists who fully supported stimulus in 2009 considered the 2021 fiscal expansion either unnecessary or excessively large.

Figure 6 shows two indicators that played an important role in policy discussions at both times. One is the unemployment rate. The other is the *quits rate*, the fraction of workers voluntarily leaving their jobs each month. This rate is widely viewed as an indication of how good the labor market is: workers are reluctant to quit if they believe new jobs are very hard to find. For this reason, the quits rate is a useful backup to the unemployment rate: if you're unsure whether the unemployment rate is giving an accurate read on the situation, you can check whether the quits rate is telling the same story.

What you can see from Figure 6 is that in early 2009 the United States showed all the signs of a deeply depressed economy, in the grip of an accelerating plunge, with unemployment high and rising and the quits rate low and falling. In 2021, however, the data were telling the opposite story: unemployment was falling fast—by year's end it would hit a 50-year low—while quits were extremely high, suggesting that jobs were even more plentiful than the unemployment rate indicated.

This difference meant that the case for expansionary fiscal policy was much weaker in 2021 than it had been in 2009. In fact, by late 2021, many economists believed that the economy was experiencing an inflationary gap, which suggested that if anything fiscal policy should have become contractionary. Unfortunately, the politics of such a move would have been impossible, so that the burden of fighting inflation, as we explain in Chapter 15, fell on monetary policy.

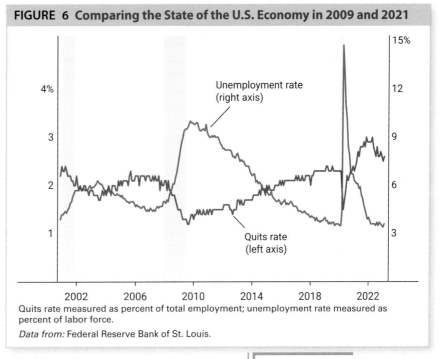

FIGURE 6 Comparing the State of the U.S. Economy in 2009 and 2021

Quits rate measured as percent of total employment; unemployment rate measured as percent of labor force.

Data from: Federal Reserve Bank of St. Louis.

>> Check Your Understanding 13-1

Solutions appear at back of book.

1. In each of the following cases, determine whether the policy is expansionary or contractionary fiscal policy.
   a. Several military bases around the country, which together employ tens of thousands of people, are closed.
   b. The number of weeks an unemployed person is eligible for unemployment benefits is increased.
   c. The federal tax on gasoline is increased.
2. Explain why federal disaster relief, which quickly disburses funds to victims of natural disasters such as hurricanes, floods, and large-scale crop failures, will stabilize the economy more effectively after a disaster than relief that must be legislated.
3. Is the following statement true or false? Explain. "When the government expands, the private sector shrinks; when the government shrinks, the private sector expands."

Fiscal Policy and the Multiplier

An expansionary fiscal policy, like the 2009 stimulus, pushes the aggregate demand curve to the right. A contractionary fiscal policy pushes the aggregate demand curve to the left. For policy makers, however, knowing the direction of the shift isn't enough: they need estimates of *how much* a given policy will shift the aggregate demand curve. To get these estimates, they use the concept of the multiplier, which we learned about in Chapter 11.

Multiplier Effects of an Increase in Government Purchases of Goods and Services

Suppose that a government decides to spend $50 billion building bridges and roads. The government's purchases of goods and services will directly increase total spending on final goods and services by $50 billion. But as we learned in Chapter 11, there will also be an indirect effect: the government's purchases will start a chain reaction throughout the economy. The firms that produce the goods and services purchased by the government earn revenues that flow to households

>> **Quick Review**

• The main channels of fiscal policy are taxes and government spending. Government spending takes the form of purchases of goods and services as well as transfers.

• In the United States, most government transfers are accounted for by **social insurance** programs designed to alleviate economic hardship—principally Social Security, Medicare, Medicaid, and the Affordable Care Act (ACA).

• The government controls *G* directly and influences *C* and *I* through taxes and transfers.

• **Expansionary fiscal policy** is implemented by an increase in government spending, a cut in taxes, or an increase in government transfers. **Contractionary fiscal policy** is implemented by a reduction in government spending, an increase in taxes, or a reduction in government transfers.

• Arguments against the effectiveness of expansionary fiscal policy based on crowding out are valid only when the economy is at or close to full employment. The argument that expansionary fiscal policy won't work because of Ricardian equivalence—that consumers will cut back spending today to offset expected future tax increases—appears to be untrue in practice. What is clearly true is that time lags can reduce the effectiveness of fiscal policy and potentially render it counterproductive.

Expansionary or contractionary fiscal policy will start a chain reaction throughout the economy.

in the form of wages, profits, interest, and rent. This increase in disposable income leads to a rise in consumer spending. The rise in consumer spending, in turn, induces firms to increase output, leading to a further rise in disposable income, which leads to another round of consumer spending increases, and so on.

As we know, the *multiplier* is the ratio of the change in real GDP caused by an autonomous change in aggregate spending to the size of that autonomous change. An increase in government purchases of goods and services is a prime example of such an autonomous increase in aggregate spending.

In Chapter 11 we considered a simple case in which there are no taxes or international trade, so that any change in GDP accrues entirely to households. We also assumed that the aggregate price level is fixed, so that any increase in nominal GDP is also a rise in real GDP, and that the interest rate is fixed. In that case the multiplier is $1/(1 - MPC)$. Recall that MPC is the *marginal propensity to consume*, the fraction of an additional dollar in disposable income that is spent. For example, if the marginal propensity to consume is 0.5, the multiplier is $1/(1 - 0.5) = 1/0.5 = 2$. Given a multiplier of 2, a \$50 billion increase in government purchases of goods and services would increase real GDP by \$100 billion. Of that \$100 billion, \$50 billion is the initial effect from the increase in G, and the remaining \$50 billion is the subsequent effect arising from the increase in consumer spending.

What happens if government purchases of goods and services are instead reduced? The math is exactly the same, except that there's a minus sign in front: if government purchases of goods and services fall by \$50 billion and the marginal propensity to consume is 0.5, real GDP falls by \$100 billion.

Multiplier Effects of Changes in Government Transfers and Taxes

Expansionary or contractionary fiscal policy need not take the form of changes in government purchases of goods and services. Governments can also change transfer payments or taxes. In general, however, a change in government transfers or taxes shifts the aggregate demand curve by *less* than an equal-sized change in government purchases, resulting in a smaller effect on real GDP.

To see why, imagine that instead of spending \$50 billion on building bridges, the government simply hands out \$50 billion in the form of government transfers. In this case, there is no direct effect on aggregate demand, as there was with government purchases of goods and services. Real GDP goes up because households spend some of that \$50 billion—but they won't spend it all.

Table 1 shows a hypothetical comparison of two expansionary fiscal policies assuming an MPC equal to 0.5: one in which the government directly purchases \$50 billion in goods and services and one in which the government makes transfer payments instead, sending out \$50 billion in checks to consumers. In each case there is a first-round effect on real GDP, either from purchases by the government or from purchases by the consumers who received the checks, followed by a series of additional rounds as rising real GDP raises disposable income.

However, the first-round effect of the transfer program is smaller. Because we have assumed that the MPC is 0.5, only \$25 billion of the \$50 billion is spent, with the other \$25 billion saved. And as a result, all the further rounds are smaller, too. In

TABLE 1 Hypothetical Effects of a Fiscal Policy When $MPC = 0.5$		
Effect on real GDP	**\$50 billion rise in government purchases of goods and services**	**\$50 billion rise in government transfer payments**
First round	\$50 billion	\$25 billion
Second round	\$25 billion	\$12.5 billion
Third round	\$12.5 billion	\$6.25 billion
•	•	•
•	•	•
•	•	•
Total effect	\$100 billion	\$50 billion
Total effect in terms of multiplier	$\Delta Y = \Delta G \times 1/(1 - MPC)$	$\Delta Y = \Delta TR \times MPC - 1/(1 - MPC)$

the end, the transfer payment increases real GDP by only $50 billion, equal to $MPC \times 1/(1 - MPC)$. In comparison, a $50 billion increase in government purchases produces a $100 billion increase in real GDP, equal to $1/(1 - MPC)$.

Overall, when expansionary fiscal policy takes the form of a rise in transfer payments, real GDP may rise by either more or less than the initial government outlay—that is, the multiplier may be either more or less than 1 depending upon the size of the *MPC*. In Table 1, with an *MPC* equal to 0.5, the multiplier is exactly 1: a $50 billion rise in transfer payments increases real GDP by $50 billion. If the *MPC* is less than 0.5, so that a smaller share of the initial transfer is spent, the multiplier on that transfer is *less* than 1. If a larger share of the initial transfer is spent, the multiplier is *more* than 1.

A tax cut has an effect similar to the effect of a transfer. It increases disposable income, leading to a series of increases in consumer spending. But the overall effect is smaller than that of an equal-sized increase in government purchases of goods and services: the autonomous increase in aggregate spending is smaller because households save part of the amount of the tax cut.

We should also note that taxes introduce a further complication—they typically change the size of the multiplier. That's because in the real world governments rarely impose **lump-sum taxes,** in which the amount of tax a household owes is independent of its income. With lump-sum taxes there is no change in the multiplier. Instead, the great majority of tax revenue is raised via taxes that are not lump-sum, and so tax revenue depends on the level of real GDP. As we'll discuss shortly, and analyze in detail in this chapter's appendix, non-lump-sum taxes reduce the size of the multiplier.

In practice, economists often argue that the size of the multiplier determines *who* among the population should get tax cuts or increases in government transfers. For example, compare the effects of an increase in unemployment benefits to a cut in taxes on profits distributed to shareholders as dividends. Consumer surveys suggest that the average unemployed worker will spend a higher share of any increase in their disposable income than would the average recipient of dividend income. That is, people who are unemployed tend to have a higher *MPC* than people who own a lot of stocks because the latter tend to be wealthier and tend to save more of any increase in disposable income. If that's true, a dollar spent on unemployment benefits increases aggregate demand more than a dollar's worth of dividend tax cuts.

How Taxes Affect the Multiplier

When we introduced the analysis of the multiplier in Chapter 11, we simplified matters by assuming that a $1 increase in real GDP raises disposable income by $1. In fact, however, government taxes capture some part of the increase in real GDP that occurs in each round of the multiplier process, since most government taxes depend positively on real GDP. As a result, disposable income increases by considerably less than $1 once we include taxes in the model.

The increase in government tax revenue when real GDP rises isn't the result of a deliberate decision or action by the government. It's a consequence of the way the tax laws are written, which causes most sources of government revenue to increase *automatically* when real GDP goes up. For example, income tax receipts increase when real GDP rises because the amount each individual owes in taxes depends positively on their income, and households' taxable incomes rise when real GDP rises. Sales tax receipts increase when real GDP rises because people with more income spend more on goods and services. And corporate profit tax receipts increase when real GDP rises because profits increase when the economy expands.

The effect of these automatic increases in tax revenue is to reduce the size of the multiplier. Remember, the multiplier is the result of a chain reaction in which

lump-sum taxes a tax that is the same for everyone, regardless of any actions people take.

automatic stabilizers government spending and taxation rules that cause fiscal policy to be automatically expansionary when the economy contracts and automatically contractionary when the economy expands without requiring any deliberate actions by policy makers. Taxes that depend on disposable income are the most important example of automatic stabilizers.

discretionary fiscal policy fiscal policy that is the direct result of deliberate actions by policy makers rather than automatic adjustments or rules.

higher real GDP leads to higher disposable income, which leads to higher consumer spending, which leads to further increases in real GDP. The fact that the government siphons off some of any increase in real GDP means that at each stage of this process, the increase in consumer spending is smaller than it would be if taxes weren't part of the picture. The result is to reduce the multiplier.

In fact, the effect of taxes on the multiplier is very similar to the effect of international trade, which also reduces the multiplier. In one case, the multiplier process is weakened because at each stage some spending "leaks" into imports; in the other case, income "leaks" into taxes. The appendix to this chapter shows how to derive the multiplier when taxes that depend positively on real GDP are taken into account.

Many macroeconomists believe it's a good thing that taxes reduce the multiplier. In the previous chapter we argued that most, though not all, recessions are the result of negative demand shocks. The same mechanism that makes tax revenue increase when the economy expands makes tax revenue decrease when the economy contracts. Since tax receipts decrease when real GDP falls, the effects of these negative demand shocks are smaller than they would be in a world in which there were no taxes. The decrease in tax revenue reduces the adverse effect of the initial fall in aggregate demand.

The automatic decrease in government tax revenue generated by a fall in real GDP—caused by a decrease in the amount of taxes households pay—acts like an automatic expansionary fiscal policy implemented in the face of a recession. Similarly, when the economy expands, the government finds itself automatically pursuing contractionary fiscal policy—a tax increase. Government spending and taxation rules that cause fiscal policy to be automatically expansionary when the economy contracts and automatically contractionary when the economy expands, without requiring any deliberate action by policy makers, are called **automatic stabilizers.**

The rules that govern tax collection aren't the only automatic stabilizers, although they are the most important ones. Some types of government transfers also play a stabilizing role. For example, more people receive unemployment insurance when the economy is depressed than when it is booming. The same is true of Medicaid and food stamps. So transfer payments tend to rise when the economy is contracting and fall when the economy is expanding. Like changes in tax revenue, these automatic changes in transfers tend to reduce the size of the multiplier because the total change in disposable income that results from a given rise or fall in real GDP is smaller.

As in the case of government tax revenue, many macroeconomists believe that it's a good thing that government transfers reduce the multiplier. Expansionary and contractionary fiscal policies that are the result of automatic stabilizers are widely considered helpful to macroeconomic stabilization because they blunt the extremes of the business cycle.

But what about fiscal policy that *isn't* the result of automatic stabilizers? **Discretionary fiscal policy** is the direct result of deliberate actions by policy makers rather than automatic adjustment. For example, during a recession, the government may pass legislation that cuts taxes and increases government spending in order to stimulate the economy. In general, economists tend to support the use of discretionary fiscal policy only in the case of a severe recession or sustained economic weakness.

During the Great Depression, the Works Progress Administration (WPA), an example of discretionary fiscal policy, put millions of unemployed Americans to work constructing bridges, roads, buildings, dams, and parks.

AP Images

ECONOMICS >> *in Action*

Austerity and the Multiplier

We've explained the logic of the fiscal multiplier, but what empirical evidence do economists have about multiplier effects in practice? Until relatively recently, the answer would have been that we didn't have nearly as much evidence as we'd like.

The problem was that large changes in fiscal policy are fairly rare, and usually happen at the same time other things are taking place, making it hard to separate the effects of spending and taxes from those of other factors. For example, the U.S. government drastically increased spending during World War II. But it also instituted rationing of many consumer goods and restricted construction of new homes in order to conserve resources for the war effort. So it is hard to distinguish the effects of the increase in government spending from the transformation of a peacetime economy to a war economy.

However, more recent events offer considerable new evidence. In the wake of the Global Financial Crisis of 2008, several European governments found themselves facing debt crises. As loans they had taken out came due, these governments were either unable to raise new funds or were forced to pay extremely high interest rates. As a result, they had to turn to the rest of Europe for aid. In an attempt to reduce budget deficits, a condition of this aid was *austerity*—sharp cuts in spending plus tax increases. Austerity is a form of contractionary fiscal policy. So by comparing the economic performance of countries forced into austerity with the performance of countries that weren't, we get a relatively clear view of the effects of changes in spending and taxes.

Figure 7 compares the amount of austerity imposed in a number of countries between 2009 and 2013 to the growth in their GDP over the same period. (We end the analysis in 2013 because European debt markets calmed down in late 2012, and the pressure for harsh austerity was greatly reduced.) Austerity is measured on the horizontal axis by the change in the *cyclically adjusted budget balance,* defined later in this chapter. As you can see, Greece stands out. It was forced to impose severe spending cuts and suffered a huge fall in output. But even without Greece there is a clear negative relationship. A line fitted through the scatterplot has a slope of −1.5. That is, the figure suggests that spending cuts and tax increases had an average multiplier of 1.5. Put another way, a contractionary fiscal policy that took $1 out of the economy resulted in a $1.50 fall in GDP.

Economists have offered a number of qualifications and caveats to this result, given that this wasn't truly a controlled experiment. Yet recent experience strongly supports the proposition that fiscal policy does indeed move GDP in the predicted direction, with a multiplier of more than 1.

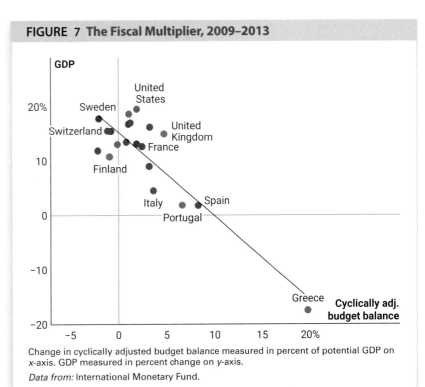

FIGURE 7 The Fiscal Multiplier, 2009–2013

Change in cyclically adjusted budget balance measured in percent of potential GDP on x-axis. GDP measured in percent change on y-axis.

Data from: International Monetary Fund.

>> Check Your Understanding 13-2

Solutions appear at back of book.

1. Explain why a $500 million increase in government purchases of goods and services will generate a larger rise in real GDP than a $500 million increase in government transfers.

2. Explain why a $500 million reduction in government purchases of goods and services will generate a larger fall in real GDP than a $500 million reduction in government transfers.

3. The country of Boldovia has no unemployment insurance benefits and a tax system using only lump-sum taxes. The neighboring country of Moldovia has generous unemployment benefits and a tax system in which residents must pay a percentage of their income. Which country will experience greater variation in real GDP in response to positive and negative demand shocks? Explain.

The Budget Balance

Headlines about the government's budget tend to focus on just one point: whether the government is running a surplus or a deficit and, in either case, how big. People usually think of surpluses as good: when the federal government ran a record surplus in 2000, many people regarded it as a cause for celebration. Conversely, people usually think of deficits as bad: when the U.S. federal government ran record deficits from 2009 to 2011, many people regarded it as a cause for concern.

How do surpluses and deficits fit into the analysis of fiscal policy? Are deficits ever a good thing and surpluses a bad thing? To answer those questions, let's look at the causes and consequences of surpluses and deficits.

The Budget Balance as a Measure of Fiscal Policy

What do we mean by surpluses and deficits? The budget balance, which was defined in Chapter 10, is the difference between the government's revenue, in the form of tax revenue, and its spending, both on goods and services and on government transfers, in a given year. That is, the budget balance—savings by government—is defined by Equation 2 (which is the same as Equation 7 in Chapter 10):

(2) $S_{Government} = T - G - TR$

where T is the value of tax revenues, G is government purchases of goods and services, and TR is the value of government transfers. As we've learned, a budget surplus is a positive budget balance and a budget deficit is a negative budget balance.

Other things equal, expansionary fiscal policies—increased government purchases of goods and services, higher government transfers, or lower taxes—reduce the budget balance for that year. That is, expansionary fiscal policies make a budget surplus smaller or a budget deficit bigger. Conversely, contractionary fiscal policies—reduced government purchases of goods and services, lower government transfers, or higher taxes—increase the budget balance for that year, making a budget surplus bigger or a budget deficit smaller.

You might think this means that changes in the budget balance can be used to measure fiscal policy. In fact, economists often do just that: they use changes in the budget balance as a "quick-and-dirty" way to assess whether current fiscal policy is expansionary or contractionary. But they always keep in mind two reasons this quick-and-dirty approach is sometimes misleading:

1. Two different changes in fiscal policy that have equal-sized effects on the budget balance may have quite unequal effects on the economy. As we have already seen, changes in government purchases of goods and services have a

larger effect on real GDP than equal-sized changes in taxes and government transfers.

2. Often, changes in the budget balance are themselves the result, not the cause, of fluctuations in the economy.

To understand the second point, we need to examine the effects of the business cycle on the budget.

The Business Cycle and the Cyclically Adjusted Budget Balance

Historically there has been a strong relationship between the federal government's budget balance and the business cycle. The budget tends to move into deficit when the economy experiences a recession, but deficits tend to get smaller or even turn into surpluses when the economy is expanding. Figure 8 shows the federal budget deficit as a percentage of GDP. Shaded areas indicate recessions; unshaded areas indicate expansions. As you can see, the federal budget deficit increased around the time of each recession and usually declined during expansions. In fact, in the late stages of the long expansion from 1991 to through early 2001, the deficit actually became negative—the budget deficit became a budget surplus.

The relationship between the business cycle and the budget balance is even clearer if we compare the budget deficit as a percentage of GDP with the unemployment rate, as we do in Figure 9. The budget deficit almost always rises when the unemployment rate rises and falls when the unemployment rate falls.

Is this relationship between the business cycle and the budget balance evidence that policy makers engage in discretionary fiscal policy, using expansionary fiscal policy during recessions and contractionary fiscal policy during expansions? Not necessarily. To a large extent the relationship in Figure 9 reflects automatic stabilizers at work. As we saw earlier in the discussion of automatic stabilizers, government tax revenue tends to rise and some government transfers, like unemployment benefit payments, tend to fall when the economy expands. Conversely, government tax revenue tends to fall and some government transfers tend to rise when the economy contracts. So the budget tends to move toward surplus during

FIGURE 8 The U.S. Federal Budget Deficit and the Business Cycle, 1964–2022

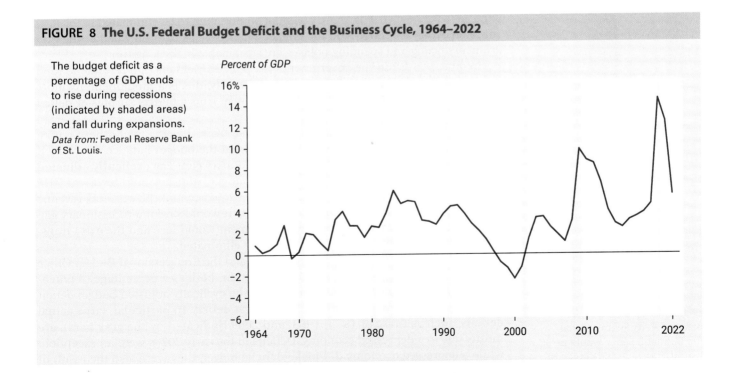

The budget deficit as a percentage of GDP tends to rise during recessions (indicated by shaded areas) and fall during expansions.

Data from: Federal Reserve Bank of St. Louis.

FIGURE 9 The U.S. Federal Budget Deficit and the Unemployment Rate, 1964–2022

There is a close relationship between the budget balance and the business cycle: a recession moves the budget balance toward deficit, but an expansion moves it toward surplus. Here, the unemployment rate serves as an indicator of the business cycle, and we should expect to see a higher unemployment rate associated with a higher budget deficit. This is confirmed by the figure: the budget deficit as a percentage of GDP moves closely in tandem with the unemployment rate.

Budget deficit is measured as a percent of GDP. Unemployment measured as the average annual unemployment rate.

Data from: Federal Reserve Bank of St. Louis.

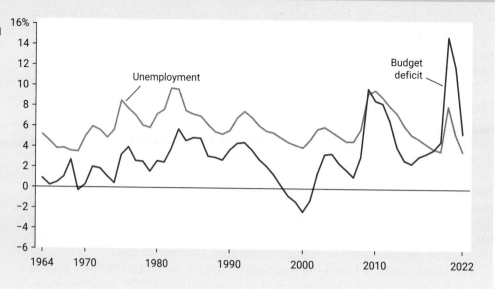

expansions and toward deficit during recessions even without any deliberate action on the part of policy makers.

In assessing budget policy, it's often useful to separate movements in the budget balance due to the business cycle from movements due to discretionary fiscal policy changes. The former are affected by automatic stabilizers and the latter by deliberate changes in government purchases, government transfers, or taxes. It's important to realize that business-cycle effects on the budget balance are temporary: both recessionary gaps (in which real GDP is below potential output) and inflationary gaps (in which real GDP is above potential output) tend to be eliminated in the long run. Removing their effects on the budget balance sheds light on whether the government's taxing and spending policies are sustainable in the long run.

In other words, do the government's tax policies yield enough revenue to fund its spending in the long run? As we'll learn shortly, this is a fundamentally more important question than whether the government runs a budget surplus or deficit in the current year.

To separate the effect of the business cycle from the effects of other factors, many governments produce an estimate of what the budget balance would be if there were neither a recessionary nor an inflationary gap. The **cyclically adjusted budget balance** is an estimate of what the budget balance would be if real GDP were exactly equal to potential output. It takes into account the extra tax revenue the government would collect and the transfers it would save if a recessionary gap were eliminated—or the revenue the government would lose and the extra transfers it would make if an inflationary gap were eliminated.

Figure 10 shows the actual budget deficit and the Congressional Budget Office estimate of the cyclically adjusted budget deficit, both as a percentage of potential GDP, from 1965 to 2022. As you can see, the cyclically adjusted budget deficit doesn't fluctuate as much as the actual budget deficit. In particular, large actual deficits, such as those of 1975, 1983, and 2009 (indicated by the gray bars), are mostly due to a depressed economy. Deficits in the early 2020s were an exception: while a depressed economy did make deficits bigger, they were also the result of extraordinary pandemic-related spending.

cyclically adjusted budget balance an estimate of what the budget balance would be if real GDP were exactly equal to potential output.

FIGURE 10 **The Actual Budget Deficit versus the Cyclically Adjusted Budget Deficit, 1965–2022**

The cyclically adjusted budget deficit is an estimate of what the budget deficit would be if the economy was at potential output. It fluctuates less than the actual budget deficit because years of large budget deficits also tend to be years when the economy has a large recessionary gap. The large actual deficits in 1975, 1983, 2009, and 2020 (which are reported in the following year) are indicated by the vertical bars. These deficits were mostly due to a depressed economy.

Data from: Congressional Budget Office.

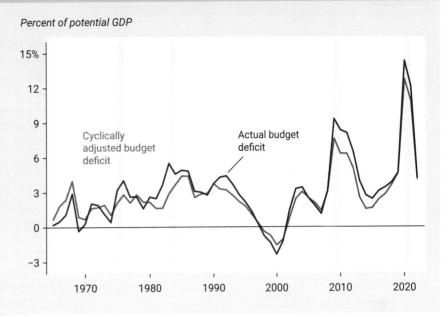

Should the Budget Be Balanced?

Persistent budget deficits can cause problems for both the government and the economy. Yet politicians are often tempted to run deficits because this allows them to cater to voters by cutting taxes without cutting spending or by increasing spending without increasing taxes. As a result, there are occasional attempts by policy makers to force fiscal discipline by introducing legislation—even a constitutional amendment—forbidding the government from running budget deficits. This is usually stated as a requirement that the budget be balanced—that revenues at least equal spending each fiscal year. Would it be a good idea to require a balanced budget annually?

Most economists don't think so. They believe that the government should only balance its budget on average—that it should be allowed to run deficits in bad years, offset by surpluses in good years. They don't believe the government should be forced to run a balanced budget *every year* because this would undermine the role of taxes and transfers as automatic stabilizers.

As we've learned, the tendency of tax revenue to fall and transfers to rise when the economy contracts helps to limit the size of recessions. But falling tax revenue and rising transfer payments generated by a downturn in the economy push the budget toward deficit. If constrained by a balanced-budget rule, the government would have to respond to this deficit with contractionary fiscal policies that would tend to deepen a recession.

Yet policy makers concerned about excessive deficits sometimes feel that rigid rules prohibiting—or at least setting an upper limit on—deficits are necessary. In fact, as the following Economics in Action explains, state and local governments do have such rules, which had a major impact on fiscal policy during the Great Recession and in its aftermath.

ECONOMICS >> *in Action*
Trying to Balance Budgets in a Recession

When the Great Recession struck, the U.S. federal government's budget deficit increased from just $160 billion to $1.4 trillion, partly because of stimulus

FIGURE 11 State and Local Government Employment, 2000–2023

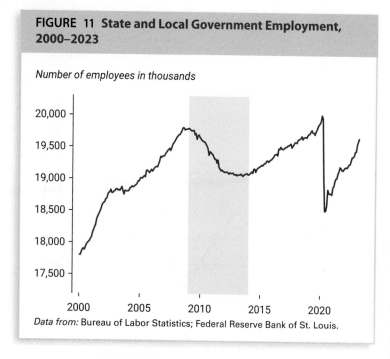

Number of employees in thousands

Data from: Bureau of Labor Statistics; Federal Reserve Bank of St. Louis.

measures but mainly because of automatic stabilizers: revenue fell sharply, while some expenditures, especially unemployment benefits, rose. Many observers worried about this deficit, but most economists thought that trying to balance the budget in the face of a recession would actually make that recession worse.

When it comes to government spending in America, however, the federal government isn't the only player. State and local governments account for about 40% of total government spending, and most government employment. (Most government employees are in positions that deliver essential services, such as schoolteachers, police officers, and firefighters.) And almost all of these state and local governments have rules requiring that they balance their budgets all the time.

There are a number of reasons for these rules, which make sense for each individual state or city. Taken together, however, the rules mean that for a large part of government in the United States, automatic stabilizers don't work. In fact, state and local governments cut back sharply in the face of a depressed economy, especially after 2010, when federal aid from the 2009 stimulus ended. Figure 11 shows the number of state and local employees from 2000 to 2023; as you can see, from 2009 until 2013 (the period shaded in gray), there were large cuts, mainly layoffs of teachers, in the face of falling revenues.

These actions at the state and local levels didn't fully offset the effects of automatic stabilizers at the federal level, but they still probably caused the recession to be deeper and the recovery slower than it would have been if we didn't have multiple levels of government, with the lower levels required to run balanced budgets.

>> **Check Your Understanding 13-3**
Solutions appear at back of book.

1. Why is the cyclically adjusted budget balance a better measure of whether government policies are sustainable in the long run than the actual budget balance is?

2. Explain why states required by their constitutions to balance their budgets are likely to experience more severe economic fluctuations than states not held to that requirement.

‖ Long-Run Implications of Fiscal Policy

At the end of 2009, the government of Greece ran into a financial wall. Like most other governments in Europe (and the U.S. government, too), the Greek government was running a large budget deficit, which meant that it needed to keep borrowing more funds, both to cover its expenses and to pay off existing loans as they came due. But governments, like countries or individuals, can only borrow if lenders believe it's likely that they will eventually be willing or able to repay their debts. By 2009, many lenders had lost faith in Greece's financial future, and they were no longer willing to lend to the Greek government. Those few who were willing to lend demanded very high interest rates to compensate them for the risk of loss.

Figure 12 compares interest rates on 10-year bonds issued by the governments of Greece and Germany. At the beginning of 2007, Greece could borrow at almost the same rate as Germany, widely considered a very safe borrower. In 2009 its

FIGURE 12 Greek and German Long-Term Interest Rates

As late as 2008, the government of Greece could borrow at interest rates only slightly higher than those facing Germany, widely considered a very safe borrower. But in early 2009, as it became clear that both Greek debt and deficits were larger than previously reported, lenders lost confidence in the government's ability to repay its debts and sent Greek borrowing costs skyrocketing.

Data from: Federal Reserve Bank of St. Louis; OECD "Main Economic Indicators Complete Database."

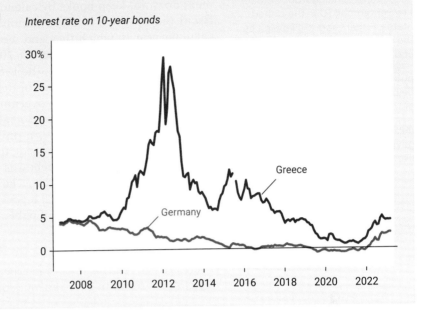

Interest rate on 10-year bonds

borrowing costs started to climb, and by the end of 2011 Greece had to pay an interest rate around 10 times the rate Germany paid.

What precipitated the crisis? In 2009, it became clear that the Greek government had used creative accounting to hide just how much debt it had already taken on. Government debt is, after all, a promise to make future payments to lenders. By 2010, it seemed likely that the Greek government had already promised more than it could possibly deliver.

Lenders became deeply worried that the level of Greek government debt was unsustainable—that is, it was unlikely to repay what was owed. As a result, Greece found itself largely shut out of private debt markets. In order to prevent a government collapse, it received emergency loans from other European nations and the International Monetary Fund. But these loans came with the requirement that the Greek government undertake austerity, by making severe spending cuts and sharply raising taxes. Austerity in Greece wreaked havoc with the economy, imposed severe economic hardship on citizens, and led to massive social unrest.

The 2009 crisis in Greece shows why no discussion of fiscal policy is complete without taking into account the long-run implications of government budget surpluses and deficits, especially the implications for government debt. We now turn to those long-run implications.

Deficits, Surpluses, and Debt

When a family spends more than it earns over the course of a year, it has to raise the extra funds either by selling assets or by borrowing. And if a family borrows year after year, it will eventually end up with a lot of debt.

The same is true for governments. With a few exceptions, governments don't raise large sums by selling assets such as national parkland. Instead, when a government spends more than the tax revenue it receives—when it runs a budget deficit—it almost always borrows the extra funds. And governments that run persistent budget deficits end up with substantial debts.

PITFALLS

DEFICITS VERSUS DEBT

Deficits and *debt* aren't the same thing.

A *deficit* is the difference between the amount of money a government spends and the amount it receives in taxes over a given period—usually, though not always, a year. Deficit numbers always come with a statement about the time period to which they apply, as in "the U.S. budget deficit *in fiscal 2022* was $1,376 billion."

A *debt* is the sum of money a government owes at a particular point in time. Debt numbers usually come with a specific date, as in "U.S. public debt *at the end of fiscal 2022* was $24.3 trillion."

Deficits and debt are linked, because government debt grows when governments run deficits. But they are different concepts that can even tell different stories. For example, Italy had a fairly small deficit by historical standards in 2022, but had a very high debt, a legacy of past policies.

fiscal year the time period used for much of government accounting, running from October 1 to September 30 in the United States. Fiscal years are labeled by the calendar year in which they end.

public debt government debt held by individuals and institutions outside the government.

debt spiral when the interest on government debt drives that debt even higher.

To interpret the numbers that follow, you need to know a slightly peculiar feature of federal government accounting. For historical reasons, the U.S. government does not keep books by calendar years. Instead, budget totals are kept by **fiscal years,** which run from October 1 to September 30 and are labeled by the calendar year in which they end. For example, fiscal 2022 began on October 1, 2021, and ended on September 30, 2022.

At the end of fiscal 2022, the U.S. federal government had total debt equal to $30.8 trillion. However, part of that debt represented special accounting rules specifying that the federal government as a whole owes funds to certain government programs, especially Social Security. We'll explain those rules shortly. For now, however, let's focus on **public debt:** federal government debt held by individuals and institutions outside the government. At the end of fiscal 2022, the federal government's public debt was "only" $24.3 trillion, or 97% of GDP. Federal public debt at the end of 2022 was larger than at the end of 2021 because the government ran a deficit in 2022: a government that runs persistent budget deficits will experience a rising level of public debt. Why is this a problem?

Potential Dangers Posed by Rising Government Debt

There are two reasons to be concerned when a government runs persistent budget deficits that result in government debt that rises over time.

1. Crowding Out When the economy is at full employment and the government borrows funds in the financial markets, it is competing with firms that plan to borrow funds for investment spending. As a result, the government's borrowing may crowd out private investment spending, increasing interest rates and reducing the economy's long-run rate of growth.

2. Financial Pressure and Default Today's deficits, by increasing the government's debt, place financial pressure on future budgets. The impact of current deficits on future budgets is straightforward. Like individuals, governments must pay their bills, including interest payments on their accumulated debt. When a government is deeply in debt, those interest payments can be substantial. In fiscal 2022, the U.S. federal government paid $718 billion or 2.9% of GDP in interest on its debt. But only $476 billion or 1.9% of GDP was paid on publicly held debt. The more heavily indebted government of Italy paid interest of well over 5% of its GDP in 2022, according to estimates.

Other things equal, a government paying large sums in interest must raise more revenue from taxes or spend less than it would otherwise be able to afford—or it must borrow even more to cover the gap. And a government that borrows to pay interest on its outstanding debt may push itself even deeper into debt—a process known as a **debt spiral.** This process can eventually push a government to the point where lenders question its ability to repay. Like a consumer who has maxed out their credit cards, it will find that lenders are unwilling to lend any more funds. The result can be that the government defaults on its debt—it stops paying what it owes. Default is often followed by deep financial and economic turmoil.

Americans aren't used to the idea of government default, but it does happen. In the 1990s Argentina, a relatively high-income developing country, was widely praised for its economic policies—and it was able to borrow large sums from foreign lenders. By 2001, however, Argentina's interest payments were spiraling out of control, and the country defaulted. It eventually reached a settlement with most of its lenders under which it paid less than a third of the amount originally due.

Default creates havoc in a country's financial markets and badly shakes public confidence in both the government and the economy. Argentina's debt default was accompanied by a crisis in the country's banking system and a very severe recession. And even if a highly indebted government avoids default, a heavy debt burden typically forces it to slash spending or raise taxes, politically unpopular

GLOBAL COMPARISON   AMERICAN DEBT IN PERSPECTIVE

The U.S. government debt is enormous — at the end of 2022 the federal government owed the public almost $25 trillion, while state and local governments owed about $3 trillion more. But the U.S. economy is also enormous. How large is our debt relative to the size of the economy, and how does that ratio compare with historical debt levels, both for the United States and for other countries?

The answer is that by historical standards, U.S. debt is high even as a percentage of gross domestic product — roughly as high as it was at the end of World War II. But other nations have gone far deeper into debt without experiencing crises.

The figure shows the ratio of government debt for the United States since 1939, and compares it with data for two other nations: Japan since 1990 (when the Japanese government began running large deficits that continue to this day) and the United Kingdom, where a special report by Parliament provides estimates all the way back to the eighteenth century.

The United States, not surprisingly, emerged from World War II — which was largely paid for by borrowing — with a high level of debt relative to GDP. The debt ratio then fell steadily for several decades, but surged during the global financial crisis and again during the coronavirus pandemic, so that as a percentage of GDP it is roughly what it was at the end of World War II.

So U.S. debt currently is historically high, especially since the United States hasn't fought a major war recently (although both the financial crisis and the pandemic were emergencies that, in fiscal

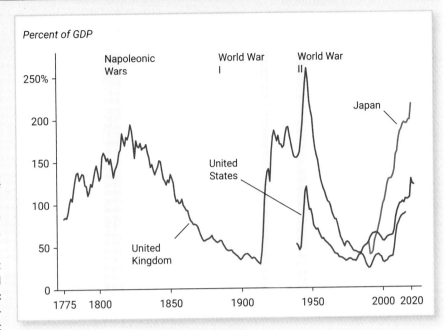

Percent of GDP

terms, were something like wars). But the U.S. debt position looks less exceptional compared with other nations' histories. Japan's debt as a percentage of GDP is more than twice that of the United States. British debt reached extraordinary levels after three major wars: the Napoleonic wars of the late eighteenth and early nineteenth centuries, then World War I and World War II.

Interestingly, neither Japan nor the United Kingdom experienced crises of confidence over the ability to pay their debts, a fact that suggests that wealthy nations with stable governments have a great deal of leeway when it comes to borrowing. This doesn't mean that the United States can't have such a crisis, but it does mean that you can't make that judgment simply by pointing to the size of the debt.

Data from: Office of Management and Budget; Federal Reserve Bank of St. Louis; Bank of England; World Bank.

measures that can also damage the economy. In some cases, austerity measures intended to reassure lenders that the government can indeed pay end up depressing the economy so much that lender confidence continues to fall.

If it has its own currency, a government that has trouble borrowing can print money to pay its bills. But doing so can lead to another problem: inflation. In fact, budget problems are the main cause of very severe inflation. Governments do not want to find themselves in a position where the choice is between defaulting on their debts and inflating those debts away by printing money.

Concerns about the long-run effects of deficits need not rule out the use of expansionary fiscal policy to stimulate the economy when it is depressed. However, these concerns do mean that governments should try to offset budget deficits in bad years with budget surpluses in good years. In other words, governments should run a budget that is approximately balanced over time. Have they actually done so?

debt–GDP ratio government debt as a percentage of GDP, frequently used as a measure of a government's ability to pay its debts.

Deficits and Debt in Practice

Figure 13 shows the U.S. federal government's budget deficit and how its debt has changed since 1940. Panel (a) shows the federal deficit as a percentage of GDP. As you can see, the federal government ran huge deficits during World War II. It briefly ran surpluses after the war, but it has normally run deficits ever since, especially after 1980. This seems inconsistent with the advice that governments should offset deficits in bad times with surpluses in good times.

However, panel (b) of Figure 13 shows that for most of the period these persistent deficits didn't lead to runaway debt. To assess the ability of governments to pay their debt, we use the **debt–GDP ratio,** the government's debt as a percentage of GDP. We use this measure, rather than simply looking at the size of the debt, because GDP, which measures the size of the economy as a whole, is a good indicator of the potential taxes the government can collect. If the government's debt grows more slowly than GDP, the burden of paying that debt is actually falling compared with the government's potential tax revenue.

What we see from panel (b) is that although the federal debt grew in almost every year, the debt–GDP ratio fell for 30 years after the end of World War II. This shows that the debt–GDP ratio can fall, even when debt is rising, as long as GDP grows faster than debt. The accompanying For Inquiring Minds explains how sufficiently high levels of growth and/or inflation can allow a government that runs persistent budget deficits to nevertheless have a declining debt–GDP ratio.

Still, a government that runs persistent *large* deficits will have a rising debt–GDP ratio when debt grows faster than GDP. In the aftermath of the financial crisis of 2008, the U.S. government began running deficits much larger than anything seen since World War II, and the debt–GDP ratio began rising sharply. Similar surges in the debt–GDP ratio could be seen in a number of other countries after 2008. Economists and policy makers agreed that this was not a sustainable

FIGURE 13 U.S. Federal Deficits and Debt

(a) The U.S. Federal Budget Deficit Since 1940

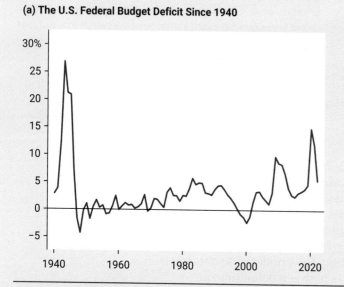

(b) The U.S. Public Debt–GDP Ratio Since 1940

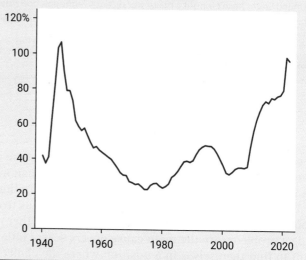

Panel (a) shows the U.S. federal budget deficit as a percentage of GDP from 1940 to 2022. The U.S. government ran huge deficits during World War II and has run smaller deficits ever since. Panel (b) shows the U.S. debt–GDP ratio. Comparing panels (a) and (b), you can see that in many years the debt–GDP ratio has declined in spite of government deficits. This seeming paradox reflects the fact that the debt–GDP ratio can fall, even when debt is rising, as long as GDP grows faster than debt.

Budget deficit (percent of GDP) on *y*-axis; Public debt (percent of GDP) on *y*-axis.

Data from: Office of Management and Budget; Federal Reserve Bank of St. Louis.

As you can see from Figure 13, the U.S. government paid for World War II by borrowing on a huge scale. By the war's end, the public debt was more than 100% of GDP, and many people worried about how it could ever be paid off.

The truth is that it never was paid off. In 1946 public debt was $242 billion; that number dipped slightly in the next few years, as the United States ran postwar budget surpluses, but the government budget went back into deficit in 1950 with the start of the Korean War. By 1962, the public debt was back up to $248 billion.

But by that time nobody was worried about the fiscal health of the U.S. government because the debt–GDP ratio had fallen by more than half. The reason? Vigorous economic growth, plus mild inflation, led to a rapid rise in GDP. The experience was a clear lesson in the peculiar fact that modern governments can run deficits forever, as long as they aren't too large.

trend, and that governments would need to get their spending and revenues back in line.

Implicit Liabilities

Looking at Figure 13, you might be tempted to conclude that until the 2008 crisis struck, the U.S. federal budget was in fairly decent shape: the return to budget deficits after 2001 caused the debt–GDP ratio to rise a bit, but that ratio was still low compared with both historical experience and some other wealthy countries. In fact, however, experts on long-run budget issues view the situation of the United States (and other countries such as Japan and Italy) with some alarm. The reason is the problem of *implicit liabilities*. **Implicit liabilities** are spending promises made by governments that are effectively a debt despite the fact that they are not included in the usual debt statistics.

The implicit liabilities of the U.S. government arise mainly from transfer programs that are aimed at providing security in retirement and protection from large health care bills:

- Social Security is the main source of retirement income for most older Americans.
- Medicare pays most of older Americans' medical costs.
- Medicaid provides health care to lower-income families.
- The Affordable Care Act subsidizes health insurance premiums for many low-to moderate-income families who are ineligible for Medicaid.

In each of these cases, the government has promised to provide transfer payments to future as well as current beneficiaries. So these programs represent a future debt that must be honored, even though the debt does not currently show up in the usual statistics. Together, these programs currently account for approximately half of federal spending.

The implicit liabilities created by these transfer programs worry fiscal experts. Figure 14 shows why. It shows actual 2023 spending on Social Security and major health care programs, measured as a percentage of GDP, together with Congressional Budget Office projections for average spending in 2053. According to these projections, spending on Social Security will rise substantially over the next few decades and spending on the major health care programs will soar. Why?

In the case of Social Security, the answer is demography. Social Security is a pay-as-you-go system: current workers pay payroll taxes that fund the benefits of current retirees. So the ratio of the number of retirees drawing benefits to the number of workers paying into Social Security has a major impact on the system's finances.

implicit liabilities spending promises made by governments that are effectively a debt despite the fact that they are not included in the usual debt statistics. In the United States, the largest implicit liabilities arise from Social Security and Medicare, which promise transfer payments to current and future retirees (Social Security) and to the elderly (Medicare).

FIGURE 14 Future Demands on the Federal Budget

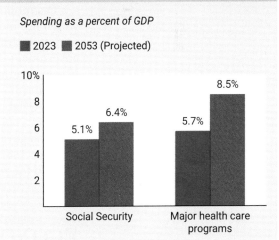

This figure shows actual spending on social insurance programs as a percentage of GDP in 2023 and Congressional Budget Office projections for these same programs in 2053. Partly as a result of an aging population, these programs will become much more expensive over time. But, it is the significant increases in health care spending that will pose the most serious problem for the federal budget in the future.
Data from: Congressional Budget Office.

There was a huge surge in the U.S. birth rate between 1946 and 1964, the years of what is commonly called the *baby boom*. Some baby boomers are still of working age—which means they are paying taxes, not collecting benefits. But many have retired, and as more and more of them do so, they will stop earning taxable income and start collecting benefits.

As a result, the ratio of retirees receiving benefits to workers paying into the Social Security system will rise. In 2018, there were 36 retirees receiving benefits for every 100 workers paying into the system. But, by 2050, according to the Social Security Administration, that number will rise to 45. So as baby boomers move into retirement, benefit payments will continue to rise relative to the size of the economy.

The aging of the baby boomers, by itself, poses only a moderately sized long-run fiscal problem. The projected rise in health care spending is a much more serious concern. These projections also reflect the aging of the population, both because more people will be eligible for Medicare and because older people tend to have higher medical costs. But the main story behind projections of higher health care spending is the long-run tendency of such spending to rise faster than overall spending, for both government-funded and privately funded health care.

To some extent, the implicit liabilities of the U.S. government are already reflected in debt statistics. We mentioned earlier that the government had a total debt of $30.8 trillion at the end of fiscal 2022 but that only $24.3 trillion of that total was owed to the public. The main explanation for that discrepancy is that both Social Security and part of Medicare (the hospital insurance program) are supported by *dedicated taxes:* their expenses are paid out of special taxes on wages. At times, these dedicated taxes yield more revenue than is needed to pay current benefits.

In particular, since the mid-1980s the Social Security system has been taking in more revenue than it currently needs in order to prepare for the retirement of the baby boomers. This surplus in the Social Security system has been used to accumulate a *Social Security trust fund*, which was $2.8 trillion at the end of fiscal 2022.

The money in the trust fund is held in the form of U.S. government bonds, which are included in the $30.8 trillion in total debt. You could say that there's something funny about counting bonds in the Social Security trust fund as part of government debt. After all, these bonds are owed by one part of the government (the government outside the Social Security system) to another part of the government (the Social Security system itself). But the debt corresponds to a real, if implicit, liability: promises by the government to pay future retirement benefits. So many economists argue that the gross debt of $30.8 trillion, the sum of public debt and government debt held by Social Security and other trust funds, is a more accurate indication of the government's fiscal health than the smaller amount owed to the public alone.

ECONOMICS >> *in Action*
Who's Afraid of a Debt Spiral?

As we explained in the text, one concern about the long-run effects of budget deficits is that they may start to feed on themselves, via a debt spiral. Deficits lead to higher debt; higher debt leads to higher interest payments, which increases the deficit, which leads to even higher debt, and so on. So debt can snowball.

But how worried should we be about debt spirals? In January 2019 Olivier Blanchard, the former chief economist of the International Monetary Fund and one of the world's most respected macroeconomists, startled his colleagues at the annual meeting of the American

TABLE 2 Interest Rates versus Growth		
	Average 10-year interest rate	Nominal GDP growth rate
1990–2019	4.41	4.51
2010–2019	2.40	3.97

Economic Association, where he gave the presidential address. Blanchard argued that fears of a debt spiral, and concerns about government debt in general, are greatly exaggerated.

Blanchard's argument emphasized a point we also made in the text, about the effects of growth and inflation on the debt–GDP ratio, which is a much better indicator of a government's fiscal health than the simple dollar value of debt. As we noted, rising nominal GDP, which reflects both inflation and real growth, causes the debt–GDP ratio to "melt" away unless the budget deficit is large.

What Blanchard pointed out was that while a rise in debt increases the government's interest payments, it also accelerates the rate of melting, basically because there is more debt to melt. You only get a debt spiral if the higher interest payments caused by higher debt exceed this melting effect. The key question is whether the interest rate the government has to pay is more or less than the rate of growth in nominal GDP.

And as Blanchard noted, the experience of the United States and other advanced economies over the past 30 years, and especially over the previous decade, was that interest rates are generally less than nominal growth rates. This point is illustrated in Table 2, which compares the average 10-year interest rate on U.S. government bonds with nominal GDP growth over time. Furthermore, the gap between growth and interest rates is even larger in many other advanced countries.

Blanchard also argued that even this comparison overstates the risk of a debt spiral, because some of the money the government pays out in interest comes back to it in tax payments from bondholders.

While Blanchard's speech came as something of a bombshell, many other economists have recently made similar arguments. Nobody is arguing that we should completely ignore debt. But there doesn't seem to be much reason to fear a runaway debt spiral.

>> Check Your Understanding 13-4

Solutions appear at back of book.

1. Explain how each of the following events would affect the public debt or implicit liabilities of the U.S. government, other things equal. Would the public debt or implicit liabilities be greater or smaller?
   a. A higher growth rate of real GDP
   b. Retirees living longer
   c. A decrease in tax revenue
   d. Government borrowing to pay interest on its current public debt

2. Suppose the economy is in a slump and the current public debt is quite large. Explain the trade-off of short-run versus long-run objectives that policy makers face when deciding whether or not to engage in deficit spending.

3. Explain how a contractionary fiscal policy like austerity can make it more likely that a government is unable to pay its debts.

>> Quick Review

- Large and persistent budget deficits lead to increases in **public debt.**

- Public debt that rises year after year can lead to financial pressure and government default. In less extreme cases, it can crowd out investment spending, reducing long-run growth. This suggests that budget deficits in bad **fiscal years** should be offset with budget surpluses in good fiscal years.

- A **debt spiral** occurs when a government must borrow to pay for past interest expenses, causing overall debt to increase. However, if a country has rising GDP, economists believe it may safely run annual deficits as long as the **debt–GDP ratio** is stable or falling because GDP is growing faster than the debt.

- In addition to their official public debt, modern governments have implicit liabilities. The U.S. government has large **implicit liabilities** in the form of Social Security, Medicare, Medicaid, and the Affordable Care Act (ACA). With large implicit liabilities, a stable debt–GDP ratio may give a misleading sense of security.

BMW Goes Electric

Sean Rayford/ASSOCIATED PRESS

In November 2022 the German-based auto manufacturer BMW, which already produces cars in the United States, announced plans to spend $1.7 billion on new factories in South Carolina: $1 billion on a plant producing electric vehicles and $700 million on a plant producing batteries. What motivated these plans? Fiscal policy.

The fiscal policy in question was not, as it happened, the American Rescue Plan featured in this chapter's opening story. Instead, it was a later piece of legislation, the Inflation Reduction Act or IRA, enacted in August 2022.

The IRA was not designed to provide fiscal stimulus: it was a mix of new spending provisions, especially tax credits and subsidies for investments in green energy, and tax increases, overwhelmingly on high-income Americans. When the bill was passed official estimates said that the tax increases would be larger than the new

spending, so that the bill would reduce the deficit and on balance act as contractionary fiscal policy. Hence the bill's name, although its real goal was mainly to reduce the rate of climate change by encouraging a shift away from fossil fuels.

Within a few months of the bill's passage, however, it was becoming clear that businesses were taking advantage of the new incentives even more enthusiastically than expected. BMW's expansion plans were only 2 of almost 100 new plants announced by the end of January 2023, with many more expected. In March 2023, Goldman Sachs predicted that the act would eventually lead to $1.2 trillion in federal outlays—about three times the original projection—and would induce another $3 trillion in private investment.

From the point of view of fighting long-term climate change, this massive response was very good news. From the point of view of short-term macroeconomic policy, however, the surge in business investment unleashed by the IRA was a bit of a problem. By 2023, the U.S. economy seemed to be suffering from an inflationary gap, and the IRA seemed likely to make that gap wider.

QUESTIONS FOR THOUGHT

1. Explain how originally the passage of the IRA would have reduced inflation.

2. In the chapter, we talked about the problem of lags in discretionary fiscal policy. In this case, explain how lags could be potentially beneficial.

3. Is the depth of a recession a good or a bad time to undertake an energy project? Why or why not? What are the concerns of implementing discretionary expansionary fiscal policy in an inflationary gap?

SUMMARY

1. The government plays a large role in the economy, collecting a large share of GDP in taxes and spending a large share both to purchase goods and services and to make transfer payments, largely for **social insurance.** *Fiscal policy* is the use of taxes, government transfers, or government purchases of goods and services to shift the aggregate demand curve.

2. Government purchases of goods and services directly affect aggregate demand, and changes in taxes and government transfers affect aggregate demand indirectly by changing households' disposable incomes. **Expansionary fiscal policy** shifts the aggregate demand curve rightward; **contractionary fiscal policy** shifts the aggregate demand curve leftward.

3. Only when the economy is at full employment is there potential for crowding out of private spending and private investment spending by expansionary fiscal policy. The argument that expansionary fiscal policy won't work because of Ricardian equivalence—that consumers will cut back spending today to offset expected future tax increases—appears to be untrue in practice. What is clearly true is that very active fiscal policy may make the economy less stable due to time lags in policy formulation and implementation.

4. Fiscal policy has a multiplier effect on the economy, the size of which depends on the fiscal policy. Except in the case of lump-sum taxes, taxes reduce the size of the multiplier. Expansionary fiscal policy leads to an increase in real GDP, and contractionary fiscal policy leads to a reduction in real GDP. Because part of any change in taxes or transfers is absorbed by savings in the first round of spending, changes in government purchases of goods and services have a more powerful effect on the economy than equal-sized changes in taxes or transfers.

5. Rules governing taxes—with the exception of **lump-sum taxes**—and some transfers act as **automatic stabilizers,** reducing the size of the multiplier and automatically reducing the size of fluctuations in the business cycle. In contrast, **discretionary fiscal policy** arises from deliberate actions by policy makers rather than from the business cycle.

6. Some of the fluctuations in the budget balance are due to the effects of the business cycle. In order to separate the effects of the business cycle from the effects of discretionary fiscal policy, governments determine the **cyclically adjusted budget balance,** an estimate of the budget balance if the economy were at potential output.

7. U.S. government budget accounting is calculated on the basis of **fiscal years.** Persistently large budget deficits have long-run consequences because they lead to an increase in **public debt.** As a result, two potential dangers may arise: crowding out, which reduces long-run economic growth, and financial pressure leading to default, which brings economic and financial turmoil. A **debt spiral** will increase public debt if countries need to take on additional debt to pay past interest expenses.

8. A widely used measure of fiscal health is the **debt–GDP ratio.** This number can remain stable or fall even in the face of persistent budget deficits if GDP rises over time. With large **implicit liabilities,** a stable debt–GDP ratio may give a misleading sense of security. The largest implicit liabilities of the U.S. government come from Social Security, Medicare, Medicaid, and the Affordable Care Act (ACA), the costs of which are increasing due to the aging of the population and rising medical costs.

KEY TERMS

Social insurance, p. 385
Expansionary fiscal policy, p. 387
Contractionary fiscal policy, p. 387
Lump-sum taxes, p. 393
Automatic stabilizers, p. 394

Discretionary fiscal policy, p. 394
Cyclically adjusted budget balance, p. 398
Fiscal year, p. 402
Public debt, p. 402

Debt spiral, p. 402
Debt–GDP ratio, p. 404
Implicit liabilities, p. 405

PRACTICE QUESTIONS

1. The fiscal programs instituted in response to the coronavirus pandemic—the 2020 CARES Act and the 2021 American Rescue Plan—were huge, amounting in combination to around $4 trillion. Although unemployment temporarily surged in 2020, these plans provided considerable fiscal stimulus. Simultaneously, the global pandemic caused a supply side shock as supply chains experienced delays as households stocked up on basic necessities. In terms of aggregate demand and aggregate supply, explain why this combination may have caused rising inflation.

2. With the CARES Act costing more than $2 trillion and the federal government facing a significant decline in tax revenue, explain the effectiveness of fiscal policy using the three claims outlined in the chapter.

3. The government's budget surplus in Macroland has risen consistently over the past five years. Two government policy makers disagree as to why this has happened. One argues that a rising budget surplus indicates a growing economy; the other argues that it shows that the government is using contractionary fiscal policy. Can you determine which policy maker is correct? If not, why not?

PROBLEMS

1. The accompanying diagram shows the current macroeconomic situation for the economy of Albernia. You have been hired as an economic consultant to help the economy move to potential output, Y_P.

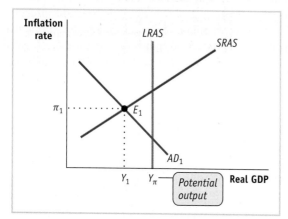

a. Is Albernia facing a recessionary or inflationary gap?

b. Which type of fiscal policy—expansionary or contractionary—would move the economy of Albernia to potential output, Y_P? What are some examples of such policies?

c. Illustrate the macroeconomic situation in Albernia with a diagram after the successful fiscal policy has been implemented.

2. The accompanying diagram shows the current macroeconomic situation for the economy of Brittania; real GDP is Y_1, and the inflation rate is π_1. You have been hired as an economic consultant to help the economy move to potential output, Y_P.

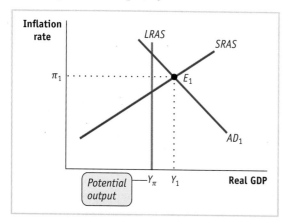

a. Is Brittania facing a recessionary or inflationary gap?

b. Which type of fiscal policy—expansionary or contractionary—would move the economy of Brittania to potential output, Y_P? What are some examples of such policies?

c. Illustrate the macroeconomic situation in Brittania with a diagram after the successful fiscal policy has been implemented.

3. An economy is in long-run macroeconomic equilibrium when each of the following aggregate demand shocks occurs. What kind of gap—inflationary or recessionary—will the economy face after the shock, and what type of fiscal policies would help move the economy back to potential output? How would your recommended fiscal policy shift the aggregate demand curve?

a. A stock market boom increases the value of stocks held by households.

b. Firms come to believe that a recession in the near future is likely.

c. Anticipating the possibility of war, the government increases its purchases of military equipment.

d. The quantity of money in the economy declines and interest rates increase.

4. During a 2008 interview, then German Finance Minister Peer Steinbruck said, "We have to watch out that in Europe and beyond, nothing like a combination of downward economic [growth] and high inflation rates emerges—something that experts call stagflation." Such a situation can be depicted by the movement of the short-run aggregate supply curve from its original position, $SRAS_1$, to its new position, $SRAS_2$, with the new equilibrium point E_2 in the accompanying figure. In this question, we try to understand why stagflation is particularly hard to fix using fiscal policy.

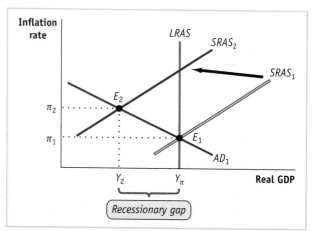

a. What would be the appropriate fiscal policy response to this situation if the primary concern of the government was to maintain economic growth?

Illustrate the effect of the policy on the equilibrium point and the inflation rate using the diagram.

b. What would be the appropriate fiscal policy response to this situation if the primary concern of the government was to maintain price stability? Illustrate the effect of the policy on the equilibrium point and the inflation rate using the diagram.

c. Discuss the effectiveness of the policies in parts a and b in fighting stagflation.

5. Show why a $10 billion reduction in government purchases of goods and services will have a larger effect on real GDP than a $10 billion reduction in government transfers by completing the accompanying table for an economy with a marginal propensity to consume (*MPC*) of 0.6. The first and second rows of the table are filled in for you: on the left side of the table, in the first row, the $10 billion reduction in government purchases decreases real GDP and disposable income, *YD*, by $10 billion, leading to a reduction in consumer spending of $6 billion (*MPC* × change in disposable income) in row 2. However, on the right side of the table, the $10 billion reduction in transfers has no effect on real GDP in round 1 but does lower *YD* by $10 billion, resulting in a decrease in consumer spending of $6 billion in round 2.

a. When government purchases decrease by $10 billion, what is the sum of the changes in real GDP after the 10 rounds?

b. When the government reduces transfers by $10 billion, what is the sum of the changes in real GDP after the 10 rounds?

c. Using the formula for the multiplier for changes in government purchases and for changes in transfers, calculate the total change in real GDP due to the $10 billion decrease in government purchases and the $10 billion reduction in transfers. What explains the difference? [*Hint:* The multiplier for government purchases of goods and services is 1/(1 − *MPC*). But since each $1 change in government transfers only leads to an initial change in real GDP of *MPC* × $1, the multiplier for government transfers is *MPC*/(1 − *MPC*).]

6. In each of the following cases, either a recessionary or inflationary gap exists. Assume that the aggregate supply curve is horizontal, so that the change in real GDP arising from a shift of the aggregate demand curve equals the size of the shift of the curve. Calculate both the change in government purchases of goods and services and the change in government transfers necessary to close the gap.

a. Real GDP equals $100 billion, potential output equals $160 billion, and the *MPC* is 0.75.

b. Real GDP equals $250 billion, potential output equals $200 billion, and the *MPC* is 0.5.

c. Real GDP equals $180 billion, potential output equals $100 billion, and the *MPC* is 0.8.

7. Most macroeconomists believe it is a good thing that taxes act as automatic stabilizers and lower the size of the multiplier. However, a smaller multiplier means that the change in government purchases of goods and services, government transfers, or taxes needed to close an inflationary or recessionary gap is larger. How can you explain this apparent inconsistency?

8. Figure 10 shows the actual budget deficit and the cyclically adjusted budget deficit as a percentage of GDP in the United States from 1965 to 2022. Assuming that potential output was unchanged, use this figure to determine which of the years from 1990 to 2022 the government used expansionary fiscal policy and in which years it used contractionary fiscal policy.

9. You are an economic adviser to a candidate for national office. She asks you for a summary of the economic consequences of a balanced-budget rule for the federal government and for your recommendation on whether she should support such a rule. How do you respond?

10. In 2022, the policy makers of the economy of Eastlandia projected the debt–GDP ratio and the ratio of the budget deficit to GDP for the economy for the next 10 years under different scenarios for growth in the government's deficit. Real GDP is currently $1,000 billion per year and is expected to grow by 3% per year,

Rounds	Decrease in G = −$10 billion (billions of dollars)			Decrease in TR = −$10 billion (billions of dollars)		
	Change in G or C	Change in real GDP	Change in YD	Change in TR or C	Change in real GDP	Change in YD
1	ΔG = −$10.00	−$10.00	−$10.00	ΔTR = −$10.00	$0.00	−$10.00
2	ΔC = −6.00	−6.00	−6.00	ΔC = −6.00	−6.00	−6.00
3	ΔC = ?	?	?	ΔC = ?	?	?
4	ΔC = ?	?	?	ΔC = ?	?	?
5	ΔC = ?	?	?	ΔC = ?	?	?
6	ΔC = ?	?	?	ΔC = ?	?	?
7	ΔC = ?	?	?	ΔC = ?	?	?
8	ΔC = ?	?	?	ΔC = ?	?	?
9	ΔC = ?	?	?	ΔC = ?	?	?
10	ΔC = ?	?	?	ΔC = ?	?	?

the public debt is $300 billion at the beginning of the year, and the deficit is $30 billion in 2022.

Year	Real GDP (billions of dollars)	Debt (billions of dollars)	Budget deficit (billions of dollars)	Debt (percent of real GDP)	Budget deficit (percent of real GDP)
2022	$1,000	$300	$30	?	?
2023	1,030	?	?	?	?
2024	1,061	?	?	?	?
2025	1,093	?	?	?	?
2026	1,126	?	?	?	?
2027	1,159	?	?	?	?
2028	1,194	?	?	?	?
2029	1,230	?	?	?	?
2030	1,267	?	?	?	?
2031	1,305	?	?	?	?
2032	1,344	?	?	?	?

a. Complete the accompanying table to show the debt–GDP ratio and the ratio of the budget deficit to GDP for the economy if the government's budget deficit remains constant at $30 billion over the next 10 years. (Remember that the government's debt will grow by the previous year's deficit.)

b. Redo the table to show the debt–GDP ratio and the ratio of the budget deficit to GDP for the economy if the government's budget deficit grows by 3% per year over the next 10 years.

c. Redo the table again to show the debt–GDP ratio and the ratio of the budget deficit to GDP for the economy if the government's budget deficit grows by 20% per year over the next 10 years.

d. What happens to the debt–GDP ratio and the ratio of the budget deficit to GDP for the economy over time under the three different scenarios?

11. Your study partner argues that the distinction between the government's budget deficit and debt is similar to the distinction between consumer savings and wealth. Your study partner also argues that if you have large budget deficits, you must have a large debt. In what ways is your study partner correct and in what ways incorrect?

12. ⎡〰〰〰⎤ Access the Discovering Data exercise for Chapter 13 online to answer these questions.

a. Which of these six countries—United States, France, Italy, Greece, Germany, and the United Kingdom—had the largest amount of government debt as a percent of GDP as of 2019? Which had the smallest?

b. Calculate the percent change in government debt from 2007 through 2019 for the same six countries. Which country experienced the largest percent increase in government debt from 2007 through 2019? Which experienced the smallest?

c. Using the six countries as a reference point, what conclusions can you draw about the relationship between government debt and economic growth?

13. In which of the following cases does the size of the government's debt and the size of the budget deficit indicate potential problems for the economy?

a. The government's debt is relatively low, but the government is running a large budget deficit as it builds a high-speed rail system to connect the major cities of the nation.

b. The government's debt is relatively high due to a recently ended deficit-financed war, but the government is now running only a small budget deficit.

c. The government's debt is relatively low, but the government is running a budget deficit to finance the interest payments on the debt.

d. The government's debt is relatively high and the government is running a budget deficit to finance new infrastructure spending.

14. How did or would the following affect the current public debt and implicit liabilities of the U.S. government?

a. In 2003, Congress passed and President George W. Bush signed the Medicare Modernization Act, which provides seniors and individuals with disabilities with a prescription drug benefit. Some of the benefits under this law took effect immediately, but other benefits will not begin until sometime in the future.

b. The age at which retired persons can receive full Social Security benefits is raised to age 70 for future retirees.

c. Social Security benefits for future retirees are limited to those with low incomes.

d. Because the cost of health care is increasing faster than the overall inflation rate, annual increases in Social Security benefits are increased by the annual increase in health care costs rather than the overall inflation rate.

e. The Affordable Care Act (ACA), which went into effect in 2014, created incentives for hospitals to find ways to save the government money.

15. Unlike households, governments are often able to sustain large debts. For example, in 2022, the U.S. government's total debt reached $30.8 trillion, approximately equal to 123.4% of GDP. At the time, according to the U.S. Treasury, the average interest rate paid by the government on its debt was 2.6%. However, running budget deficits becomes hard when very large debts are outstanding.

a. Calculate the dollar cost of the annual interest on the government's total debt assuming the interest rate and debt figures cited above.

b. If the government operates on a balanced budget before interest payments are taken into account, at what rate must GDP grow in order for the debt–GDP ratio to remain unchanged?

c. Calculate the total increase in national debt if the government incurs a deficit of $600 billion in 2023.

d. At what rate would nominal GDP have to grow in order for the debt–GDP ratio to remain unchanged when the deficit in 2023 is $600 billion?

e. Why is the debt–GDP ratio the preferred measure of a country's debt rather than the dollar value of the debt? Why is it important for a government to keep this number under control?

16. The accompanying table shows how consumers' marginal propensities to consume in a particular economy are related to their level of income.

Income range	Marginal propensity to consume
$0–$20,000	0.9
$20,001–$40,000	0.8
$40,001–$60,000	0.7
$60,001–$80,000	0.6
Above $80,000	0.5

a. Suppose the government engages in increased purchases of goods and services. For each of the income groups in the table, what is the value of the multiplier—that is, what is the "bang for the buck" from each dollar the government spends on government purchases of goods and services in each income group?

b. If the government needed to close a recessionary or inflationary gap, at which group should it primarily aim its fiscal policy of changes in government purchases of goods and services? ■

Taxes and the Multiplier

In the chapter, we described how taxes that depend positively on real GDP reduce the size of the multiplier and act as an automatic stabilizer for the economy. Let's look a little more closely at the mathematics of how this works.

Specifically, let's assume that the government "captures" a fraction t of any increase in real GDP in the form of taxes, where t, the tax rate, is a fraction between 0 and 1. And let's repeat the exercise we carried out in Chapter 11, where we consider the effects of a $100 billion increase in investment spending. The same analysis holds for *any* autonomous increase in aggregate spending—in particular, it is also true for increases in government purchases of goods and services.

The $100 billion increase in investment spending initially raises real GDP by $100 billion (the first round). In the absence of taxes, disposable income would rise by $100 billion. But because part of the rise in real GDP is collected in the form of taxes, disposable income only rises by $(1 - t) \times \$100$ billion. The second-round increase in consumer spending, which is equal to the marginal propensity to consume (MPC) multiplied by the rise in disposable income, is $(MPC \times (1 - t)) \times \$100$ billion. This leads to a third-round increase in consumer spending of $(MPC \times (1 - t)) \times (MPC \times (1 - t)) \times \$100$ billion, and so on. So the total effect on real GDP is

Increase in investment spending $= \$100$ billion
$+$ Second-round increase in consumer spending $= (MPC \times (1 - t)) \times \$100$ billion
$+$ Third-round increase in consumer spending $= (MPC \times (1 - t))^2 \times \$100$ billion
$+$ Fourth-round increase in consumer spending $= (MPC \times (1 - t))^3 \times \$100$ billion

$\vdots \qquad\qquad\qquad\qquad \vdots$

$$\text{Total increase in real GDP} = [1 + (MPC \times (1 - t)) + (MPC \times (1 - t))^2 + (MPC \times (1 - t))^3 + \cdots] \times \$100 \text{ billion}$$

As explained in Chapter 11, an infinite series of the form $1 + x + x^2 + \cdots$, with $0 < x < 1$, is equal to $1/(1 - x)$. In this example, $x = (MPC \times (1 - t))$. So the total effect of a $100 billion increase in investment spending, taking into account all the subsequent increases in consumer spending, is to raise real GDP by:

$$\frac{1}{1 - (MPC \times (1 - t))} \times \$100 \text{ billion}$$

When we calculated the multiplier assuming away the effect of taxes, we found that it was $1/(1 - MPC)$. But when we assume that a fraction t of any change in real GDP is collected in the form of taxes, the multiplier is:

$$\text{Multiplier} = \frac{1}{1 - (MPC \times (1 - t))}$$

This is always a smaller number than $1/(1 - MPC)$, and its size diminishes as t grows. Suppose, for example, that $MPC = 0.6$. In the absence of taxes, this implies a multiplier of $1/(1 - 0.6) = 1/0.4 = 2.5$. But now let's assume that $t = 1/3$, that is, that 1/3 of any increase in real GDP is collected by the government. Then the multiplier is:

$$\frac{1}{1 - (0.6 \times (1 - 1/3))} = \frac{1}{1 - (0.6 \times 2/3)} = \frac{1}{1 - 0.4} = \frac{1}{0.6} = 1.667$$

PROBLEMS

1. An economy has a marginal propensity to consume of 0.6, real GDP equals $500 billion, and the government collects 20% of GDP in taxes. If government purchases increase by $10 billion, show the rounds of increased spending that take place by completing the accompanying table. The first and second rows are filled in for you. In the first row, the increase in government purchases of $10 billion raises real GDP by $10 billion, taxes increase by $2 billion, and *YD* increases by $8 billion; in the second row, the increase in *YD* of $8 billion increases consumer spending by $4.80 billion (*MPC* × change in disposable income).

Rounds	Change in *G* or *C*		Change in real GDP	Change in taxes	Change in *YD*
	(billions of dollars)				
1	Δ*G* =	$10.00	$10.00	$2.00	$8.00
2	Δ*C* =	4.80	4.80	0.96	3.84
3	Δ*C* =	?	?	?	?
4	Δ*C* =	?	?	?	?
5	Δ*C* =	?	?	?	?
6	Δ*C* =	?	?	?	?
7	Δ*C* =	?	?	?	?
8	Δ*C* =	?	?	?	?
9	Δ*C* =	?	?	?	?
10	Δ*C* =	?	?	?	?

a. What is the total change in real GDP after the 10 rounds? What is the value of the multiplier? What would you expect the total change in real GDP to be, based on the multiplier formula? How do your two answers compare?

b. Redo the accompanying table, assuming the marginal propensity to consume is 0.75 and the government collects 10% of the rise in real GDP in taxes. What is the total change in real GDP after 10 rounds? What is the value of the multiplier? How do your two answers compare?

2. Calculate the change in government purchases of goods and services necessary to close the recessionary or inflationary gaps in the following cases. Assume that the short-run aggregate supply curve is horizontal, so that the change in real GDP arising from a shift of the aggregate demand curve equals the size of the shift of the curve.

a. Real GDP equals $100 billion, potential output equals $160 billion, the government collects 20% of any change in real GDP in the form of taxes, and the marginal propensity to consume is 0.75.

b. Real GDP equals $250 billion, potential output equals $200 billion, the government collects 10% of any change in real GDP in the form of taxes, and the marginal propensity to consume is 0.5.

c. Real GDP equals $180 billion, potential output equals $100 billion, the government collects 25% of any change in real GDP in the form of taxes, and the marginal propensity to consume is 0.8. ∎

14

Money, Banking, and the Federal Reserve System

 NOT SO FUNNY MONEY

"THE PRODUCT IS CAREFULLY CREATED in rural facilities throughout the Peruvian countryside using cheap labor, then hoarded in stash houses controlled by violent gangs in Lima. Once there, the goods are packed into parcels, loaded onto planes or hidden inside luggage, pottery, hollowed-out Bibles, sneakers, children's toys or massive shipping containers bound for major U.S. ports of entry, such as Miami." So began a *Washington Post* report on Operation Sunset, a huge raid carried out by Peruvian authorities in cooperation with the U.S. Secret Service in 2016. But what was the target of this raid? It wasn't a drug bust; it was a fake money bust.

In recent years, Peru has become a major source for the production of counterfeit U.S. currency; the so-called "Peruvian note" is considered to be the best counterfeit in the business. Workers employed by criminal syndicates meticulously add decorative details to printed bills by hand, creating high-quality fakes that are very hard to detect.

The funny thing is that elaborately decorated pieces of paper have little or no intrinsic value. Indeed, a $100 bill printed with blue or orange ink wouldn't be worth the paper it was printed on.

But if the ink on that piece of paper is just the right shade of green, people will think that it's *money* and will accept it as payment for very real goods and services, because they believe, correctly, that they can do the same thing: exchange that piece of green paper for real goods and services.

In fact, here's a riddle: If a fake $100 bill from Peru enters the United States and is successfully exchanged for a good or service with nobody ever realizing it's a fake, who gets hurt? Accepting a fake $100 bill isn't like buying a car that turns out to be a lemon or a meal that turns out to be inedible. As long as the bill's counterfeit nature remains undiscovered, it will pass from hand to hand just like a real $100 bill.

The answer to the riddle is that the actual victims of the counterfeiting are U.S. taxpayers, because counterfeit dollars reduce the revenues available to pay for the operations of the U.S. government. The Treasury Department believes that only around 0.01% of the currency in circulation, about $200 million, is fake, but that could still mean that taxpayers have been defrauded of hundreds of millions of dollars. Accordingly, the Secret Service diligently monitors the integrity of U.S. currency, promptly investigating any reports of counterfeit dollars. The efforts of the Secret Service attest to the fact that money isn't like ordinary goods and services, and it certainly is not like pieces of colored paper.

In this chapter we'll look at what money is, the role that it plays, the workings of a modern monetary system, and the institutions that sustain and regulate it, including the *Federal Reserve*. ●

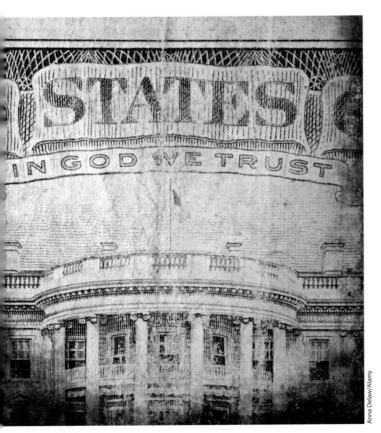

Anna Delaw/Alamy

Money is the essential channel that links the various parts of the modern economy.

WHAT YOU WILL LEARN

- What are the various roles that **money** plays and what forms does it take?
- Why is the level of the **money supply** so important to the state of the economy?
- How do the actions of private banks and the Federal Reserve determine the money supply?
- How does the Federal Reserve use **open-market operations** to change the **monetary base**?

money any asset that can easily be used to purchase goods and services.

currency in circulation actual cash held by the public.

checkable bank deposits bank accounts that can be accessed by using checks, debit cards, and digital payments.

money supply the total value of financial assets in the economy that are considered money.

‖ The Meaning of Money

In everyday conversation, we often use the word *money* to mean wealth. If you ask, "How much money does Jeff Bezos, the founder of Amazon, have?" the answer will be something like, "Oh, $172 billion or so, but who's counting?" That is, the number will include the value of the stocks, bonds, real estate, and other assets he owns.

But the economist's definition of money doesn't include all forms of wealth. The dollar bills in your wallet are money; other forms of wealth—such as stocks, bonds, and real estate—aren't money. What, according to economists, distinguishes money from other forms of wealth?

What Is Money?

Money is defined in terms of what it does: **money** is any asset that can easily be used to purchase goods and services. In Chapter 10, we defined an asset as *liquid* if it can easily be converted into cash. Money consists of cash itself, which is liquid by definition, as well as other assets that are highly liquid.

You can see the distinction between money and other assets by asking yourself how you pay for your morning jolt of java. The cashier will accept dollar bills in return for a double mocha latte—but they won't accept stock certificates or a collection of vintage baseball cards. If you want to convert stock certificates or vintage baseball cards into a latte, you have to sell them—trade them for money—and then use the money to buy your drink.

Without a liquid asset like money, making purchases would be much harder.

Of course, the vast majority of stores allow you to buy goods with a debit card linked to your bank account, and many of us pay larger bills (like tuition) with checks written on our accounts. Does that make your bank account money, even if you haven't converted it into cash? Yes. **Currency in circulation**—actual cash in the hands of the public—is considered money. So are **checkable bank deposits**—bank accounts that can be accessed using debit cards, digital payments, and checks.

Some definitions of money include assets other than currency and checkable bank deposits. There are two widely used definitions of the **money supply,** the total value of financial assets in the economy that are considered money.

1. The narrower definition of money considers only the most liquid assets to be money: currency in circulation, checkable bank deposits, and savings accounts.
2. The broader definition includes the two categories just noted plus other assets that are "almost" checkable, mainly holdings in money market funds that can easily be transferred into your bank account with a click of a mouse or a tap on your smartphone. Both definitions of the money supply, however, make a distinction between those assets that can easily be used to purchase goods and services and those that can't.

Money plays a crucial role in generating *gains from trade* because it makes indirect exchange possible. Think of what happens when a cardiac surgeon buys a new refrigerator. The surgeon has valuable services to offer—namely, heart operations. The owner of the store has valuable goods to offer—refrigerators and other appliances. It would be extremely difficult for both parties if, instead of using money, they had to directly barter the goods and services they sell. In a barter system, a cardiac surgeon and an appliance store owner could trade only if the store owner happened to want a heart operation and the surgeon happened to want a new refrigerator.

This is known as the problem of finding a *double coincidence of wants:* in a barter system, two parties can trade only when each wants what the other has to offer. Money solves this problem: individuals can trade what they have to offer for money and trade money for what they want.

Because the ability to make transactions with money rather than relying on bartering makes it easier to achieve gains from trade, the existence of money increases welfare, even though money does not directly produce anything.

Let's take a closer look at the roles money plays in the economy.

medium of exchange an asset that individuals acquire for the purpose of trading for goods and services rather than for their own consumption.

Roles of Money

Money plays three main roles in any modern economy: it is a *medium of exchange,* a *store of value,* and a *unit of account.*

1. Medium of Exchange Our cardiac surgeon/refrigerator example illustrates the role of money as a **medium of exchange**—an asset that individuals use to trade for goods and services rather than for consumption. People can't eat dollar bills; rather, they use dollar bills to trade for goods and services.

In normal times, the official money of a given country—the dollar in the United States, the peso in Mexico, and so on—is also the medium of exchange in virtually all transactions in that country. During troubled economic times, however, other goods or assets often play that role instead. For example, during economic turmoil people often turn to other countries' moneys as the medium of exchange: U.S. dollars have played this role in troubled Latin American countries, as have euros in troubled Eastern European countries. In a famous example, cigarettes functioned as the medium of exchange in World War II prisoner-of-war camps: even nonsmokers traded goods and services for cigarettes because the cigarettes could in turn be easily traded for other items. Inmates at federal penitentiaries,

---

🌐 GLOBAL COMPARISON   THE CASH OF NATIONS

When did you last pay for something using cash—that is, literally hand over green pieces of paper bearing portraits of historical figures? For many of us, the answer may be that it was days, weeks, and, for some, months ago. These days, many of our day-to-day purchases are made using some form of digital payment, whether it involves a card or a smartphone.

So is cash on its way out? The answer, somewhat surprisingly, is that it depends on what country you live in. One simple measure of the prevalence of cash transactions is the ratio of the value of currency in circulation to GDP, the value of goods and services produced in a nation. The accompanying figure shows this ratio for three countries, Sweden, the United States, and Japan.

At one extreme, Sweden is very nearly a cashless society: most shops don't accept cash, and half of the country's bank branches don't even handle cash. At the other extreme, Japanese still carry around a lot of cash. The United States is somewhere in the middle.

What's odd about this is that all three countries are technologically sophisticated, to about the same degree. Why are they so different when it comes to cash?

In the case of Japan, the answer seems to be mainly cultural: for a variety of reasons, Japanese citizens are still accustomed to using currency and are reluctant to go digital even though their society is every bit as addicted to smartphones as ours.

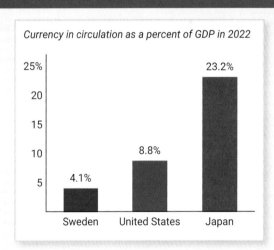

Currency in circulation as a percent of GDP in 2022

The U.S. case is different: as upcoming For Inquiring Minds explains, a large fraction of U.S. currency is actually held outside the country, mainly in the form of $100 bills.

Sweden, arguably, is what the monetary future will look like; it is, in fact, considering eliminating cash altogether. And even in the United States a growing number of businesses have stopped accepting cash. But not everyone is happy with that future. Recently, New York City passed a law requiring that stores continue to accept cash as payment, arguing that cashless stores effectively discriminate against people too poor to have a card linked to a bank account.

Data from: Bank for International Settlements, International Monetary Fund.

store of value an asset that is a means of holding purchasing power over time.

unit of account a measure used to set prices and make economic calculations.

commodity money a medium of exchange that is a good, normally gold or silver, that has intrinsic value in other uses.

commodity-backed money a medium of exchange that has no intrinsic value, whose ultimate value is guaranteed by a promise that it can be converted into valuable goods on demand.

where smoking is now banned, reportedly use packages of ramen noodles for many transactions. During the extreme German inflation of 1923, goods such as eggs and lumps of coal became, briefly, mediums of exchange.

2. Store of Value To act as a medium of exchange, money must also be a **store of value**—a means of holding purchasing power over time. To see why this is necessary, imagine trying to operate an economy in which ice cream cones were the medium of exchange. Such an economy would quickly suffer from, well, monetary meltdown: your medium of exchange would likely turn into a sticky puddle before you could use it to buy something else. (As we'll see in Chapter 16, one of the problems caused by high inflation is that, in effect, it causes the value of money to "melt.") Of course, money is by no means the only store of value. Any asset that holds its purchasing power over time is a store of value. So the store-of-value role is a necessary but not distinctive feature of money.

3. Unit of Account Finally, money normally serves as the **unit of account**—the commonly accepted measure individuals use to set prices and make economic calculations. To understand the importance of this role, consider a historical fact: during the Middle Ages, peasants typically were required to provide landowners with goods and labor rather than money. A peasant might, for example, be required to work on the landowner's land one day a week and hand over one-fifth of their harvest.

Today, rents, like other prices, are almost always specified in money terms. That makes things much clearer: imagine how hard it would be to decide which apartment to rent if landlords today followed medieval practice. Suppose, for example, that one landlord says he'll let you have a place if you clean his house twice a week and bring him a pound of steak every day, whereas a second landlord wants you to clean her house just once a week but wants four pounds of chicken every day. Who's offering the better deal? It's hard to say. If, instead, the first landlord wants $600 a month and the other wants $700, the comparison is easy. In other words, without a commonly accepted measure, the terms of a transaction are harder to determine, making it more difficult to make transactions and achieve gains from trade.

Types of Money

In some form or another, money has been in use for thousands of years. For most of that time, people used **commodity money:** the medium of exchange was a good, normally gold or silver, that had intrinsic value in other uses. These alternative uses gave commodity money value independent of its role as a medium of exchange. For example, cigarettes, which served as money in World War II prisoner-of-war camps, were also valuable because many prisoners smoked. Gold was valuable because it was used for jewelry and ornamentation, aside from the fact that it was minted into coins.

By 1776, the year in which the United States declared independence and Adam Smith published *The Wealth of Nations,* there was widespread use of paper money in addition to gold or silver coins. Unlike modern dollar bills, however, this paper money consisted of notes issued by private banks, which promised to exchange their notes for gold or silver coins on demand. So the paper currency that initially replaced commodity money was **commodity-backed money,** a medium of exchange with no intrinsic value whose ultimate value was guaranteed by a promise that it could always be converted into valuable goods on demand.

The big advantage of commodity-backed money over simple commodity money, like gold and silver coins, was that it

joecicak/Getty Images

Goods with value, like gold and silver, were used as a medium of exchange for centuries.

Library of Congress, Prints & Photographs Division, Reproduction number LC-DIG-ds-11255 (digital file from original item)

By issuing paper notes to function as money instead of gold and silver coins, banks were able to free up valuable resources.

tied up fewer valuable resources. Although a note-issuing bank still had to keep some gold and silver on hand, it had to keep only enough to satisfy demands for redemption of its notes. And it could rely on the fact that on a normal day only a fraction of its paper notes would be redeemed. So the bank needed to keep only a portion of the total value of its notes in circulation in the form of gold and silver in its vaults. It could then lend out the remaining gold and silver to those who wished to use it. This allowed society to use the remaining gold and silver for other purposes, all with no loss in the ability to achieve gains from trade.

In a famous passage in *The Wealth of Nations,* Adam Smith described paper money as a "waggon-way through the air." Smith was making an analogy between money and an imaginary highway that did not absorb valuable land beneath it. An actual highway provides a useful service but at a cost: land that could be used to grow crops is instead paved over. If the highway could be built through the air, it wouldn't destroy useful land. As Smith understood, when banks replaced gold and silver money with paper notes, they accomplished a similar feat: they reduced the amount of real resources used by society to provide the functions of money.

At this point you may ask: why make any use at all of gold and silver in the monetary system, even to back paper money? In fact, today's monetary system goes even further than the system Smith admired, having eliminated any role for gold and silver. A U.S. dollar bill isn't commodity money, and it isn't even commodity-backed. Rather, its value arises entirely from the fact that it is generally accepted as a means of payment, a role that is ultimately decreed by the U.S. government. Money whose value derives entirely from its official status as a means of exchange is known as **fiat money** because it exists by government fiat, a historical term for a policy declared by a ruler.

Fiat money has two major advantages over commodity-backed money. First, it is even more of a "waggon-way through the air"—creating it doesn't use up any real resources beyond the paper it's printed on. Second, the supply of money can be adjusted based on the needs of the economy, instead of being determined by the amount of gold and silver that prospectors happen to discover.

Fiat money, though, poses some risks. In the opening story, we described one such risk—counterfeiting. Counterfeiters usurp a privilege of the U.S. government, which has the sole legal right to print dollar bills. And the benefit that counterfeiters get by exchanging fake bills for real goods and services comes at the expense of the U.S. federal government, which covers a small but nontrivial part of its own expenses by issuing new currency to meet a growing demand for money.

Another large risk is that governments that can create money whenever they feel like it will be tempted to abuse the privilege. In Chapter 16, we'll learn how governments sometimes rely too heavily on printing money to pay their bills, leading to high inflation. In this chapter, however, we'll stay focused on the question of what money is and how it is managed.

Measuring the Money Supply

The Federal Reserve calculates the size of two **monetary aggregates,** overall measures of the money supply, which differ in how strictly money is defined. The two aggregates are known, rather cryptically, as M1 and M2. (There used to be a third aggregate named—you guessed it—M3, but in 2006 the Federal Reserve stopped measuring it, having determined that it was no longer useful.)

M1, the narrowest definition, contains only currency in circulation (also known as cash), checkable deposits, and other liquid deposits (notably savings accounts). M2 adds other kinds of assets, often referred to as **near-moneys**—financial assets that aren't directly usable as a medium of exchange but can be readily converted into cash or checkable bank deposits. The main example is money market funds, which can be transferred over to bank accounts within a day. Because currency and checkable deposits are directly usable as a medium of exchange, M1 is the most liquid measure of money.

fiat money a medium of exchange whose value derives entirely from its official status as a means of payment.

monetary aggregate an overall measure of the money supply. The most common monetary aggregates in the United States are M1, which includes currency in circulation, traveler's checks, and checkable bank deposits, and M2, which includes M1 as well as near-moneys.

near-moneys financial assets that can't be directly used as a medium of exchange but can be readily converted into cash or checkable bank deposits.

PITFALLS

WHAT'S NOT IN THE MONEY SUPPLY

Financial assets like stocks and bonds are not part of the money supply under any definition because they're not liquid enough.

M1 consists, roughly speaking, of assets you can use to buy groceries or a cup of coffee: currency and bank deposits. M2 is broader, because it includes things like money market funds that can easily and quickly be converted into M1. For example, you can generally transfer funds between your money market fund and your checking account or using an app on your smartphone.

By contrast, converting a stock or a bond into cash requires selling the stock or bond—something that usually takes some time and involves paying a broker's fee. That makes these assets much less liquid than bank deposits. So stocks and bonds, unlike bank deposits, aren't considered money.

FIGURE 1 Monetary Aggregates, March 2023

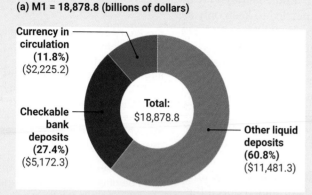

(a) M1 = 18,878.8 (billions of dollars)

Currency in circulation (11.8%) ($2,225.2)

Checkable bank deposits (27.4%) ($5,172.3)

Total: $18,878.8

Other liquid deposits (60.8%) ($11,481.3)

(b) M2 = $20,823.1 (billions of dollars)

Money market funds (6.4%) ($1,341.1)

Time deposits (2.9%) ($603.2)

Total: $20,823.1

M1 (90.1%) ($18,878.8)

The Federal Reserve uses two definitions of the money supply, M1 and M2. As panel (a) shows, most of M1 consists of checkable and other liquid deposits with currency in circulation making up all of the rest. M2, as panel (b) shows, has a broader definition: it includes M1 plus other deposits and deposit-like assets. (Numbers may not add to 100% due to rounding.)

Data from: Federal Reserve Bank of St. Louis.

Figure 1 shows the actual composition of M1 and M2 as of March 2023, in billions of dollars. M1 was valued at $18.9 trillion, with about $2.2 trillion accounted for by currency in circulation and the rest accounted for by bank deposits. M2 was larger, $21.1 trillion, with most of the difference consisting of assets in money market funds. These near-moneys pay interest—cash (currency in circulation) does not—and they typically pay higher interest rates than any offered on checkable bank deposits.

FOR INQUIRING MINDS   All About the Benjamins

There is nearly $2.3 trillion of U.S. currency in circulation in the United States, around $6,000 for every man, woman, and child. Most individuals don't carry this amount in their wallets—the average American holds only about $60 in cash, probably because people increasingly make purchases using debit cards and smartphone apps. So where is all that cash sitting?

Some of it can be found in cash registers. Businesses as well as individuals need to hold cash. However, a large proportion of these huge currency holdings—at least 45%—is in the hands of foreign residents who so distrust their own national currencies that the U.S. dollar has become a widely accepted medium of exchange and store of value.

Cash is also widely used to keep transactions hidden — by criminals such as drug dealers, or businesspeople looking to avoid paying taxes on their income. The prevalence of illegal transactions may explain why around four-fifths of the value of U.S. currency in circulation takes the form of $100 bills — sometimes called "Benjamins," because they bear the portrait of Benjamin Franklin — which many legitimate businesses won't even accept.

The desire to shield transactions from the eyes of authorities helps to explain the growth of "cryptocurrencies," most famously Bitcoin, a virtual currency created in 2009. Cryptocurrencies are basically computing algorithms that create electronic tokens that are accepted by some as currency. So far, at least, cryptocurrencies aren't being widely used as a means of payment except for illegal transactions.

But what leads people to place faith in a virtual currency — to accept it in place of "real" money? As with the dollar, faith in cryptocurrencies comes from the belief that someone else, at a later date, will accept them in exchange for something real. One difference, however, is that dollars are, in a sense, ultimately backed by their official status, which means that the U.S. government accepts them as payment for taxes; cryptocurrencies have no such guarantee, which may account for the fact that their purchasing power has been wildly volatile.

ECONOMICS >> *in Action*
The History of the Dollar

U.S. dollar bills are pure fiat money: they have no intrinsic value, and they are not backed by anything that does. But U.S. money wasn't always like that. In the early days of European settlement, the colonies that would become the United States used commodity money, partly consisting of gold and silver coins minted in Europe. But because such coins were scarce on this side of the Atlantic, the colonists relied on a variety of other forms of commodity money. For example, settlers in Virginia used tobacco as money and settlers in the Northeast used *wampum,* made from a clamshell.

Later in U.S. history, commodity-backed paper money came into widespread use. But this wasn't paper money as we now know it, issued by the U.S. government and bearing the signature of the Secretary of the Treasury. Before the Civil War, the U.S. government didn't issue any paper money. Instead, dollar bills were issued by private banks, which promised that their bills could be redeemed for gold or silver coins on demand. These promises weren't always credible because banks sometimes failed, leaving holders of their bills with worthless pieces of paper. Understandably, people were reluctant to accept currency from any bank rumored to be in financial trouble. In this private money system, some dollars were less valuable than others.

A curious legacy of that time was notes issued by the Citizens' Bank of Louisiana, based in New Orleans, that became among the most widely used bank notes in the southern states. These notes were printed in English on one side and French on the other. (At the time, many people in New Orleans, originally a colony of France, spoke French.) Thus, the $10 bill read *Ten* on one side and *Dix,* the French word for *ten,* on the other. These $10 bills became known as *dixies,* probably the source of the nickname of the U.S. South.

The U.S. government began issuing official paper money, called *greenbacks,* in 1862 as a way to pay for the ongoing Civil War. At first, greenbacks had no fixed value in terms of commodities. After 1873, the U.S. government guaranteed the value of a dollar in terms of gold, effectively turning dollars into commodity-backed money.

In 1933, when President Franklin D. Roosevelt broke the link between dollars and gold, his own federal budget director—who feared that the public would lose confidence in the dollar if it wasn't ultimately backed by gold—declared ominously, "This will be the end of Western civilization." It wasn't. The link between the dollar and gold was restored a few years later, then dropped again—seemingly for good—in August 1971. Despite the warnings of doom, the U.S. dollar went on to become the world's most widely used currency.

>> *Check Your Understanding* 14-1

Solutions appear at back of book.

1. Suppose you have a gift card, good for certain products at participating stores. Is this gift card money? Why or why not?

2. Although most bank accounts pay some interest, depositors can get a higher interest rate by buying a certificate of deposit, or CD. The difference between a CD and a checking account is that the depositor pays a penalty for withdrawing the money before the CD comes due—a period of months or even years. Small CDs are counted in M2 but not in M1. Explain why they are not part of M1.

3. Explain why a system of commodity-backed money uses resources more efficiently than a system of commodity money.

|| **The Monetary Role of Banks**

Only a fraction of M1, the narrowest definition of the money supply, consists of currency in circulation—$1 bills, $5 bills, and so on. It's obvious where currency comes from: it's printed by the U.S. Treasury. But the rest of M1 consists of checkable deposits and savings accounts. So bank deposits are a major component of

bank reserves currency held by banks in their vaults plus their deposits at the Federal Reserve.

T-account a simple tool that summarizes a business's financial position by showing, in a single table, the business's assets and liabilities, with assets on the left and liabilities on the right.

the money supply. And this fact brings us to our next topic: the monetary role of banks.

What Banks Do

As we learned in Chapter 10, a bank is a *financial intermediary* that uses liquid assets in the form of bank deposits to finance the illiquid investments of borrowers. Banks can create liquidity because it isn't necessary for a bank to keep all of the funds deposited with it in the form of highly liquid assets. Except in the case of a *bank run*—which we'll get to shortly—all of a bank's depositors won't want to withdraw their funds at the same time. So a bank can provide its depositors with liquid assets yet still invest much of the depositors' funds in illiquid assets, such as mortgages and business loans.

Banks can't, however, lend out all the funds placed in their hands by depositors because they have to satisfy any depositor who wants to withdraw their funds. In order to meet these demands, a bank must keep substantial quantities of liquid assets on hand. In the modern U.S. banking system, these assets take the form either of currency in the bank's vault or deposits held in the bank's own account at the Federal Reserve. As we'll see shortly, the latter can be converted into currency more or less instantly. Currency in bank vaults and bank deposits held at the Federal Reserve are called **bank reserves.** Because bank reserves are in bank vaults and at the Federal Reserve, not held by the public, they are not part of currency in circulation.

To understand the role of banks in determining the money supply, we start by introducing a simple tool for analyzing the financial position of a bank or business: a **T-account.** A T-account summarizes the financial position of a bank or business in a single table by showing assets on the left and liabilities on the right.

Figure 2 shows the T-account for a hypothetical business that *isn't* a bank—Samantha's Smoothies. According to Figure 2, Samantha's Smoothies owns a building worth $30,000 and has $15,000 worth of smoothie-making equipment. These are assets, so they're on the left side of the table. To finance its opening, the business borrowed $20,000 from a local bank. That's a liability, so the loan is on the right side of the table. By looking at the T-account, you can immediately see what Samantha's Smoothies owns and what it owes. Oh, and it's called a T-account because the lines in the table make a T-shape.

Samantha's Smoothies is an ordinary, nonbank business. Now let's look at the T-account for a hypothetical bank, First Street Bank, which is the repository of $1 million in bank deposits.

Figure 3 shows First Street Bank's financial position. The loans First Street Bank has made are on the left side because they're assets: they represent funds that those who have borrowed from the bank are expected to repay. The bank's only other assets, in this simplified example, are its reserves, which, as we've learned, can take the form either of cash in the bank's vault or deposits at the Federal Reserve. On the right side are the bank's liabilities, which in this example

---

FIGURE 2 A T-Account for Samantha's Smoothies

A T-account summarizes a business's financial position. Its assets, in this case consisting of a building and some smoothie-making machinery, are on the left side. Its liabilities, consisting of the money it owes to a local bank, are on the right side.

Assets		Liabilities	
Building	$30,000	Loan from bank	$20,000
Smoothie-making machines	$15,000		

FIGURE 3 Assets and Liabilities of First Street Bank		

First Street Bank's assets consist of $1,200,000 in loans and $100,000 in reserves. Its liabilities consist of $1,000,000 in deposits—money owed to people who have placed funds in First Street's hands.

Assets		Liabilities	
Loans	$1,200,000	Deposits	$1,000,000
Reserves	$100,000		

consist entirely of deposits made by customers at First Street Bank. These are liabilities because they represent funds that must ultimately be repaid to depositors.

Notice that in this example First Street Bank's assets are larger than its liabilities. And that's the way it is supposed to be. Banks are required by law to maintain assets that are larger than their liabilities by a specific percentage.

We will assume that First Street Bank holds reserves equal to 10% of its customers' bank deposits. The fraction of bank deposits that a bank holds as reserves is its **reserve ratio.** In the modern U.S. system, the Federal Reserve—which, among other things, regulates banks operating in the United States—sets a minimum required reserve ratio that banks must maintain. To understand why banks are regulated, let's consider a problem banks can face: bank runs.

The Problem of Bank Runs

A bank can lend out most of the funds deposited in its care because in normal times only a small fraction of its depositors want to withdraw their funds on any given day. But what would happen if, for some reason, all or at least a large fraction of its depositors tried to withdraw their funds during a short period of time, such as over a couple of days?

If a significant share of its depositors demanded their money back at the same time, the bank wouldn't be able to raise enough cash to meet those demands. The reason for this cash shortfall is that banks convert most of their depositors' funds into loans made to borrowers. That's how banks earn revenue—by charging interest on loans.

Bank loans, however, are illiquid: they can't easily be converted into cash on short notice. To see why, imagine that First Street Bank has lent $100,000 to Drive-a-Peach Used Cars, a local dealership. To raise cash to meet demands for withdrawals, First Street Bank can sell its loan to Drive-a-Peach to someone else—another bank or an individual investor. But if First Street Bank tries to sell the loan quickly, potential buyers will be wary: they will suspect that First Street Bank wants to sell the loan because there is something wrong and the loan might not be repaid. As a result, First Street Bank can sell the loan quickly only by offering it for sale at a deep discount—say, a discount of 40%, for a sale price of $60,000.

The upshot is that if a significant number of First Street Bank's depositors suddenly decided to withdraw their funds, the bank's efforts to raise the necessary cash quickly would force it to sell off its assets very cheaply. Inevitably, this leads to a *bank failure:* the bank would be unable to pay off its depositors in full.

What might start this whole process? That is, what might lead First Street Bank's depositors to rush to pull their money out? A plausible answer is a spreading rumor that the bank is in financial trouble. Even if depositors aren't sure the rumor is true, they are likely to play it safe and get their money out while they still can. And it gets worse: a depositor who simply thinks that *other* depositors are going to panic and try to get their money out will realize that this could "break the bank." So this depositor joins the rush. In other words, fear about a bank's

reserve ratio the fraction of bank deposits that a bank holds as reserves. In the United States, the minimum required reserve ratio is set by the Federal Reserve.

bank run a phenomenon in which many of a bank's depositors try to withdraw their funds because of fears of a bank failure.

deposit insurance a guarantee that a bank's depositors will be paid even if the bank can't come up with the funds, up to a maximum amount per account.

financial condition can be a self-fulfilling prophecy: depositors who believe that other depositors will rush to the exit will rush to the exit themselves.

A **bank run,** then, is a phenomenon in which many of a bank's depositors try to withdraw their funds due to fears of a bank failure. Moreover, bank runs aren't bad only for the bank in question and its depositors. Historically, they have often proved contagious, with a run on one bank leading to a loss of faith in other banks, causing additional bank runs.

The upcoming Economics in Action describes an actual case of a bank run, the rush of depositors out of Silicon Valley Bank in March 2023. Although this bank run shocked investors and led to runs on several other banks, such events are rare in the modern world. Why? Because the United States and most other modern governments established a system of bank regulations that protect depositors and prevent most bank runs.

Bank Regulation

Should you worry about losing money in the United States due to a bank run? As long as it's a conventional bank and your account is worth less than $250,000, the answer is no. After the banking crises of the 1930s, the United States and most other countries put into place a system designed to protect depositors and the economy as a whole against bank runs. This system has four main features: *deposit insurance, capital requirements, reserve requirements,* and, in addition, banks have access to the *discount window,* a source of cash when it's needed.

1. Deposit Insurance Almost all banks in the United States advertise themselves as a "member of the FDIC"—the Federal Deposit Insurance Corporation. The FDIC provides **deposit insurance,** a guarantee that depositors will be paid from FDIC funds, even if the bank is unable to satisfy withdrawals, up to a maximum amount per account. The FDIC currently guarantees the first $250,000 per depositor, per insured bank.

It is worth noting that deposit insurance doesn't just protect depositors if a bank fails. It also greatly reduces the potential for bank failures from bank runs by limiting the main reason for bank runs: since most depositors know their funds are safe even if a bank should fail, they have no incentive to rush to withdraw their accounts because of a rumor that the bank is in trouble. We'll explain in the Economics in Action why Silicon Valley Bank was an exception.

2. Capital Requirements Although deposit insurance protects the banking system against bank runs, it creates a well-known incentive problem. Because depositors are protected from loss, they have no incentive to monitor their bank's financial health, allowing risky behavior by the bank to go undetected. At the same time, the owners of banks have an incentive to engage in overly risky investment behavior, such as making questionable loans at high interest rates. That's because if all goes well, the owners profit. But if things go badly, the government covers the losses through federal deposit insurance.

To reduce the incentive for excessive risk taking, regulators require that bank owners hold substantially more assets than the value of bank deposits. That way, the bank still has assets larger than its deposits even if some of its loans go bad, and losses will accrue against the bank's assets, not the government. The excess of a bank's assets over its bank deposits and other liabilities is called the *bank's capital.* Bank capital is sometimes referred to as the bank's *net worth* or *owner's equity.* For example, First Street Bank has capital of $300,000, equal to ($1,200,000 + $100,000) − $1,000,000. This is equivalent to $300,000/($1,200,000 + $100,000) = 23% of the total value of its assets. In practice, banks' capital is required to equal at least 7% of the value of their assets.

3. Reserve Requirements Another regulation used to reduce the risk of bank runs is **reserve requirements,** rules set by the Federal Reserve that specify the minimum reserve ratio for banks. For example, in the United States, the minimum reserve ratio for checkable bank deposits is 10%.

4. The Discount Window One final protection against bank runs is the fact that the Federal Reserve, which we discuss more thoroughly later in this chapter, stands ready to lend money to banks in trouble, an arrangement known as the **discount window.** The ability to borrow money means a bank can avoid being forced to sell its assets at fire-sale prices in order to satisfy the demands of a sudden rush of depositors demanding cash. Instead, it can turn to the Fed and borrow the funds it needs to pay off depositors.

reserve requirements rules of the Federal Reserve that set the minimum reserve ratio for banks. For checkable bank deposits in the United States, the minimum reserve ratio is set at 10%.

discount window a protection against bank runs in which the Federal Reserve stands ready to lend money to banks in trouble.

Limits to Regulation's Reach: Shadow Banking For the most part, the modern U.S. banking system is well-protected against old-fashioned bank runs. Unfortunately, as many investors learned to their horror in 2008, although old-fashioned bank runs may have become rare, new-fashioned bank runs—which look very different, but have many of the same effects—can still happen.

How is that possible? The answer lies in a variety of financial arrangements that aren't exactly banking in the traditional sense, but serve more or less the same purposes as conventional banking, and can pose serious risks. These arrangements, referred to as *shadow banking,* are undertaken by nondepository financial firms, including investment banks, insurance companies, hedge fund companies, and money market fund companies. Because they don't accept deposits, firms in the shadow banking sector aren't fully covered by the protections or regulations that have made conventional, depository banking so safe. We'll say more about shadow banking later in the chapter.

ECONOMICS >> *in Action*
The Fall of Silicon Valley Bank

The biggest bank run in history, at least in dollar terms, happened on March 9, 2023. Over the course of that day, nervous depositors pulled $42 billion out of Silicon Valley Bank, a medium-sized institution (as compared with giants such as Citigroup or Bank of America) that catered to venture capitalists and the technology industry. Unlike old-fashioned bank runs, there were no scenes of panicky clients banging on the bank's doors; all the action took place over the internet. Nonetheless, the Federal Deposit Insurance Corporation (FDIC) closed the bank the next morning.

What happened to Silicon Valley Bank? Somewhat surprisingly, it hadn't made a lot of risky loans. Instead, it placed much of its depositors' money in long-term U.S. government bonds, which basically pose no risk of default. However, interest rates had risen sharply since the bank bought many of those bonds, which meant that the market value of the bonds had fallen. (If you spent $1 million buying 10-year bonds that offered an interest rate of 2%, but a year later the going rate on new 10-year bonds is 4%, people won't be willing to pay $1 million for your old bonds.)

Even so, it's still not clear whether the bank would have failed without the bank run. The interest it was earning on its bonds was still more than the interest it was paying depositors, so if it could have simply held on to the

Silicon Valley Bank depositors rushed to pull their money out of the troubled bank in March 2023.

Justin Sullivan/Getty Images

bonds it might have been okay. But to come up with cash to pay off depositors, it had to sell bonds at a loss and quickly went bust.

But why were depositors rushing to get their money out? Aren't deposits insured? Yes, but only up to $250,000. And Silicon Valley Bank catered to businesses with accounts much bigger than that limit. For example, the cryptocurrency company Circle had an account at Silicon Valley worth $3.3 *billion*. Because most of its customers had huge accounts, an amazing 93.9% of Silicon Valley Bank's deposits weren't covered by federal insurance.

As it turned out, even these uninsured deposits ended up being protected. Legally, the FDIC has the right to make depositors whole even if their deposits exceed $250,000, if it determines that failing to do so would threaten to undermine the banking system. It invoked this "systemic risk exception" to fully compensate all of Silicon Valley Bank's depositors, although the bank's stockholders lost all their money and its executives lost their jobs.

>> Check Your Understanding 14-2
Solutions appear at back of book.

1. Suppose you are a depositor at First Street Bank. You hear a rumor that the bank has suffered serious losses on its loans. Every depositor knows that the rumor isn't true, but each thinks that most other depositors believe the rumor. Why, in the absence of deposit insurance, could this lead to a bank run? How does deposit insurance change the situation?

2. A con artist has a great idea: they'll open a bank without investing any capital and lend all the deposits at high interest rates to real estate developers. If the real estate market booms, the loans will be repaid and they'll make high profits. If the real estate market goes bust, the loans won't be repaid and the bank will fail—but they will not lose any of their own wealth. How would modern bank regulation frustrate this scheme?

‖ Determining the Money Supply

Without banks, there would be no checkable deposits, so the quantity of currency in circulation would equal the money supply. In that case, the money supply would be solely determined by whoever controls government minting and printing presses. But banks do exist, and through their creation of checkable bank deposits they affect the money supply in two ways.

1. Banks reduce the money supply by removing some currency from circulation: dollar bills that are sitting in bank vaults, as opposed to sitting in people's wallets, aren't part of the money supply.

2. Much more importantly, banks increase the money supply by making loans, the total value of which is much larger than their reserves. As a result, they make the money supply larger than just the value of currency in circulation.

Our next topic is how banks create money and what determines the amount of money they create.

How Banks Create Money

To see how banks create money, let's examine what happens when someone decides to deposit currency in a bank. Consider the example of Silas, a miser, who keeps a shoebox full of cash under his bed. Suppose Silas realizes that it would be safer, as well as more convenient, to deposit that cash in the bank and to use his debit card when shopping. Assume that he deposits $1,000 into a checkable account at First Street Bank. What effect will Silas's actions have on the money supply?

FIGURE 4   Effect on the Money Supply of Turning Cash into a Checkable Deposit at First Street Bank

(a) Initial Effect Before Bank Makes a New Loan

Assets		Liabilities	
Loans	No change	Checkable deposits	+$1,000
Reserves	+$1,000		

(b) Effect When Bank Makes a New Loan

Assets		Liabilities
Loans	+$900	No change
Reserves	−$900	

When Silas deposits $1,000 (which had been stashed under his bed) into a checkable bank account, there is initially no effect on the money supply: currency in circulation falls by $1,000, but checkable bank deposits rise by $1,000. The corresponding entries on the bank's T-account, depicted in panel (a), show deposits initially rising by $1,000 and the bank's reserves initially rising by $1,000. In the second stage, depicted in panel (b), the bank holds 10% of Silas's deposit ($100) as reserves and lends out the rest ($900) to Maya. As a result, its reserves fall by $900 and its loans increase by $900. Its liabilities, including Silas's $1,000 deposit, are unchanged. The money supply, the sum of checkable bank deposits and currency in circulation, has now increased by $900—the $900 now held by Maya.

Panel (a) of Figure 4 shows the initial effect of his deposit. First Street Bank credits Silas with $1,000 in his account, so the economy's checkable bank deposits rise by $1,000. Meanwhile, Silas's cash goes into the vault, raising First Street's reserves by $1,000 as well.

This initial transaction has no effect on the money supply. Currency in circulation, part of the money supply, falls by $1,000. Checkable bank deposits, also part of the money supply, rise by the same amount.

But this is not the end of the story, because First Street Bank can now lend out part of Silas's deposit. Assume that it holds 10% of Silas's deposit—$100—in reserves and lends the rest out in cash to Silas's neighbor, Maya. The effect of this second stage is shown in panel (b). First Street's deposits remain unchanged, and so does the value of its assets. But the composition of its assets changes: by making the loan, it reduces its reserves by $900, so that they are only $100 larger than they were before Silas made his deposit. In the place of the $900 reduction in reserves, the bank has acquired an IOU, its $900 cash loan to Maya.

So by putting $900 of Silas's cash back into circulation by lending it to Maya, First Street Bank has, in fact, increased the money supply. That is, the sum of currency in circulation and checkable bank deposits has risen by $900 compared to what it had been when Silas's cash was still under his bed. Although Silas is still the owner of $1,000, now in the form of a checkable deposit, Maya has the use of $900 in cash from her borrowings.

And this may not be the end of the story. Suppose that Maya uses her cash to buy a television from Acme Merchandise. What does Anne Acme, the store's owner, do with the cash? If she holds on to it, the money supply doesn't increase any further. But suppose she deposits the $900 into a checkable bank deposit—say, at Second Street Bank. Second Street Bank, in turn, will keep only part of that deposit in reserves, lending out the rest, creating still more money.

Assume that Second Street Bank, like First Street Bank, keeps 10% of any bank deposit in reserves and lends out the rest. Then it will keep $90 in reserves and lend

TABLE 1   How Banks Create Money

	Currency in circulation	Checkable bank deposits	Money supply
First stage Silas keeps his cash under his bed.	$1,000	$0	$1,000
Second stage Silas deposits cash in First Street Bank, which lends out $900 to Maya, who then pays it to Anne Acme.	900	1,000	1,900
Third stage Anne Acme deposits $900 in Second Street Bank, which lends out $810 to another borrower.	810	1,900	2,710

excess reserves a bank's reserves over and above the reserves required by law or regulation.

out $810 of Anne's deposit to another borrower, further increasing the money supply.

Table 1 shows the process of money creation we have described so far. To simplify the table we will assume that, at first, the money supply consists only of Silas's $1,000. After he deposits the cash into a checkable bank deposit and the bank makes a loan, the money supply rises to $1,900. After the second deposit and the second loan, the money supply rises to $2,710. And the process will, of course, continue from there. (Although we have considered the case in which Silas places his cash in a checkable bank deposit, the results would be the same if he put it into any type of near-money.)

This process of money creation may sound familiar. In Chapter 11, we described the *multiplier process:* an initial increase in real GDP leads to a rise in consumer spending, which leads to a further rise in real GDP, which leads to a further rise in consumer spending, and so on. What we have here is another kind of multiplier—the *money multiplier.* We'll now see what determines the size of this multiplier.

Reserves, Bank Deposits, and the Money Multiplier

In tracing out the effect of Silas's deposit in Table 1, we assumed that the funds a bank lends out always end up being deposited either in the same bank or in another bank—so funds disbursed as loans come back to the banking system, even if not to the lending bank itself.

In reality, some of these loaned funds may be held by borrowers in their wallets and not deposited in a bank, meaning that some of the loaned amount "leaks" out of the banking system. Such leaks reduce the size of the money multiplier, just as leaks of real income into savings reduce the size of the real GDP multiplier. (Bear in mind, however, that the leak here comes from the fact that borrowers keep some of their funds in currency, rather than the fact that consumers save some of their income.)

But let's set that complication aside for a moment and consider how the money supply is determined in a checkable-deposits-only monetary system, where funds are always deposited in bank accounts and none are held in wallets as currency. That is, in our checkable-deposits-only monetary system, any and all funds borrowed from a bank are immediately deposited into a checkable bank account. We'll assume that banks are required to satisfy a minimum reserve ratio of 10% and that every bank lends out all of its **excess reserves,** reserves over and above the amount needed to satisfy the minimum reserve ratio.

Now suppose that for some reason a bank suddenly finds itself with $1,000 in excess reserves. What happens? The answer is that the bank will lend out that $1,000, which will end up as a checkable bank deposit somewhere in the banking system, launching a money multiplier process very similar to the process shown in Table 1.

In the first stage, the bank lends out its excess reserves of $1,000, which becomes a checkable bank deposit somewhere. The bank that receives the $1,000 deposit keeps 10%, or $100, as reserves and lends out the remaining 90%, or $900, which again becomes a checkable bank deposit somewhere. The bank receiving this $900 deposit again keeps 10%, which is $90, as reserves and lends out the remaining $810. The bank receiving this $810 keeps $81 in reserves and lends out the remaining $729, and so on. As a result of this process, the total increase in checkable bank deposits is equal to a sum that looks like:

$$\$1,000 + \$900 + \$810 + \$729 + \cdots$$

"There's money in there that could be used for other purposes."

We'll use the symbol *rr* for the reserve ratio. More generally, the total increase in checkable bank deposits that is generated when a bank lends out $1,000 in excess reserves is:

(1) Increase in checkable bank deposits from $1,000 in excess reserves =
$$\$1,000 + (\$1,000 \times (1 - rr)) + (\$1,000 \times (1 - rr)^2) + (\$1,000 \times (1 - rr)^3) + \cdots$$

As we saw in Chapter 11, an infinite series of this form can be simplified to:

(2) Increase in checkable bank deposits from $1,000 in excess reserves =
$1,000/*rr*

Given a reserve ratio of 10%, or 0.1, a $1,000 increase in excess reserves will increase the total value of checkable bank deposits by $1,000/0.1 = $10,000. In fact, in a checkable-deposits-only monetary system, the total value of checkable bank deposits will be equal to the value of bank reserves divided by the reserve ratio. Or to put it a different way, if the reserve ratio is 10%, each $1 of reserves held by a bank supports $1/*rr* = $1/0.1 = $10 of checkable bank deposits.

The Money Multiplier in Reality

In reality, the determination of the money supply is more complicated than our simple model suggests because it depends not only on the ratio of reserves to bank deposits but also on the fraction of the money supply that individuals choose to hold in the form of currency. In fact, we already saw this in our example of Silas depositing the cash under his bed: when he chose to hold a checkable bank deposit instead of currency, he set in motion an increase in the money supply.

To define the money multiplier in practice, it's important to recognize that the Federal Reserve controls the *sum* of bank reserves and currency in circulation, called the *monetary base,* but it does not control the allocation of that sum between bank reserves and currency in circulation. Consider Silas and his deposit one more time: by taking the cash from under his bed and depositing it in a bank, he reduced the quantity of currency in circulation but increased bank reserves by an equal amount—leaving the *monetary base,* on net, unchanged. The **monetary base,** which is the quantity the monetary authorities control, is the sum of currency in circulation and reserves held by banks.

The monetary base is different from the money supply in two ways.

1. Bank reserves, which are part of the monetary base, aren't considered part of the money supply. A $1 bill in someone's wallet is considered money because it's available for an individual to spend, but a $1 bill held as bank reserves in a bank vault or deposited at the Federal Reserve isn't considered part of the money supply because it's not available for spending.

2. Checkable and other liquid deposits, which are part of the money supply because they are available for spending, aren't part of the monetary base.

Figure 5 illustrates the two concepts. The circle on the left represents the monetary base, consisting of bank reserves plus currency in circulation. The circle on the right represents the money supply, consisting mainly of currency in circulation plus checkable or other liquid bank deposits. As the figure indicates, currency in circulation is part of both the monetary base and the money supply. But bank reserves aren't part of the money supply, and checkable or other liquid bank deposits aren't part of the monetary base. In practice, most of the monetary base actually consists of currency in circulation, which also makes up approximately 10% of the money supply.

Now we can formally define the **money multiplier:** it's the ratio of the money supply to the monetary base. Before the financial crisis of 2008, it was about 1.6, as calculated from official Federal Reserve statistics. After the crisis, it fell to about 0.7. Even before the crisis it was a lot smaller than 1/0.1 = 10, which would

monetary base the sum of currency in circulation and bank reserves.

money multiplier the ratio of the money supply to the monetary base.

FIGURE 5 The Monetary Base and the Money Supply

The monetary base is equal to bank reserves plus currency in circulation. It is different from the money supply, consisting mainly of checkable or other liquid bank deposits plus currency in circulation. Each dollar of bank reserves backs several dollars of bank deposits. As a result, in normal economic times, the money supply is larger than the monetary base, making the circle at right larger than the circle on the left. However, in extraordinary economic times, as in the aftermath of the 2008 financial crisis, the monetary base grew, overtaking the money supply, making the circle at right smaller than the circle on the left.

The collapse of Lehman Brothers and the ensuing financial crisis prompted the Federal Reserve to dramatically increase the monetary base in order to stabilize the economy.

be the money multiplier in a checkable-deposits-only system with a reserve ratio of 10% (the minimum required ratio for most checkable deposits in the United States).

The reason the actual money multiplier has been smaller than 10 is that people hold significant amounts of cash, and a dollar of currency in circulation, unlike a dollar in reserves, doesn't support multiple dollars of the money supply. In fact, before the crisis currency in circulation accounted for more than 90% of the monetary base.

At the beginning of 2009, currency in circulation had dropped to only 40% of the monetary base. In 2020, before the pandemic, the percentage had only increased slightly, to 52%. What happened, basically, is that the Federal Reserve dramatically expanded the monetary base in response to the financial crisis. The Fed undertook this action in an effort to stabilize the economy after Lehman Brothers, a key financial institution, failed in September 2008.

However, banks saw few opportunities for safe, profitable lending at the time. So rather than lending out the increase in the monetary base, they parked it at the Federal Reserve in the form of deposits that counted as part of the monetary base. As a result, currency in circulation no longer dominated the monetary base, as the surge in deposits at the Fed made the monetary base larger than M1. As a result, the money multiplier, measured as the ratio of currency and checkable deposits to the monetary base, fell to less than 1 as banks held much more than the required 10% in reserves at the Fed. While not as dramatic as the Great Recession, during the Covid-19 pandemic the Federal Reserve again took dramatic action by expanding the monetary base. Currency in circulation fell to 35% of the monetary base and the money multiplier was once again under 1. By March of 2023, the multiplier had increased to 1.3 but currency in circulation was still well below the values seen before the Great Recession, 40% of the monetary base.

ECONOMICS >> *in Action*
Multiplying Money Down

In our hypothetical example illustrating how banks create money, we described Silas the miser taking the currency from under his bed and turning it into a checkable bank deposit. This led to an increase in the money supply as banks engaged in successive waves of lending backed by Silas's funds. It follows that if something happened to make Silas revert to old habits, taking his money out of the bank and putting it back under his bed, the result would be less lending and, ultimately, a decline in the money supply. That's exactly what happened as a result of the bank runs of the 1930s.

Table 2 shows what happened between 1929 and 1933, as bank failures shook the public's confidence in the banking system:

- The second column shows the public's holdings of currency. This increased sharply, as many Americans decided that money under the bed was safer than money in the bank after all.
- The third column shows the value of checkable bank deposits. This fell sharply, through the multiplier process, when individuals pulled their cash out of banks. Loans also fell because banks that survived the waves of bank runs increased their excess reserves, just in case another wave began.
- The fourth column shows the value of M1, the first of the monetary aggregates we described earlier. It fell sharply because the total reduction in checkable or near-checkable bank deposits was much larger than the increase in currency in circulation.

TABLE 2 The Effects of Bank Runs, 1929–1933

	Currency in circulation	Checkable bank deposits	M1
	(billions of dollars)		
1929	$3.90	$22.74	$26.64
1933	5.09	14.82	19.91
Percent change	+31%	−35%	+25%

Data from: U.S. Census Bureau (1975), *Historical Statistics of the United States.*

>> Check Your Understanding 14-3

Solutions appear at back of book.

1. Assume that total reserves are equal to $200 and total checkable bank deposits are equal to $1,000. Also assume that the public does not hold any currency. Now suppose that the required reserve ratio falls from 20% to 10%. Trace out how this leads to an expansion in bank deposits.
2. Take the example of Silas depositing his $1,000 in cash into First Street Bank and assume that the required reserve ratio is 10%. But now assume that each time someone receives a bank loan, they keep half the loan in cash. Explain the resulting expansion in the money supply.

>> Quick Review

- Banks create money when they lend out **excess reserves,** generating a multiplier effect on the money supply.
- In a checkable-deposits-only system, $1 of bank reserves supports $1/*rr* checkable deposits. So the money supply would be equal to bank reserves divided by the reserve ratio. In reality, however, the public holds some funds as cash rather than in checkable deposits.
- The Fed controls the **monetary base,** equal to bank reserves plus currency in circulation. The **money multiplier** is equal to the money supply divided by the monetary base. It is smaller than $1/*rr* because people hold some funds as cash.

The Federal Reserve System

Who's in charge of ensuring that banks maintain enough reserves? Who decides how large the monetary base will be? The answer, in the United States, is an institution known as the Federal Reserve, or the Fed. The Federal Reserve is a **central bank**—an institution that oversees and regulates the banking system and controls the monetary base.

Other central banks include the Bank of England, the People's Bank of China, the Bank of Japan, and the European Central Bank, or ECB. The ECB acts as a common central bank for 19 European countries: Austria, Belgium, Cyprus, Estonia, Finland, France, Germany, Greece, Ireland, Italy, Latvia, Lithuania, Luxembourg, Malta, the Netherlands, Portugal, Slovakia, Slovenia, and Spain. The world's oldest central bank is Sweden's Sveriges Riksbank, which awards the Nobel Prize in economics.

The Structure of the Fed

The legal status of the Fed, which was created in 1913, is unusual: it is not exactly part of the U.S. government, but it is not really a private institution either. Strictly speaking, the Federal Reserve system consists of two parts: the Board of Governors and the 12 regional Federal Reserve Banks.

central bank an institution that oversees and regulates the banking system and controls the monetary base.

The Board of Governors, which oversees the entire system from its offices in Washington, D.C., is constituted like a government agency: its seven members are appointed by the president and must be approved by the Senate. However, they are appointed for 14-year terms, to insulate them from political pressure in their conduct of monetary policy. (Why this is a potential problem will become clear in the next chapter, when we discuss inflation.)

Although the chair is appointed more frequently—every four years—chairs are often reappointed and serve much longer terms. For example, William McChesney Martin was chair of the Fed from 1951 until 1970. Alan Greenspan, appointed in 1987, served as the Fed's chair until 2006. Ben Bernanke, Greenspan's successor, served until 2014. Janet Yellen, who followed Bernanke, became the first chair to not be reappointed to a second term. Jerome Powell was her successor at the Fed.

The 12 Federal Reserve Banks each serve a region of the country, providing various banking and supervisory services. One of their jobs, for example, is to audit the books of private-sector banks to ensure their financial health. Each regional bank is run by a board of directors chosen from the local banking and business community. The Federal Reserve Bank of New York plays a special role: it carries out *open-market operations,* usually the main tool of monetary policy. Figure 6 shows the 12 Federal Reserve districts and the city in which each regional Federal Reserve Bank is located.

Decisions about monetary policy are made by the Federal Open Market Committee, which consists of the Board of Governors plus five of the regional bank presidents. The president of the Federal Reserve Bank of New York is always on the committee, and the other four seats rotate among the 11 other regional bank presidents. The chair of the Board of Governors normally also serves as the chair of the Open Market Committee.

The effect of this complex structure is to create an institution that is ultimately accountable to the voting public because the Board of Governors is chosen by the president and confirmed by the Senate, all of whom are themselves elected officials. But the long terms served by board members, as well as the indirectness of their appointment process, largely insulate them from short-term political pressures.

What the Fed Does: Reserve Requirements and the Discount Rate

The Fed has three main policy tools at its disposal: *reserve requirements,* the *discount rate,* and, most importantly, *open-market operations.*

FIGURE 6 The Federal Reserve System

The Federal Reserve System consists of the Board of Governors in Washington, D.C., plus 12 regional Federal Reserve Banks. This map shows each of the 12 Federal Reserve districts.

Data from: Board of Governors of the Federal Reserve System.

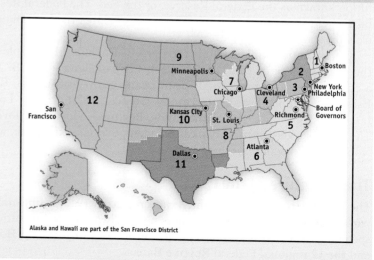

Alaska and Hawaii are part of the San Francisco District

In our discussion of bank runs, we noted that the Fed sets a minimum reserve ratio requirement, currently equal to 10% for checkable bank deposits. Banks that fail to maintain at least the required reserve ratio on average over a two-week period face penalties.

What does a bank do if it looks as if it has insufficient reserves to meet the Fed's reserve requirement? Normally, it borrows additional reserves from other banks via the **federal funds market,** a financial market that allows banks that fall short of the reserve requirement to borrow reserves (usually just overnight) from banks that are holding excess reserves. The interest rate in this market is determined by supply and demand—but the supply and demand for bank reserves are both strongly affected by Federal Reserve actions. As we'll see in the next chapter, the **federal funds rate,** the interest rate at which funds are borrowed and lent in the federal funds market, plays a key role in modern monetary policy.

Alternatively, banks in need of reserves can borrow from the Fed itself via the *discount window*. The **discount rate** is the rate of interest the Fed charges on those loans. Normally, the discount rate is set 1 percentage point above the federal funds rate in order to discourage banks from turning to the Fed when they are in need of reserves. Beginning in the fall of 2007, however, the Fed reduced the spread between the federal funds rate and the discount rate as part of its response to an ongoing financial crisis, described in the upcoming Economics in Action. As a result, by the spring of 2008 the discount rate was only 0.25 percentage points above the federal funds rate. And in early 2020, just before the coronavirus crisis struck, the discount rate was still only 0.60 percentage points above the federal funds rate.

In order to alter the money supply, the Fed can change reserve requirements, the discount rate, or both. If the Fed reduces reserve requirements, banks will normally lend a larger percentage of their deposits, leading to more loans and an increase in the money supply via the money multiplier. Alternatively, if the Fed increases reserve requirements, banks are forced to reduce their lending, leading to a fall in the money supply via the money multiplier.

If the Fed reduces the spread between the discount rate and the federal funds rate, the cost to banks of being short of reserves falls. Banks respond by increasing their lending, and the money supply increases via the money multiplier. If the Fed increases the spread between the discount rate and the federal funds rate, bank lending falls—and so will the money supply via the money multiplier.

Under current practice, however, the Fed doesn't use changes in reserve requirements to actively manage the money supply. The last significant change in reserve requirements was in 1992. During the Great Recession, the Federal Reserve underwent a significant shift in its policy regarding bank reserves. Departing from setting the reserve requirement, the Fed adopted a new strategy: offering interest on reserve balances (IORB), banks receive an interest rate on the funds they hold in their reserve account with the Federal Reserve. This change introduced a voluntary mechanism as banks adjust their reserve holdings in response to alterations in the IORB set by the Fed.

The implementation of interest on reserve balances (IORB) assumes a critical role in the Fed's toolkit for regulating bank lending. The IORB establishes a minimum interest rate, or floor, below which banks are reluctant to lend. Suppose the Fed sets the IORB at 4%. Financial institutions would not be inclined to offer loans to customers at rates lower than this threshold. Should the Fed desire to curtail lending it can raise the IORB and banks would respond by holding more funds as reserves. If the Fed increases the IORB to 6%, the bank would now only offer loans to customers at interest rates above 6%. If their customers are unwilling to borrow at higher rates, the bank would simply deposit these funds in their reserve account and enjoy a 6% interest rate on those reserves.

The introduction of interest on reserve balances (IORB) marks a pivotal development in the Federal Reserve's strategy for influencing bank behavior and

federal funds market a financial market that allows banks that fall short of reserve requirements to borrow funds from banks with excess reserves.

federal funds rate the interest rate at which funds are borrowed and lent in the federal funds market.

discount rate the rate of interest the Federal Reserve charges on loans to banks that fall short of reserve requirements.

open-market operation a
purchase or sale of U.S. Treasury
bills by the Federal Reserve,
normally through a transaction
with a commercial bank.

shaping lending practices. In addition to changing interest on reserve balances, monetary policy is also conducted through the Fed's third policy tool: open-market operations.

Open-Market Operations and Reverse Repo Operations

Like the banks it oversees, the Federal Reserve has assets and liabilities. The Fed's assets normally consist of holdings of debt issued by the U.S. government, mainly short-term U.S. government bonds with a maturity of less than one year, known as U.S. Treasury bills. Remember, the Fed isn't exactly part of the U.S. government, so U.S. Treasury bills held by the Fed are a liability of the government but an asset of the Fed. The Fed's liabilities consist of currency in circulation and bank reserves. Figure 7 summarizes the normal assets and liabilities of the Fed in the form of a T-account.

In an **open-market operation** the Federal Reserve buys or sells U.S. Treasury bills, normally through a transaction with *commercial banks* (banks that accept deposits and make loans) and *investment banks* (banks that create and trade assets but don't accept deposits). The Fed never buys U.S. Treasury bills directly from the federal government. There's a good reason for this: when a central bank buys government debt directly from the government, it is lending directly to the government—in effect, the central bank is printing money to finance the government's budget deficit. This has historically been a formula for disastrously high levels of inflation.

The two panels of Figure 8 show the changes in the financial position of both the Fed and commercial banks that result from open-market operations. When the Fed buys U.S. Treasury bills from a commercial bank, it pays by crediting the bank's reserve account by an amount equal to the value of the Treasury bills. This is illustrated in panel (a): the Fed buys $100 million of U.S. Treasury bills from commercial banks, which increases the monetary base by $100 million because it increases bank reserves by $100 million. When the Fed sells U.S. Treasury bills to commercial banks, it debits the banks' accounts, reducing their reserves. This is shown in panel (b), where the Fed sells $100 million of U.S. Treasury bills. Here, bank reserves and the monetary base decrease.

You might wonder where the Fed gets the funds to purchase U.S. Treasury bills from banks. The answer is that it simply creates them with a mouse click that credits the banks' accounts with extra reserves. (The Fed prints money to pay for Treasury bills only when banks want the additional reserves in the form of currency.) Remember, the modern dollar is fiat money, which isn't backed by anything. So the Fed can create additional monetary base at its own discretion.

The change in bank reserves caused by an open-market operation doesn't directly affect the money supply. Instead, it starts the money multiplier in motion. After the $100 million increase in reserves shown in panel (a) of Figure 8, commercial banks will (under normal circumstances) lend out all of their additional reserves, immediately increasing the money supply by $100 million. Some of those loans would be deposited back into the banking system, increasing reserves again and permitting a further round of loans, and so on, leading to a rise in the money

FIGURE 7 The Federal Reserve's Assets and Liabilities

The Federal Reserve holds its assets mostly in short-term government bonds called U.S. Treasury bills. Its liabilities are the monetary base—currency in circulation plus bank reserves.

Assets	Liabilities
Government debt (Treasury bills)	Monetary base (currency in circulation + bank reserves)

FIGURE 8 Open-Market Operations by the Federal Reserve

(a) An Open-Market Purchase of $100 Million

	Assets		Liabilities	
Federal Reserve	Treasury bills	+$100 million	Monetary base	+$100 million

	Assets		Liabilities
Commercial banks	Treasury bills	−$100 million	No change
	Reserves	+$100 million	

(b) An Open-Market Sale of $100 Million

	Assets		Liabilities	
Federal Reserve	Treasury bills	−$100 million	Monetary base	−$100 million

	Assets		Liabilities
Commercial banks	Treasury bills	+$100 million	No change
	Reserves	−$100 million	

In panel (a), the Federal Reserve increases the monetary base by purchasing U.S. Treasury bills from private commercial banks in an open-market operation. Here, a $100 million purchase of U.S. Treasury bills by the Federal Reserve is paid for by a $100 million addition to private bank reserves, generating a $100 million increase in the monetary base. This will ultimately lead to an increase in the money supply via the money multiplier as banks lend out some of these new reserves. In panel (b), the Federal Reserve reduces the monetary base by selling U.S. Treasury bills to private commercial banks in an open-market operation. Here, a $100 million sale of U.S. Treasury bills leads to a $100 million reduction in private bank reserves, resulting in a $100 million decrease in the monetary base. This will ultimately lead to a fall in the money supply via the money multiplier as banks reduce their loans in response to a fall in their reserves.

supply. An open-market sale has the reverse effect: bank reserves fall, requiring banks to reduce their loans, leading to a fall in the money supply.

While many banks are receive interest on reserve balances, there are many financial institutions that do not have the ability to deposit funds in reserve accounts (what are these institutions...) with the Fed. While the interest rate paid on reserve balances places a floor on the overnight federal funds rates for institutions with access to the Federal Reserve system, it is possible institutions outside the Federal Reserve system would lend at rates below the target federal funds rate. For these institutions, the Federal Reserve created the Overnight Reverse Repurchase Agreement Facility (ON RRP). The ON RRP enables financial institutions, without access to reserve accounts, the ability to deposit funds overnight with the Fed and in exchange will receive a short-term U.S. treasury bill as collateral. The financial institution and the Fed agree to reverse the transaction the following morning. Meanwhile, the financial institution earns an interest rate nearly the same as what other banks receive on reserve balances.

It is fairly straightforward to see why the ON RRP facility is necessary. Suppose there is a financial institution outside the Federal Reserve system holding significant cash, above their reserve requirement. This could result in these financial institutions lending at rates below the federal funds rates, effectively undermining the Fed's monetary policy objectives.

Although economists often say, loosely, that the Fed controls the money supply—checkable deposits plus currency in circulation, that statement is not completely accurate. *The Fed literally only controls the monetary base—bank reserves plus currency in circulation. But by increasing or reducing the monetary base, the Fed can exert a powerful influence on both the money supply and interest rates.* This influence is the basis of monetary policy, the subject of the next chapter.

The Fed owns a lot of assets—Treasury bills—that it bought from commercial banks in exchange for additions to the monetary base in the form of credits to banks' reserve accounts. These assets pay interest. (It does pay a modest interest rate on bank reserves that exceed the legal minimum.) Yet the Fed's liabilities consist mainly of the monetary base, liabilities on which the Fed normally *doesn't* pay interest. So the Fed is, in effect, an institution that has the privilege of borrowing funds at a zero interest rate and lending them out at a positive interest rate. That sounds like a pretty profitable business. And the U.S. taxpayers get the profits.

The Fed keeps some of the interest it receives to finance its operations but turns most of it over to the U.S. Treasury. For example, in 2022 the total income of the Federal Reserve system was $58.8 billion, almost all in the form of interest on its assets, while it sent slightly more, $54.9 billion, in remittances to the Treasury. (The Fed was able to pay more than its income, and also cover its operating expenses, because it was selling off some of the assets it had acquired in its response to the financial crisis.)

Let's consider our opening story again and the impact of those forged dollars printed in Peru. When, say, a fake $20 bill enters circulation, it has the same economic effect as a real $20 bill printed by the U.S. government. That is, as long as nobody catches the forgery, the fake bill serves, for all practical purposes, as part of the monetary base.

Meanwhile, the Fed decides on the size of the monetary base based on economic considerations—in particular, the Fed normally doesn't let the monetary base get too large because that can cause higher inflation. So every fake $20 bill that enters circulation means that the Fed prints one less real $20 bill. When the Fed prints a $20 bill legally, however, it gets Treasury bills in return—and the interest on those bills helps pay U.S. government expenses. So a counterfeit $20 bill reduces the amount of Treasury bills the Fed can acquire and thereby reduces the interest payments going to the Fed and the U.S. Treasury. Taxpayers, then, bear the real cost of counterfeiting.

The European Central Bank

We've seen that the Fed is only one of a number of central banks around the world, and it's much younger than Sweden's Sveriges Riksbank and Britain's Bank of England. In general, other central banks operate in much the same way as the Fed. That's especially true of the only other central bank that rivals the Fed in terms of importance to the world economy: the European Central Bank.

The European Central Bank (ECB) was created in January 1999 when 11 European nations abandoned their national currencies, adopted the euro as their common currency, and placed their joint monetary policy in the ECB's hands. More countries have joined since then, with Lithuania becoming the nineteenth European nation to adopt the euro in 2015. The ECB instantly became an extremely important institution: although no single European nation has an economy anywhere near as large as that of the United States, the combined economies of the eurozone, the group of countries that have adopted the euro as their currency, are roughly as big as the U.S. economy. As a result, the ECB and the Fed are the two giants of the monetary world.

Like the Fed, the ECB has a special status: it's not a private institution, but it's not exactly a government agency either. In fact, it can't be a government agency because there is no pan-European government! Luckily for puzzled Americans, there are strong analogies between European central banking and the Federal Reserve system.

First of all, the ECB, which is located in Frankfurt, Germany, isn't really the counterpart of the whole Federal Reserve system: it's the equivalent of the Board of Governors in Washington, D.C. The European counterparts of the regional Federal Reserve Banks are Europe's national central banks: the Bank of France, the Bank of Italy, and so on. Until 1999, each of these national banks was its country's equivalent to the Fed. For example, the Bank of France controlled the French monetary base.

Today these national banks, like regional Feds, provide various financial services to local banks and businesses and conduct open-market operations, but the making of monetary policy has moved upstream to the ECB. Still, the various European national central banks aren't small institutions: in total, they employ more than 50,000 people.

In the eurozone, each country chooses who runs its own national central bank. The ECB's Executive Board is the counterpart of the Fed's Board of Governors; its members are chosen by unanimous consent of the eurozone national governments. The counterpart of the Federal Open Market Committee is the ECB's Governing Council. Just as the Fed's Open Market Committee consists of the Board of Governors plus a rotating group of regional Fed presidents, the ECB's Governing Council consists of the Executive Board plus the heads of the national central banks.

Like the Fed, the ECB is ultimately answerable to voters, and it tries to maintain its independence from short-term political pressures.

ECONOMICS >> *in Action*
The Fed's Balance Sheet, Normal and Abnormal

Figure 7 showed a simplified version of the Fed's balance sheet. Here, liabilities consisted entirely of the monetary base and assets consisted entirely of Treasury bills. This is an oversimplification because the Fed's operations are more complicated in reality and its balance sheet contains a number of additional things. But, in normal times, Figure 7 is a reasonable approximation: the monetary base typically accounts for 90% of the Fed's liabilities, and 90% of its assets are in the form of claims on the U.S. Treasury (as in Treasury bills).

But in late 2007, it became painfully clear that we were no longer in normal times. The source of the turmoil was the bursting of a huge housing bubble, which led to massive losses for financial institutions that had made mortgage loans or held mortgage-related assets. This led to a widespread loss of confidence in the financial system.

Not only were conventional deposit-taking commercial banks in trouble, but so were nondepository financial institutions like investment banks and insurance companies, which make up the shadow banking sector. Because they carried a lot of debt, faced huge losses from the collapse of the housing bubble, and held illiquid assets, panic hit the shadow banking sector. Within hours the financial system was frozen as financial institutions experienced what were essentially bank runs.

For example, in 2008, many investors became worried about the health of Bear Stearns, a Wall Street investment bank that engaged in complex financial deals, buying and selling financial assets with borrowed funds. When confidence in Bear Stearns dried up, the firm was unable to raise the funds needed to deliver on its end of these deals and it quickly spiraled into collapse. This was followed by the collapse of another investment bank, Lehman Brothers, and set off widespread panic in financial markets.

The Fed sprang into action to contain what was becoming a meltdown across the entire financial sector. It greatly expanded its discount window—making huge loans to deposit-taking banks as well as nondepository financial institutions. This gave financial institutions the liquidity that the financial market had denied them. And as these firms took advantage of the ability to borrow cheaply from the Fed, they pledged their assets on hand as collateral—a motley collection of real estate loans, business loans, and so on.

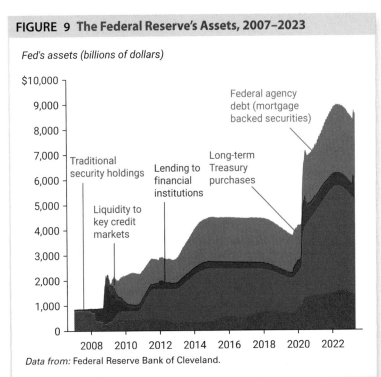

FIGURE 9 The Federal Reserve's Assets, 2007–2023

Data from: Federal Reserve Bank of Cleveland.

Examining Figure 9, we see that starting in mid-2008, the Fed sharply reduced its holdings of traditional securities like Treasury bills, as its "lending to financial institutions" skyrocketed—referring to discount window lending, but also to loans the Fed made directly to firms like Bear Stearns. "Liquidity to key credit markets" covers purchases by the Fed of assets like corporate bonds, which was necessary to keep interest rates on loans to firms from soaring. Finally, "Federal agency debt" is the debt of Fannie Mae and Freddie Mac, the government-sponsored home mortgage agencies, which the Fed was also compelled to buy in order to prevent collapse in the mortgage market.

As the crisis subsided in late 2009, the Fed didn't return to its traditional asset holdings. Instead, it shifted into long-term Treasury bills and increased its purchases of federal agency debt. When the coronavirus pandemic struck in March 2020, threatening to cause another financial meltdown, the Fed moved even further away from tradition, buying trillions more in long-term assets and even pushing some corporate bonds.

>> Check Your Understanding 14-4

Solutions appear at back of book.

1. Assume that any money lent by a bank is always deposited back in the banking system as a checkable deposit, that the reserve ratio is 10%, and that banks don't hold excess reserves. Explain the effects of a $100 million open-market purchase of U.S. Treasury bills by the Fed on the value of checkable bank deposits. What is the size of the money multiplier?

The Evolution of the U.S. Banking System

Up to this point, we have been describing the U.S. banking system and how it works. To fully understand that system, however, it is helpful to understand how and why it was created—a story that is closely intertwined with the story of how and when things went wrong. The key elements of twenty-first century U.S. banking weren't created out of thin air: efforts to change both the regulations that govern banking and the Federal Reserve system that resulted from the 2008 crisis have propelled financial reform to the forefront. This reform promises to continue reshaping the financial system well into future years.

The Crisis in U.S. Banking in the Early Twentieth Century

The creation of the Federal Reserve system in 1913 marked the beginning of the modern era of U.S. banking. From 1864 until 1913, U.S. banking was dominated by a federally regulated system of national banks. They alone were allowed to issue currency, and the currency notes they issued were printed by the federal government with uniform size and design. How much currency a national bank could issue depended on its capital. Although this system was an improvement on the earlier period in which banks issued their own notes with no uniformity and virtually no regulation, the national banking regime still suffered numerous bank failures and major financial crises—at least one and often two per decade.

The main problem afflicting the system was that the money supply was not sufficiently responsive: it was difficult to shift currency around the country to respond quickly to local economic changes. (In particular, there was often a tug-of-war between New York City banks and rural banks for adequate amounts of currency.) Rumors that a bank had insufficient currency to satisfy demands for withdrawals would quickly lead to a bank run. A bank run would then spark a contagion, setting off runs at other nearby banks, sowing widespread panic and devastation in the local economy. In response, bankers in some locations pooled their resources to create local clearinghouses that would jointly guarantee a member's liabilities in the event of a panic, and some state governments began offering deposit insurance on their banks' deposits.

Despite these recurrent crises, calls for monetary reform went unheeded until the Panic of 1907, which led to a four-year national recession, drove home just how vulnerable the system had become.

This crisis originated in institutions in New York known as *trusts*, bank-like institutions that accepted deposits but that were originally intended to manage only inheritances and estates for wealthy clients. Because these trusts were supposed to engage only in low-risk activities, they were less regulated, had lower reserve requirements, and had lower cash reserves than national banks, allowing them to pay their depositors higher returns. As a result, trusts grew rapidly: by 1907, the total assets of trusts in New York City were as large as those of national banks. Meanwhile, the trusts declined to join the New York Clearinghouse, a consortium of New York City national banks that guaranteed one another's soundness.

The Panic of 1907 began with the failure of the Knickerbocker Trust, a large New York City trust that failed when it suffered massive losses in unsuccessful stock market speculation. Quickly, other New York trusts came under pressure, and frightened depositors began queuing in long lines to withdraw their funds. The New York Clearinghouse declined to step in and lend to the trusts, and even healthy trusts came under serious assault. Within two days, a dozen major trusts had gone under. Credit markets froze, and the stock market fell dramatically as stock traders were unable to get credit to finance their trades and business confidence evaporated.

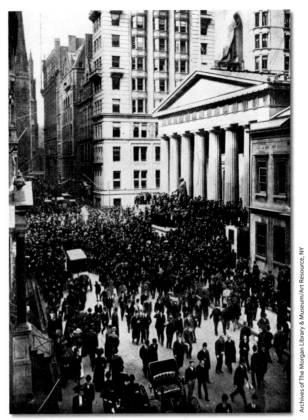

In both the Panic of 1907 and the financial crisis of 2008, large losses from risky speculation destabilized the banking system.

Fortunately, New York City's wealthiest man, the banker J. P. Morgan, quickly stepped in to stop the panic. Understanding that the crisis was spreading and would soon engulf healthy institutions, trusts and banks alike, he worked with other bankers, wealthy men such as John D. Rockefeller, and the U.S. Secretary of the Treasury to shore up the reserves of banks and trusts so they could withstand the onslaught of withdrawals. Once people were assured that they could withdraw their money, the panic ceased. Although the panic itself lasted little more than a week, it and the stock market collapse decimated the economy. A four-year recession ensued, with production falling 11% and unemployment rising from 3% to 8%.

Responding to Banking Crises: The Creation of the Federal Reserve

Concerns over the frequency of banking crises and the unprecedented role of J. P. Morgan in saving the financial system prompted the federal government to initiate banking reform. In 1913, the national banking system was eliminated and the Federal Reserve system was created as a way to compel all deposit-taking institutions to hold adequate reserves and to open their accounts to inspection by regulators. The Panic of 1907 convinced many that the time for centralized control of bank reserves had come. In addition, the Federal Reserve was given the sole right to issue currency in order to make the money supply sufficiently responsive to satisfy economic conditions around the country.

Although the new regime standardized and centralized the holding of bank reserves, it did not eliminate the potential for bank runs because banks' reserves were still less than the total value of their deposits. The potential for more bank runs became a reality during the Great Depression. Plunging commodity prices hit U.S. farmers particularly hard, precipitating a series of bank runs in 1930, 1931, and 1933, each of which started at midwestern banks and then spread throughout the country.

After the failure of a particularly large bank in 1930, federal officials realized that the economy-wide effects compelled them to take a less hands-off approach and to intervene more vigorously. In 1932, the Reconstruction Finance Corporation (RFC) was established and given the authority to make loans to banks in order to stabilize the banking sector. Also, the Glass-Steagall Act of 1933, which created federal deposit insurance and increased the ability of banks to borrow from the Federal Reserve system, was passed. However, the beast had not yet been tamed. Banks became fearful of borrowing from the RFC because doing so signaled weakness to the public.

As noted earlier, the new president, Franklin D. Roosevelt, was inaugurated during the catastrophic bank run of 1933. He immediately declared a "bank holiday," closing all banks until regulators could get a handle on the problem.

In March 1933, emergency measures were adopted that gave the RFC extraordinary powers to stabilize and restructure the banking industry by providing capital to banks through either loans or outright purchases of bank shares. With the new rules, regulators closed nonviable banks and recapitalized viable ones by allowing the RFC to buy preferred shares in banks (shares that gave the U.S. government more rights than regular shareholders) and by greatly expanding banks' ability to borrow from the Federal Reserve. By 1933, the RFC had invested nearly $19 billion (2020 dollars) in bank capital—one-third of the total capital of all banks in the United States at that time—and purchased shares in almost one-half of all banks. The RFC loaned more than $37 billion (2020 dollars) to banks during this period.

Economic historians uniformly agree that the banking crises of the early 1930s greatly exacerbated the severity of the Great Depression, rendering monetary policy ineffective as the banking sector broke down and currency, withdrawn from banks and stashed under beds, reduced the money supply.

Although the powerful actions of the RFC stabilized the banking industry, new legislation was needed to prevent future banking crises. The Glass-Steagall Act of 1933 separated banks into two categories, **commercial banks,** depository banks that are covered by deposit insurance, and nondepository **investment banks,** which engaged in creating and trading financial assets such as stocks and corporate bonds and were not covered by deposit insurance.

Regulation Q prevented commercial banks from paying interest on checking accounts in the belief that this would promote unhealthy competition between banks. In addition, investment banks were much more lightly regulated than commercial banks. The most important measure for the prevention of bank runs, however, was the adoption of federal deposit insurance (with an original limit of $2,500 per deposit).

These measures were clearly successful, and the United States enjoyed a long period of financial and banking stability. As memories of the bad old days dimmed, Depression-era bank regulations were lifted. In 1980, Regulation Q was eliminated; by 1999, the Glass-Steagall Act had been so weakened that offering services like trading financial assets was no longer off-limits to commercial banks.

The Savings and Loan Crisis of the 1980s

Along with banks, the banking industry also included **savings and loans** (also called S&Ls or **thrifts**), institutions designed to accept savings and turn them into long-term mortgages for home-buyers. S&Ls were covered by federal deposit insurance and were tightly regulated for safety. However, trouble hit in the 1970s, as high inflation led savers to withdraw their funds from low-interest-paying S&L

commercial bank a bank that accepts deposits and is covered by deposit insurance.

investment bank a bank that trades in financial assets and does not accept deposits, so it is not covered by deposit insurance.

savings and loan (thrift) deposit-taking banks, usually specialized in issuing home loans.

accounts and put them into higher-interest-paying money market accounts. In addition, the high inflation rate severely eroded the value of the S&Ls' assets, the long-term mortgages they held on their books.

To improve S&Ls' competitive position vis-à-vis banks, Congress eased regulations to allow S&Ls to undertake much more risky investments in addition to long-term home mortgages. However, the new freedom did not bring with it increased oversight, leaving S&Ls with less oversight than banks. Not surprisingly, during the real estate boom of the 1970s and 1980s, S&Ls engaged in overly risky real estate lending. Also, corruption occurred as some S&L executives used their institutions as private piggy banks.

During the late 1970s and early 1980s, political interference from Congress kept insolvent S&Ls open when a bank in a comparable situation would have been quickly shut down by regulators. By the early 1980s, numerous S&Ls had failed. Because accounts were covered by federal deposit insurance, the liabilities of a failed S&L became liabilities of the federal government, and depositors had to be paid from taxpayer funds. From 1986 through 1995, the federal government closed over 1,000 failed S&Ls, costing U.S. taxpayers over $124 billion.

In a classic case of shutting the barn door after the horse has escaped, in 1989 Congress put in place comprehensive oversight of S&L activities. It also empowered Fannie Mae and Freddie Mac to take over much of the home mortgage lending previously done by S&Ls. *Fannie Mae* and *Freddie Mac* are quasi-governmental agencies created during the Great Depression to make homeownership more affordable for low- and moderate-income households. The S&L crisis led to a steep slowdown in the finance and real estate industries, leading to the recession of the early 1990s.

Back to the Future: The Financial Crisis of 2008 and Its Aftermath

The bank regulations introduced in the 1930s led to a long era of relative financial stability. But by the early twenty-first century a new problem had emerged: these regulations didn't cover **shadow banking**—activities, as we explained earlier, that don't look like traditional banking but serve similar purposes while posing significant risks. In 2008, shadow banking was at the center of a crisis that in important ways resembled the crisis of the 1930s.

Shadow Banking and Its Vulnerabilities

The details of shadow banking can be complex. However, much of the shadow banking system involves financial intermediaries—nondepository financial firms like investment banks, insurance companies, hedge funds, and money market funds. These firms borrow short-term—often taking out loans that must be repaid the next day—and use the borrowed funds to buy relatively illiquid assets to put up as collateral. This looks like banking to those lending funds to intermediaries, because their loans are a lot like bank deposits. For example, a corporation with extra cash on hand might lend that extra cash on an overnight basis to a Wall Street investment bank. That way it can get a higher interest rate than if it parked the funds in ordinary bank deposits, and under normal circumstances it can still count on having access to the money with only one day's notice.

Meanwhile, the financial intermediary doesn't have to keep enough cash on hand to repay all of its debts every day. Many of the lenders will simply roll over their loans each day, relending the funds. And when a lender does demand repayment, the borrower will simply raise the cash from another lender. So the shadow banking firm's relationship to its lenders is a lot like a conventional bank's relationship with its depositors, except for two significant differences: there is no deposit insurance and there is much less regulation of the intermediary's actions.

shadow banking bank-like activities undertaken by nondepository financial firms such as investment banks and hedge funds, but without regulatory oversight and protection.

subprime lending lending to home-buyers who don't meet the usual criteria for qualifying for a loan.

securitization the pooling of loans and mortgages made by a financial institution and the sale of shares in such a pool to other investors.

It is a system that can work seamlessly in normal times, but it can also go terribly wrong as it did when the housing bubble it helped to create burst in 2007, leading to the Great Recession.

Subprime Lending and the Housing Bubble

The story of the 2008 crisis begins with low interest rates: by 2003, U.S. interest rates were at historically low levels, partly because of Federal Reserve policy and partly because of large inflows of capital from other countries, especially China. These low interest rates helped cause a boom in housing, which in turn pulled the U.S. economy out of recession. As housing boomed, however, financial institutions took on greater risks that were not well understood.

Traditionally, people were only able to borrow money to buy homes if they could show that they had sufficient income to meet the mortgage payments. Home loans to people who don't meet the usual criteria for borrowing, called **subprime lending,** were only a minor part of overall lending. But in the booming housing market of 2003 to 2006, subprime lending started to seem like a safe bet. According to conventional thinking, since housing prices kept rising, borrowers who were unable to make their mortgage payments could always pay off their mortgages by selling their homes. As a result, subprime lending exploded.

For the most part, these subprime loans were not made by traditional banks that lend out depositors' money. Instead, most of the loans were made by *loan originators,* companies specializing in making subprime loans and quickly selling them off to other investors in the shadow banking market. Large-scale sales of subprime mortgages were made possible by **securitization:** the assembly of pools of loans and sale of shares of the income from these pools. Again, according to conventional thinking at the time, these shares were considered relatively safe investments, based on the belief that large numbers of home-buyers were unlikely to default on their payments at the same time.

"Honey we're homeless."

Leo Cullum/CartoonStock

But that's exactly what happened. The housing boom turned out to be a bubble, and when home prices started falling in late 2006, significant numbers of subprime borrowers were unable either to meet their mortgage payments or sell their houses for enough to pay off their mortgages. As a result, they defaulted and investors in securities backed by subprime mortgages suffered heavy losses.

These securities were largely held by shadow banking institutions, but also by some traditional, depository banks. Like the trusts that played a key role in the Panic of 1907, these largely unregulated shadow banks offered higher returns to investors but left them extremely vulnerable in a crisis. Without the safety net of deposit insurance, mortgage-related losses led to a collapse of trust in the financial system.

Figure 10 shows one measure of the severity of the loss of trust: the quantity of *asset-backed commercial paper,* an important asset class in shadow banking. In the mid-2000s this paper—backed by short-term loans taken out using assets often created by securitization of mortgages and other debts—grew rapidly in volume. After the housing bust, it went into rapid decline, a sign of extreme financial stress. Although this was not a 1930s-style crash in the money supply in an official sense, it functioned in much the same way because commercial paper was an essential source of liquidity in the financial system.

Crisis and Response

Starting in 2007, the bursting of the housing bubble, followed by large losses on the part of financial firms and the collapse in trust in the financial system, led to major disruptions for the economy as a whole. All firms—financial and nonfinancial—found it difficult to borrow, even for short-term operations. Individuals found home loans unavailable and credit card limits reduced. Prices of many assets tumbled, severely reducing household wealth.

FIGURE 10 Measuring Lost Trust

In the mid-2000s the use of asset-backed commercial paper, short-term loans created by securitization of mortgages and other debts, and an important component of shadow banking, grew rapidly in volume. But it went into rapid decline after the housing boom went bust, a sign of extreme financial stress as liquidity in the financial system dried up.

Data from: Federal Reserve Bank of St. Louis.

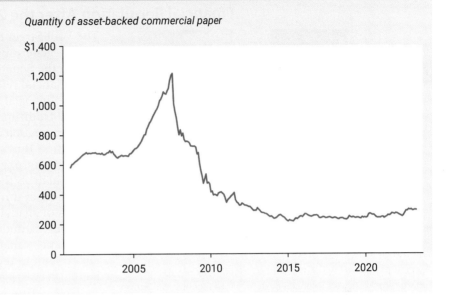

Quantity of asset-backed commercial paper

Overall, the negative economic effect of the financial crisis bore a strong and extremely troubling resemblance to the banking crisis of the early 1930s, which sparked the Great Depression. Policy makers, noticing the resemblance, tried to prevent a repeat performance. Beginning in August 2007, the Federal Reserve provided liquidity to stop a cascade of defaults, by lending funds to a wide range of institutions and buying commercial paper. The Fed and the Treasury Department also stepped in to rescue individual firms that were deemed too crucial to be allowed to fail, such as the investment bank Bear Stearns and the insurance company AIG.

In September 2008, however, under political pressure to punish "irresponsible bankers," policy makers allowed one major investment bank, Lehman Brothers, to fail. They quickly regretted the decision. Within days of Lehman's failure, widespread panic gripped the financial markets. In response, the U.S. government intervened further to support the financial system. The U.S. Treasury injected capital directly into banks—supplying them with cash in return for shares. The effect was to partly *nationalize* the financial system (take public ownership). The Federal Reserve engaged in novel forms of open-market operations, such as providing massive liquidity through discount window lending and buying a large quantity of other assets—mainly long-term government debt and the debt of Fannie Mae and Freddie Mac (as shown in Figure 9 by the huge surge in Fed assets after September 2008).

The Aftermath of the Crisis After many terrifying months, in the fall of 2010 the financial system stabilized, and major institutions had repaid much of the money the federal government had injected during the crisis. However, the recovery of the banks was not matched by a successful turnaround for the overall economy. Although the recession that began in December 2007 officially ended in June 2009, with unemployment reaching a high of 10% in October 2009, unemployment fell very slowly afterward. It took nearly nine years, until May 2016, for the unemployment rate to fall back to where it had been before the start of the Great Recession.

Like earlier crises, the crisis of 2008 led to changes in banking regulation, most notably the Dodd-Frank financial regulatory reform act discussed in the following *Economics in Action.*

ECONOMICS >> *in Action*
Financial Regulation After the 2008 Crisis

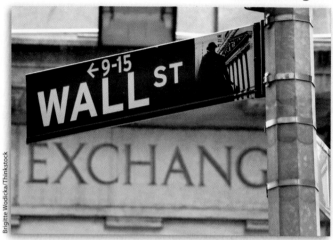

Brigitte Wodicka/Thinkstock

The Dodd-Frank Act extended old-fashioned bank regulation to today's more complex financial system. More recently, the Trump administration has rolled back some of its provisions.

The Wall Street Reform and Consumer Protection Act of 2010—generally known as Dodd-Frank, after its sponsors in the Senate and House, respectively—was the biggest financial reform enacted since the 1930s. How did it change financial regulation?

For traditional depository banks, the main change was the creation of a new agency, the Consumer Financial Protection Bureau. Its mission was to protect borrowers from being exploited through seemingly attractive financial deals they didn't understand.

The main thrust of Dodd-Frank, however, was the regulation of shadow banking institutions. Under the law, a financial institution could be designated as "systematically important"—that is, like Lehman Brothers, it was important enough to the financial system that it could trigger a banking crisis, even though it wasn't a depository bank.

Under Dodd-Frank, these systemically important institutions were subjected to depository bank–style regulation, such as relatively high capital requirements and limits on risk taking. In addition, the federal government asserted *resolution authority*, the right to seize troubled nondepository financial institutions in much the same way that it seized troubled banks.

Dodd-Frank also mandated that most *derivatives*, complex financial instruments that also played a significant role in the 2008 crisis, could be bought and sold on public exchanges in order to make them more transparent and reduce risk.

Overall, the purpose of Dodd-Frank was to extend the spirit of old-fashioned bank regulation to the more complex financial system of the twenty-first century. How well is it working? Relatively well, according to the evidence so far:

- The new rules on systemically important institutions seem to have reduced the incentive to create shadow banks that bypass regulations on conventional banks. An example is the case of GE Capital, an unregulated bank once owned by General Electric. Although it was the main source of profits for its parent company, General Electric sold it off in the wake of Dodd-Frank.

- Resolution authority seems to have led to a reduction in the so-called *too big to fail subsidy:* the lower cost of borrowing enjoyed by big financial institutions compared to smaller ones because it was assumed that only the big ones would be bailed out in a crisis.

- The Consumer Financial Protection Bureau was widely considered to have been quite effective at punishing and deterring financial fraud. Its power and effectiveness were, however, greatly curtailed after 2017, when the newly elected Trump administration moved to reduce the agency's independence and reduce its role.

That said, we won't know how effective Dodd-Frank has been until the next period of financial turbulence.

>> Quick Review

- The Federal Reserve system was created in response to the Panic of 1907.

- Widespread bank runs in the early 1930s resulted in greater bank regulation and the creation of federal deposit insurance. Banks were separated into two categories: **commercial** (covered by deposit insurance) and **investment** (not covered).

- In the **savings and loan (thrift)** crisis of the 1970s and 1980s, insufficiently regulated S&Ls incurred huge losses from risky speculation in housing.

- Unregulated **shadow banking** activities created a vulnerability in the financial system. In the mid-2000s, **securitization** spread loans from **subprime lending** throughout the shadow banking sector, and among some traditional banks, leading to a financial crisis when the housing bubble burst. The Federal Reserve and U.S. Treasury undertook extraordinary steps to stabilize financial markets.

- In 2010, Congress passed the Dodd-Frank Act. The law extended both financial regulations — to avoid another financial crisis — and protections against consumer financial fraud.

>> Check Your Understanding 14-5
Solutions appear at back of book.

1. What are the similarities between the Panic of 1907, the S&L crisis, and the crisis of 2008?

2. Why did the creation of the Federal Reserve fail to prevent the bank runs of the Great Depression? What measures stopped the bank runs?

3. Why were extraordinary measures needed to deal with the financial crisis of 2008?

The Perfect Gift: Cash or a Gift Card?

Kenishirotie/Alamy Stock Photo

It's always nice when someone gives you a gift. Over the past few years, more people have been showing their appreciation by giving gift cards, often prepaid plastic cards issued by a retailer that can be redeemed for merchandise in the store or online. The best-selling single item for more than 80% of the top 100 U.S. retailers, according to the website GiftCardUSA, is their gift cards.

What could be more simple and useful than allowing the recipient to choose what they want? And isn't a gift card more personal than cash or a check?

Yet a number of firms are now making a profit from the fact that gift card recipients are often willing to sell their cards at a discount—sometimes at a fairly sizable discount—to turn them into cold, impersonal dollars and cents. Meanwhile, other people are willing to buy those cards, and turn them into goods they want, at a discount.

CardCash is one such site. At the time of writing, it offers to pay cash to a seller of a Walmart gift card equivalent to 88% of the card's face value. For example, the seller of a Walmart card with a value of $100 would receive $88. Cardcash.com profits by reselling the card at a premium over what it paid. So it would sell a Walmart gift card for more than 88% of its face value. The amount of cash offered to sellers of cards will vary by retailer. CardCash offers cash equal to only 75% of a Gap card's face value, for example.

Many consumers will sell at a sizable discount to turn gift cards into cash. But retailers promote the use of gift cards over cash because much of the value of gift cards issued never gets used, a phenomenon known as *breakage*.

How does breakage occur? People lose cards. Or they spend only $47 of a $50 gift card, and never return to spend that last $3. Also, retailers have imposed fees on the use of cards or made them subject to expiration dates, which customers forget about. Sometimes they even forget that they have a gift card. And if a retailer goes out of business, the value of outstanding gift cards disappears with it.

In addition to breakage, retailers benefit when customers intent on using up the value of their gift card find that it is too difficult to spend exactly the amount of the card. Instead, they end up spending even more than the card's face value, sometimes even more than they would have without the gift card.

Gift cards are so beneficial to retailers that instead of rewarding customer loyalty with rebate checks (once a common practice) many have switched loyalty programs to dispensing gift cards. Today retailers are hoping loyal customers reward them with a gift of their own. During the coronavirus shutdown, shuttered restaurants needed cash, quickly, so they turned to selling gift cards. Restaurants were even adding a 20% bonus if you purchased a $50 or $100 gift card. Restaurants were hoping that receiving the cash upfront would help cover their expenses and the cards they dispensed would help retain customer loyalty.

QUESTIONS FOR THOUGHT

1. Why are gift card owners willing to sell their cards for a cash amount less than their face value?

2. Why do gift cards for Walmart sell for a smaller discount than those for the Gap?

3. Use your answer from Question 2 to explain why cash never "sells" at a discount.

4. Explain why retailers prefer to reward loyal customers with gift cards instead of rebate checks.

5. There are now laws restricting retailers' ability to impose fees and expiration dates on their gift cards and mandate greater disclosure of their terms. Why do you think Congress enacted this legislation?

SUMMARY

1. **Money** is any asset that can easily be used to purchase goods and services. **Currency in circulation** and **checkable bank deposits** are both considered part of the **money supply.** Money plays three roles: it is a **medium of exchange** used for transactions, a **store of value** that holds purchasing power over time, and a **unit of account** in which prices are stated.

2. Over time, **commodity money,** which consists of goods possessing value aside from their role as money, such as gold and silver coins, was replaced by **commodity-backed money,** such as paper currency backed by gold. Today the dollar is pure **fiat money,** whose value derives solely from its official role.

3. The Federal Reserve calculates two measures of the money supply. M1 is the narrowest **monetary aggregate,** containing only currency in circulation, and checkable bank deposits. M2 includes a wider range of assets called **near-moneys,** mainly other forms of bank deposits, that can easily be converted into checkable bank deposits.

4. Banks allow depositors immediate access to their funds, but they also lend out most of the funds deposited in their care. To meet demands for cash, they maintain **bank reserves** composed of both currency held in vaults and deposits at the Federal Reserve. The **reserve ratio** is the ratio of bank reserves to bank deposits. A **T-account** summarizes a bank's financial position, with loans and reserves counted as assets and deposits counted as liabilities.

5. Banks have sometimes been subject to **bank runs,** most notably in the early 1930s. To avert this danger, depositors are now protected by **deposit insurance,** bank owners face capital requirements that reduce the incentive to make overly risky loans with depositors' funds, and banks must satisfy **reserve requirements.**

6. When currency is deposited in a bank, it starts a multiplier process in which banks lend out **excess reserves,** leading to an increase in the money supply—so banks create money. If the entire money supply consisted of checkable bank deposits, the money supply would be equal to the value of reserves divided by the reserve ratio. In reality, much of the **monetary base** consists of currency in circulation, and the **money multiplier** is the ratio of the money supply to the monetary base.

7. The monetary base is controlled by the Federal Reserve, the **central bank** of the United States. The Fed regulates banks and sets reserve requirements. To meet those requirements, banks borrow and lend reserves in the **federal funds market** at the **federal funds rate.** Through the **discount window** facility, banks can borrow from the Fed at the **discount rate.**

8. **Open-market operations** by the Fed are the principal tool of monetary policy: the Fed can increase or reduce the monetary base by buying U.S. Treasury bills from banks or selling U.S. Treasury bills to banks.

9. In response to the Panic of 1907, the Fed was created to centralize the holding of reserves, inspect banks' books, and make the money supply sufficiently responsive to varying economic conditions.

10. The Great Depression sparked widespread bank runs in the early 1930s, which greatly worsened and lengthened it. Federal deposit insurance was created, and the government recapitalized banks by lending to them and by buying shares of banks. By 1933, banks had been separated into two categories: **commercial banks** (which accept deposits and are covered by deposit insurance) and **investment banks** (which don't accept deposits and are not covered). Public acceptance of deposit insurance finally stopped the bank runs of the Great Depression.

11. The **savings and loan (thrift)** crisis of the 1980s arose because insufficiently regulated S&Ls engaged in overly risky speculation and incurred huge losses. Depositors in failed S&Ls were compensated with taxpayer funds because they were covered by deposit insurance. The crisis caused steep losses in the financial and real estate sectors, resulting in a recession in the early 1990s.

12. The emergence of **shadow banking,** bank-like activities undertaken by nondepository financial firms not subject to regulatory oversight or protection, made the financial system once again vulnerable to bank-run type panics. In the mid-2000s, **securitization** of mortgage loans from **subprime lending** spread through the shadow banking sector and among some traditional depository banks. When the housing bubble burst in 2007, losses by financial institutions led to panic and a widespread collapse of the financial system in 2008. To prevent another Great Depression, the Federal Reserve and U.S. Treasury undertook extraordinary actions to provide support to the financial system, such as injecting capital into banks through the purchase of bank shares, providing massive liquidity through discount window lending, and buying large amounts of long-term government debt and government-sponsored agency debt. By 2010, the financial system had stabilized but the economy did not fully recover until 2016.

13. In 2010, Congress passed a financial regulation reform act, known as Dodd-Frank, in order to prevent another crisis. Its main purpose was to extend old-fashioned bank regulation to today's more complex financial system. It also extended protection for consumers against financial fraud.

KEY TERMS

Money, p. 418
Currency in circulation, p. 418
Checkable bank deposits, p. 418
Money supply, p. 418
Medium of exchange, p. 419
Store of value, p. 420
Unit of account, p. 420
Commodity money, p. 420
Commodity-backed money, p. 420
Fiat money, p. 421
Monetary aggregate, p. 421

Near-moneys, p. 421
Bank reserves, p. 424
T-account, p. 424
Reserve ratio, p. 425
Bank run, p. 426
Deposit insurance, p. 426
Reserve requirements, p. 427
Discount window, p. 427
Excess reserves, p. 430
Monetary base, p. 431
Money multiplier, p. 431

Central bank, p. 433
Federal funds market, p. 435
Federal funds rate, p. 435
Discount rate, p. 435
Open-market operation, p. 436
Commercial bank, p. 442
Investment bank, p. 442
Savings and loan (thrift), p. 442
Shadow banking, p. 443
Subprime lending, p. 444
Securitization, p. 444

PRACTICE QUESTIONS

1. Your roommate is considering purchasing cryptocurrency, as they believe it can be used in place of money. Can cryptocurrency function as money?

2. During the economic collapse of 2020 many people had concerns about the stability of the financial system. As employment fell, many residents were unable to make mortgage, rent, car, or credit card payments. Many wondered: would we see another financial panic, like what occurred following the housing collapse in 2009? Explain how changes in regulations following the Great Recession helped prevent another bank run.

3. How did the Federal Reserve respond to the economic crash of 2020? Using Figure 9, explain how the Federal Reserve's response was similar to the response following the bursting of the housing bubble.

PROBLEMS

1. For each of the following transactions, what is the initial effect (increase or decrease) on M1? On M2?

   a. You sell a few shares of stock and put the proceeds into your savings account.

   b. You sell a few shares of stock and put the proceeds into your checking account.

   c. You transfer money from your money market account to your checking account.

   d. You discover $0.25 under the floor mat in your car and deposit it in your checking account.

   e. You discover $0.25 under the floor mat in your car and deposit it in your savings account.

2. There are three types of money: commodity money, commodity-backed money, and fiat money. Which type of money is used in each of the following situations?

   a. Bottles of rum were used to pay for goods in colonial Australia.

   b. Salt was used in many European countries as a medium of exchange.

   c. For a brief time, Germany used paper money (the "Rye Mark") that could be redeemed for a certain amount of rye, a type of grain.

   d. The town of Ithaca, New York, prints its own currency, the Ithaca HOURS, which can be used to purchase local goods and services.

3. The following table shows the components of M1 and M2 in billions of dollars for the month of December in the years 2020 to 2022 reported by the Federal Reserve Bank of St. Louis. Complete the table by calculating M1, M2, currency in circulation as a percentage of M1, and currency in circulation as a percentage of M2. What trends or patterns about M1, M2, currency in circulation as a percentage of M1, and currency in circulation as a percentage of M2 do you see? What might account for these trends?

Year	Currency in circulation	Checkable deposits	Other liquid assets	Time deposits	Money market funds	M1	M2	Currency in circulation as a percentage of M1	Currency in circulation as a percentage of M2
2020	$1,981.7	$3,588.5	$12,429.2	$243.4	$1,049.5	?	?	?	?
2021	2,139.1	4,985.6	13,539.8	83.8	995.1	?	?	?	?
2022	2,213.9	5,213.6	12,418.8	397.5	1,185.3	?	?	?	?

Data from: Federal Reserve Bank of St. Louis.

4. Indicate whether each of the following is part of M1, M2, or neither:

  a. $95 on your campus meal card

  b. $0.55 in the change cup of your car

  c. $1,663 in your savings account

  d. $459 in your checking account

  e. 100 shares of stock worth $4,000

  f. A $1,000 line of credit on your Target credit card

5. Tracy Williams deposits $500 that was in her sock drawer into a checking account at the local bank. The reserve ratio is 10%.

  a. How does the deposit initially change the T-account of the local bank? How does it change the money supply?

  b. If the bank maintains a reserve ratio of 10%, how will it respond to the new deposit?

  c. If every time the bank makes a loan, the loan results in a new checkable bank deposit in a different bank equal to the amount of the loan, by how much could the total money supply in the economy expand in response to Tracy's initial cash deposit of $500?

  d. If every time the bank makes a loan, the loan results in a new checkable bank deposit in a different bank equal to the amount of the loan and the bank maintains a reserve ratio of 5%, by how much could the money supply expand in response to Tracy's initial cash deposit of $500?

6. Ryan Cozzens withdraws $400 from his checking account at the local bank and keeps it in his wallet.

  a. How will the withdrawal change the T-account of the local bank and the money supply?

  b. If the bank maintains a reserve ratio of 10%, how will it respond to the withdrawal? Assume that the bank responds to insufficient reserves by reducing the amount of deposits it holds until its level of reserves satisfies its required reserve ratio. The bank reduces its deposits by calling in some of its loans, forcing borrowers to pay back these loans by taking cash from their checking deposits (at the same bank) to make repayment.

  c. If every time the bank decreases its loans, checkable bank deposits fall by the amount of the loan, by how much will the money supply in the economy contract in response to Ryan's withdrawal of $400?

  d. If every time the bank decreases its loans, checkable bank deposits fall by the amount of the loan and the bank maintains a reserve ratio of 20%, by how much will the money supply contract in response to a withdrawal of $400?

7. The government of Eastlandia uses measures of monetary aggregates similar to those used by the United States, and the central bank of Eastlandia imposes a required reserve ratio of 10%. Given the following information, answer the questions below. Bank deposits at the central bank = $200 million

Currency held by public = $150 million

Currency in bank vaults = $100 million

Checkable bank deposits = $500 million

  a. What is M1?

  b. What is the monetary base?

  c. Are the commercial banks holding excess reserves?

  d. Can the commercial banks increase checkable bank deposits? If yes, by how much can checkable bank deposits increase?

8. In Westlandia, the public holds 50% of M1 in the form of currency, and the required reserve ratio is 20%. Estimate how much the money supply will increase in response to a new cash deposit of $500 by completing the accompanying table. (*Hint:* The first row shows that the bank must hold $100 in minimum reserves—20% of the $500 deposit—against this deposit, leaving $400 in excess reserves that can be loaned out. However, since the public wants to hold 50% of the loan in currency, only $400 × 0.5 = $200 of the loan will be deposited in round 2 from the loan granted in round 1.) How does your answer compare to an economy in which the total amount of the loan is deposited in the banking system and the public doesn't hold any of the loan in currency? What does this imply about the relationship between the public's desire for holding currency and the money multiplier?

Round	Deposits	Required reserves	Excess reserves	Loans	Held as currency
1	$500.00	$100.00	$400.00	$400.00	$200.00
2	200.00	?	?	?	?
3	?	?	?	?	?
4	?	?	?	?	?
5	?	?	?	?	?
6	?	?	?	?	?
7	?	?	?	?	?
8	?	?	?	?	?
9	?	?	?	?	?
Total after 10 rounds	?	?	?	?	?

9. What will happen to the money supply under the following circumstances in a checkable-deposits-only system?

  a. The required reserve ratio is 25%, and a depositor withdraws $700 from their checkable bank deposit and holds it as cash.

  b. The required reserve ratio is 5%, and a depositor withdraws $700 from their checkable bank deposit and holds it as cash.

  c. The required reserve ratio is 20%, and a customer deposits $750 to their checkable bank deposit and holds it as cash.

  d. The required reserve ratio is 10%, and a customer deposits $600 to their checkable bank deposit and holds it as cash.

10. Although the U.S. Federal Reserve doesn't use changes in reserve requirements to manage the money supply, the central bank of Albernia does. The commercial banks of Albernia have $100 million in reserves and $1,000 million in checkable deposits; the initial required reserve ratio is 10%. The commercial banks follow a policy of holding no excess reserves. The public holds no currency, only checkable deposits in the banking system.

   a. How will the money supply change if the required reserve ratio falls to 5%?

   b. How will the money supply change if the required reserve ratio rises to 25%?

11. Using Figure 6, find the Federal Reserve district in which you live. Go to www.federalreserve.gov/fomc/ and determine if the president of the regional Federal Reserve bank in your district is currently a voting member of the Federal Open Market Committee (FOMC).

12. Show the changes to the T-accounts for the Federal Reserve and for commercial banks when the Federal Reserve sells $30 million in U.S. Treasury bills. If the public holds a fixed amount of currency (so that all new loans create an equal amount of checkable bank deposits in the banking system) and the minimum reserve ratio is 5%, by how much will checkable bank deposits in the commercial banks change? By how much will the money supply change? Show the final changes to the T-account for the commercial banks when the money supply changes by this amount.

13. The Congressional Research Service estimates that at least $45 million of counterfeit U.S. $100 notes produced by the North Korean government are in circulation.

   a. Why do U.S. taxpayers lose because of North Korea's counterfeiting?

   b. As of March 2022, the interest rate earned on one-year U.S. Treasury bills was 4.8%. At a 4.8% rate of interest, what is the amount of money U.S. taxpayers are losing per year because of these $45 million in counterfeit notes?

14. As shown in Figure 9, the portion of the Federal Reserve's assets made up of U.S. Treasury bills has declined since 2007. Go to www.federalreserve.gov. On the top of the page, under "Data" and "Money Stock and Reserve Balances," select the link "Factors Affecting Reserve Balances – H.4.1." Click on the link for the current release.

   a. Under "Condition Statement of Federal Reserve Banks," find the row "Reserve Bank Credit." What is the total amount of reserve bank credit under "Average of Daily Figures" for the most current week ended? What is the amount displayed for "U.S.

Treasury securities"? What percentage of the Federal Reserve's total reserve bank credit is currently made up of U.S. Treasury bills?

   b. Do the Federal Reserve's assets consist primarily of U.S. Treasury securities, as they did in January 2007, the beginning of the graph in Figure 9, or does the Fed still own a large number of other assets, as it did in early 2023, the end of the graph in Figure 9?

15. The accompanying figure shows new U.S. housing starts, in thousands of units per month, between January 1980 and March 2023. The figure shows a large drop in new housing starts from 1984 to 1991 and 2006 to 2009. New housing starts are related to the availability of mortgages.

   a. What caused the drop in new housing starts from 1984 to 1991?

   b. What caused the drop in new housing starts from 2006 to 2009?

   c. How could better regulation of financial institutions have prevented these two instances?

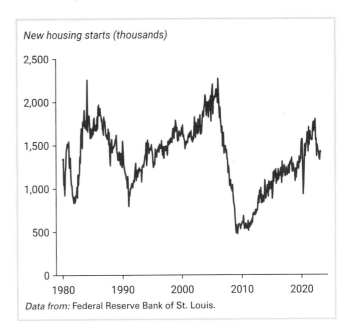

New housing starts (thousands)

Data from: Federal Reserve Bank of St. Louis.

16. Show the changes to the T-accounts for the Federal Reserve and for commercial banks when the Federal Reserve buys $50 million in U.S. Treasury bills. If the public holds a fixed amount of currency (so that all loans create an equal amount of deposits in the banking system), the minimum reserve ratio is 10%, and banks hold no excess reserves, by how much will deposits in the commercial banks change? By how much will the money supply change? Show the final changes to the T-account for commercial banks when the money supply changes by this amount. ∎

15 Monetary Policy

THE MOST POWERFUL PERSON IN GOVERNMENT

"... JOB GAINS HAVE BEEN ROBUST IN RECENT MONTHS, and the unemployment rate has remained low. Inflation remains elevated, reflecting supply and demand imbalances related to the pandemic, higher energy prices, and broader price pressures.

"The invasion of Ukraine by Russia is causing tremendous human and economic hardship ... In addition, COVID-related lockdowns in China are likely to exacerbate supply chain disruptions ...

"The Committee seeks to achieve maximum employment and inflation at the rate of 2 percent over the longer run. In support of these goals, the Committee decided to raise the target range for the federal funds rate to 1-1/2 to 1-3/4 percent and anticipates that ongoing increases in the target range will be appropriate."

So read a statement issued on June 15, 2022, by the people who set U.S. monetary policy. They had begun raising the interest rates they control in March 2022; by May 2023 their target would be 5 percentage points higher than it had been before the rate hikes began.

These repeated announcements constituted a major shift in U.S. economic policy. But who was doing the shifting? Neither Congress nor the president has any direct role in setting interest rates. That role falls, instead, to the Board of Governors of the Federal Reserve, an independent agency that was chaired at the time by Jerome Powell. And there is an old saw to the effect that the Fed chair, not the president, is the most powerful person in government.

Yet, at the Federal Reserve, unlike at the nearby White House, there is no pomp and circumstance: no aides dashing around, no splendidly dressed military guards, no ornate paintings on the walls, and no Secret Service. Instead, workers at the Fed are casually dressed — and often look like graduate students. For example, each day at the Federal Reserve Bank of New York, where the Fed's financial operations are performed, billions of dollars' worth of long-term U.S. government bonds are bought and sold in a small room with just five employees. Struck by the ordinariness of it all, one journalist wrote, "Can a spectacle so lacking in the indicia of importance — no pageantry, no emotions, not even speaking — really be the beating heart of capitalism?"

The answer is yes. The source of the power of the Fed chair and the Board of Governors comes from their ability to set *monetary policy*. It's hard to overstate the importance of the Fed's monetary policy to the U.S. economy — for price stability, for job creation, and for the smooth functioning of the financial system. Roughly half the recessions that have occurred since World War II can be attributed, at least partly, to policies undertaken by the Federal Reserve to fight inflation. And during many other periods, Fed policy played a critical role in fighting slumps and promoting recovery. During the financial crisis of 2008 and the ensuing Great Recession, the Fed was at the very center of the fight to keep the economy from plunging into an abyss.

How does the Fed accomplish all this? Through changes in the money supply and interest rates, which are implemented by its unassuming-looking employees trading billions of dollars daily in U.S. government bonds.

In this chapter, we'll learn how monetary policy works — how actions by the Federal Reserve can have a powerful effect on the economy. We'll start by looking at the *demand for money* from households and firms. Then we'll see how the Fed's ability to change the *supply of money* allows it to move interest rates in the short run and thereby affect real GDP. We'll look at U.S. monetary policy in practice and compare it to the monetary policy of other central banks. We'll conclude by examining monetary policy's long-run effects. ●

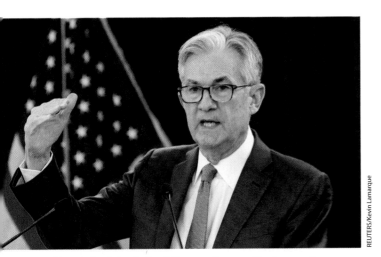

The chair of the Federal Reserve is arguably the most powerful position in the U.S. government.

WHAT YOU WILL LEARN

- What is the **money demand curve?**
- Why does the **liquidity preference model** determine the interest rate in the short run?
- How does the Federal Reserve implement monetary policy?
- Why is monetary policy the main tool for stabilizing the economy?
- Why do economists believe in **monetary neutrality?**

certificate of deposit (CD)
a bank-issued asset in which customers deposit funds for a specified amount of time and earn a specified interest rate.

‖ The Demand for Money

In the previous chapter, we learned about the various types of monetary aggregates: M1, the most commonly used definition of the money supply, consists of currency in circulation (cash) plus checkable bank deposits; and M2, a broader definition of the money supply, consists of M1 plus deposits that can easily be transferred into checkable deposits. We also learned why people hold money—to make it easier to purchase goods and services. Now we'll go deeper, examining what determines how much money individuals and firms want to hold at any given time.

The Opportunity Cost of Holding Money

Most economic decisions involve trade-offs at the margin. That is, individuals decide how much of a good to consume by determining whether the benefit they'd gain from consuming a bit more of any given good is worth the cost. The same decision process is used when deciding how much money to hold.

There is a price to be paid for the convenience of holding money.

Individuals and firms find it useful to hold some of their assets in the form of money because of the convenience that cash provides: money can be used to make purchases directly, but other assets can't. But there is a price to be paid for that convenience: money normally yields no rate of return, or a lower rate of return, than nonmonetary assets.

As an example of how convenience makes it worth incurring some opportunity costs, consider the substantial sums that Americans hold in cash and in zero-interest bank accounts linked to debit cards or money transmitters like PayPal and Venmo. By doing so, they forgo the interest that could have been earned by putting those funds into an interest-bearing asset like a certificate of deposit. A **certificate of deposit, or CD,** is a bank-issued asset that allows customers to deposit their funds for a specified amount of time, and, in return, the bank pays a specified interest rate. For example, as of March 2023 the bank Capital One was offering a two-year CD paying 4.3% annually. But CDs also carry a penalty if funds are withdrawn before the specified amount of time—which often runs from one to five years—has elapsed.

So making sense of the demand for money is about understanding how individuals and firms trade off the benefit of holding monetary assets that provide convenience but little or no interest (like cash and low-interest bank accounts) versus the benefit of holding nonmonetary assets—that provide more interest but less convenience (like CDs). And that trade-off is affected by the interest rate. (As before, when we say *the interest rate* it is with the understanding that we mean a nominal interest rate—that is, it's unadjusted for inflation.) Next, we'll examine how that trade-off changed dramatically from February 2022 to February 2023, when there was a big rise in interest rates.

Table 1 illustrates the opportunity cost of holding money in a specific month, February 2023. The first row shows the interest rate on one-month Treasury bills—that is, the interest rate individuals could get if they were willing to lend funds to the U.S. government for one month.

In February 2023, one-month Treasury bills yielded 4.51%. The second row shows the interest rate on interest-bearing demand deposits. Funds in these accounts were more accessible than those in Treasury bills, but the price of that convenience was a much lower interest rate, only 0.10%. Finally, the last row shows the interest rate on currency—cash in your wallet—which was, of course, zero.

TABLE 1 Selected Interest Rates, February 2023

One-month Treasury bills	4.51%
Interest-bearing demand deposits	0.10%
Currency	0

Data from: Federal Reserve Bank of St. Louis, FDIC.

Table 1 shows the opportunity cost of holding money at one point in time, but the opportunity cost of holding money changes when the overall level of interest rates changes. Specifically, when the overall level of interest rates falls, the opportunity cost of holding money falls, too.

Table 2 illustrates this point by showing how selected interest rates changed between February 2022 and February 2023; as we've already seen, over that period the Fed was raising rates in an effort to bring inflation down. A comparison between interest rates in those two months illustrates what happens when the opportunity cost of holding money rises sharply. Over the course of a year the federal funds rate, which is the rate the Fed controls most directly, rose by 4.5 percentage points. The interest rate on one-month Treasuries rose by almost the same amount. These interest rates are **short-term interest rates**—rates on financial assets that come due, or mature, within less than a year.

As short-term interest rates rose, the interest rate on money didn't rise by the same amount. The interest rate on currency, of course, remained at zero. The interest rate paid on demand deposits rose slightly to 0.10%. As a comparison of the two columns of Table 2 shows, the opportunity cost of holding money rose. The last two rows of Table 2 summarize this comparison: they give the differences between the interest rates on Treasuries and demand deposits and between the interest rates on Treasuries and currency.

These differences—the opportunity cost of holding money rather than interest-bearing assets—rose sharply between February 2022 and February 2023. This reflects a general result: *the higher the short-term interest rate, the higher the opportunity cost of holding money; the lower the short-term interest rate, the lower the opportunity cost of holding money.*

The fact that the federal funds rate in Table 2 and the interest rate on Treasuries rose by almost the same percentage is not an accident: all short-term interest rates tend to move together, with rare exceptions. The reason short-term interest rates tend to move together is that short-term assets are in effect competing for the same business. Any short-term asset that offers a lower-than-average interest rate will be sold by investors, who will move their wealth into a higher-yielding short-term asset. The selling of the asset, in turn, forces its interest rate up, because investors must be rewarded with a higher rate in order to induce them to buy it.

Conversely, investors will move their wealth into any short-term financial asset that offers an above-average interest rate. The purchase of the asset drives its interest rate down when sellers find they can lower the rate of return on the asset and still find willing buyers. So, interest rates on short-term financial assets tend to be roughly the same because no asset will consistently offer a higher-than-average or a lower-than-average interest rate.

Table 2 contains only short-term interest rates. At any given moment, **long-term interest rates**—rates of interest on financial assets that mature, or come due, a number of years into the future—may be different from short-term interest rates. The difference between short-term and long-term interest rates is sometimes important as a practical matter.

Moreover, it's short-term rates rather than long-term rates that affect money demand, because the decision to hold money involves trading off the convenience of holding cash versus the payoff from holding assets that mature in the short term—a year or less. For the moment, however, let's ignore the distinction between short-term and long-term rates and assume that there is only one interest rate.

TABLE 2 Interest Rates and the Opportunity Cost of Holding Money

	February 2022	February 2023
Federal funds rate	0.08%	4.57%
One-month Treasury bills	0.04%	4.51%
Interest-bearing demand deposits	0.06%	0.10%
Currency	0	0
Treasury bills minus interest-bearing demand deposits (percentage points)	−0.02	4.41
Treasury bills minus currency (percentage points)	0.04	4.51

Data from: Federal Reserve Bank of St. Louis, FDIC.

short-term interest rates the interest rate on financial assets that mature within less than a year.

long-term interest rates the interest rate on financial assets that mature a number of years into the future.

money demand curve a graphical representation of the relationship between the interest rate and the quantity of money demanded. The money demand curve slopes downward because, other things equal, a higher interest rate increases the opportunity cost of holding money.

The Money Demand Curve

Because the overall level of interest rates affects the opportunity cost of holding money, the quantity of money individuals and firms want to hold is, other things equal, negatively related to the interest rate. In Figure 1, the horizontal axis shows the quantity of money demanded and the vertical axis shows the interest rate, r, which you can think of as a representative short-term interest rate such as the rate on one-month CDs. (As we discussed in Chapter 10, it is the nominal interest rate, not the real interest rate, that influences people's money allocation decisions. Hence, r in Figure 1 and all subsequent figures is the nominal interest rate.)

The relationship between the interest rate and the quantity of money demanded by the public is illustrated by the **money demand curve**, MD, in Figure 1. The money demand curve slopes downward because, other things equal, a higher interest rate increases the opportunity cost of holding money, leading the public to reduce the quantity of money it demands. For example, if the interest rate is very low—say, 1%—the interest forgone by holding money is relatively small. As a result, individuals and firms will tend to hold relatively large amounts of money to avoid the cost and nuisance of converting other assets into money when making purchases.

By contrast, if the interest rate is relatively high—say, 15%, a level it reached in the United States in the early 1980s—the opportunity cost of holding money is high. People will respond by keeping only small amounts in cash and deposits, converting assets into money only when needed.

You might ask why we draw the money demand curve with the interest rate—as opposed to rates of return on other assets, such as stocks or real estate—on the vertical axis. The answer is that for most people the relevant question in deciding how much money to hold is whether to put the funds in the form of other assets that can be turned fairly quickly and easily into money. Many online brokers offer $0 trades. Stocks don't fit that definition because converting stocks to cash can take considerable time, incur substantial fees, or both, and also because stock values fluctuate. Real estate doesn't fit the definition either because selling real estate involves even larger fees and can take a long time as well. So the relevant comparison is with assets that are "close to" money—assets like CDs that are less liquid than money but more liquid than stocks or real estate. And as we've already seen, the interest rates on all these assets normally move closely together.

FIGURE 1 The Money Demand Curve

The money demand curve illustrates the relationship between the interest rate and the quantity of money demanded. It slopes downward: a higher interest rate leads to a higher opportunity cost of holding money and reduces the quantity of money demanded. Correspondingly, a lower interest rate reduces the opportunity cost of holding money and increases the quantity of money demanded.

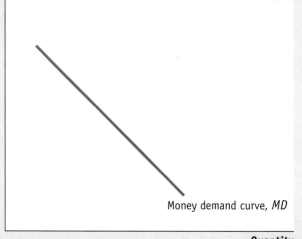

Shifts of the Money Demand Curve

A number of factors other than the interest rate affect the demand for money. When one of these factors changes, the money demand curve shifts. Figure 2 shows shifts of the money demand curve: an increase in the demand for money corresponds to a rightward shift of the *MD* curve, raising the quantity of money demanded at any given interest rate; a decrease in the demand for money corresponds to a leftward shift of the *MD* curve, reducing the quantity of money demanded at any given interest rate.

The most important factors causing the money demand curve to shift are changes in the aggregate price level, changes in real GDP, changes in credit markets and banking technology, and changes in institutions.

Changes in the Aggregate Price Level Americans keep a lot more cash on hand and funds in their checking accounts today than they did in the 1950s. One reason is that they have to if they want to be able to buy anything: almost everything costs more now than it did when you could get a burger, fries, and a drink at McDonald's for 45 cents and a gallon of gasoline for 29 cents. So, other things equal, higher prices increase the demand for money (a rightward shift of the *MD* curve), and lower prices decrease the demand for money (a leftward shift of the *MD* curve).

We can actually be more specific than this: other things equal, the demand for money is *proportional* to the price level. That is, if the aggregate price level rises by 20%, the quantity of money demanded at any given interest rate, such as r_1 in Figure 2, also rises by 20% — the movement from M_1 to M_2. Why? Because if the price of everything rises by 20%, it takes 20% more money to buy the same basket of goods and services. And if the aggregate price level falls by 20%, at any given interest rate the quantity of money demanded falls by 20% — shown by the movement from M_1 to M_3 at the interest rate r_1. As we'll see later, the fact that money demand is proportional to the price level has important implications for the long-run effects of monetary policy.

Changes in Real GDP Households and firms hold money as a way to facilitate purchases of goods and services. The larger the quantity of goods and services

---

FIGURE 2 Increases and Decreases in the Demand for Money

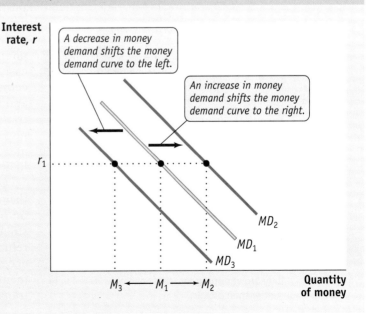

The demand curve for money shifts when non-interest-rate factors that affect the demand for money change. An increase in money demand shifts the money demand curve to the right, from MD_1 to MD_2, and the quantity of money demanded rises at any given interest rate. A decrease in money demand shifts the money demand curve to the left, from MD_1 to MD_3, and the quantity of money demanded falls at any given interest rate.

A decrease in money demand shifts the money demand curve to the left.

An increase in money demand shifts the money demand curve to the right.

they buy, the larger the quantity of money they will want to hold at any given interest rate. So, an increase in real GDP—the total quantity of goods and services produced and sold in the economy—shifts the money demand curve rightward. A fall in real GDP shifts the money demand curve leftward.

Since the start of coronavirus pandemic merchants have seen a spike in contactless forms of payment like ApplePay and Google Pay.

Changes in Credit Markets and Banking Technology As late as the 1960s, almost all small purchases—lunch, groceries, and more—were made using cash because alternatives were few. Since then, however, the need for cash has been greatly reduced by a series of innovations, from widely available credit cards to debit cards to apps like Venmo that let you pay with your smartphone (see the Business Case at end of chapter to learn more about money transmitters like PayPal and Venmo). ATMs and then online banking also made it much easier to transfer funds between accounts, so it became less necessary to hold a surplus of funds in checking accounts in order to make payments. Since the coronavirus pandemic, consumers have preferred contactless payment and have dumped cash in favor of digital platforms like ApplePay or Google Pay. All of these developments make it easier for people to make purchases and reduce the demand for money, shifting the demand curve for money to the left.

Changes in Institutions Changes in institutions can increase or decrease the demand for money. For example, until Regulation Q was eliminated in 1980, U.S. banks weren't allowed to offer interest on checking accounts. So the interest you would forgo by holding funds in a checking account instead of an interest-bearing asset made the opportunity cost of holding funds in checking accounts very high. When banking regulations changed, allowing banks to pay interest on checking account funds, the demand for money rose and shifted the money demand curve to the right.

ECONOMICS >> *in Action*
A Yen for Cash

Japan, say financial experts, is still a "cash society." Visitors from the United States or Europe are surprised at how little use the Japanese make of credit cards

No matter what they are shopping for, Japanese consumers tend to pay with cash rather than plastic.

or debit cards. They do make many purchases with smartphones, yet they still carry remarkably large amounts of cash around in their wallets. Yet Japan is one of the most economically and technologically advanced countries, and superior to the United States in some areas, such as transportation. So why do the citizens of this economic powerhouse often still do business the way Americans and Europeans did a generation ago? The answer highlights the factors affecting the demand for money.

One reason the Japanese use cash so much is that their institutions never made the switch to heavy reliance on plastic. For complex reasons, Japan's retail sector is still dominated by small mom-and-pop stores, which are reluctant to pay the up-front costs that would let them accept credit cards, let alone smartphone apps, as payment. Japan's banks have also been slow about pushing transaction technology; visitors are often surprised to find that ATMs outside of major metropolitan areas close early in the evening rather than staying open all night.

But there's another reason the Japanese hold so much cash: there's little opportunity cost to doing so. Short-term interest rates in Japan have been below 1% since the mid-1990s. It also helps that the Japanese crime rate is quite low, so you are unlikely to have your wallet stolen. So why not hold cash?

>> Check Your Understanding 15-1

Solutions appear at back of book.

1. Explain how each of the following would affect the quantity of money demanded. Does the change cause a movement along the money demand curve or a shift of the money demand curve?
   a. Short-term interest rates rise from 5% to 30%.
   b. All prices fall by 10%.
   c. New "just walk out technology" automatically charges supermarket purchases to credit cards, eliminating the need to stop at the cash register.
   d. In order to avoid paying a sharp increase in taxes, residents of Laguria shift their assets into overseas bank accounts. These accounts are harder for tax authorities to trace but also harder for their owners to tap and convert funds into cash.

2. Which of the following will increase the opportunity cost of holding cash? Which will reduce it? Explain.
   a. In order to attract new customers, the new electronic payment firm, PayBuddy, announces it will pay 0.5% interest on cash balances in a PayBuddy account.
   b. To attract more deposits, banks raise the interest paid on six-month CDs.
   c. In an effort to increase holiday sales, stores offer one-year zero-interest deals on purchases made with store credit cards.

‖ Money and Interest Rates

We started this chapter by quoting from a Federal Reserve press release announcing a change in the target federal funds rate. We learned about the federal funds rate in Chapter 14: it's the rate at which banks lend reserves to each other to meet the required reserve ratio. As the statement implies, at each of its eight-times-a-year meetings, and also sometimes on special occasions between meetings, a group called the Federal Open Market Committee sets a target value for the federal funds rate. It's then up to Fed officials to achieve that target. This is done by the Open Market Desk at the Federal Reserve Bank of New York, which buys and sells short-term U.S. government debt, known as Treasury bills, to achieve that target.

As we've already seen, other short-term interest rates move with the federal funds rate. So when the Fed raised its target for the federal funds rate in June 2022, many other short-term interest rates also rose by about the same amount.

How does the Fed go about achieving a *target federal funds rate?* And more to the point, how is the Fed able to affect interest rates at all?

The Equilibrium Interest Rate

Recall that, for simplicity, we're assuming there is only one interest rate paid on nonmonetary financial assets, both in the short run and in the long run. To understand how the interest rate is determined, consider Figure 3, which illustrates the **liquidity preference model of the interest rate;** this model says that the interest rate is determined by the supply and demand for money in the market for money. Figure 3 combines the money demand curve, *MD*, with the **money supply curve,** *MS*, which shows how the quantity of money supplied by the Federal Reserve varies with the interest rate.

liquidity preference model of the interest rate a model of the market for money in which the interest rate is determined by the supply and demand for money.

money supply curve a graphical representation of the relationship between the quantity of money supplied by the Federal Reserve and the interest rate.

FIGURE 3 Equilibrium in the Money Market

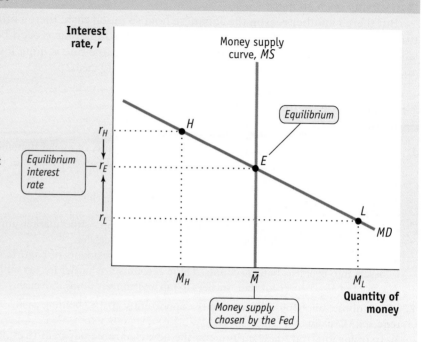

The money supply curve, *MS*, is vertical at the money supply chosen by the Federal Reserve, $\overline{M}$. The money market is in equilibrium at the interest rate r_E: the quantity of money demanded by the public is equal to $\overline{M}$, the quantity of money supplied.

At a point such as *L*, the interest rate, r_L, is below r_E and the corresponding quantity of money demanded, M_L, exceeds the money supply, $\overline{M}$. In an attempt to shift their wealth out of nonmoney interest-bearing financial assets and raise their money holdings, investors drive the interest rate up to r_E. At a point such as *H*, the interest rate r_H exceeds r_E and the corresponding quantity of money demanded, M_H, is less than the money supply, $\overline{M}$. In an attempt to shift out of money holdings into nonmoney interest-bearing financial assets, investors drive the interest rate down to r_E.

The Federal Reserve can increase or decrease the money supply: it usually does this through *open-market operations*, buying or selling Treasury bills, through overnight reverse repurchase agreements (ON-RRP), but it can also lend via the discount window, change reserve requirements, or change the interest rate paid on bank reserves. Let's assume for simplicity that the Fed, using one or more of these methods, simply chooses the level of the money supply that it believes will achieve its interest rate target. Then the money supply curve is a vertical line, *MS* in Figure 3, with a horizontal intercept corresponding to the money supply chosen by the Fed, $\overline{M}$. The money market equilibrium is at *E*, where *MS* and *MD* cross. At this point the quantity of money demanded equals the money supply, $\overline{M}$, leading to an equilibrium interest rate of r_E.

To understand why r_E is the equilibrium interest rate, consider what happens if the money market is at a point like *L*, where the interest rate, r_L, is below r_E. At r_L the public wants to hold the quantity of money M_L, an amount larger than the actual money supply, $\overline{M}$. This means that at point *L*, the public wants to shift some of its wealth out of interest-bearing assets such as CDs into money.

This result has two implications.

1. The quantity of money demanded is *more* than the quantity of money supplied.
2. The quantity of interest-bearing nonmoney assets demanded is *less* than the quantity supplied.

So those trying to sell nonmoney assets will find that they have to offer a higher interest rate to attract buyers. As a result, the interest rate will be driven up from r_L until the public wants to hold the quantity of money that is actually available, $\overline{M}$. That is, the interest rate will rise until it is equal to r_E.

Now consider what happens if the money market is at a point such as *H* in Figure 3, where the interest rate r_H is above r_E. In that case the quantity of money demanded, M_H, is less than the quantity of money supplied, $\overline{M}$. Correspondingly, the quantity of interest-bearing nonmoney assets demanded is greater than the quantity supplied. Those trying to sell interest-bearing nonmoney assets will find that they can offer a lower interest rate and still find willing buyers. This leads to a fall in the interest rate from r_H. It falls until the public wants to hold the quantity of money that is actually available, $\bar{M}$. Again, the interest rate will end up at r_E.

Two Models of Interest Rates?

You might have noticed that this is the second time we have discussed the determination of the interest rate. In Chapter 10, we studied the *loanable funds model* of the interest rate; according to that model, the interest rate is determined by the equalization of the supply of funds from lenders and the demand for funds by borrowers in the market for loanable funds. But here we have described a seemingly different model in which the interest rate is determined by the equalization of the supply and demand for money in the money market. Which of these models is correct?

The answer is both. We explain how the models are consistent with each other in the appendix to this chapter. For now, let's put the loanable funds model to one side and concentrate on the liquidity preference model of the interest rate. The most important insight from this model is that it shows us how monetary policy—actions by the Federal Reserve and other central banks—works.

Monetary Policy and the Interest Rate

Let's examine how the Federal Reserve can use changes in the money supply to change the interest rate. Figure 4 shows what happens when the Fed increases the money supply from $\bar{M}_1$ to $\bar{M}_2$. The economy is originally in equilibrium at E_1, with an equilibrium interest rate of r_1 and money supply, $\bar{M}_1$. An increase in the money supply by the Fed to $\bar{M}_2$ shifts the money supply curve to the right, from MS_1 to MS_2, and leads to a fall in the equilibrium interest rate to r_2. Why? Because r_2 is the only interest rate at which the public is willing to hold the quantity of money actually supplied, $\bar{M}_2$.

So an increase in the money supply drives the interest rate down. Conversely, a reduction in the money supply drives the interest rate up. By adjusting the money supply up or down, the Fed can set the interest rate.

In practice, at each meeting the Federal Open Market Committee decides on the interest rate to prevail for the next six weeks, until its next meeting. The Fed sets a **target federal funds rate,** a desired level for the federal funds rate. This

> **target federal funds rate** the Federal Reserve's desired level for the federal funds rate. The Federal Reserve adjusts the money supply through the purchase and sale of Treasury bills until the actual rate equals the desired rate.

FIGURE 4 The Effect of an Increase in the Money Supply on the Interest Rate

The Federal Reserve can lower the interest rate by increasing the money supply. Here, the equilibrium interest rate falls from r_1 to r_2 in response to an increase in the money supply from $\bar{M}_1$ to $\bar{M}_2$. In order to induce people to hold the larger quantity of money, the interest rate must fall from r_1 to r_2.

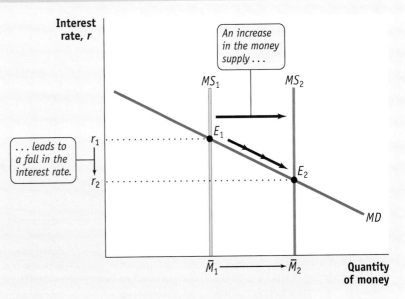

SETTING INTEREST RATES OR THE MONEY SUPPLY: DIFFERENT LOOK, SAME STORY

Over the years, the Federal Reserve has changed the way in which monetary policy is implemented. In the late 1970s and early 1980s, it set a target level for the money supply and altered the monetary base to achieve that target. Under this operating procedure, the federal funds rate fluctuated freely. Today the Fed does the opposite: setting a target for the federal funds rate, allowing the money supply to fluctuate as it pursues that target.

A common mistake is to assume that these changes in the way the Fed operates alter the way the money market works. You may have heard the claim that the interest rate no longer reflects the supply and demand for money because the Fed sets the interest rate.

In fact, the money market works as it always has: the interest rate is determined by the supply and demand for money. The only difference is that now the Fed adjusts the supply of money to achieve its target interest rate. It's important not to confuse a change in the Fed's operating procedure with a change in the way the economy works.

target is then enforced by the Open Market Desk of the Federal Reserve Bank of New York—in those small rooms we mentioned in the opening story—which adjusts the money supply through the purchase and sale of Treasury bills and adjustments to the interest paid on bank reserves until the actual federal funds rate equals the target rate. The other tools of monetary policy, lending through the discount window and changes in reserve requirements, aren't used on a regular basis (although the Fed used discount window lending in its efforts to address the 2008 financial crisis).

Figure 5 shows how this works. In both panels, r_T is the target federal funds rate. In panel (a), the initial money supply curve is MS_1 with money supply $\bar{M}_1$, and the equilibrium interest rate, r_1, is above the target rate. To lower the interest rate to r_T, the Fed makes an open-market purchase of Treasury bills that leads to an increase in the money supply via the money multiplier. This is illustrated in panel (a) by the rightward shift of the money supply curve from MS_1 to MS_2 and an increase in the money supply to $\bar{M}_2$. This drives the equilibrium interest rate down to the target rate, r_T.

Panel (b) shows the opposite case. Again, the initial money supply curve is MS_1 with money supply $\bar{M}_1$. But this time the equilibrium interest rate, r_1, is below the target federal funds rate, r_T. In this case, the Fed will make an open-market sale of Treasury bills, leading to a fall in the money supply to $\bar{M}_2$ via the money multiplier. The money supply curve shifts leftward from MS_1 to MS_2, driving the equilibrium interest rate up to the target federal funds rate, r_T.

Long-Term Interest Rates

In February 2022, just before the Fed began raising rates to fight inflation, short-term interest rates were quite similar in the world's wealthy economies, because

FIGURE 5 Setting the Federal Funds Rate

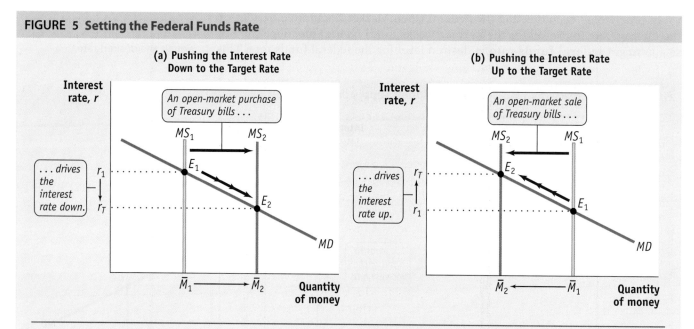

The Federal Reserve sets a target for the federal funds rate and uses open-market operations to achieve that target. In both panels the target rate is r_T. In panel (a) the initial equilibrium interest rate, r_1, is above the target rate. The Fed increases the money supply by making an open-market purchase of Treasury bills, pushing the money supply curve rightward, from MS_1 to MS_2, and driving the interest rate down to r_T. In panel (b) the initial equilibrium interest rate, r_1, is below the target rate. The Fed reduces the money supply by making an open-market sale of Treasury bills, pushing the money supply curve leftward, from MS_1 to MS_2, and driving the interest rate up to r_T.

they were all close to zero. But long-term interest rates—rates on bonds or loans that mature in several years—were quite different. The interest rate on 10-year German government bonds was 0.35%, but the corresponding rate for the United States was 1.93%.

Why were these long-term rates so different? Because long-term rates reflect expected future monetary policy, which in turn largely depend on the future economic outlook.

Consider the case of Min, who has already decided to place $10,000 in U.S. government bonds for the next two years. However, she hasn't decided whether to put the money in one-year bonds, at a 4% rate of interest, or two-year bonds, at a 5% rate of interest. If she buys the one-year bond, then in one year, Min will receive the $10,000 she paid for the bond (the *principal*) plus interest earned. If instead she buys the two-year bond, Min will have to wait until the end of the second year to receive her principal and her interest.

You might think that the two-year bonds are a clearly better deal—but they may not be. Suppose that Min expects the rate of interest on one-year bonds to rise sharply next year. If she puts her funds in one-year bonds this year, she will be able to reinvest the money at a much higher rate next year. And this could give her a two-year rate of return that is higher than if she put her funds into the two-year bonds today.

For example, if the rate of interest on one-year bonds rises from 4% this year to 8% next year, putting her funds in a one-year bond today and in another one-year bond a year from now will give her an annual rate of return over the next two years of about 6%, better than the 5% rate on two-year bonds.

The same considerations apply to all investors deciding between short-term and long-term bonds. If they expect short-term interest rates to rise, investors may buy short-term bonds even if long-term bonds bought today offer a higher interest rate today. If they expect short-term interest rates to fall, investors may buy long-term bonds even if short-term bonds bought today offer a higher interest rate today.

As the example suggests, long-term interest rates largely reflect the average expectation in the market about what's going to happen to short-term rates in the future. What happened in 2022 was that investors expected the U.S. economy to continue growing in the near future, which led to the expectation that the Fed would raise short-term interest rates.

Expected monetary policy is not, however, the whole story: risk is also a factor. Let's return to Min's decision: whether to buy one-year or two-year bonds. Suppose that there is some chance she will need to cash in her investment after just one year—say, to meet an emergency medical bill. If she buys two-year bonds, she would have to sell those bonds to meet the unexpected expense. But what price will she get for those bonds? It depends on what has happened to interest rates in the rest of the economy. As we've learned, bond prices and interest rates move in opposite directions: if interest rates rise, bond prices fall, and vice versa.

This means that Min will face extra risk if she buys two-year rather than one-year bonds, because if a year from now bond prices fall and she must sell her bonds in order to raise cash, she will lose money on the bonds. Owing to this risk factor, long-term interest rates are, on average, higher than short-term rates in order to compensate long-term bond purchasers for the higher risk they face (although this relationship is reversed when short-term rates are unusually high).

As we will soon see, the fact that long-term rates don't necessarily move with short-term rates is sometimes an important consideration for monetary policy.

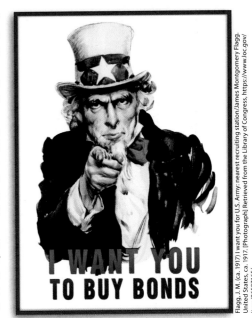

Flagg, J. M. (ca. 1917) I want you for U.S. Army: nearest recruiting station/James Montgomery Flagg. United States, ca. 1917. [Photograph] Retrieved from the Library of Congress, https://www.loc.gov/ item/96507165/.

Advertising during the two world wars increased the demand for government long-term bonds from savers who might have been otherwise reluctant to tie up their funds for several years.

ECONOMICS >> *in Action*
Up the Down Staircase

We began this chapter with the Fed's June 2022 announcement that it was raising its target interest rate. By historical standards, however, it was raising rates from a

FIGURE 6 The Fed's Target, 2007–2023

Data from: Federal Reserve Bank of St. Louis.

very low level. As Figure 6 shows, in early 2007, before the financial crisis, the target rate was 5.25%. But when the financial crisis hit in 2008, the Fed drastically cut rates in an effort to fight the Great Recession, and kept them close to zero for seven years.

Why did the Fed keep rates so low? Because a severe recession followed by a slow recovery kept unemployment—also shown in the figure—very high, while inflation stayed low, for a very long time. In effect, the Fed believed that it needed to keep the pedal to the metal.

By mid-2022, however, U.S. economy was in a very different place, with unemployment close to a 50-year low, but inflation higher than it had been since the early 1980s. So the Federal Open Market Committee began raising rates.

Interestingly, many investors appeared to believe that the big rise in short-term rates would be only temporary. Long-term interest rates, such as the interest rate on 10-year U.S. government bonds, are normally higher than short-term rates, but in early 2023 they were significantly lower than short-term rates, reflecting the widespread belief that once inflation subsided the Fed would at least partially reverse its rate hikes.

>> Check Your Understanding 15-2

Solutions appear at back of book.

1. There is an increase in the demand for money at every interest rate. Draw a diagram showing the effect of this on the equilibrium interest rate for a given money supply.

2. Now assume that the Fed is following a policy of targeting the federal funds rate. What will the Fed do in the situation described in Question 1 to keep the federal funds rate unchanged? Illustrate with a diagram.

3. Malia must decide whether to buy a one-year bond today and another one a year from now, or to buy a two-year bond today. In which of the following scenarios is she better off taking the first action? The second action?
   a. This year, the interest on a one-year bond is 4%; next year, it will be 10%. The interest rate on a two-year bond is 5%.
   b. This year, the interest rate on a one-year bond is 4%; next year, it will be 1%. The interest rate on a two-year bond is 3%.

‖ Monetary Policy and Aggregate Demand

We saw how fiscal policy can be used to stabilize the economy in Chapter 13. Now we will see how monetary policy, which we defined earlier as changes in the money supply, and the interest rate, together, can play the same role.

Expansionary and Contractionary Monetary Policy

In Chapter 12, we learned that monetary policy shifts the aggregate demand curve. We can now explain how that works: through the effect of monetary policy on the interest rate.

Figure 7 illustrates the process. Suppose, first, that the Federal Reserve wants to reduce interest rates, so it expands the money supply. As you can see in the

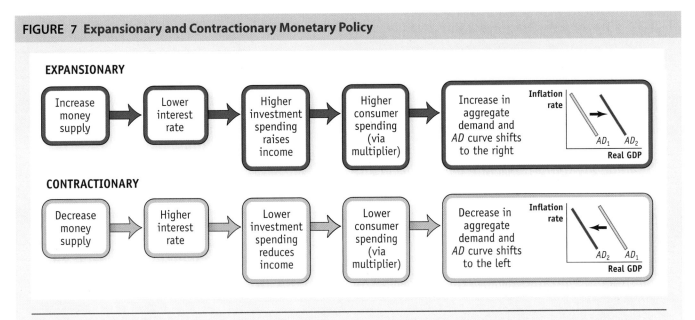

FIGURE 7 Expansionary and Contractionary Monetary Policy

The top portion of the diagram shows what happens when the Fed adopts an expansionary monetary policy and increases the money supply. Interest rates fall, leading to higher investment spending, which raises income, which, in turn, raises consumer spending and shifts the *AD* curve to the right. The bottom portion shows what happens when the Fed adopts a contractionary monetary policy and reduces the money supply. Interest rates rise, leading to lower investment spending and a reduction in income. This lowers consumer spending and shifts the *AD* curve to the left.

top portion of the figure, a lower interest rate will lead, other things equal, to more investment spending. This will in turn lead to higher consumer spending, through the multiplier process, and to an increase in aggregate output demanded. In the end, the total quantity of goods and services demanded at any given inflation rate rises when the quantity of money increases, and the *AD* curve shifts to the right. Monetary policy that increases the demand for goods and services is known as **expansionary monetary policy.** (It is also commonly called *loose monetary policy.*)

Suppose, alternatively, that the Federal Reserve wants to increase interest rates, so it contracts the money supply. You can see this process illustrated in the bottom portion of the diagram. Contraction of the money supply leads to a higher interest rate. The higher interest rate leads to lower investment spending, then to lower consumer spending, and then to a decrease in aggregate output demanded. So, the total quantity of goods and services demanded falls when the money supply is reduced, and the *AD* curve shifts to the left. Monetary policy that decreases the demand for goods and services is called **contractionary monetary policy.** (It is also commonly called *tight monetary policy.*)

"I told you the Fed should have tightened."

expansionary monetary policy monetary policy that, through the lowering of the interest rate, increases aggregate demand and therefore output.

contractionary monetary policy monetary policy that, through the raising of the interest rate, reduces aggregate demand and therefore output.

Monetary Policy in Practice

How does the Fed decide whether to use expansionary or contractionary monetary policy? And how does it decide how much is enough? As we've learned, policy makers try to both fight recessions and ensure *price stability:* low (though usually not zero) inflation. Actual monetary policy reflects a combination of these goals.

In general, the Fed and other central banks tend to engage in expansionary monetary policy when actual real GDP is below potential output. Panel (a) of

FIGURE 8 Tracking Monetary Policy Using the Output Gap and Inflation

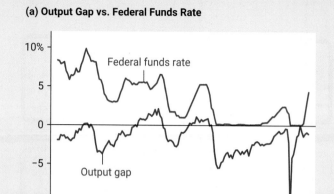

(a) Output Gap vs. Federal Funds Rate

(b) Inflation Rate vs. Federal Funds Rate

Panel (a) shows that the federal funds rate usually rises when the output gap is rising, and falls when the output gap is

falling. Panel (b) illustrates that the federal funds rate tends to be high when inflation is high and low when inflation is low.
Data from: Federal Reserve Bank of St. Louis.

Figure 8 shows the U.S. output gap, defined in Chapter 12 as the percentage difference between actual real GDP and potential output, versus the federal funds rate since 1985. (Recall that the output gap is positive when actual real GDP exceeds potential output.) As you can see, the Fed tends to raise interest rates when the output gap is rising (when the economy is developing an inflationary gap) and cut rates when the output gap is falling. (The exception is the period from 2009 to 2016, and again in 2020, when the federal funds rate was stuck near zero, a phenomenon, called the *zero lower bound on interest rates*.)

The big exception was the late 1990s, when the Fed left rates steady for several years even as the economy developed a positive output gap (which went along with a low unemployment rate). One reason the Fed was willing to keep interest rates low in the late 1990s was that inflation was low.

Panel (b) of Figure 8 compares the inflation rate, measured as the rate of change in consumer prices excluding food and energy, with the federal funds rate. You can see how low inflation during the mid-1990s, the early 2000s, and the late 2000s helped encourage loose monetary policy in the late 1990s, in 2002–2003, and again beginning in 2008, while inducing tighter monetary policy in 2022.

The Taylor Rule Method of Setting Monetary Policy

In 1993, Stanford economist John Taylor suggested that monetary policy should follow a simple rule that takes into account concerns about both the business cycle and inflation. He also suggested that actual monetary policy often looks as if the Federal Reserve was, in fact, more or less following the proposed rule. A **Taylor rule for monetary policy** is a rule for setting interest rates that takes into account the inflation rate and the output gap or, in some cases, the unemployment rate.

A widely cited example of a Taylor rule is a relationship among Fed policy, inflation, and unemployment estimated by economists at the Federal Reserve

Taylor rule for monetary policy a rule that sets the federal funds rate according to the level of the inflation rate and either the output gap or the unemployment rate.

FIGURE 9 The Taylor Rule and the Federal Funds Rate

The purple line shows the federal funds rate predicted by the San Francisco Fed's version of the Taylor rule, which relates the interest rate to the inflation rate and the unemployment rate. The blue line shows the actual federal funds rate. The actual rate tracked the predicted rate quite closely through the end of 2008. After that, however, the Taylor rule called for negative interest rates, which is a difficult and problematic goal to achieve.

Data from: Bureau of Labor Statistics; Congressional Budget Office; Federal Reserve Bank of St. Louis; Glenn D. Rudebusch, "The Fed's Monetary Policy Response to the Current Crisis," FRBSF Economic Letter #2009–17 (May 22, 2009).

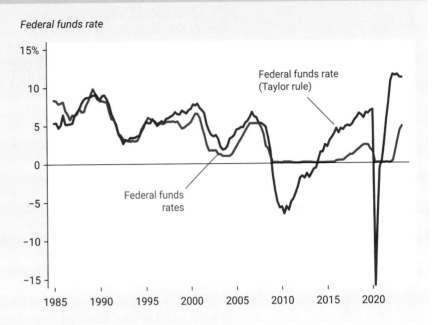

Bank of San Francisco. These economists found that between 1988 and 2008 the Fed's behavior was well summarized by the following Taylor rule:

Federal funds rate = 2.07 + 1.28 × inflation rate − 1.95 × unemployment gap

where the inflation rate was measured by the change over the previous year in consumer prices excluding food and energy, and the unemployment gap was the difference between the actual unemployment rate and Congressional Budget Office estimates of the natural rate of unemployment.

Figure 9 compares the federal funds rate predicted by this rule with the actual federal funds rate from 1985 to 2023. As you can see, the Fed's decisions were quite close to those predicted by this particular Taylor rule from 1985 through the end of 2008. We'll talk about what happened after 2008 shortly.

Inflation Targeting

Until January 2012, the Fed did not explicitly commit itself to achieving a particular inflation rate. However, in January 2012, the Fed announced that it would set its policy to maintain an approximately 2% inflation rate per year. With that statement, the Fed joined a number of other central banks that have explicit inflation targets. So, rather than using a Taylor rule to set monetary policy, they instead announce the inflation rate that they want to achieve—the *inflation target*—and set policy in an attempt to hit that target. This method of setting monetary policy, called **inflation targeting,** involves having the central bank announce the inflation rate it is trying to achieve and set policy in an attempt to hit that target. The central bank of New Zealand, which was the first country to adopt inflation targeting, specified a range for that target of 1% to 3%.

Other central banks commit themselves to achieving a specific number. For example, the Bank of England has committed to keeping inflation at 2%. In practice, there doesn't seem to be much difference between these versions: central banks with a target range for inflation seem to aim for the middle of that range, and central banks with a fixed target tend to give themselves considerable wiggle room.

One major difference between inflation targeting and the Taylor rule method is that inflation targeting is forward-looking rather than backward-looking. That is,

inflation targeting an approach to monetary policy that requires that the central bank try to keep the inflation rate near a predetermined target rate.

the Taylor rule method adjusts monetary policy in response to *past* inflation, but inflation targeting is based on a forecast of future inflation.

Advocates of inflation targeting argue that it has two key advantages over the Taylor rule: *transparency* and *accountability*. First, economic uncertainty is reduced because the central bank's plan is transparent: the public knows the objective of an inflation-targeting central bank. Second, the central bank's success can be judged by seeing how closely actual inflation rates have matched the inflation target, making central bankers accountable.

Critics of inflation targeting argue that it's too restrictive because there are times when other concerns—like the stability of the financial system—should take priority over achieving any particular inflation rate. Indeed, starting in late 2013 the Taylor rule rate and the federal funds rate diverged significantly, as the Fed kept the interest rate close to zero while the Taylor rule rate climbed. The Fed's actions were motivated by the fear that an interest rate rise could push the persistently weak economy back into turmoil and recession.

Many American macroeconomists have had positive things to say about inflation targeting—including Ben Bernanke (the Fed chair from 2006 through early 2014). And in January 2012, the Fed declared that what it means by the "price stability" it seeks is 2% inflation, although there was no explicit commitment about when this inflation rate would be achieved.

The Zero Lower Bound Problem

As Figure 9 shows, a Taylor rule based on inflation and the unemployment rate does a good job of predicting Federal Reserve policy from 1985 through 2008. After that, however, things go awry, and for a simple reason: with very high unemployment and low inflation, the same Taylor rule called for an interest rate significantly less than zero, which is a difficult and problematic goal to achieve.

Negative interest rates are a problem because people always have the alternative of holding cash, which offers a zero interest rate. Why, then, would they ever buy a bond yielding an interest rate less than zero?

Until 2014, most economists believed that it was basically impossible for interest rates to go below zero. That year, however, the central bank of Switzerland did the previously unthinkable, setting rates slightly below zero. It turns out that even at a slightly negative interest rate, there are limits to how much cash the public is willing to hold, because storing cash is expensive: you need vaults that are secure against loss, both from potential theft and from threats like money-eating mice.

GLOBAL COMPARISON   INFLATION TARGETS

This figure shows the target inflation rates of six central banks that have adopted inflation targeting. The central bank of New Zealand introduced inflation targeting in 1990. Today it has an inflation target range of 1% to 3%. The central banks of Canada, Sweden, and Norway have the same target range but also specify 2% as the precise target. The Bank of England, Britain's central bank, specifies an inflation target of 2%. Since 2012, the U.S. Federal Reserve also targets inflation at 2%.

In practice, these differences in detail don't seem to lead to significantly different results. New Zealand aims for the middle of its range, at 2% inflation; Britain, Norway, and the United States allow considerable wiggle room around their target inflation rates.

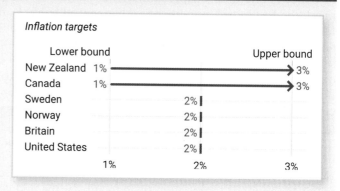

Data from: IMF, Reserve Bank of New Zealand, Bank of Canada, Riksbank, Bank of England, Norges Bank, and Federal Reserve System.

(Yes, rodent control turns out to play some role in monetary policy.) By 2016, the Swiss equivalent of the federal funds rate was –0.75%, and both the European Central Bank and the Bank of Japan also had slightly negative rates. (Japan's situation, which economists refer to as being *up against the zero bound,* is addressed in Chapter 16.)

So, the zero lower bound isn't an absolute limit. Still, no central bank has tried to push rates significantly below zero, say down to –3% or –6%, which is what the Taylor rule suggested for the United States in 2009 and 2010. This is explained partly because rates that low would lead to the hoarding of cash. Also, negative interest rates are widely believed to cause big problems for the banking system, with adverse effects on the economy as a whole. This set of circumstances leads to what is called the **zero lower bound for interest rates:** interest rates cannot fall much below zero without causing significant problems.

As a result, the Fed has never been willing to push rates below zero. This in turn means that when inflation is low and the economy is operating far below potential, normal monetary policy—open-market purchases of short-term government debt to expand the money supply—runs out of room to operate because short-term interest rates are already at or near zero. Economists refer to this situation as *running up against the zero lower bound.*

In November 2010, the Fed began an attempt to circumvent the problem caused by its inability to reduce interest rates further despite economic weakness. This attempt went by the somewhat obscure name *quantitative easing.* Instead of purchasing only short-term government debt, it began buying longer-term government debt—five-year or six-year bonds, rather than three-month Treasury bills. And, as we know, long-term interest rates don't exactly follow short-term rates. At the time the Fed began this program, short-term rates were near zero, but rates on longer-term bonds were between 2% and 3%. The Fed hoped that direct purchases of these longer-term bonds would drive down interest rates on long-term debt, exerting an expansionary effect on the economy.

Later the Fed expanded the program further, also purchasing mortgage-backed securities, which normally offer somewhat higher rates than U.S. government debt. Here, too, the hope was that these rates could be driven down, with an expansionary effect on the economy. As with ordinary open-market operations, quantitative easing was undertaken by the Federal Reserve Bank of New York.

Was this policy effective? The Federal Reserve believes that it helped the economy. However, the pace of recovery remained disappointingly slow. Starting in 2016, the Fed began to slowly raise rates by an amount less than a Taylor rule would have predicted, reflecting the sluggish pace of the recovery. And it reversed course in 2019, even before the coronavirus pandemic sent the economy reeling.

zero lower bound for interest rates statement of the fact that interest rates cannot fall below zero without causing significant problems.

ECONOMICS >> *in Action*
What the Fed Wants, the Fed Gets

What's the evidence that the Fed can actually cause an economic contraction or expansion? You might think that finding such evidence is just a matter of looking at what happens to the economy when interest rates go up or down. But it turns out that there's a big problem with that approach: the Fed usually changes interest rates in an attempt to tame the business cycle, raising rates if the economy is expanding and reducing rates if the economy is slumping. So in the actual data, it often looks as if low interest rates go along with a weak economy and high rates go along with a strong economy.

In a famous paper titled "Does Monetary Policy Matter?," macroeconomists Christina Romer and David Romer solved this problem by focusing on episodes in which monetary policy wasn't a reaction to the business cycle. Specifically, they

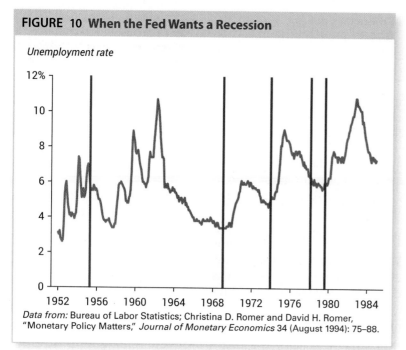

FIGURE 10 When the Fed Wants a Recession

Unemployment rate

Data from: Bureau of Labor Statistics; Christina D. Romer and David H. Romer, "Monetary Policy Matters," *Journal of Monetary Economics* 34 (August 1994): 75–88.

used minutes from the Federal Open Market Committee and other sources to identify episodes "in which the Federal Reserve in effect decided to attempt to create a recession to reduce inflation." As we'll learn in Chapter 16, rather than just using monetary policy as a tool of macroeconomic stabilization, sometimes it is used to eliminate *embedded inflation*—inflation that people believe will persist into the future. In such a case, the Fed needs to create a recessionary gap—not just eliminate an inflationary gap—to wring embedded inflation out of the economy.

Figure 10 shows the unemployment rate between 1952 and 1984 and also identifies five dates on which, according to Romer and Romer, the Fed decided that it wanted a recession (the vertical lines). In four out of the five cases, the decision to contract the economy was followed, after a modest lag, by a rise in the unemployment rate. On average, Romer and Romer found the unemployment rate rises by 2 percentage points after the Fed decides that unemployment needs to go up.

So yes, the Fed gets what it wants.

>> Quick Review

• The Federal Reserve can use **expansionary monetary policy** to increase aggregate demand and **contractionary monetary policy** to reduce aggregate demand. The Federal Reserve and other central banks generally try to tame the business cycle while keeping the inflation rate low but positive.

• Under a **Taylor rule for monetary policy,** the target federal funds rate rises when there is high inflation and either a positive output gap or very low unemployment; it falls when there is low or negative inflation and either a negative output gap or high unemployment.

• In contrast, some central banks set monetary policy by **inflation targeting,** a forward-looking policy rule, rather than by using the Taylor rule, a backward-looking policy rule. Although inflation targeting has the benefits of transparency and accountability, some think it is too restrictive. Until 2008, the Fed followed a loosely defined Taylor rule. Starting in early 2012, it began inflation targeting with a target of 2% per year.

• There is a **zero lower bound for interest rates**—they cannot fall much below zero without causing significant problems—that limits the effectiveness of monetary policy.

• Because it is subject to fewer lags than fiscal policy, monetary policy is the main tool for macroeconomic stabilization.

>> Check Your Understanding 15-3

Solutions appear at back of book.

1. Suppose the economy is currently suffering from an output gap and the Federal Reserve uses an expansionary monetary policy to close that gap. Describe the short-run effect of this policy on the following.
   a. The money supply curve
   b. The equilibrium interest rate
   c. Investment spending
   d. Consumer spending
   e. Aggregate output

2. In setting monetary policy, which central bank—one that operates according to a Taylor rule or one that operates by inflation targeting—is likely to respond more directly to a financial crisis? Explain.

‖ Money, Output, and Prices in the Long Run

Through its expansionary and contractionary effects, monetary policy is generally the policy tool of choice to help stabilize the economy. However, not all actions by central banks are productive. In particular, central banks sometimes print money, not to fight a recessionary gap but to help the government pay its bills, an action that typically destabilizes the economy.

What happens when a change in the money supply pushes the economy away from, rather than toward, long-run equilibrium? As we've learned, the economy is self-correcting in the long run: a demand shock has only a temporary effect on aggregate output. If the demand shock is the result of a change in the money supply, we can make a stronger statement: in the long run, changes in the quantity of money affect the aggregate price level, but they do not change real aggregate output or the interest rate. To see why, let's look at what happens if the central bank permanently increases the money supply.

Short-Run and Long-Run Effects of an Increase in the Money Supply

To analyze the long-run effects of monetary policy, it's helpful to think of the central bank as choosing a target for the money supply rather than the interest rate. In assessing the effects of an increase in the money supply, we return to the analysis of the long-run effects of an increase in aggregate demand, first introduced in Chapter 12.

We learned in Chapter 12 that an increase in aggregate demand raises output in the short run, but has no effect on output in the long run. This is true for any kind of increase in aggregate demand, but we can say more when the demand increase is caused by a rise in the money supply. If we assume that the increase in the money supply is a one-time event—that it won't be followed, say, by a series of future monetary expansions—we can make a broader statement: in the long run, an increase in the money supply won't have any real effects at all. This proposition is known as *monetary neutrality*.

Monetary Neutrality

How much does a change in the money supply change the aggregate price level in the long run? The answer is that a change in the money supply leads to an equal proportional change in the aggregate price level in the long run. For example, if the money supply falls 25%, the aggregate price level falls 25% in the long run; if the money supply rises 50%, the aggregate price level rises 50% in the long run.

How do we know this? Consider the following thought experiment: suppose all prices in the economy—prices of final goods and services and also factor prices, such as nominal wage rates—double. And suppose the money supply doubles at the same time. What difference does this make to the economy in real terms? The answer is none. All real variables in the economy—such as real GDP and the real value of the money supply (the amount of goods and services it can buy)—are unchanged. So there is no reason for anyone to behave any differently.

We can state this argument in reverse: if the economy starts out in long-run macroeconomic equilibrium and the money supply changes, restoring long-run macroeconomic equilibrium requires restoring all real values to their original values. This includes restoring the real value of the money supply to its original level. So if the money supply falls 25%, the aggregate price level must fall 25%; if the money supply rises 50%, the aggregate price level must rise 50%; and so on.

This analysis demonstrates the concept known as **monetary neutrality,** in which changes in the money supply have no real effects on the economy. In the long run, the only effect of an increase in the money supply is to raise the aggregate price level by an equal percentage. Economists argue that *money is neutral in the long run.*

This is, however, a good time to recall the dictum of John Maynard Keynes: "In the long run we are all dead." In the long run, changes in the money supply don't have any effect on real GDP, interest rates, or anything else except the price level. But it would be foolish to conclude from this statement that the Fed is irrelevant. Monetary policy does have powerful real effects on the economy in the short run, often making the difference between recession and expansion. And that matters a lot for society's welfare.

Changes in the Money Supply and the Interest Rate in the Long Run

In the short run, an increase in the money supply leads to a fall in the interest rate, and a decrease in the money supply leads to a rise in the interest rate. In the long run, however, changes in the money supply don't affect the interest rate.

Figure 11 shows why. It shows the money supply curve and the money demand curve before and after the Fed increases the money supply. We assume that the economy is initially at E_1, in long-run macroeconomic equilibrium at potential

monetary neutrality the concept that changes in the money supply have no real effects on the economy in the long run and only result in a proportional change in the price level.

FIGURE 11 The Long-Run Determination of the Interest Rate

The economy is initially at E_1, a long-run macroeconomic equilibrium. In the short run, an increase in the money supply, from $\overline{M}_1$ to $\overline{M}_2$ pushes the interest rate down from r_1 to r_2. The economy moves to E_2, a short-run equilibrium. In the long run, however, the aggregate price level rises in proportion to the increase in the money supply, leading to an increase in money demand at any given interest rate in proportion to the increase in the aggregate price level, as shown by the shift from MD_1 to MD_2. The result is that the quantity of money demanded at any given interest rate rises by the same amount as the quantity of money supplied. The economy moves to long-run equilibrium at E_3 and the interest rate returns to r_1.

output, and with money supply $\overline{M}_1$. The initial equilibrium interest rate, determined by the intersection of the money demand curve MD_1 and the money supply curve MS_1, is r_1.

Now suppose the money supply increases from $\overline{M}_1$ to $\overline{M}_2$. In the short run, the economy moves from E_1 to E_2 and the interest rate falls from r_1 to r_2. Over time, however, the aggregate price level rises, and this raises money demand, shifting the money demand curve rightward from MD_1 to MD_2. The economy moves to a new long-run equilibrium at E_3, and the interest rate rises to its original level at r_1.

And it turns out that the long-run equilibrium interest rate is the original interest rate, r_1. We know this for two reasons. First, due to monetary neutrality, in the long run the aggregate price level rises by the same proportion as the money supply; so if the money supply rises by, say, 50%, the aggregate price level will also rise by 50%. Second, the demand for money is, other things equal, proportional to the aggregate price level.

So a 50% increase in the money supply raises the aggregate price level by 50%, which increases the quantity of money demanded at any given interest rate by 50%. As a result, the quantity of money demanded at the initial interest rate, r_1, rises exactly as much as the money supply—so that r_1 is still the equilibrium interest rate. In the long run, then, changes in the money supply do not affect the interest rate.

ECONOMICS >> *in Action*
International Evidence of Monetary Neutrality

These days monetary policy is quite similar among developed countries. Each major nation (or, in the case of the euro, the euro area) has a central bank that is insulated from political pressure. All of these central banks try to keep the aggregate price level roughly stable, which usually means inflation of at most 2% to 3% per year.

But if we look at a longer period and a wider group of countries, we see large differences in the growth of the money supply. Between 1986 and 2021, the money supply rose only a few percent per year in some countries, such as Switzerland

and the United States, but rose much more rapidly in some lower income countries, such as Mexico and Turkey. These differences allow us to see whether it is really true that increases in the money supply lead, in the long run, to equal percent rises in the aggregate price level.

Figure 12 shows the annual percentage increases in the money supply and average annual increases in the aggregate price level—that is, the average rate of inflation—for a sample of countries during the period 1986–2021, with each point representing a country. If the relationship between increases in the money supply and changes in the aggregate price level were exact, the points would lie precisely on a 45-degree line.

In fact, the relationship isn't exact, because other factors besides money affect the aggregate price level. But the scatter of points clearly lies close to a 45-degree line, showing a more or less proportional relationship between money and the aggregate price level. That is, the data support the concept of monetary neutrality in the long run.

FIGURE 12 The Long-Run Relationship Between Money and Inflation

Inflation and money growth are in percent, annual average.
Data from: Federal Reserve Bank of St. Louis.

>> Check Your Understanding 15-4

Solutions appear at back of book.

1. Assume the central bank increases the quantity of money by 25%, even though the economy is initially in both short-run and long-run macroeconomic equilibrium. Describe the effects, in the short run and in the long run (giving numbers where possible), on the following.
   a. Aggregate output
   b. Aggregate price level
   c. Interest rate
2. Why does monetary policy affect the economy in the short run but not in the long run?

>> Quick Review

• According to the concept of **monetary neutrality,** changes in the money supply do not affect real GDP, they only affect the aggregate price level. Economists believe that money is neutral in the long run.

• In the long run, the equilibrium interest rate in the economy is unaffected by changes in the money supply.

Parking Your Money at PayPal

Andrew Harrer/Bloomberg/Getty Images

Officially, PayPal, the electronic funds-transfer firm—which is also the owner of the popular mobile-phone payment service Venmo—isn't considered a bank. Instead, regulators consider it a *money transmitter,* an entity that sends your money someplace rather than holding it and keeping it safe.

However, as users accumulate substantial sums in their Venmo PayPal accounts, that distinction has started to look questionable. Venmo users, in particular, often seem willing to let incoming payments sit in their accounts until the funds are spent, the way people once kept cash in their wallets. As a result, PayPal's accounts were estimated to total more than $36.5 billion in 2022. If those billions were considered bank deposits, PayPal would be considered among the 60 largest banks in the United States.

At first glance, leaving significant sums in PayPal accounts seems counterintuitive for two reasons. First, these accounts aren't protected by federal deposit insurance. Second, they pay no interest. But upon closer examination, this behavior makes good economic sense. People will typically hold only a tiny fraction of their wealth in their PayPal account, thereby making the lack of federal deposit insurance an acceptable risk. And interest rates on bank accounts are so low at the time of this writing (around 0.06% in March 2022) that losing that interest is a reasonable price to pay to avoid the hassle of moving funds back and forth between a bank account and a PayPal or Venmo account.

The result is that many people are behaving like one user quoted by the *Wall Street Journal,* who now waits a while before transferring funds out of her Venmo account to her regular bank account: "I'm starting to intentionally keep my money in there a little bit longer."

But will PayPal/Venmo or something like it begin to make major inroads into traditional banking? Some analysts think so. Others suggest, however, that payment systems like Zelle, developed by conventional banks, and eventually rising interest rates will lure customers back to conventional bank deposits. Time will tell.

QUESTIONS FOR THOUGHT

1. PayPal accounts aren't counted as part of the money supply. Should they be? Why or why not?

2. In 2010, only around 25% of mobile phones in the United States were smartphones. By 2023, almost everyone had a smartphone. How does this situation play into the PayPal story, and how does it fit into the broader pattern of monetary history?

3. Explain how the action of raising interest rates by the Federal Open Market Committee affect the future of PayPal and similar services?

SUMMARY

1. The **money demand curve** arises from a trade-off between the opportunity cost of holding money and the liquidity that money provides. Americans hold substantial sums in cash and in zero-interest bank accounts linked to debit cards or money transmitters like PayPal and Venmo. By doing so they forgo the interest that could have been earned by putting those funds into an interest-bearing asset like a **certificate of deposit (CD).** The opportunity cost of holding money depends on **short-term interest rates,** not **long-term interest rates.** Changes in the aggregate price level, real GDP, technology, and institutions shift the money demand curve.

2. According to the **liquidity preference model of the interest rate,** the interest rate is determined in the money market by the money demand curve and the **money supply curve.** The Federal Reserve can change the interest rate in the short run by shifting the money supply curve. In practice, the Fed uses open-market operations to achieve a **target federal funds rate,** which other short-term interest rates generally track. Although long-term interest rates don't necessarily move with short-term interest rates, they reflect expectations about what's going to happen to short-term rates in the future.

3. **Expansionary monetary policy** reduces the interest rate by increasing the money supply. This increases investment spending and consumer spending, which in turn increases aggregate demand and real GDP in the short run. **Contractionary monetary policy** raises the interest rate by reducing the money supply. This reduces investment spending and consumer spending, which in turn reduces aggregate demand and real GDP in the short run.

4. The Federal Reserve and other central banks try to stabilize the economy, limiting fluctuations of actual output around potential output, while also keeping inflation low but positive. Under a **Taylor rule for monetary policy,** the target federal funds rate rises when there is high inflation and either a positive output gap or very low unemployment; it falls when there is low or negative inflation and either a negative output gap or high unemployment. Some central banks, including the Fed, engage in **inflation targeting,** which is a forward-looking policy rule, whereas the Taylor rule method is a backward-looking policy rule. Because monetary policy is subject to fewer implementation lags than fiscal policy, it is the preferred policy tool for stabilizing the economy. However, because interest rates cannot fall much below zero without causing significant problems, there is a **zero lower bound for interest rates.** As a result, the effectiveness of monetary policy is limited.

5. In the long run, changes in the money supply affect the aggregate price level but not real GDP or the interest rate. Data show that the concept of **monetary neutrality** holds: changes in the money supply have no real effect on the economy in the long run.

KEY TERMS

PRACTICE QUESTIONS

1. The rise of electronic payment systems has encouraged more peer-to-peer lending programs. These programs connect lenders and borrowers outside the traditional banking system. As the Federal Reserve relies on changes to the money supply through open-market operations and ultimately bank lending, how will a rise of peer-to-peer lending networks affect the Federal Reserve's ability to conduct effective monetary policy?

2. John Maynard Keynes said, "In the long run we are all dead." How is this quote consistent with the concept of money neutrality? How is it inconsistent?

3. According to the European Central Bank website, the treaty establishing the European Community "makes clear that ensuring price stability is the most important contribution that monetary policy can make to achieve a favourable economic environment and a high level of employment." If price stability is the only goal of monetary policy, explain how monetary policy would be conducted during recessions. Analyze both the case of a recession that is the result of a demand shock and the case of a recession that is the result of a supply shock.

PROBLEMS

1. Access the Discovering Data exercise for Chapter 15, Problem 1 online to answer the following questions.

   a. What is the target federal funds rate?

   b. Is the target federal funds rate different from the target federal funds rate in the previous FOMC statement? If yes, by how much does it differ?

   c. Does the statement comment on current macroeconomic conditions in the United States? How does it describe the U.S. economy?

2. How will the following events affect the demand for money? In each case, specify whether there is a shift of the demand curve or a movement along the demand curve and its direction.

   a. There is a fall in the interest rate from 12% to 10%.

   b. Thanksgiving arrives and, with it, the beginning of the holiday shopping season.

   c. Increasingly, merchants are adopting electronic payment systems that allow more consumers to use PayPal and Apple Pay to make purchases.

   d. The Fed engages in an open-market purchase of U.S. Treasury bills.

3. a. Go to www.treasurydirect.gov. Under "Auctions," go to "Recent Auction Results." Click on "20 Most Recent Auctions." Under the tab "Bills," find the investment rate for the most recently issued 52-week T-bills?

   b. Go to the website of your favorite bank. What is the interest rate for one-year CDs?

   c. Why are the rates for one-year CDs higher than for 52-week Treasury bills?

4. Go to www.treasurydirect.gov. Under "Auctions," go to "Recent Auction Results." Click on "20 Most Recent Auctions." Find the most recent auction results for notes (treasury bonds with maturities from 2 to 10 years).

   a. What are the interest rates on 2-year and 10-year notes?

   b. How do the interest rates on the 2-year and 10-year notes relate to each other? Why is the interest rate on the 10-year note higher (or lower) than the interest rate on the 2-year note?

5. An economy is facing the recessionary gap shown in the accompanying diagram. To eliminate the gap, should the central bank use expansionary or contractionary monetary policy? How will the interest rate, investment spending, consumer spending, real GDP, and the inflation rate change as monetary policy closes the recessionary gap?

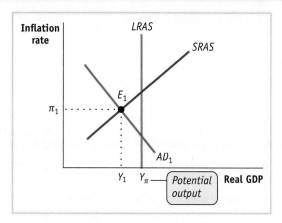

6. An economy is facing the inflationary gap shown in the accompanying diagram. To eliminate the gap, should the central bank use expansionary or contractionary monetary policy? How will the interest rate, investment spending, consumer spending, real GDP, and the inflation rate change as monetary policy closes the inflationary gap?

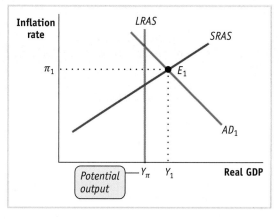

7. In the economy of Eastlandia, the money market is initially in equilibrium when the economy begins to slide into a recession.

   a. Using the accompanying diagram, explain what will happen to the interest rate if the central bank of Eastlandia keeps the money supply constant at $\overline{M}_1$.

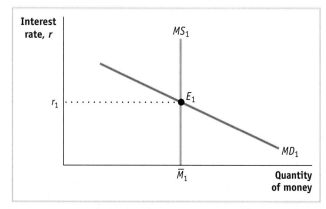

b. If the central bank is instead committed to maintaining an interest rate target of r_1, then as the economy slides into a recession, how should the central bank react? Using your diagram from part a, demonstrate the central bank's reaction.

8. Suppose that the money market in Westlandia is initially in equilibrium and the central bank decides to decrease the money supply.

   a. Using a diagram like the one in Problem 7, explain what will happen to the interest rate in the short run.

   b. What will happen to the interest rate in the long run?

9. An economy is in long-run macroeconomic equilibrium with an unemployment rate of 5% when the government passes a law requiring the central bank to use monetary policy to lower the unemployment rate to 3% and keep it there. How could the central bank achieve this goal in the short run? What would happen in the long run? Illustrate with a diagram.

10. The effectiveness of monetary policy depends on how easy it is for changes in the money supply to change interest rates. By changing interest rates, monetary policy affects investment spending and the aggregate demand curve. The economies of Albernia and Brittania have very different money demand curves, as shown in the accompanying diagram. In which economy will changes in the money supply be a more effective policy tool? Why?

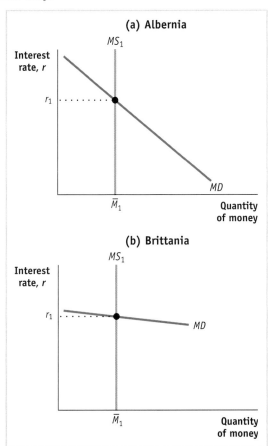

(a) Albernia

(b) Brittania

11. During the Great Depression, businesspeople in the United States were very pessimistic about the future of economic growth and reluctant to increase investment spending even when interest rates fell. How did this limit the potential for monetary policy to help alleviate the Depression?

12. Access the Discovering Data exercise for Chapter 15, Problem 12 online to answer the following questions.

   a. How does the relationship between the effective federal funds rate and the Taylor rule change throughout the Great Recession?

   b. Compare the long-term and short-term interest rate before and after the Great Recession.

13. Because of the economic slowdown associated with the 2007–2009 recession, the Federal Open Market Committee of the Federal Reserve, between September 18, 2007, and December 16, 2008, lowered the federal funds rate in a series of steps from a high of 5.25% to a rate between zero and 0.25%. The idea was to provide a boost to the economy by increasing aggregate demand.

   a. Use the liquidity preference model to explain how the Federal Open Market Committee lowers the interest rate in the short run. Draw a typical graph that illustrates the mechanism. Label the vertical axis "Interest rate" and the horizontal axis "Quantity of money." Your graph should show two interest rates, r_1 and r_2.

   b. Explain why the reduction in the interest rate causes aggregate demand to increase in the short run.

   c. Suppose that in 2022 the economy is at potential output but that this is somehow overlooked by the Fed, which continues its monetary expansion. Demonstrate the effect of the policy measure on the *AD* curve. Use the *LRAS* curve to show that the effect of this policy measure on the *AD* curve, other things equal, causes the aggregate price level to rise in the long run. Label the vertical axis "Aggregate price level" and the horizontal axis "Real GDP." ■

Reconciling the Two Models of the Interest Rate

In the liquidity preference model of the interest rate developed in Chapter 15, at the equilibrium interest rate the quantity of money demanded equals the quantity of money supplied. Yet, in the loanable funds model of the interest rate developed in Chapter 10, the equilibrium interest rate matches the quantity of loanable funds supplied by savers with the quantity of loanable funds demanded for investment spending. Can these two models of the interest rate be reconciled? Yes, they can. We will do this in two steps, focusing first on the short run and then on the long run.

The Interest Rate in the Short Run

As explained in the chapter, a fall in the interest rate leads to a rise in investment spending, I, which then leads to a rise in both real GDP and consumer spending, C. The rise in real GDP doesn't lead only to a rise in consumer spending, however. It also leads to a rise in savings: at each stage of the multiplier process, part of the increase in disposable income is saved. How much do savings rise?

In Chapter 10, we introduced the *savings–investment spending identity:* total savings in the economy is always equal to investment spending. *This tells us that when a fall in the interest rate leads to higher investment spending, the resulting increase in real GDP generates exactly enough additional savings to match the rise in investment spending.* To put it another way, after a fall in the interest rate, the quantity of savings supplied rises exactly enough to match the quantity of savings demanded. Understanding this relationship is the key to reconciling the two models of the interest rate.

Figure A-1 illustrates how the two models of the interest rate are reconciled in the short run. Panel (a) shows the liquidity preference model of the interest rate where MS_1 and MD_1 are the initial supply and demand curves for money, and r_1, the initial equilibrium interest rate, equalizes the quantity of money supplied to the quantity of money demanded in the money market. Panel (b) shows the loanable funds model of the interest rate where S_1 is the initial supply curve, D is the demand curve for loanable funds, and r_1, the initial equilibrium interest rate, equalizes the quantity of loanable funds supplied to the quantity of loanable funds demanded in the market for loanable funds.

In Figure A-1, both the money market and the market for loanable funds are initially in equilibrium at E_1 with the same interest rate, r_1. You might think that this would only happen by accident, but in fact it will always be true. To see why, consider what happens in panel (a), the money market, when the Fed increases the money supply from $\overline{M}_1$ to $\overline{M}_2$, pushing the money supply curve rightward, to MS_2, reducing the equilibrium interest rate in the market to r_2, and moving the economy to a short-run equilibrium at E_2.

What happens in panel (b), the market for loanable funds? In the short run, the fall in the interest rate due to the increase in the money supply leads to a rise in real GDP, which generates a rise in savings through the multiplier process. This rise in savings shifts the supply curve for loanable funds rightward, from S_1 to S_2, moving the equilibrium in the loanable funds market from E_1 to E_2 and reducing the equilibrium interest rate in the loanable funds market. Since the rise in

FIGURE A-1 The Short-Run Determination of the Interest Rate

(a) The Liquidity Preference Model of the Interest Rate

In the short run, an increase in the money supply reduces the interest rate . . .

(b) The Loanable Funds Model of the Interest Rate

. . . which leads to a short-run increase in real GDP and an increase in the supply of loanable funds.

Panel (a) shows the liquidity preference model of the interest rate: the equilibrium interest rate matches the money supply to the quantity of money demanded. In the short run, the interest rate is determined in the money market, where an increase in the money supply, from $\overline{M}_1$ to $\overline{M}_2$, pushes the equilibrium interest rates down, from r_1 to r_2. Panel (b) shows the loanable funds model of the interest rate. The fall in the interest rate in the money market leads, through the multiplier effect, to an increase in real GDP and savings; to a rightward shift of the supply curve of loanable funds, from S_1 to S_2; and to a fall in the interest rate, from r_1 to r_2. As a result, the new equilibrium interest rate in the loanable funds market matches the new equilibrium interest rate in the money market at r_2.

savings must exactly match the rise in investment spending, the equilibrium rate in the loanable funds market must fall to r_2, the same as the new equilibrium interest rate in the money market.

In the short run, then, the supply and demand for money determine the interest rate, and the loanable funds market follows the lead of the money market until the equilibrium interest rate in the loanable funds market is the same as the equilibrium interest rate in the money market.

Notice our use of the phrase *in the short run*. Changes in aggregate demand affect aggregate output only in the short run. In the long run, aggregate output is equal to potential output. So our story about how a fall in the interest rate leads to a rise in aggregate output, which leads to a rise in savings, applies only to the short run.

In the long run, as we'll see next, the determination of the interest rate is quite different, because the roles of the two markets are reversed. In the long run, the loanable funds market determines the equilibrium interest rate, and it is the market for money that follows the lead of the loanable funds market.

The Interest Rate in the Long Run

In the short run an increase in the money supply leads to a fall in the interest rate, and a decrease in the money supply leads to a rise in the interest rate. In the long run, however, changes in the money supply don't affect the interest rate.

Figure A-2 shows why. As in Figure A-1, panel (a) shows the liquidity preference model of the interest rate and panel (b) shows the supply and demand for loanable funds. We assume that in both panels the economy is initially at E_1, in long-run

FIGURE A-2 The Long-Run Determination of the Interest Rate

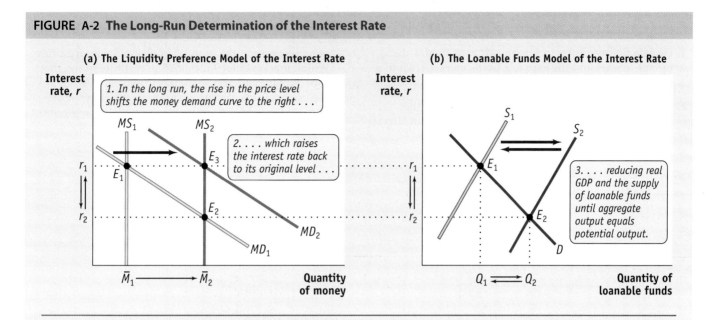

Panel (a) shows the liquidity preference model long-run adjustment to an increase in the money supply from $\bar{M}_1$ to $\bar{M}_2$; panel (b) shows the corresponding long-run adjustment in the loanable funds market. Both panels start from E_1, a long-run macroeconomic equilibrium at potential output and with interest rate r_1. As we discussed in Figure A-1, the increase in the money supply reduces the interest rate from r_1 to r_2, increases real GDP, and increases savings in the short run. This is shown in panels (a) and (b) as the movement from E_1 to E_2. In the long run, however, the increase in the money supply

raises wages and other nominal prices. This shifts the money demand curve in panel (a) from MD_1 to MD_2, leading to an increase in the interest rate from r_2 to r_1 as the economy moves from E_2 to E_3. The rise in the interest rate causes a fall in real GDP and a fall in savings, shifting the loanable funds supply curve back to S_1 from S_2 and moving the loanable funds market from E_2 back to E_1. In the long run, the equilibrium interest rate is determined by matching the supply of loanable funds to the demand for loanable funds that results when real GDP equals potential output.

macroeconomic equilibrium at potential output with the money supply equal to $\bar{M}_1$. The demand curve for loanable funds is D, and the initial supply curve for loanable funds is S_1. The initial equilibrium interest rate in both markets is r_1.

Now suppose the money supply rises from $\bar{M}_1$ to $\bar{M}_2$. As in Figure A-1, this initially reduces the interest rate to r_2. According to the neutrality of money, in the long run the aggregate price level rises by the same proportion as the increase in the money supply. And we also know that a rise in the aggregate price level increases money demand by the same proportion. So in the long run the money demand curve shifts out to MD_2 as money demand responds to higher prices, and moves the equilibrium interest rate back to its original level, r_1.

Panel (b) of Figure A-2 shows what happens in the market for loanable funds. As before, an increase in the money supply leads to a short-run rise in real GDP, and this shifts the supply of loanable funds rightward from S_1 to S_2. In the long run, however, real GDP falls back to its original level as wages and other nominal prices rise. As a result, the supply of loanable funds, S, which initially shifted from S_1 to S_2, shifts back to S_1.

In the long run, then, changes in the money supply do not affect the interest rate. So what determines the interest rate in the long run, r_1, in Figure A-2? The answer is the supply and demand for loanable funds. More specifically, in the long run the equilibrium interest rate matches the supply and demand for loanable funds that arise at potential output.

PROBLEMS

1. Using a figure similar to Figure A-1, explain how the money market and the loanable funds market react to a reduction in the money supply in the short run.

2. Contrast the short-run effects of an increase in the money supply on the interest rate to the long-run effects of an increase in the money supply on the interest rate. Which market determines the interest rate in the short run? Which market does so in the long run? What are the implications of your answers for the effectiveness of monetary policy in influencing real GDP in the short run and the long run? ■

16

Inflation, Disinflation, and Deflation

THAT AND 900,000 BOLIVARS WILL GET YOU A CUP OF COFFEE

IN 2015, THE SOUTH AMERICAN NATION of Venezuela essentially stopped releasing economic statistics, probably in an attempt to hide how badly things were going—and in particular, to avoid admitting the extent of the country's runaway inflation. But it's unlikely that anyone was fooled.

Independent observers came up with their own measures of inflation; for example, Bloomberg News began releasing a "café con leche index" based on the price of Venezuela's favorite drink. And private citizens, well aware that the value of bolivars, the nation's currency, was plunging, made every effort to get rid of the currency as soon as it came into their hands. Shopkeepers wouldn't put money in the cash register, they would run out to spend it on new supplies. Enterprising individuals would buy goods subject to price controls and smuggle them out to sell in neighboring countries. And everyone tried to exchange bolivars for U.S. dollars on the black market.

In 2019, Venezuela's central bank, the equivalent of the Federal Reserve, finally relented and released inflation numbers, which confirmed what everyone already knew. In 2016, the inflation rate was

"only" 274%; by 2018, it had reached 130,000%. (Inflation fell slightly in 2019, but few expected the reprieve to last.)

Venezuela's experience was shocking, but not unprecedented. In 2008, Zimbabwe briefly reached 500 billion percent inflation before abandoning its currency altogether. In 1994, the inflation rate in Armenia hit 27,000%. In 1991, Nicaraguan inflation exceeded 60,000%. And Zimbabwe's experience was more or less matched by history's most famous example of extreme inflation, which took place in Germany in 1922–1923. Toward the end of the German hyperinflation, prices were rising 16% a *day*, which—through compounding—meant an increase of approximately 500 billion percent over the course of five months.

Germans became so reluctant to hold paper money, which lost value by the hour, that eggs and lumps of coal began to circulate as currency. Firms would pay their workers several times a day so that they could spend their earnings before they lost value (lending new meaning to the term *hourly wage*). Legend has it that customers sitting down at a bar would order two beers at a time, out of fear that the price of a beer would rise before they could order a second round!

The United States has never experienced that kind of inflation. The worst U.S. inflation in modern times took place at the end of the 1970s. From 1978 to 1980, the U.S. inflation rate more than doubled, from 6.4% to 14.5%. Yet inflation at even that rate was profoundly troubling to the American public, and the policies the Federal Reserve pursued in order to get U.S. inflation back down to an acceptable rate led to a severe recession.

What causes inflation to rise and fall? In this chapter, we'll look at the underlying reasons for inflation. We'll see that the underlying causes of very high inflation, the type of inflation suffered by Venezuela, are quite different from the causes of more moderate inflation. We'll also learn why *disinflation*, a reduction in the inflation rate, is often very difficult. Finally, we'll discuss the special problems associated with a falling price level, or deflation. ●

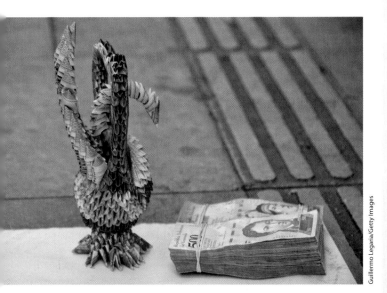

Stacks of currency, worth a lot less than they were even a month earlier.

Guillermo Legaria/Getty Images

WHAT YOU WILL LEARN

- Why can printing money lead to high rates of inflation and hyperinflation?
- How does the **Phillips curve** describe the short-run trade-off between inflation and unemployment?
- Why does the trade-off between inflation and unemployment cease in the long run?
- Why can even moderate levels of inflation be hard to end?
- Why is deflation a problem for economic policy makers?

‖ Money and Inflation

Moderate levels of inflation such as those experienced in the United States—even the double-digit inflation of the late 1970s—can have complex causes. But very high inflation is always associated with rapid increases in the money supply.

To understand why, we need to revisit the effect of changes in the money supply on the overall price level. Then we'll turn to the reasons governments sometimes increase the money supply very rapidly.

The Classical Model of Money and Prices

In the previous chapter we learned that in the short run, expansionary monetary policy increases real GDP by lowering the interest rate and stimulating investment spending and consumer spending. However, in the long run, as prices rise, real GDP falls back to its original level. So in the long run, monetary policy is neutral—it does not change real GDP.

Monetary policy does, however, affect the price level. In particular, as we noted at the end of Chapter 15, in the long run an increase in the money supply will lead to an equal percent rise in the overall price level. That is, the prices of all goods and services in the economy, including nominal wages and the prices of intermediate goods, rise by the same percentage as the money supply.

As a result, a change in the *nominal* money supply, M, leads in the long run to a change in the aggregate price level that leaves the *real* quantity of money, M/P, at its original level, with no long-run effect on aggregate demand or real GDP. For example, when Turkey dropped six zeros from its currency, the Turkish lira, in January 2005, Turkish real GDP did not change. The only thing that changed was the number of zeros in prices: instead of something costing 2,000,000 lira, it cost 2 lira.

This is, to repeat, what happens in the long run. When analyzing high inflation, however, macroeconomists often find it useful to ignore the distinction between the short run and the long run. Instead, they work with a simplified model in which the effect of a change in the money supply on the aggregate price level takes place instantaneously rather than over a long period of time. You might be concerned about this assumption, given that in previous chapters we've emphasized the difference between the short run and the long run. However, for reasons we'll explain shortly, this is a reasonable assumption to make in the case of high inflation.

A simplified model in which the real quantity of money, M/P, is always at its long-run equilibrium level is known as the **classical model of the price level** because it was commonly used by "classical" economists who wrote before the work of John Maynard Keynes.

The classical model performs poorly during periods of low inflation, because it may take a while for workers and firms to react to a monetary expansion by raising wages and prices. In the face of high inflation, however, economists have observed that the short-run stickiness of nominal wages and prices tends to vanish. Workers and businesses, sensitized to inflation, are quick to raise their wages and prices in response to changes in the money supply. This implies that under high inflation, there is a quicker adjustment of wages and prices of intermediate goods than occurs in the case of low inflation. So the short-run aggregate supply curve shifts leftward more quickly, and there is a more rapid return to long-run equilibrium under high inflation. As a result, the classical model of the price level is much more likely to be a good approximation of reality for economies experiencing persistently high inflation.

The consequence of this rapid adjustment of all prices in the economy is that in countries with persistently high inflation, changes in the money supply are quickly translated into changes in the inflation rate. Let's look at Venezuela.

classical model of the price level a simplified financial model of the price level in which the real quantity of money, M/P, is always at its long-run equilibrium level. This model ignores the distinction between the short run and the long run but is useful for analyzing the case of high inflation.

FIGURE 1 Money Supply Growth and Inflation in Venezuela

This figure shows *monthly* rates of change in Venezuela's monetary base and consumer prices as the country spiraled into hyperinflation. Surges in the monetary base were quickly reflected in surges in the price level.

Data from: Central Bank of Venezuela.

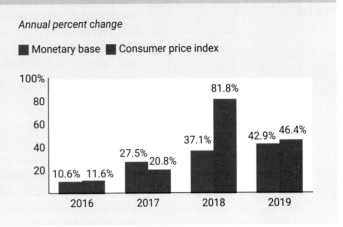

Annual percent change

■ Monetary base ■ Consumer price index

Year	Monetary base	Consumer price index
2016	10.6%	11.6%
2017	27.5%	20.8%
2018	37.1%	81.8%
2019	42.9%	46.4%

Figure 1 shows the *monthly* rate of growth in the money supply (as measured by the monetary base) and the monthly rate of change of consumer prices from 2016 through 2019. We use monthly rates of change partly because that is how people in very-high-inflation economies tend to think about inflation, partly because otherwise inflation at "only" a few hundred percent per year would be invisible. As you can see, the surge in the growth rate of the money supply coincided with a surge in the inflation rate.

What leads a country to increase its money supply so much that the result is an inflation rate in the thousands of percent per year?

The Inflation Tax

Modern economies use fiat money—pieces of paper that have no intrinsic value but are accepted as a medium of exchange. In the United States and most other wealthy countries, the decision about how many pieces of paper to issue is placed in the hands of a central bank that is somewhat independent of the political process. However, this independence can always be taken away if politicians decide to seize control of monetary policy.

So what is to prevent a government from paying for some of its expenses not by raising taxes or borrowing but simply by printing money? Nothing. In fact, governments, including the U.S. government, do it all the time. How can the U.S. government do this, given that the Federal Reserve issues money, not the U.S. Treasury? The answer is that the Treasury and the Federal Reserve work in concert. The Treasury issues debt to finance the government's purchases of goods and services, and the Fed *monetizes* the debt by creating money and buying the debt back from the public through open-market purchases of Treasury bills. In effect, the U.S. government can and does raise revenue by printing money.

For example, in August 2008, the U.S. monetary base—bank reserves plus currency in circulation—was $18 billion larger than it had been a year earlier. This occurred because, over the course of that year, the Federal Reserve had issued $20 billion in money or its electronic

inflation tax the reduction in the value of money held by the public as a result of inflation.

equivalent and put it into circulation through open-market operations. To put it another way, the Fed created money out of thin air and used it to buy valuable government securities from the private sector. It's true that the U.S. government pays interest on debt owned by the Federal Reserve—but the Fed, by law, hands the interest payments it receives on government debt back to the Treasury, keeping only enough to fund its own operations. In effect, then, the Federal Reserve's actions enabled the government to pay off $18 billion in outstanding government debt by printing money.

An alternative way to look at this is to say that the right to print money is itself a source of revenue. Economists refer to the revenue generated by the government's right to print money as *seigniorage*, an archaic term that goes back to the Middle Ages. It refers to the right to stamp gold and silver into coins, and charge a fee for doing so, that medieval lords—*seigniors,* in Medieval France—reserved for themselves.

Seigniorage normally accounts for only a tiny fraction (less than 1%) of the U.S. government's budget. Furthermore, concerns about seigniorage don't have any influence on the Federal Reserve's decisions about how much money to print; the Fed is worried about inflation and unemployment, not revenue. But this hasn't always been true, even in the United States: both the North and the South relied on seigniorage to help cover budget deficits during the Civil War. And there have been many occasions in history when governments turned to their printing presses as a crucial source of revenue.

According to the usual scenario, a government finds itself running a large budget deficit, but lacks either the competence or the political will to eliminate this deficit by raising taxes or cutting spending. Furthermore, the government can't borrow to cover the gap because potential lenders won't extend loans given the fear that the government's weakness will continue and leave it unable to repay its debts.

In such a situation, governments end up printing money to cover the budget deficit. But by printing money to pay its bills, a government increases the quantity of money in circulation. And as we've just seen, increases in the money supply sooner or later translate into equally large increases in the aggregate price level. So printing money to cover a budget deficit leads to inflation.

Who ends up paying for the goods and services the government purchases with newly printed money? The people who currently hold money pay. They pay because inflation erodes the purchasing power of their money holdings. In other words, a government imposes an **inflation tax,** the reduction in the value of the money held by the public, by printing money to cover its budget deficit and creating inflation.

It's helpful to think about what this tax represents. If the inflation rate is 5%, then a year from now $1 will buy goods and services worth only $0.95 today. So a 5% inflation rate in effect imposes a tax rate of 5% on the value of all money held by the public.

But why would any government push the inflation tax to rates of hundreds or thousands of percent? We turn next to the logic of hyperinflation.

The Logic of Hyperinflation

Inflation imposes a tax on individuals who hold money. And, like most taxes, it will lead people to change their behavior. In particular, when inflation is high, people will try to avoid holding money and will instead substitute real goods as well as interest-bearing assets for money. In the opening story we described how, during the German hyperinflation, people began using eggs or lumps of coal as a medium of exchange. They did this because lumps of coal maintained their real value over time, but money didn't. Indeed, during the peak of German hyperinflation, people often burned paper money, which was less valuable than wood.

Moreover, people don't just reduce their nominal money holdings—they reduce their *real* money holdings, cutting the amount of money they hold so much that it actually has less purchasing power than the amount of money they would hold if inflation were low. They do this by using the money to buy goods that last over time or assets that hold their value, like gold. Why? Because the more real money holdings they have, the greater the real amount of resources the government captures from them through the inflation tax.

We are now ready to understand how countries can get themselves into situations of extreme inflation. High inflation arises when the government must print a large quantity of money, imposing a large inflation tax, to cover a large budget deficit.

Now, the seigniorage collected by the government over a short period—say, one month—is equal to the change in the money supply over that period. Let's use M to represent the money supply and use the symbol Δ to mean "monthly change in." Then:

(1) Seigniorage $= \Delta M$

In the 1920s, hyperinflation made German currency worth so little that children made kites from banknotes.

The money value of seigniorage, however, isn't very informative by itself. After all, the whole point of inflation is that a given amount of money buys less and less over time. So it's more useful to look at *real* seigniorage, the revenue created by printing money divided by the price level, P:

(2) Real seigniorage $= \Delta M/P$

Equation 2 can be rewritten by dividing and multiplying by the current level of the money supply, M, giving us:

(3) Real seigniorage $= (\Delta M/M) \times (M/P)$

or

Real seigniorage = Rate of growth of the money supply $\times$ Real money supply

But as we've just explained, in the face of high inflation the public reduces the real amount of money it holds, so the far right-hand term in Equation 3, M/P, gets smaller. Suppose that the government needs to print enough money to pay for a given quantity of goods and services—that is, it needs to collect a given *real* amount of seigniorage. Then, as the real money supply, M/P, falls as people hold smaller amounts of real money, the government has to respond by accelerating the rate of growth of the money supply, $\Delta M/M$. This will lead to an even higher rate of inflation. And people will respond to this new higher rate of inflation by reducing their real money holdings, M/P, yet again.

As the process becomes self-reinforcing, it can easily spiral out of control. Although the amount of real seigniorage that the government must ultimately collect to pay off its deficit does not change, the inflation rate the government needs to impose to collect that amount rises. So the government is forced to increase the money supply more rapidly, leading to an even higher rate of inflation, and so on.

Here's an analogy: imagine a city government that tries to raise a lot of money with a special fee on parking. The fee will raise the cost of parking in the city, and this will cause people to turn to easily available substitutes, such as walking or taking the bus. As the number of parked cars declines, the government finds that its tax revenue declines, and it must impose a higher fee to raise the same amount of revenue as before. You can imagine the ensuing vicious circle: the government imposes fees on parking, which leads to less parking, which causes the government to raise the fee on parking, which leads to even less parking, and so on.

Substitute the real money supply for parking and the inflation rate for the fee on parking, and you have the story of hyperinflation. A race develops between the government printing presses and the public: the presses churn out money at a faster and faster rate to try to compensate for the fact that the public is reducing its real money holdings. At some point the inflation rate explodes into hyperinflation, and people are unwilling to hold any money at all (and resort to trading in eggs and lumps of coal). The government is then forced to abandon its use of the inflation tax and shut down the printing presses.

ECONOMICS >> *in Action*
Behind Venezuela's Inflation

FIGURE 2 Real Oil Prices, 2010–2023

U.S. Dollars (January 2005 = 100)

Data from: U.S. Energy Information Administration.

Venezuela offers the most recent example of a country experiencing very high inflation. Figure 1 showed that surges in Venezuela's money supply growth were matched by almost simultaneous surges in its inflation rate. But why did Venezuela's government pursue policies that led to runaway inflation?

Venezuela used to be relatively rich compared with other major Latin American nations. This wealth, however, rested on a very narrow base: the Venezuelan economy was almost completely reliant on oil exports. And many Venezuelans felt that they weren't getting their fair share of the country's income, that it was being siphoned off for the benefit of a small, wealthy minority.

In 1999 Hugo Chavez, a left-wing populist, took power with the promise to use Venezuela's oil wealth to help the poor and working class. For a number of years he delivered at least partly on that promise, increasing spending on social programs and presiding over what appears to have been a substantial reduction in poverty. However, he did nothing to diversify Venezuela away from its dependence on oil.

Chavez died in 2013, and his successor, Nicolas Maduro, soon found himself in trouble, largely because of a collapse in global oil prices. Figure 2 shows the real price of oil—that is, the price adjusted for inflation—in the United States since 2010. Prices plunged in 2013, largely because fracking led to a surge in the supply of oil and other hydrocarbons, mainly natural gas. And Venezuela's government, deeply dependent on oil revenue, no longer had the money to pay for Chavez's programs.

Instead of cutting back or seeking new revenue sources, however, the Maduro government tried to close the budget gap by printing money. When this, predictably, led to inflation, the Venezuelan government tried to suppress the inflation with price controls, leading to widespread shortages that probably made the inflation worse.

While there are many unique details to the Venezuela story, overall it fits the classic pattern, in which a government that can't or won't pay for its operations turns to the printing press, and stumbles its way into hyperinflation.

>> *Quick Review*

• The **classical model of the price level** does not distinguish between the short and the long run. It explains how increases in the money supply feed directly into inflation. It is a good description of reality only for countries with persistently high inflation or hyperinflation.

• Governments sometimes print money to cover a budget deficit. The resulting loss in the value of money is called the **inflation tax.**

• A high inflation rate causes people to reduce their real money holdings, leading to the printing of more money and higher inflation in order to collect the inflation tax. This can cause a self-reinforcing spiral into hyperinflation.

>> *Check Your Understanding* 16-1
Solutions appear at back of book.

1. Suppose there is a large increase in the money supply in an economy that previously had low inflation. As a consequence, aggregate output expands in the short run. What does this say about situations in which the classical model of the price level applies?

2. Suppose that all wages and prices in an economy are indexed to inflation—that is, wages and prices are automatically adjusted to incorporate the latest inflation figures. Can there still be an inflation tax?

‖ Moderate Inflation and Disinflation

The governments of wealthy, politically stable countries, like the United States and Britain, don't find themselves forced to print money to pay their bills. Yet over the past 40 years, both countries, along with a number of other nations, have experienced uncomfortable episodes of inflation. In the United States, the inflation rate peaked at 14% at the beginning of the 1980s. In Britain, the inflation rate reached 26% in 1975. There was a second, smaller bout of inflation after 2021, with U.S. inflation at an annual rate peaking at 9% in June 2022 before declining. Why did policy makers allow this to happen?

The answer, in brief, is that in the short run, policies that produce a booming economy also tend to lead to higher inflation, and policies that reduce inflation tend to depress the economy. This creates both temptations and dilemmas for governments.

First, imagine yourself as a politician facing an election in a year or two, and suppose that inflation is fairly low at the moment. You might well be tempted to pursue expansionary policies that will push the unemployment rate down as a way to please voters, even if your economic advisers warn that this will eventually lead to higher inflation. You might also be tempted to find different economic advisers who will tell you not to worry: in politics, as in ordinary life, wishful thinking often prevails over realistic analysis.

Conversely, imagine yourself as a politician in an economy suffering from inflation. Your economic advisers will probably tell you that the only way to bring inflation down is to push the economy into a recession, which will lead to temporarily higher unemployment. Are you willing to pay that price? Maybe not.

This political dilemma—inflationary policies often produce short-term political gains, but disinflationary policies to bring inflation down carry short-term political costs—explains how countries with no need to impose an inflation tax can end up with serious inflation problems. For example, that 26% rate of inflation in Britain was largely the result of the British government's decision in 1971 to pursue highly expansionary monetary and fiscal policies in order to gain a political advantage. British politicians disregarded warnings that these policies would be inflationary and were extremely reluctant to reverse course when it became clear that the warnings had been accurate.

To be fair, the inflationary episode of the early 2020s, which affected many nations, had causes that went beyond political opportunism. Some of the inflation reflected disruptions associated first with the coronavirus pandemic, then with the war between Russia and Ukraine. Also, governments spent very large sums in 2020 and 2021 in an attempt to mitigate the hardship associated with the pandemic; although this spending wasn't mainly intended to serve as economic stimulus, it nonetheless amounted to strongly expansionary fiscal policy.

But why do expansionary policies lead to inflation? To answer that question, we need to look first at the relationship between output and unemployment.

The Output Gap and the Unemployment Rate

In Chapter 12 we introduced the concept of *potential output,* the level of real GDP that the economy would produce once all prices had fully adjusted. Potential output typically grows steadily over time, reflecting long-run growth. However, as we learned from the *AD–AS* model, actual aggregate output fluctuates around potential output in the short run: a recessionary gap arises when actual aggregate output falls short of potential output. An inflationary gap arises when actual aggregate output exceeds potential output.

Recall that the percentage difference between the actual level of real GDP and potential output is called the *output gap*. A positive or negative output gap occurs when an economy is producing more than or less than what would be "expected" because all prices, including wages in the labor market, have not yet adjusted. And wages, as we've learned, are the prices in the labor market.

Meanwhile, we learned in Chapter 8 that the unemployment rate is composed of both cyclical unemployment and natural unemployment (natural unemployment is the portion of the unemployment rate unaffected by the business cycle). So there is a relationship between the unemployment rate and the output gap. This relationship is defined by two rules:

1. When actual aggregate output is equal to potential output, the actual unemployment rate is equal to the natural rate of unemployment.

2. When the output gap is positive (an inflationary gap), the unemployment rate is *below* the natural rate. When the output gap is negative (a recessionary gap), the unemployment rate is *above* the natural rate.

In other words, fluctuations of aggregate output around the long-run trend of potential output correspond to fluctuations of the unemployment rate around the natural rate.

This makes sense. When the economy is producing less than potential output—when the output gap is negative—it is not making full use of its productive resources. Among the resources that are not fully utilized is labor, the economy's most important resource. So we would expect a negative output gap to be associated with unusually high unemployment. Conversely, when the economy is producing more than potential output, it is temporarily using resources at higher-than-normal rates. With this positive output gap, we would expect to see lower-than-normal unemployment.

Figure 3 confirms this rule. Panel (a) shows the actual and natural rates of unemployment, as estimated by the Congressional Budget Office (CBO). Panel (b) shows two series. One is cyclical unemployment: the difference between the actual unemployment rate and the CBO estimate of the natural rate of unemployment, measured on the left. The other is the CBO estimate of the output gap, measured on the right. To make the relationship clearer, the output gap series is inverted—shown upside down—so that the line goes down if actual output rises above potential output and up if actual output falls below potential output.

As you can see, the two series move together quite closely, showing the strong relationship between the output gap and cyclical unemployment. Years of high cyclical unemployment, like 1982, 1992, 2009, or 2020, were also years of a strongly negative output gap. Years of low cyclical unemployment, like the late 1960s or late 1990s into the early 2000s, were also years of a strongly positive output gap.

The Short-Run Phillips Curve

We've just seen that expansionary policies lead to a lower unemployment rate. Our next step in understanding the temptations and dilemmas facing governments is to show that there is a short-run trade-off between unemployment and inflation—lower unemployment tends to lead to higher inflation, and vice versa. The key concept is that of the *Phillips curve*.

The origins of this concept lie in a famous 1958 paper by the New Zealand–born economist A. W. H. Phillips. Looking at historical data for Britain, he found that when the unemployment rate was high, the wage rate tended to fall, and when the unemployment rate was low, the wage rate tended to rise. Using data from Britain, the United States, and elsewhere, other economists soon found a similar apparent relationship between the unemployment rate and the rate of inflation—that is, the rate of change in the aggregate price level. For example, Figure 4 shows the U.S. unemployment rate and the rate of consumer price inflation over each subsequent year from 1955 to 1968, with each dot representing one year's data.

FIGURE 3 Cyclical Unemployment and the Output Gap

Panel (a) shows the actual U.S. unemployment rate from 1949 through February 2020, together with the Congressional Budget Office estimate of the natural rate of unemployment. The actual rate fluctuates around the natural rate, often for extended periods. Panel (b) shows cyclical unemployment — the difference between the actual unemployment and the natural rate of unemployment — and the output gap, also estimated by the CBO. The unemployment rate is measured on the left vertical axis, and the output gap is measured with an inverted scale on the right vertical axis. With an inverted scale, it moves in the same direction as the unemployment rate: when the output gap is positive, the actual unemployment rate is below its natural rate. And when the output gap is negative, the actual unemployment rate is above its natural rate. The two series track one another closely, showing the strong relationship between the output gap and cyclical unemployment.

Average quarterly unemployment rate measured in percent on *y*-axis.

Data from: (a) Federal Reserve Bank of St. Louis and Bureau of Economic Analysis. (b) Federal Reserve of St. Louis; Bureau of Economic Analysis; and Congressional Budget Office.

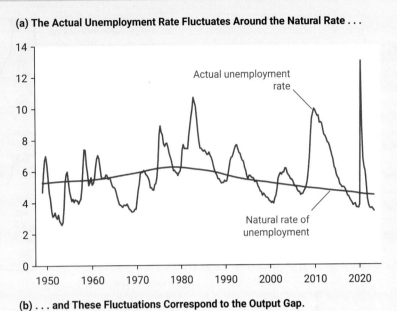

(a) The Actual Unemployment Rate Fluctuates Around the Natural Rate . . .

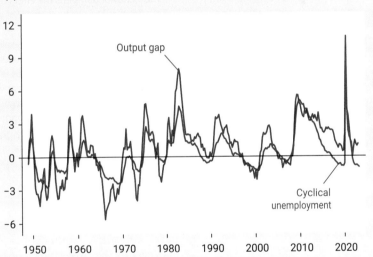

(b) . . . and These Fluctuations Correspond to the Output Gap.

Looking at evidence like Figure 4, many economists concluded that there is a negative short-run relationship between the unemployment rate and the inflation rate, which is called the **short-run Phillips curve,** or *SRPC*. (We'll explain the difference between the short-run and the long-run Phillips curve soon.) Figure 5 shows a hypothetical short-run Phillips curve.

Early estimates of the short-run Phillips curve for the United States were very simple: they showed a negative relationship between the unemployment rate and the inflation rate, without taking account of any other variables. During the 1950s and 1960s, this simple approach seemed, for a while, to be adequate. And this simple relationship is clear in the data in Figure 4.

Even at the time, however, some economists argued that a more accurate short-run Phillips curve would include other factors. In Chapter 12 we discussed the effect of *supply shocks,* such as sudden changes in the price of oil, which shift the short-run aggregate supply curve. Such shocks also shift the short-run Phillips curve: surging oil prices were an important factor in the inflation of the 1970s

short-run Phillips curve a graphical representation of the negative short-run relationship between the unemployment rate and the inflation rate.

FOR INQUIRING MINDS Okun's Law

Although cyclical unemployment and the output gap move together, cyclical unemployment seems to move *less* than the output gap. For example, the output gap reached −8% in 1982, but the cyclical unemployment rate reached only 4%. This observation is the basis of an important relationship originally discovered by the economist Arthur Okun.

Modern estimates of **Okun's law** — the negative relationship between the output gap and the cyclical unemployment rate — typically find that a rise in the output gap of 1 percentage point reduces the unemployment rate by about $\frac{1}{2}$ of a percentage point.

For example, suppose that the natural rate of unemployment is 5.2% and that the economy is currently producing at only 98% of potential output. In that case, the output gap is −2%, and Okun's law predicts an unemployment rate of $5.2\% - \frac{1}{2} \times (-2\%) = 6.2\%$.

The fact that a 1% rise in output reduces the unemployment rate by only $\frac{1}{2}$ of 1% may seem puzzling: you might have expected to see a one-to-one relationship between the output gap and unemployment. Doesn't a 1% rise in aggregate output require a 1% increase in employment? And shouldn't that take 1% off the unemployment rate?

The answer is no: there are several well-understood reasons why the relationship isn't one-to-one. For one thing, companies often meet changes in demand in part by changing the number of hours their existing employees work. For example, a company that experiences a sudden increase in demand for its products may cope by asking (or requiring) its workers to put in longer hours, rather than by hiring more workers. Conversely, a company that sees sales drop will often reduce workers' hours rather than lay off employees. This behavior dampens the effect of output fluctuations on the number of workers employed.

Also, the number of workers looking for jobs is affected by the availability of jobs. Suppose that the number of jobs falls by 1 million. Measured unemployment will rise by less than 1 million because some unemployed workers become discouraged and give up actively looking for work. (Recall that workers aren't counted as unemployed unless they are actively seeking work.)

Conversely, if the economy adds 1 million jobs, some people who haven't been actively looking for work will begin doing so. As a result, measured unemployment will fall by less than 1 million.

Finally, the rate of growth of labor productivity generally accelerates during booms and slows down or even turns negative during busts. The reasons for this phenomenon are the subject of some dispute among economists. The consequence, however, is that the effects of booms and busts on the unemployment rate are dampened.

Okun's law the negative relationship between the output gap and the unemployment rate, whereby each additional percentage point of output gap reduces the unemployment rate by about 1/2 of a percentage point.

expected rate of inflation the inflation rate that businesses and workers are expecting in the near future.

and also played an important role in the acceleration of inflation in 2007–2008. In general, a negative supply shock shifts *SRPC* up as the inflation rate increases for every level of the unemployment rate, and a positive supply shock shifts it down as the inflation rate falls for every level of the unemployment rate. Both outcomes are shown in Figure 5.

A negative supply shock shifts the *SRPC* up, and a positive supply shock shifts the *SRPC* down. But supply shocks are not the only factors that can change the inflation rate. In the early 1960s, Americans had little experience with inflation because inflation rates had been low for decades. But by the late 1960s, after inflation had been steadily increasing for a number of years, Americans had come to expect future inflation. In 1968, two economists — Milton Friedman of the University of Chicago and Edmund Phelps of Columbia University — independently set forth a crucial hypothesis: that expectations about future inflation directly affect the present inflation rate. Today most economists accept that the *expected inflation rate* — the rate of inflation that employers and workers expect in the near future — is the most important factor, other than the unemployment rate, affecting inflation.

Inflation Expectations and the Short-Run Phillips Curve

The **expected rate of inflation** is the rate of inflation that employers and workers expect in the near future. One of the crucial discoveries of modern

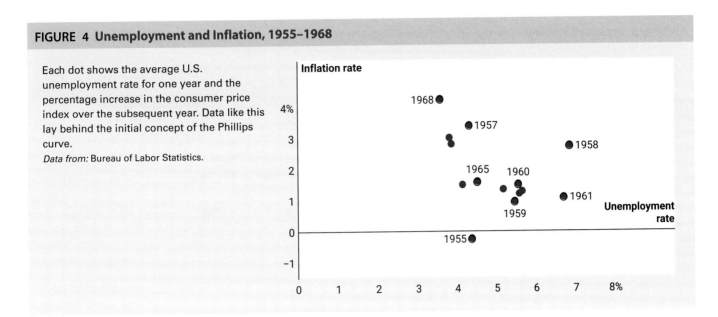

FIGURE 4 Unemployment and Inflation, 1955–1968

Each dot shows the average U.S. unemployment rate for one year and the percentage increase in the consumer price index over the subsequent year. Data like this lay behind the initial concept of the Phillips curve.

Data from: Bureau of Labor Statistics.

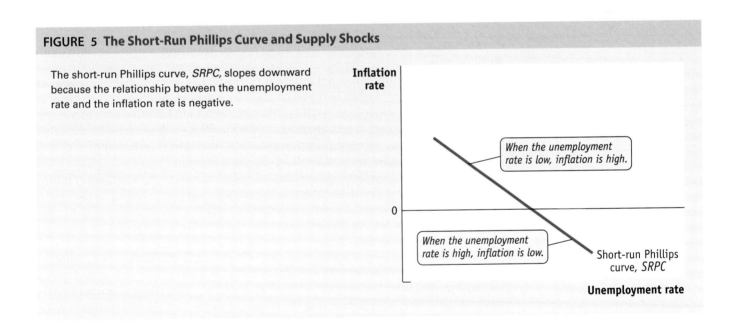

FIGURE 5 The Short-Run Phillips Curve and Supply Shocks

The short-run Phillips curve, *SRPC,* slopes downward because the relationship between the unemployment rate and the inflation rate is negative.

When the unemployment rate is low, inflation is high.

When the unemployment rate is high, inflation is low.

Short-run Phillips curve, *SRPC*

macroeconomics is that changes in the expected rate of inflation affect the short-run trade-off between unemployment and inflation and shift the short-run Phillips curve.

Why do changes in expected inflation affect the short-run Phillips curve? Put yourself in the position of a worker and employer about to sign a contract setting the worker's wages over the next year. For a number of reasons, the wage rate they agree to will be higher if everyone expects high inflation (including rising wages) than if everyone expects prices to be stable. The worker will want a wage rate that takes into account future declines in the purchasing power of earnings. They will also want a wage rate that won't fall behind the wages of other workers. And the employer will be more willing to agree to a wage increase now if hiring workers later will be even more expensive. Also, rising prices will make paying a higher wage rate more affordable for the employer because the employer's output will sell for more.

FIGURE 6 Expected Inflation and the Short-Run Phillips Curve

An increase in expected inflation shifts the short-run Phillips curve up. $SRPC_0$ is the initial short-run Phillips curve with an expected inflation rate of 0%; $SRPC_2$ is the short-run Phillips curve with an expected inflation rate of 2%. Each additional percentage point of expected inflation raises the actual inflation rate at any given unemployment rate by 1 percentage point.

For these reasons, an increase in expected inflation shifts the short-run Phillips curve upward: the actual rate of inflation at any given unemployment rate is higher when the expected inflation rate is higher. In fact, macroeconomists believe that the relationship between changes in expected inflation and changes in actual inflation is one-to-one. That is, when the expected inflation rate increases, the actual inflation rate at any given unemployment rate will increase by the same amount. When the expected inflation rate falls, the actual inflation rate at any given level of unemployment will fall by the same amount.

Figure 6 shows how the expected rate of inflation affects the short-run Phillips curve. First, suppose that the expected rate of inflation is 0%. $SRPC_0$ is the short-run Phillips curve when the public expects 0% inflation. According to $SRPC_0$, the actual inflation rate will be 0% if the unemployment rate is 6%; it will be 2% if the unemployment rate is 4%.

Alternatively, suppose the expected rate of inflation is 2%. In that case, employers and workers will build this expectation into wages and prices: at any given unemployment rate, the actual inflation rate will be 2 percentage points higher than it would be if people expected 0% inflation. $SRPC_2$, which shows the Phillips curve when the expected inflation rate is 2%, is $SRPC_0$ shifted upward by 2 percentage points at every level of unemployment. According to $SRPC_2$, the actual inflation rate will be 2% if the unemployment rate is 6%; it will be 4% if the unemployment rate is 4%.

What determines the expected rate of inflation? In general, people base their expectations about inflation on experience. If the inflation rate has hovered around 0% in the last few years, people will expect it to be around 0% in the near future. But if the inflation rate has averaged around 5% lately, people will expect inflation to be around 5% in the near future.

Since expected inflation is an important part of the modern discussion about the short-run Phillips curve, you might wonder why it was not in the original formulation of the Phillips curve. The answer lies in history. Think back to what we said about the early 1960s: at that time, people were accustomed to low inflation rates and reasonably expected that future inflation rates would also be low. It was only after 1965 that persistent inflation became a fact of life. So only then did economists begin to argue that expected inflation should play an important role in price setting.

Sure enough, the seemingly clear relationship between inflation and unemployment fell apart after 1969. Figure 7 plots the track of U.S. unemployment and

FIGURE 7 Unemployment and Inflation, 1961–1990

In the 1970s, the short-run Phillips curve relationship that seemed to hold during the 1950s and 1960s broke down as the U.S. economy experienced a combination of high unemployment and high inflation. Economists believe this was the result of both negative supply shocks and the cumulative effect of several years of higher than expected inflation. Inflation came down during the 1980s, and the 1990s were a time of both low unemployment and low inflation.

Data from: Federal Reserve Bank of St. Louis; Bureau of Labor Statistics.

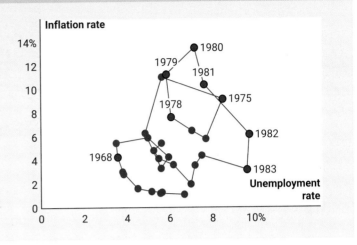

inflation rates from 1961 to 1990. As you can see, the track looks more like a tangled piece of yarn than like a smooth curve.

Through much of the 1970s and early 1980s, the economy suffered from a combination of above-average unemployment rates coupled with inflation rates unprecedented in modern American history. This condition came to be known as *stagflation*—for stagnation combined with high inflation. In the late 1990s, by contrast, the economy was experiencing a blissful combination of low unemployment and low inflation. What explains these developments?

Part of the answer can be attributed to a series of negative supply shocks that the U.S. economy suffered during the 1970s. The price of oil, in particular, soared as wars and revolutions in the Middle East led to a reduction in oil supplies and as oil-exporting countries deliberately curbed production to drive up prices. Compounding the oil price shocks, there was also a slowdown in labor productivity growth. Both of these factors shifted the short-run Phillips curve upward. During the 1990s, by contrast, supply shocks were positive. Prices of oil and other raw materials were generally falling, and productivity growth accelerated. As a result, the short-run Phillips curve shifted downward.

Equally important, however, was the role of expected inflation. As mentioned earlier in the chapter, inflation accelerated during the 1960s. During the 1970s, the public came to expect high inflation, and this also shifted the short-run Phillips curve up. It took a sustained and costly effort during the 1980s to get inflation back down. The result, however, was that expected inflation was very low by the late 1990s, allowing actual inflation to be low even with low rates of unemployment.

In fact, most macroeconomists believe that in the 1990s we recreated conditions somewhat similar to those that prevailed in the 1950s and 1960s: people expected inflation to remain low and stable. As some analysts put it, inflation expectations became "anchored" at an annual rate of around 2%. As a result, the relationship between unemployment and inflation began to look a lot like the original Phillips curve.

ECONOMICS >> *in Action*
The Spanish Squeeze

The relationship between unemployment and inflation isn't exact; few relationships in economics are. By February 2020 the U.S. unemployment rate had

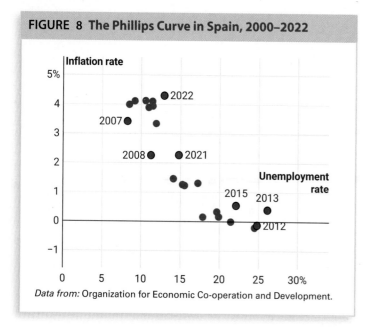

FIGURE 8 The Phillips Curve in Spain, 2000–2022

Data from: Organization for Economic Co-operation and Development.

dropped to just 3.5%, well below its level before the 2008 financial crisis, yet inflation remained low. Economists weren't sure why, although some suggested that the unemployment rate wasn't as good an indicator of labor market tightness as it used to be.

We would still expect, however, to see really big moves in the unemployment rate reflected in the inflation rate. And this is in fact what we see looking at countries that experienced very high unemployment after the 2008 financial crisis.

Spain is an example of a country that has experienced dramatic ups and downs since the start of the twenty-first century. From 2000 to 2007 it experienced a huge boom, driven by an enormous housing bubble, bigger than the one experienced in the United States. When this bubble burst, Spain fell into a deep slump, made worse by large cuts in government spending intended to reassure investors worried about Spain's government debt. As a result, the unemployment rate shot up, reaching an amazing 26% in 2013. After that, and until Covid struck, Spain achieved a gradual recovery.

Did the big swings in Spain's unemployment rate lead to changes in the inflation rate? Yes. Figure 8 shows Spanish unemployment versus inflation (as measured by the GDP deflator) from 2000 to 2019. The low-unemployment-rate years were marked by relatively high inflation, the ultra-high-unemployment-rate years by very low inflation.

You may have noticed that for Spain, "low unemployment" still meant unemployment rates of 8% to 10%, high by U.S. standards. Indeed, Spain seems to have high measured unemployment even when the economy appears to be booming. One reason is that quite a few "unemployed" Spaniards actually do have jobs, but are working off the books to avoid taxes and regulations.

>> Check Your Understanding 16-2

Solutions appear at back of book.

1. Explain how the short-run Phillips curve illustrates the negative relationship between cyclical unemployment and the actual inflation rate for a given level of the expected inflation rate.

2. Which way does the short-run Phillips curve move in response to a fall in commodities prices? To a surge in commodities prices? Explain.

‖ Inflation and Unemployment in the Long Run

The short-run Phillips curve says that at any given point in time, there is a trade-off between unemployment and inflation. According to this view, policy makers have a choice: they can choose whether or not to accept the price of high inflation in order to achieve low unemployment. In fact, during the 1960s, many economists believed that this trade-off represented a real choice.

However, this view was greatly altered by the later recognition that expected inflation affects the short-run Phillips curve. In the short run, expectations often diverge from reality. In the long run, however, any consistent rate of inflation will be reflected in expectations. If inflation is consistently high, as it was in the 1970s, people will come to expect more of the same; if inflation is consistently low, as it has been in recent years, that, too, will become part of expectations.

So what does the trade-off between inflation and unemployment look like in the long run, when actual inflation is incorporated into expectations? Most macroeconomists believe that there is, in fact, no long-run trade-off. That is, it is not possible to achieve lower unemployment in the long run by accepting higher inflation. To see why, we need to introduce another concept: the *long-run Phillips curve.*

The Long-Run Phillips Curve

Figure 9 reproduces the two short-run Phillips curves from Figure 6, $SRPC_0$ and $SRPC_2$. It also adds an additional short-run Phillips curve, $SRPC_4$, representing a 4% expected rate of inflation. In a moment, we'll explain the significance of the vertical long-run Phillips curve, $LRPC$.

Suppose that the economy has, in the past, had a 0% inflation rate. In that case, the current short-run Phillips curve will be $SRPC_0$, reflecting a 0% expected inflation rate. If the unemployment rate is 6%, the actual inflation rate will be 0%.

Also suppose that policy makers decide to trade off lower unemployment for a higher rate of inflation. They use monetary policy, fiscal policy, or both to drive the unemployment rate down to 4%. This puts the economy at point A on $SRPC_0$, leading to an actual inflation rate of 2%.

Over time, the public will come to expect a 2% inflation rate. *This increase in inflationary expectations will shift the short-run Phillips curve upward* to $SRPC_2$. Now, when the unemployment rate is 6%, the actual inflation rate will be 2%. Given this new short-run Phillips curve, policies adopted to keep the unemployment rate at 4% will lead to a 4% actual inflation rate—point B on $SRPC_2$—rather than point A with a 2% actual inflation rate.

Eventually, the 4% actual inflation rate gets built into expectations about the future inflation rate, and the short-run Phillips curve shifts upward yet again to $SRPC_4$. To keep the unemployment rate at 4% would now require accepting a 6% actual inflation rate, point C on $SRPC_4$, and so on. In short, a persistent attempt to trade off lower unemployment for higher inflation leads to *accelerating* inflation over time.

To avoid accelerating inflation over time, the unemployment rate must be high enough that the actual rate of inflation matches the expected rate of inflation.

This is the situation at E_0 on $SRPC_0$: when the expected inflation rate is 0% and the unemployment rate is 6%, the actual inflation rate is 0%. It is also the

FIGURE 9 The NAIRU and the Long-Run Phillips Curve

$SRPC_0$ is the short-run Phillips curve when the expected inflation rate is 0%. At a 4% unemployment rate, the economy is at point A with an actual inflation rate of 2%. The higher inflation rate will be incorporated into expectations, and the $SRPC$ will shift upward to $SRPC_2$. If policy makers act to keep the unemployment rate at 4%, the economy will be at point B and the actual inflation rate will rise to 4%. Inflationary expectations will be revised upward again, and $SRPC$ will shift to $SRPC_4$. At a 4% unemployment rate, the economy will be at point C and the actual inflation rate will rise to 6%. Here, an unemployment rate of 6% is the NAIRU, or nonaccelerating inflation rate of unemployment. As long as unemployment is at the NAIRU, the actual inflation rate will match expectations and remain constant. An unemployment rate below 6% requires ever-accelerating inflation. The long-run Phillips curve, $LRPC$, which passes through E_0, E_2, and E_4, is vertical: no long-run trade-off between unemployment and inflation exists.

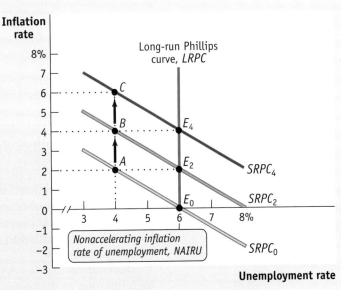

nonaccelerating inflation rate of unemployment (NAIRU) the unemployment rate at which, other things equal, inflation does not change over time.

long-run Phillips curve a graphical representation of the relationship between unemployment and inflation in the long run after expectations of inflation have had time to adjust to experience.

situation at E_2 on $SRPC_2$: when the expected inflation rate is 2% and the unemployment rate is 6%, the actual inflation rate is 2%. And it is the situation at E_4 on $SRPC_4$: when the expected inflation rate is 4% and the unemployment rate is 6%, the actual inflation rate is 4%. This relationship between accelerating inflation and the unemployment rate is known as the *natural rate hypothesis*.

The unemployment rate at which inflation does not change over time—6% in Figure 9—is known as the **nonaccelerating inflation rate of unemployment,** or **NAIRU** for short. Keeping the unemployment rate below the NAIRU leads to ever-accelerating inflation and cannot be maintained. Most macroeconomists believe that there is a NAIRU and that there is no long-run trade-off between unemployment and inflation.

We can now explain the significance of the vertical line *LRPC*. It is the **long-run Phillips curve,** the relationship between unemployment and inflation in the long run, after expectations of inflation have had time to adjust to experience. It is vertical because any unemployment rate below the NAIRU leads to ever-accelerating inflation. In other words, the long-run Phillips curve shows that there are limits to expansionary policies, because an unemployment rate below the NAIRU cannot be maintained in the long run. Moreover, there is a corresponding point we have not yet emphasized: any unemployment rate above the NAIRU leads to decelerating inflation.

The Natural Rate of Unemployment, Revisited

Recall that the natural rate of unemployment is the portion of the unemployment rate unaffected by the swings of the business cycle. Now we have introduced the concept of the *NAIRU*. How do these two concepts relate to each other?

The answer is that the NAIRU is another name for the natural rate. The level of unemployment the economy needs in order to avoid accelerating inflation is equal to the natural rate of unemployment.

In fact, economists estimate the natural rate of unemployment by looking for evidence about the NAIRU from the behavior of the inflation rate and the unemployment rate over the course of the business cycle. For example, the way major European countries learned, to their dismay, that their natural rates of unemployment had risen 9% or more by around 1990, was through unpleasant experience. In the late 1980s, and again in the late 1990s, European inflation began to accelerate as European unemployment rates, which had been above 9%, began to fall, approaching 8%.

In Figure 3, we cited Congressional Budget Office estimates of the U.S. natural rate of unemployment. The CBO has a model that predicts changes in the inflation rate based on the deviation of the actual unemployment rate from the natural rate. Given data on actual unemployment and inflation, this model can be used to deduce estimates of the natural rate—and that's where the CBO numbers come from. In 2023, the CBO estimate of the U.S. natural rate was 4.4%.

The Costs of Disinflation

Through experience, policy makers have found that bringing inflation down can be a much harder task than increasing it. The reason is that once the public has come to expect continuing inflation, bringing inflation down is painful.

A persistent attempt to keep unemployment below the natural rate leads to accelerating inflation that becomes incorporated into expectations. To reduce inflationary expectations, policy makers need to run the process in reverse, adopting contractionary policies that keep the unemployment rate above the natural rate for an extended period of time. The process of bringing down inflation that has become embedded in expectations is known as *disinflation*, a concept discussed in Chapter 8.

Disinflation can be very expensive. As we've noted, the United States had very high inflation at the beginning of the 1980s, but brought the inflation rate down to around 4% by the middle of that decade. However, the process of disinflation

GLOBAL COMPARISON   DISINFLATION AROUND THE WORLD

The disinflation of the 1980s wasn't unique to the United States. A number of other advanced countries also experienced high inflation during the 1970s, then brought inflation down during the 1980s at the cost of a severe recession. This figure shows the annual rate of inflation in Britain, Italy, and the United States from 1970 to 2022. All three nations experienced high inflation rates following the two oil price shocks of 1973 and 1979, with the U.S. inflation rate the least severe of the three. All three nations then weathered severe recessions in order to bring inflation down. Since the 1980s, inflation has remained low and stable in all wealthy nations.

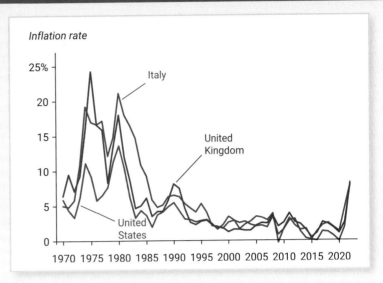

Average annual inflation rate measured in percent on *y*-axis.

Data from: World Development Indicators, World Bank.

was very painful. Figure 7 shows the U.S. inflation rate and unemployment rate from the beginning of 1980 to the end of 1984. Inflation came way down, but only at the cost of a brutal recession that sent the unemployment rate to 10.8%. In fact, unemployment stayed high for a long time: the unemployment rate didn't get below 6% until 1987.

Some economists argue that the costs of disinflation can be reduced if policy makers explicitly state their determination to reduce inflation. A clearly announced, credible policy of disinflation, they contend, can reduce expectations of future inflation and so shift the short-run Phillips curve downward. Some economists believe that the clear determination of the Federal Reserve to combat the inflation of the 1970s was credible enough that the costs of disinflation, huge though they were, were lower than they might otherwise have been.

ECONOMICS >> *in Action*
A Tale of Two Disinflations

U.S. inflation stayed low for a generation after the great disinflation of the 1980s. In 2021–2022, however, it took off again. In fact, at its peak inflation in the 2020s wasn't that much lower than it had been in 1980. In June 2022, consumer prices were 9% higher than they had been a year earlier; using modern methodology (the U.S. Bureau of Labor Statistics calculated inflation slightly differently four decades ago) the corresponding inflation rate was 14.2% in February 1980. As we've mentioned, this sudden burst of inflation probably reflected a combination of disruptions associated with the coronavirus pandemic and large government spending undertaken in an effort to limit hardship from the pandemic.

Whatever its causes, the return of inflation profoundly disturbed both policy makers and the general public, and the Federal Reserve responded by tightening monetary policy in an attempt to bring inflation back down. The big question was whether disinflation would prove as costly in the 2020s as it had been in the 1980s.

Some economists argued that disinflation would indeed require an extended period of very high unemployment. However, there were some reasons to believe that controlling inflation would be much less costly (although not necessarily

FIGURE 10 The Great Disinflation

■ Annual inflation rate ■ Expected inflation rate

Annual inflation rate is measured as the annual rate of change of the consumer price index. Expected inflation rate is measured as households expected inflation over the next five years.

Data from: Bureau of Labor Statistics; University of Michigan Survey of Consumers.

easy) this time around. Crucially, high inflation didn't seem to have become embedded in expectations the way it had in the 1980s.

Figure 10 compares the situation near the peak of both inflationary episodes: February 1980 and June 2022. In each case, the first bar shows the percentage increase in consumer prices over the previous year, while the second bar shows consumer expectations of inflation over the next five years, as measured by the long-running Michigan Survey of Consumers.

In 1980, almost everyone—consumers, businesses, and economists alike—expected inflation to remain around 10% for the indefinite future. This expectation was reflected in decisions about prices and wages—for example, a number of companies with unionized workers were granting contracts that guaranteed wage hikes of 9% or more for several years, because they expected their competitors to be doing the same. To get inflation down, policy makers had to break these expectations.

By contrast, in 2022 most people expected high inflation to be temporary, suggesting that a moderate cooling off of the economy might be enough to bring inflation under control.

At the time of writing, disinflation did seem to be proceeding at a much lower cost than that experienced in the 1980s. As of April 2023, inflation over the previous 6 months was running at an annual rate of only 5%, far below its 2022 peak, while there hadn't yet been any significant rise in unemployment. It wasn't yet clear, however, how hard it would be to get inflation down to roughly 2% which was the Federal Reserve's target.

>> Quick Review

• Policies that keep the unemployment rate below the **NAIRU, the nonaccelerating rate of inflation,** will lead to accelerating inflation as inflationary expectations adjust to higher levels of actual inflation. The NAIRU is equal to the natural rate of unemployment.

• The **long-run Phillips curve** is vertical and shows that an unemployment rate below the NAIRU cannot be maintained in the long run. As a result, there are limits to expansionary policies.

• *Disinflation* imposes high costs — unemployment and lost output — on an economy. Governments adopt it to avoid the costs of persistently high inflation.

>> Check Your Understanding 16-3
Solutions appear at back of book.

1. Why is there no long-run trade-off between unemployment and inflation?

2. British economists believe that the natural rate of unemployment in their country rose sharply during the 1970s, from around 3% to as much as 10%. During that period, Britain experienced a sharp acceleration of inflation, which for a time went above 20%. How might these facts be related?

3. Why is disinflation so costly for an economy? Are there ways to reduce these costs?

|| Deflation

Before World War II, *deflation*—a falling aggregate price level—was almost as common as inflation. (We introduced deflation in Chapter 6.) In fact, the U.S. consumer price index on the eve of World War II was 30% lower than it had been in 1920. After World War II, inflation became the norm in all countries. But in the 1990s, deflation reappeared in Japan and proved difficult to reverse. Concerns about potential deflation played a crucial role in U.S. monetary policy in the early 2000s and again in the aftermath of the 2008 financial crisis.

Why is deflation a problem? And why is it hard to end?

Debt Deflation

Deflation, like inflation, produces both winners and losers—but in the opposite direction. Due to the falling price level, a dollar in the future has a higher real value than a dollar today. So lenders, who are owed money, gain under deflation because the real value of borrowers' payments increases. Borrowers lose because the real burden of their debt rises.

In a famous analysis at the beginning of the Great Depression, Irving Fisher (who first analyzed the *Fisher effect* of expected inflation on interest rates, described in Chapter 10) claimed that the effects of deflation on borrowers and lenders can worsen an economic slump. Deflation, in effect, takes real resources away from borrowers and redistributes them to lenders.

Fisher argued that borrowers, who lose from deflation, are typically short of cash and will be forced to cut their spending sharply when their debt burden rises. Lenders, however, are unlikely to increase spending sharply when the values of the loans they own rise. The overall effect, said Fisher, is that deflation reduces aggregate demand, deepening an economic slump, which, in a vicious circle, may lead to further deflation. The effect of deflation in reducing aggregate demand, known as **debt deflation,** probably played a significant role in the Great Depression.

Effects of Expected Deflation

Like expected inflation, expected deflation affects the nominal interest rate. Look back at Chapter 10, Figure 9, which demonstrated how expected inflation affects the equilibrium interest rate: the equilibrium nominal interest rate is 4% if the expected inflation rate is 0%. But, if the expected inflation rate is –3% — if the public expects deflation at 3% per year — the equilibrium nominal interest rate would fall to 1%.

But what would happen if the expected rate of inflation is –6%? Would the nominal interest rate fall to –2%, in which lenders are paying borrowers 2% on their debt? Probably not, because they could do better by simply holding cash. As explained in Chapter 15, we now know that there isn't a strict zero lower bound because holding lots of cash is inconvenient. But the nominal rate clearly can't go more than a small amount below zero.

This restriction — called the *zero lower bound problem* — can limit the effectiveness of monetary policy. Suppose the economy is depressed, with output below potential output and the unemployment rate above the natural rate. Normally the central bank can respond by cutting interest rates to increase aggregate demand. If the nominal interest rate is already zero, however, the central bank cannot push it down any further. The central bank is up against the zero lower bound for the nominal interest rate. Banks refuse to lend and consumers and firms refuse to spend because, with a negative inflation rate and a 0% nominal interest rate, holding cash yields a positive real return: with falling prices, a given amount of cash buys more over time. Any further increases in the monetary base will either be held in bank vaults or held as cash by individuals and firms, without being spent.

A situation in which conventional monetary policy to fight a slump — cutting interest rates — can't be used because nominal interest rates can't be cut further is known as a **liquidity trap.** A liquidity trap can occur whenever there is a sharp reduction in demand for loanable funds — which is exactly what happened during the Great Depression. Figure 11 shows the interest rate on short-term U.S. government debt from 1920 to 2020. As you can see, during the period from 1933 to the post–World War II recovery, the U.S. economy was either close to or up against the zero lower bound. After World War II, when inflation became the norm around the world, the zero lower bound largely vanished as a problem, as the public came to expect inflation rather than deflation. As a result, economists largely lost interest in the issue.

But, as you can see, the zero lower bound emerged again as a result of the financial crisis of 2008, and again during the coronavirus pandemic. Once more, the interest rate on three-month U.S. Treasury bills was virtually zero. Yet for reasons not entirely clear, the United States did not experience deflation during the Great Recession. Sticky wages may have been the cause, since the United States

debt deflation the reduction in aggregate demand arising from the increase in the real burden of outstanding debt caused by deflation; occurs because borrowers, whose real debt rises as a result of deflation, are likely to cut spending sharply, and lenders, whose real assets are now more valuable, are less likely to increase spending.

liquidity trap the economy is in a liquidity trap when monetary policy is ineffective because nominal interest rates are up against the zero bound.

FIGURE 11 The Zero Lower Bound in the U.S. Economy

This figure shows U.S. short-term interest rates, specifically the interest rate on three-month Treasury bills, from 1920 to 2022. As shown by the shaded bar at left, for much of the 1930s, interest rates were very close to zero, leaving little room for expansionary monetary policy. After World War II, persistent inflation generally kept interest rates well above zero. However, in late 2008, in the wake of the housing bubble bursting and the financial crisis, the interest rate on three-month Treasury bills was again virtually zero and stayed there for almost eight years — shown by the shaded bar at right. During the pandemic, interest rates fell to close to zero yet again until they began to rise in early 2022.

Data from: National Bureau of Economic Research; Federal Reserve Bank of St. Louis.

did not experience a significant fall in nominal wages although unemployment shot up.

The recent history of the Japanese economy, shown in Figure 12, provides the best modern illustration of the problem of deflation and the liquidity trap. In the 1990s, after the bursting of a huge housing and stock bubble, the Japanese economy entered a period of sustained weakness in which wages and prices fell. In an effort to fight the economic weakness, the Bank of Japan—the equivalent of the Federal Reserve—repeatedly cut interest rates. Eventually, it arrived at the ZIRP: the *zero interest rate policy*. The call money rate, the equivalent of the U.S. federal funds rate, was literally set equal to zero. Because the economy was still depressed, it would have been desirable to cut interest rates even further. But that wasn't possible: Japan was up against the zero lower bound. And it was still there in 2020, nearly 25 years later!

FIGURE 12 Deflation and the Liquidity Trap in the Japanese Economy

A prolonged economic slump in Japan led to deflation from the late 1990s on. The Bank of Japan responded by cutting interest rates — but eventually ran up against the zero lower bound where it remained in 2020, nearly 25 years later.

Inflation measured as annual rate of change in percent; interest rate is the overnight rate from the Bank of Japan.

Data from: Organization for Economic Co-operation and Development.

In the aftermath of the 2008 financial crisis, the world's most important central banks—the U.S. Federal Reserve and the European Central Bank—found themselves facing much of the same problems as the Bank of Japan had faced since the 1990s: their economies remained depressed despite policy interest rates close to zero and inflation persistently below target.

ECONOMICS >> *in Action*
Is the Zero Lower Bound History?

The Federal Reserve cut the federal funds rate—the short-term interest rate it controls, and the usual tool for monetary policy—close to zero in 2008, and the Fed kept it there for most of the next 13 years, raising rates briefly in the late 2010s but dropping them back again. As Figure 13 shows, however, the Fed began raising rates rapidly in 2022, to fight inflation. This raised a strongly debated question: would ultra-low interest rates return once inflation was back under control?

After keeping interest rates very low for years, the Fed raised them sharply beginning in 2022. But would they stay high or go back down?

Reasonable economists took both sides of this question. As most acknowledged, there was a reason to keep interest rates very low after 2008: The economy seemed to need very low rates to stay anywhere near full employment, possibly because slowing population growth was depressing investment spending and creating a savings glut. This situation changed with the burst of government spending and inflation associated with the coronavirus pandemic. But many economists argued that the prepandemic fundamentals would reassert themselves within a few years.

Others argued that the fundamentals might have changed. Probably the most interesting argument for permanently higher interest rates involved a surprising source: climate policy. The Inflation Reduction Act of 2022, which despite its name was mainly a climate bill, introduced a wide range of subsidies to firms and consumers that adopted green technologies—shifting to renewable energy, buying electric vehicles, and so on. By 2023, it was already apparent that these incentives were giving rise to a surge in business investment, in everything from solar installations to battery factories. If this surge were to persist, it would absorb the previous savings glut for years to come, precluding any return to very low interest rates.

The truth, of course, is that nobody knows the answer. But the debate over the future of interest rates helps illuminate the reasons the zero lower bound was a problem in the past, and might become one again in the future.

FIGURE 13 Will Ultra-Low Interest Rates Return?

Data from: Federal Reserve Bank of St. Louis.

>> *Check Your Understanding* 16-4
Solutions appear at back of book.

1. Why won't anyone lend money at a negative nominal rate of interest? How can this pose problems for monetary policy?

>> *Quick Review*

• Unexpected deflation helps lenders and hurts borrowers. This can lead to **debt deflation,** which has a contractionary effect on aggregate demand.

• Deflation makes it more likely that interest rates will end up against the zero lower bound. When this happens, the economy is in a **liquidity trap,** and monetary policy is ineffective.

Hyperinflation as a Business Opportunity

Carolina Cabral/Getty Images

We often say that modern governments with fiat currencies simply print their own currencies. But sometimes that's not literally true—what they actually do is hire private companies to print money for them. That's what happened in November 2019, when Venezuela signed a contract with Goznak, a Russian money-printing company, to churn out 300 million bolivar bills, in denominations running from 10,000 to 50,000 bolivars.

Venezuela's use of a foreign money-printer isn't actually that unusual. Printing currency that isn't easy to counterfeit requires a fair bit of technical expertise and specialized equipment, so many countries contract the work out. Even Britain subcontracts the printing of pound banknotes to De La Rue, a 200-year-old company that, for example, supplied currency for the pre-Communist government of China.

Indeed, Venezuela has relied on De La Rue in the past. But as of 2019, it still owed the company money for past work, and none of De La Rue's usual competitors were willing to take the business. Hence the choice of Goznak, which happens to be owned by the Russian government.

There were two unusual things about the Goznak contract. One was the fact that the order was quite small—just $143 million in face value, which isn't much even for a country the size of Venezuela. Yet this amounted to about one-fifth of the value of Venezuelan currency in circulation at the time. The other was the unusually high fee—about 5% of the value of the notes. This high fee partly reflected the low purchasing power of the notes: the cost of printing a 10,000 bolivar note is presumably not very different from the cost of printing, say, a $20 bill, but even at the time the Venezuelan note was worth only around $0.14.

Still, business is business, and Goznak's contract showed that even bad times offer opportunities.

QUESTIONS FOR THOUGHT

1. Why was Venezuela so desperate to hire someone to print more money?

2. Why did such a small order for new currency account for such a large fraction of the existing money supply?

3. How would you classify the fees paid to Goznak under the general category of costs of inflation?

SUMMARY

1. In analyzing high inflation, economists use the **classical model of the price level,** which says that changes in the money supply lead to proportional changes in the aggregate price level even in the short run.

2. Governments sometimes print money in order to finance budget deficits. When they do, they impose an **inflation tax,** generating tax revenue equal to the inflation rate times the money supply, on those who hold money. Revenue from the real inflation tax, the inflation rate times the real money supply, is the real value of resources captured by the government. In order to avoid paying the inflation tax, people reduce their real money holdings and force the government to increase inflation to capture the same amount of real inflation tax revenue. In some cases, this leads to a vicious circle of a shrinking real money supply and a rising rate of inflation, leading to hyperinflation and a fiscal crisis.

3. The output gap is the percentage difference between the actual level of real GDP and potential output. A positive output gap is associated with lower-than-normal unemployment; a negative output gap is associated with higher-than-normal unemployment. The relationship between the output gap and cyclical unemployment is described by **Okun's law.**

4. Countries that don't need to print money to cover government deficits can still stumble into moderate inflation, either because of political opportunism or because of wishful thinking.

5. At a given point in time, there is a downward-sloping relationship between unemployment and inflation known as the **short-run Phillips curve.** This curve is shifted by changes in the **expected rate of inflation.** The **long-run Phillips curve,** which shows the relationship between unemployment and inflation once expectations have had time to adjust, is vertical. It defines the **nonaccelerating inflation rate of unemployment,** or **NAIRU,** which is equal to the natural rate of unemployment. *Stagflation,* a combination of high unemployment and high inflation, reflects an upward shift of the short-run Phillips curve.

6. Once inflation has become embedded in expectations, getting inflation back down can be difficult because *disinflation* can be very costly, requiring the sacrifice of large amounts of aggregate output and imposing high levels of unemployment. However, policy makers in the United States and other wealthy countries were willing to pay that price of bringing down the high inflation of the 1970s.

7. Deflation poses several problems. It can lead to **debt deflation,** in which a rising real burden of outstanding debt intensifies an economic downturn. Also, nominal interest rates are more likely to run up against the zero lower bound in an economy experiencing deflation. When this happens, the economy enters a **liquidity trap,** rendering conventional monetary policy ineffective.

KEY TERMS

Classical model of the price level, p. 484
Inflation tax, p. 486
Short-run Phillips curve, p. 491
Okun's law, p. 492
Expected rate of inflation, p. 492
Nonaccelerating inflation rate of unemployment (NAIRU), p. 498
Long-run Phillips curve, p. 498
Debt deflation, p. 501
Liquidity trap, p. 501

PRACTICE QUESTIONS

1. Throughout the textbook, we relied on a traditional upward-sloping short-run aggregate supply curve. But across the profession there is a large debate around the actual slope of the short-run aggregate supply curve. Many economists believe the *SRAS* curve is much "flatter" than depicted in the book. Explain how a flatter *SRAS* curve affects the Phillips curve and the short-run trade-off between inflation and unemployment following expansionary monetary and fiscal policy.

2. During the onset of the economic shutdown tied to COVID-19, many economists were debating the effects the economic shutdown and subsequent policy efforts would have on future inflation. Explain how each of the following events will affect the short-run Phillips curve. Treat each part as a unique event.
   a. A decline in consumer spending in expectation of a slowdown in future economic activity.
   b. An increase in expansionary fiscal and monetary policy.
   c. A shutdown of global production has made it difficult for producers to maintain production for essential goods, causing production costs to increase.

3. You recently read two quotes, one from an article in *National Review:* "Then there are the costs of shortening the global supply chains and perhaps

re-domesticating some production. Entirely without economic theory, simply from observing how the world economy." The author came to an inevitable conclusion, "There will be inflation. How much inflation? ... I'd say low double digits in the United States by the first months of 2022."

And the other from Olivier Blanchard, past chief economist for the International Monetary Fund, "Will falling commodity prices, stumbling oil prices, and a depressed labour market bring low inflation and perhaps even deflation, or will very large increases in fiscal deficits and central bank balance sheets bring inflation?" Blanchard went on to conclude, "The challenge for monetary and fiscal policy is thus likely to be to sustain demand and avoid deflation rather than the reverse."

Given the extreme range of opinions, how would you assess each statement over the next one to two years?

PROBLEMS

1. In the economy of Scottopia, policy makers want to lower the unemployment rate and raise real GDP by using monetary policy. Using the accompanying diagram, show why this policy will ultimately result in a higher aggregate price level but no change in real GDP.

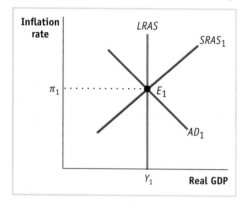

2. In the following examples, would the classical model of the price level be a useful model for analyzing how the economy behaves?

   a. The economy has high unemployment and no history of inflation.

   b. The economy has just experienced five years of hyperinflation.

   c. Although the economy experienced inflation in the 10% to 20% range three years ago, prices have recently been stable and the unemployment rate has approximated the natural rate of unemployment.

3. [icon] Access the Discovering Data exercise for Chapter 16 online to answer the following questions.

   a. How much did the monetary base change in the last year?

   b. How did the change in the monetary base help in the government's efforts to finance its deficit?

   c. Why is it important for the central bank to be independent of government policy makers?

4. Answer the following questions about the (real) inflation tax, assuming that the price level starts at 1.

   a. Maria keeps $1,000 in her sock drawer for a year. Over the year, the inflation rate is 10%. What is the real inflation tax paid by Maria for this year?

   b. Maria continues to keep the $1,000 in her drawer for a second year. What is the real value of this $1,000 at the beginning of the second year? Over the year, the inflation rate is again 10%. What is the real inflation tax paid by Maria for the second year?

   c. For a third year, Maria keeps the $1,000 in the drawer. What is the real value of this $1,000 at the beginning of the third year? Over the year, the inflation rate is again 10%. What is the real inflation tax paid by Maria for the third year?

   d. After three years, what is the cumulative real inflation tax paid?

   e. Redo parts a through d with an inflation rate of 25%. Why is hyperinflation such a problem?

5. The inflation tax is often used as a significant source of revenue in developing countries where the tax collection and reporting system is not well developed and tax evasion may be high.

   a. Use the numbers in the accompanying table to calculate the inflation tax in the United States and India (Rp = rupees).

	Inflation in 2022	Money supply in 2022 (billions)	Central government receipts in 2022 (billions)
India	5.56%	Rp55,878	Rp18,251
United States	5.70%	$19,846	$7,602

Data from: Bureau of Economic Analysis; Controller General of Accounts (India); Reserve Bank of India; International Monetary Fund; The World Bank.

   b. How large is the inflation tax for the two countries when calculated as a percentage of government receipts?

6. Concerned about the crowding-out effects of government borrowing on private investment spending, a candidate for president argues that the United States should just print money to cover the government's budget deficit. What are the advantages and disadvantages of such a plan?

7. The accompanying scatter diagram shows the relationship between the unemployment rate and the output gap in the United States from 1996 to 2022. Draw a straight line through the scatter of dots in the figure. Assume that this line represents Okun's law:

$$\text{Unemployment rate} = b - (m \times \text{Output gap})$$

where b is the vertical intercept and $-m$ is the slope.

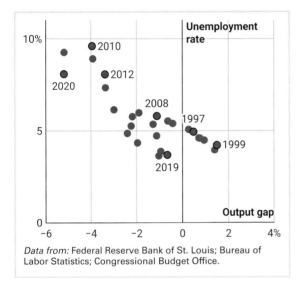

Data from: Federal Reserve Bank of St. Louis; Bureau of Labor Statistics; Congressional Budget Office.

What is the unemployment rate when aggregate output equals potential output? What would the unemployment rate be if the output gap were 2%? What if the output gap were −3%? What do these results tell us about the coefficient m in Okun's law?

8. After experiencing a recession for the past two years, the residents of Albernia were looking forward to a decrease in the unemployment rate. Yet after six months of strong positive economic growth, the unemployment rate has fallen only slightly below what it was at the end of the recession. How can you explain why the unemployment rate did not fall as much although the economy was experiencing strong economic growth? (*Hint:* Reread the For Inquiring Minds box on Okun's law for help with answering this question.)

9. a. Go to www.bls.gov. Click on link "Subjects"; on the left, under "Inflation & Prices," click on the link "Consumer Price Index," then under the heading "CPI Data," select "Tables" and then "Archived CPI Detailed Report." Download the file for "2009 Detailed Reports" and open file cpid09av.pdf. What is the value of the percent change in the CPI from 2008 to 2009?

b. Now go to www.treasury.gov and under the tab "Data" and "Interest Rates" select "Daily Treasury Bill Rates" and select "2009" under "Select Time Period." Examine the data in "4 Weeks Bank Discount." What is the maximum? The minimum? Then do the same for 2007. How do the data for 2009 and 2007 compare? How would you relate this to your answer in part a? From the data on Treasury bill interest rates, what would you infer about the level of the inflation rate in 2007 compared to 2009? (You can check your answer by going back to the www.bls.gov website to find the percent change in the CPI from 2006 to 2007.)

c. How would you characterize the change in the U.S. economy from 2007 to 2009? What were the implications for the effectiveness of monetary policy?

10. The economy of Brittania has been suffering from high inflation with an unemployment rate equal to its natural rate. Policy makers would like to disinflate the economy with the lowest economic cost possible. Assume that the state of the economy is not the result of a negative supply shock. How can they try to minimize the unemployment cost of disinflation? Is it possible for there to be no cost of disinflation?

11. Who are the winners and losers when a mortgage company lends $100,000 to the Miller family to buy a house worth $105,000 and during the first year prices unexpectedly fall by 10%? What would you expect to happen if the deflation continued over the next few years? How would continuing deflation affect borrowers and lenders throughout the economy as a whole?

12. Due to historical differences, countries often differ in how quickly a change in actual inflation is incorporated into a change in expected inflation. In a country such as Japan, which has had very little inflation in recent memory, it will take longer for a change in the actual inflation rate to be reflected in a corresponding change in the expected inflation rate. In contrast, in a country such as Zimbabwe, which has recently had very high inflation, a change in the actual inflation rate will immediately be reflected in a corresponding change in the expected inflation rate. What does this imply about the short-run and long-run Phillips curves in these two types of countries? What does this imply about the effectiveness of monetary and fiscal policy to reduce the unemployment rate? ■

17 Macroeconomics: Events and Ideas

SYMPATHY FOR THE DEFICIT

IN FISCAL 2019, THE U.S. FEDERAL GOVERNMENT ran a budget deficit of almost $1 trillion, 4.7% of GDP. It wasn't the biggest deficit in U.S. history. However, in the past deficits that size occurred only during wars and economic emergencies like the aftermath of the 2008 financial crisis. To run such a big deficit in the face of low unemployment and healthy growth was unprecedented.

You might have expected, then, to see economists warning about fiscal irresponsibility. In fact, however, 2019 also happened to be a year in which several prominent macroeconomists published articles arguing that government debt is a much less pressing problem than many people imagine. In January 2019, Olivier Blanchard, the former chief economist of the International Monetary Fund and about as mainstream and widely respected as any modern macroeconomist, devoted his presidential lecture to the American Economic Association to the issue of public debt, and concluded that it may not do much, if any, damage.

A few weeks later Jason Furman and Lawrence Summers, who had been top economists in the Obama administration, published an article titled "Who's afraid of budget deficits?" that concluded, "It's time for Washington to put away its deficit obsession and focus on bigger things."

Indeed, when budget deficits exploded in 2020 as a result of plunging revenue and emergency spending to cope with the coronavirus, economists surveyed by the University of Chicago supported a program providing income support to unemployed workers, even though this program was adding hundreds of billions to government spending.

Why have influential economists developed a soft spot for budget deficits? The answer, as is often the case in macroeconomics, is that they were strongly influenced by events — in this case, both the financial crisis of 2008 and the era of very low interest rates that began during the crisis but continued right through 2020.

Macroeconomic ideas evolve because circumstances change. Solutions that were appropriate when gold and silver were the only monies available are inappropriate in an age of debit cards, Venmo, and digital currency. However, macroeconomic ideas also evolve because there is a steady accumulation of research and evidence that can be applied to the kinds of economic phenomenon that recur over time. The lessons learned in one decade are made available for the benefit of future generations.

To understand the state of macroeconomic thinking today, then, requires a trip through economic history and an understanding of the way economic ideas have evolved in the face of events.

In this chapter, we'll trace the development of macroeconomic ideas over the past 90 years: the rise of Keynesian economics in response to the Great Depression, the challenges to policy activism that arose in response to the stagflation of the 1970s, the revisions to economic thinking induced by changes in the economic environment since the Great Recession, and the intellectual fallout from the resurgence of inflation in 2021–2022. ●

Speaking at the American Economic Association's Annual Meeting, President Olivier Blanchard discusses fallacies around issuing public debt.

WHAT YOU WILL LEARN

- Why was classical macroeconomics inadequate for the problems posed by the Great Depression?
- How did John Maynard Keynes and the experience of the Great Depression legitimize **macroeconomic policy activism?**
- Why did the original focus of **Keynesian economics** on fiscal policy give way to an emphasis on monetary policy?
- Why did economists come temporarily to have great faith in the power of independent central banks to stabilize the economy?
- How have events since 2008 undermined that faith, and also changed views on deficits and debt?

Classical Macroeconomics

The term *macroeconomics* appears to have been coined in 1933 by the Norwegian economist Ragnar Frisch. The date, during the worst year of the Great Depression, is no accident. Still, there were economists analyzing what we now consider macroeconomic issues—the behavior of the aggregate price level and aggregate output—before then.

Money and the Price Level

In Chapter 16, we described the *classical model of the price level*. According to the classical model, prices are flexible, making the aggregate supply curve vertical even in the short run. In this model, an increase in the money supply leads, other things equal, to an equal proportional rise in the aggregate price level, with no effect on aggregate output. As a result, increases in the money supply lead to inflation, and that's all. Before the 1930s, the classical model of the price level dominated economic thinking about the effects of monetary policy.

Did classical economists really believe that changes in the money supply affected only aggregate prices, without any effect on aggregate output? Probably not. Historians of economic thought argue that before 1930 most economists were aware that changes in the money supply affect aggregate output as well as aggregate prices in the short run—or, to use modern terms, they were aware that the short-run aggregate supply curve slopes upward. But they regarded such short-run effects as unimportant, stressing that it was the long run that mattered. It was this attitude that led the British economist John Maynard Keynes to scoff at the exclusive focus on the long run: he famously quipped that "in the long run, we are all dead."

The Business Cycle

Despite their lack of interest in the short run, classical economists were aware that the economy did not grow smoothly. Some economic historians argue that the first true recession in the modern sense took place in Britain in 1825–1826, when an overheated boom in canal-building collapsed. As the Industrial Revolution spread beyond Britain, so did the business cycle, which eventually became the object of systematic, quantitative study, pioneered by the American economist Wesley Mitchell. In 1920, Mitchell founded the National Bureau of Economic Research (NBER), an independent, nonprofit organization that to this day has the official role of declaring the beginnings of recessions and expansions. Thanks to Mitchell's work, the *measurement* of business cycles was well advanced by 1930. But there was no widely accepted *theory* of what caused business cycles or what to do about them.

In the absence of any clear theory, conflicts arose among policy makers over how to respond to a recession. Some economists favored expansionary monetary and fiscal policies to fight a recession. Others believed that such policies would worsen the slump or merely postpone the inevitable. For example, in 1934 Harvard's Joseph Schumpeter, now famous for his early recognition of the importance of technological change, warned that any attempt to alleviate the Great Depression with expansionary monetary policy "would, in the end, lead to a collapse worse than the one it was called in to remedy." When the Great Depression hit, policy was paralyzed by this lack of consensus.

Necessity was, however, the mother of invention. As we'll see next, the Great Depression provided an opportunity for economists to develop theories that could serve as a guide to policy.

The Great Depression and the Keynesian Revolution

The Great Depression demonstrated, once and for all, that economists cannot safely ignore the short run. Not only was the economic pain severe; it threatened to destabilize societies and political systems. In particular, the economic plunge helped Adolf Hitler rise to power in Germany, setting the stage for World War II.

The whole world wanted to know how this economic disaster could be happening and what should be done about it. But because there was no widely accepted theory of the business cycle, economists gave conflicting and often harmful advice. Some believed that only a huge change in the economic system—such as having the government take over much of private industry and replace markets with a command economy—could end the slump. Others argued that slumps were natural—even beneficial, helping to correct past excesses—and that nothing should be done.

Some economists, however, argued that slumps were destructive and should be cured. Moreover, they could be cured without compromising the market economy. The most compelling advocate for this view was John Maynard Keynes, who compared the problems of the U.S. and British economies in 1930 to those of a car with a defective starter. Getting the economy running, he argued, would require only a modest repair, not a complete overhaul.

Nice metaphor. But what did he mean, specifically?

Keynes's Theory

In 1936, Keynes presented his analysis of the Great Depression—his explanation of what was wrong with the economy's starter—in a book titled *The General Theory of Employment, Interest, and Money*. In 1946, the great American economist and Nobel Prize–winner Paul Samuelson wrote that "it is a badly written book, poorly organized. . . . Flashes of insight and intuition intersperse tedious algebra. . . . We find its analysis to be obvious and at the same time new. In short, it is a work of genius." Samuelson was correct on both counts: *The General Theory* isn't easy reading, yet it stands with Adam Smith's *The Wealth of Nations* as one of the most influential books on economics ever written.

As Samuelson's description indicates, Keynes's book offers a vast stew of ideas. *Keynesian economics* is principally based on two innovations. First, Keynes emphasized the importance of short-run effects of changes in aggregate demand on aggregate output, unlike the classicists who focused exclusively on the long-run determination of the aggregate price level.

Until *The General Theory* appeared most economists had treated short-run macroeconomics as a minor issue. Keynes shifted the focus of attention of economists away from the unreachable long run to the world in which people actually live, one in which the short-run aggregate supply curve slopes upward and shifts in the aggregate demand curve affect aggregate output and employment as well as inflation.

Figure 1 illustrates the difference between Keynesian and classical macroeconomics. Both panels of the figure show the short-run aggregate supply curve, *SRAS;* in both it is assumed that for some reason demand falls and the aggregate demand curve shifts leftward from AD_1 to AD_2—say, for example, in response to a fall in stock market prices that leads households to reduce consumer spending.

Panel (a) shows the classical view: in it, the short-run aggregate supply curve is vertical. Therefore the fall in aggregate demand leads to a fall in inflation, from π_1 to π_2, but leaves aggregate output unchanged. Panel (b) shows the Keynesian view: in it, the short-run aggregate supply curve slopes upward. So a fall in aggregate demand leads to both a fall in inflation, from π_1 to π_2, and a fall in aggregate output, from Y_1 to Y_2.

As we've already explained, many classical macroeconomists would have agreed that panel (b) portrayed an accurate story in the short run—but they regarded the short run as unimportant. Keynes strongly disagreed, arguing that short-run economic problems caused great social distress and were in fact fixable. (Just to be clear, there isn't any diagram that looks like panel (b) of Figure 1 in Keynes's *General Theory*. But Keynes's discussion of aggregate supply, translated into modern terminology, clearly implies an upward-sloping *SRAS* curve.)

FIGURE 1 Classical versus Keynesian Macroeconomics

(a) The Classical View

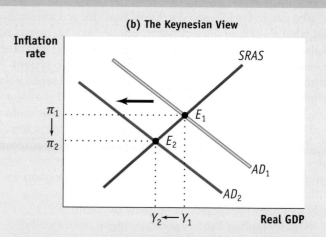

(b) The Keynesian View

One important difference between classical and Keynesian economics involves the short-run aggregate supply curve. Panel (a) shows the classical view: the *SRAS* curve is vertical, so shifts in aggregate demand affect inflation but not aggregate output. Panel (b) shows the Keynesian view: in the short run the *SRAS* curve slopes upward, so shifts in aggregate demand affect aggregate output as well as inflation.

Keynes's second innovation concerned the question of what factors shifted the aggregate demand curve and caused business cycles. Classical economists attributed shifts in the demand curve almost exclusively to changes in the money supply. Keynes, by contrast, argued that other factors, especially changes in "animal spirits"—these days usually referred to with the bland term *business confidence*—are mainly responsible for business cycles.

Before Keynes, economists argued that as long as the money supply stayed constant, changes in factors like business confidence would have no effect on either inflation or aggregate output. Keynes offered a very different picture in which, for example, pessimism about future profits can lead to a fall in investment spending, and this can cause a recession.

Keynesian economics, a view of the business cycle informed by these innovations, has penetrated deeply into the public consciousness, to the extent that many people who have never heard of Keynes, or have heard of him but think they disagree with his theory, use Keynesian ideas all the time. For example, suppose that a business commentator says something like this: "Businesses are holding back on investment spending because they're worried about low consumer demand, and that's why recovery has stalled." Whether the commentator knows it or not, that statement is pure Keynesian economics.

Keynes himself more or less predicted that someday people would make use of his ideas without knowing that they were *Keynesians*. As he famously wrote in *The General Theory,* "Practical men, who believe themselves to be quite exempt from any intellectual influences, are usually the slaves of some defunct economist."

Policy to Fight Recessions

The greatest consequence of Keynes's work was that it legitimized **macroeconomic policy activism**—the use of monetary and fiscal policy to smooth out the business cycle.

It's true that some economists had called for macroeconomic activism before Keynes, in particular advocating monetary expansion to fight economic downturns. And some economists had even argued, as Keynes did, that temporary

Keynesian economics a school of thought emerging out of the works of John Maynard Keynes; according to Keynesian economics, a depressed economy is the result of inadequate spending and government intervention can help a depressed economy through monetary policy and fiscal policy.

macroeconomic policy activism the use of monetary policy and fiscal policy to smooth out the business cycle.

Some political commentators use the term *Keynesian economics* as a synonym for left-wing economics. Because Keynes offered a rationale for some kinds of government activism, these commentators have gone on to claim that he was a leftist of some kind, maybe even a social-ist. But the truth is more complicated.

As we explained, Keynesian ideas have actually been accepted among economists and policy makers across a broad range of the political spectrum. In 2004, the U.S. pres-ident, George W. Bush, was a conservative, as was his top economist, N. Gregory Mankiw. But Mankiw is also a well-known promoter of Keynesian ideas.

In fact, Keynes was no socialist — and not much of a leftist. At the time *The General Theory* was published, the Depression had con-vinced many intellectuals that socialism was the only solution to the economy's woes. They believed that the Great Depression was the final crisis of the capitalist economic sys-tem and that only a government takeover of

industry could save the economy. Keynes, in contrast, argued that socialism was not the answer. Instead, he said, all the capitalist market system needed was a narrow technical fix. In essence, his ideas were pro-capitalist and politically conservative.

What is true is that the rise of Keynesian economics in the 1940s, 1950s, and 1960s accompanied a general enlargement of the role of government in the economy, and those who favored a larger role for govern-ment tended to be enthusiastic Keynesians. Conversely, a swing of the pendulum back toward free-market policies in the 1970s and 1980s was accompanied by a series of challenges to Keynesian ideas, which we will describe in this chapter.

Recent history shows that it is quite easy to find respected economists and policy makers who have conservative political preferences and who simultaneously respect Keynes's fundamental contributions to mac-roeconomics. It is equally possible to find

those of a liberal bent who question some of Keynes's ideas.

The ideas of John Maynard Keynes have been accepted across the political spectrum.

budget deficits were a good thing in times of recession. But macroeconomic pol-icy activism at the time was considered deeply controversial and those who advo-cated it were fiercely attacked.

As a result, when some governments during the 1930s followed policies that we would now call Keynesian, they were carried out in a half-hearted way and were insufficient to turn the Great Depression around. In the United States, the administration of Franklin Roosevelt engaged in modest deficit spending in an effort to create jobs, actions which seemed to gain some traction in improv-ing the economy. But, in 1937 Roosevelt gave in to advice from non-Keynesian economists who urged him to balance the federal budget and raise interest rates, even though the economy was still deeply depressed. The result was a renewed slump.

Over time, however, Keynesian ideas spread, and they were widely accepted among economists after World War II. There were, however, a series of challenges to those ideas, which led to a considerable shift in views even among those econo-mists who continued to believe that Keynes was broadly right about the causes of recessions. Next we'll learn about those challenges and the schools, *new classical economics* and *new Keynesian economics,* that emerged.

ECONOMICS >> *in Action*
The End of the Great Depression

It would make a good story if Keynes's ideas had led to a change in economic policy that brought the Great Depression to an end. Unfortunately, that's not what happened. Yet the way the Depression finally ended helped convince the econom-ics profession that Keynes was basically right.

What economists learned from Keynes's work was that economic recovery requires aggressive fiscal expansion — deficit spending on a sufficiently large

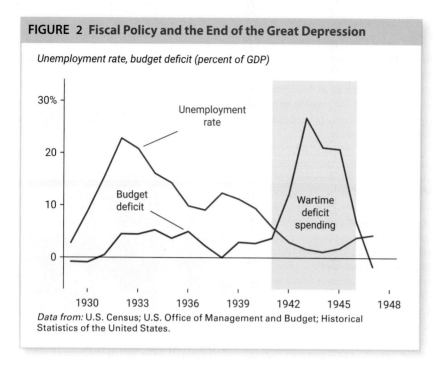

FIGURE 2 Fiscal Policy and the End of the Great Depression

Unemployment rate, budget deficit (percent of GDP)

Data from: U.S. Census; U.S. Office of Management and Budget; Historical Statistics of the United States.

scale to create jobs and push up aggregate demand. And that happened in the United States not because of intentional economic policy, but as the result of a very large war that required an enormous amount of government spending, World War II. The overwhelming evidence that it was government expenditures for World War II that lifted the economy out of the Great Depression finally ended the debate over the validity of Keynes's views.

Figure 2 shows the U.S. unemployment rate and the federal budget deficit as a share of GDP from 1929 to 1947. As you can see, deficit spending during the 1930s was on a modest scale. In 1940, as the risk of war grew larger, the United States began a large military buildup, building tanks, planes, military bases, and the like, moving the budget deep into deficit. After the attack on Pearl Harbor on December 7, 1941, the country began deficit spending on an enormous scale: in fiscal 1943, which began in July 1942, the deficit was 30% of GDP. Today that would be equivalent to a deficit of $6 trillion.

What was clear to economists and policy makers was that this enormous surge in government spending led the economy, mired in the Great Depression for well over a decade, to finally recover in a sustainable way. World War II wasn't intended as a Keynesian fiscal policy. And it is hard to believe that any event, short of a world war, would have compelled the U.S. government to spend so much money. Yet unintentional as it was, World War II spending demonstrated that expansionary fiscal policy can lift the economy out of a deep slump.

>> Check Your Understanding 17-1

Solutions appear at back of book.

1. In their famous book *A Monetary History of the United States, 1867–1960,* the economists Milton Friedman and Anna Schwartz argued that the Federal Reserve was responsible for the Great Depression, because it failed to pursue a sufficiently expansionary monetary policy. Why would a classical economist have thought that action by the Federal Reserve would not have made a difference in the length or depth of the Great Depression?

2. In a press release during the Great Recession, the National Federation of Independent Business, which calculates the Small Business Optimism Index, stated "The Small Business Optimism Index rose just 0.1 points in January. . . . Historically, optimism remains at recession levels. While small business owners appeared less pessimistic about the outlook for business conditions and real sales growth, that optimism did not materialize in hiring or increased inventories plans." Would this statement seem familiar to a Keynesian economist? Which conclusion would a Keynesian economist draw for the need for public policy?

‖ Challenges to Keynesian Economics

Keynes's ideas fundamentally changed the way economists think about business cycles. They did not, however, go unquestioned. In the wake of the success of government expenditures in ending the Great Depression, Keynesian economics faced a new series of challenges. As a result, by the 1980s the consensus of macroeconomists retreated somewhat from the strong version of Keynesianism that prevailed in the 1950s. In particular, many economists began to suggest limits to the effectiveness of macroeconomic policy activism.

The Revival of Monetary Policy

Many macroeconomists agree with Keynes's view that during a depression monetary policy would be relatively ineffective. We met this phenomenon in Chapter 16 in what we called the *liquidity trap*, a situation in which monetary policy is ineffective because the interest rate cannot be pushed any lower. In the 1930s, when Keynes wrote, interest rates were, in fact, very close to zero.

When the era of near-zero interest rates came to an end after World War II and the economy had recovered, the pendulum had swung so far in favor of Keynesian economics that many economists continued to emphasize fiscal policy and downplay the usefulness of monetary policy. Eventually, however, the pendulum swung partly back as macroeconomists reassessed the importance of monetary policy.

A key milestone in this reassessment was the 1963 publication of *A Monetary History of the United States, 1867–1960*, by Milton Friedman, of the University of Chicago, and Anna Schwartz, of the National Bureau of Economic Research. Friedman and Schwartz showed that business cycles had historically been associated with fluctuations in the money supply. In particular, the money supply fell sharply during the onset of the Great Depression. Friedman and Schwartz persuaded many, though not all, economists that the Great Depression could have been avoided if the Federal Reserve had acted to prevent the monetary contraction by increasing the monetary base. They persuaded most economists that monetary policy should play a key role in economic management.

Milton Friedman and co-author Anna Schwartz played a key role in convincing macroeconomists of the importance of monetary policy.

The revival of interest in monetary policy was significant because it suggested that the burden of managing the economy could be shifted away from fiscal policy—meaning that economic management could largely be taken out of the hands of politicians. This feature was attractive to many because fiscal policy necessarily involves political choices. If the government tries to stimulate the economy by cutting taxes, it must decide whose taxes will be cut. If it tries to stimulate the economy with government spending, it must decide what to spend the money on. As a result, management of the economy would often be bogged down by the political process if fiscal policy were the only tool available.

Monetary policy, in contrast, does not involve such political choices: when the central bank cuts interest rates to fight a recession, it cuts everyone's interest rate at the same time. So a shift from relying on fiscal policy to relying on monetary policy makes macroeconomics a more technical, less political undertaking. In fact, as we've learned, monetary policy in most major economies is set by an independent central bank that is insulated from the political process.

Monetarism

After the publication of *A Monetary History*, Friedman led a movement that sought to eliminate all forms of macroeconomic policy activism—fiscal and monetary. Instead, he asserted that the best way to manage the economy was with non-activist or *nondiscretionary* monetary policy. **Monetarism** asserts that GDP will grow steadily if the money supply grows steadily. According to the monetarist policy prescription, the central bank should target a constant rate of growth of the money supply, such as 3% per year, and maintain that target regardless of any fluctuations in the economy.

monetarism a theory of business cycles, associated primarily with Milton Friedman, that asserts that GDP will grow steadily if the money supply grows steadily.

discretionary monetary policy
policy actions, either changes
in interest rates or changes in
the money supply, undertaken
by the central bank based on its
assessment of the state of the
economy.

monetary policy rule a formula
that determines the central bank's
actions.

It's important to realize that monetarism retained many Keynesian ideas. Like
Keynes, Friedman asserted that the short run is important and that short-run
changes in aggregate demand affect aggregate output as well as aggregate prices.
Like Keynes, he argued that macroeconomic policy should have been much more
expansionary during the Great Depression, even if he believed that only monetary
policy was needed.

Monetarists argued, however, that in most cases activist macroeconomic policy
to smooth out the business cycle actually makes things worse. In Chapter 13, we
described how lags can cause problems for *discretionary fiscal policy.* For example, a government that tries to respond to recessions by increasing spending sometimes finds that by the time it realizes that a recession is underway, takes action,
and gets results, the recession is over, and the spending increase feeds a boom
instead of fighting a slump. According to monetarists, **discretionary monetary
policy,** changes in the interest rate or the money supply by the central bank in
order to stabilize the economy, faces similar problems and can easily make the
economy less stable.

Friedman also argued that if the central bank followed his advice, adopting a
non-activist monetary policy and refusing to change the money supply in response
to fluctuations in the economy, fiscal policy would be much less effective than
Keynesians believed due to *crowding out*—when government spending crowds
out private investment spending. In Chapter 10, we analyzed how this can occur:
government spending leads to deficits, which drive up interest rates and reduce
investment spending. Friedman and others pointed out that if the money supply is
held fixed while the government pursues an expansionary fiscal policy, crowding
out will occur as the interest rate rises, limiting the effect of the fiscal expansion
on aggregate demand.

As already noted, Friedman didn't favor activist monetary policy either,
arguing that the problems of time lags that limit the ability of discretionary fiscal policy to stabilize the economy also apply to discretionary monetary policy.
Friedman's solution was to make monetary policy nondiscretionary, to put it on
autopilot. The central bank, he argued, should follow a **monetary policy rule,** a
formula that determines its actions and leaves it relatively little discretion. During
the 1960s and 1970s, most monetarists favored a monetary policy rule of slow,
steady growth in the money supply.

Monetarism strongly influenced U.S. monetary policy in the late 1970s and
early 1980s as the Fed tried to keep the rate of growth in the money supply constant. It quickly became clear, however, that this didn't ensure steady growth in
the economy.

Consequently, traditional monetarists—those who believe that GDP will grow
steadily if the money supply grows steadily—are hard to find among today's
macroeconomists. However, Friedman's argument that monetary policy can do
the job of stabilizing the economy, and that fiscal policy has little role to play,
became widespread among economists until it was called into question by the
2008 crisis and its aftermath.

Limits to Macroeconomic Policy: Inflation and the Natural Rate of Unemployment

The problem of time lags in the implementation of activist macroeconomic policy
was not the only criticism leveled at Keynesian economics. Another serious concern arose over its effect on inflation. During the 1940s and 1950s, many Keynesian
economists believed that expansionary fiscal policy could be used to achieve full
employment on a permanent basis. By the 1960s, however, many economists realized that persistently expansionary policies could cause problems with inflation.
Yet they still believed that governments could choose to keep unemployment low
if they were willing to accept higher inflation.

In 1968, however, Milton Friedman and Edmund Phelps of Columbia University, working independently, argued that there isn't actually a long-run trade-off between unemployment and inflation. (Incidentally, Friedman made his argument in a famous 1969 presidential address to the American Economic Association—the same occasion that Olivier Blanchard used to downplay concerns about public debt 50 years later.) According to Friedman and Phelps's **natural rate hypothesis,** any attempt to keep unemployment below a minimum level would lead not just to inflation but to ever-rising inflation. The important point to recognize here is that, if true, the natural rate hypothesis implies that Keynesian policies can't accomplish as much as macroeconomists previously believed. Because the government can't keep unemployment below the natural rate, its task is not to keep unemployment low but to keep it *stable around the natural rate*—to prevent large fluctuations in unemployment above or below the natural rate.

And the natural rate hypothesis was, in fact, accepted by most economists after the 1970s. The Friedman–Phelps hypothesis made a strong prediction: that the apparent trade-off between unemployment and inflation would not survive an extended period of rising prices. Once inflation was embedded into the public's expectations, it would continue even in the face of high unemployment.

Sure enough, that's exactly what happened in the 1970s. This accurate prediction was one of the triumphs of macroeconomic analysis. It convinced the great majority of economists that the natural rate hypothesis was correct, although some macroeconomists believe that at very low rates of inflation or deflation the hypothesis doesn't work.

Rational Expectations and New Classical Economics

As we have seen, one key difference between classical economics and Keynesian economics is that classical economists believed that the short-run aggregate supply curve is vertical, while Keynesian economics claims that the aggregate supply curve slopes upward in the short run. A consequence of the upward-sloping supply curve is that demand shocks—shifts in the aggregate demand curve—cause fluctuations in aggregate output.

In the 1970s and 1980s, the classical view that shifts in the aggregate demand curve affect only the aggregate price level, not aggregate output, was revived in an approach known as **new classical macroeconomics.** It evolved in two stages. First, some economists challenged traditional arguments about the slope of the short-run aggregate supply curve based on the concept of *rational expectations.* Second, some economists suggested that changes in productivity cause economic fluctuations, a view known as *real business cycle theory.*

In the 1970s, a concept known as *rational expectations* had a powerful impact on macroeconomics. **Rational expectations,** originally introduced by John Muth in 1961, claims that individuals and firms make decisions optimally, using all available information.

For example, workers and employers bargaining over long-term wage contracts need to take account of the expected inflation rate over the life of that contract. The concept of rational expectations says that in making estimates of future inflation, they won't just look at past rates of inflation; they will also take into account currently available information about monetary and fiscal policy. Suppose that prices didn't rise last year, but that the monetary and fiscal policies announced by policy makers have made it clear that there will be substantial inflation over the next few years. According to rational expectations, long-term wage contracts will be adjusted today to reflect this future inflation, even though prices haven't yet risen.

Adopting the premise of rational expectations can significantly alter beliefs about the effectiveness of activist macroeconomic policy. According to the original version of the natural rate hypothesis, a government attempt to persistently

natural rate hypothesis the hypothesis that because inflation is eventually embedded into expectations, to avoid accelerating inflation over time the unemployment rate should be kept stable around the natural rate.

new classical macroeconomics an approach to the business cycle that returns to the classical view that shifts in the aggregate demand curve affect only the aggregate price level, not aggregate output.

rational expectations a theory of expectation formation that holds that individuals and firms make decisions optimally, using all available information.

During the 1970s a group of economic writers began propounding what came to be known as *supply-side economics*. Proponents of this view believed that reducing tax rates, and so increasing the incentives to work and invest, would have a powerful positive effect on the growth rate of potential output. The supply-siders urged the government to cut taxes without worrying about matching spending cuts: economic growth, they argued, would offset any negative effects from budget deficits.

Some supply-siders even argued that a cut in tax *rates* would have such a miraculous effect on economic growth that tax *revenues*—the total amount taxpayers pay to the government—would actually rise. That is, some supply-siders argued that the United States was on the wrong side of the *Laffer curve,* a hypothetical relationship between tax rates and total tax revenue that

slopes upward at low tax rates but turns downward when tax rates are very high. Supply-side economics became popular with politicians, and in 1980 Ronald Reagan made supply-side economics the basis of his presidential campaign.

Because supply-side economics emphasizes supply rather than demand, and because the supply-siders are harshly critical of Keynesian economics, it would appear that it belongs in our discussion of new classical macroeconomics. But, in fact, supply-side economics is generally dismissed by economic researchers.

The main reason for this dismissal is lack of supporting evidence. Almost all economists agree that tax cuts increase incentives to work and invest. But attempts to estimate these incentive effects indicate that at current U.S. tax levels, the positive incentive effects aren't nearly strong enough

to support the strong claims made by supply-siders. In particular, the supply-side doctrine implies that large tax cuts, such as the Reagan tax cuts of the early 1980s, should sharply raise potential output, while tax hikes, like the Clinton tax hikes of 1993, should slow potential growth. Yet estimates by the Congressional Budget Office and others showed no sign of either.

Years later, in 2012, the state of Kansas provided the best evidence so far against the usefulness of supply-side economics. That year, Kansas passed large cuts in state taxes. Yet its economy tanked, with economic growth and job creation falling far below the national average, and its state deficit skyrocketed. In 2017, facing a state financial crisis and voters angry over cuts to state services, Kansas ended its experiment in supply-side economics and raised taxes.

push the unemployment rate below the natural rate would work in the short run but will eventually fail because higher inflation will get built into expectations. According to rational expectations, we should remove the word *eventually* and replace it with *immediately:* if the government tries to lower unemployment today at the cost of higher inflation in the future, inflation will shoot up immediately without even a temporary fall in unemployment. So, under rational expectations, government intervention fails in the short run and the long run.

In the 1970s, Robert Lucas of the University of Chicago used the logic of rational expectations to argue that monetary policy can change the level of output and unemployment only if it comes as a surprise to the public. In 1995, Lucas won the Nobel Prize in economics for this work, which remains widely admired. However, many—perhaps most—macroeconomists, especially those advising policy makers, now believe that his conclusions were overstated. The Federal Reserve certainly thinks that it can play a useful role in economic stabilization.

Why, in the view of many macroeconomists, doesn't Lucas's **rational expectations model** of macroeconomics accurately describe how the economy actually behaves? **New Keynesian economics,** a set of ideas that became influential in the 1990s, provides an explanation. It argues that market imperfections interact to make many prices in the economy temporarily sticky. And with sticky prices, expected inflation can't rise quickly enough to offset activist macroeconomic policy.

Over time, new Keynesian ideas combined with actual experience have reduced the practical influence of the rational expectations concept. However, some macroeconomists went even further than Lucas, arguing that demand shocks play no role in recessions. In the 1980s, a number of economists argued that slowdowns in productivity growth, which they attributed to pauses in technological progress, are the main cause of recessions. **Real business cycle theory** claims that fluctuations in the rate of growth of productivity cause the business cycle.

This theory was strongly influential for some years, reflected by the fact that two of the founders of real business cycle theory, Finn Kydland of Carnegie Mellon University and Edward Prescott of the Federal Reserve Bank of

rational expectations model a model of the economy in which expected changes in monetary policy have no effect on unemployment and output and only affect the price level.

new Keynesian economics a theory that argues that market imperfections can lead to price stickiness for the economy as a whole.

real business cycle theory a theory of business cycles that asserts that fluctuations in the growth rate of total factor productivity cause the business cycle.

Minneapolis, won the 2004 Nobel Prize in economics. The current status of real business cycle theory, however, is similar to that of rational expectations. It is widely recognized for making a valuable contribution to our understanding of the economy, and for cautioning against an overemphasis on aggregate demand.

But many of the real business cycle theorists themselves now acknowledge that the actual economic data indicate that their models need an upward-sloping aggregate supply curve—and that this gives aggregate demand a potential role in determining aggregate output.

The Political Business Cycle

One final challenge to Keynesian economics focused not on the validity of the economic analysis but on its political consequences. A number of economists and political scientists pointed out that activist macroeconomic policy lends itself to political manipulation.

Statistical evidence suggests that election results are strongly affected by the state of the economy in the months just before the election. In the United States, if the economy is growing rapidly and the unemployment rate is falling in the six months or so before Election Day, the incumbent party tends to be reelected even if the economy performed poorly in the preceding three years. This creates an obvious temptation to abuse activist macroeconomic policy: pump up the economy in an election year, and pay the price in higher inflation and/or higher unemployment later. The consequence will be unnecessary instability in the economy, a **political business cycle** caused by the use of macroeconomic policy to serve political ends.

An often-cited example is the combination of expansionary fiscal and monetary policy that led to rapid growth in the U.S. economy just before the 1972 election and a sharp acceleration in inflation after the election. Kenneth Rogoff, a highly respected macroeconomist who served as chief economist at the International Monetary Fund, has proclaimed Richard Nixon, the president at the time, "the all-time hero of political business cycles."

As we've learned, one way to avoid a political business cycle is to place monetary policy in the hands of an independent central bank, insulated from political pressure. The political business cycle is also a reason to limit the use of discretionary fiscal policy to extreme circumstances like a liquidity trap.

political business cycle a business cycle that results from the use of macroeconomic policy to serve political ends.

Political manipulation in order to win votes is a danger of activist macroeconomic policy.

ECONOMICS >> *in Action*
Did the Fed Cause the Great Depression?

The Great Depression gave birth to Keynesian economics and convinced most economists of the need for activist macroeconomic policy. But Friedman and Schwartz's influential *A Monetary History* argued that the Federal Reserve could have prevented the Great Depression if only it had done its job. Some of Friedman's later writings strengthen this view and claim the Fed *caused* the depression.

Did the Fed, in fact, cause the Great Depression or at least allow it to happen through negligence?

The case against the Fed rests largely on the fact that the overall money supply, as measured by M2, fell sharply from 1929 to 1933 as the economy plunged. This monetary contraction is shown in Figure 3, where M2 is shown as an index with 1929 = 100. The Friedman–Schwartz view was that the Fed could have prevented the fall in M2 and hence stopped the depression from happening.

However, the Fed doesn't directly control monetary aggregates like M2, which consist mainly of bank deposits. What the Fed controls directly is the monetary base—currency in circulation plus bank reserves. And as Figure 3 also shows, the monetary base actually rose sharply in the early years of the Great Depression.

FIGURE 3 Monetary Policy During the Great Depression

During the Great Depression the Federal Reserve increased the monetary base by over 50% but the overall money supply, measured by M2, declined by 30% before stabilizing in 1933 and slightly increasing in 1934 and 1935. Most economists believe the divergence in M2 and the monetary base stemmed from the widespread bank failures.

Data from: Friedman, Milton, and Anna Jacobson Schwartz (1970). "Monetary Statistics of the United States: Estimates, Sources, Methods."

Index (1929 = 100) on y-axis

>> *Quick Review*

• Early Keynesianism downplayed the effectiveness of monetary as opposed to fiscal policy, but later macroeconomists realized that monetary policy is effective except in the case of a liquidity trap.

• According to **monetarism,** due to time lags, both discretionary fiscal policy and **discretionary monetary policy** do more harm than good, and a simple **monetary policy rule** is the best way to stabilize the economy. This doctrine was popular for a time but has fallen out of favor as its predictions failed to materialize.

• The **natural rate hypothesis,** now very widely accepted, places sharp limits on what macroeconomic policy can achieve. It implies that policy should aim to stabilize the unemployment rate around the natural rate.

• **New classical macroeconomics** revived some pre-Keynesian views about monetary policy. The **rational expectations model** cast doubt on whether monetary policy can work even in the short run, while **real business cycle theory** suggested that productivity shocks are responsible for recessions. These views, however, were countered by **new Keynesian economics,** and have had little influence on policy.

• Concerns about a **political business cycle** suggest that the central bank should be independent and that discretionary fiscal policy should be avoided except in extreme circumstances like a liquidity trap.

Why did M2 fall so much even though the monetary base was rising? The main explanation was that a wave of bank runs destroyed confidence in banks' safety: many people chose to convert their deposits into currency, and surviving banks cut back on lending, accumulating reserves instead, so that they would have cash on hand in the event of a run.

Under these conditions, it's not at all clear that the Fed could have prevented the plunge in M2. Interest rates were very low, giving banks little incentive to lend, so even if the Fed had engaged in large open-market operations, adding to bank reserves, the money might well have just sat there.

In fact, that's what happened after the 2008 financial crisis, when the Fed massively increased the monetary base but saw only a small rise in M2.

In short, it's doubtful whether the Fed could have prevented the Great Depression, and it certainly didn't cause it.

>> *Check Your Understanding* **17-2**
Solutions appear at back of book.

1. What are the limits of macroeconomic policy activism?

2. Starting in 2008, as the economy entered the Great Recession, unemployment soared while interest rates and investment spending fell sharply. The Fed accelerated the growth of the monetary base in response.
   a. Do you think Milton Friedman would have agreed with the Fed's policy?
   b. Monetarists, like Friedman, generally believe that discretionary monetary policy and fiscal policy are ineffective. Do you think their objections to fiscal and monetary policy were valid during the Great Recession? Note that unemployment did not return to its pre-recession level until 2016.

3. In late 2008, as it became clear that the United States was experiencing a recession, the Fed reduced its target for the federal funds rate to near zero, as part of a larger aggressively expansionary monetary policy stance (including what the Fed called *quantitative easing*). Most observers agreed that the Fed's aggressive monetary expansion helped reduce the length and severity of the Great Recession.
   a. What would rational expectations theorists say about this conclusion?
   b. What would real business cycle theorists say?

From Great Moderation to Secular Stagnation

The 1970s and the first half of the 1980s were a stormy period for the U.S. economy (and for other major economies, too). There was a severe recession in 1974–1975, then two back-to-back recessions in 1979–1982 that sent the unemployment rate to almost 11%. At the same time, the inflation rate soared into double digits—and then plunged. As we have seen, these events left a strong mark on macroeconomic thought.

After about 1985, however, the economy settled down. The recession of 1990–1991 was much milder than the 1974–1975 recession or the double-dip slump from 1979 to 1982, and the inflation rate generally stayed below 4%. The period of relative calm in the economy from 1985 to 2007 came to be known as the **Great Moderation.** And the calmness of the economy was to a large extent marked by a similar calm in macroeconomic policy discussion. In fact, it seemed that a broad consensus had emerged about several key macroeconomic issues.

However, the global financial crisis of 2008 and its aftermath undermined any sense that policy makers had things under control, and also led to a rethinking of macroeconomic policy—a rethinking that in some ways brought macroeconomists back to a more traditional Keynesian view.

To tackle the Great Recession, policy makers were able to use the macroeconomic tools that evolved from the experience of the Great Depression.

The Limits of Monetary Policy

In the end, Milton Friedman was unable to convince policy makers that monetarism was a good idea—simply ensuring that the money supply was growing at a steady rate was not enough to stabilize the economy. During the Great Moderation, however, both economists and policy makers generally believed that monetary policy in general was highly effective, and that apolitical technocrats at the Fed and other central banks could do the job of stabilizing the economy.

Events since 2008 have, however, undermined confidence in the ability of central bankers to keep the economy on an even keel. Figure 4, which shows the

Great Moderation the period from 1985 to 2007 when the U.S. economy experienced small fluctuations and low inflation.

FIGURE 4 Monetary Policy in Recent Recessions

The Federal Reserve responds actively to economic downturns. During each of these four recessions, the Federal Reserve acted quickly to cut interest rates.
Data from: Federal Reserve Bank of St. Louis.

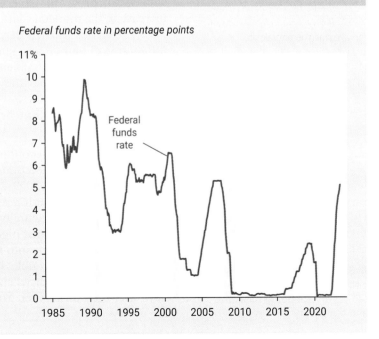

FIGURE 5 Big Money, Small Inflation in the United States, 2007–2023

Quantitative easing led to a huge rise in the U.S. monetary base after the Great Recession, and some economists warned that this would in turn lead to high inflation. The Fed, however, argued that inflation risks were low, and, as you can see from the figure, was vindicated by events: the consumer price index stayed virtually flat, reflecting a very low inflation rate from 2008 onward.

Data from: Federal Reserve Bank of St. Louis.

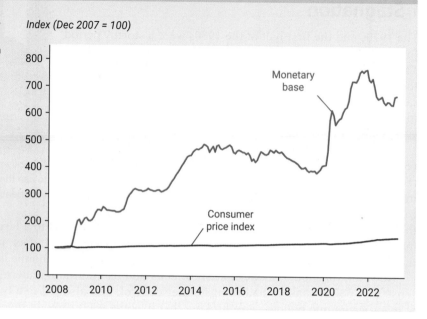

federal funds rate since the beginning of the Great Moderation, illustrates the problem. Normal monetary policy involves raising or lowering the federal funds rate through open-market operations, and the Fed has in fact cut that rate by about 5 percentage points each time recession has struck.

In 2008, however, cutting the federal funds rate all the way to zero wasn't enough to prevent a severe recession—and recovery from that recession was disappointingly slow. In other words, conventional monetary policy didn't seem up to the job it was supposed to do.

In fact, even unconventional monetary policy seemed to fall short. Normally the Fed only buys short-term government debt. In 2010, however, it tried to boost the economy by buying other assets, including long-term government debt and the debt of government agencies that lend money to home-buyers. As Figure 5 shows, this program, generally referred to as *quantitative easing*, led to a huge increase in the monetary base.

Some critics warned that the surge in the monetary base would lead to high inflation. As Figure 5 also shows, this didn't happen. On the other hand, it didn't lead to an economic boom either. Fed officials believe that the program had some positive effects, but if so, they weren't dramatic.

The Revival of Fiscal Policy

Events after 2008 showed that monetary policy wasn't as reliable a recession-fighting tool as many economists had believed. This led to a revival of interest in fiscal policy. The United States engaged in significant expansionary fiscal policy, or **fiscal stimulus,** in 2009–2010, because the economy was still contracting even though the Fed had cut interest rates all the way to zero.

Does fiscal policy actually work? Some observers pointed to the fact that U.S. unemployment remained high after the 2009 stimulus as evidence that it doesn't, but this argument runs into the problem that the stimulus was a response to an economy already in trouble. Consider an analogy with visits to the doctor: people tend to see their doctor when they get sick, and many of them are still sick a few days after their office visit. You wouldn't want to cite this as evidence that doctors are useless.

fiscal stimulus expansionary fiscal policy that takes the form of temporary spending measures and temporary tax cuts.

A better test came over the period from 2010–2013, when a number of countries shifted from stimulus to harsh **austerity policies**—attempts to reduce their budget deficits by cutting spending and raising taxes. These policies were largely inspired by events in Greece, which saw interest rates soar in 2010 as investors lost confidence in the Greek government's ability to pay its debts.

Fearing a similar fate, many countries, including the United States, engaged in fiscal austerity, but the degree of austerity varied a great deal from country to country. For example, Spain imposed budget cuts equal to around 8% of GDP, while Belgium, which actually had a higher level of debt relative to GDP, imposed almost no cuts.

An influential study from the International Monetary Fund showed a strong correlation between budget cuts and economic growth compared with earlier forecasts: the deeper the budget cuts, the worse the economic performance. Indeed, each dollar of budget cuts seemed to reduce GDP by around $1.50. Together with other evidence, this experience convinced many economists that fiscal policy does indeed have strong effects in a world of low interest rates, with little evidence of crowding out.

As a result, macroeconomists have a much stronger interest in fiscal policy as a tool for stabilizing the economy than they did during the Great Moderation.

Expansionary fiscal policy, however, means higher budget deficits. Shouldn't this be a source of concern? The answer, as we suggested in this chapter's opening story, is that many (though not all) macroeconomists have become less concerned about debt than they once were. This reduced concern has a lot to do with the same phenomenon that has reduced confidence in the effectiveness of monetary policy: persistently low interest rates.

austerity policies a policy that tries to limit government borrowing by cutting spending and raising taxes.

Policy in a Low-Interest-Rate World

We saw in Figure 4 that the Fed cut interest rates all the way to zero in the face of the 2008 financial crisis, and found that even this wasn't enough to avoid a severe recession followed by a sluggish recovery. At first, however, most economists—and Federal Reserve officials—believed that the Fed would be able to raise interest rates to historically normal levels once the crisis had passed. But as you can also see in Figure 4, the Fed ended up keeping rates close to zero for

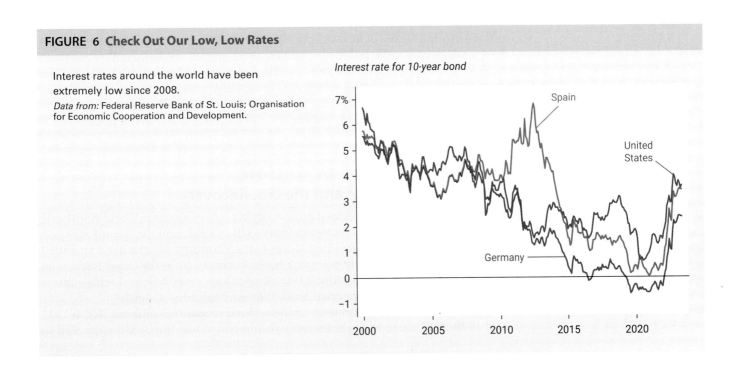

FIGURE 6 Check Out Our Low, Low Rates

Interest rates around the world have been extremely low since 2008.

Data from: Federal Reserve Bank of St. Louis; Organisation for Economic Cooperation and Development.

secular stagnation a state in which the interest rate that would be needed to achieve full employment is consistently below zero. Proponents of this view, known as *secular stagnationists*, advocate an active fiscal policy and unconventional monetary policy.

multiple years, then raised them only slightly, and began cutting again in 2019 amid signs of economic weakness. The coronavirus pandemic forced the Fed to return to their zero interest rate policy.

The persistence of low interest rates wasn't just a U.S. phenomenon. Figure 6 shows 10-year interest rates, which are often used as an indicator of long-term borrowing costs, for three countries since 2000: the United States, Germany, and Spain. As you can see, interest rates in both the United States and Germany have been on a declining trend—in Germany they're actually negative. Spain saw a temporary rise in rates after the Greek debt crisis caused a panic about other European nations' debt, but the panic soon subsided and by early 2016 Spain's borrowing costs were even lower than those of the United States.

Why have interest rates fallen so much and so persistently? A number of economists, invoking a concept from the 1930s, suggest that underlying factors such as declining population growth and, perhaps, a slowdown in technological progress had put the world's major economies in or on the edge of **secular stagnation,** a state in which the interest rate that is needed to achieve full employment is consistently close to zero.

If very low interest rates are the new normal, as they appear to be, this has two major consequences for economic policy: we shouldn't worry much about debt, and we should worry a lot about fiscal responses to downturns.

We began this chapter by talking about Olivier Blanchard's presidential address to the American Economic Association, in which he argued that fears about debt have been overstated. Low interest rates were central to his argument.

In the past, he noted, people have worried that debt might snowball over time, as interest payments on debt lead to higher deficits, which increase debt, leading to higher interest payments, and so on. As Blanchard noted, however, what matters for the economy is not the absolute size of the debt but the ratio of debt to GDP. And in recent decades interest rates have been well below the economy's growth rate. What this means is that instead of feeding on itself, a high ratio of debt to GDP tends to shrink over time unless the government runs a large non-interest-rate deficit. You might say, we don't need to worry about snowballing debt because the snowball tends to melt.

Indeed, there may be a good case for increasing government debt through further borrowing, if the borrowing is used to pay for things like infrastructure that will strengthen the economy in the future.

At the same time, an economy in which interest rates are persistently low is also an economy in which even medium-size adverse shocks may be too big to offset with monetary policy, simply because the Fed and its counterparts don't have enough room to cut. This suggests that we should strengthen the economy's *automatic stabilizers,* the tax and spending responses that help fight recessions even without new legislation. Some economists also argue that a moderate degree of persistent deficit spending may be a good thing, especially if it involves public investment, because it means that some fiscal stimulus is already in place.

ECONOMICS >> *in Action*
Debt Fears, Austerity, and the U.S. Recovery

The United States has experienced three really big recessions since World War II: one in 1974–1975, a double-dip recession from 1979 to 1982, and the Great Recession of 2007–2009. After the first two slumps, the economy experienced so-called V-shaped recoveries, quickly bouncing back. Recovery from the Great Recession, however, was much more gradual; it took about six years before the unemployment rate fell close to its pre-crisis level. Why was recovery sluggish?

One answer is that the causes of these three recessions differed: 1974–1975 and 1979–1982 were brought on by high interest rates, imposed by the Fed to

FIGURE 7 Austerity, American Style

Persistent cuts in government spending after 2011 may have delayed U.S. recovery from the Great Recession.

Note: Real GDP growth measured as percent change from quarter one year ago. Fiscal impact measured as contribution real GDP growth if negative, government is subtracting from GDP growth.

Data from: Federal Reserve Bank of St. Louis; Hutchins Center on Fiscal and Monetary Policy.

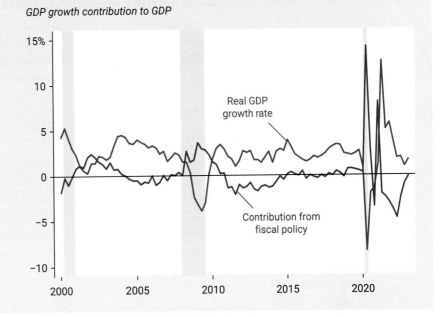

control inflation, while 2007–2009 was the result of a financial crisis, whose adverse effects were much harder to reverse. But fiscal policy also probably played an important role.

True, the U.S. government enacted a major fiscal stimulus in 2009. But the effects of that stimulus began to fade out in late 2010. And by that time much of Washington's political establishment had decided that public debt was a major danger—that the Greek crisis was a warning to everyone—and began pushing for fiscal austerity in the form of spending cuts.

U.S. fiscal austerity was never as extreme as austerity in, say, Spain, let alone Greece. But it was significant. The Hutchins Center at Washington's Brookings Institution provides regular estimates of what it calls its "fiscal impact measure," which "shows how much local, state, and federal tax and spending policy adds to or subtracts from overall economic growth." Figure 7 shows this measure along with real GDP growth over the past 20 years. According to this estimate, austerity imposed steady growth, shown as a negative, from early 2011 through 2015.

How much difference did this drag make to the pace of recovery? If the Hutchins estimate is correct, without austerity the United States might well have experienced a full recovery, with unemployment falling below 5%, by sometime in 2012.

So the United States seems to have paid a large price for austerity imposed in the name of limiting government debt. If economists who now say that debt fears were overblown are right, this was a huge policy mistake.

>> Check Your Understanding 17-3

Solutions appear at back of book.

1. Why did the Great Recession lead to the decline of the Great Moderation consensus? What is the current state of consensus among most economists?

2. Why was there such a fierce debate over both the Fed's unconventional monetary policy and the appropriate level of the Fed's inflation target?

>> Quick Review

• The **Great Moderation,** the period of economic calm from 1985 to 2007, led many economists to believe that monetary policy was sufficient to stabilize the economy. However, the 2008 financial crisis, in which the Fed cut rates to zero and even this wasn't enough to prevent a severe recession, undermined this belief.

• The appearance of limits to monetary policy led to renewed interest in fiscal policy, with a temporary turn to **fiscal stimulus** to fight the Great Recession. However, concerns about government debt led many countries to reverse this policy from 2010 onward, engaging in **austerity policies** instead. The adverse effects of austerity on growth, somewhat ironically, showed that fiscal policy is effective.

• Interest rates have remained very low since the 2008 financial crisis. Some economists believe that we are suffering from **secular stagnation:** declining population growth and slower technological progress led to a state of persistent economic weakness.

• In a low-interest-rate world, former concerns about government debt appear to have been overstated, and there is a much stronger case for fiscal stimulus, especially to fight recessions, but possibly even in normal times.

The Coronavirus Pandemic and the Economics of Disruption

In February 2020, the U.S. economy entered a recession that was both very severe and very short. You can see both the severity and the brevity of the slump by looking at Figure 8, which shows one widely used measure of the state of the labor market, the employed share of adults in their prime working years, ages 25 to 54.

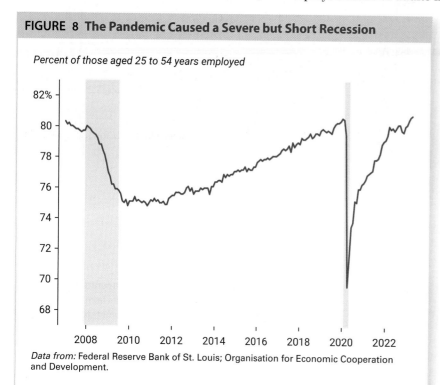

FIGURE 8 The Pandemic Caused a Severe but Short Recession

Percent of those aged 25 to 54 years employed

Data from: Federal Reserve Bank of St. Louis; Organisation for Economic Cooperation and Development.

This measure plunged even more in 2020 than it did in the Great Recession. But where recovery from the Great Recession was sluggish and took many years, recovery from the 2020 slump was very quick.

It's not too hard to understand why the experience was so different. The 2020 slump wasn't a normal recession: it was brought on by the coronavirus pandemic and the public health response. In particular, many countries, the United States included, temporarily banned or restricted activities that were thought to pose high risks of spreading the coronavirus—for example, for a time most indoor dining was prohibited. Even activities that weren't officially banned—including things like visits to the dentist!—slumped because consumers stayed home out of concerns over the health risks of public activities. Once many restrictions were lifted and fears subsided, in part because of the rapid development of vaccines, employment quickly returned to normal.

Yet as we noted in Chapter 16, the rapid economic recovery was accompanied by a surge in inflation. You might think that these dramatic events would, like previous crises, have led to a major rethinking of macroeconomics. For the most part, however, this doesn't seem to have happened.

There were, of course, major policy debates: Was public aid intended to cushion the financial impact of the pandemic excessive? Did the Federal Reserve wait too long to begin raising interest rates? However, economists on both sides of these debates for the most part worked with similar models. Their disagreements were largely about specific numbers, for example the size of the fiscal multiplier, rather than fundamental economic concepts.

To the extent that the economics of the pandemic affected macroeconomic thinking, the main change was a new appreciation that the economy isn't as flexible as we might like, at least in the short run.

Macroeconomics normally focuses on aggregates—aggregate output, the aggregate price level—rather than on the output or prices of particular goods and services. Normally this makes a lot of sense, because the economy can and does change the mix of things it produces, normally with little difficulty. Not that long ago people who watched movies at home usually relied on DVDs; in April 2023 Netflix, which began as a company that rented DVDs, discontinued the service, and now delivers entertainment solely by streaming. Some people miss the company's once-famous red envelopes, but few would argue that their disappearance significantly affected economic growth.

However, rapid shifts in supply or demand for particular goods may be harder to accommodate. Policy makers have long known this. That's why the Fed usually bases its policy on measures of "core" inflation that exclude food and energy prices, which are known to be highly volatile for reasons that may have little to do with broader economic considerations. For example, a surge in gasoline prices caused by a war in an oil-producing region needn't mean that the economy is suffering from an inflationary gap. Excluding these prices, the Fed believes, gives a better picture of the balance between aggregate supply and aggregate demand.

The pandemic, however, produced large disruptions in the supply and demand for goods whose prices are usually fairly stable. For example, concerns about infection temporarily led people to avoid consuming services that need to be delivered in person, purchasing physical goods as substitutes. Famously, for a while fitness-minded Americans stopped going to the gym and bought exercise equipment, like Peloton stationary bicycles, instead.

People waited for months for Peloton bikes during the pandemic.

It turned out, however, that supply chains—the activities that bring physical goods to consumers, even if they've purchased those goods online—have limited capacity. The sudden shifts in demand associated with the pandemic put supply chains under severe strain. Most spectacularly, many manufactured goods reach U.S. consumers via containerized shipping—but the sudden increase in demand for goods left hundreds of large ships steaming back and forth in front of major ports, waiting for a chance to unload, and also created a worldwide shortage of shipping containers. The result, as shown in Figure 9, was that ocean shipping costs suddenly increased by a factor of 5, only to slump back to prepandemic levels as the economy normalized.

Other pandemic-related changes were less dramatic, but nonetheless had large effects on measured inflation. The pandemic drastically accelerated the movement toward working from home, and people responded by seeking more home to work from—looking for more personal space in homes that had also become offices. The result was a temporary surge in apartment rents, which are a major

FIGURE 9 Rapid Shifts in Demand Caused Temporary Bottlenecks

Shipping prices increased by a factor of five during the pandemic. Shipping prices didn't return to pre-pandemic levels until early 2023.

Data from: Drewry and Statista.

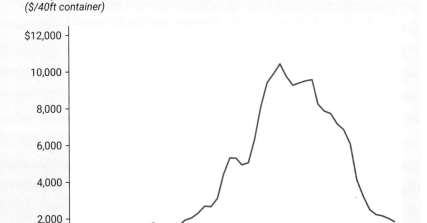

FIGURE 10 Working from Home and Housing Costs

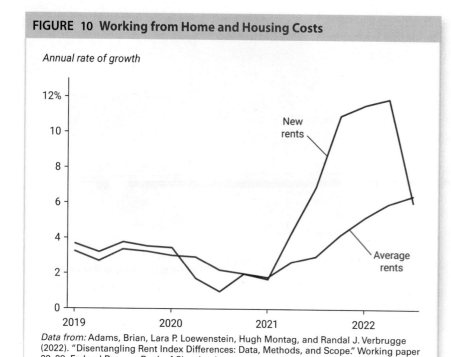

Annual rate of growth

Data from: Adams, Brian, Lara P. Loewenstein, Hugh Montag, and Randal J. Verbrugge (2022). "Disentangling Rent Index Differences: Data, Methods, and Scope." Working paper 22–38. Federal Reserve Bank of Cleveland.

factor in official estimates of the cost of shelter—and shelter accounts for about a third of the Consumer Price Index.

As we said, none of this had huge effects on macroeconomic theory. For the most part, macroeconomists argued that pandemic-related disruptions were similar in their effect to adverse supply shocks, which have long been part of standard economic analysis. But while the economic fallout from the pandemic had a relatively small impact on macroeconomic theory, it created difficulties for policy makers. In particular, there was a fierce argument about how much inflation was caused by excessive demand, how much by temporary pandemic disruptions.

At the time of writing, this argument was still raging. Both sides agreed, however, that the question was empirical and would eventually be resolved by events. Few were calling the basic aggregate supply-aggregate demand framework into question.

ECONOMICS >> *in Action*
The Pandemic and Housing Inflation

The price of shelter—mainly the cost of housing, although it also includes hotel rooms—plays a large part in measures of the aggregate price level. In fact, it's about a third of the Consumer Price Index. Housing prices, in turn, have two main components: payments by consumers who rent houses and apartments, and owners' equivalent rent, an estimate of what homeowners would be paying if they rented their homes (or, equivalently, the rent they are effectively paying themselves). Equivalent rent is imputed by looking at how much people who do rent their housing actually pay.

The pandemic, it turns out, was associated with a surge in rents. The main reason, several studies suggest, was the rise in working from home: many white-collar workers can do at least part of their jobs without going into the office, for example holding meetings on Zoom or other conferencing platforms. Fear of infection gave a huge jumpstart to working from home, much of which appears likely to persist now that people have seen that it works.

But if you're going to work from home, it's helpful to have someplace to do it from—if not a dedicated home office, a room or at least an alcove where you can do conference calls without being in the middle of your family, or overhearing the conference calls others in your household are holding at the same time. So demand for housing shot up. As Figure 10 shows, rental rates shot up in 2021, rising at more than 10 percent a year.

Actually, Figure 10 shows two measures of rental inflation: the rise in prices of newly rented units, and the rise in average rents paid. The latter lags behind new rents because most renters are on leases that last a year or more, so it takes time for a hot rental market to get fully reflected in average rents.

This lag, however, created additional difficulties in measuring the state of the economy. The shelter prices measured in the CPI reflect average rents, not new rentals. As a result, shelter inflation was hitting new highs in early 2023, even though most indications were that the big rental surge ended in early 2022.

The good news is that policy makers understood this: the Federal Reserve, in particular, was focused on measures of inflation that excluded shelter as well as food and energy. But the downside of these exclusions was that policy was being based on measures of inflation that exclude a large part of what consumers actually buy.

>> Check your Understanding 17-4

Solutions appear at back of book.

1. Why does the Fed usually focus on inflation excluding food and energy prices?
2. How did the pandemic cause shipping costs and apartment rents to surge?

>> Quick Review

• The Covid-19 pandemic led to a severe but short recession, followed by a rapid recovery. However, this recovery was accompanied by a surge in inflation.

• Unlike previous crises, the pandemic-related slump doesn't seem to have induced large changes in basic macroeconomic theory — in how economists think about the economy.

• However, the pandemic highlighted the difficulties the economy can have in responding to rapid changes in the mix of goods and services people want to consume, and big swings in prices like the cost of shipping and apartment rents made it more difficult than usual for policy makers to assess the economic situation.

SUMMARY

1. Classical macroeconomics asserted that monetary policy affected only the aggregate price level, not aggregate output, and that the short run was unimportant. By the 1930s, measurement of business cycles was a well-established subject, but there was no widely accepted theory of business cycles.

2. **Keynesian economics** attributed the business cycle to shifts of the aggregate demand curve, often the result of changes in business confidence. Keynesian economics also offered a rationale for **macroeconomic policy activism.**

3. In the decades that followed Keynes's work, economists came to agree that monetary policy as well as fiscal policy is effective under certain conditions. **Monetarism,** a doctrine that called for a **monetary policy rule** as opposed to **discretionary monetary policy** and argued for steady growth in the money supply, was influential for a time but was eventually rejected by many macroeconomists.

4. The **natural rate hypothesis** became almost universally accepted, limiting the role of macroeconomic policy to stabilizing the economy rather than seeking a permanently lower unemployment rate. Fears of a **political business cycle** led to a consensus that monetary policy should be insulated from politics.

5. The concept of **rational expectations** claims that individuals and firms make decisions using all available information. According to the **rational expectations model** of the economy, only unexpected changes in monetary policy affect aggregate output and employment; expected changes merely alter the price level.

Real business cycle theory claims that changes in the rate of growth of total factor productivity are the main cause of business cycles. Both of these versions of **new classical macroeconomics** received wide attention and respect, but policy makers and many economists haven't accepted the conclusion that monetary and fiscal policy are ineffective in changing aggregate output.

6. **New Keynesian economics** argues that market imperfections can lead to price stickiness, so that changes in aggregate demand have effects on aggregate output after all.

7. The **Great Moderation** from 1985 to 2007 made many economists confident that monetary policy alone can stabilize the economy. But the Great Recession revealed the limits to monetary policy and the potential usefulness of **fiscal stimulus.** On the other hand, after the Greek debt crisis many countries, worried about their levels of government debt, turned to **austerity policies** that appear to have hurt growth and delayed recovery.

8. The persistence of very low interest rates has led to concerns that we face **secular stagnation:** declining population growth and a slowdown in technological progress lead to a state of persistent economic weakness. In any case, low interest rates suggest that governments should focus less on debt, and perhaps engage in more deficit spending.

9. The Covid-19 pandemic caused a severe but brief recession. For the most part, these events didn't have large effects on macroeconomic theory. They did, however, highlight the economy's limited flexibility in the face of drastic change, and made it harder for policymakers to figure out the true economic situation.

KEY TERMS

Keynesian economics, p. 512
Macroeconomic policy activism, p. 512
Monetarism, p. 515
Discretionary monetary policy, p. 516
Monetary policy rule, p. 516
Natural rate hypothesis, p. 517

New classical macroeconomics, p. 517
Rational expectations, p. 517
Rational expectations model, p. 518
New Keynesian economics, p. 518
Real business cycle theory, p. 518
Political business cycle, p. 519

Great Moderation, p. 521
Fiscal stimulus, p. 522
Austerity policies, p. 523
Secular stagnation, p. 524

PRACTICE QUESTIONS

1. Figure 1 highlights the differences in the *SRAS* for classical and Keynesian economists. What would the different *SRAS* imply about the Phillips curve? Following the Great Recession most research has found a "flattening of the Phillips curve": what does this imply about the two schools of thought?

2. "We are all Keynesians now," is a quote that is often attributed to President Richard Nixon. While the

origins of the exact quote remain up for debate, how does this quote, in terms to fiscal stimulus and austerity policies, apply to the lesson we've learned following the Great Recession and the economic shutdown tied to the coronavirus pandemic?

3. At the start of the economic shutdown tied to the coronavirus pandemic, the Congressional Budget Office projected the publicly held federal debt to GDP ratio to

GDP ratio would reach 98.2% by the end of 2023, an increase of 14 percentage points from their previous projection. Going forward, what lessons can be applied from the record-level debt following World War II? What are the primary factors that will determine if debt snowballs out of control or will slowly melt?

PROBLEMS

1. Since the crash of its stock market in 1989, the Japanese economy has seen little economic growth and some deflation. The accompanying table from the Organization for Economic Cooperation and Development (OECD) shows some key macroeconomic data for Japan for 1991 (a "normal" year) and 1995–2003.

a. From the data, determine the type of policies Japan's policy makers undertook at that time to promote growth.

b. We can safely consider a short-term interest rate that is less than 0.1% to effectively be a 0% interest rate. What is this situation called? What does it imply about the effectiveness of monetary policy? Of fiscal policy?

Year	Real GDP annual growth rate	Short-term interest rate	Government debt (percent of GDP)	Government budget deficit (percent of GDP)
1991	3.4%	7.38%	64.8%	−1.81%
1995	1.9	1.23	87.1	4.71
1996	3.4	0.59	93.9	5.07
1997	1.9	0.60	100.3	3.79
1998	−1.1	0.72	112.2	5.51
1999	0.1	0.25	125.7	7.23
2000	2.8	0.25	134.1	7.48
2001	0.4	0.12	142.3	6.13
2002	−0.3	0.06	149.3	7.88
2003	2.5	0.04	157.5	7.67

2. The National Bureau of Economic Research (NBER) maintains the official chronology of past U.S. business cycles. Go to its website at www.nber.org/cycles/cyclesmain.html to answer the following questions.

a. How many business cycles have occurred since the end of World War II in 1945?

b. What was the average duration of a business cycle when measured from the end of one expansion (its peak) to the end of the next? That is, what was the average duration of a business cycle in the period from 1945 to 2009?

c. When was the last announcement by the NBER's Business Cycle Dating Committee, and what was it?

3. The fall of its military rival, the Soviet Union, in 1989 allowed the United States to significantly reduce its defense spending in subsequent years. Using the data in the following table from the Economic Report of the President, replicate Figure 2 for the 1990–2000 period. Given the strong economic growth in the United States during the late 1990s, why would a Keynesian see the reduction in defense spending during the 1990s as a good thing?

Year	Budget deficit (percent of GDP)	Unemployment rate
1990	3.9%	5.6%
1991	4.5	6.8
1992	4.7	7.5
1993	3.9	6.9
1994	2.9	6.1
1995	2.2	5.6
1996	1.4	5.4
1997	0.3	4.9
1998	−0.8	4.5
1999	−1.4	4.2
2000	−2.4	4.0

4. In the modern world, central banks are free to increase or reduce the money supply as they see fit. However, some people harken back to the "good old days" of the gold standard. Under the gold standard, the money supply could expand only when the amount of available gold increased.

a. Under the gold standard, if a growing economy led to a rising demand for money, what would have had to happen to keep prices stable?

b. Why would modern macroeconomists consider the gold standard a bad idea?

5. The chapter notes that Kenneth Rogoff proclaimed Richard Nixon "the all-time hero of political business cycles." Using the following table of data from the Economic Report of the President, explain why Nixon may have earned that title. (*Note:* Nixon entered office in January 1969 and was reelected in November 1972. He resigned in August 1974.)

Year	Government receipts (billions of dollars)	Government spending (billions of dollars)	Government budget balance (billions of dollars)	M1 growth	M2 growth	3-month Treasury bill rate
1969	$186.9	$183.6	$3.2	3.3%	3.7%	6.68%
1970	192.8	195.6	−2.8	5.1	6.6	6.46
1971	187.1	210.2	−23.0	6.5	13.4	4.35
1972	207.3	230.7	−23.4	9.2	13.0	4.07
1973	230.8	245.7	−14.9	5.5	6.6	7.04

6. The economy of Albernia is facing a recessionary gap, and the leader of that nation calls together its best economists representing the classical, Keynesian, monetarist, real business cycle, Great Moderation consensus, expansionary austerity, and secular stagnationist views of the macroeconomy. Explain what policies each economist would recommend and why.

7. Which of the following policy recommendations are consistent with the classical, Keynesian, monetarist, and/or Great Moderation view, versus secular stagnationist views of the macroeconomy?

a. Since the long-run growth of GDP is 2%, the money supply should grow at 2%.

b. Decrease government spending in order to decrease inflationary pressure.

c. Increase the money supply in order to alleviate a recessionary gap.

d. Always maintain a balanced budget.

e. Decrease the budget deficit as a percent of GDP when facing a recessionary gap.

f. Pursue large, expansionary fiscal policies during a liquidity trap.

8. Using a graph of *AD/AS* and money supply and money demand, show how a monetarist can argue that a contractionary fiscal policy need not lead to a fall in real GDP given a fixed money supply. Explain.

9. In response to the Great Recession, the Federal Reserve took drastic and largely untested measures to stabilize both the financial system and the macroeconomy. These measures caused the monetary base to increase from approximately $850 billion to over $4 trillion. What would an economist from each of the following viewpoints—classical, Keynesian, monetarist, real business cycle, Great Moderation consensus, and secular stagnationists—predict about the effect of these policies, and why? Indicate whether each school would support the Fed's actions.

10. Using our aggregate demand and aggregate supply framework individually analyze each of the following events. What is the initial effects on real GDP and inflation for each event?

a. Public aid intended to cushion the financial impact of the pandemic.

b. Federal Reserve lowered overnight bank lending rates to zero.

c. A decrease in labor supply.

d. Significant increase in shipping costs for raw materials.

Given your responses above, assess the following possible results (1) the U.S. economy to experience stagflation, rising inflation and unemployment and (2) the U.S. economy will overhead with rising inflation and declining unemployment. Based on current data, what likely happened? ■

18 > International Macroeconomics

PROPPING UP THE TURKISH LIRA

IN FEBRUARY 2023, a severe earthquake struck southern Turkey and northern Syria, killing tens of thousands and leaving an estimated 1.5 million people homeless. The Turkish government and international relief agencies rushed in to help the survivors. But the biggest immediate outlay of funds by Turkish authorities didn't go to earthquake victims. Instead, they rushed to spend about $7 billion of their foreign exchange reserves — a hoard of assets in other countries' currencies, mainly dollars and euros — buying up their own currency, the Turkish lira, in an attempt to keep its value from plunging in the quake's aftermath.

What this emergency intervention illustrated was the importance of a dimension of macroeconomics that we haven't emphasized so far — the fact that modern national economies trade large quantities of goods, services, and assets with the rest of the world. *International macroeconomics* is a branch of macroeconomics that deals with the relationships between national economies (it is sometimes referred to as *open-economy macroeconomics*). As the Turkish story illustrates, economic interactions with the rest of the world can have a profound impact on a domestic economy.

In this chapter we'll learn about some of the key issues in international macroeconomics: the determinants of a country's *balance of payments,* the factors affecting *exchange rates,* the different forms of *exchange rate policy* adopted by various countries, and the relationship between exchange rates and macroeconomic policy. ●

Turkey was devastated by a severe earthquake in early 2023, but most of the government aid went to prevent the value of the Turkish lira from plummeting.

WHAT YOU WILL LEARN

- What are the **balance of payments accounts?**
- What determines international capital flows?
- What roles do the **foreign exchange market** and the **exchange rate** play?
- How do **real exchange rates** affect the **current account?**
- Why do countries choose different **exchange rate regimes,** such as **fixed exchange rates** and **floating exchange rates?**
- How should domestic macroeconomic policy be adjusted as a consequence of international economic considerations?

balance of payments accounts
a summary of a country's transactions with other countries for a given year, including two main elements: the balance of payments on current account and the balance of payments on financial account.

|| Capital Flows and the Balance of Payments

In 2022, people living in the United States sold trillions of dollars' worth of stuff to people living in other countries and bought trillions of dollars' worth of stuff in return. What kind of stuff? All kinds. Residents of the United States (including firms operating in the United States) sold airplanes, bonds, software licenses, wheat, and many other items to residents of other countries. U.S. residents bought cars, stocks, oil, and many other items from residents of other countries.

How can we keep track of these transactions? In Chapter 7 we learned that economists keep track of the domestic economy using the national income and product accounts. Economists keep track of international transactions using a different but related set of numbers, the *balance of payments accounts.*

Balance of Payments Accounts

A country's **balance of payments accounts** are a summary of the country's transactions with other countries for a given year.

To understand the basic idea behind the balance of payments accounts, let's consider a small-scale example: not a country, but a family farm. Let's say that we know the following about how last year went financially for the Costas, who own a small artichoke farm in California:

- They made $100,000 by selling artichokes.
- They spent $70,000 on running the farm, including purchases of new farm machinery, and another $40,000 buying food, paying utility bills, replacing their worn-out car, and so on.
- They received $500 in interest on their bank account but paid $10,000 in interest on their mortgage.
- They took out a new $25,000 loan to help pay for farm improvements but didn't use all the money immediately. So they put the remaining $5,500 in the bank.

How could we summarize the Costas' transactions for the year? One way would be with a table like Table 1, which shows sources of cash coming in and uses of cash going out, characterized under a few broad headings. The first row of Table 1 shows sales and purchases of goods and services: sales of artichokes; purchases of groceries, heating oil, that new car, and so on. The second row shows interest payments: the interest the Costas received from their bank account and the interest they paid on their mortgage. The third row shows loans and deposits: cash coming in from a loan and cash deposited in the bank.

In each row we show the net inflow of cash from that type of transaction. So the net in the first row is –$10,000, because the Costas spent $10,000 more than they earned. The net in the second row is –$9,500, the difference between the interest the Costas received on their bank account and the interest they paid on the mortgage. The net in the third row is $19,500: the Costas brought in $25,000 with their new loan but put only $5,500 of that sum in the bank.

The last row shows the sum of cash coming in from all sources and the sum of all cash used. These sums are equal, by definition: every dollar has a source, and every dollar received gets used somewhere. (What if the Costas hid money under the mattress? Then that would be counted as another "use" of cash.)

A country's balance of payments accounts is a table that summarizes the country's transactions with the rest of the world for a given year in a manner very similar to the way we just summarized the Costas' financial year.

TABLE 1 The Costas' Financial Year

	Sources of cash	Uses of cash	Net
Sales and purchases of goods and services	Artichoke sales: $100,000	Farm operation and living expenses: $110,000	–$10,000
Interest payments	Interest received on bank account: $500	Interest paid on mortgage: $10,000	–$9,500
Loans and deposits	Funds received from new loan: $25,000	Funds deposited in bank: $5,500	+$19,500
Total	$125,500	$125,500	$0

Table 2 shows a simplified version of the U.S. balance of payments accounts for 2022. Where the Costas family's accounts show sources and uses of cash, a country's balance of payments accounts show payments from foreigners—sources of cash for the United States as a whole—and payments to foreigners—uses of cash for the United States as a whole.

Row 1 of Table 2 shows payments that arise from U.S. sales to foreigners and U.S. purchases from foreigners of goods and services in 2022. For example, the number in the second column of row 1, $3,012 billion, incorporates items such as the value of U.S. wheat exports and the fees foreigners paid to U.S. consulting companies in 2022. The number in the third column of row 1, $3,957 billion, incorporates items such as the value of U.S. oil imports and the fees U.S. companies paid to Indian call centers—the people who often answer your 1-800 calls—in 2022.

Row 2 shows U.S. *factor income* in 2022—the income that foreigners paid to U.S. residents for the use of U.S.-owned factors of production, as well as income paid by Americans to foreigners for the use of foreign-owned factors of production. Factor income mostly consists of investment income, such as interest paid by Americans on loans from overseas, profits of U.S.-owned corporations that operate overseas, and the like. For example, the profits earned by Disneyland Paris, which is owned by the U.S.-based Walt Disney Company, are included in the $1,217 billion figure in the second column of row 2. The profits earned by the U.S. operations of Japanese auto companies are included in the $1,040 billion figure shown in the third column of row 2. Factor income also includes some labor income. For example, the wages of an American engineer who worked temporarily on a construction site in Dubai are counted in the $1,217 billion figure in the second column.

Row 3 shows *international transfers* for the United States in 2022—funds sent by U.S. residents to residents of other countries and vice versa. The figure in the second column of row 3, $180 billion, includes payments sent home by skilled U.S. workers who work abroad. The third column accounts for the major portion of international transfers. That figure, $356 billion, is composed mainly of remittances that immigrants who reside in the United States, such as the millions of Mexican-born workers employed in the United States, send to their families in their country of origin.

Row 4 of the table shows net payments accruing from sales and purchases of assets between U.S. residents and foreigners in 2022. Such payments involve a wide variety of transactions, from Chinese companies purchasing U.S. firms to U.S. purchases of European stocks and bonds. The details of these transactions are complex, and if you add up all purchases the value is very large, which is why we focus only on the net value. Overall, according to official figures, and as you can see in the table, U.S. residents sold $597 billion more in assets than they purchased.

In laying out Table 2, we have separated rows 1, 2, and 3 into one group, to distinguish them from row 4, reflecting a fundamental difference in how these two groups of transactions affect the future. When a U.S. resident sells a good such as wheat to a foreigner, that's the end of the transaction. But a financial asset, such as a bond, is different: it is a promise to pay interest and principal in the future. So when a U.S. resident sells a bond to a foreigner, that sale creates a liability: the U.S. resident will have to pay interest and repay principal in the future. The balance of payments accounts distinguish between transactions that don't create liabilities and those that do.

TABLE 2 The U.S. Balance of Payments in 2022 (billions of dollars)

		Payments from foreigners	Payments to foreigners	Net
1	Sales and purchases of goods and services	$3,012	$3,957	−$945
2	Factor income	1,217	1,040	177
3	Transfers	180	356	−176
	Current account (1 + 2 + 3)			−944
4	Asset sales and purchases (financial account)	1,516	919	597
	Financial account (4)			**597**
	Statistical discrepancy	−	−	−347

Data from: Bureau of Economic Analysis.

balance of payments on current account (current account) transactions that don't create liabilities; a country's balance of payments on goods and services plus net international transfer payments and factor income.

balance of payments on goods and services the difference between the value of exports and the value of imports of a country during a given period.

merchandise trade balance (trade balance) the difference between a country's exports and imports of goods alone—not including services.

balance of payments on financial account (financial account) international transactions that involve the sale or purchase of assets, and therefore create future liabilities.

Transactions that don't create liabilities are considered part of the **balance of payments on current account,** often referred to simply as the **current account:** the balance of payments on goods and services plus net international transfer payments and factor income. This corresponds to rows 1, 2, and 3 in Table 2. In practice, row 1 of the table, amounting to –$945 billion, corresponds to the most important part of the current account: the **balance of payments on goods and services,** the difference between the value of exports and the value of imports during a given period.

In economic news reports, you may see references to another measure, the **merchandise trade balance,** sometimes referred to as the **trade balance,** for short. It is the difference between a country's exports and imports of goods alone—not including services. Economists sometimes focus on the merchandise trade balance, even though it's an incomplete measure, because data on international trade in services aren't as accurate as data on trade in physical goods, and they are also slower to arrive.

Transactions that involve the sale or purchase of assets, and therefore do create future liabilities, are considered part of the **balance of payments on financial account,** or the **financial account** for short, for a given period. This corresponds to row 4 in Table 2, which was $597 billion in 2022. (Until a few years ago, economists often referred to the financial account as the *capital account.* We'll use the modern term, but you may run across the older term.)

So how does it all add up? The rows shaded purple in Table 2 show the bottom lines: the overall U.S. current account and financial account for 2022. As you can see:

- The United States ran a *current account deficit:* the amount it paid to foreigners for goods, services, factors, and transfers was more than the amount it received.

- Simultaneously, it ran a *financial account surplus:* the value of the assets it sold to foreigners was more than the value of the assets it bought from foreigners.

- In the official data, the U.S. current account deficit and financial account surplus didn't offset each other: the financial account surplus in 2022 was $347

FOR INQUIRING MINDS   **GDP, GNP, and the Current Account**

When we discussed national income accounting in Chapter 7, we derived the basic equation relating GDP to the components of spending:

$$Y = C + I + G + X - IM$$

where X and IM are exports and imports, respectively, of goods and services. But as we've learned, the balance of payments on goods and services is only one component of the current account balance. Why doesn't the national income equation use the current account as a whole?

The answer is that gross domestic product, Y, is the value of goods and services produced domestically. So it doesn't include international factor income and international transfers, two sources of income that are included in the calculation of the current account balance. The profits of Ford Motors U.K. aren't included in the U.S. GDP, and

the funds Latin American immigrants send home to their families aren't subtracted from GDP.

Shouldn't we have a broader measure that does include these sources of income? Actually, gross *national* product—GNP—does include international factor income. Estimates of U.S. GNP differ slightly from estimates of GDP because GNP adds in items such as the earnings of U.S. companies abroad and subtracts items such as the interest payments on bonds owned by residents of China and Japan. There isn't, however, any regularly calculated measure that includes transfer payments.

Why do economists usually use GDP rather than a broader measure? Two reasons. First, the original purpose of the national accounts was to track production rather than income. Second, data on international factor income and transfer payments are generally

considered somewhat unreliable. So if you're trying to keep track of movements in the economy, it usually makes sense to focus on GDP, because it doesn't include these unreliable data. (As the Economics in Action on "leprechaun economics" shows, however, sometimes GDP has problems, too.)

The funds Latin American immigrants send abroad are included in GDP because they were earned for services performed in the United States.

billion smaller than the current account deficit (shown in the final row of the table). But that was just a statistical error, reflecting the imperfection of official data. (The discrepancy may have reflected foreign purchases of U.S. assets that official data somehow missed.)

In fact, it's a basic rule of balance of payments accounting that the current account and the financial account must sum to zero:

(1) Current account (CA) + Financial account $(FA) = 0$

or

$$CA = -FA$$

Why must Equation 1 be true? We already saw the fundamental explanation in Table 1, which showed the accounts of the Costas family: in total, the sources of cash must equal the uses of cash. The same applies to balance of payments accounts. Figure 1, a variant on the circular-flow diagram we have found useful in discussing domestic macroeconomics, may help you visualize how this adding up works. Instead of showing the flow of money *within* a national economy, Figure 1 shows the flow of money *between* national economies.

Money flows into the United States from the rest of the world as payment for U.S. exports of goods and services, as payment for the use of U.S.-owned factors of production, and as transfer payments. These flows, indicated by the lower blue arrow, are the positive components of the U.S. current account. Money also flows into the United States from foreigners who purchase U.S. assets. They make up the positive component of the U.S. financial account and are shown by the lower green arrow.

At the same time, money flows from the United States to the rest of the world as payment for U.S. imports of goods and services, as payment for the use of foreign-owned factors of production, and as transfer payments. These flows, indicated by the upper blue arrow, are the negative components of the U.S. current account. Money also flows from the United States to purchase foreign assets. They make up the negative component of the U.S. financial account and are shown by the upper green arrow.

FIGURE 1 The Balance of Payments

The blue arrows represent payments that are counted in the current account. The green arrows represent payments that are counted in the financial account. Because the total flow into the United States must equal the total flow out of the United States, the sum of the current account plus the financial account is zero.

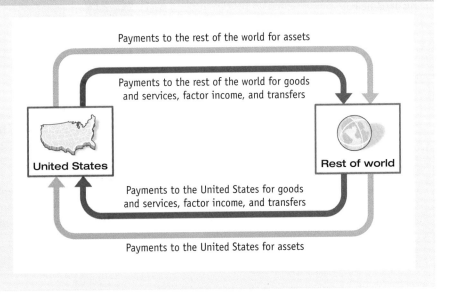

As in all circular-flow diagrams, the flow into a box and the flow out of a box are equal. This means that the sum of the blue and green arrows going into the United States (at the bottom of the diagram) is equal to the sum of the blue and green arrows going out of the United States (at the top of the diagram). That is:

(2)

Positive current account entries + Positive financial account entries =
(lower blue arrow) (lower green arrow)

Negative current account entries + Negative financial account entries
(upper blue arrow) (upper green arrow)

Equation 2 can be rearranged as follows:

(3)

Positive current account entries – Negative current account entries +

Positive financial account entries – Negative financial account entries = 0

Equation 3 is equivalent to Equation 1: once we have summed up the positive and negative entries within each account, the current account plus the financial account is equal to zero.

But what determines the current account and the financial account?

Modeling the Financial Account

A country's financial account measures its net sales of assets to foreigners. There is, however, another way to think about the financial account: it's a measure of *capital inflows*, of foreign savings that are available to finance domestic investment spending.

GLOBAL COMPARISON **BIG SURPLUSES**

As we've seen, the United States generally runs a large deficit in its current account. In fact, the United States leads the world in its current account deficit; other countries run bigger deficits as a share of GDP, but they have much smaller economies, so the U.S. deficit is much bigger in absolute terms.

For the world as a whole, however, deficits on the part of some countries must be matched with surpluses on the part of other countries. So who are the surplus nations offsetting U.S. deficits, and what if anything do they have in common?

The accompanying figure shows the average current account surplus of the five countries that ran the largest surpluses over the period from 2012 to 2021. You may not be surprised to see China on this list. For a time China had a deliberate policy of keeping its currency weak relative to other currencies.

Germany, Japan, the Netherlands, and South Korea run current account surpluses for more or less the same reasons: they are rich nations with high savings rates, giving them a lot of money to invest. They also have slow long-run growth, which reduces the opportunities for domestic investment. So, much of their savings goes abroad, which means that they run deficits on the financial account and surpluses on the current account.

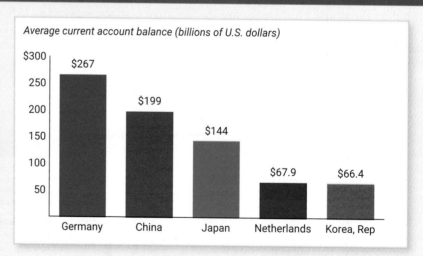

Average current account balance (billions of U.S. dollars)

The current account surpluses of Germany, which tops the list, and the Netherlands have also grown thanks to the declining value of the euro. A lower euro has reduced the cost of their manufacturing goods on world markets, allowing them to export more.

Overall, the surplus countries are a diverse group. If your picture of the world is simply one of U.S. deficits versus Chinese surpluses, you're missing a large part of the story.

Note: Average current account balance (billions of U.S. dollars) on *y*-axis. Data are from 2021.
Data from: International Monetary Fund.

What determines these capital inflows?

Part of the explanation will have to wait until later because some international capital flows are carried out by governments and central banks, which sometimes act very differently from private investors. But we can gain insight into the motivations for capital flows that are the result of private decisions by using the *loanable funds model* developed in Chapter 10 and, in particular, in Chapter 10, Figures 7 and 8. In using this model to analyze the financial account, we make two important simplifications:

1. We assume that all international capital flows are in the form of loans. In reality, capital flows take many forms, including purchases of shares of stock in foreign companies and foreign real estate as well as *direct foreign investment*, in which companies build factories or acquire other productive assets abroad.

2. We ignore the effects of expected changes in exchange rates, the relative values of different national currencies. We analyze the determination of exchange rates shortly.

Recall Figure 7 in Chapter 10 from our discussion of the global loanable funds market. It shows a hypothetical world consisting of two countries, the United States and Britain, which would have different equilibrium interest rates—6% in the United States, 2% in Britain—in the absence of international capital flows. But this difference in interest rates will not persist if it is easy for British lenders to make their funds available to U.S. borrowers. In fact, if British lenders consider loans to Americans just as good as domestic loans, interest rates will fall in the United States and rise in Britain until they are the same in both countries, with the United States, in effect, importing loanable funds from Britain. This equalization of interest rates (at 4%) is shown in Chapter 10, Figure 8.

However, given our two simplifying assumptions, the loanable funds the United States imports from Britain (which are Britain's excess savings or capital outflows), are precisely the U.S. balance of payments on the financial account! So the financial account is determined by the supply and demand for loanable funds: capital moves from places where it would be cheap in the absence of international capital flows to places where it would be expensive in the absence of such flows.

Underlying Determinants of International Capital Flows

While the loanable funds model tells us the direction of capital flows—from countries in which capital is cheap to countries in which capital is expensive—it doesn't explain why. That is, why is capital cheap in one country but expensive in another?

International differences in investment opportunities generate international differences in the demand for capital. A country with a rapidly growing economy, other things equal, will offer more investment opportunities and a higher return to investors than a country with a slowly growing economy. So a country with a rapidly growing economy will typically have a higher demand for capital than the country with a slowly growing economy. As a result, capital tends to flow from slowly growing to rapidly growing economies.

International differences in the supply of funds reflect differences in savings across countries. These may be the result of differences in private savings rates, which vary among countries. They may also reflect differences in savings by governments. In particular, government budget deficits, which reduce overall national savings, can lead to capital inflows.

Now we can put together the demand for capital generated by investment opportunities within a country, with the supply for capital generated by savings within a country, to explain differences in interest rates across countries. Other things equal, countries with a high demand for capital and/or a low supply of capital will have higher interest rates. As a result, they will be the recipients of capital inflows.

Conversely, other things equal, countries with a low demand for funds and/or a high supply of funds will have lower interest rates. As a result, they will be the sources of capital outflows. The classic example of international capital flows is the flow of capital from Britain to the United States and other New World economies from 1870 to 1914. During that era, the United States was rapidly industrializing and had a high demand for capital. But Britain, which already industrialized, had a slowly growing economy with a large amount of accumulated savings.

Two-Way Capital Flows

In fact, it is the direction of *net* capital flows—the excess of inflows into a country over outflows, or vice versa—that is explained by the loanable funds model. The direction of *net* flows, other things equal, is determined by differences in interest rates between countries. However, *gross* flows take place in both directions: for example, the United States both sells assets to foreigners and buys assets from foreigners. Why does capital move in both directions?

The answer to this question is that in the real world, as opposed to the simple model just described, there are other motives for international capital flows besides seeking a higher rate of interest.

Individual investors often seek to diversify against risk by buying stocks in several countries. Stocks in Europe may do well when stocks in the United States do badly, or vice versa, so investors in Europe try to reduce their risk by buying some U.S. stocks, as U.S. investors try to reduce their risk by buying some European stocks. The result is capital flows in both directions.

Meanwhile, corporations often engage in international investment as part of their business strategy—for example, auto companies may find that they can compete better in an overseas market if they assemble some of their cars in that location. Such business investments can also lead to two-way capital flows, as, say, European car makers build plants in the United States even as U.S. computer companies open facilities in Europe.

Finally, some countries, including the United States, are international banking centers: people from all over the world put money in U.S. financial institutions, which then invest many of those funds overseas.

The result of these two-way flows is that modern economies are typically both debtors (countries that owe money to the rest of the world) and creditors (countries to which the rest of the world owes money). Due to years of both capital inflows and outflows, at the end of 2022, the United States had accumulated foreign assets worth $31.7 trillion, and foreigners had accumulated assets in the United States worth $47.8 trillion.

Many American companies have opened plants in China to access the growing Chinese market and take advantage of low labor costs.

ECONOMICS >> *in Action*

Leprechaun Economics

One factor we didn't mention in our discussion of international capital flows was taxation. Yet tax rates on corporate profits vary considerably between nations. France, for example, has a corporate tax rate of 28%, while Ireland's rate is only 12.5%. These tax differences create an incentive for multinational corporations to report large investments in low-tax countries.

Notice how we worded this: it gives corporations an incentive to *report* large investments in countries like Ireland. Consider the operations of Apple's Irish subsidiary, which buys parts from Apple operations in other countries and sells much of what it makes to other Apple branches; it also pays royalties to the home company for its use of Apple patents. How profitable is that subsidiary? It's hard to say, because both the prices it receives and the prices it pays largely reflect internal Apple decisions rather than some independent market.

So it's easy for Apple to record very large profits on its Irish operations; as long as it doesn't send the profits home, these profits are considered to have been invested in Ireland, even though there isn't any real investment taking place.

Tax avoidance doesn't just distort balance of payments statistics. It can also distort national income accounting, especially for smaller countries. In 2015 Ireland reported that its real GDP rose 26%, which was obviously not the economy's true growth rate. What happened was that several big companies changed their accounting, choosing to attribute more of their value added to Ireland. One of this book's authors immediately dubbed the bizarre reported figure "leprechaun economics," a term quickly picked up by the Irish, who fortunately have a good sense of humor about themselves (and who have developed alternative measures that give a better picture of the economy's true growth.)

Unfortunately, joking aside, this kind of profit shifting has become a major problem for tax collection. The IMF estimates that "phantom" capital flows, done solely to avoid taxes, account for about 40% of international corporate investment. This represents a serious revenue loss for many governments.

>> Check Your Understanding 18-1

Solutions appear at back of book.

1. Which of the balance of payments accounts do the following events affect?
   a. Boeing, a U.S.-based company, sells a newly built airplane to China.
   b. Chinese investors buy stock in Boeing from U.S. residents.
   c. A Chinese company buys a used airplane from American Airlines and ships it to China.
   d. A Chinese investor who owns property in the United States buys a corporate jet, which they will keep in the United States so they can travel around America.

2. What effect do you think the collapse of the U.S. housing bubble in 2008, and the ensuing Great Recession, had on international capital flows into the United States?

The Role of the Exchange Rate

We've just seen how differences in the supply of loanable funds from savings and the demand for loanable funds for investment spending lead to international capital flows. We've also learned that a country's balance of payments on current account plus its balance of payments on financial account add to zero: a country that receives net capital inflows must run a matching current account deficit, and a country that generates net capital outflows must run a matching current account surplus.

The behavior of the financial account—reflecting inflows or outflows of capital—is best described by equilibrium in the global loanable funds market. At the same time, the balance of payments on goods and services, the main component of the current account, is determined by decisions in the international markets for goods and services.

So given that the financial account reflects the movement of capital and the current account reflects the movement of goods and services, what ensures that the balance of payments really does balance? That is, what ensures that the two accounts actually offset each other?

Not surprisingly, a price is what makes these two accounts balance. Specifically, that price is the *exchange rate*, which is determined in the *foreign exchange market.*

foreign exchange market the market in which currencies can be exchanged for each other.

exchange rates the price at which currencies trade, determined by the foreign exchange market.

appreciates a rise in the value of one currency in terms of other currencies.

depreciates a fall in the value of one currency in terms of other currencies.

Understanding Exchange Rates

In general, goods, services, and assets produced in a country must be paid for in that country's currency. U.S. products must be paid for in dollars; European products must be paid for in euros; Japanese products must be paid for in yen. Occasionally, sellers will accept payment in foreign currency, but they will then exchange that currency for domestic money.

International transactions, then, require a market—the **foreign exchange market**—in which currencies can be exchanged for each other. This market determines **exchange rates,** the prices at which currencies trade. (The foreign exchange market is, in fact, not located in any one geographic spot. Rather, it is a global electronic market that traders around the world use to buy and sell currencies.)

Table 3 shows exchange rates among the world's three most important currencies as of 11 P.M., EDT, on June 7, 2023. Each entry shows the price of the "row" currency in terms of the "column" currency. For example, at that time US\$1 exchanged for €0.9345, so it took €0.9345 to buy US\$1. Similarly, it took US\$1.07 to buy €1. These two numbers reflect the same rate of exchange between the euro and the U.S. dollar: 1/1.07 = 0.9345.

There are two ways to write any given exchange rate. In this case, there were €0.9345 to US\$1 and US\$1.07 to €1. Which is the correct way to write it? The answer is that there is no fixed rule. In most countries, people tend to express the exchange rate as the price of a dollar in domestic currency. However, this rule isn't universal, and the U.S. dollar–euro rate is commonly quoted both ways. The important thing is to be sure you know which one you are using, as explained in the accompanying Pitfalls.

When discussing movements in exchange rates, economists use specialized terms to avoid confusion. When a currency becomes more valuable in terms of other currencies, economists say that the currency **appreciates.** When a currency becomes less valuable in terms of other currencies, it **depreciates.** Suppose, for example, that the value of €1 went from \$1 to \$1.25, which means that the value of US\$1 went from €1 to €0.80 (because 1/1.25 = 0.80). In this case, we would say that the euro appreciated and the U.S. dollar depreciated.

By the way, although *appreciate* and *depreciate* are the technical, more or less official terms for a rise or fall of a currency against other currencies, you will also often hear it said that an appreciating currency is getting "stronger," or a depreciating currency is getting "weaker." It's important to realize that these terms, while widely used, shouldn't be taken as value judgments: a strong dollar isn't necessarily a good thing and a weak dollar isn't necessarily a bad thing.

Movements in exchange rates, other things equal, affect the relative prices of goods, services, and assets in different countries. Suppose, for example, that the price of a U.S. hotel room is US\$100 and the price of a French hotel room is €100. If the exchange rate is €1 = US\$1, these hotel rooms have the same price. If the exchange rate is €1.25 = US\$1, the French hotel room is 20% cheaper than the U.S. hotel room. If the exchange rate is €0.80 = US\$1, the French hotel room is 25% more expensive than the U.S. hotel room.

But what determines exchange rates? Supply and demand in the foreign exchange market.

The Equilibrium Exchange Rate

Imagine, for the sake of simplicity, that there are only two currencies in the world: U.S. dollars and euros. Europeans wanting to purchase

TABLE 3 Exchange Rates, June 7, 2023, 6 P.M.

	U.S. dollars	Yen	Euros
One U.S. dollar exchanged for	1	140.09	0.9345
One yen exchanged for	0.0071	1	0.0067
One euro exchanged for	1.07	149.92	1

WHICH WAY IS UP?

Someone says that "The U.S. exchange rate is up." What exactly does that mean?

It isn't clear. Sometimes the exchange rate is measured as the price of a dollar in terms of foreign currency, sometimes as the price of foreign currency in terms of dollars. So the statement could mean either that the dollar appreciated or that it depreciated!

You have to be particularly careful when using published statistics. Most countries other than the United States state their exchange rates in terms of the price of a dollar in their domestic currency—for example, Turkish officials will say that the exchange rate is 19, meaning 19 lira per dollar. But Britain, for historical reasons, usually states its exchange rate the other way. On June 7, 2023, US\$1 was worth £0.8046, and £1 was worth US\$1.2429. More often than not, this number is reported as an exchange rate of 1.2429. In fact, on occasion, professional economists and consultants embarrass themselves by getting the direction in which the pound is moving wrong!

By the way, Americans generally follow other countries' lead: we usually say that the exchange rate against Turkey is 19 lira per dollar but that the exchange rate against Britain is 1.24 dollars per pound. But this rule isn't reliable; exchange rates against the euro are often stated both ways.

So before using exchange rate data, always ask yourself: which way is the exchange rate being measured?

FIGURE 2 The Foreign Exchange Market

The foreign exchange market matches up the demand for a currency from foreigners who want to buy domestic goods, services, and assets with the supply of a currency from domestic residents who want to buy foreign goods, services, and assets. Here the equilibrium in the market for dollars is at point *E*, corresponding to an equilibrium exchange rate of €0.80 per US$1.

U.S. goods, services, and assets come to the foreign exchange market, wanting to exchange euros for U.S. dollars. That is, Europeans demand U.S. dollars from the foreign exchange market and, correspondingly, supply euros to that market. Americans wanting to buy European goods, services, and assets come to the foreign exchange market to exchange U.S. dollars for euros. That is, Americans supply U.S. dollars to the foreign exchange market and, correspondingly, demand euros from that market. (International transfers and payments of factor income also enter into the foreign exchange market, but to make things simple we'll ignore these.)

Figure 2 shows how the foreign exchange market works. The quantity of dollars demanded and supplied at any given euro–U.S. dollar exchange rate is shown on the horizontal axis, and the euro–U.S. dollar exchange rate is shown on the vertical axis. The exchange rate plays the same role as the price of a good or service in an ordinary supply and demand diagram.

The figure shows two curves, the demand curve for U.S. dollars and the supply curve for U.S. dollars. The key to understanding the slopes of these curves is that the level of the exchange rate affects exports and imports. When a country's currency appreciates (becomes more valuable), exports fall and imports rise. When a country's currency depreciates (becomes less valuable), exports rise and imports fall.

To understand why the demand curve for U.S. dollars slopes downward, recall that the exchange rate, other things equal, determines the prices of U.S. goods, services, and assets relative to those of European goods, services, and assets.

If the U.S. dollar rises against the euro (the dollar appreciates), U.S. products will become more expensive to Europeans relative to European products. So Europeans will buy less from the United States and will acquire fewer dollars in the foreign exchange market: the quantity of U.S. dollars demanded falls as the number of euros needed to buy a U.S. dollar rises.

If the U.S. dollar falls against the euro (the dollar depreciates), U.S. products will become relatively cheaper for Europeans. Europeans will respond by buying more from the United States and acquiring more dollars in the foreign exchange market: the quantity of U.S. dollars demanded rises as the number of euros needed to buy a U.S. dollar falls.

equilibrium exchange rate the exchange rate at which the quantity of a currency demanded in the foreign exchange market is equal to the quantity supplied.

A similar argument explains why the supply curve of U.S. dollars in Figure 2 slopes upward: the more euros required to buy a U.S. dollar, the more dollars Americans will supply. Again, the reason is the effect of the exchange rate on relative prices. If the U.S. dollar rises against the euro, European products look cheaper to Americans—who will demand more of them. This will require Americans to convert more dollars into euros.

The **equilibrium exchange rate** is the exchange rate at which the quantity of U.S. dollars demanded in the foreign exchange market is equal to the quantity of U.S. dollars supplied. In Figure 2, the equilibrium is at point *E*, and the equilibrium exchange rate is €0.80. That is, at an exchange rate of €0.80 per US$1, the quantity of U.S. dollars supplied to the foreign exchange market is equal to the quantity of U.S. dollars demanded.

To understand the significance of the equilibrium exchange rate, it's helpful to consider a numerical example of what equilibrium in the foreign exchange market looks like. A hypothetical example is shown in Table 4. The first row shows European purchases of U.S. dollars, either to buy U.S. goods and services or to buy U.S. assets. The second row shows U.S. sales of U.S. dollars, either to buy European goods and services or to buy European assets. At the equilibrium exchange rate, the total quantity of U.S. dollars Europeans want to buy is equal to the total quantity of U.S. dollars Americans want to sell.

Remember that the balance of payments accounts divide international transactions into two types. Purchases and sales of goods and services are counted in the current account. (Again, we're leaving out transfers and factor income to keep things simple.) Purchases and sales of assets are counted in the financial account. At the equilibrium exchange rate, then, we have the situation shown in Table 4: the sum of the balance of payments on the current account plus the balance of payments on the financial account is zero.

Now let's briefly consider how a shift in the demand for U.S. dollars affects equilibrium in the foreign exchange market. Suppose that for some reason capital flows from Europe to the United States increase due to a

TABLE 4 A Hypothetical Equilibrium in the Foreign Exchange Market

	Current account	Financial account	Totals
European purchases of U.S. dollars (trillions of dollars)	To buy U.S. goods and services: 1.0	To buy U.S. assets: 1.0	2.0
U.S. sales of U.S. dollars (trillions of dollars)	To buy European goods and services: 1.5	To buy European assets: 0.5	2.0
U.S. balance of payments	−0.5	+0.5	

FIGURE 3 An Increase in the Demand for U.S. Dollars

An increase in the demand for U.S. dollars might result from a change in the preferences of European investors. The demand curve for U.S. dollars shifts from D_1 to D_2. So the equilibrium number of euros per U.S. dollar rises — the dollar appreciates against the euro. As a result, the balance of payments on current account falls as the balance of payments on financial account rises.

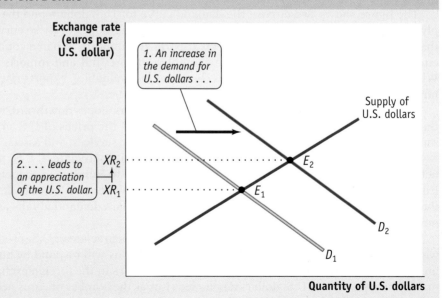

1. An increase in the demand for U.S. dollars . . .

2. . . . leads to an appreciation of the U.S. dollar.

change in the preferences of European investors. The effects are shown in Figure 3. The demand for U.S. dollars in the foreign exchange market increases as European investors convert euros into dollars to fund their new investments in the United States. This is shown by the shift of the demand curve from D_1 to D_2. As a result, the U.S. dollar appreciates against the euro: the number of euros per U.S. dollar at the equilibrium exchange rate rises from XR_1 to XR_2.

What are the consequences of this increased capital inflow for the balance of payments? The total quantity of U.S. dollars supplied to the foreign exchange market still must equal the total quantity of U.S. dollars demanded. So the increased capital inflow to the United States—an increase in the balance of payments on the financial account—must be matched by a decline in the balance of payments on the current account. What causes the balance of payments on the current account to decline? The appreciation of the U.S. dollar. A rise in the number of euros per U.S. dollar leads Americans to buy more European goods and services and Europeans to buy fewer U.S. goods and services.

Table 5 shows a hypothetical example of how this might work. Europeans are buying more U.S. assets, increasing the balance of payments on the financial account from 0.5 to 1.0. This is offset by a reduction in European purchases of U.S. goods and services and a rise in U.S. purchases of European goods and services, both the result of the dollar's appreciation.

So any change in the U.S. balance of payments on financial account generates an equal and opposite reaction in the balance of payments on current account. Movements in the exchange rate ensure that changes in the financial account and in the current account offset each other.

TABLE 5 A Hypothetical Example of Effects of Increased Capital Inflows

	Current account	Financial account	Totals
European purchases of U.S. dollars (trillions of dollars)	To buy U.S. goods and services: 0.75 (down 0.25)	To buy U.S. assets: 1.5 (up 0.5)	2.25
U.S. sales of U.S. dollars (trillions of dollars)	To buy European goods and services: 1.75 (up 0.25)	To buy European assets: 0.5 (no change)	2.25
U.S. balance of payments	−1.0 (down 0.5)	+1.0 (up 0.5)	

Let's briefly run this process in reverse. Suppose there is a reduction in capital flows from Europe to the United States—again due to a change in the preferences of European investors. The demand for U.S. dollars in the foreign exchange market falls, and the dollar depreciates: the number of euros per U.S. dollar at the equilibrium exchange rate falls. This leads Americans to buy fewer European products and Europeans to buy more U.S. products. Ultimately, this generates an increase in the U.S. balance of payments on current account. So a fall in capital flows into the United States leads to a weaker dollar, which in turn generates an increase in U.S. net exports.

Inflation and Real Exchange Rates

In 1993 one U.S. dollar exchanged, on average, for 3.1 Mexican pesos. By 2023 the peso had fallen against the dollar by nearly 80%, with an average exchange rate of more than 17.5 pesos per dollar. Did Mexican products also become drastically cheaper relative to U.S. products over that 27-year period? Did the price of Mexican products expressed in terms of U.S. dollars also fall by nearly 80%? The answer to both questions is no, because Mexico had much higher inflation than the United States over that period. In fact, the relative price of U.S. and Mexican products fluctuated both up and down between 1993 and 2023, with no clear trend.

To take account of the effects of differences in inflation rates, economists calculate **real exchange rates,** exchange rates adjusted for international differences in aggregate price levels. Suppose that the exchange rate we are looking at is the number of Mexican pesos per U.S. dollar. Let P_{US} and P_{Mex} be indexes of the aggregate price levels in the United States and Mexico, respectively. Then the real exchange rate between the Mexican peso and the U.S. dollar is defined as:

(4) Real exchange rate = Mexican pesos per U.S. dollar $\times \dfrac{P_{US}}{P_{Mex}}$

real exchange rates the exchange rate adjusted for international differences in aggregate price levels.

To distinguish it from the real exchange rate, the exchange rate unadjusted for aggregate price levels is sometimes called the *nominal* exchange rate.

To understand the significance of the difference between the real and nominal exchange rates, let's consider the following example. Suppose that the Mexican peso depreciates against the U.S. dollar, with the exchange rate going from 10 pesos per U.S. dollar to 15 pesos per U.S. dollar, a 50% change. But suppose that at the same time the price of everything in Mexico, measured in pesos, increases by 50%, so that the Mexican price index rises from 100 to 150. At the same time, suppose that there is no change in U.S. prices, so that the U.S. price index remains at 100. Then the initial real exchange rate is:

$$\text{Pesos per dollar before depreciation} \times \frac{P_{US}}{P_{Mex}} = 10 \times \frac{100}{100} = 10$$

After the peso depreciates and the Mexican price level increases, the real exchange rate is:

$$\text{Pesos per dollar after depreciation} \times \frac{P_{US}}{P_{Mex}} = 15 \times \frac{100}{100} = 15$$

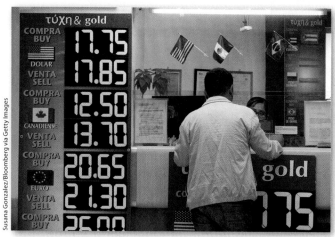

It's the real exchange rate, not the nominal exchange rate, that counts in decisions about buying and selling abroad.

In this example, the peso has depreciated substantially in terms of the U.S. dollar, but the *real* exchange rate between the peso and the U.S. dollar hasn't changed at all. And because the real peso–U.S. dollar exchange rate hasn't changed, the nominal depreciation of the peso against the U.S. dollar will have no effect either on the quantity of goods and services exported by Mexico to the United States or on the quantity of goods and services imported by Mexico from the United States.

To see why, consider again the example of a hotel room. Suppose that this room initially costs 1,000 pesos per night, which is $100 at an exchange rate of 10 pesos per dollar. After both Mexican prices and the number of pesos per dollar rise by 50%, the hotel room costs 1,500 pesos per night—but 1,500 pesos divided by 15 pesos per dollar is $100, so the Mexican hotel room still costs $100. As a

FIGURE 4 Real versus Nominal Exchange Rates, 1993–2023

Between November 1993 and February 2023, the price of a dollar in Mexican pesos increased dramatically. But because Mexico had higher inflation than the United States, the real exchange rate, which measures the relative price of Mexican goods and services, ended up roughly where it started.
Data from: Federal Reserve Bank of St. Louis.

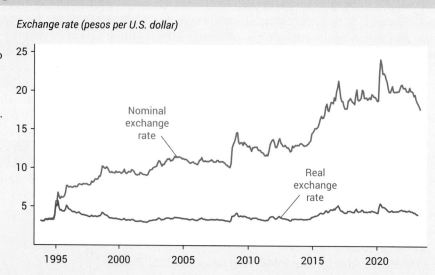

Susana Gonzalez/Bloomberg via Getty Images

result, a U.S. tourist considering a trip to Mexico will have no reason to change plans.

The same is true for all goods and services that enter into trade: *the current account responds only to changes in the real exchange rate, not the nominal exchange rate.* A country's products become cheaper to foreigners only when that country's currency depreciates in real terms, and those products become more expensive to foreigners only when the currency appreciates in real terms. As a consequence, economists who analyze movements in exports and imports of goods and services focus on the real exchange rate, not the nominal exchange rate.

Figure 4 illustrates just how important it can be to distinguish between nominal and real exchange rates. The line labeled "Nominal exchange rate" shows the number of pesos it took to buy a U.S. dollar from 1993 to 2023. As you can see, the peso depreciated massively over that period. But the line labeled "Real exchange rate" shows the real exchange rate: it was calculated using Equation 4, with price indexes for both Mexico and the United States set so that 1993 = 100. In real terms, the peso depreciated between 1994 and 1995, but not by nearly as much as the nominal depreciation. By 2013, the real peso–U.S. dollar exchange rate was just about back where it started, although it rose again over the next two years.

purchasing power parity (between two countries' currencies) the nominal exchange rate at which a given basket of goods and services would cost the same amount in each country.

Purchasing Power Parity

A useful tool for analyzing exchange rates, closely connected to the concept of the real exchange rate, is known as *purchasing power parity*. The **purchasing power parity** between two countries' currencies is the nominal exchange rate at which a given basket of goods and services would cost the same amount in each country. Suppose, for example, that a basket of goods and services that costs $100 in the United States costs 1,000 pesos in Mexico. Then the purchasing power parity is 10 pesos per U.S. dollar: at that exchange rate, 1,000 pesos = $100, so the market basket costs the same amount in both countries.

FOR INQUIRING MINDS   Burgernomics

The Economist magazine publishes an annual comparison of the cost in different countries of one particular consumption item that is found around the world—a McDonald's Big Mac. The magazine finds the price of a Big Mac in local currency, then computes two numbers: the price of a Big Mac in U.S. dollars using the prevailing exchange rate and the exchange rate at which the price of a Big Mac would equal the U.S. price.

If purchasing power parity held for Big Macs, the dollar price of a Big Mac would be the same everywhere. If purchasing power parity is a good theory for the long run, the exchange rate at which a Big Mac's price matches the U.S. price should offer some guidance about where the exchange rate will eventually end up.

Table 6 shows The *Economist* estimates for selected countries as of July 2022, ranked in increasing order of the dollar price of a Big Mac. The countries with the cheapest Big

Macs, and therefore by this measure with the most undervalued currencies, are Mexico, India, and China, all three developing countries. And topping the list, with a Big Mac some 20% more expensive than in the United States, is Switzerland—which has taken extraordinary action in an effort to depreciate its currency.

TABLE 6 Purchasing Power Parity and the Price of a Big Mac				
	Big Mac price		**Local currency per dollar**	
Country	**In local currency**	**In U.S. dollars**	**Implied PPP**	**Actual exchange rate**
India	Rupee 190	$2.39	37.09	9.95
Japan	¥ 390	2.83	75.73	137.87
Mexico	Peso 70	3.43	13.59	20.41
China	Yuan 24	3.56	4.66	6.75
Brazil	Real 19.90	4.25	4.45	5.39
Britain	£ 3.69	4.44	0.72	0.83
Euro area	€ 4.65	4.77	0.90	0.98
United States	$5.15	5.15	1.00	1.00
Switzerland	SFr 6.50	6.71	1.26	0.97

Data from: The Economist.

FIGURE 5 Purchasing Power Parity versus the Nominal Exchange Rate, 1990–2022

The purchasing power parity between the United States and Canada — the exchange rate at which a basket of goods and services would have cost the same amount in both countries — changed very little over the period shown, staying near C$1.20 per US$1. But the nominal exchange rate fluctuated widely.

Data from: OECD.

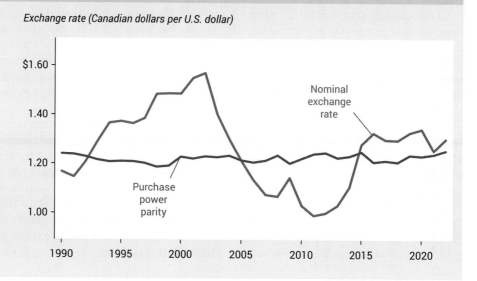

Calculations of purchasing power parities are usually made by estimating the cost of buying broad market baskets containing many goods and services — everything from cars and groceries to housing and internet service. But as the For Inquiring Minds, "Burgernomics," illustrates, nominal exchange rates almost always differ from purchasing power parities. Some of these differences are systematic: in general, aggregate price levels are lower in poor countries than in rich countries because services tend to be cheaper in poor countries. But even among countries at roughly the same level of economic development, nominal exchange rates vary quite a lot from purchasing power parity.

Figure 5 shows the nominal exchange rate between the Canadian dollar and the U.S. dollar, measured as the number of Canadian dollars per U.S. dollar, 1990 to 2022, together with an estimate of the purchasing power parity exchange rate between the United States and Canada over the same period. The purchasing power parity didn't change much over the whole period because the United States and Canada had about the same rate of inflation. For most of the 1990s through 2005, the nominal exchange rate was above the purchasing power parity, so a market basket was much cheaper in Canada than in the United States. But from 2005 to 2015, the Canadian dollar had appreciated, making a market basket more expensive in Canada.

Over the long run, however, purchasing power parities are pretty good at predicting actual changes in nominal exchange rates. In particular, nominal exchange rates between countries at similar levels of economic development tend to fluctuate around levels that lead to similar costs for a given market basket.

ECONOMICS >> *in Action*
Strong Dollar Woes

Does the exchange rate really matter for business? To answer this question, let's consider what happened to U.S. corporations from 2014 to 2015.

Over the course of these two years, the dollar strengthened sharply against many currencies, especially the euro and the Japanese yen. The dollar's rise largely reflected the weaknesses of other economies: troubles in Europe and Japan kept interest rates and investment demand low, and capital flowed to the United States, which was experiencing steady job growth and overall was doing a much better job recovering from the Great Recession.

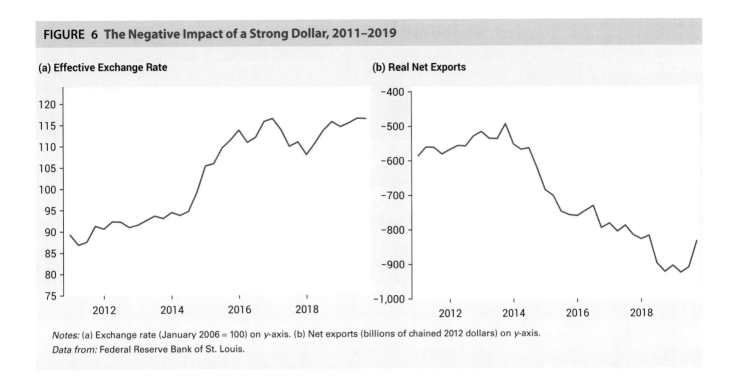

FIGURE 6 The Negative Impact of a Strong Dollar, 2011–2019

(a) Effective Exchange Rate

(b) Real Net Exports

Notes: (a) Exchange rate (January 2006 = 100) on *y*-axis. (b) Net exports (billions of chained 2012 dollars) on *y*-axis.
Data from: Federal Reserve Bank of St. Louis.

While the strong dollar reflected (relatively) good news for the U.S. economy as a whole, it was bad news for U.S. companies that sell a lot to overseas markets—companies like Procter and Gamble, which sells toothpaste and other toiletries around the world, or, Kimberly-Clark, whose Huggies diapers protect many foreign babies' bottoms. Such companies reported large hits to their profits, and began either losing ground to foreign competitors or shifting some of their own production abroad.

Figure 6 illustrates the overall picture. It compares the U.S. *effective exchange rate*, a measure of the average value of the dollar against other currencies, with *real net exports*, exports minus imports, measured in 2012 dollars. From early 2014 to early 2016 the dollar rose about 15% on average, then stayed at this higher level during the pandemic, while real net exports moved considerably deeper into deficit.

In other words, the exchange rate does matter a lot for businesses that compete with foreign rivals. Earlier we noted that while it's common to describe an appreciating currency as "getting stronger," that doesn't mean it's a good thing. And the stronger dollar of 2014 to 2015 definitely wasn't a good thing for some U.S. companies.

>> Check Your Understanding 18-2

Solutions appear at back of book.

1. Mexico discovers huge reserves of oil and starts exporting oil to the United States. Describe how this would affect the following.
   a. The nominal peso–U.S. dollar exchange rate
   b. Mexican exports to the United States of other goods and services
   c. Mexican imports from the United States of goods and services

2. A basket of goods and services that costs $100 in the United States costs 800 pesos in Mexico, and the current nominal exchange rate is 10 pesos per U.S. dollar. Over the next five years, the cost of that market basket rises to $120 in the United States and to 1,200 pesos in Mexico, although the nominal exchange rate remains at 10 pesos per U.S. dollar. Calculate the following.
   a. The real exchange rate now and five years from now, if today's price index in both countries is 100
   b. Purchasing power parity today and five years from now

>> Quick Review

• Currencies are traded in the **foreign exchange market,** which determines **exchange rates.**

• Exchange rates can be measured in two ways. To avoid confusion, economists say that a currency **appreciates** or **depreciates.** The **equilibrium exchange rate** matches the supply and demand for currencies on the foreign exchange market.

• To take account of differences in national price levels, economists calculate **real exchange rates.** The current account responds only to changes in the real exchange rate, not the nominal exchange rate.

• **Purchasing power parity** is the nominal exchange rate that equalizes the price of a market basket in two countries. While the nominal exchange rate almost always differs from purchasing power parity, purchasing power parity is a good predictor of actual changes in the nominal exchange rate.

exchange rate regime a rule governing policy toward the exchange rate.

fixed exchange rate an exchange rate regime in which the government keeps the exchange rate against some other currency at or near a particular target.

floating exchange rate an exchange rate regime in which the government lets market forces determine the exchange rate.

‖ Exchange Rate Policy

The nominal exchange rate, like other prices, is determined by supply and demand. Unlike the price of wheat or oil, however, the exchange rate is the price of a country's money (in terms of another country's money). Money isn't a good or service produced by the private sector; it's an asset whose quantity is determined by government policy. As a result, governments have much more power to influence nominal exchange rates than they have to influence ordinary prices.

The nominal exchange rate is a very important price for many countries because it determines the price of imports and the price of exports. In economies where exports and imports are large percentages of GDP, movements in the exchange rate can have major effects on aggregate output and the aggregate price level. What do governments do with their power to influence this important price?

The answer is, it depends. At different times and in different places, governments have adopted a variety of *exchange rate regimes*. Let's talk about these regimes, how they are enforced, and how governments choose a regime. (From now on, we'll adopt the convention that we mean the nominal exchange rate when we refer to the exchange rate.)

Exchange Rate Regimes

An **exchange rate regime** is a rule governing policy toward the exchange rate. There are two main kinds of exchange rate regimes. A country has a **fixed exchange rate** when the government keeps the exchange rate against some other currency at or near a particular target. For example, Hong Kong has an official policy of setting an exchange rate of HK$7.80 per US$1. In contrast, a country has a **floating exchange rate** when the government lets market forces determine the exchange rate. This is the policy followed by Britain, Canada, and the United States.

Fixed exchange rates and floating exchange rates aren't the only possibilities. At various times, countries have adopted compromise policies that lie somewhere between fixed and floating exchange rates. These include exchange rates that are fixed at any given time but are adjusted frequently, exchange rates that aren't fixed but are managed by the government to avoid wide swings, and exchange rates that float within a *target zone* but are prevented from leaving that zone. In this chapter, however, we'll focus on the two main exchange rate regimes.

The immediate puzzle posed by a fixed exchange rate is how a government can fix the exchange rate when the exchange rate is determined by supply and demand.

How Can an Exchange Rate Be Held Fixed?

To understand how it is possible for a country to fix its exchange rate, let's consider a hypothetical country, Genovia, which for some reason has decided to fix the value of its currency, the geno, at US$1.50.

The obvious problem is that $1.50 may not be the equilibrium exchange rate in the foreign exchange market: the equilibrium rate may be either higher or lower than the target exchange rate. Figure 7 shows the foreign exchange market for genos, with the quantities of genos supplied and demanded on the horizontal axis and the exchange rate of the geno, measured in U.S. dollars per geno, on the vertical axis. Panel (a) shows the case in which the equilibrium value of the geno is *below* the target exchange rate. Panel (b) shows the case in which the equilibrium value of the geno is *above* the target exchange rate.

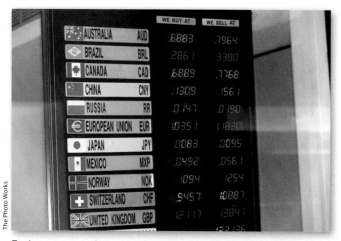

Exchange rates play a very important role in the global economy.

The Photo Works

Consider first the case in which the equilibrium value of the geno is below the target exchange rate. As panel (a) shows, at the target exchange rate of $1.50 per geno, there is a surplus of genos in the foreign exchange market, which would normally push the value of the geno down. How can the Genovian government support the value of the geno to keep the rate where it wants? There are three possible answers, all of which have been used by governments at some point.

One way the Genovian government can support the geno is to soak up the surplus of genos by buying its own currency in the foreign exchange market. A government purchase or sale of currency in the foreign exchange market is called an **exchange market intervention.** To buy genos in the foreign exchange market, of course, the Genovian government must have U.S. dollars to exchange for genos. In fact, most countries maintain **foreign exchange reserves,** stocks of foreign currency (usually U.S. dollars or euros) that they can use to buy their own currency to support its price.

We mentioned earlier in the chapter that an important part of international capital flows is the result of purchases and sales of foreign assets by governments and central banks. Now we can see why governments sell foreign assets: they are supporting their currency through exchange market intervention. As we'll see in a moment, governments that keep the value of their currency *down* through exchange market intervention must *buy* foreign assets. First, however, let's talk about the other ways governments fix exchange rates.

A second way for the Genovian government to support the geno is to try to shift the supply and demand curves for the geno in the foreign exchange market. Governments usually do this by changing monetary policy. For example, to support the geno the Genovian central bank can raise the Genovian interest rate. This will increase capital flows into Genovia, increasing the demand for genos, at the same time that it reduces capital flows out of Genovia, reducing the supply of

exchange market intervention
government purchases or sales of currency in the foreign exchange market.

foreign exchange reserves
stocks of foreign currency that governments can use to buy their own currency on the foreign exchange market.

FIGURE 7 Exchange Market Intervention

In both panels, the imaginary country of Genovia is trying to keep the exchange rate of the geno fixed at US$1.50 per geno. In panel (a), the equilibrium exchange rate is below $1.50, leading to a surplus of genos on the foreign exchange market. To keep the geno from falling below $1.50, the Genovian government can buy genos and sell U.S. dollars. In panel (b), the equilibrium exchange rate is above $1.50, leading to a shortage of genos on the foreign exchange market. To keep the geno from rising above $1.50, the Genovian government can sell genos and buy U.S. dollars.

foreign exchange controls
licensing systems that limit the right of individuals to buy foreign currency.

genos. So, other things equal, an increase in a country's interest rate will increase the value of its currency.

Third, the Genovian government can support the geno by reducing the supply of genos to the foreign exchange market. It can do this by requiring domestic residents who want to buy foreign currency to get a license and giving these licenses only to people engaging in approved transactions (such as the purchase of imported goods the Genovian government thinks are essential). Licensing systems that limit the right of individuals to buy foreign currency are called **foreign exchange controls.** Other things equal, foreign exchange controls increase the value of a country's currency.

So far we've been discussing a situation in which the government is trying to prevent a depreciation of the geno. Suppose, instead, that the situation is as shown in panel (b) of Figure 7, where the equilibrium value of the geno is *above* the target exchange rate of $1.50 per geno and there is a shortage of genos. To maintain the target exchange rate, the Genovian government can apply the same three basic options in the reverse direction. It can intervene in the foreign exchange market, in this case *selling* genos and acquiring U.S. dollars, which it can add to its foreign exchange reserves. It can *reduce* interest rates to increase the supply of genos and reduce the demand. Or it can impose foreign exchange controls that limit the ability of foreigners to buy genos. All of these actions, other things equal, will reduce the value of the geno.

As we said, all three techniques have been used to manage fixed exchange rates. But we haven't said whether fixing the exchange rate is a good idea. In fact, the choice of exchange rate regime poses a dilemma for policy makers, because fixed and floating exchange rates each have both advantages and disadvantages.

The Exchange Rate Regime Dilemma

Few questions in macroeconomics produce as many arguments as that of whether a country should adopt a fixed or a floating exchange rate. And there are so many arguments because both sides have a case.

To understand the case for a fixed exchange rate, consider for a moment how easy it is to conduct business across state lines in the United States. There are a number of things that make interstate commerce trouble-free, but one of them is the absence of any uncertainty about the value of money: a dollar is a dollar, in both New York City and Los Angeles.

By contrast, a dollar isn't a dollar in transactions between New York City and Toronto. The exchange rate between the Canadian dollar and the U.S. dollar fluctuates, sometimes widely. If a U.S. firm promises to pay a Canadian firm a given number of U.S. dollars a year from now, the value of that promise in Canadian currency can vary by 10% or more. This uncertainty has the effect of deterring trade between the two countries. So, one benefit of a fixed exchange rate is certainty about the future value of a currency.

There is also, in some cases, an additional benefit to adopting a fixed exchange rate: by committing itself to a fixed rate, a country is also committing itself not to engage in inflationary policies. For example, in 1991 Argentina, which has a long history of irresponsible policies leading to severe inflation, adopted a fixed exchange rate of US$1 per Argentine peso in an attempt to commit itself to noninflationary policies in the future. (Argentina's fixed exchange rate regime collapsed disastrously in late 2001. But that's another story.)

The point is that there is some economic value in having a stable exchange rate. Indeed, as the accompanying For Inquiring Minds explains, the presumed benefits of stable exchange rates motivated the international system of fixed exchange rates created after World War II. It was also a major reason for the creation of the euro.

FOR INQUIRING MINDS **From Bretton Woods to the Euro**

In 1944, while World War II was still raging, representatives of Allied nations met in Bretton Woods, New Hampshire, to establish a postwar international monetary system of fixed exchange rates among major currencies. The system was highly successful at first, but it broke down in 1971. After a confusing interval during which policy makers tried unsuccessfully to establish a new fixed exchange rate system, by 1973 most economically advanced countries had moved to floating exchange rates.

In Europe, however, many policy makers were unhappy with floating exchange rates, which they believed created too much uncertainty for business. From the late 1970s onward they tried several times to create a system of more or less fixed exchange rates in Europe, culminating in an arrangement known as the Exchange Rate Mechanism. (The Exchange Rate Mechanism was, strictly speaking, a target zone system — European exchange rates were free to move within a narrow band, but not outside it.) And in 1991 they agreed to move to the ultimate in fixed exchange rates: a common European currency, the euro. To the surprise of many analysts, they pulled it off: today most of Europe has abandoned national currencies for the euro.

Figure 8 illustrates the history of European exchange rate arrangements. It shows the exchange rate between the French franc and the German mark, measured as francs per mark, from 1971 until their replacement by the euro. The exchange rate fluctuated widely at first. The plateaus you can see in the data — eras when the exchange rate fluctuated only modestly — are periods when attempts to restore fixed exchange rates were

in process. The Exchange Rate Mechanism, after a couple of false starts, became effective in 1987, stabilizing the exchange rate at about 3.4 francs per mark. (The wobbles in the early 1990s reflect two *currency crises* — episodes in which widespread expectations of imminent devaluations led to large but temporary capital flows.)

In 1999, the exchange rate was *locked* — no further fluctuations were allowed as the countries prepared to switch from francs and

marks to the euro. At the end of 2001, the franc and the mark ceased to exist.

The transition to the euro has not been without costs. Countries that adopted the euro sacrificed some important policy tools: they could no longer tailor monetary policy to their specific economic circumstances, and they could no longer lower their costs relative to other European nations simply by letting their currencies depreciate.

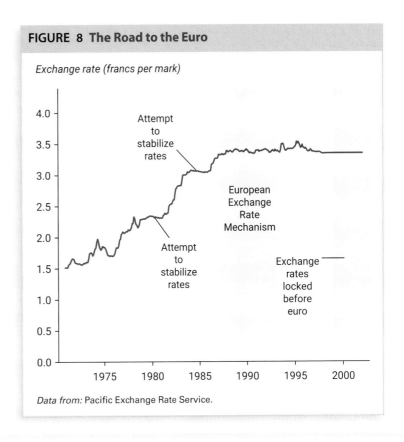

FIGURE 8 The Road to the Euro

Data from: Pacific Exchange Rate Service.

However, there are also costs to fixing the exchange rate. To stabilize an exchange rate through intervention, a country must keep large quantities of foreign currency on hand — usually a low-return investment. Furthermore, even large reserves can be quickly exhausted when there are large capital flows out of a country. If a country chooses to stabilize an exchange rate by adjusting monetary policy rather than through intervention, it must divert monetary policy from other goals, notably stabilizing the economy and managing the inflation rate. Finally, foreign exchange controls, like import quotas and tariffs, distort incentives for importing and exporting goods and services. They can also create substantial costs in terms of red tape and corruption.

So there's a dilemma. Should a country let its currency float, which leaves monetary policy available for macroeconomic stabilization but creates uncertainty for business? Or should it fix the exchange rate, which eliminates the uncertainty but means giving up monetary policy, adopting exchange controls, or both?

Different countries reach different conclusions at different times. Most European countries, except for Britain, have long believed that exchange rates among major European economies, which do most of their international trade with each other, should be fixed. But Canada seems happy with a floating exchange rate with the United States, even though the United States accounts for most of Canada's trade.

Fortunately we don't have to resolve this dilemma. For the rest of the chapter, we'll take exchange rate regimes as given and ask how they affect macroeconomic policy.

ECONOMICS >> *in Action*
Turkey's Lira Problem

We opened this chapter by describing how Turkey engaged in large-scale foreign exchange market intervention to prop up the value of its currency after the 2023 earthquake. Why did Turkish authorities feel the need to do this?

Turkey doesn't have a fixed exchange rate. In fact, the Turkish lira has been steadily declining against both the dollar and the euro for many years, largely because Turkey has consistently had higher inflation than the United States or the euro area, so the lira has had to depreciate just to keep the real exchange rate constant. Figure 9 shows the rate of change in Turkey's exchange rate, measured in lira per dollar, and Turkey's consumer price index. As you can see in the figure, however, the pace of lira depreciation really picked up in 2021, with Turkish inflation soaring soon afterward.

Specifically, the lira plunged in the fall of 2021. The immediate reason was that investors lost confidence in the country's economic management: faced with rising inflation, Recep Erdogan, the country's president, decided—overruling most economists' advice—that he should cut interest rates, not increase them. This loss of confidence led to capital outflows and a plunging lira. The fall in the lira then helped cause inflation to accelerate even more.

All of this happened *before* the 2023 earthquake. But with inflation already running at around 80%, it seems likely that Turkish policy makers worried that a plunge in the lira following the quake might send inflation even higher, and possibly unleash a vicious cycle of inflation and depreciation. So one of their first policy actions after the earthquake was large-scale intervention in the foreign exchange market to prop up the lira's value.

At the time of writing, it wasn't clear how this story would end. With a presidential election looming, the Turkish government was continuing to draw on its foreign exchange reserves to support the lira. Many news reports speculated that the lira would be allowed to fall after the election, no matter who won. But in any case the story shows how important exchange rates can be to macroeconomic policy, especially in smaller economies.

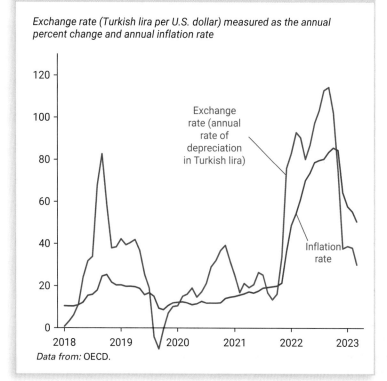

FIGURE 9 Inflation and Depreciation in Turkey from 2018 through 2023

Exchange rate (Turkish lira per U.S. dollar) measured as the annual percent change and annual inflation rate

Exchange rate (annual rate of depreciation in Turkish lira)

Inflation rate

Data from: OECD.

1. Draw a diagram, similar to Figure 7, representing the foreign exchange situation of China when it kept the exchange rate fixed. Express the exchange rate as U.S. dollars per yuan. Then show with a diagram how each of the following policy changes will eliminate the disequilibrium in the market.
    a. China no longer fixing its exchange rate, allowing it to float freely
    b. Placing restrictions on foreigners who want to invest in China
    c. Removing restrictions on Chinese who want to invest abroad
    d. Imposing taxes on Chinese exports, such as shipments of clothing, that are causing a political backlash in the importing countries

Exchange Rates and Macroeconomic Policy

When the euro was created in 1999, there were celebrations across the nations of Europe where it was seen as a step toward a brighter future. But there were a few notable exceptions. You see, some countries chose not to adopt the new currency. The most important of these was Britain, but other European countries, such as Sweden, also decided that the euro was not for them.

Why did Britain say no? Part of the answer was national pride: if Britain gave up the pound, it would also have to give up currency that bears the portrait of the monarch. But there were also serious economic concerns about giving up the pound in favor of the euro. British economists who favored adoption of the euro argued that if Britain used the same currency as its neighbors, the country's international trade would expand and its economy would become more productive. But other economists pointed out that adopting the euro would take away Britain's ability to have an independent monetary policy and might lead to macroeconomic problems.

As this discussion suggests, the fact that modern economies are open to international trade and capital flows adds a new level of complication to our analysis of macroeconomic policy. Let's look at three policy issues raised by international aspects of macroeconomics:

1. Devaluation and revaluation of fixed exchange rates
2. Monetary policy under floating exchange rates
3. International business cycles

Devaluation and Revaluation of Fixed Exchange Rates

Historically, fixed exchange rates haven't been permanent commitments. Sometimes countries with a fixed exchange rate switch to a floating rate. In other cases, they retain a fixed rate but change the target exchange rate. Such adjustments in the target were common during the Bretton Woods era described in the preceding For Inquiring Minds. For example, in 1967 Britain changed the exchange rate of the pound against the U.S. dollar from US$2.80 per £1 to US$2.40 per £1. A modern example is Argentina, which maintained a fixed exchange rate against the dollar from 1991 to 2001 but switched to a floating exchange rate at the end of 2001.

A reduction in the value of a currency that is set under a fixed exchange rate regime is called a **devaluation.** As we've already learned, a *depreciation* is a downward move in a currency. A devaluation is a depreciation that is due to a revision in a fixed exchange rate target. An increase in the value of a currency that is set under a fixed exchange rate regime is called a **revaluation.**

A devaluation, like any depreciation, makes domestic goods cheaper in terms of foreign currency, which leads to higher exports. At the same time, it makes foreign goods more expensive in terms of domestic currency, which reduces imports. The effect is to

devaluation a reduction in the value of a currency that is set under a fixed exchange rate regime.

revaluation an increase in the value of a currency that is set under a fixed exchange rate regime.

increase the balance of payments on current account. Similarly, a revaluation makes domestic goods more expensive in terms of foreign currency, which reduces exports, and makes foreign goods cheaper in domestic currency, which increases imports. So a revaluation reduces the balance of payments on current account.

Devaluations and revaluations serve two purposes under fixed exchange rates. First, they can be used to eliminate shortages or surpluses in the foreign exchange market. For example, in 2010 some economists and politicians were urging China to revalue the yuan because they believed that China's exchange rate policy unfairly aided Chinese exports.

Second, devaluation and revaluation can be used as tools of macroeconomic policy. A devaluation, by increasing exports and reducing imports, increases aggregate demand. So a devaluation can be used to reduce or eliminate a recessionary gap. A revaluation has the opposite effect, reducing aggregate demand. So a revaluation can be used to reduce or eliminate an inflationary gap.

Monetary Policy Under Floating Exchange Rates

Under a floating exchange rate regime, a country's central bank retains its ability to pursue independent monetary policy: it can increase aggregate demand by cutting the interest rate or decrease aggregate demand by raising the interest rate. But the exchange rate adds another dimension to the effects of monetary policy. To see why, let's return to the hypothetical country of Genovia and ask what happens if the central bank cuts the interest rate.

Just as in an economy without international linkages, a lower interest rate leads to higher investment spending and higher consumer spending. But the decline in the interest rate also affects the foreign exchange market. Foreigners have less incentive to move funds into Genovia because they will receive a lower interest rate on their loans. As a result, they have less need to exchange U.S. dollars for genos, so the demand for genos falls. At the same time, Genovians have *more* incentive to move funds abroad because the interest rate on loans at home has fallen, making investments outside the country more attractive. As a result, they need to exchange more genos for U.S. dollars, so the supply of genos rises.

Figure 10 shows the effect of an interest rate reduction on the foreign exchange market. The demand curve for genos shifts leftward, from D_1 to D_2, and the supply curve shifts rightward, from S_1 to S_2. The equilibrium exchange rate, as measured

FIGURE 10 Monetary Policy and the Exchange Rate

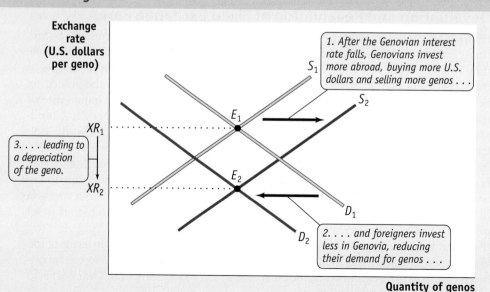

Here we show what happens in the foreign exchange market if Genovia cuts its interest rate. Residents of Genovia have a reduced incentive to keep their funds at home, so they invest more abroad. As a result, the supply of genos shifts rightward, from S_1 to S_2. Meanwhile, foreigners have less incentive to put funds into Genovia, so the demand for genos shifts leftward, from D_1 to D_2. The geno depreciates: the equilibrium exchange rate falls from XR_1 to XR_2.

Exchange rate (U.S. dollars per geno)

1. After the Genovian interest rate falls, Genovians invest more abroad, buying more U.S. dollars and selling more genos . . .

3. . . . leading to a depreciation of the geno.

2. . . . and foreigners invest less in Genovia, reducing their demand for genos . . .

Quantity of genos

in U.S. dollars per geno, falls from XR_1 to XR_2. That is, a reduction in the Genovian interest rate causes the geno to *depreciate*.

The depreciation of the geno, in turn, affects aggregate demand. We've already seen that a devaluation—a depreciation that is the result of a change in a fixed exchange rate—increases exports and reduces imports, thereby increasing aggregate demand. A depreciation that results from an interest rate cut has the same effect: it increases exports and reduces imports, increasing aggregate demand.

In other words, monetary policy under floating rates has effects beyond those we've described before. In the absence of international trade and capital flows, a reduction in the interest rate leads to a rise in aggregate demand because it leads to more investment spending and consumer spending. In an economy with a floating exchange rate, the interest rate reduction leads to increased investment spending and consumer spending, but it also increases aggregate demand in another way: it leads to a currency depreciation, which increases exports and reduces imports, and further increases aggregate demand.

International Business Cycles

Up to this point, we have discussed macroeconomics as if all demand shocks originate from the domestic economy. In reality, however, economies sometimes face shocks coming from abroad. For example, recessions in the United States have historically led to recessions in Mexico.

The key point is that changes in aggregate demand affect the demand for goods and services produced abroad as well as at home: other things equal, a recession leads to a fall in imports and an expansion leads to a rise in imports. And one country's imports are another country's exports. This link between aggregate demand in different national economies is one reason business cycles in different countries sometimes—but not always—seem to be synchronized. Prime examples are the Great Depression of the 1930s, the Great Recession of 2008, and the 2020 slump brought on by the coronavirus pandemic, all of which affected countries around the world.

The extent of this link depends, however, on the exchange rate regime. To see why, think about what happens if a recession abroad reduces the demand for Genovia's exports. A reduction in foreign demand for Genovian goods and services is also a reduction in demand for genos in the foreign exchange market. If Genovia has a fixed exchange rate, it responds to this decline with exchange market intervention. But if Genovia has a floating exchange rate, the geno depreciates. Because Genovian goods and services become cheaper to foreigners when the demand for exports falls, the quantity of goods and services exported doesn't fall by as much as it would under a fixed rate. At the same time, the fall in the geno makes imports more expensive to Genovians, leading to a fall in imports. Both effects limit the decline in Genovia's aggregate demand compared to what it would have been under a fixed exchange rate.

One of the virtues of a floating exchange rate, according to advocates of such exchange rates, is that they help insulate countries from recessions originating abroad. This theory looked pretty good in the early 2000s: Britain, with a floating exchange rate, managed to stay out of a recession that affected the rest of Europe, and Canada, which also has a floating rate, suffered a less severe recession than the United States.

In the Great Recession, however, a financial crisis that began in the United States led to a recession in virtually every country. In this case, it appears that "financial contagion"—the spread of market disruption via international linkages among financial markets—was much stronger than any insulation from overseas disturbances provided by floating exchange rates.

Finally, the coronavirus slump was global in large part because of literal contagion: nations around the world put much of their economies on temporary lockdown in an attempt to limit the spread of COVID-19.

ECONOMICS >> *in Action*
The Little Currency That Could

Iceland, with a population around 334,000, is a tiny country. And in 2008, it had a very big economic problem. Between 2003 and 2007 the country's main banks expanded very aggressively, mainly with money borrowed from banks in other countries, and the banking boom led in turn to a booming local economy. But then the boom went bust, as did the banks, and Iceland needed to go back to more mundane ways of making a living, like fishing and tourism. To do this it needed to reduce costs, mainly by cutting wages. It wasn't the only country in this position. Other nations that had borrowed a lot of money, like Greece, also needed to make big adjustments.

But there was one big difference between Iceland and Greece (aside from the weather): Greece no longer had its own currency, because it had adopted the euro, whereas Iceland, tiny though it was, still had its own currency, the krona (plural kronur)—and Icelandic wages are set in kronur, not euros or dollars.

This made the process of cutting wages very different in Iceland than it was in euro-using countries. In Greece, employers actually had to tell workers that they would be paid less—something companies are reluctant to do, because at best it creates bad feelings and at worst it leads to strikes. Iceland, however, could gain competitiveness without wage cuts, simply by letting the krona fall.

Figure 11 shows how the different options played out. The red line shows average wages in the euro area as a whole, with 2007 = 100, while the purple line shows Greek wages over the same period. As you can see, Greece did manage to cut wages gradually over time while wages in other European nations rose, so the Greek economy gradually became more competitive. It was, however, a slow and extremely painful process.

The other two lines show Iceland's story. The blue line shows wages in Iceland's own currency, kronur. These continued to rise; there were no nominal wage cuts. The green line shows Icelandic wages in euros, which fell dramatically thanks to the depreciation of the krona.

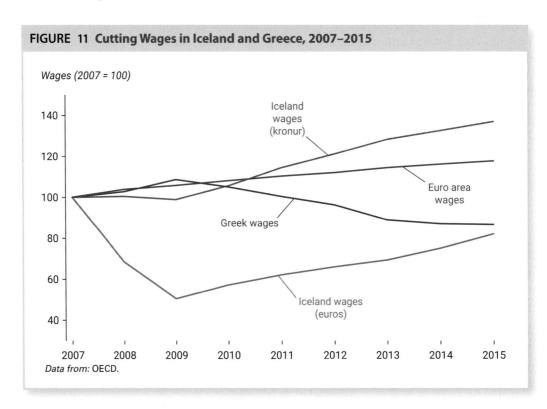

FIGURE 11 Cutting Wages in Iceland and Greece, 2007–2015

Data from: OECD.

It would be wrong to say that this process was painless—Icelandic workers saw the prices of imported goods rise, reducing their purchasing power. But it wasn't nearly as painful as Greece's adjustment. In Greece, unemployment rose year after year, peaking at 28% in late 2013 before it began inching down. In Iceland, by contrast, the jobs crisis only lasted about two years, and by late 2014 the unemployment rate was under 5%.

Overall, Iceland's experience was an object lesson in the advantages of having your own currency—even when your country is no bigger than a medium-sized U.S. town.

>> Check Your Understanding 18-4

Solutions appear at back of book.

1. Look at the data in Figure 8. Where do you see devaluations and revaluations of the franc against the mark?

2. In the late 1980s Canadian economists argued that the high interest rate policies of the Bank of Canada weren't just causing high unemployment—they were also making it hard for Canadian manufacturers to compete with the United States. Explain this complaint, using our analysis of how monetary policy works under floating exchange rates.

>> Quick Review

• Countries can change fixed exchange rates. A **devaluation,** a reduction in the value of the currency, can help reduce surpluses in the foreign exchange market and can increase aggregate demand. A **revaluation,** an increase in the value of the currency, can help reduce shortages in the foreign exchange market and can reduce aggregate demand.

• In an open economy with a floating exchange rate, interest rates also affect the exchange rate, and so monetary policy affects aggregate demand through the effects of the exchange rate on imports and exports.

• Because one country's imports are another country's exports, business cycles are sometimes synchronized across countries. However, floating exchange rates may reduce this link.

German Cars, Made in Spain

ANDER GILLENEA/Getty Images

The town of Pamplona, Spain, is famous for the "running of the bulls," a summer event in which thrill-seekers attempt to outrun a group of bulls through a cordoned-off section of the town's ancient center. But that is an annual event, and while it does draw in tourists, the town's residents have to make a living all year long. And what many of them actually live off, directly or indirectly, is something you probably don't associate with Spain: automotive manufacturing.

Pamplona is home to a large assembly plant owned by Volkswagen, one of many car producers operating in Spain. Volkswagen, like other automotive firms—especially but not only German corporations—began investing large sums expanding its Spanish operations in the early 2010s. You probably don't think of Spain as an auto-industry powerhouse, since there are no Spanish-owned car companies. But multinational auto companies have flocked to Spain, making it Europe's second-largest producer of cars, behind only Germany.

The Spanish auto industry mainly produces cars for consumers in other countries; 80% of its output is exported. So why are companies like Volkswagen moving production to Spain? In a word, costs.

Spain, like Germany, uses the euro. When it faced a severe recession that drove the unemployment rate to 26%, it couldn't devalue its currency the way Iceland did. However, as we noted in the Economics in Action in Chapter 16, Spanish inflation dropped drastically in the face of high unemployment, while prices in other countries, including Germany, continued to rise. Spanish wages also lagged. From 2010 until 2022, the hourly cost of labor in Spain grew only half as fast as it did in Germany.

Spain's relative wage restraint seems to have mattered a lot for its auto industry. And the booming auto industry has been one of the biggest forces behind Spain's economic recovery.

QUESTIONS FOR THOUGHT

1. How does the story of Spain's auto industry relate to our discussion of the determinants of the current account on p. 542?

2. Spain's adjustment since the early 2010s is sometimes described as "internal devaluation." What do you think that means?

3. Spain's rising auto exports are entirely due to the investments of non-Spanish companies. How might this affect changes in Spain's current account?

SUMMARY

1. A country's **balance of payments accounts** summarize its transactions with the rest of the world. The **balance of payments on current account,** or **current account,** includes the **balance of payments on goods and services** together with balances on factor income and transfers. The **merchandise trade balance,** or **trade balance,** is a frequently cited component of the balance of payments on goods and services. The **balance of payments on financial account,** or **financial account,** measures capital flows. By definition, the balance of payments on current account plus the balance of payments on financial account is zero.

2. The loanable funds model shows that the direction of net capital flows—the excess of inflows over outflows, or vice versa—across countries is determined by differences in interest rates that arise from differences in investment opportunities and savings behavior. Capital flows move to equalize interest rates across countries. In the real world, countries experience two-way capital flows—gross flows of capital in and out—because factors other than interest rate differences affect investors' decisions. Those factors are risk considerations, business strategy, and banking industry expertise.

3. Currencies are traded in the **foreign exchange market;** the prices at which they are traded are **exchange rates.** When a currency rises against another currency, it **appreciates;** when it falls, it **depreciates.** The **equilibrium exchange rate** matches the quantity of that currency supplied to the foreign exchange market to the quantity demanded.

4. To correct for international differences in inflation rates, economists calculate **real exchange rates,** which multiply the exchange rate between two countries' currencies by the ratio of the countries' price levels. The current account responds only to changes in the real exchange rate, not the nominal exchange rate. **Purchasing power parity** is the exchange rate that makes the cost of a basket of goods and services equal in two countries. While purchasing power parity and the nominal exchange rate almost always differ,

purchasing power parity is a good predictor of actual changes in the nominal exchange rate.

5. Countries adopt different **exchange rate regimes,** rules governing exchange rate policy. The main types are **fixed exchange rates,** where the government takes action to keep the exchange rate at a target level, and **floating exchange rates,** where the exchange rate is free to fluctuate. Countries can fix exchange rates using **exchange market intervention,** which requires them to hold **foreign exchange reserves** that they use to buy any surplus of their currency. Alternatively, they can change domestic policies, especially monetary policy, to shift the demand and supply curves in the foreign exchange market. Finally, they can use **foreign exchange controls.**

6. Exchange rate policy poses a dilemma: there are economic payoffs to stable exchange rates, but the policies used to fix the exchange rate have costs. Exchange market intervention requires large reserves, and exchange controls distort incentives. If monetary policy is used to help fix the exchange rate, it isn't available to use for domestic policy.

7. Fixed exchange rates aren't always permanent commitments: countries with a fixed exchange rate sometimes engage in **devaluations,** reductions in the target value of the currency, or **revaluations,** increases in the target value of the currency. In addition to helping eliminate a surplus of domestic currency on the foreign exchange market, a devaluation increases aggregate demand. Similarly, a revaluation reduces shortages of domestic currency and reduces aggregate demand.

8. Under floating exchange rates, expansionary monetary policy works in part through the exchange rate: cutting domestic interest rates leads to a depreciation, and through that to higher exports and lower imports, which increases aggregate demand. Contractionary monetary policy has the reverse effect.

9. The fact that one country's imports are another country's exports creates a link between the business cycle in different countries. Floating exchange rates, however, may reduce the strength of that link.

KEY TERMS

Balance of payments accounts, p. 534
Balance of payments on current account (current account), p. 536
Balance of payments on goods and services, p. 536
Merchandise trade balance (trade balance), p. 536
Balance of payments on financial account (financial account), p. 536

Foreign exchange market, p. 542
Exchange rates, p. 542
Appreciates, p. 542
Depreciates, p. 542
Equilibrium exchange rate, p. 544
Real exchange rate, p. 545
Purchasing power parity, p. 547
Exchange rate regime, p. 550

Fixed exchange rate, p. 550
Floating exchange rate, p. 550
Exchange market intervention, p. 551
Foreign exchange reserves, p. 551
Foreign exchange controls, p. 552
Devaluation, p. 555
Revaluation, p. 555

PRACTICE QUESTIONS

1. You recently read a headline that states: "The U.S. loses $500 billion a year to trade with China." This amount would be included as part of the U.S. current account deficit. How is this headline misleading? How do these transactions affect the loanable funds framework?

2. During his presidency, Donald Trump attempted to alleviate the U.S. trade deficit by passing a series of tariffs on Chinese exports. Prior to President Trump taking office, the U.S. had an average tariff rate of 3.1% on Chinese exports but by February of 2020 the average tariff rate had increased to 19.3%. During the same time period, the U.S. dollar appreciated from 6.27 Chinese yuan to 7.10 yuan per U.S. dollar. Using the foreign exchange market, explain how the implementation of the tariffs would change the yuan/dollar exchange rate. Is this consistent with what we observed in the data?

3. With oil priced in U.S. dollars, most Middle Eastern and other oil-producing countries have a fixed exchange rate peg to the U.S. dollar. What are the pros and cons of these countries pegging their currency to the U.S. dollar?

PROBLEMS

1. How would the following transactions be categorized in the U.S. balance of payments accounts? Would they be entered in the current account (as a payment to or from a foreigner) or the financial account (as a sale of assets to or purchase of assets from a foreigner)? How will the balance of payments on the current and financial accounts change?

   a. A French importer buys a case of California wine for $500.

   b. An American who works for a French company deposits her paycheck, drawn on a Paris bank, into her San Francisco bank.

   c. An American buys a bond from a Japanese company for $10,000.

   d. An American charity sends $100,000 to Africa to help local residents buy food after a harvest shortfall.

2. The accompanying diagram shows foreign-owned assets in the United States and U.S.-owned assets abroad, both as a percentage of foreign GDP. As you can see from the diagram, both increased around fivefold from 1980 to 2022.

Percentage of world GDP

Notes: Share of U.S.-owned assets abroad and foreign-owned assets in the United States.

Data from: Bureau of Economic Analysis.

   a. As U.S.-owned assets abroad increased as a percentage of foreign GDP, does this mean that the United States, over the period, experienced net capital outflows?

   b. Does this diagram indicate that world economies were more tightly linked in 2022 than they were in 1980?

3. In the economy of Scottopia in 2022, exports equaled $400 billion of goods and $300 billion of services, imports equaled $500 billion of goods and $350 billion of services, and the rest of the world purchased $250 billion of Scottopia's assets. What was the merchandise trade balance for Scottopia? What was the balance of payments on current account in Scottopia? What was the balance of payments on financial account? What was the value of Scottopia's purchases of assets from the rest of the world?

4. In the economy of Popania in 2022, total Popanian purchases of assets in the rest of the world equaled $300 billion, purchases of Popanian assets by the rest of the world equaled $400 billion, and Popania exported goods and services equal to $350 billion. What was Popania's balance of payments on financial account in 2022? What was its balance of payments on current account? What was the value of its imports?

5. Suppose that Northlandia and Southlandia are the only two trading countries in the world, that each nation runs a balance of payments on both current and financial accounts equal to zero, and that each nation sees the other's assets as identical to its own. Using the accompanying diagrams, explain how the demand and supply of loanable funds, the interest rate, and the balance of payments on current and financial accounts will change in each country if international capital flows are possible.

(a) Northlandia

(b) Southlandia

6. Based on the exchange rates for the trading days of 2022 and 2023 shown in the accompanying table, did the U.S. dollar appreciate or depreciate over the year? Did the movement in the value of the U.S. dollar make American goods and services more or less attractive to foreigners?

June 1, 2022	June 1, 2023
US$1.25 to buy 1 British pound sterling	US$1.25 to buy 1 British pound sterling
29.20 Taiwan dollars to buy US$1	30.69 Taiwan dollars to buy US$1
US$0.79 to buy 1 Canadian dollar	US$0.74 to buy 1 Canadian dollar
129.90 Japanese yen to buy US$1	138.85 Japanese yen to buy US$1
US$1.06 to buy 1 euro	US$1.07 to buy 1 euro
0.96 Swiss franc to buy US$1	0.91 Swiss franc to buy US$1

7. Go to http://fx.sauder.ubc.ca. Using the table labeled "The Most Recent Cross-Rates of Major Currencies," determine whether the British pound (GBP), the Canadian dollar (CAD), the Japanese yen (JPY), the euro (EUR), and the Swiss franc (CHF) have appreciated or depreciated against the U.S. dollar (USD) since June 1, 2023. The exchange rates on June 1, 2023 are listed in the table in Problem 6.

8. In January 2001, the U.S. federal funds rate was 6.5%, falling to 2% in November 2004. During the same period, the marginal lending rate at the European Central Bank fell from 5.75% to 3%.

  a. Considering the change in interest rates over the period and using the loanable funds model, would you have expected funds to flow from the United States to Europe or from Europe to the United States over this period?

  b. The accompanying diagram shows the exchange rate between the euro and the U.S. dollar from January 1, 2001, through September 2008. Is the movement of the exchange rate over the period January 2001 to November 2004 consistent with the movement in funds predicted in part a?

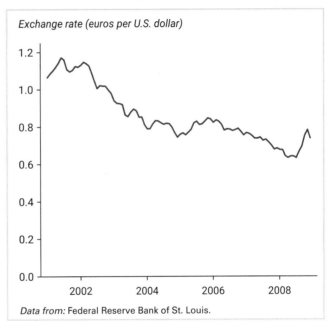

Exchange rate (euros per U.S. dollar)

Data from: Federal Reserve Bank of St. Louis.

9. In each of the following scenarios, suppose that the two nations are the only trading nations in the world. Given inflation and the change in the nominal exchange rate, which nation's goods become more attractive?

  a. Inflation is 10% in the United States and 5% in Japan; the U.S. dollar–Japanese yen exchange rate remains the same.

  b. Inflation is 3% in the United States and 8% in Mexico; the price of the U.S. dollar falls from 12.50 to 10.25 Mexican pesos.

  c. Inflation is 5% in the United States and 3% in the euro area; the price of the euro falls from $1.30 to $1.20.

  d. Inflation is 8% in the United States and 4% in Canada; the price of the Canadian dollar rises from US$0.60 to US$0.75.

10. Starting from a position of equilibrium in the foreign exchange market under a fixed exchange rate regime, how must a government react to an increase in the demand for the nation's goods and services by the rest of the world to keep the exchange rate at its fixed value?

11. Suppose that Albernia's central bank has fixed the value of its currency, the bern, to the U.S. dollar (at a rate of US$1.50 to 1 bern) and is committed to that exchange rate. Initially, the foreign exchange market for the bern is also in equilibrium, as shown in the accompanying diagram. However, both Albernians and Americans begin to believe that there are big risks in holding Albernian assets; as a result, they become unwilling to hold Albernian assets unless they receive a higher rate of return on them than they do on U.S. assets. How would this affect the diagram? If the Albernian central bank tries to keep the exchange rate fixed using monetary policy, how will this affect the Albernian economy?

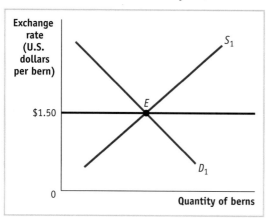

12. Access the Discovering Data exercise for Chapter 18 online to answer the following questions.

    a. Using the most current data available, how has the exchange rate changed for Mexico, the United Kingdom, and Switzerland?

    b. By how much did each of these three currencies appreciate and depreciate against the U.S. dollar?

    c. How will the exchange rate change in each of the three countries affect their exports to the United States?

13. Your study partner asks you, "If central banks lose the ability to use discretionary monetary policy under fixed exchange rates, why would nations agree to a fixed exchange rate system?" How do you respond?

14. Suppose the United States and Japan are the only two trading countries in the world. What will happen to the value of the U.S. dollar if the following occur, other things equal?

    a. Japan relaxes some of its import restrictions.

    b. The United States imposes some import tariffs on Japanese goods.

    c. Interest rates in the United States rise dramatically.

    d. A report indicates that Japanese cars last much longer than previously thought, especially compared with U.S. cars. ∎

Solutions to *Check Your Understanding* Questions

This section offers suggested answers to the *Check Your Understanding* questions found within chapters.

CHAPTER ONE

1-1 Check Your Understanding

1. **a.** This illustrates the concept of opportunity cost. Given that a person can only eat so much at one sitting, having a slice of chocolate cake requires that you forgo eating something else, such as a slice of coconut cream pie.

    b. This illustrates the concept that resources are scarce. Even if there were more resources in the world, the total amount of those resources would be limited. As a result, scarcity would still arise. For there to be no scarcity, there would have to be unlimited amounts of everything (including unlimited time in a human life), which is clearly impossible.

    c. This illustrates the concept that people usually exploit opportunities to make themselves better off. Students will seek to make themselves better off by signing up for the tutorials of teaching assistants with good reputations and avoiding those teaching assistants with poor reputations. It also illustrates the concept that resources are scarce. If there were unlimited spaces in tutorials with good teaching assistants, they would not fill up.

    d. This illustrates the concept of marginal analysis. Your decision about allocating your time is a "how much" decision: how much time spent exercising versus how much time spent studying. You make your decision by comparing the benefit of an additional hour of exercising to its cost, the effect on your grades of one less hour spent studying.

2. **a.** Yes. The increased time spent commuting is a cost you will incur if you accept the new job. That additional time spent commuting—or equivalently, the benefit you would get from spending that time doing something else—is an opportunity cost of the new job.

    b. Yes. One of the benefits of the new job is that you will be making $50,000. But if you take the new job, you will have to give up your current job; that is, you have to give up your current salary of $45,000. So $45,000 is one of the opportunity costs of taking the new job.

    c. No. A more spacious office is an additional benefit of your new job and does not involve forgoing something else. So it is not an opportunity cost.

1-2 Check Your Understanding

1. **a.** This illustrates the concept that there are gains from trade. Students trade tutoring services based on their different abilities in academic subjects.

    b. This illustrates the concept that when markets don't achieve efficiency, government intervention can improve society's welfare. In this case the market, left alone, will permit bars and nightclubs to impose costs on their neighbors in the form of loud music, costs that the bars and nightclubs have no incentive to take into account. This is an inefficient outcome because society as a whole can be made better off if bars and nightclubs are induced to reduce their noise.

    c. This illustrates the concept that resources should be used as efficiently as possible to achieve society's goals. By closing neighborhood clinics and shifting funds to the main hospital, better health care can be provided at a lower cost.

    d. This illustrates the concept that markets move toward equilibrium. Here, because books with the same amount of wear and tear sell for about the same price, no buyer or seller can be made better off by engaging in a different trade than they undertook. This means that the market for used textbooks has moved to an equilibrium.

2. **a.** This does not describe an equilibrium situation. Many students should want to change their behavior and switch to eating at the restaurants. An equilibrium will be established when students are equally as well off eating at the restaurants as eating at the dining hall—which would happen if, say, prices at the dining hall were higher than at the restaurants.

    b. This does describe an equilibrium situation. By changing your behavior and riding the bus, you would not be made better off. Therefore, you have no incentive to change your behavior.

1-3 Check Your Understanding

1. **a.** This illustrates the principle that increases in the economy's potential lead to economic growth over time. Cheaper solar panels will lower the cost of energy, increasing the economy's potential and economic growth. Solar panel manufacturers will be better off but firms producing competing energy will be worse off.

    b. This illustrates the principle that overall spending sometimes gets out of line with the economy's productive capacity; when it does, government policy can change spending. The tax cut would increase people's after-tax incomes, leading to higher consumer spending.

    c. This illustrates the principle that one person's spending is another person's income. As oil companies decrease their spending on labor by laying off workers and paying remaining workers lower wages, those workers' incomes fall. In turn, those workers decrease their consumer spending, causing restaurants and other consumer businesses to lose income.

CHAPTER TWO

2-1 Check Your Understanding

1. **a.** False. An increase in the resources available to Boeing for use in producing Dreamliners and small jets changes the production possibility frontier by shifting it outward. This is because Boeing can now produce more small jets and Dreamliners than before. In the accompanying figure, the line labeled "Boeing's original PPF" represents Boeing's original production possibility frontier, and the line labeled "Boeing's new PPF" represents the new production possibility frontier that results from an increase in resources available to Boeing.

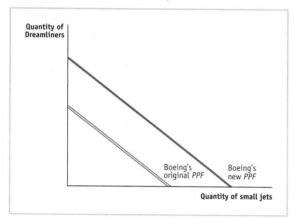

b. True. A technological change that allows Boeing to build more small jets for any amount of Dreamliners built results in a change in its production possibility frontier. This is illustrated in the accompanying figure: the new production possibility frontier is represented by the line labeled "Boeing's new PPF," and the original production frontier is represented by the line labeled "Boeing's original PPF." Since the maximum quantity of Dreamliners that Boeing can build is the same as before, the new production possibility frontier intersects the vertical axis at the same point as the original frontier. But since the maximum possible quantity of small jets is now greater than before, the new frontier intersects the horizontal axis to the right of the original frontier.

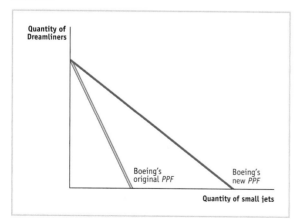

c. False. The production possibility frontier illustrates how much of one good an economy must give up to get more of another good only when resources are used efficiently in production. If an economy is producing

inefficiently—that is, inside the frontier—then it does not have to give up a unit of one good in order to get another unit of the other good. Instead, by becoming more efficient in production, this economy can have more of both goods.

2. **a.** The United States has an absolute advantage in automobile production because it takes fewer Americans (6) to produce a car in one day than Italians (8). The United States also has an absolute advantage in washing machine production because it takes fewer Americans (2) to produce a washing machine in one day than Italians (3).

b. In Italy the opportunity cost of a washing machine in terms of an automobile is $\frac{3}{8}$: $\frac{3}{8}$ of a car can be produced with the same number of workers and in the same time it takes to produce 1 washing machine. In the United States the opportunity cost of a washing machine in terms of an automobile is $\frac{2}{6} = \frac{1}{3}$: $\frac{1}{3}$ of a car can be produced with the same number of workers and in the same time it takes to produce 1 washing machine. Since $\frac{1}{3} < \frac{3}{8}$, the United States has a comparative advantage in the production of washing machines: to produce a washing machine, only $\frac{1}{3}$ of a car must be given up in the United States but $\frac{3}{8}$ of a car must be given up in Italy. This means that Italy has a comparative advantage in automobiles. This can be checked as follows. The opportunity cost of an automobile in terms of a washing machine in Italy is $\frac{8}{3}$, equal to $2\frac{2}{3}$: $2\frac{2}{3}$ washing machines can be produced with the same number of workers and in the time it takes to produce 1 car in Italy. And the opportunity cost of an automobile in terms of a washing machine in the United States is $\frac{6}{2}$, equal to 3:3 washing machines can be produced with the same number of workers and in the time it takes to produce 1 car in the United States. Since $2\frac{2}{3} < 3$, Italy has a comparative advantage in producing automobiles.

c. The greatest gains are realized when each country specializes in producing the good for which it has a comparative advantage. Therefore, the United States should specialize in washing machines and Italy should specialize in automobiles.

3. At a trade of 10 U.S. large jets for 15 Brazilian small jets, Brazil gives up less for a large jet than it would if it were building large jets itself. Without trade, Brazil gives up 3 small jets for each large jet it produces. With trade, Brazil gives up only 1.5 small jets for each large jet from the United States. Likewise, the United States gives up less for a small jet than it would if it were producing small jets itself. Without trade, the United States gives up $\frac{3}{4}$ of a large jet for each small jet. With trade, the United States gives up only $\frac{2}{3}$ of a large jet for each small jet from Brazil.

4. An increase in the amount of money spent by households results in an increase in the flow of goods to households. This, in turn, generates an increase in demand for factors of production by firms. So, there is an increase in the number of jobs in the economy.

2-2 Check Your Understanding

1. **a.** This is a normative statement because it stipulates what should be done. In addition, it may have no "right" answer. That is, should people be prevented from all dangerous personal behavior if they enjoy that behavior—like

skydiving? Your answer will depend on your point of view.

b. This is a positive statement because it is a description of fact.

2. a. True. Economists often have different value judgments about the desirability of a particular social goal. But despite those differences in value judgments, they will tend to agree that society, once it has decided to pursue a given social goal, should adopt the most efficient policy to achieve that goal. Therefore economists are likely to agree on adopting policy choice B.

b. False. Disagreements between economists are more likely to arise because they base their conclusions on different models or because they have different value judgments about the desirability of the policy.

CHAPTER THREE

3-1 Check Your Understanding

1. a. The quantity of umbrellas demanded is higher at any given price on a rainy day than on a dry day. This is a rightward shift of the demand curve, since at any given price the quantity demanded rises. This implies that any specific quantity can now be sold at a higher price.

b. The quantity of summer Caribbean cruises demanded rises in response to a price reduction. This is a movement along the demand curve for summer Caribbean cruises.

c. The demand for roses increases the week of Valentine's Day. This is a rightward shift of the demand curve.

d. The quantity of gasoline demanded falls in response to a rise in price. This is a movement along the demand curve.

3-2 Check Your Understanding

1. a. The quantity of houses supplied rises as a result of an increase in prices. This is a movement along the supply curve.

b. The quantity of strawberries supplied is higher at any given price. This is a rightward shift of the supply curve.

c. The quantity of labor supplied is lower at any given wage. This is a leftward shift of the supply curve compared to the supply curve during school vacation. So, in order to attract workers, fast-food chains have to offer higher wages.

d. The quantity of labor supplied rises in response to a rise in wages. This is a movement along the supply curve.

e. The quantity of cabins supplied is higher at any given price. This is a rightward shift of the supply curve.

3-3 Check Your Understanding

1. a. The supply curve shifts rightward. At the original equilibrium price of the year before, the quantity of grapes supplied exceeds the quantity demanded. This is a case of surplus. The price of grapes will fall.

b. The demand curve shifts leftward. At the original equilibrium price, the quantity of hotel rooms supplied exceeds the quantity demanded. This is a case of surplus. The rates for hotel rooms will fall.

c. The demand curve for second-hand snowblowers shifts rightward. At the original equilibrium price, the quantity of second-hand snowblowers demanded

exceeds the quantity supplied. This is a case of shortage. The equilibrium price of second-hand snowblowers will rise.

3-4 Check Your Understanding

1. a. The market for large cars: this is a rightward shift in demand caused by a decrease in the price of a complement, gasoline. As a result of the shift, the equilibrium price of large cars will rise and the equilibrium quantity of large cars bought and sold will also rise.

b. The market for fresh paper made from recycled stock: this is a rightward shift in supply due to a technological innovation. As a result of this shift, the equilibrium price of fresh paper made from recycled stock will fall and the equilibrium quantity bought and sold will rise.

c. The market for movies at a local movie theater: this is a leftward shift in demand caused by a fall in the price of a substitute, on-demand films. As a result of this shift, the equilibrium price of movie tickets will fall and the equilibrium number of people who go to the movies will also fall.

2. Upon the announcement of the new chip, the demand curve for computers using the earlier chip shifts leftward, as demand decreases, and the supply curve for these computers shifts rightward, as supply increases.

a. If demand decreases relatively more than supply increases, then the equilibrium quantity falls, as shown here:

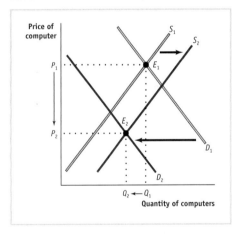

If supply increases relatively more than demand decreases, then the equilibrium quantity rises, as shown here:

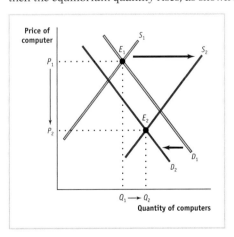

b. In both cases, the equilibrium price falls.

‖ CHAPTER FOUR

4-1 Check Your Understanding

1. **a.** Fewer homeowners are willing to rent out their driveways because the price ceiling has reduced the payment they receive. This is an example of a fall in price leading to a fall in the quantity supplied. It is shown in the accompanying diagram by the movement from point *E* to point *A* along the supply curve, a reduction in quantity of 400 parking spaces.

   b. The quantity demanded increases by 400 spaces as the price decreases. At a lower price, more fans are willing to drive and rent a parking space. It is shown in the diagram by the movement from point *E* to point *B* along the demand curve.

   c. Under a price ceiling, the quantity demanded exceeds the quantity supplied; as a result, shortages arise. In this case, there will be a shortage of 800 parking spaces. It is shown by the horizontal distance between points *A* and *B*.

   d. Price ceilings result in wasted resources. The additional time fans spend to guarantee a parking space is wasted time.

   e. Price ceilings lead to inefficient allocation of a good—here, the parking spaces—to consumers.

   f. Price ceilings lead to black markets.

2. **a.** False. By lowering the price that producers receive, a price ceiling leads to a decrease in the quantity supplied.

   b. True. A price ceiling leads to a lower quantity supplied than in an efficient, unregulated market. As a result, some people who would have been willing to pay the market price, and so would have gotten the good in an unregulated market, are unable to obtain it when a price ceiling is imposed.

   c. True. Those producers who still sell the product now receive less for it and are therefore worse off. Other producers will no longer find it worthwhile to sell the product at all and so will also be made worse off.

4-2 Check Your Understanding

1. **a.** Some gas station owners will benefit from getting a higher price. Q_F indicates the sales made by these owners. But some will lose; there are those who make sales at the market equilibrium price of P_E but do not make sales at the regulated price of P_F. These missed sales are indicated on the graph by the fall in the quantity demanded along the demand curve, from point *E* to point *A*.

   b. Those who buy gas at the higher price of P_F will probably receive better service; this is an example of *inefficiently high quality* caused by a price floor as gas station owners compete on quality rather than price. But opponents are correct to claim that consumers are generally worse off—those who buy at P_F would have been happy to buy at P_E, and many who were willing to buy at a price between P_E and P_F are now unwilling to buy. This is indicated on the graph by the fall in the quantity demanded along the demand curve, from point *E* to point *A*.

   c. Proponents are wrong because consumers and some gas station owners are hurt by the price floor, which creates "missed opportunities"—desirable transactions between consumers and station owners that never take place. Moreover, the inefficiency of wasted resources arises as consumers spend time and money driving to other states. The price floor also tempts people to engage in black market activity. With the price floor, only Q_F units are sold. But at prices between P_E and P_F, there are drivers who cumulatively want to buy more than Q_F and owners who are willing to sell to them, a situation likely to lead to illegal activity.

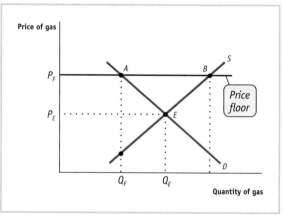

4-3 Check Your Understanding

1. **a.** The price of a ride is $7 since the quantity demanded at this price is 6 million: $7 is the *demand price* of 6 million rides. This is represented by point *A* in the accompanying figure.

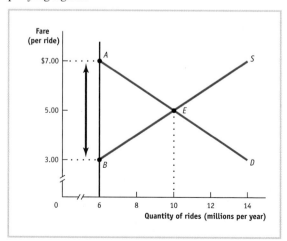

b. At 6 million rides, the supply price is $3 per ride, represented by point *B* in the figure. The wedge between the demand price of $7 per ride and the supply price of $3 per ride is the quota rent per ride, $4. This is represented in the figure above by the vertical distance between points *A* and *B*.

c. At 9 million rides, the demand price is $5.50 per ride, indicated by point *C* in the accompanying figure, and the supply price is $4.50 per ride, indicated by point *D*. The quota rent is the difference between the demand price and the supply price: $1.

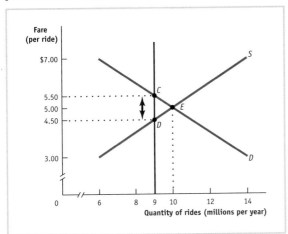

2. The accompanying figure shows a decrease in demand by 4 million rides, represented by a leftward shift of the demand curve from D_1 to D_2: at any given price, the quantity demanded falls by 4 million rides. (For example, at a price of $5, the quantity demanded falls from 10 million to 6 million rides per year.) This eliminates the effect of a quota limit of 8 million rides. At point E_2, the new market equilibrium, the equilibrium quantity is equal to the quota limit; as a result, the quota has no effect on the market.

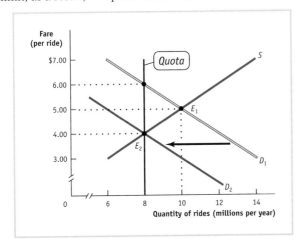

‖ CHAPTER FIVE

5-1 Check Your Understanding

1. a. To determine comparative advantage, we must compare the two countries' opportunity costs for a given good. Take the opportunity cost of 1 ton of corn in terms of bicycles. In China, the opportunity cost of 1 bicycle is

0.01 ton of corn; so the opportunity cost of 1 ton of corn is 1/0.01 bicycles = 100 bicycles. The United States has the comparative advantage in corn since its opportunity cost in terms of bicycles is 50, a smaller number. Similarly, the opportunity cost in the United States of 1 bicycle in terms of corn is 1/50 ton of corn = 0.02 ton of corn. This is greater than 0.01, the Chinese opportunity cost of 1 bicycle in terms of corn, implying that China has a comparative advantage in bicycles.

b. Given that the United States can produce 200,000 bicycles if no corn is produced, it can produce 200,000 bicycles × 0.02 ton of corn/bicycle = 4,000 tons of corn when no bicycles are produced. Likewise, if China can produce 3,000 tons of corn if no bicycles are produced, it can produce 3,000 tons of corn × 100 bicycles/ton of corn = 300,000 bicycles if no corn is produced. These points determine the vertical and horizontal intercepts of the U.S. and Chinese production possibility frontiers, as shown in the accompanying diagram.

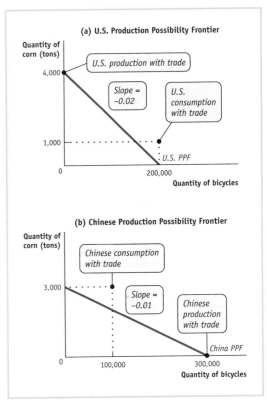

c. The diagram shows the production and consumption points of the two countries. Each country is clearly better off with international trade because each now consumes a bundle of the two goods that lies outside its own production possibility frontier, indicating that these bundles were unattainable in autarky.

2. a. According to the Heckscher–Ohlin model, this pattern of trade occurs because the United States has a relatively larger endowment of factors of production, such as human capital and physical capital, that are suited to the production of movies, but France has a relatively larger endowment of factors of production suited to wine-making, such as vineyards and the human capital of vintners.

b. According to the Heckscher–Ohlin model, this pattern of trade occurs because the United States has a relatively larger endowment of factors of production, such as human and physical capital, that are suited to making machinery, but Brazil has a relatively larger endowment of factors of production suited to shoe-making, such as unskilled labor and leather.

5-2 Check Your Understanding

1. In the accompanying diagram, P_A is the U.S. price of grapes in autarky and P_W is the world price of grapes under international trade. With trade, U.S. consumers pay a price of P_W for grapes and consume quantity Q_D, U.S. grape producers produce quantity Q_S, and the difference, $Q_D - Q_S$, represents imports of Mexican grapes. As a consequence of the strike by truckers, imports are halted, the price paid by American consumers rises to the autarky price, P_A, and U.S. consumption falls to the autarky quantity, Q_A.

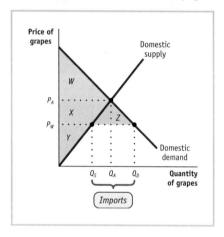

a. Before the strike, U.S. consumers enjoyed consumer surplus equal to areas $W + X + Z$. After the strike, their consumer surplus shrinks to W. So consumers are worse off, losing consumer surplus represented by $X + Z$.

b. Before the strike, U.S. producers had producer surplus equal to the area Y. After the strike, their producer surplus increases to $Y + X$. So U.S. producers are better off, gaining producer surplus represented by X.

c. U.S. total surplus falls as a result of the strike by an amount represented by area Z, the loss in consumer surplus that does not accrue to producers.

2. Mexican grape producers are worse off because they lose sales of exported grapes to the United States, and Mexican grape pickers are worse off because they lose the wages that were associated with the lost sales. The lower demand for Mexican grapes caused by the strike implies that the price Mexican consumers pay for grapes falls, making them better off. U.S. grape pickers are better off because their wages increase as a result of the increase of $Q_A - Q_S$ in U.S. sales.

5-3 Check Your Understanding

1. a. If the tariff is $0.50, the price paid by domestic consumers for a pound of imported butter is $0.50 + $0.50 = $1.00, the same price as a pound of domestic butter. Imported butter will no longer have a price advantage over domestic butter, imports will cease, and domestic producers

will capture all the feasible sales to domestic consumers, selling amount Q_A in the accompanying figure. If the tariff is $0.25, the price paid by domestic consumers for a pound of imported butter is $0.50 + $0.25 = $0.75, $0.25 cheaper than a pound of domestic butter. American butter producers will gain sales in the amount of $Q_2 - Q_1$ as a result of the $0.25 tariff. But this is smaller than the amount they would have gained under the $0.50 tariff, the amount $Q_A - Q_1$.

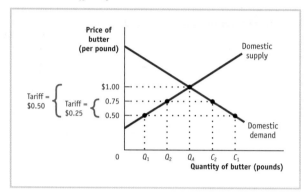

b. As long as the tariff is at least $0.50, increasing it more has no effect. At a tariff of $0.50, all imports are effectively blocked.

2. All imports are effectively blocked at a tariff of $0.50. So such a tariff corresponds to an import quota of 0.

5-4 Check Your Understanding

1. There are many fewer businesses that use steel as an input than there are consumers who buy sugar or clothing. So it will be easier for such businesses to communicate and coordinate among themselves to lobby against tariffs than it will be for consumers. In addition, each business will perceive that the cost of a steel tariff is quite costly to its profits, but an individual consumer is either unaware of or perceives little loss from tariffs on sugar or clothing.

2. Countries are often tempted to protect domestic industries by claiming that an import poses a quality, health, or environmental danger to domestic consumers. A WTO official should examine whether domestic producers are subject to the same stringency in the application of quality, health, or environmental regulations as foreign producers. If they are, then it is more likely that the regulations are for legitimate, non–trade protection purposes; if they are not, then it is more likely that the regulations are intended as trade protection measures.

CHAPTER SIX

6-1 Check Your Understanding

1. a. This is a microeconomic question because it addresses decisions made by consumers about a particular product.

b. This is a macroeconomic question because it addresses consumer spending in the overall economy.

c. This is a macroeconomic question because it addresses changes in the overall economy.

d. This is a microeconomic question because it addresses changes in a particular market, in this case the market for economists.

e. This is a microeconomic question because it addresses choices made by consumers and producers about which mode of transportation to use.

f. This is a microeconomic question because it addresses changes in a particular market.

g. This is a macroeconomic question because it addresses changes in a measure of the economy's overall price level.

2. a. When people can't get credit to finance their purchases, they will be unable to spend money. This will weaken the economy, and as others see the economy weaken, they will also cut back on their spending in order to save for future bad times. As a result, the credit shortfall will spark a compounding effect through the economy as people cut back their spending, making the economy worse, leading to more cutbacks in spending, and so on.

b. If you believe the economy is self-regulating, then you would advocate doing nothing in response to the slump.

c. If you believe in Keynesian economics, you would advocate that policy makers undertake monetary and fiscal policies to stimulate spending in the economy.

6-2 Check Your Understanding

1. We talk about business cycles for the economy as a whole because recessions and expansions are not confined to a few industries—they reflect downturns and upturns for the economy as a whole. In downturns, almost every sector of the economy reduces output and the number of people employed. Moreover, business cycles are an international phenomenon, sometimes moving in rough synchrony across countries.

2. A recession can hurt people throughout society. They cause large numbers of workers to lose their jobs and make it hard to find new jobs. Recessions hurt the standard of living of many families and are usually associated with a rise in the number of people living below the poverty line, an increase in the number of people who lose their houses because they can't afford their mortgage payments, and a fall in the percentage of Americans with health insurance. Recessions also hurt the profits of firms.

6-3 Check Your Understanding

1. Countries with high rates of population growth will have to maintain higher long-run growth rates of overall output than countries with low rates of population growth in order to achieve an increased standard of living per person, because aggregate output will have to be divided among a larger number of people.

2. No, Argentina is not poorer than it was in the past. Both Argentina and Canada have experienced long-run growth. However, after World War II, Argentina did not make as much progress as Canada, perhaps because of political instability and bad macroeconomic policies. Also, Canada's economy grew much faster than Argentina's. Although Canada is now about three times as rich as Argentina, Argentina still experienced long-run growth.

6-4 Check Your Understanding

1. a. As some prices have risen but other prices have fallen, there may be overall inflation or deflation. The answer is ambiguous.

b. As all prices have risen significantly, this sounds like inflation.

c. As most prices have fallen and others have not changed, this sounds like deflation.

6-5 Check Your Understanding

1. a. This situation reflects comparative advantage. Canada's comparative advantage results from the development of oil—Canada now has an abundance of oil.

b. This situation reflects comparative advantage. China's comparative advantage results from an abundance of labor; China is good at labor-intensive activities such as assembly.

c. This situation reflects macroeconomic forces. Germany has been running huge trade surpluses because of underlying decisions regarding savings and investment spending with its savings in excess of its investment spending.

d. This situation reflects macroeconomic forces. The United States was able to begin running large trade deficits because the technology boom made the United States an attractive place to invest, with investment spending outstripping U.S. savings.

CHAPTER SEVEN

7-1 Check Your Understanding

1. Let's start by considering the relationship between the total value added of all domestically produced final goods and services and aggregate spending on domestically produced final goods and services. These two quantities are equal because every final good and service produced in the economy is either purchased by someone or added to inventories. And additions to inventories are counted as spending by firms. Next, consider the relationship between aggregate spending on domestically produced final goods and services and total factor income. These two quantities are equal because all spending that is channeled to firms to pay for purchases of domestically produced final goods and services is revenue for firms. Those revenues must be paid out by firms to their factors of production in the form of wages, profit, interest, and rent. Taken together, this means that all three methods of calculating GDP are equivalent.

2. Firms make sales to other firms, households, the government, and the rest of the world. Households are linked to firms through the sale of factors of production to firms, through purchases from firms of final goods and services, and through lending funds to firms in the financial markets. Households are linked to the government through their payment of taxes, their receipt of transfers, and their lending of funds to the government via the financial markets. Finally, households are linked to the rest of the world through their purchases of imports and transactions with foreigners in financial markets.

3. You would be counting the value of the steel twice—once as it was sold by National Steel to National Motors and once as part of the car sold by National Motors.

7-2 Check Your Understanding

1. a. In 2022 nominal GDP was $(1,000,000 \times \$0.40) + (800,000 \times \$0.60) = \$400,000 + \$480,000 = \$880,000$. A 25% rise in the price of french fries from 2022 to

2023 means that the 2023 price of french fries was $1.25 \times \$0.40 = \$0.50$. A 10% fall in servings sold means that $1,000,000 \times 0.9 = 900,000$ servings were sold in 2023. As a result, the total value of sales of french fries in 2023 was $900,000 \times \$0.50 = \$450,000$. A 15% fall in the price of onion rings from 2022 to 2023 means that the 2023 price of onion rings was $0.85 \times \$0.60 = \$0.51$. A 5% rise in servings sold means that $800,000 \times 1.05 = 840,000$ servings were sold in 2023. As a result, the total value of sales of onion rings in 2023 was $840,000 \times \$0.51 = \$428,400$. Nominal GDP in 2023 was $\$450,000 + \$428,400 = \$878,400$. To find real GDP in 2023, we must calculate the value of sales in 2023 using 2022 prices: $(900,000$ french fries $\times \$0.40) + (840,000$ onion rings $\times \$0.60) = \$360,000 + \$504,000 = \$864,000$.

b. The change in nominal GDP from 2022 to 2023 was $(($$878,400 - $880,000)/$880,000) \times 100 = -0.18\%$, a decline. But a comparison using real GDP shows a decline of $(($864,000 - $880,000)/$880,000) \times 100 = -1.8\%$. That is, a calculation based on real GDP shows a drop 10 times larger (1.8%) than a calculation based on nominal GDP (0.18%). In this case, the calculation based on nominal GDP underestimates the true magnitude of the change.

2. A price index based on 2016 prices will contain a relatively high price of electronics and a relatively low price of housing compared to a price index based on 2022 prices. This means that a 2016 price index used to calculate real GDP in 2018 will magnify the value of electronics production in the economy, but a 2022 price index will magnify the value of housing production in the economy.

7-3 Check Your Understanding

1. This market basket costs, pre-frost, $(100 \times \$0.20) + (50 \times \$0.60) + (200 \times \$0.25) = \$20 + \$30 + \$50 = \$100$. The same market basket, post-frost, costs $(100 \times \$0.40) + (50 \times \$1.00) + (200 \times \$0.45) = \$40 + \$50 + \$90 = \$180$. So the price index is $(\$100/\$100) \times 100 = 100$ before the frost and $(\$180/\$100) \times 100 = 180$ after the frost, implying a rise in the price index of 80%. This increase in the price index is less than the 84.2% increase calculated in the text. The reason for this difference is that the new market basket of 100 oranges, 50 grapefruit, and 200 lemons contains proportionately more of the items that have experienced relatively lower price increases (the lemons, whose price has increased by 80%) and proportionately fewer of the items that have experienced relatively large price increases (the oranges, whose price has increased by 100%). This shows that the price index can be very sensitive to the composition of the market basket. If the market basket contains a large proportion of goods whose prices have risen faster than the prices of other goods, it will lead to a higher estimate of the increase in the price level. If it contains a large proportion of goods whose prices have risen more slowly than the prices of other goods, it will lead to a lower estimate of the increase in the price level.

2. **a.** A market basket determined 10 years ago would contain fewer cars than at present. Given that the average price of a car has grown faster than the average prices of other goods, this basket will underestimate the true increase in the cost of living because it contains relatively too few cars.

   b. A market basket determined 20 years ago will not contain broadband internet access. So it cannot track the fall in prices of internet access over the past few years. As a result, it will overestimate the true increase in the cost of living.

3. Using Equation 7-3, the inflation rate from 2021 to 2022 is $(298.99/280.88) - 1 = 0.0645$ or 6.45%.

CHAPTER EIGHT

8-1 Check Your Understanding

1. Software improvements developed by employment websites that enable job-seekers to find jobs more quickly will reduce the unemployment rate over time. However, websites that induce discouraged workers to begin actively looking for work again will lead to an increase in the unemployment rate over time.

2. **a.** Rosa is not counted as unemployed because she is not actively looking for work, but she is counted in broader measures of labor underutilization as a discouraged worker.

   b. Anthony is not counted as unemployed; he is considered employed because he has a job.

   c. Kanako is unemployed; she is not working and is actively looking for work.

   d. Sergio is not unemployed, but underemployed; he is working part time for economic reasons. He is counted in broader measures of labor underutilization.

   e. Natasha is not unemployed, but she is a marginally attached worker. She is counted in broader measures of labor underutilization.

3. Both parts a and b are consistent with the relationship, illustrated in Figure 5, between above-average or below-average growth in real GDP and changes in the unemployment rate: during years of above-average growth, the unemployment rate falls, and during years of below-average growth, the unemployment rate rises. However, part c is not consistent: it implies that a recession is associated with a fall in the unemployment rate, which is incorrect.

8-2 Check Your Understanding

1. **a.** When the pace of technological advancement quickens, there will be higher rates of job creation and destruction as old industries disappear and new ones emerge. As a result, frictional unemployment will be higher as workers leave jobs in declining industries in search of jobs in expanding industries.

   b. When the pace of technological advancement quickens, there will be greater mismatch between the skills employees have and the skills employers are looking for, leading to higher structural unemployment.

   c. When the unemployment rate is low, frictional unemployment will account for a larger share of total unemployment because other sources of unemployment will be diminished. So the share of total unemployment composed of the frictionally unemployed will rise.

2. A binding minimum wage represents a price floor below which wages cannot fall. As a result, actual wages cannot move toward equilibrium. So a minimum wage causes the quantity of labor supplied to exceed the quantity of labor demanded. Because this surplus of labor reflects unemployed workers, it affects the unemployment rate.

Collective bargaining has a similar effect—unions are able to raise the wage above the equilibrium level to a level like W_U in the accompanying diagram. This will act like a minimum wage by causing the number of job-seekers to be larger than the number of workers firms are willing to hire. Collective bargaining causes the unemployment rate to be higher than it otherwise would be, as shown in the accompanying diagram.

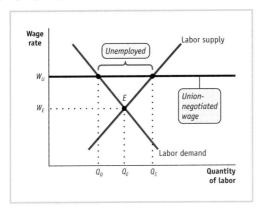

3. An increase in unemployment benefits at the peak of the business cycle reduces the cost to individuals of being unemployed, causing them to spend more time searching for new jobs. So the natural rate of unemployment would increase.

8-3 Check Your Understanding

1. Shoe-leather costs as a result of inflation will be lower because it is now less costly for individuals to manage their assets in order to economize on their money holdings. This reduction in the costs associated with converting other assets into money translates into lower shoe-leather costs.

2. A sudden increase in inflation will benefit borrowers and hurt lenders. In this case, anyone that had borrowed prior to the spike in inflation would be better off. This would include households that took out mortgages, new car loans, recent graduates repaying student loans, and the U.S. government. Those harmed by the sudden increase would be the debt holders, mainly financial institutions and savers.

‖ CHAPTER NINE

9-1 Check Your Understanding

1. Economic progress raises the living standards of the average resident of a country. An increase in overall real GDP does not accurately reflect an increase in an average resident's living standard because it does not account for growth in the number of residents. If, for example, real GDP rises by 10% but population grows by 20%, the living standard of the average resident falls: after the change, the average resident has only $(110/120) \times 100 = 91.6\%$ as much real income as before the change. Similarly, an increase in nominal GDP per capita does not accurately reflect an increase in living standards because it does not account for any change in prices. For example, a 5% increase in nominal GDP per capita generated by a 5% increase in prices implies that there has been no change in living standards. Real GDP per capita is the only

measure that accounts for both changes in the population and changes in prices.

2. Using the Rule of 70, the number of years it will take for China to double its real GDP per capita is $(70/7.8) = 8.97$, or approximately 9 years; India, $(70/4.1) = 17.07$, or approximately 17 years; Ireland, $(70/3.7) = 18.92$, or approximately 19 years; Bangladesh, $(70/3) = 23.33$, or approximately 23 years; the United States, $(70/1.6) = 43.75$, or approximately 44 years; France, $(70/1.3) = 53.85$, or approximately 54 years; and Argentina $(70/0.5) = 140$ years. Since the Rule of 70 can only be applied to a positive growth rate, we cannot apply it to the case of Venezuela, which experienced negative growth. If India continues to have a higher growth rate of real GDP per capita than the United States, then India's real GDP per capita will eventually surpass that of the United States.

3. The United States began growing rapidly over a century ago, but China and India have begun growing rapidly only recently. As a result, the living standard of the typical Chinese or Indian household has not yet caught up with that of the typical U.S. household.

9-2 Check Your Understanding

1. **a.** Significant technological progress will result in a positive growth rate of productivity even though physical capital per worker and human capital per worker are unchanged.

   b. The growth rate of productivity will fall but remain positive due to diminishing returns to physical capital.

2. **a.** If output has grown 3% per year and the labor force has grown 1% per year, then productivity—output per person—has grown at approximately $3\% - 1\% = 2\%$ per year.

   b. If physical capital has grown 4% per year and the labor force has grown 1% per year, then physical capital per worker has grown at approximately $4\% - 1\% = 3\%$ per year.

   c. According to estimates, each 1% rise in physical capital, other things equal, increases productivity by 0.3%. So, as physical capital per worker has increased by 3%, productivity growth that can be attributed to an increase in physical capital per worker is $0.3 \times 3\% = 0.9\%$. As a percentage of total productivity growth, this is $0.9\%/2\% \times 100\% = 45\%$.

   d. If the rest of productivity growth is due to technological progress, then technological progress has contributed $2\% - 0.9\% = 1.1\%$ to productivity growth. As a percentage of total productivity growth, this is $1.1\%/2\% \times 100\% = 55\%$.

3. It will take a period of time for workers to learn how to use the new computer system and to adjust their routines. And because there are often setbacks in learning a new system, such as accidentally erasing your computer files, productivity at Multinomics, Inc. may decrease for a period of time.

9-3 Check Your Understanding

1. A country that has high domestic savings is able to achieve a high rate of investment spending as a percent of GDP. This, in turn, allows the country to achieve a high growth rate.

2. It is likely that the United States will experience a greater pace of innovation and development of new drugs because

closer links between private companies and academic research centers will lead to research and development more directly focused on producing new drugs rather than on pure research.

3. It is likely that these events resulted in a fall in the country's growth rate because the lack of property rights would have dissuaded people from making investments in a productive capacity.

9-4 Check Your Understanding

1. The conditional version of the convergence hypothesis says that countries grow faster, other things equal, when they start from relatively low GDP per capita. From this we can infer that they grow more slowly, other things equal, when their real GDP per capita is relatively higher. This points to lower future Asian growth. However, other things might not be equal: if Asian economies continue investing in human capital, if savings rates continue to be high, if governments invest in infrastructure, and so on, growth might continue at an accelerated pace.

2. The regions of East Asia, Western Europe, and the United States support the convergence hypothesis because a comparison among them shows that the growth rate of real GDP per capita falls as real GDP per capita rises. Eastern Europe, West Asia, Latin America, and Africa do not support the hypothesis because they all have much lower real GDP per capita than the United States but have either approximately the same growth rate (West Asia and Eastern Europe) or a lower growth rate (Africa and Latin America).

3. The evidence suggests that both sets of factors matter: better infrastructure is important for growth, but so is political and financial stability. Policies should try to address both areas.

9-5 Check Your Understanding

1. Economists are typically more concerned about environmental degradation than resource scarcity. The reason is that in modern economies the price response tends to alleviate the limits imposed by resource scarcity through conservation and the development of alternatives. However, because environmental degradation involves a cost imposed by individuals or firms on others without the requirement to pay compensation (known as a *negative externality*), effective government intervention is required to address it. As a result, economists are more concerned about the limits to growth imposed by environmental degradation because a market response would be inadequate.

2. Growth increases a country's greenhouse gas emissions. The current best estimates are that a large reduction in emissions will result in only a modest reduction in growth. The international burden sharing of greenhouse gas emissions reduction is contentious because rich countries are reluctant to pay the costs of reducing their emissions only to see newly emerging countries like China rapidly increase their emissions. Yet most of the current accumulation of gases is due to the past actions of rich countries. Poorer countries like China are equally reluctant to sacrifice their growth to pay for the past actions of rich countries.

CHAPTER TEN

10-1 Check Your Understanding

1. **a.** As there is a net capital inflow into the economy, the supply of loanable funds increases. This is illustrated by the shift of the supply curve from S_1 to S_2 in the accompanying diagram. As the equilibrium moves from E_1 to E_2, the equilibrium interest rate falls from r_1 to r_2, and the equilibrium quantity of loanable funds increases from Q_1 to Q_2.

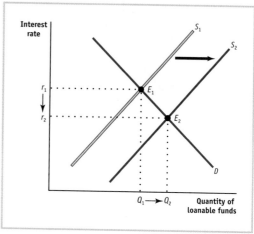

b. Savings fall due to the higher proportion of retired people, and the supply of loanable funds decreases. This is illustrated by the leftward shift of the supply curve from S_1 to S_2 in the accompanying diagram. The equilibrium moves from E_1 to E_2, the equilibrium interest rate rises from r_1 to r_2, and the equilibrium quantity of loanable funds falls from Q_1 to Q_2.

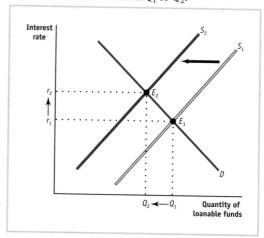

2. We know from the loanable funds market that as the interest rate rises, households want to save more and consume less. But at the same time, an increase in the interest rate lowers the number of investment spending projects with returns at least as high as the interest rate. The statement "households will want to save more money than businesses will want to invest" cannot represent an equilibrium in the loanable funds market because it says that the quantity of loanable funds offered exceeds the quantity of loanable funds demanded. If that were to occur, the interest rate

must fall to make the quantity of loanable funds offered equal to the quantity of loanable funds demanded.

3. **a.** The real interest rate will not change. According to the Fisher effect, an increase in expected inflation drives up the nominal interest rate, leaving the real interest rate unchanged.

   b. The nominal interest rate will rise by 3%. Each additional percentage point of expected inflation drives up the nominal interest rate by 1 percentage point.

   c. As we saw in Figure 9, as long as inflation is expected, it does not affect the equilibrium quantity of loanable funds. Both the supply and demand curves for loanable funds are pushed upward, leaving the equilibrium quantity of loanable funds unchanged.

10-2 Check Your Understanding

1. The transaction costs for (a) a bank deposit and (b) a share of a mutual fund are approximately equal because each can typically be accomplished by making a phone call, going online, or visiting a branch office. Transaction costs are highest for (c) a share of a family business, since finding a buyer for the share consumes time and resources. The level of risk is lowest for (a) a bank deposit, since these deposits are insured by the Federal Deposit Insurance Corporation (FDIC) up to $250,000; somewhat higher for (b) a share of a mutual fund, since despite diversification, there is still risk associated with holding mutual funds; and highest for (c) a share of a family business, since this investment is not diversified. The level of liquidity is highest for (a) a bank deposit, since withdrawals can usually be made immediately; somewhat lower for (b) a share of a mutual fund, since it may take a few days between selling your shares and the payment being processed; and lowest for (c) a share of a family business, since it can only be sold with the unanimous agreement of other members and it will take some time to find a buyer.

2. Economic development and growth are the result of, among other factors, investment spending on physical capital. Since investment spending is equal to savings, the greater the amount saved, the higher investment spending will be, and so the higher growth and economic development will be. So the existence of institutions that facilitate savings will help a country's growth and economic development. As a result, a country with a financial system that provides low transaction costs, opportunities for diversification of risk, and high liquidity to its savers will experience faster growth and economic development than a country that doesn't.

10-3 Check Your Understanding

1. **a.** Today's stock prices reflect the market's expectation of future stock prices, and according to the efficient markets hypothesis, stock prices always take account of all available information. The fact that this year's profits are low is not new information, so it is already built into the share price. However, when it becomes known that the company's profits will be high next year, the price of a share of its stock will rise today, reflecting this new information.

   b. The expectations of investors about high profits were already built into the stock price. Since profits will be lower than expected, the market's expectations about the company's future stock price will be revised downward. This new information will lower the stock price.

   c. When other companies in the same industry announce that sales are unexpectedly slow this year, investors are likely to conclude that sales will also be unexpectedly slow for this company. As a result, investors will revise their expectations of future profits and of the future stock price downward. This new information will result in a lower stock price today.

   d. This announcement will either have no effect on the company's stock price or will increase it only slightly. It does not add any new information, beyond removing some uncertainty about whether the profit forecast was correct. It should therefore result in either no increase or only a small increase in the stock price.

2. The efficient markets hypothesis states that all available information is immediately taken into account in stock prices. So if investors consistently bought stocks the day after the Dow rose by 1%, a smart investor would *sell* on that day because demand—and so stock prices—would be high. If a profit can be made that way, eventually many investors would be selling, and it would no longer be true that investors always bought stocks the day after the Dow rose by 1%.

CHAPTER ELEVEN

11-1 Check Your Understanding

1. A decline in investment spending, like a rise in investment spending, has a multiplier effect on real GDP—the only difference in this case is that real GDP falls instead of rises. The fall in I leads to an initial fall in real GDP, which leads to a fall in disposable income, which leads to lower consumer spending, which leads to another fall in real GDP, and so on. So consumer spending falls as an indirect result of the fall in investment spending.

2. When MPC is 0.5, the multiplier is equal to $1/(1 − 0.5) = 1/0.5 = 2$. When MPC is 0.8, the multiplier is equal to $1/(1 − 0.8) = 1/0.2 = 5$.

3. The greater the share of GDP that is saved rather than spent, the lower the MPC. Disposable income that goes to savings is like a "leak" in the system, reducing the amount of spending that fuels a further expansion. So it is likely that Amerigo will have the larger multiplier.

11-2 Check Your Understanding

1. **a.** Angelina's autonomous consumer spending is $8,000. When her current disposable income rises by $10,000, her consumer spending rises by $12,000 − $8,000 = $4,000. So her MPC is $4,000/$10,000 = 0.4 and her consumption function is $c = \$8,000 + 0.4 \times YD$. Felicia's autonomous consumer spending is $6,500. When her current disposable income rises by $10,000, her consumer spending rises by $14,500 − $6,500 = $8,000. So her MPC is $8,000/$10,000 = 0.8 and her consumption function is $c = \$6,500 + 0.8 \times YD$. Marina's autonomous consumer spending is $7,250. When her current disposable income rises by $10,000, her consumer spending rises by $14,250 − $7,250 = $7,000. So her MPC is $7,000/$10,000 = 0.7 and her consumption function is $c = \$7,250 + 0.7 \times YD$.

   b. The aggregate autonomous consumer spending in this economy is $8,000 + $6,500 + $7,250 = $21,750.

A \$30,000 increase in disposable income ($3 \times \$10,000$) leads to a $\$4,000 + \$8,000 + \$7,000 = \$19,000$ increase in consumer spending. So the economy-wide *MPC* is $\$19,000/\$30,000 = 0.63$ and the aggregate consumption function is $C = \$21,750 + 0.63 \times YD$.

2. If you expect your future disposable income to fall, you would like to save some of today's disposable income to tide you over in the future. But you cannot do this if you cannot save. If you expect your future disposable income to rise, you would like to spend some of tomorrow's higher income today. But you cannot do this if you cannot borrow. If you cannot save or borrow, your expected future disposable income will have no effect on your consumer spending today. In fact, your *MPC* must always equal 1: you must consume all your current disposable income today, and you will be unable to smooth your consumption over time.

11-3 Check Your Understanding

1. **a.** An unexpected increase in consumer spending will result in a reduction in inventories as producers sell items from their inventories to satisfy this short-term increase in demand. This is negative unplanned inventory investment: it reduces the value of producers' inventories.

   b. A rise in the cost of borrowing is equivalent to a rise in the interest rate: fewer investment spending projects are now profitable to producers, whether they are financed through borrowing or retained earnings. As a result, producers will reduce the amount of planned investment spending.

   c. A sharp increase in the rate of real GDP growth leads to a higher level of planned investment spending by producers, according to the accelerator principle, as they increase production capacity to meet higher demand.

   d. As sales fall, producers sell less, and their inventories grow. This leads to positive unplanned inventory investment.

2. Since the marginal propensity to consume is less than 1—because consumers normally spend part but not all of an additional dollar of disposable income—consumer spending does not fully respond to fluctuations in current disposable income. This behavior diminishes the effect of fluctuations in the economy on consumer spending. In contrast, by the accelerator principle, investment spending is directly related to the expected future growth rate of GDP. As a result, investment spending will magnify fluctuations in the economy: a higher expected future growth rate of real GDP leads to higher planned investment spending; a lower expected future growth rate of real GDP leads to lower planned investment spending.

3. When consumer spending is sluggish, firms with excess production capacity will cut back on planned investment spending because they think their existing capacities are sufficient for expected future sales. Similarly, when consumer spending is sluggish and firms have a large amount of unplanned inventory investment, they are likely to cut back their production of output because they think their existing inventories are sufficient for expected future sales. So an inventory overhang is likely to depress current economic activity as firms cut back on their planned investment spending and on their output.

11-4 Check Your Understanding

1. A slump in planned investment spending will lead to a fall in real GDP in response to an unanticipated increase in inventories. The fall in real GDP will translate into a fall in households' disposable income, and households will respond by reducing consumer spending. The decrease in consumer spending leads producers to further decrease output, further lowering disposable income and leading to further reductions in consumer spending. So although the slump originated in investment spending, it will cause a reduction in consumer spending.

2. **a.** After an autonomous fall in planned aggregate spending, the economy is no longer in equilibrium: real GDP is greater than planned aggregate spending. The accompanying figure shows this autonomous fall in planned aggregate spending by the shift of the aggregate spending curve from AE_1 to AE_2. The difference between the two results in positive unplanned inventory investment: there is an unanticipated increase in inventories. Firms will respond by reducing production. This will eventually move the economy to a new equilibrium. In the accompanying figure, this is illustrated by the movement from the initial income–expenditure equilibrium at E_1 to the new income–expenditure equilibrium at E_2. As the economy moves to its new equilibrium, real GDP falls from its initial income–expenditure equilibrium level at Y_1^* to its new lower level, Y_2^*.

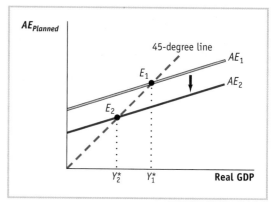

   b. We know that the change in income–expenditure equilibrium GDP is given by Equation 11-17: $\Delta Y^* = \text{Multiplier} \times \Delta AAE_{Planned}$. Here, the multiplier is equal to $1/(1 - 0.5) = 1/0.5 = 2$. So a \$300 million autonomous reduction in planned aggregate spending will lead to a $2 \times \$300$ million $= \$600$ million (\$0.6 billion) fall in income–expenditure equilibrium GDP. The new Y^* will be \$500 billion – \$0.6 billion = \$499.4 billion.

CHAPTER TWELVE

12-1 Check Your Understanding

1. **a.** This is a shift of the aggregate demand curve. A decrease in the quantity of money raises the interest rate, since people now want to borrow more and lend less. A higher interest rate reduces investment and consumer spending at any given aggregate price level. So the aggregate demand curve shifts to the left.

   b. This is a movement up along the aggregate demand curve. As the aggregate price level rises, the real value of money holdings falls. This is the interest rate effect of a change in the aggregate price level: as the value of money falls, people want to hold more money. They do so by borrowing more and lending less. This leads to a rise in the interest rate and a reduction in consumer and investment spending. So it is a movement along the aggregate demand curve.

  c. This is a shift of the aggregate demand curve. Expectations of a poor job market, and so lower average disposable incomes, will reduce people's consumer spending today at any given aggregate price level. So the aggregate demand curve shifts to the left.

  d. This is a shift of the aggregate demand curve. A fall in tax rates raises people's disposable income. At any given aggregate price level, consumer spending is now higher. So the aggregate demand curve shifts to the right.

  e. This is a movement down along the aggregate demand curve. As the aggregate price level falls, the real value of assets rises. This is the wealth effect of a change in the aggregate price level: as the value of assets rises, people will increase their consumption plans. This leads to higher consumer spending. So it is a movement along the aggregate demand curve.

12-2 Check Your Understanding

1. **a.** This represents a movement along the *SRAS* curve because the CPI—like the GDP deflator—is a measure of the aggregate price level, the overall price level of final goods and services in the economy.

  b. This represents a shift of the *SRAS* curve because oil is a commodity. The *SRAS* curve will shift to the right because production costs are now lower, leading to a higher quantity of aggregate output supplied at any given aggregate price level.

  c. This represents a shift of the *SRAS* curve because it involves a change in nominal wages. An increase in legally mandated benefits to workers is equivalent to an increase in nominal wages. As a result, the *SRAS* curve will shift leftward because production costs are now higher, leading to a lower quantity of aggregate output supplied at any given aggregate price level.

2. You would need to know what happened to the aggregate price level. If the increase in the quantity of aggregate output supplied was due to a movement along the *SRAS* curve, the aggregate price level would have increased at the same time as the quantity of aggregate output supplied increased. If the increase in the quantity of aggregate output supplied was due to a rightward shift of the *LRAS* curve, the aggregate price level might not rise. Alternatively, you could make the determination by observing what happened to aggregate output in the long run. If it fell back to its initial level in the long run, then the temporary increase in aggregate output was due to a movement along the *SRAS* curve. If it stayed at the higher level in the long run, the increase in aggregate output was due to a rightward shift of the *LRAS* curve.

12-3 Check Your Understanding

1. **a.** An increase in the minimum wage raises the nominal wage and, as a result, shifts the short-run aggregate supply curve to the left. As a result of this negative supply shock, the aggregate price level rises and aggregate output falls.

  b. Increased investment spending shifts the aggregate demand curve to the right. As a result of this positive demand shock, both the aggregate price level and aggregate output rise.

  c. An increase in taxes and a reduction in government spending both result in negative demand shocks, shifting the aggregate demand curve to the left. As a result, both the aggregate price level and aggregate output fall.

  d. This is a negative supply shock, shifting the short-run aggregate supply curve to the left. As a result, the aggregate price level rises and aggregate output falls.

2. As the rise in productivity increases potential output, the long-run aggregate supply curve shifts to the right. If, in the short run, there is now a recessionary gap (aggregate output is less than potential output), nominal wages will fall, shifting the short-run aggregate supply curve to the right. This results in a fall in the aggregate price level and a rise in aggregate output. As prices fall, we move along the aggregate demand curve due to the wealth and interest rate effects of a change in the aggregate price level. Eventually, as long-run macroeconomic equilibrium is reestablished, aggregate output will rise to be equal to potential output.

12-4 Check Your Understanding

1. **a.** An economy is overstimulated when an inflationary gap is present. This will arise if an expansionary monetary or fiscal policy is implemented when the economy is currently in long-run macroeconomic equilibrium. This shifts the aggregate demand curve to the right, in the short run raising the aggregate price level and aggregate output and creating an inflationary gap. Eventually nominal wages will rise and shift the short-run aggregate supply curve to the left, and aggregate output will fall back to potential output. This is the scenario envisaged by the speaker.

  b. No, this is not a valid argument. When the economy is not currently in long-run macroeconomic equilibrium, an expansionary monetary or fiscal policy does not lead to the outcome described above. Suppose a negative demand shock has shifted the aggregate demand curve to the left, resulting in a recessionary gap. An expansionary monetary or fiscal policy can shift the aggregate demand curve back to its original position in long-run macroeconomic equilibrium. In this way, the short-run fall in aggregate output and deflation caused by the original negative demand shock can be avoided. So, if used in response to demand shocks, fiscal or monetary policy is an effective policy tool.

2. Those within the Fed who advocated lowering interest rates were focused on boosting aggregate demand in order to counteract the negative demand shock caused by the collapse of the housing bubble. Lowering interest rates will result in a rightward shift of the aggregate demand curve, increasing aggregate output but raising the aggregate price level. Those within the Fed who advocated holding interest rates steady were focused on the fact that fighting the slump in aggregate demand in the face of a negative supply shock could result in a rise in inflation. Holding interest rates steady relies on the ability of the economy to self-correct in the long run, with the aggregate price level and aggregate output only gradually returning to their levels before the negative supply shock.

CHAPTER THIRTEEN

13-1 Check Your Understanding

1. **a.** This is contractionary fiscal policy because it is a reduction in government purchases of goods and services.

   b. This is expansionary fiscal policy because it is an increase in government transfers that will increase disposable income.

   c. This is contractionary fiscal policy because it is an increase in taxes that will reduce disposable income.

2. Federal disaster relief that is quickly disbursed is more effective than legislated aid because there is very little time lag between the time of the disaster and the time it is received by victims. So it will stabilize the economy after a disaster. In contrast, legislated aid is likely to entail a time lag in its disbursement, potentially destabilizing the economy.

3. This statement implies that expansionary fiscal policy will result in crowding out of the private sector, and that the opposite, contractionary fiscal policy, will lead the private sector to grow. Whether this statement is true or not depends on whether the economy is at full employment; it is only then that we should expect expansionary fiscal policy to lead to crowding out. If, instead, the economy has a recessionary gap, then we should expect instead that the private sector grows along with the fiscal expansion, and contracts along with a fiscal contraction.

13-2 Check Your Understanding

1. A $500 million increase in government purchases of goods and services directly increases aggregate spending by $500 million, which then starts the multiplier in motion. It will increase real GDP by $500 million $\times 1/(1 - MPC)$. A $500 million increase in government transfers increases aggregate spending only to the extent that it leads to an increase in consumer spending. Consumer spending rises by $MPC \times \$1$ for every $1 increase in disposable income, where MPC is less than 1. So a $500 million increase in government transfers will cause a rise in real GDP only MPC times as much as a $500 million increase in government purchases of goods and services. It will increase real GDP by $500 million $\times MPC/(1 - MPC)$.

2. This is the same issue as in Problem 1, but in reverse. If government purchases of goods and services fall by $500 million, the initial fall in aggregate spending is $500 million. If there is a $500 million reduction in government transfers, the initial fall in aggregate spending is $MPC \times \$500$ million, which is less than $500 million.

3. Boldovia will experience greater variation in its real GDP than Moldovia because Moldovia has automatic stabilizers while Boldovia does not. In Moldovia the effects of slumps will be lessened by unemployment insurance benefits that will support residents' incomes, while the effects of booms will be diminished because tax revenues will go up. In contrast, incomes will not be supported in Boldovia during slumps because there is no unemployment insurance. In addition, because Boldovia has lump-sum taxes, its booms will not be diminished by increases in tax revenue.

13-3 Check Your Understanding

1. The actual budget balance takes into account the effects of the business cycle on the budget deficit. During recessionary gaps, it incorporates the effect of lower tax revenues and higher transfers on the budget balance; during inflationary gaps, it incorporates the effect of higher tax revenues and reduced transfers. In contrast, the cyclically adjusted budget balance factors out the effects of the business cycle and assumes that real GDP is at potential output. Since, in the long run, real GDP tends to potential output, the cyclically adjusted budget balance is a better measure of the long-run sustainability of government policies.

2. In recessions, real GDP falls. This implies that consumers' incomes, consumer spending, and producers' profits also fall. So in recessions, states' tax revenue (which depends in large part on consumers' incomes, consumer spending, and producers' profits) falls. In order to balance the state budget, states have to cut spending or raise taxes. But that deepens the recession. Without a balanced-budget requirement, states could use expansionary fiscal policy during a recession to lessen the fall in real GDP.

13-4 Check Your Understanding

1. **a.** A higher growth rate of real GDP implies that tax revenue will increase. If government spending remains constant and the government runs a budget surplus, the size of the public debt will be less than it would otherwise have been.

   b. If retirees live longer, the average age of the population increases. As a result, the implicit liabilities of the government increase because spending on programs for older Americans, such as Social Security and Medicare, will rise.

   c. A decrease in tax revenue without offsetting reductions in government spending will cause the public debt to increase.

   d. Public debt will increase as a result of government borrowing to pay interest on its current public debt.

2. In order to stimulate the economy in the short run, the government can use fiscal policy to increase real GDP. This entails borrowing, increasing the size of the public debt further and leading to undesirable consequences: in extreme cases, governments can be forced to default on their debts. Even in less extreme cases, a large public debt is undesirable because government borrowing crowds out borrowing for private investment spending. This reduces the amount of investment spending, reducing the long-run growth of the economy.

3. A contractionary fiscal policy like austerity reduces government spending, which in turn reduces income and reduces tax revenue. With less tax revenue, the government is less able to pay its debts. Also, a failing economy causes lenders to have less confidence that a government is able to pay its debts and leads them to raise interest rates on the debt. Higher interest rates on the debt make it even less likely the government can repay.

CHAPTER FOURTEEN

14-1 Check Your Understanding

1. The defining characteristic of money is its liquidity: how easily it can be used to purchase goods and services. Although a gift card can easily be used to purchase a very defined set of goods or services (the goods or services available at the store issuing the gift card), it cannot be used to

purchase any other goods or services. A gift card is therefore not money, since it cannot easily be used to purchase all goods and services.

2. Again, the important characteristic of money is its liquidity: how easily it can be used to purchase goods and services. M1, the narrowest definition of the money supply, contains only currency in circulation and checkable bank deposits. CDs aren't checkable—and they can't be made checkable without incurring a cost because there's a penalty for early withdrawal. This makes them less liquid than the assets counted in M1.

3. Commodity-backed money uses resources more efficiently than simple commodity money, like gold and silver coins, because commodity-backed money ties up fewer valuable resources. Although a bank must keep some of the commodity—generally gold and silver—on hand, it only has to keep enough to satisfy demand for redemptions. It can then lend out the remaining gold and silver, which allows society to use these resources for other purposes, with no loss in the ability to achieve gains from trade.

14-2 Check Your Understanding

1. Even though you know that the rumor about the bank is not true, you are concerned about other depositors pulling their money out of the bank. And you know that if enough other depositors pull their money out, the bank will fail. In that case, it is rational for you to pull your money out before the bank fails. All depositors will think like this, so even if they all know that the rumor is false, they may still rationally pull their money out, leading to a bank run. Deposit insurance leads depositors to worry less about the possibility of a bank run. Even if a bank fails, the FDIC will currently pay each depositor up to $250,000 per account. This will make you much less likely to pull your money out in response to a rumor. Since other depositors will think the same, there will be no bank run.

2. The aspects of modern bank regulation that would frustrate this scheme are *capital requirements* and *reserve requirements*. Capital requirements mean that a bank has to have a certain amount of capital—the difference between its assets (loans plus reserves) and its liabilities (deposits). So the con artist could not open a bank without putting any of their own wealth in because the bank needs a certain amount of capital—that is, it needs to hold more assets (loans plus reserves) than deposits. So the con artist would be at risk of losing their own wealth if their loans turn out badly.

14-3 Check Your Understanding

1. Since they only have to hold $100 in reserves, instead of $200, banks now lend out $100 of their reserves. Whoever borrows the $100 will deposit it in a bank, which will lend out $100 × (1 − rr) = $100 × 0.9 = $90. Whoever borrows the $90 will put it into a bank, which will lend out $90 × 0.9 = $81 , and so on. Overall, deposits will increase by $100/0.1 = $1, 000.

2. Silas puts $1,000 in the bank, of which the bank lends out $1,000 × (1 − rr) = $1,000 × 0.9 = $900. Whoever borrows the $900 will keep $450 in cash and deposit $450 in a bank. The bank will lend out $450 × 0.9 = $405. Whoever borrows the $405 will keep $202.50 in cash and deposit $202.50 in a

bank. The bank will lend out $202.50 × 0.9 = $182.25, and so on. Overall, this leads to an increase in deposits of $1,000 + $450 + $202.50 + ⋯. But it decreases the amount of currency in circulation: the amount of cash is reduced by the $1,000 Silas puts into the bank. This is offset, but not fully, by the amount of cash held by each borrower. The amount of currency in circulation therefore changes by −$1,000 + $450 + $202.50 + ⋯. The money supply therefore increases by the sum of the increase in deposits and the change in currency in circulation, which is $1,000 − $1,000 + $450 + $450 + $202.50 + $202.50 + ⋯ and so on.

14-4 Check Your Understanding

1. An open-market purchase of $100 million by the Fed increases banks' reserves by $100 million as the Fed credits their accounts with additional reserves. In other words, this open-market purchase increases the monetary base (currency in circulation plus bank reserves) by $100 million. Banks lend out the additional $100 million. Whoever borrows the money puts it back into the banking system in the form of deposits. Of these deposits, banks lend out $100 million × (1 − rr) = $100 million × 0.9 = $90 million. Whoever borrows the money deposits it back into the banking system. And banks lend out $90 million × 0.9 = $81 million, and so on. As a result, bank deposits increase by $100 million + $90 million + $81 million + ⋯ = $100 million/rr = $100 million/0.1 = $1,000 million = $1 billion. Since in this simplified example all money lent out is deposited back into the banking system, there is no increase of currency in circulation, so the increase in bank deposits is equal to the increase in the money supply. In other words, the money supply increases by $1 billion. This is greater than the increase in the monetary base by a factor of 10: in this simplified model in which deposits are the only component of the money supply and in which banks hold no excess reserves, the money multiplier is 1/rr = 10.

14-5 Check Your Understanding

1. The Panic of 1907, the S&L crisis, and the crisis of 2008 all involved losses by shadow bank–like financial institutions that were less regulated than traditional depository banks. In the crises of 1907 and 2008, there was a widespread loss of confidence in the financial sector and a collapse of credit markets. Like the crisis of 1907 and the S&L crisis, the crisis of 2008 exerted a powerful negative effect on the economy.

2. The creation of the Federal Reserve failed to prevent bank runs because it did not eradicate the fears of depositors that a bank collapse would cause them to lose their money. The bank runs eventually stopped after federal deposit insurance was instituted and the public came to understand that their deposits were now protected.

3. Extraordinary measures were needed to address the financial crisis of 2008 because the failure of unregulated shadow banks, like Lehman Brothers, led to increased panic in markets as asset prices tumbled and credit markets froze for households and businesses. The failure of shadow banks also put the entire financial system at risk of failure, both the financially sound traditional depository banks and nondepository financial institutions, that were eventually deemed too critical to the economy to fail.

|| CHAPTER FIFTEEN

15-1 Check Your Understanding

1. **a.** By increasing the opportunity cost of holding money, a high interest rate reduces the quantity of money demanded. This is a movement up and to the left along the money demand curve.

    b. A 10% fall in prices reduces the quantity of money demanded at any given interest rate, shifting the money demand curve leftward.

    c. This technological change reduces the quantity of money demanded at any given interest rate. So it shifts the money demand curve leftward.

    d. This will increase the demand for money at any given interest rate. With more of the economy's assets in overseas bank accounts that are difficult to access, people will want to hold more cash to finance purchases. The money demand curve shifts to the right.

2. **a.** The 0.5% interest paid on cash balances will reduce the opportunity cost of holding cash for PayBuddy customers because they now forgo less by holding cash.

    b. An increase in the interest paid on six-month CDs raises the opportunity cost of holding cash because holding cash requires forgoing the higher interest paid.

    c. One year of zero-interest financing on holiday purchases increases the opportunity cost of holding cash. A holiday shopper need not convert interest-paying assets into cash in order to avoid paying interest on credit card purchases. So what a shopper forgoes by paying for holiday purchases with cash instead of charging it on a credit card has increased.

15-2 Check Your Understanding

1. In the accompanying diagram, the increase in the demand for money is shown as a rightward shift of the money demand curve, from MD_1 to MD_2. This raises the equilibrium interest rate from r_1 to r_2

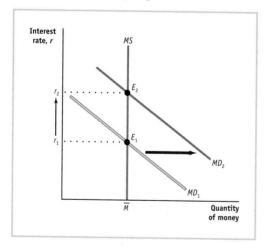

2. In order to prevent the interest rate from rising, the Federal Reserve must make an open-market purchase of Treasury bills, shifting the money supply curve rightward. This is shown in the accompanying diagram as the move from MS_1 to MS_2.

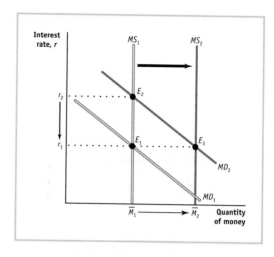

3. **a.** Malia is better off buying a one-year bond today and a one-year bond next year because this allows her to get the higher interest rate one year from now.

    b. Malia is better off buying a two-year bond today because it gives her a higher interest rate in the second year than if she bought two one-year bonds.

15-3 Check Your Understanding

1. **a.** The money supply curve shifts to the right.

    b. The equilibrium interest rate falls.

    c. Investment spending rises, due to the fall in the interest rate.

    d. Consumer spending rises, due to the multiplier process.

    e. Aggregate output rises because of the rightward shift of the aggregate demand curve.

2. The central bank that uses a Taylor rule is likely to respond more directly to a financial crisis than one that uses inflation targeting because with a Taylor rule the central bank does not have to set policy to meet a prespecified inflation target. Additionally, under the Taylor rule, central banks will respond directly to a change in the unemployment rate because in a financial crisis unemployment is more likely to increase than inflation is to decrease.

15-4 Check Your Understanding

1. **a.** Aggregate output rises in the short run, then falls back to equal potential output in the long run.

    b. The aggregate price level rises in the short run, but by less than 25%. It rises further in the long run, for a total increase of 25%.

    c. The interest rate falls in the short run, then rises back to its original level in the long run.

2. In the short run, a change in the interest rate alters the economy because it affects investment spending, which in turn affects aggregate demand and real GDP through the multiplier process. However, in the long run, changes in consumer spending and investment spending will eventually result in changes in nominal wages and the nominal prices of other factors of production. For example, an expansionary monetary policy will eventually cause a rise in factor prices; a contractionary policy will eventually cause a fall in factor prices. In response, the short-run

aggregate supply curve will shift to move the economy back to long-run equilibrium. So in the long run, monetary policy has no effect on the economy.

CHAPTER SIXTEEN

16-1 Check Your Understanding

1. The inflation rate is more likely to quickly reflect changes in the money supply when the economy has had an extended period of high inflation. That's because an extended period of high inflation sensitizes workers and firms to raise nominal wages and prices of intermediate goods when the aggregate price level rises. As a result, there will be little or no increase in real output in the short run after an increase in the money supply, and the increase in the money supply will simply be reflected in an equal-sized percent increase in prices. In an economy where people are not sensitized to high inflation because of low inflation in the past, an increase in the money supply will lead to an increase in real output in the short run. This illustrates the fact that the classical model of the price level best applies to economies with persistently high inflation, not those with little or no history of high inflation even though they may currently have high inflation.

2. Yes, there can still be an inflation tax because the tax is levied on people who hold money. As long as people hold money, regardless of whether prices are indexed or not, the government is able to use seigniorage to capture real resources from the public.

16-2 Check Your Understanding

1. When real GDP equals potential output, cyclical unemployment is zero and the unemployment rate is equal to the natural rate. Assuming a 0% expected inflation rate, this also corresponds to a 6% unemployment rate on curve E_1 in Figure 6. Any unemployment in excess of this 6% rate, or less than the 6% rate, represents cyclical unemployment. An increase in aggregate demand leads to a fall in the unemployment rate below the natural rate (negative cyclical unemployment) and an increase in the inflation rate. A reduction in aggregate demand leads to a rise in the unemployment rate above the natural rate (positive cyclical unemployment) and a fall in the inflation rate. So for a given expected inflation rate, the short-run Phillips curve illustrates the relationship between cyclical unemployment and the actual inflation rate.

2. A fall in commodities prices leads to a positive supply shock, which lowers the aggregate price level and reduces inflation. As a result, any given level of unemployment can be sustained with a lower inflation rate now—meaning that the short-run Phillips curve has shifted downward. In contrast, a surge in commodities prices leads to a negative supply shock, which raises the aggregate price level and increases inflation. Any given level of unemployment can be sustained only with a higher inflation rate—meaning that the short-run Phillips curve has shifted upward.

16-3 Check Your Understanding

1. There is no long-run trade-off between unemployment and inflation because once expectations of inflation adjust, wages will also adjust, returning employment and the unemployment rate to their equilibrium (natural) levels.

This implies that once expectations of inflation fully adjust to any change in actual inflation, the unemployment rate will return to the natural rate of unemployment, or NAIRU. This also implies that the long-run Phillips curve is vertical.

2. There are two possible explanations for this. First, negative supply shocks (for example, increases in the price of oil) will cause an increase in unemployment and an increase in inflation. Second, it is possible that British policy makers attempted to lower the unemployment rate below the natural rate of unemployment. Any attempt to lower the unemployment rate below the natural rate will result in an increase in inflation.

3. Disinflation is costly because to reduce the inflation rate, aggregate output in the short run must typically fall below potential output. This, in turn, results in an increase in the unemployment rate above the natural rate. In general, we would observe a reduction in real GDP. The costs of any disinflation will be lower if the central bank is credible and it announces in advance its policy to reduce inflation. In this situation, the adjustment to the disinflationary policy will be more rapid, resulting in a smaller loss of aggregate output.

16-4 Check Your Understanding

1. If the nominal interest rate is negative, an individual is better off simply holding cash, which has a 0% nominal rate of return. If the options facing an individual are to lend and receive a negative nominal interest rate or to hold cash and receive a 0% nominal interest rate, the individual will hold cash. Such a scenario creates the possibility of a liquidity trap, in which monetary policy is ineffective because the nominal interest rate cannot fall more than a small amount below zero. Once the nominal interest rate falls to zero, further increases in the money supply will lead firms and individuals to simply hold the additional cash.

CHAPTER SEVENTEEN

17-1 Check Your Understanding

1. A classical economist would have said that although expansionary monetary policy would probably have some effect in the short run, the short run was unimportant. Instead, a classical economist would have stressed the long run, claiming expansionary monetary policy would result only in an increase in the aggregate price level without affecting aggregate output.

2. The statement would seem very familiar to a Keynesian economist. According to Keynes, business confidence (which he called "animal spirits") is mainly responsible for recessions. If business confidence is low, a Keynesian economist would think of this as a case for macroeconomic policy activism: that the government should use expansionary monetary and fiscal policy to help the economy recover.

17-2 Check Your Understanding

1. Fiscal policy is limited by time lags in recognizing economic problems, forming a response, passing legislation, and implementing the policies. Monetary policy is also limited by time lags, but these lags are not as severe as those for fiscal policy because the Federal Reserve tends

to act more quickly than Congress. Attempts to reduce unemployment below the natural rate via both fiscal and monetary policy are limited by predictions of the natural rate hypothesis: that these attempts will result in accelerating inflation. Also, both fiscal and monetary policy are limited by concerns about the political business cycle: that they will be used to satisfy political ends and will end up destabilizing the economy.

2. **a.** It's likely that Milton Friedman would have agreed with the Fed policy of accelerating the growth of M1, because we know that Friedman believed that the Fed should have undertaken a more expansionary monetary policy in the wake of the Great Depression. Although he may have expressed caution over using discretionary policy.

   b. The monetarist objections to fiscal policy are based on the problems of time lags in its implementation and crowding out. Monetarists also believe time lags undermine the effectiveness of monetary policy, but to a lesser extent than with fiscal policy. However, none of these objections applied during the Great Recession. Because it lasted so long, both fiscal policy and monetary policy were effective despite time lags. And because interest rates and investment spending plunged, crowding out by fiscal policy was not a problem.

3. **a.** Rational expectations theorists would argue that only unexpected changes in the money supply would have any short-run effect on economic activity. They would also argue that expected changes in the money supply would affect only the aggregate price level, with no short-run effect on aggregate output. So such theorists would give credit to the Fed for limiting the severity of the Great Recession only if the Fed's monetary policy had been more aggressive than individuals expected during this period.

   b. Real business cycle theorists would argue that the Fed's policy had no effect on ending the Great Recession because they believe that fluctuations in aggregate output are caused largely by changes in total factor productivity.

17-3 Check Your Understanding

1. The liquidity trap brought on by the Great Recession greatly diminished the Great Moderation consensus, which considered monetary policy to be the main policy tool, and monetary policy was now largely ineffective. The continuing disagreements over fiscal policy were brought to the forefront. The dismal experience of European countries that had adopted fiscal austerity, when compared to the faster recovery of the United States, which had adopted fiscal expansionary policies, has led most economists to more or less agree with the Keynesian view about the effects of fiscal policy.

2. The Fed was criticized by some individuals who thought it was doing too much and by secular stagnationists who thought it was doing too little. Some individuals believed that the huge increase in the monetary base and quantitative easing would lead to high inflation. Secular stagnationists believed the economy was in a liquidity trap and in a state of secular stagnation. Therefore, the stagnationists advocated for a higher inflation target that would allow the Fed to push the real interest rate down while the nominal rate was near zero.

17-4 Check Your Understanding

1. Food and energy prices tend to be volatile and unrelated to economic policy. Turmoil in the Middle East will cause the price of oil to increase and droughts in California would do the same for food prices. By focusing on "core" inflation the Fed can better estimate how shifts in aggregate demand and aggregate supply affect inflation.

2. The pandemic forced more people to work from home which required them to purchase home office furniture. But the buying frenzy didn't stop there. With nearly all forms of recreation shutdown households increased their purchases of exercise equipment, TVs, outdoor furniture, and other recreational equipment.

CHAPTER EIGHTEEN

18-1 Check Your Understanding

1. **a.** The sale of the new airplane to China represents an export of a good to China and so enters the current account.

   b. The sale of Boeing stock to Chinese investors is a sale of a U.S. asset and so enters the financial account.

   c. Even though the plane already exists, when it is shipped to China it is an export of a good from the United States. So the sale of the plane enters the current account.

   d. Because the plane stays in the United States, the Chinese investor is buying a U.S. asset. So this is identical to the answer to part b: the sale of the jet enters the financial account.

2. The collapse of the U.S. housing bubble and the ensuing recession led to a dramatic fall in interest rates in the United States because of the deeply depressed economy. Consequently, capital inflows into the United States dried up.

18-2 Check Your Understanding

1. **a.** The increased purchase of Mexican oil will cause U.S. individuals (and firms) to increase their demand for the peso. To purchase pesos, individuals will increase their supply of U.S. dollars to the foreign exchange market, causing a rightward shift in the supply curve of U.S. dollars. This will cause the peso price of the dollar to fall (the amount of pesos per dollar will fall). The peso has appreciated and the U.S. dollar has depreciated as a result.

   b. This appreciation of the peso means it will take more U.S. dollars to obtain the same quantity of Mexican pesos. If we assume that the price level (measured in Mexican pesos) of other Mexican goods and services does not change, other Mexican goods and services become more expensive to U.S. households and firms. The dollar cost of other Mexican goods and services will rise as the peso appreciates. So Mexican exports to the United States of goods and services other than oil will fall.

   c. Assuming that the U.S. price level (measured in U.S. dollars) does not change, the appreciation of the peso will make U.S. goods and services cheaper in terms of pesos. So Mexican imports from the United States of goods and services will rise.

2. a. The real exchange rate equals

$$\text{Pesos per U.S. dollar} \times \frac{\text{Aggregate price level in the U.S.}}{\text{Aggregate price level in Mexico}}$$

Today, the aggregate price levels in both countries are both equal to 100. The real exchange rate today is $10 \times (100/100) = 10$. The aggregate price level in five years in the United States will be $100 \times (120/100) = 120$, and in Mexico it will be $100 \times (1,200/800) = 150$. The real exchange rate in five years, assuming the nominal exchange rate does not change, will be $10 \times (120/150) = 8$.

b. Today, a basket of goods and services that costs $100 costs 800 pesos, so the purchasing power parity is 8 pesos per U.S. dollar. In five years, a basket that costs $120 will cost 1,200 pesos, so the purchasing power parity will be 10 pesos per U.S. dollar.

18-3 Check Your Understanding

1. The accompanying diagram shows the supply of and demand for the yuan, with the U.S. dollar price of the yuan on the vertical axis. In 2005, prior to the revaluation, the exchange rate was pegged at 8.28 yuan per U.S. dollar or, equivalently, 0.121 U.S. dollars per yuan ($0.121). At the target exchange rate of $0.121, the quantity of yuan demanded exceeded the quantity of yuan supplied, creating the shortage depicted in the diagram. Without any intervention by the Chinese government, the U.S. dollar price of the yuan would have been bid up, causing an appreciation of the yuan. The Chinese government, however, intervened to prevent this appreciation.

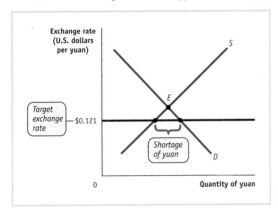

a. If the exchange rate is allowed to move freely, the U.S. dollar price of the exchange rate will move toward the equilibrium exchange rate (labeled XR^* in the accompanying diagram). This will occur as a result of the shortage, when buyers of the yuan will bid up its U.S. dollar price. As the exchange rate increases, the quantity of yuan demanded will fall and the quantity of yuan supplied will increase. If the exchange rate increases to XR^*, the disequilibrium will be entirely eliminated.

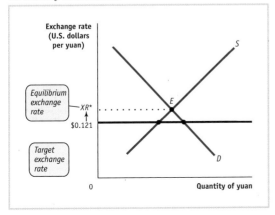

b. Placing restrictions on foreigners who want to invest in China will reduce the demand for the yuan, causing the demand curve to shift in the accompanying diagram from D_1 to a position like D_2. This will cause a reduction in the shortage of the yuan. If demand fell to D_3, the disequilibrium will be completely eliminated.

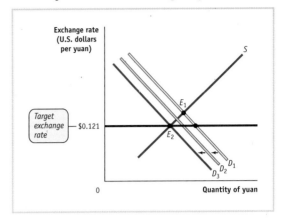

c. Removing restrictions on Chinese who wish to invest abroad will cause an increase in the supply of the yuan and a rightward shift in the supply curve. This increase in supply will also cause a reduction in the size of the shortage. If, for example, supply increased from S_1 to S_2, the disequilibrium will be eliminated completely in the accompanying diagram.

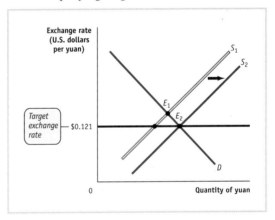

d. Imposing a tax on exports (Chinese goods sold to foreigners) will raise the price of these goods and decrease the amount of Chinese goods purchased. This will also decrease the demand for the yuan. The graphical analysis here is virtually identical to that found in the figure accompanying part b.

18-4 Check Your Understanding

1. The devaluations and revaluations most likely occurred in those periods when there was a sudden change in the franc–mark exchange rate: 1974, 1976, the early 1980s, 1986, and 1993–1994.

2. The high Canadian interest rates would likely have caused an increase in capital inflows to Canada. To obtain these assets (which yielded a relatively higher interest rate) in Canada, investors would first have had to obtain Canadian dollars. The increase in the demand for the Canadian dollar would have caused the Canadian dollar to appreciate. This appreciation of the Canadian currency would have raised the price of Canadian goods to foreigners (measured in terms of the foreign currency). This would have made it more difficult for Canadian firms to compete in other markets.

Glossary

A

absolute advantage the advantage a country has in producing a good or service if the country can produce more output per worker than other countries. Likewise, an individual has an absolute advantage in producing a good or service if they are better at producing it than other people. Having an absolute advantage is not the same thing as having a comparative advantage.

absolute value the value of a number without regard to a plus or minus sign.

accelerator principle the proposition that a higher growth rate in real GDP results in a higher level of planned investment spending, and a lower growth rate in real GDP leads to lower planned investment spending.

actual investment spending the sum of planned investment spending and unplanned inventory investment.

AD–AS model the basic model used to understand fluctuations in aggregate output and the inflation rate. It uses the aggregate supply curve and the aggregate demand curve together to analyze the behavior of the economy in response to shocks or government policy.

aggregate consumption function the relationship for the economy as a whole between aggregate current disposable income and aggregate consumer spending.

aggregate demand curve a graphical representation that shows the relationship between the inflation rate and the quantity of aggregate output demanded by households, firms, the government, and the rest of the world. The aggregate demand curve has a negative slope as the inflation rate declines the quantity of aggregate demand increases.

aggregate output the total quantity of final goods and services the economy produces for a given time period, usually a year. Real GDP is the numerical measure of aggregate output typically used by economists.

aggregate price level a single number that represents the overall price level for final goods and services in the economy.

aggregate production function a hypothetical function that shows how productivity (real GDP per worker) depends on the quantities of physical capital per worker and human capital per worker as well as the state of technology.

aggregate spending the total flow of funds into markets for domestically produced final goods and services; the sum of consumer spending, investment spending, government purchases of goods and services, and exports minus imports.

aggregate supply curve a graphical representation that shows the relationship between the inflation rate and the total quantity of aggregate output supplied.

appreciation a rise in the value of one currency in terms of other currencies.

austerity policy a policy that tries to limit government borrowing by cutting spending and raising taxes.

autarky a situation in which a country does not trade with other countries.

automatic stabilizers government spending and taxation rules that cause fiscal policy to be automatically expansionary when the economy contracts and automatically contractionary when the economy expands without requiring any deliberate actions by policy makers. Taxes that depend on disposable income are the most important example of automatic stabilizers.

autonomous change in aggregate spending an initial rise or fall in aggregate spending at a given level of real GDP.

B

balance of payments accounts a summary of a country's transactions with other countries for a given year, including two main elements: the balance of payments on current account and the balance of payments on financial account.

balance of payments on current account (current account) transactions that don't create liabilities; a country's balance of payments on goods and services plus net international transfer payments and factor income.

balance of payments on financial account (financial account) international transactions that involve the sale or purchase of assets, and therefore create future liabilities.

balance of payments on goods and services the difference between the value of exports and the value of imports of a country during a given period.

bank a financial intermediary that provides liquid assets in the form of bank deposits to lenders and uses those funds to finance the illiquid investments or investment spending needs of borrowers.

bank deposit a claim on a bank that obliges the bank to give the depositor their cash when demanded.

bank reserves currency held by banks in their vaults plus their deposits at the Federal Reserve.

bank run a phenomenon in which many of a bank's depositors try to withdraw their funds because of fears of a bank failure.

bar graph a graph that uses bars of varying heights or lengths to show the comparative sizes of different observations of a variable.

barter trade in the form of the direct exchange of goods or services for other goods or services that people want.

budget balance the difference between tax revenue and government spending. A positive budget balance is referred to as a budget surplus; a negative budget balance is referred to as a budget deficit.

budget deficit the difference between tax revenue and government spending when government spending exceeds tax revenue; dissaving by the government in the form of a budget deficit is a negative contribution to national savings.

budget surplus the difference between tax revenue and government spending when tax revenue exceeds government spending; saving by the government in the form of a budget surplus is a positive contribution to national savings.

business cycle the short-run alternation between economic downturns, known as recessions, and economic upturns, known as expansions.

business-cycle peak the point in time at which the economy shifts from expansion to recession.

business-cycle trough the point in time at which the economy shifts from recession to expansion.

C

causal relationship the relationship between two variables in which the value taken by one variable directly influences or determines the value taken by the other variable.

central bank an institution that oversees and regulates the banking system and controls the monetary base.

certificate of deposit (CD) a bank-issued asset in which customers deposit funds for a specified amount of time and earn a specified interest rate.

chained dollars method of calculating real GDP that splits the difference between growth rates calculated using early base years and the growth rate calculated using a late base year.

checkable bank deposits bank accounts that can be accessed by using checks, debit cards, and digital payments.

circular-flow diagram a diagram that represents the transactions in an economy by two kinds of flows around a circle: flows of physical things such as goods or labor in one direction and flows of money to pay for these physical things in the opposite direction.

classical model of the price level a simplified financial model of the price level in which the real quantity of money, M/P, is always at its long-run equilibrium level. This model ignores the distinction between the short run and the long run but is useful for analyzing the case of high inflation.

commercial bank a bank that accepts deposits and is covered by deposit insurance.

commodity-backed money a medium of exchange that has no intrinsic value, whose ultimate value is guaranteed by a promise that it can be converted into valuable goods on demand.

commodity money a medium of exchange that is a good, normally gold or silver, that has intrinsic value in other uses.

comparative advantage the advantage a country has in producing a good or service if its opportunity cost of producing the good or service is lower than other countries' cost. Likewise, an individual has a comparative advantage in producing a good or service if their opportunity

cost of producing the good or service is lower than it is for other people.

competitive market a market in which there are many buyers and sellers of the same good or service, none of whom can influence the price at which the good or service is sold.

complements pairs of goods for which a rise in the price of one good leads to a decrease in the demand for the other good.

consumer price index (CPI) a measure of prices; calculated by surveying market prices for a market basket intended to represent the consumption of a typical urban American family of four. The CPI is the most commonly used measure of prices in the United States.

consumer spending household spending on goods and services from domestic and foreign firms.

consumer surplus a term often used to refer both to individual consumer surplus and to total consumer surplus.

consumption function an equation showing how an individual household's consumer spending varies with the household's current disposable income.

contractionary fiscal policy fiscal policy that reduces aggregate demand by decreasing government purchases, increasing taxes, or decreasing transfers.

contractionary monetary policy monetary policy that, through the raising of the interest rate, reduces aggregate demand and therefore output.

convergence hypothesis a principle of economic growth that holds that international differences in real GDP per capita tend to narrow over time because countries that start with lower real GDP per capita tend to have higher growth rates.

cost (of seller) the lowest price at which a seller is willing to sell a good.

crowding out the negative effect of budget deficits on private investment, which occurs because government borrowing drives up interest rates.

currency in circulation actual cash held by the public.

curve a line on a graph, which may be curved or straight, that depicts a relationship between two variables.

cyclical unemployment the difference between the actual rate of unemployment and the natural rate of unemployment due to downturns in the business cycle.

cyclically adjusted budget balance an estimate of what the budget balance would be if real GDP were exactly equal to potential output.

D

debt deflation the reduction in aggregate demand arising from the increase in the real burden of outstanding debt caused by deflation; occurs because borrowers, whose real debt rises as a result of deflation, are likely to cut spending sharply, and lenders, whose real assets are now more valuable, are less likely to increase spending.

debt–GDP ratio government debt as a percentage of GDP, frequently used as a measure of a government's ability to pay its debts.

debt spiral when the interest on government debt drives that debt even higher.

default the failure of a bond issuer to make payments as specified by the bond contract.

deflation a fall in the overall level of prices.

demand curve a graphical representation of the demand schedule. It shows the relationship between quantity demanded and price.

demand price the price of a given quantity at which consumers will demand that quantity.

demand schedule a list or table showing how much of a good or service consumers will want to buy at different prices.

demand shock an event that shifts the aggregate demand curve. A positive demand shock is associated with higher demand for aggregate output at any inflation rate and shifts the curve to the right. A negative demand shock is associated with lower demand for aggregate output at any inflation rate and shifts the curve to the left.

dependent variable the determined variable in a causal relationship.

deposit insurance a guarantee that a bank's depositors will be paid even if the bank can't come up with the funds, up to a maximum amount per account.

depreciation a fall in the value of one currency in terms of other currencies.

devaluation a reduction in the value of a currency that is set under a fixed exchange rate regime.

diminishing returns to physical capital in an aggregate production function when the amount of human capital per worker and the state of technology are held fixed, each successive increase in the amount of physical capital per worker leads to a smaller increase in productivity.

discount rate the rate of interest the Federal Reserve charges on loans to banks that fall short of reserve requirements.

discount window a protection against bank runs in which the Federal Reserve stands ready to lend money to banks in trouble.

discouraged workers individuals who want to work but who have stated to government researchers that they aren't currently searching for a job because they see little prospect of finding one given the state of the job market.

discretionary fiscal policy fiscal policy that is the direct result of deliberate actions by policy makers rather than automatic adjustments or rules.

discretionary monetary policy policy actions, either changes in interest rates or changes in the money supply, undertaken by the central bank based on its assessment of the state of the economy.

disinflation the process of bringing down inflation that has become embedded in expectations.

diversification investment in several different assets with unrelated, or independent, risks, so that the possible losses are independent events.

domestic demand curve a demand curve that shows how the quantity of a good demanded by domestic consumers depends on the price of that good.

domestic supply curve a supply curve that shows how the quantity of a good supplied by domestic producers depends on the price of that good.

E

economic growth the growing ability of the economy to produce goods and services, leading to higher living standards.

economics the social science that studies the production, distribution, and consumption of goods and services.

economy a system for coordinating society's productive activities.

efficiency wages wages that employers set above the equilibrium wage rate as an incentive for workers to deliver better performance.

efficient description of a market or economy that takes all opportunities to make some people better off without making other people worse off.

efficient markets hypothesis a principle of asset price determination that holds that asset prices embody all publicly available information. The hypothesis implies that stock prices should be unpredictable, or follow a random walk, since changes should occur only in response to new information about fundamentals.

employment the total number of people currently employed for pay in the economy, either full time or part time.

equilibrium an economic situation in which no individual would be better off doing something different.

equilibrium exchange rate the exchange rate at which the quantity of a currency demanded in the foreign exchange market is equal to the quantity supplied.

equilibrium interest rate a situation where the interest rate at which the quantity of loanable funds supplied equals the quantity of loanable funds demanded.

equilibrium price the price at which the market is in equilibrium, that is, the quantity of a good or service demanded equals the quantity of that good or service supplied; also referred to as the market-clearing price.

equilibrium quantity the quantity of a good or service bought and sold at the equilibrium (or market-clearing) price.

equity fairness; everyone gets their fair share. Since people can disagree about what is "fair," equity is not as well defined a concept as efficiency.

European Union (EU) a customs union among 27 European nations.

excess reserves a bank's reserves over and above the reserves required by law or regulation.

exchange market intervention government purchases or sales of currency in the foreign exchange market.

exchange rate the price at which currencies trade, determined by the foreign exchange market.

exchange rate regime a rule governing policy toward the exchange rate.

expansion a period of economic upturn in which output and employment are rising; most economic numbers are following their normal upward trend; also referred to as a recovery.

expansionary fiscal policy fiscal policy that increases aggregate demand by increasing government purchases, decreasing taxes, or increasing transfers.

expansionary monetary policy monetary policy that, through the lowering of the interest rate, increases aggregate demand and therefore output.

expected rate of inflation the inflation rate that businesses and workers are expecting in the near future.

exporting industries industries that produce goods and services that are sold abroad.

exports goods and services sold to other countries.

F

factor intensity a measure of which factor is used in relatively greater quantities than other factors in production. For example, oil refining is capital-intensive compared to auto seat production because oil refiners use a higher ratio of capital to labor than do producers of auto seats.

factor markets markets in which firms buy the resources they need to produce goods and services.

factors of production the resources used to produce goods and services.

federal funds market a financial market that allows banks that fall short of reserve requirements to borrow funds from banks with excess reserves.

federal funds rate the interest rate at which funds are borrowed and lent in the federal funds market.

fiat money a medium of exchange whose value derives entirely from its official status as a means of payment.

final goods and services goods and services sold to the final, or end, user.

financial asset a paper claim that entitles the buyer to future income from the seller. Loans, stocks, bonds, and bank deposits are types of financial assets.

financial intermediary an institution, such as a mutual fund, pension fund, life insurance company, or bank, that transforms the funds it gathers from many individuals into financial assets.

financial markets the banking, stock, and bond markets, which channel private savings and foreign lending into investment spending, government borrowing, and foreign borrowing.

financial risk uncertainty about future outcomes that involve financial losses or gains.

firm an organization that produces goods and services for sale.

fiscal policy changes in government spending and taxes designed to affect overall spending.

fiscal stimulus expansionary fiscal policy that takes the form of temporary spending measures and temporary tax cuts.

fiscal year the time period used for much of government accounting, running from October 1 to September 30 in the United States. Fiscal years are labeled by the calendar year in which they end.

Fisher effect the principle by which an increase in expected future inflation drives up the nominal interest rate, leaving the expected real interest rate unchanged.

fixed exchange rate an exchange rate regime in which the government keeps the exchange rate against some other currency at or near a particular target.

floating exchange rate an exchange rate regime in which the government lets market forces determine the exchange rate.

forecast a simple prediction of the future.

foreign exchange controls licensing systems that limit the right of individuals to buy foreign currency.

foreign exchange market the market in which currencies can be exchanged for each other.

foreign exchange reserves stocks of foreign currency that governments can use to buy their own currency on the foreign exchange market.

free trade occurs in an economy when the government does not attempt either to reduce or to increase the levels of exports and imports that occur naturally as a result of supply and demand.

frictional unemployment unemployment due to time workers spend in job search.

G

gains from trade gains achieved by dividing tasks and trading; in this way people can get more of what they want through trade than they could if they tried to be self-sufficient.

GDP deflator a price measure for a given year that is equal to 100 times the ratio of nominal GDP to real GDP in that year.

GDP per capita GDP divided by the size of the population; equivalent to the average GDP per person.

global loanable funds market a situation in which international capital flows are so large that they equalize interest rates across countries.

globalization the phenomenon of growing economic linkages among countries.

government borrowing the total amount of funds borrowed by federal, state, and local governments in the financial markets.

government purchases of goods and services total purchases by federal, state, and local governments on goods and services.

Great Moderation the period from 1985 to 2007 when the U.S. economy experienced small fluctuations and low inflation.

gross domestic product (GDP) the total value of all final goods and services produced in the economy during a given period, usually a year.

growth accounting accounting that estimates the contribution of each of the major factors (physical and human capital, labor, and technology) in the aggregate production function.

H

Heckscher–Ohlin model a model of international trade in which a country has a comparative advantage in a good whose production is intensive in the factors that are abundantly available in that country.

horizontal axis the horizontal number line of a graph along which values of the x-variable are measured; also referred to as the **x-axis.**

horizontal intercept the point at which a curve hits the horizontal axis; it indicates the value of the x-variable when the value of the y-variable is zero.

household a person or a group of people that share their income.

human capital the improvement in labor created by the education and knowledge embodied in the workforce.

hyperglobalization the phenomenon of extremely high levels of international trade.

I

illiquid describes an asset that cannot be quickly converted into cash with relatively little loss of value.

implicit liabilities spending promises made by governments that are effectively a debt despite the fact that they are not included in the usual debt statistics. In the United States, the largest implicit liabilities arise from Social Security and Medicare, which promise transfer payments to current and future retirees (Social Security) and to the elderly (Medicare).

import-competing industries industries that produce goods and services that are also imported.

import quota a legal limit on the quantity of a good that can be imported.

imports goods and services purchased from other countries.

incentive anything that offers rewards to people to change their behavior.

income distribution the way in which total income is divided among the owners of the various factors of production.

income–expenditure equilibrium a situation in which aggregate output, measured by real GDP, is equal to planned aggregate spending and firms have no incentive to change output.

income–expenditure equilibrium GDP the level of real GDP at which real GDP equals planned aggregate spending.

independent variable the determining variable in a causal relationship.

individual choice the decision by an individual of what to do, which necessarily involves a decision of what not to do.

individual consumer surplus the net gain to an individual buyer from the purchase of a good; equal to the difference between the buyer's willingness to pay and the price paid.

individual demand curve a graphical representation of the relationship between quantity demanded and price for an individual consumer.

individual producer surplus the net gain to an individual seller from selling a good; equal to the difference between the price received and the seller's cost.

individual supply curve a graphical representation of the relationship between quantity supplied and price for an individual producer.

inefficient allocation of sales among sellers a form of inefficiency in which sellers who would be willing to sell a good at the lowest price are unable to make sales while sales go to sellers who are only willing to sell at a higher price; often the result of a price floor.

inefficient allocation to consumers a form of inefficiency in which some people who want the good badly and are willing to pay a high price don't get it, and some who care relatively little about the good and are only willing to pay a low price do get it; often a result of a price ceiling.

inefficiently high quality a form of inefficiency in which sellers offer high-quality goods at a high price even though buyers would prefer a lower quality at a lower price; often the result of a price floor.

inefficiently low quality a form of inefficiency in which sellers offer low-quality goods at a low price even though buyers would prefer a higher quality at a higher price; often a result of a price ceiling.

inferior good a good for which a rise in income decreases the demand for the good.

inflation a rise in the overall level of prices.

inflation rate the annual percent change in a price index—typically the consumer price index. The inflation rate is positive when the aggregate price level is rising (inflation) and negative when the aggregate price level is falling (deflation).

inflation targeting an approach to monetary policy that requires that the central bank try to keep the inflation rate near a predetermined target rate.

inflation tax the reduction in the value of money held by the public as a result of inflation.

inflationary gap the gap that exists when aggregate output is above potential output.

infrastructure physical capital, such as roads, power lines, ports, information networks, and other parts of an economy, that provides the underpinnings, or foundation, for economic activity.

input a good or service used to produce another good or service.

interaction (of choices) my choices affect your choices, and vice versa; a feature of most economic situations. The results of this interaction are often quite different from what the individuals intend.

interest rate the price, calculated as a percentage of the amount borrowed, charged by the lender.

intermediate goods and services goods and services—bought from one firm by another firm—that are inputs for production of final goods and services.

international trade agreements treaties in which a country promises to engage in less trade protection against the exports of other countries in return for a promise by other countries to do the same for its own exports.

inventories stocks of goods and raw materials held to facilitate business operations.

inventory investment the value of the change in total inventories held in the economy during a given period. Unlike other types of investment spending, inventory investment can be negative if inventories fall.

investment bank a bank that trades in financial assets and does not accept deposits, so it is not covered by deposit insurance.

investment spending spending on productive physical capital—such as machinery and construction of buildings—and on changes to inventories.

invisible hand a phrase used by Adam Smith to refer to the way in which an individual's pursuit of self-interest can lead, without the individual intending it, to good results for society as a whole.

J

job search the time spent by workers in looking for employment.

jobless recovery a period in which real GDP growth rate is positive but the unemployment rate is still rising.

K

Keynesian cross a diagram that identifies income–expenditure equilibrium as the point where the planned aggregate spending line crosses the 45-degree line.

Keynesian economics a school of thought emerging out of the works of John Maynard Keynes; according to Keynesian economics, a depressed economy is the result of inadequate spending and government intervention can help a depressed economy through monetary policy and fiscal policy.

L

labor force the sum of employment and unemployment; that is, the number of people who are currently working plus the number of people who are currently looking for work.

labor force participation rate the percentage of the population age 16 or older that is in the labor force.

labor productivity output per worker; also referred to as simply productivity. Increases in labor productivity are the only source of long-run economic growth.

law of demand the principle that a higher price for a good or service, other things equal, leads people to demand a smaller quantity of that good or service.

liability a requirement to pay income in the future.

license the right, conferred by the government or an owner, to supply a good.

life insurance company a financial intermediary that sells policies guaranteeing a payment to a policyholder's beneficiaries when the policyholder dies.

linear relationship the relationship between two variables in which the slope is constant and therefore is depicted on a graph by a curve that is a straight line.

liquid describes an asset that can be quickly converted into cash with relatively little loss of value.

liquidity preference model of the interest rate a model of the market for money in which the interest rate is determined by the supply and demand for money.

liquidity trap the economy is in a liquidity trap when monetary policy is ineffective because nominal interest rates are up against the zero bound.

loan a lending agreement between an individual lender and an individual borrower. Loans are usually tailored to the individual borrower's needs and ability to pay but carry relatively high transaction costs.

loanable funds market a hypothetical market that brings together those who want to lend money (savers) and those

who want to borrow (firms with investment spending projects).

loan-backed securities assets created by pooling individual loans and selling shares in that pool.

long-run aggregate supply curve a graphical representation that shows the relationship between the inflation rate and the quantity of aggregate output supplied that would exist if all prices, including nominal wages, were fully flexible. The long-run aggregate supply curve is vertical because the inflation rate has no effect on aggregate output in the long run; in the long run, aggregate output is determined by the economy's potential output.

long-run economic growth the sustained rise in the quantity of goods and services the economy produces.

long-run macroeconomic equilibrium the point at which the short-run macroeconomic equilibrium is on the long-run aggregate supply curve; so short-run equilibrium aggregate output is equal to potential output.

long-run Phillips curve a graphical representation of the relationship between unemployment and inflation in the long run after expectations of inflation have had time to adjust to experience.

long-term interest rate the interest rate on financial assets that mature a number of years into the future.

lump-sum tax a tax that is the same for everyone, regardless of any actions people take.

M

macroeconomic policy activism the use of monetary policy and fiscal policy to smooth out the business cycle.

macroeconomics the branch of economics that is concerned with the overall ups and downs in the economy.

marginal analysis the study of marginal decisions.

marginal decision a decision made at the "margin" of an activity to do a bit more or a bit less of that activity.

marginal propensity to consume (*MPC*) the increase in consumer spending when disposable income rises by $1. Because consumers normally spend part but not all of an additional dollar of disposable income, *MPC* is between 0 and 1.

marginal propensity to save (*MPS*) the fraction of an additional dollar of disposable income that is saved; *MPS* is equal to $1 - MPC$.

marginally attached workers nonworking individuals who say they would like a job and have looked for work in the recent past but are not currently looking for work.

market basket a hypothetical consumption bundle of consumer purchases of goods and services, used to measure changes in overall price level.

market-clearing price the price at which the market is in equilibrium, that is, the quantity of a good or service demanded equals the quantity of that good or service supplied; also referred to as the equilibrium price.

market economy an economy in which decisions about production and consumption are made by individual producers and consumers.

market failure the failure of a market to be efficient.

markets for goods and services markets in which firms sell goods and services that they produce to households.

maximum the highest point on a nonlinear curve, where the slope of the curve changes from positive to negative.

medium of exchange an asset that individuals acquire for the purpose of trading for goods and services rather than for their own consumption.

menu cost the real cost of changing a listed price.

merchandise trade balance (trade balance) the difference between a country's exports and imports of goods alone—not including services.

microeconomics the branch of economics that studies how people make decisions and how these decisions interact.

minimum the lowest point on a nonlinear curve, where the slope of the curve changes from negative to positive.

minimum wage a legal floor on the wage rate, which is the market price of labor.

model a simplified representation of a real situation that is used to better understand real-life situations.

monetarism a theory of business cycles, associated primarily with Milton Friedman, that asserts that GDP will grow steadily if the money supply grows steadily.

monetary aggregate an overall measure of the money supply. The most common monetary aggregates in the United States are M1, which includes currency in circulation, traveler's checks, and checkable bank deposits, and M2, which includes M1 as well as near-moneys.

monetary base the sum of currency in circulation and bank reserves.

monetary neutrality the concept that changes in the money supply have no real effects on the economy in the long run and only result in a proportional change in the price level.

monetary policy changes in the quantity of money in circulation designed to alter interest rates and affect the level of overall spending.

monetary policy rule a formula that determines the central bank's actions.

money any asset that can easily be used to purchase goods and services.

money demand curve a graphical representation of the relationship between the interest rate and the quantity of money demanded. The money demand curve slopes downward because, other things equal, a higher interest rate increases the opportunity cost of holding money.

money multiplier the ratio of the money supply to the monetary base.

money supply the total value of financial assets in the economy that are considered money.

money supply curve a graphical representation of the relationship between the quantity of money supplied by the Federal Reserve and the interest rate.

movement along the demand curve a change in the quantity demanded of a good that results from a change in the good's price.

movement along the supply curve a change in the quantity supplied of a good that results from a change in the good's price.

multiplier the ratio of total change in real GDP caused by an autonomous change in aggregate spending to the size of that autonomous change.

mutual fund a financial intermediary that creates a stock portfolio by buying and holding shares in companies and then selling shares of this portfolio to individual investors.

N

national income and product accounts (national accounts) a method of calculating and keeping track of consumer spending, sales of producers, business investment spending, government purchases, and a variety of other flows of money between different sectors of the economy.

national savings the sum of private savings and the government's budget balance; the total amount of savings generated within the economy.

natural rate hypothesis the hypothesis that because inflation is eventually embedded into expectations, to avoid accelerating inflation over time the unemployment rate should be kept stable around the natural rate.

natural rate of unemployment the normal unemployment rate around which the actual unemployment rate fluctuates; the unemployment rate that arises from the effects of frictional and structural unemployment.

near-moneys financial assets that can't be directly used as a medium of exchange but can be readily converted into cash or checkable bank deposits.

negative relationship a relationship between two variables in which an increase in the value of one variable is associated with a decrease in the value of the other variable. It is illustrated by a curve that slopes downward from left to right.

net capital inflow the total inflow of funds into a country minus the total outflow of funds out of a country.

net exports the difference between the value of exports and the value of imports. A positive value for net exports indicates that a country is a net exporter of goods and services; a negative value indicates that a country is a net importer of goods and services.

new classical macroeconomics an approach to the business cycle that returns to the classical view that shifts in the aggregate demand curve affect only the aggregate price level, not aggregate output.

new Keynesian economics a theory that argues that market imperfections can lead to price stickiness for the economy as a whole.

nominal GDP the value of all final goods and services produced in the economy during a given year, calculated using the prices current in the year in which the output is produced.

nominal interest rate the interest rate in dollar terms.

nominal wage the dollar amount of any given wage paid.

nonaccelerating inflation rate of unemployment (NAIRU) the unemployment rate at which, other things equal, inflation does not change over time.

nonlinear curve a curve in which the slope is not the same between every pair of points.

nonlinear relationship the relationship between two variables in which the slope is not constant and therefore is depicted on a graph by a curve that is not a straight line.

normal good a good for which a rise in income increases the demand for that good—the "normal" case.

normative economics the branch of economic analysis that makes prescriptions about the way the economy should work.

North American Free Trade Agreement (NAFTA) a trade agreement among the United States, Canada, and Mexico. Revised in 2018 as USMCA.

O

offshore outsourcing the practice in which businesses hire people in another country to perform various tasks.

Okun's law the negative relationship between the output gap and the unemployment rate, whereby each additional percentage point of output gap reduces the unemployment rate by about 1/2 of a percentage point.

omitted variable an unobserved variable that, through its influence on other variables, creates the erroneous appearance of a direct causal relationship among those variables.

open economy an economy that trades goods and services with other countries.

open-market operation a purchase or sale of U.S. Treasury bills by the Federal Reserve, normally through a transaction with a commercial bank.

opportunity cost the real cost of an item: what you must give up in order to get it.

origin the point where the axes of a two-variable graph meet.

other things equal assumption in the development of a model, the assumption that all other relevant factors remain unchanged.

output gap the percentage difference between actual aggregate output and potential output.

P

pension fund a type of mutual fund that holds assets in order to provide retirement income to its members.

physical asset a claim on a tangible object that can be used to generate future income.

physical capital human-made resources such as buildings and machines.

pie chart a circular graph that shows how some total is divided among its components, usually expressed in percentages.

planned aggregate spending the total amount of planned spending in the economy; includes consumer spending and planned investment spending.

planned investment spending the investment spending that firms intend to undertake during a given period. Planned investment spending may differ from actual investment spending due to unplanned inventory investment.

political business cycle a business cycle that results from the use of macroeconomic policy to serve political ends.

positive economics the branch of economic analysis that describes the way the economy actually works.

positive relationship a relationship between two variables in which an increase in the value of one variable is associated with an increase in the value of the other variable. It is illustrated by a curve that slopes upward from left to right.

potential output the level of real GDP the economy would produce if all prices, including nominal wages, were fully flexible.

price ceiling a maximum price sellers are allowed to charge for a good or service; a form of price control.

price controls legal restrictions on how high or low a market price may go.

price floor a minimum price buyers are required to pay for a good or service; a form of price control.

price index a measure of the cost of purchasing a given market basket in a given year, where that cost is normalized so that it is equal to 100 in the selected base year; a measure of overall price level.

price stability a situation in which the overall cost of living is changing slowly or not at all.

producer price index (PPI) a measure of the cost of a typical basket of goods and services purchased by producers. Because these commodity prices respond quickly to changes in demand, the PPI is often regarded as a leading indicator of changes in the inflation rate.

producer surplus a term often used to refer both to individual producer surplus and to total producer surplus.

production possibility frontier a model that illustrates the trade-offs facing an economy that produces only two goods. It shows the maximum quantity of one good that can be produced for any given quantity produced of the other.

productivity output per worker; a shortened form of the term *labor productivity*.

protection an alternative term for trade protection; policies that limit imports.

public debt government debt held by individuals and institutions outside the government.

purchasing power parity (between two countries' currencies) the nominal exchange rate at which a given basket of goods and services would cost the same amount in each country.

Q

quantity control an upper limit, set by the government, on the quantity of some good that can be bought or sold; also referred to as a quota.

quantity demanded the actual amount of a good or service consumers are willing to buy at some specific price.

quantity supplied the actual amount of a good or service producers are willing to sell at some specific price.

quota an upper limit, set by the government, on the quantity of some good that can be bought or sold; also referred to as a quantity control.

quota limit the total amount of a good under a quota or quantity control that can be legally transacted.

quota rent the difference between the demand price and the supply price at the quota limit; this difference, the earnings that accrue to the licenseholder from ownership of the right to sell the good, is equal to the market price of the license when the licenses are traded.

R

random walk the movement over time of an unpredictable variable.

rational expectations a theory of expectation formation that holds that individuals and firms make decisions optimally, using all available information.

rational expectations model a model of the economy in which expected changes in monetary policy have no effect on unemployment and output and only affect the price level.

real business cycle theory a theory of business cycles that asserts that fluctuations in the growth rate of total factor productivity cause the business cycle.

real exchange rates the exchange rate adjusted for international differences in aggregate price levels.

real GDP the total value of all final goods and services produced in the economy during a given year, calculated using the prices of a selected base year.

real income income divided by the price level.

real interest rate the nominal interest rate minus the inflation rate.

real wage the wage rate divided by the price level.

recession a downturn in the economy when output and employment are falling; also referred to as a contraction.

recessionary gap the gap that exists when aggregate output is below potential output.

research and development (R&D) spending to create new technologies and prepare them for practical use.

reserve ratio the fraction of bank deposits that a bank holds as reserves. In the United States, the minimum required reserve ratio is set by the Federal Reserve.

reserve requirements rules of the Federal Reserve that set the minimum reserve ratio for banks. For checkable bank deposits in the United States, the minimum reserve ratio is set at 10%.

resource something that can be used to produce something else; includes natural resources (from the physical environment) and human resources (labor, skill, intelligence).

revaluation an increase in the value of a currency that is set under a fixed exchange rate regime.

reverse causality the error committed when the true direction of causality between two variables is reversed, and the independent variable and the dependent variable are incorrectly identified.

Ricardian model of international trade a model that analyzes international trade under the assumption that opportunity costs are constant.

Rule of 70 a mathematical formula that states that the time it takes real GDP per capita, or any other variable that grows gradually over time, to double is approximately 70 divided by that variable's annual growth rate.

S

savings and loan (thrift) deposit-taking banks, usually specialized in issuing home loans.

savings–investment spending identity an accounting fact that states that savings and investment spending are always equal for the economy as a whole.

scarce in short supply; a resource is scarce when there is not enough of the resource available to satisfy all the various ways a society wants to use it.

scatter diagram a graph that shows points that correspond to actual observations of the x- and y-variables; a curve is usually fitted to the scatter of points to indicate the trend in the data.

secular stagnation a state in which the interest rate that would be needed to achieve full employment is consistently below zero. Proponents of this view, known as *secular stagnationists*, advocate an active fiscal policy and unconventional monetary policy.

securitization the pooling of loans and mortgages made by a financial institution and the sale of shares in such a pool to other investors.

self-correcting describes an economy in which shocks to aggregate demand affect aggregate output in the short run but not in the long run.

self-regulating economy describes an economy in which problems such as unemployment are resolved without government intervention, through the working of the invisible hand, and in which government attempts to improve the economy's performance would be ineffective at best, and would probably make things worse.

shadow banking bank-like activities undertaken by nondepository financial firms such as investment banks and hedge funds, but without regulatory oversight and protection.

shadow market a market in which goods or services are bought and sold illegally, either because it is illegal to sell them at all or because the prices charged are legally prohibited by a price ceiling; also known as a black market.

shift of the demand curve a change in the quantity demanded at any given price, represented graphically by the shift of the original demand curve to a new position, denoted by a new demand curve.

shift of the supply curve a change in the quantity supplied of a good or service at any given price. It is represented by the change of the original supply curve to a new position, denoted by a new supply curve.

shoe-leather costs (of inflation) the increased costs of transactions caused by inflation.

shortage the insufficiency of a good or service that occurs when the quantity demanded exceeds the quantity supplied; shortages occur when the price is below the equilibrium price.

short-run aggregate supply curve a graphical representation that shows the positive relationship between the inflation rate and the quantity of aggregate output supplied that exists in the short run, the time period when many production costs, particularly nominal wages, can be taken as fixed. The short-run aggregate supply curve has a positive slope because a rise in the inflation rate leads to a rise in profits, and therefore output, when production costs are fixed.

short-run equilibrium aggregate output the quantity of aggregate output produced in short-run macroeconomic equilibrium.

short-run equilibrium inflation rate the inflation rate in the short-run macroeconomic equilibrium.

short-run macroeconomic equilibrium the point at which the quantity of aggregate output supplied is equal to the quantity demanded.

short-run Phillips curve a graphical representation of the negative short-run relationship between the unemployment rate and the inflation rate.

short-term interest rate the interest rate on financial assets that mature within less than a year.

slope a measure of how steep a line or curve is. The slope of a line is measured by "rise over run"—the change in the y-variable between two points on the line divided by the change in the x-variable between those same two points.

social insurance government programs—like Social Security, Medicare, unemployment insurance, and food stamps—intended to protect families against economic hardship.

specialization the situation in which each person specializes in the task that they are good at performing.

stabilization policy the use of government policy to reduce the severity of recessions and to rein in excessively strong expansions. There are two main tools of stabilization policy: monetary policy and fiscal policy.

stagflation the combination of inflation and falling aggregate output.

sticky wages nominal wages that are slow to fall even in the face of high unemployment and slow to rise even in the face of labor shortages.

store of value an asset that is a means of holding purchasing power over time.

structural unemployment unemployment that results when there are more people seeking jobs in a particular labor market than there are jobs available at the current wage rate, even when the economy is at the peak of the business cycle.

subprime lending lending to homebuyers who don't meet the usual criteria for qualifying for a loan.

substitutes pairs of goods for which a rise in the price of one of the goods leads to an increase in the demand for the other good.

supply and demand model a model of how a competitive market behaves.

supply curve a graphical representation of the supply schedule, showing the relationship between quantity supplied and price.

supply price the price of a given quantity at which producers will supply that quantity.

supply schedule a list or table showing how much of a good or service producers will supply at different prices.

supply shock an event that shifts the short-run aggregate supply curve. A negative supply shock raises production costs and reduces the quantity supplied at any inflation rate, shifting the curve leftward. A positive supply shock decreases production costs and increases the quantity supplied at any inflation rate, shifting the curve rightward.

surplus the excess of a good or service that occurs when the quantity supplied exceeds the quantity demanded; surpluses occur when the price is above the equilibrium price.

sustainable long-run economic growth long-run growth that can continue in the face of the limited supply of natural resources and with less negative impact on the environment.

T

T-account a simple tool that summarizes a business's financial position by showing, in a single table, the business's assets and liabilities, with assets on the left and liabilities on the right.

tangent line a straight line that just touches, or is tangent to, a nonlinear curve at a particular point; the slope of the tangent line is equal to the slope of the nonlinear curve at that point.

target federal funds rate the Federal Reserve's desired level for the federal funds rate. The Federal Reserve adjusts the money supply through the purchase and sale of Treasury bills until the actual rate equals the desired rate.

tariff a tax levied on imports.

Taylor rule for monetary policy a rule that sets the federal funds rate according to the level of the inflation rate and either the output gap or the unemployment rate.

technological progress an advance in the technical means of production of goods and services.

technology the technical means for producing goods and services.

time-series graph a two-variable graph that has dates on the horizontal axis and values of a variable that occurred on those dates on the vertical axis.

total consumer surplus the sum of the individual consumer surpluses of all the buyers of a good in a market.

total factor productivity the amount of output that can be produced with a given amount of factor inputs.

total producer surplus the sum of the individual producer surpluses of all the sellers of a good in a market.

total surplus the total net gain to consumers and producers from trading in a market; it is the sum of the producer surplus and the consumer surplus.

trade the practice, in a market economy, in which individuals provide goods and services to others and receive goods and services in return.

trade deficit the deficit that results when the value of the goods and services bought from foreigners is more than the value of the goods and services sold to consumers abroad.

trade-off a comparison of costs and benefits of doing something.

trade protection policies that limit imports.

trade surplus the surplus that results when the value of goods and services bought from foreigners is less than the value of the goods and services sold to them.

trade war occurs when countries deliberately try to impose pain on their trading partners, as a way to extract policy concessions.

transaction costs the expenses of negotiating and executing a deal that often prevent a mutually beneficial trade from occurring.

truncated cut; in a truncated axis, some of the range of values are omitted, usually to save space.

U

underemployment the number of people who work part time because they cannot find full-time jobs.

unemployment the total number of people who are actively looking for work but aren't currently employed.

unemployment rate the percentage of the total number of people in the labor force who are unemployed, calculated as unemployment/(unemployment + employment).

union an organization of workers that bargains collectively with employers to raise wages and improve working conditions.

United States-Mexico-Canada Agreement or USMCA a revised trade agreement between the United States, Canada, and Mexico to replace NAFTA.

unit of account a measure used to set prices and make economic calculations.

unit-of-account costs (of inflation) costs arising from the way inflation makes money a less reliable unit of measurement.

unplanned inventory investment an unintended swing in inventory that occurs when actual sales are higher or lower than expected sales.

V

value added (of a producer) the value of a producer's sales minus the value of its purchases of intermediate goods and services.

variable a quantity that can take on more than one value.

vertical axis the vertical number line of a graph along which values of the y-variable are measured; also referred to as the **y-axis**.

vertical intercept the point at which a curve hits the vertical axis; it shows the value of the y-variable when the value of the x-variable is zero.

W

wasted resources a form of inefficiency in which people expend money, effort, and time to cope with the shortages caused by a price ceiling.

wealth (of a household) the value of accumulated savings.

wedge the difference between the demand price of the quantity transacted and the supply price of the quantity transacted for a good when the supply of the good is legally restricted. Often created by a quantity control, or quota. The price paid by buyers ends up being higher than that received by sellers.

willingness to pay the maximum price at which a consumer is prepared to pay for a good.

world price the price at which that good can be bought or sold abroad.

World Trade Organization (WTO) an international organization of member countries that oversees international trade agreements and rules on disputes between countries over those agreements.

Z

zero lower bound for interest rates statement of the fact that interest rates cannot fall below zero without causing significant problems.

Index

monetary policy, 173, 453–477
aggregate demand and, 353, 355, 464–470
business cycle and, 178, 469–470, 515
contractionary (tight), 464–465
demand for money and, 454–459
discretionary, 516
exchange rates and, 551–552, 553, 556–557
expansionary (loose), 464–465
Great Depression-era, 519–520
inflation targeting and, 467–468
influence of, 469–470
interest rates and, 453, 461–462, 523–524. *See also* interest rate(s)
limits of, 521–522
long run implications of, 470–473
monetarist views on, 515–516, 521
monetary neutrality and, 471, 472–473
money supply and. *See* money supply
nondiscretionary, 515–516
power to decide, 453, 469–470. *See also* Federal Reserve System
in practice, 465–466
quantitative easing as, 469, 522
revival of interest in, 515
Taylor rule for, 466–467
zero lower bound problem and, 466, 468–469, 501, 524
monetary policy rule, 516
monetization of debt, 273, 485–486
money, 418–423. *See also* currency(ies); dollar (U.S.); monetary policy
aggregate price level changes and, 349–350, 457
bank creation of, 423, 428–430
in circulation, 418, 419, 422, 429, 431–433
commodity, 420, 423
commodity-backed, 420–421, 423
counterfeit, 417, 421, 438
definition of, 418–419
demand for, 454–460
fiat, 421
gains from trade and, 418–419
interest rates and, 459–464. *See also* interest rate(s)

opportunity cost of holding, 454–455, 459
printing of, 403, 485–486, 488, 504
roles of, 419–420
supply of. *See* money supply
types of, 420–421
unit-of-account role of, 231–232, 420
money demand curve (MD), 456–459
interest rate and, 459–460
shifts of, 457–458
money multiplier, 430–433
money supply, 418, 421–422, 428–433
bank creation of money and, 428–430
bank runs and, 433
changes in, interest rate effects of, 461–462, 471–472
classical macroeconomics and, 510
components of, 421
Fed's tools for increasing or decreasing, 434–437, 460
Great Depression and, 519–520
increase in, short- and long-run effects of, 471–472
inflation and, 473, 484–488, 522
measuring of, 421–422
monetarism on, 515–516, 521
monetary base and, 431–432, 437, 438, 522
monetary neutrality and, 471, 472–473
money multiplier and, 430–433
nominal, 484
money supply curve (MS), 459–460
money transmitters, 454, 474
Morgan, J. P., 441
mortgages
delinquencies in, 301–302
government-sponsored, 440, 443, 445
inflation effects on, 232–233
mortgage-backed securities with, 293, 469
subprime lending and, 444
movement along the aggregate demand curve, 351–352
movements along the demand curve, 79–80, 92
movements along the supply curve, 70–71, 73, 91
MPC (marginal propensity to consume), 316–318, 392
MPS (marginal propensity to save), 316–317

MS (money supply curve), 459–460. *See also* money supply
multiplier, 315, 316–319, 330, 391–395
algebraic derivation of, 345
austerity and, 395
changes in government transfers and taxes and, 392–393
definition of, 318, 392
fiscal policy and, 391–395
increase in government purchases of goods and services and, 391–392
international trade and, 339
inventory adjustment and, 334–337, 339–340
money, 430–433
paradox of thrift and, 336–337
taxes and, 392–394, 415–416
Mumbai, India, rent controls in, 108
Muth, John, 517
mutual funds, 293–294

N

NAFTA (North American Free Trade Agreement), 153
NAFTA-USMCA, 153
NAIRU (nonaccelerating inflation rate of unemployment), 497, 498
NASDAQ, 297, 303
national accounts, 190. *See also* national income and product accounts
National Bureau of Economic Research (NBER), 176, 178, 510
National Cash Register Corporation, 268
national income and product accounts, 190–197
circular-flow diagram and, 190–191
gross domestic product and, 191–197
nationalization, partial, of financial system, Great Recession and, 445
national savings, 275
National Science Foundation, 256
national security argument for trade protection, 152
natural rate hypothesis, 498, 517–518
natural rate of unemployment, 220–228
changes in, 226–227
cyclical unemployment and, 225

definition of, 225
frictional unemployment and, 221–222
job creation and job destruction and, 220–221
long-run Phillips curve and, 498
NAIRU related to, 498
structural unemployment and, 222–225, 228
natural resources
overexploitation of, as market failure, 4
productivity and, 251–252
scarcity of, 8
sustainable long-run economic growth and, 264–265
NBER (National Bureau of Economic Research), 176, 178, 510
NCR Corp., 268
near-moneys, 421
negative relationships, 54
net capital inflow, 276, 283
net exports, 197
real, 549
Netflix, 526
Netherlands, current account surplus of, 538
net present value, 310–311
new classical macroeconomics, 517–519
new Keynesian economics, 518
New York City
parking in, 11, 15
rent controls in, 103, 104–106, 108, 110
taxicab medallions in, 117–122
traffic congestion in, 4, 11, 17–18, 85
Uber in, 96
U.S. banking system and, 440–441
New York Clearinghouse, 441
New Zealand, inflation targeting in, 468
Nicaragua, inflation in, 483
Nigeria
economic growth of, 259, 260–261
natural resources and real GDP per capita of, 251
Nike, 163
Nixon, Richard, 519
nominal exchange rates, 546–547, 550
nominal GDP, 198, 200, 203
nominal interest rate, 232, 286–287, 454
nominal money supply, 484
nominal wage, 356
downward rigidity of, 371
sticky, 357, 358, 360